23e

College Accounting

CHAPTERS 1-27

James A. Heintz, DBA, CPA
Professor of Accounting
School of Business
University of Kansas
Lawrence, Kansas

Robert W. Parry, Jr., Ph.D.
Professor of Accounting
Kelley School of Business
Indiana University
Bloomington, Indiana

CENGAGE

Australia • Brazil • Mexico • Singapore • United Kingdom • United States

**_College Accounting_, 23rd Edition,
Chapters 1-27
James A. Heintz and Robert W. Parry**

Senior Vice President, Higher Ed Product,
    Content, and Market Development: Erin Joyner

Product Director: Jason Fremder

Product Manager: Christopher Rader

Learning Designer: Kristen Meere

Senior Digital Delivery Leads: Sally Nieman and
    Tim Ross

Senior Content Manager: Tim Bailey

Product Assistant: Aiyana Moore

Executive Marketing Manager: Nathan Anderson

Production Service/Composition: SPi Global

Senior Designer: Bethany Bourgeois

Cover and Internal Designer:
    Ke Design/Ted Knapke

Cover Image: iStock.com/cifotart

Design Images:

   "A Broader View" Feature: Johannes
   Kornelius/Shutterstock.com

   "Your Perspective" Feature:
   leungchopan/Shutterstock.com

   Theme image used on title page, front and
   back matter tabs, and part openers:
   ra2studio/Shutterstock.com

Intellectual Property Analyst: Reba Frederics

Intellectual Property Project Manager:
Carly Belcher

For product information and technology assistance, contact us at
Cengage Customer & Sales Support, 1-800-354-9706 or **support.cengage.com**.

For permission to use material from this text or product,
submit all requests online at **www.cengage.com/permissions**.

Microsoft Excel® is a registered trademark of Microsoft Corporation.
© 2018 Microsoft.

Library of Congress Control Number: 2018954951

ISBN: 978-1-337-79475-6

Cengage
20 Channel Center Street
Boston, MA 02210
USA

Cengage is a leading provider of customized learning solutions with employees residing in nearly 40 different countries and sales in more than 125 countries around the world. Find your local representative at **www.cengage.com**.

Cengage products are represented in Canada by Nelson Education, Ltd.

To learn more about Cengage platforms and services, register or access your online learning solution, or purchase materials for your course, visit **www.cengage.com**.

Printed at CLDPC, USA, 04-21

James A. Heintz

James A. Heintz was a Professor of Accounting for 15 years, including 13 years as the Director of Accounting and Information Systems, in the School of Business at the University of Kansas. He is now Professor Emeritus at Kansas. Prior to joining the University of Kansas, he was Accounting Department Head at the University of Connecticut for eight years, and Assistant, Associate, and Full Professor at Indiana University for 20 years. He also taught for many years for the University of Kansas and the University of Iowa in a study abroad program in Northern Italy. His doctorate is from Washington University in St. Louis, and he is a CPA. He was Price Waterhouse Faculty Fellow at Indiana, Arthur Andersen Faculty Fellow at Connecticut, and Deloitte & Touche Faculty Fellow at Kansas. Professor Heintz has won numerous school and university teaching awards, including five teaching awards from Doctoral Student Associations. He has served in various capacities on 27 doctoral dissertation committees. Professor Heintz has published numerous articles in accounting and business journals, such as *The Accounting Review; Auditing: A Journal of Practice and Theory; Accounting Horizons; Accounting and Business Research; Journal of Business Finance and Accounting;* and *International Journal of Accounting Education and Research.* He served on the editorial board of *Auditing: A Journal of Practice and Theory* for seven years and was president of the Accounting Programs Leadership Group of the AAA. He also has participated in external reviews of accounting programs at 12 major universities.

Robert W. Parry

Robert W. Parry is Professor Emeritus of Accounting at Indiana University's Kelley School of Business in Bloomington, Indiana. An accomplished teacher, Professor Parry has taught accounting at virtually all levels. While earning his MBA, he taught accounting at Bishop Klonowski High School in Scranton, Pennsylvania. While earning his Ph.D., he taught introductory financial and managerial accounting at Northampton County Community College and Lehigh University. At Indiana, he taught in the Undergraduate, MBA, MBA in Accounting, Master of Science in Accounting, the online Kelley Direct MBA Program, and Ph.D. Programs. In addition, he has taught accounting in the Consortium of Universities for International Studies in Asolo, Italy. During his 35 years at Indiana University, he won or was nominated for a total of 27 teaching excellence awards, including recognition twice by *Business Week* as one of the country's Outstanding MBA Faculty. In addition, he was awarded the Indiana University Distinguished Service Award for his efforts in planning and deploying a new, integrated MBA Core Program. He also received the Kelley School of Business Innovative Teaching Award for his role in designing and implementing the curriculum for the Master of Science in Accounting Program.

Parry has conducted research in the areas of public finance, governmental accounting, and accounting education. His work has been published in many journals, including *Public Finance Quarterly, Public Budgeting and Financial Management, Financial Analysts Journal, Accounting Horizons, Management Accounting, Research in Accounting Regulation, Research in Governmental and Non-Profit Accounting, Issues in Accounting Education,* and *Journal of Accounting Education.* Professor Parry was a lead author on the *Service Efforts and Accomplishments* research report published by the Governmental Accounting Standards Board. He also served on many committees of the American Accounting Association, including President of the Government and Nonprofit Accounting Section.

Rob and his wife, Jane, enjoy golf, ballroom dancing, hiking, kayaking, travel, and working in the yard. They have two children, Mitchell and Jessica, and four grandchildren, Anya Catrin Parry, Rohan Macsen Parry, Damon Robert Williams, and Mitchell David Williams.

Where *Accounting Education* and the *Real World* Meet

As the leading choice in college accounting, Heintz & Parry's *College Accounting 23e* combines a proven, step-by-step approach and excellent examples with a tightly integrated online homework tool that makes accounting understandable to every student, regardless of their accounting background or business experience. The Heintz & Parry program, well-known for its quality, consistency, and technology, focuses on the practical skills students need to transition from the classroom to the workplace. With even more practice opportunities and independent study resources than ever before, the 23rd edition delivers the tools students need to succeed.

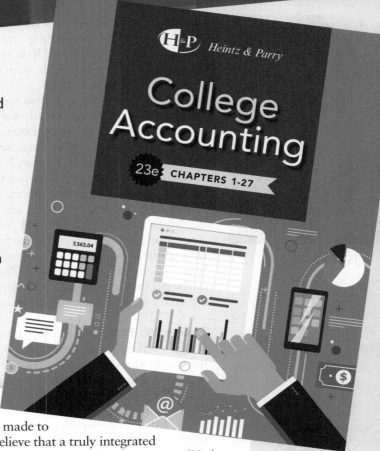

As the authors of *College Accounting 23e*, we are excited about this new edition and the enhancements made to the CengageNOWv2 online homework system. We believe that a truly integrated textbook and online homework system that serves as an extension of the classroom will help students be more successful in the college accounting course and better prepared for the real world.

Many of the end-of-chapter exercises and problems in CNOWv2 have "Show Me How" videos. If you are having difficulty with an assignment, a video icon indicates that additional help is available in CengageNOWv2. There, you can click on the icon. A voice-over, PowerPoint video presentation will pop up with an explanation of how to solve a similar exercise. We think these videos are similar to a quick visit to our offices. Hope you find them helpful.

Chapters 1–27: 9781337794
Chapters 1–15: 9781337794
Chapters 1–9: 9781337794

Throughout the revision process, we spent much of our time participating in the CengageNOWv2 development. We viewed it as essential to clearly connect CengageNOWv2 with the *College Accounting 23e* text by ensuring consistent terminology use, meaningful feedback for the students, and examples consistent with those in the textbook.

We hope this preface will serve as a guide to help you gain the most knowledge from this text and its supporting materials.

Sincerely,

Jim Heintz and Rob Parry

iv

Where *Accounting Education* and Digital Learning Meet

College Accounting 23e combined with CengageNOWv2 elevates student thinking with unique content that addresses each phase of the learning process. The text combined with the digital content in **CengageNOWv2** offers students clearly defined tools to optimize their learning experience. Included are many proven resources including algorithmic activities, test bank, course management tools, reporting and assessment options, and much more.

Recent CengageNOWv2 Enhancements

- **Refreshed Design:** This refreshed look will help you and your students focus easily and quickly on what is important, while maintaining the same functionality that CengageNOW users know and love.

- **Integration with Popular Learning Management Systems:** Single login, deep linking, and grade return! (Check with your local Learning Consultant for more details!)

- **Upload Files Capability:** You can now upload files in CengageNOWv2 for student use—including videos, Excel files, Word files, and more.

- **Email Instructor Feature:** Students can now send you a screenshot of the question they are working on directly through CengageNOWv2 and ask specific questions about where they are stuck.

- **Better Date Management:** When modifying assignment due dates for a whole course, the system will now automatically adjust due dates based on a new start date, making it easier to reuse a course from one term to the next and adjust for snow days.

- **Streamlined Assignment Creation Process:** A simplified and streamlined Assignment Creation process allows instructors to quickly set up and manage assignments from a single page!

- **New Report Options:** New reporting options allow you to get better reports on your students' progress.

- **New Student Registration Process:** When you create a course, a URL will be generated that will automatically take students right into the instructor's course without them having to enter the course key!

Blank Sheet of Paper Experience A less-leading Blank Sheet of Paper Experience discourages overreliance on the system.

- The use of drop down menus and Smart Entry (type-ahead) has been eliminated.

- Students must refer to the Chart of Accounts and decide for themselves which account is impacted.

- The number of accounts in each transaction is not given away.

- Whether the account should be debited or credited is not given away.

- Transactions may be entered in any order (as long as the entries are correct).

- Check My Work feedback only reports on what students have actually attempted, which prevents students from "guessing" their way through the assignment.

> " Jim and I love the "Blank Sheet of Paper Experience" for the Mastery Problems and select end-of-chapter problems. This addition in CengageNOWv2 gives students the chance to complete the problems online without the technology giving away the correct responses. "
>
> *Rob Parry*

Where *Accounting Education* and Digital Learning Meet

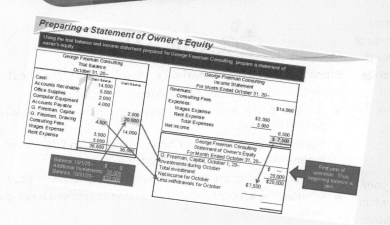

Mastery Problems available in Blank Sheet of Paper offer students a real-world opportunity to test their expertise in each chapter's content. Check My Work feedback provides truly helpful guidance to assist in the completion of a question before the student submits the assignment for grading. This feature can be turned on or off by the instructor.

- **Easy-to-use course management options** offer flexibility and continuity from one semester to the next.
- The most **robust** and **flexible assignment options** in the industry.
- **Cengage Learning Testing Powered by Cognero** is a flexible, online system that allows you to:
  - author, edit, and manage test bank content from multiple Cengage Learning solutions
  - create multiple test versions in an instant
  - deliver tests from your LMS, your classroom, or wherever you want
- Each problem is tagged by topic, learning objectives, level of difficulty, Bloom's Taxonomy, AICPA, ACBSP, and general business program standards allowing you to **analyze student work from the gradebook and generate reports on learning outcomes**.

> *If a student needs help with end-of-chapter materials, in Show Me How videos, Rob and I show students how to solve sample problems and exercises.*
>
> *Jim Heintz*

Cengage Unlimited is a first of-its-kind digital subscription designed specifically to lower costs. Students get access to everything Cengage has to offer on demand—in one place. That's 20,000 eBooks, 2,300 digital learning products, and dozens of study tools across 70 disciplines and over 675 courses. Currently available in select markets. Details at www.cengage.com/unlimited

CENGAGE UNLIMITED

Where *Accounting Education* and *Digital Learning Meet*

A Note to Faculty Colleagues on Revenue Recognition and Spreadsheets

Revenue Recognition

In this edition, we have expanded our discussion of sales returns and allowances to address the new revenue recognition standard issued by the FASB and IASB. This standard emphasizes the concept of recognizing revenue once the "performance obligation" has been satisfied. Of course, if a customer has the right to return merchandise, the performance obligation has not been fully satisfied at the time of the initial sale. Businesses have always recorded the *actual* returns and allowances and reported the related impact on the financial statements. The new standard requires firms to account for *actual <u>and</u> expected* returns and allowances: those that were returned this year and those expected to be returned next year as a result of this year's sales. We illustrate this process under the periodic and perpetual inventory systems. Here, let us share our approach to addressing this issue.

Periodic Inventory System—Under the periodic inventory system, Merchandise Inventory is not updated for inventory transactions during the year. We simply make an adjustment to the account at the end of the year. We make the same assumption for Estimated Returns Inventory and Customer Refunds Payable, new accounts introduced in this edition to address the new revenue recognition standard. No entries are made to these accounts during the year. Further, we assume Estimated Returns Inventory is adjusted the same way we have always adjusted Merchandise Inventory, by first removing the old inventory and then entering the new inventory in a two-step process. Customer Refunds Payable is also adjusted (up or down) at the end of each year to properly reflect the estimated refunds to be granted next year as a result of this year's sales.

Perpetual Inventory System—Under the perpetual inventory system, entries are made to Merchandise Inventory throughout the year. Thus, assuming no shrinkage, the balance of this account should reflect the merchandise inventory held by the business at any point in time. We make the same assumption for Estimated Returns Inventory. At the end of each year, this account is adjusted to reflect an estimate of the cost of the inventory sold this year, but expected to be returned next year. This is done by debiting Estimated Returns Inventory and crediting Cost of Goods Sold. When customers return inventory sold in the prior year we debit Merchandise Inventory and credit Estimated Returns Inventory.

Similarly, we adjust Customer Refunds Payable at the end of each year to reflect the customer refunds expected to be paid next year as a result of this year's sales. This is done by debiting Sales Returns and Allowances and crediting Customer Refunds Payable. When customers return inventory sold in the prior year, we debit Customer Refunds Payable and credit Cash.

New Six-Column Spreadsheet

In Chapters 5 and 6 you will see the familiar 10-column work sheet. However, in Chapter 14, we introduce a new six-column spreadsheet. This is done to recognize the important role computer spreadsheets play in accounting. We have eliminated the Income Statement and Balance Sheet columns and rely on the Adjusted Trial Balance columns for the preparation of financial statements. Further, we illustrate how net income can be calculated using the Adjusted Trial Balance Columns on the spreadsheet.

Where *Accounting Education, the Classroom, and the Workplace Meet*

Real-World Examples, bringing accounting concepts to life.

College Accounting, 23e maintains its dedication to its proven step-by-step style, clear explanations, excellent examples, and a relevant approach. Practical learning aids and fine-tuned pedagogy highlight and build upon key content to reinforce the accounting principles.

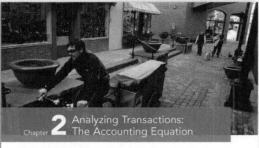

Chapter 2 — Analyzing Transactions: The Accounting Equation

LEARNING OBJECTIVES

Careful study of this chapter should enable you to:

LO1 Define the accounting elements.
LO2 Construct the accounting equation.
LO3 Analyze business transactions.
LO4 Show the effects of business transactions on the accounting equation.
LO5 Prepare and describe the purposes of a simple income statement, statement of owner's equity, and balance sheet.
LO6 Define the three basic phases of the accounting process.

At Rob's Bike Courier Service in Fort Collins, Colorado, Rob believes "less is more." His small company doesn't "have a fleet of vehicles, just some pretty cool bicycles." His mission is providing successful bike delivery service, perfect for both traditional business delivery services and residential errands. Since January of 2005, Rob's Bike Courier Service has been the alternative to gas-powered vehicle delivery. Thus, besides great rates and friendly, reliable service, Rob offers earth-friendly service.

Currently, he delivers wholesale bagels from a mid-town baker to several downtown coffee shops. He does the same for another pastry chef. Rob also picks up recycling materials, offers bike towing services, and will go to a customer's home to fix flat bike tires and make repairs.

Though his company is small, Rob still needs an accounting system to maintain records of his business transactions and to prepare financial statements. Currently, he uses Quickbooks®, an accounting program used by many small companies. In Chapters 2 through 6, we learn how to account for a service business like Rob's by using an example of a similar company: Mitchell's Campus Delivery.

■ **Chapter openers** feature small companies from throughout the United States, setting the stage for why each chapter's content is relevant and important in the business world.

YOUR PERSPECTIVE

Procurement Clerk

In many large businesses the task of keeping track of purchases and supplies is done by a *procurement clerk*. Procurement clerks compile requests for materials and prepare purchase orders. They also handle questions concerning orders as well as order changes or cancelations. They make sure the purchases arrive on time and that the items meet the required specifications. Upon receiving an order, procurement clerks prepare a receiving report or stamp the vendor's invoice to show that the item has been received. As this chapter explains, the receiving report is an important part of good internal control over purchases and payments.

■ **Your Perspective** showcases everyday student jobs, such as a procurement clerk, cashier, or lodging manager to illustrate how accounting relates to tasks that students encounter on a daily basis. The jobs highlighted in the "Your Perspective" features throughout this textbook are described in detail in the *U.S. Bureau of Labor Statistics' Occupational Outlook Handbook* (OOH). For more information about each job, type the job title in the "Search Handbook" box in the OOH website.

A BROADER VIEW

All Kinds of Businesses Need Accounting Systems

Even small businesses like those that provide guided horseback tours of the Rocky Mountains need good accounting systems. Proper records must be maintained for the cost of the horses, feed, food served, tour guides' salaries, and office expenses. Without this information, the company would not know how much to charge and whether a profit is made on these trips.

JACK HOLLINGSWORTH/CORBIS

■ **A Broader View** feature provides captivating examples of actual business events or situations that relate to each chapter's accounting topics. Students more easily retain topics when they understand the connection to the business world.

ETHICS ❤ ETHICS CASE

Electronics, Inc. is a high-volume, wholesale merchandising company. Most inventory turns over four or five times a year. The company has had 50 units of a particular brand of computers on hand for over a year. These computers have and probably will not sell unless they are discounted 60 to 70%. The accountant is carrying them on the books at cost and intends to recognize the loss when they are sold. This way, she can avoid a significant write-down in inventory on the current year's financial statements.

1. Is the accountant correct in her treatment of the inventory? Why or why not?
2. If the computers cost $1,000 each and their market value is 40% of their cost, journalize the entry necessary for the write-down.
3. In groups of three or four, make a list of reasons why inventories of electronic equipment might have to be written down.

■ **Ethics Cases** provide future business leaders with a clear understanding of the important ethical implications in modern accounting procedures and decisions. These cases highlight work-related ethical dilemmas and invite further analysis by the student independently or through classroom discussions.

Where *Accounting Education,* the *Classroom,* and the *Workplace* Meet

Superior Pedagogy, designed to keep students on track and truly help them succeed.

- **Learning Objectives** connect the chapter coverage from beginning to end.

  Problems in CengageNOWv2 are linked to the eBook, by Learning Objective, to guide students as they complete their homework.

- ■ **Excellent Examples, Clear Illustrations,** and **Step-by-Step Instructions** guide students visually through the steps of learning accounting. Heintz & Parry are well known for thorough, relevant, and visually simple examples.

- ■ **Color-Coding System** helps students understand how accounts are classified and assists them with following the key transactions presented, clarifying the impact of transactions on the accounting equation.

CHECKPOINT ✔

Complete Checkpoint-2 on page 305 to test your basic understanding of LO4.

Self-Study featuring Checkpoint Exercises offers the best in ongoing, self-review. These end-of-chapter summaries provide a strong framework for study, recap chapter content, emphasize **Key Points to Remember**, and provide **Demonstration Problems** and solutions. Checkpoint call-outs, at the end of each learning objective, direct students to the **Self-Study Test Questions and Checkpoint Exercises,** allowing students to check their understanding of each learning objective.

The Adaptive Study Plan within CengageNOWv2 allows students to focus their study on the areas they are weakest. First, students take a **quiz** to assess where they are now. An **Adaptive Study Plan** will be crafted based on their results. After working through the study plan resources, students can take **another quiz** to see how they have improved.

Where *Accounting Education*, the *Classroom*, and the *Workplace* Meet

Real-World Preparation, giving students the experience to apply accounting knowledge and prepare them for real-world success.

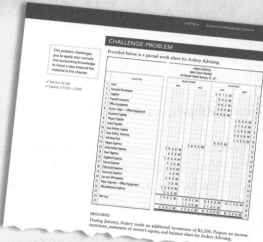

- **End-of-Chapter** material provides students the opportunity to apply chapter content to current business situations, strengthening decision-making skills, and reinforcing the ability to follow proper procedures as they progress through the course. **Mastery and Challenge Problems** give students the opportunity to apply their cumulative accounting knowledge and move a step beyond the material in the chapter, sharpening their problem solving and critical thinking skills.

- **Comprehensive Problems** tie content together, giving students a chance to apply accounting procedures, which helps them understand the processes they studied in a series of chapters (1–6, 7–15, and 16–19). As students complete the End-of-Chapter Material and Comprehensive Problems, **"Check My Work" feedback** (available in CengageNOWv2) reminds students of the things they need to consider when thinking through the problem. This creates an online instructional tool to help students reach deeper understanding.

  CENGAGENOW

CHECK LIST
☐ Managing
☐ Planning
☐ Drafting
☐ Break
☐ Revising
☐ Managing

MANAGING YOUR WRITING

You are a public accountant with many small business clients. During a recent visit to a client's business, the bookkeeper approached you with a problem. The columns of the trial balance were not equal. You helped the bookkeeper find and correct the error, but believe you should go one step further. Write a memo to all of your clients that explains the purpose of the double-entry framework, the importance of maintaining the equality of the accounting equation, the errors that might cause an inequality, and suggestions for finding the errors.

- **Managing Your Writing** teaches students how to be efficient and effective writers. Writing assignments at the end of each chapter are accompanied by a **Checklist of tips** presented in Chapter 1, serving as a reminder to students to seek the additional help as they complete their assignment.

"In addition to examining and preparing financial documentation, accountants and auditors must explain their findings. This includes preparing written reports and meeting face-to-face with organization managers and individual clients."

Bureau of Labor Statistics, U.S. Department of Labor, Occupational Outlook Handbook, Accountants and Auditors, on the Internet at https://www.bls.gov/ooh/business-and-financial/accountants-and-auditors.htm (visited June 11, 2018).

Where *Accounting Education*, the *Classroom*, and the *Workplace* Meet

Real-World Technology, **providing students the employability skills and confidence needed for workplace success.**

■ **Excel Online** Cengage and Microsoft have partnered in CNOWv2 to provide students with a uniform, authentic Excel experience. It provides instant feedback, built-in video tips, and easily accessible spreadsheet work. These features allow you to spend more time teaching college accounting applications, and less time troubleshooting Excel.

These new algorithmic activities offer pre-populated data directly in Microsoft Excel Online. Each student receives their own version of the problem to perform the necessary data calculations in Excel Online. Their work is constantly saved in Cengage cloud storage as a part of homework assignments in CNOWv2. It's easily retrievable so students can review their answers without cumbersome file management and numerous downloads/uploads.

COMPREHENSIVE PROBLEM 1:
The Accounting Cycle

Bob Night opened The General's Favorite Fishing Hole. The fishing camp is open from April through September and attracts many famous college basketball coaches during the off-season. Guests typically register for one week, arriving on Sunday afternoon and returning home the following Saturday afternoon. The registration fee includes room and board, the use of fishing boats, and professional instruction in fishing techniques. The chart of accounts for the camping operations is provided below.

The General's Favorite Fishing Hole
Chart of Accounts

This comprehensive problem is intended to serve as a mini-practice set without the source documents. As such, students should plan on about three to four hours to complete this problem.

Assets		Revenues	
101	Cash	401	Registration Fees
142	Office Supplies		
144	Food Supplies	Expenses	
145	Prepaid Insurance	511	Wages Expense
181	Fishing Boats	521	Rent Expense
181.1	Accum. Depr.—Fishing Boats	523	Office Supplies Expense
		524	Food Supplies Expense
Liabilities		525	Phone Expense
202	Accounts Payable	533	Utilities Expense
219	Wages Payable	535	Insurance Expense
		536	Postage Expense
Owner's Equity		542	Depr. Exp.—Fishing Boats
311	Bob Night, Capital		
312	Bob Night, Drawing		
313	Income Summary		

The following transactions took place during April 20--.

Apr. 1 Night invested cash in business, $90,000.
1 Paid insurance premium for six-month camping season, $9,000.
2 Paid rent for lodge and campgrounds for the month of April, $40,000.
2 Deposited registration fees, $35,000.
2 Purchased 10 fishing boats on account for $60,000. The boats have estimated useful lives of five years, at which time they will be donated to a local day camp. Arrangements were made to pay for the boats in July.
3 Purchased food supplies from Acme Super Market on account, $7,000.
5 Purchased office supplies from Gordon Office Supplies on account, $500.
7 Deposited registration fees, $38,600.
10 Purchased food supplies from Acme Super Market on account, $8,200.
10 Paid wages to fishing guides, $10,000.
14 Deposited registration fees, $30,500.

(continued)
223

■ **Comprehensive Problems are available to be solved using QuickBooks®,** as well as using the manual method.

■ **Excel templates** are provided for selected exercises and problems. To help students stay on track, certain cells are coded to display a red asterisk when an incorrect answer is entered.

> 66 Employment of accountants and auditors is expected to grow 10% from 2016 to 2026 ... with about 139,900 new jobs expected over the projections decade. 99
>
> Bureau of Labor Statistics, National Employment Matrix as of January 30, 2018.

Many of the end-of-chapter exercises and problems have "Show Me How" videos in CNOWv2. If the student is having difficulty with an assignment, the video icon indicates that additional help is available in CengageNOWv2. There, the student can click on the icon. A voice-over, PowerPoint video presentation will pop up with an explanation of how to solve a similar exercise. We think these videos are similar to a quick office visit.

Chapter 1: Introduction to Accounting

- Updated Jets.com opener.
- Updated statistics on job opportunities for Figures 1-6 and 1-7.
- Updated accounting position descriptions and salary information.

Chapter 2: Analyzing Transactions: The Accounting Equation

- Updated "A Broader View" on AT&T.
- Updated transactions for Mitchell's Campus Delivery.
- New margin note on revenue recognition.
- Updated financial statements to reflect revised transactions.

Chapter 3: The Double-Entry Framework

- Updated information on AppRiver opener.
- Updated transactions for Mitchell's Campus Delivery.
- Updated financial statements to reflect revised transactions.

Chapter 4: Journalizing and Posting Transactions

- Revised entries for Mitchell's Campus Delivery.
- Enhanced discussion on making corrections in the accounting system.

Chapter 5: Adjusting Entries and the Work Sheet

- Updated chapter opener on Floyd's 99 Barbershop.
- Enhanced discussion of the revenue recognition principle to reflect new accounting standard.
- Updated adjustments and adjusting entries for Mitchell's Campus Delivery.
- Enhanced discussion of the accrual basis of accounting.
- New work sheet illustrations in Figures 5-16, 5-17, and 5-18.

Chapter 6: Financial Statements and the Closing Process

- Updated financial statement to reflect revised transactions for Mitchell's Campus Delivery.
- Updated closing entries and post-closing trial balance for Mitchell's Campus Delivery.

Chapter 7: Accounting for Cash

- Updated chapter opener on H20Audio.
- Increased coverage of electronic banking and security issues.
- Revised "Your Perspective" regarding cashier.
- Updated "A Broader View" with new fraud information.

Chapter 8: Payroll Accounting: Employee Earnings and Deductions

- Updated chapter opener on Intechra Group.
- Updated text and end-of-chapter materials for new FIT withholding tables and Social Security maximum.
- Increased wage and salary amounts to more current pay scales.

Chapter 9: Payroll Accounting: Employer Taxes and Reports
- Emphasized IRS preference for electronic filing and payment of taxes.
- Provided full explanation and new illustration of lookback period for tax deposits.
- Provided new Form 941.

Chapter 10: Accounting for Sales and Cash Receipts
- Provided new chapter opener on Kalso Earth Shoes.
- Explained and illustrated new accounts, transactions, and adjustments for new FASB revenue standard.
- Provided new "Your Perspective" regarding Financial Clerk.

Chapter 11: Accounting for Purchases and Cash Payments
- Updated chapter opener on Innovar Environmental.
- Added description of use of voucher system for internal control over purchases and cash payments.

Chapter 12: Special Journals
- Revised chapter opener on Nutra Planet.
- Explained and illustrated alternative form of purchases journal.

Chapter 13: Accounting for Merchandise Inventory
- Updated opening story on Marsh Supermarkets.
- New margin note on returned merchandise inventory account.
- New foreshadowing of adjustment for inventory expected to be returned in the next accounting period.

Chapter 14: Adjustments for a Merchandising Business
- Revised learning objectives, LO3 and LO5.
- Revised introduction to the chapter to alert reader to the use of a new spreadsheet to assist in the adjusting process and preparation of financial statements.
- New discussion of end-of-period adjustments for customer refunds expected to be paid next period as a result of sales made in the current period under the periodic inventory system (FASB ASC 606).
- New discussion of end-of-period adjustments for the estimated cost of merchandise inventory sold this year, but expected to be returned next year under the periodic inventory system (FASB ASC 606).
- New accounts introduced: Estimated Returns Inventory and Customer Refunds Payable.
- New spreadsheet, six column format, for preparing adjustments.
- New discussion of end-of-period adjustments for customer refunds expected to be paid next period as a result of sales made in the current period under the perpetual inventory system (FASB ASC 606).
- New discussion of end-of-period adjustments for the estimated cost of merchandise inventory sold this year, but expected to be returned next year under the perpetual inventory system (FASB ASC 606).
- New, or heavily revised, end of chapter assignments that address new revenue recognition standard:
  o Demonstration Problem.
  o Multiple Choice Questions: 1, 2, 3, and 5.
  o Review Questions: 6 and 7.
  o Exercises: 14-2A/B, 14-4A/B, 14-7A/B, 14-8A/B, and 14-11A/B.
  o Problems: 14-13A/B and 14-14A/B.
  o Mastery Problem.

Chapter 15: Financial Statements and Year-End Accounting for a Merchandising Business

- New use of Adjusted Trial Balance columns in a six-column spreadsheet to prepare financial statements.
- Revised spreadsheet, financial statements, closing entries, post-closing trial balance, and discussion of reversing entries for Sunflower Cycle to include new accounts (Estimated Returns Inventory and Customer Refunds Payable) and to address new revenue recognition standard.
- New, or heavily revised, end of chapter assignments that address new revenue recognition standard:
  - o Demonstration Problem.
  - o Checkpoint Exercises: 1, 2, 3, 4, and 5.
  - o Exercises: 15-2A/B, 15-3A/B, 15-4A/B, and 15-5A/B.
  - o Problems: 15-8A/B, 15-9A/B, and 15-10A/B.
  - o Mastery Problem.

Chapter 16: Accounting for Accounts Receivable

- Revised "Your Perspective" regarding Bill and Account Collector.

Chapter 17: Accounting for Notes and Interest

- Updated chapter opener on College Boxes.
- Revised explanation of all components of promissory note.
- Revised explanation and demonstration of interest, due dates, and time line figures/illustrations of borrowing and discounting.

Chapter 18: Accounting for Long-Term Assets

- New margin note on assets that are not depreciated or amortized.
- Updated discussion of depreciation for federal income taxes to address tax reforms enacted in 2017.
- Enhanced discussion of role of "commercial substance" when determining the gain or loss on the exchange of plant assets.
- Updated "A Broader View" on buying a car.
- New, or revised, end-of-chapter assignments that address depreciation methods under the tax reforms passed in 2017:
  - o Review Questions 8 and 9.
  - o Managing Your Writing assignment.

Chapter 19: Accounting for Partnerships

- Updated "A Broader View" on PwC.
- Enhanced discussion of accounting for the admission of a new partner.
- Mastery Problem revised to reflect new discussion on admission of a new partner.

Chapter 20: Corporations: Organization and Capital Stock

- Revised chapter opener on Gotham Dream Cars.
- Added margin note on multiple classes of common stock.
- Updated "A Broader View" with new company and country information.

Chapter 21: Corporations: Taxes, Earnings, Distributions, and the Statement of Retained Earnings

- Revised chapter opener on Bamko.
- Revised text and end-of-chapter materials for new corporate income tax rate.
- Provided new illustration of the effect of stock dividends.

Chapter 22: Corporations: Bonds

- Updated chapter opener on InTouch Health.
- Revised comparison of bonds and common stock.
- Revised "A Broader View" on Horizon Lines.

Chapter 23: Statement of Cash Flows

- Updated chapter opener on Costume Craze.
- New margin note to remind students of new revenue recognition standard.
- Enhanced discussion of economic importance of cash provided from operating activities.
- New margin note to clarify impact of increases in accounts receivable and wages payable on cash from operating activities.
- New margin note to remind students that gains and losses on the early retirement of bonds were addressed in Chapter 22.
- Updated "A Broader View" providing an analysis of the differences between net income and cash from operating activities for Eli Lilly Company from 2006 to 2017.
- New margin note clarifying role of assumptions made to calculate cash received from customers.
- New margin note clarifying role of assumptions made to calculate cash paid to suppliers for merchandise.

Chapter 24: Analysis of Financial Statements

- Updated chapter opener for Skullcandy.
- Enhanced discussion of asset turnover ratio.
- "A Broader View" was revised to focus on how a similar return on assets is generated by very different businesses: IBM and Walmart.
- Enhanced discussion of limitations of financial statement analysis.

Chapter 25: Departmental Accounting

- Updated chapter opener on VIZIO.
- Provided new explanation of three types of responsibility centers, with emphasis on profit centers.
- Provided additional explanation and interpretation of use of direct operating margin in running a business.
- Revised "Your Perspective" Department Manager to create "Your Perspective" Lodging Manager.

Chapter 26: Manufacturing Accounting: The Job Order Cost System

- Updated chapter opener on Lusive Decor.
- Revised comparison of cost of goods sold section for merchandiser vs. manufacturer.
- Revised comparison of current asset section for merchandiser vs. manufacturer.

Chapter 27: Adjustments, Financial Statements, and Year-End Accounting for a Manufacturing Business

- Updated chapter opener on SRS.
- Completely revised chapter and end of chapter materials for use of 6-column spreadsheet in place of old 10-column work sheet, and application of new FASB revenue standard affecting accounts, transactions, adjustments, and financial statements.
- Updated "A Broader View" with new Boeing information.

Student Supplements and Resources

QuickBooks Data Files for Comprehensive Problems

These data sets allow you to complete the requirements of the Comprehensive Problems using QuickBooks software. Al templates can be downloaded for free from the student website located at Cengage.com.

Excel Templates

These templates are provided for selected end-of-chapter exercises and problems, designated by an icon in the text. They are designed to help you set up and work the assignment. To help you stay on track, certain cells are coded to display a red asterisk when an incorrect answer is entered. Your instructor may ask you to use the template for homework assignments. All templates can be downloaded for free from the student website located at Cengage.com.

Student Website

Now, mastering accounting concepts is easier than ever with the rich array of learning resources at the Heintz & Parry student website found at Cengage.com. Designed specifically to help you learn the most from your course and earn the grade you want, this website's interactive study center features chapter-by-chapter PowerPoint® student slides, online quizzes, flashcards, outlines, key terms, and a final exam, as well as links to accounting resources and more.

Study Guide and Working Papers

The study guide and working papers for the text assignments are provided together in one resource for your convenience. Written by the text authors to ensure accuracy and consistent quality, this resource provides chapter outlines linked to learning objectives and a set of "C" assignments that include review questions, exercises, and problems to enhance your learning experience. Students can purchase the study guide and working papers at Cengage.com.
Chapters 1–9: (ISBN: 978-1-337-91355-3)
Chapters 1–15: (ISBN: 978-1-337-91356-0)
Chapters 16–27: (ISBN: 978-1-337-91357-7)

Trey's Fast Cleaning Service Practice Set

This practice set features a sole proprietorship service business simulation. It reviews the accounting cycle and accounting for cash (appropriate for use after Chapter 7). Students can purchase this practice set through Cengage.com.

Coolspring Furniture Practice Set

Practice your accounting success, including working with payroll taxes, within this sole proprietorship merchandising business (appropriate for use after Chapter 12). Students can purchase this practice set through Cengage.com.

Using QuickBooks Accountant for Accounting

This book teaches fundamental accounting concepts and principles while developing students' proficiency with the market-leading accounting software, QuickBooks Accountant by Intuit. This well-organized and concise text teaches the technology and application of accounting skills by illustrating how accounting information is created and used. **2018 edition**: (ISBN: 978-0-357-04207-6)

Instructor Supplements

CengageNOWv2

CengageNOWv2 is a powerful course management and online homework resource that provides control and customization to optimize the student learning experience. Included are many proven resources including algorithmic activities, test bank, course management tools, reporting and assessment options, and much more.

Instructor Resource Guide

The Instructor Resource Guide is available in electronic format and contains a correlation grid with changes from the 22nd edition to the 23rd edition, enhanced chapter outlines with teaching tips, suggested in-class exercises, figure references, and homework suggestions.

Solutions Manual

The Solutions Manual is prepared by the text authors. It is available in electronic format and contains carefully verified solutions for all text assignments, including Review Questions, all Exercises and Problem sets, Challenge and Mastery problems, Comprehensive Problems 1–3, as well as suggested answers to the Ethics Cases and the Managing Your Writing exercises.

Test Bank

The Test Bank has been revised and verified and tagging standards have been added including level of difficulty, learning objectives, Bloom's Taxonomy, AICPA, ACBSP, and general business program standards (BUSPROG) to allow greater guidance in developing assessments and evaluating student progress. The Test Bank is available in electronic format on the Instructor Website.

Cognero Information Testing Software

Cengage Learning Testing powered by Cognero is a flexible, online system that allows you to author, edit, and manage test bank content from multiple Cengage Learning solutions, create multiple test versions in an instant, and deliver tests from your LMS, your classroom, or wherever you want.
(ISBN: 978-1-337-91350-8)

Study Guide and Working Papers

Written by the text authors to ensure accuracy and quality consistent with the text, the study guide and the working papers for the text assignments are provided together in one convenient resource. Students can reinforce their learning experience with chapter outlines that are linked to learning objectives and a set of "C" assignments that include review questions, exercises, and problems. The working papers are tailored to the text's end-of-chapter assignments. (Solutions for the working papers are included in the Solutions Manual. Solutions for study guide assignments are available on the Instructor Website.)
Chapters 16–27: (ISBN: 978-1-337-91357-7)
Chapters 1–15: (ISBN: 978-1-337-91356-0)
Chapters 1–9: (ISBN: 978-1-337-91355-3)

Study Guide Solutions

Solutions to all Study Guide set "C" assignments are available on the Instructor Website.

Trey's Fast Cleaning Service Practice Set

Put your students to work within a sole proprietorship business in this dynamic simulation for use after text Chapter 7. Students will review the basics of accrual accounting, including the accounting cycle and accounting for cash.

Coolspring Furniture Practice Set

This practice set features a sole proprietorship merchandising business and can be completed using either the general journal alone or special journals. The practice set is appropriate for use after Chapter 12 of the text and covers the topic of payroll.

Instructor Website

Instructors can log into the password-protected website through http://login.cengage.com. This site places all the teaching resources in one place. It includes the Instructor's Resource Guide, PowerPoint® lecture presentations, Test Bank in PDF format, Solutions to the spreadsheet templates, Study Guide Solutions in Word format, and the Solutions Manual in Word format.

DEDICATION

We are grateful to our wives, Celia Heintz and Jane Parry, and our children, Andrea Heintz Tangari, John Heintz, Jessica Parry, and Mitch Parry, for their love, support, and assistance during the preparation of the 23rd edition. We especially want to thank Jessica Parry and Chris Williams for granting permission to use Professor Parry's grandson's name, Mitchell Williams throughout the first six chapters.

ACKNOWLEDGEMENTS

We thank the following individuals for their helpful contributions to this revision of *College Accounting*.

Abe Qastin, *Lakeland College*

Adam Baker, *Minnesota State Community and Technical College*

Alex Gialanella, *Manhattanville College*

Alyson Crow, *Temple College*

Amanda Hardin, *Mississippi Delta Community College*

Amy Chataginer, *Mississippi Gulf Coast Community College*

Amy Smith, *Pearl River Community College*

Anna Boulware, *St. Charles Community College*

Anne Bikofsky, *College of Westchester*

Anne Borsellino, *McLennan Community College*

Barbara L. Squires, *Corning Community College*

Barbara Prince, *Anoka Ramsey Community College, Cambridge*

Barbara Squires, *Corning Community College*

Belinda Chastain, *Spartanburg Community College*

Beth Berry, *Glendale Community College*

Bhaskar Singh, *College of Menominee Nation*

Bob Urell, *Irvine Valley College*

Bonnie Hopson, *Athens Technical College*

Brad Davis, *Santa Rosa Junior College*

Brian Fink, *Danville Area Community College*

Britt Blackwell, *Central Community College*

Carol Ann Kirby, *Portland Community College*

Carol Ottaway, *Chemeketa Community College*

Cheryl Corke, *Genesee Community College*

Christy Chauvin, *Delgado Community College*

Chuck Smith, *Iowa Western Community College*

Cynthia E. Moody-Paige, *Erwin Technical Center*

Dale Walker, *Arkansas State University—Little Rock Air Force Base*

Daniel J. Kerch, *Pennsylvania Highlands Community College*

Dawn Stevens, *Northwest Mississippi Community College*

Deanna Knight, *Daytona State College*

Debbie Adkins, *University of Phoenix*

Diana Sullivan, *Portland Community College*

Dianne Henline, *Texarkana College*

Dmitriy Kalyagin, *Chabot College*

Dominique Svarc, *Harper College*

Don Williams, *Feather River College*

Eilene LePelley, *Lane Community College*

Ellen Orr, *Seminole State College of Florida*

Eric Stadnik, *Santa Rosa Junior College*

Eugene Schneider, *ASA Institute of Business and Technology*

George Holder, *Cloud County Community College*

Glenn Pate, *Palm Beach State College*

Gloria Sanchez, *Mt. San Jacinto College*

Greg Lauer, *North Iowa Area Community College*

H. Gin Chong, *Prairie View A&M University*

Jackie Marshall, *Ohio Business College*

James M. Emig, *Villanova University*

Jan Hogue, *Laurel Technical Institute*

Jean Rodgers, *Wenatchee Valley College*

Jeanette Milius, *Iowa Western Community College*

Jeff Hsu, *St. Louis Community College at Meramec*

Jennifer Garcia, *Blinn College*

Jim Bauer, *Archbishop Moeller High School*

Jody Dunaway, *Herzing University*

Joe Adamo, *Cazenovia College*

John Allen Fortner, *Daytona State College*

John Fasler, *Whatcom Community College*

John Fortner, *Daytona State College*

John Nader, *Davenport University*

John Seilo, *Orange Coast College*

Johnny Howard, *Arkansas State University—Mountain Home*

Jolena Grande, *Cypress College*

Joseph M. Nicassio, *Westmoreland County Community College*

Judith Toland, *Bucks County Community College*

Judy Boozer, *Lane Community College*

Judy Hurtt, *East Central Community College*

Julia Angel, *North Arkansas College*

June Hanson, *Upper Iowa University*

Junnae Landry, *Pratt Community College*

Karen Alexander, *College of The Albemarle*

Karen M. Kydd, *Husson University*

Karen Welch, *Tennessee College of Applied Technology—Jackson*

Kathleen Fratianne, *Blackhawk Technical College*

Kathleen Smith, *Tennessee College of Applied Technology*

Kathy Beith, *Milan Institute*

Kathy Bowen, *Murray State College*

Keith Blankenship, *South College-Asheville*

Kerry Stager, *Lake Area Technical Institute*

Kim Anderson, *Elgin Community College*

Kim Hurt, *Central Community College*

Kim Potts, *North Arkansas College*

Kippi Harraid, *Trinity Valley Community College*

Kirk Canzano, *Long Beach City College*

La Vonda Ramey, *Schoolcraft College*

Laurie Gambrell, *Copiah-Lincoln Community College*

Lawrence A. Roman, *Cuyahoga Community College*

Leonia Houston, *Holmes Community College*

Leslie Schmidt, *Front Range Community College*

Linda Arndt, *LCO College*

Lingling Zhang, *American River College*

Lisa Briggs, *Columbus State Community College*

Lisa Nash, *Vincennes University*

Lisa Novak, *Mott Community College*

Lori Grady, *Bucks County Community College*

Lorna Hofer, *Lake Area Technical Institute*

Luis Plascencia, *Harold Washington College*

M. Jeff Quinlan, *Madison Area Technical College*

Mabel Machin, *Valencia College*

Marcia Shulman, *New York University*

Marilyn St. Clair, *Weatherford College*

Marina Grau, *Houston Community College*

Mark Gale, *Cosumnes River College*

Mark Wells, *Big Sandy Community and Technical College*

Meg Costello Lambert, *Oakland Community College-Auburn Hills Campus*

Melvin Williams, *College of the Mainland*

Michael Dole, *Marquette University*

Michele Wehrle, *Community College of Allegheny County*

Mike Belleman, *St Clair County Community College*

Mike Boren, *Tooele Applied Technology College*

Molly McFadden-May, *Tulsa Community College—Metro*

Monica Quattlebaum, *Phillips Community College of the University of Arkansas*

Morgan Rockett, *Moberly Area Community College*

Nancy Lee Howard, *Mt. Hood Community College*

Nelly Cintron Lorenzo, *Valencia College-West Campus*

Norma Cerpa, *Custom Training Solutions*

Nova Randolph, *Shawnee Community College*

Pam Perry, *Hinds Community College*

Patricia Worsham, *Norco College*

Patrick Borja, *Citrus College*

Perry Sellers, *Lone Star College System*

R. Stephen Holman, *Elizabethtown Community and Technical College*

Richard J. Pettit, *Mountain View College*

Rick Street, *Spokane Community College*

Robert Brooks, *San Bernardino Valley College*

Robert Derstine, *West Chester University*

Robin Fuller, *Mississippi Gulf Coast Community College*

Roger McMillian, *Mineral Area College*

Ronald Edward Camp, *Trinity Valley Community College*

Ronald Pearson, *Bay College*

Rosemary C. Garcia, *New Mexico State University, Doña Ana Community College*

Rosemary Nurre, *College Of San Mateo*

Ruth Gregory, *East Central Community College*

Sandra Sturdy, *Bay College*

Scott Birk, *Portland Community College*

Scott Wallace, *Blue Mountain Community College*

Sharon R. Morgan, *Western Nevada College*

Shawn Abbott, *College of the Siskiyous*

Sherry Laskie, *Milan Institute*

Shirley A. Montagne, *Community College of Vermont*

Sonora White, *Caddo Kiowa Technology Center*

Spencer Miller, *Eastern Idaho Technical College*

Stella Sorovigas, *Lansing Community College*

Stephanie Cox, *Louisiana Delta Community College*

Steven Ernest, *Baton Rouge Community College*

Sue Sandblom, *Scottsdale Community College*

Sue Savino, *Copiah Lincoln Community College*

Sueann Hely, *West Kentucky Community and Technical College*

Susan Davis, *Green River Community College*

Susan Greene, *Cloud County Community College*

Susan Mundy, *City University of Seattle*

Tatyana Pashnyak, *Bainbridge State College*

Teresa Worthy, *Gaston College*

Therese Rice, *North Hennepin Community College*

Thomas Gross, *Herzing University*

Tilda A. Woody, *Navajo Technical University*

Tim Green, *North Georgia Technical College*

Tim Whited, *American National University*

Tom Snare, *South Hills School of Business and Technology*

Toni Hartley, *Laurel Business Institute*

Tricia Popowsky, *Redlands Community College*

Tynia Kessler, *Lake Land College*

Vickie Boeder, *Madison Area Technical College—Watertown*

Vicky Lassiter, *Wayne Community College*

Wayne Corlis, *Mid Michigan Community College*

Wendy Eismont, *South Hills School of Business and Technology*

Whit Hunt, *South Plains College*

Special recognition goes to the following supplemental preparers for their revision work on the instructor and student materials:

Mark D. Sears

Alice Sineath, *Forsyth Technical Community College*

Domenic Tavella, *Carlow University*

We would like to thank the following individuals for their detailed verification of the homework:

Robin Browning

Alice Sineath, *Forsyth Technical Community College*

Erin Dischler, *Milwaukee Area Technical College*

Domenic Tavella, *Carlow University*

Brenda McVey, *Green River Community College*

We are honored to serve as the authors of the all-time and current best-selling college accounting text. As has been true for almost three decades, we are delighted with the editorial and marketing support provided by Cengage. Without their support and the constructive comments and suggestions made by our loyal friends using our text, this success would not have been possible. We are anxious to receive your comments on this edition, because we want to make the next one even better.

James A. Heintz
jheintz@ku.edu

Rob Parry
parry@indiana.edu

BRIEF CONTENTS

CONTENTS

Part ① Accounting for a Service Business

Part ② Accounting for Cash and Payroll

CHAPTER **7**

Accounting for Cash   231

CHAPTER **8**

Payroll Accounting: Employee Earnings and Deductions   282

Part ③ Accounting for a Merchandising Business

CHAPTER **14**

Adjustments for a Merchandising Business   525

CHAPTER **15**

Financial Statements and Year-End Accounting for a Merchandising Business   566

Part 4 Specialized Accounting Procedures for Merchandising Businesses and Partnerships

CHAPTER 19
Accounting for Partnerships 728

Part 5 — Accounting for Corporations and Manufacturing Businesses

CHAPTER 20
Corporations: Organization and Capital Stock 779

CHAPTER **27**

Adjustments, Financial Statements, and Year-End Accounting for a Manufacturing Business 1059

Index 1104

Module: Accounting for a Professional Service Business: The Combination Journal. *Module available online only at Cengage.com*

1 Accounting for a Service Business

Add some color to your learning!

Throughout the text, you will be introduced to many important terms and types of accounts. To help you learn the different terms and types of accounts, we have coded many of them using the following color key in Part 1:

Assets Contra-Assets Liabilities Capital Drawing Revenues Expenses Income Summary (Net Income/Net Loss)

Chapter **1** Introduction to Accounting

Need a private jet to get away for the weekend, attend a business meeting, or visit Mom? Call Jets.com. Established in 1999, Jets.com serves as a broker for private jet services. Call or go online, and its technology will automatically send your trip request/itinerary to a network of approved operators who will locate available aircraft. Operators will competitively bid for your business, resulting in significant savings and increased aircraft options for you.

In addition to a system that links customers with private jet service, Jets.com needs a system to account for its business transactions. Thus, it employs accounting professionals who understand the accounting process and generally accepted accounting principles.

Welcome to the world of accounting. We are delighted that you have decided to join us. A solid foundation in accounting concepts and techniques will serve you well. This is true whether you accept a professional position in accounting, work for or own a business, or simply seek a better understanding of your personal finances.

Oh, and what does it cost to take a private jet to the Super Bowl? Rates run from $5,500 to $15,000 per hour on one of the busiest weekends of the year.

LEARNING OBJECTIVES

Careful study of this chapter should enable you to:

LO1 Describe the purpose of accounting.

LO2 Describe the accounting process.

LO3 Define GAAP and describe the process used by FASB to develop these principles.

LO4 Define three types of business ownership structures.

LO5 Classify different types of businesses by activities.

LO6 Identify career opportunities in accounting.

VIKTOR KOCHETKOV/SHUTTERSTOCK.COM

3

Accounting is the language of business. You must learn this language to understand the impact of economic events on a specific company. Common, everyday terms have very precise meanings when used in accounting. For example, you have probably heard terms like asset, liability, revenue, expense, and net income. Take a moment to jot down how you would define each of these terms. After reading and studying Chapter 2, compare your definitions with those developed in this text. This comparison will show whether you can trust your current understanding of accounting terms. Whether you intend to pursue a career in accounting or simply wish to understand the impact of business transactions, you need a clear understanding of this language.

| LO1 | The Purpose of Accounting |

Describe the purpose of accounting.

The purpose of accounting is to provide financial information about the current operations and financial condition of a business to individuals, agencies, and organizations. As shown in Figure 1-1, owners, managers, creditors, and government agencies all need accounting information. Other users of accounting information include customers, clients, labor unions, stock exchanges, and financial analysts.

FIGURE 1-1 Users of Accounting Information

USER	INFORMATION NEEDED	DECISIONS MADE BY USERS
Owners—Present and future	Company's profitability and current financial condition.	If business is good, owners may consider making additional investments for growth. If business is poor, they may want to talk to management to find out why and may consider closing the business.
Managers—May or may not own business	Detailed measures of business performance.	Managers need to make operating decisions. How much and what kinds of inventory should be carried? Is business strong enough to support higher wages for employees?
Creditors—Present and future	Company's profitability, debt outstanding, and assets that could be used to secure debt.	Should a loan be granted to this business? If so, what amount of debt can the business support, and what interest rate should be charged?
Government Agencies—National, state, and local	Company's profitability, cash flows, and overall financial condition.	The IRS enforces U.S. tax laws to determine how much income tax the business must pay. Local governments may be willing to adjust property taxes paid by the business to encourage it to stay in town.

| LO2 | The Accounting Process |

Describe the accounting process.

Accounting is a system of gathering financial information about a business and reporting this information to users. The six major steps of the accounting process are analyzing, recording, classifying, summarizing, reporting, and interpreting (Figure 1-2). Computers are often used in the recording, classifying, summarizing, and reporting steps. Whether or not computers are used, the accounting concepts and techniques are the same. Information entered into the computer system must reflect a proper application of these concepts. Otherwise, the output will be meaningless.

FIGURE 1-2   The Accounting Process

Analyzing → Recording → Classifying → Summarizing → Reporting → Interpreting

- **Analyzing** is looking at events that have taken place and thinking about how they affect the business. This first step in the accounting process usually occurs when the business receives some type of information, such as a bill, that needs to be properly entered into the business's records. This first step also involves deciding if the piece of information should result in an accounting entry or not.

- **Recording** is entering financial information about events into the accounting system. Although this can be done with paper and pencil, most businesses use computers to perform routine record-keeping operations.

- **Classifying** is sorting and grouping similar items together rather than merely keeping a simple, diary-like record of numerous events.

- **Summarizing** is the aggregation of many similar events to provide information that is easy to understand. For example, a firm may buy and sell baseballs during the year. Summarizing provides information on the total baseballs bought and sold and the change in the number of baseballs held from the beginning to the end of the period.

- **Reporting** is telling the results. In accounting, it is common to use tables of numbers to report results.

- **Interpreting** is deciding the meaning and importance of the information in various reports. This may include ratio analysis to help explain how pieces of information relate to one another.

LO3   Generally Accepted Accounting Principles (GAAP)

Define GAAP and describe the process used by FASB to develop these principles.

Soon after the stock market crash of 1929, the federal government established the Securities and Exchange Commission (SEC). The purpose of this government agency is to help develop standards for reporting financial information to stockholders. The SEC currently has authority over companies publicly traded on the major stock exchanges (New York and NASDAQ). It has the power to require these firms to follow certain rules when preparing their financial statements. These rules are referred to as generally accepted accounting principles (GAAP).

Rather than developing GAAP on its own, the SEC encouraged the creation of a private standard-setting body. It did so because it believed the private sector had better access to the resources and talent necessary to develop these standards. Since 1973, the Financial Accounting Standards Board (FASB) has filled this role. In developing accounting standards, FASB follows a specific process and relies on the advice of many organizations. When an accounting issue is identified, the following steps are followed:

1. The issue is placed on FASB's agenda. This lets everyone know that the Board plans to develop a standard addressing this issue.

2. After researching an issue, FASB issues a Preliminary Views document. This document identifies the pros and cons of various accounting treatments for an event and invites others to comment.

3. To gather additional views on the issue, the Board will often hold public hearings around the country. Interested parties are invited to express their opinions at these hearings.

SOURCE: FINANCIAL ACCOUNTING STANDARDS BOARD

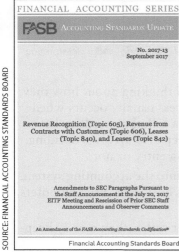

4. Following these hearings, the Board issues an **Exposure Draft.** This document explains the rules that FASB believes firms should follow in accounting for this event.

5. After considering feedback on the Exposure Draft, the Board issues a final **Accounting Standards Update** which amends the **Financial Accounting Standards Board Accounting Standards Codification.** This Codification is an electronic database that provides one authoritative source for the standards that must be followed by U.S. companies.

Throughout this process, many parties participate by testifying at public hearings or by sending letters to the Board explaining why they agree or disagree with the proposed standard. These parties include the American Institute of Certified Public Accountants (AICPA), the American Accounting Association (AAA), the Institute of Management Accountants (IMA), Financial Executives International (FEI), corporate executives and accountants, representatives from the investment community, analysts, bankers, industry associations, and the SEC and other government agencies. Clearly, FASB considers the views of a wide range of parties. By doing so, it maximizes the likelihood of developing and gaining acceptance of the most appropriate accounting and disclosure requirements.

The International Accounting Standards Board (IASB) issues accounting standards followed by many firms in countries outside the United States. These are called International Financial Reporting Standards (IFRS). In recent years, the IASB and FASB have worked together to try to minimize the differences in these standards. These standards may eventually converge into one set of standards used around the world.

LO4   Three Types of Ownership Structures

Define three types of business ownership structures.

One or more persons may own a business. Businesses are classified according to who owns them and the specific way they are organized. Three types of ownership structures are (1) sole proprietorship, (2) partnership, and (3) corporation (Figure 1-3). Accountants provide information to owners of all three types of ownership structures.

FIGURE 1-3 Types of Ownership Structures—Advantages and Disadvantages

TYPES OF OWNERSHIP STRUCTURES		
Sole Proprietorship	**Partnership**	**Corporation**
• One owner • Owner assumes all risk • Owner makes all decisions	• Two or more partners • Partners share risks • Partners may disagree on how to run business	• Stockholders • Stockholders have limited risk • Stockholders may have little influence on business decisions

Most businesses in the United States operate as sole proprietorships or partnerships. However, corporations earn the highest amount of revenue.

Sole Proprietorship

A **sole proprietorship** is owned by one person. The owner is usually called a proprietor. The proprietor often manages the business. The owner assumes all risks for the business, and personal assets can be taken to pay creditors. The advantage of a sole proprietorship is that the owner can make all decisions.

Partnership

A partnership is owned by more than one person. One or more partners may manage the business. Like proprietors, partners assume the risks for the business, and their assets may be taken to pay creditors. An advantage of a partnership is that owners share risks and decision making. A disadvantage is that partners may disagree about the best way to run the business.

Corporation

The largest corporations in the United States are known as the "Fortune 500."

A corporation is owned by stockholders (or shareholders). Corporations may have many owners, and they usually employ professional managers. The owners' risk is usually limited to their initial investment, and they often have very little influence on the business decisions.

LO5	Types of Businesses

Classify different types of businesses by activities.

Businesses are classified according to the type of service or product provided. Some businesses provide a service. Others sell a product. A business that provides a service is called a service business. A business that buys a product from another business to sell to customers is called a merchandising business. A business that makes a product to sell is called a manufacturing business. You will learn about all three types of businesses in this book. Figure 1-4 lists examples of types of businesses organized by activity.

FIGURE 1-4 Types and Examples of Businesses Organized by Activities

SERVICE	MERCHANDISING	MANUFACTURING
Travel Agency	Department Store	Automobile Manufacturer
Computer Consultant	Pharmacy	Furniture Maker
Physician	Grocery Store	Toy Factory

A BROADER VIEW

All Kinds of Businesses Need Accounting Systems

Even small businesses like those that provide guided horseback tours of the Rocky Mountains need good accounting systems. Proper records must be maintained for the cost of the horses, feed, food served, tour guides' salaries, and office expenses. Without this information, the company would not know how much to charge and whether a profit is made on these trips.

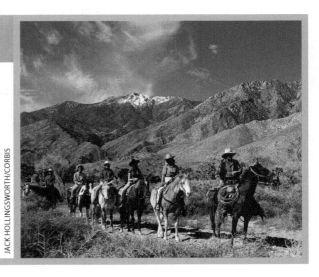

JACK HOLLINGSWORTH/CORBIS

LO6	**Career Opportunities in Accounting**

Identify career opportunities in accounting.

Accounting offers many career opportunities. The positions described below require varying amounts of education, experience, and technological skill.

Accounting Clerks

Businesses with large quantities of accounting tasks to perform daily often employ accounting clerks to record, sort, and file accounting information. Often, accounting clerks will specialize in cash, payroll, accounts receivable, accounts payable, inventory, or purchases. As a result, they are involved with only a small portion of the total accounting responsibilities for the firm. Accounting clerks usually have at least one year of accounting education.

Bookkeepers and Para-Accountants

Bookkeepers generally supervise the work of accounting clerks, help with daily accounting work, and summarize accounting information. In small-to-medium-sized businesses, the bookkeeper may also help managers and owners interpret the accounting information. Bookkeepers usually have one to two years of accounting education and experience as an accounting clerk.

Para-accountants provide many accounting, auditing, or tax services under the direct supervision of an accountant. A typical para-accountant has a two-year degree or significant accounting and bookkeeping experience.

Accountants

The difference between accountants and bookkeepers is not always clear, particularly in smaller companies where bookkeepers also help interpret the accounting information. In large companies, the distinction is clearer. Bookkeepers focus on the processing of accounting data. Accountants design the accounting information system and focus on analyzing and interpreting information. They also look for important trends in the data and study the impact of alternative decisions.

Most accountants enter the field with a college degree in accounting. In fact, since many states require 150 credit hours to sit for the CPA exam, many students are also earning a master's degree in accounting before entering the profession. Accountants are employed in public accounting, private (managerial) accounting, and governmental and not-for-profit accounting (Figure 1-5).

FIGURE 1-5 Accounting Careers

ACCOUNTING CAREERS		
Public Accounting • Auditing • Taxation • Management Advisory Services	**Private Accounting** • Accounting Information Systems • Financial Accounting • Cost Accounting • Budgeting • Tax Accounting • Internal Auditing	**Governmental and Not-for-Profit Accounting**

Public Accounting

Public accountants offer services in much the same way as doctors and lawyers. The public accountant can achieve professional recognition as a Certified Public Accountant (CPA). This is done by meeting certain educational and experience requirements as determined by each state and passing a uniform examination prepared by the American Institute of Certified Public Accountants.

Many CPAs work alone, while others work for local, regional, national, or international accounting firms that vary in scope and size. The largest public accounting firms in the United States are known as the "Big Four." They are Deloitte, Ernst & Young, KPMG, and PricewaterhouseCoopers.

Services offered by public accountants are listed below.

- Auditing. Auditing involves the application of standard review and testing procedures to be certain that proper accounting policies and practices have been followed. The purpose of the audit is to provide an independent opinion that the financial information about a business is fairly presented in a manner consistent with generally accepted accounting principles.
- Taxation. Tax specialists advise on tax planning, prepare tax returns, and represent clients before governmental agencies such as the Internal Revenue Service.
- Management Advisory Services. Given the financial training and business experience of public accountants, many businesses seek their advice on a wide variety of managerial issues. Often, accounting firms are involved in designing computerized accounting systems.
- Forensic Accounting. Forensic accounting is a rapidly growing segment of accounting practice. It includes fraud detection, fraud prevention, litigation support, business valuations, expert witness services, and other investigative activities. Public accounting firms offer forensic accounting services, but forensic accountants also work for insurance companies, banks, law enforcement agencies, and other organizations. By meeting certain requirements, and passing the Certified Fraud Examiner exam, a forensic accountant may earn a Certified Fraud Examiner (CFE) designation.

In 2002, the Sarbanes-Oxley Act (SOX) was passed by Congress to help improve reporting practices of public companies. The act was in response to accounting scandals at firms like Enron, WorldCom, Cendant, Xerox, and others. Key provisions of SOX are listed below.

- The Public Company Accounting Oversight Board (PCAOB) was created to enforce SOX rules and regulations. The PCAOB also has authority to set auditing standards for public company audits and to perform inspections of auditing firms.
- For the largest companies, external auditors are required to report on the effectiveness of a public company's accounting procedures.
- Auditing firms are prohibited from offering many nonaudit services to their public audit clients.
- Auditing firms must rotate lead audit partners off audit engagements every five years.
- The CEO and CFO must personally certify that the financial statements are accurate.

It is difficult to guarantee that information provided in financial statements is always complete and accurate. These measures are a step in the right direction. If our economy and financial markets are to function properly, information provided in financial statements must be reliable.

Private (Managerial) Accounting

Many accountants are employees of private business firms. The controller oversees the entire accounting process and is the principal accounting officer of the company. Private or managerial accountants perform a wide variety of services for the business. These services are listed below.

- Accounting Information Systems. Accountants in this area design and implement manual and computerized accounting systems.

- Financial Accounting. Based on the accounting data prepared by the bookkeepers and accounting clerks, accountants prepare various reports and financial statements and help in analyzing operating, investing, and financing decisions.

- Cost Accounting. The cost of producing specific products or providing services must be measured. Further analysis is also done to determine whether the products are produced and services are provided in the most cost-effective manner.

- Budgeting. In the budgeting process, accountants help managers develop a financial plan.

- Tax Accounting. Instead of hiring a public accountant, a company may have its own accountants. They focus on tax planning, preparation of tax returns, and dealing with the Internal Revenue Service and other governmental agencies.

- Internal Auditing. Internal auditors review the operating and accounting control procedures adopted by management to make sure the controls are adequate and are being followed. They also monitor the accuracy and timeliness of the reports provided to management and to external parties.

A managerial accountant can achieve professional status as a Certified Management Accountant (CMA). This is done by passing a uniform examination offered by the Institute of Management Accountants. An internal auditor can achieve professional recognition as a Certified Internal Auditor (CIA) by passing the uniform examination offered by the Institute of Internal Auditors.

Governmental and Not-for-Profit Accounting

Thousands of governmental and not-for-profit organizations (states, cities, schools, churches, and hospitals) gather and report financial information. These organizations employ a large number of accountants. Since these entities are not profit oriented, the rules are somewhat different for governmental and not-for-profit organizations. However, many accounting procedures are similar to those found in profit-seeking enterprises.

Job Opportunities

Job growth in some areas will be much greater than in others. Employment advertisements often indicate that accountants and accounting clerks are expected to have computer skills. Computer skills definitely increase the opportunities available to you in your career. Almost every business needs accountants, accounting clerks, and bookkeepers. Figure 1-6 shows the expected growth for different industry sectors. Notice that growth will be greatest in health care services. Chapters 2 through 9 introduce accounting skills that you will need to work in a service business, like health care. Chapter 10 begins the discussion of merchandising businesses. Accounting for manufacturing businesses is addressed in the last chapters of the book.

Figure 1-7 shows an overall increase in projected demand for accounting skills. Demand for billing and posting clerks, accountants and auditors, and budget analysts is expected to increase by 14.1%, 10.0%, and 6.5% respectively from 2016 to 2026. Demand for bookkeepers, accounting, and auditing clerks is projected to dip by 1.5%.

Figure 1-8 provides various job descriptions in the accounting profession along with the range of salaries paid.

FIGURE 1-6 Expected Job Growth by Industry 2016–2026 (in thousands)

3,998.30 ♦♦♦
Health Care and Social Assistance

2,159.70 ♦♦♦♦♦♦♦♦♦♦♦♦♦♦♦♦♦♦♦♦♦♦♦♦♦
Professional and Business Services

1,319.00 ♦♦♦♦♦♦♦♦♦♦♦♦♦♦♦♦
Leisure and Hospitality

864.70 ♦♦♦♦♦♦♦♦♦♦
Construction

788.70 ♦♦♦♦♦♦♦♦♦
State and Local Government

506.50 ♦♦♦♦♦♦
Educational Services

479.80 ♦♦♦♦♦
Financial Activities

412.30 ♦♦♦♦♦
Retail Trade

364.30 ♦♦♦♦
Transportation and Warehousing

145.80 ♦♦
Wholesale Trade

90.80 ♦
Mining

The growth in the number of new jobs from 2016 to 2026 will vary according to industry. As shown above, health care industries are expected to account for a large portion of the new jobs projected through 2026. Other industries are shown for comparison purposes. Note that professional and business services also appear to provide good opportunities. Total employment for all industry sectors is projected to grow by 7.4% over the decade, resulting in 11.5 million new jobs.

Source: Bureau of Labor Statistics News Release, January 30, 2018: Employment Projections—2016–2026. *(https://www.bls.gov/news.release/pdf/ecopro.pdf)*

FIGURE 1-7 Expected Demand

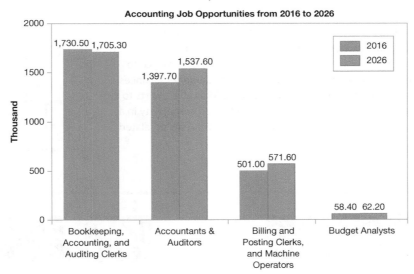

Accounting Job Opportunities from 2016 to 2026

The highest number of jobs available is expected to be for bookkeepers, accounting and auditing clerks, though a 1.5 percent dip in these jobs over the decade is projected. As shown below, jobs for accountants and auditors are expected to increase by 10 percent. The projected growth, or decline, for each area from 2016 to 2026 is shown below.

	Thousands	Percentage
Accountants and auditors	139.9	10.0%
Budget analysts	3.8	6.5%
Bookkeeping, accounting, and auditing clerks	−25.2	−1.5%
Billing and posting clerks, and machine operators	70.6	14.1%

Source: Bureau of Labor Statistics, National Employment Matrix as of January 30, 2018. *(https://www.bls.gov/emp/ep_table_102.htm)*

FIGURE 1-8 Accounting Positions according to Salary.com, 2018

Accounting Clerk I

Performs routine accounting activities such as maintenance of the general ledger, preparation of various accounting statements and financial reports. Posts journal entries and verifies billings, invoices and checks. Assists in completing moderately complex calculations. Reconciles accounts and bank statements. Has a basic understanding of bookkeeping and accounting principles. Is proficient with spreadsheets and other software tools. Typically requires a high school diploma. Typically reports to a supervisor or manager. Possesses a moderate understanding of general aspects of the job. Works under the close direction of senior personnel in the functional area. May require 0-1 year of general work experience.

Bookkeeper

Maintains and records a complete and systematic set of business transactions. Balances ledgers, reconciles accounts, and prepares reports to show receipts, expenditures, accounts receivable, and payable. Follows bookkeeping procedures established by the organization. May require an associate's degree or its equivalent. Typically reports to a supervisor or a manager. Gaining or has attained full proficiency in a specific area of discipline. Works under moderate supervision. Typically requires 1-3 years of related experience.

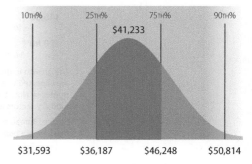

Budet Analyst I

Analyzes an organization's accounting records to determine financial resources required. Plans, analyzes, and prepares the organization's budget activities according to previous budget figures and estimated revenue. Makes recommendations for budget allocations to ensure conformance to budgetary limits. Keeps track of expenses, inventories, and budget balances. Prepares financial reports. Requires a bachelor's degree. Typically reports to a supervisor or manager. Works on projects/matters of limited complexity in a support role. Work is closely managed. Typically requires 0-2 years of related experience.

YOUR PERSPECTIVE

Industrial Engineering Technician

Accounting is the language of business and the eyes and ears of management. No matter the job, it likely provides accounting information that management uses to make important operating decisions. Even a technology-oriented job, such as *industrial engineering technician*, involves accounting. These technicians assist engineers in devising systems that make products or provide services. They also perform duties that provide accounting information such as analyzing production costs and managing supply chain costs to control inventory.

Accounts Payable Manager

Manages all activities in the accounts payable function. Ensures timely payments of vendor invoices and expense vouchers and maintains accurate records and control reports. Reviews applicable accounting reports and accounts payable register to ensure accuracy. Typically requires a bachelor's degree. Typically reports to a head of a unit/department. Manages subordinate staff in the day-to-day performance of their jobs. True first level manager. Ensures that project/department milestones/goals are met and adhering to approved budgets. Has full authority for personnel actions. Extensive knowledge of department processes. Typically requires 5 years experience in the related area as an individual contributor. 1 to 3 years supervisory experience may be required.

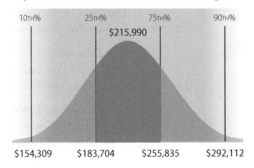

Accounts Payable manager – *U.S. National Averages*

Top Audit Executive

Oversees all aspects of an organization's auditing function. Plans and directs all accounting and financial data. Designs internal auditing procedures and ensures they are followed. Monitors procedures for effectiveness and provides recommendations for improvement. Requires a bachelor's degree. Typically reports to top management. Manages a business unit, division, or corporate function with major organizational impact. Establishes overall direction and strategic initiatives for the given major function or line of business. Has acquired the business acumen and leadership experience to become a top function or division head.

Top Audit Executive – *U.S. National Averages*

Controller

Leads and directs an organization's accounting functions. Establishes and maintains the organization's overall accounting systems, procedures, and policies. Directs all analysis and reporting of financial information including budgets, planning, and required filings and reports. Presents findings and recommendations to management. Requires a bachelor's degree of accounting or finance. Typically reports to Chief Financial Officer (CFO). Typically requires CPA. Manages a departmental function within a broader corporate function. Develops major goals to support broad functional objectives. Approves policies developed within various sub-functions and departments. Comprehensive knowledge of the overall departmental function. Typically requires 8+ years of managerial experience.

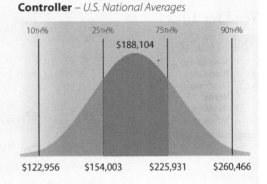

Controller – *U.S. National Averages*

Source: Salary.com, March 2018.

Managing Your Writing

Regardless of the type of career you desire, writing skills are important in business and your personal life. Becoming a good writer requires practice and a strategy for the process used to prepare memos, letters, and other documents. On pages 14 and 15, Ken Davis, *Professor Emeritus of English at Indiana University*, offers an excellent approach to managing your writing. Take a moment to read Ken's tips. Then, practice his approach by completing the writing assignments as you finish each chapter.

From: Ken Davis
Subject: Managing Your Writing
To: Accounting Students

Here's a secret: the business writing that you and I do—the writing that gets the world's work done—requires no special gift. It can be managed, like any other business process.

Managing writing is largely a matter of managing time. Writing is a process, and like any process it can be done efficiently or inefficiently. Unfortunately, most of us are pretty inefficient writers. That's because we try to get each word, each sentence, right the first time. Given a letter to write, we begin with the first sentence. We think about that sentence, write it, revise it, even check its spelling, before going on to the second sentence. In an hour of writing, we might spend 45 or 50 minutes doing this kind of detailed drafting. We spend only a few minutes on overall planning at the beginning and only a few minutes on overall revising at the end.

That approach to writing is like building a house by starting with the front door: planning, building, finishing—even washing the windows—before doing anything with the rest of the house. No wonder most of us have so much trouble writing.

Efficient, effective writers take better charge of their writing time. They *manage* their writing. Like building contractors, they spend time planning before they start construction. Once construction has started, they don't try to do all of the finishing touches as they go.

As the following illustration shows, many good writers break their writing process into three main stages: planning, drafting, and revising. They spend more time at the first and third stages than at the second. They also build in some "management" time at the beginning and the end, and some break time in the middle. To manage *your* writing time, try the following steps.

To Do List

CHECK LIST

☐ **Managing**
☐ **Planning**
☐ **Drafting**
☐ **Break**
☐ **Revising**
☐ **Managing**

At the **Managing Stage** *(perhaps two or three minutes for a one-hour writing job):*

Remind yourself that writing *can* be managed and that it's largely a matter of managing time. Plan your next hour.

At the **Planning Stage** *(perhaps 20 minutes out of the hour):*

1. Find the "we." Define the community to which you and your reader belong. Then ask, "How are my reader and I alike and different?"—in knowledge, attitudes, and circumstances.

2. Define your purpose. Remember the advice a consultant once gave Stanley Tool executives: "You're not in the business of making drills: you're in the business of making holes." Too many of us lose sight of the difference between making drills and making holes when we write letters and memos. We focus on the piece of writing—the tool itself—not its purpose. The result: our writing often misses the chance to be as effective as it could be. When you're still at the planning stage, focus on the outcome you want, not on the means you will use to achieve it.

3. Get your stuff together. Learn from those times when you've turned a one-hour home-improvement project into a three- or four-hour job by having to make repeated trips to the hardware store for tools or parts. Before you start the drafting stage of writing, collect the information you need.

4. Get your ducks in a row. Decide on the main points you want to make. Then, make a list or rough outline placing your points in the most logical order.

At the **Drafting Stage** *(perhaps 5 minutes out of the hour):*

5. Do it wrong the first time. Do a "quick and dirty" draft, without editing. Think of your draft as a "prototype," written not for the end user but for your own testing and improvement. Stopping to edit while you draft breaks your train of thought and keeps you from being a good writer. (*Hint:* If you are writing at a computer, try turning off the monitor during the drafting stage.)

At the **Break Stage** *(perhaps 5 minutes):*

6. Take a break and change hats. Get away from your draft, even if for only a few minutes. Come back with a fresh perspective—the reader's perspective.

At the **Revising Stage** *(perhaps 25 minutes):*

7. Signal your turns. Just as if you were driving a car, you're leading your reader through new territory. Use "turn signals"—*and, in addition, but, however, or, therefore, because, for example*—to guide your reader from sentence to sentence.

8. Say what you mean. Put the point of your sentences in the subjects and verbs. For example, revise "There are drawbacks to using this accounting method" to "This accounting method has some drawbacks." You'll be saying what you mean, and you'll be a more effective communicator.

9. Pay by the word. Reading your memo requires work. If your sentences are wordy and you are slow to get to the point, the reader may decide that it is not worth the effort. Pretend you are paying the reader by the word to read your memo. Then, revise your memo to make it as short and to the point as possible.

10. Translate into English. Keep your words simple. (Lee Iacocca put both these tips in one "commandment of good management": "Say it in English and keep it short.") Remember that you write to express, not impress.

11. Finish the job. Check your spelling, punctuation, and mechanics.

Finally, at the **Managing Stage** *(2 to 3 minutes):*

12. Evaluate your writing process. Figure out how to improve it next time.

By following these 12 steps, you can take charge of your writing time. Begin today to *manage your writing.* As a United Technologies Corporation advertisement in *The Wall Street Journal* admonished, "If you want to manage somebody, manage yourself. Do that well and you'll be ready to stop managing and start leading."

Dr. Kenneth W. Davis is Professor Emeritus of English at Indiana University, and a writing trainer and coach.

SELF-STUDY

LEARNING OBJECTIVES	Key Points to Remember
LO1 **Describe the purpose of accounting.**	The purpose of accounting is to provide financial information about a business to individuals and organizations.
LO2 **Describe the accounting process.**	The six major steps of the accounting process are analyzing, recording, classifying, summarizing, reporting, and interpreting.
LO3 **Define GAAP and describe the process used by FASB to develop these principles.**	Generally accepted accounting principles (GAAP) are the rules that businesses must follow when preparing financial statements. FASB takes the following steps to develop an accounting standard: 1. The issue is placed on the Board's agenda. 2. After researching the issue, a Preliminary Views document is issued. 3. Public hearings are held. 4. An Exposure Draft is issued. 5. The Board issues an Accounting Standards Update which amends the FASB Accounting Standards Codification.
LO4 **Define three types of business ownership structures.**	Three types of business ownership structures are the sole proprietorship, the partnership, and the corporation.
LO5 **Classify different types of businesses by activities.**	Different types of businesses classified by activities are a service business, a merchandising business, and a manufacturing business.
LO6 **Identify career opportunities in accounting.**	Career opportunities in accounting include work in public accounting, private accounting, and governmental and not-for-profit accounting.

KEY TERMS

accountant (8) Designs the accounting information system and focuses on analyzing and interpreting information.

accounting (4) A system of gathering financial information about a business and reporting this information to users.

accounting clerk (8) Records, sorts, and files accounting information.

accounting information systems (10) Accountants in this area design and implement manual and computerized accounting systems.

Accounting Standards Update (6) A standard issued by the Financial Accounting Standards Board. These standards must be followed when preparing financial statements. The updates are included in the FASB Accounting Standards Codification.

analyzing (5) Looking at events that have taken place and thinking about how they affect the business.

auditing (9) Reviewing and testing to be certain that proper accounting policies and practices have been followed.

bookkeeper (8)   Generally supervises the work of accounting clerks, helps with daily accounting work, and summarizes accounting information.

budgeting (10)   The process in which accountants help managers develop a financial plan.

Certified Fraud Examiner (CFE) (9)   A forensic accountant who has passed the exam offered by the Association of Certified Fraud Examiners.

Certified Internal Auditor (CIA) (10)   An internal auditor who has achieved professional recognition by passing the uniform examination offered by the Institute of Internal Auditors.

Certified Management Accountant (CMA) (10)   An accountant who has passed an examination offered by the Institute of Management Accountants.

Certified Public Accountant (CPA) (9)   A public accountant who has met certain educational and experience requirements and has passed an examination prepared by the American Institute of Certified Public Accountants.

classifying (5)   Sorting and grouping similar items together rather than merely keeping a simple, diary-like record of numerous events.

Controller (10)   The accountant who oversees the entire accounting process and is the principal accounting officer of a company.

corporation (7)   A type of ownership structure in which stockholders own the business. The owners' risk is usually limited to their initial investment, and they usually have very little influence on the business decisions.

cost accounting (10)   Determining the cost of producing specific products or providing services and analyzing for cost effectiveness.

Exposure Draft (6)   This document explains the rules that FASB believes firms should follow in accounting for a particular event. Based on the responses to the Exposure Draft, the Board will decide if any changes are necessary before issuing a final standard.

financial accounting (10)   Includes preparing various reports and financial statements and analyzing operating, investing, and financing decisions.

Financial Accounting Standards Board Accounting Standards Codification (6)   This Codification is an electronic database that provides one authoritative source for the standards which must be followed by U.S. companies.

forensic accounting (9)   A specialized field that combines fraud detection, fraud prevention, litigation support, expert witnessing, business valuations, and other investigative activities.

generally accepted accounting principles (GAAP) (5)   Procedures and guidelines developed by the Financial Accounting Standards Board to be followed in the accounting and reporting process.

internal auditing (10)   Reviewing the operating and accounting control procedures adopted by management to make sure the controls are adequate and being followed; assuring that accurate and timely information is provided.

interpreting (5)   Deciding the meaning and importance of the information in various reports.

management advisory services (9)   Providing advice to businesses on a wide variety of managerial issues.

manufacturing business (7)   A business that makes a product to sell.

merchandising business (7)   A business that buys products to sell.

para-accountant (8)   A paraprofessional who provides many accounting, auditing, or tax services under the direct supervision of an accountant.

partnership (7)   A type of ownership structure in which more than one person owns the business.

Preliminary Views (5)   The first document issued by FASB when developing an accounting standard. This document identifies the pros and cons of various accounting treatments for an event and invites others to comment.

public hearing (5)   Following the issuance of a discussion memorandum, public meetings are often held by FASB to gather opinions on the accounting issue.

recording (5)   Entering financial information about events affecting the company into the accounting system.

reporting (5)   Telling the results of the financial information.

Sarbanes-Oxley Act (SOX) (9)   An act passed by Congress to help improve reporting practices of public companies.

service business (7)   A business that provides a service.

sole proprietorship (6)   A type of ownership structure in which one person owns the business.

summarizing (5)   Bringing the various items of information together to determine a result.

tax accounting (10)   Services focused on tax planning, preparing tax returns, and dealing with the Internal Revenue Service and other governmental agencies.

taxation (9)   See tax accounting.

APPLYING YOUR KNOWLEDGE

CengageNowv2 provides "Show Me How" videos for selected exercises and problems. Additional resources, such as Excel templates for completing selected exercises and problems, are available for download from the companion website at Cengage.com.

REVIEW QUESTIONS

LO1   1. What is the purpose of accounting?

LO1   2. Identify four user groups normally interested in financial information about a business.

LO2   3. Identify the six major steps of the accounting process and explain each step.

LO3   4. What are generally accepted accounting principles (GAAP)?

LO3   5. Describe the steps followed by the Financial Accounting Standards Board when developing an accounting standard.

LO3   6. What is the name of the organization that issues accounting standards followed by many firms in countries outside the United States?

LO4   7. Identify the three types of ownership structures and discuss the advantages and disadvantages of each.

LO5   8. Identify three types of businesses according to activities.

LO6   9. What are the main functions of an accounting clerk?

LO6   10. Name and describe four areas of specialization for a public accountant.

LO6   11. What is the purpose of the Sarbanes-Oxley Act?

LO6   12. Name and describe six areas of specialization for a managerial accountant.

SERIES A EXERCISES

E 1-1A   (LO1)   PURPOSE OF ACCOUNTING Match the following users with the information needed.

1. Owners
2. Managers
3. Creditors
4. Government agencies

a. Whether the firm can pay its bills on time
b. Detailed, up-to-date information to measure business performance (and plan for future operations)
c. To determine taxes to be paid and whether other regulations are met
d. The firm's current financial condition

E 1-2A   (LO2)   ACCOUNTING PROCESS List the six major steps of the accounting process in order (1–6) and define each.

_____	Recording
_____	Summarizing
_____	Reporting
_____	Analyzing
_____	Interpreting
_____	Classifying

SERIES B EXERCISES

E 1-1B   (LO1)   PURPOSE OF ACCOUNTING Describe the kind of information needed by the users listed.

Owners (present and future)

Managers

Creditors (present and future)

Government agencies

E 1-2B   (LO2)   ACCOUNTING PROCESS Match the following steps of the accounting process with their definitions.

Analyzing
Recording
Classifying
Summarizing
Reporting
Interpreting

a. Telling the results
b. Looking at events that have taken place and thinking about how they affect the business
c. Deciding the importance of the various reports
d. Aggregating many similar events to provide information that is easy to understand
e. Sorting and grouping like items together
f. Entering financial information into the accounting system

CHECK LIST
☐ **Managing**
☐ **Planning**
☐ **Drafting**
☐ **Break**
☐ **Revising**
☐ **Managing**

MANAGING YOUR WRITING

Take a moment to think about what it would be like to run your own business. If you started a business, what would it be? Prepare a one-page memo that describes the type of business you would enjoy the most. Would it be a service, merchandising, or manufacturing business? Explain what form of ownership you would prefer and why.

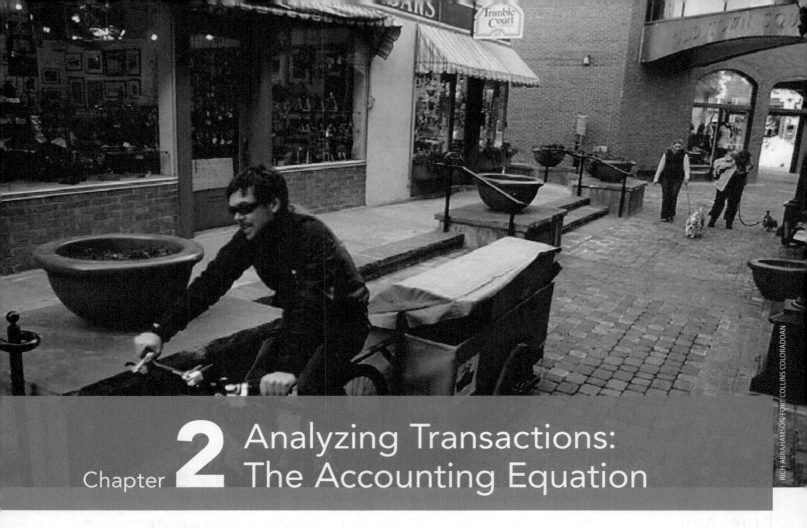

RICH ABRAHAMSON/FORT COLLINS COLORADOAN

Chapter 2 Analyzing Transactions: The Accounting Equation

LEARNING OBJECTIVES

Careful study of this chapter should enable you to:

LO1 Define the accounting elements.

LO2 Construct the accounting equation.

LO3 Analyze business transactions.

LO4 Show the effects of business transactions on the accounting equation.

LO5 Prepare and describe the purposes of a simple income statement, statement of owner's equity, and balance sheet.

LO6 Define the three basic phases of the accounting process.

At Rob's Bike Courier Service in Fort Collins, Colorado, Rob believes "less is more." His small company doesn't "have a fleet of vehicles, just some pretty cool bicycles." His mission is providing successful bike delivery service, perfect for both traditional business delivery services and residential errands. Since January of 2005, Rob's Bike Courier Service has been the alternative to gas-powered vehicle delivery. Thus, besides great rates and friendly, reliable service, Rob offers earth-friendly service.

Currently, he delivers wholesale bagels from a mid-town baker to several downtown coffee shops. He does the same for another pastry chef. Rob also picks up recycling materials, offers bike towing services, and will go to a customer's home to fix flat bike tires and make repairs.

Though his company is small, Rob still needs an accounting system to maintain records of his business transactions and to prepare financial statements. Currently, he uses Quickbooks®, an accounting program used by many small companies. In Chapters 2 through 6, we learn how to account for a service business like Rob's by using an example of a similar company: Mitchell's Campus Delivery.

The entire accounting process is based on one simple equation, called the accounting equation. In this chapter, you will learn how to use this equation to analyze business transactions. You will also learn how to prepare financial statements that report the effect of these transactions on the financial condition of a business.

LO1 | The Accounting Elements

Define the accounting elements.

Before the accounting process can begin, the entity to be accounted for must be defined. A business entity is an individual, association, or organization that engages in economic activities and controls specific economic resources. This definition allows the personal and business finances of an owner to be accounted for separately.

Three basic accounting elements exist for every business entity: assets, liabilities, and owner's equity. These elements are defined below.

Assets

LEARNING KEY

Pay close attention to the definitions for the basic accounting elements. A clear understanding of these definitions will help you analyze even the most complex business transactions.

Assets are items that are owned by a business and will provide future benefits. Examples of assets include cash, merchandise, furniture, fixtures, machinery, buildings, and land. Businesses may also have an asset called accounts receivable. This asset represents the amount of money owed to the business by its customers as a result of making sales "on account," or "on credit." Making sales on account simply means that the customers have promised to pay sometime in the future.

Liabilities

Liabilities represent something owed to another business entity. The amount owed represents a probable future outflow of assets as a result of a past event or transaction. Liabilities are debts or obligations of the business that can be paid with cash, goods, or services.

The most common liabilities are accounts payable and notes payable. An account payable is an unwritten promise to pay a supplier for assets purchased or services received. Acquiring assets or services by promising to make payments in the future is referred to as making a purchase "on account," or "on credit." Formal written promises to pay suppliers or lenders specified sums of money at definite future times are known as notes payable.

Owner's Equity

LEARNING KEY

The business entity's assets and liabilities are separate from the owner's nonbusiness assets and liabilities.

Owner's equity is the amount by which the business assets exceed the business liabilities. Other terms used for owner's equity include net worth and capital. If there are no business liabilities, the owner's equity is equal to the total assets.

The owner of a business may have business assets and liabilities as well as nonbusiness assets and liabilities. For example, the business owner probably owns a home, clothing, and a car, and perhaps owes the dentist for dental service. These are personal, nonbusiness assets and liabilities. According to the business entity concept, nonbusiness assets and liabilities are not included in the business entity's accounting records.

CHECKPOINT ✔

Complete Checkpoint-1 on page 41 to test your basic understanding of LO1.

If the owner invests money or other assets in the business, the item invested is reclassified from a nonbusiness asset to a business asset. If the owner withdraws money or other assets from the business for personal use, the item withdrawn is reclassified from a business asset to a nonbusiness asset. These distinctions are important and allow the owner to make decisions based on the financial condition and results of the business apart from nonbusiness activities.

A BROADER VIEW

Assets and the Cost of Products We Buy

Next time you buy something, think of all the assets a company needs to produce that product. If the product comes from a capital-intensive industry, one that requires heavy investments in assets, the company must price the product high enough to cover the cost of using the assets and replacing them when they wear out. For example, AT&T recently reported that the cost of property, plant, and equipment used for operating purposes came to over $319 billion.

CHAMPIOFOTO/SHUTTERSTOCK.COM

LO2

The Accounting Equation

Construct the accounting equation.

The relationship between the three basic accounting elements—assets, liabilities, and owner's equity—can be expressed in the form of a simple equation known as the **accounting equation.**

Assets	=	Liabilities	+	Owner's Equity

This equation reflects the fact that both outsiders and insiders have an interest in the assets of a business.

• Liabilities represent the outside interests of creditors.

• Owner's equity represents the inside interests of owners.

Or, viewed another way,

The left side of the equation shows the assets.

The right side of the equation shows where the money came from to buy the assets.

When two elements are known, the third can always be calculated. For example, assume that assets on December 31 total $60,400. On that same day, the business liabilities consist of $5,400 owed for equipment. Owner's equity is calculated by subtracting total liabilities from total assets, $60,400 − $5,400 = $55,000.

Assets	=	Liabilities	+	Owner's Equity
$60,400	=	$5,400	+	$55,000
$60,400	=	**$60,400**		

If during the next accounting period, assets increased by $10,000 and liabilities increased by $3,000, owner's equity must have increased by $7,000 ($10,000 − $3,000) as shown on the next page.

LEARNING KEY 🔑

If you know two accounting elements, you can calculate the third element.

Total assets	$60,400
Total liabilities	−5,400
Owner's equity	$55,000

	Assets	=	Liabilities	+	Owner's Equity
BB	$60,400		$5,400		$55,000
	+10,000	=	+3,000	+	+7,000
EB	$70,400	=	$8,400	+	$62,000
	$70,400	=		$70,400	

BB: Beginning balance
EB: Ending balance

CHECKPOINT ✔

Complete Checkpoint-2 on page 41 to test your basic understanding of LO2.

Note also that after computing the ending balances for assets, liabilities, and owner's equity, the accounting equation remains in balance.

LO3   Analyzing Business Transactions

Analyze business transactions.

A business transaction is an economic event that has a direct impact on the business. A business transaction almost always requires an exchange between the business and another outside entity. We must be able to measure this exchange in dollars. Examples of business transactions include buying goods and services, selling goods and services, buying and selling assets, making loans, and borrowing money.

All business transactions affect the accounting equation through specific accounts. An account is a separate record used to summarize changes in each asset, liability, and the owner's equity of a business. Account titles provide a description of the particular type of asset, liability, or owner's equity affected by a transaction.

Three basic questions must be answered when analyzing the effects of a business transaction on the accounting equation. These questions help address the steps in the accounting process discussed in Chapter 1.

1. What happened?
   • Make certain you understand the event that has taken place.

2. Which accounts are affected?
   • Identify the accounts that are affected.
   • Classify these accounts as assets, liabilities, or owner's equity.

3. How is the accounting equation affected?
   • Determine which accounts have increased or decreased.
   • Make certain that the accounting equation remains in balance after the transaction has been entered.

LO4   Effect of Transactions on the Accounting Equation

Show the effects of business transactions on the accounting equation.

In Chapters 2 through 6, we will focus on learning how to account for a business similar to Rob's Bike Courier Service, discussed in the chapter opener. In these chapters, we will focus on Mitchell's Campus Delivery. By studying Mitchell's business transactions and accounting techniques, you will learn about business and accounting. A major advantage of studying accounting is that it helps you learn a great deal about business.

As explained earlier, we must first understand the economic substance of events. Then, we must determine how that information is entered into the accounting system. *If Mitch does not understand the economic events affecting his delivery business and their impact on the accounting equation, the events will not be correctly entered into the accounting system.*

Each transaction affects at least two accounts and one or more of the three basic accounting elements. A transaction increases or decreases specific asset, liability, or owner's equity accounts. Assume that the following transactions occurred during June 20--, the first month of operations for Mitchell's Campus Delivery.

Transaction (a): Investment by owner

> Remember, capital does not mean cash. The cash is shown in the cash account.

An Increase in an Asset Offset by an Increase in Owner's Equity. Mitch Williams opened a bank account with a deposit of $5,000 for his business. The new business now has $5,000 of the asset Cash. Since Mitch contributed the asset, the owner's equity element, Mitchell Williams, Capital, increases by the same amount.

Assets (Items Owned)	=	Liabilities (Amounts Owed)	+	Owner's Equity (Owner's Investment)
Cash	=			Mitchell Williams, Capital
(a) $5,000	=			$5,000

Transaction (b): Purchase of an asset for cash

An Increase in an Asset Offset by a Decrease in Another Asset. Mitch decided that the fastest and easiest way to get around campus and find parking is on a motor scooter. Thus, he bought a motor scooter (delivery equipment) for $2,000 cash. Mitch exchanged one asset, cash, for another, delivery equipment. This transaction reduces Cash and creates a new asset, Delivery Equipment.

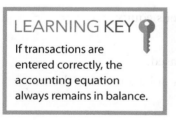

LEARNING KEY

If transactions are entered correctly, the accounting equation always remains in balance.

Assets (Items Owned)			=	Liabilities (Amounts Owed)	+	Owner's Equity (Owner's Investment)
Cash	+	Delivery Equipment	=			Mitch Williams, Capital
$5,000						$5,000
(b) −2,000		+$2,000				
$3,000	+	$2,000	=			$5,000
$5,000			=			$5,000

Transaction (c): Purchase of an asset on account

An Increase in an Asset Offset by an Increase in a Liability. Mitch hired a friend to work for him, which meant that a second scooter would be needed. Given Mitch's limited cash, he bought a secondhand model for $1,800. The seller agreed to allow Mitch to spread the payments over the next three months. This transaction increased an asset, Delivery Equipment, by $1,800 and increased the liability, Accounts Payable, by an equal amount.

Assets (Items Owned)		=	Liabilities (Amounts Owed)	+	Owner's Equity (Owner's Investment)
Cash	+ Delivery Equipment	=	Accounts Payable	+	Mitchell Williams, Capital
(c) $3,000	$2,000 +1,800		+$1,800		$5,000
$3,000	+ $3,800	=	$1,800	+	$5,000
$6,800		=	$6,800		

Transaction (d): Payment on a loan

A Decrease in an Asset Offset by a Decrease in a Liability. Mitch paid the first install-ment on the scooter of $600 [see transaction (c)]. This payment decreased the asset, Cash, and the liability, Accounts Payable, by $600.

Assets (Items Owned)		=	Liabilities (Amounts Owed)	+	Owner's Equity (Owner's Investment)
Cash	+ Delivery Equipment	=	Accounts Payable	+	Mitchell Williams, Capital
(d) $3,000 −600	$3,800		$1,800 −600		$5,000
$2,400	+ $3,800	=	$1,200	+	$5,000
$6,200		=	$6,200		

Expanding the Accounting Equation: Revenues, Expenses, and Withdrawals

In the preceding sections, three key accounting elements of every business entity were defined and explained: assets, liabilities, and owner's equity. To complete the explanation of the accounting process, three additional elements must be added to the discussion: revenues, expenses, and withdrawals.

Revenues

> More precisely, revenue is recognized when a "performance obligation" is satisfied. We will address the details of revenue recognition later in the text.

Revenues represent the amount a business charges customers for products sold or services performed. Customers generally pay with cash or a credit card, or they promise to pay at a later date. Most businesses recognize revenues when earned, even if cash has not yet been received. Separate accounts are used to recognize dif-ferent types of revenue. Examples include Delivery Fees; Consulting Fees; Rent Revenue, if the business rents space to others; Interest Revenue, for interest earned on bank deposits; and Sales, for sales of merchandise. *Revenues increase both assets and owner's equity.*

Expenses

Expenses represent the *decrease* in assets (or *increase* in liabilities) as a result of a company's efforts to produce revenues. Common examples of expenses are rent, salaries, supplies consumed, and taxes. As with revenues, separate accounts are used to keep the accounting records for each different type of expense. Expenses are "incurred" as

- assets are consumed (such as supplies), or
- services are provided (by employees, for example) to the business.

LEARNING KEY

It is important to remember that expenses do not always reduce cash and revenues do not always increase cash right away.

The two main purposes of recognizing an expense are (a) to keep track of the amount and types of expenses incurred and (b) to show the reduction in owner's equity. Again, an expense can cause a reduction in assets or an increase in liabilities. Wages earned by employees is a good example.

- If paid, the expense reduces owner's equity and an asset, Cash.
- If not paid, the expense reduces owner's equity and increases a liability, Wages Payable.

Either way, owner's equity is reduced. If total revenues are greater than total expenses for the period, the excess is the net income, or net profit, for the period. On the other hand, if total expenses are greater than total revenues for the period, the excess is a net loss for the period.

Revenues	$9,000	Revenues	$ 3,000
Expenses	5,000	Expenses	5,000
Net income	$4,000	Net loss	$(2,000)

The owner can determine the time period used in the measurement of net income or net loss. It may be a month, a quarter (three months), a year, or some other time period. The concept that income determination can be made on a periodic basis is known as the accounting period concept. Any accounting period of 12 months is called a fiscal year. The fiscal year frequently coincides with the calendar year.

Withdrawals

LEARNING KEY

Owner's Equity

Decrease	Increase
Expenses	Revenues
Drawing	Owner's Investments

Withdrawals, or drawing, reduce owner's equity as a result of the owner taking cash or other assets out of the business for personal use. Since earnings are expected to offset withdrawals, this reduction is viewed as temporary.

The accounting equation is expanded to include revenues, expenses, and withdrawals. Note that revenues increase owner's equity, while expenses and drawing reduce owner's equity.

Assets (Items Owned)			=	Liabilities (Amounts Owed)	+	Owner's Equity				
						(Owner's Investment)		+	(Earnings)	
Cash	+	Delivery Equipment	=	Accounts Payable	+	Mitchell Williams, Capital	− Mitchell Williams, Drawing	+	Revenues −	Expenses
Balance $2,400	+	$3,800	=	$1,200	+	$5,000				
$6,200			=			$6,200				

Effect of Revenue, Expense, and Withdrawal Transactions on the Accounting Equation

To show the effects of revenue, expense, and withdrawal transactions, the example of Mitchell's Campus Delivery will be continued. Assume that the following transactions took place in Mitchell's business during June 20--.

Transaction (e): Delivery revenues earned in cash

An Increase in an Asset Offset by an Increase in Owner's Equity Resulting from Revenue. Mitch received $2,100 cash from clients for delivery services. This transaction increased the asset, Cash, and increased owner's equity by $2,100. The increase in owner's equity is shown by increasing the revenue account, Delivery Fees, by $2,100.

	Assets (Items Owned)		=	Liabilities (Amounts Owed)	+	Owner's Equity					
						(Owner's Investment)			(Earnings)		
	Cash	+ Delivery Equipment	=	Accounts Payable	+	Mitchell Williams, Capital	− Mitchell Williams, Drawing	+	Revenues	− Expenses	Description
	$2,400	$3,800		$1,200		$5,000					
(e)	+2,100								+$2,100		Deliv. Fees
	$4,500	+ $3,800	=	$1,200	+	$5,000		+	$2,100		
	$8,300		=			$8,300					

Transaction (f): Paid rent for month

A Decrease in an Asset Offset by a Decrease in Owner's Equity Resulting from an Expense. Mitch rents a small office near campus. He paid $1,000 for office rent for June. This transaction decreased both Cash and owner's equity by $1,000. The decrease in owner's equity is shown by increasing an expense called Rent Expense by $1,000. An increase in an expense decreases owner's equity.

	Assets (Items Owned)		=	Liabilities (Amounts Owed)	+	Owner's Equity					
						(Owner's Investment)			(Earnings)		
	Cash	+ Delivery Equipment	=	Accounts Payable	+	Mitchell Williams, Capital	− Mitchell Williams, Drawing	+	Revenues	− Expenses	Description
	$4,500	+ $3,800		$1,200		$5,000			$2,100		
(f)	−1,000									+$1,000	Rent Exp.
	$3,500	+ $3,800	=	$1,200	+	$5,000		+	$2,100	− $1,000	
	$7,300		=			$7,300					

Transaction (g): Paid phone bill

A Decrease in an Asset Offset by a Decrease in Owner's Equity Resulting from an Expense. Mitch paid $100 in cash for phone service. This transaction, like the previous one, decreased both Cash and owner's equity. This decrease in owner's equity is shown by increasing an expense called Phone Expense by $100.

	Assets (Items Owned)		=	Liabilities (Amounts Owed)	+	Owner's Equity					
						(Owner's Investment)			(Earnings)		
	Cash	+ Delivery Equipment	=	Accounts Payable	+	Mitchell Williams, Capital	− Mitchell Williams, Drawing	+	Revenues	− Expenses	Description
	$3,500	$3,800		$1,200		$5,000			$2,100	$1,000	
(g)	−100									+100	Phone Expense
	$3,400	+ $3,800	=	$1,200	+	$5,000		+	$2,100	− $1,100	
	$7,200		=			$7,200					

LEARNING KEY

Revenue is recognized when it is earned even though cash is not received.

Transaction (h): Delivery revenues earned on account

An Increase in an Asset Offset by an Increase in Owner's Equity Resulting from Revenue. Mitch extends credit to regular customers. Often, delivery services are performed for which payment will be received later. Since revenues are recognized when earned, an increase in owner's equity must be reported by increasing the revenue account. Since no cash is received at this time, Cash cannot be increased. Instead, an increase is reported for another asset, Accounts Receivable. *The total of Accounts Receivable at any point in time reflects the amount owed to Mitch by his customers.* Deliveries made on account amounted to $2,400. Accounts Receivable and Delivery Fees are increased.

	Assets (Items Owned)			=	Liabilities (Amounts Owed)	+	Owner's Equity (Owner's Investment) +			(Earnings)		
	Cash +	Accounts Receivable	+ Delivery Equipment	=	Accounts Payable	+	Mitchell Williams, Capital	– Mitchell Williams, Drawing	+	Revenues	– Expenses	Description
	$3,400		$3,800		$1,200		$5,000			$2,100	$1,100	
(h)		+$2,400								+2,400		**Deliv. Fees**
	$3,400 +	$2,400	+ $3,800	=	$1,200	+	$5,000		+	$4,500	– $1,100	
	$9,600			=					**$9,600**			

Transaction (i): Purchase of supplies

An Increase in an Asset Offset by a Decrease in an Asset. Mitch bought pens, paper, delivery envelopes, and other supplies for $80 cash. These supplies should last for several months. Since they will generate future benefits, the supplies should be recorded as an asset. The accounting equation will show an increase in an asset, Supplies, and a decrease in Cash.

	Assets (Items Owned)				=	Liabilities (Amounts Owed)	+	Owner's Equity (Owner's Investment) +			(Earnings)		
	Cash +	Accounts Receivable	+ Supplies	+ Delivery Equipment	=	Accounts Payable	+	Mitchell Williams, Capital	– Mitchell Williams, Drawing	+ Revenues	– Expenses	Description
	$3,400	$2,400		$3,800		$1,200		$5,000		$4,500	$1,100	
(i)	–80		+$80									
	$3,320 +	$2,400	+ $80	+ $3,800	=	$1,200	+	$5,000		+ $4,500	– $1,100	
	$9,600				=				**$9,600**			

As shown in transactions (i) and (j), transactions do not always affect both sides of the accounting equation.

Transaction (j): Cash receipts from prior sales on account

An Increase in an Asset Offset by a Decrease in an Asset. Mitch received $1,900 in cash for delivery services performed for customers earlier in the month [see transaction (h)]. Receipt of this cash increases the cash account and reduces the amount due from customers reported in the accounts receivable account. *Notice that owner's equity is not affected in this transaction. Owner's equity increased in transaction (h) when revenue was recognized as it was earned, rather than now when cash is received.*

	Assets (Items Owned)				=	Liabilities (Amounts Owed)	+	Owner's Equity (Owner's Investment) + (Earnings)				
Cash	+ Accounts Receivable	+ Supplies	+ Delivery Equipment	=		Accounts Payable	+ Mitchell Williams Capital	− Mitchell Williams Drawing	+ Revenues	− Expenses	Description
$3,320	$2,400	$80	$3,800			$1,200	$5,000		$4,500	$1,100	
(j) +1,900	−1,900										
$5,220 +	$ 500 +	$80 +	$3,800	=		$1,200 +	$5,000	+	$4,500 −	$1,100	
	$9,600			=				**$9,600**			

Transaction (k): Purchase of an asset on account making a partial payment

An Increase in an Asset Offset by a Decrease in an Asset and an Increase in a Liability. With business increasing, Mitch hired a second employee and bought a third motor scooter. The scooter cost $1,000. Mitch paid $300 in cash and will spread the remaining payments over the next four months. The asset Delivery Equipment increases by $1,000, Cash decreases by $300, and the liability Accounts Payable increases by $700. *Note that this transaction changes three accounts. Even so, the accounting equation remains in balance.*

	Assets (Items Owned)				=	Liabilities (Amounts Owed)	+	Owner's Equity (Owner's Investment) + (Earnings)				
Cash	+ Accounts Receivable	+ Supplies	+ Delivery Equipment	=		Accounts Payable	+ Mitchell Williams Capital	− Mitchell Williams Drawing	+ Revenues	− Expenses	Description
$5,220	$500	$80	$3,800			$1,200	$5,000		$4,500	$1,100	
(k) −300			+1,000			+700					
$4,920 +	$500 +	$80 +	$4,800	=		$1,900 +	$5,000	+	$4,500 −	$1,100	
	$10,300			=				**$10,300**			

Transaction (l): Payment of insurance premium

An Increase in an Asset Offset by a Decrease in an Asset. Since Mitch plans to graduate and sell the business next January, he paid $700 for a seven-month liability insurance policy. Insurance is paid in advance and will provide future benefits. Thus, it is treated as an asset. We must expand the equation to include another asset, Prepaid Insurance, and show that Cash has been reduced.

	Assets (Items Owned)					=	Liabilities (Amounts Owed)	+	Owner's Equity (Owner's Investment) + (Earnings)				
Cash	+ Accounts Receivable	+ Supplies	+ Prepaid Insurance	+ Delivery Equipment	=		Accounts Payable	+ Mitchell Williams Capital	− Mitchell Williams Drawing	+ Revenues	− Expenses	Description
$4,920	$500	$80		$4,800			$1,900	$5,000		$4,500	$1,100	
(l) −700			$700									
$4,220 +	$500 +	$80 +	$700 +	$4,800	=		$1,900 +	$5,000	+	$4,500 −	$1,100	
	$10,300				=				**$10,300**			

Transaction (m): Payment of wages

A Decrease in an Asset Offset by a Decrease in Owner's Equity Resulting from an Expense. Mitch paid his part-time employees $1,650 in wages. This represents an additional business expense. As with other expenses, Cash is reduced and owner's equity is reduced by increasing an expense.

Assets (Items Owned)					=	Liabilities (Amounts Owed)	+	Owner's Investment	+	Earnings		
Cash +	Accounts Receivable +	Supplies +	Prepaid Insurance +	Delivery Equipment =		Accounts Payable	+	Mitchell Williams, Capital	– Mitchell Williams, Drawing	+ Revenues	– Expenses	Description
$4,220	$500	$80	$700	$4,800		$1,900		$5,000		$4,500	$1,100	
(m) –1,650											+1,650	Wages Exp.
$2,570 +	$500 +	$80 +	$700 +	$4,800 =		$1,900	+	$5,000		+ $4,500	– $2,750	
		$8,650							$8,650			

Transaction (n): Deliveries made for cash and on account

An Increase in Two Assets Offset by an Increase in Owner's Equity. Total delivery fees for the remainder of the month amounted to $3,500: $900 in cash and $2,600 on account. Since all of these delivery fees have been earned, the revenue account increases by $3,500. Also, Cash increases by $900 and Accounts Receivable increases by $2,600. Thus, revenues increase assets and owner's equity. Note, once again, that recording these revenues impacts three accounts while the equation remains in balance.

Assets (Items Owned)					=	Liabilities (Amounts Owed)	+	Owner's Investment	+	Earnings		
Cash +	Accounts Receivable +	Supplies +	Prepaid Insurance +	Delivery Equipment =		Accounts Payable	+	Mitchell Williams, Capital	– Mitchell Williams, Drawing	+ Revenues	– Expenses	Description
$2,570	$ 500	$80	$700	$4,800		$1,900		$5,000		$4,500	$2,750	
(n) +900	+2,600									+3,500		Deliv. Fees
$3,470 +	$3,100 +	$80 +	$700 +	$4,800 =		$1,900	+	$5,000		+ $8,000	– $2,750	
		$12,150							$12,150			

Transaction (o): Withdrawal of cash from business

A Decrease in an Asset Offset by a Decrease in Owner's Equity Resulting from a Withdrawal by the Owner. At the end of the month, Mitch took $3,000 in cash from the business to pay for textbooks, extra class fees, and living expenses. Since these expenditures are not related to his delivery business, this is a withdrawal. Withdrawals can be viewed as the opposite of investments by the owner. Both owner's equity and Cash decrease.

Assets (Items Owned)					=	Liabilities (Amounts Owed)	+	Owner's Investment	+	Earnings		
Cash +	Accounts Receivable +	Supplies +	Prepaid Insurance +	Delivery Equipment =		Accounts Payable	+	Mitchell Williams, Capital	– Mitchell Williams, Drawing	+ Revenues	– Expenses	Description
$3,470	$3,100	$80	$700	$4,800		$1,900		$5,000		$8,000	$2,750	
(o) –3,000									+$3,000			
$ 470 +	$3,100 +	$80 +	$700 +	$4,800 =		$1,900	+	$5,000 –	$3,000	+ $8,000	– $2,750	
		$9,150							$9,150			

FIGURE 2-1 Summary of Transactions Illustrated

Trans-action	Cash +	Accounts Receivable +	Supplies +	Prepaid Insurance +	Delivery Equipment =	Accounts Payable +	Mitchell Williams, Capital –	Mitchell Williams, Drawing +	Revenues –	Expenses	Description
Assets (Items Owned)						**Liabilities** (Amounts Owed)	**Owner's Equity** (Owner's Investment) +		(Earnings)		
Balance (a)	5,000						5,000				
Balance (b)	5,000						5,000				
	(2,000)				2,000						
Balance (c)	3,000				2,000		5,000				
					1,800	1,800					
Balance (d)	3,000				3,800	1,800	5,000				
	(600)					(600)					
Balance (e)	2,400				3,800	1,200	5,000				
	2,100								2,100		Deliv. Fees
Balance (f)	4,500				3,800	1,200	5,000		2,100		
	(1,000)									1,000	Rent Exp.
Balance (g)	3,500				3,800	1,200	5,000		2,100	1,000	
	(100)									100	Phone Exp.
Balance (h)	3,400				3,800	1,200	5,000		2,100	1,100	
		2,400							2,400		Deliv. Fees
Balance (i)	3,400	2,400			3,800	1,200	5,000		4,500	1,100	
	(80)		80								
Balance (j)	3,320	2,400	80		3,800	1,200	5,000		4,500	1,100	
	1,900	(1,900)									
Balance (k)	5,220	500	80		3,800	1,200	5,000		4,500	1,100	
	(300)				1,000	700					
Balance (l)	4,920	500	80		4,800	1,900	5,000		4,500	1,100	
	(700)			700							
Balance (m)	4,220	500	80	700	4,800	1,900	5,000		4,500	1,100	
	(1,650)									1,650	Wages Exp.
Balance (n)	2,570	500	80	700	4,800	1,900	5,000		4,500	2,750	
	900	2,600							3,500		Deliv. Fees
Balance (o)	3,470	3,100	80	700	4,800	1,900	5,000		8,000	2,750	
	(3,000)							3,000			
Balance	**470** +	**3,100** +	**80** +	**700** +	**4,800** =	**1,900** +	**5,000** –	**3,000** +	**8,000** –	**2,750**	

Cash	$ 470	Accounts Payable	$1,900
Accounts Receivable	3,100	Mitchell Williams, Capital	5,000
Supplies	80	Mitchell Williams, Drawing	(3,000)
Prepaid Insurance	700	Delivery Fees	8,000
Delivery Equipment	4,800	Rent Expense	(1,000)
Total Assets	**$9,150**	Phone Expense	(100)
		Wages Expense	(1,650)
		Total Liabilities and Owner's Equity	**$9,150**

Amounts in ( ) are subtracted

As with the running totals in the table, the listing immediately below the table provides proof that the accounting equation is in balance.

CHECKPOINT ✔

Complete Checkpoint-3 on page 41 to test your basic understanding of LO3/4.

Figure 2-1 shows a summary of the transactions. Use this summary to test your understanding of transaction analysis by describing the economic event represented by each transaction. At the bottom of Figure 2-1, the asset accounts and their totals are compared with the liability and owner's equity accounts and their totals.

LO5 | Financial Statements

Prepare and describe the purposes of a simple income statement, statement of owner's equity, and balance sheet.

Three financial statements commonly prepared by a business entity are the income statement, statement of owner's equity, and balance sheet. The transaction information gathered and summarized in the accounting equation may be used to prepare these financial statements. Figure 2-2 shows the following:

1. A summary of the specific revenue and expense transactions and the ending totals for the asset, liability, capital, and drawing accounts from the accounting equation
2. The financial statements and their linkages with the accounting equation and each other

Note that each of the financial statements in Figure 2-2 has a heading consisting of the following:

HEADING FOR FINANCIAL STATEMENTS	
1. The name of the company	Mitchell's Campus Delivery
2. The title of the statement	Income Statement, Statement of Owner's Equity, or Balance Sheet
3. The time period covered or the date of the statement	For Month Ended June 30, 20--, or June 30, 20--

The income statement and statement of owner's equity provide information concerning events covering a period of time, in this case, *the month ended* June 30, 20--. The balance sheet, on the other hand, offers a picture of the business on *a specific date*, June 30, 20--.

GUIDELINES FOR PREPARING FINANCIAL STATEMENTS
1. Financial statements are prepared primarily for users not associated with the company. To make a good impression and enhance understanding, financial statements must follow a standard form with careful attention to placement, spacing, and indentations.
2. All statements have a heading with the name of the company, name of the statement, and accounting period or date.
3. Single rules (underlines) indicate that the numbers above the line have been added or subtracted. Double rules (double underlines) indicate a total.
4. Dollar signs are used at the top of columns and for the first amount entered in a column beneath a ruling.
5. On the income statement, some companies list expenses from highest to lowest dollar amount, with miscellaneous expense listed last.
6. On the balance sheet, assets are listed from most liquid to least liquid. **Liquidity** measures the ease with which the asset will be converted to cash. Liabilities are listed from most current to least current.

The Income Statement

The income statement, sometimes called the profit and loss statement or operating statement, reports the profitability of business operations for a specific period of time. Mitchell's income statement shows the revenues earned for the month of June.

FIGURE 2-2 Summary and Financial Statements

Trans-action	Cash	+	Accounts Receivable	+	Supplies	+	Prepaid Insurance	+	Delivery Equipment	=	Accounts Payable	+	Mitchell Williams, Capital	−	Mitchell Williams, Drawing	+	Revenues	−	Expenses	Description
										Assets (Items Owned) = **Liabilities (Amounts Owed)** + **Owner's Equity (Owner's Investment)** + **(Earnings)**										
(e)																	2,100			Deliv. Fees
(f)																			1,000	Rent Exp.
(g)																			100	Phone Exp.
(h)																	2,400			Deliv. Fees
(m)																			1,650	Wages Exp.
(n)																	3,500			Deliv. Fees
Balance	470	+	3,100	+	80	+	700	+	4,800	=	1,900	+	5,000	−	3,000	+	8,000	−	2,750	

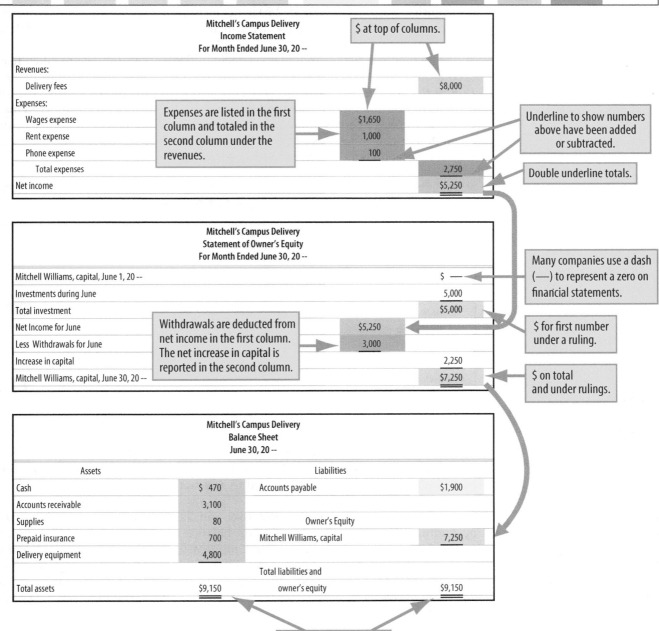

Mitchell's Campus Delivery
Income Statement
For Month Ended June 30, 20 --

Revenues:		
Delivery fees		$8,000
Expenses:		
Wages expense	$1,650	
Rent expense	1,000	
Phone expense	100	
Total expenses		2,750
Net income		$5,250

$ at top of columns.

Expenses are listed in the first column and totaled in the second column under the revenues.

Underline to show numbers above have been added or subtracted.

Double underline totals.

Mitchell's Campus Delivery
Statement of Owner's Equity
For Month Ended June 30, 20 --

Mitchell Williams, capital, June 1, 20 --		$ —
Investments during June		5,000
Total investment		$5,000
Net Income for June	$5,250	
Less Withdrawals for June	3,000	
Increase in capital		2,250
Mitchell Williams, capital, June 30, 20 --		$7,250

Withdrawals are deducted from net income in the first column. The net increase in capital is reported in the second column.

Many companies use a dash (—) to represent a zero on financial statements.

$ for first number under a ruling.

$ on total and under rulings.

Mitchell's Campus Delivery
Balance Sheet
June 30, 20 --

Assets		Liabilities	
Cash	$ 470	Accounts payable	$1,900
Accounts receivable	3,100		
Supplies	80	Owner's Equity	
Prepaid insurance	700	Mitchell Williams, capital	7,250
Delivery equipment	4,800		
		Total liabilities and	
Total assets	$9,150	owner's equity	$9,150

Double underline totals.

Next, the expenses incurred as a result of the efforts made to earn these revenues are deducted. If the revenues are greater than the expenses, net income is reported. If the expenses are greater than the revenue, a net loss is reported.

By carefully studying the income statement, it is clear that Mitch earns revenues in only one way: by making deliveries. If other types of services were offered, these revenues would also be identified on the statement. Further, the reader can see the kinds of expenses that were incurred. The reader can make a judgment as to whether these seem reasonable given the amount of revenue earned. Finally, the most important number on the statement is the net income. This is known as the "bottom line."

The Statement of Owner's Equity

The statement of owner's equity illustrated in Figure 2-2 reports on these activities for the month of June. Mitch started his business with an investment of $5,000. During the month of June, he earned $5,250 in net income and withdrew $3,000 for personal expenses. Mitch's $5,000 original investment, plus the net increase of $2,250, results in his ending capital of $7,250.

Note that Mitchell's original investment and later withdrawal are taken from the accounting equation. *The net income figure could have been computed from information in the accounting equation. However, it is easier to simply transfer net income as reported on the income statement to the statement of owner's equity.* This is an important linkage between the income statement and statement of owner's equity.

If Mitch had a net loss of $500 for the month, the statement of owner's equity would be prepared as shown in Figure 2-3.

FIGURE 2-3 Statement of Owner's Equity with Net Loss

Mitchell's Campus Delivery Statement of Owner's Equity For Month Ended June 30, 20 --		
Mitchell Williams, capital, June 1, 20 --		$ —
Investments during June		5,000
Total investment		$5,000
Less: Net loss for June	$500	
Withdrawals for June	3,000	
Decrease in capital		(3,500)
Mitchell Williams, capital, June 30, 20 --		$1,500

The Balance Sheet

The balance sheet reports a firm's assets, liabilities, and owner's equity on a specific date. It is called a balance sheet because it confirms that the accounting equation has remained in balance. It is also referred to as a statement of financial position or statement of financial condition.

As illustrated in Figure 2-2, the asset and liability accounts are taken from the accounting equation and reported on the balance sheet. *The total of Mitchell's capital account on June 30 could have been computed from the owner's equity accounts in the accounting equation ($5,000 − $3,000 + $8,000 − $2,750 = $7,250). However, it is simpler to take the June 30, 20--, capital as computed on the statement of owner's equity and transfer it to the balance sheet.* This is an important linkage between these two statements.

LO6   Overview of the Accounting Process

Define the three basic phases of the accounting process.

Figure 2-4 shows the three basic phases of the accounting process in terms of input, processing, and output.

- Input. Business transactions provide the necessary *input*.
- Processing. Recognizing the effect of these transactions on the assets, liabilities, owner's equity, revenues, and expenses of a business is the *processing* function.
- Output. The financial statements are the *output*.

FIGURE 2-4 Input, Processing, and Output

SELF-STUDY

LEARNING OBJECTIVES	Key Points to Remember
LO1 Define the accounting elements.	The three key accounting elements are assets, liabilities, and owner's equity. Owner's equity is expanded in LO4 to include revenues, expenses, and drawing.
LO2 Construct the accounting equation.	The accounting equation is Assets = Liabilities + Owner's Equity
LO3 Analyze business transactions.	Three questions must be answered in analyzing business transactions: 1. What happened? 2. Which accounts are affected? 3. How is the accounting equation affected?
LO4 Show the effects of business transactions on the accounting equation.	Each transaction affects at least two accounts and one or more of the three basic accounting elements. The transactions described in this chapter can be classified into five groups: 1. Increase in an asset offset by an increase in owner's equity. 2. Increase in an asset offset by a decrease in another asset.

(*continued*)

LEARNING OBJECTIVES	**Key Points to Remember**
LO4 (concluded)	3. Increase in an asset offset by an increase in a liability.
	4. Decrease in an asset offset by a decrease in a liability.
	5. Decrease in an asset offset by a decrease in owner's equity.
LO5 Prepare and describe the purposes of a simple income statement, statement of owner's equity, and balance sheet.	The purposes of the income statement, statement of owner's equity, and balance sheet can be summarized as follows:

STATEMENT	PURPOSE
Income statement	Reports net income or loss
	Revenues − Expenses = Net Income or Loss
Statement of owner's equity	Shows changes in the owner's capital account
	Beginning Capital + Investments + Net Income − Withdrawals = Ending Capital
Balance sheet	Verifies balance of accounting equation
	Assets = Liabilities + Owner's Equity

LO6 Define the three basic phases of the accounting process.	The three basic phases of the accounting process are shown below. • **Input.** Business transactions provide the necessary input. • **Processing.** Recognizing the effect of these transactions on the assets, liabilities, owner's equity, revenues, and expenses of a business is the processing function. • **Output.** The financial statements are the output.

DEMONSTRATION PROBLEM

Kenny Young has started his own business, Home and Away Inspections. He inspects property for buyers and sellers of real estate. Young rents office space and has a part-time assistant to answer the phone and help with inspections. The transactions for the month of September are as follows:

(a) On the first day of the month, Young invested cash by making a deposit in a bank account for the business, $15,000.
(b) Paid rent for September, $300.
(c) Bought a used truck for cash, $8,000.
(d) Purchased tools on account from Crafty Tools, $3,000.
(e) Paid electricity bill, $50.
(f) Paid two-year premium for liability insurance on truck, $600.
(g) Received cash from clients for services performed, $2,000.
(h) Paid part-time assistant (wages) for first half of month, $200.
(i) Performed inspection services for clients on account, $1,000.
(j) Paid phone bill, $35.
(k) Bought office supplies costing $300. Paid $100 cash and will pay the balance next month, $200.
(l) Received cash from clients for inspections performed on account in (i), $300.
(m) Paid part-time assistant (wages) for last half of month, $250.
(n) Made partial payment on tools bought in (d), $1,000.

(o) Earned additional revenues amounting to $2,000: $1,400 in cash and $600 on account.

(p) Young withdrew cash at the end of the month for personal expenses, $500.

REQUIRED

1. Enter the transactions in an accounting equation similar to the one illustrated below.

Assets (Items Owned)						=	Liabilities (Amounts Owed)	+	Owner's Equity (Owner's Investment) + (Earnings)				
Cash +	Accounts Receivable +	Supplies +	Prepaid Insurance +	Tools +	Truck =		Accounts Payable	+	Kenny Young, Capital	– Kenny Young, Drawing	+ Revenues	– Expenses	Description

2. Compute the ending balances for all accounts.
3. Prepare an income statement for Home and Away Inspections for the month of September 20--.
4. Prepare a statement of owner's equity for Home and Away Inspections for the month of September 20--.
5. Prepare a balance sheet for Home and Away Inspections as of September 30, 20--.

SOLUTION 1, 2.

	Assets (Items Owned)						=	Liabilities (Amounts Owed)	+	Owner's Equity (Owner's Investment)+ (Earnings)				
	Cash +	Accounts Receivable +	Supplies +	Prepaid Insurance +	Tools +	Truck =		Accounts Payable	+	Kenny Young, Capital	– Kenny Young, Drawing	+ Revenues	– Expenses	Description
(a)	15,000									15,000				
(b)	(300)												300	Rent Exp.
(c)	(8,000)					8,000								
(d)					3,000			3,000						
(e)	(50)												50	Utilities Exp.
(f)	(600)			600										
(g)	2,000											2,000		Inspect. Fees
(h)	(200)												200	Wages Exp.
(i)		1,000										1,000		Inspect. Fees
(j)	(35)												35	Phone Exp.
(k)	(100)		300					200						
(l)	300	(300)												
(m)	(250)												250	Wages Exp.
(n)	(1,000)							(1,000)						
(o)	1,400	600										2,000		Inspect. Fees
(p)	(500)										500			
Bal.	**7,665** +	**1,300** +	**300** +	**600** +	**3,000** +	**8,000** =		**2,200**	+	**15,000** –	**500** +	**5,000**	– **835**	

SOLUTION 3.

Home and Away Inspections Income Statement For Month Ended September 30, 20 --		
Revenues:		
Inspection fees		$ 5,000
Expenses:		
Wages expense	$450	
Rent expense	300	
Utilities expense	50	
Phone expense	35	
Total expenses		835
Net income		$ 4,165

SOLUTION 4.

Home and Away Inspections Statement of Owner's Equity For Month Ended September 30, 20 - -		
Kenny Young, capital, September 1, 20 - -		$ ——
Investment during September		15,000
Total investment		$15,000
Net income for September	$4,165	
Less withdrawals for September	500	
Increase in capital		3,665
Kenny Young, capital, September 30, 20 - -		$18,665

SOLUTION 5.

Home and Away Inspections Balance Sheet September 30, 20 --			
Assets		Liabilities	
Cash	$ 7,665	Accounts payable	$ 2,200
Accounts receivable	1,300		
Supplies	300	Owner's Equity	
Prepaid insurance	600	Kenny Young, capital	18,665
Tools	3,000		
Truck	8,000		
		Total liabilities and	
Total assets	$20,865	owner's equity	$20,865

KEY TERMS

account (23)   A separate record used to summarize changes in each asset, liability, and owner's equity of a business.

account title (23)   Provides a description of the particular type of asset, liability, owner's equity, revenue, or expense.

accounting equation (22)   The accounting equation consists of the three basic accounting elements: Assets = Liabilities + Owner's Equity.

accounting period concept (26)   The concept that income determination can be made on a periodic basis.

accounts payable (21)   An unwritten promise to pay a supplier for assets purchased or services received.

accounts receivable (21)   An amount owed to a business by its customers as a result of the sale of goods or services.

asset (21)   An item that is owned by a business and will provide future benefits.

balance sheet (34)   Reports assets, liabilities, and owner's equity on a specific date. It is called a balance sheet because it confirms that the accounting equation is in balance.

business entity (21)   An individual, association, or organization that engages in economic activities and controls specific economic resources.

business entity concept (21)   The concept that nonbusiness assets and liabilities are not included in the business entity's accounting records.

business transaction (23)   An economic event that has a direct impact on the business.

capital (21)   Another term for owner's equity, the amount by which the business assets exceed the business liabilities.

drawing (26)   Withdrawals that reduce owner's equity as a result of the owner taking cash or other assets out of the business for personal use.

expenses (25)   The decrease in assets (or increase in liabilities) as a result of efforts to produce revenues.

fiscal year (26)   Any accounting period of 12 months' duration.

income statement (32)   Reports the profitability of business operations for a specific period of time.

input (35)   Business transactions provide the necessary input for the accounting information system.

liability (21)   Something owed to another business entity.

liquidity (32)   A measure of the ease with which an asset will be converted to cash.

net income (26)   The excess of total revenues over total expenses for the period.

net loss (26)   The excess of total expenses over total revenues for the period.

net worth (21)   Another term for owner's equity, the amount by which the business assets exceed the business liabilities.

notes payable (21)   A formal written promise to pay a supplier or lender a specified sum of money at a definite future time.

operating statement (32)   Another name for the income statement, which reports the profitability of business operations for a specific period of time.

output (35)   The financial statements are the output of the accounting information system.

owner's equity (21)   The amount by which the business assets exceed the business liabilities.

processing (35)   Recognizing the effect of transactions on the assets, liabilities, owner's equity, revenues, and expenses of a business.

profit and loss statement (32)   Another name for the income statement, which reports the profitability of business operations for a specific period of time.

revenues (25)   The amount a business charges customers for products sold or services performed.

statement of financial condition (34)   Another name for the balance sheet, which reports assets, liabilities, and owner's equity on a specific date.

statement of financial position (34)   Another name for the balance sheet, which reports assets, liabilities, and owner's equity on a specific date.

statement of owner's equity (34)   Reports beginning capital plus net income less withdrawals to compute ending capital.

withdrawals (26)   Reduce owner's equity as a result of the owner taking cash or other assets out of the business for personal use.

SELF-STUDY TEST QUESTIONS

True/False

1. **LO1**   Assets are items that are owned by the business and are expected to provide future benefits.

2. **LO1**   Accounts Payable is an example of an asset account.

3. **LO1**   According to the business entity concept, nonbusiness assets and liabilities are not included in the business's accounting records.

4. **LO2**   The accounting equation (Assets = Liabilities + Owner's Equity) must always be in balance.

5. **LO2**   When an asset increases, a liability must also increase.

6. **LO3**   Expenses represent outflows of assets or increases in liabilities as a result of efforts to produce revenues.

7. **LO5**   When total revenues exceed total expenses, the difference is called net loss.

Multiple Choice

1. **LO4**   An increase to which of these accounts will increase owner's equity?
   (a) Accounts Payable   (c) Client Fees
   (b) Drawing   (d) Rent Expense

2. **LO4**   When delivery revenue is earned in cash, which accounts increase or decrease?
   (a) Cash increases; Revenue increases.
   (b) Cash decreases; Revenue increases.
   (c) Cash decreases; Revenue decreases.
   (d) Cash does not change; owner's equity increases.

3. **LO4** When delivery revenue is earned on account, which accounts increase or decrease?
(a) Cash increases; Revenue increases.
(b) Accounts Receivable increases; Revenue increases.
(c) Accounts Receivable increases; Revenue decreases.
(d) Accounts Receivable decreases; Revenue decreases.

4. **LO4** When payment is made on an existing debt, which accounts increase or decrease?
(a) Cash increases; Accounts Receivable increases.
(b) Cash decreases; Accounts Payable increases.
(c) Cash increases; Accounts Payable increases.
(d) Cash decreases; Accounts Payable decreases.

5. **LO5** Which of the following accounts does not appear on the income statement?
(a) Delivery Fees   (c) Drawing
(b) Wages Expense   (d) Rent Expense

CHECKPOINT ✔

Checkpoint Exercises

1. **LO1** Label each of the following accounts as an asset (A), a liability (L), or owner's equity (OE), using the following format:

Account	Classification
Accounts Receivable	_____
Accounts Payable	_____
Judy Smith, Capital	_____

2. **LO2** What is missing from the accounting equation below?

$$\underline{\quad ? \quad} = \text{Liabilities} + \text{Owner's Equity}$$

3. **LO3/4** What are the effects of the following transactions on the accounting equation? Indicate an increase (+) or decrease (−) under the affected asset, liability, and owner's equity headings.

Transaction	Assets	Liabilities	Owner's Equity
a. Purchase of an asset on account.	_____	_____	_____
b. Made payment on account for transaction (a).	_____	_____	_____

4. **LO5** Classify the following accounts as assets (A), liabilities (L), owner's equity (OE), revenue (R), or expense (E). Indicate the financial statement on which the account belongs—income statement (IS), statement of owner's equity (SOE), or balance sheet (BS).

Account	Classification	Financial Statement
Accounts Payable	_____	_____
Peggy Welsch, Drawing	_____	_____
Rent Expense	_____	_____
Sales	_____	_____
Equipment	_____	_____

The answers to the Self-Study Test Questions are at the end of the chapter (page 49).

CengageNowv2 provides "Show Me How" videos for selected exercises and problems. Additional resources, such as Excel templates for completing selected exercises and problems, are available for download from the companion website at Cengage.com.

REVIEW QUESTIONS

LO1 1. Why is it necessary to distinguish between business assets and liabilities and nonbusiness assets and liabilities of a single proprietor?

LO1/4 2. Name and define the six major elements of the accounting equation.

LO3 3. List the three basic questions that must be answered when analyzing the effects of a business transaction on the accounting equation.

LO5 4. What is the function of an income statement?

LO5 5. What is the function of a statement of owner's equity?

LO5 6. What is the function of a balance sheet?

LO6 7. What are the three basic phases of the accounting process?

SERIES A EXERCISES

E 2-1A (LO1)

ACCOUNTING ELEMENTS Label each of the following accounts as an asset (A), a liability (L), or owner's equity (OE), using the following format:

Item	Account	Classification
Money in bank	Cash	
Office supplies	Supplies	
Money owed	Accounts Payable	
Office chairs	Office Furniture	
Net worth of owner	John Smith, Capital	
Money withdrawn by owner	John Smith, Drawing	
Money owed by customers	Accounts Receivable	

E 2-2A (LO2)

THE ACCOUNTING EQUATION Using the accounting equation, compute the missing elements.

Assets	=	Liabilities	+	Owner's Equity
_____	=	$27,000	+	$17,000
$32,000	=	$18,000	+	_____
$27,000	=	_____	+	$20,000

E 2-3A (LO3/4)

✓ Assets following (d): $32,200

EFFECTS OF TRANSACTIONS (BALANCE SHEET ACCOUNTS) John Sullivan started a business. During the first month (February 20--), the following transactions occurred. Show the effect of each transaction on the accounting equation: *Assets = Liabilities + Owner's Equity*. After each transaction, show the new totals.

(a) Invested cash in the business, $27,000.

(b) Bought office equipment on account, $7,500.

(c) Bought office equipment for cash, $1,600.

(d) Paid cash on account to supplier in transaction (b), $2,300.

E 2-4A   (LO3/4)
✓ Assets following (k): $31,586

EFFECTS OF TRANSACTIONS (REVENUE, EXPENSE, WITHDRAWALS) This exercise is an extension of Exercise 2-3A. Let's assume John Sullivan completed the following additional transactions during February. Show the effect of each transaction on the basic elements of the expanded accounting equation: *Assets = Liabilities + Owner's Equity (Capital − Drawing + Revenues − Expenses)*. After transaction (k), report the totals for each element. Demonstrate that the accounting equation has remained in balance.

(e) Received cash from a client for professional services, $1,500.

(f) Paid office rent for February, $600.

(g) Paid February phone bill, $64.

(h) Withdrew cash for personal use, $1,000.

(i) Performed services for clients on account, $750.

(j) Paid wages to part-time employee, $1,200.

(k) Received cash for services performed on account in transaction (i), $400.

E 2-5A   (LO1/5)

FINANCIAL STATEMENT ACCOUNTS Label each of the following accounts as an asset (A), liability (L), owner's equity (OE), revenue (R), or expense (E). Indicate the financial statement on which the account belongs—income statement (IS), statement of owner's equity (SOE), or balance sheet (BS)—in a format similar to the following.

Account	Classification	Financial Statement
Cash		
Rent Expense		
Accounts Payable		
Service Fees		
Supplies		
Wages Expense		
Ramon Martinez, Drawing		
Ramon Martinez, Capital		
Prepaid Insurance		
Accounts Receivable		

E 2-6A   (LO5)
✓ Capital, 6/30: $22,000

STATEMENT OF OWNER'S EQUITY REPORTING NET INCOME Betsy Ray started an accounting service on June 1, 20--, by investing $20,000. Her net income for the month was $10,000, and she withdrew $8,000. Prepare a statement of owner's equity for the month of June.

E 2-7A   (LO5)
✓ Capital, 6/30: $9,000

STATEMENT OF OWNER'S EQUITY REPORTING NET LOSS Based on the information provided in Exercise 2-6A, prepare a statement of owner's equity assuming Ray had a net loss of $3,000.

SERIES A PROBLEMS

P 2-8A   (LO1/2)
✓ 3: $32,040 = $12,910 + $19,130

THE ACCOUNTING EQUATION Dr. John Salvaggi is a chiropractor. As of December 31, he owned the following property that related to his professional practice.

Cash	$ 3,500
Office Equipment	6,400
X-ray Equipment	10,220
Laboratory Equipment	6,840

He also owes the following business suppliers:

Chateau Gas Company	$ 3,430
Aloe Medical Supply Company	4,120

REQUIRED

1. From the preceding information, compute the accounting elements and enter them in the accounting equation shown as follows.

Assets	=	Liabilities	+	Owner's Equity
_____	=	_____	+	_____

2. During January, the assets increase by $8,540, and the liabilities increase by $3,360. Compute the resulting accounting equation.
3. During February, the assets decrease by $3,460, and the liabilities increase by $2,000. Compute the resulting accounting equation.

P 2-9A   (LO3/4)
✓ Total cash following (g): $12,950

EFFECT OF TRANSACTIONS ON ACCOUNTING EQUATION Jay Pembroke started a business. During the first month (April 20--), the following transactions occurred.

(a) Invested cash in business, $18,000.
(b) Bought office supplies for $4,600: $2,000 in cash and $2,600 on account.
(c) Paid one-year insurance premium, $1,200.
(d) Earned revenues totaling $3,300: $1,300 in cash and $2,000 on account.
(e) Paid cash on account to the company that supplied the office supplies in transaction (b), $2,300.
(f) Paid office rent for the month, $750.
(g) Withdrew cash for personal use, $100.

REQUIRED

Show the effect of each transaction on the individual accounts of the expanded accounting equation: *Assets = Liabilities + Owner's Equity (Capital − Drawing + Revenues − Expenses)*. After transaction (g), report the totals for each element. Demonstrate that the accounting equation has remained in balance.

P 2-10A   (LO5)
✓ Net income: $2,550

INCOME STATEMENT Based on Problem 2-9A, prepare an income statement for Jay Pembroke for the month of April 20--.

P 2-11A   (LO5)
✓ Capital, 4/30: $20,450

STATEMENT OF OWNER'S EQUITY Based on Problem 2-9A, prepare a statement of owner's equity for Jay Pembroke for the month of April 20--.

P 2-12A   (LO5)
✓ Total assets, 4/30: $20,750

BALANCE SHEET Based on Problem 2-9A, prepare a balance sheet for Jay Pembroke as of April 30, 20--.

SERIES B EXERCISES

E 2-1B   (LO1)

ACCOUNTING ELEMENTS Label each of the following accounts as an asset (A), liability (L), or owner's equity (OE) using the following format.

Account	Classification
Cash	
Accounts Payable	
Supplies	
Bill Jones, Drawing	
Prepaid Insurance	
Accounts Receivable	
Bill Jones, Capital	

E 2-2B   (LO2)

THE ACCOUNTING EQUATION Using the accounting equation, compute the missing elements.

Assets	=	Liabilities	+	Owner's Equity
_____	=	$20,000	+	$ 5,000
$30,000	=	$15,000	+	_____
$20,000	=	_____	+	$10,000

E 2-3B   (LO3/4)
✓ Assets following (d): $32,500

EFFECTS OF TRANSACTIONS (BALANCE SHEET ACCOUNTS) Jon Wallace started a business. During the first month (March 20--), the following transactions occurred. Show the effect of each transaction on the accounting equation: *Assets = Liabilities + Owner's Equity*. After each transaction, show the new account totals.

(a) Invested cash in the business, $30,000.

(b) Bought office equipment on account, $4,500.

(c) Bought office equipment for cash, $1,600.

(d) Paid cash on account to supplier in transaction (b), $2,000.

E 2-4B   (LO3/4)
✓ Assets following (k): $34,032

EFFECTS OF TRANSACTIONS (REVENUE, EXPENSE, WITHDRAWALS) This exercise is an extension of Exercise 2-3B. Let's assume Jon Wallace completed the following additional transactions during March. Show the effect of each transaction on the basic elements of the expanded accounting equation: *Assets = Liabilities + Owner's Equity (Capital − Drawing + Revenues − Expenses)*. After transaction (k), report the totals for each element. Demonstrate that the accounting equation has remained in balance.

(e) Performed services and received cash, $3,000.

(f) Paid rent for March, $1,000.

(g) Paid March phone bill, $68.

(*continued*)

(h) Jon Wallace withdrew cash for personal use, $800.

(i) Performed services for clients on account, $900.

(j) Paid wages to part-time employee, $500.

(k) Received cash for services performed on account in transaction (i), $500.

E 2-5B (LO1/5)

FINANCIAL STATEMENT ACCOUNTS Label each of the following accounts as an asset (A), liability (L), owner's equity (OE), revenue (R), or expense (E). Indicate the financial statement on which the account belongs—income statement (IS), statement of owner's equity (SOE), or balance sheet (BS)—in a format similar to the following.

Account	Classification	Financial Statement
Cash		
Rent Expense		
Accounts Payable		
Service Fees		
Supplies		
Wages Expense		
Amanda Wong, Drawing		
Amanda Wong, Capital		
Prepaid Insurance		
Accounts Receivable		

E 2-6B (LO5)
✓ Capital, 6/30: $14,000

STATEMENT OF OWNER'S EQUITY REPORTING NET INCOME Efran Lopez started a financial consulting service on June 1, 20--, by investing $15,000. His net income for the month was $6,000, and he withdrew $7,000 for personal use. Prepare a statement of owner's equity for the month of June.

E 2-7B (LO5)
✓ Capital, 6/30: $6,000

STATEMENT OF OWNER'S EQUITY REPORTING NET LOSS Based on the information provided in Exercise 2-6B, prepare a statement of owner's equity assuming Lopez had a net loss of $2,000.

SERIES B PROBLEMS

P 2-8B (LO1/2)
✓ 3: $25,235 = $10,165 + $15,070

THE ACCOUNTING EQUATION Dr. Patricia Parsons is a dentist. As of January 31, Parsons owned the following property that related to her professional practice:

Cash	$3,560
Office Equipment	4,600
X-ray Equipment	8,760
Laboratory Equipment	5,940

She also owes the following business suppliers:

Cupples Gas Company	$1,815
Swan Dental Lab	2,790

REQUIRED

1. From the preceding information, compute the accounting elements and enter them in the accounting equation as shown below.

Assets	=	Liabilities	+	Owner's Equity
_____	=	_____	+	_____

2. During February, the assets increase by $4,565, and the liabilities increase by $3,910. Compute the resulting accounting equation.

3. During March, the assets decrease by $2,190, and the liabilities increase by $1,650. Compute the resulting accounting equation.

P 2-9B   (LO3/4)
✓ Total cash following (g): $11,300

EFFECT OF TRANSACTIONS ON ACCOUNTING EQUATION David Segal started a business. During the first month (October 20--), the following transactions occurred.

(a) Invested cash in the business, $15,000.

(b) Bought office supplies for $3,800: $1,800 in cash and $2,000 on account.

(c) Paid one-year insurance premium, $1,000.

(d) Earned revenues amounting to $2,700: $1,700 in cash and $1,000 on account.

(e) Paid cash on account to the company that supplied the office supplies in transaction (b), $1,800.

(f) Paid office rent for the month, $650.

(g) Withdrew cash for personal use, $150.

REQUIRED

Show the effect of each transaction on the individual accounts of the expanded accounting equation: *Assets = Liabilities + Owner's Equity (Capital − Drawing + Revenues − Expenses)*. After transaction (g), report the totals for each element. Demonstrate that the accounting equation has remained in balance.

P 2-10B   (LO5)
✓ Net income: $2,050

INCOME STATEMENT Based on Problem 2-9B, prepare an income statement for David Segal for the month of October 20--.

P 2-11B   (LO5)
✓ Capital, 10/31: $16,900

STATEMENT OF OWNER'S EQUITY Based on Problem 2-9B, prepare a statement of owner's equity for David Segal for the month of October 20--.

P 2-12B   (LO5)
✓ Total assets, 10/31: $17,100

BALANCE SHEET Based on Problem 2-9B, prepare a balance sheet for David Segal as of October 31, 20--.

CHECK LIST
- ☐ **Managing**
- ☐ **Planning**
- ☐ **Drafting**
- ☐ **Break**
- ☐ **Revising**
- ☐ **Managing**

MANAGING YOUR WRITING

Write a brief memo that explains the differences and similarities between expenses and withdrawals.

MASTERY PROBLEM

✓ Cash following (p): $3,105
✓ Revenue following (p): $2,100

Lisa Vozniak started her own business, We Do Windows. She offers interior and exterior window cleaning for local area residents. Lisa rents a garage to store her tools and cleaning supplies and has a part-time assistant to answer the phone and handle third-story work. (Lisa is afraid of heights.) The transactions for the month of July are as follows:

(a) Lisa invested cash by making a deposit in a bank account for the business, $8,000.

(b) Paid rent for July, $150.

(c) Purchased a used van for cash, $5,000.

(d) Purchased tools on account from Clean Tools, $600.

(e) Purchased cleaning supplies that cost $300. Paid $200 cash and will pay the balance next month, $100.

(f) Paid part-time assistant (wages) for first half of month, $100.

(g) Paid for advertising, $75.

(h) Paid two-year premium for liability insurance on van, $480.

(i) Received cash from clients for services performed, $800.

(j) Performed cleaning services for clients on account, $500.

(k) Paid phone bill, $40.

(l) Received cash from clients for window cleaning performed on account in transaction (j), $200.

(m) Paid part-time assistant (wages) for last half of month, $150.

(n) Made partial payment on tools purchased in transaction (d), $200.

(o) Earned additional revenues amounting to $800: $600 in cash and $200 on account.

(p) Vozniak withdrew cash at the end of the month for personal expenses, $100.

REQUIRED

1. Enter the above transactions in an accounting equation similar to the one illustrated below.

Assets (Items Owned)						=	Liabilities (Amounts Owed)	+	Owner's Equity (Owner's Investment) + (Earnings)				
Cash +	Accounts Receivable +	Supplies +	Prepaid Insurance +	Tools +	Van =		Accounts Payable	+	Lisa Vozniak, Capital	– Lisa Vozniak, Drawing	+ Revenues	– Expenses	Description

2. After transaction (p), compute the balance of each account.

3. Prepare an income statement for We Do Windows for the month of July 20--.

4. Prepare a statement of owner's equity for We Do Windows for the month of July 20--.

5. Prepare a balance sheet for We Do Windows as of July 31, 20--.

This problem challenges you to apply your cumulative accounting knowledge to move a step beyond the material in the chapter.

CHALLENGE PROBLEM

✓ Cash difference: $2,165

In this chapter, you learned about three important financial statements: the income statement, statement of owner's equity, and balance sheet. As mentioned in the margin note on page 34, most firms also prepare a statement of cash flows. Part of this statement reports the cash received from customers and cash paid for goods and services.

REQUIRED

Take another look at the Demonstration Problem for Kenny Young's "Home and Away Inspections." Note that when revenues are measured based on the amount earned, and expenses are measured based on the amount incurred, net income for the period was $4,165. Now, compute the difference between cash received from customers and cash paid to suppliers of goods and services by completing the form provided below. Are these measures different? Which provides a better measure of profitability?

Cash from customers	_____
Cash paid for wages	_____
Cash paid for rent	_____
Cash paid for utilities	_____
Cash paid for insurance	_____
Cash paid for supplies	_____
Cash paid for phone	_____
Total cash paid for operating items	_____
Difference between cash received from customers and cash paid for goods and services	_____

ANSWERS TO SELF-STUDY TEST QUESTIONS

True/False

1. T
2. F (Accounts Payable is a liability.)
3. T
4. T
5. F (Other changes could occur: capital could increase, revenue could increase, etc.)
6. T
7. F (net income)

Multiple Choice

1. c　2. a　3. b　4. d　5. c

Checkpoint Exercises

1.
Account	Classification
Accounts Receivable	A
Accounts Payable	L
Judy Smith, Capital	OE

2. Assets = Liabilities + Owner's Equity

3.
Transaction	Assets	Liabilities	Owner's Equity
a. Purchase of an asset on account.	+	+	
b. Made payment on account for transaction (a).	−	−	

4.
Account	Classification	Financial Statement
Accounts Payable	L	BS
Peggy Welsch, Drawing	OE	SOE
Rent Expense	E	IS
Sales	R	IS
Equipment	A	BS

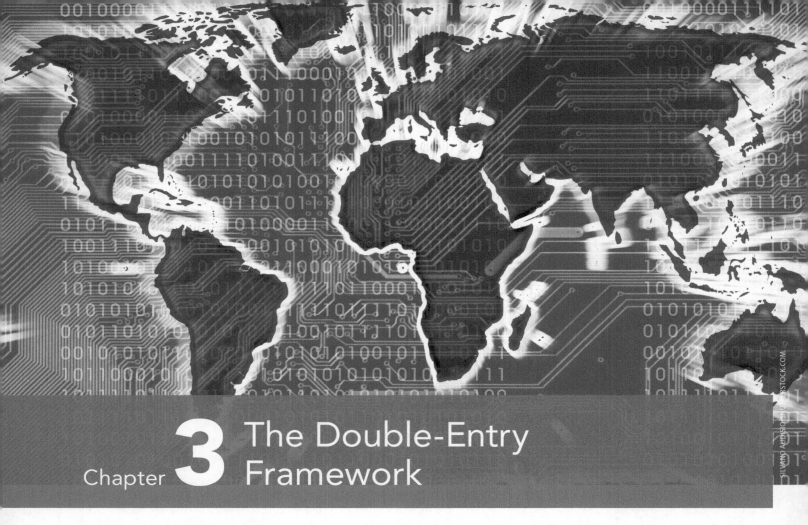

Chapter **3** The Double-Entry Framework

LEARNING OBJECTIVES

Careful study of this chapter should enable you to:

LO1 Define the parts of a T account.

LO2 Foot and balance a T account.

LO3 Describe the effects of debits and credits on specific types of accounts.

LO4 Use T accounts to analyze transactions.

LO5 Prepare a trial balance and explain its purposes and linkages with the financial statements.

Tired of receiving spam e-mail messages? Or, are you worried about your computer picking up a virus, or being hacked? Businesses have the same concerns. In response to demand for email and web security, AppRiver was founded in April of 2002 to provide simple, yet powerful protection from Internet-based threats to businesses of any size. The company is based in Gulf Breeze, Florida, and maintains multiple data centers at secure locations in the United States, Europe, and Asia. AppRiver's 200 employees protect more than 60,000 companies around the world by providing spam and virus protection, email encryption, and web security.

Just as internet security is important to you in your personal life and to businesses, the same can be said about accounting. A solid understanding of financial accounting will help you manage your personal finances and help you understand business transactions in your professional life. In this chapter, you will learn about the double-entry framework used by businesses to enter transactions into an accounting system. You could use the same concepts for your personal transactions or for a business you might start.

The terms asset, liability, owner's equity, revenue, and expense were explained in Chapter 2. Examples showed how individual business transactions change one or more of these basic accounting elements. Each transaction had a dual effect. An increase or decrease in any asset, liability, owner's equity, revenue, or expense was *always* accompanied by an offsetting change within the basic accounting elements. The fact that each transaction has a dual effect upon the accounting elements provides the basis for what is called double-entry accounting. To understand double-entry accounting, it is important to learn how T accounts work and the role of debits and credits in accounting.

LO1 — The T Account

Define the parts of a T account.

The assets of a business may consist of a number of items, such as cash, accounts receivable, equipment, buildings, and land. The liabilities may consist of one or more items, such as accounts payable and notes payable. Similarly, owner's equity may consist of the owner's investments and various revenue and expense items. A separate account is used to record the increases and decreases in each type of asset, liability, owner's equity, revenue, and expense.

The T account gets its name from the fact that it resembles the letter T. The three major parts of an account are as follows:

> **LEARNING KEY** 🔑
>
> Debit means left and credit means right.

1. the title,
2. the debit, or left side, and
3. the credit, or right side.

	Title	
Debit = Left		Credit = Right

The debit side is always on the left, and the credit side is always on the right. This is true for all types of asset, liability, owner's equity, revenue, and expense accounts.

Sometimes new accounting students think that a debit is bad because it sounds like "debt." Similarly, credit sounds like a good thing, especially when the bank says they will credit your account. Please clear your mind of these thoughts. *In accounting, debit simply means left and credit means right.*

LO2 — Balancing a T Account

Foot and balance a T account.

To determine the balance of a T account at any time, simply total the dollar amounts on the debit and credit sides. These totals are known as footings. The difference between the footings is called the balance of the account. This amount is then written on the side with the larger footing.

In Chapter 2, the accounting equation was used to analyze business transactions. This required columns in which to record the increases and decreases in various accounts. Let's compare this approach with the use of a T account for the transactions affecting cash. When a T account is used, increases in cash are recorded on the debit side and decreases are recorded on the credit side. Transactions for Mitchell's Campus Delivery are shown in Figure 3-1.

FIGURE 3-1 Cash T Account

COLUMNAR SUMMARY (From Chapter 2, page 31)		T ACCOUNT FORM			
Transaction	**Cash**	Cash			
(a)	5,000	(a) 5,000		(b)	2,000
(b)	(2,000)	(e) 2,100		(d)	600
(d)	(600)	(j) 1,900		(f)	1,000
(e)	2,100	(n) 900		(g)	100
(f)	(1,000)	footing ⟶ **9,900**		(i)	80
(g)	(100)			(k)	300
(i)	(80)			(l)	700
(j)	1,900			(m)	1,650
(k)	(300)			(o)	3,000
(l)	(700)	Balance ⟶ 470		**9,430** ⟵ footing	
(m)	(1,650)				
(n)	900				
(o)	(3,000)				
Balance	470				

> **CHECKPOINT ✔**
> Complete Checkpoint-1 on page 74 to test your basic understanding of LO2.

LO3   Debits and Credits

Describe the effects of debits and credits on specific types of accounts.

To *debit* an account means to enter an amount on the left or debit side of the account. To *credit* an account means to enter an amount on the right or credit side of the account. *Debits may increase or decrease the balances of specific accounts. This is also true for credits. To learn how to use debits and credits, it is best to focus on the accounting equation.*

> Abbreviations: Often debit and credit are abbreviated as: Dr. = Debit, Cr. = Credit (based on the Latin terms "debere" and "credere")

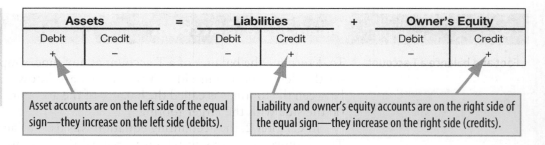

Assets		=	Liabilities		+	Owner's Equity	
Debit	Credit		Debit	Credit		Debit	Credit
+	–		–	+		–	+

Asset accounts are on the left side of the equal sign—they increase on the left side (debits).

Liability and owner's equity accounts are on the right side of the equal sign—they increase on the right side (credits).

Assets

Assets are on the left side of the accounting equation. Therefore, increases are entered on the left (debit) side of an asset account, and decreases are entered on the right (credit) side.

Liabilities and Owner's Equity

Liabilities and owner's equity are on the right side of the equation. Therefore, increases are entered on the right (credit) side, and decreases are entered on the left (debit) side.

The Owner's Equity Umbrella

Owner's equity includes four types of accounts: Owner's Capital, Revenues, Expenses, and Drawing. Expanding the accounting equation helps illustrate the use of debits and credits. Since these accounts affect owner's equity, they are shown under the "umbrella" of owner's equity in the accounting equation in Figure 3-2. It is helpful to think of the Owner's Capital account as hovering over the revenue, expense, and drawing accounts like an umbrella. Since revenues increase Owner's Capital, the revenue account is shown under the credit side of Owner's Capital. Since expenses and drawing reduce Owner's Capital, they are shown under the debit side of Owner's Capital.

FIGURE 3-2 The Accounting Equation and the Owner's Equity Umbrella

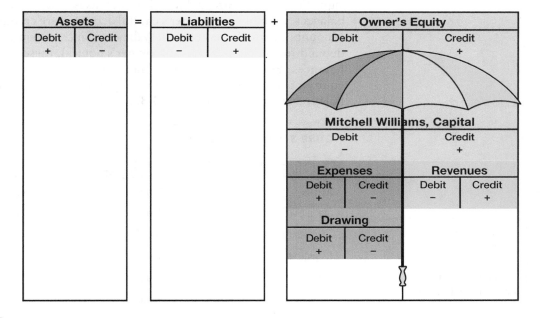

Owner's Capital

The owner's capital account, Mitchell Williams, Capital, in Figure 3-2 reports the amount the owner has invested in the business. These investments increase the owner's equity and are credited to the owner's capital account.

Revenues

Revenues increase owner's equity. Revenues could be recorded directly on the credit side of the owner's capital account. However, readers of financial statements are interested in the specific types of revenues earned. Therefore, specific revenue accounts, like Delivery Fees, Sales, and Service Fees, are used. These specific accounts are credited when revenue is earned.

Remember: An increase in an expense decreases owner's equity.

Expenses

Expenses decrease owner's equity. Expenses could be recorded on the debit side of the owner's capital account. However, readers of financial statements want to see the types of expenses incurred during the accounting period. Thus, specific expense accounts are maintained for items like rent, wages, advertising, and utilities. These specific accounts are debited as expenses are incurred.

Drawing

Withdrawals of cash and other assets by the owner for personal reasons decrease owner's equity. Withdrawals could be debited directly to the owner's capital account. However, readers of financial statements want to know the amount of withdrawals for the accounting period. Thus, as shown in Figure 3-2, withdrawals are debited to a separate account, Drawing.

Normal Balances

A normal balance is the side of an account that is used to increase the account. Thus, the normal balances for the accounts illustrated in Figure 3-2 are shown with a "+" sign. Since assets are debited for increases, these accounts normally have debit balances. Liability and owner's capital accounts are credited for increases; thus, these accounts normally have credit balances. Since expense and drawing accounts are debited for increases (reducing owner's equity), these accounts normally have debit balances. Finally, revenue accounts are credited for increases (increasing owner's equity); thus, these accounts normally have credit balances. A summary of normal balances is provided in Figure 3-3.

FIGURE 3-3 Normal Balances

ACCOUNT	INCREASE	DECREASE	NORMAL BALANCE
Assets	Debit	Credit	Debit
Liabilities	Credit	Debit	Credit
Owner's Capital	Credit	Debit	Credit
Revenues	Credit	Debit	Credit
Expenses	Debit	Credit	Debit
Drawing	Debit	Credit	Debit

CHECKPOINT ✔
Complete Checkpoint-2 on page 74 to test your basic understanding of LO3.

LO4   Transaction Analysis

Use T accounts to analyze transactions.

LEARNING KEY 🔑
Since the accounting equation must stay in balance, there must be at least one debit and at least one credit for each transaction.

In Chapter 2, you learned how to analyze transactions by using the accounting equation. Here, we continue to use the accounting equation, but add debits and credits by using T accounts. As shown in Figure 3-4, the three basic questions that must be answered when analyzing a transaction are essentially the same but are expanded slightly to address the use of the owner's equity umbrella and T accounts. You must determine the location of the account within the accounting equation and/or the owner's equity umbrella. You must also determine whether the accounts should be debited or credited.

FIGURE 3-4 Steps in Transaction Analysis

1. **What happened?**
   Be sure you understand the event that has taken place.

2. **Which accounts are affected?**
   Once you understand what happened, you must:

   • Identify the accounts that are affected.
   • Classify these accounts as assets, liabilities, owner's equity, revenues, or expenses.
   • Identify the location of the accounts in the accounting equation and/or the owner's equity umbrella—left or right.

3. **How is the accounting equation affected?**

   • Determine whether the accounts have increased or decreased.
   • Determine whether the accounts should be debited or credited.
   • Make certain the accounting equation remains in balance after the transaction has been entered.
   (1) Assets = Liabilities + Owner's Equity
   (2) Debits = Credits for every transaction

Debits and Credits: Asset, Liability, and Owner's Equity Accounts

Transactions (a) through (d) from Mitchell's Campus Delivery (Chapter 2) demonstrate the double-entry process for transactions affecting asset, liability, and owner's equity accounts.

As you study each transaction, answer the three questions: (1) What happened? (2) Which accounts are affected? and (3) How is the accounting equation affected? The transaction statement tells you what happened. The analysis tells which accounts are affected. The illustration shows you how the accounting equation is affected.

Transaction (a): Investment by owner

Mitchell Williams, opened a bank account with a deposit of $5,000 for his business (Figure 3-5).

Analysis. As a result of this transaction, the business acquired an asset, Cash. In exchange for the asset, the business gave Mitchell Williams, owner's equity. The owner's equity account is called Mitchell Williams, Capital. The transaction is entered as an increase in an asset and an increase in owner's equity. Debit Cash and credit Mitchell Williams, Capital for $5,000.

FIGURE 3-5 Transaction (a): Investment by Owner

Assets		=	Liabilities		+	Owner's Equity	
Debit +	Credit −		Debit −	Credit +		Debit −	Credit +
Cash						**Mitchell Williams, Capital**	
(a) 5,000							(a) 5,000
$5,000		=	$0		+	$5,000	
$5,000		=		$5,000			

Transaction (b): Purchase of an asset for cash

Mitch bought a motor scooter (delivery equipment) for $2,000 cash (Figure 3-6).

Analysis. Mitch exchanged one asset, Cash, for another, Delivery Equipment. Debit Delivery Equipment and credit Cash for $2,000. Notice that the total assets are still $5,000 as they were following transaction (a). Transaction (b) shifted assets from cash to delivery equipment, but total assets remained the same.

FIGURE 3-6 Transaction (b): Purchase of an Asset for Cash

Assets		=	Liabilities		+	Owner's Equity	
Debit +	Credit −		Debit −	Credit +		Debit −	Credit +
Cash						Mitchell Williams, Capital	
Bal. 5,000							Bal. 5,000
	(b) 2,000						
Bal. 3,000							
Delivery Equipment							
(b) 2,000							
$5,000		=	$0		+	$5,000	
$5,000		=			$5,000		

Transaction (c): Purchase of an asset on account

Mitch bought a second motor scooter on account for $1,800 (Figure 3-7). Recall from Chapter 2 that "on account" means Mitch will pay for the asset later.

Analysis. The asset, Delivery Equipment, increases by $1,800 and the liability, Accounts Payable, increases by the same amount. Thus, debit Delivery Equipment and credit Accounts Payable for $1,800.

FIGURE 3-7 Transaction (c): Purchase of an Asset on Account

Assets		=	Liabilities		+	Owner's Equity	
Debit +	Credit −		Debit −	Credit +		Debit −	Credit +
Cash			Accounts Payable			Mitchell Williams, Capital	
Bal. 3,000				(c) 1,800			Bal. 5,000
Delivery Equipment							
Bal. 2,000							
(c) 1,800							
Bal. 3,800							
$6,800		=	$1,800		+	$5,000	
$6,800		=			$6,800		

Transaction (d): Payment on account

Mitch made the first $600 payment on the scooter purchased in transaction (c) (Figure 3-8).

Analysis. This payment decreases the asset, Cash, and decreases the liability, Accounts Payable. Debit Accounts Payable and credit Cash for $600.

FIGURE 3-8 Transaction (d): Payment on Account

Assets		=	Liabilities		+	Owner's Equity	
Debit +	Credit −		Debit −	Credit +		Debit −	Credit +

Cash			Accounts Payable			Mitchell Williams, Capital	
Bal. 3,000	(d) 600		(d) 600	Bal. 1,800			Bal. 5,000
Bal. 2,400				Bal. 1,200			

Delivery Equipment	
Bal. 3,800	

$6,200	=	$1,200	+	$5,000
$6,200	=	**$6,200**		

Notice that for transactions (a) through (d), the debits equal credits and the accounting equation is in balance. Review transactions (a) through (d). Again, identify the accounts that were affected and how they were classified (assets, liabilities, or owner's equity). Finally, note each account's location within the accounting equation.

Debits and Credits: Including Revenues, Expenses, and Drawing

Transactions (a) through (d) involved only assets, liabilities, and the owner's capital account. To complete the illustration of Mitchell's Campus Delivery, the equation is expanded to include revenues, expenses, and drawing. Remember, revenues increase owner's equity and are shown under the credit side of the capital account. Expenses and drawing decrease owner's equity and are shown under the debit side of the capital account. The expanded equation is shown in Figure 3-9.

FIGURE 3-9 The Expanded Accounting Equation

Assets		=	Liabilities		+	Owner's Equity	
Debit +	Credit −		Debit −	Credit +		Debit −	Credit +

Drawing		Expenses		Revenues	
Debit +	Credit −	Debit +	Credit −	Debit −	Credit +

Transaction (e): Delivery revenues earned in cash

Mitch made deliveries and received $2,100 cash from clients (Figure 3-10).

Analysis. The asset, Cash, and the revenue, Delivery Fees, increase. Debit Cash and credit Delivery Fees for $2,100.

FIGURE 3-10 Transaction (e): Delivery Revenues Earned in Cash

Assets		=	Liabilities		+	Owner's Equity	
Debit +	Credit −		Debit −	Credit +		Debit −	Credit +

Cash
Bal. 2,400
(e) 2,100
Bal. 4,500

Delivery Equipment
Bal. 3,800

Accounts Payable
Bal. 1,200

Mitchell Williams, Capital
Bal. 5,000

Drawing		Expenses		Revenues	
Debit +	Credit −	Debit +	Credit −	Debit −	Credit +

Delivery Fees
(e) 2,100

$8,300 = $1,200 + $7,100

$8,300 = $8,300

Transaction (f): Paid rent for month

Mitch paid $1,000 for office rent for June (Figure 3-11).

Analysis. Rent Expense increases and Cash decreases. Debit Rent Expense and credit Cash for $1,000.

A debit to an expense account *increases* that expense and *decreases* owner's equity. Notice that the placement of the plus and minus signs for expenses is opposite the placement of the signs for owner's equity. Note also that expenses are located on the left (debit) side of the owner's equity umbrella.

FIGURE 3-11 Transaction (f): Paid Rent for Month

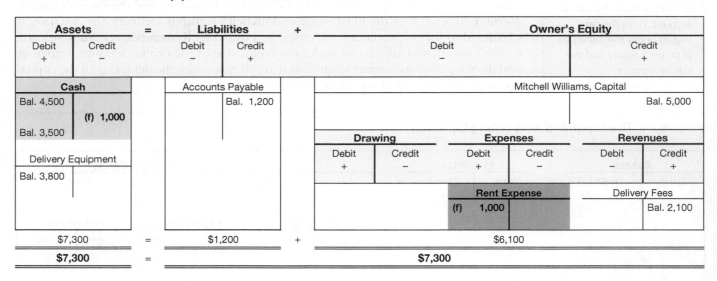

Transaction (g): Paid phone bill

Mitch paid for phone service, $100 (Figure 3-12).

Analysis. This transaction, like the previous one, increases an expense and decreases an asset. Debit Phone Expense and credit Cash for $100.

FIGURE 3-12 Transaction (g): Paid Phone Bill

Assets		=	Liabilities		+	Owner's Equity		
Debit +	Credit −		Debit −	Credit +		Debit −		Credit +

Cash			Accounts Payable			Mitchell Williams, Capital	
Bal. 3,500				Bal. 1,200			Bal. 5,000
	(g) 100						
Bal. 3,400							

Delivery Equipment					Drawing		Expenses		Revenues	
Bal. 3,800					Debit +	Credit −	Debit +	Credit −	Debit −	Credit +

Rent Expense / Delivery Fees

Rent Expense		Delivery Fees	
Bal. 1,000			Bal. 2,100

Phone Expense	
(g) 100	

$7,200	=	$1,200	+	$6,000
$7,200	=			**$7,200**

Transaction (h): Delivery revenues earned on account

Mitch made deliveries on account for $2,400 (Figure 3-13).

Analysis. As discussed in Chapter 2, delivery services are performed for which payment will be received later. This is called offering services "on account" or "on credit." Instead of receiving cash, Mitch receives a promise that his customers will pay cash in the future. Therefore, the asset, Accounts Receivable, increases. Since revenues are recognized when earned, the revenue account, Delivery Fees, also increases. Debit Accounts Receivable and credit Delivery Fees for $2,400.

FIGURE 3-13 Transaction (h): Delivery Revenues Earned on Account

Assets		=	Liabilities		+	Owner's Equity		
Debit +	Credit −		Debit −	Credit +		Debit −		Credit +

Cash			Accounts Payable			Mitchell Williams, Capital	
Bal. 3,400				Bal. 1,200			Bal. 5,000

Accounts Receivable					Drawing		Expenses		Revenues	
(h) 2,400					Debit +	Credit −	Debit +	Credit −	Debit −	Credit +

Delivery Equipment					Rent Expense		Delivery Fees	
Bal. 3,800					Bal. 1,000			Bal. 2,100
								(h) 2,400
								Bal. 4,500

Phone Expense	
Bal. 100	

$9,600	=	$1,200	+	$8,400
$9,600	=			**$9,600**

Review transactions (e) through (h). Note the following:

- Expense and revenue transactions do not always affect cash.
- The debits equal credits, and the accounting equation is in balance after each transaction.

Upcoming transactions (i) and (l) both involve an exchange of cash for another asset. As you analyze these two transactions, you may wonder why prepaid insurance and supplies are assets while the rent and phone bill in transactions (f) and (g) are expenses. Prepaid insurance and supplies are assets because they will provide benefits for more than one month. Mitch pays his rent and his phone bill each month so they are classified as expenses. If Mitch paid his rent only once every three months, he would need to set up an asset account called Prepaid Rent. He would debit this account when he paid the rent.

Transaction (i): Purchase of Supplies

Mitch bought pens, paper, delivery envelopes, and other supplies for $80 cash (Figure 3-14).

Analysis. These supplies will last for several months. Since they will generate future benefits, the supplies should be recorded as an asset. An asset, Supplies, increases, and an asset, Cash, decreases. Debit Supplies and credit Cash for $80.

FIGURE 3-14 Transaction (i): Purchase of Supplies

A BROADER VIEW

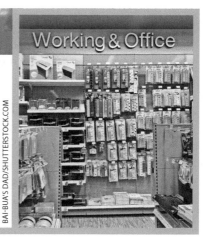

Working & Office

BAI-BUA'S DAD/SHUTTERSTOCK.COM

Supplies—Asset or Expense?

When businesses buy office supplies from Staples or other suppliers, the supplies are initially recorded as assets. This is done because the supplies will provide future benefits. Those still remaining in inventory at the end of the accounting period are reported on the balance sheet as assets. Supplies actually used during the period are recognized as an expense on the income statement. We will discuss how to account for the expense in Chapter 5.

Transaction (j): Cash receipts from prior sales on account

Mitch received $1,900 in cash for delivery services performed for customers earlier in the month [see transaction (h)] (Figure 3-15).

Analysis. This transaction increases Cash and reduces the amount due from customers reported in Accounts Receivable. Debit Cash and credit Accounts Receivable $1,900.

As you analyze transaction (j), notice which accounts are affected and the location of these accounts in the accounting equation. Mitch received cash, but this transaction did not affect revenue. The revenue was recorded in transaction (h). Transaction (j) is an exchange of one asset (Accounts Receivable) for another asset (Cash).

FIGURE 3-15 Transaction (j): Cash Receipts from Prior Sales on Account

Assets		=	Liabilities		+	Owner's Equity	
Debit +	Credit −		Debit −	Credit +		Debit −	Credit +

Cash		Accounts Payable		Mitchell Williams, Capital	
Bal. 3,320			Bal. 1,200		Bal. 5,000
(j) 1,900					
Bal. 5,220					

Accounts Receivable	
Bal. 2,400	
	(j) 1,900
Bal. 500	

Drawing		Expenses		Revenues	
Debit +	Credit −	Debit +	Credit −	Debit −	Credit +

Supplies	
Bal. 80	

Rent Expense		Delivery Fees	
Bal. 1,000			Bal. 4,500

Delivery Equipment	
Bal. 3,800	

Phone Expense	
Bal. 100	

$9,600	=	$1,200	+	$8,400
$9,600	=		**$9,600**	

As you analyze transactions (k) through (o), make certain that you understand what has happened in each transaction. Identify the accounts that are affected and the locations of these accounts within the accounting equation. Notice that the accounting equation remains in balance after every transaction and debits equal credits for each transaction.

Transaction (k): Purchase of an asset on credit making a partial payment

Mitch bought a third motor scooter for $1,000. Mitch made a down payment of $300 and spread the remaining payments over the next four months (Figure 3-16).

Analysis. The asset, Delivery Equipment, increases by $1,000, Cash decreases by $300, and the liability, Accounts Payable, increases by $700. Thus, debit Delivery Equipment for $1,000, credit Cash for $300, and credit Accounts Payable for $700. This transaction requires one debit and two credits. Even so, total debits ($1,000) equal the total credits ($700 + $300) and the accounting equation remains in balance.

FIGURE 3-16 Transaction (k): Purchase of an Asset on Credit Making a Partial Payment

Assets		=	Liabilities		+	Owner's Equity	
Debit +	Credit −		Debit −	Credit +		Debit −	Credit +

Cash		**Accounts Payable**		**Mitchell Williams, Capital**	
Bal. 5,220			Bal. 1,200		Bal. 5,000
	(k) 300		(k) 700		
Bal. 4,920			Bal. 1,900		

Accounts Receivable	
Bal. 500	

Drawing		**Expenses**		**Revenues**	
Debit +	Credit −	Debit +	Credit −	Debit −	Credit +

Supplies	
Bal. 80	

Rent Expense		Delivery Fees	
Bal. 1,000			Bal. 4,500

Phone Expense	
Bal. 100	

Delivery Equipment	
Bal. 3,800	
(k) 1,000	
Bal. 4,800	

$10,300	=	$1,900	+	$8,400
$10,300	=			$10,300

Transaction (l): Payment of insurance premium

Mitch paid $700 for an eight-month liability insurance policy (Figure 3-17).

Analysis. Since insurance is paid in advance and will provide future benefits, it is treated as an asset. Therefore, one asset, Prepaid Insurance, increases and another, Cash, decreases. Debit Prepaid Insurance and credit Cash for $700.

Transaction (m): Payment of wages

Mitch paid his part-time employees $1,650 in wages (Figure 3-18).

Analysis. This is an additional business expense. Wages Expense increases and Cash decreases. Debit Wages Expense and credit Cash for $1,650.

FIGURE 3-17 Transaction (l): Payment of Insurance Premium

Assets		=	Liabilities		+	Owner's Equity	
Debit +	Credit −		Debit −	Credit +		Debit −	Credit +

Cash		Accounts Payable		Mitchell Williams, Capital	
Bal. 4,920			Bal. 1,900		Bal. 5,000
	(l) 700				
Bal. 4,220					

Accounts Receivable	
Bal. 500	

Supplies	
Bal. 80	

Prepaid Insurance	
(l) 700	

Delivery Equipment	
Bal. 4,800	

Drawing		Expenses		Revenues	
Debit +	Credit −	Debit +	Credit −	Debit −	Credit +

Rent Expense		Delivery Fees	
Bal. 1,000			Bal. 4,500

Phone Expense	
Bal. 100	

$10,300	=	$1,900	+	$8,400
$10,300	=			**$10,300**

FIGURE 3-18 Transaction (m): Payment of Wages

Assets		=	Liabilities		+	Owner's Equity	
Debit +	Credit −		Debit −	Credit +		Debit −	Credit +

Cash		Accounts Payable		Mitchell Williams, Capital	
Bal. 4,220			Bal. 1,900		Bal. 5,000
	(m) 1,650				
Bal. 2,570					

Accounts Receivable	
Bal. 500	

Supplies	
Bal. 80	

Prepaid Insurance	
Bal. 700	

Delivery Equipment	
Bal. 4,800	

Drawing		Expenses		Revenues	
Debit +	Credit −	Debit +	Credit −	Debit −	Credit +

Rent Expense		Delivery Fees	
Bal. 1,000			Bal. 4,500

Phone Expense	
Bal. 100	

Wages Expense	
(m) 1,650	

$8,650	=	$1,900	+	$6,750
$8,650	=			**$8,650**

Transaction (n): Deliveries made for cash and credit

Total delivery fees for the remainder of the month amounted to $3,500: $900 in cash and $2,600 on account (Figure 3-19 as shown below).

Analysis. Since the delivery fees have been earned, the revenue account increases by $3,500. Also, Cash increases by $900 and Accounts Receivable increases by $2,600. Note once again that one event impacts three accounts. This time we have debits of $900 to Cash and $2,600 to Accounts Receivable and a credit of $3,500 to Delivery Fees. As before, the total debits ($900 + $2,600) equal the total credits ($3,500) and the accounting equation remains in balance.

FIGURE 3-19 Transaction (n): Deliveries Made for Cash and Credit

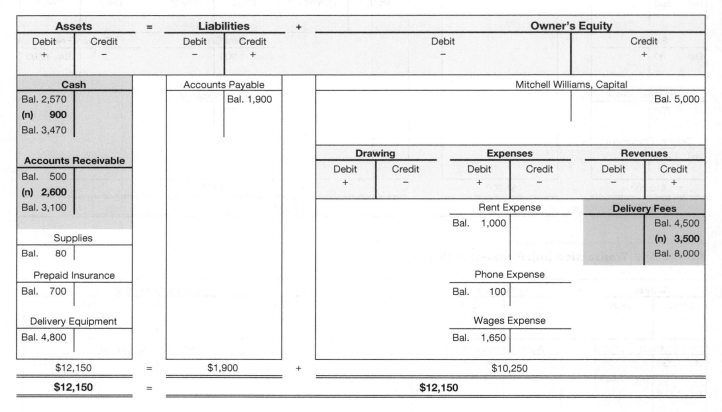

Transaction (o): Withdrawal of cash from business

At the end of the month, Mitch withdrew $3,000 in cash from the business to pay for textbooks, extra class fees, and living expenses (Figure 3-20 on the next page).

Analysis. Cash withdrawals decrease owner's equity and decrease cash. Debit Mitchell Williams, Drawing and credit Cash for $3,000.

Withdrawals are reported in the drawing account. Withdrawals by an owner are the opposite of an investment. You could debit the owner's capital account for withdrawals. However, using a specific account tells the user of the accounting information how much was withdrawn for the period.

FIGURE 3-20 Transaction (o): Withdrawal of Cash from Business

Assets		=	Liabilities		+	Owner's Equity	
Debit +	Credit −		Debit −	Credit +		Debit −	Credit +

Cash			Accounts Payable			Mitchell Williams, Capital	
Bal. 3,470				Bal. 1,900			Bal. 5,000
	(o) 3,000						
Bal. 470							

Accounts Receivable		
Bal. 3,100		

		Drawing		Expenses		Revenues	
		Debit +	Credit −	Debit +	Credit −	Debit −	Credit +

Supplies			Mitchell Williams, Drawing		Rent Expense		Delivery Fees	
Bal. 80			(o) 3,000		Bal. 1,000			Bal. 8,000

Prepaid Insurance			Phone Expense	
Bal. 700			Bal. 100	

Delivery Equipment			Wages Expense	
Bal. 4,800			Bal. 1,650	

$9,150	=	$1,900	+	$7,250
$9,150	**=**		**$9,150**	

Summary of Transactions

In illustrating transactions (a) through (o), each T account for Mitchell's Campus Delivery shows a balance before and after each transaction. To focus your attention on the transaction being explained, only a single entry was shown. In practice, this is not done. Instead, each account gathers all transactions for a period. Mitchell's accounts, with all transactions listed, are shown in Figure 3-21. Note the following four items:

1. The footings are directly under the debit (left) and credit (right) sides of the T account for those accounts with more than one debit or credit.

2. The balance is shown on the side with the larger footing.

3. The footing serves as the balance for accounts with entries on only one side of the account.

4. If an account has only a single entry, it is not necessary to enter a footing or balance.

CHECKPOINT ✔

Complete Checkpoint-3 on page 74 to test your basic understanding of LO4.

FIGURE 3-21 Summary of Transactions (a) Through (o)

Assets		=	Liabilities		+	Owner's Equity	
Debit +	Credit −		Debit −	Credit +		Debit −	Credit +

Cash			Accounts Payable			Mitchell Williams, Capital	
(a) 5,000	(b) 2,000		(d) 600	(c) 1,800			(a) 5,000
(e) 2,100	(d) 600			(k) 700			
(j) 1,900	(f) 1,000			**2,500**			
(n) 900	(g) 100			Bal. 1,900			
9,900	(i) 80						

			Drawing		Expenses		Revenues	
	(k) 300		Debit +	Credit −	Debit +	Credit −	Debit −	Credit +
	(l) 700							
	(m) 1,650		Mitchell Williams, Drawing		Rent Expense		Delivery Fees	
	(o) 3,000		(o) 3,000		(f) 1,000			(e) 2,100
	9,430							(h) 2,400
Bal. 470								(n) 3,500
								Bal. 8,000

Accounts Receivable					Phone Expense	
(h) 2,400	(j) 1,900				(g) 100	
(n) 2,600						
5,000						
Bal. 3,100						

Supplies					Wages Expense	
(i) 80					(m) 1,650	

Prepaid Insurance	
(l) 700	

Delivery Equipment	
(b) 2,000	
(c) 1,800	
(k) 1,000	
Bal. 4,800	

$9,150	=	$1,900	+	$7,250
$9,150	=			**$9,150**

LO5   **The Trial Balance**

Prepare a trial balance and explain its purposes and linkages with the financial statements.

Recall the following two very important rules in double-entry accounting:

1. The sum of the debits must equal the sum of the credits.

    At least two accounts are affected by each transaction. This rule is so important that many computer accounting programs will not permit a transaction to be entered into the accounting system unless the debits equal the credits.

2. The accounting equation must remain in balance.

    In illustrating the transactions for Mitchell's Campus Delivery, the equality of the accounting equation was verified after each transaction. Because of the large number of transactions entered each day, this is not done in practice. Instead, a trial balance is prepared periodically to determine the equality of the debits and credits. A trial balance is a list of all accounts showing the title and balance of each account. By totaling the debits and credits, their equality can be tested.

A trial balance of Mitchell's accounts, taken on June 30, 20--, is shown in Figure 3-22. This date is shown on the third line of the heading. The trial balance shows that the debit and credit totals are equal in amount. This is proof that (1) in entering transactions (a) through (o), the total of the debits was equal to the total of the credits, and (2) the accounting equation has remained in balance.

A trial balance is not a formal statement or report. Normally, only the accountant sees it. As shown in Figure 3-23, a trial balance can be used as an aid in preparing the financial statements.

Since a trial balance is not a formal statement, dollar signs are not used. Formal statements include: Income Statement, Statement of Owner's Equity, Balance Sheet, and Statement of Cash Flows.

FIGURE 3-22 Trial Balance

<table>
<tr><td colspan="2" align="center">Mitchell's Campus Delivery
Trial Balance
June 30, 20 --</td></tr>
<tr><td>ACCOUNT TITLE</td><td>DEBIT BALANCE</td><td>CREDIT BALANCE</td></tr>
<tr><td>Cash</td><td>4 7 0 00</td><td></td></tr>
<tr><td>Accounts Receivable</td><td>3 1 0 0 00</td><td></td></tr>
<tr><td>Supplies</td><td>8 0 00</td><td></td></tr>
<tr><td>Prepaid Insurance</td><td>7 0 0 00</td><td></td></tr>
<tr><td>Delivery Equipment</td><td>4 8 0 0 00</td><td></td></tr>
<tr><td>Accounts Payable</td><td></td><td>1 9 0 0 00</td></tr>
<tr><td>Mitchell Williams, Capital</td><td></td><td>5 0 0 0 00</td></tr>
<tr><td>Mitchell Williams, Drawing</td><td>3 0 0 0 00</td><td></td></tr>
<tr><td>Delivery Fees</td><td></td><td>8 0 0 0 00</td></tr>
<tr><td>Rent Expense</td><td>1 0 0 0 00</td><td></td></tr>
<tr><td>Phone Expense</td><td>1 0 0 00</td><td></td></tr>
<tr><td>Wages Expense</td><td>1 6 5 0 00</td><td></td></tr>
<tr><td></td><td>14 9 0 0 00</td><td>14 9 0 0 00</td></tr>
</table>

FIGURE 3-23 Linkages Between the Trial Balance and Financial Statements

<table>
<tr><td colspan="2" align="center">Mitchell's Campus Delivery
Trial Balance
June 30, 20 --</td></tr>
<tr><td>ACCOUNT TITLE</td><td>DEBIT BALANCE</td><td>CREDIT BALANCE</td></tr>
<tr><td>Cash</td><td>4 7 0 00</td><td></td></tr>
<tr><td>Accounts Receivable</td><td>3 1 0 0 00</td><td></td></tr>
<tr><td>Supplies</td><td>8 0 00</td><td></td></tr>
<tr><td>Prepaid Insurance</td><td>7 0 0 00</td><td></td></tr>
<tr><td>Delivery Equipment</td><td>4 8 0 0 00</td><td></td></tr>
<tr><td>Accounts Payable</td><td></td><td>1 9 0 0 00</td></tr>
<tr><td>Mitchell Williams, Capital</td><td></td><td>5 0 0 0 00</td></tr>
<tr><td>Mitchell Williams, Drawing</td><td>3 0 0 0 00</td><td></td></tr>
<tr><td>Delivery Fees</td><td></td><td>8 0 0 0 00</td></tr>
<tr><td>Rent Expense</td><td>1 0 0 0 00</td><td></td></tr>
<tr><td>Phone Expense</td><td>1 0 0 00</td><td></td></tr>
<tr><td>Wages Expense</td><td>1 6 5 0 00</td><td></td></tr>
<tr><td></td><td>14 9 0 0 00</td><td>14 9 0 0 00</td></tr>
</table>

(continued)

If the beginning capital balance was $5,000 and Mitch made no additional investments, the statement would be prepared as follows:

Mitchell's Campus Delivery
Statement of Owner's Equity
For Month Ended June 30, 20 --

Mitchell Williams, capital, June 1, 20 --		$5,000
Net income for 20 --	$5,250	
Less withdrawals for 20 --	3,000	
Increase in capital		2,250
Mitchell Williams, capital, June 30, 20 --		$7,250

FIGURE 3-23 Linkages Between the Trial Balance and Financial Statements (*concluded*)

Mitchell's Campus Delivery
Income Statement
For Month Ended June 30, 20 --

Revenue:			
Delivery fees			$8,000
Expenses:			
Wages expense		$1,650	
Rent expense		1,000	
Phone expense		100	
Total expenses			2,750
Net income			$5,250

Mitchell's Campus Delivery
Statement of Owner's Equity
For Month Ended June 30, 20 --

Mitchell Williams, capital, June 1, 20 --		$ —
Investments during June		5,000
Total investment		$5,000
Net income for 20 --	$5,250	
Less withdrawals for 20 --	3,000	
Increase in capital		2,250
Mitchell Williams, capital, June 30, 20 --		$7,250

Mitchell's Campus Delivery
Balance Sheet
June 30, 20 --

Assets		Liabilities	
Cash	$ 470	Accounts payable	$1,900
Accounts receivable	3,100		
Supplies	80	Owner's Equity	
Prepaid insurance	700	Mitchell Williams, capital	7,250
Delivery equipment	4,800		
Total assets	$9,150	Total liabilities and owner's equity	$9,150

CHECKPOINT ✔

Complete Checkpoint-4 on page 74 to test your basic understanding of LO5.

SELF-STUDY

LEARNING OBJECTIVES	Key Points to Remember
LO1 Define the parts of a T account.	The parts of a T account are 1. the title, 2. the debit, or left side, and 3. the credit, or right side.

Title	
Debit = Left	Credit = Right

LEARNING OBJECTIVES	**Key Points to Remember**
LO2 **Foot and balance a T account.**	Rules for footing and balancing T accounts are:

LO2 **Foot and balance a T account.**

Rules for footing and balancing T accounts are:

1. The footings are directly under the debit (left) and credit (right) sides of the T account for those accounts with more than one debit or credit.
2. The balance is shown on the side with the larger footing.
3. The footing serves as the balance for accounts with entries on only one side of the account.
4. If an account has only a single entry, it is not necessary to enter a footing or balance.

LO3 **Describe the effects of debits and credits on specific types of accounts.**

Rules for debits and credits. (See illustration below.)

1. Assets are on the left side of the accounting equation. Therefore, increases are entered on the left (debit) side of an asset account and decreases are entered on the right (credit) side.
2. Liabilities and owner's equity are on the right side of the accounting equation. Therefore, increases are entered on the right (credit) side and decreases are entered on the left (debit) side.
3. Revenues increase owner's equity. Therefore, increases are entered on the right (credit) side and decreases are entered on the left (debit) side.
4. Expenses and drawing decrease owner's equity. Therefore, increases are entered on the left (debit) side and decreases are entered on the right (credit) side.

Accounting Equation with Owner's Equity Umbrella

LO4 **Use T accounts to analyze transactions.**

Picture the accounting equation in your mind as you analyze transactions. When entering transactions in T accounts:

1. The sum of the debits must equal the sum of the credits.
2. At least two accounts are affected by each transaction.
3. When finished, the accounting equation must remain in balance.

LO5 **Prepare a trial balance and explain its purposes and linkages with the financial statements.**

A trial balance shows that the debit and credit totals are equal. A trial balance also can be used in preparing the financial statements.

DEMONSTRATION PROBLEM

Celia Pints opened We-Buy, You-Pay Shopping Services. For a fee that is based on the amount of research and shopping time required, Pints and her associates will shop for almost anything from groceries to home furnishings. Business is particularly heavy around Christmas and in early summer. The business operates from a rented store front. The associates receive a commission based on the revenues they produce and a mileage reimbursement for the use of their personal automobiles for shopping trips. Pints decided to use the following accounts to record transactions.

Assets	Owner's Equity
Cash	Celia Pints, Capital
Accounts Receivable	Celia Pints, Drawing
Office Equipment	Revenue
Computer Equipment	Shopping Fees
Liabilities	Expenses
Accounts Payable	Rent Expense
Notes Payable	Phone Expense
	Commissions Expense
	Utilities Expense
	Travel Expense

The following transactions are for the month of December 20--.

(a) Pints invested cash in the business, $30,000.
(b) Bought office equipment for $10,000. Paid $2,000 in cash and promised to pay the balance over the next four months.
(c) Paid rent for December, $500.
(d) Provided shopping services for customers on account, $5,200.
(e) Paid phone bill, $90.
(f) Borrowed cash from the bank by signing a note payable, $5,000.
(g) Bought a computer and printer, $4,800.
(h) Collected cash from customers for services performed on account, $4,000.
(i) Paid commissions to associates for revenues generated during the first half of the month, $3,500.
(j) Paid utility bill, $600.
(k) Paid cash on account for the office equipment purchased in transaction (b), $2,000.
(l) Earned shopping fees of $13,200: $6,000 in cash and $7,200 on account.
(m) Paid commissions to associates for last half of month, $7,000.
(n) Paid mileage reimbursements for the month, $1,500.
(o) Paid cash on note payable to bank, $1,000.
(p) Pints withdrew cash for personal use, $2,000.

REQUIRED

1. Enter the transactions for December in T accounts. Use the accounting equation as a guide for setting up the T accounts.
2. Foot the T accounts and determine their balances as necessary.
3. Prepare a trial balance of the accounts as of December 31 of the current year.
4. Prepare an income statement for the month ended December 31 of the current year.
5. Prepare a statement of owner's equity for the month ended December 31 of the current year.
6. Prepare a balance sheet as of December 31 of the current year.

SOLUTION 1, 2.

Assets		=	Liabilities		+	Owner's Equity		
Debit +	Credit −		Debit −	Credit +		Debit −		Credit +

Assets

Cash
- (a) 30,000 | (b) 2,000
- (f) 5,000 | (c) 500
- (h) 4,000 | (e) 90
- (l) 6,000 | (g) 4,800
- **45,000** | (i) 3,500
- | (j) 600
- | (k) 2,000
- | (m) 7,000
- | (n) 1,500
- | (o) 1,000
- | (p) 2,000
- | **24,990**
- Bal. 20,010

Accounts Receivable
- (d) 5,200 | (h) 4,000
- (l) 7,200 |
- **12,400**
- Bal. 8,400

Office Equipment
- (b) 10,000

Computer Equipment
- (g) 4,800

Liabilities

Accounts Payable
- (k) 2,000 | (b) 8,000
- | Bal. 6,000

Notes Payable
- (o) 1,000 | (f) 5,000
- | Bal. 4,000

Owner's Equity

Celia Pints, Capital
- | (a) 30,000

Drawing		Expenses		Revenues	
Debit +	Credit −	Debit +	Credit −	Debit −	Credit +

Celia Pints, Drawing
- (p) 2,000

Rent Expense
- (c) 500

Shopping Fees
- | (d) 5,200
- | (l) 13,200
- | Bal. 18,400

Phone Expense
- (e) 90

Commissions Expense
- (i) 3,500
- (m) 7,000
- Bal. 10,500

Utilities Expense
- (j) 600

Travel Expense
- (n) 1,500

$43,210	=	$10,000	+	$33,210
$43,210	=			**$43,210**

SOLUTION 3.

We-Buy, You-Pay Shopping Services Trial Balance December 31, 20 --											
ACCOUNT TITLE	DEBIT BALANCE					CREDIT BALANCE					
Cash	20	0	1	0	00						
Accounts Receivable	8	4	0	0	00						
Office Equipment	10	0	0	0	00						
Computer Equipment	4	8	0	0	00						
Accounts Payable						6	0	0	0	00	
Notes Payable						4	0	0	0	00	
Celia Pints, Capital						30	0	0	0	00	
Celia Pints, Drawing	2	0	0	0	00						
Shopping Fees						18	4	0	0	00	
Rent Expense		5	0	0	00						
Phone Expense			9	0	00						
Commissions Expense	10	5	0	0	00						
Utilities Expense		6	0	0	00						
Travel Expense	1	5	0	0	00						
	58	4	0	0	00	58	4	0	0	00	

SOLUTION 4.

We-Buy, You-Pay Shopping Services Income Statement For Month Ended December 31, 20 --		
Revenue:		
Shopping fees		$18,400
Expenses:		
Commissions expense	$10,500	
Travel expense	1,500	
Utilities expense	600	
Rent expense	500	
Phone expense	90	
Total expenses		13,190
Net income		$ 5,210

SOLUTION 5.

We-Buy, You-Pay Shopping Services Statement of Owner's Equity For Month Ended December 31, 20 --		
Celia Pints, capital, December 1, 20 --		$ —
Investments during December		30,000
Total investment		$30,000
Net income for December	$5,210	
Less withdrawals for December	2,000	
Increase in capital		3,210
Celia Pints, capital, December 31, 20 --		$33,210

SOLUTION 6.

We-Buy, You-Pay Shopping Services Balance Sheet December 31, 20 --			
Assets		**Liabilities**	
Cash	$20,010	Accounts payable	$ 6,000
Accounts receivable	8,400	Notes payable	4,000
Office equipment	10,000	Total liabilities	$10,000
Computer equipment	4,800		
		Owner's Equity	
		Celia Pints, capital	33,210
Total assets	$43,210	Total liabilities and owner's equity	$43,210

KEY TERMS

balance (51)   The difference between the footings of an account.

credit (52)   To enter an amount on the right side of an account.

credit balance (54)   The normal balance of liability, owner's equity, and revenue accounts.

debit (52)   To enter an amount on the left side of an account.

debit balance (54)   The normal balance of asset, expense, and drawing accounts.

double-entry accounting (51)   A system in which each transaction has a dual effect on the accounting elements.

footings (51)   The total dollar amounts on the debit and credit sides of an account.

normal balance (54)   The side of an account that is increased.

trial balance (67)   A list of all accounts, showing the title and balance of each account, used to prove that the sum of the debits equals the sum of the credits.

SELF-STUDY TEST QUESTIONS

True/False

1. **LO3**   To debit an account is to enter an amount on the left side of the account.

2. **LO3**   Liability accounts normally have debit balances.

3. **LO3**   Increases in owner's equity are entered as credits.

4. **LO3**   Revenue accounts normally have debit balances.

5. **LO3**   To credit an account is to enter an amount on the right side of the account.

6. **LO3**   A debit to an asset account will decrease it.

Multiple Choice

1. **LO3**   A common example of an asset is
   (a) Professional Fees.
   (b) Rent Expense.
   (c) Accounts Receivable.
   (d) Accounts Payable.

2. **LO3**   The accounting equation may be expressed as
   (a) Assets = Liabilities − Owner's Equity.
   (b) Assets = Liabilities + Owner's Equity.
   (c) Liabilities = Owner's Equity − Assets.
   (d) all of the above.

3. **LO3**   Liability, owner's equity, and revenue accounts normally have
   (a) debit balances.
   (b) large balances.
   (c) negative balances.
   (d) credit balances.

4. **LO4**   To record the payment of rent expense, an accountant would
   (a) debit Cash; credit Rent Expense.
   (b) debit Rent Expense; debit Cash.
   (c) debit Rent Expense; credit Cash.
   (d) credit Rent Expense; credit Cash.

5. **LO4**   An investment of cash by the owner will
   (a) increase assets and owner's equity.
   (b) increase assets and liabilities.
   (c) increase liabilities and owner's equity.
   (d) increase owner's equity and decrease liabilities.

Checkpoint Exercises

1. **LO2** Foot and balance the accounts receivable T account shown below.

Accounts Receivable	
100	50
200	30

2. **LO3** Complete the following questions using either "debit" or "credit":

   (a) The asset account Supplies is increased with a _____.
   (b) The owner's capital account is increased with a _____.
   (c) The rent expense account is increased with a _____.

3. **LO4** Analyze the following transaction using the T accounts provided below. Robb Todd purchased equipment for $300 cash.

Cash		Equipment	

4. **LO5** The following accounts have normal balances. Prepare a trial balance. Accounts Payable, $20; Accounts Receivable, $90; Capital, $40; Sales, $200; Cash, $100; Rent Expense, $70.

The answers to the Self-Study Test Questions are at the end of the chapter (page 84).

APPLYING YOUR KNOWLEDGE

CengageNowv2 provides "Show Me How" videos for selected exercises and problems. Additional resources, such as Excel templates for completing selected exercises and problems, are available for download from the companion website at Cengage.com.

REVIEW QUESTIONS

LO1	1.	What are the three major parts of a T account?
LO1	2.	What is the left side of the T account called? the right side?
LO2	3.	What is a footing?
LO3	4.	What is the relationship between the revenue and expense accounts and the owner's equity account?
LO5	5.	What is the function of the trial balance?

SERIES A EXERCISES

E 3-1A   (LO2)
✓ Cash bal.: $1,200 (Dr.)

FOOT AND BALANCE A T ACCOUNT Foot and balance the cash T account shown below.

Cash	
500	100
400	200
600	

E 3-2A   (LO3)   DEBIT AND CREDIT ANALYSIS Complete the following statements using either "debit" or "credit":

(a) The cash account is increased with a _____.

(b) The owner's capital account is increased with a _____.

(c) The delivery equipment account is increased with a _____.

(d) The cash account is decreased with a _____.

(e) The liability account Accounts Payable is increased with a _____.

(f) The revenue account Delivery Fees is increased with a _____.

(g) The asset account Accounts Receivable is increased with a _____.

(h) The rent expense account is increased with a _____.

(i) The owner's drawing account is increased with a _____.

E 3-3A   (LO2/3/4)
✓ Cash bal. after (c): $3,100 (Dr.)

ANALYSIS OF T ACCOUNTS Richard Gibbs began a business called Richard's Shoe Repair.

1. Create T accounts for Cash; Supplies; Richard Gibbs, Capital; and Utilities Expense. Identify the following transactions by letter and place them on the proper side of the T accounts:

(a) Invested cash in the business, $6,500.

(b) Purchased supplies for cash, $700.

(c) Paid utility bill, $2,700.

2. Foot the T account for cash and enter the ending balance.

E 3-4A   (LO3)   NORMAL BALANCE OF ACCOUNT Indicate the normal balance (debit or credit) for each of the following accounts:

1. Cash   5. Supplies

2. Wages Expense   6. Owner's Capital

3. Accounts Payable   7. Equipment

4. Owner's Drawing

E 3-5A   (LO4)   TRANSACTION ANALYSIS Linda Kipp started a business on May 1, 20--. Analyze the following transactions for the first month of business using T accounts. Label each T account with the title of the account affected and then place the transaction letter and the dollar amount on the debit or credit side.

(a) Invested cash in the business, $5,000.

(b) Bought equipment for cash, $700.

(c) Bought equipment on account, $600.

(d) Paid cash on account for equipment purchased in transaction (c), $400.

(e) Withdrew cash for personal use, $900.

E 3-6A   (LO2)
✓ Cash bal. after (e): $3,000 (Dr.)

FOOT AND BALANCE T ACCOUNTS Foot and balance the T accounts prepared in Exercise 3-5A if necessary.

E 3-7A   (LO2/4)
✓ Cash bal. after (k): $24,400 (Dr.)

ANALYSIS OF TRANSACTIONS Charles Chadwick opened a business called Charlie's Detective Service in January 20--. Set up T accounts for the following accounts: Cash; Accounts Receivable; Office Supplies; Computer Equipment; Office Furniture; Accounts Payable; Charles Chadwick, Capital; Charles Chadwick, Drawing; Professional Fees; Rent Expense; and Utilities Expense.

The following transactions occurred during the first month of business. Record these transactions in T accounts. After all transactions are recorded, foot and balance the accounts if necessary.

(a) Invested cash in the business, $30,000.
(b) Bought office supplies for cash, $300.
(c) Bought office furniture for cash, $5,000.
(d) Purchased computer and printer on account, $8,000.
(e) Received cash from clients for services, $3,000.
(f) Paid cash on account for computer and printer purchased in transaction (d), $4,000.
(g) Earned professional fees on account during the month, $9,000.
(h) Paid cash for office rent for January, $1,500.
(i) Paid utility bills for the month, $800.
(j) Received cash from clients billed in transaction (g), $6,000.
(k) Withdrew cash for personal use, $3,000.

E 3-8A (LO5)
✓ Trial bal. total debits: $46,000

TRIAL BALANCE Based on the transactions recorded in Exercise 3-7A, prepare a trial balance for Charlie's Detective Service as of January 31, 20--.

E 3-9A (LO5)
✓ Trial bal. total debits: $42,800

TRIAL BALANCE The following accounts have normal balances. Prepare a trial balance for Kenny's Lawn Service as of September 30, 20--.

Cash	$10,000
Accounts Receivable	6,000
Supplies	1,600
Prepaid Insurance	1,200
Mowing Equipment	16,000
Accounts Payable	4,000
Kenny Young, Capital	20,000
Kenny Young, Drawing	2,000
Mowing Fees	18,800
Wages Expense	4,200
Rent Expense	1,800

E 3-10A, E 3-11A, E 3-12A

Provided below is a trial balance for Juanita's Delivery Service. **Use this trial balance for Exercises 3-10A, 3-11A, and 3-12A.**

Juanita's Delivery Service Trial Balance September 30, 20 --										
ACCOUNT TITLE	DEBIT BALANCE					CREDIT BALANCE				
Cash	5	0	0	0	00					
Accounts Receivable	3	0	0	0	00					
Supplies		8	0	0	00					
Prepaid Insurance		6	0	0	00					
Delivery Equipment	8	0	0	0	00					
Accounts Payable						2	0	0	0	00
Juanita Raye, Capital						10	0	0	0	00
Juanita Raye, Drawing	1	0	0	0	00					
Delivery Fees						9	4	0	0	00
Wages Expense	2	1	0	0	00					
Rent Expense		9	0	0	00					
	21	4	0	0	00	21	4	0	0	00

E 3-10A   (LO5)
✓ Net income: $6,400

INCOME STATEMENT From the information in the trial balance presented above, prepare an income statement for Juanita's Delivery Service for the month ended September 30, 20--.

E 3-11A   (LO5)
✓ Capital, 9/30: $15,400

STATEMENT OF OWNER'S EQUITY From the information in the trial balance presented above, prepare a statement of owner's equity for Juanita's Delivery Service for the month ended September 30, 20--. Assume this is not the first month of operations and the owner did not invest in the business during September.

E 3-12A   (LO5)
✓ Total assets, 9/30: $17,400

BALANCE SHEET   From the information in the trial balance presented for Juanita's Delivery Service on page 76, prepare a balance sheet for Juanita's Delivery Service as of September 30, 20--.

SERIES A PROBLEMS

P 3-13A   (LO2/4/5)
✓ Cash bal. after (p): $21,805 (Dr.)
✓ Trial bal. total debits: $44,900

T ACCOUNTS AND TRIAL BALANCE Wilhelm Kohl started a business in May 20-- called Kohl's Home Repair. Kohl hired a part-time college student as an assistant. Kohl has decided to use the following accounts for recording transactions:

Assets	Owner's Equity
Cash	Wilhelm Kohl, Capital
Accounts Receivable	Wilhelm Kohl, Drawing
Office Supplies	Revenue
Prepaid Insurance	Service Fees
Equipment	Expenses
Van	Rent Expense
Liabilities	Wages Expense
Accounts Payable	Phone Expense
	Gas and Oil Expense

The following transactions occurred during May:

(a) Invested cash in the business, $25,000.

(b) Purchased a used van for cash, $6,000.

(c) Purchased equipment on account, $4,000.

(d) Received cash for services rendered, $7,500.

(e) Paid cash on account owed from transaction (c), $2,300.

(f) Paid rent for the month, $850.

(g) Paid phone bill, $230.

(h) Earned revenue on account, $4,500.

(i) Purchased office supplies for cash, $160.

(j) Paid wages to an assistant, $800.

(k) Purchased a one-year insurance policy, $1,100.

(l) Received cash from services performed in transaction (h), $3,400.

(m) Paid cash for gas and oil expense on the van, $155.

(n) Purchased additional equipment for $4,200, paying $1,500 cash and spreading the remaining payments over the next 10 months.

(o) Earned service fees for the remainder of the month of $3,500: $1,900 in cash and $1,600 on account.

(p) Withdrew cash at the end of the month, $2,900.

REQUIRED

1. Enter the transactions in T accounts, identifying each transaction with its corresponding letter.
2. Foot and balance the accounts where necessary.
3. Prepare a trial balance as of May 31, 20--.

P 3-14A (LO5)
✓ Net income: $13,465
✓ Owner's equity, 5/31: $35,565
✓ Total assets, 5/31: $39,965

NET INCOME AND CHANGE IN OWNER'S EQUITY Refer to the trial balance of Kohl's Home Repair in Problem 3-13A to determine the following information. Use the format provided below.

1. a. Total revenue for the month   _____

   b. Total expenses for the month   _____

   c. Net income for the month   _____

2. a. Wilhelm Kohl's original investment
      in the business   _____
      + Net income for the month   _____
      − Owner's drawing   _____
      Increase (decrease) in capital   _____
      = Ending owner's equity   _____

   b. End of month accounting equation:

Assets	=	Liabilities	+	Owner's Equity
_____	=	_____	+	_____

P 3-15A (LO5)
✓ NI: $13,465
✓ Capital, 5/31/20--: $35,565
✓ Total assets 5/31/20--: $39,965

FINANCIAL STATEMENTS Refer to the trial balance in Problem 3-13A and to the analysis of the change in owner's equity in Problem 3-14A.

REQUIRED

1. Prepare an income statement for Kohl's Home Repair for the month ended May 31, 20--.
2. Prepare a statement of owner's equity for Kohl's Home Repair for the month ended May 31, 20--.
3. Prepare a balance sheet for Kohl's Home Repair as of May 31, 20--.

SERIES B EXERCISES

E 3-1B (LO2)
✓ Accts. Pay: $400 (Cr.)

FOOT AND BALANCE A T ACCOUNT Foot and balance the accounts payable T account shown below.

Accounts Payable	
300	450
250	350
	150

E 3-2B (LO3)

DEBIT AND CREDIT ANALYSIS Complete the following statements using either "debit" or "credit":

(a) The asset account Prepaid Insurance is increased with a _____.
(b) The owner's drawing account is increased with a _____.

(c) The asset account Accounts Receivable is decreased with a _____.

(d) The liability account Accounts Payable is decreased with a _____.

(e) The owner's capital account is increased with a _____.

(f) The revenue account Professional Fees is increased with a _____.

(g) The expense account Repair Expense is increased with a _____.

(h) The asset account Cash is decreased with a _____.

(i) The asset account Delivery Equipment is decreased with a _____.

E 3-3B **(LO2/3/4)**
✓ Cash bal. after (c): $3,900 (Dr.)

ANALYSIS OF T ACCOUNTS Roberto Alvarez began a business called Roberto's Fix-It Shop.

1. Create T accounts for Cash; Supplies; Roberto Alvarez, Capital; and Utilities Expense. Identify the following transactions by letter and place them on the proper side of the T accounts:

   (a) Invested cash in the business, $6,000.

   (b) Purchased supplies for cash, $1,200.

   (c) Paid utility bill, $900.

2. Foot the T account for cash and enter the ending balance.

E 3-4B **(LO3)**

NORMAL BALANCE OF ACCOUNT Indicate the normal balance (debit or credit) for each of the following accounts:

1. Cash

2. Rent Expense

3. Notes Payable

4. Owner's Drawing

5. Accounts Receivable

6. Owner's Capital

7. Tools

E 3-5B **(LO4)**

TRANSACTION ANALYSIS George Atlas started a business on June 1, 20--. Analyze the following transactions for the first month of business using T accounts. Label each T account with the title of the account affected and then place the transaction letter and the dollar amount on the debit or credit side.

(a) Invested cash in the business, $7,000.

(b) Purchased equipment for cash, $900.

(c) Purchased equipment on account, $1,500.

(d) Paid cash on account for equipment purchased in transaction (c), $800.

(e) Withdrew cash for personal use, $1,100.

E 3-6B **(LO2)**
✓ Cash bal. after (e): $4,200 (Dr.)

FOOT AND BALANCE T ACCOUNTS Foot and balance the T accounts prepared in Exercise 3-5B if necessary.

E 3-7B **(LO2/4)**
✓ Cash bal. after (k): $9,000 (Dr.)

ANALYSIS OF TRANSACTIONS Nicole Lawrence opened a business called Nickie's Neat Ideas in January 20--. Set up T accounts for the following accounts: Cash; Accounts Receivable; Office Supplies; Computer Equipment; Office Furniture; Accounts Payable; Nicole Lawrence, Capital; Nicole Lawrence, Drawing; Professional Fees; Rent Expense; and Utilities Expense.

The following transactions occurred during the first month of business. Record these transactions in T accounts. After all transactions have been recorded, foot and balance the accounts if necessary.

(a) Invested cash in the business, $18,000.

(b) Purchased office supplies for cash, $500.

(c) Purchased office furniture for cash, $8,000.

(d) Purchased computer and printer on account, $5,000.

(e) Received cash from clients for services, $4,000.

(f) Paid cash on account for computer and printer purchased in transaction (d), $2,000.

(g) Earned professional fees on account during the month, $7,000.

(h) Paid office rent for January, $900.

(i) Paid utility bills for the month, $600.

(j) Received cash from clients that were billed previously in transaction (g), $3,000.

(k) Withdrew cash for personal use, $4,000.

E 3-8B   (LO5)
✓ Trial bal. total debits: $32,000

TRIAL BALANCE Based on the transactions recorded in Exercise 3-7B, prepare a trial balance for Nickie's Neat Ideas as of January 31, 20--.

E 3-9B   (LO5)
✓ Trial bal. total debits: $55,000

TRIAL BALANCE The following accounts have normal balances. Prepare a trial balance for Betty's Cleaning Service as of September 30, 20--.

Cash	$14,000	Betty Par, Capital	$24,000
Accounts Receivable	8,000	Betty Par, Drawing	4,000
Supplies	1,200	Cleaning Fees	25,000
Prepaid Insurance	1,800	Wages Expense	6,000
Cleaning Equipment	18,000	Rent Expense	2,000
Accounts Payable	6,000		

E 3-10B, E 3-11B, E 3-12B

Provided below is a trial balance for Bill's Delivery Service. **Use this trial balance for Exercises 3-10B, 3-11B, and 3-12B.**

Bill's Delivery Service
Trial Balance
September 30, 20 --

ACCOUNT TITLE	DEBIT BALANCE	CREDIT BALANCE
Cash	7 0 0 0 00	
Accounts Receivable	4 0 0 0 00	
Supplies	6 0 0 00	
Prepaid Insurance	9 0 0 00	
Delivery Equipment	9 0 0 0 00	
Accounts Payable		3 0 0 0 00
Bill Swift, Capital		12 0 0 0 00
Bill Swift, Drawing	2 0 0 0 00	
Delivery Fees		12 5 0 0 00
Wages Expense	3 0 0 0 00	
Rent Expense	1 0 0 0 00	
	27 5 0 0 00	27 5 0 0 00

E 3-10B   (LO5)
✓ Net income: $8,500

INCOME STATEMENT From the information in the trial balance presented above, prepare an income statement for Bill's Delivery Service for the month ended September 30, 20--.

3-11B   (LO5)
✓ Capital, 9/30: $18,500

STATEMENT OF OWNER'S EQUITY From the information in the trial balance presented above, prepare a statement of owner's equity for Bill's Delivery Service for the month ended September 30, 20--. Assume this is not the first month of operations and the owner did not invest in the business during September.

E 3-12B   (LO5)
✓ Total assets, 9/30: $21,500

BALANCE SHEET From the information in the trial balance presented for Bill's Delivery Service on page 80, prepare a balance sheet for Bill's Delivery Service as of September 30, 20--.

SERIES B PROBLEMS

P 3-13B   (LO2/4/5)
✓ Cash bal. after (p): $20,200 (Dr.)
✓ Trial bal. total debits: $44,300

T ACCOUNTS AND TRIAL BALANCE Sue Jantz started a business in August 20-- called Jantz Plumbing Service. Jantz hired a part-time college student as an administrative assistant. Jantz has decided to use the following accounts:

Assets	Owner's Equity
Cash	Sue Jantz, Capital
Accounts Receivable	Sue Jantz, Drawing
Office Supplies	Revenue
Prepaid Insurance	Service Fees
Plumbing Equipment	Expenses
Van	Rent Expense
Liabilities	Wages Expense
Accounts Payable	Phone Expense
	Advertising Expense

The following transactions occurred during August:

(a) Invested cash in the business, $30,000.

(b) Purchased a used van for cash, $8,000.

(c) Purchased plumbing equipment on account, $4,000.

(d) Received cash for services rendered, $3,000.

(e) Paid cash on account owed from transaction (c), $1,000.

(f) Paid rent for the month, $700.

(g) Paid phone bill, $100.

(h) Earned revenue on account, $4,000.

(i) Purchased office supplies for cash, $300.

(j) Paid wages to student, $500.

(k) Purchased a one-year insurance policy, $800.

(l) Received cash from services performed in transaction (h), $3,000.

(m) Paid cash for advertising expense, $2,000.

(n) Purchased additional plumbing equipment for $2,000, paying $500 cash and spreading the remaining payments over the next six months.

(o) Earned revenue from services for the remainder of the month of $2,800: $1,100 in cash and $1,700 on account.

(p) Withdrew cash at the end of the month, $3,000.

REQUIRED

1. Enter the transactions in T accounts, identifying each transaction with its corresponding letter.
2. Foot and balance the accounts where necessary.
3. Prepare a trial balance as of August 31, 20--.

P 3-14B   (LO5)

✓ Net income: $6,500
✓ Owner's equity, 8/31: $33,500
✓ Total assets, 8/31: $38,000

NET INCOME AND CHANGE IN OWNER'S EQUITY   Refer to the trial balance of Jantz Plumbing Service in Problem 3-13B to determine the following information. Use the format provided below.

1. a. Total revenue for the month   _____
   b. Total expenses for the month   _____
   c. Net income for the month   _____
2. a. Sue Jantz's original investment in the business   _____
      + Net income for the month   _____
      − Owner's drawing   _____   _____
      Increase (decrease) in capital   _____
      = Ending owner's equity   _____
   b. End of month accounting equation:

Assets	=	Liabilities	+	Owner's Equity
_____	=	_____	+	_____

P 3-15B   (LO5)

✓ NI: $6,500
✓ Capital, 8/31/20--: $33,500
✓ Total assets, 8/31/20--: $38,000

FINANCIAL STATEMENTS   Refer to the trial balance in Problem 3-13B and to the analysis of the change in owner's equity in Problem 3-14B.

REQUIRED

1. Prepare an income statement for Jantz Plumbing Service for the month ended August 31, 20--.
2. Prepare a statement of owner's equity for Jantz Plumbing Service for the month ended August 31, 20--.
3. Prepare a balance sheet for Jantz Plumbing Service as of August 31, 20--.

CHECK LIST

☐ Managing
☐ Planning
☐ Drafting
☐ Break
☐ Revising
☐ Managing

✓ Cash bal. after (p): $1,980 (Dr.)
✓ Trial bal. debit total: $5,840
✓ Net income: $500
✓ Total assets: $4,300

MANAGING YOUR WRITING

Write a one-page memo to your instructor explaining how you could use the double-entry system to maintain records of your personal finances. What types of accounts would you use for the accounting elements?

MASTERY PROBLEM

Craig Fisher started a lawn service called Craig's Quick Cut to earn money over the summer months. Fisher has decided to use the following accounts for recording transactions:

(continued)

Assets

    Cash

    Accounts Receivable

    Mowing Equipment

    Lawn Tools

Liabilities

    Accounts Payable

    Notes Payable

Owner's Equity

    Craig Fisher, Capital

    Craig Fisher, Drawing

Revenue

    Lawn Fees

Expenses

    Rent Expense

    Wages Expense

    Phone Expense

    Gas and Oil Expense

    Transportation Expense

Transactions for the month of June are listed below.

(a) Invested cash in the business, $3,000.

(b) Bought mowing equipment for $1,000: paid $200 in cash and promised to pay the balance over the next four months.

(c) Paid garage rent for June, $50.

(d) Provided lawn services for customers on account, $520.

(e) Paid phone bill, $30.

(f) Borrowed cash from the bank by signing a note payable, $500.

(g) Bought lawn tools, $480.

(h) Collected cash from customers for services performed on account in transaction (d), $400.

(i) Paid associates for lawn work done during the first half of the month, $350.

(j) Paid for gas and oil for the equipment, $60.

(k) Paid cash on account for the mowing equipment purchased in transaction (b), $200.

(l) Earned lawn fees of $1,320: $600 in cash and $720 on account.

(m) Paid associates for last half of month, $700.

(n) Reimbursed associates for costs incurred using their own vehicles for transportation, $150.

(o) Paid on note payable to bank, $100.

(p) Withdrew cash for personal use, $200.

REQUIRED

1. Enter the transactions for June in T accounts. Use the accounting equation as a guide for setting up the T accounts.

2. Foot and balance the T accounts where necessary.

3. Prepare a trial balance of the accounts as of June 30, 20--.

4. Prepare an income statement for the month ended June 30, 20--.

5. Prepare a statement of owner's equity for the month ended June 30, 20--.

6. Prepare a balance sheet as of June 30, 20--.

This problem challenges you to apply your cumulative accounting knowledge to move a step beyond the material in the chapter.

✓ Capital, 8/31/20--: $600

CHALLENGE PROBLEM

Your friend Chris Stevick started a part-time business in June and has been keeping her own accounting records. She has been preparing monthly financial statements. At the end of August, she stopped by to show you her performance for the most recent month. She prepared the following income statement and balance sheet:

Income Statement		Balance Sheet	End of Month	Beginning of Month
Revenues	$500	Cash	$600	$400
Expenses	200	Capital	600	400
Net income	$300			

Chris has also heard that there is a statement of owner's equity, but she is not familiar with that statement. She asks if you can help her prepare one. After confirming that she has no assets other than cash, no liabilities, and made no additional investments in the business in August, you agree.

REQUIRED

1. Prepare the statement of owner's equity for your friend's most recent month.
2. What suggestions might you give to Chris that would make her income statement more useful?

ANSWERS TO SELF-STUDY TEST QUESTIONS

True/False

1. T
2. F (Liability accounts normally have credit balances.)
3. T
4. F (credit balances)
5. T
6. F (increase)

Multiple Choice

1. c   2. b   3. d   4. c   5. a

Checkpoint Exercises

1.
Accounts Receivable	
100	50
200	30
300	**80**
Bal. 220	

2. (a) The asset account Supplies is increased with a debit.
(b) The owner's capital account is increased with a credit.
(c) The rent expense account is increased with a debit.

3.
Cash		Equipment	
300		300	

4.
Trial Balance		
Cash	100	
Accounts Receivable	90	
Accounts Payable		20
Capital		40
Sales		200
Rent Expense	70	
	260	260

Chapter 4 Journalizing and Posting Transactions

Campus Advantage (CA) provides a comprehensive range of student residential services in the following areas: management, development, acquisition, and consulting. It specializes in the creation of modern, full-service facilities that are secure, private, and equipped with all of the tools that today's students need for success. Its communities are no-hassle alternatives to dorm living with full dining service options. CA has facilities across the country, but each student residence reflects the unique identity of the school and community it serves. University Crossing, CA furnished, luxury, student apartments in Manhattan, Kansas, are just minutes from Kansas State University.

As with all businesses, CA relies on an accounting system to maintain a record of transactions from the source document through the preparation of the trial balance and financial statements. In this chapter, we discuss source documents, the chart of accounts, and the process used to journalize and post transactions. And, just in case an error is made, we address how to find and correct errors.

LEARNING OBJECTIVES

Careful study of this chapter should enable you to:

LO1 Describe the flow of data from source documents to the trial balance.

LO2 Describe and explain the purpose of source documents.

LO3 Describe the chart of accounts as a means of classifying financial information.

LO4 Journalize transactions.

LO5 Post to the general ledger and prepare a trial balance.

LO6 Explain how to find and correct errors.

The double-entry framework of accounting was explained and illustrated in Chapter 3. To demonstrate the use of debits and credits, business transactions were entered directly into T accounts. Now we will take a more detailed look at the procedures used to account for business transactions.

| LO1 | Flow of Data |

Describe the flow of data from source documents to the trial balance.

This chapter traces the flow of financial data from the source documents through the accounting information system. This process includes the following steps:

1. Analyze what happened by using information from source documents and the firm's chart of accounts.
2. Enter business transactions in the general journal in the form of journal entries.
3. Post these journal entries to the accounts in the general ledger.
4. Prepare a trial balance.

The flow of data from the source documents through the preparation of a trial balance is shown in Figure 4-1.

FIGURE 4-1 Flow of Data from Source Documents through Trial Balance

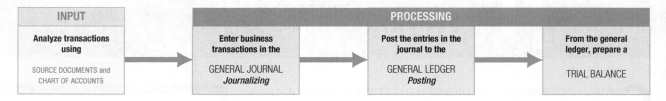

| LO2 | Source Documents |

Describe and explain the purpose of source documents.

Almost any document that provides information about a business transaction can be called a **source document**. A source document triggers the analysis of what happened. It begins the process of entering transactions in the accounting system. Examples of source documents are shown in Figure 4-2. These source documents provide information that is useful in determining the effect of business transactions on specific accounts.

In addition to serving as input for transaction analysis, source documents serve as objective evidence of business transactions. If anyone questions the accounting records, these documents may be used as objective, verifiable evidence of the accuracy of the accounting records. For this reason, source documents are filed for possible future reference. *Having objective, verifiable evidence that a transaction occurred is an important accounting concept.*

FIGURE 4-2 Source Documents

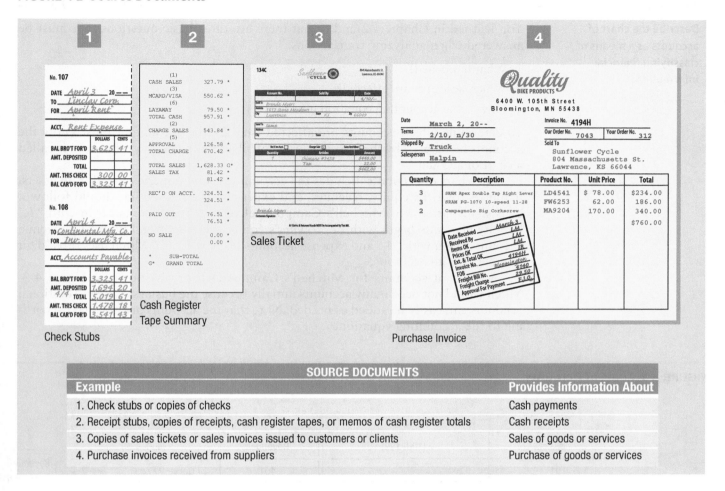

Check Stubs

Cash Register
Tape Summary

Sales Ticket

Purchase Invoice

SOURCE DOCUMENTS	
Example	**Provides Information About**
1. Check stubs or copies of checks	Cash payments
2. Receipt stubs, copies of receipts, cash register tapes, or memos of cash register totals	Cash receipts
3. Copies of sales tickets or sales invoices issued to customers or clients	Sales of goods or services
4. Purchase invoices received from suppliers	Purchase of goods or services

A BROADER VIEW

Electronic Source Documents

With the ability to go shopping in cyberspace, more transactions are being initiated electronically. This means that more and more "source documents" will be in an electronic form.

SCOTT OLSON/GETTY IMAGES

CHECKPOINT ✔

Complete Checkpoint-1 on page 113 to test your basic understanding of LO2.

LO3

The Chart of Accounts

Describe the chart of accounts as a means of classifying financial information.

You learned in Chapters 2 and 3 that there are three basic questions that must be answered when analyzing transactions.

1. What happened?
2. Which accounts are affected?
3. How is the accounting equation affected?

To determine which accounts are affected (step 2), the accountant must know the accounts being used by the business. A list of all accounts used by a business is called a chart of accounts.

The chart of accounts includes the account titles in numeric order for all assets, liabilities, owner's equity, revenues, and expenses. The numbering should follow a consistent pattern. In Mitchell's Campus Delivery, asset accounts begin with "1," liability accounts begin with "2," owner's equity accounts begin with "3," revenue accounts begin with "4," and expense accounts begin with "5." Mitch uses three-digit numbers for all accounts.

A chart of accounts for Mitchell's Campus Delivery is shown in Figure 4-3. Mitch would not need many accounts initially because the business is new. Additional accounts can easily be added as needed. Note that the accounts are arranged according to the accounting equation.

FIGURE 4-3 Chart of Accounts

MITCHELL'S CAMPUS DELIVERY CHART OF ACCOUNTS				
Assets	**(100–199)**		**Revenues**	**(400–499)**
101	Cash		401	Delivery Fees
122	Accounts Receivable			
141	Supplies		**Expenses**	**(500–599)**
145	Prepaid Insurance		511	Wages Expense
185	Delivery Equipment		521	Rent Expense
			525	Phone Expense
Liabilities	**(200–299)**			
202	Accounts Payable			
Owner's Equity	**(300–399)**			
311	Mitchell Williams, Capital			
312	Mitchell Williams, Drawing			

Assets begin with 1

Liabilities begin with 2

Owner's Equity begin with 3

Revenues begin with 4

Expenses begin with 5

LO4	The General Journal

Journalize transactions.

A day-by-day listing of the transactions of a business is called a journal. The purpose of a journal is to provide a record of all transactions completed by the business. The journal shows the date of each transaction, titles of the accounts to be debited and credited, and the amounts of the debits and credits.

A journal is commonly referred to as a book of original entry because it is here that the first formal accounting record of a transaction is made. Although many types of journals are used in business, the simplest journal form is a two-column general journal (Figure 4-4). Any kind of business transaction may be entered into a general journal.

A two-column general journal is so-named because it has only two amount columns, one for debit amounts and one for credit amounts. Journal pages are numbered in the upper right-hand corner. The five column numbers in Figure 4-4 are explained in Figure 4-5.

> **LEARNING KEY** 🔑
>
> A journal provides a day-by-day listing of all transactions completed by the business.

FIGURE 4-4 Two-Column General Journal

FIGURE 4-5 The Columns in a Two-Column General Journal

Column **1** Date	The year is entered in small figures at the top of the column immediately below the column heading. The year is repeated only at the top of each new page. The month is entered for the first entry on the page and for the first transaction of the month. The day of the month is recorded for every transaction, even if it is the same as the prior entry.
Column **2** Description	The *Description* or *Explanation* column is used to enter the titles of the accounts affected by each transaction and to provide a very brief description of the transaction. Each transaction affects two or more accounts. The account(s) to be debited are entered first at the extreme left of the column. The account(s) to be credited are listed after the debits and indented. The description should be entered immediately following the last credit entry with an additional indentation.
Column **3** Posting Reference	No entries are made in the *Posting Reference* column during journalizing. Entries are made in this column when the debits and credits are copied to the proper accounts in the ledger. This process will be explained in detail later in this chapter.
Column **4** Debit Amount	The *Debit amount column* is used to enter the amount to be debited to an account. The amount should be entered on the same line as the title of that account.
Column **5** Credit Amount	The *Credit amount column* is used to enter the amount to be credited to an account. The amount should be entered on the same line as the title of that account.

Journalizing

> **LEARNING KEY** 🔑
>
> When journalizing, the exact account titles shown in the chart of accounts must be used. Refer to the chart of accounts in Figure 4-3 as you review the entries for Mitchell's Campus Delivery.

Entering the transactions day-by-day in a journal is called journalizing. For every transaction, the entry should include the date, the title of each account affected, the amounts, and a brief description.

To illustrate the journalizing process, transactions for the first month of operations of Mitchell's Campus Delivery will be journalized. The transactions are listed in Figure 4-6. Since you analyzed these transactions in Chapters 2 and 3, the journalizing process should be easier to understand. Let's start with a close look at the steps followed when journalizing the first transaction, Mitchell's initial investment of $5,000.

FIGURE 4-6 Summary of Transactions

		SUMMARY OF TRANSACTIONS MITCHELL'S CAMPUS DELIVERY
	Transaction	
(a)	June 1	Mitchell Williams invested cash in his business, $5,000.
(b)	3	Bought delivery equipment for cash, $2,000.
(c)	5	Bought delivery equipment on account from Big Red Scooters, $1,800.
(d)	6	Paid first installment from transaction (c) to Big Red Scooters, $600.
(e)	6	Received cash for delivery services rendered, $2,100.
(f)	7	Paid cash for June office rent, $1,000.
(g)	15	Paid phone bill, $100.
(h)	15	Made deliveries on account for a total of $2,400: Library ($400) and the School of Music ($2,000).
(i)	16	Bought supplies for cash, $80.
(j)	20	Received $1,900 in cash for services performed in transaction (h): $400 from the Library and $1,500 from the School of Music.
(k)	25	Bought a third scooter from Big Red Scooters, $1,000. Paid $300 cash, with the remaining payments expected over the next four months.
(l)	26	Paid cash for a seven-month liability insurance policy, $700. Coverage began on June 1.
(m)	27	Paid wages of part-time employees, $1,650.
(n)	30	Earned delivery fees for the remainder of the month amounting to $3,500. $900 in cash and $2,600 on account. Deliveries on account: Library ($250) and Athletic Ticket Office ($2,350).
(o)	30	Mitch withdrew cash for personal use, $3,000.

Transaction (a)

June 1 Mitchell Williams opened a bank account with a deposit of $5,000 for his business.

STEP 1   Enter the date. Since this is the first entry on the journal page, the year is entered on the first line of the Date column (in small print at the top of the line). The month and day are entered on the same line, below the year, in the Date column.

		GENERAL JOURNAL			PAGE 1
	DATE	DESCRIPTION	POST. REF.	DEBIT	CREDIT
1	20-- June 1				
2					

STEP 2 **Enter the debit.** Cash is entered on the first line at the extreme left of the Description column. The amount of the debit, $5,000, is entered on the same line in the Debit column. Since this is not a formal financial statement, dollar signs are not used.

In Chapter 3, we simply debited the T account.

	Cash	
(a) 5,000		

		GENERAL JOURNAL				PAGE 1	
	DATE	DESCRIPTION	POST. REF.	DEBIT		CREDIT	
1	20-- June 1	Cash		5 0 0 0 00			1
2							2

STEP 3 **Enter the credit.** The title of the account to be credited, Mitchell Williams, Capital, is entered on the second line, **indented one-half inch from the left side of the Description column.** The amount of the credit, $5,000, is entered on the same line in the Credit column.

In Chapter 3, we simply credited the T account.

Mitchell Williams, Capital	
	(a) 5,000

		GENERAL JOURNAL				PAGE 1	
	DATE	DESCRIPTION	POST. REF.	DEBIT		CREDIT	
1	20-- June 1	Cash		5 0 0 0 00			1
2		Mitchell Williams, Capital				5 0 0 0 00	2

STEP 4 **Enter the explanation.** The explanation of the entry is entered on the next line, **indented an additional one-half inch.** The second line of the explanation, if needed, is also indented the same distance as the first.

		GENERAL JOURNAL				PAGE 1	
	DATE	DESCRIPTION	POST. REF.	DEBIT		CREDIT	
1	20-- June 1	Cash		5 0 0 0 00			1
2		Mitchell Williams, Capital				5 0 0 0 00	2
3		Owner's original investment in					3
4		delivery business					4

Enter the next transaction. To enter transaction (b), the purchase of a motor scooter (delivery equipment) for $2,000 cash, we skip a line and follow the same four steps. Note that the month and year do not need to be repeated. The day of the month must, however, be entered.

		GENERAL JOURNAL				PAGE 1	
	DATE	DESCRIPTION	POST. REF.	DEBIT		CREDIT	
1	20-- June 1	Cash		5 0 0 0 00			1
2		Mitchell Williams, Capital				5 0 0 0 00	2
3		Owner's original investment in					3
4		delivery business					4
5							5
6	3	Delivery Equipment		2 0 0 0 00			6
7		Cash				2 0 0 0 00	7
8		Purchased delivery equipment for cash					8

Skip a line →

The journal entries for the month of June are shown in Figure 4-7. Note that the entries on June 25 and June 30 affect more than two accounts. Entries requiring more than one debit and/or one credit are called compound entries. The entry on June 25 has two credits. The credits are listed after the debit, indented and listed one under the other. The entry on June 30 has two debits. They are aligned with the left margin of the Description column and listed one under the other. In both cases, the debits equal the credits.

FIGURE 4-7 General Journal Entries

GENERAL JOURNAL   PAGE 1

	DATE		DESCRIPTION	POST. REF.	DEBIT	CREDIT	
1	20– June	1	Cash *List debits first.*		5 0 0 0 00		1
2			Mitchell Williams, Capital			5 0 0 0 00	2
3			Owner's original investment in *Explanation is third and indented.*				3
4			delivery business				4
5							5
6		3	Delivery Equipment		2 0 0 0 00		6
7			Cash			2 0 0 0 00	7
8			Purchased delivery equipment for cash				8
9							9
10		5	Delivery Equipment		1 8 0 0 00		10
11			Accounts Payable			1 8 0 0 00	11
12			Purchased delivery equipment on account				12
13			from Big Red Scooters				13
14							14
15		6	Accounts Payable		6 0 0 00		15
16			Cash			6 0 0 00	16
17			Made partial payment to Big Red Scooters				17
18							18
19		6	Cash		2 1 0 0 00		19
20			Delivery Fees			2 1 0 0 00	20
21			Received cash for delivery services				21
22							22
23		7	Rent Expense		1 0 0 0 00		23
24			Cash			1 0 0 0 00	24
25			Paid office rent for June				25
26							26
27		15	Phone Expense		1 0 0 00		27
28			Cash			1 0 0 00	28
29			Paid phone bill for June				29
30							30
31		15	Accounts Receivable		2 4 0 0 00		31
32			Delivery Fees			2 4 0 0 00	32
33			Deliveries made on account for				33
34			Library ($400) and School of Music ($2,000)				34
35							35

List credits second and indented.

Space to make entries easier to read. To prevent improper changes to entries, the extra spacing might not be used in practice.

(*Continued*)

FIGURE 4-7 General Journal Entries (*concluded*)

	DATE		DESCRIPTION	POST. REF.	DEBIT		CREDIT		
1	20-- June	16	Supplies		8 0 00				1
2			Cash				8 0 00		2
3			Purchased supplies for cash						3
4									4
5		20	Cash		1 9 0 0 00				5
6			Accounts Receivable				1 9 0 0 00		6
7			Received cash on account from						7
8			Library ($400) and School of Music ($1,500)						8
9									9
10		25	Delivery Equipment		1 0 0 0 00				10
11			Accounts Payable				7 0 0 00		11
12			Cash				3 0 0 00		12
13			Purchased scooter with down payment;						13
14			balance on account with Big Red Scooters						14
15									15
16		26	Prepaid Insurance		7 0 0 00				16
17			Cash				7 0 0 00		17
18			Paid premium for seven-month						18
19			insurance policy						19
20									20
21		27	Wages Expense		1 6 5 0 00				21
22			Cash				1 6 5 0 00		22
23			Paid employees						23
24									24
25		30	Cash		9 0 0 00				25
26			Accounts Receivable		2 6 0 0 00				26
27			Delivery Fees				3 5 0 0 00		27
28			Deliveries made for cash and on account to						28
29			Library ($250) and						29
30			Athletic Ticket Office ($2,350)						30
31									31
32		30	Mitchell Williams, Drawing		3 0 0 0 00				32
33			Cash				3 0 0 0 00		33
34			Owner's withdrawal						34

GENERAL JOURNAL — PAGE 2

Line up credits — Compound entry — *Debits = Credits*

Line up debits — Compound entry — *Debits = Credits*

CHECKPOINT ✔
Complete Checkpoint-2 on page 113 to test your basic understanding of LO4.

LO5	**The General Ledger**

Post to the general ledger and prepare a trial balance.

The journal provides a day-by-day record of business transactions. To determine the current balance of specific accounts, however, the information in the journal must be transferred to accounts similar to the T accounts illustrated in Chapter 3. This process is called posting.

A complete set of all the accounts used by a business is known as the **general ledger**. The general ledger accumulates a complete record of the debits and credits made to each account as a result of entries made in the journal. The accounts are numbered and arranged in the same order as the chart of accounts. That is, accounts are numbered and grouped by classification: assets, liabilities, owner's equity, revenues, and expenses.

General Ledger Account

For purposes of illustration, the T account was introduced in Chapter 3. In practice, businesses are more likely to use a version of the account called the **general ledger account**. Figure 4-8 compares the cash T account from Chapter 3 for Mitchell's Campus Delivery and a general ledger account summarizing the same cash transactions.

A four-column general ledger account contains columns for the debit or credit transaction and columns for the debit or credit running balance. In addition, there are columns for the date, description of the item, and posting reference.

The Item column is used to provide descriptions of special entries. For example, "Balance" is written in this column when the balance of an account is transferred to a new page. In addition, "Correcting," "Adjusting," "Closing," or "Reversing" may be written in this column when these types of entries are made. Correcting entries are described later in the chapter. Adjusting, closing, and reversing entries are illustrated in Chapters 5, 6, and 15, respectively.

The Posting Reference (Post. Ref.) column is used to indicate the journal page from which an entry was posted, or a check mark (✓) is inserted to indicate that no posting was required.

As shown in Figure 4-8, the primary advantage of the T account is that the debit and credit sides of the account are easier to identify. Thus, for demonstration purposes

FIGURE 4-8 Comparison of T Account and General Ledger Account

Cash (T Account)

(a)	5,000	(b)	2,000
(e)	2,100	(d)	600
(j)	1,900	(f)	1,000
(n)	900	(g)	100
	9,900	(i)	80
		(k)	300
		(l)	700
		(m)	1,650
		(o)	3,000
Bal.	470		9,430

GENERAL LEDGER

ACCOUNT: Cash   ACCOUNT NO. 101

DATE	ITEM	POST. REF.	DEBIT	CREDIT	BALANCE DEBIT	BALANCE CREDIT
20-- June 1			5 0 0 0 00		5 0 0 0 00	
3				2 0 0 0 00	3 0 0 0 00	
6				6 0 0 00	2 4 0 0 00	
6			2 1 0 0 00		4 5 0 0 00	
7				1 0 0 0 00	3 5 0 0 00	
15				1 0 0 00	3 4 0 0 00	
16				8 0 00	3 3 2 0 00	
20			1 9 0 0 00		5 2 2 0 00	
25				3 0 0 00	4 9 2 0 00	
26				7 0 0 00	4 2 2 0 00	
27				1 6 5 0 00	2 5 7 0 00	
30			9 0 0 00		3 4 7 0 00	
30				3 0 0 0 00	4 7 0 00	

└─ Transaction Amount ─┘ └─ Running Balance ─┘

and analyzing what happened, T accounts are very helpful. However, computing the balance of a T account is cumbersome. The primary advantage of the general ledger account is that it maintains a running balance.

Note that the heading for the general ledger account has the account title and an account number. The account number is taken from the chart of accounts and is used in the posting process.

Posting to the General Ledger

The process of copying the debits and credits from the journal to the ledger accounts is known as posting. All amounts entered in the journal must be posted to the general ledger accounts. Posting from the journal to the ledger is done daily or at frequent intervals.

To illustrate the posting process, the first journal entry for Mitchell's Campus Delivery will be posted step by step. There are five steps in the process of posting each debit and credit. First, let's post the debit to Cash (Figure 4-9).

FIGURE 4-9 Posting a Debit

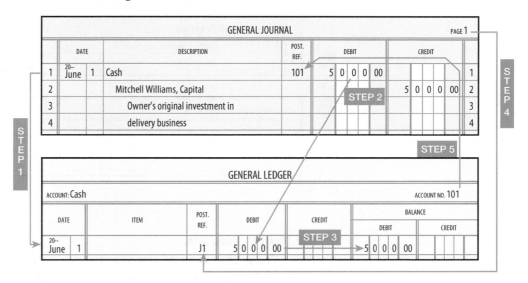

In the ledger account:

STEP 1 **Enter the date of the transaction in the Date column.** Enter the year, "20--," the month, "June," and the day, "1," in the Date column of the cash account.

STEP 2 **Enter the debit.** Copy the $5,000 debit to Cash in the journal to the Debit column of the ledger. Since this is not a formal financial statement, dollar signs are not used.

STEP 3 **Enter the balance of the account.** Enter the $5,000 balance in the Balance columns under Debit. (If the balance of the account is zero, draw a line through the Debit and Credit columns.)

STEP 4 **Enter the journal page in the Posting Reference column.** Enter "J1" in the Posting Reference column since the posting came from page 1 of the journal.

The Item column is left blank, except for special reasons such as indicating the beginning balance, adjusting, correcting, closing, or reversing entries.

In the journal:

STEP 5   Enter the ledger account number in the Posting Reference column. Enter the account number for Cash, 101 (see chart of accounts in Figure 4-3 on page 88), in the Posting Reference column of the journal on the same line as the debit to Cash for $5,000.

Step 5 is the last step in the posting process. After this step is completed, the posting references will indicate which journal entries have been posted to the ledger accounts. This is very helpful, particularly if you are interrupted during the posting process. The information in the Posting Reference columns of the journal and ledger provides a link between the journal and ledger known as a cross-reference.

Now let's post the credit portion of the first entry (Figure 4-10).

FIGURE 4-10 Posting a Credit

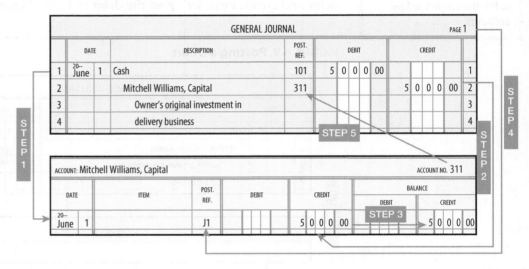

In the ledger account:

STEP 1   Enter the date of the transaction in the Date column. Enter the year, "20--," the month, "June," and the day, "1," in the Date column of the account Mitchell Williams, Capital.

STEP 2   Enter the credit. Copy the $5,000 credit to Mitchell Williams, Capital in the journal to the Credit column in the ledger.

STEP 3   Enter the balance of the account. Enter the $5,000 balance in the Balance columns under Credit. (If the balance of the account is zero, draw a line through the Debit and Credit columns.)

STEP 4   Enter the journal page in the Posting Reference column. Enter "J1" in the Posting Reference column since the posting came from page 1 of the journal.

The Item column is left blank, except for special reasons such as indicating the beginning balance, adjusting, correcting, closing, or reversing entries.

In the journal:

STEP 5 **Enter the ledger account number in the Posting Reference column.**
Enter the account number for Mitchell Williams, Capital, 311, in the Posting Reference column. Again, this last step indicates that the credit has been posted to the general ledger.

After posting the journal entries for Mitchell's Campus Delivery for the month of June, the general journal and general ledger should appear as illustrated in Figures 4-11 and 4-12 on pages 97–100. *Note that the Posting Reference column of the journal has been filled in because the entries have been posted.*

FIGURE 4-11 General Journal After Posting

	DATE		DESCRIPTION	POST. REF.	DEBIT	CREDIT	
1	20-- June	1	Cash	101	5 0 0 0 00		1
2			Mitchell Williams, Capital	311		5 0 0 0 00	2
3			Owner's original investment in				3
4			delivery business				4
5							5
6		3	Delivery Equipment	185	2 0 0 0 00		6
7			Cash	101		2 0 0 0 00	7
8			Purchased delivery equipment for cash				8
9							9
10		5	Delivery Equipment	185	1 8 0 0 00		10
11			Accounts Payable	202		1 8 0 0 00	11
12			Purchased delivery equipment on account				12
13			from Big Red Scooters				13
14							14
15		6	Accounts Payable	202	6 0 0 00		15
16			Cash	101		6 0 0 00	16
17			Made partial payment to Big Red Scooters				17
18							18
19		6	Cash	101	2 1 0 0 00		19
20			Delivery Fees	401		2 1 0 0 00	20
21			Received cash for delivery services				21
22							22
23		7	Rent Expense	521	1 0 0 0 00		23
24			Cash	101		1 0 0 0 00	24
25			Paid office rent for June				25
26							26
27		15	Phone Expense	525	1 0 0 00		27
28			Cash	101		1 0 0 00	28
29			Paid phone bill for June				29
30							30
31		15	Accounts Receivable	122	2 4 0 0 00		31
32			Delivery Fees	401		2 4 0 0 00	32
33			Deliveries made on account for				33
34			Library ($400) and School of Music ($2,000)				34
35							35

GENERAL JOURNAL   PAGE 1

FIGURE 4-11 General Journal After Posting (*concluded*)

	DATE		DESCRIPTION	POST. REF.	DEBIT					CREDIT					
1	20-- June	16	Supplies	141			8	0	00						1
2			Cash	101								8	0	00	2
3			Purchased supplies for cash												3
4															4
5		20	Cash	101	1	9	0	0	00						5
6			Accounts Receivable	122						1	9	0	0	00	6
7			Received cash on account from												7
8			Library ($400) and School of Music ($1,500)												8
9															9
10		25	Delivery Equipment	185	1	0	0	0	00						10
11			Accounts Payable	202							7	0	0	00	11
12			Cash	101							3	0	0	00	12
13			Purchased scooter with down payment;												13
14			balance on account with Big Red Scooters												14
15															15
16		26	Prepaid Insurance	145			7	0	0	00					16
17			Cash	101							7	0	0	00	17
18			Paid premium for seven-month												18
19			insurance policy												19
20															20
21		27	Wages Expense	511	1	6	5	0	00						21
22			Cash	101						1	6	5	0	00	22
23			Paid employees												23
24															24
25		30	Cash	101		9	0	0	00						25
26			Accounts Receivable	122	2	6	0	0	00						26
27			Delivery Fees	401						3	5	0	0	00	27
28			Deliveries made for cash and on account to												28
29			Library ($250) and												29
30			Athletic Ticket Office ($2,350)												30
31															31
32		30	Mitchell Williams, Drawing	312	3	0	0	0	00						32
33			Cash	101						3	0	0	0	00	33
34			Owner's withdrawal												34

FIGURE 4-12 General Ledger After Posting

GENERAL LEDGER

ACCOUNT: Cash   ACCOUNT NO. 101

DATE		ITEM	POST. REF.	DEBIT	CREDIT	BALANCE	
						DEBIT	CREDIT
20-- June	1		J1	5 0 0 0 00		5 0 0 0 00	
	3		J1		2 0 0 0 00	3 0 0 0 00	
	6		J1		6 0 0 00	2 4 0 0 00	
	6		J1	2 1 0 0 00		4 5 0 0 00	
	7		J1		1 0 0 0 00	3 5 0 0 00	
	15		J1		1 0 0 00	3 4 0 0 00	
	16		J2		8 0 00	3 3 2 0 00	
	20		J2	1 9 0 0 00		5 2 2 0 00	
	25		J2		3 0 0 00	4 9 2 0 00	
	26		J2		7 0 0 00	4 2 2 0 00	
	27		J2		1 6 5 0 00	2 5 7 0 00	
	30		J2	9 0 0 00		3 4 7 0 00	
	30		J2		3 0 0 0 00	4 7 0 00	

> For asset, expense, and drawing accounts, a running balance is maintained by adding the debit or subtracting the credit from the previous balance.

ACCOUNT: Accounts Receivable   ACCOUNT NO. 122

DATE		ITEM	POST. REF.	DEBIT	CREDIT	BALANCE	
						DEBIT	CREDIT
20-- June	15		J1	2 4 0 0 00		2 4 0 0 00	
	20		J2		1 9 0 0 00	5 0 0 00	
	30		J2	2 6 0 0 00		3 1 0 0 00	

ACCOUNT: Supplies   ACCOUNT NO. 141

DATE		ITEM	POST. REF.	DEBIT	CREDIT	BALANCE	
						DEBIT	CREDIT
20-- June	16		J2	8 0 00		8 0 00	

ACCOUNT: Prepaid Insurance   ACCOUNT NO. 145

DATE		ITEM	POST. REF.	DEBIT	CREDIT	BALANCE	
						DEBIT	CREDIT
20-- June	26		J2	7 0 0 00		7 0 0 00	

ACCOUNT: Delivery Equipment   ACCOUNT NO. 185

DATE		ITEM	POST. REF.	DEBIT	CREDIT	BALANCE	
						DEBIT	CREDIT
20-- June	3		J1	2 0 0 0 00		2 0 0 0 00	
	5		J1	1 8 0 0 00		3 8 0 0 00	
	25		J2	1 0 0 0 00		4 8 0 0 00	

FIGURE 4-12 General Ledger After Posting (*concluded*)

> For liability, revenue, and capital accounts, a running balance is maintained by adding the credit or subtracting the debit from the previous balance.

ACCOUNT: Accounts Payable   ACCOUNT NO. 202

DATE		ITEM	POST. REF.	DEBIT	CREDIT	BALANCE DEBIT	BALANCE CREDIT
20-- June	5		J1		1 8 0 0 00		1 8 0 0 00
	6		J1	6 0 0 00			1 2 0 0 00
	25		J2		7 0 0 00		1 9 0 0 00

ACCOUNT: Mitchell Williams, Capital   ACCOUNT NO. 311

DATE		ITEM	POST. REF.	DEBIT	CREDIT	BALANCE DEBIT	BALANCE CREDIT
20-- June	1		J1		5 0 0 0 00		5 0 0 0 00

ACCOUNT: Mitchell Williams, Drawing   ACCOUNT NO. 312

DATE		ITEM	POST. REF.	DEBIT	CREDIT	BALANCE DEBIT	BALANCE CREDIT
20-- June	30		J2	3 0 0 0 00		3 0 0 0 00	

ACCOUNT: Delivery Fees   ACCOUNT NO. 401

DATE		ITEM	POST. REF.	DEBIT	CREDIT	BALANCE DEBIT	BALANCE CREDIT
20-- June	6		J1		2 1 0 0 00		2 1 0 0 00
	15		J1		2 4 0 0 00		4 5 0 0 00
	30		J2		3 5 0 0 00		8 0 0 0 00

ACCOUNT: Wages Expense   ACCOUNT NO. 511

DATE		ITEM	POST. REF.	DEBIT	CREDIT	BALANCE DEBIT	BALANCE CREDIT
20-- June	27		J2	1 6 5 0 00		1 6 5 0 00	

ACCOUNT: Rent Expense   ACCOUNT NO. 521

DATE		ITEM	POST. REF.	DEBIT	CREDIT	BALANCE DEBIT	BALANCE CREDIT
20-- June	7		J1	1 0 0 0 00		1 0 0 0 00	

ACCOUNT: Phone Expense   ACCOUNT NO. 525

DATE		ITEM	POST. REF.	DEBIT	CREDIT	BALANCE DEBIT	BALANCE CREDIT
20-- June	15		J1	1 0 0 00		1 0 0 00	

The Trial Balance

In Chapter 3, a trial balance was used to prove that the totals of the debit and credit balances in the T accounts were equal. In this chapter, a trial balance is used to prove the equality of the debits and credits in the ledger accounts. A trial balance can be prepared daily, weekly, monthly, or whenever desired. Before preparing a trial balance, all transactions should be journalized and posted so that the effect of all transactions will be reflected in the ledger accounts.

The trial balance for Mitchell's Campus Delivery shown in Figure 4-13 was prepared from the balances in the general ledger in Figure 4-12. The accounts are listed in the order used in the chart of accounts. This order is also often used when preparing financial statements. In Chapter 2, we pointed out that many firms list expenses from highest to lowest amounts. Some firms list expenses according to the chart of accounts, which is the method we will follow.

LEARNING KEY 🔑

The chart of accounts determines the order for listing accounts in the general ledger and trial balance. This order may also be used when preparing financial statements.

FIGURE 4-13 Trial Balance

ACCOUNT TITLE	ACCOUNT NO.	DEBIT BALANCE	CREDIT BALANCE
Mitchell's Campus Delivery			
Trial Balance			
June 30, 20 - -			
Cash	101	4 7 0 00	
Accounts Receivable	122	3 1 0 0 00	
Supplies	141	8 0 00	
Prepaid Insurance	145	7 0 0 00	
Delivery Equipment	185	4 8 0 0 00	
Accounts Payable	202		1 9 0 0 00
Mitchell Williams, Capital	311		5 0 0 0 00
Mitchell Williams, Drawing	312	3 0 0 0 00	
Delivery Fees	401		8 0 0 0 00
Wages Expense	511	1 6 5 0 00	
Rent Expense	521	1 0 0 0 00	
Phone Expense	525	1 0 0 00	
		14 9 0 0 00	14 9 0 0 00

CHECKPOINT ✓

Complete Checkpoint-3 on page 113 to test your basic understanding of LO5.

Even though the trial balance indicates that the ledger is in balance, the ledger can still contain errors. For example, if a journal entry was made debiting or crediting the wrong accounts, or if an item was posted to the wrong account, the ledger will still be in balance. It is important, therefore, to be very careful in preparing the journal entries and in posting them to the ledger accounts.

| LO6 | **Finding and Correcting Errors in the Trial Balance** |

Explain how to find and correct errors.

Tips are available to help if your trial balance has an error. Figure 4-14 offers hints for finding the error when your trial balance does not balance.

FIGURE 4-14 Tips for Finding Errors in the Trial Balance

1. Double check your addition. Review balances to see if they are too large or small, relative to other accounts, or entered in the wrong column.

2. Find the difference between the debits and the credits.

   a. If the difference is equal to the amount of a specific transaction, perhaps you forgot to post the debit or credit portion of this transaction.

   b. Divide the difference by 2. If the difference is evenly divisible by 2, you may have posted two debits or two credits for a transaction. If a debit was posted as a credit, it would mean that one transaction had two credits and no debits. The difference between the total debits and credits would be twice the amount of the debit that was posted as a credit.

   c. Divide the difference by 9. If the difference is evenly divisible by 9, you may have committed a **slide error** or a **transposition error**. A slide occurs when debit or credit amounts "slide" a digit or two to the left or right when entered. For example, if *$250* was entered as *$25*:

   | $250 | — | $25 | = | $225 |
   | $225 | ÷ | 9 | = | $25 |

   The difference is evenly divisible by 9.

   A transposition occurs when two digits are reversed. For example, if *$250* was entered as *$520*:

   | $520 | — | $250 | = | $270 |
   | $270 | ÷ | 9 | = | $30 |

   Again, the difference is evenly divisible by 9.

If the tips in Figure 4-14 don't work, you must retrace your steps through the accounting process. Double check your addition for the ledger accounts. Also trace all postings. Be patient as you search for your error. Use this process as an opportunity to reinforce your understanding of the flow of information through the accounting system. Much can be learned while looking for an error.

Once you have found an error, it is important to make the correction in a manner that is easy for others to observe and understand. Although you may want to erase when correcting your homework, this is not acceptable in practice. An erasure may suggest that you are trying to hide something. Instead, you should make a correcting entry.

Correcting Entries

If an incorrect entry has been journalized and posted to the wrong account, a correcting entry should be made. For example, assume that a $400 payment for Rent Expense was incorrectly debited to Repair Expense and correctly credited to

Cash. This requires a correcting entry and explanation as shown in Figure 4-15. Figure 4-16 shows the effects of the correcting entry on the ledger accounts. Generally, "Correcting" is written in the Item column of the general ledger account.

When using a computerized accounting system, the journal entries are automatically posted to the ledger. To correct an error, the correcting entry method should be used.

FIGURE 4-15 Correcting Entry Method

	DATE		DESCRIPTION	POST. REF.	DEBIT	CREDIT	
			GENERAL JOURNAL			PAGE 6	
1	20— Sept.	25	Rent Expense	521	4 0 0 00		1
2			Repair Expense	537		4 0 0 00	2
3			To correct error in which payment for rent				3
4			was debited to Repair Expense				4
5							5

FIGURE 4-16 Effects of Correcting Entry on Ledger Accounts

GENERAL LEDGER

ACCOUNT: Rent Expense ACCOUNT NO. 521

DATE		ITEM	POST. REF.	DEBIT	CREDIT	BALANCE DEBIT	BALANCE CREDIT
20— Sept.	25	Correcting	J6	4 0 0 00		4 0 0 00	

ACCOUNT: Repair Expense ACCOUNT NO. 537

DATE		ITEM	POST. REF.	DEBIT	CREDIT	BALANCE DEBIT	BALANCE CREDIT
20— Sept.	10		J5	5 0 00		5 0 00	
	15		J5	4 0 0 00		4 5 0 00	
	25	Correcting	J6		4 0 0 00	5 0 00	

CHECKPOINT ✔

Complete Checkpoint-4 on page 113 to test your basic understanding of LO6.

SELF-STUDY

LEARNING OBJECTIVES	Key Points to Remember
LO1 Describe the flow of data from source documents to the trial balance.	The flow of data from the source documents to the trial balance is as follows: 1. Analyze business transactions. 2. Journalize transactions in the general journal. 3. Post journal entries to the general ledger. 4. Prepare a trial balance.

LO2 Describe and explain the purpose of source documents.	Source documents trigger the analysis of business transactions and the entries into the accounting system.
LO3 Describe the chart of accounts as a means of classifying financial information.	The chart of accounts includes the account titles in numerical order for all assets, liabilities, owner's equity, revenues, and expenses. The chart of accounts is used in classifying information about transactions.
LO4 Journalize transactions.	A journal provides a day-by-day listing of transactions. The journal shows the date, titles of the accounts to be debited or credited, and the amounts of the debits and credits. The steps in the journalizing process are as follows: 1. Enter the date. 2. Enter the debit. Accounts to be debited are entered first. 3. Enter the credit. Accounts to be credited are entered after the debits and are indented one-half inch. 4. Enter the explanation. A brief explanation of the transaction should be entered in the description column on the line following the last credit. The explanation should be indented an additional one-half inch.
LO5 Post to the general ledger and prepare a trial balance.	The general ledger is a complete set of all accounts used by the business. The steps in posting from the general journal to the general ledger are as follows: In the general ledger: 1. Enter the date of each transaction. 2. Enter the amount of each debit or credit in the Debit or Credit column. 3. Enter the new balance. 4. Enter the journal page number from which each transaction is posted in the Posting Reference column.

(continued)

LEARNING OBJECTIVES	Key Points to Remember
LO5 (concluded)	In the journal: 5. Enter the account number to which each transaction is posted in the Posting Reference column. The trial balance provides a check to make sure the total of all debit balances in the ledger accounts equals the total of all credit balances in the ledger accounts.
LO6 Explain how to find and correct errors.	Errors may be found by verifying your addition, by dividing the difference between the debits and credits by 2 or 9, and by retracing your steps through the accounting process. If an incorrect entry has been made and posted, a correcting entry must be made.

DEMONSTRATION PROBLEM

George Fielding is a financial planning consultant. He provides budgeting, estate planning, tax planning, and investing advice for professional golfers. He developed the following chart of accounts for his business:

Assets		Revenues	
101	Cash	401	Professional Fees
142	Office Supplies		
		Expenses	
Liabilities		511	Wages Expense
202	Accounts Payable	521	Rent Expense
		525	Phone Expense
Owner's Equity		533	Utilities Expense
311	George Fielding, Capital	534	Charitable Contributions Expense
312	George Fielding, Drawing	538	Automobile Expense

The following transactions took place during the month of December of the current year:

Dec.	1	Fielding invested cash to start the business, $20,000.
	3	Paid Bollhorst Real Estate for December office rent, $1,000.
	4	Received cash from Aaron Patton, a client, for services, $2,500.
	6	Paid T. Z. Anderson Electric for December heating and light, $75.
	7	Received cash from Andrew Conder, a client, for services, $2,000.
	12	Paid Fichter's Super Service for gasoline and oil purchases for the company car, $60.

(continued)

Dec. 14   Paid Hillenburg Staffing for temporary secretarial services during the past two weeks, $600.

17   Bought office supplies from Bowers Office Supply on account, $280.

20   Paid Mitchell Phone Co. for business calls during the past month, $100.

21   Fielding withdrew cash for personal use, $1,100.

24   Made donation to the National Multiple Sclerosis Society, $100.

27   Received cash from Billy Walters, a client, for services, $2,000.

28   Paid Hillenburg Staffing for temporary secretarial services during the past two weeks, $600.

29   Made payment on account to Bowers Office Supply, $100.

REQUIRED

1. Record the preceding transactions in a general journal.
2. Post the entries to the general ledger.
3. Prepare a trial balance.
4. Prepare an income statement, statement of owner's equity, and balance sheet for the month of December.

SOLUTION 1, 2.

	DATE		DESCRIPTION	POST. REF.	DEBIT	CREDIT	
			GENERAL JOURNAL			PAGE 1	
1	20-- Dec.	1	Cash	101	20 0 0 0 00		1
2			George Fielding, Capital	311		20 0 0 0 00	2
3			Owner's original investment in				3
4			consulting business				4
5							5
6		3	Rent Expense	521	1 0 0 0 00		6
7			Cash	101		1 0 0 0 00	7
8			Paid rent for December				8
9							9
10		4	Cash	101	2 5 0 0 00		10
11			Professional Fees	401		2 5 0 0 00	11
12			Received cash for services rendered				12
13							13
14		6	Utilities Expense	533	7 5 00		14
15			Cash	101		7 5 00	15
16			Paid utilities				16
17							17
18		7	Cash	101	2 0 0 0 00		18
19			Professional Fees	401		2 0 0 0 00	19
20			Received cash for services rendered				20
21							21

(continued)

GENERAL JOURNAL — PAGE 1

	DATE		DESCRIPTION	POST. REF.	DEBIT	CREDIT	
22	20-- Dec.	12	Automobile Expense	538	6 0 0 00		22
23			Cash	101		6 0 0 00	23
24			Paid for gas and oil				24
25							25
26		14	Wages Expense	511	6 0 0 00		26
27			Cash	101		6 0 0 00	27
28			Paid temporary secretaries				28
29							29
30		17	Office Supplies	142	2 8 0 00		30
31			Accounts Payable	202		2 8 0 00	31
32			Purchased office supplies on account from				32
33			Bowers Office Supply				33
34							34
35							35

GENERAL JOURNAL — PAGE 2

	DATE		DESCRIPTION	POST. REF.	DEBIT	CREDIT	
1	20-- Dec.	20	Phone Expense	525	1 0 0 00		1
2			Cash	101		1 0 0 00	2
3			Paid phone bill				3
4							4
5		21	George Fielding, Drawing	312	1 1 0 0 00		5
6			Cash	101		1 1 0 0 00	6
7			Owner's withdrawal				7
8							8
9		24	Charitable Contributions Expense	534	1 0 0 00		9
10			Cash	101		1 0 0 00	10
11			Contribution to National Multiple				11
12			Sclerosis Society				12
13							13
14		27	Cash	101	2 0 0 0 00		14
15			Professional Fees	401		2 0 0 0 00	15
16			Received cash for services rendered				16
17							17
18		28	Wages Expense	511	6 0 0 00		18
19			Cash	101		6 0 0 00	19
20			Paid temporary secretaries				20
21							21
22		29	Accounts Payable	202	1 0 0 00		22
23			Cash	101		1 0 0 00	23
24			Payment on account to Bowers Office Supply				24

SOLUTION 2.

GENERAL LEDGER

ACCOUNT: Cash ACCOUNT NO. 101

DATE		ITEM	POST. REF.	DEBIT	CREDIT	BALANCE DEBIT	BALANCE CREDIT
20-- Dec.	1		J1	20 0 0 0 00		20 0 0 0 00	
	3		J1		1 0 0 0 00	19 0 0 0 00	
	4		J1	2 5 0 0 00		21 5 0 0 00	
	6		J1		7 5 00	21 4 2 5 00	
	7		J1	2 0 0 0 00		23 4 2 5 00	
	12		J1		6 0 00	23 3 6 5 00	
	14		J1		6 0 0 00	22 7 6 5 00	
	20		J2		1 0 0 00	22 6 6 5 00	
	21		J2		1 1 0 0 00	21 5 6 5 00	
	24		J2		1 0 0 00	21 4 6 5 00	
	27		J2	2 0 0 0 00		23 4 6 5 00	
	28		J2		6 0 0 00	22 8 6 5 00	
	29		J2		1 0 0 00	22 7 6 5 00	

ACCOUNT: Office Supplies ACCOUNT NO. 142

DATE		ITEM	POST. REF.	DEBIT	CREDIT	BALANCE DEBIT	BALANCE CREDIT
20-- Dec.	17		J1	2 8 0 00		2 8 0 00	

ACCOUNT: Accounts Payable ACCOUNT NO. 202

DATE		ITEM	POST. REF.	DEBIT	CREDIT	BALANCE DEBIT	BALANCE CREDIT
20-- Dec.	17		J1		2 8 0 00		2 8 0 00
	29		J2	1 0 0 00			1 8 0 00

ACCOUNT: George Fielding, Capital ACCOUNT NO. 311

DATE		ITEM	POST. REF.	DEBIT	CREDIT	BALANCE DEBIT	BALANCE CREDIT
20-- Dec.	1		J1		20 0 0 0 00		20 0 0 0 00

(continued)

ACCOUNT: George Fielding, Drawing — ACCOUNT NO. 312

DATE	ITEM	POST. REF.	DEBIT	CREDIT	BALANCE DEBIT	BALANCE CREDIT
20-- Dec. 21		J2	1 1 0 0 00		1 1 0 0 00	

ACCOUNT: Professional Fees — ACCOUNT NO. 401

DATE	ITEM	POST. REF.	DEBIT	CREDIT	BALANCE DEBIT	BALANCE CREDIT
20-- Dec. 4		J1		2 5 0 0 00		2 5 0 0 00
7		J1		2 0 0 0 00		4 5 0 0 00
27		J2		2 0 0 0 00		6 5 0 0 00

ACCOUNT: Wages Expense — ACCOUNT NO. 511

DATE	ITEM	POST. REF.	DEBIT	CREDIT	BALANCE DEBIT	BALANCE CREDIT
20-- Dec. 14		J1	6 0 0 00		6 0 0 00	
28		J2	6 0 0 00		1 2 0 0 00	

ACCOUNT: Rent Expense — ACCOUNT NO. 521

DATE	ITEM	POST. REF.	DEBIT	CREDIT	BALANCE DEBIT	BALANCE CREDIT
20-- Dec. 3		J1	1 0 0 0 00		1 0 0 0 00	

ACCOUNT: Phone Expense — ACCOUNT NO. 525

DATE	ITEM	POST. REF.	DEBIT	CREDIT	BALANCE DEBIT	BALANCE CREDIT
20-- Dec. 20		J2	1 0 0 00		1 0 0 00	

ACCOUNT: Utilities Expense								ACCOUNT NO. 533	
DATE	ITEM	POST. REF.	DEBIT	CREDIT	BALANCE				
					DEBIT		CREDIT		
20-- Dec. 6		J1	7 5 00		7 5 00				

ACCOUNT: Charitable Contributions Expense								ACCOUNT NO. 534	
DATE	ITEM	POST. REF.	DEBIT	CREDIT	BALANCE				
					DEBIT		CREDIT		
20-- Dec. 24		J2	1 0 0 00		1 0 0 00				

ACCOUNT: Automobile Expense								ACCOUNT NO. 538	
DATE	ITEM	POST. REF.	DEBIT	CREDIT	BALANCE				
					DEBIT		CREDIT		
20-- Dec. 12		J1	6 0 00		6 0 00				

SOLUTION 3.

George Fielding, Financial Planning Consultant
Trial Balance
December 31, 20 --

ACCOUNT TITLE	ACCOUNT NO.	DEBIT BALANCE	CREDIT BALANCE
Cash	101	22 7 6 5 00	
Office Supplies	142	2 8 0 00	
Accounts Payable	202		1 8 0 00
George Fielding, Capital	311		20 0 0 0 00
George Fielding, Drawing	312	1 1 0 0 00	
Professional Fees	401		6 5 0 0 00
Wages Expense	511	1 2 0 0 00	
Rent Expense	521	1 0 0 0 00	
Phone Expense	525	1 0 0 00	
Utilities Expense	533	7 5 00	
Charitable Contributions Expense	534	1 0 0 00	
Automobile Expense	538	6 0 00	
		26 6 8 0 00	26 6 8 0 00

(continued)

SOLUTION 4.

George Fielding, Financial Planning Consultant		
Income Statement		
For Month Ended December 31, 20 --		
Revenue:		
Professional fees		$6,500
Expenses:		
Wages expense	$1,200	
Rent expense	1,000	
Phone expense	100	
Utilities expense	75	
Charitable contributions expense	100	
Automobile expense	60	
Total expenses		2,535
Net income		$3,965

George Fielding, Financial Planning Consultant		
Statement of Owner's Equity		
For Month Ended December 31, 20 --		
George Fielding, capital, December 1, 20 --		$ —
Investments during December		20,000
Total investment		$20,000
Net income for December	$3,965	
Less withdrawals for December	1,100	
Increase in capital		2,865
George Fielding, Capital, December 31, 20 --		$22,865

George Fielding, Financial Planning Consultant			
Balance Sheet			
December 31, 20 --			
Assets		Liabilities	
Cash	$22,765	Accounts payable	$ 180
Office Supplies	280	Owner's equity	
		George Fielding, capital	22,865
Total assets	$23,045	Total liabilities and owner's equity	$23,045

KEY TERMS

book of original entry (89)   The journal or the first formal accounting record of a transaction.

chart of accounts (88)   A list of all accounts used by a business.

compound entry (92)   A general journal entry that affects more than two accounts.

correcting entry (102)   An entry to correct an incorrect entry that has been journalized and posted to the wrong account.

cross-reference (96)   The information in the Posting Reference columns of the journal and ledger that provides a link between the journal and ledger.

general ledger (94)   A complete set of all the accounts used by a business. The general ledger accumulates a complete record of the debits and credits made to each account as a result of entries made in the journal.

general ledger account (94)   An account with columns for the debit or credit transaction and columns for the debit or credit running balance.

journal (89)   A day-by-day listing of the transactions of a business.

journalizing (89)   Entering the transactions in a journal.

posting (95)   Copying the debits and credits from the journal to the ledger accounts.

slide error (102)   An error that occurs when debit or credit amounts "slide" a digit or two to the left or right.

source document (86)   Any document that provides information about a business transaction.

transposition error (102)   An error that occurs when two digits are reversed.

trial balance (101)   A list used to prove that the totals of the debit and credit balances in the ledger accounts are equal.

two-column general journal (89)   A journal with only two amount columns, one for debit amounts and one for credit amounts.

SELF-STUDY TEST QUESTIONS

True/False

1. **LO2** Source documents serve as historical evidence of business transactions.

2. **LO3** The chart of accounts lists capital accounts first, followed by liabilities, assets, expenses, and revenue.

3. **LO4** No entries are made in the Posting Reference column at the time of journalizing.

4. **LO4** When entering the credit item in a general journal, it should be listed after all debits and indented.

5. **LO6** When an incorrect entry has been journalized and posted to the wrong account, a correcting entry should be made.

Multiple Choice

1. **LO2** Which of the following is not a source document?
   (a) Check stub
   (b) Cash register tape
   (c) Journal entry
   (d) Purchase invoice

2. **LO3** A revenue account will begin with the number _____ in the chart of accounts.
   (a) 1   (c) 3
   (b) 2   (d) 4

3. **LO4**   To purchase an asset such as office equipment on account, you would credit which account?
   (a) Cash
   (b) Accounts Receivable
   (c) Accounts Payable
   (d) Capital

4. **LO4**   When fees are earned and the customer promises to pay later, which account is debited?
   (a) Cash
   (b) Accounts Receivable
   (c) Accounts Payable
   (d) Capital

5. **LO6**   When the correct numbers are used but are in the wrong order, the error is called a
   (a) transposition.
   (b) slide.
   (c) reversal.
   (d) correcting entry.

Checkpoint Exercises

1. **LO2**   A check stub serves as a source document for what kind of transaction?

2. **LO4**   Indicate the information that would be entered for each of the lettered items in the general journal provided below.

									GENERAL JOURNAL										PAGE	
		DATE				DESCRIPTION					POST. REF.		DEBIT				CREDIT				
1	A B		C	D							G		H								1
2					E						J							I			2
3					F																3
4																					4
5																					5

3. **LO5**   Indicate the information that would be entered for each of the lettered items in the general ledger account provided below.

						GENERAL LEDGER								
ACCOUNT: A											ACCOUNT NO. B			
DATE		ITEM		POST. REF.		DEBIT		CREDIT		BALANCE				
										DEBIT		CREDIT		
C D	E	F		G		H		I		J		K		

4. **LO6**   Dunkin Company made the following entry for the payment of $500 cash for rent expense:

   Rent Expense   500
        Rent Payable   500

   Prepare a correcting entry.

The answers to the Self-Study Test Questions are at the end of the chapter (pages 128–129).

APPLYING YOUR KNOWLEDGE

REVIEW QUESTIONS

LO1 1. Trace the flow of accounting information through the accounting system.

LO2 2. Name a source document that provides information about each of the following types of business transactions:
  a. Cash payment
  b. Cash receipt
  c. Sale of goods or services
  d. Purchase of goods or services

LO3 3. Explain the purpose of a chart of accounts.

LO3 4. Name the five types of financial statement classifications for which it is ordinarily desirable to keep separate accounts.

LO4 5. Where is the first formal accounting record of a business transaction usually made?

LO4 6. Describe the four steps required to journalize a business transaction in a general journal.

LO5 7. In what order are the accounts customarily placed in the ledger?

LO5 8. Explain the primary advantage of a general ledger account.

LO5 9. Explain the five steps required when posting the journal to the ledger.

LO5 10. What information is entered in the Posting Reference column of the journal as an amount is posted to the proper account in the ledger?

LO6 11. Explain why the ledger can still contain errors even though the trial balance is in balance. Give examples of two such types of errors.

LO6 12. What is a slide error?

LO6 13. What is a transposition error?

LO6 14. What is a correcting entry?

SERIES A EXERCISES

E 4-1A (LO2)

SOURCE DOCUMENTS Source documents trigger the analysis of events requiring an accounting entry. Match the following source documents with the type of information they provide.

1. Check stubs or check register
2. Purchase invoice from suppliers (vendors)
3. Sales tickets or invoices to customers
4. Receipts or cash register tapes

a. A good or service has been sold.
b. Cash has been received by the business.
c. Cash has been paid by the business.
d. Goods or services have been purchased by the business.

E 4-2A   (LO4)

GENERAL JOURNAL ENTRIES For each of the following transactions, list the account to be debited and the account to be credited in the general journal.

1. Invested cash in the business, $5,000.
2. Paid office rent, $500.
3. Purchased office supplies on account, $300.
4. Received cash for services rendered (fees), $400.
5. Paid cash on account, $50.
6. Rendered services on account, $300.
7. Received cash for an amount owed by a customer, $100.

E 4-3A   (LO5)
✓ Final Cash bal.: $4,950

GENERAL LEDGER ACCOUNTS Set up T accounts for each of the general ledger accounts needed for Exercise 4-2A and post debits and credits to the accounts. Foot the accounts and enter the balances. Prove that total debits equal total credits.

E 4-4A   (LO4)

GENERAL JOURNAL ENTRIES Diane Bernick has opened Bernick's Consulting. Journalize the following transactions that occurred during January of the current year. Use the following journal pages: January 1–10, page 1; and January 11–29, page 2. Use the following chart of accounts:

Chart of Accounts

Assets
101   Cash
142   Office Supplies
181   Office Equipment

Liabilities
202   Accounts Payable

Owner's Equity
311   Diane Bernick, Capital
312   Diane Bernick, Drawing

Revenues
401   Consulting Fees

Expenses
511   Wages Expense
521   Rent Expense
525   Phone Expense
533   Utilities Expense
549   Miscellaneous Expense

Jan. 1	Bernick invested cash in the business, $12,000.
2	Paid office rent, $750.
3	Purchased office equipment on account, $1,300.
5	Received cash for services rendered, $950.
8	Paid phone bill, $85.
10	Paid for a magazine subscription (miscellaneous expense), $20.
11	Purchased office supplies on account, $250.
15	Made a payment on account (see Jan. 3 transaction), $200.
18	Paid part-time employee, $600.
21	Received cash for services rendered, $800.
25	Paid utilities bill, $105.
27	Bernick withdrew cash for personal use, $400.
29	Paid part-time employee, $600.

E 4-5A (LO5)
✓ Final Cash bal.: $10,990
✓ Trial bal. total debits: $15,100

GENERAL LEDGER ACCOUNTS; TRIAL BALANCE Set up general ledger accounts using the chart of accounts provided in Exercise 4-4A. Post the transactions from Exercise 4-4A to the general ledger accounts and prepare a trial balance.

E 4-6A (LO5)
✓ Total assets, Jan. 31: $12,540

FINANCIAL STATEMENTS From the information in Exercises 4-4A and 4-5A, prepare an income statement, a statement of owner's equity, and a balance sheet.

E 4-7A (LO5)
✓ Total assets, July 31: $7,100

FINANCIAL STATEMENTS From the following trial balance taken after one month of operation, prepare an income statement, a statement of owner's equity, and a balance sheet.

TJ's Paint Service **Trial Balance** **July 31, 20 - -**										
ACCOUNT TITLE	ACCOUNT NO.	DEBIT BALANCE					CREDIT BALANCE			
Cash	101	4	3	0	0	00				
Accounts Receivable	122	1	1	0	0	00				
Supplies	141		8	0	0	00				
Paint Equipment	183		9	0	0	00				
Accounts Payable	202						2	1	5	0	00
TJ Ulza, Capital	311						3	2	0	5	00
TJ Ulza, Drawing	312		5	0	0	00				
Painting Fees	401						3	6	0	0	00
Wages Expense	511		9	0	0	00				
Rent Expense	521		2	5	0	00				
Phone Expense	525			5	0	00				
Transportation Expense	526			6	0	00				
Utilities Expense	533			7	0	00				
Miscellaneous Expense	549			2	5	00				
		8	9	5	5	00	8	9	5	5	00

E 4-8A (LO6)

FINDING AND CORRECTING ERRORS On May 25, after the transactions had been posted, Joe Adams discovered that the following entry contains an error. The cash received represents a collection on account, rather than new service fees. Correct the error in the general journal using a correcting entry.

22																		22
23	20-- May	23	Cash	101	1	0	0	0	00									23
24			Service Fees	401						1	0	0	0	00				24
25			Received cash for services previously earned															25

SERIES A PROBLEMS

P 4-9A **(LO4/5)**
✓ Cash bal., Jan. 31: $10,021
✓ Trial bal. total debits: $13,460

JOURNALIZING AND POSTING TRANSACTIONS Annette Creighton opened Creighton Consulting. She rented a small office and paid a part-time worker to answer the phone and make deliveries. Her chart of accounts is as follows:

Chart of Accounts

Assets		Revenues	
101	Cash	401	Consulting Fees
142	Office Supplies		
181	Office Equipment	Expenses	
		511	Wages Expense
Liabilities		512	Advertising Expense
202	Accounts Payable	521	Rent Expense
		525	Phone Expense
Owner's Equity		526	Transportation Expense
311	Annette Creighton, Capital	533	Utilities Expense
312	Annette Creighton, Drawing	549	Miscellaneous Expense

Creighton's transactions for the first month of business are as follows:

Jan. 1   Creighton invested cash in the business, $10,000.

  1   Paid rent, $500.

  2   Purchased office supplies on account, $300.

  4   Purchased office equipment on account, $1,500.

  6   Received cash for services rendered, $580.

  7   Paid phone bill, $42.

  8   Paid utilities bill, $38.

  10   Received cash for services rendered, $360.

  12   Made payment on account, $50.

  13   Paid for car rental while visiting an out-of-town client (transportation expense), $150.

  15   Paid part-time worker, $360.

  17   Received cash for services rendered, $420.

  18   Creighton withdrew cash for personal use, $100.

  20   Paid for a newspaper ad, $26.

  22   Reimbursed part-time employee for cab fare incurred delivering materials to clients (transportation expense), $35.

  24   Paid for books on consulting practices (miscellaneous expense), $28.

  25   Received cash for services rendered, $320.

  27   Made payment on account for office equipment purchased, $150.

  29   Paid part-time worker, $360.

  30   Received cash for services rendered, $180.

(*continued*)

REQUIRED

1. Set up general ledger accounts from the chart of accounts.
2. Journalize the transactions for January in a two-column general journal. Use the following journal page numbers: January 1–10, page 1; January 12–24, page 2; January 25–30, page 3.
3. Post the transactions to the general ledger.
4. Prepare a trial balance.
5. Prepare an income statement and a statement of owner's equity for the month of January and a balance sheet as of January 31, 20--.

P 4-10A   (LO4/5)
✓ Cash bal., June 30: $3,958
✓ Trial bal. total debits: $22,358

JOURNALIZING AND POSTING TRANSACTIONS Jim Andrews opened a delivery business in March. He rented a small office and has a part-time assistant. His trial balance shows accounts for the first three months of business.

ACCOUNT TITLE	ACCOUNT NO.	DEBIT BALANCE	CREDIT BALANCE
Jim's Quick Delivery — Trial Balance — May 31, 20 - -			
Cash	101	3 8 2 6 00	
Accounts Receivable	122	1 2 1 2 00	
Office Supplies	142	6 4 8 00	
Office Equipment	181	2 1 0 0 00	
Delivery Truck	185	8 0 0 0 00	
Accounts Payable	202		6 0 0 0 00
Jim Andrews, Capital	311		4 4 7 8 00
Jim Andrews, Drawing	312	1 8 0 0 00	
Delivery Fees	401		9 8 8 0 00
Wages Expense	511	1 2 0 0 00	
Advertising Expense	512	9 0 00	
Rent Expense	521	9 0 0 00	
Phone Expense	525	1 2 6 00	
Electricity Expense	533	9 8 00	
Charitable Contributions Expense	534	6 0 00	
Gas and Oil Expense	538	1 8 6 00	
Miscellaneous Expense	549	1 1 2 00	
		20 3 5 8 00	20 3 5 8 00

Andrews' transactions for the month of June are as follows:

June 1   Paid rent, $300.
2   Performed delivery services for $300: $100 in cash and $200 on account.
4   Paid for newspaper advertising, $15.
6   Purchased office supplies on account, $180.
7   Received cash for delivery services rendered, $260.
9   Paid cash on account (truck payment), $200.
10   Purchased a copier (office equipment) for $700: paid $100 in cash and put $600 on account.

June 11	Made a contribution to the Red Cross (charitable contributions), $20.	
12	Received cash for delivery services rendered, $380.	
13	Received cash on account for services previously rendered, $100.	
15	Paid a part-time worker, $200.	
16	Paid electric bill, $36.	
18	Paid phone bill, $46.	
19	Received cash on account for services previously rendered, $100.	
20	Andrews withdrew cash for personal use, $200.	
21	Paid for gas and oil, $32.	
22	Made payment on account (for office supplies), $40.	
24	Received cash for services rendered, $340.	
26	Paid for a magazine subscription (miscellaneous expense), $15.	
27	Received cash for services rendered, $180.	
27	Received cash on account for services previously rendered, $100.	
29	Paid for gasoline, $24.	
30	Paid a part-time worker, $200.	

REQUIRED

1. Set up general ledger accounts by entering the balances as of June 1.
2. Journalize the transactions for June in a two-column general journal. Use the following journal pages: June 1–10, page 7; June 11–20, page 8; June 21–30, page 9.
3. Post the entries to the general ledger.
4. Prepare a trial balance.

P 4-11A   (LO6)

CORRECTING ERRORS Assuming that all entries have been posted, prepare correcting entries for each of the following errors.

1. The following entry was made to record the purchase of $700 in supplies on account:

Supplies	142	700	
Cash	101		700

2. The following entry was made to record the payment of $450 in wages:

Rent Expense	521	450	
Cash	101		450

3. The following entry was made to record a $300 payment to a supplier on account:

Supplies	142	100	
Cash	101		100

SERIES B EXERCISES

E 4-1B (LO2)

SOURCE DOCUMENTS What type of information is found on each of the following source documents?

1. Cash register tape
2. Sales ticket (issued to customer)
3. Purchase invoice (received from supplier or vendor)
4. Check stub

E 4-2B (LO4)

GENERAL JOURNAL ENTRIES For each of the following transactions, list the account to be debited and the account to be credited in the general journal.

1. Invested cash in the business, $1,000.
2. Performed services on account, $200.
3. Purchased office equipment on account, $500.
4. Received cash on account for services previously rendered, $200.
5. Made a payment on account, $100.

E 4-3B (LO5)
✓ **Final Cash bal.: $1,100**

GENERAL LEDGER ACCOUNTS Set up T accounts for each of the general ledger accounts needed for Exercise 4-2B and post debits and credits to the accounts. Foot the accounts and enter the balances. Prove that total debits equal total credits.

E 4-4B (LO4)

GENERAL JOURNAL ENTRIES Sengel Moon opened The Bike Doctor. Journalize the following transactions that occurred during the month of October of the current year. Use the following journal pages: October 1–12, page 1; and October 14–29, page 2. Use the following chart of accounts:

Chart of Accounts

Assets		Revenues	
101	Cash	401	Repair Fees
141	Bicycle Parts		
142	Office Supplies		
		Expenses	
		511	Wages Expense
Liabilities		521	Rent Expense
202	Accounts Payable	525	Phone Expense
		533	Utilities Expense
Owner's Equity		549	Miscellaneous Expense
311	Sengel Moon, Capital		
312	Sengel Moon, Drawing		

Oct. 1 Moon invested cash in the business, $15,000.
  2 Paid shop rental for the month, $300.
  3 Purchased bicycle parts on account, $2,000.
  5 Purchased office supplies on account, $250.
  8 Paid phone bill, $38.
  9 Received cash for services, $140.
  11 Paid a sports magazine subscription (miscellaneous expense), $15.

Oct. 12   Made payment on account (see Oct. 3 transaction), $100.

14   Paid part-time employee, $300.

15   Received cash for services, $350.

16   Paid utilities bill, $48.

19   Received cash for services, $250.

23   Moon withdrew cash for personal use, $50.

25   Made payment on account (see Oct. 5 transaction), $50.

29   Paid part-time employee, $300.

E 4-5B   (LO5)
✓ Final Cash bal.: $14,539
✓ Trial bal. total debits: $17,840

GENERAL LEDGER ACCOUNTS; TRIAL BALANCE Set up general ledger accounts using the chart of accounts provided in Exercise 4-4B. Post the transactions from Exercise 4-4B to the general ledger accounts and prepare a trial balance.

E 4-6B   (LO5)
✓ Total assets, Oct. 31: $16,789

FINANCIAL STATEMENTS From the information in Exercises 4-4B and 4-5B, prepare an income statement, a statement of owner's equity, and a balance sheet.

E 4-7B   (LO5)
✓ Total assets, Mar. 31: $11,900

FINANCIAL STATEMENTS From the following trial balance taken after one month of operation, prepare an income statement, a statement of owner's equity, and a balance sheet.

AT Speaker's Bureau Trial Balance March 31, 20 - -													
ACCOUNT TITLE	ACCOUNT NO.	DEBIT BALANCE					CREDIT BALANCE					
Cash	101	6	6	0	0	00					
Accounts Receivable	122	2	8	0	0	00					
Office Supplies	142	1	0	0	0	00					
Office Equipment	181	1	5	0	0	00					
Accounts Payable	202						3	0	0	0	00
AT Speaker, Capital	311						6	0	9	8	00
AT Speaker, Drawing	312		8	0	0	00					
Speaking Fees	401						4	8	0	0	00
Wages Expense	511		4	0	0	00					
Rent Expense	521		2	0	0	00					
Phone Expense	525			3	5	00					
Travel Expense	526		4	5	0	00					
Utilities Expense	533			8	8	00					
Miscellaneous Expense	549			2	5	00					
		13	8	9	8	00	13	8	9	8	00

E 4-8B   (LO6)

FINDING AND CORRECTING ERRORS On April 25, after the transactions had been posted, Mary Smith discovered the following entry contains an error. When her customer received services, Cash was debited, but the service was provided on account. Correct the error in the journal using a correcting entry.

27														27
28	20-- Apr.	21	Cash	101	3	0	0	00						28
29			Service Fees	401					3	0	0	00		29
30			Revenue earned from services											30
31			previously rendered											31

SERIES B PROBLEMS

P 4-9B (LO4/5)
✓ Cash bal., May 31: $4,500
✓ Trial bal. total debits: $8,790

JOURNALIZING AND POSTING TRANSACTIONS Benito Mendez opened Mendez Appraisals. He rented office space and has a part-time secretary to answer the phone and make appraisal appointments. His chart of accounts is as follows:

Chart of Accounts

Assets		Revenues	
101	Cash	401	Appraisal Fees
122	Accounts Receivable		
142	Office Supplies	Expenses	
181	Office Equipment	511	Wages Expense
		512	Advertising Expense
Liabilities		521	Rent Expense
202	Accounts Payable	525	Phone Expense
		526	Transportation Expense
Owner's Equity		533	Electricity Expense
311	Benito Mendez, Capital	549	Miscellaneous Expense
312	Benito Mendez, Drawing		

Mendez's transactions for the first month of business are as follows:

May 1	Mendez invested cash in the business, $5,000.
2	Paid rent, $500.
3	Purchased office supplies, $100.
4	Purchased office equipment on account, $2,000.
5	Received cash for services rendered, $280.
8	Paid phone bill, $38.
9	Paid electric bill, $42.
10	Received cash for services rendered, $310.
13	Paid part-time employee, $500.
14	Paid car rental for out-of-town trip, $200.
15	Paid for newspaper ad, $30.
18	Received cash for services rendered, $620.
19	Paid mileage reimbursement for part-time employee's use of personal car for business deliveries (transportation expense), $22.
21	Mendez withdrew cash for personal use, $50.
23	Made payment on account for office equipment purchased earlier, $200.

May 24   Earned appraisal fee, which will be paid in a week, $500.

     26   Paid for newspaper ad, $30.

     27   Paid for local softball team sponsorship (miscellaneous expense), $15.

     28   Paid part-time employee, $500.

     29   Received cash on account, $250.

     30   Received cash for services rendered, $280.

     31   Paid cab fare (transportation expense), $13.

REQUIRED

1. Set up general ledger accounts from the chart of accounts.
2. Journalize the transactions for May in a two-column general journal. Use the following journal page numbers: May 1–10, page 1; May 13–24, page 2; May 26–31, page 3.
3. Post the transactions to the general ledger.
4. Prepare a trial balance.
5. Prepare an income statement and a statement of owner's equity for the month of May, and a balance sheet as of May 31, 20--.

P 4-10B (LO4/5)

✓ Cash bal., Nov. 30: $7,012
✓ Trial bal. total debits: $16,105

JOURNALIZING AND POSTING TRANSACTIONS   Ann Taylor owns a suit tailoring shop. She opened business in September. She rented a small work space and has an assistant to receive job orders and process claim tickets. Her trial balance shows her account balances for the first two months of business.

Taylor Tailoring Trial Balance October 31, 20 --													
ACCOUNT TITLE	ACCOUNT NO.	DEBIT BALANCE					CREDIT BALANCE					
Cash	101	6	2	1	1	00						
Accounts Receivable	122		4	8	4	00						
Tailoring Supplies	141	1	0	0	0	00						
Tailoring Equipment	183	3	8	0	0	00						
Accounts Payable	202						4	1	2	5	00	
Ann Taylor, Capital	311						6	1	3	0	00	
Ann Taylor, Drawing	312		8	0	0	00						
Tailoring Fees	401						3	6	0	0	00	
Wages Expense	511		8	0	0	00						
Advertising Expense	512			3	4	00						
Rent Expense	521		6	0	0	00						
Phone Expense	525			6	0	00						
Electricity Expense	533			4	4	00						
Miscellaneous Expense	549			2	2	00						
		13	8	5	5	00	13	8	5	5	00	

(continued)

Taylor's transactions for November are as follows:

Nov. 1   Paid rent, $300.

2   Purchased tailoring supplies on account, $150.

3   Purchased a new button hole machine on account, $300.

5   Earned first week's revenue, $400: $100 in cash and $300 on account.

8   Paid for newspaper advertising, $13.

9   Paid phone bill, $28.

10   Paid electric bill, $21.

11   Received cash on account from customers, $200.

12   Earned second week's revenue, $450: $200 in cash and $250 on account.

15   Paid assistant, $400.

16   Made payment on account, $100.

17   Paid for magazine subscription (miscellaneous expense), $12.

19   Earned third week's revenue, $450: $300 in cash, $150 on account.

23   Received cash on account from customers, $300.

24   Paid for newspaper advertising, $13.

26   Paid for postage (miscellaneous expense), $12.

27   Earned fourth week's revenue, $600: $200 in cash and $400 on account.

30   Received cash on account from customers, $400.

REQUIRED

1. Set up general ledger accounts by entering the balances as of November 1, 20--.
2. Journalize the transactions for November in a two-column general journal. Use the following journal page numbers: November 1–11, page 7; November 12–24, page 8; November 26–30, page 9.
3. Post the entries to the general ledger.
4. Prepare a trial balance.

P 4-11B   (LO6)

CORRECTING ERRORS   Assuming that all entries have been posted, prepare correcting entries for each of the following errors.

1. The following entry was made to record the purchase of $400 in equipment on account:

| Supplies | 142 | 400 | |
| Cash | 101 | | 400 |

2. The following entry was made to record the payment of $200 for advertising:

| Repair Expense | 537 | 200 | |
| Cash | 101 | | 200 |

3. The following entry was made to record a $600 payment to a supplier on account:

Prepaid Insurance	145	400	
Cash	101		400

CHECK LIST
- ☐ **Managing**
- ☐ **Planning**
- ☐ **Drafting**
- ☐ **Break**
- ☐ **Revising**
- ☐ **Managing**

MANAGING YOUR WRITING

You are a public accountant with many small business clients. During a recent visit to a client's business, the bookkeeper approached you with a problem. The columns of the trial balance were not equal. You helped the bookkeeper find and correct the error, but believe you should go one step further. Write a memo to all of your clients that explains the purpose of the double-entry framework, the importance of maintaining the equality of the accounting equation, the errors that might cause an inequality, and suggestions for finding the errors.

MASTERY PROBLEM

✓ Cash bal., June 30: $45,495
✓ Trial bal. total debits: $96,200

Barry Bird opened the Barry Bird Basketball Camp for children ages 10 through 18. Campers typically register for one week in June or July, arriving on Sunday and returning home the following Saturday. College players serve as cabin counselors and assist the local college and high school coaches who run the practice sessions. The registration fee includes a room, meals at a nearby restaurant, and basketball instruction. In the off-season, the facilities are used for weekend retreats and coaching clinics. Bird developed the following chart of accounts for his service business:

Chart of Accounts

Assets
101 Cash
142 Office Supplies
183 Athletic Equipment
184 Basketball Facilities

Liabilities
202 Accounts Payable

Owner's Equity
311 Barry Bird, Capital
312 Barry Bird, Drawing

Revenues
401 Registration Fees

Expenses
511 Wages Expense
512 Advertising Expense
524 Food Expense
525 Phone Expense
533 Utilities Expense
536 Postage Expense

(continued)

The following transactions took place during the month of June:

June 1 Bird invested cash in the business, $10,000.

1 Purchased basketballs and other athletic equipment, $3,000.

2 Paid Hite Advertising for flyers that had been mailed to prospective campers, $5,000.

2 Collected registration fees, $15,000.

2 Rogers Construction completed work on a new basketball court that cost $12,000. Arrangements were made to pay the bill in July.

5 Purchased office supplies on account from Gordon Office Supplies, $300.

6 Received bill from Magic's Restaurant for meals served to campers on account, $5,800.

7 Collected registration fees, $16,200.

10 Paid wages to camp counselors, $500.

14 Collected registration fees, $13,500.

14 Received bill from Magic's Restaurant for meals served to campers on account, $6,200.

17 Paid wages to camp counselors, $500.

18 Paid postage, $85.

21 Collected registration fees, $15,200.

22 Received bill from Magic's Restaurant for meals served to campers on account, $6,500.

24 Paid wages to camp counselors, $500.

28 Collected registration fees, $14,000.

30 Received bill from Magic's Restaurant for meals served to campers on account, $7,200.

30 Paid wages to camp counselors, $500.

30 Paid Magic's Restaurant on account, $25,700.

30 Paid utility bill, $500.

30 Paid phone bill, $120.

30 Bird withdrew cash for personal use, $2,000.

REQUIRED

1. Enter the transactions in a general journal. Use the following journal pages: June 1–6, page 1; June 7–22, page 2; June 24–30, page 3.

2. Post the entries to the general ledger.

3. Prepare a trial balance.

CHALLENGE PROBLEM

> This problem challenges you to apply your cumulative accounting knowledge to move a step beyond the material in the chapter.

✓ Total debits: $19,150

Journal entries and a trial balance for Fred Phaler Consulting follow. As you will note, the trial balance does not balance, suggesting that there are errors. Recall that the chapter offers tips on identifying individual posting errors. These techniques are not as effective when there are two or more errors. Thus, you will need to first carefully inspect the trial balance to see if you can identify any obvious errors due to amounts that either look out of proportion or are simply reported in the wrong place. Then, you will need to carefully evaluate the other amounts by using the techniques offered in the text, or tracing the journal entries to the amounts reported on the trial balance. (*Hint:* Four errors were made in the posting process and preparation of the trial balance.)

	DATE		DESCRIPTION	POST. REF.	DEBIT	CREDIT	
1	20-- June	1	Cash	101	10 0 0 0 00		1
2			Fred Phaler, Capital	311		10 0 0 0 00	2
3							3
4		2	Rent Expense	521	5 0 0 00		4
5			Cash	101		5 0 0 00	5
6							6
7		3	Cash	101	4 0 0 0 00		7
8			Professional Fees	401		4 0 0 0 00	8
9							9
10		4	Utilities Expense	533	1 0 0 00		10
11			Cash	101		1 0 0 00	11
12							12
13		7	Cash	101	3 0 0 0 00		13
14			Professional Fees	401		3 0 0 0 00	14
15							15
16		12	Automobile Expense	526	5 0 00		16
17			Cash	101		5 0 00	17
18							18
19		14	Wages Expense	511	5 0 0 00		19
20			Cash	101		5 0 0 00	20
21							21
22		14	Office Supplies	142	2 5 0 00		22
23			Accounts Payable	202		2 5 0 00	23
24							24
25		20	Phone Expense	525	1 0 0 00		25
26			Cash	101		1 0 0 00	26
27							27
28		21	Fred Phaler, Drawing	312	1 2 0 0 00		28
29			Cash	101		1 2 0 0 00	29
30							30
31		24	Accounts Receivable	122	2 0 0 0 00		31
32			Professional Fees	401		2 0 0 0 00	32
33							33
34		25	Accounts Payable	202	1 0 0 00		34
35			Cash	101		1 0 0 00	35
36							36
37		30	Wages Expense	511	3 0 0 00		37
38			Cash	101		3 0 0 00	38

GENERAL JOURNAL PAGE 1

(continued)

Fred Phaler Consulting
Trial Balance
June 30, 20 - -

ACCOUNT TITLE	ACCOUNT NO.	DEBIT BALANCE					CREDIT BALANCE				
Cash	101						13	9	0	0	00
Accounts Receivable	122	2	0	0	0	00					
Office Supplies	142		2	5	0	00					
Accounts Payable	202		1	0	0	00					
Fred Phaler, Capital	311						10	0	0	0	00
Fred Phaler, Drawing	312	2	1	0	0	00					
Professional Fees	401						9	0	0	0	00
Wages Expense	511		8	0	0	00					
Rent Expense	521		5	0	0	00					
Phone Expense	525		1	0	0	00					
Automobile Expense	526	50	0	0	0	00					
Utilities Expense	533		1	0	0	00					
		55	9	5	0	00	32	9	0	0	00

REQUIRED

1. Find the errors.
2. Explain what caused the errors.
3. Prepare a corrected trial balance.

ANSWERS TO SELF-STUDY TEST QUESTIONS

True/False

1. T
2. F (A, L, OE, R, E)
3. T
4. T
5. T

Multiple Choice

1. c   2. d   3. c   4. b   5. a

Checkpoint Exercises

1. A   cash payment.
2. A   Year in which entry was made. (Needed for first transaction on this page.)

B   Month in which entry was made. (Needed for first transaction on this page.)

C   Day of the month entry was made. (Needed for every transaction.)

D   Account debited.

E   Account credited.

F   Description of transaction.

G   Account number for account debited to indicate the debit has been posted.

H   Amount for account debited.

I   Amount for account credited.

J   Account number for account credited to indicate the credit has been posted.

3. A Account title.

  B Account number.

  C Year of transaction. (Needed for first transaction on this page.)

  D Month of transaction. (Needed for first transaction on this page.)

  E Day of month transaction was made. (Needed for every transaction.)

  F Generally left blank, except for special reasons such as indicating the beginning balance, adjusting, correcting, closing, or reversing entries.

  G Journal page from which entry was posted.

  H Dollar amount of debit.

  I Dollar amount of credit.

  J Balance if account has a debit balance.

  K Balance if account has a credit balance.

4.

	DATE	DESCRIPTION	POST. REF.	DEBIT	CREDIT	
1		Rent Payable		5 0 0 00		1
2		Cash			5 0 0 00	2
3		To correct error in which payment for rent				3
4		was credited to Rent Payable rather than Cash.				4
5						5

GENERAL JOURNAL — PAGE 1

Chapter 5 Adjusting Entries and the Work Sheet

LEARNING OBJECTIVES

Careful study of this chapter should enable you to:

LO1 Prepare end-of-period adjustments.

LO2 Post adjusting entries to the general ledger.

LO3 Prepare a work sheet.

LO4 Describe methods for finding errors on the work sheet.

LO5 Journalize adjusting entries from the work sheet.

LO6 Explain the cash, modified cash, and accrual bases of accounting.

Floyd's 99 Barbershop, founded in 2001, is a contemporary full-service barbershop/hair-care concept offering haircuts, coloring, styling, and shaves. In a setting where *Hard Rock* meets haircuts, customers listen to custom designed Floyd's 99 Radio, watch TV, surf the Internet, and get a signature shoulder massage and hot lather neck shave all as a part of their overall haircut experience. As they like to say, "Floyd's 99 is NOT your grandfather's barbershop." Headquartered in Greenwood Village, Colorado, Floyd's 99 has 113 shops in 13 states, primarily Colorado, California, Texas, Illinois, and Maryland.

As a rapidly growing company, Floyd's 99 uses the accrual basis of accounting, which requires making end-of-period adjusting entries. In this chapter, you will learn why adjusting entries are important, how they are made, and how they affect the financial statements. In addition, you will learn how to use a work sheet to help in the preparation of adjusting entries and the financial statements.

Up to this point, you have learned how to journalize business transactions, post to the ledger, and prepare a trial balance. Now it is time to learn how to make end-of-period adjustments to the accounts listed in the trial balance. This chapter explains the need for adjustments and illustrates how they are made with or without the use of a work sheet.

LO1	**End-of-Period Adjustments**

Prepare end-of-period adjustments.

Throughout the accounting period, business transactions are entered in the accounting system. These transactions are based on exchanges between the business and other companies and individuals. During the accounting period, other changes occur that affect the business's financial condition. For example, equipment is wearing out, prepaid insurance and supplies are being used up, and employees are earning wages that have not yet been paid. Since these events have not been entered into the accounting system, adjusting entries must be made prior to the preparation of financial statements.

> **LEARNING KEY** 🔑
>
> Transactions are entered as they occur throughout the year. Adjustments are made at the end of the accounting period for items that do not involve exchanges with an outside party.

These adjustments are guided by three important principles. The revenue recognition principle states that revenues should be recognized when earned, regardless of when cash is received from the customer. Revenues are considered earned when a service has been provided or a product has been sold. Similarly, the expense recognition principle states that expenses should be recognized when incurred, regardless of when cash is paid. Expenses are generally considered incurred when services are received or assets are consumed as a result of efforts made to generate revenues. The proper matching of revenues earned during an accounting period with the expenses incurred to produce the revenues is often referred to as the matching principle. This approach offers the best measure of net income. The income statement reports earnings for a specific period of time, and the balance sheet reports the assets, liabilities, and owner's equity on a specific date. Thus, to follow these three principles, the accounts must be brought up to date before financial statements are prepared. This requires adjusting some of the accounts listed in the trial balance. Figure 5-1 lists reasons to adjust the trial balance.

FIGURE 5-1 Reasons to Adjust the Trial Balance

> 1. To report all revenues earned during the accounting period.
>
> 2. To report all expenses incurred to produce the revenues earned in the accounting period.
>
> 3. To accurately report the assets on the balance sheet date. Some assets may have been used up during the accounting period.
>
> 4. To accurately report the liabilities on the balance sheet date. Expenses may have been incurred but not yet paid.

> **LEARNING KEY** 🔑
>
> Matching revenues earned with expenses incurred to produce those revenues offers the best measure of net income.

Generally, adjustments are made and financial statements prepared at the end of a 12-month period called a fiscal year. This period does not need to be the same as a calendar year. In fact, many businesses schedule their fiscal year-end for a time when business is slow. In this chapter, we continue the illustration of Mitchell's Campus Delivery and will prepare adjustments at the end of the first month of operations. We will focus on the following accounts: Supplies, Prepaid Insurance, Wages Expense, and Delivery Equipment.

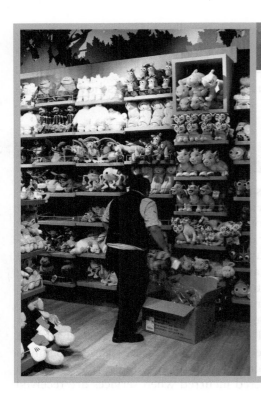

A BROADER VIEW

Adjusting Entries

Are adjusting entries important? The Walt Disney Company and Mattel, Inc. probably think so. The Walt Disney Company granted Mattel the right to make and sell toys based on Disney characters. In return, Mattel agreed to make payments to Disney as the toys were sold. One of the issues in a court case was whether Mattel should have made an adjusting entry when it fell behind on these payments. The entry would have been:

Royalty Expense	17,000,000	
Accounts Payable (Disney)		17,000,000

This adjusting entry would have reduced Mattel's fourth-quarter earnings for that year by more than 15%. Following an investigation by the Securities and Exchange Commission, Mattel eventually agreed to make an adjustment to later financial statements.

CC/DREAMSTIME.COM

Supplies

During June, Mitch purchased supplies consisting of paper, pens, and delivery envelopes for $80. *Since these supplies were expected to provide future benefits, Supplies, an asset, was debited at the time of the purchase.* No other entries were made to the supplies account during June. As reported on the trial balance in Figure 5-2, the $80 balance remains in the supplies account at the end of the month.

FIGURE 5-2 Trial Balance

			ACCOUNT TITLE	ACCOUNT NO	DEBIT BALANCE					CREDIT BALANCE				
			Mitchell's Campus Delivery Trial Balance June 30, 20 - -											
Cash				101		4	7	0	00					
Accounts Receivable				122	3	1	0	0	00					
Supplies				141			8	0	00					
Prepaid Insurance				145		7	0	0	00					
Delivery Equipment				185	4	8	0	0	00					
Accounts Payable				202							1	9	0	0	00
Mitchell Williams, Capital				311							5	0	0	0	00
Mitchell Williams, Drawing				312	3	0	0	0	00					
Delivery Fees				401							8	0	0	0	00
Wages Expense				511	1	6	5	0	00					
Rent Expense				521	1	0	0	0	00					
Phone Expense				525		1	0	0	00					
					14	9	0	0	00		14	9	0	0	00

As supplies are used, an expense is incurred. However, it is not practical to make a journal entry to recognize this expense and the reduction in the supplies account every time someone uses an envelope. It is more efficient to wait until the end of the accounting period to make one adjusting entry to reflect the expense incurred for the use of supplies for the entire month.

At the end of the month, an inventory, or physical count, of the remaining supplies is taken. The inventory shows that supplies costing $20 were still unused at the end of June. Since Mitch bought supplies costing $80, and only $20 worth remain, supplies costing $60 must have been used ($80 – $20 = $60). Thus, supplies expense for the month is $60.

Since $60 worth of supplies have been used, Supplies Expense is debited and Supplies (asset) is credited for $60. This entry is illustrated in Figure 5-3 in T account and general journal form. Thus, as shown in Figure 5-4, supplies with a cost of $20 will be reported as an asset on the balance sheet and a supplies expense of $60 will be reported on the income statement. The adjusting entry affected an income statement account (Supplies Expense) and a balance sheet account (Supplies).

FIGURE 5-3 Adjustment for Supplies

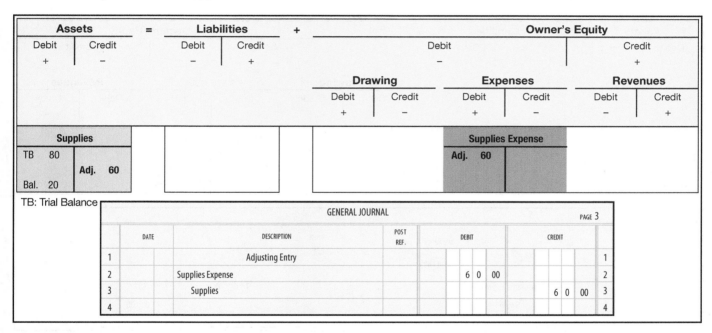

FIGURE 5-4 Effect of Adjusting Entry for Supplies on Financial Statements

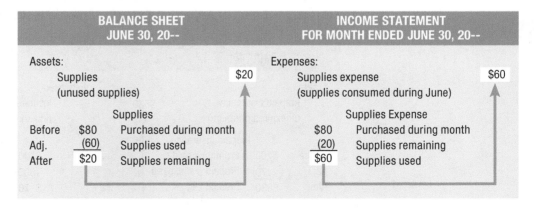

Prepaid Insurance

On June 18, Mitch paid $700 for a ten-month liability insurance policy with coverage beginning on June 1. *Prepaid Insurance, an asset, was debited because the insurance policy is expected to provide future benefits in the form of insurance coverage, or a cash refund if the policy is canceled.* The $700 balance is reported on the trial balance. As the insurance policy expires with the passage of time, the asset should be reduced and an expense recognized.

Since the $700 premium covers ten months, the cost of the expired coverage for June is $70 ($700 ÷ 10 months). As shown in Figure 5-5, the adjusting entry is to debit Insurance Expense for $70 and credit Prepaid Insurance for $70. Figure 5-6 shows that the unexpired portion of the insurance premium will be reported on the balance sheet as Prepaid Insurance of $630. The expired portion will be reported on the income statement as Insurance Expense of $70.

FIGURE 5-5 Adjustment for Expired Insurance

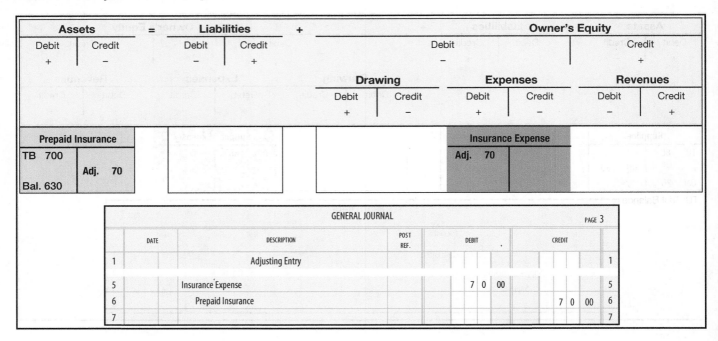

FIGURE 5-6 Effect of Adjusting Entry for Prepaid Insurance on Financial Statements

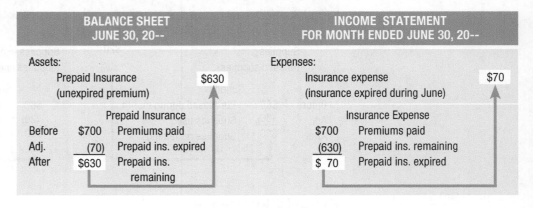

Wages Expense

Mitch paid his part-time employees $1,650 on June 27. Since then, they have earned an additional $400, but have not yet been paid. The additional wages expense must be recognized.

Since the employees have not been paid, Wages Payable, a liability, should be established. Thus, Wages Expense is debited and Wages Payable is credited for $400 in Figure 5-7. Note in Figure 5-8 that Wages Expense of $2,050 is reported on the income statement and Wages Payable of $400 is reported on the balance sheet.

FIGURE 5-7 Adjustment for Unpaid Wages

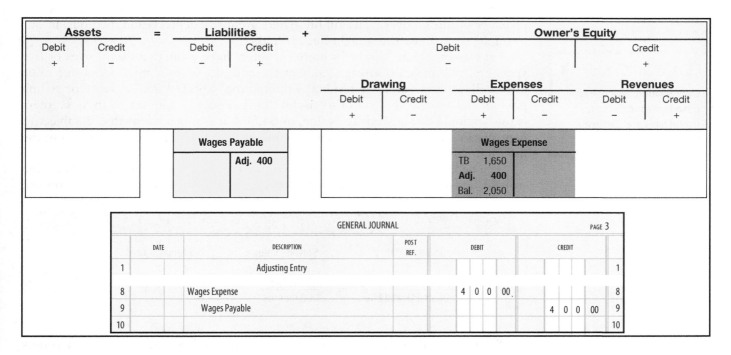

FIGURE 5-8 Effect of Adjusting Entry for Wages on Financial Statements

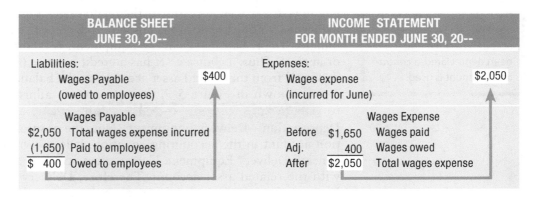

To learn about other depreciation methods, see the appendix to this chapter.

Depreciation Expense

During the month of June, Mitch purchased three motor scooters. Since the scooters will provide future benefits, they were recorded as assets in the delivery equipment account. Under the historical cost principle, many assets are required to be recorded at their actual cost, in this case $4,800. This cost remains on the books as long as the business owns the asset. No adjustments are made for changes in the market value of the asset. It does not matter whether the firm got a "good buy" or paid "too much" when the asset was purchased.

The period of time that an asset is expected to help produce revenues is called its useful life. The asset's useful life expires as a result of wear and tear or because it no longer satisfies the needs of the business. For example, as miles are added to the scooters, they will become less reliable and will eventually fail to run. As this happens, depreciation expense should be recognized and the value of the asset should be reduced. Depreciation is a method of *matching* an asset's original cost against the revenues produced over its useful life. There are many depreciation methods. In our example, we will use the straight-line method.

Let's assume that Mitchell's motor scooters have estimated useful lives of five years and will have no salvage value at the end of that time period. Salvage value (also called scrap value, or residual value) is the expected market value or selling price of the asset at the end of its useful life. The depreciable cost of these scooters is the original cost, less salvage value, or $4,800. It is this amount that is subject to depreciation. Let's also assume that a full month's depreciation is recognized in the month in which an asset is purchased.

The depreciable cost is spread over 60 months (5 years × 12 months). Thus, the straight-line depreciation expense for the month of June is $80 ($4,800 ÷ 60 months).

STRAIGHT-LINE DEPRECIATION		
Original Cost − Salvage Value = Depreciable Cost		
$\dfrac{\text{Depreciable Cost}}{\text{Estimated Useful Life}}$ =	$\dfrac{\$4,800}{60 \text{ months}}$ =	$80 per month

When we made adjustments for supplies and prepaid insurance, the asset accounts were credited to show that they had been consumed. Assets of a durable nature that are expected to provide benefits over several years or more, called plant assets, require a different approach. The business maintains a record of the original cost and the amount of depreciation taken since the asset was acquired. By comparing these two amounts, the reader can estimate the relative age of the assets. Thus, instead of crediting Delivery Equipment for the amount of depreciation, a contra-asset account, Accumulated Depreciation—Delivery Equipment, is credited. "Contra" means opposite or against. Thus, a contra-asset has a credit balance (the opposite of an asset) and is deducted from the related asset account on the balance sheet.

As shown in Figure 5-9, the appropriate adjusting entry consists of a debit to Depreciation Expense—Delivery Equipment and a credit to Accumulated Depreciation—Delivery Equipment. Note the position of the accumulated depreciation account in the accounting equation. It is shown in the assets section, directly beneath Delivery Equipment. Contra-asset accounts should always be shown along with the related asset account. Therefore, Delivery Equipment and Accumulated Depreciation—Delivery Equipment are shown together.

FIGURE 5-9 **Adjustment for Depreciation of Delivery Equipment**

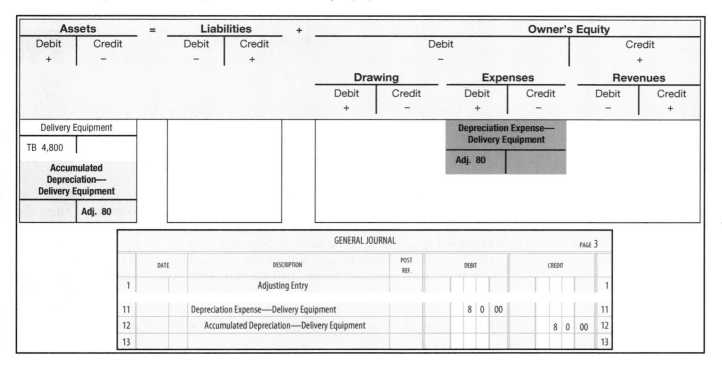

The same concept is used on the balance sheet. Note in Figure 5-10 that Accumulated Depreciation is reported immediately beneath Delivery Equipment as a deduction. The difference between these accounts is known as the book value, or undepreciated cost, of the delivery equipment. Book value simply means the value carried on the books or in the accounting records. It does *not* represent the market value, or selling price, of the asset.

LEARNING KEY 🔑

There is no individual account that reports book value. It must be computed.

Cost of Plant Assets
− Accumulated Depreciation
= Book Value

FIGURE 5-10 **Effect of Adjusting Entry for Depreciation on Financial Statements for June**

BALANCE SHEET JUNE 30, 20--			INCOME STATEMENT FOR MONTH ENDED JUNE 30, 20--	
Assets:			Expenses:	
Delivery equipment	$4,800		Depreciation expense	$80
Less: Accumulated			(Expired cost for June)	
depreciation	80	$4,720		
		(Book value)		

If no delivery equipment is bought or sold during the next month, the same adjusting entry would be made at the end of July. If an income statement for the month of July and a balance sheet as of July 31 were prepared, the amounts shown in Figure 5-11 would be reported for the delivery equipment.

FIGURE 5-11 **Effect of Adjusting Entry for Depreciation on Financial Statements for July**

BALANCE SHEET JULY 31, 20--			INCOME STATEMENT FOR MONTH ENDED JULY 31, 20--	
Assets:			Expenses:	
Delivery equipment	$4,800		Depreciation expense	$80
Less: Accumulated			(Expired cost for July)	
depreciation	160	$4,640		
		(Book value)		

The cost ($4,800) remains unchanged, but the accumulated depreciation has increased to $160. This represents *the depreciation that has accumulated* since the delivery equipment was purchased ($80 in June and $80 in July). The depreciation expense for July is $80, the same as reported for June. Depreciation expense is reported for a specific time period. It does not accumulate across reporting periods.

If financial statements are prepared at the end of the year, December 31, 20--, the results for the seven months of operations would be presented as shown in Figure 5-12. Depreciation expense for the year is $560 ($80 × 7 months), and the accumulated depreciation would be the same because this is the first year of operation.

Cost	$4,800	= $ 80
Useful life	60 months	
Dep./month		$ 80
Months in service		× 7
Dep. June–Dec.		$560

FIGURE 5-12 **Straight-Line Depreciation for Seven Months**

BALANCE SHEET DECEMBER 31, 20--			INCOME STATEMENT FOR YEAR ENDED DECEMBER 31, 20--	
Assets:			Expenses:	
Delivery equipment	$4,800		Depreciation expense	$560
Less: Accumulated			(Expired cost for June	
depreciation	560	$4,240	through December)	
		(Book value)		

Expanded Chart of Accounts

CHECKPOINT ✔

Complete Checkpoint-1 on page 158 to test your basic understanding of LO1.

Several new accounts were needed to make the adjusting entries. New accounts are easily added to the chart of accounts, as shown in Figure 5-13. Note the close relationship between assets and contra-assets in the numbering of the accounts. Contra-accounts carry the same number as the related asset account with a ".1" suffix. For example, Delivery Equipment is account number 185 and the contra-asset account, Accumulated Depreciation—Delivery Equipment, is account number 185.1.

LO2

Posting Adjusting Entries

Post adjusting entries to the general ledger.

Adjusting entries are posted to the general ledger in the same manner as all other entries, except that "*Adjusting*" is written in the Item column of the general ledger. Figure 5-14 shows the posting of the adjusting entries. The posting reference numbers are inserted as each entry is posted.

FIGURE 5-13 **Expanded Chart of Accounts**

MITCHELL'S CAMPUS DELIVERY CHART OF ACCOUNTS			
Assets		**Revenues**	
101	Cash	401	Delivery Fees
122	Accounts Receivable		
141	Supplies	**Expenses**	
145	Prepaid Insurance	511	Wages Expense
185	Delivery Equipment	521	Rent Expense
185.1	Accumulated Depr.—	523	Supplies Expense
	Delivery Equipment	525	Phone Expense
		535	Insurance Expense
Liabilities		541	Depr. Expense —
202	Accounts Payable		Delivery Equipment
219	Wages Payable		
Owner's Equity			
311	Mitchell Williams, Capital		
312	Mitchell Williams, Drawing		

FIGURE 5-14 **Posting the Adjusting Entries**

(continued)

FIGURE 5-14 Posting the Adjusting Entries (*concluded*)

CHECKPOINT ✔

Complete Checkpoint-2 on page 158 to test your basic understanding of LO2.

LO3

The Work Sheet

Prepare a work sheet.

A work sheet pulls together all of the information needed to enter adjusting entries and prepare the financial statements. Work sheets are not financial statements, are not a formal part of the accounting system, and are not a required part of the accounting process. However, many accountants prepare them because they are very helpful in planning the adjustments and preparing the financial statements. Ordinarily, only the accountant uses a work sheet. For this reason, a work sheet is usually prepared as an Excel spreadsheet. When accounting software is used, a work sheet is not needed. We walk you through the manual creation of a work sheet in this section and throughout Chapter 6 to help you understand how work sheets are set up and used by accountants.

The 10-Column Work Sheet

Although a work sheet can take several forms, a common format has a column for account titles and 10 amount columns grouped into five pairs of debits and credits. The work sheet format and the five steps in preparing the work sheet are illustrated in Figure 5-15. As with financial statements, the work sheet has a heading consisting of the name of the company, name of the working paper, and the date of the accounting period just ended. The five major column headings for the work sheet are Trial Balance, Adjustments, Adjusted Trial Balance, Income Statement, and Balance Sheet.

FIGURE 5-15 Steps in Preparing the Work Sheet

Preparing the Work Sheet

Let's apply the five steps required for the preparation of a work sheet to Mitchell's Campus Delivery.

STEP 1   Prepare the Trial Balance. As shown in Figure 5-16, the first pair of amount columns is for the trial balance. The trial balance assures the equality of the debits and credits before the adjustment process begins. The columns should be double ruled to show that they are equal.

Note that all accounts listed in the expanded chart of accounts are included in the Trial Balance columns of the work sheet. This is done even though some accounts have zero balances. The accounts with zero balances could be added to the bottom of the list as they are needed for adjusting entries. However, it is easier to include them now, especially if preparing the work sheet on an electronic spreadsheet. Listing the accounts within their proper classifications (assets, liabilities, etc.) also makes it easier to extend the amounts to the proper columns.

STEP 2   Prepare the Adjustments. As shown in Figure 5-16, the second pair of amount columns is used to prepare the adjusting entries. Enter the adjustments directly in these columns. When an account is debited or credited, the amount is entered on the same line as the name of the account and in the appropriate Adjustments Debit or Credit column. A small letter in parentheses identifies each adjusting entry made on the work sheet.

> **LEARNING KEY** 🔑
>
> For adjustments (a), (b), and (d), we are simply recognizing that assets have been used. When this happens, the asset must be decreased and an expense recognized. Note that the reported amount for delivery equipment is reduced by crediting a contra-asset.

Adjustment (a):

Supplies costing $60 were used during June.

	Debit	Credit
Supplies Expense	60	
Supplies		60

Adjustment (b):

One month's insurance premium has expired.

	Debit	Credit
Insurance Expense	70	
Prepaid Insurance		70

Adjustment (c):

Employees earned $400 that has not yet been paid.

	Debit	Credit
Wages Expense	400	
Wages Payable		400

> **LEARNING KEY** 🔑
>
> Adjustment (c) recognizes an economic event that has not required an actual transaction yet. Employees earned wages, but have not been paid. The adjustment recognizes an expense and a liability.

Adjustment (d):

Depreciation on the motor scooters is recognized.

	Debit	Credit
Depreciation Expense—Delivery Equipment	80	
Accumulated Depreciation—Delivery Equipment		80

When all adjustments have been entered on the work sheet, each column should be totaled to assure that the debits equal the credits for all entries. After balancing the columns, they should be double ruled.

FIGURE 5-16 Step 1: Prepare the Trial Balance; Step 2: Prepare the Adjustments

Mitchell's Campus Delivery
Work Sheet
For Month Ended June 30, 20 - -

	ACCOUNT TITLE	TRIAL BALANCE DEBIT	TRIAL BALANCE CREDIT	ADJUSTMENT DEBIT	ADJUSTMENT CREDIT	ADJUSTED TRIAL BALANCE DEBIT	ADJUSTED TRIAL BALANCE CREDIT	INCOME STATEMENT DEBIT	INCOME STATEMENT CREDIT	BALANCE SHEET DEBIT	BALANCE SHEET CREDIT	
1	Cash	4 7 0 00										1
2	Accounts Receivable	3 1 0 00										2
3	Supplies	8 0 00			(a) 6 0 00							3
4	Prepaid Insurance	7 0 0 00			(b) 7 0 00							4
5	Delivery Equipment	4 8 0 0 00										5
6	Accum. Depr.—Delivery Equipment				(d) 8 0 00							6
7	Accounts Payable		1 9 0 0 00									7
8	Wages Payable				(c) 4 0 0 00							8
9	Mitchell Williams, Capital		5 0 0 0 00									9
10	Mitchell Williams, Drawing	3 0 0 0 00										10
11	Delivery Fees		8 0 0 0 00									11
12	Wages Expense	1 6 5 0 00		(c) 4 0 0 00								12
13	Rent Expense	1 0 0 0 00										13
14	Supplies Expense			(a) 6 0 00								14
15	Phone Expense	1 0 0 00										15
16	Insurance Expense			(b) 7 0 00								16
17	Depr. Expense—Delivery Equipment			(d) 8 0 00								17
18		14 9 0 0 00	14 9 0 0 00	6 1 0 00	6 1 0 00							18
19	Net income											19
20												20

STEP 1

STEP 2

Step 1: Prepare the Trial Balance.
• Write the heading, account titles, and the debit and credit amounts from the general ledger.
• Place a single rule across the Trial Balance columns and total the debit and credit amounts.
• Place a double rule under the totals for each column.
• Total debits must equal total credits.

Step 2: Prepare the Adjustments.
• Record the adjustments.
  Hint: Make certain that each adjustment is on the same line as the account name and in the appropriate column.
• Identify each adjusting entry by a letter in parentheses.
  Hint: Identify each adjusting entry by a letter in parentheses.
• Rule the Adjustments columns.
• Total the Debit and Credit columns and double rule the columns.
• Total debits must equal total credits.

STEP 3 **Prepare the Adjusted Trial Balance.** As shown in Figure 5-17, the third pair of amount columns on the work sheet is the Adjusted Trial Balance columns.

- When an account balance is not affected by entries in the Adjustments columns, the amount in the Trial Balance columns is extended directly to the Adjusted Trial Balance columns.
- *When affected by an entry in the Adjustments columns, the account balance to be entered in the Adjusted Trial Balance columns increases or decreases by the amount of the adjusting entry.*

For example, in Mitchell's business, Supplies are listed in the Trial Balance Debit column as $80. Since the entry of $60 is in the Adjustments Credit column, the amount extended to the Adjusted Trial Balance Debit column is $20 ($80 − $60).

Wages Expense is listed in the Trial Balance Debit column as $1,650. Since $400 is in the Adjustments Debit column, the amount extended to the Adjusted Trial Balance Debit column is $2,050 ($1,650 + $400).

After all extensions have been made, the Adjusted Trial Balance columns are totaled to prove the equality of the debits and the credits. Once balanced, the columns are double ruled.

STEP 4 **Extend Adjusted Balances to the Income Statement and Balance Sheet Columns.** As shown in Figure 5-18, each account listed in the Adjusted Trial Balance must be extended to either the Income Statement or Balance Sheet columns. The Income Statement columns show the amounts that will be reported in the income statement. All revenue accounts are extended to the Income Statement Credit column and expense accounts are extended to the Income Statement Debit column.

The asset, liability, drawing, and capital accounts are extended to the Balance Sheet columns. Although called the Balance Sheet columns, these columns of the work sheet show the amounts that will be reported in the balance sheet and the statement of owner's equity. The asset and drawing accounts are extended to the Balance Sheet Debit column. The liability and owner's capital accounts are extended to the Balance Sheet Credit column.

> **LEARNING KEY** 🔑
>
> The Balance Sheet columns show the amounts for both the balance sheet and the statement of owner's equity.

STEP 5 **Complete the Work Sheet.** To complete the work sheet, first total the Income Statement columns. If the total of the credits (revenues) exceeds the total of the debits (expenses), the difference represents net income. If the total of the debits exceeds the total of the credits, the difference represents a net loss.

The Income Statement columns of Mitchell's work sheet in Figure 5-18 show total credits of $8,000 and total debits of $3,360. The difference, $4,640, is the net income for the month of June. This amount should be added to the Debit column to balance the Income Statement columns. "Net Income" should be written on the same line in the Account Title column. If the business had a net loss, the amount of the loss would be added to the Income Statement Credit column and the words "Net Loss" would be written in the Account Title column. Once balanced, the columns should be double ruled.

> **LEARNING KEY** 🔑
>
> In the Balance Sheet columns of the work sheet, total debits minus total credits equals net *income* if greater than zero and equals net loss if less than zero.

Finally, the Balance Sheet columns are totaled. The difference between the totals of these columns also is the amount of net income or net loss for the accounting period. If the total debits exceed the total credits, the difference is net income. If the total credits exceed the total debits, the difference is a net loss. This difference should be the same as the difference we found for the Income Statement columns.

FIGURE 5-17 Step 3: Prepare the Adjusted Trial Balance

Mitchell's Campus Delivery
Work Sheet
For Month Ended June 30, 20- -

	TRIAL BALANCE		ADJUSTMENT		ADJUSTED TRIAL BALANCE		INCOME STATEMENT		BALANCE SHEET	
ACCOUNT TITLE	DEBIT	CREDIT	DEBIT	CREDIT	DEBIT	CREDIT	DEBIT	CREDIT	DEBIT	CREDIT
1 Cash	4 7 0 00				4 7 0 00					
2 Accounts Receivable	3 1 0 0 00				3 1 0 0 00					
3 Supplies	8 0 0 00			(a) 6 0 0 00	2 0 0 00					
4 Prepaid Insurance	7 0 0 00			(b) 7 0 00	6 3 0 00					
5 Delivery Equipment	4 8 0 0 00				4 8 0 0 00					
6 Accum. Depr.—Delivery Equipment				(d) 8 0 00		8 0 00				
7 Accounts Payable		1 9 0 0 00				1 9 0 0 00				
8 Wages Payable				(c) 4 0 0 00		4 0 0 00				
9 Mitchell Williams, Capital		5 0 0 0 00				5 0 0 0 00				
10 Mitchell Williams, Drawing	3 0 0 0 00				3 0 0 0 00					
11 Delivery Fees		8 0 0 0 00				8 0 0 0 00				
12 Wages Expense	1 6 5 0 00		(c) 4 0 0 00		2 0 5 0 00					
13 Rent Expense	1 0 0 0 00				1 0 0 0 00					
14 Supplies Expense			(a) 6 0 0 00		6 0 0 00					
15 Phone Expense	1 0 0 00				1 0 0 00					
16 Insurance Expense			(b) 7 0 00		7 0 00					
17 Depr. Expense—Delivery Equipment			(d) 8 0 00		8 0 00					
18	14 9 0 0 00	14 9 0 0 00	6 1 0 00	6 1 0 00	15 3 8 0 00	15 3 8 0 00				
19 Net income										

STEP 1   STEP 2   STEP 3

Callouts:
- No adjustment: simply extend balance to appropriate column.
- A debit and a credit: subtract.
- A single debit or credit: extend to appropriate column.
- Two debits: add.
- When columns are balanced, use double ruling.

Step 3: Prepare the Adjusted Trial Balance.
- Extend those debits and credits that are not adjusted directly to the appropriate Adjusted Trial Balance column.
- Enter the adjusted balances in the appropriate Adjusted Trial Balance column.
  Hint: If an account has a debit and a credit, subtract the adjustment. If an account has two debits or two credits, add the adjustment.
- Single rule the Adjusted Trial Balance columns. Total and double rule the Debit and Credit columns.
- Total debits must equal total credits.

FIGURE 5-18 Step 4: Extend Adjusted Balances to the Inc. Stmt. & Balance Sheet Columns; Step 5: Complete the Work Sheet

Mitchell's Campus Delivery
Work Sheet
For Month Ended June 30, 20- -

	ACCOUNT TITLE	TRIAL BALANCE DEBIT	TRIAL BALANCE CREDIT	ADJUSTMENT DEBIT	ADJUSTMENT CREDIT	ADJUSTED TRIAL BALANCE DEBIT	ADJUSTED TRIAL BALANCE CREDIT	INCOME STATEMENT DEBIT	INCOME STATEMENT CREDIT	BALANCE SHEET DEBIT	BALANCE SHEET CREDIT	
1	Cash	4 7 0 00				4 7 0 00				4 7 0 00		1
2	Accounts Receivable	3 1 0 0 00				3 1 0 0 00				3 1 0 0 00		2
3	Supplies	8 0 00			(a) 6 0 00	2 0 00				2 0 00		3
4	Prepaid Insurance	7 0 0 00			(b) 7 0 00	6 3 0 00				6 3 0 00		4
5	Delivery Equipment	4 8 0 0 00				4 8 0 0 00				4 8 0 0 00		5
6	Accum. Depr.—Delivery Equipment				(d) 8 0 00		8 0 00				8 0 00	6
7	Accounts Payable		1 9 0 0 00				1 9 0 0 00				1 9 0 0 00	7
8	Wages Payable				(c) 4 0 0 00		4 0 0 00				4 0 0 00	8
9	Mitchell Williams, Capital		5 0 0 0 00				5 0 0 0 00				5 0 0 0 00	9
10	Mitchell Williams, Drawing	3 0 0 0 00				3 0 0 0 00				3 0 0 0 00		10
11	Delivery Fees		8 0 0 0 00				8 0 0 0 00		8 0 0 0 00			11
12	Wages Expense	1 6 5 0 00		(c) 4 0 0 00		2 0 5 0 00		2 0 5 0 00				12
13	Rent Expense	1 0 0 0 00				1 0 0 0 00		1 0 0 0 00				13
14	Supplies Expense			(a) 6 0 00		6 0 00		6 0 00				14
15	Phone Expense	1 0 0 00				1 0 0 00		1 0 0 00				15
16	Insurance Expense			(b) 7 0 00		7 0 00		7 0 00				16
17	Depr. Expense—Delivery Equipment			(d) 8 0 00		8 0 00		8 0 00				17
18		14 9 0 0 00	14 9 0 0 00	6 1 0 00	6 1 0 00	15 3 8 0 00	15 3 8 0 00	3 3 6 0 00	8 0 0 0 00	12 0 2 0 00	7 3 8 0 00	18
19	Net income							4 6 4 0 00			4 6 4 0 00	19
20								8 0 0 0 00	8 0 0 0 00	12 0 2 0 00	12 0 2 0 00	20
21												21
22												22

STEP 1   STEP 2   STEP 3   STEPS 4 AND 5

Step 4: Extend Adjusted Balances to the Income Statement and Balance Sheet Columns.
- Extend all revenue accounts to the Income Statement Credit column.
- Extend all expense accounts to the Income Statement Debit column.
- Extend the asset and drawing accounts to the Balance Sheet Debit column.
- Extend the liability and owner's capital accounts to the Balance Sheet Credit columns.

Step 5: Complete the Work Sheet.
- Rule and total the Income Statement and Balance Sheet columns.
- Calculate the difference between the Income Statement Debit and Credit columns.
- Calculate the difference between the Balance Sheet Debit and Credit columns.
  Hint: If the Income Statement credits exceed debits, net income has occurred; otherwise a net loss has occurred. If the Balance Sheet debits exceed the credits, the difference is net income; otherwise a net loss has occurred.
- Add the net income to the Income Statement Debit column or add the net loss to the Income Statement Credit column. Add the net income to the Balance Sheet credit column or the net loss to the Balance Sheet Debit column. Write "Net income" or "Net Loss" in the Account Title column.
  Hint: The difference between the Balance Sheet columns should be the same as the difference between the Income Statement columns.
- Total and double rule the columns.

The Balance Sheet columns of Mitchell's work sheet show total debits of $12,020 and total credits of $7,380. The difference of $4,640 represents the net income for the month. This amount is added to the Credit column to balance the Balance Sheet columns. If the business had a net loss, this amount would be added to the Balance Sheet Debit column. Once balanced, the columns should be double ruled.

A trick for remembering the appropriate placement of the net income and net loss is the following: Net Income *apart*; Net Loss *together*. Figure 5-19 illustrates this learning aid.

CHECKPOINT ✔

Complete Checkpoint-3 on page 158 to test your basic understanding of LO3.

FIGURE 5-19 Net Income Apart, Net Loss Together

LO4

Finding Errors on the Work Sheet

Describe methods for finding errors on the work sheet.

If any of the columns on the work sheet do not balance, you must find the error before you continue. Once you are confident that the work sheet is accurate, you are ready to journalize the adjusting entries and prepare financial statements. Figure 5-20 offers tips for finding errors on the work sheet.

FIGURE 5-20 Finding Errors on the Work Sheet

TIPS FOR FINDING ERRORS ON THE WORK SHEET
1. Check the addition of all columns.
2. Check the addition and subtraction required when extending to the Adjusted Trial Balance columns.
3. Make sure the adjusted account balances have been extended to the appropriate columns.
4. Make sure that the net income or net loss has been added to the appropriate columns.

CHECKPOINT ✔

Complete Checkpoint-4 on page 158 to test your basic understanding of LO4.

LO5

Journalizing Adjusting Entries from the Work Sheet

Journalize adjusting entries from the work sheet.

Keep in mind that the work sheet simply helps the accountant organize the end-of-period work. *Writing the adjustments on the work sheet has no effect on the ledger accounts in the accounting system. The only way to change the balance of a ledger account is to make a journal entry.* Once the work sheet has been completed, simply copy the adjustments from the work sheet to the journal, as shown in Figure 5-21.

FIGURE 5-21 Journalizing Adjusting Entries from the Work Sheet

Mitchell's Campus Delivery
Work Sheet (Partial)
For Month Ended June 30, 20--

	ACCOUNT TITLE	TRIAL BALANCE DEBIT	TRIAL BALANCE CREDIT	ADJUSTMENTS DEBIT	ADJUSTMENTS CREDIT	
1	Cash	4 7 0 00				1
2	Accounts Receivable	3 1 0 0 00				2
3	Supplies	8 0 00			(a) 6 0 00	3
4	Prepaid Insurance	7 0 0 00			(b) 7 0 00	4
5	Delivery Equipment	4 8 0 0 00				5
6	Accum. Depr.—Delivery Equipment				(d) 8 0 00	6
7	Accounts Payable		1 9 0 0 00			7
8	Wages Payable				(c) 4 0 0 00	8
9	Mitchell Williams, Capital		5 0 0 0 00			9
10	Mitchell Williams, Drawing	3 0 0 0 00				10
11	Delivery Fees		8 0 0 0 00			11
12	Wages Expense	1 6 5 0 00		(c) 4 0 0 00		12
13	Rent Expense	1 0 0 0 00				13
14	Supplies Expense			(a) 6 0 00		14
15	Phone Expense	1 0 0 00				15
16	Insurance Expense			(b) 7 0 00		16
17	Depr. Expense—Delivery Equipment			(d) 8 0 00		17
18		14 9 0 0 00	14 9 0 0 00	6 1 0 00	6 1 0 00	18

	GENERAL JOURNAL				PAGE 3	
	DATE	DESCRIPTION	POST. REF.	DEBIT	CREDIT	
1		Adjusting Entries				1
2	20-- June 30	Supplies Expense	523	6 0 00		2
3		Supplies	141		6 0 00	3
4						4
5	30	Insurance Expense	535	7 0 00		5
6		Prepaid Insurance	145		7 0 00	6
7						7
8	30	Wages Expense	511	4 0 0 00		8
9		Wages Payable	219		4 0 0 00	9
10						10
11	30	Depr. Expense—Delivery Equipment	541	8 0 00		11
12		Accum. Depr.—Delivery Equipment	185.1		8 0 00	12

(a) rows 2–3, (b) rows 5–6, (c) rows 8–9, (d) rows 11–12

CHECKPOINT ✔

Complete Checkpoint-5 on page 159 to test your basic understanding of LO5.

Mitchell's adjusting entries are illustrated in Figure 5-21 as they would appear in a general journal. Note that the last day of the accounting period, June 30, has been entered in the date column and "*Adjusting Entries*" is written in the Description column prior to the first adjusting entry. No explanation is required in the Description column for individual adjusting entries. We simply label them as adjusting entries.

LO6	Methods of Accounting: Cash, Modified Cash, and Accrual

Explain the cash, modified cash, and accrual bases of accounting.

The accrual basis of accounting offers the best matching of revenues and expenses and is required under generally accepted accounting principles. GAAP financial statements prepared using the accrual method are particularly important when major businesses want to raise large amounts of money. Investors and creditors expect GAAP financial statements and generally will not invest or make loans without them.

However, many small professional service organizations are not concerned with raising large amounts of money from investors and creditors. These organizations include CPAs, doctors, dentists, lawyers, engineers, and architects. Since these organizations do not need to prepare GAAP financial statements, they often use the cash or modified cash basis. If one of these organizations needs to borrow money from a bank that requires GAAP financial statements, an accountant can convert the financial statements to the accrual basis.

Under the accrual basis of accounting, revenues are recorded when earned. Revenues are considered earned when a service has been provided or a product has been sold, regardless of when cash is received from the customer. If cash is not received, a receivable is set up.

The accrual basis also assumes that expenses are recorded when incurred. Expenses are incurred when a service is received or an asset consumed in an effort to generate revenues. This is done regardless of when cash is paid. If cash is not paid when a service is received, a payable is set up. When assets are consumed, prepaid assets are decreased or long-term assets are depreciated. Since the accrual basis accounts for long-term assets, prepaid assets, receivables, and payables, it is the most comprehensive system and best method of measuring income for the vast majority of businesses.

LEARNING KEY 🔑

Accrual Basis

Accounting for: Revenues and Expenses	Accounting for: Assets and Liabilities	
Record revenue when earned.	Accounts receivable:	Yes
Record expenses when incurred.	Accounts payable:	Yes
	Prepaid assets:	Yes
	Long-term assets:	Yes

Under the cash basis of accounting, revenues are recorded when cash is received and expenses are recorded when cash is paid. This method will provide results that are similar to the accrual basis if there are few receivables, payables, and assets. However, as shown in Figure 5-22, the cash and accrual bases can result in very different measures of net income if a business has significant amounts of receivables, payables, and assets.

LEARNING KEY 🔑

Cash Basis

Accounting for: Revenues and Expenses	Accounting for: Assets and Liabilities	
Record revenue when cash is received.	Accounts receivable:	No
Record expenses when cash is paid.	Accounts payable:	No
	Prepaid assets:	No
	Long-term assets:	No

FIGURE 5-22 Cash versus Accrual Accounting

		Method of Accounting			
		Accrual Basis		Cash Basis	
Transaction		Expense	Revenue	Expense	Revenue
(a)	Provided services on account, $600.		$600		
(b)	Paid wages earned this period, $300	$300		$300	
(c)	Received cash for services performed on account last month, $200				$ 200
(d)	Received cleaning bill for month, $250	250			
(e)	Paid on account for last month's advertising, $100			100	
(f)	Purchase of supplies, $50			50	
(g)	Supplies used during month, $40	40			
		$590	$600	$450	$ 200

Revenue	$600	$ 200
Expense	590	450
Net Income (Loss)	$ 10	$(250)

Revenues are recognized when:	earned	cash is received
Expenses are recognized when:	incurred	cash is paid

> The modified cash basis is the same as the accrual basis, except receivables and payables are not recognized for revenues and operating expenses.

A third method of accounting combines aspects of the cash and accrual methods. With the **modified cash basis of accounting**, a business uses the cash basis for recording revenues and most expenses. Exceptions are made when cash is paid for assets with useful lives greater than one accounting period. For example, under a strict cash basis, if cash is paid for equipment, buildings, supplies, or insurance, the amount is immediately recorded as an expense. This approach could cause major distortions when measuring net income. Under the modified cash basis, cash payments like these are recorded as assets, and adjustments are made each period as under the accrual basis. Liabilities associated with the acquisition of these assets are also recognized.

Although similar to the accrual basis, the modified cash basis does not account for receivables or for payables for services received. Thus, the modified cash basis is a combination of the cash and accrual methods of accounting. The differences and similarities among the cash, modified cash, and accrual methods of accounting are demonstrated in Figure 5-23.

LEARNING KEY 🔑

Modified Cash Basis

Accounting for:
Revenues and Expenses

Record revenue when cash is received.
Record expenses when cash is paid, except for assets with useful lives greater than one accounting period. Accrual accounting is used for prepaid assets (insurance and supplies) and long-term assets.

Accounting for:
Assets and Liabilities

Accounts receivable:	No
Accounts payable	
for purchase of assets:	Yes
for services received:	No
Prepaid assets:	Yes
Long-term assets:	Yes

FIGURE 5-23 Comparison of Cash, Modified Cash, and Accrual Methods

	ENTRIES MADE UNDER EACH ACCOUNTING METHOD		
Event	**Cash**	**Modified Cash**	**Accrual**
Revenues:			
Perform services for cash	Cash Professional Fees	Cash Professional Fees	Cash Professional Fees
Perform services on account	No entry	No entry	Accounts Receivable Professional Fees
Expenses:			
Pay cash for operating expenses: wages, advertising, rent, phone, etc.	Expense Cash	Expense Cash	Expense Cash
Pay cash for prepaid items: insurance, supplies, etc.	Expense Cash	Prepaid Asset Cash	Prepaid Asset Cash
Pay cash for property, plant, and equipment (PP&E)	Expense Cash	PP&E Asset Cash	PP&E Asset Cash
Receive bill for services received	No entry	No entry	Expense Accounts Payable
End-of-period adjustments:			
Wages earned by employees but not paid	No entry	No entry	Wages Expense Wages Payable
Prepaid items used	No entry	Expense Prepaid Asset	Expense Prepaid Asset
Depreciation on property, plant, and equipment	No entry	Depreciation Expense Accumulated Depreciation	Depreciation Expense Accumulated Depreciation
Other:			
Purchase of assets on account	No entry	Asset Accounts Payable	Asset Accounts Payable
Payments for assets purchased on account	Expense Cash	Accounts Payable Cash	Accounts Payable Cash

LEARNING KEY 🔑

The shaded areas in Figure 5-23 show that sometimes the modified cash basis is the same as the cash basis and sometimes it is the same as the accrual basis. For some transactions, all methods are the same.

CHECKPOINT ✔

Complete Checkpoint-6 on page 159 to test your basic understanding of LO6.

If all businesses were the same, only one method of accounting would be needed. However, businesses vary in their need for major assets like buildings and equipment, the amount of customer receivables, and payables to suppliers. For example, if a business were rather small with no major assets, receivables, or payables, it would be simpler to use the cash basis of accounting. In addition, under these circumstances, the difference in net income under the accrual and cash bases of accounting would be small. Most individuals fit this description and use the cash basis on their tax returns.

Businesses with buildings and equipment, but few receivables and payables, might use the modified cash basis. Again, the accounting would be a little simpler and differences between net income computed under the modified cash and accrual bases would be small. Finally, businesses with buildings and equipment, and receivables and payables, should use the accrual basis of accounting to achieve the best matching of revenues and expenses.

SELF-STUDY

LEARNING OBJECTIVES	Key Points to Remember
LO1 **Prepare end-of-period adjustments.**	End-of-period adjustments are necessary to bring the general ledger accounts up to date prior to preparing financial statements. Reasons to adjust the trial balance are as follows: 1. To report all revenues earned during the accounting period. 2. To report all expenses incurred to produce the revenues during the accounting period. 3. To accurately report the assets on the balance sheet. Some assets may have expired, depreciated, or been used up during the accounting period. 4. To accurately report the liabilities on the balance sheet date. Expenses may have been incurred, but not yet paid.
LO2 **Post adjusting entries to the general ledger.**	Adjusting entries are posted to the general ledger in the same manner as all other entries, except that "Adjusting" is written in the Item column of the general ledger.
LO3 **Prepare a work sheet.**	Steps in preparing the work sheet are as follows: 1. Prepare the trial balance. 2. Prepare the adjustments. 3. Prepare the adjusted trial balance. 4. Extend the adjusted account balances to the Income Statement and Balance Sheet columns. 5. Total the Income Statement and Balance Sheet columns to compute the net income or net loss.
LO4 **Describe methods for finding errors on the work sheet.**	Tips for finding errors on the work sheet include the following: 1. Check the addition of all columns. 2. Check the addition and subtraction required when extending to the Adjusted Trial Balance columns. 3. Make sure the adjusted account balances have been extended to the appropriate columns. 4. Make sure that the net income or net loss has been added to the appropriate columns.
LO5 **Journalize adjusting entries from the work sheet.**	The adjustments are copied from the work sheet to the journal. The last day of the accounting period is entered in the Date column and "Adjusting Entries" is written in the Description column.
LO6 **Explain the cash, modified cash, and accrual bases of accounting.**	Cash Basis—Record revenues when cash is received and expenses when cash is paid. Accrual Basis—Record revenues when earned and expenses as incurred. Modified Cash Basis—Same as accrual, except no accounts receivable and no accounts payable for operating expenses.

DEMONSTRATION PROBLEM

Justin Park is a lawyer specializing in corporate tax law. He began his practice on January 1. A chart of accounts and trial balance taken on December 31, 20--, are provided below and on page 154.

Information for year-end adjustments is as follows:

(a) Office supplies on hand at year-end amounted to $300.

(b) On January 1, 20--, Park purchased office equipment costing $15,000 with an expected life of five years and no salvage value.

(c) Computer equipment costing $6,000 with an expected life of three years and no salvage value was purchased on July 1, 20--. Assume that Park computes depreciation to the nearest full month.

(d) A premium of $1,200 for a one-year insurance policy was paid on December 1, 20--.

(e) Wages earned by Park's part-time secretary, which have not yet been paid, amount to $300.

REQUIRED

1. Prepare the work sheet for the year ended December 31, 20--.
2. Prepare adjusting entries in a general journal.

JUSTIN PARK LEGAL SERVICES CHART OF ACCOUNTS			
Assets		**Revenue**	
101	Cash	401	Client Fees
142	Office Supplies		
145	Prepaid Insurance	**Expenses**	
181	Office Equipment	511	Wages Expense
181.1	Accumulated Depr.—	521	Rent Expense
	Office Equipment	523	Office Supplies Expense
187	Computer Equipment	525	Phone Expense
187.1	Accumulated Depr.—	533	Utilities Expense
	Computer Equipment	535	Insurance Expense
Liabilities		541	Depr. Expense—
201	Notes Payable		Office Equipment
202	Accounts Payable	542	Depr. Expense—
219	Wages Payable		Computer Equipment
Owner's Equity			
311	Justin Park, Capital		
312	Justin Park, Drawing		

(*continued*)

Justin Park Legal Services Trial Balance December 31, 20 --												
ACCOUNT TITLE	ACCOUNT NO.	\multicolumn{5}{c}{DEBIT BALANCE}	\multicolumn{5}{c}{CREDIT BALANCE}	
Cash	101	7	0	0	0	00						
Office Supplies	142		8	0	0	00						
Prepaid Insurance	145	1	2	0	0	00						
Office Equipment	181	15	0	0	0	00						
Computer Equipment	187	6	0	0	0	00						
Notes Payable	201						5	0	0	0	00	
Accounts Payable	202						5	0	0	0	00	
Justin Park, Capital	311						11	4	0	0	00	
Justin Park, Drawing	312	5	0	0	0	00						
Client Fees	401						40	0	0	0	00	
Wages Expense	511	12	0	0	0	00						
Rent Expense	521	5	0	0	0	00						
Phone Expense	525	1	0	0	0	00						
Utilities Expense	533	3	9	0	0	00						
		56	9	0	0	00	56	9	0	0	00	

The solution to part (1) is found on page 155.
2.

GENERAL JOURNAL													PAGE 11	
	\multicolumn{2}{c}{DATE}	DESCRIPTION	POST. REF.	\multicolumn{4}{c}{DEBIT}	\multicolumn{4}{c}{CREDIT}		
1			Adjusting Entries											1
2	20-- Dec.	31	Office Supplies Expense			5	0	0	00					2
3			Office Supplies								5	0	0	00	3
4														4
5		31	Depr. Expense—Office Equipment		3	0	0	0	00					5
6			Accum. Depr.—Office Equipment							3	0	0	0	00	6
7														7
8		31	Depr. Expense—Computer Equipment		1	0	0	0	00					8
9			Accum. Depr.—Computer Equipment							1	0	0	0	00	9
10														10
11		31	Insurance Expense			1	0	0	00					11
12			Prepaid Insurance								1	0	0	00	12
13														13
14		31	Wages Expense			3	0	0	00					14
15			Wages Payable								3	0	0	00	15

SOLUTION 1.

Justin Park Legal Services
Work Sheet
For Year Ended December 31, 20--

#	ACCOUNT TITLE	TRIAL BALANCE DEBIT	TRIAL BALANCE CREDIT	ADJUSTMENTS DEBIT	ADJUSTMENTS CREDIT	ADJUSTED TRIAL BALANCE DEBIT	ADJUSTED TRIAL BALANCE CREDIT	INCOME STATEMENT DEBIT	INCOME STATEMENT CREDIT	BALANCE SHEET DEBIT	BALANCE SHEET CREDIT
1	Cash	7 0 0 0 00				7 0 0 0 00				7 0 0 0 00	
2	Office Supplies	8 0 0 00			(a) 5 0 0 00	3 0 0 00				3 0 0 00	
3	Prepaid Insurance	1 2 0 0 00			(d) 1 0 0 00	1 1 0 0 00				1 1 0 0 00	
4	Office Equipment	15 0 0 0 00				15 0 0 0 00				15 0 0 0 00	
5	Accum. Depr.—Office Equip.				(b) 3 0 0 00		3 0 0 00				3 0 0 00
6	Computer Equipment	6 0 0 0 00				6 0 0 0 00				6 0 0 0 00	
7	Accum. Depr.—Computer Equip.				(c) 1 0 0 00		1 0 0 00				1 0 0 00
8	Notes Payable		5 0 0 0 00				5 0 0 0 00				5 0 0 0 00
9	Accounts Payable		5 0 0 00				5 0 0 00				5 0 0 00
10	Wages Payable				(e) 3 0 0 00		3 0 0 00				3 0 0 00
11	Justin Park, Capital		11 4 0 0 00				11 4 0 0 00				11 4 0 0 00
12	Justin Park, Drawing	5 0 0 0 00				5 0 0 0 00				5 0 0 0 00	
13	Client Fees		40 0 0 0 00				40 0 0 0 00		40 0 0 0 00		
14	Wages Expense	12 0 0 0 00		(e) 3 0 0 00		12 3 0 0 00		12 3 0 0 00			
15	Rent Expense	5 0 0 0 00				5 0 0 0 00		5 0 0 0 00			
16	Office Supplies Expense			(a) 5 0 0 00		5 0 0 00		5 0 0 00			
17	Phone Expense	1 0 0 0 00				1 0 0 0 00		1 0 0 0 00			
18	Utilities Expense	3 9 0 0 00				3 9 0 0 00		3 9 0 0 00			
19	Insurance Expense			(d) 1 0 0 00		1 0 0 00		1 0 0 00			
20	Depr. Expense—Office Equip.			(b) 3 0 0 00		3 0 0 00		3 0 0 00			
21	Depr. Expense—Computer Equip.			(c) 1 0 0 00		1 0 0 00		1 0 0 00			
22		56 9 0 0 00	56 9 0 0 00	4 9 0 0 00	4 9 0 0 00	61 2 0 0 00	61 2 0 0 00	26 8 0 0 00	40 0 0 0 00	34 4 0 0 00	21 2 0 0 00
23	Net Income							13 2 0 0 00			13 2 0 0 00
24								40 0 0 0 00	40 0 0 0 00	34 4 0 0 00	34 4 0 0 00

KEY TERMS

accrual basis of accounting (149) A method of accounting under which revenues are recorded when earned and expenses are recorded when incurred.

Adjusted Trial Balance columns (144) The third pair of amount columns on the work sheet. They are used to prove the equality of the debits and credits in the general ledger accounts after making all end-of-period adjustments.

adjusting entries (131) Journal entries made at the end of an accounting period to reflect changes in account balances that are not the direct result of an exchange with an outside party.

Balance Sheet columns (144) The work sheet columns that show the amounts that will be reported in the balance sheet and the statement of owner's equity.

book value (137) The difference between the asset account and its related accumulated depreciation account. The value reflected by the accounting records.

cash basis of accounting (149) A method of accounting under which revenues are recorded when cash is received and expenses are recorded when cash is paid.

contra-asset (136) An account with a credit balance that is deducted from the related asset account on the balance sheet.

depreciable cost (136) The cost of an asset that is subject to depreciation.

depreciation (136) A method of matching an asset's original cost against the revenues produced over its useful life.

expense recognition principle (131) Expenses should be recognized when incurred, regardless of when cash is paid. Expenses are generally considered to be incurred when services are received or assets consumed.

fiscal year (131) A 12-month period for which financial reports are prepared.

historical cost principle (136) A principle that requires many assets to be recorded at their actual cost.

Income Statement columns (144) The work sheet columns that show the amounts that will be reported in the income statement.

market value (136) The amount an item can be sold for under normal economic conditions.

matching principle (131) The proper matching of revenues earned during an accounting period with the expenses incurred to produce the revenues is often referred to as the matching principle.

modified cash basis of accounting (150) A method of accounting that combines aspects of the cash and accrual methods. It uses the cash basis for recording revenues and most expenses. Exceptions are made when cash is paid for assets with useful lives greater than one accounting period.

plant assets (136) Assets of a durable nature that will be used for operations over several years. Examples include buildings and equipment.

revenue recognition principle (131) Revenues should be recognized when earned, regardless of when cash is received from the customer. Revenues are considered earned when a service has been provided or a product has been sold.

salvage value (136) The expected market value of an asset at the end of its useful life.

straight-line method (136) A depreciation method in which the depreciable cost is divided by the estimated useful life.

undepreciated cost (137) The difference between the asset account and its related accumulated depreciation account. Also known as book value.

useful life (136)   The period of time that an asset is expected to help produce revenues.

work sheet (140)   A form used to pull together all of the information needed to enter adjusting entries and prepare the financial statements.

SELF-STUDY TEST QUESTIONS

True/False

1. **LO1**   The matching principle in accounting requires the matching of debits and credits.

2. **LO1**   Adjusting entries are required at the end of the accounting period because of mistakes in the journal and ledger.

3. **LO1**   As part of the adjustment of supplies, an expense account is debited and Supplies is credited for the amount of supplies used during the accounting period.

4. **LO1**   Depreciable cost is the difference between the original cost of the asset and its accumulated depreciation.

5. **LO1**   The purpose of depreciation is to record the asset's market value in the accounting records.

Multiple Choice

1. **LO1**   The purpose of depreciation is to
   (a) spread the cost of an asset over its useful life.
   (b) show the current market value of an asset.
   (c) set up a reserve fund to purchase a new asset.
   (d) expense the asset in the year it was purchased.

2. **LO1**   Depreciable cost is the
   (a) difference between original cost and accumulated depreciation.
   (b) difference in actual cost and true market value.
   (c) difference between original cost and estimated salvage value.
   (d) difference between estimated salvage value and actual salvage value.

3. **LO1**   Book value is the
   (a) difference between market value and estimated value.
   (b) difference between market value and historical cost.
   (c) difference between original cost and salvage value.
   (d) difference between original cost and accumulated depreciation.

4. **LO1**   The adjustment for wages earned by employees but not yet paid is
   (a) debit Wages Payable and credit Wages Expense.
   (b) debit Wages Expense and credit Cash.
   (c) debit Wages Expense and credit Wages Payable.
   (d) debit Wages Expense and credit Accounts Receivable.

5. **LO3**   The first step in preparing a work sheet is to
   (a) prepare the trial balance.
   (b) prepare the adjustments.
   (c) prepare the adjusted trial balance.
   (d) extend the amounts from the Adjusted Trial Balance to the Income Statement and Balance Sheet columns.

CHECKPOINT ✔

Checkpoint Exercises

1. **LO1**   On December 31, the trial balance indicates that the supplies account has a balance, prior to the adjusting entry, of $100. A physical count of the supplies inventory shows that $70 of supplies remain. What adjustment should be made to the supplies account?

2. **LO2**   When posting adjusting entries to the general ledger, what is written in the Item column?

3. **LO3**   Indicate the heading for the columns of the work sheet A through F below.

A	B		C		D		E		F	
	DEBIT	CREDIT	DEBIT	CREDIT	DEBIT	CREDIT	DEBIT	CREDIT	DEBIT	CREDIT
1										
2										

4. **LO4**   Find the error(s) in the work sheet below.

	ACCOUNT TITLE	TRIAL BALANCE DEBIT	TRIAL BALANCE CREDIT	ADJUSTMENTS DEBIT	ADJUSTMENTS CREDIT	ADJUSTED TRIAL BALANCE DEBIT	ADJUSTED TRIAL BALANCE CREDIT	INCOME STATEMENT DEBIT	INCOME STATEMENT CREDIT	BALANCE SHEET DEBIT	BALANCE SHEET CREDIT	
1	Cash	3 7 0 00				3 7 0 00				3 7 0 00		1
2	Accounts Receivable	6 5 0 00				6 5 0 00				6 5 0 00		2
3	Supplies	8 0 00			(a) 6 0 00	1 4 0 00				1 4 0 00		3
4	Prepaid Insurance	2 0 0 00			(b) 2 5 00	1 7 5 00				1 7 5 00		4
5	Delivery Equipment	3 6 0 0 00				3 6 0 0 00				3 6 0 0 00		5
6	Accum. Depr.—Delivery Equipment				(d) 1 0 0 00		1 0 0 00				1 0 0 00	6
7	Accounts Payable		1 8 0 0 00				1 8 0 0 00				1 8 0 0 00	7
8	Wages Payable				(c) 5 0 00		5 0 00				5 0 00	8
9	Mitchell Williams, Capital		2 0 0 0 00				2 0 0 0 00				2 0 0 0 00	9
10	Mitchell Williams, Drawing	1 5 0 00				1 5 0 00				1 5 0 00		10
11	Delivery Fees		2 1 5 0 00				2 1 5 0 00		2 1 5 0 00			11
12	Wages Expense	6 5 0 00		(c) 5 0 00		7 0 0 00		7 0 0 00				12
13	Rent Expense	2 0 0 00				2 0 0 00		2 0 0 00				13
14	Supplies Expense			(a) 6 0 00		6 0 00		6 0 00				14
15	Phone Expense	5 0 00				5 0 00		5 0 00				15
16	Insurance Expense			(b) 2 5 00		2 5 00		2 5 00				16
17	Depr. Expense—Delivery Equipment			(d) 1 0 0 00		1 0 0 00		1 0 0 00				17
18		5 9 5 0 00	5 9 5 0 00	2 3 5 00	2 3 5 00	6 2 2 0 00	6 1 0 0 00	1 1 3 5 00	2 1 5 0 00	5 0 8 5 00	3 9 5 0 00	18
19								1 0 1 5 00			1 1 3 5 00	19
20								2 1 5 0 00	2 1 5 0 00	5 0 8 5 00	5 0 8 5 00	20
21												21
22												22
23												23
24												24

5. **LO5**   Using the following partial work sheet prepared on December 31, 20--, journalize the adjusting entry.

	ACCOUNT TITLE	TRIAL BALANCE		ADJUSTMENTS	
		DEBIT	CREDIT	DEBIT	CREDIT
1	Cash	3 7 0 00			
2	Accounts Receivable	6 5 0 00			
3	Supplies	8 0 00			
4	Prepaid Insurance	2 0 0 00			(b) 5 0 00
5	Delivery Equipment	3 6 0 0 00			
6	Accum. Depr.—Delivery Equipment				
7	Accounts Payable		1 8 0 0 00		
8	Wages Payable				
9	Mitchell Williams, Capital		2 0 0 0 00		
10	Mitchell Williams, Drawing	1 5 0 00			
11	Delivery Fees		2 1 5 0 00		
12	Wages Expense	6 5 0 00			
13	Rent Expense	2 0 0 00			
14	Supplies Expense				
15	Phone Expense	5 0 00			
16	Insurance Expense			(b) 5 0 00	
17	Depr. Expense—Delivery Equipment				
18		5 9 5 0 00	5 9 5 0 00	5 0 00	5 0 00
19					

6. **LO6**   Bill Roberts provided legal advice to a client for $500 on account. Roberts paid a legal assistant $50 for research on this engagement and used office supplies costing $10. If these are the only transactions for the period, compute net income under the cash, accrual, and modified cash bases.

The answers to the Self-Study Test Questions are at the end of the chapter (pages 177–178).

APPLYING YOUR KNOWLEDGE

CengageNowv2 provides "Show Me How" videos for selected exercises and problems. Additional resources, such as Excel templates for completing selected exercises and problems, are available for download from the companion website at Cengage.com.

REVIEW QUESTIONS

LO1   1.   Explain the revenue recognition principle.

LO1   2.   Explain the expense recognition principle.

LO1   3.   Explain the matching principle.

LO1   4.   Explain the historical cost principle.

LO1	5.	Describe a plant asset.
LO1	6.	What is a contra-asset?
LO1	7.	What is the useful life of an asset?
LO1	8.	What is the purpose of depreciation?
LO1	9.	What is an asset's depreciable cost?
LO1	10.	What is the book value of an asset?
LO3	11.	Explain the purpose of the work sheet.
LO3	12.	Identify the five major column headings on a work sheet.
LO3	13.	List the five steps taken in preparing a work sheet.
LO4	14.	Describe four tips for finding errors on the work sheet.
LO6	15.	Explain when revenues are recorded under the cash basis, modified cash basis, and accrual basis of accounting.
LO6	16.	Explain when expenses are recorded under the cash basis, modified cash basis, and accrual basis of accounting.

SERIES A EXERCISES

E 5-1A   (LO1)

ADJUSTMENT FOR SUPPLIES On December 31, the trial balance indicates that the supplies account has a balance, prior to the adjusting entry, of $320. A physical count of the supplies inventory shows that $90 of supplies remain. Analyze this adjustment for supplies using T accounts, and then formally enter this adjustment in the general journal.

E 5-2A   (LO1)

ADJUSTMENT FOR INSURANCE On December 1, a six-month liability insurance policy was purchased for $900. Analyze the required adjustment as of December 31 using T accounts, and then formally enter this adjustment in the general journal.

E 5-3A   (LO1)

ADJUSTMENT FOR WAGES On December 31, the trial balance shows wages expense of $600. An additional $200 of wages was earned by the employees, but has not yet been paid. Analyze this adjustment for wages using T accounts, and then formally enter this adjustment in the general journal.

E 5-4A   (LO1)

ADJUSTMENT FOR DEPRECIATION OF ASSET On December 1, delivery equipment was purchased for $7,200. The delivery equipment has an estimated useful life of four years (48 months) and no salvage value. Using the straight-line depreciation method, analyze the necessary adjusting entry as of December 31 (one month) using T accounts, and then formally enter this adjustment in the general journal.

E 5-5A   (LO1)

CALCULATION OF BOOK VALUE On June 1, 20--, a depreciable asset was acquired for $6,840. The asset has an estimated useful life of six years (72 months) and no salvage value. Using the straight-line depreciation method, calculate the book value as of December 31, 20--.

E 5-6A   (LO1)   ANALYSIS OF ADJUSTING ENTRY FOR SUPPLIES Analyze each situation and indicate the correct dollar amount for the adjusting entry. (Trial balance is abbreviated as TB.)

1. Ending inventory of supplies is $260.

(Balance Sheet) Supplies		(Income Statement) Supplies Expense
TB 580		
Bal. _____		

2. Amount of supplies used is $230.

(Balance Sheet) Supplies		(Income Statement) Supplies Expense
TB 435		
Bal. _____		

E 5-7A   (LO1)   ANALYSIS OF ADJUSTING ENTRY FOR INSURANCE Analyze each situation and indicate the correct dollar amount for the adjusting entry.

1. Amount of insurance expired is $970.

(Balance Sheet) Prepaid Insurance		(Income Statement) Insurance Expense
TB 1,450		
Bal. _____		

2. Amount of unexpired insurance is $565.

(Balance Sheet) Prepaid Insurance		(Income Statement) Insurance Expense
TB 1,350		
Bal. _____		

E 5-8A   (LO2)   POSTING ADJUSTING ENTRIES Two adjusting entries are in the following general journal. Post these adjusting entries to the four general ledger accounts. The following account numbers were taken from the chart of accounts: 141, Supplies; 219, Wages Payable; 511, Wages Expense; and 523, Supplies Expense. If you are not using the working papers that accompany this text, enter the following balances before posting the entries: Supplies, $200 Debit; and Wages Expense, $1,200 Debit.

(*continued*)

			GENERAL JOURNAL							PAGE 9		
	DATE		DESCRIPTION	POST. REF.	DEBIT				CREDIT			
1			Adjusting Entries									1
2	20-- Dec.	31	Supplies Expense			8	5	00				2
3			Supplies							8	5	00	3
4												4
5		31	Wages Expense		2	2	0	00				5
6			Wages Payable						2	2	0	00	6

E 5-9A   (LO3)
✓ Adjustments col. total: $1,550

WORK SHEET AND ADJUSTING ENTRIES A partial work sheet for Jim Jacobs' Furniture Repair is shown as follows. Indicate by letters (a) through (d) the four adjustments in the Adjustments columns of the work sheet, properly matching each debit and credit. Complete the Adjustments columns.

Jim Jacobs' Furniture Repair
Work Sheet (Partial)
For Year Ended December 31, 20 - -

	ACCOUNT TITLE	TRIAL BALANCE				ADJUSTMENTS				ADJUSTED TRIAL BALANCE				
		DEBIT		CREDIT		DEBIT		CREDIT		DEBIT		CREDIT		
1	Cash	1 0 0 00								1 0 0 00				1
2	Supplies	8 5 0 00								2 0 0 00				2
3	Prepaid Insurance	9 0 0 00								3 0 0 00				3
4	Delivery Equipment	3 6 0 0 00								3 6 0 0 00				4
5	Accum. Depr.—Delivery Equipment			6 0 0 00								8 0 0 00		5
6	Wages Payable											1 0 0 00		6
7	Jim Jacobs, Capital			4 0 0 0 00								4 0 0 0 00		7
8	Repair Fees			1 6 5 0 00								1 6 5 0 00		8
9	Wages Expense	6 0 0 00								7 0 0 00				9
10	Advertising Expense	2 0 0 00								2 0 0 00				10
11	Supplies Expense									6 5 0 00				11
12	Insurance Expense									6 0 0 00				12
13	Depr. Expense—Delivery Equipment									2 0 0 00				13
14		6 2 5 0 00		6 2 5 0 00						6 5 5 0 00		6 5 5 0 00		14

E 5-10A   (LO5)

JOURNALIZING ADJUSTING ENTRIES From the Adjustments columns in Exercise 5-9A, journalize the four adjusting entries, as of December 31, in proper general journal format.

E 5-11A   (LO3)   EXTENDING ADJUSTED BALANCES TO THE INCOME STATEMENT AND BALANCE SHEET COLUMNS Indicate with an "X" whether each account total should be extended to the Income Statement Debit or Credit or to the Balance Sheet Debit or Credit columns on the work sheet.

	Income Statement Debit	Income Statement Credit	Balance Sheet Debit	Balance Sheet Credit
Cash	_____	_____	_____	_____
Accounts Receivable	_____	_____	_____	_____
Supplies	_____	_____	_____	_____
Prepaid Insurance	_____	_____	_____	_____
Delivery Equipment	_____	_____	_____	_____
Accum. Depr.—Delivery Equipment	_____	_____	_____	_____
Accounts Payable	_____	_____	_____	_____
Wages Payable	_____	_____	_____	_____
Owner, Capital	_____	_____	_____	_____
Owner, Drawing	_____	_____	_____	_____
Delivery Fees	_____	_____	_____	_____
Wages Expense	_____	_____	_____	_____
Rent Expense	_____	_____	_____	_____
Supplies Expense	_____	_____	_____	_____
Insurance Expense	_____	_____	_____	_____
Depr. Exp.—Delivery Equipment	_____	_____	_____	_____

E 5-12A   (LO3)   ANALYSIS OF NET INCOME OR NET LOSS ON THE WORK SHEET Indicate with an "X" in which columns, Income Statement Debit or Credit or Balance Sheet Debit or Credit, a net income or a net loss would appear on a work sheet.

	Income Statement Debit	Income Statement Credit	Balance Sheet Debit	Balance Sheet Credit
Net Income	_____	_____	_____	_____
Net Loss	_____	_____	_____	_____

E 5-13A   (LO6)
✓ See Figure 5-23 in text

CASH, MODIFIED CASH, AND ACCRUAL BASES OF ACCOUNTING Prepare the entry for each of the following transactions, using the (a) cash basis, (b) modified cash basis, and (c) accrual basis of accounting.

1. Purchase supplies on account.
2. Make payment on asset previously purchased.
3. Purchase supplies for cash.
4. Purchase insurance for cash.
5. Pay cash for wages.
6. Pay cash for phone expense.
7. Pay cash for new equipment.

End-of-Period Adjusting Entries:

8. Wages earned but not paid.
9. Prepaid item purchased, partly used.
10. Depreciation on long-term assets.

SERIES A PROBLEMS

P 5-14A **(LO1/3)**
✓ Adjustments col. total: $2,145
✓ Net income: $810

ADJUSTMENTS AND WORK SHEET SHOWING NET INCOME The trial balance after one month of operation for Mason's Delivery Service as of September 30, 20--, is shown below. Data to complete the adjustments are as follows:

(a) Supplies inventory as of September 30, $90.

(b) Insurance expired (used), $650.

(c) Depreciation on delivery equipment, $600.

(d) Wages earned by employees but not paid as of September 30, $350.

REQUIRED

1. Enter the adjustments in the Adjustments columns of the work sheet.
2. Complete the work sheet.

Mason's Delivery Service
Work Sheet (Partial)
For Month Ended September 30, 20 - -

	ACCOUNT TITLE	TRIAL BALANCE DEBIT	TRIAL BALANCE CREDIT	ADJUSTMENTS DEBIT	ADJUSTMENTS CREDIT	
1	Cash	1 6 0 0 00				1
2	Accounts Receivable	9 4 0 00				2
3	Supplies	6 3 5 00				3
4	Prepaid Insurance	1 2 0 0 00				4
5	Delivery Equipment	6 4 0 0 00				5
6	Accum. Depr.—Delivery Equipment					6
7	Accounts Payable		1 2 2 0 00			7
8	Wages Payable					8
9	Jill Mason, Capital		8 0 0 0 00			9
10	Jill Mason, Drawing	1 4 0 0 00				10
11	Delivery Fees		6 2 0 0 00			11
12	Wages Expense	1 5 0 0 00				12
13	Advertising Expense	4 6 0 00				13
14	Rent Expense	8 0 0 00				14
15	Supplies Expense					15
16	Phone Expense	1 6 5 00				16
17	Insurance Expense					17
18	Repair Expense	2 3 0 00				18
19	Oil and Gas Expense	9 0 00				19
20	Depr. Expense—Delivery Equipment					20
21		15 4 2 0 00	15 4 2 0 00			21

P 5-15A **(LO1/3)**
✓ Adjustments col. total: $1,380
✓ Net loss: $2,495

ADJUSTMENTS AND WORK SHEET SHOWING A NET LOSS Jason Armstrong started a business called Campus Delivery Service. After the first month of operations, the trial balance as of November 30, 20--, is as shown on the next page.

REQUIRED

1. Analyze the following adjustments and enter them on the work sheet.
   (a) Ending inventory of supplies on November 30, $185.
   (b) Unexpired (remaining) insurance as of November 30, $800.
   (c) Depreciation expense on van, $300.
   (d) Wages earned but not paid as of November 30, $190.

2. Complete the work sheet.

		Campus Delivery Service												
		Work Sheet (Partial)												
		For Month Ended November 30, 20 - -												
	ACCOUNT TITLE	TRIAL BALANCE				ADJUSTMENTS								
		DEBIT		CREDIT		DEBIT		CREDIT						
1	Cash	9 8 0 00												1
2	Accounts Receivable	5 9 0 00												2
3	Supplies	5 7 5 00												3
4	Prepaid Insurance	1 3 0 0 00												4
5	Van	5 8 0 0 00												5
6	Accum. Depr.—Van													6
7	Accounts Payable			9 6 0 00										7
8	Wages Payable													8
9	Jason Armstrong, Capital			10 0 0 0 00										9
10	Jason Armstrong, Drawing	6 0 0 00												10
11	Delivery Fees			2 6 0 0 00										11
12	Wages Expense	1 8 0 0 00												12
13	Advertising Expense	3 8 0 00												13
14	Rent Expense	9 0 0 00												14
15	Supplies Expense													15
16	Phone Expense	2 2 0 00												16
17	Insurance Expense													17
18	Repair Expense	3 1 5 00												18
19	Oil and Gas Expense	1 0 0 00												19
20	Depr. Expense—Van													20
21		13 5 6 0 00		13 5 6 0 00										21

P 5-16A   **(LO2/5)**   JOURNALIZE AND POST ADJUSTING ENTRIES FROM THE WORK SHEET Refer to Problem 5-15A and the following additional information:

Account Name	Account Number	Balance in Account Before Adjusting Entry
Supplies	141	$ 575
Prepaid Insurance	145	1,300
Accum. Depr.—Van	185.1	0
Wages Payable	219	0
Wages Expense	511	1,800
Supplies Expense	523	0
Insurance Expense	535	0
Depr. Expense—Van	541	0

(continued)

REQUIRED

1. Journalize the adjusting entries on page 5 of the general journal.
2. Post the adjusting entries to the general ledger. (If you are not using the working papers that accompany this text, enter the balances provided in this problem before posting the adjusting entries.)

P 5-17A (LO4)
✓ Adjustments col. total: $1,160
✓ Net income: $1,575

CORRECTING WORK SHEET WITH ERRORS A beginning accounting student tried to complete a work sheet for Joyce Lee's Tax Service. The following adjusting entries were to have been analyzed and entered onto the work sheet. The work sheet is shown on page 167.

(a) Ending inventory of supplies as of March 31, $160.
(b) Unexpired insurance as of March 31, $520.
(c) Depreciation of office equipment, $275.
(d) Wages earned, but not paid as of March 31, $110.

REQUIRED

The accounting student made a number of errors. Review the work sheet for addition mistakes, transpositions, and other errors and make all necessary corrections.

SERIES B EXERCISES

E 5-1B (LO1)

ADJUSTMENT FOR SUPPLIES On July 31, the trial balance indicates that the supplies account has a balance, prior to the adjusting entry, of $430. A physical count of the supplies inventory shows that $120 of supplies remain. Analyze the adjustment for supplies using T accounts, and then formally enter this adjustment in the general journal.

E 5-2B (LO1)

ADJUSTMENT FOR INSURANCE On July 1, a six-month liability insurance policy was purchased for $750. Analyze the required adjustment as of July 31 using T accounts, and then formally enter this adjustment in the general journal.

E 5-3B (LO1)

ADJUSTMENT FOR WAGES On July 31, the trial balance shows wages expense of $800. An additional $150 of wages was earned by the employees but has not yet been paid. Analyze the required adjustment using T accounts, and then formally enter this adjustment in the general journal.

E 5-4B (LO1)

ADJUSTMENT FOR DEPRECIATION OF ASSET On July 1, delivery equipment was purchased for $4,320. The delivery equipment has an estimated useful life of three years (36 months) and no salvage value. Using the straight-line depreciation method, analyze the necessary adjusting entry as of July 31 (one month) using T accounts, and then formally enter this adjustment in the general journal.

E 5-5B (LO1)

CALCULATION OF BOOK VALUE On January 1, 20--, a depreciable asset was acquired for $5,760. The asset has an estimated useful life of four years (48 months) and no salvage value. Use the straight-line depreciation method to calculate the book value as of July 1, 20--.

PROBLEM 5-17A

Joyce Lee's Tax Service
Work Sheet
For Month Ended March 31, 20--

#	ACCOUNT TITLE	TRIAL BALANCE DEBIT	TRIAL BALANCE CREDIT	ADJUSTMENTS DEBIT	ADJUSTMENTS CREDIT	ADJUSTED TRIAL BALANCE DEBIT	ADJUSTED TRIAL BALANCE CREDIT	INCOME STATEMENT DEBIT	INCOME STATEMENT CREDIT	BALANCE SHEET DEBIT	BALANCE SHEET CREDIT
1	Cash	1 7 2 5 00				1 7 2 5 00				1 7 5 2 00	
2	Accounts Receivable	9 6 0 00				9 6 0 00				9 6 0 00	
3	Supplies	5 2 5 00			(a) 1 6 0 00	3 6 5 00				3 6 5 00	
4	Prepaid Insurance	9 3 0 00			(b) 4 1 0 00	5 4 0 00				5 4 0 00	
5	Office Equipment	5 4 5 0 00			(c) 2 7 5 00	5 1 7 5 00				5 1 7 5 00	
6	Accum. Depr.– Office Equipment										
7	Accounts Payable		4 8 0 00				4 8 0 00				4 8 0 00
8	Wages Payable				(d) 1 1 0 00		1 1 0 00		1 1 0 00		
9	Joyce Lee, Capital		7 5 0 0 00				7 5 0 0 00				7 5 0 0 00
10	Joyce Lee, Drawing	1 1 2 5 00				1 1 2 5 00					
11	Professional Fees		5 7 0 0 00				5 7 0 0 00		5 7 0 0 00		
12	Wages Expense	1 4 2 0 00		(d) 1 1 0 00		1 4 2 0 00		1 4 2 0 00			1 5 8 0 00
13	Advertising Expense	3 5 0 00				3 5 0 00		3 5 0 00			
14	Rent Expense	7 0 0 00				7 0 0 00		7 0 0 00			
15	Supplies Expense			(a) 1 6 0 00		1 6 0 00		1 6 0 00			
16	Phone Expense	1 3 0 00				1 3 0 00		1 3 0 00			
17	Utilities Expense	1 9 0 00				1 9 0 00		1 9 0 00			
18	Insurance Expense			(b) 4 1 0 00		4 1 0 00		4 1 0 00			
19	Depr. Expense–Office Equipment			(c) 2 7 5 00		2 7 5 00		2 7 5 00			
20	Miscellaneous Expense	1 7 5 00				1 7 5 00		1 7 5 00			
21											
22		13 6 8 0 00	13 6 8 0 00	9 5 5 00	9 5 5 00	13 1 6 0 00	13 7 9 0 00	4 5 6 6 00	5 8 1 0 00	9 5 0 8 00	7 9 8 0 00
23								1 2 4 4 00			1 5 2 8 00
24								5 8 1 0 00	5 8 1 0 00	9 5 0 8 00	9 5 0 8 00
25											
26											
27											
28											
29											
30											

Contains Errors (watermark)

This work sheet contains errors.

E 5-6B   (LO1)   ANALYSIS OF ADJUSTING ENTRY FOR SUPPLIES Analyze each situation and indicate the correct dollar amount for the adjusting entry.

1. Ending inventory of supplies is $95.

(Balance Sheet) Supplies		(Income Statement) Supplies Expense	
TB	540		
Bal. _____			

2. Amount of supplies used is $280.

(Balance Sheet) Supplies		(Income Statement) Supplies Expense	
TB	330		
Bal. _____			

E 5-7B   (LO1)   ANALYSIS OF ADJUSTING ENTRY FOR INSURANCE Analyze each situation and indicate the correct dollar amount for the adjusting entry.

1. Amount of insurance expired (used) is $830.

(Balance Sheet) Prepaid Insurance		(Income Statement) Insurance Expense	
TB	960		
Bal. _____			

2. Amount of unexpired (remaining) insurance is $340.

(Balance Sheet) Prepaid Insurance		(Income Statement) Insurance Expense	
TB	1,135		
Bal. _____			

E 5-8B   (LO2)   POSTING ADJUSTING ENTRIES Two adjusting entries are shown in the following general journal. Post these adjusting entries to the four general ledger accounts. The following account numbers were taken from the chart of accounts: 145, Prepaid Insurance; 183.1, Accumulated Depreciation—Cleaning Equipment; 541, Depreciation Expense—Cleaning Equipment; and 535, Insurance Expense. If you are not using the working papers that accompany this text, enter the following balances before posting the entries: Prepaid Insurance, $960 Debit; Accumulated Depreciation—Cleaning Equipment, $870 Credit.

GENERAL JOURNAL													PAGE 7	
	DATE		DESCRIPTION	POST. REF.		DEBIT					CREDIT			
1			Adjusting Entries											1
2	20-- July	31	Insurance Expense			3	2	0	00					2
3			Prepaid Insurance								3	2	0	00	3
4														4
5		31	Depr. Expense—Cleaning Equipment			1	4	5	00					5
6			Accum. Depr.—Cleaning Equipment								1	4	5	00	6

E 5-9B **(LO3)**
✓ Adjustments col. total: $1,530

WORK SHEET AND ADJUSTING ENTRIES A partial work sheet for Jasmine Kah's Auto Detailing is shown below. Indicate by letters (a) through (d) the four adjustments in the Adjustments columns of the work sheet, properly matching each debit and credit. Complete the Adjustments columns.

Jasmine Kah's Auto Detailing
Work Sheet (Partial)
For Month Ended June 30, 20 - -

	ACCOUNT TITLE	TRIAL BALANCE								ADJUSTMENTS								ADJUSTED TRIAL BALANCE								
		DEBIT				CREDIT				DEBIT				CREDIT				DEBIT				CREDIT				
1	Cash		1	5	0	00													1	5	0	00					1
2	Supplies		5	2	0	00														9	0	00					2
3	Prepaid Insurance		7	5	0	00													2	0	0	00					3
4	Cleaning Equipment	5	4	0	0	00												5	4	0	0	00					4
5	Accum. Depr.— Cleaning Equipment						8	5	0	00													1	1	5	0	00	5
6	Wages Payable																							2	5	0	00	6
7	Jasmine Kah, Capital						4	6	0	0	00												4	6	0	0	00	7
8	Detailing Fees						2	2	2	0	00												2	2	2	0	00	8
9	Wages Expense		7	0	0	00													9	5	0	00					9
10	Advertising Expense		1	5	0	00													1	5	0	00					10
11	Supplies Expense																			4	3	0	00					11
12	Insurance Expense																			5	5	0	00					12
13	Depr. Expense—Cleaning Equipment																			3	0	0	00					13
14		7	6	7	0	00	7	6	7	0	00								8	2	2	0	00	8	2	2	0	00	14

E 5-10B **(LO5)**

JOURNALIZING ADJUSTING ENTRIES From the Adjustments columns in Exercise 5-9B, journalize the four adjusting entries as of June 30, in proper general journal format.

E 5-11B **(LO3)**

EXTENDING ADJUSTED BALANCES TO THE INCOME STATEMENT AND BALANCE SHEET COLUMNS Indicate with an "X" whether each account total should be extended to the Income Statement Debit or Credit or to the Balance Sheet Debit or Credit columns on the work sheet.

(continued)

	Income Statement Debit	Credit	Balance Sheet Debit	Credit
Cash	_____	_____	_____	_____
Accounts Receivable	_____	_____	_____	_____
Supplies	_____	_____	_____	_____
Prepaid Insurance	_____	_____	_____	_____
Automobile	_____	_____	_____	_____
Accum. Depr.—Automobile	_____	_____	_____	_____
Accounts Payable	_____	_____	_____	_____
Wages Payable	_____	_____	_____	_____
Owner, Capital	_____	_____	_____	_____
Owner, Drawing	_____	_____	_____	_____
Service Fees	_____	_____	_____	_____
Wages Expense	_____	_____	_____	_____
Supplies Expense	_____	_____	_____	_____
Utilities Expense	_____	_____	_____	_____
Insurance Expense	_____	_____	_____	_____
Depr. Exp.—Automobile	_____	_____	_____	_____

E 5-12B   (LO3)   ANALYSIS OF NET INCOME OR NET LOSS ON THE WORK SHEET   Insert the dollar amounts where the net income or net loss would appear on the work sheet.

	Income Statement Debit	Credit	Balance Sheet Debit	Credit
Net Income: $2,500	_____	_____	_____	_____
Net Loss: $1,900	_____	_____	_____	_____

E 5-13B   (LO6)
✓ See Figure 5-23 in text

CASH, MODIFIED CASH, AND ACCRUAL BASES OF ACCOUNTING   For each journal entry shown below, indicate the accounting method(s) for which the entry would be appropriate. If the journal entry is not appropriate for a particular accounting method, explain the proper accounting treatment for that method.

1. Office Equipment
    Cash
        Purchased equipment for cash

2. Office Equipment
    Accounts Payable
        Purchased equipment on account

3. Cash
    Revenue
        Cash receipts for week

4. Accounts Receivable
    Revenue
        Services performed on account

5. Prepaid Insurance
    Cash
        Purchased prepaid asset

6. Supplies
    Accounts Payable
        Purchased prepaid asset

7. Phone Expense
　　Cash
　　　　Paid phone bill
8. Wages Expense
　　Cash
　　　　Paid wages for month
9. Accounts Payable
　　Cash
　　　　Made payment on account

Adjusting Entries:

10. Supplies Expense
　　　Supplies
11. Wages Expense
　　　Wages Payable
12. Depreciation Expense—Office Equipment
　　　Accumulated Depreciation—Office Equipment

SERIES B PROBLEMS

P 5-14B   (LO1/3)
✓ Adjustments col. total: $805
✓ Net income: $2,410

ADJUSTMENTS AND WORK SHEET SHOWING NET INCOME Louie Long started a business called Louie's Lawn Service. The trial balance as of March 31, after the first month of operation, is as follows:

| | | | | | TRIAL BALANCE | | | | | | | ADJUSTMENTS | | | | | | | |
			DEBIT				CREDIT				DEBIT				CREDIT				
	Louie's Lawn Service Work Sheet For Month Ended March 31, 20 --																		
	ACCOUNT TITLE																		
1	Cash	1	3	7	5	00													1
2	Accounts Receivable		8	8	0	00													2
3	Supplies		4	9	0	00													3
4	Prepaid Insurance		8	0	0	00													4
5	Lawn Equipment	5	7	0	0	00													5
6	Accum. Depr.—Lawn Equipment																		6
7	Accounts Payable							7	8	0	00								7
8	Wages Payable																		8
9	Louie Long, Capital						6	5	0	0	00								9
10	Louie Long, Drawing	1	2	5	0	00													10
11	Lawn Service Fees						6	1	0	0	00								11
12	Wages Expense	1	1	4	5	00													12
13	Advertising Expense		5	4	0	00													13
14	Rent Expense		7	2	5	00													14
15	Supplies Expense																		15
16	Phone Expense		1	6	0	00													16
17	Insurance Expense																		17
18	Repair Expense		2	5	0	00													18
19	Depr. Expense—Lawn Equipment																		19
20	Miscellaneous Expense			6	5	00													20
21		13	3	8	0	00	13	3	8	0	00								21

(continued)

REQUIRED

1. Analyze the following adjustments and enter them on a work sheet.
   (a) Ending supplies inventory as of March 31, $165.
   (b) Insurance expired (used), $100.
   (c) Depreciation of lawn equipment, $200.
   (d) Wages earned but not paid as of March 31, $180.

2. Complete the work sheet.

P 5-15B   (LO1/3)
✓ Adjustments col. total: $990
✓ Net loss: $1,625

ADJUSTMENTS AND WORK SHEET SHOWING A NET LOSS Val Nolan started a business called Nolan's Home Appraisals. The trial balance as of October 31, after the first month of operations, is as follows:

Nolan's Home Appraisals
Work Sheet
For Month Ended October 31, 20 - -

	ACCOUNT TITLE	TRIAL BALANCE DEBIT	TRIAL BALANCE CREDIT	ADJUSTMENTS DEBIT	ADJUSTMENTS CREDIT	
1	Cash	8 3 0 00				1
2	Accounts Receivable	7 6 0 00				2
3	Supplies	6 2 5 00				3
4	Prepaid Insurance	9 5 0 00				4
5	Automobile	6 5 0 0 00				5
6	Accum. Depr.—Automobile					6
7	Accounts Payable		1 5 0 0 00			7
8	Wages Payable					8
9	Val Nolan, Capital		9 9 0 0 00			9
10	Val Nolan, Drawing	1 1 0 0 00				10
11	Appraisal Fees		3 0 0 0 00			11
12	Wages Expense	1 5 6 0 00				12
13	Advertising Expense	4 2 0 00				13
14	Rent Expense	1 0 5 0 00				14
15	Supplies Expense					15
16	Phone Expense	2 5 5 00				16
17	Insurance Expense					17
18	Repair Expense	2 7 0 00				18
19	Oil and Gas Expense	8 0 00				19
20	Depr. Expense—Automobile					20
21		14 4 0 0 00	14 4 0 0 00			21

REQUIRED

1. Analyze the following adjustments and enter them on the work sheet.
   (a) Supplies inventory as of October 31, $210.
   (b) Unexpired (remaining) insurance as of October 31, $800.
   (c) Depreciation of automobile, $250.
   (d) Wages earned but not paid as of October 31, $175.

2. Complete the work sheet.

P 5-16B (LO2/5)   JOURNALIZE AND POST ADJUSTING ENTRIES FROM THE WORK SHEET Refer to Problem 5-15B and the following additional information:

Account Name	Account Number	Balance in Account Before Adjusting Entry
Supplies	141	$ 625
Prepaid Insurance	145	950
Accum. Depr.—Automobile	185.1	0
Wages Payable	219	0
Wages Expense	511	1,560
Supplies Expense	523	0
Insurance Expense	535	0
Depr. Expense—Automobile	541	0

REQUIRED

1. Journalize the adjusting entries on page 3 of the general journal.
2. Post the adjusting entries to the general ledger. (If you are not using the working papers that accompany this text, enter the balances provided in this problem before posting the adjusting entries.)

P 5-17B (LO4)
✓ Adjustments col. total: $1,640
✓ Net income: $1,405

CORRECTING WORK SHEET WITH ERRORS A beginning accounting student tried to complete a work sheet for Dick Ady's Bookkeeping Service. The following adjusting entries were to have been analyzed and entered in the work sheet:

(a) Ending inventory of supplies on July 31, $130.
(b) Unexpired insurance on July 31, $420.
(c) Depreciation of office equipment, $325.
(d) Wages earned, but not paid as of July 31, $95.

REQUIRED
Review the work sheet shown on page 174 for addition mistakes, transpositions, and other errors and make all necessary corrections.

MANAGING YOUR WRITING

CHECK LIST
☐ Managing
☐ Planning
☐ Drafting
☐ Break
☐ Revising
☐ Managing

Delia Alvarez, owner of Delia's Lawn Service, wants to borrow money to buy new lawn equipment. A local bank has asked for financial statements. Alvarez has asked you to prepare financial statements for the year ended December 31, 20--. You have been given the unadjusted trial balance on page 175 and suspect that Alvarez expects you to base your statements on this information. You are concerned, however, that some of the account balances may need to be adjusted. Write a memo to Alvarez explaining what additional information you need before you can prepare the financial statements. Alvarez is not familiar with accounting issues. Therefore, explain in your memo why you need this information, the potential impact of this information on the financial statements, and the importance of making these adjustments before approaching the bank for a loan.

(continued)

PROBLEM 5-17B

Dick Ady's Bookkeeping Service
Work Sheet
For Month Ended July 31, 20--

	ACCOUNT TITLE	TRIAL BALANCE DEBIT	TRIAL BALANCE CREDIT	ADJUSTMENTS DEBIT	ADJUSTMENTS CREDIT	ADJUSTED TRIAL BALANCE DEBIT	ADJUSTED TRIAL BALANCE CREDIT	INCOME STATEMENT DEBIT	INCOME STATEMENT CREDIT	BALANCE SHEET DEBIT	BALANCE SHEET CREDIT
1	Cash	1 3 6 5 00				1 3 6 5 00				1 3 6 5 00	
2	Accounts Receivable	8 4 5 00				8 4 5 00			8 4 5 00		
3	Supplies	6 2 0 00			(a) 4 9 0 00	1 3 0 00				1 3 0 00	
4	Prepaid Insurance	1 1 5 00			(b) 4 2 0 00	7 3 0 00				7 3 0 00	
5	Office Equipment	6 4 0 0 00			(c) 3 2 5 00	6 7 2 5 00				6 7 2 5 00	
6	Accum. Depr.—Office Equipment										
7	Accounts Payable		7 3 5 00				7 3 5 00				7 3 5 00
8	Wages Payable				(d) 9 5 00		9 5 00				5 9 00
9	Dick Ady, Capital		7 8 0 0 00				7 8 0 0 00				7 8 0 0 00
10	Dick Ady, Drawing	1 2 0 0 00				1 2 0 0 00				1 2 0 0 00	
11	Professional Fees		6 3 5 0 00				6 3 5 0 00		6 3 5 0 00		
12	Wages Expense	1 4 9 5 00		(d) 9 5 00		1 5 9 0 00		1 5 9 0 00			
13	Advertising Expense	3 8 0 00				3 8 0 00		3 8 0 00			
14	Rent Expense	8 5 0 00				8 5 0 00		8 5 0 00			
15	Supplies Expense			(a) 4 9 0 00		4 9 0 00		4 9 0 00			
16	Phone Expense	2 0 5 00				2 0 5 00		2 5 0 00			
17	Utilities Expense	2 8 5 00				2 8 5 00		2 8 5 00			
18	Insurance Expense			(b) 4 2 0 00		4 2 0 00		4 2 0 00			
19	Depr. Expense—Office Equipment			(c) 3 2 5 00		3 2 5 00		3 2 5 00			
20	Miscellaneous Expense	9 0 00				9 0 00		9 0 00			
21		14 8 8 5 00	14 8 8 5 00	1 3 3 0 00	1 3 3 0 00	15 6 3 0 00	14 9 8 0 00	4 8 8 0 00	7 1 9 5 00	10 1 4 1 00	8 5 9 4 00
22	Net Income							2 3 1 5 00			1 5 4 7 00
23								7 1 9 5 00	7 1 9 5 00	10 1 4 1 00	10 1 4 1 00
24											
25											
26											
27											
28											
29											
30											

Contains Errors

Delia's Lawn Service Trial Balance December 31, 20 - -											
ACCOUNT TITLE	**ACCOUNT NO.**	\multicolumn{4}{c}{**DEBIT BALANCE**}				\multicolumn{4}{c}{**CREDIT BALANCE**}
Cash	101		7	7	0	00					
Accounts Receivable	122	1	7	0	0	00					
Supplies	142		2	8	0	00					
Prepaid Insurance	145		4	0	0	00					
Lawn Equipment	183	13	8	0	0	00					
Accounts Payable	202							2	2	0	0	00
Delia Alvarez, Capital	311							3	0	0	0	00
Delia Alvarez, Drawing	312		3	5	0	00					
Lawn Cutting Fees	401						52	4	0	0	00
Wages Expense	511	35	8	5	0	00					
Rent Expense	521	1	2	0	0	00					
Gas and Oil Expense	538	3	2	5	0	00					
		57	6	0	0	00	57	6	0	0	00

MASTERY PROBLEM

✓ **Adjusted Trial Bal. total: $58,500**
✓ **Net income: $13,630**

Kristi Williams offers family counseling services specializing in financial and marital problems. A chart of accounts and a trial balance taken on December 31, 20--, follow.

KRISTI WILLIAMS FAMILY COUNSELING SERVICES CHART OF ACCOUNTS			
Assets		**Revenue**	
101	Cash	401	Client Fees
142	Office Supplies		
145	Prepaid Insurance	**Expenses**	
181	Office Equipment	511	Wages Expense
181.1	Accumulated Depr.—	521	Rent Expense
	Office Equipment	523	Office Supplies Expense
187	Computer Equipment	533	Utilities Expense
187.1	Accumulated Depr.—	535	Insurance Expense
	Computer Equipment	541	Depr. Expense—
Liabilities			Office Equipment
201	Notes Payable	542	Depr. Expense—
202	Accounts Payable		Computer Equipment
		549	Miscellaneous Expense
Owner's Equity			
311	Kristi Williams, Capital		
312	Kristi Williams, Drawing		

(*continued*)

Kristi Williams Family Counseling Services Trial Balance December 31, 20 - -													
ACCOUNT TITLE	ACCOUNT NO.	DEBIT BALANCE					CREDIT BALANCE						
Cash	101	8	7	3	0	00						
Office Supplies	142		7	0	0	00						
Prepaid Insurance	145		6	0	0	00						
Office Equipment	181	18	0	0	0	00						
Computer Equipment	187	6	0	0	0	00						
Notes Payable	201						8	0	0	0	00		
Accounts Payable	202							5	0	0	00		
Kristi Williams, Capital	311						11	4	0	0	00		
Kristi Williams, Drawing	312	3	0	0	0	00						
Client Fees	401						35	8	0	0	00		
Wages Expense	511	9	5	0	0	00						
Rent Expense	521	6	0	0	0	00						
Utilities Expense	533	2	1	7	0	00						
Miscellaneous Expense	549	1	0	0	0	00						
		55	7	0	0	00	55	7	0	0	00		

Information for year-end adjustments is as follows:

(a) Office supplies on hand at year-end amounted to $100.

(b) On January 1, 20--, Williams purchased office equipment that cost $18,000. It has an expected useful life of 10 years and no salvage value.

(c) On July 1, 20--, Williams purchased computer equipment costing $6,000. It has an expected useful life of three years and no salvage value. Assume that Williams computes depreciation to the nearest full month.

(d) On December 1, 20--, Williams paid a premium of $600 for a six-month insurance policy.

REQUIRED

1. Prepare the work sheet for the year ended December 31, 20--.
2. Prepare adjusting entries in a general journal.

CHALLENGE PROBLEM

> This problem challenges you to apply your cumulative accounting knowledge to move a step beyond the material in the chapter.

Your friend, Diane Kiefner, teaches elementary school and operates her own wilderness kayaking tours in the summers. She thinks she has been doing fine financially, but has never really measured her profits. Until this year, her business has always had more money at the end of the summer than at the beginning. She enjoys kayaking and as long as she came out a little ahead, that was fine. Unfortunately, Diane had to dip into her savings to make up for "losses" on her kayaking tours this past summer. Hearing that you have been studying accounting, she brought a list of cash receipts and expenditures and would like you to try to figure out what happened.

Cash balance beginning of summer		$15,000
Cash receipts from kayakers over the summer	$10,000	
Cash expenditures over the summer	13,500	
Amount taken from savings		(3,500)
Cash balance end of summer		$11,500

When asked for more details on the expenditures and the kayaking gear that you saw in her garage, Diane provided the following information:

Expenditures were made on the following items:

Brochures used to advertise her services (Diane only used about 1/4 of them and plans to use the remainder over the next three summers.)	$1,000
Food for trips (nothing left)	2,000
Rent on equipment used by kayakers on trips	3,000
Travel expenses	4,000
A new kayak and paddles (At the beginning of the summer, Diane bought a new kayak and paddles. Up to this time, she had always borrowed her father's. Diane expects to use the equipment for about five years. At that time, she expects it to have no value.)	3,500

A trial balance based on this information follows. As you will note, Diane's trial balance is not consistent with some of the concepts discussed in this chapter.

Diane Kiefner's Wilderness Kayaking Tours
Work Sheet
For Summer Ended 20 - -

	ACCOUNT TITLE	TRIAL BALANCE		ADJUSTMENTS		ADJUSTED TRIAL BALANCE		INCOME STATEMENT		BALANCE SHEET		
		DEBIT	CREDIT	DEBIT	CREDIT	DEBIT	CREDIT	DEBIT	CREDIT	DEBIT	CREDIT	
1	Cash	11 5 0 0 00										1
2	Diane Kiefner, Capital		15 0 0 0 00									2
3	Tour Revenue		10 0 0 0 00									3
4	Advertising Supplies Expense	1 0 0 0 00										4
5	Food Expense	2 0 0 0 00										5
6	Equipment Rental Expense	3 0 0 0 00										6
7	Travel Expense	4 0 0 0 00										7
8	Kayak Expense	3 5 0 0 00										8
9		25 0 0 0 00	25 0 0 0 00									9

REQUIRED

1. Complete Diane's work sheet by making appropriate adjustments and extensions. *Note*: (a) You may need to add new accounts. (b) Some of the adjustments you need to make are actually "corrections of errors" Diane has made in classifying certain items.

2. What is your best measure of Diane's net income for the summer of 20--?

ANSWERS TO SELF-STUDY TEST QUESTIONS

True/False

1. F (match revenues and expenses)
2. F (to bring accounts up to date)
3. T
4. F (depreciable cost = cost − salvage value)
5. F (to match cost of asset against revenues it will help generate)

Multiple Choice

1. a   **2.** c   **3.** d   **4.** c   **5.** a

Checkpoint Exercises

1. Supplies should be reduced (credited) for $30.

2. Adjusting.

3. A. Account Title
   B. Trial Balance
   C. Adjustments
   D. Adjusted Trial Balance
   E. Income Statement
   F. Balance Sheet

4. Errors are highlighted in yellow.

	ACCOUNT TITLE	TRIAL BALANCE		ADJUSTMENTS		ADJUSTED TRIAL BALANCE		INCOME STATEMENT		BALANCE SHEET		
		DEBIT	CREDIT	DEBIT	CREDIT	DEBIT	CREDIT	DEBIT	CREDIT	DEBIT	CREDIT	
1	Cash	3 7 0 00				3 7 0 00				3 7 0 00		1
2	Accounts Receivable	6 5 0 00				6 5 0 00				6 5 0 00		2
3	Supplies	8 0 00			(a) 6 0 00	1 4 0 00				1 4 0 00		3
4	Prepaid Insurance	2 0 0 00			(b) 2 5 00	1 7 5 00				1 7 5 00		4
5	Delivery Equipment	3 6 0 0 00				3 6 0 0 00				3 6 0 0 00		5
6	Accum. Depr.—Delivery Equipment				(d) 1 0 0 00		1 0 0 00				1 0 0 00	6
7	Accounts Payable		1 8 0 0 00				1 8 0 0 00				1 8 0 0 00	7
8	Wages Payable				(c) 5 0 00		5 0 00				5 0 00	8
9	Mitchell Williams, Capital		2 0 0 0 00				2 0 0 0 00				2 0 0 0 00	9
10	Mitchell Williams, Drawing	1 5 0 00				1 5 0 00				1 5 0 00		10
11	Delivery Fees		2 1 5 0 00				2 1 5 0 00		2 1 5 0 00			11
12	Wages Expense	6 5 0 00		(c) 5 0 00		7 0 0 00		7 0 0 00				12
13	Rent Expense	2 0 0 00				2 0 0 00		2 0 0 00				13
14	Supplies Expense			(a) 6 0 00		6 0 00		6 0 00				14
15	Phone Expense	5 0 00				5 0 00		5 0 00				15
16	Insurance Expense			(b) 2 5 00		2 5 00		2 5 00				16
17	Depr. Expense—Delivery Equipment			(d) 1 0 0 00		1 0 0 00		1 0 0 00				17
18		5 9 5 0 00	5 9 5 0 00	2 3 5 00	2 3 5 00	6 2 2 0 00	6 1 0 0 00	1 1 3 5 00	2 1 5 0 00	5 0 8 5 00	3 9 5 0 00	18
19	Net Income							1 0 1 5 00			1 1 3 5 00	19
20								2 1 5 0 00	2 1 5 0 00	5 0 8 5 00	5 0 8 5 00	20
21												21

5.

Adjusting Entry

		Debit	Credit
Dec. 31	Insurance Expense	50.00	
	Prepaid Insurance		50.00

6.

Transaction	Cash Basis	Accrual Basis	Modified Cash Basis
Services on account	$ —	$500	$ —
Payment for legal research assistance	(50)	(50)	(50)
Office supplies used		(10)	(10)
Net Income (Net Loss)	$(50)	$440	$(60)

Depreciation Methods

LEARNING OBJECTIVES

Careful study of this appendix should enable you to:

LO1 Prepare a depreciation schedule using the straight-line method.

LO2 Prepare a depreciation schedule using the sum-of-the-years'-digits method.

LO3 Prepare a depreciation schedule using the double-declining-balance method.

LO4 Prepare a depreciation schedule for tax purposes using the Modified Accelerated Cost Recovery System.

In Chapter 5, we introduced the straight-line method of depreciation. Here, we will review this method and illustrate three others: sum-of-the-years'-digits; double-declining-balance; and, for tax purposes, the Modified Accelerated Cost Recovery System. For all illustrations, we will assume that a delivery van was purchased for $40,000. It has a five-year useful life and salvage value of $4,000.

LO1

Prepare a depreciation schedule using the straight-line method.

Straight-Line Method

Under the straight-line depreciation method, an equal amount of depreciation will be taken each period. First, compute the depreciable cost by subtracting the salvage value from the cost of the asset. This is done because we expect to sell the asset for $4,000 at the end of its useful life. Thus, the total cost to be recognized as an expense over the five years is $36,000, not $40,000.

Cost	–	Salvage Value	=	Depreciable Cost
$40,000	–	$4,000	=	$36,000

Next, we divide the depreciable cost by the expected life of the asset, five years.

$$\text{Depreciation Expense per Year} = \frac{\text{Depreciable Cost}}{\text{Years of Life}}$$

$$\$7{,}200 \text{ per year} = \frac{\$36{,}000}{5 \text{ years}}$$

When preparing a depreciation schedule, it is often convenient to use a depreciation rate per year. In this case, it would be 20% (100% ÷ 5 years of life). Figure 5A-1 shows the depreciation expense, accumulated depreciation, and book value for each of the five years.

FIGURE 5A-1 Depreciation Schedule Using Straight-Line Method

Straight-Line Depreciation Expense

					STRAIGHT-LINE DEPRECIATION		
Year	Depreciable Cost	×	Rate	=	Depreciation Expense	Accumulated Depreciation (End of Year)	Book Value (End of Year)
1	$36,000		20%		$7,200	$ 7,200	$32,800
2	36,000		20%		7,200	14,400	25,600
3	36,000		20%		7,200	21,600	18,400
4	36,000		20%		7,200	28,800	11,200
5	36,000		20%		7,200	36,000	4,000

Cost	$40,000		100%		Same amount each year	Accum. Depr. increases by the same amount each year, $7,200.	Cost
− Salvage Value	4,000		5 Years				− Accum. Depr.
Depreciable Cost	$36,000		= 20%				Book Value

LO2

Sum-of-the-Years'-Digits

Prepare a depreciation schedule using the sum-of-the-years'-digits method.

Under the sum-of-the-years'-digits depreciation method, depreciation is determined by multiplying the depreciable cost by a schedule of fractions. The numerator of the fraction for a specific year is the number of years of remaining useful life for the asset, measured from the beginning of the year. The denominator for all fractions is determined by adding the digits that represent the years of the estimated life of the asset. The calculation of the sum-of-the-years'-digits for our delivery van with a five-year useful life is shown below.

Sum-of-the-Years'-Digits = 5 + 4 + 3 + 2 + 1 = 15

A depreciation schedule using these fractions is shown in Figure 5A-2.

FIGURE 5A-2 Depreciation Schedule Using Sum-of-the-Years'-Digits Method

Sum-of-the-Years'-Digits Depreciation Expense

					SUM-OF-THE-YEARS'-DIGITS		
Year	Depreciable Cost	×	Rate	=	Depreciation Expense	Accumulated Depreciation (End of Year)	Book Value (End of Year)
1	$36,000		5/15		$12,000	$12,000	$28,000
2	36,000		4/15		9,600	21,600	18,400
3	36,000		3/15		7,200	28,800	11,200
4	36,000		2/15		4,800	33,600	6,400
5	36,000		1/15		2,400	36,000	4,000

Cost	$40,000		Remaining life from beginning of period		Expense gets smaller each year	Accum. Depr. increases by amount of current year's depreciation expense.	Cost
− Salvage Value	4,000						− Accum. Depr.
Depreciable Cost	$36,000		SYD				Book Value

LO3

Double-Declining-Balance Method

Prepare a depreciation schedule using the double-declining-balance method.

Under the double-declining-balance depreciation method, the book value is multiplied by a fixed rate, often double the straight-line rate. The van has a five-year life, so the straight-line rate is $1 \div 5$, or 20%. Double the straight-line rate is $2 \times 20\%$, or 40%. The double-declining-balance depreciation schedule is shown in Figure 5A-3. Note that the rate is applied to the book value of the asset. Once the book value is reduced to the expected salvage value, $4,000, no more depreciation may be recognized.

FIGURE 5A-3 Depreciation Schedule Using Double-Declining-Balance Method

	DOUBLE-DECLINING-BALANCE METHOD					
Year	Book Value (Beginning of Year)	× Rate	=	Depreciation Expense	Accumulated Depreciation (End of Year)	Book Value (End of Year)
1	$40,000	40%		$16,000	$16,000	$24,000
2	24,000	40%		9,600	25,600	14,400
3	14,400	40%		5,760	31,360	8,640
4	8,640	40%		3,456	34,816	5,184
5	5,184			1,184	36,000	4,000

Cost
– Accum. Depr.
Book Value

Double the Straight Line
Rate 1/5 x 2
= 2/5 = 40%

LEARNING KEY 🔑

Double means double the straight-line rate. Declining-balance means that the rate is multiplied by the book value (not depreciable cost) at the beginning of each year. This amount is declining each year.

LO4

Prepare a depreciation schedule for tax purposes using the Modified Accelerated Cost Recovery System.

Modified Accelerated Cost Recovery System

For assets purchased since 1986, many firms use the Modified Accelerated Cost Recovery System (MACRS) for tax purposes. Under this method, the Internal Revenue Service (IRS) classifies various assets according to useful life and sets depreciation rates for each year of the asset's life. These rates are then multiplied by the cost of the asset. Even though the van is expected to have a useful life of five years, and a salvage value of $4,000, the IRS schedule, shown in Figure 5A-4, spreads the depreciation over a six-year period and assumes no salvage value.

FIGURE 5A-4 Depreciation Schedule Using Modified Accelerated Cost Recovery System

	MODIFIED ACCELERATED COST RECOVERY SYSTEM					
Year	Cost	× Rate	=	Depreciation Expense	Accumulated Depreciation (End of Year)	Book Value (End of Year)
1	$40,000	20.00%		$ 8,000	$ 8,000	$32,000
2	40,000	32.00%		12,800	20,800	19,200
3	40,000	19.20%		7,680	28,480	11,520
4	40,000	11.52%		4,608	33,088	6,912
5	40,000	11.52%		4,608	37,696	2,304
6	40,000	5.76%		2,304	40,000	0

Rate set by
IRS

Cost
–Accum. Depr.
Book Value

LEARNING OBJECTIVES	Key Points to Remember
LO1 **Prepare a depreciation schedule using the straight-line method.**	Under straight-line depreciation, an equal amount of depreciation is taken each period. Depreciation expense for each year is computed as follows: Cost − Salvage Value $=$ Depreciable Cost/Expected Years of Life $=$ Depreciation Expense per Year
LO2 **Prepare a depreciation schedule using the sum-of-the-years'-digits method.**	Under the sum-of-the-years'-digits method, the depreciable cost is multiplied by a fraction. The fraction consists of the following: $$\frac{\text{Remaining Years of Life Measured from the Beginning of the Current Year}}{\text{Sum-of-the-Years'-Digits}}$$ If an asset has a life of three years, the sum-of-the-years'-digits is equal to: $$3+2+1=6$$ Depreciation would be computed as follows: Year 1: 3/6 × Depreciable Cost Year 2: 2/6 × Depreciable Cost Year 3: 1/6 × Depreciable Cost
LO3 **Prepare a depreciation schedule using the double-declining-balance method.**	Under this method, the book value (the declining balance) is multiplied by a fixed rate, often double the straight-line rate.
LO4 **Prepare a deprecia-tion schedule for tax purposes using the Modified Accelerated Cost Recovery System.**	Under this method, the IRS provides the depreciation rates to be applied to the cost of the asset. Simply multiply the rate provided by the IRS by the cost of the asset.

KEY TERMS

double-declining-balance depreciation method (181)   A depreciation method that recognizes depreciation each year by multiplying a rate (typically double the straight-line rate) by the book value of the asset.

Modified Accelerated Cost Recovery System (MACRS) (181)   A depreciation method in which rates determined by the IRS are multiplied by the cost of the asset to determine depreciation expense for the year.

straight-line depreciation method (179)   A depreciation method that recognizes an equal amount of depreciation each year.

sum-of-the-years'-digits (180)   If an asset has a five-year life, the sum-of-the-years'-digits is computed as follows: 5+4+3+2+1 =15.

sum-of-the-years'-digits depreciation method (180)   A depreciation method that recognizes depreciation each year by multiplying a fraction by the depreciable cost. The numerator of the fraction is the remaining life of the asset, measured from the beginning of the year. The denominator is the sum-of-the-years'-digits.

REVIEW QUESTIONS

1. List three depreciation methods used for financial reporting.

2. Which depreciation method is used for tax purposes?

SERIES A EXERCISES

E 5Apx-1A   (LO1)
✓ Accum. depr. end of Yr. 2: $10,000

STRAIGHT-LINE DEPRECIATION A small delivery truck was purchased on January 1 at a cost of $25,000. It has an estimated useful life of four years and an estimated salvage value of $5,000. Prepare a depreciation schedule showing the depreciation expense, accumulated depreciation, and book value for each year under the straight-line method.

E 5Apx-2A   (LO2)
✓ Accum. depr. end of Yr. 2: $14,000

SUM-OF-THE-YEARS'-DIGITS DEPRECIATION Using the information given in Exercise 5Apx-1A, prepare a depreciation schedule showing the depreciation expense, accumulated depreciation, and book value for each year under the sum-of-the-years'-digits method.

E 5Apx-3A   (LO3)
✓ Accum. depr. end of Yr. 2: $18,750

DOUBLE-DECLINING-BALANCE DEPRECIATION Using the information given in Exercise 5Apx-1A, prepare a depreciation schedule showing the depreciation expense, accumulated depreciation, and book value for each year under the double-declining-balance method.

E 5Apx-4A   (LO4)
✓ Accum. depr. end of Yr. 2: $13,000

MODIFIED ACCELERATED COST RECOVERY SYSTEM Using the information given in Exercise 5Apx-1A and the rates shown in Figure 5A-4, prepare a depreciation schedule showing the depreciation expense, accumulated depreciation, and book value for each year under the Modified Accelerated Cost Recovery System. For tax purposes, assume that the truck has a useful life of five years. (The IRS schedule will spread depreciation over six years.)

SERIES B EXERCISES

E 5Apx-1B   (LO1)
✓ Accum. depr. end of Yr. 2: $1,800

STRAIGHT-LINE DEPRECIATION A computer was purchased on January 1 at a cost of $5,000. It has an estimated useful life of five years and an estimated salvage value of $500. Prepare a depreciation schedule showing the depreciation expense, accumulated depreciation, and book value for each year under the straight-line method.

E 5Apx-2B   (LO2)
✓ Accum. depr. end of Yr. 2: $2,700

SUM-OF-THE-YEARS'-DIGITS DEPRECIATION Using the information given in Exercise 5Apx-1B, prepare a depreciation schedule showing the depreciation expense, accumulated depreciation, and book value for each year under the sum-of-the-years'-digits method.

E 5Apx-3B   (LO3)
✓ Accum. depr. end of Yr. 2: $3,200

DOUBLE-DECLINING-BALANCE DEPRECIATION Using the information given in Exercise 5Apx-1B, prepare a depreciation schedule showing the depreciation expense, accumulated depreciation, and book value for each year under the double-declining-balance method.

E 5Apx-4B   (LO4)
✓ Accum. depr. end of Yr. 2: $2,600

MODIFIED ACCELERATED COST RECOVERY SYSTEM Using the information given in Exercise 5Apx-1B and the rates shown in Figure 5A-4, prepare a depreciation schedule showing the depreciation expense, accumulated depreciation, and book value for each year under the Modified Accelerated Cost Recovery System. For tax purposes, assume that the computer has a useful life of five years. (The IRS schedule will spread depreciation over six years.)

Chapter 6 Financial Statements and the Closing Process

LEARNING OBJECTIVES

Careful study of this chapter should enable you to:

LO1 Prepare financial statements with the aid of a work sheet.

LO2 Journalize and post closing entries.

LO3 Prepare a post-closing trial balance.

LO4 List and describe the steps in the accounting cycle.

Indy Express Band is central Indiana's premier variety band. It offers a popular mix of musical styles from Top 40 to Big Band. The eight-piece band is led by Greg Imboden, fronted by Cozette Myers, driven by a three-piece horn section, and backed by a tight rhythm section. The **Indy Express Band** is perfect for a wedding reception, corporate function, conference event, dinner dance, or charity ball. Members of **Indy Express Band** have provided music for entertainers such as Jay Leno, Rod Stewart, Natalie Cole, Dionne Warwick, and Al Jarreau.

In addition to playing at weddings and other events, the band generally performs on New Year's Eve, the same day many businesses prepare closing entries. In this chapter, we complete the accounting cycle by demonstrating how to make closing entries and prepare the post-closing trial balance.

The work sheet, introduced in Chapter 5, is used for three major end-of-period activities:

1. journalizing adjusting entries,

2. preparing financial statements, and

3. journalizing closing entries.

This chapter illustrates the use of the work sheet for preparing financial statements and closing entries. In addition, the post-closing trial balance is explained and illustrated. All of these activities take place at the end of the firm's fiscal year. However, to continue our illustration of Mitchell's Campus Delivery, we demonstrate these activities at the end of the first month of operations.

LO1	The Financial Statements

Prepare financial statements with the aid of a work sheet.

The work sheet prepared in Chapter 5 supplies most of the information needed to prepare an income statement, a statement of owner's equity, and a balance sheet. The statements and work sheet columns from which they are derived for Mitchell's Campus Delivery are shown in Figures 6-1 and 6-2.

As you refer to the financial statements in Figures 6-1 and 6-2, notice the placement of dollar signs, single rulings, and double rulings. Dollar signs are placed at the top of each column and beneath rulings. Single rulings indicate addition or subtraction, and double rulings are placed under totals. Notice that each statement heading contains three lines: (1) company name, (2) statement title, and (3) period ended or date.

The Income Statement

> Multiple columns are used on the financial statements to make them easier to read. There are no debit or credit columns on the financial statements.

Figure 6-1 shows how the Income Statement columns of the work sheet provide the information needed to prepare an income statement. Revenue is shown first, followed by an itemized and totaled list of expenses. Then, net income is calculated to double check the accuracy of the work sheet. It is presented with a double ruling as the last item in the statement.

The expenses could be listed in the same order that they appear in the chart of accounts or in descending order by dollar amount. The second approach helps the reader identify the most important expenses.

The Statement of Owner's Equity

> LEARNING KEY 🔑
>
> The owner's capital account in the general ledger must be reviewed to determine if additional investments were made during the accounting period.

The Balance Sheet columns of the work sheet provide most of the information needed to prepare a statement of owner's equity. Figure 6-2 shows that Mitchell's capital account balance and the drawing account balance are in the Balance Sheet columns. Be careful, however, when using the capital account balance reported on the work sheet. This account balance is the beginning balance *plus any investments made during the period*. Recall that Mitchell's beginning capital balance was zero. During June, he made an investment of $5,000. Thus, as reported previously, the beginning balance on the statement of owner's equity must be zero with the $5,000 reported as an investment during June. The net income for the month can be found either on

FIGURE 6-1 Linkages Between the Work Sheet and Income Statement

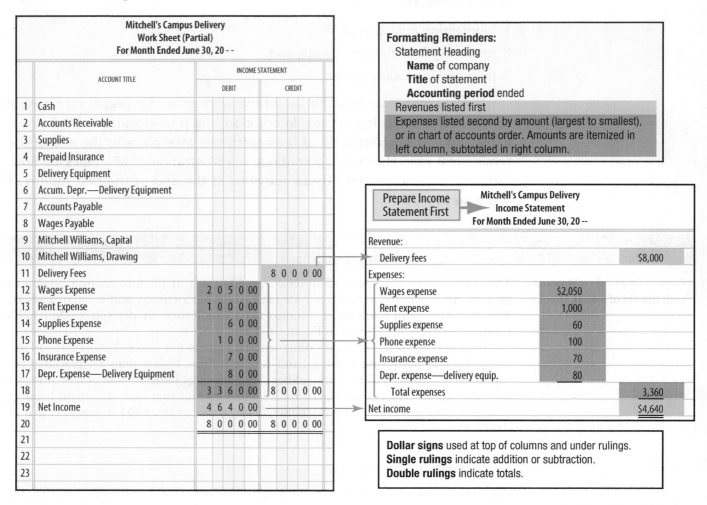

the work sheet at the bottom of the Income Statement (see Figure 6-1) and Balance Sheet columns or on the income statement itself. With these items of information, the statement of owner's equity can be prepared.

The Balance Sheet

As shown in Figure 6-2, the work sheet and the statement of owner's equity are used to prepare Mitchell's balance sheet. The asset and liability amounts can be found in the Balance Sheet columns of the work sheet. The ending balance in Mitchell Williams Capital has been computed on the statement of owner's equity. This amount should be copied from the statement of owner's equity to the balance sheet.

Two important features of the balance sheet in Figure 6-2 should be noted. First, it is a report form of balance sheet, which means that the liabilities and owner's equity sections are shown below the assets section. It differs from an account form of balance sheet in which the assets are on the left and the liabilities and owner's equity sections are on the right. (See Mitchell's balance sheet illustrated in Figure 2-2 on page 33 in Chapter 2.)

Second, it is a classified balance sheet, which means that similar items are grouped together on the balance sheet. Assets are classified as current assets and property, plant, and equipment. Similarly, liabilities are broken down into current and long-term sections. The following major balance sheet classifications are generally used.

FIGURE 6-2 Linkages Between the Work Sheet, Statement of Owner's Equity, and Balance Sheet

Statement Heading
 Name of company
 Title of statement
 Date for BS and accounting period ended for SOE
Current assets: cash and items that will be converted to cash or consumed within a year.
Property, plant, and equipment: durable assets that will help produce revenues for several years.
Current liabilities: amounts owed that will be paid within a year (will require the use of current assets).

Note: The statement of owner's equity is prepared before the balance sheet. The S.O.E. is shown below the B.S. to enhance the illustration of the linkages between the work sheet and financial statements.

Mitchell's Campus Delivery
Work Sheet (Partial)
For Month Ended June 30, 20 - -

	ACCOUNT TITLE	BALANCE SHEET DEBIT	BALANCE SHEET CREDIT
1	Cash	4 7 0 00	
2	Accounts Receivable	3 1 0 0 00	
3	Supplies	2 0 00	
4	Prepaid Insurance	6 3 0 00	
5	Delivery Equipment	4 8 0 0 00	
6	Accum. Depr.—Delivery Equip.		8 0 00
7	Accounts Payable		1 9 0 0 00
8	Wages Payable		4 0 0 00
9	Mitchell Williams, Capital		5 0 0 0 00
10	Mitchell Williams, Drawing	3 0 0 0 00	
11	Delivery Fees		
12	Wages Expense		
13	Rent Expense		
14	Supplies Expense		
15	Phone Expense		
16	Insurance Expense		
17	Depr. Expense—Delivery Equip.		
18		12 0 2 0 00	7 3 8 0 00
19	Net Income		4 6 4 0 00
20		12 0 2 0 00	12 0 2 0 00
21			

Prepare BS Third

Mitchell's Campus Delivery
Balance Sheet
June 30, 20 --

Assets
Current assets:
Cash	$ 470	
Accounts receivable	3,100	
Supplies	20	
Prepaid insurance	630	
Total current assets		$4,220

Property, plant, and equipment:
Delivery equipment	$4,800	
Less accumulated depreciation	80	4,720
Total assets		$8,940

Liabilities
Current liabilities:
Accounts payable	$1,900	
Wages payable	400	
Total current liabilities		$2,300

Owner's Equity
| Mitchell Williams, capital | | 6,640 |
| Total liabilities and owner's equity | | $8,940 |

Prepare SOE Second

Mitchell's Campus Delivery
Statement of Owner's Equity
For Month Ended June 30, 20 --

Mitchell Williams, capital, June 1, 20--		$ —
Investments during June		5,000
Total investment		$5,000
Net income for June	$4,640	
Less: withdrawals for June	3,000	
Increase in capital		1,640
Mitchell Williams, capital, June 30, 20--		$6,640

Ending capital is not taken from the work sheet. It is computed on the statement of owner's equity.
Dollar signs used at top of columns and under rulings.
Single rulings indicate addition or subtraction.
Double rulings indicate totals.

Current Assets

Current assets include cash and assets that will be converted into cash or consumed within either one year or the normal operating cycle of the business, whichever is longer. Examples include cash, accounts receivable, supplies, and prepaid insurance. As shown in Figure 6-3, an operating cycle is the period of time required to purchase supplies and services and convert them back into cash.

FIGURE 6-3 Operating Cycle

Operating Cycle for a Service Business

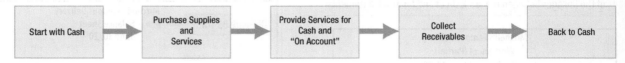

Property, Plant, and Equipment

Property, plant, and equipment, also called plant assets or long-term assets, represent assets that are expected to serve the business for many years. Examples include land, buildings, and equipment.

Current Liabilities

Current liabilities are due within either one year or the normal operating cycle of the business, whichever is longer. They will be paid out of current assets. Accounts payable and wages payable are classified as current liabilities.

Long-Term Liabilities

Long-term liabilities, or long-term debt, are obligations that are not expected to be paid within a year and do not require the use of current assets. A mortgage on an office building is an example of a long-term liability. Mitch has no long-term debts. If he did, they would be listed on the balance sheet in the long-term liabilities section immediately following the current liabilities.

Additional Investments by the Owner (Revisited)

If the owner of a business made additional investments during the accounting period, the owner's capital reported in the Balance Sheet columns of the work sheet represents the beginning balance plus any additional investments made during the accounting period. Thus, it may not represent the beginning balance of the capital account and should not be used to prepare the statements. If this amount were used as the beginning balance on the statement of owner's equity, it would not equal the ending balance from last period and would create confusion for those comparing the two statements. In addition, the statement would not reflect all of the activities affecting the owner's capital account during the period.

Therefore, we must also review the owner's capital account in the general ledger to get the information needed to prepare the statement of owner's equity. Figure 6-4 illustrates this situation for another business, Ramon's Shopping Service. The $5,000 balance of July 1, 20--, in Ramon Balboa's general ledger capital account is used as the beginning balance on the statement of owner's equity. Note that this is also the ending balance on June 30, 20--. The additional investment of $3,000 made on July 5 and posted to Balboa's general ledger capital account is reported by writing "Investments during period" on the line immediately after the beginning balance. The beginning balance plus investments during the period equals the total investment by the owner in the business and is the amount reported in the Balance Sheet columns of the work sheet. From this point, the preparation of the statement is the same as for businesses without additional investments.

FIGURE 6-4 Statement of Owner's Equity with Additional Investment

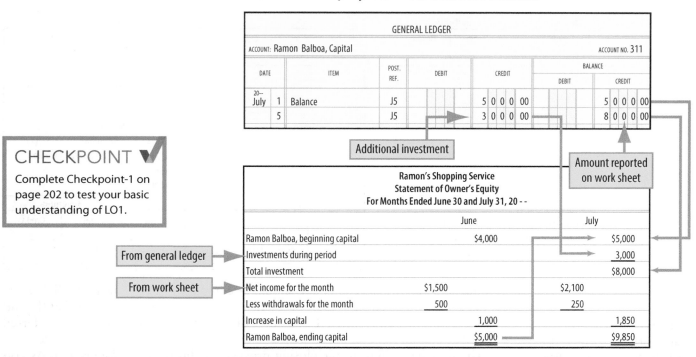

CHECKPOINT ✔

Complete Checkpoint-1 on page 202 to test your basic understanding of LO1.

LO2

Journalize and post closing entries.

> **LEARNING KEY** 🔑
>
> Permanent accounts contain the results of all transactions since the business started. Their balances are carried forward to each new accounting period.

> **LEARNING KEY** 🔑
>
> Temporary accounts contain information for one accounting period. These accounts are closed at the end of each accounting period.

The Closing Process

Assets, liabilities, and the owner's capital account accumulate information across accounting periods. For example, the cash balance at the end of one accounting period must be the same as the cash balance at the beginning of the next period. Thus, the balance reported for Cash is a result of all cash transactions since the business first opened. This is true for all accounts reported on the balance sheet. For this reason, they are called **permanent accounts**.

Revenue, expense, and drawing accounts accumulate information *for only a specific accounting period.* When preparing the financial statements, only revenues, expenses, and withdrawals for *this year* should be reported. Revenues, expenses, and withdrawals from prior years should not be included in *this year's* financial statements. Similarly, *this year's* revenues, expenses, and withdrawals should not be included in next year's financial statements. Thus, at the end of the fiscal year, these accounts must be *closed.* The **closing process** gives these accounts zero balances so they are prepared to accumulate new information for the next accounting period. Since these accounts are closed at the end of each period, they are called **temporary accounts**.

The accounting records are closed "as of" December 31, or another fiscal year-end chosen by the business. The actual adjusting entries, closing entries, and financial statements are generally prepared several weeks after the official closing date. However, it is important to include all transactions occurring prior to year-end in the *current* year's financial statements. Similarly, transactions taking place after year-end must be included in the *next* year's financial statements. Improper timing of the recognition of transactions taking place around the end of the year can have major effects on the reported profits. For example, some businesses have been found to "leave the books open" for a few days to include a major sale, or other profitable transactions, that actually took place after the end of the fiscal year. Thus, proper treatment of transactions taking place around the end of the year is carefully monitored by auditors.

The closing process is most clearly demonstrated by returning to the accounting equation and T accounts. As shown in Figure 6-5, revenue, expense, and drawing

FIGURE 6-5 The Closing Process

accounts impact owner's equity and should be considered "under the umbrella" of the capital account. The effect of these accounts on owner's equity is formalized at the end of the accounting period when the balances of the temporary accounts are transferred to the owner's capital account (a permanent account) during the closing process.

The four basic steps in the closing process are illustrated in Figure 6-5. As you can see, a new account, Income Summary, is used in the closing process. This account may also be called *Expense and Revenue Summary*. This temporary account is used to close the revenue and expense accounts. After closing the revenues and expenses to Income Summary, the balance of this account is equal to the net income. This is why it is called Income Summary. Income Summary is opened during the closing process. Then it is closed to the owner's capital account. It does not appear on any financial statement. The four steps in the closing process are explained below.

Steps in the Closing Process

STEP 1   Close Revenue Accounts to Income Summary. Revenues have credit balances and increase owner's equity. Therefore, the revenue account is debited to create a zero balance. Income Summary is credited for the same amount.

STEP 2   Close Expense Accounts to Income Summary. Expenses have debit balances and reduce owner's equity. Therefore, the expense accounts are credited to create a zero balance. Income Summary must be debited for the total of the expenses.

STEP 3   Close Income Summary to the Owner's Capital Account. The balance in Income Summary represents the net income (credit balance) or net loss (debit balance). If net income has been earned, Income Summary is debited to create a zero balance, and the owner's capital account is credited. If a net loss has been incurred, the owner's capital account is debited and Income Summary is credited to create a zero balance. Figure 6-6 shows examples for closing net income and net loss.

STEP 4   Close Drawing to the Owner's Capital Account. Drawing has a debit balance and reduces owner's equity. Therefore, it is credited to create a zero balance. The owner's capital account is debited.

Upon completion of these four steps, all temporary accounts have zero balances. The earnings and withdrawals for the period have been transferred to the owner's capital account. Closing entries for Mitchell's Campus Delivery, in T account form, are illustrated in Figure 6-7.

The Income Summary account is not really needed for the closing process. Revenue and expense accounts can be closed directly to the owner's capital account. One benefit of using the Income Summary account is that its balance before closing to the capital account equals the net income or net loss for the period. Thus, it can serve as a check of the accuracy of the closing entries for revenues and expenses.

LEARNING KEY

The owner can make withdrawals from the business at any time, as long as the assets are available. These withdrawals have nothing to do with measuring the profitability of the firm. Thus, they are closed directly to the owner's capital account.

FIGURE 6-6 Step 3: Closing Net Income and Closing Net Loss

NET INCOME			
Capital			
	1,000		STEP 3
			(Net Income)
Income Summary			
(Expenses)	4,000	5,000	(Revenues)
STEP 3 to close	1,000	1,000	(Bal. before closing)
	—	—	

NET LOSS			
Capital			
STEP 3	2,000		
(Net Loss)			
Income Summary			
(Expenses)	6,000	4,000	(Revenues)
(Bal. before closing)	2,000	2,000	STEP 3 to close
	—	—	

Dashes (—) in the T Accounts indicate zero balances

FIGURE 6-7 Closing Entries in T Account Form

Dashes (—) in the T Accounts indicate zero balances

Journalize Closing Entries

Of course, to actually change the ledger accounts, the closing entries must be journalized and posted to the general ledger. As shown in Figure 6-8, the balances of the accounts to be closed are readily available from the Income Statement and Balance Sheet columns of the work sheet. These balances are used to illustrate the closing entries for Mitchell's Campus Delivery, in general journal form. Remember: Closing entries are made at the end of the *fiscal year*. Closing entries made at the end of June are illustrated here so you can see the completion of the accounting cycle for Mitchell's Campus Delivery. Like adjusting entries, the closing entries are made on the last day of the accounting period. "Closing Entries" is written in the Description column before the first entry and no explanations are required. Note that it is best to make one compound entry to close the expense accounts.

Post the Closing Entries

> Computer programs post the closing entries to the owner's capital account automatically.

The account numbers have been entered in the Posting Reference column of the journal to show that the entries have been posted to the ledger accounts illustrated in Figure 6-9. Note that "Closing" has been written in the Item column of each account to identify the closing entries. Zero account balances are recorded by entering dashes in both the Balance Debit and Credit columns.

FIGURE 6-8 Closing Entries in Journal Form

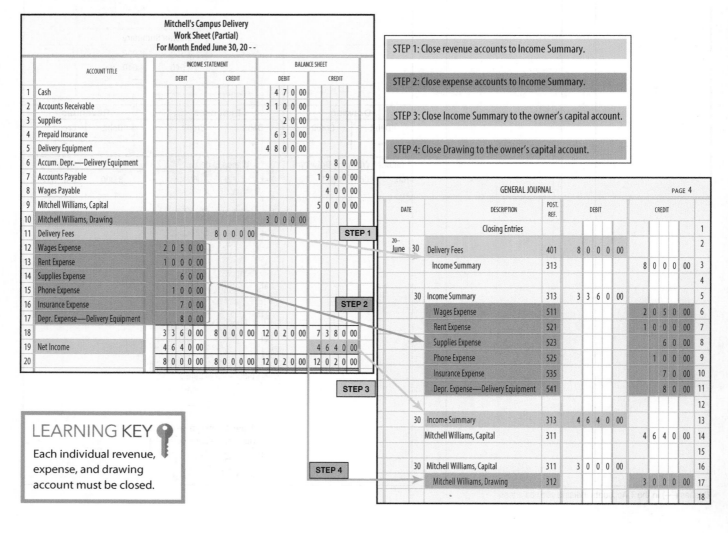

LEARNING KEY

Each individual revenue, expense, and drawing account must be closed.

YOUR PERSPECTIVE

Bookkeeping, Accounting, and Auditing Clerks

Bookkeeping clerks are responsible for maintaining an organization's general ledger, recording transactions, and posting debits and credits. They produce the organization's financial statements, prepare bank deposits, and confirm account reconciliations. Other duties may include handling payroll, purchasing, and invoicing, and tracking overdue accounts. Accounting clerks, typically found in larger organizations, perform specialized duties

and have titles such as accounts payable or accounts receivable clerk, which reflect the type of work they do. Auditing clerks check the accuracy of figures, posted transactions, and accounting reports. If small errors are found, the auditing clerk may make the corrections. However, in the case of major errors, senior management would be informed.

These jobs are extremely important because the financial information maintained is reported in the organization's financial statements. The information must be prepared accurately and in a timely manner because it is used to make critical business decisions.

FIGURE 6-9 Closing Entries Posted to the General Ledger

(continued)

FIGURE 6-9 Closing Entries Posted to the General Ledger (*concluded*)

ACCOUNT: Wages Expense — ACCOUNT NO. 511

DATE		ITEM	POST. REF.	DEBIT	CREDIT	BALANCE DEBIT	BALANCE CREDIT
20-- June	27		J2	1 6 5 0 00		1 6 5 0 00	
	30	Adjusting	J3	4 0 0 00		2 0 5 0 00	
	30	Closing	J4		2 0 5 0 00		

ACCOUNT: Rent Expense — ACCOUNT NO. 521

DATE		ITEM	POST. REF.	DEBIT	CREDIT	BALANCE DEBIT	BALANCE CREDIT
20-- June	7		J1	1 0 0 0 00		1 0 0 0 00	
	30	Closing	J4		1 0 0 0 00		

ACCOUNT: Supplies Expense — ACCOUNT NO. 523

DATE		ITEM	POST. REF.	DEBIT	CREDIT	BALANCE DEBIT	BALANCE CREDIT
20-- June	30	Adjusting	J3	6 0 00		6 0 00	
	30	Closing	J4		6 0 00		

ACCOUNT: Phone Expense — ACCOUNT NO. 525

DATE		ITEM	POST. REF.	DEBIT	CREDIT	BALANCE DEBIT	BALANCE CREDIT
20-- June	15		J1	1 0 0 00		1 0 0 00	
	30	Closing	J4		1 0 0 00		

ACCOUNT: Insurance Expense — ACCOUNT NO. 535

DATE		ITEM	POST. REF.	DEBIT	CREDIT	BALANCE DEBIT	BALANCE CREDIT
20-- June	30	Adjusting	J3	7 0 00		7 0 00	
	30	Closing	J4		7 0 00		

ACCOUNT: Depreciation Expense—Delivery Equipment — ACCOUNT NO. 541

DATE		ITEM	POST. REF.	DEBIT	CREDIT	BALANCE DEBIT	BALANCE CREDIT
20-- June	30	Adjusting	J3	8 0 00		8 0 00	
	30	Closing	J4		8 0 00		

CHECKPOINT ✓

Complete Checkpoint-2 on page 202 to test your basic understanding of LO2.

LO3   **Post-Closing Trial Balance**

Prepare a post-closing trial balance.

After posting the closing entries, a post-closing trial balance should be prepared to prove the equality of the debit and credit balances in the general ledger accounts. The ending balance of each general ledger account that remains open at the end of the year is listed. Remember: Only the permanent accounts remain open after the closing process is completed. Figure 6-10 shows the post-closing trial balance for Mitchell's ledger.

Note that all amounts reflected on the post-closing trial balance are the same as reported in the Balance Sheet columns of the work sheet except Drawing and Owner's Capital. Drawing was closed. Owner's Capital was updated to reflect revenues, expenses, and drawing for the accounting period.

LEARNING KEY 🔑

Once the closing entries are posted, the general ledger capital account balance will agree with the amount reported on the balance sheet.

CHECKPOINT ✔

Complete Checkpoint-3 on page 202 to test your basic understanding of LO3.

FIGURE 6-10 Post-Closing Trial Balance

ACCOUNT TITLE	ACCOUNT NO.	DEBIT BALANCE					CREDIT BALANCE				
Mitchell's Campus Delivery Post-Closing Trial Balance June 30, 20 - -											
Cash	101		4	7	0	00					
Accounts Receivable	122	3	1	0	0	00					
Supplies	141			2	0	00					
Prepaid Insurance	145		6	3	0	00					
Delivery Equipment	185	4	8	0	0	00					
Accumulated Depreciation—Delivery Equipment	185.1								8	0	00
Accounts Payable	202						1	9	0	0	00
Wages Payable	219							4	0	0	00
Mitchell Williams, Capital	311						6	6	4	0	00
		9	0	2	0	00	9	0	2	0	00

A BROADER VIEW

Importance of Earnings to the Stock Market

Investors in the stock market pay close attention to earnings reported on the income statement. If earnings are different from what investors are expecting, the price of the stock may go up or down. For example, AT&T's share prices dipped simply because they missed expected earnings by a penny per share.

LO4   The Accounting Cycle

List and describe the steps in the accounting cycle.

The steps involved in accounting for all of the business activities during an accounting period are called the accounting cycle. The cycle begins with the analysis of source documents and ends with a post-closing trial balance. A brief summary of the steps in the cycle follows.

Steps in the Accounting Cycle

During Accounting Period

LEARNING KEY 🔑

Properly analyzing and journalizing transactions is very important. A mistake made in step 1 is carried through the entire accounting cycle.

STEP 1   Analyze source documents.

STEP 2   Journalize the transactions.

STEP 3   Post to the general ledger accounts.

End of Accounting Period

STEP 4   Prepare a trial balance.

STEP 5   Determine and prepare the needed adjustments on the work sheet.

STEP 6   Complete an end-of-period work sheet.

STEP 7   Journalize and post the adjusting entries.

STEP 8   Prepare an income statement, a statement of owner's equity, and a balance sheet.

STEP 9   Journalize and post the closing entries.

STEP 10   Prepare a post-closing trial balance.

Steps 4 through 10 in the preceding list are performed *as of* the last day of the accounting period. This does not mean that they are actually done on the last day. The accountant may not be able to do any of these things until the first few days (sometimes weeks) of the next period. Nevertheless, the work sheet, statements, and entries are prepared as of the closing date.

SELF-STUDY

LEARNING OBJECTIVES	Key Points to Remember
LO1 **Prepare financial statements with the aid of a work sheet.**	The work sheet is used as an aid in preparing 1. adjusting entries, 2. financial statements, and 3. closing entries. The following classifications are used for accounts reported on the balance sheet. • *Current assets* include cash and assets that will be converted into cash or consumed within either one year or the normal operating cycle of the business, whichever is longer. An *operating cycle* is the time required to purchase supplies and services and convert them back into cash. • *Property, plant, and equipment*, also called *plant assets* or *long-term assets*, represent assets that are expected to serve the business for many years. • *Current liabilities* are liabilities that are due within either one year or the normal operating cycle of the business, whichever is longer, and that are to be paid out of current assets. • *Long-term liabilities*, or *long-term debt*, are obligations that are not expected to be paid within a year and do not require the use of current assets.
LO2 **Journalize and post closing entries.**	Steps in the closing process are: 1. Close revenue accounts to Income Summary. 2. Close expense accounts to Income Summary. 3. Close Income Summary to the owner's capital account. 4. Close Drawing to the owner's capital account.

(continued)

LEARNING OBJECTIVES **Key Points to Remember**

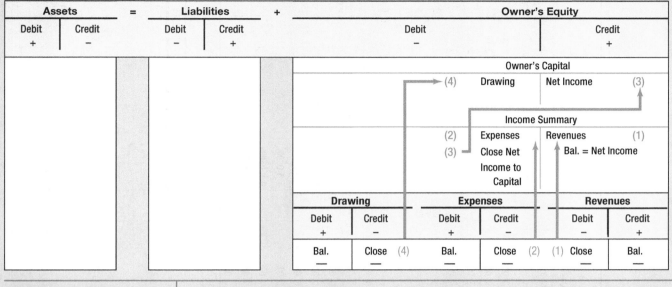

LO3 Prepare a post-closing trial balance.

After posting the closing entries, a post-closing trial balance should be prepared to prove the equality of the debit and credit balances in the general ledger accounts. The accounts shown in the post-closing trial balance are the permanent accounts.

LO4 List and describe the steps in the accounting cycle.

Steps in the accounting cycle are:

During Accounting Period

1. Analyze source documents.
2. Journalize the transactions.
3. Post to the general ledger accounts.

End of Accounting Period

4. Prepare a trial balance.
5. Determine and prepare the needed adjustments on the work sheet.
6. Complete an end-of-period work sheet.
7. Journalize and post the adjusting entries.
8. Prepare an income statement, a statement of owner's equity, and a balance sheet.
9. Journalize and post the closing entries.
10. Prepare a post-closing trial balance.

DEMONSTRATION PROBLEM

Timothy Chang owns and operates Hard Copy Printers. A work sheet for the year ended December 31, 20--, is provided on the next page. Chang made no additional investments during the year.

REQUIRED

1. Prepare financial statements.
2. Prepare closing entries.

Hard Copy Printers
Work Sheet
For Year Ended December 31, 20--

	ACCOUNT TITLE	TRIAL BALANCE DEBIT	TRIAL BALANCE CREDIT	ADJUSTMENTS DEBIT	ADJUSTMENTS CREDIT	ADJUSTED TRIAL BALANCE DEBIT	ADJUSTED TRIAL BALANCE CREDIT	INCOME STATEMENT DEBIT	INCOME STATEMENT CREDIT	BALANCE SHEET DEBIT	BALANCE SHEET CREDIT	
1	Cash	1 1 8 0 00				1 1 8 0 00				1 1 8 0 00		1
2	Paper Supplies	3 6 0 0 00			(a) 3 5 5 0 00	5 0 00				5 0 00		2
3	Prepaid Insurance	1 0 0 0 00			(b) 5 0 5 00	4 9 5 00				4 9 5 00		3
4	Printing Equipment	5 8 0 0 00				5 8 0 0 00				5 8 0 0 00		4
5	Accum. Depr.—Printing Equipment				(d) 1 2 0 0 00		1 2 0 0 00				1 2 0 0 00	5
6	Accounts Payable		5 0 0 00				5 0 0 00				5 0 0 00	6
7	Wages Payable				(c) 3 0 00		3 0 00				3 0 00	7
8	Timothy Chang, Capital		10 0 0 0 00				10 0 0 0 00				10 0 0 0 00	8
9	Timothy Chang, Drawing	13 0 0 0 00				13 0 0 0 00				13 0 0 0 00		9
10	Printing Fees		35 1 0 0 00				35 1 0 0 00		35 1 0 0 00			10
11	Wages Expense	11 9 7 0 00		(c) 3 0 00		12 0 0 0 00		12 0 0 0 00				11
12	Rent Expense	7 5 0 0 00				7 5 0 0 00		7 5 0 0 00				12
13	Paper Supplies Expense			(a) 3 5 5 0 00		3 5 5 0 00		3 5 5 0 00				13
14	Phone Expense	5 5 0 00				5 5 0 00		5 5 0 00				14
15	Utilities Expense	1 0 0 0 00				1 0 0 0 00		1 0 0 0 00				15
16	Insurance Expense			(b) 5 0 5 00		5 0 5 00		5 0 5 00				16
17	Depr. Expense—Printing Equipment			(d) 1 2 0 0 00		1 2 0 0 00		1 2 0 0 00				17
18		45 6 0 0 00	45 6 0 0 00	5 2 8 5 00	5 2 8 5 00	46 8 3 0 00	46 8 3 0 00	26 3 0 5 00	35 1 0 0 00	20 5 2 5 00	11 7 3 0 00	18
19	Net Income							8 7 9 5 00			8 7 9 5 00	19
20								35 1 0 0 00	35 1 0 0 00	20 5 2 5 00	20 5 2 5 00	20
21												21
22												22
23												23
24												24
25												25
26												26
27												27
28												28
29												29
30												30

SOLUTION 1.

Hard Copy Printers
Income Statement
For Year Ended December 31, 20 --

Revenue:		
Printing fees		$35,100
Expenses:		
Wages expense	$12,000	
Rent expense	7,500	
Paper supplies expense	3,550	
Phone expense	550	
Utilities expense	1,000	
Insurance expense	505	
Depreciation expense—printing equipment	1,200	
Total expenses		26,305
Net income		$ 8,795

Hard Copy Printers
Statement of Owner's Equity
For Year Ended December 31, 20 --

Timothy Chang, capital, January 1, 20 --		$10,000
Net income for 20 --	$ 8,795	
Less withdrawals for 20 --	13,000	
Decrease in capital		(4,205)
Timothy Chang, capital, December 31, 20 --		$ 5,795

Hard Copy Printers
Balance Sheet
December 31, 20 - -

Assets		
Current assets:		
Cash	$ 1,180	
Paper supplies	50	
Prepaid insurance	495	
Total current assets		$ 1,725
Property, plant, and equipment:		
Printing equipment	$ 5,800	
Less accumulated depreciation	1,200	4,600
Total assets		$ 6,325
Liabilities		
Current liabilities:		
Accounts payable	$ 500	
Wages payable	30	
Total current liabilities		$ 530
Owner's Equity		
Timothy Chang, capital		5,795
Total liabilities and owner's equity		$ 6,325

SOLUTION 2.

	DATE		DESCRIPTION	POST. REF.	DEBIT					CREDIT					
			GENERAL JOURNAL										PAGE 4		
1			Closing Entries												1
2	20-- Dec.	31	Printing Fees		35	1	0	0	00						2
3			Income Summary							35	1	0	0	00	3
4															4
5		31	Income Summary		26	3	0	5	00						5
6			Wages Expense							12	0	0	0	00	6
7			Rent Expense							7	5	0	0	00	7
8			Paper Supplies Expense							3	5	5	0	00	8
9			Phone Expense								5	5	0	00	9
10			Utilities Expense							1	0	0	0	00	10
11			Insurance Expense								5	0	5	00	11
12			Depr. Expense—Printing Equipment							1	2	0	0	00	12
13															13
14		31	Income Summary		8	7	9	5	00						14
15			Timothy Chang, Capital							8	7	9	5	00	15
16															16
17		31	Timothy Chang, Capital		13	0	0	0	00						17
18			Timothy Chang, Drawing							13	0	0	0	00	18
19															19

KEY TERMS

account form of balance sheet (186) A balance sheet in which the assets are on the left and the liabilities and the owner's equity sections are on the right.

accounting cycle (195) The steps involved in accounting for all of the business activities during an accounting period.

classified balance sheet (186) A balance sheet with separate categories for current assets; property, plant, and equipment; current liabilities; and long-term liabilities.

closing process (189) The process of giving zero balances to the temporary accounts so that they can accumulate information for the next accounting period.

current assets (188) Cash and assets that will be converted into cash or consumed within either one year or the normal operating cycle of the business, whichever is longer.

current liabilities (188) Liabilities that are due within either one year or the normal operating cycle of the business, whichever is longer, and that are to be paid out of current assets.

Income Summary (190) A temporary account used in the closing process to summarize the effects of all revenue and expense accounts.

long-term assets (188) See property, plant, and equipment.

long-term debt (188) See long-term liabilities.

long-term liabilities (188) Obligations that are not expected to be paid within a year and do not require the use of current assets. Also called long-term debt.

operating cycle (188)   The period of time required to purchase supplies and services and convert them back into cash.

permanent accounts (189)   Accounts that accumulate information across accounting periods; all accounts reported on the balance sheet.

plant assets (188)   See property, plant, and equipment.

post-closing trial balance (194)   Prepared after posting the closing entries to prove the equality of the debit and credit balances in the general ledger accounts.

property, plant, and equipment (188)   Assets that are expected to serve the business for many years. Also called plant assets or long-term assets.

report form of balance sheet (186)   A balance sheet in which the liabilities and the owner's equity sections are shown below the assets section.

temporary accounts (189)   Accounts that do not accumulate information across accounting periods but are closed, such as the drawing account and all income statement accounts.

SELF-STUDY TEST QUESTIONS

True/False

1. **LO1**   Expenses are listed on the income statement as they appear in the chart of accounts or in descending order (by dollar amount).

2. **LO1**   Additional investments of capital during the month are not reported on the statement of owner's equity.

3. **LO1**   The income statement cannot be prepared using the work sheet alone.

4. **LO1**   A classified balance sheet groups similar items, such as current assets together.

5. **LO2**   Temporary accounts are closed at the end of each accounting period.

Multiple Choice

1. **LO2**   Which of these types of accounts is considered a "permanent" account?
   (a) Revenue   (c) Drawing
   (b) Asset   (d) Expense

2. **LO2**   Which of these accounts is considered a "temporary" account?
   (a) Cash   (c) J. Jones, Capital
   (b) Accounts Payable   (d) J. Jones, Drawing

3. **LO2**   Which of these is the first step in the closing process?
   (a) Close revenue account(s).   (c) Close the Income Summary account.
   (b) Close expense accounts.   (d) Close the drawing account.

4. **LO3**   The _____ is prepared after closing entries are posted to prove the equality of debit and credit balances.
   (a) balance sheet   (c) post-closing trial balance
   (b) income statement   (d) statement of owner's equity

5. **LO4**   Steps that begin with analyzing source documents and conclude with the post-closing trial balance are called the
   (a) closing process.   (c) adjusting entries.
   (b) accounting cycle.   (d) posting process.

Checkpoint Exercises

1. **LO1**   Joe Fisher operates Fisher Consulting. A partial work sheet for August 20-- is provided below. Fisher made no additional investments during the month. Prepare an income statement, statement of owner's equity, and balance sheet.

Fisher Consulting
Work Sheet (Partial)
For Month Ended August 31, 20 - -

	ACCOUNT TITLE	INCOME STATEMENT DEBIT	INCOME STATEMENT CREDIT	BALANCE SHEET DEBIT	BALANCE SHEET CREDIT	
1	Cash			2 5 0 0 00		1
2	Accounts Receivable			8 0 0 00		2
3	Equipment			3 8 0 0 00		3
4	Accum. Depr.— Equipment				2 0 0 00	4
5	Accounts Payable				1 0 0 0 00	5
6	Joe Fisher, Capital				3 0 0 0 00	6
7	Joe Fisher, Drawing			3 0 0 00		7
8	Professional Fees		5 0 0 0 00			8
9	Wages Expense	1 0 0 0 00				9
10	Rent Expense	7 0 0 00				10
11	Depreciation Expense	1 0 0 00				11
12		1 8 0 0 00	5 0 0 0 00	7 4 0 0 00	4 2 0 0 00	12
13	Net Income	3 2 0 0 00			3 2 0 0 00	13
14		5 0 0 0 00	5 0 0 0 00	7 4 0 0 00	7 4 0 0 00	14
15						15
16						16

2. **LO2**   Using the work sheet provided in Checkpoint Exercise 1, prepare closing entries in general journal form.

3. **LO3**   Using the work sheet provided in Checkpoint Exercise 1 and financial statements prepared for that exercise, prepare a post-closing trial balance.

The answers to the Self-Study Test Questions are at the end of the chapter (pages 215–217).

APPLYING YOUR KNOWLEDGE

REVIEW QUESTIONS

LO1   1. Identify the source of the information needed to prepare the income statement.

LO1   2. Describe two approaches to listing the expenses in the income statement.

LO1   3. Identify the sources of the information needed to prepare the statement of owner's equity.

LO1 4. If additional investments were made during the year, what information in addition to the work sheet would be needed to prepare the statement of owner's equity?

LO1 5. Identify the sources of the information needed to prepare the balance sheet.

LO2 6. What is a permanent account? On which financial statement are permanent accounts reported?

LO2 7. Name three types of temporary accounts.

LO2 8. List the four steps for closing the temporary accounts.

LO2 9. Describe the net effect of the four closing entries on the balance of the owner's capital account. Where else is this same amount calculated?

LO3 10. What is the purpose of the post-closing trial balance?

LO4 11. List the 10 steps in the accounting cycle.

SERIES A EXERCISES

E 6-1A (LO1)
✓ Net income: $2,220

E 6-2A (LO1)
✓ Capital 1/31: $5,420

E 6-3A (LO1)
✓ Total assets: $6,720

INCOME STATEMENT From the partial work sheet for Major Advising below, prepare an income statement.

STATEMENT OF OWNER'S EQUITY From the partial work sheet below, prepare a statement of owner's equity, assuming no additional investment was made by the owner.

BALANCE SHEET From the statement of owner's equity prepared in E 6-2A and the partial work sheet below, prepare a balance sheet.

(FOR EXERCISES 6-1A, 6-2A, 6-3A, AND 6-4A)

Major Advising — Work Sheet (Partial) — For Month Ended January 31, 20 - -

	ACCOUNT TITLE	IS DEBIT	IS CREDIT	BS DEBIT	BS CREDIT	
1	Cash			1 3 3 9 00		1
2	Accounts Receivable			9 3 5 00		2
3	Supplies			3 4 6 00		3
4	Prepaid Insurance			8 0 0 00		4
5	Office Equipment			3 5 0 0 00		5
6	Accum. Depr.—Office Equipment				2 0 0 00	6
7	Accounts Payable				1 0 0 0 00	7
8	Wages Payable				3 0 0 00	8
9	Ed Major, Capital				4 1 0 0 00	9
10	Ed Major, Drawing			9 0 0 00		10
11	Advising Fees		4 1 4 0 00			11
12	Wages Expense	7 0 0 00				12
13	Advertising Expense	9 0 00				13
14	Rent Expense	5 0 0 00				14
15	Supplies Expense	1 5 0 00				15
16	Phone Expense	6 7 00				16
17	Electricity Expense	4 8 00				17
18	Insurance Expense	8 9 00				18
19	Gas and Oil Expense	5 3 00				19
20	Depr. Expense—Office Equipment	2 0 0 00				20
21	Miscellaneous Expense	2 3 00				21
22		1 9 2 0 00	4 1 4 0 00	7 8 2 0 00	5 6 0 0 00	22
23	Net Income	2 2 2 0 00			2 2 2 0 00	23
24		4 1 4 0 00	4 1 4 0 00	7 8 2 0 00	7 8 2 0 00	24

E 6-4A **(LO2)**
✓ Capital 1/31: $5,420

CLOSING ENTRIES (NET INCOME) Set up T accounts for Major Advising based on the work sheet in Exercise 6-1A and the chart of accounts provided below. Enter the existing balance for each account. Prepare closing entries in general journal form. Then post the closing entries to the T accounts.

Chart of Accounts

Assets		Revenues	
101	Cash	401	Advising Fees
122	Accounts Receivable		
141	Supplies	Expenses	
145	Prepaid Insurance	511	Wages Expense
181	Office Equipment	512	Advertising Expense
181.1	Accum. Depr.—Office Equip.	521	Rent Expense
		524	Supplies Expense
Liabilities		525	Phone Expense
202	Accounts Payable	533	Electricity Expense
219	Wages Payable	535	Insurance Expense
		538	Gas and Oil Expense
Owner's Equity		541	Depr. Exp.—Office Equip.
311	Ed Major, Capital	549	Miscellaneous Expense
312	Ed Major, Drawing		
313	Income Summary		

E 6-5A **(LO2)**

CLOSING ENTRIES (NET INCOME) Using the following partial listing of T accounts, prepare closing entries in general journal form dated April 30, 20--. Then post the closing entries to the T accounts.

Cash	101		Income Summary	313		Supplies Expense	524
Bal. 500						Bal. 500	

Accounts Receivable	122		Golf Instruction Fees	401		Insurance Expense	535
Bal. 1,500				Bal. 4,000		Bal 100	

Wages Payable	219		Wages Expense	511		Postage Expense	536
	Bal. 400		Bal. 800			Bal. 50	

Chris Williams, Capital	311		Advertising Expense	512		Gas and Oil Expense	538
	Bal. 9,000		Bal. 200			Bal. 150	

Chris Williams, Drawing	312		Travel Expense	515		Miscellaneous Expense	549
Bal. 1,000			Bal. 600			Bal. 80	

E 6-6A   (LO2)
✓ Capital 1/31: $2,597

CLOSING ENTRIES (NET LOSS) Using the following partial listing of T accounts, prepare closing entries in general journal form dated January 31, 20--. Then post the closing entries to the T accounts.

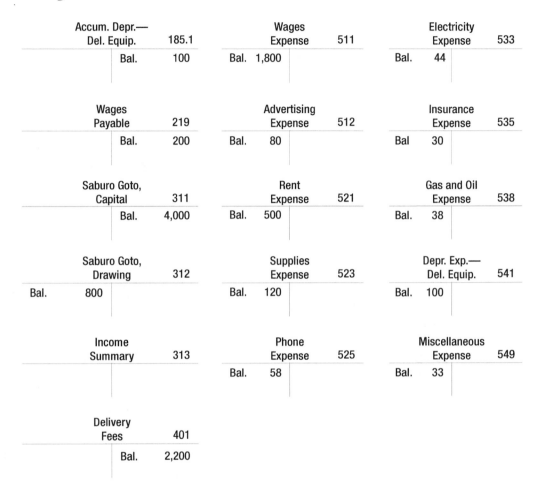

Accum. Depr.—Del. Equip.	185.1		
		Bal.	100

Wages Payable	219		
		Bal.	200

Saburo Goto, Capital	311		
		Bal.	4,000

Saburo Goto, Drawing	312		
Bal.	800		

Income Summary	313		

Delivery Fees	401		
		Bal.	2,200

Wages Expense	511		
Bal.	1,800		

Advertising Expense	512		
Bal.	80		

Rent Expense	521		
Bal.	500		

Supplies Expense	523		
Bal.	120		

Phone Expense	525		
Bal.	58		

Electricity Expense	533		
Bal.	44		

Insurance Expense	535		
Bal	30		

Gas and Oil Expense	538		
Bal.	38		

Depr. Exp.—Del. Equip.	541		
Bal.	100		

Miscellaneous Expense	549		
Bal.	33		

SERIES A PROBLEMS

P 6-7A   (LO1)
✓ Net income: $838
✓ Capital 1/31: $7,738
✓ Total assets 1/31: $9,338

FINANCIAL STATEMENTS Page 206 shows a work sheet for Megaffin's Repairs. No additional investments were made by the owner during the month.

REQUIRED

1. Prepare an income statement.
2. Prepare a statement of owner's equity.
3. Prepare a balance sheet.

PROBLEM 6-7A

Megaffin's Repairs
Work Sheet
For Month Ended January 31, 20--

	ACCOUNT TITLE	TRIAL BALANCE DEBIT	TRIAL BALANCE CREDIT	ADJUSTMENTS DEBIT	ADJUSTMENTS CREDIT	ADJUSTED TRIAL BALANCE DEBIT	ADJUSTED TRIAL BALANCE CREDIT	INCOME STATEMENT DEBIT	INCOME STATEMENT CREDIT	BALANCE SHEET DEBIT	BALANCE SHEET CREDIT	
1	Cash	3 6 7 3 00				3 6 7 3 00				3 6 7 3 00		1
2	Accounts Receivable	1 4 5 0 00				1 4 5 0 00				1 4 5 0 00		2
3	Supplies	7 0 0 00			3 0 0 00	4 0 0 00				4 0 0 00		3
4	Prepaid Insurance	9 0 0 00			2 3 0 00	6 7 0 00				6 7 0 00		4
5	Delivery Equipment	3 2 0 0 00				3 2 0 0 00				3 2 0 0 00		5
6	Accum. Depr.—Delivery Equipment				5 5 00		5 5 00				5 5 00	6
7	Accounts Payable		1 2 0 0 00				1 2 0 0 00				1 2 0 0 00	7
8	Wages Payable				4 0 0 00		4 0 0 00				4 0 0 00	8
9	Don Megaffin, Capital		8 0 0 0 00				8 0 0 0 00				8 0 0 0 00	9
10	Don Megaffin, Drawing	1 1 0 0 00				1 1 0 0 00				1 1 0 0 00		10
11	Repair Fees		4 7 0 0 00				4 7 0 0 00		4 7 0 0 00			11
12	Wages Expense	1 7 5 0 00		4 0 0 00		2 1 5 0 00		2 1 5 0 00				12
13	Advertising Expense	2 0 0 00				2 0 0 00		2 0 0 00				13
14	Rent Expense	6 4 0 00				6 4 0 00		6 4 0 00				14
15	Supplies Expense			3 0 0 00		3 0 0 00		3 0 0 00				15
16	Phone Expense	5 0 00				5 0 00		5 0 00				16
17	Insurance Expense			2 3 0 00		2 3 0 00		2 3 0 00				17
18	Gas and Oil Expense	2 0 0 00				2 0 0 00		2 0 0 00				18
19	Depr. Expense—Delivery Equipment			5 5 00		5 5 00		5 5 00				19
20	Miscellaneous Expense	3 7 00				3 7 00		3 7 00				20
21		13 9 0 0 00	13 9 0 0 00	9 8 5 00	9 8 5 00	14 3 5 5 00	14 3 5 5 00	3 8 6 2 00	4 7 0 0 00	10 4 9 3 00	9 6 5 5 00	21
22	Net Income							8 3 8 00			8 3 8 00	22
23								4 7 0 0 00	4 7 0 0 00	10 4 9 3 00	10 4 9 3 00	23
24												24
25												25
26												26
27												27
28												28
29												29
30												30

P 6-8A   (LO2/3)

✓ Capital 1/31: $7,738

✓ Post-closing trial balance total debits: $9,393

CLOSING ENTRIES AND POST-CLOSING TRIAL BALANCE Refer to the work sheet in Problem 6-7A for Megaffin's Repairs. The trial balance amounts (before adjustments) have been entered in the ledger accounts provided in the working papers. If you are not using the working papers that accompany this book, set up ledger accounts and enter these balances as of January 31, 20--. A chart of accounts is provided below.

Megaffin's Repairs
Chart of Accounts

Assets		Revenues	
101	Cash	401	Repair Fees
122	Accounts Receivable		
141	Supplies	Expenses	
145	Prepaid Insurance	511	Wages Expense
185	Delivery Equipment	512	Advertising Expense
185.1	Accum. Depr.—Delivery Equip.	521	Rent Expense
		523	Supplies Expense
Liabilities		525	Phone Expense
202	Accounts Payable	535	Insurance Expense
219	Wages Payable	538	Gas and Oil Expense
		541	Depr. Exp.—Delivery Equip.
Owner's Equity		549	Miscellaneous Expense
311	Don Megaffin, Capital		
312	Don Megaffin, Drawing		
313	Income Summary		

REQUIRED

1. Journalize (page 10) and post the adjusting entries.

2. Journalize (page 11) and post the closing entries.

3. Prepare a post-closing trial balance.

P 6-9A   (LO1)

✓ Capital 1/31: $6,820

STATEMENT OF OWNER'S EQUITY The capital account for Autumn Chou, including an additional investment, and a partial work sheet are shown below and on page 208.

REQUIRED

Prepare a statement of owner's equity.

GENERAL LEDGER							
ACCOUNT: Autumn Chou, Capital						ACCOUNT NO. 311	
DATE	ITEM	POST. REF.	DEBIT	CREDIT	BALANCE		
						DEBIT	CREDIT
20-- Jan. 1	Balance	✔					4 8 0 0 00
18		J1		1 2 0 0 00			6 0 0 0 00

Autumn's Home Designs
Work Sheet (Partial)
For Month Ended January 31, 20 --

	ACCOUNT TITLE	INCOME STATEMENT DEBIT	INCOME STATEMENT CREDIT	BALANCE SHEET DEBIT	BALANCE SHEET CREDIT	
1	Cash			3 2 0 0 00		1
2	Accounts Receivable			1 6 0 0 00		2
3	Supplies			8 0 0 00		3
4	Prepaid Insurance			9 0 0 00		4
5	Office Equipment			2 5 0 0 00		5
6	Accum. Depr.—Office Equipment				5 0 00	6
7	Accounts Payable				1 9 5 0 00	7
8	Wages Payable				1 8 0 00	8
9	Autumn Chou, Capital				6 0 0 0 00	9
10	Autumn Chou, Drawing			1 0 0 0 00		10
11	Design Fees		4 8 6 6 00			11
12	Wages Expense	1 9 0 0 00				12
13	Advertising Expense	2 1 00				13
14	Rent Expense	6 0 0 00				14
15	Supplies Expense	2 0 0 00				15
16	Phone Expense	8 5 00				16
17	Electricity Expense	4 8 00				17
18	Insurance Expense	6 0 00				18
19	Gas and Oil Expense	3 2 00				19
20	Depr. Expense—Office Equipment	5 0 00				20
21	Miscellaneous Expense	5 0 00				21
22		3 0 4 6 00	4 8 6 6 00	10 0 0 0 00	8 1 8 0 00	22
23	Net Income	1 8 2 0 00			1 8 2 0 00	23
24		4 8 6 6 00	4 8 6 6 00	10 0 0 0 00	10 0 0 0 00	24

SERIES B EXERCISES

E 6-1B (LO1) ✓ Net income: $1,826

INCOME STATEMENT From the partial work sheet for Adams' Shoe Shine on the next page, prepare an income statement.

E 6-2B (LO1) ✓ Capital 6/30: $5,826

STATEMENT OF OWNER'S EQUITY From the partial work sheet on the next page, prepare a statement of owner's equity, assuming no additional investment was made by the owner.

E 6-3B (LO1) ✓ Total assets: $7,936

BALANCE SHEET From the statement of owner's equity prepared in E 6-2B and the partial work sheet on the next page, prepare a balance sheet for Adams' Shoe Shine.

(FOR EXERCISES 6-1B, 6-2B, 6-3B, AND 6-4B)

	ACCOUNT TITLE	INCOME STATEMENT DEBIT	INCOME STATEMENT CREDIT	BALANCE SHEET DEBIT	BALANCE SHEET CREDIT	
			Adams' Shoe Shine Work Sheet (Partial) For Month Ended June 30, 20 - -			
1	Cash			3 2 6 2 00		1
2	Accounts Receivable			1 2 4 4 00		2
3	Supplies			8 0 0 00		3
4	Prepaid Insurance			6 4 0 00		4
5	Office Equipment			2 1 0 0 00		5
6	Accum. Depr.—Office Equipment				1 1 0 00	6
7	Accounts Payable				1 8 5 0 00	7
8	Wages Payable				2 6 0 00	8
9	Mary Adams, Capital				6 0 0 0 00	9
10	Mary Adams, Drawing			2 0 0 0 00		10
11	Service Fees		4 8 1 3 00			11
12	Wages Expense	1 0 8 0 00				12
13	Advertising Expense	3 4 00				13
14	Rent Expense	9 0 0 00				14
15	Supplies Expense	3 2 2 00				15
16	Phone Expense	1 3 3 00				16
17	Utilities Expense	1 0 2 00				17
18	Insurance Expense	1 2 0 00				18
19	Gas and Oil Expense	8 8 00				19
20	Depr. Expense—Office Equipment	1 1 0 00				20
21	Miscellaneous Expense	9 8 00				21
22		2 9 8 7 00	4 8 1 3 00	10 0 4 6 00	8 2 2 0 00	22
23	Net Income	1 8 2 6 00			1 8 2 6 00	23
24		4 8 1 3 00	4 8 1 3 00	10 0 4 6 00	10 0 4 6 00	24

E 6-4B   (LO2)
✓ Capital 6/30: $5,826

CLOSING ENTRIES (NET INCOME) Set up T accounts for Adams' Shoe Shine based on the work sheet above and the chart of accounts provided below. Enter the existing balance for each account. Prepare closing entries in general journal form. Then post the closing entries to the T accounts.

Chart of Accounts

Assets		Revenues	
101	Cash	401	Service Fees
122	Accounts Receivable		
141	Supplies	Expenses	
145	Prepaid Insurance	511	Wages Expense
181	Office Equipment	512	Advertising Expense
181.1	Accum. Depr.—Office Equip.	521	Rent Expense
		523	Supplies Expense
Liabilities		525	Phone Expense
202	Accounts Payable	533	Utilities Expense
219	Wages Payable	535	Insurance Expense
		538	Gas and Oil Expense
Owner's Equity		542	Depr. Exp.—Office Equip.
311	Mary Adams, Capital	549	Miscellaneous Expense
312	Mary Adams, Drawing		
313	Income Summary		

E 6-5B   (LO2)

CLOSING ENTRIES (NET INCOME) Using the following partial listing of T accounts, prepare closing entries in general journal form dated May 31, 20--. Then post the closing entries to the T accounts.

Cash 101		Income Summary 313		Supplies Expense 524	
Bal. 600				Bal. 900	

Accounts Receivable 122		Lawn Service Fees 401		Insurance Expense 535	
Bal. 1,800			Bal. 5,000	Bal. 300	

Wages Payable 219		Wages Expense 511		Postage Expense 536	
	Bal. 500	Bal. 400		Bal. 40	

Mark Thrasher, Capital 311		Advertising Expense 512		Gas and Oil Expense 538	
	Bal. 8,000	Bal. 600		Bal. 700	

Mark Thrasher, Drawing 312		Travel Expense 515		Miscellaneous Expense 549	
Bal. 800		Bal. 100		Bal. 200	

E 6-6B   (LO2)
✓ Capital 6/30: $3,826

CLOSING ENTRIES (NET LOSS) Using the following partial listing of T accounts, prepare closing entries in general journal form dated June 30, 20--. Then post the closing entries to the T accounts.

Accum. Depr.— Office Equip. 181.1		Wages Expense 511		Utilities Expense 533	
	Bal. 110	Bal. 1,080		Bal. 102	

Wages Payable 219		Advertising Expense 512		Insurance Expense 535	
	Bal. 260	Bal. 34		Bal. 120	

Raquel Zapata, Capital 311		Rent Expense 521		Gas and Oil Expense 538	
	Bal. 6,000	Bal. 900		Bal. 88	

Raquel Zapata, Drawing 312		Supplies Expense 523		Depr. Exp.— Office Equip. 541	
Bal. 2,000		Bal. 322		Bal. 110	

Income Summary 313		Phone Expense 525		Miscellaneous Expense 549	
		Bal. 133		Bal. 98	

Referral Fees 401	
	Bal. 2,813

SERIES B PROBLEMS

P 6-7B   (LO1)
✓ Net income: $1,450
✓ Capital 6/30: $7,650
✓ Total assets: $9,350

FINANCIAL STATEMENTS A work sheet for Juanita's Consulting is shown on the following page. There were no additional investments made by the owner during the month.

REQUIRED

1. Prepare an income statement.
2. Prepare a statement of owner's equity.
3. Prepare a balance sheet.

P 6-8B   (LO2/3)
✓ Capital 6/30: $7,650
✓ Post-closing trial bal.
  total debits: $9,460

CLOSING ENTRIES AND POST-CLOSING TRIAL BALANCE Refer to the work sheet for Juanita's Consulting in Problem 6-7B. The trial balance amounts (before adjustments) have been entered in the ledger accounts provided in the working papers. If you are not using the working papers that accompany this book, set up ledger accounts and enter these balances as of June 30, 20--. A chart of accounts is provided below.

Juanita's Consulting
Chart of Accounts

Assets		Revenues	
101	Cash	401	Consulting Fees
122	Accounts Receivable		
141	Supplies	Expenses	
145	Prepaid Insurance	511	Wages Expense
181	Office Equipment	512	Advertising Expense
181.1	Accum. Depr.—Office Equip.	521	Rent Expense
		523	Supplies Expense
Liabilities		525	Phone Expense
202	Accounts Payable	533	Electricity Expense
219	Wages Payable	535	Insurance Expense
		538	Gas and Oil Expense
Owner's Equity		541	Depr. Exp.—Office Equip.
311	Juanita Alvarez, Capital	549	Miscellaneous Expense
312	Juanita Alvarez, Drawing		
313	Income Summary		

REQUIRED

1. Journalize (page 10) and post the adjusting entries.
2. Journalize (page 11) and post the closing entries.
3. Prepare a post-closing trial balance.

PROBLEM 6-7B

Juanita's Consulting
Work Sheet
For Month Ended June 30, 20—

	ACCOUNT TITLE	TRIAL BALANCE DEBIT	TRIAL BALANCE CREDIT	ADJUSTMENTS DEBIT	ADJUSTMENTS CREDIT	ADJUSTED TRIAL BALANCE DEBIT	ADJUSTED TRIAL BALANCE CREDIT	INCOME STATEMENT DEBIT	INCOME STATEMENT CREDIT	BALANCE SHEET DEBIT	BALANCE SHEET CREDIT	
1	Cash	5 2 8 5 00				5 2 8 5 00				5 2 8 5 00		1
2	Accounts Receivable	1 0 7 5 00				1 0 7 5 00				1 0 7 5 00		2
3	Supplies	7 5 0 00			(a) 2 5 0 00	5 0 0 00				5 0 0 00		3
4	Prepaid Insurance	5 0 0 00			(b) 1 0 0 00	4 0 0 00				4 0 0 00		4
5	Office Equipment	2 2 0 0 00				2 2 0 0 00				2 2 0 0 00		5
6	Accum. Depr.—Office Equipment				(d) 1 1 0 00		1 1 0 00				1 1 0 00	6
7	Accounts Payable		1 5 0 0 00				1 5 0 0 00				1 5 0 0 00	7
8	Wages Payable				(c) 2 0 0 00		2 0 0 00				2 0 0 00	8
9	Juanita Alvarez, Capital		7 0 0 0 00				7 0 0 0 00				7 0 0 0 00	9
10	Juanita Alvarez, Drawing	8 0 0 00				8 0 0 00				8 0 0 00		10
11	Consulting Fees		4 2 0 4 00				4 2 0 4 00		4 2 0 4 00			11
12	Wages Expense	1 4 0 0 00		(c) 2 0 0 00		1 6 0 0 00		1 6 0 0 00				12
13	Advertising Expense	6 0 0 00				6 0 0 00		6 0 0 00				13
14	Rent Expense	5 0 0 00				5 0 0 00		5 0 0 00				14
15	Supplies Expense			(a) 2 5 0 00		2 5 0 00		2 5 0 00				15
16	Phone Expense	4 6 00				4 6 00		4 6 00				16
17	Electricity Expense	3 9 00				3 9 00		3 9 00				17
18	Insurance Expense			(b) 1 0 0 00		1 0 0 00		1 0 0 00				18
19	Gas and Oil Expense	2 8 00				2 8 00		2 8 00				19
20	Depr. Expense—Office Equipment			(d) 1 1 0 00		1 1 0 00		1 1 0 00				20
21	Miscellaneous Expense	2 1 00				2 1 00		2 1 00				21
22		12 7 0 4 00	12 7 0 4 00	6 6 0 00	6 6 0 00	13 0 1 4 00	13 0 1 4 00	2 7 5 4 00	4 2 0 4 00	10 2 6 0 00	8 8 1 0 00	22
23	Net Income							1 4 5 0 00			1 4 5 0 00	23
24								4 2 0 4 00	4 2 0 4 00	10 2 6 0 00	10 2 6 0 00	24
25												25
26												26
27												27
28												28
29												29
30												30

P 6-9B   (LO1)
✓ Capital 1/31: $9,975

STATEMENT OF OWNER'S EQUITY The capital account for Minta's Editorial Services, including an additional investment, and a partial work sheet are shown below.

GENERAL LEDGER

ACCOUNT: Minta Berry, Capital   ACCOUNT NO. 311

DATE		ITEM	POST. REF.	DEBIT	CREDIT	BALANCE DEBIT	BALANCE CREDIT
20-- Jan.	1	Balance	✔				3 6 0 0 00
	22		J1		2 9 0 0 00		6 5 0 0 00

Minta's Editorial Services
Work Sheet (Partial)
For Month Ended January 31, 20 --

	ACCOUNT TITLE	INCOME STATEMENT DEBIT	INCOME STATEMENT CREDIT	BALANCE SHEET DEBIT	BALANCE SHEET CREDIT	
1	Cash			3 8 0 0 00		1
2	Accounts Receivable			2 2 0 0 00		2
3	Supplies			1 0 0 0 00		3
4	Prepaid Insurance			9 5 0 00		4
5	Computer Equipment			4 5 0 0 00		5
6	Accum. Depr.—Computer Equipment				2 2 5 00	6
7	Accounts Payable				2 1 0 0 00	7
8	Wages Payable				1 5 0 00	8
9	Minta Berry, Capital				6 5 0 0 00	9
10	Minta Berry, Drawing			1 7 0 0 00		10
11	Editing Fees		7 0 1 2 00			11
12	Wages Expense	6 0 0 00				12
13	Advertising Expense	4 9 00				13
14	Rent Expense	4 5 0 00				14
15	Supplies Expense	2 8 8 00				15
16	Phone Expense	4 4 00				16
17	Utilities Expense	3 8 00				17
18	Insurance Expense	1 2 5 00				18
19	Depr. Expense—Computer Equipment	2 2 5 00				19
20	Miscellaneous Expense	1 8 00				20
21		1 8 3 7 00	7 0 1 2 00	14 1 5 0 00	8 9 7 5 00	21
22	Net Income	5 1 7 5 00			5 1 7 5 00	22
23		7 0 1 2 00	7 0 1 2 00	14 1 5 0 00	14 1 5 0 00	23

REQUIRED
Prepare a statement of owner's equity.

MANAGING YOUR WRITING

At lunch, two bookkeepers got into a heated discussion about whether closing entries should be made before or after preparing the financial statements. They have come to you to resolve this issue and have agreed to accept your position. Write a memo explaining the purpose of closing entries and whether they should be made before or after preparing the financial statements.

MASTERY PROBLEM

✓ Total assets: $4,740
✓ E. Soltis, capital, Dec. 31: $4,475

Elizabeth Soltis owns and operates Aunt Ibby's Styling Salon. A year-end work sheet is provided on the next page. Using this information, prepare adjusting entries, financial statements, and closing entries. Soltis made no additional investments during the year.

MASTERY PROBLEM

Aunt Ibby's Styling Salon
Work Sheet
For Year Ended December 31, 20--

	ACCOUNT TITLE	TRIAL BALANCE DEBIT	TRIAL BALANCE CREDIT	ADJUSTMENTS DEBIT	ADJUSTMENTS CREDIT	ADJUSTED TRIAL BALANCE DEBIT	ADJUSTED TRIAL BALANCE CREDIT	INCOME STATEMENT DEBIT	INCOME STATEMENT CREDIT	BALANCE SHEET DEBIT	BALANCE SHEET CREDIT	
1	Cash	9 4 0 00				9 4 0 00				9 4 0 00		1
2	Styling Supplies	1 5 0 0 00			(a)1 4 5 0 00	5 0 00				5 0 00		2
3	Prepaid Insurance	8 0 0 00			(b) 6 5 0 00	1 5 0 00				1 5 0 00		3
4	Salon Equipment	4 5 0 0 00				4 5 0 0 00				4 5 0 0 00		4
5	Accum. Depr.—Salon Equipment				(d) 9 0 0 00		9 0 0 00				9 0 0 00	5
6	Accounts Payable		2 2 5 00				2 2 5 00				2 2 5 00	6
7	Wages Payable				(c) 4 0 00		4 0 00				4 0 00	7
8	Elizabeth Soltis, Capital		2 7 6 5 00				2 7 6 5 00				2 7 6 5 00	8
9	Elizabeth Soltis, Drawing	12 0 0 0 00				12 0 0 0 00				12 0 0 0 00		9
10	Styling Fees		32 0 0 0 00				32 0 0 0 00		32 0 0 0 00			10
11	Wages Expense	8 0 0 0 00		(c) 4 0 00		8 0 4 0 00		8 0 4 0 00				11
12	Rent Expense	6 0 0 0 00				6 0 0 0 00		6 0 0 0 00				12
13	Styling Supplies Expense			(a) 1 4 5 0 00		1 4 5 0 00		1 4 5 0 00				13
14	Phone Expense	4 5 0 00				4 5 0 00		4 5 0 00				14
15	Utilities Expense	8 0 0 00				8 0 0 00		8 0 0 00				15
16	Insurance Expense			(b) 6 5 0 00		6 5 0 00		6 5 0 00				16
17	Depr. Expense—Salon Equipment			(d) 9 0 0 00		9 0 0 00		9 0 0 00				17
18		34 9 9 0 00	34 9 9 0 00	3 0 4 0 00	3 0 4 0 00	35 9 3 0 00	35 9 3 0 00	18 2 9 0 00	32 0 0 0 00	17 6 4 0 00	3 9 3 0 00	18
19	Net Income							13 7 1 0 00			13 7 1 0 00	19
20								32 0 0 0 00	32 0 0 0 00	17 6 4 0 00	17 6 4 0 00	20
21												21
22												22
23												23
24												24
25												25
26												26
27												27
28												28
29												29
30												30

CHALLENGE PROBLEM

This problem challenges you to apply your cumulative accounting knowledge to move a step beyond the material in the chapter.

✓ Net loss: $2,100
✓ Capital, 1/31/20--: ($700)

Provided below is a partial work sheet for Ardery Advising.

Ardery Advising
Work Sheet (Partial)
For Month Ended January 31, 20 - -

	ACCOUNT TITLE	INCOME STATEMENT DEBIT	INCOME STATEMENT CREDIT	BALANCE SHEET DEBIT	BALANCE SHEET CREDIT	
1	Cash			2 4 1 2 00		1
2	Accounts Receivable			8 9 6 00		2
3	Supplies			4 8 2 00		3
4	Prepaid Insurance			9 0 0 00		4
5	Office Equipment			3 0 0 0 00		5
6	Accum. Depr.—Office Equipment				2 0 0 0 00	6
7	Accounts Payable				2 1 9 0 00	7
8	Wages Payable				1 2 0 0 00	8
9	Notes Payable				3 0 0 0 00	9
10	Sam Ardery, Capital				2 2 0 0 00	10
11	Sam Ardery, Drawing			8 0 0 00		11
12	Advising Fees		3 8 0 2 00			12
13	Wages Expense	1 8 0 0 00				13
14	Advertising Expense	4 0 0 00				14
15	Rent Expense	1 5 0 0 00				15
16	Supplies Expense	1 2 0 00				16
17	Phone Expense	3 0 0 00				17
18	Electricity Expense	4 4 00				18
19	Insurance Expense	2 0 0 00				19
20	Gas and Oil Expense	3 8 00				20
21	Depr. Expense—Office Equipment	1 0 0 0 00				21
22	Miscellaneous Expense	5 0 0 00				22
23		5 9 0 2 00	3 8 0 2 00	8 4 9 0 00	10 5 9 0 00	23
24	Net Loss		2 1 0 0 00	2 1 0 0 00		24
25		5 9 0 2 00	5 9 0 2 00	10 5 9 0 00	10 5 9 0 00	25

REQUIRED

During January, Ardery made an additional investment of $1,200. Prepare an income statement, statement of owner's equity, and balance sheet for Ardery Advising.

ANSWERS TO SELF-STUDY TEST QUESTIONS

CHECKPOINT

Checkpoint Exercises

1.

Fisher Consulting		
Income Statement		
For Month Ended August 31, 20 --		
Revenue:		
Professional fees		$5,000
Expenses:		
Wages expense	$1,000	
Rent expense	700	
Depreciation expense	100	
Total expenses		1,800
Net income		$3,200

Fisher Consulting		
Statement of Owner's Equity		
For Month Ended August 31, 20 --		
Joe Fisher, capital, August 1, 20 - -		$3,000
Net income for August	$3,200	
Less withdrawals for August	300	
Increase in capital		2,900
Joe Fisher, capital, August 31, 20 - -		$5,900

Fisher Consulting		
Balance Sheet		
August 31, 20 --		
Assets		
Current assets:		
Cash	$2,500	
Accounts receivable	800	
Total current assets		$3,300
Property, plant, and equipment:		
Equipment	$3,800	
Less accumulated depreciation	200	3,600
Total assets		$6,900
Liabilities		
Current liabilities:		
Accounts payable		$1,000
Owner's Equity		
Joe Fisher, capital, August 31, 20--		5,900
Total liabilities and owner's equity		$6,900

2.

DATE		DESCRIPTION	POST. REF.	DEBIT					CREDIT				
		Closing Entries											
20-- Aug.	31	Professional Fees		5	0	0	0	00					
		Income Summary							5	0	0	0	00
	31	Income Summary		1	8	0	0	00					
		Wages Expense							1	0	0	0	00
		Rent Expense								7	0	0	00
		Depreciation Expense								1	0	0	00
	31	Income Summary		3	2	0	0	00					
		Joe Fisher, capital							3	2	0	0	00
	31	Joe Fisher, Capital			3	0	0	00					
		Joe Fisher, Drawing								3	0	0	00

3.

Joe Fisher, Consulting
Post-Closing Trial Balance
August 31, 20 - -

ACCOUNT TITLE	ACCOUNT NO	DEBIT BALANCE					CREDIT BALANCE				
Cash		2	5	0	0	00					
Accounts Receivable			8	0	0	00					
Equipment		3	8	0	0	00					
Accumulated Depr.—Equipment								2	0	0	00
Accounts Payable							1	0	0	0	00
Joe Fisher, Capital							5	9	0	0	00
		7	1	0	0	00	7	1	0	0	00

CHAPTER 6 APPENDIX

Statement of Cash Flows

Thus far, we have discussed three financial statements: the income statement, the statement of owner's equity, and the balance sheet. A fourth statement, the statement of cash flows, is also very important. It explains what the business did to generate cash and how the cash was used. This is done by categorizing all cash transactions into three types of activities: operating, investing, and financing.

LEARNING OBJECTIVES

Careful study of this appendix should enable you to:

LO1 Classify business transactions as operating, investing, or financing.

LO2 Prepare a statement of cash flows by analyzing and categorizing a series of business transactions.

LO1	Types of Business Activities

Classify business transactions as operating, investing, or financing.

Cash flows from operating activities are related to the revenues and expenses reported on the income statement. Examples include cash received for services performed and the payment of cash for expenses.

Investing activities are those transactions involving the purchase and sale of long-term assets, lending money, and collecting the principal on the related loans.

Financing activities are those transactions dealing with the exchange of cash between the business and its owners and creditors. Examples include cash received from the owner to finance the operations and cash paid to the owner as withdrawals. Financing activities also include borrowing cash and repaying the loan principal.

Figure 6A-1 provides a review of the transactions for Mitchell's Campus Delivery for the month of June. The transactions are classified as operating, investing, or financing, and an explanation for the classification is provided.

LEARNING KEY

There are three types of business activities: operating, investing, and financing.

LEARNING KEY

Lending money to another entity is an outflow of cash from investing activities. The collection of the principal when the loan is due is an inflow of cash from investing activities. Borrowing cash is an inflow from financing activities. Repayment of the loan principal is an outflow from financing activities.

FIGURE 6A-1 Summary of Transactions for Mitchell's Campus Delivery

SUMMARY OF TRANSACTIONS FOR MITCHELL'S CAMPUS DELIVERY	TYPE OF TRANSACTION	EXPLANATION
(a) Mitchell Williams invested cash in his business, $5,000.	Financing	Cash received from the owner is an inflow from financing activities. Don't be fooled by the word "invested." From the company's point of view, this is a way to *finance* the business.
(b) Purchased delivery equipment for cash, $2,000.	Investing	Purchases of long-term assets are investments.
(c) Purchased delivery equipment on account from Big Red Scooters, $1,800. (*Note:* Big Red has loaned Mitch $1,800.)	No cash involved	This transaction will not affect the main sections of the statement of cash flows. (This is a noncash investing and financing activity.)
(d) Paid first installment to Big Red Scooters, $600. [See transaction (c).]	Financing	Repayments of loans are financing activities.
(e) Received cash for delivery services rendered, $2,100.	Operating	Cash received as a result of providing services is classified as an operating activity.
(f) Paid cash for June office rent, $1,000.	Operating	Cash payments for expenses are classified as operating activities.
(g) Paid phone bill, $100.	Operating	Cash payments for expenses are classified as operating activities.
(h) Made deliveries on account for a total of $2,400. $400 for the Library and $2,000 for the School of Music.	No cash involved	This transaction will not affect the statement of cash flows.
(i) Purchased supplies for cash, $80.	Operating	Cash payments for expenses are classified as operating activities. Most of these supplies were used up. Those that remain will be used in the near future. These are not long-term assets and, thus, do not qualify as investments.
(j) Received $1,900 in cash for services performed in transaction (h): $400 from the Library and $1,500 from the School of Music.	Operating	Cash received as a result of providing services is classified as an operating activity.
(k) Purchased a third scooter from Big Red Scooters, $1,000. A down payment of $300 was made with the remaining payments expected over the next four months.	Investing	Purchases of long-term assets are investments. Only the $300 cash paid will be reported on the statement of cash flows.
(l) Paid cash for a seven-month liability insurance policy, $700. Coverage began on June 1.	Operating	Cash payments for expenses are classified as operating activities. Prepaid Insurance is not considered a long-term asset and, thus, does not qualify as an investment.
(m) Paid wages of part-time employees, $1,650.	Operating	Cash payments for expenses are classified as operating activities.
(n) Earned delivery fees for the remainder of the month amounting to $3,500. $900 in cash and $2,600 on account. Deliveries on account: Library ($250) and Athletic Ticket Office ($2,350).	Operating	Cash received ($900) as a result of providing services is classified as an operating activity.
(o) Mitch withdrew cash for personal use, $3,000.	Financing	Cash payments to owners are classified as a financing activity.

LO2 Preparing the Statement of Cash Flows

Prepare a statement of cash flows by analyzing and categorizing a series of business transactions.

The classifications of the cash transactions for Mitchell's Campus Delivery are summarized in the expanded cash T account shown in Figure 6A-2. Using this information, we can prepare a statement of cash flows. As shown in Figure 6A-3, the heading is similar to that used for the income statement. Since the statement of cash flows reports on the flow of cash for a period of time, the statement is dated for the month ended June 30, 20--.

The main body of the statement is arranged in three sections: operating, investing, and financing activities. First, cash received from customers is listed under operating activities. Then, cash payments for operating activities are listed and totaled. The net amount is reported as net cash provided by operating activities. Since this is

FIGURE 6A-2 Cash T Account for Mitchell's Campus Delivery with Classifications of Cash Transactions

Event	**Classification**	**Amount**	**Amount**	**Classification**	**Event**	
(a) Investment by Mitch.	Financing	5,000	2,000	Investing	Purchased delivery equipment.	(b)
(e) Cash received for services.	Operating	2,100	600	Financing	Made payment on loan.	(d)
(j) Cash received for services.	Operating	1,900	1,000	Operating	Paid office rent.	(f)
(n) Cash received for services.	Operating	900	100	Operating	Paid phone bill.	(g)
		9,900	80	Operating	Purchased supplies.	(i)
			300	Investing	Purchased delivery equipment.	(k)
			700	Operating	Paid for insurance.	(l)
			1,650	Operating	Paid wages.	(m)
			3,000	Financing	Withdrawal by owner.	(o)
			9,430			
	Bal.	470				

FIGURE 6A-3 Statement of Cash Flows for Mitchell's Campus Delivery

Mitchell's Campus Delivery Statement of Cash Flows For Month Ended June 30, 20 - -		
Cash flows from operating activities:		
Cash received from customers for delivery services		$4,900
Cash paid for wages	$ (1,650)	
Cash paid for rent	(1,000)	
Cash paid for supplies	(80)	
Cash paid for phone	(100)	
Cash paid for insurance	(700)	
Total cash paid for operations		(3,530)
Net cash provided by operating activities		$1,370
Cash flows from investing activities:		
Cash paid for delivery equipment	$ (2,300)	
Net cash used for investing activities		(2,300)
Cash flows from financing activities:		
Cash investment by owner	$ 5,000	
Cash withdrawal by owner	(3,000)	
Payment made on loan	(600)	
Net cash provided by financing activities		1,400
Net increase in cash		$ 470

LEARNING KEY

To prove the accuracy of the statement of cash flows, compare the net increase or decrease reported on the statement with the change in the balance of the cash account.

the main purpose of the business, it is important to be able to generate positive cash flows from operating activities.

The next two sections list the inflows and outflows from investing and financing activities. Debits to the cash account are inflows and credits are outflows. Note that there was an outflow, or net use of cash, from investing activities resulting from the purchase of the motor scooters. In addition, cash was provided from financing activities because Mitchell's initial investment more than covered his withdrawal and the payment on the loan. These investing and financing activities are typical for a new business.

The sum of the inflows and outflows from operating, investing, and financing activities equals the net increase (or decrease) in the cash account during the period. Since this is a new business, the cash account had a beginning balance of zero. The ending balance is $470. This agrees with the net increase in cash of $470 reported on the statement of cash flows.

This appendix introduces you to the purpose and format of the statement of cash flows. Here, we classified entries made to the cash account as operating, investing, or financing. These classifications were then used to prepare the statement. Businesses have thousands of entries to the cash account. Thus, this approach to preparing the statement is not really practical. Other approaches to preparing the statement will be discussed in Chapter 23. However, the purpose and format of the statements are the same.

LEARNING OBJECTIVES	**Key Points to Remember**
LO1 Classify business transactions as operating, investing, or financing.	The purpose of the statement of cash flows is to report what the firm did to generate cash and how the cash was used. Business transactions are classified as operating, investing, and financing activities. *Operating activities* are those transactions related to the revenues and expenses reported on the income statement. *Investing activities* are those transactions involving the purchase and sale of long-term assets, lending money, and collecting the principal on the related loans. *Financing activities* are those transactions dealing with the exchange of cash between the business and its owners and creditors.
LO2 Prepare a statement of cash flows by analyzing and categorizing a series of business transactions.	The main body of the statement of cash flows consists of three sections: operating, investing, and financing activities.

Name of Business
Statement of Cash Flows
For Period Ended Date

Cash flows from operating activities:		
Cash received from customers		$ x,xxx
List cash paid for various expenses	$ (xxx)	
Total cash paid for operations		(x,xxx)
Net cash provided by (used for) operating activities		$ xxx
Cash flows from investing activities:		
List cash received from the sale of long-term assets and other investing activities	$ x,xxx	
List cash paid for the purchase of long-term assets and other investing activities	(x,xxx)	
Net cash provided by (used for) investing activities		x,xxx
Cash flows from financing activities:		
List cash received from owners and creditors	$ x,xxx	
List cash paid to owners and creditors	(xxx)	
Net cash provided by (used for) financing activities		x,xxx
Net increase (decrease) in cash		$ xxx

KEY TERMS

financing activities (218)   Those transactions dealing with the exchange of cash between the business and its owners and creditors.

investing activities (218)   Those transactions involving the purchase and sale of long-term assets, lending money, and collecting the principal on the related loans.

operating activities (218)   Those transactions related to the revenues and expenses reported on the income statement.

REVIEW QUESTIONS

LO1   1. Explain the purpose of the statement of cash flows.
LO1   2. Define and provide examples of the three types of business activities.

SERIES A EXERCISE

E 6Apx-1A   (LO1)

CLASSIFYING BUSINESS TRANSACTIONS Dolores Lopez opened a new consulting business. The following transactions occurred during January of the current year. Classify each transaction as an operating, an investing, or a financing activity.

(a) Invested cash in the business, $10,000.
(b) Paid office rent, $500.
(c) Purchased office equipment. Paid $1,500 cash and agreed to pay the balance of $2,000 in four monthly installments.
(d) Received cash for services rendered, $900.
(e) Paid phone bill, $65.
(f) Made payment on loan in transaction (c), $500.
(g) Paid wages to part-time employee, $500.
(h) Received cash for services rendered, $800.
(i) Paid electricity bill, $85.
(j) Withdrew cash for personal use, $100.
(k) Paid wages to part-time employee, $500.

SERIES A PROBLEM

P 6Apx-2A   (LO2)
✓ Operating activities: $50
✓ Investing activities: ($1,500)
✓ Financing activities: $9,400

PREPARING A STATEMENT OF CASH FLOWS Prepare a statement of cash flows based on the transactions reported in Exercise 6Apx-1A.

SERIES B EXERCISE

E 6Apx-1B   (LO1)

CLASSIFYING BUSINESS TRANSACTIONS Bob Jacobs opened an advertising agency. The following transactions occurred during January of the current year. Classify each transaction as an operating, an investing, or a financing activity.

(a) Invested cash in the business, $5,000.
(b) Purchased office equipment. Paid $2,500 cash and agreed to pay the balance of $2,000 in four monthly installments.
(c) Paid office rent, $400.
(d) Received cash for services rendered, $700.
(e) Paid phone bill, $95.
(f) Received cash for services rendered, $600.
(g) Made payment on loan in transaction (b), $500.
(h) Paid wages to part-time employee, $800.
(i) Paid electricity bill, $100.
(j) Withdrew cash for personal use, $500.
(k) Paid wages to part-time employee, $600.

SERIES B PROBLEM

P 6Apx-2B   (LO2)
✓ Operating activities: ($695)
✓ Investing activities: ($2,500)
✓ Financing activities: $4,000

PREPARING A STATEMENT OF CASH FLOWS Prepare a statement of cash flows based on the transactions reported in Exercise 6Apx-1B.

COMPREHENSIVE PROBLEM 1:

The Accounting Cycle

Bob Night opened The General's Favorite Fishing Hole. The fishing camp is open from April through September and attracts many famous college basketball coaches during the off-season. Guests typically register for one week, arriving on Sunday afternoon and returning home the following Saturday afternoon. The registration fee includes room and board, the use of fishing boats, and professional instruction in fishing techniques. The chart of accounts for the camping operations is provided below.

This comprehensive problem is intended to serve as a mini-practice set without the source documents. As such, students should plan on about three to four hours to complete this problem.

The General's Favorite Fishing Hole
Chart of Accounts

Assets		Revenues	
101	Cash	401	Registration Fees
142	Office Supplies		
144	Food Supplies	Expenses	
145	Prepaid Insurance	511	Wages Expense
181	Fishing Boats	521	Rent Expense
181.1	Accum. Depr.—Fishing Boats	523	Office Supplies Expense
		524	Food Supplies Expense
Liabilities		525	Phone Expense
202	Accounts Payable	533	Utilities Expense
219	Wages Payable	535	Insurance Expense
		536	Postage Expense
Owner's Equity		542	Depr. Exp.—Fishing Boats
311	Bob Night, Capital		
312	Bob Night, Drawing		
313	Income Summary		

The following transactions took place during April 20--.

Apr. 1 Night invested cash in business, $90,000.

1 Paid insurance premium for six-month camping season, $9,000.

2 Paid rent for lodge and campgrounds for the month of April, $40,000.

2 Deposited registration fees, $35,000.

2 Purchased 10 fishing boats on account for $60,000. The boats have estimated useful lives of five years, at which time they will be donated to a local day camp. Arrangements were made to pay for the boats in July.

3 Purchased food supplies from Acme Super Market on account, $7,000.

5 Purchased office supplies from Gordon Office Supplies on account, $500.

7 Deposited registration fees, $38,600.

10 Purchased food supplies from Acme Super Market on account, $8,200.

10 Paid wages to fishing guides, $10,000.

14 Deposited registration fees, $30,500.

(*continued*)

Apr. 16	Purchased food supplies from Acme Super Market on account, $9,000.
17	Paid wages to fishing guides, $10,000.
18	Paid postage, $150.
21	Deposited registration fees, $35,600.
24	Purchased food supplies from Acme Super Market on account, $8,500.
24	Paid wages to fishing guides, $10,000.
28	Deposited registration fees, $32,000.
29	Paid wages to fishing guides, $10,000.
30	Purchased food supplies from Acme Super Market on account, $6,000.
30	Paid Acme Super Market on account, $32,700.
30	Paid utilities bill, $2,000.
30	Paid phone bill, $1,200.
30	Bob Night withdrew cash for personal use, $6,000.

Adjustment information for the end of April is provided below.

(a) Office supplies remaining on hand, $100.

(b) Food supplies remaining on hand, $8,000.

(c) Insurance expired during the month of April, $1,500.

(d) Depreciation on the fishing boats for the month of April, $1,000.

(e) Wages earned, but not yet paid, at the end of April, $500.

REQUIRED

1. Enter the transactions in a general journal. Enter transactions from April 1–5 on page 1, April 7–18 on page 2, April 21–29 and the first two entries for April 30 on page 3, and the remaining entries for April 30 on page 4.

2. Post the entries to the general ledger. (If you are not using the working papers that accompany this text, you will need to enter the account titles and account numbers in the general ledger accounts.)

3. Prepare a trial balance on a work sheet.

4. Complete the work sheet.

5. Journalize the adjusting entries (page 5).

6. Post the adjusting entries to the general ledger.

7. Prepare the income statement.

8. Prepare the statement of owner's equity.

9. Prepare the balance sheet.

10. Journalize the closing entries (pages 5 and 6).

11. Post the closing entries to the general ledger.

12. Prepare a post-closing trial balance.

The Accounting Cycle

During the month of May 20--, The General's Favorite Fishing Hole engaged in the following transactions. These transactions required an expansion of the chart of accounts as shown below.

This comprehensive problem is intended to serve as a mini-practice set without the source documents. As such, students should plan on about three to four hours to complete this problem.

Assets		Revenues	
101	Cash	401	Registration Fees
122	Accounts Receivable	404	Vending Commission Revenue
142	Office Supplies		
144	Food Supplies	Expenses	
145	Prepaid Insurance	511	Wages Expense
146	Prepaid Subscriptions	512	Advertising Expense
161	Land	521	Rent Expense
171	Buildings	523	Office Supplies Expense
171.1	Accum. Depr.—Buildings	524	Food Supplies Expense
181	Fishing Boats	525	Phone Expense
181.1	Accum. Depr.—Fishing Boats	533	Utilities Expense
182	Surround Sound System	535	Insurance Expense
182.1	Accum. Depr.—Surround Sound Sys.	536	Postage Expense
183	Big Screen TV	537	Repair Expense
183.1	Accum. Depr.—Big Screen TV	540	Depr. Exp.—Buildings
		541	Depr. Exp.—Surround Sound Sys.
Liabilities		542	Depr. Exp.—Fishing Boats
202	Accounts Payable	543	Depr. Exp.—Big Screen TV
219	Wages Payable	546	Satellite Programming Exp.
		548	Subscriptions Expense
Owner's Equity			
311	Bob Night, Capital		
312	Bob Night, Drawing		
313	Income Summary		

May 1   In order to provide snacks for guests on a 24-hour basis, Night signed a contract with Snack Attack. Snack Attack will install vending machines with food and drinks and pay a 10% commission on all sales. Estimated payments are made at the beginning of each month. Night received a check for $200, the estimated commission on sales for May.

    2   Night purchased a surround sound system and big screen TV with a digital satellite system for the guest lounge. The surround sound system cost $3,600 and has an estimated useful life of five years and no salvage value. The TV cost $8,000, has an estimated useful life of eight years, and has a salvage value of $800. Night paid cash for both items.

    2   Paid for May's programming on the new digital satellite system, $125.

(continued)

May	3	Night's office manager returned $100 worth of office supplies to Gordon Office Supply. Night received a $100 reduction on the account.
	3	Deposited registration fees, $52,700.
	3	Paid rent for lodge and campgrounds for the month of May, $40,000.
	3	In preparation for the purchase of a nearby campground, Night invested an additional $600,000.
	4	Paid Gordon Office Supply on account, $400.
	4	Purchased the assets of a competing business and paid cash for the following: land, $100,000; lodge, $530,000; and fishing boats, $9,000. The lodge has a remaining useful life of 50 years and a $50,000 salvage value. The boats have remaining lives of five years and no salvage value.
	5	Paid May's insurance premium for the new camp, $1,000. (See above transaction.)
	5	Purchased food supplies from Acme Super Market on account, $22,950.
	5	Purchased office supplies from Gordon Office Supplies on account, $1,200.
	7	Night paid $40 each for one-year subscriptions to *Fishing Illustrated*, *Fishing Unlimited*, and *Fish Master*. The magazines are published monthly.
	10	Deposited registration fees, $62,750.
	13	Paid wages to fishing guides, $30,000. (Don't forget wages payable from prior month.)
	14	A guest became ill and was unable to stay for the entire week. A refund was issued in the amount of $1,000.
	17	Deposited registration fees, $63,000.
	19	Purchased food supplies from Acme Super Market on account, $18,400.
	21	Deposited registration fees, $63,400.
	23	Paid $2,500 for May's advertising spots on National Sports Talk Radio.
	25	Paid repair fee for damaged boat, $850.
	27	Paid wages to fishing guides, $30,000.
	28	Paid $1,800 for May's advertising spots on billboards.
	29	Purchased food supplies from Acme Super Market on account, $14,325.
	30	Paid utilities bill, $3,300.
	30	Paid phone bill, $1,800.
	30	Paid Acme Super Market on account, $47,350.
	31	Bob Night withdrew cash for personal use, $7,500.

Adjustment information at the end of May is provided below.

(a) Total vending machine sales were $2,300 for the month of May. A 10% commission is earned on these sales.

(b) Straight-line depreciation is used for the 10 boats purchased on April 2 for $60,000. The useful life for these assets is five years and there is no salvage value. A full month's depreciation was taken in April on these boats. Straight-line depreciation is also used for the two boats purchased in May. Make one adjusting entry for all depreciation on the boats.

(c) Straight-line depreciation is used to depreciate the surround sound system.

(d) Straight-line depreciation is used to depreciate the big screen TV.

(e) Straight-line depreciation is used for the building purchased in May.

(f) On April 2, Night paid $9,000 for insurance during the six-month camping season. May's portion of this premium was used up during this month.

(g) Night received his May issues of *Fishing Illustrated, Fishing Unlimited*, and *Fish Master*.

(h) Office supplies remaining on hand, $150.

(i) Food supplies remaining on hand, $5,925.

(j) Wages earned, but not yet paid, at the end of May, $6,000.

REQUIRED

1. Enter the transactions in a general journal. Enter transactions from May 1–4 on page 7, May 5–28 on page 8, and the remaining entries on page 9. To save time and space, don't enter descriptions for the journal entries.

2. Post the entries to the general ledger. (If you are not using the working papers that accompany this text, you will need to enter the account titles, account numbers, and balances from April 30 in the general ledger accounts.)

3. Prepare a trial balance on a work sheet.

4. Complete the work sheet.

5. Journalize the adjusting entries on page 10 of the general journal.

6. Post the adjusting entries to the general ledger.

7. Prepare the income statement.

8. Prepare the statement of owner's equity.

9. Prepare the balance sheet.

10. Journalize the closing entries on page 11 of the general journal.

11. Post the closing entries to the general ledger.

12. Prepare a post-closing trial balance.

2 Accounting for Cash and Payroll

Add some color to your learning!

Throughout the text, you will be introduced to many important terms and types of accounts. To help you learn the different terms and types of accounts, we have coded many of them using the following color key in Part 2:

Assets
Contra-Assets
Liabilities
Capital
Drawing
Revenues
Contra-Revenues
Expenses
Contra-Costs (Contra-Purchases)
Income Summary (Net Income/Net Loss)

Chapter 7 Accounting for Cash

H20 Audio was founded in 2003 with its home office in San Diego, California. Its key products include waterproof, weatherproof, and sweatproof audio equipment designed to enable athletes to use their electronics across virtually all sports, especially underwater. H20 Audio sells its merchandise online, in major electronics stores, in sports shops, and in other retailers throughout the United States and in more than 30 other countries. The company started quite small, but it grew rapidly. In one four-year period, its revenues increased more than 800%.

Two of the challenges for a company growing as fast as H20 Audio are managing and protecting its cash. H20 Audio has multiple checking accounts, receives cash receipts from multiple sources, and makes cash payments for many different bills. The company must have clear procedures and complete and accurate records in order to properly control cash and to plan for future needs. In this chapter, you will learn some of the ways to manage this critical business asset.

LEARNING OBJECTIVES

Careful study of this chapter should enable you to:

LO1 Describe how to open and use a checking account.

LO2 Prepare a bank reconciliation and related journal entries.

LO3 Establish and use a petty cash fund.

LO4 Establish a change fund and use the cash short and over account.

Cash is an asset that is quite familiar and important to all of us. We generally think of cash as the bills and coins in our pockets and the money we have in our checking accounts. To a business, cash also includes checks received from customers, money orders, and bank cashier's checks.

Because it plays such a central role in operating a business, cash must be carefully managed and controlled. A business should have a system of internal control—a set of policies and procedures designed to ensure proper accounting for transactions. For good internal control of cash transactions, all cash received should be deposited daily in a bank. All disbursements, except for payments from petty cash, should be made by check.

| LO1 | **Checking Account** |

Describe how to open and use a checking account.

The key documents and forms required in opening and using a checking account are the signature card, deposit tickets, checks, and bank statements.

Opening a Checking Account

The USA PATRIOT Act was passed in 2001. The primary purpose of the act was to help detect and prevent terrorism. As a result of the act, all banks must have a CIP that provides clear identification of every account holder of the bank.

Every bank is required to maintain a Customer Identification Program (CIP) that provides clear identification of every account holder. The specific documents required from the customer vary depending on the bank's program and services provided to the customer. For example, for a checking account, each person authorized to sign checks must complete and sign a signature card (Figure 7-1 on page 233). The bank can use this card to verify the depositor's signature on banking transactions. The taxpayer identification number (TIN) is the depositor's Social Security number or employer identification number (EIN). This number is shown on the card to identify the depositor for income tax purposes. An EIN can be obtained from the Internal Revenue Service.

Making Deposits

Because of the high volume of transactions that they process, banks normally review signatures only on checks for large amounts and a sample of others. This makes it important for you to review your monthly bank statement.

A deposit ticket (Figure 7-2 on page 234) is a form showing a detailed listing of items being deposited. Bills, coins, and checks are listed separately. Each check can be identified by its ABA (American Bankers Association) Number. This number is the small fraction printed in the upper right-hand corner of each check (see Figure 7-4 on page 236). Part of this number also appears in a magnetic ink character recognition (MICR) code on the lower left side of the front of each check. The code is used to sort and route checks throughout the U.S. banking system. Normally, only the numerator of the fraction is used in identifying checks on the deposit ticket. Alternatively, the individual checks can be identified by the name of the writer of the check.

The depositor delivers or mails the deposit ticket and all items being deposited to the bank. The bank then gives or mails a receipt to the depositor. The deposit also can be made after business hours by using the night depository provided by most banks. The deposit is put in a locked bag, which is placed in a secure drawer or chute at the bank, for processing the following morning.

When checks are deposited, there commonly is a delay before the funds are available for withdrawal. The delay can vary from one to eleven days, depending on the newness of the account, size and source of the checks, and many other factors.

Deposits can also be made at ATMs and through mobile apps. These methods are discussed later in the chapter.

Endorsements

Each check being deposited (or cashed) must be endorsed by the payee, the party to whom the check is payable. The endorsement consists of stamping or writing the

FIGURE 7-1 Signature Card

ACCOUNT NUMBER

ACCOUNT OWNER(S) NAME & ADDRESS

OWNERSHIP OF ACCOUNT - PERSONAL PURPOSE
- ☐ INDIVIDUAL   ☐ _____
- ☐ JOINT - WITH SURVIVORSHIP (and not as tenants in common)
- ☐ JOINT - NO SURVIVORSHIP (as tenants in common)
- ☐ TRUST - SEPARATE AGREEMENT

☐ REVOCABLE TRUST   OR   ☐ PAY-ON-DEATH
DESIGNATION AS DEFINED IN THIS AGREEMENT
Name and Address of Beneficiaries:

TYPE OF ACCOUNT
- ☐ NEW   ☐ EXISTING
- ☐ CHECKING   ☐ SAVINGS
- ☐ MONEY MARKET ☐ CERTIFICATE OF DEPOSIT
- ☐ NOW   ☐ _____

This is your (check one):
    ☐ Permanent   ☐ Temporary   account agreement

Number of signatures required for withdrawal _____
FACSIMILE SIGNATURE(S) ALLOWED?   ☐ YES ☐ NO

X _____

OWNERSHIP OF ACCOUNT - BUSINESS PURPOSE
- ☐ SOLE PROPRIETORSHIP
- ☐ CORPORATION: ☐ FOR PROFIT   ☐ NOT FOR PROFIT
- ☐ PARTNERSHIP
- ☐ _____
- BUSINESS: _____
- COUNTRY & STATE
- OF ORGANIZATION: _____
- AUTHORIZATION DATED: _____

DATE OPENED _____ BY_____
INITIAL DEPOSIT $ _____
    ☐ CASH ☐ CHECK ☐ _____
HOME PHONE# _____
BUSINESS PHONE# _____
DRIVER'S LICENSE# _____
E-MAIL _____
EMPLOYER _____
MOTHER'S MAIDEN NAME _____
Name and address of someone who will always know your location: _____
_____
_____

SIGNATURE(S) - The undersigned certifies the accuracy of the information he/she has provided and acknowledges receipt of a completed copy of this form. The undersigned authorizes the financial institution to verify credit and employment history and/or have a credit reporting agency prepare a credit report on the undersigned, as individuals. The undersigned also acknowledge the receipt of a copy and agree to the terms of the following agreement(s) and/or disclosure(s):

- ☐ Terms & Conditions ☐ Truth in Savings ☐ Funds Availability
- ☐ Electronic Fund Transfers ☐ Privacy ☐ Substitute Checks
- ☐ Common Features ☐ _____

X _____

I.D. # _____ D.O.B. _____

X _____

I.D. # _____ D.O.B. _____

BACKUP WITHHOLDING CERTIFICATIONS
TIN: _____

☐ **TAXPAYER I.D. NUMBER -** The Taxpayer Identification Number shown above(TIN) is my correct taxpayer identification number.

☐ **BACKUP WITHHOLDING -** I am not subject to backup withholding either because I have not been notified that I am subject to backup withholding as a result of a failure to report all interest or dividends, or the Internal Revenue Service has notified me that I am no longer subject to backup withholding.

☐ **EXEMPT RECIPIENTS -** I am an exempt recipient under the Internal Revenue Service Regulations.

SIGNATURE: I certify under penalties of perjury the statements checked in this section and that I am a U.S. citizen or other U.S. person (as defined in the instructions).

X _____
                    (Date)

X _____

I.D. # _____ D.O.B. _____

X _____

I.D. # _____ D.O.B. _____

☐ Authorized Signer (Individual Accounts Only)

X _____

I.D. # _____ D.O.B. _____

FIGURE 7-2 Deposit Ticket

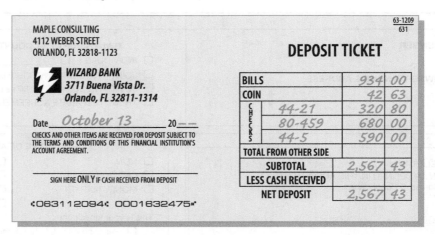

payee's name and sometimes other information on the back of the check, in the space provided near the left end. There are two basic types of endorsements.

1. **Blank endorsement**—the payee simply signs the back of the check. This makes the check payable to any bearer.
2. **Restrictive endorsement**—the payee adds words such as "Pay to the order of (specific) bank," or "Pay to Daryl Beck" to restrict the payment of the check to a specific party. By adding words such as "For deposit only," the payee can restrict the payment of the check for a specific purpose.

Businesses commonly use a rubber stamp to endorse checks for deposit. The check shown in Figure 7-3 has been stamped with a restrictive endorsement.

FIGURE 7-3 Restrictive Endorsement

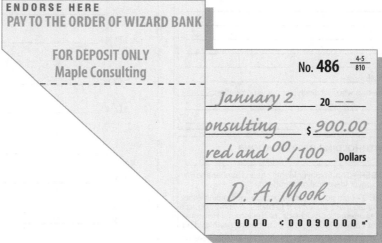

Automated Teller Machines

Postage stamps can be purchased at some ATMs. For deposits, some ATMs can provide an image of any checks being deposited.

Most banks now make **automated teller machines (ATMs)** available at all times to depositors for making deposits or withdrawals. Each depositor has a plastic card and a personal identification number (PIN). The depositor inserts the card, keys in the PIN, indicates whether the transaction is a withdrawal or a deposit, and enters the amount. The machine has a drawer or door for withdrawal or deposit.

Most ATMs are now on a system such as Cirrus that allows noncustomers to use other ATMs in both the United States and foreign countries. There are also "cash machines" that supply only cash and do not take deposits. These are often found at airports and convenience stores.

The convenience of ATMs and other forms of electronic banking discussed later in this chapter comes with a challenge: security. It is very important to keep PIN numbers and other forms of passwords safe, to protect your assets.

It is also important for the depositor to keep an accounting record of ATM withdrawals and deposits. This is done on the check stub or register described in the following section, and with an appropriate journal entry.

Writing Checks

A check is a document ordering a bank to pay cash from a depositor's account. There are three parties to every check.

1. Drawer—the depositor who orders the bank to pay the cash.
2. Drawee—the bank on which the check is drawn.
3. Payee—the party to whom the check is payable.

Checks used by businesses are usually bound in the form of a book. In some checkbooks, each check is attached to a check stub (Figure 7-4) that contains space to record all relevant information about the check. Other checkbooks are accompanied by a small register book in which the relevant information is noted. If a financial computer software package is used, both the check and the register can be prepared electronically.

Note that the check stubs in Figure 7-4 contain space to record amounts deposited. It generally is a good idea also to indicate the date of the deposit, as shown on check stub No. 108.

Use the following three steps in preparing a check:

STEP 1   Complete the check stub or register.

STEP 2   Enter the date, payee name, and amount on the check.

STEP 3   Sign the check.

The check stub is completed first so that the drawer retains a record of each check issued. This information is needed to determine the proper journal entry for the transaction.

The "payee's" name is entered on the first long line on the check, followed by the amount in figures. The amount in words is then entered on the second long line. If the amount in figures does not agree with the amount in words, the bank usually contacts the drawer for the correct amount or returns the check unpaid.

The most critical point in preparing a check is signing it, and this should be done last. The signature authorizes the bank to pay cash from the drawer's account. The check signer should make sure that all other aspects of the check are correct before signing it.

The numbers at the bottom of the check are preprinted on every check. They indicate the bank routing number used by the Federal Reserve Bank, the bank account number, and the check number. This information and the code in the upper right-hand corner of the check are used to process the check through the banking system.

Bank Statement

A statement of account issued by a bank to each depositor once a month is called a bank statement. Banks prepare bank statements using various formats. Figure 7-5 is a simple bank statement for a checking account. The statement shows the following:

1. The balance at the beginning of the period.
2. Deposits and other amounts added during the period.
3. Checks and other amounts subtracted during the period.
4. Other electronic transactions.
5. The balance at the end of the period.

> When a check needs to be voided, follow these procedures: 1. tear off or completely cross out (deface) the signature, 2. write "Void" by the check number on the check stub or check register, and 3. file the voided check numerically with the other records of canceled checks.

> LEARNING KEY
>
> The check should not be signed until the check signer has verified that all aspects of the check are correct.

FIGURE 7-4 Checks and Check Stubs

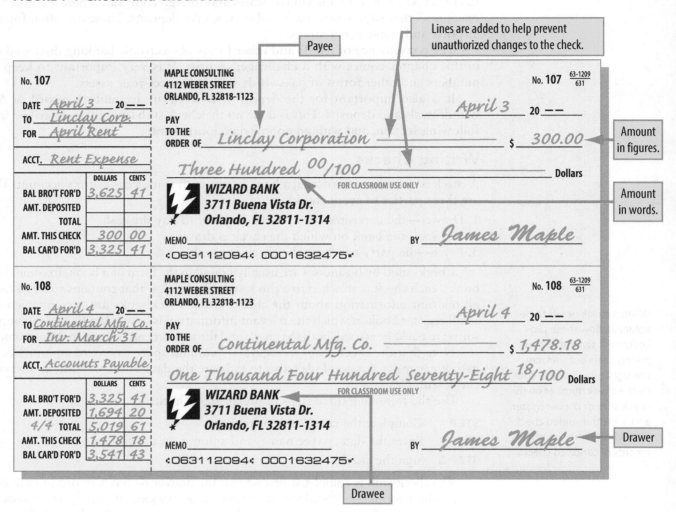

Complete Checkpoint-1 on page 253 to test your basic understanding of LO1.

CHECKPOINT ✔

With the bank statement, the bank normally sends the following to the depositor:

1. Listing of **canceled checks**—a list of the depositor's checks paid by the bank during the period. The bank may send "imaged" sheets showing only the faces of the checks or the checks themselves, although this is increasingly uncommon today.
2. Any other forms representing items added to or subtracted from the account.

LO2

Prepare a bank reconciliation and related journal entries.

Reconciling the Bank Statement

On any given day, the balance in the cash account on the depositor's books (the book balance) is unlikely to be the same as that on the bank's books (the bank balance). This difference can be due to errors, but it usually is caused by timing. Transactions generally are recorded by the business at a time that is different from when the bank records them.

Deposits

Suppose there are cash receipts of $600 on April 30. These cash receipts would be recorded on the depositor's books on April 30, and a deposit of $600 would be transmitted to the bank. The deposit would not clear however, until at least the following

FIGURE 7-5 Bank Statement

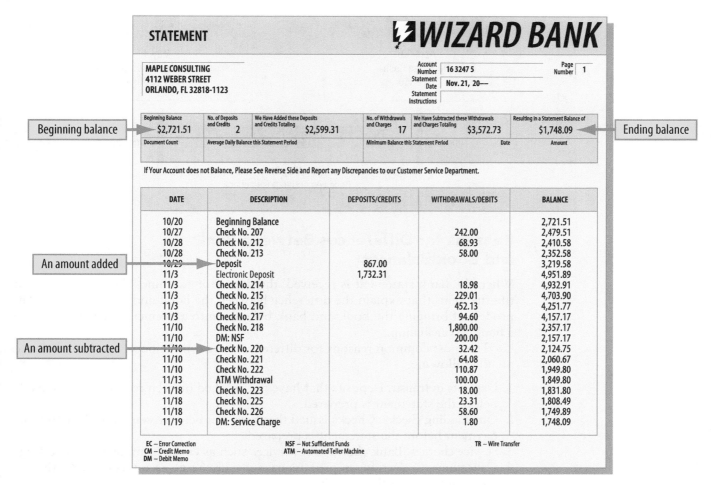

Beginning balance

Ending balance

An amount added

An amount subtracted

day, May 1. This timing difference in recording the $600 of cash receipts is illustrated in Figure 7-6. Notice that on April 30, the balances in the depositor's books and in the bank's books would be different. The depositor's book balance would be $600 more than the bank's book balance.

FIGURE 7-6 Depositor and Bank Records—Deposits

Cash Payments

Similar timing differences occur with cash payments. Suppose a check for $350 is written on April 30. This cash payment would be recorded on the depositor's books on April 30 and the check mailed to the payee. The check probably would not be received by the payee until May 3. If the payee deposited the check promptly, it still would not clear the bank until May 4. This timing difference in recording the $350 cash payment is illustrated in Figure 7-7. Notice once again that on April 30, the balances in the depositor's books and in the bank's books would be different. The depositor's book balance would be $350 less than the bank's book balance.

FIGURE 7-7 Depositor and Bank Records—Cash Payments

Reasons for Differences Between Bank and Book Balances

When the bank statement is received, the depositor examines the records to identify the items that explain the difference between the book and bank balances. This process of bringing the book and bank balances into agreement is called preparing a bank reconciliation.

The most common reasons for differences between the book and bank balances are the following:

1. **Deposits in transit.** Deposits that have not reached or been recorded by the bank before the statement is prepared.
2. **Outstanding checks.** Checks issued that have not been presented to the bank for payment before the statement is prepared.
3. **Service charges.** Bank charges for services such as check printing and processing.
4. **Collections.** Collections of promissory notes or charge accounts made by the bank on behalf of the depositor.
5. **Not sufficient funds (NSF) checks.** Checks deposited by the depositor that are not paid because the drawer did not have sufficient funds.
6. **Errors.** Errors made by the bank or the depositor in recording cash transactions.

Steps in Preparing the Bank Reconciliation

Use the following three steps in preparing the bank reconciliation:

STEP 1 Identify deposits in transit and any related errors.

STEP 2 Identify outstanding checks and any related errors.

STEP 3 Identify additional reconciling items.

Deposits in Transit and Related Errors

Follow these steps:

STEP 1 Compare deposits listed on the bank statement with deposits in transit on last month's bank reconciliation. All of last month's deposits in transit should appear on the current month's bank statement.

STEP 2 Compare the remaining deposits on the bank statement with deposits listed in the accounting records. Any deposits listed in the accounting records but not on the bank statement are deposits in transit on the current bank reconciliation.

STEP 3 Compare the individual deposit amounts on the bank statement and in the accounting records. If they differ, the error needs to be corrected.

Outstanding Checks and Related Errors

Follow these steps:

STEP 1 Compare canceled checks with the bank statement and the accounting records. If the amounts differ, the error needs to be corrected.

STEP 2 As each canceled check is compared with the accounting records, place a check mark on the check stub or other accounting record to indicate that the check has cleared.

STEP 3 Any checks written that have not been checked off represent outstanding checks on the bank reconciliation. This includes outstanding checks from last month's bank reconciliation that have not yet cleared.

Additional Reconciling Items

Compare any additions and deductions on the bank statement that are not deposits or checks with the accounting records. Items that the bank adds to the account are called credit memos. Items that the bank deducts from the account are called debit memos. Remember that a depositor's account is a liability to the bank. Thus, a credit memo increases this liability; a debit memo reduces the liability. Any of these items not appearing in the accounting records represent additional items on the bank reconciliation.

> Some banks pay interest on checking account balances. This reconciling item would be handled in the same manner as a bank credit memo.

Illustration of a Bank Reconciliation

A general format for the bank reconciliation is shown in Figure 7-8. Not every item shown in this illustration would be in every bank reconciliation, but this format is helpful in determining where to put items. A bank reconciliation form also can be found on the back of most bank statements. Figure 7-9 is an example of such a form with instructions. Some banks also include a reconciliation form on their website.

To illustrate the preparation of a bank reconciliation, we will use the Maple Consulting bank statement shown in Figure 7-5. That statement shows a balance of $1,748.09 as of November 21. The balance in Maple's check stubs and general ledger

FIGURE 7-8 Bank Reconciliation Format

BANK RECONCILIATION		
Bank statement balance		$xxxx
Add: Deposits in transit	$xxxx	
Bank errors (that understate balance)	xxxx	xxxx
		$xxxx
Deduct: Outstanding checks	$xxxx	
Bank errors (that overstate balance)	xxxx	xxxx
Adjusted bank balance		$xxxx
Book balance		$xxxx
Add: Bank credit memos	$xxxx	
Book errors (that understate balance)	xxxx	xxxx
		$xxxx
Deduct: Bank debit memos	$xxxx	
Book errors (that overstate balance)	xxxx	xxxx
Adjusted book balance		$xxxx

FIGURE 7-9 Reconciliation Form From Bank Statement

Outstanding Deposits

Date	Amount
Total	$

Outstanding Withdrawals

Date	Amount
Total	$

1. List any deposits that do not appear on your statement in the Outstanding Deposits section at the left. Record the total.

2. Check off in your book register all checks, withdrawals (including Check Card and ATM) and automatic payments that appear on your statement. Withdrawals that are NOT checked off should be recorded in the Outstanding Withdrawals section at the left. Record the total.

3. Enter the ending balance shown on this statement. $_____

4. Enter the total deposits recorded in the Outstanding Deposits section. $_____

5. Total the amounts in steps 3 and 4. $_____

6. Enter the total withdrawals recorded in the Outstanding Withdrawals section. $_____

7. Subtract the amount in step 6 from the amount in step 5. This is your balance. $_____

8. Enter in your register and subtract from your register balance any checks, withdrawals, or other debits (including fees, if any) that appear on your statement but have not been recorded in your register.

9. Enter in your register and add to your register balance any deposits or other credits (including interest, if any) that appear in your statement but have not been recorded in your register.

10. The balance in your register should be the same as the balance shown in step 7. If it does not match, review and check all figures used, and check the addition and subtraction in your register. If necessary, review and balance your statement from the previous month.

FIGURE 7-10 Bank Reconciliation

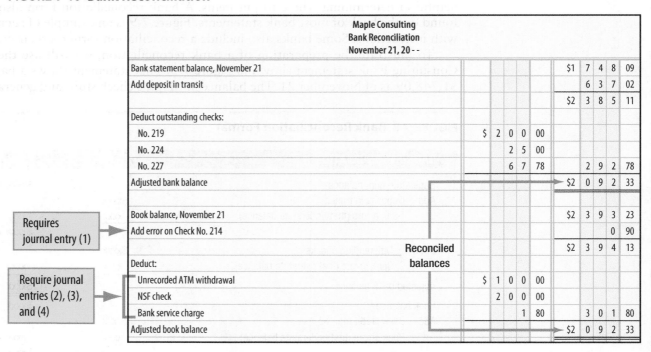

Maple Consulting									
Bank statement balance, November 21						$1	7	4 8	09
Add deposit in transit							6	3 7	02
						$2	3	8 5	11
Deduct outstanding checks:									
No. 219	$	2	0 0	00					
No. 224			2 5	00					
No. 227			6 7	78			2	9 2	78
Adjusted bank balance						$2	0	9 2	33
Book balance, November 21						$2	3	9 3	23
Add error on Check No. 214								0	90
						$2	3	9 4	13
Deduct:									
Unrecorded ATM withdrawal	$	1	0 0	00					
NSF check		2	0 0	00					
Bank service charge			1	80			3	0 1	80
Adjusted book balance						$2	0	9 2	33

Requires journal entry (1)

Require journal entries (2), (3), and (4)

Reconciled balances

cash account is $2,393.23. The three steps described on page 238 were used to identify the following items, and the reconciliation in Figure 7-10 was prepared.

1. A deposit of $637.02 recorded on November 21 had not been received by the bank. Maple has received the funds but the amount has not yet been counted by the bank. This deposit in transit is added to the bank statement balance.

2. Check numbers 219, 224, and 227 are outstanding. The funds have been disbursed by Maple but have not yet been paid out by the bank. The amount of these outstanding checks is subtracted from the bank statement balance.

3. Check number 214 was written for $18.98 but was entered on the check stub and on the books as $19.88. This $0.90 error is added to the book balance because $0.90 too much had been deducted from the book balance.

4. Maple made an ATM withdrawal of $100 on November 13 for personal use but did not record the withdrawal on the books. The bank has reduced Maple's balance by this amount. Thus, this amount is deducted from the book balance.

5. The bank returned an NSF check of $200. This was a check received by Maple from a customer. The bank has reduced Maple's balance by $200, but Maple has not yet recorded it. This amount is deducted from the book balance.

6. The bank service charge was $1.80. The bank has reduced Maple's balance by this amount, but Maple has not yet recorded it. This amount is deducted from the book balance.

Journal Entries

Only two kinds of items appearing on a bank reconciliation require journal entries.

1. Errors in the depositor's books.
2. Bank additions and deductions that do not already appear in the books.

> **LEARNING KEY**
>
> Journal entries are needed to correct errors in the books and to record bank additions and deductions that are not in the books.

Note the four items in the lower portion of the bank reconciliation in Figure 7-10. A journal entry always is required for each item in this book balance portion of the bank reconciliation. The four journal entries for Maple Consulting are shown below, using entry numbers matching those noted in Figure 7-10.

The $0.90 item is an error in the accounting records that occurred when the check amount was incorrectly entered. Assume that $18.98 was in payment of an account payable which had been incorrectly debited for $19.88. The entry to correct this error is as follows:

4	(1)	Cash				0	90						4
5		Accounts Payable								0	90		5
6		Error in recording check											6

The $100 ATM withdrawal has been deducted from Maple's account by the bank. Maple has not yet recorded the withdrawal. Maple withdrew the funds for personal use, so the following journal entry is required:

8	(2)	James Maple, Drawing		1	0	0	00						8
9		Cash							1	0	0	00	9
10		Unrecorded ATM withdrawal											10

The $200 NSF check is a deduction by the bank for a check deposited by Maple that proved to be worthless. This amount must be deducted from the book balance. Assuming that $200 was received from a customer on account, the following journal entry is required:

12	(3)	Accounts Receivable		2	0	0	00						12
13		Cash							2	0	0	00	13
14		Unrecorded NSF check											14

The $1.80 bank service charge is a fee for bank services received by Maple. The bank has deducted this amount from Maple's account. Bank service charges are usually small and are charged to Miscellaneous Expense.

16		(4) Miscellaneous Expense						1	80					16
17		Cash								1	80			17
18		Bank service charge												18

Figure 7-11 contains a detailed list of items that require journal entries.

FIGURE 7-11 Bank Reconciliation Items that Require Journal Entries

ADDITIONS TO CASH BALANCE	DEDUCTIONS FROM CASH BALANCE

* Unrecorded deposits (including ATM)
* Note collected by bank
* Interest earned
* Errors:
  1. Added too little as a deposit
  2. Deducted too much as a check
	* Unrecorded ATM withdrawals
	* NSF checks
	* Bank service charges
	* Deposits recorded twice
	* Unrecorded checks
	* Loan payments
	* Interest payments
	* Errors:
	  1. Added too much as a deposit
	  2. Deducted too little as a check

Electronic Banking

Thus far in the chapter, we have explained and illustrated mainly a world of paper deposits, payments, and bank statements. Such a world still exists. But while many businesses and individuals still write and receive checks, the paper world of banking is shrinking rapidly. In fact, virtually every aspect of banking processes can be handled electronically.

Electronic Funds Transfer

Both deposits and payments can be made with electronic funds transfer (EFT), using a computer rather than paper checks. Your net pay can be sent electronically by your employer to your bank, and you can review the summary of your compensation and various deductions on your computer. You can take a picture of a check with your smart phone and send it to the bank as a deposit. You can transfer funds between savings and checking accounts electronically. You can buy lunch or groceries, or withdraw money from a bank machine using your debit card. Payments on your credit card account or for utility bills can be made electronically. And your bank statement probably is sent to you electronically by your bank.

Businesses also are making increasing use of EFT in handling cash transactions. For example, as noted above, employee wages can be paid using EFT. Bills from suppliers also can be paid by EFT. Payments from customers frequently are in electronic form. And funds can be transferred electronically among multiple accounts at different banks.

Bank Reconciliations

Even the idea of the monthly bank reconciliation requires adjustment in an electronic banking world. In a paper world, you deposit paper checks, write paper checks, and keep paper records of your financial activities. Once a month, the bank sends you a bank statement and you "reconcile" your transactions and balance with the bank's records. In the electronic banking world, you can use your smartphone to regularly (daily?) view the effects of your transactions on your balance. There is no waiting until month-end to compare your records with the bank's. With fully electronic banking, the monthly reconciliation can be replaced by a regular "monitoring" of the account. If the bank's processing of a transaction is different from yours, you can

CHECKPOINT ✓

Complete Checkpoint-2 on page 254 to test your basic understanding of LO2.

see it immediately and correct your records or contact the bank. There should be very little news in a monthly bank statement in an electronic banking world.

Heavy use of EFT will present record keeping challenges. Many of the documents handled in a purely manual environment disappear when EFT is used. Bank accounts are just one of many areas where computers require accountants to think in new ways. Regardless of what system is used, the key point to remember is that the accounting records must be correctly updated.

A BROADER VIEW

Fraud—A Real Threat to Small Business

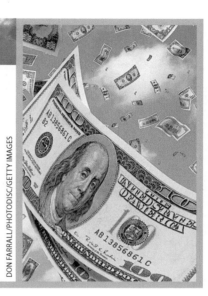

Every two years, the Association of Certified Fraud Examiners (ACFE) surveys its members on the occupational fraud they have investigated during the preceding two years. The most recent survey showed that more than 30% of the frauds occurred in small businesses. In addition, the median loss suffered by small businesses was $150,000. The most commonly cited factor that allowed the fraud to occur was a lack of adequate internal control. And the majority of the asset misappropriation cases involved theft or misuse of cash.

These survey findings show the importance of the kinds of internal controls over cash described in this chapter and the appendix.

DON FARRALL/PHOTODISC/GETTY IMAGES

LO3

The Petty Cash Fund

Establish and use a petty cash fund.

For good control over cash, payments generally should be made by check. Unfortunately, payments of very small amounts by check can be both inconvenient and inefficient. For example, the time and cost required to write a check for $0.70 to mail a letter might be greater than the cost of the postage. Therefore, businesses customarily establish a petty cash fund to pay for small items with cash. "Petty" means small, and both the amount of the fund and the maximum amount of any bill that can be paid from the fund are small.

Establishing a Petty Cash Fund

To establish a petty cash fund, a check is written to the petty cash custodian for the amount to be set aside in the fund. The amount may be $50, $100, $200, or any amount considered necessary. The journal entry to establish a petty cash fund of $100 would be as follows:

4		Petty Cash		1	0	0	00						4
5		Cash							1	0	0	00	5
6		Establish petty cash fund											6

Petty Cash is an asset that is listed immediately below Cash on the balance sheet.

The custodian cashes the check and places the money in a petty cash box. For good control, the custodian should be the only person authorized to make payments from the fund. The custodian should be able to account for the full amount of the fund at any time.

Making Payments from a Petty Cash Fund

A receipt called a petty cash voucher (Figure 7-12) should be prepared for every payment from the fund. The voucher shows the name of the payee, the purpose of the payment, and the account to be charged for the payment. Each voucher should be signed by the custodian and by the person receiving the cash. The vouchers should be numbered consecutively so that all vouchers can be accounted for. At any time, the sum of the current vouchers and the unused cash should equal the original amount of the fund.

FIGURE 7-12 Petty Cash Voucher

PETTY CASH VOUCHER		
	NO. 2	
	DATE December 8, 20 — —	
PAID TO James Maple		
FOR Client Luncheon	$	¢
CHARGE TO Travel & Entertainment Expense	25	75
REMITTANCE RECEIVED	APPROVED BY	
James Maple	Tina Blank	

Petty Cash Payments Record

When a petty cash fund is maintained, a formal record is often kept of all payments from the fund. The petty cash payments record (Figure 7-13) is a special multi-column record that supplements the regular accounting records. It is not a journal. The headings of the Distribution of Payments columns may vary, depending upon the types of expenditures.

The petty cash payments record of Maple Consulting is shown in Figure 7-13. A narrative of the petty cash transactions shown in Figure 7-13 is as follows:

Dec. 1 Maple issued a check for $200 payable to Tina Blank, Petty Cash Custodian. Blank cashed the check and placed the money in a secure cash box.

A notation of the amount received is made in the Description column of the petty cash payments record. In addition, this transaction is entered in the journal as follows:

8	Dec. 1	Petty Cash		2	0	0	00					8
9		Cash							2	0	0	00	9
10		Establish petty cash fund											10

During the month of December, the following payments were made from the petty cash fund:

Dec. 5 Paid $32.80 to Jerry's Auto for servicing the company automobile. Voucher No. 1.

8 Reimbursed Maple $25.75 for the amount spent for lunch with a client. Voucher No. 2.

9 Gave Maple $30 for personal use. Voucher No. 3.

There is no special Distribution column for entering amounts withdrawn by the owner for personal use. Therefore, this payment is entered by writing the account name in the Account column and $30 in the Amount column at the extreme right of the petty cash payments record.

FIGURE 7-13 Maple Consulting's Petty Cash Payments Record

PETTY CASH PAYMENTS FOR THE MONTH OF December 20—   PAGE 1

DAY	DESCRIPTION		VOU. NO.	TOTAL AMOUNT	AUTO EXP.	POST. EXP.	TRAVEL/ ENTERT. EXP.	MISC. EXP.	ACCOUNT	AMOUNT	
1	Received in fund	200.00									1
5	Automobile repairs		1	3 2 80	3 2 80						2
8	Client luncheon		2	2 5 75			2 5 75				3
9	James Maple, personal use		3	3 0 00					James Maple, Drawing	3 0 00	4
15	Printer repairs		4	3 8 25				3 8 25			5
17	Traveling expenses		5	1 4 50			1 4 50				6
19	Washing automobile		6	8 00	8 00						7
22	Postage expense		7	9 50		9 50					8
29	Postage stamps		8	3 0 00		3 0 00					9
				1 8 8 80	4 0 80	3 9 50	4 0 25	3 8 25		3 0 00	10
31	Balance	11.20									11
31	Replenished fund	188.80									12
	Total	200.00									13
											14
											15
											16
											17
18											18
19											19
20											20
21											21
22											22
23											23
24											24
25											25
26											26
27											27
28											28

DISTRIBUTION OF PAYMENTS

Total must equal original fund balance.

Credit to replenish petty cash fund and reduce Cash.

Debits to replenish petty cash fund and recognize expenses paid out of petty cash.

15 Paid $38.25 for printer repairs. Voucher No. 4.

17 Reimbursed Maple $14.50 for travel expenses. Voucher No. 5.

19 Paid $8 to Big Red Car Care for washing the company automobile. Voucher No. 6.

22 Paid $9.50 for mailing a package. Voucher No. 7.

29 Paid $30 for postage stamps. Voucher No. 8.

Replenishing the Petty Cash Fund

The petty cash fund should be replenished whenever the fund runs low and at the end of each accounting period, so that the accounts are brought up to date. The amount columns of the petty cash payments record are totaled to verify that the total of the Total Amount column equals the total of the Distribution columns. The amount columns are then ruled as shown in Figure 7-13.

The information in the petty cash payments record is then used to replenish the petty cash fund. On December 31, a check for $188.80 is issued to the petty cash custodian. The journal entry to record the replenishment of the fund is as follows:

18	Dec.	31	Automobile Expense		4	0	80						18
19			Postage Expense		3	9	50						19
20			Travel and Entertainment Expense		4	0	25						20
21			Miscellaneous Expense		3	8	25						21
22			James Maple, Drawing		3	0	00						22
23			Cash						1	8	8	80	23
24			Replenishment of petty cash fund										24

Note two important aspects of the functioning of a petty cash fund.

1. Once the fund is established by debiting Petty Cash and crediting Cash, no further entries are made to Petty Cash. Notice in the journal entry to replenish the fund that the debits are to appropriate expense and drawing accounts and the credit is to Cash. Only if the amount of the fund itself is being changed would there be a debit or credit to Petty Cash.

2. The petty cash payments record is strictly a supplement to the regular accounting records. Because it is not a journal, no posting is done from this record. A separate entry must be made in the journal to replenish the fund and update the expense accounts.

LEARNING KEY

Once the petty cash fund is established, an entry is made to Petty Cash only if the amount of the fund is being changed.

CHECKPOINT

Complete Checkpoint-3 on page 254 to test your basic understanding of LO3.

LO4

The Change Fund and Cash Short and Over

Establish a change fund and use the cash short and over account.

Businesses generally must be able to make change when customers use cash to pay for goods or services received. To do so, generally it is a good idea to establish a change fund. A change fund is a supply of bills and coins kept in a cash register or cash drawer for use in handling cash sales.

Establishing and Operating the Change Fund

The journal entries for establishing and maintaining a change fund are very similar to the ones just used for petty cash. To establish a change fund of $200 on June 1, the following entry would be made:

8	June 1	Change Fund		2	0	0	00							8
9		Cash								2	0	0	00	9
10		Establish change fund												10

At the end of the day, cash received during the day is deposited, but the change fund is held back for use the following business day. For example, if cash of $1,250 was received on June 3 for services provided, the cash drawer would contain $1,450, as follows:

Change fund	$ 200
Cash sales	1,250
Total cash on hand	$1,450

The $1,250 would be deposited in the bank, and the following journal entry would be made:

12	June 3	Cash		1	2	5	0	00						12
13		Service Fees							1	2	5	0	00	13
14		Cash received for services												14

LEARNING KEY
Once the change fund is established, an entry is made to Change Fund only if the amount of the fund is being changed.

Notice the additional similarity between the change fund and the petty cash fund. Once the change fund is established by a debit to Change Fund and a credit to Cash, no further entries are made to the change fund. Only if the amount of the change fund itself is being changed would there be a debit or credit to Change Fund.

Cash Short and Over

An unavoidable part of the change-making process is that errors can occur. It is important to know whether such errors have occurred and how to account for them.

Businesses commonly use cash registers with tapes that accumulate a record of the day's receipts. The amount of cash according to the tapes plus the amount of the change fund can be compared with the amount of cash in the register to determine any error. For example, assume a cash shortage is identified for June 19.

Change fund	$ 200
Receipts per register tapes	963
Total	$1,163
Cash count	1,161
Cash shortage	$ 2

Similarly, assume a cash overage is identified for June 20.

Change fund	$ 200
Receipts per register tapes	814
Total	$1,014
Cash count	1,015
Cash overage	$ 1

We account for such errors by using an account called Cash Short and Over. In T account form, Cash Short and Over appears as follows:

Cash Short and Over

Shortage (Expense)	Overage (Revenue)

The register tapes on June 19 showed receipts of $963 and the change fund was $200, but only $1,161 in cash was counted. The journal entry on June 19 to record the revenues and cash shortage (remember that we hold back the change fund) would be as follows:

18	June	19	Cash			9	6	1	00								18
19			Cash Short and Over					2	00								19
20			Service Fees									9	6	3	00		20
21			Record service fees and cash shortage														21

The entry on June 20 to record the revenues and cash overage (holding back the change fund) would be as follows:

23	June	20	Cash			8	1	5	00								23
24			Service Fees									8	1	4	00		24
25			Cash Short and Over											1	00		25
26			Record service fees and cash overage														26

CHECKPOINT ✔

Complete Checkpoint-4 on page 254 to test your basic understanding of LO4.

The cash short and over account is used to accumulate cash shortages and overages throughout the accounting period. At the end of the period, a debit balance in the account (a net shortage) is treated as an expense. A credit balance in the account (a net overage) is treated as revenue.

YOUR PERSPECTIVE

Cashier

Anyone who has ever worked in a retail environment knows that cash is a precious asset. *Cashiers* are responsible for safeguarding this cash in stores and restaurants. At the beginning of each shift, the cashier begins by counting the change fund in the assigned register. The change fund is a supply of currency and coins kept in a cash register or drawer used in handling cash sales. This is one way the business maintains control over cash. At the end of the shift, the cashier recounts the cash and compares it to the register tape to determine any shortages or overages. This is important because the business needs to know if errors have occurred and to decide how to account for them.

SELF-STUDY

LEARNING OBJECTIVES	Key Points to Remember
LO1 Describe how to open and use a checking account.	Three steps to follow in preparing a check are as follows: 1. Complete the check stub or register. 2. Enter the date, payee name, and amount on the check. 3. Sign the check.

LEARNING OBJECTIVES	**Key Points to Remember**
LO2 Prepare a bank reconciliation and related journal entries.	The most common reasons for differences between the book and bank cash balances are as follows: 1. Deposits in transit 2. Outstanding checks 3. Bank service charges 4. Bank collections for the depositor 5. NSF checks 6. Errors by the bank or the depositor Three steps to follow in preparing a bank reconciliation are as follows: 1. Identify deposits in transit and any related errors. 2. Identify outstanding checks and any related errors. 3. Identify additional reconciling items. Only two kinds of items on a bank reconciliation require journal entries. 1. Errors in the depositor's books. 2. Bank additions and deductions that do not already appear in the books.
LO3 Establish and use a petty cash fund.	Two important aspects of the functioning of a petty cash fund are as follows: 1. Once the fund is established, subsequent entries do not affect the petty cash account balance, unless the size of the fund itself is being changed. 2. The petty cash payments record is supplemental to the regular accounting records. No posting is done from this record.
LO4 Establish a change fund and use the cash short and over account.	A change fund is established by debiting Change Fund and crediting Cash. Cash shortages and overages are accounted for using the cash short and over account. A debit balance in this account represents expense; a credit balance represents revenue.

DEMONSTRATION PROBLEM

Jason Kuhn's check stubs indicated a balance of $4,565.12 for Kuhn's Wilderness Outfitters on March 31. This included a record of a deposit of $926.10 mailed to the bank on March 30, but not credited to Kuhn's account until April 1. In addition, the following checks were outstanding on March 31:

No. 462	$524.26
No. 465	$213.41
No. 473	$543.58
No. 476	$351.38
No. 477	$197.45

The bank statement showed a balance of $5,419 as of March 31. The bank statement included a service charge of $4.10 with the date of March 29. In matching the canceled checks and record of deposits with the stubs, it was discovered that

Check No. 456, a payment on account to Office Suppliers, Inc., for $39 was errone-
ously recorded on the stub as $93. This caused the bank balance on that stub and
those following to be $54 too small. It was also discovered that an ATM withdrawal
of $100 for personal use was not recorded on the books.

Kuhn maintains a $200 petty cash fund. His petty cash payments record showed
the following totals at the end of March of the current year:

Automobile expense	$ 32.40
Postage expense	27.50
Charitable contributions expense	35.00
Phone expense	6.20
Travel and entertainment expense	38.60
Miscellaneous expense	17.75
Jason Kuhn, drawing	40.00
Total	$197.45

This left a balance of $2.55 in the petty cash fund, and the fund was replenished.

REQUIRED

1. Prepare a bank reconciliation for Jason Kuhn as of March 31, 20--.
2. Journalize the entries that should be made by Kuhn on his books as of March
   31, 20--, (a) as a result of the bank reconciliation and (b) to replenish the petty
   cash fund.
3. Show proof that, after these entries, the total of the cash and petty cash
   account balances equals $4,715.02.

SOLUTION 1.

Kuhn's Wilderness Outfitters
Bank Reconciliation
March 31, 20 --

Bank statement balance, March 31						$5	4	1 9	00
Add deposit in transit							9	2 6	10
						$6	3	4 5	10
Deduct outstanding checks:									
No. 462	$ 5	2	4	26					
No. 465	2	1	3	41					
No. 473	5	4	3	58					
No. 476	3	5	1	38					
No. 477	1	9	7	45	1	8 3	0	08
Adjusted bank balance						$4	5	1 5	02
Book balance, March 31						$4	5	6 5	12
Add error on Check No. 456								5 4	00
						$4	6	1 9	12
Deduct: Bank service charge	$		4	10					
Unrecorded ATM withdrawal	1	0	0	00			1 0	4	10
Adjusted book balance						$4	5	1 5	02

SOLUTION 2a.

3												3
4	Mar.	31	Miscellaneous Expense			4	10					4
5			Cash							4	10	5
6			Bank service charge									6
7												7
8			Cash		5	4	00					8
9			Accounts Payable—Office Suppliers, Inc.						5	4	00	9
10			Error on Check No. 456									10
11												11
12			Jason Kuhn, Drawing	1	0	0	00					12
13			Cash					1	0	0	00	13
14			Unrecorded ATM withdrawal									14
15												15
b.		31	Automobile Expense		3	2	40					16
17			Postage Expense		2	7	50					17
18			Charitable Contributions Expense		3	5	00					18
19			Phone Expense			6	20					19
20			Travel and Entertainment Expense		3	8	60					20
21			Miscellaneous Expense		1	7	75					21
22			Jason Kuhn, Drawing		4	0	00					22
23			Cash					1	9	7	45	23
24			Replenishment of petty cash fund									24
25												25

SOLUTION 3.

Cash in bank:

Check stub balance, March 31	$4,565.12	
Plus error on Ck. No. 456	54.00	
Less bank charges	(104.10)	
Adjusted cash in bank		$4,515.02

Cash on hand:

Petty cash fund	$ 2.55	
Add replenishment	197.45	
Adjusted cash on hand		200.00
Total cash in bank and petty cash on hand		$4,715.02

KEY TERMS

ABA (American Bankers Association) Number (232)　The small fraction printed in the upper right-hand corner of each check.

automated teller machine (ATM) (234)　A machine used by depositors to make withdrawals or deposits at any time.

bank reconciliation (238)　A report used to bring the book and bank balances into agreement.

bank statement (235)　A statement of account issued by a bank to each depositor once a month.

blank endorsement (234)   An endorsement where the payee simply signs the back of the check, making the check payable to any bearer.

canceled check (236)   A depositor's check paid by the bank during the bank statement period.

cash (232)   To a business, cash includes bills, coins, checks received from customers, money orders, and bank cashier's checks.

change fund (246)   A supply of bills and coins kept in a cash register or cash drawer for use in handling cash sales.

check (235)   A document ordering a bank to pay cash from a depositor's account.

check stub (235)   In some checkbooks, a document attached to a check that contains space for relevant information about the check.

collections (238)   Collections of promissory notes or charge accounts made by the bank on behalf of the depositor.

credit memo (239)   An item that the bank adds to the account.

Customer Identification Program (CIP) (232)   A program every bank is required to maintain that provides clear identification of every account holder.

debit memo (239)   An item that the bank deducts from the account.

deposit ticket (232)   A form showing a detailed listing of items being deposited.

deposits in transit (238)   Deposits that have not reached or been recorded by the bank before the bank statement is prepared.

drawee (235)   The bank on which the check is drawn.

drawer (235)   The depositor who orders the bank to pay the cash.

electronic funds transfer (EFT) (242)   A process using a computer rather than paper checks to complete transactions with the bank.

endorsement (232)   Stamping or writing the payee's name and sometimes other information on the back of the check.

errors (238)   Errors made by the bank or the depositor in recording cash transactions.

internal control (232)   A set of procedures designed to ensure proper accounting for transactions.

magnetic ink character recognition (MICR) code (232)   The character code used to print identifying information on the lower left front side of each check.

not sufficient funds (NSF) check (238)   A check deposited by the depositor that is not paid because the drawer did not have sufficient funds.

outstanding check (238)   A check issued that has not been presented to the bank for payment before the statement is prepared.

payee (235)   The person being paid the cash.

petty cash fund (243)   A fund established to pay for small items with cash.

petty cash payments record (244)   A special multi-column record that supplements the regular accounting records.

petty cash voucher (244)   A receipt that is prepared for every payment from the petty cash fund.

restrictive endorsement (234)   An endorsement where the payee adds words such as "Pay to the order of (specific) bank" or "For deposit only" to restrict the payment of the check.

service charge (238)   A bank charge for services such as check printing and processing.

signature card (232)   A card that is completed and signed by each person authorized to sign checks.

SELF-STUDY TEST QUESTIONS

True/False

1. **LO2** The primary purpose of a bank reconciliation is to detect and correct errors made by the bank in its records.

2. **LO2** NSF checks are subtracted from the bank statement balance on the bank reconciliation.

3. **LO2** The bank service charge requires a journal entry to record its effects on the cash account.

4. **LO2** Unrecorded ATM withdrawals are added to the book balance on the bank reconciliation.

5. **LO3** The petty cash record is a journal of original entry (entries are posted from it to the general ledger accounts).

Multiple Choice

1. **LO2** Which of these could be *added* to the ending book balance?
   - (a) Service charges
   - (b) NSF check
   - (c) Checkbook errors that understate balance
   - (d) Outstanding checks

2. **LO2** Which of these is *subtracted* from the ending book balance?
   - (a) Deposits in transit
   - (b) Service charges
   - (c) Note collection
   - (d) Bank errors

3. **LO2** Which of these is *added* to the ending bank statement balance?
   - (a) Outstanding checks
   - (b) Service charges
   - (c) Checkbook errors
   - (d) Deposits in transit

4. **LO3** To establish a petty cash fund, which account is debited?
   - (a) Cash
   - (b) Petty Cash
   - (c) Miscellaneous Expense
   - (d) Revenue

5. **LO4** When the cash short and over account has a debit balance at the end of the month, it is considered
   - (a) an expense.
   - (b) an asset.
   - (c) revenue.
   - (d) a liability.

CHECKPOINT

Checkpoint Exercises

1. **LO1** Match the following words with their definitions by entering the correct number in the spaces below.

   1. deposit ticket
   2. ATM
   3. check
   4. bank statement
   5. blank endorsement

   _____ a. A document ordering a bank to pay cash from a depositor's account.

   _____ b. An endorsement where the payee simply signs the back of the check, making the check payable to any bearer.

   _____ c. Automated teller machine—a machine used by depositors to make withdrawals or deposits at any time.

_____ d. A statement of account issued by a bank to each depositor once a month.

_____ e. A form showing a detailed listing of items being deposited.

2. **LO2** Indicate how each of the following items should be treated in a bank reconciliation by entering the correct letter in the spaces provided.

a. Add to bank statement balance
b. Subtract from bank statement balance
c. Add to book balance
d. Subtract from book balance

_____ 1. Interest earned on checking account balance

_____ 2. Error in checkbook whereby a check for $82 was entered in the checkbook as $28

_____ 3. Deposit in transit

_____ 4. Outstanding checks

3. **LO3** A petty cash fund established for $200 had the following cash payments during the month:

Phone expense	$23.50
Automobile expense	49.10
H. Appy, drawing	50.00

Prepare the journal entry to replenish the petty cash fund at the end of the month.

4. **LO4** The cash register tape for June 30 showed cash receipts of $876, and the cash in the register drawer was $1,070. A change fund of $200 is maintained.

Prepare the journal entry for service fees and cash short and over at June 30.

The answers to the Self-Study Test Questions are at the end of the chapter (page 266).

APPLYING YOUR KNOWLEDGE

REVIEW QUESTIONS

LO1 1. Why must a signature card be filled out and signed to open a checking account?

LO1 2. Explain the difference between a blank endorsement and a restrictive endorsement.

LO1 3. Who are the three parties to every check?

LO1 4. What are the three steps to follow in preparing a check?

LO2 5. What are the most common reasons for differences between the book and bank cash balances?

LO2 6. What are the three steps to follow in preparing a bank reconciliation?

LO2	7.	What two kinds of items on a bank reconciliation require journal entries?
LO2	8.	Name five common uses of electronic funds transfer.
LO3	9.	What is the purpose of a petty cash fund?
LO3	10.	What should be prepared every time a petty cash payment is made?
LO3	11.	At what two times should the petty cash fund be replenished?
LO3	12.	From what source is the information obtained for issuing a check to replenish the petty cash fund?
LO4	13.	At what two times would an entry be made affecting the change fund?
LO4	14.	What does a debit balance in the cash short and over account represent? What does a credit balance in this account represent?

SERIES A EXERCISES

E 7-1A   (LO1)

CHECKING ACCOUNT TERMS Match the following words with their definitions:

1. An endorsement where the payee simply signs on the back of the check
2. An endorsement that contains words like "For Deposit Only" together with the signature
3. A card filled out and signed by each person authorized to sign checks on an account
4. The depositor who orders the bank to pay cash from the depositor's account
5. The bank on which the check is drawn
6. The person being paid the cash
7. A check that has been paid by the bank and is being returned to the depositor

a. signature card
b. canceled check
c. blank endorsement
d. drawer
e. restrictive endorsement
f. drawee
g. payee

E 7-2A   (LO1)
✓ Net deposit: $962.20

PREPARE DEPOSIT TICKET Based on the following information, prepare a deposit ticket:

Date:		· January 15, 20--
Bills:		$396.00
Coin:		23.20
Checks:	No. 4-12	372.00
	No. 80-318	127.00
	No. 3-8	44.00

E 7-3A   (LO1)

PREPARE CHECK AND STUB Based on the following information, prepare a check and stub:

Date:	January 15, 20--
Balance brought forward:	$2,841.50
Deposit:	(from Exercise 7-2A)
Check to:	J. M. Suppliers
Amount:	$150.00
For:	Office Supplies
Signature:	Sign your name

E 7-4A   (LO2)

BANK RECONCILIATION PROCEDURES In a format similar to the following, indicate whether the action at the left will result in an addition to (+) or subtraction from (−) the ending bank balance or the ending book balance.

	Ending Bank Balance	Ending Book Balance
1. Deposits in transit to the bank	_____	_____
2. Error in checkbook: check recorded as $32 but was actually for $23	_____	_____
3. Service fee charged by the bank	_____	_____
4. Outstanding checks	_____	_____
5. NSF check deposited earlier	_____	_____
6. Error in checkbook: check recorded as $22 but was actually for $220	_____	_____
7. Bank credit memo advising a note was collected for us	_____	_____

E 7-5A   (LO2)
✓ NSF check: Dr. Accounts Receivable, $468

PREPARE JOURNAL ENTRIES FOR BANK RECONCILIATION Based on the following bank reconciliation, prepare the journal entries:

Carmen Lui Associates Bank Reconciliation July 31, 20 - -							
Bank statement balance, July 31					$3	3 1 6	80
Add deposits in transit	$ 3 0 0	00					
	1 1 8	00			4 1 8	00	
					$3	7 3 4	80
Deduct outstanding checks:							
No. 296	$ 4 2 4	20					
No. 299	2 2	60					
No. 301	3 9	90			4 8 6	70	
Adjusted bank balance					$3	2 4 8	10
Book balance, July 31					$3	7 0 0	50
Add error on Check No. 291*						2 7	60
					$3	7 2 8	10
Deduct: NSF check	$ 4 6 8	00					
Bank service charge	1 2	00			4 8 0	00	
Adjusted book balance					$3	2 4 8	10
*Accounts Payable was debited in original entry.							

E 7-6A   (LO3)
✓ Replenishment: Cr. Cash, $228.10

PETTY CASH JOURNAL ENTRIES Based on the following petty cash information, prepare (a) the journal entry to establish a petty cash fund and (b) the journal entry to replenish the petty cash fund.

On January 1, 20--, a check was written in the amount of $300 to establish a petty cash fund. During January, the following vouchers were written for cash removed from the petty cash drawer:

Voucher No.	Account Debited	Amount
1	Phone Expense	$21.20
2	Automobile Expense	39.60
3	James Lucas, Drawing	85.00
4	Postage Expense	15.30
5	Charitable Contributions Expense	20.00
6	Miscellaneous Expense	47.00

E 7-7A   (LO4)
✓ Apr. 16: Cr. Cash Short and Over, $1.75

CASH SHORT AND OVER ENTRIES Based on the following information, prepare the weekly entries for cash receipts from service fees and cash short and over. A change fund of $100 is maintained.

Date	Change Fund	Cash Register Receipt Amount	Actual Cash Counted
Apr. 2	$100	$268.50	$366.50
9	100	237.75	333.50
16	100	309.25	411.00
23	100	226.50	324.00
30	100	318.00	422.00

SERIES A PROBLEMS

P 7-8A   (LO2)
✓ Adjusted book balance: $5,023

BANK RECONCILIATION AND RELATED JOURNAL ENTRIES The book balance in the checking account of Johnson Enterprises as of October 31 is $5,718. The bank statement shows an ending balance of $5,217. The following information is discovered by (1) comparing last month's deposits in transit and outstanding checks with this month's bank statement, (2) comparing deposits and checks written per books and per bank in the current month, and (3) noting service charges and other debit and credit memos shown on the bank statement.

Deposits in transit:	10/29	$210.00
	10/30	406.00
Outstanding checks:	No. 1635	56.40
	No. 1639	175.00
	No. 1641	135.50
	No. 1653	443.10
Unrecorded ATM withdrawal:*		200.00
Bank service charge:		37.00
NSF check:		476.00
Error on Check No. 1624	Checkbook shows it was for $75, but it was actually written for $57. Accounts Payable was debited.	

*Funds were withdrawn by Enoch Johnson for personal use.

(*continued*)

1. Prepare a bank reconciliation as of October 31, 20--.

2. Prepare the required journal entries.

P 7-9A   (LO2)

✓ Adjusted bank balance: $3,069.95

BANK RECONCILIATION AND RELATED JOURNAL ENTRIES The book balance in the checking account of Lyle's Salon as of November 30 is $3,282.95. The bank statement shows an ending balance of $2,127. By examining last month's bank reconciliation, comparing the deposits and checks written per books and per bank in November, and noting the service charges and other debit and credit memos shown on the bank statement, the following were found:

(a) An ATM withdrawal of $150 on November 18 by Lyle for personal use was not recorded on the books.

(b) A bank debit memo issued for an NSF check from a customer of $19.50.

(c) A bank credit memo issued for interest of $19 earned during the month.

(d) On November 30, a deposit of $1,177 was made, which is not shown on the bank statement.

(e) A bank debit memo issued for $17.50 for bank service charges.

(f) Checks No. 549, 561, and 562 for the amounts of $185, $21, and $9.40, respectively, were written during November but have not yet been received by the bank.

(g) The reconciliation from the previous month showed outstanding checks totaling $271.95. One of those checks, No. 471 for $18.65, has not yet been received by the bank.

(h) Check No. 523 written to a creditor in the amount of $372.90 was recorded in the books as $327.90.

REQUIRED

1. Prepare a bank reconciliation as of November 30.

2. Prepare the required journal entries.

P 7-10A   (LO3)

✓ Replenishment: Cr. Cash, $149

PETTY CASH RECORD AND JOURNAL ENTRIES On May 1, a petty cash fund was established for $150. The following vouchers were issued during May:

Date	Voucher No.	Purpose	Amount
May 1	1	Postage due	$ 3.50
3	2	Office supplies	11.00
5	3	Auto repair (miscellaneous)	43.00
7	4	Drawing (Joy Adams)	25.00
11	5	Donation (Red Cross)	10.00
15	6	Travel expenses	28.00
22	7	Postage stamps	3.50
26	8	Phone call	5.00
30	9	Donation (Boy Scouts)	20.00

REQUIRED

1. Prepare the journal entry to establish the petty cash fund.

2. Record the vouchers in the petty cash record. Total and rule the petty cash record.

3. Prepare the journal entry to replenish the petty cash fund. Make the appropriate entry in the petty cash record.

P 7-11A (LO4)
✓ July 23: Dr. Cash Short and Over, $2.50

CASH SHORT AND OVER ENTRIES Listed below are the weekly cash register tape amounts for service fees and the related cash counts during the month of July. A change fund of $100 is maintained.

Date	Change Fund	Cash Register Receipt Amount	Actual Cash Counted
July 2	$100	$289.50	$387.00
9	100	311.50	411.50
16	100	306.00	408.50
23	100	317.50	415.00
30	100	296.00	399.50

REQUIRED

1. Prepare the journal entries to record the cash service fees and cash short and over for each of the five weeks.
2. Post to the cash short and over account (use Account No. 516).
3. Determine the ending balance of the cash short and over account. Does it represent an expense or revenue?

SERIES B EXERCISES

E 7-1B (LO1)

CHECKING ACCOUNT TERMS Match the following words with their definitions:

1. Banking number used to identify checks for deposit tickets
2. A card filled out to open a checking account
3. A machine from which withdrawals can be taken or deposits made to accounts
4. A place where relevant information is recorded about a check
5. A set of procedures designed to ensure proper accounting for transactions
6. A statement of account issued to each depositor once a month
7. A detailed listing of items being deposited to an account

a. bank statement
b. deposit ticket
c. signature card
d. internal control
e. check stub
f. ATM
g. ABA number

E 7-2B (LO1)
✓ Total deposit: $645

PREPARE DEPOSIT TICKET Based on the following information, prepare a deposit ticket:

Date: November 15, 20--

Bills:		$283
Coin:		19
Checks:	No. 3-22	201
	No. 19-366	114
	No. 3-2	28

(continued)

E 7-3B (LO1)

PREPARE CHECK AND STUB Based on the following information, prepare a check and stub:

Date:	November 15, 20--
Balance brought forward:	$3,181
Deposit:	(from Exercise 7-2B)
Check to:	R. J. Smith Co.
Amount:	$120
For:	Payment on account
Signature:	Sign your name

E 7-4B (LO2)

BANK RECONCILIATION PROCEDURES In a format similar to the following, indicate whether the action at the left will result in an addition to (+) or subtraction from (−) the ending bank balance or the ending book balance.

	Ending Bank Balance	Ending Book Balance
1. Service fee of $12 charged by the bank	_____	_____
2. Outstanding checks	_____	_____
3. Error in checkbook: check recorded as $36 was actually for $28	_____	_____
4. NSF check deposited earlier	_____	_____
5. Bank credit memo advising a note was collected for us	_____	_____
6. Deposits in transit to the bank	_____	_____
7. Error in checkbook: check recorded as $182 was actually for $218	_____	_____

E 7-5B (LO2)

✓ NSF check: Dr. Accounts Receivable, $66

PREPARE JOURNAL ENTRIES FOR BANK RECONCILIATION Based on the following bank reconciliation, prepare the journal entries:

Ruggero Celini Associates Bank Reconciliation July 31, 20 --								
Bank statement balance, July 31						$1	7 8 4	00
Add deposits in transit	$ 4	1 8	50					
	1	0 0	50			5	1 9	00
						$2	3 0 3	00
Deduct outstanding checks:								
No. 185	$ 2	0 6	50					
No. 203	3	1 7	40					
No. 210		5 6	10			5	8 0	00
Adjusted bank balance						$1	7 2 3	00
Book balance, July 31						$1	7 9 2	00
Add: Error on Check No. 191*	$	1 0	00					
Interest earned		2	00				1 2	00
						$1	8 0 4	00
Deduct: NSF check	$	6 6	00					
Bank service charge		1 5	00				8 1	00
Adjusted book balance						$1	7 2 3	00
*Accounts Payable was debited in original entry.								

E 7-6B (LO3)
✓ Replenishment: Cr. Cash, $190

PETTY CASH JOURNAL ENTRIES Based on the following petty cash information, prepare (a) the journal entry to establish a petty cash fund and (b) the journal entry to replenish the petty cash fund.

On October 1, 20--, a check was written in the amount of $200 to establish a petty cash fund. During October, the following vouchers were written for cash taken from the petty cash drawer:

Voucher No.	Account Debited	Amount
1	Postage Expense	$13
2	Miscellaneous Expense	17
3	John Flanagan, Drawing	45
4	Phone Expense	36
5	Charitable Contributions Expense	50
6	Automobile Expense	29

E 7-7B (LO4)
✓ June 15: Dr. Cash Short and Over, $2

CASH SHORT AND OVER ENTRIES Based on the following information, prepare the weekly entries for cash receipts from service fees and cash short and over. A change fund of $100 is maintained.

Date	Change Fund	Cash Register Receipt Amount	Actual Cash Counted
June 1	$100	$330.00	$433.00
8	100	297.00	400.00
15	100	233.00	331.00
22	100	302.00	396.50
29	100	316.00	412.00

SERIES B PROBLEMS

P 7-8B (LO2)
✓ Adjusted book balance: $2,674

BANK RECONCILIATION AND RELATED JOURNAL ENTRIES The book balance in the checking account of Kyri Enterprises as of November 30 is $2,964. The bank statement shows an ending balance of $2,525. The following information is discovered by (1) comparing last month's deposits in transit and outstanding checks with this month's bank statement, (2) comparing deposits and checks written per books and per bank in the current month, and (3) noting service charges and other debit and credit memos shown on the bank statement.

Deposits in transit:	11/29	$125
	11/30	200
Outstanding checks:	No. 322	17
	No. 324	105
	No. 327	54
Unrecorded ATM withdrawal:*		100
Bank service charge:		25
NSF check:		185

Error on Check No. 321   Checkbook shows it was for $64, but it was actually written for $44. Accounts Payable was debited.

*Funds were withdrawn by Susan Kyri for personal use.

(*continued*)

REQUIRED

1. Prepare a bank reconciliation as of November 30, 20--.

2. Prepare the required journal entries.

P 7-9B (LO2)
✓ Adjusted bank balance: $4,518.70

BANK RECONCILIATION AND RELATED JOURNAL ENTRIES The book balance in the checking account of Tori's Health Center as of April 30 is $4,690.30. The bank statement shows an ending balance of $3,275.60. By examining last month's bank reconciliation, comparing the deposits and checks written per books and per bank in April, and noting the service charges and other debit and credit memos shown on the bank statement, the following were found:

(a) An ATM withdrawal of $200 on April 20 by Tori for personal use was not recorded on the books.

(b) A bank debit memo issued for an NSF check from a customer of $29.10.

(c) A bank credit memo issued for interest of $28 earned during the month.

(d) On April 30, a deposit of $1,592 was made, which is not shown on the bank statement.

(e) A bank debit memo issued for $24.50 for bank service charges.

(f) Checks No. 481, 493, and 494 for the amounts of $215, $71, and $24.30, respectively, were written during April but have not yet been received by the bank.

(g) The reconciliation from the previous month showed outstanding checks totaling $418.25. One of these checks, No. 397 for $38.60, has not yet been received by the bank.

(h) Check No. 422 written to a creditor in the amount of $217.90 was recorded in the books as $271.90.

REQUIRED

1. Prepare a bank reconciliation as of April 30.

2. Prepare the required journal entries.

P 7-10B (LO3)
✓ Replenishment: Cr. Cash, $87

PETTY CASH RECORD AND JOURNAL ENTRIES On July 1, a petty cash fund was established for $100. The following vouchers were issued during July:

Date	Voucher No.	Purpose	Amount
July 1	1	Office supplies	$ 3.00
3	2	Donation (Goodwill)	15.00
5	3	Travel expenses	5.00
7	4	Postage due	2.00
8	5	Office supplies	4.00
11	6	Postage due	3.50
15	7	Phone call	5.00
21	8	Travel expenses	11.00
25	9	Withdrawal by owner (L. Ortiz)	20.00
26	10	Copier repair (miscellaneous)	18.50

REQUIRED

1. Prepare the journal entry to establish the petty cash fund.

2. Record the vouchers in the petty cash record. Total and rule the petty cash record.

3. Prepare the journal entry to replenish the petty cash fund. Make the appropriate entry in the petty cash record.

P 7-11B **(LO4)**

✓ Aug. 8: Dr. Cash Short and Over, $3.50

CASH SHORT AND OVER ENTRIES Listed below are the weekly cash register tape amounts for service fees and the related cash counts during the month of July. A change fund of $200 is maintained.

Date	Change Fund	Cash Register Receipt Amount	Actual Cash Counted
Aug. 1	$200	$292.50	$495.00
8	200	305.00	501.50
15	200	286.00	486.00
22	200	330.25	532.75
29	200	299.20	495.00

REQUIRED

1. Prepare the journal entries to record the cash service fees and cash short and over for each of the five weeks.

2. Post to the cash short and over account (use Account No. 516).

3. Determine the ending balance of the cash short and over account. Does it represent an expense or revenue?

CHECK LIST
- ☐ **Managing**
- ☐ **Planning**
- ☐ **Drafting**
- ☐ **Break**
- ☐ **Revising**
- ☐ **Managing**

MANAGING YOUR WRITING

The current month's bank statement for your account arrives in the mail. In reviewing the statement, you notice a deposit listed for $400 that you did not make. It has been credited in error to your account.

Discuss whether you have an ethical or legal obligation to inform the bank of the error. What action should you take?

ETHICS

ETHICS CASE

Ben Thomas works as a teller for First National Bank. When he arrived at work on Friday, the branch manager, Frank Mills, asked him to get his cash drawer out early because the head teller, Naomi Ray, was conducting a surprise cash count for all the tellers. Surprise cash counts are usually done four or five times a year by the branch manager or the head teller and once or twice a year by internal auditors. Ben's drawer was $100 short and his reconciliation tape showed that he was in balance on Thursday night. Naomi asked Ben for an explanation, and Ben immediately took $100 out of his pocket and handed it to her. He went on to explain he needed the cash to buy prescriptions for his son and pay for groceries and intended to put the $100 back in his cash drawer on Monday, which was pay day. He also told Naomi that this was the first time he had ever "borrowed" money from his cash drawer and that he would never do it again.

1. What are the ethical considerations in this case from both Ben's and Naomi's perspectives?

2. What options does Naomi have to address this problem?

3. Assume Naomi chooses to inform the branch manager. Write a short incident report describing the findings.

4. In small groups, come up with as many ideas as possible on how to safeguard cash on hand in a bank (petty cash, teller drawer cash, and vault cash) from employee theft and mismanagement.

MASTERY PROBLEM

✓ Adjusted bank balance: $4,324.05

Turner Excavation maintains a checking account and has decided to open a petty cash fund. The following petty cash fund transactions occurred during July:

July   2   Established a petty cash fund by issuing Check No. 301 for $100.

   5   Paid $25 from the petty cash fund for postage. Voucher No. 1.

   7   Paid $30 from the petty cash fund for delivery of flowers (Miscellaneous Expense). Voucher No. 2.

   8   Paid $20 from the petty cash fund to repair a tire on the company truck. Voucher No. 3.

   12   Paid $22 from the petty cash fund for a newspaper advertisement. Voucher No. 4.

   13   Issued Check No. 303 to replenish the petty cash fund. (Total and rule the petty cash payments record. Record the balance and the amount needed to replenish the fund in the Description column of the petty cash payments record.)

   20   Paid $26 from the petty cash fund to reimburse an employee for expenses incurred to repair the company truck. Voucher No. 5.

   24   Paid $12.50 from the petty cash fund for phone calls made from a phone booth. Voucher No. 6.

   28   Paid $25 from the petty cash fund as a contribution to the YMCA. Voucher No. 7.

   31   Issued Check No. 308 to replenish the petty cash fund. (Total and rule the petty cash payments record. Record the balance and the amount needed to replenish the fund in the Description column of the petty cash payments record.)

   The following additional transactions occurred during July:

July   5   Issued Check No. 302 to pay office rent, $650.

   15   Issued Check No. 304 for office equipment, $525.

   17   Issued Check No. 305 for the purchase of supplies, $133.

   18   Issued Check No. 306 to pay attorney fees, $1,000.

   30   Issued Check No. 307 to pay newspaper for an advertisement, $200.20.

REQUIRED

1. Record the petty cash transactions in a petty cash payments record.

2. Make all required general journal entries for the cash transactions. (*Note:* The petty cash fund was established and replenished twice during July.)

3. The bank statement on page 265 was received in the mail. Deposits were made on July 6 for $3,500 and on July 29 for $2,350. The book balance on July 31 is $4,331.55. Notice the discrepancy in Check No. 302 that cleared the bank for $655. This check was written on July 5 for rent expense, but was incorrectly entered on the check stub and in the journal as $650. Prepare a bank reconciliation and make any necessary journal entries as of July 31.

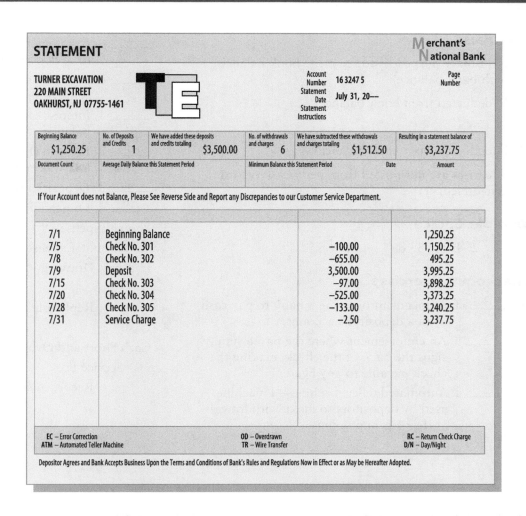

CHALLENGE PROBLEM

This problem challenges you to apply your cumulative accounting knowledge to move a step beyond the material in the chapter.

✓ 2. Item 4: Dr. Depositor Accounts, $350

Susan Panera is preparing the June 30 bank reconciliation for Panera Bakery. She discovers the following items that explain the difference between the cash balance on her books and the balance as reported by Lawrence Bank:

1. An ATM withdrawal of $200 for personal use was not recorded by Susan.
2. A deposit of $850 was recorded by Susan but has not been received by Lawrence Bank as of June 30.
3. A check written in payment on account to Jayhawk Supply for $340 was recorded by Susan as $430 and by Lawrence Bank as $530.
4. An ATM deposit of $350 was recorded twice by Lawrence Bank.
5. An electronic funds transfer of $260 to Sunflower Mills as a payment on account was not recorded by Susan.
6. Checks No. 103 for $235 and No. 110 for $127 had not cleared Lawrence Bank as of June 30.

REQUIRED

1. Prepare the journal entries required to correct Panera Bakery's books as of June 30.
2. Prepare the journal entries required to correct Lawrence Bank's books as of June 30.

ANSWERS TO SELF-STUDY TEST QUESTIONS

True/False

1. F (primary purpose is to reconcile book balance with bank balance)
2. F (deducted from book balance)
3. T
4. F (deducted from book balance)
5. F (entries are not posted from petty cash record to general ledger)

Multiple Choice

1. c   2. b   3. d   4. b   5. a

Checkpoint Exercises

1. __3__ a. A document ordering a bank to pay cash from a depositor's account.
   __5__ b. An endorsement where the payee simply signs the back of the check, making the check payable to any bearer.
   __2__ c. Automated teller machine—a machine used by depositors to make withdrawals or deposits at any time.
   __4__ d. A statement of account issued by a bank to each depositor once a month.
   __1__ e. A form showing a detailed listing of items being deposited.

2. __c__ 1. Interest earned on checking account balance
   __d__ 2. Error in checkbook whereby a check for $82 was entered in the checkbook as $28
   __a__ 3. Deposit in transit
   __b__ 4. Outstanding checks

3. Phone Expense   23.50
   Automobile Expense   49.10
   H. Appy, Drawing   50.00
      Cash   122.60
      Replenished petty cash fund

4. Cash   870.00
   Cash Short and Over   6.00
      Service Fees   876.00
      Recorded service fees and cash shortage

266

Internal Controls

In Chapter 7, we introduced the concept of internal control and provided some examples of good internal control over cash transactions. Here, we examine internal control in greater depth.

We do the following:

1. Explain why internal control has achieved greater importance today.
2. Identify the key components of internal control.
3. Give examples of internal control over cash receipts.
4. Describe internal control of cash payments using a voucher system.

LO1 — Importance of Internal Control

Explain the importance of internal control.

To be successful, management must have adequate control of the operations of the business. For example, the records of business activities must be reliable and timely, so that management has the information it needs to take necessary actions. The assets of the business must be known and protected. Employees must follow the rules and procedures defined by management. Accurate information must be available to report to owners, lenders, and regulatory bodies, such as the IRS. Without good internal control, it simply would not be possible to effectively and efficiently run a business.

The importance of strong internal control for managing a business has been known for years. But in 2002, the importance of internal control was raised to a whole new level. In July 2002, Congress passed the Sarbanes-Oxley Act (SOX). SOX applies to all **publicly held companies**—companies whose stock is traded on the major stock exchanges. Section 404 (a) of SOX requires these companies to report annually on the effectiveness of internal control over financial reporting. For decades, these corporations have been required to provide audited financial statements. Now, they must also report on the quality of their internal control system. Figure 7A-1 provides an example of management's Section 404 (a) report for Microsoft.

One of the interesting effects of SOX is how widely its rules are being felt. Officially, SOX applies to all publicly held companies and their external auditors. But SOX is causing many other companies and managements to look closely at the quality of their internal controls. The logic is simple: if internal controls are so important for publicly held companies, they probably deserve attention in other companies as well. Clearly, internal controls are a hot topic today.

FIGURE 7A-1 Section 404 Internal Control Report

> **REPORT OF MANAGEMENT ON INTERNAL CONTROL OVER FINANCIAL REPORTING**
>
> Our management [of Microsoft] is responsible for establishing and maintaining adequate internal control over financial reporting for the company. Internal control over financial reporting is a process to provide reasonable assurance regarding the reliability of our financial reporting for external purposes in accordance with accounting principles generally accepted in the United States of America. Internal control over financial reporting includes maintaining records that in reasonable detail accurately and fairly reflect our transactions; providing reasonable assurance that transactions are recorded as necessary for preparation of our financial statements; providing reasonable assurance that receipts and expenditures of company assets are made in accordance with management authorization; and providing reasonable assurance that unauthorized acquisition, use, or disposition of company assets that could have a material effect on our financial statements would be prevented or detected on a timely basis. Because of its inherent limitations, internal control over financial reporting is not intended to provide absolute assurance that a misstatement of our financial statements would be prevented or detected.
>
> Management conducted an evaluation of the effectiveness of our internal control over financial reporting based on the framework in Internal Control—Integrated Framework issued by the Committee of Sponsoring Organizations (2013) of the Treadway Commission. Based on this evaluation, management concluded that the company's internal control over financial reporting was effective as of June 30, 2016. There were no changes in our internal control over financial reporting during the quarter ended June 30, 2016 that have materially affected, or are reasonably likely to materially affect, our internal control over financial reporting. Deloitte & Touche LLP has audited our internal control over financial reporting as of June 30, 2016; their report follows.

LO2 — Key Components of Internal Control

Define internal control and describe its key components.

Internal control is really important. So what exactly do we mean by internal control? Both the concept and attempts to define it have existed for many years. For our purposes, the following is a good definition:

> Internal control is a system developed by a company to provide reasonable assurance of achieving (1) effective and efficient operations, (2) reliable financial reporting, and (3) compliance with laws and regulations.

Several internal control frameworks have been developed that are consistent with this definition. The most widely accepted framework in the United States contains the following five components:

- Control environment
- Risk assessment
- Control activities
- Information and communication system
- Monitoring processes

Control Environment

The control environment is the policies, procedures, and attitudes of the top management and owners of the business. It is often referred to as the "tone at the top." It includes the organization structure, management's philosophy and operating style, integrity and ethical values, and commitment to competent, trustworthy employees. The control environment provides the foundation for all other components of internal control.

Risk Assessment

Risk assessment is management's process for identifying, analyzing, and responding to its business risks. All businesses face various and changing risks from both external and internal sources. These risks include error and fraud. As part of the risk assessment component of internal control, management must deal with these risks. For example, if a business sells products like computers that are affected by rapid technology changes, its marketing and inventory plans should carefully guard against obsolete inventory. If a business has high employee turnover, its employee screening and training programs should be very thorough and up to date. If a business is growing rapidly, it should regularly review its internal controls to see that they fit the size and activities of the business.

Control Activities

Control activities are the policies and procedures established to help management meet its control objectives. Control activities can be classified in various ways. Four types of control activities are particularly important for our purposes.

1. Segregation of duties
2. Authorization procedures and related responsibilities
3. Adequate documents and records
4. Protection of assets and records

   Segregation of duties means that:

   1. Different employees should be responsible for different parts of a transaction and

   2. Employees who account for transactions should not also have custody of the assets.

For example, one employee should be responsible for ordering goods and another employee should be responsible for issuing the check to pay for them. One employee should be responsible for recording the purchase of goods and another employee should be responsible for receiving and placing the goods in inventory. This segregation of duties provides a built-in check by one employee on another. One employee cannot obtain goods for personal use without being caught by another employee.

In computerized systems, programs and data files often combine the duties of several employees. For example, programs can order goods automatically at a preset level from approved vendors, and payments then can be made based on an electronic billing. This requires a different segregation of duties. Three functions must be segregated: (1) system design and programming, (2) system operations, and (3) data file and program storage.

Authorization procedures and related responsibilities means that every business activity should be properly authorized. In addition, it should be possible to identify who is responsible for every activity that has occurred. For example, to acquire new equipment, a signed document should authorize the purchase. After the purchase is made, this signed document shows who is responsible for the action.

In computerized systems, as noted above, the combination of processing programs and data files can initiate transactions. Therefore, special authorization procedures are needed. Once a program is operating, no changes should be allowed in that program without authorization. Similarly, no changes should be allowed in a data file without authorization. It is essential to protect both the programs and data files from unauthorized access.

Adequate documents and records means that accounting documents and records should be used so that all business transactions are recorded. For example, every purchase that occurs should be supported by a document. These documents should be:

- prenumbered,
- used in sequence, and
- subsequently accounted for.

In this way, the business can be sure that it has made a record of each transaction.

One of the benefits of a computerized system is that the programs can automatically account for the sequence of transactions or documents. Numbers and sequences of sales, purchases, employees for payroll, and payments can be accounted for. If there is any break in the proper numbering sequence, an error message is created.

A computerized system also requires additional documentation. For example, complete documentation is needed of all code, development, and testing of programs before they are put in operation.

Protection of assets and records means that assets and records should be physically and logically protected. For assets, this generally means physical protection. Some examples are vaults for cash, securities, and precious gems, or secure storage rooms for inventory. For records, this can mean storing journals, ledgers, and key documents in physically secure locations. In computerized systems, both physical and logical protection are needed. For example, an online retailer needs assurance that transactions are valid and accurate, customer credit card information is protected, and its website is secure. Passwords are a common form of logical protection of data files and processing programs.

Information and Communication System

The information and communication system is the set of procedures, processes, and records used to initiate, process, record, and report the business's transactions. In addition, the system accounts for the related assets and liabilities. Typically, the system has several subcomponents for different business processes, such as:

- sales,
- cash receipts,
- purchases, and
- cash payments.

The journals and ledgers we learned to use in the previous chapters would be part of an information and communication system.

A computerized system provides great opportunities in this area of internal control. Because of the power of the computer, data files can be compared across departments or other business units to identify problem areas. Data can be screened to ensure their quality, and input from customers and suppliers can be gathered and analyzed.

Monitoring Processes

Monitoring processes are the methods used by management to determine that the controls are operating properly, and that the controls are modified in response to changes in assessed risks. Figure 7A-2 provides some examples of such processes. Monitoring can be part of the ongoing activities of the business or a separate process. One ongoing activity could be comparisons of financial reports with expectations. If financial reports differ from expectations, it could indicate internal control failures. Follow-up on customer complaints regarding account balances might also uncover internal control weaknesses. The most common form of separate process is the work of the internal audit department. Internal auditors evaluate the design of the internal control system in light of the business risks. They also perform specific tests to determine whether internal controls are operating properly. If a business is not large enough to have an internal audit department, these responsibilities must be assumed by top management.

Computers also can help with the monitoring process. Large volumes of data can be analyzed at very low cost. For example, an entire data file of payment transactions can be examined to identify large amounts, duplicates, and unknown suppliers.

FIGURE 7A-2 Sample Monitoring Processes

- Comparison of results with expectations
- Review of customer correspondence
- Internal audit

LO3 | Internal Controls Over Cash Receipts

Describe selected internal controls over cash receipts.

The main purposes of internal controls over cash receipts are to make sure that

- all cash received by the business is recorded in the accounts, and
- the cash is promptly deposited in the business bank account.

The exact form of some of these controls will vary depending on whether the cash is received directly from customers for sales, or is received by mail as a collection on account. Some of the key internal controls are shown in Figure 7A-3 and described in the following paragraphs.

FIGURE 7A-3 Sample Controls over Cash Receipts

Do these three amounts agree?

Cash receipts per register record = Cash receipts per register drawer = Cash receipts per bank deposit

Do these two amounts agree?

Cash receipts per remittance list = Cash receipts per bank deposit

Do transactions and balances per books and bank agree?

Monthly bank reconciliation

If cash is received directly from customers, the use of a cash register or terminal with a printed receipt is essential. Only authorized employees should be allowed to operate the register. The register should generate an internal record of all transactions entered, including a total of cash receipts. This amount should be reconciled with the actual cash (and checks) in the register drawer. Any differences greater than a small amount to allow for errors in making change should be investigated. All cash receipts should be deposited daily in the business bank account. The total deposited and the total cash receipts according to the register should be reconciled and any differences investigated.

If cash is received as collections on account, the mail room should be supervised and employees who handle the cash (checks) should have no access to the accounting records. One reason for separating the handling of cash from the accounting records is to prevent lapping. **Lapping** means stealing cash received on account from one customer and hiding the theft by applying the cash received on account from another customer to the first customer's account. For example, assume customer A sends a check for $500 as a payment on account and that the employee keeps the $500 for him/herself. This causes customer A's account to be in error by $500. So when customer B makes a $500 payment on account, the employee applies this cash receipt to customer A's account. The dishonest employee must continue lapping the accounts receivable in this manner to continue to conceal the theft.

When the mail is opened, a remittance list should be prepared showing all amounts received and from whom they are received. Checks should be immediately endorsed "For deposit" to the business bank account.

The remittance list is sent to the accounting department for use in recording the collections in the journal and ledgers. The cash is sent to the cash receipts department to deposit in the business bank account. The total of the remittance list and the amount of the bank deposit should be independently verified and any differences investigated.

An additional internal control common to both systems described above is the independent monthly preparation of a bank reconciliation. Procedures for preparing the bank reconciliation are described in Chapter 7. The cash receipts, cash payments, and beginning and ending balances per bank and per books must be reconciled. The reconciliation should be prepared by employees who have no access to cash. Any differences should be investigated.

Many businesses have multiple bank accounts and transfer cash among them. When there are multiple bank accounts, it is possible to overstate the cash balance by engaging in kiting. **Kiting** consists of recording a transfer of cash *into* one bank account in the current period, but not recording the transfer *out of* another bank account until the following period. For example, assume that a $1,000 check is written on bank account A on June 30, but not recorded as a cash payment until July 1. This check is deposited in bank account B and recorded as a cash receipt on June 30. By recording the transaction in this manner, the cash balance in both bank accounts includes the $1,000 at June 30. The total cash balance is thus overstated by $1,000 on June 30.

One of the reasons internal controls over cash are so important is that they help businesses manage their cash resources. Naturally, it is important to plan to have sufficient cash to meet current obligations. But it is also important not to allow too much cash to lie idle. Management should carefully monitor and plan for its cash needs. Strong internal controls help with this process.

LO4   Internal Controls Over Cash Payments

Describe selected internal controls over cash payments and the use of a voucher system.

The main purpose of internal controls over cash payments is to make sure cash is paid only for goods and services received by the business, consistent with its best interests. To achieve this objective, controls are needed from the beginning of the process of acquiring goods and services through the payment of cash for those goods and services. An effective way to do so is with a voucher system.

Voucher System

Three of the four control activities described above can be combined to control cash payments by using a voucher system. A voucher system is a control technique that requires every acquisition and subsequent payment to be supported by an approved voucher. A voucher is a document which shows that an acquisition is proper and that payment is authorized.

The Purchasing Process

Figure 7A-4 is a simplified illustration of how the purchasing portion of a voucher system operates. An authorized person or department prepares a purchase requisition to indicate the need for goods. The purchasing department reviews and approves the purchase requisition and prepares a purchase order to send to the supplier. When the goods are received, a receiving report is prepared. A copy of each of these documents is sent to the vouchers payable section in the accounting department.

When the purchase invoice arrives, it is compared with the purchase requisition, purchase order, and receiving report. If the purchase invoice is

- for the goods ordered (purchase requisition and purchase order),
- at the correct price (purchase order),
- and for the correct quantity (receiving report),

then a voucher like the one in Figure 7A-5 on page 274 is prepared. This is the first key control provided by the voucher system. If any aspect of the purchase is improper, it will be caught when the voucher is prepared.

FIGURE 7A-4 Voucher System—Purchasing Process

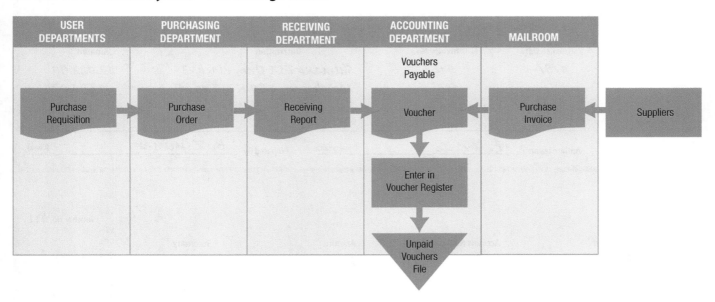

The front of the voucher usually shows the voucher number, date, supplier, and what was purchased. The back indicates the accounts to be debited and the payment date, check number, and amount.

After the voucher is prepared and approved, it is entered in a special journal called a voucher register. A voucher register is used to record purchases of all types of assets and services.

After the voucher is entered in the voucher register, the voucher and supporting documents (purchase requisition, purchase order, receiving report, and purchase invoice) are stapled together. This "voucher packet" is then filed in an unpaid vouchers file, normally by due date. Alternatively, vouchers can be filed by supplier name. Filing by due date is preferred because this helps management plan for cash needs. It also helps ensure that vouchers are paid on the due date and cash discounts are taken.

The completed voucher provides the basis for paying the supplier's invoice on the due date. This is the second key control provided by the voucher system. No payment may be made without an approved voucher.

Notice how three of the four control activities that are part of an internal control system can be seen in this system.

- *Duties are segregated* because different employees order, receive, and record the purchases.
- *Authorization* is required to order the goods and to prepare the voucher.
- The *documents and records* include purchase requisitions, purchase orders, receiving reports, and vouchers that are prenumbered and accounted for. This means that every recorded purchase is supported by the following five documents:

  1. Voucher
  2. Purchase invoice

FIGURE 7A-5 Voucher

			Voucher No. **111**
Sunflower **CYCLE** 804 Massachusetts St., Lawrence, KS 66044	Date *4/11/--* To: *King Creek Corp. 1545 Power Rd. Mesa, AZ 85206*	Terms: *1/15/, n/30*	Due: *4/24/--*

Invoice Date	Invoice No.	Description	Amount
4/9/--	*4123*	*Shimano FSX One, Black-3*	*$2,022.00*
		Motobecane 550 HT, Red-4	*1,636.00*
			$3,658.00

Authorization *A. White* (Supervisor)	Prepared By *B. Zimmer* (Clerk)

					Voucher No. **111**
Account Debited *Purchases*	**Account No.** *501*	**Amount** *$3,658.00*	**Summary** *Invoice* *Discount* *Net*	*$3,658.00* *36.58* *$3,621.42*	

Payment Date *4/24/--*	Check No. *331*	Amount *$3,621.42*
Approved Distribution *J. G.*		Payment

Back

3. Receiving report

4. Purchase order

5. Purchase requisition

This provides management with strong assurance that purchasing activities are properly controlled.

The Payment Process

Figure 7A-6 is a simplified illustration of the payment process when a voucher system is used. On the due date, the voucher is pulled from the unpaid vouchers file. The voucher is given to the person responsible for preparing and signing checks (the cashier in this illustration). The cashier reviews each voucher and supporting documents to see that the expenditure is proper. The cashier then prepares and signs the check and sends it to the supplier. It is important for internal control that no check be prepared without a supporting voucher and that the check be mailed as soon as it is signed.

Ordinary checks may be used to make payments, but under the voucher system, voucher checks often are used. A voucher check is a check with space for entering data about the voucher being paid. Figure 7A-7 on page 276 shows a voucher check used to pay Voucher No. 111 (Figure 7A-5).

The voucher check has two parts:

1. The check itself, which is similar to an ordinary check

2. An attached statement, which indicates the invoice being paid and any deductions

In addition, the voucher check stub identifies the voucher number being paid.

> **LEARNING KEY** 🔑
>
> For good internal control of cash payments, it is important for the check to be mailed as soon as it is signed.

FIGURE 7A-6 Voucher System—Payment Process

1. Pull Voucher and Supporting Documents; Send to Cashier.
2. Review Voucher and Documents; Prepare and Sign Check.
3. Send Check to Supplier.
4. Cancel Voucher and Documents.
5. Return Voucher and Documents to Vouchers Payable; Record Payment in Voucher Register.
6. File Voucher and Documents in Paid Vouchers File.
7. Record Payment in Check Register.

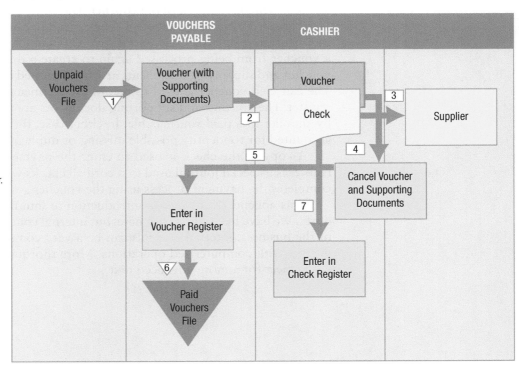

FIGURE 7A-7 Voucher Check

After the voucher has been paid, the cashier completes the "Payment" information and approval on the back of the voucher. The voucher and supporting documents are then canceled to indicate payment. The canceling can be done with a rubber stamp, by perforating, or by simply writing "paid" on all relevant documents. This prevents a voucher from being processed again to create a duplicate payment. The canceled voucher and supporting documents are then returned to the vouchers payable section. The canceled voucher is used to record the payment of the voucher in the voucher register. The voucher and supporting documents are then filed either numerically or by supplier in a **paid vouchers file**. In either case, the numerical sequence should be accounted for to identify possible missing or duplicate vouchers.

A copy of the check is used to enter the payment in a check register. A **check register** is a special journal used to record all checks written in a voucher system. This completes the payment process using the voucher system.

This appendix provides an introduction to internal control concepts and procedures. We have focused on cash here, but internal controls are important in every area of the business. Internal controls can be a very complicated subject, particularly in dealing with computerized operations. More thorough analysis of internal controls is a subject for a more advanced text.

LEARNING OBJECTIVES	**Key Points to Remember**
LO1 **Explain the importance of internal control.**	Internal controls help assure management that it has reliable records to run the business and prepare needed reports. In addition, SOX requires publicly held companies to report annually on the quality of their internal control system.
LO2 **Define internal control and describe its key components.**	Internal control is a system developed by a company to provide reasonable assurance of achieving (1) effective and efficient operations, (2) reliable financial reporting, and (3) compliance with laws and regulations. The key components are as follows: • Control environment • Risk assessment • Control activities • Information and communication system • Monitoring processes
LO3 **Describe selected internal controls over cash receipts.**	If cash is received directly from customers, a cash register should be used. The record of cash receipts per the register should be reconciled with the actual cash in the drawer. If cash is received by mail, a remittance list should be prepared and sent to accounting. The checks should be endorsed immediately "For deposit" and sent to the cash receipts department for deposit in the bank. The remittance list and bank deposit should be independently reconciled.
LO4 **Describe selected internal controls over cash payments and the use of a voucher system.**	Every acquisition and subsequent payment should be supported by an approved voucher. The voucher should be supported by a purchase requisition, purchase order, receiving report, and purchase invoice. On the due date, checks are written only for approved vouchers, and vouchers and supporting documents are canceled to prevent reuse.

KEY TERMS

check register (276)   A special journal used to record all checks written in a voucher system.

kiting (272)   Recording a transfer of cash *into* one bank account in the current period, but not recording the transfer *out of* another bank account until the following period.

lapping (272)   Stealing cash received on account from one customer and hiding the theft by applying the cash received on account from another customer to the first customer's account.

paid vouchers file (276)   A file in which paid vouchers and supporting documents are placed, organized either numerically or by supplier.

publicly held companies (267)   Companies whose stock is traded on the major stock exchanges.

unpaid vouchers file (274)   A file in which unpaid voucher packets are placed, normally organized by due date.

voucher (273)   A document that shows that an acquisition is proper and that payment is authorized.

voucher check (275)   A check with space for entering data about the voucher being paid.

voucher register (273)   A special journal used to record purchases of all types of assets and services.

voucher system (273)   A control technique that requires that every acquisition and subsequent payment be supported by an approved voucher.

REVIEW QUESTIONS

LO1   1.   What does Section 404 of the Sarbanes-Oxley Act require?

LO2   2.   What is the meaning of internal control?

LO2   3.   What are the five components of internal control?

LO2   4.   What are the four types of control activities?

LO3   5.   What are the main purposes of internal controls over cash receipts?

LO4   6.   What is the main purpose of internal controls over cash payments?

LO4   7.   What is a voucher system?

LO4   8.   In a voucher system, each recorded purchase is supported by what five documents?

LO4   9.   What is the purpose of canceling the voucher and supporting documents when a payment is made?

SERIES A EXERCISES

E 7Apx-1A   (LO2)   INTERNAL CONTROL COMPONENTS   The most widely accepted internal control framework in the United States contains the following five components. Describe each of them.

1. Control environment
2. Risk assessment
3. Control activities
4. Information and communication system
5. Monitoring processes

E 7Apx-2A   (LO2)   INTERNAL CONTROL PROCEDURES AND PROCESSES   In the left column below, five different internal control procedures and processes are described. In the right column, the five components of internal control are listed. Match the procedures and processes with the components by placing the letter of the appropriate component on the blank provided.

1. _____ A company publishes and uses a code of ethical conduct.
2. _____ The accounting system automatically generates monthly sales reports for each product line.
3. _____ A company has established an internal audit department.
4. _____ All purchases above $5,000 must be approved in writing by the head of the purchasing department.
5. _____ A company invests heavily in employee training programs because of the technical nature of its products.

a. Control environment
b. Risk assessment
c. Control activities
d. Information and communication system
e. Monitoring processes

E 7Apx-3A **(LO4)**   PURCHASING PROCESS USING A VOUCHER SYSTEM In the following flowchart, identify the documents, records, and procedures that illustrate the purchasing process in a voucher system.

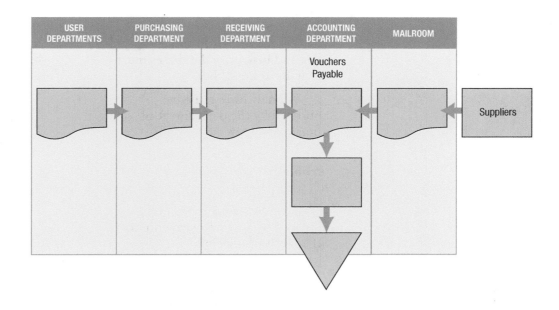

SERIES A PROBLEM

P 7Apx-4A **(LO2/3/4)**   USING INTERNAL CONTROLS TO PREVENT ERRORS The following misstatements occurred in the records of ICW Company. For each misstatement, suggest a control to prevent it from happening.

1. A bill from a supplier was paid even though the shipment was not received.

2. A supplier's bill was paid twice for the same purchase.

3. A plant employee increased his pay rate by entering the computer system using a plant terminal and altering the payroll records.

4. The cash receipts clerk kept a portion of the regular bank deposits for personal use and concealed the theft by manipulating the monthly bank reconciliation she prepared.

SERIES B EXERCISES

E 7Apx-1B **(LO2)**   INTERNAL CONTROL COMPONENTS Four types of internal control activities are listed below. Describe each of them.

1. Segregation of duties

2. Authorization procedures and related responsibilities

3. Adequate documents and records

4. Protection of assets and records

E 7Apx-2B   (LO2)

INTERNAL CONTROL PROCEDURES AND PROCESSES In the left column below, four different internal control procedures are described. In the right column, the four basic types of internal control activities are listed. Match the procedures with the activities by placing the letter of the appropriate activity on the blank provided.

1. _____ All passwords for access to sales and inventory databases must be changed monthly.

2. _____ All new hires must be approved by the department of human resources.

3. _____ All sales invoices are prenumbered and accounted for.

4. _____ Bank reconciliations are prepared by an employee with no other cash responsibilities.

a. Segregation of duties
b. Authorization procedures and related responsibilities
c. Adequate documents and records
d. Protection of assets and records

E 7Apx-3B   (LO4)

PAYMENT PROCESS USING A VOUCHER SYSTEM In the following flowchart, identify the documents, records, and procedures that illustrate the payment process using a voucher system.

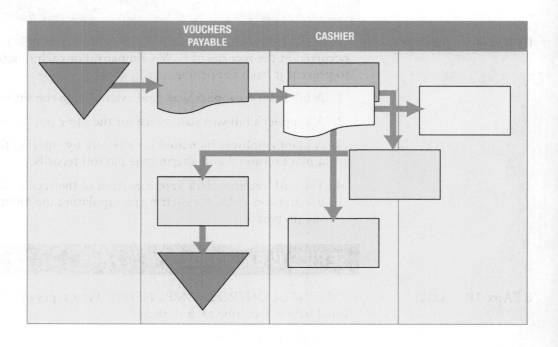

SERIES B PROBLEM

P 7Apx-4B   (LO2/3/4)   USING INTERNAL CONTROLS TO PREVENT ERRORS The following misstatements occurred in the records of MW Company. For each misstatement, suggest a control to prevent it from happening.

1. A bill from a supplier was paid for goods that had not been ordered.

2. A supplier's bill for 50 boxes of materials was paid even though only 40 boxes were received.

3. Expensive product components were stolen by an employee from a loading dock area after hours.

4. No bill was sent to a customer for a shipment because the shipping document was lost after the shipment was made.

Chapter 8 Payroll Accounting: Employee Earnings and Deductions

LEARNING OBJECTIVES

Careful study of this chapter should enable you to:

LO1 Distinguish between employees and independent contractors.

LO2 Calculate employee earnings and deductions.

LO3 Describe and prepare payroll records.

LO4 Account for employee earnings and deductions.

LO5 Describe various payroll record-keeping methods.

When a company upgrades its computers and needs to dump its old ones, it might be time to call Intechra Group. Intechra Group provides computer hardware, software, and database disposal and recycling services nationwide. Founded in 1987, the company grew rapidly in response to environmental and privacy concerns about the use of IT assets. In 2010, Intechra was acquired by Arrow Electronics and now functions as a subsidiary of Arrow. Intechra is one of the largest electronics life-cycle management companies in the United States and currently processes more than ten million pounds of electronics annually. With more than 10,000 employees, it offers both on-site services and secure transport of assets to its locations. Consistent with environmental concerns, the entire recycling operation is performed under a zero-landfill policy for e-waste.

A company such as Intechra requires a variety of employees—from highly technical to basic materials handling staff—with very different rates of pay. For legal and operating efficiency reasons, a company must accurately track and control its payroll costs. It needs to know not only what to pay its people, but also what taxes to withhold from their wages. In this chapter, you will learn how to identify and account for payroll expenses for multiple employees.

Chapters 8 and 9 provide a basic introduction to payroll accounting. To assume responsibility for this area in a business, a full course in payroll accounting should be taken.

The only contact most of us have with payroll is receiving a paycheck. Few of us have seen the large amount of record keeping needed to produce that paycheck.

Employers maintain complete payroll accounting records for two reasons. First, payroll costs are major expenditures for most companies. Payroll accounting records provide data useful in analyzing and controlling these expenditures. Second, federal, state, and local laws require employers to keep payroll records. Companies must accumulate payroll data both for the business as a whole and for each employee.

There are two major types of payroll taxes: those paid by the employee and those paid by the employer. In this chapter, we discuss employee taxes. In Chapter 9, we address payroll taxes paid by the employer.

LO1   Employees and Independent Contractors

Distinguish between employees and independent contractors.

Not every person who performs services for a business is considered an employee. An employee works under the control and direction of an employer. Examples include secretaries, maintenance workers, salesclerks, and plant supervisors. In contrast, an independent contractor performs a service for a fee and does not work under the control and direction of the company paying for the service. Examples of independent contractors include public accountants, real estate agents, and lawyers.

The distinction between an employee and an independent contractor is important for payroll purposes. Government laws and regulations regarding payroll are much more complex for employees than for independent contractors. Employers must deduct certain taxes, maintain payroll records, and file numerous reports for all employees. Only one form (Form 1099) must be filed for independent contractors. The payroll accounting procedures described in this chapter apply only to employer/employee relationships.

LO2   Employee Earnings and Deductions

Calculate employee earnings and deductions.

Three steps are required to determine how much to pay an employee for a pay period:

1. Calculate total earnings.
2. Determine the amounts of deductions.
3. Subtract deductions from total earnings to compute net pay.

Salaries and Wages

Compensation for managerial or administrative services usually is called salary. A salary normally is expressed in biweekly (every two weeks), monthly, or annual terms. Compensation for skilled or unskilled labor usually is referred to as wages. Wages ordinarily are expressed in terms of hours, weeks, or units produced. The terms "salaries" and "wages" often are used interchangeably in practice.

The Fair Labor Standards Act (FLSA), often called the Federal Wage and Hour Law, requires employers to pay overtime at 1½ times the regular rate to any hourly employee who works over 40 hours in a week. Some companies pay a higher rate for hours worked on Saturday or Sunday, but this is not required by the FLSA. Some salaried employees are exempt from the FLSA rules and are not paid overtime.

Computing Total Earnings

Compensation usually is based on the time worked during the payroll period. Sometimes it is based on sales or units of output during the period. When compensation is based on time, a record must be kept of the time worked by each employee. Time cards (Figure 8-1) are helpful for this purpose. In large businesses with computer-based timekeeping systems, plastic cards or badges with special magnetic strips or bar codes (Figure 8-2) can be used. Employees use the cards to clock in and out at terminals with card readers. For increased security, these terminals also are available with fingerprint readers.

FIGURE 8-1 Time Card

Westly, Inc.
Time Card — Hourly Payroll

Emp. Name **Kuzmik, Helen**   Base Dept.: **Sales**

Emp. ID: **359-47-1138**   Pay Per. End: **12/19/20--**

| | | | | | HOURS | | | |
Date	Time In	Time Out	Time In	Time Out	Reg	OT	DT	Total
12/13	8:00	12:30	13:00	17:30	8	1		9
12/14	8:00	12:30	13:00	17:30	8	1		9
12/15	8:00	12:30	13:00	17:30	8	1		9
12/16	8:00	12:30	13:00	17:30	8	1		9
12/17	8:00	12:30	13:00	17:30	8	1		9
12/18	10:00	15:00				5		5
12/19	13:00	17:00					4	4
TOTAL					40	10	4	54

Remarks_____

_____

Approval_____ TM _____
          Dept. Head

To illustrate the computation of total earnings, look at the time card of Helen Kuzmik in Figure 8-1. The card shows that Kuzmik worked 54 hours for the week.

Regular hours	40 hours
Overtime	10
Double time	4
Total hours worked	54 hours

Kuzmik's regular rate of pay is $14 per hour. She is paid 1½ times the regular rate for hours in excess of 8 on Monday through Friday and any hours worked on

FIGURE 8-2 Time Cards and Clock Terminal

Saturday, and twice the regular rate for hours on Sunday. Kuzmik's total earnings for the week ended December 19 are computed as follows:

40 hours × $14	$560
10 hours × $21 (1½ × $14 = $21)	210
4 hours (on Sunday) × $28 (2 × $14 = $28)	112
Total earnings for the week	$882

Salaried employees who are not exempt from the FSLA rules may also be entitled to premium pay for overtime. If this is the case, it is necessary to compute the regular hourly rate of pay before computing the overtime rate. To illustrate, assume that Linda Swaney has a salary of $2,600 a month plus 1½ times the regular hourly rate for hours in excess of 40 per week. Swaney's overtime rate of pay is computed as follows:

$2,600 × 12 months	$31,200 annual pay
$31,200 ÷ 52 weeks	$600.00 pay per week
$600.00 ÷ 40 hours	$15.00 pay per regular hour
$15.00 × 1½	$22.50 overtime pay per hour

If Swaney worked 50 hours during the week ended December 19, her total earnings for the week would be computed as follows:

40 hours × $15.00	$600.00
10 hours × $22.50	225.00
Total earnings for the week	$825.00

> There are 52 weeks in each year but not 4 weeks in each month. That is why monthly salaries must be annualized in order to determine the hourly rate.

Deductions from Total Earnings

An employee's total earnings are called **gross pay**. Various deductions are made from gross pay to yield take-home or **net pay**. Deductions from gross pay fall into three major categories:

1. Federal (and possibly state and city) income tax withholding
2. Employee FICA tax withholding
3. Voluntary deductions

Income Tax Withholding

Federal law requires employers to withhold certain amounts from the total earnings of each employee. These withholdings are applied toward the payment of the employee's federal income tax. Four factors determine the amount to be withheld from an employee's gross pay each pay period:

1. Total earnings
2. Marital status
3. Number of withholding allowances claimed
4. Length of the pay period

Withholding Allowances. Each employee is required to furnish the employer an Employee's Withholding Allowance Certificate, Form W-4 (Figure 8-3). The marital status of the employee and the number of allowances claimed on Form W-4 determine the dollar amount of earnings subject to withholding. A **withholding allowance** exempts a specific dollar amount of an employee's gross pay from federal income tax withholding. In general, each employee is permitted one personal withholding allowance, one for a spouse who does not also claim an allowance, and one for each dependent.

FIGURE 8-3 Employee's Withholding Allowance Certificate (Form W-4)

A withholding certificate completed by Ken Istone is shown in Figure 8-3. Istone is married, has a spouse who does not claim an allowance, and has two dependent children. On line 5 of the W-4 form, Istone claims four allowances, calculated as follows:

Personal allowance	1
Spouse allowance	1
Allowances for dependents	2
Total withholding allowances	4

Wage-Bracket Method. Employers generally use the **wage-bracket method** or the **percentage method** to determine the amount of tax to be withheld from an employee's pay. We will illustrate the wage-bracket method here. The employee's gross pay for a specific time period is traced into the appropriate wage-bracket table provided by the Internal Revenue Service (IRS). These tables cover various time periods, and there are separate tables for single and married taxpayers. Copies are provided in *Circular E—Employer's Tax Guide*, also known as Publication 15, which may be obtained from any local IRS office or at the IRS Internet site.

Portions of weekly income tax wage-bracket withholding tables for single and married persons are illustrated in Figure 8-4. Assume that Ken Istone (who claims 4 allowances) had gross earnings of $640 for the week ending December 19, 20--. The amount to withhold for Istone is determined by using the following steps, as shown in Figure 8-4 for married persons (on page 289):

1. Find the row for wages of "at least $635, but less than $645."
2. Find the column headed "4 withholding allowances."
3. Where the row and column cross, $10 is given as the amount to be withheld.

For state or city income taxes, withholding generally is handled in one of two ways: (1) forms and tables similar to those provided by the IRS are used or (2) an amount equal to a percentage of the federal withholding amount is withheld.

Employee FICA Tax Withholding

The Federal Insurance Contributions Act requires employers to withhold **FICA taxes** from employees' earnings. FICA taxes include amounts for both Social Security and Medicare programs. Social Security provides pensions and disability benefits. Medicare provides health insurance.

Congress has frequently changed the tax rates and the maximum amounts of earnings subject to FICA taxes. For this text, we assume the Social Security rate is 6.2% on maximum earnings of $128,400. The Medicare rate is 1.45% on all earnings; there is no maximum.

To illustrate the calculation of FICA taxes, assume the following earnings for Sarah Cadrain:

	Earnings	
Pay Period	Week	Year-to-Date
Dec. 6–12	$2,000	$127,340
Dec. 13–19	$2,060	$129,400

For the week of December 6–12, FICA taxes on Cadrain's earnings would be:

Gross Pay	×	Tax Rate		=	Tax
$2,000		Social Security	6.2%		$124.00
		Medicare	1.45%		29.00
					$153.00

Circular E and many other IRS publications and forms can be found at the IRS Web site: www.irs.gov. These materials are essential for working in payroll accounting.

LEARNING KEY

To determine the amount to withhold:

1. Find the row for wages.
2. Find the column for withholding allowances.
3. Find the amount where they cross.

An additional Medicare tax of 0.9% is imposed on employee earnings of more than $200,000 for single filers, and more than $250,000 for joint filers.

FIGURE 8-4 Federal Withholding Tax Table: Single Persons

SINGLE Persons—WEEKLY Payroll Period
(For Wages Paid through December 31, 2018)

And the wages are—		And the number of withholding allowances claimed is—										
At least	But less than	0	1	2	3	4	5	6	7	8	9	10
		The amount of income tax to be withheld is—										
$360	$370	$32	$22	$13	$5	$0	$0	$0	$0	$0	$0	$0
370	380	33	23	14	6	0	0	0	0	0	0	0
380	390	34	24	15	7	0	0	0	0	0	0	0
390	400	35	26	16	8	0	0	0	0	0	0	0
400	410	36	27	17	9	1	0	0	0	0	0	0
410	420	38	28	18	10	2	0	0	0	0	0	0
420	430	39	29	20	11	3	0	0	0	0	0	0
430	440	40	30	21	12	4	0	0	0	0	0	0
440	450	41	32	22	13	5	0	0	0	0	0	0
450	460	42	33	23	14	6	0	0	0	0	0	0
460	470	44	34	24	15	7	0	0	0	0	0	0
470	480	45	35	26	16	8	0	0	0	0	0	0
480	490	46	36	27	17	9	1	0	0	0	0	0
490	500	47	38	28	18	10	2	0	0	0	0	0
500	510	48	39	29	20	11	3	0	0	0	0	0
510	520	50	40	30	21	12	4	0	0	0	0	0
520	530	51	41	32	22	13	5	0	0	0	0	0
530	540	52	42	33	23	14	6	0	0	0	0	0
540	550	53	44	34	24	15	7	0	0	0	0	0
550	560	54	45	35	26	16	8	1	0	0	0	0
560	570	56	46	36	27	17	9	2	0	0	0	0
570	580	57	47	38	28	18	10	3	0	0	0	0
580	590	58	48	39	29	20	11	4	0	0	0	0
590	600	59	50	40	30	21	12	5	0	0	0	0
600	610	60	51	41	32	22	13	6	0	0	0	0
610	620	62	52	42	33	23	14	7	0	0	0	0
620	630	63	53	44	34	24	15	8	0	0	0	0
630	640	64	54	45	35	26	16	9	1	0	0	0
640	650	65	56	46	36	27	17	10	2	0	0	0
650	660	66	57	47	38	28	19	11	3	0	0	0
660	670	68	58	48	39	29	20	12	4	0	0	0
670	680	69	59	50	40	30	21	13	5	0	0	0
680	690	70	60	51	41	32	22	14	6	0	0	0
690	700	71	62	52	42	33	23	15	7	0	0	0
700	710	72	63	53	44	34	25	16	8	0	0	0
710	720	74	64	54	45	35	26	17	9	1	0	0
720	730	75	65	56	46	36	27	18	10	2	0	0
730	740	76	66	57	47	38	28	19	11	3	0	0
740	750	77	68	58	48	39	29	20	12	4	0	0
750	760	78	69	59	50	40	31	21	13	5	0	0
760	770	80	70	60	51	41	32	22	14	6	0	0
770	780	81	71	62	52	42	33	23	15	7	0	0
780	790	82	72	63	53	44	34	25	16	8	0	0
790	800	83	74	64	54	45	35	26	17	9	1	0
800	810	84	75	65	56	46	37	27	18	10	2	0
810	820	86	76	66	57	47	38	28	19	11	3	0
820	830	88	77	68	58	48	39	29	20	12	4	0
830	840	90	78	69	59	50	40	31	21	13	5	0
840	850	92	80	70	60	51	41	32	22	14	6	0

FIGURE 8-4 Federal Withholding Tax Table: (*concluded*) Married Persons

MARRIED Persons—WEEKLY Payroll Period
(For Wages Paid through December 31, 2018)

At least	But less than	0	1	2	3	(2) 4	5	6	7	8	9	10
		\multicolumn{11}{The amount of income tax to be withheld is—}										
$425	$435	$21	$13	$5	$0	$0	$0	$0	$0	$0	$0	$0
435	445	22	14	6	0	0	0	0	0	0	0	0
445	455	23	15	7	0	0	0	0	0	0	0	0
455	465	24	16	8	0	0	0	0	0	0	0	0
465	475	25	17	9	1	0	0	0	0	0	0	0
475	485	26	18	10	2	0	0	0	0	0	0	0
485	495	27	19	11	3	0	0	0	0	0	0	0
495	505	28	20	12	4	0	0	0	0	0	0	0
505	515	29	21	13	5	0	0	0	0	0	0	0
515	525	30	22	14	6	0	0	0	0	0	0	0
525	535	31	23	15	7	0	0	0	0	0	0	0
535	545	32	24	16	8	0	0	0	0	0	0	0
545	555	33	25	17	9	1	0	0	0	0	0	0
555	565	34	26	18	10	2	0	0	0	0	0	0
565	575	35	27	19	11	3	0	0	0	0	0	0
575	585	36	28	20	12	4	0	0	0	0	0	0
585	595	37	29	21	13	5	0	0	0	0	0	0
595	605	38	30	22	14	6	0	0	0	0	0	0
605	615	39	31	23	15	7	0	0	0	0	0	0
615	625	40	32	24	16	8	0	0	0	0	0	0
625	635	42	33	25	17	9	1	0	0	0	0	0
(1) 635	645	43	34	26	18	(3) 10	2	0	0	0	0	0
645	655	44	35	27	19	11	3	0	0	0	0	0
655	665	45	36	28	20	12	4	0	0	0	0	0
665	675	46	37	29	21	13	5	0	0	0	0	0
675	685	48	38	30	22	14	6	0	0	0	0	0
685	695	49	39	31	23	15	7	0	0	0	0	0
695	705	50	40	32	24	16	8	0	0	0	0	0
705	715	51	42	33	25	17	9	1	0	0	0	0
715	725	52	43	34	26	18	10	2	0	0	0	0
725	735	54	44	35	27	19	11	3	0	0	0	0
735	745	55	45	36	28	20	12	4	0	0	0	0
745	755	56	46	37	29	21	13	5	0	0	0	0
755	765	57	48	38	30	22	14	6	0	0	0	0
765	775	58	49	39	31	23	15	7	0	0	0	0
775	785	60	50	40	32	24	16	8	0	0	0	0
785	795	61	51	42	33	25	17	9	1	0	0	0
795	805	62	52	43	34	26	18	10	2	0	0	0
805	815	63	54	44	35	27	19	11	3	0	0	0
815	825	64	55	45	36	28	20	12	4	0	0	0
825	835	66	56	46	37	29	21	13	5	0	0	0
835	845	67	57	48	38	30	22	14	6	0	0	0
845	855	68	58	49	39	31	23	15	7	0	0	0
855	865	69	60	50	40	32	24	16	8	0	0	0
865	875	70	61	51	42	33	25	17	9	1	0	0
875	885	72	62	52	43	34	26	18	10	2	0	0
885	895	73	63	54	44	35	27	19	11	3	0	0
895	905	74	64	55	45	36	28	20	12	4	0	0
905	915	75	66	56	46	37	29	21	13	5	0	0
1,315	1,325	124	115	105	96	86	77	67	57	48	38	30
1,325	1,335	126	116	106	97	87	78	68	59	49	39	31
1,335	1,345	127	117	108	98	88	79	69	60	50	41	32
1,345	1,355	128	118	109	99	90	80	71	61	51	42	33
1,355	1,365	129	120	110	100	91	81	72	62	53	43	34
1,365	1,375	130	121	111	102	92	83	73	63	54	44	35
1,375	1,385	132	122	112	103	93	84	74	65	55	45	36
1,385	1,395	133	123	114	104	95	85	75	66	56	47	37
1,395	1,405	134	124	115	105	96	86	77	67	57	48	38
1,405	1,415	135	126	116	106	97	87	78	68	59	49	39
1,415	1,425	136	127	117	108	98	89	79	69	60	50	41
1,425	1,435	138	128	118	109	99	90	80	71	61	51	42
1,435	1,445	139	129	120	110	101	91	81	72	62	53	43
1,445	1,455	140	130	121	111	102	92	83	73	63	54	44
1,455	1,465	141	132	122	112	103	93	84	74	65	55	45
1,465	1,475	142	133	123	114	104	95	85	75	66	56	47
1,475	1,485	144	134	124	115	105	96	86	77	67	57	48
1,485	1,495	145	135	126	116	107	97	87	78	68	59	49
1,495	1,505	146	136	127	117	108	98	89	79	69	60	50
1,505	1,515	147	138	128	118	109	99	90	80	71	61	51

When the Social Security program was established in 1937, the tax was 1% on earnings up to $3,000 per year!

During the week of December 13–19, Cadrain's earnings for the calendar year went over the $128,400 Social Security maximum by $1,000 ($129,400 – $128,400). Therefore, $1,000 of her $2,060 earnings for the week would not be subject to the Social Security tax.

Year-to-date earnings	$129,400
Social Security maximum	128,400
Amount not subject to Social Security tax	$ 1,000

The Social Security tax on Cadrain's December 13–19 earnings would be:

Gross pay	$2,060.00
Amount not subject to Social Security tax	1,000.00
Amount subject to Social Security tax	$1,060.00
Tax rate	6.2%
Social Security tax	$ 65.72

Since there is no Medicare maximum, all of Cadrain's December 13–19 earnings would be subject to the Medicare tax.

Gross pay	$2,060.00
Tax rate	1.45%
Medicare tax	$ 29.87

The total FICA tax would be:

Social Security tax	$65.72
Medicare tax	29.87
Total FICA tax	95.59

For the rest of the calendar year through December 31, Cadrain's earnings would be subject only to Medicare taxes.

Voluntary Deductions

In addition to the mandatory deductions from employee earnings for income and FICA taxes, many other deductions are possible. These deductions are usually voluntary and depend on specific agreements between the employee and employer. Examples of voluntary deductions are:

1. U.S. savings bond purchases
2. Health insurance premiums
3. Credit union deposits
4. Pension plan payments
5. Charitable contributions

If you use Microsoft® Excel to create a payroll register, a column or row *may* be off by a few cents. This usually occurs in the Social Security and Medicare tax calculations because of rounding. To get an accurate number, use the "ROUND" function in any cell with more than two non-zero decimal places.

Computing Net Pay

To compute an employee's net pay for the period, subtract all tax withholdings and voluntary deductions from the gross pay. Ken Istone's net pay for the week ended December 19 would be calculated as follows:

Gross pay		$640.00
Deductions:		
Federal income tax withholding	$10.00	
Social Security tax withholding	39.68	
Medicare tax withholding	9.28	
Health insurance premiums	10.00	
Total deductions		68.96
Net pay		$571.04

CHECKPOINT ✔

Complete Checkpoint-1 on page 305 to test your basic understanding of LO2.

LO3	**Payroll Records**

Describe and prepare payroll records.

Payroll records should provide the following information for each employee:

1. Name, address, occupation, Social Security number, marital status, and number of withholding allowances
2. Gross amount of earnings, date of payment, and period covered by each payroll
3. Gross amount of earnings accumulated for the year
4. Amounts of taxes and other items withheld

Three types of payroll records are used to accumulate this information:

1. The payroll register
2. The payroll check (or record of direct deposit) with earnings statement attached
3. The employee earnings record

These records can be prepared by either manual or automated methods. The illustrations in this chapter are based on a manual system. The forms and procedures illustrated are equally applicable to both manual and automated systems.

Payroll Register

A good example of a deduction column that could be added is State Income Tax. In the payroll register in Figure 8-5, the column could be inserted immediately after Federal Income Tax.

A payroll register is a form used to assemble the data required at the end of each payroll period. Figure 8-5 on pages 292 and 293 illustrates Westly, Inc.'s payroll register for the payroll period ended December 19, 20--. Detailed information on earnings, taxable earnings, deductions, and net pay is provided for each employee. Column headings for deductions may vary, depending on which deductions are commonly used by a particular business. The sources of key information in the register are indicated in Figure 8-5.

Note four important things about Westly's payroll register:

1. The first $128,400 of earnings of each employee is subject to Social Security tax. The Cumulative Total column, under the Earnings category, shows that Sarah Cadrain has exceeded this limit during the period. Thus, only $1,060 of her earnings for this pay period is subject to Social Security tax, as shown in the Taxable Earnings columns.
2. There are two Taxable Earnings columns: Unemployment Compensation and Social Security. Only one of these columns (Social Security) is needed to determine employee taxes. Both columns are shown here because they are a standard part of a payroll register. The Unemployment Compensation column is needed to determine this payroll tax on employers. The Social Security column is needed to determine both employee and employer Social Security taxes. The two employer taxes (Unemployment Compensation and Social Security) are discussed in Chapter 9.
3. Regular deductions are made from employee earnings for federal income tax and Social Security and Medicare taxes.
4. Voluntary deductions are made for health insurance and United Way contributions, based on agreements with individual employees.

FIGURE 8-5 **Payroll Register (left side)**

PAYROLL REGISTER

#	NAME	ALLOWANCES	MARITAL STATUS	EARNINGS			CUMULATIVE TOTAL	TAXABLE EARNINGS	
				REGULAR	OVERTIME	TOTAL		UNEMPLOYMENT COMPENSATION	SOCIAL SECURITY
1	Cadrain, Sarah	4	M	2 0 0 0 00	6 0 00	2 0 6 0 00	129 4 0 0 00	0 00	1 0 6 0 00
2	Gruder, James	1	S	7 6 0 00	1 4 0 00	9 0 0 00	43 4 0 0 00	0 00	9 0 0 00
3	Istone, Ken	4	M	6 4 0 00		6 4 0 00	32 0 2 5 00	0 00	6 4 0 00
4	Kuzmik, Helen	2	M	5 6 0 00	3 2 2 00	8 8 2 00	34 0 0 0 00	0 00	8 8 2 00
5	Lee, Hoseoup	3	M	6 2 0 00		6 2 0 00	31 3 4 0 00	0 00	6 2 0 00
6	Swaney, Linda	2	S	6 0 0 00	2 2 5 00	8 2 5 00	30 5 0 0 00	0 00	8 2 5 00
7	Tucci, Paul	3	M	6 1 0 00		6 1 0 00	30 1 0 0 00	0 00	6 1 0 00
8	Wiles, Harry	1	S	3 6 0 00		3 6 0 00	6 3 0 0 00	3 6 0 00	3 6 0 00
9				6 1 5 0 00	7 4 7 00	6 8 9 7 00	337 0 6 5 00	3 6 0 00	5 8 9 7 00
10									

Time cards, pay rates

Prior period total + current period earnings

Current below $7,000 cumul. total

Current below $128,400 cumul. total

Discussed in Chapter 9

After the data for each employee have been entered, the amount columns in the payroll register should be totaled and the totals verified as follows:

Regular earnings		$6,150.00
Overtime earnings		747.00
Gross earnings		$6,897.00
Deductions:		
Federal income tax	$444.00	
Social Security tax	365.61	
Medicare tax	100.01	
Health insurance premiums	46.00	
United Way	40.00	995.62
Net amount of payroll		$5,901.38

In a computerized accounting system, the payroll software performs this proof. An error in the payroll register could cause the payment of an incorrect amount to an employee. It also could result in sending an incorrect amount to the government or other agencies for whom funds are withheld.

Paying Employees

Employees should be paid by check or by direct deposit. Data needed to prepare a paycheck for each employee are contained in the payroll register. In a computer-based system, the paychecks and payroll register normally are prepared at the same time. The employer furnishes an earnings statement to each employee along with each paycheck. Paychecks with detachable earnings statements, like the one for Ken Istone illustrated in Figure 8-6, are widely used for this purpose. Before the check is deposited or cashed, the employee should detach the stub and keep it for his records.

FIGURE 8-5 Payroll Register (right side)

—WEEK ENDED 12/19/--

	FEDERAL INCOME TAX	SOCIAL SECURITY TAX	MEDICARE TAX	HEALTH INSURANCE	UNITED WAY	OTHER	TOTAL	NET PAY	CHECK NO.	
	175 00	65 72	29 87				270 59	1 789 41	409	1
	86 00	55 80	13 05		20 00		174 85	725 15	410	2
	10 00	39 68	9 28	10 00			68 96	571 04	411	3
	52 00	54 68	12 79	13 00	20 00		152 47	729 53	412	4
	16 00	38 44	8 99	13 00			76 43	543 57	413	5
	68 00	51 15	11 96				131 11	693 89	414	6
	15 00	37 82	8 85	10 00			71 67	538 33	415	7
	22 00	22 32	5 22				49 54	310 46	416	8
	444 00	365 61	100 01	46 00	40 00	0 00	995 62	5 901 38		9
										10

DEDUCTIONS

- Withholding Tax Table
- 6.2% × Social Security taxable earnings
- 1.45% × total earnings
- Specific employer–employee agreements
- Total earnings – total deductions

FIGURE 8-6 Paycheck and Earnings Statement

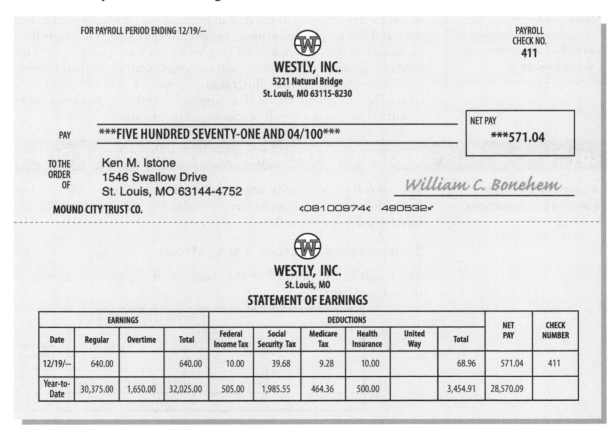

FOR PAYROLL PERIOD ENDING 12/19/--

WESTLY, INC.
5221 Natural Bridge
St. Louis, MO 63115-8230

PAYROLL CHECK NO. **411**

PAY   ***FIVE HUNDRED SEVENTY-ONE AND 04/100***

NET PAY   ***571.04

TO THE ORDER OF
Ken M. Istone
1546 Swallow Drive
St. Louis, MO 63144-4752

William C. Bonehem

MOUND CITY TRUST CO.   ⑈08100974⑈ 490532⑉

WESTLY, INC.
St. Louis, MO
STATEMENT OF EARNINGS

	EARNINGS			DEDUCTIONS						NET PAY	CHECK NUMBER
Date	Regular	Overtime	Total	Federal Income Tax	Social Security Tax	Medicare Tax	Health Insurance	United Way	Total		
12/19/--	640.00		640.00	10.00	39.68	9.28	10.00		68.96	571.04	411
Year-to-Date	30,375.00	1,650.00	32,025.00	505.00	1,985.55	464.36	500.00		3,454.91	28,570.09	

FIGURE 8-7 **Employee Earnings Record (left side)**

PERIOD ENDED	EARNINGS			CUMULATIVE TOTAL	TAXABLE EARNINGS	
	REGULAR	OVERTIME	TOTAL		UNEMPLOYMENT COMPENSATION	SOCIAL SECURITY
11/28	6 4 0 00		6 4 0 00	29 9 5 5 00		6 4 0 00
12/5	6 4 0 00	7 5 00	7 1 5 00	30 5 9 5 00		7 1 5 00
12/12	6 4 0 00	7 5 00	7 1 5 00	31 3 1 0 00		7 1 5 00
12/19	6 4 0 00		6 4 0 00	32 0 2 5 00		6 4 0 00

GENDER	DEPARTMENT	OCCUPATION	SOCIAL SECURITY NUMBER	MARITAL STATUS	ALLOWANCES
M ✔ F	Maintenance	Service	393-58-8194	M	4

When direct deposit is used, the employee does not even handle the paycheck. Rather, payment is deposited directly by the employer into the employee's bank account using an electronic funds transfer (EFT). The employee receives only the earnings statement from the check indicating the deposit has been made. Payment by check or direct deposit provides better internal accounting control than payment by cash.

Employee Earnings Record

A separate record of each employee's earnings is called an employee earnings record. An employee earnings record for Ken M. Istone for a portion of the last quarter of the calendar year is illustrated in Figure 8-7 above.

The information in this record is obtained from the payroll register. In a computer-based system, the employee earnings record can be updated at the same time the payroll register is prepared.

Istone's earnings for four weeks of the last quarter of the year are shown on this form. Note that the entry for the pay period ended December 19 is the same as that in the payroll register illustrated in Figure 8-5. This linkage between the payroll register and the employee earnings record always exists. The payroll register provides a summary of the earnings of all employees for each pay period. The earnings record provides a summary of the annual earnings of an individual employee.

The earnings record illustrated in Figure 8-7 is designed to accumulate both quarterly and annual totals. The employer needs this information to prepare several reports. These reports will be discussed in Chapter 9.

LEARNING KEY 🔑

The payroll register and employee earnings record are linked. The payroll register shows the earnings of all employees for a single pay period. The employee earnings record summarizes the earnings of an individual employee for all pay periods.

LO4 Accounting for Employee Earnings and Deductions

Account for employee earnings and deductions.

The payroll register described in the previous section provides complete payroll data for each pay period. But the payroll register is not a journal. We still need to make a journal entry for payroll.

Journalizing Payroll Transactions

The totals at the bottom of the columns of the payroll register in Figure 8-5 are reproduced here.

PAYROLL REGISTER (LEFT SIDE)					
EARNINGS			CUMULATIVE TOTAL	TAXABLE EARNINGS	
REGULAR	OVERTIME	TOTAL		UNEMPLOYMENT COMPENSATION	SOCIAL SECURITY
6 1 5 0 00	7 4 7 00	6 8 9 7 00	337 0 6 5 00	3 6 0 00	5 8 9 7 00

FIGURE 8-7 Employee Earnings Record (right side)

FOR PERIOD ENDED						20--					
				DEDUCTIONS							
FEDERAL INCOME TAX	SOCIAL SECURITY TAX	MEDICARE TAX	HEALTH INSURANCE	UNITED WAY	OTHER		TOTAL		CHECK NO.	AMOUNT	
1 0 00	3 9 68	9 28	1 0 00				6 8 96		387	5 7 1 04	
1 8 00	4 4 33	1 0 37	1 0 00				8 2 70		395	6 3 2 30	
1 8 00	4 4 33	1 0 37	1 0 00				8 2 70		403	6 3 2 30	
1 0 00	3 9 68	9 28	1 0 00				6 8 96		411	5 7 1 04	

PAY RATE	DATE OF BIRTH	DATE HIRED	NAME/ADDRESS	EMPLOYEE NUMBER
$640/wk	8/17/64	1/3/87	Ken M. Istone 1546 Swallow Drive St. Louis, MO 63144-4752	3

A BROADER VIEW

Payroll Fraud—Paying for Ghosts

A supervisor at Haas Transfer Warehouse embezzled $12,000 from the company by collecting paychecks for former employees. When an employee left the company, the supervisor continued to submit a department time report for the employee. This caused a paycheck to be generated for the "ghost" employee. The supervisor then simply kept this paycheck when others were distributed to actual employees.

This fraud shows the importance of two procedures that appear in this chapter: (1) a time card, plastic card, or badge should be used for each employee to keep an accurate record of time worked and (2) payment by direct deposit or electronic funds transfer to the employee's bank is a good internal control.

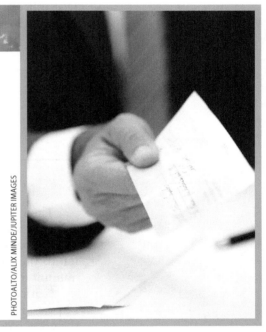

PHOTOALTO/ALIX MINDE/JUPITER IMAGES

The numbered amounts in the payroll register column totals thus provide the basis for recording the payroll. If the employee paychecks are written from the regular bank account, the following journal entry is made:

PAYROLL REGISTER (RIGHT SIDE)						20--				
				DEDUCTIONS						NET PAY
FEDERAL INCOME TAX	SOCIAL SECURITY TAX	MEDICARE TAX	HEALTH INSURANCE	UNITED WAY	OTHER		TOTAL			
4 4 4 00	3 6 5 61	1 0 0 01	4 6 00	4 0 00	0 00	0 00	9 9 5 62			5 9 0 1 38
(2)	(3)	(4)	(5)	(6)						(7)

An alternative to crediting Cash immediately for the net amount due ($5,901.38) to employees is to credit this amount to Wages and Salaries Payable. Then Wages and Salaries Payable is debited and Cash is credited when the employees are paid.

	DATE		DESCRIPTION	POST REF.	DEBIT	CREDIT	
(1) 5	Dec.	19	Wages and Salaries Expense		6 8 9 7 00		5
(2) 6			Employee Federal Income Tax Payable			4 4 4 00	6
(3) 7			Social Security Tax Payable			3 6 5 61	7
(4) 8			Medicare Tax Payable			1 0 0 01	8
(5) 9			Health Insurance Premiums Payable			4 6 00	9
(6) 10			United Way Contributions Payable			4 0 00	10
(7) 11			Cash			5 9 0 1 38	11
12			Payroll for week ended Dec. 19				12

Employee paychecks also can be written from a special payroll bank account. Large businesses with many employees commonly use a payroll bank account. If Westly used a payroll bank account, it first would have made the following entry on December 19 to transfer funds from the regular bank account to the payroll bank account:

	DATE		DESCRIPTION	POST REF.	DEBIT	CREDIT	
1	Dec.	19	Payroll Cash		5 9 0 1 38		1
2			Cash			5 9 0 1 38	2
3			Cash for Dec. 19 payroll				3

Then, the payroll entry shown above would be made, except that the credit of $5,901.38 would be to Payroll Cash rather than Cash.

If a payroll bank account is used, individual checks totaling $5,901.38 are written to the employees from that account. Otherwise, individual checks totaling that amount are written to the employees from the regular bank account.

Notice two important facts about the payroll entry. First, Wages and Salaries Expense is debited for the gross pay of the employees. The expense to the employer is the gross pay, not the employees' net pay after deductions. Second, a separate account is kept for each deduction.

The accounts needed in entering deductions depend upon the deductions involved. To understand the accounting for these deductions, consider what the employer is doing. By deducting amounts from employees' earnings, the employer is simply serving as an agent for the government and other groups. Amounts that are deducted from an employee's gross earnings must be paid by the employer to these groups. Therefore, a separate account should be kept for the liability for each type of deduction.

To help us understand the journal entry for payroll, let's use the accounting equation to examine the accounts involved. The seven accounts affected by the payroll entry above are shown in the accounting equation in Figure 8-8.

LEARNING KEY

Wages and Salaries Expense is debited for the gross pay. A separate account is kept for each earnings deduction. Cash is credited for the net pay.

FIGURE 8-8 Accounting for Payroll

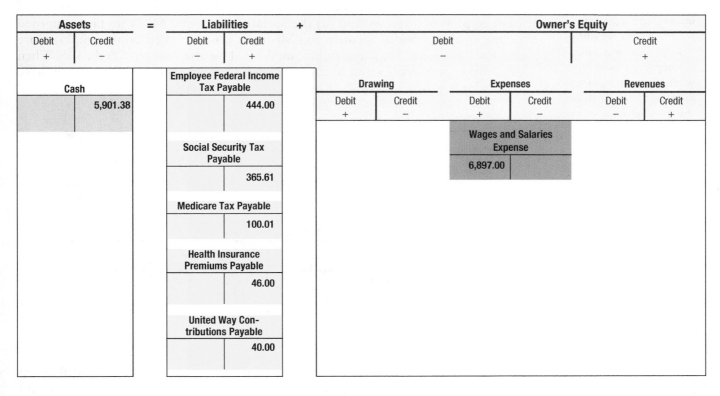

Wages and Salaries Expense

This account is debited for the gross pay of all employees for each pay period. Sometimes separate expense accounts are kept for the employees of different departments. Thus, separate accounts may be kept for Office Salaries Expense, Sales Salaries Expense, and Factory Wages Expense.

Wages and Salaries Expense	
Debit	Credit
Gross pay of employees for each pay period	

Employee Federal Income Tax Payable

This account is credited for the total federal income tax withheld from employees' earnings. The account is debited for amounts paid to the IRS. When all of the income taxes withheld have been paid, the account will have a zero balance. A state or city income tax payable account is used in a similar manner.

Employee Federal Income Tax Payable	
Debit	Credit
Payment of federal income tax previously withheld	Federal income tax withheld from employees' earnings

Social Security and Medicare Taxes Payable

Income, Social Security, and Medicare taxes are withheld from earnings when employees are **paid**. Thus, when wages and salaries are accrued at year end, these tax liabilities are not accrued.

These accounts are credited for (1) the Social Security and Medicare taxes withheld from employees' earnings and (2) the Social Security and Medicare taxes imposed on the employer. Social Security and Medicare taxes imposed on the employer are discussed in Chapter 9. The accounts are debited for amounts paid to the IRS. When all of the Social Security and Medicare taxes have been paid, the accounts will have zero balances.

Social Security Tax Payable

Debit	Credit
Payment of Social Security tax previously withheld or imposed	Social Security taxes (1) withheld from employees' earnings and (2) imposed on the employer

Medicare Tax Payable

Debit	Credit
Payment of Medicare tax previously withheld or imposed	Medicare taxes (1) withheld from employees' earnings and (2) imposed on the employer

CHECKPOINT ✔

Complete Checkpoint-2 on page 305 to test your basic understanding of LO4.

Other Deductions

Health Insurance Premiums Payable is credited for health insurance contributions deducted from an employee's pay. The account is debited for the subsequent payment of these amounts to the health insurer. United Way Contributions Payable is handled in a similar manner.

LO5 Payroll Record-Keeping Methods

Describe various payroll record-keeping methods.

You probably noticed that the same information appears in several places in the payroll records—in the payroll register, paycheck and stub, and employee earnings records. If all records are prepared by hand (a manual system), the same information would be recorded several times. Unless an employer has only a few employees, this can be very inefficient. Various approaches are available to make payroll accounting more efficient and accurate.

Both medium- and large-size businesses commonly use two approaches for payroll record keeping: payroll processing centers and electronic systems. A payroll processing center is a business that sells payroll record-keeping services. The employer provides the center with all basic employee data and each period's report of hours worked. The processing center maintains all payroll records and prepares each period's payroll checks. Payroll processing center fees tend to be much less than the cost to an employer of handling payroll internally.

An electronic system is a computer system based on a software package that performs all payroll record keeping and prepares payroll checks or EFT records. In this system, only the employee number and hours worked need to be entered into a computer each pay period, as shown in Figure 8-9. All other payroll data needed to prepare the payroll records can be stored in the computer. The computer uses the employee number and hours worked to determine the gross pay, deductions, and net pay. The payroll register, checks (or EFTs), and employee earnings records are provided as outputs.

FIGURE 8-9 Electronic Payroll System

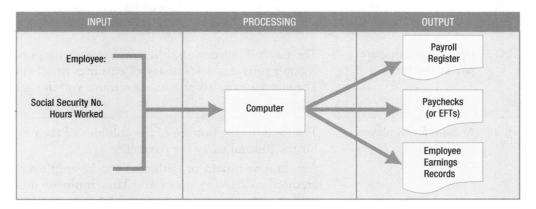

The same inputs and outputs are required in all payroll systems. Even with a computer, the data required for payroll processing have to be entered into the system at some point. The outputs—the payroll register, paychecks, and employee earnings records—are basically the same under each system.

SELF-STUDY

LEARNING OBJECTIVES	Key Points to Remember
LO1 Distinguish between employees and independent contractors.	Employees work under the control and direction of an employer. Independent contractors perform a service for a fee and do not work under the control and direction of the company paying for the service. Payroll accounting procedures apply only to employees, not to independent contractors.
LO2 Calculate employee earnings and deductions.	Three steps are required to determine how much to pay an employee for a pay period: 1. Calculate total earnings. 2. Determine the amounts of deductions. 3. Subtract deductions from total earnings to compute net pay. Deductions from gross pay fall into three categories: 1. Income tax withholding 2. Employee Social Security and Medicare taxes withholding 3. Voluntary deductions Four factors determine the amount to be withheld from an employee's gross pay each pay period: 1. Total earnings 2. Marital status 3. Number of withholding allowances claimed 4. Length of the pay period

(continued)

LEARNING OBJECTIVES	Key Points to Remember
LO3 Describe and prepare payroll records.	The payroll register and the employee earnings record are linked. The payroll register provides a summary of earnings of all employees for each pay period. The earnings record provides a summary of the annual earnings of an individual employee.
LO4 Account for employee earnings and deductions.	The totals at the bottom of the columns of the payroll register provide the basis for the journal entry for payroll. Amounts withheld or deducted by the employer from employee earnings are credited to liability accounts. The employer must pay these amounts to the proper government groups and other appropriate groups.
LO5 Describe various payroll record-keeping methods.	In a manual payroll system, the same information needs to be recorded several times. An electronic payroll system is much more efficient.

DEMONSTRATION PROBLEM

Carole Vohsen operates a pet grooming salon called Canine Coiffures. She has five employees, all of whom are paid on a weekly basis. Canine Coiffures uses a payroll register, individual employee earnings records, a journal, and a general ledger.

The payroll data for each employee for the week ended January 21, 20--, are given below. Employees are paid 1½ times the regular rate for work over 40 hours a week.

Name	Employee No.	No. of Allowances	Marital Status	Total Hours Worked Jan. 15–21	Rate	Total Earnings Jan. 1–14
DeNourie, Katie	1	2	S	44	$14.50	$1,218.00
Garriott, Pete	2	1	M	40	15.00	1,260.00
Martinez, Sheila	3	3	M	40	15.50	1,302.00
Parker, Nancy	4	2	M	42	14.00	1,176.00
Shapiro, John	5	2	S	40	14.50	1,190.00

Sheila Martinez is the manager of the Shampooing Department. Her Social Security number is 500-88-4189, and she was born April 12, 1969. She lives at 46 Darling Crossing, Norwich, CT, 06360. Martinez was hired September 1 of last year.

Canine Coiffures uses a federal income tax withholding table. A portion of this weekly table is provided in Figure 8-4 on pages 288 and 289. Social Security tax is withheld at the rate of 6.2% of the first $128,400 earned. Medicare tax is withheld at the rate of 1.45%, and city earnings tax at the rate of 1%, both applied to gross pay. Garriott and Parker each have $14 and DeNourie and Martinez each have $10 withheld for health insurance. DeNourie, Martinez, and Shapiro each have $15 withheld to be invested in the groomers' credit union. Garriott and Shapiro each have $18.75 withheld under a savings bond purchase plan.

Canine Coiffures' payroll is met by drawing checks on its regular bank account. This week, the checks were issued in sequence, beginning with No. 811.

REQUIRED

1. Prepare a payroll register for Canine Coiffures for the week ended January 21, 20--. (In the Taxable Earnings/Unemployment Compensation column, enter the same amounts as in the Social Security column.) Total the amount columns, verify the totals, and rule with single and double lines.

2. Prepare an employee earnings record for Sheila Martinez for the week ended January 21, 20--.

3. Assuming that the wages for the week ended January 21 were paid on January 23, prepare the journal entry for the payment of this payroll.

4. Post the entry in requirement (3) to the affected accounts in the ledger of Canine Coiffures. Do not enter any amounts in the Balance columns. Use account numbers as follows: Cash—101; Employee Federal Income Tax Payable—211; Social Security Tax Payable—212; Medicare Tax Payable—213; City Earnings Tax Payable—215; Health Insurance Premiums Payable—216; Credit Union Payable—217; Savings Bond Deductions Payable—218; Wages and Salaries Expense—511.

SOLUTION 1.

PAYROLL REGISTER

	NAME	EMPLOYEE NO.	ALLOWANCES	MARITAL STATUS	EARNINGS REGULAR	EARNINGS OVERTIME	EARNINGS TOTAL	CUMULATIVE TOTAL	TAXABLE EARNINGS UNEMPLOYMENT COMPENSATION	TAXABLE EARNINGS SOCIAL SECURITY
1	DeNourie, Katie	1	2	S	5 8 0 00	8 7 00	6 6 7 00	1 8 8 5 00	6 6 7 00	6 6 7 00
2	Garriott, Pete	2	1	M	6 0 0 00		6 0 0 00	1 8 6 0 00	6 0 0 00	6 0 0 00
3	Martinez, Sheila	3	3	M	6 2 0 00		6 2 0 00	1 9 2 2 00	6 2 0 00	6 2 0 00
4	Parker, Nancy	4	2	M	5 6 0 00	4 2 00	6 0 2 00	1 7 7 8 00	6 0 2 00	6 0 2 00
5	Shapiro, John	5	2	S	5 8 0 00		5 8 0 00	1 7 7 0 00	5 8 0 00	5 8 0 00
6					2 9 4 0 00	1 2 9 00	3 0 6 9 00	9 2 1 5 00	3 0 6 9 00	3 0 6 9 00
7										
8										
9										
10										

—WEEK ENDED 12/19/--

FEDERAL INCOME TAX	SOCIAL SECURITY TAX	MEDICARE TAX	CITY TAX	DEDUCTIONS HEALTH INSURANCE	CREDIT UNION	OTHER	TOTAL	NET PAY	CHECK NO.	
4 8 00	4 1 35	9 67	6 67	1 0 00	1 5 00		1 3 0 69	5 3 6 31	811	1
3 0 00	3 7 20	8 70	6 00	1 4 00		1 8 75	1 1 4 65	4 8 5 35	812	2
1 6 00	3 8 44	8 99	6 20	1 0 00	1 5 00		9 4 63	5 2 5 37	813	3
2 2 00	3 7 32	8 73	6 02	1 4 00			8 8 07	5 1 3 93	814	4
3 9 00	3 5 96	8 41	5 80		1 5 00	1 8 75	1 2 2 92	4 5 7 08	815	5
1 5 5 00	1 9 0 27	4 4 50	3 0 69	4 8 00	4 5 00	3 7 50	5 5 0 96	2 5 1 8 04		6
										7
										8
										9
										10

SOLUTION 2.

EMPLOYEE EARNINGS RECORD

20--PERIOD ENDED	EARNINGS				TAXABLE EARNINGS	
	REGULAR	OVERTIME	TOTAL	CUMULATIVE TOTAL	UNEMPLOYMENT COMPENSATION	SOCIAL SECURITY
1/7						
1/14						
1/21	6 2 0 00		6 2 0 00	1 9 2 2 00	6 2 0 00	6 2 0 00
1/28						

GENDER		DEPARTMENT	OCCUPATION	SOCIAL SECURITY NUMBER	MARITAL STATUS	ALLOWANCES
M	F ✔	Shampooing	Manager	500-88-4189	M	3

FOR PERIOD ENDED   20--

DEDUCTIONS

FEDERAL INCOME TAX	SOCIAL SECURITY TAX	MEDICARE TAX	CITY TAX	HEALTH INSURANCE	CREDIT UNION	OTHER	TOTAL	CHECK NO.	AMOUNT
1 6 00	3 8 44	8 99	6 20	1 0 00	1 5 00		9 4 63	813	5 2 5 37

PAY RATE	DATE OF BIRTH	DATE HIRED	NAME/ADDRESS	EMPLOYEE NUMBER
$15.50	4/12/69	9/1/--	Sheila Martinez 46 Darling Crossing Norwich, CT 06360	3

SOLUTION 3.

GENERAL JOURNAL   PAGE 1

	DATE		DESCRIPTION	POST. REF.	DEBIT	CREDIT	
1	20--Jan.	23	Wages and Salaries Expense	511	3 0 6 9 00		1
2			Employee Federal Income Tax Payable	211		1 5 5 00	2
3			Social Security Tax Payable	212		1 9 0 27	3
4			Medicare Tax Payable	213		4 4 50	4
5			City Earnings Tax Payable	215		3 0 69	5
6			Health Insurance Premiums Payable	216		4 8 00	6
7			Credit Union Payable	217		4 5 00	7
8			Savings Bond Deductions Payable	218		3 7 50	8
9			Cash	101		2 5 1 8 04	9
10			Payroll for week ended Jan. 21				10

SOLUTION 4.

GENERAL LEDGER

ACCOUNT: Cash   ACCOUNT NO. 101

DATE	ITEM	POST. REF.	DEBIT	CREDIT	BALANCE DEBIT	BALANCE CREDIT
20-- Jan. 23		J1		2 5 1 8 04		

ACCOUNT: Employee Federal Income Tax Payable   ACCOUNT NO. 211

DATE	ITEM	POST. REF.	DEBIT	CREDIT	BALANCE DEBIT	BALANCE CREDIT
20-- Jan. 23		J1		1 5 5 00		

ACCOUNT: Social Security Tax Payable   ACCOUNT NO. 212

DATE	ITEM	POST. REF.	DEBIT	CREDIT	BALANCE DEBIT	BALANCE CREDIT
20-- Jan. 23		J1		1 9 0 27		

ACCOUNT: Medicare Tax Payable   ACCOUNT NO. 213

DATE	ITEM	POST. REF.	DEBIT	CREDIT	BALANCE DEBIT	BALANCE CREDIT
20-- Jan. 23		J1		4 4 50		

ACCOUNT: City Earnings Tax Payable   ACCOUNT NO. 215

DATE	ITEM	POST. REF.	DEBIT	CREDIT	BALANCE DEBIT	BALANCE CREDIT
20-- Jan. 23		J1		3 0 69		

ACCOUNT: Health Insurance Premiums Payable   ACCOUNT NO. 216

DATE	ITEM	POST. REF.	DEBIT	CREDIT	BALANCE DEBIT	BALANCE CREDIT
20-- Jan. 23		J1		4 8 00		

ACCOUNT: Credit Union Payable   ACCOUNT NO. 217

DATE	ITEM	POST. REF.	DEBIT	CREDIT	BALANCE DEBIT	BALANCE CREDIT
20-- Jan. 23		J1		4 5 00		

ACCOUNT: Savings Bond Deductions Payable   ACCOUNT NO. 218

DATE	ITEM	POST. REF.	DEBIT	CREDIT	BALANCE DEBIT	BALANCE CREDIT
20-- Jan. 23		J1		3 7 50		

ACCOUNT: Wages and Salaries Expense   ACCOUNT NO. 511

DATE	ITEM	POST. REF.	DEBIT	CREDIT	BALANCE DEBIT	BALANCE CREDIT
20-- Jan. 23		J1	3 0 6 9 00			

KEY TERMS

direct deposit (294)   A payroll method in which the employee does not handle the paycheck; payment is made by the employer directly to the employee's bank account using EFT.

electronic system (298)   A computer system based on a software package that performs all payroll record keeping and prepares payroll checks.

employee (283)   Someone who works under the control and direction of an employer.

employee earnings record (294)   A separate record of each employee's earnings.

Fair Labor Standards Act (FLSA) (283)   A law that requires employers to pay overtime at 1½ times the regular rate to any hourly employee who works over 40 hours in a week.

FICA taxes (287)   Payroll taxes withheld to provide Social Security and Medicare benefits.

gross pay (286)   An employee's total earnings.

independent contractor (283)   Someone who performs a service for a fee and does not work under the control and direction of the company paying for the service.

manual system (298)   Payroll system in which all records are prepared by hand.

net pay (286)   Gross pay less mandatory and voluntary deductions.

payroll processing center (298)   A business that sells payroll record-keeping services.

payroll register (291)   A form used to assemble the data required at the end of each payroll period.

percentage method (287)   A method of determining the amount to withhold from an employee's gross pay for a specific period.

salary (283)   Compensation for managerial or administrative services.

wage-bracket method (287)   A method of determining the amount to withhold from an employee's gross pay for a specific time period. Wage-bracket tables are provided by the Internal Revenue Service.

wages (283)   Compensation for skilled or unskilled labor.

withholding allowance (286)   A specific dollar amount of an employee's gross pay that is exempt from federal income tax withholding.

SELF-STUDY TEST QUESTIONS

True/False

1. **LO1**   An independent contractor is one who works under the control and direction of an employer.

2. **LO1**   Government laws and regulations regarding payroll are more complex for employees than for independent contractors.

3. **LO2**   Compensation for skilled or unskilled labor expressed in terms of hours, weeks, or units is called salary.

4. **LO2**   An employee's total earnings is called gross pay.

5. **LO3**   A payroll register is a multi-column form used to assemble the data required at the end of each payroll period.

Multiple Choice

1. **LO2**   Jack Smith is married, has a spouse who is not employed and has five dependent children. How many withholding allowances is Smith entitled to?
   (a) 5   (c) 7
   (b) 6   (d) 8

2. **LO2**   Nancy Summers worked 44 hours during the past week. She is entitled to 1½ times her regular pay for all hours worked in excess of 40 during the week. Her regular rate of pay is $15.00. Social Security tax is withheld at the rate of 6.2% and Medicare tax is withheld at the rate of 1.45%; federal income tax withheld is $39; and $5 of union dues are withheld. Her net pay for the week is
   (a) $593.21.   (c) $690.
   (b) $651.   (d) $637.22.

3. **LO2**   Which of the following is *not* a factor that determines the amount of federal income tax to be withheld from an employee's gross pay?
   (a) marital status   (c) total earnings
   (b) number of withholding allowances claimed   (d) age of employee

4. **LO3**   A separate record of each employee's earnings is called a(n)
   (a) payroll register.   (c) W-4.
   (b) employee earnings record.   (d) earnings statement.

5. **LO4**   Social Security Tax Payable and Medicare Tax Payable are classified as
   (a) liabilities.   (c) owner's equity.
   (b) assets.   (d) expenses.

Checkpoint Exercises

1. **LO2**   Qian Wang is paid a regular rate of $14 per hour and 1½ times the regular rate for hours worked over 40 in a week. During the past week, Qian worked 45 hours.

   (a) Compute Qian's gross pay for the week.
   (b) Assume Qian is married and claims two withholding allowances. Compute the amount of federal income tax her employer should withhold for the week.

2. **LO4**   The column totals from the payroll register of Jawhawk Supplies for the week ended February 9 were as follows:

Total earnings	$4,600.00
Federal income tax	417.00
Social Security tax	285.20
Medicare tax	66.70
State income tax	46.00
Health insurance	181.00

   Prepare the journal entry to record the payroll, crediting Cash for the net pay.

The answers to the Self-Study Test Questions are at the end of the chapter (page 316).

APPLYING YOUR KNOWLEDGE

REVIEW QUESTIONS

LO1 1. Why is it important for payroll accounting purposes to distinguish between an employee and an independent contractor?

LO2 2. Name three major categories of deductions from an employee's gross pay.

LO2 3. Identify the four factors that determine the amount of federal income tax that is withheld from an employee's pay each pay period.

LO2 4. In general, an employee is entitled to withholding allowances for what purposes?

LO3 5. Identify the three payroll records usually needed by an employer.

LO3 6. Describe the information contained in the payroll register.

LO3 7. Why is it important to total and verify the totals of the payroll register after the data for each employee have been entered?

LO3 8. Distinguish between the payroll register and the employee earnings record.

LO4 9. Explain what an employer does with the amounts withheld from an employee's pay.

LO5 10. Explain why payroll processing centers and electronic systems are commonly used in payroll accounting.

SERIES A EXERCISES

E 8-1A (LO2)
✓ Gross pay: $795

COMPUTING WEEKLY GROSS PAY Ryan Lawrence's regular hourly rate is $15. He receives 1½ times the regular rate for any hours worked over 40 a week and double the rate for work on Sunday. During the past week, Lawrence worked 8 hours each day Monday through Thursday, 10 hours on Friday, and 5 hours on Sunday. Compute Lawrence's gross pay for the past week.

E 8-2A (LO2)
✓ b: $712.50

COMPUTING OVERTIME RATE OF PAY AND GROSS WEEKLY PAY Rebecca Huang receives a regular salary of $2,600 a month and is paid 1½ times the regular hourly rate for hours worked in excess of 40 per week.

(a) Calculate Huang's overtime rate of pay.

(b) Calculate Huang's total gross weekly pay if she works 45 hours during the week.

E 8-3A (LO2)
✓ e: $7

COMPUTING FEDERAL INCOME TAX Using the table in Figure 8-4 on pages 288 and 289, determine the amount of federal income tax an employer should withhold weekly for employees with the following marital status, earnings, and withholding allowances:

	Marital Status	Total Weekly Earnings	Number of Allowances	Amount of Withholding
(a)	S	$447.60	2	_____
(b)	S	451.50	1	_____
(c)	M	481.15	3	_____
(d)	S	490.52	0	_____
(e)	M	691.89	5	_____

E 8-4A (LO2)
✓ 3d row, Soc. Sec. tax: $161.20

CALCULATING SOCIAL SECURITY AND MEDICARE TAXES Assume a Social Security tax rate of 6.2% is applied to maximum earnings of $128,400 and a Medicare tax rate of 1.45% is applied to all earnings. Calculate the Social Security and Medicare taxes for the following situations:

Cumul. Pay Before Current Weekly Payroll	Current Gross Pay	Year-to-Date Earnings	Soc. Sec. Maximum	Amount Over Max. Soc. Sec.	Amount Subject to Soc. Sec.	Soc. Sec. Tax Withheld	Medicare Tax Withheld
$ 22,000	$1,700	_____	$128,400	_____	_____	_____	_____
54,000	4,200	_____	128,400	_____	_____	_____	_____
125,800	3,925	_____	128,400	_____	_____	_____	_____
127,800	4,600	_____	128,400	_____	_____	_____	_____

E 8-5A (LO2)
✓ Net pay: $639.15

COMPUTING NET PAY Mary Sue Guild works for a company that pays its employees 1½ times the regular rate for all hours worked in excess of 40 per week. Guild's pay rate is $14.50 per hour. Her wages are subject to deductions for federal income tax, Social Security tax, and Medicare tax. She is married and claims four withholding allowances. Guild has a ½-hour lunch break during an 8½-hour day. Her time card is shown below.

Name	Mary Sue Guild					
Week Ending	March 30, 20--					
Day	In	Out	In	Out	Regular	Overtime
M	7:57	12:05	12:35	4:33	8	
T	7:52	12:09	12:39	5:05	8	½
W	7:59	12:15	12:45	5:30	8	1
T	8:00	12:01	12:30	6:31	8	2
F	7:56	12:05	12:34	4:30	8	
S	8:00	10:31				2½

(continued)

Complete the following for the week:

(a) _____ regular hours × $14.50 per hour $_____

(b) _____ overtime hours × $21.75 per hour $_____

(c) Total gross wages $_____

(d) Federal income tax withholding (from tax tables in
Figure 8-4, pages 288 and 289) $_____

(e) Social Security withholding at 6.2% $_____

(f) Medicare withholding at 1.45% $_____

(g) Total withholding $_____

(h) Net pay $_____

E 8-6A   (LO4)
✓ Med. tax: $126.15

JOURNALIZING PAYROLL TRANSACTIONS On December 31, the payroll register of Hamstreet Associates indicated the following information:

Wages and Salaries Expense	$8,700.00
Employee Federal Income Tax Payable	920.00
United Way Contributions Payable	200.00
Earnings subject to Social Security tax	8,000.00

Determine the amount of Social Security and Medicare taxes to be withheld and record the journal entry for the payroll, crediting Cash for the net pay.

E 8-7A   (LO4)
✓ Cr. Cash: $4,932.37

PAYROLL JOURNAL ENTRY Journalize the following data taken from the payroll register of CopyMasters as of April 15, 20—:

Regular earnings	$5,715.00
Overtime earnings	790.00
Deductions:	
Federal income tax	625.00
Social Security tax	403.31
Medicare tax	94.32
Pension plan	80.00
Health insurance premiums	270.00
United Way contributions	100.00

SERIES A PROBLEMS

P 8-8A   (LO2/4)
✓ Net pay: $425.30

GROSS PAY, DEDUCTIONS, AND NET PAY Donald Chin works for Northwest Supplies. His rate of pay is $14.00 per hour, and he is paid 1½ times the regular rate for all hours worked in excess of 40 per week. During the last week of January of the current year, he worked 48 hours. Chin is married and claims three withholding allowances on his W-4 form. His weekly wages are subject to the following deductions:

(a) Employee federal income tax (use Figure 8-4 on pages 288 and 289)

(b) Social Security tax at 6.2%

(c) Medicare tax at 1.45%

(d) Health insurance premium, $85

(e) Credit union, $125

(f) United Way contribution, $10

REQUIRED

1. Compute Chin's regular pay, overtime pay, gross pay, and net pay.

2. Journalize the payment of his wages for the week ended January 31, crediting Cash for the net amount.

P 8-9A   **(LO2/3/4)**
✓ Cr. Cash: $2,410.41

PAYROLL REGISTER AND PAYROLL JOURNAL ENTRY Mary Losch operates a travel agency called Mary's Luxury Travel. She has five employees, all of whom are paid on a weekly basis. The travel agency uses a payroll register, individual employee earnings records, and a general journal.

Mary's Luxury Travel uses a weekly federal income tax withholding table like the one in Figure 8-4 on pages 288 and 289. The payroll data for each employee for the week ended March 22, 20—, are given below. Employees are paid 1½ times the regular rate for working over 40 hours a week.

Name	No. of Allowances	Marital Status	Total Hours Worked Mar. 16–22	Rate	Total Earnings Jan. 1–Mar. 15
Bacon, Andrea	4	M	44	$14.00	$6,300.00
Cole, Andrew	1	S	40	15.00	6,150.00
Hicks, Melvin	3	M	44	13.50	5,805.00
Leung, Cara	1	S	36	14.00	5,600.00
Melling, Melissa	2	M	40	14.50	5,945.00

Social Security tax is withheld from the first $128,400 of earnings at the rate of 6.2%. Medicare tax is withheld at the rate of 1.45%, and city earnings tax at the rate of 1%, both applied to gross pay. Bacon and Leung have $15 withheld and Cole and Hicks have $10 withheld for health insurance. Bacon and Leung have $20 withheld to be invested in the travel agency's credit union. Cole has $38.75 withheld and Hicks has $18.75 withheld under a savings bond purchase plan.

Mary's Luxury Travel's payroll is met by drawing checks on its regular bank account. The checks were issued in sequence, beginning with Check No. 423.

REQUIRED

1. Prepare a payroll register for Mary's Luxury Travel for the week ended March 22, 20--. (In the Taxable Earnings/Unemployment Compensation column, enter the same amounts as in the Social Security column.) Total the amount columns, verify the totals, and rule with single and double lines.

2. Assuming that the wages for the week ended March 22 were paid on March 24, prepare the journal entry for the payment of the payroll.

P 8-10A   **(LO3)**
✓ Soc. Sec. tax: $37.20

EMPLOYEE EARNINGS RECORD Mary's Luxury Travel in Problem 8-9A keeps employee earnings records. Andrew Cole, employee number 62, is employed as a manager in the ticket sales department. He was born on May 8, 1986, and was hired on June 1 of last year. His Social Security number is 544-67-1283. He lives at 28 Quarry Drive, Vernon, CT, 06066.

REQUIRED

For the week ended March 22, complete an employee earnings record for Andrew Cole. (Insert earnings data only for the week of March 22.)

SERIES B EXERCISES

E 8-1B   (LO2)
✓ Gross pay: $678

COMPUTING WEEKLY GROSS PAY Manuel Soto's regular hourly rate is $12. He receives 1½ times the regular rate for hours worked in excess of 40 a week and double the rate for work on Sunday. During the past week, Soto worked 8 hours each day Monday through Thursday, 11 hours on Friday, and 6 hours on Sunday. Compute Soto's gross pay for the past week.

E 8-2B   (LO2)
✓ b: $918.75

COMPUTING OVERTIME RATE OF PAY AND GROSS WEEKLY PAY Mike Fritz receives a regular salary of $3,120 a month and is paid 1½ times the regular hourly rate for hours worked in excess of 40 per week.

(a) Calculate Fritz's overtime rate of pay. (Compute to the nearest half cent.)

(b) Calculate Fritz's total gross weekly pay if he works 46 hours during the week.

E 8-3B   (LO2)
✓ e: $62

COMPUTING FEDERAL INCOME TAX Using the table in Figure 8-4 on pages 288 and 289, determine the amount of federal income tax an employer should withhold weekly for employees with the following marital status, earnings, and withholding allowances:

	Marital Status	Total Weekly Earnings	Number of Allowances	Amount of Withholding
(a)	M	$546.00	3	_____
(b)	M	490.00	1	_____
(c)	S	461.39	2	_____
(d)	M	522.88	2	_____
(e)	S	612.00	0	_____

E 8-4B   (LO2)
✓ 3rd row, Soc. Sec. tax: $179.80

CALCULATING SOCIAL SECURITY AND MEDICARE TAXES Assume a Social Security tax rate of 6.2% is applied to maximum earnings of $128,400 and a Medicare tax rate of 1.45% is applied to all earnings. Calculate the Social Security and Medicare taxes for the following situations:

Cumul. Pay Before Current Weekly Payroll	Current Gross Pay	Year-to-Date Earnings	Soc. Sec. Maximum	Amount Over Max. Soc. Sec.	Amount Subject to Soc. Sec.	Soc. Sec. Tax Withheld	Medicare Tax Withheld
$ 31,000	$1,500	_____	$128,400	_____	_____	_____	_____
53,000	2,860	_____	128,400	_____	_____	_____	_____
125,500	3,140	_____	128,400	_____	_____	_____	_____
127,600	2,920	_____	128,400	_____	_____	_____	_____

E 8-5B   (LO2)
✓ Net pay: $658.39

COMPUTING NET PAY Tom Hallinan works for a company that pays its employees 1½ times the regular rate for all hours worked in excess of 40 per week. Hallinan's pay rate is $15 per hour. His wages are subject to deductions for federal income tax, Social Security tax, and Medicare tax. He is married and claims five withholding allowances. Hallinan has a ½-hour lunch break during an 8½-hour day. His time card is on next page.

Name	Tom Hallinan					
Week Ending	March 30, 20--					
Day	In	Out	In	Out	Hours Worked	
					Regular	Overtime
M	7:55	12:02	12:32	5:33	8	1
T	7:59	12:04	12:34	6:05	8	1½
W	7:59	12:05	12:35	4:30	8	
T	8:00	12:01	12:30	5:01	8	½
F	7:58	12:02	12:31	5:33	8	1
S	7:59	9:33				1½

Complete the following for the week:

(a) _____ regular hours × $15 per hour $_____

(b) _____ overtime hours × $22.50 per hour $_____

(c) Total gross wages $_____

(d) Federal income tax withholding (from tax tables in Figure 8-4, pages 288 and 289) $_____

(e) Social Security withholding at 6.2% $_____

(f) Medicare withholding at 1.45% $_____

(g) Total withholding $_____

(h) Net pay $_____

E 8-6B   (LO4)
✓ Med. tax: $136.30

JOURNALIZING PAYROLL TRANSACTIONS On November 30, the payroll register of Webster & Smith indicated the following information:

Wages and Salaries Expense	$9,400.00
Employee Federal Income Tax Payable	985.00
United Way Contributions Payable	200.00
Earnings subject to Social Security tax	9,400.00

Determine the amount of Social Security and Medicare taxes to be withheld and record the journal entry for the payroll, crediting Cash for the net pay.

E 8-7B   (LO4)
✓ Cr. Cash: $5,696.54

PAYROLL JOURNAL ENTRY Journalize the following data taken from the payroll register of Himes Bakery as of June 12, 20--:

Regular earnings	$6,520.00
Overtime earnings	950.00
Deductions:	
Federal income tax	782.00
Social Security tax	463.14
Medicare tax	108.32
Pension plan	80.00
Health insurance premiums	190.00
United Way contributions	150.00

SERIES B PROBLEMS

P 8-8B (LO2/4)
✓ Net pay: $416.15

GROSS PAY, DEDUCTIONS, AND NET PAY Elyse Lin works for Columbia Industries. Her rate of pay is $14.50 per hour, and she is paid 1½ times the regular rate for all hours worked in excess of 40 per week. During the last week of January of the current year, she worked 46 hours. Lin is married and claims two withholding allowances on her W-4 form. Her weekly wages are subject to the following deductions:

(a) Employee federal income tax (use Figure 8-4 on pages 288 and 289)

(b) Social Security tax at 6.2%

(c) Medicare tax at 1.45%

(d) Health insurance premium, $92

(e) Credit union, $110

(f) United Way contribution, $5

REQUIRED

1. Compute Lin's regular pay, overtime pay, gross pay, and net pay.

2. Journalize the payment of her wages for the week ended January 31, crediting Cash for the net amount.

P 8-9B (LO2/3/4)
✓ Cr. Cash: $2,374.27

PAYROLL REGISTER AND PAYROLL JOURNAL ENTRY Karen Jolly operates a bakery called Karen's Cupcakes. She has five employees, all of whom are paid on a weekly basis. Karen's Cupcakes uses a payroll register, individual employee earnings records, and a general journal.

Karen's Cupcakes uses a weekly federal income tax withholding table like the one in Figure 8-4 on pages 288 and 289. The payroll data for each employee for the week ended February 15, 20--, are given below. Employees are paid 1½ times the regular rate for working over 40 hours a week.

Name	No. of Allowances	Marital Status	Total Hours Worked Feb. 9–15	Rate	Total Earnings Jan. 1–Feb. 8
Barone, William	1	S	40	$14.00	$3,360.00
Hastings, Gene	4	M	45	15.00	3,870.00
Nitobe, Isako	3	M	46	12.00	3,168.00
Smith, Judy	2	M	42	13.00	3,276.00
Tarshis, Dolores	1	S	39	14.50	3,480.00

Social Security tax is withheld from the first $128,400 of earnings at the rate of 6.2%. Medicare tax is withheld at the rate of 1.45%, and city earnings tax at the rate of 1%, both applied to gross pay. Hastings and Smith have $35 withheld and Nitobe and Tarshis have $15 withheld for health insurance. Nitobe and Tarshis have $25 withheld to be invested in the bakers' credit union. Hastings has $18.75 withheld and Smith has $43.75 withheld under a savings bond purchase plan.

Karen's Cupcakes' payroll is met by drawing checks on its regular bank account. The checks were issued in sequence, beginning with No. 365.

REQUIRED

1. Prepare a payroll register for Karen's Cupcakes for the week ended February 15, 20--. (In the Taxable Earnings/Unemployment Compensation column, enter the same amounts as in the Social Security column.) Total the amount columns, verify the totals, and rule with single and double lines.

2. Assuming that the wages for the week ended February 15 were paid on February 17, prepare the journal entry for the payment of this payroll.

P 8-10B   (LO3)
✓ Soc. Sec. tax: $34.72

EMPLOYEE EARNINGS RECORD Karen's Cupcakes in Problem 8-9B keeps employee earnings records. William Barone, employee number 19, is employed as a baker in the desserts department. He was born on August 26, 1979, and was hired on October 1 of last year. His Social Security number is 342-73-4681. He lives at 30 Timber Lane, Willington, CT, 06279.

REQUIRED

For the week ended February 15, complete an employee earnings record for William Barone. (Insert earnings data only for the week of February 15.)

CHECK LIST
- ☐ Managing
- ☐ Planning
- ☐ Drafting
- ☐ Break
- ☐ Revising
- ☐ Managing

MANAGING YOUR WRITING

The federal minimum wage originally was only 25 cents an hour. Today it is $7.25 an hour and many states have minimum wage rates much higher. Assume that Congress is considering raising the minimum wage again and your U.S. representative is asking for public opinion on this issue. Write a letter to your representative with arguments for and against a higher minimum wage.

ETHICS

ETHICS CASE

Maura Lowe is a payroll accountant for N & L Company. She prepares and processes the company's payroll on a weekly basis and has been at N & L for only three months. All employees are paid on Friday. On Wednesday afternoon, Simon Lentz, one of the company's top sales associates, asks Maura to not take out any payroll deductions from his pay this week. He explains that he is short of cash and needs the full amount of his gross salary just to put food on the table and make his past-due car payment. He promises Maura that she can catch up on the deductions over the next month. The deductions include employee income tax, Social Security tax, Medicare tax, and health insurance premiums.

1. Is Simon's request of Maura ethical? Why or why not?

2. If this were the first pay period of the year and Maura agreed not to take out deductions from Simon's pay, what effect would this have on the liabilities section of the balance sheet?

3. Write a short paragraph from Maura to Simon explaining how omitting deductions from a pay period will cause errors in the company's financial statements.

4. In small groups, discuss what action Maura should take regarding Simon's request.

MASTERY PROBLEM

✓ Cr. Cash: $4,824.92

Abigail Trenkamp owns and operates the Trenkamp Collection Agency. Listed below are the name, number of allowances claimed, marital status, information from time cards on hours worked each day, and the hourly rate of each employee. All hours worked in excess of 40 hours for Monday through Friday are paid at 1½ times the regular rate. All weekend hours are paid at double the regular rate.

Trenkamp uses a weekly federal income tax withholding table (see Figure 8-4 on pages 288 and 289). Social Security tax is withheld at the rate of 6.2% for the first $128,400 earned. Medicare tax is withheld at 1.45% and state income tax at 3.5%. Each employee has $12 withheld for health insurance. All employees use payroll deduction to the credit union for varying amounts as listed.

Trenkamp Collection Agency
Payroll Information for the Week Ended November 18, 20--

Name	Employee No.	No of Allow.	Marital Status	Hours Worked S S M T W T F							Hourly Rate	Credit Union Deposit	Total Earnings 1/1–11/11
Berling, James	1	3	M	2 2 9 8 8 9 10							$12	$149.60	$ 24,525
Merz, Linda	2	4	M	0 0 8 8 8 8 10							15	117.00	30,480
Goetz, Ken	3	2	M	0 0 6 7 8 9 10							13	91.30	23,400
Menick, Judd	4	2	S	8 8 0 0 8 8 9							13	126.50	26,325
Morales, Eva	5	3	M	0 0 8 8 8 6 8							13	117.05	24,730
Heimbrock, Jacob	6	5	M	0 0 8 8 8 8 4							42	154.25	127,440
Townsley, Sarah	7	2	M	4 0 6 6 6 6 4							12	83.05	21,425
Salzman, Beth	8	2	M	6 2 8 8 6 6 6							11	130.00	6,635
Layton, Esther	9	3	M	0 0 8 8 8 8 8							11	88.00	5,635
Thompson, David	10	5	M	0 2 10 9 7 7 10							14	128.90	25,830
Vadillo, Carmen	11	2	S	8 0 4 8 8 8 9							13	139.11	24,115

The Trenkamp Collection Agency follows the practice of drawing a single check for the net amount of the payroll and depositing the check in a special payroll account at the bank. Individual checks issued were numbered consecutively, beginning with No. 331.

REQUIRED

1. Prepare a payroll register for Trenkamp Collection Agency for the week ended November 18, 20--. (In the Taxable Earnings/Unemployment Compensation column, enter $365 for Salzman and $440 for Layton. Leave this column blank for all other employees.) Total the amount columns, verify the totals, and rule with single and double lines.

2. Assuming that the wages for the week ended November 18 were paid on November 21, prepare the journal entry for the payment of this payroll.

3. The current employee earnings record for Beth Salzman is provided in the working papers. Update Salzman's earnings record to reflect the November 18 payroll. Although this information should have been entered earlier, complete the required information on the earnings record. The necessary information is as follows:

Name	Beth F. Salzman
Address	12 Windmill Lane
	Trumbull, CT 06611
Employee No.	8
Gender	Female
Department	Administration
Occupation	Office Assistant
Social Security No.	446-46-6321
Marital Status	Married
Allowances	2
Pay Rate	$11.00 per hour
Date of Birth	4/5/84
Date Hired	7/22/--

CHALLENGE PROBLEM

This problem challenges you to apply your cumulative accounting knowledge to move a step beyond the material in the chapter.

Irina Company pays its employees weekly. The last pay period for 20-1 was on December 28. From December 28 through December 31, the employees earned $1,754, so the following adjusting entry was made:

5	20-1 Dec	31	Wages and Salaries Expense		1 7 5 4 00		5
6			Wages and Salaries Payable			1 7 5 4 00	6
7			To record accrued wages and salaries				7

The first pay period in 20-2 was on January 4. The totals line from Irina Company's payroll register for the week ended January 4, 20-2, was as follows:

✓ Dr. Wages and Salaries Expense: $1,596

PAYROLL REGISTER

			EARNINGS				TAXABLE EARNINGS	
			REGULAR	OVERTIME	TOTAL	CUMULATIVE TOTAL	UNEMPLOYMENT COMPENSATION	SOCIAL SECURITY
1	Totals		3 3 5 0 00		3 3 5 0 00	3 3 5 0 00	3 3 5 0 00	3 3 5 0 00

—WEEK ENDED January 4, 20-2

	DEDUCTIONS							NET PAY	
FEDERAL INCOME TAX	SOCIAL SECURITY TAX	MEDICARE TAX	HEALTH INSURANCE	UNITED WAY	OTHER		TOTAL		
2 4 2 00	2 0 7 70	4 8 58	5 0 00	8 0 00			6 2 8 28	2 7 2 1 72	1

REQUIRED

1. Prepare the journal entry for the payment of the payroll on January 4, 20-2.
2. Prepare T accounts for Wages and Salaries Expense and Wages and Salaries Payable showing the beginning balance, January 4, 20-2, entry, and ending balance as of January 4, 20-2.

True/False

1. F (does *not* work under control and direction)

2. T

3. F (is called wages)

4. T

5. T

Multiple Choice

1. c   **2.** a   **3.** d   **4.** b   **5.** a

Checkpoint Exercises

1.

    (a) $40 \times \$14$ = $\$560$

        $5 \times \$14 \times 1.5$ =   105

        Gross pay $\underline{\$665}$

    (b) $29

2.

Wages and Salaries Expense	4,600.00	
Employee Federal Income Tax Payable		417.00
Social Security Tax Payable		285.20
Medicare Tax Payable		66.70
State Income Tax Payable		46.00
Health Insurance Premiums Payable		181.00
Cash		3,604.10

Chapter 9 Payroll Accounting: Employer Taxes and Reports

As competition has become more global, many challenges to businesses have developed. Learning how to function in many different languages and cultures is one of these challenges. LinguaLinx is a full-service translation company that offers help with language issues. Founded in 2002, LinguaLinx has offices in the United States and the United Kingdom. It employs more than 5,000 native-speaking linguists with skills tailored to provide services in more than 100 languages. Some examples of its capabilities include simple text translation, simultaneous interpretation, sign language, copywriting, and even Braille production. It can also provide on-site language instruction classes.

LinguaLinx faces the same kinds of payroll issues as Intechra, the company described in the introduction to Chapter 8. But LinguaLinx would face the added challenge of employees in multiple countries, so it would need to know the regulations in each location. In addition, you will learn in this chapter that employers must account for not just *employee* wages and taxes but also *employer* taxes. The complexity of payroll accounting is a major reason why many businesses hire an outside company to manage their payroll. You will also learn about two of these payroll service companies in this chapter's "A Broader View."

LEARNING OBJECTIVES

Careful study of this chapter should enable you to:

LO1 Describe and calculate employer payroll taxes.

LO2 Account for employer payroll taxes expense.

LO3 Describe employer reporting and payment responsibilities.

LO4 Describe and account for workers' compensation insurance.

The taxes we discussed in Chapter 8 had one thing in common—they all were levied on the employee. The employer withheld them from employees' earnings and paid them to the government. They did not add anything to the employer's payroll expenses.

In this chapter, we will examine several taxes that are imposed directly on the employer. All of these taxes represent additional payroll expenses. You will see that the total cost of employees includes not only wages but also payroll taxes and benefits such as vacation and sick pay.

LO1	Employer Payroll Taxes

Describe and calculate employer payroll taxes.

Most employers must pay FICA, FUTA (Federal Unemployment Tax Act), and SUTA (state unemployment tax) taxes.

Employer FICA Taxes

Employer FICA taxes are levied on employers at the same rates and on the same earnings bases as the employee FICA taxes. As explained in Chapter 8, we are assuming the Social Security component is 6.2% on maximum earnings of $128,400 for each employee. Since there is no maximum on the Medicare component, this tax is 1.45% on all earnings.

The payroll register we saw in Chapter 8 is a key source of information for computing employer payroll taxes. That payroll register is reproduced in Figure 9-1. The Taxable Earnings Social Security column shows that $5,897 of employee earnings were subject to Social Security tax for the pay period. The employer's Social Security tax on these earnings is computed as follows:

FIGURE 9-1   Payroll Register (left side)

PAYROLL REGISTER

	NAME	ALLOWANCES	MARITAL STATUS	EARNINGS						TAXABLE EARNINGS	
				REGULAR	OVERTIME	TOTAL	CUMULATIVE TOTAL			UNEMPLOYMENT COMPENSATION	SOCIAL SECURITY
1	Cadrain, Sarah	4	M	2 0 0 0 00	6 0 00	2 0 6 0 00	129 4 0 0 00			0 00	1 0 6 0 00
2	Gruder, James	1	S	7 6 0 00	1 4 0 00	9 0 0 00	43 4 0 0 00			0 00	9 0 0 00
3	Istone, Ken	4	M	6 4 0 00		6 4 0 00	32 0 2 5 00			0 00	6 4 0 00
4	Kuzmik, Helen	2	M	5 6 0 00	3 2 2 00	8 8 2 00	34 0 0 0 00			0 00	8 8 2 00
5	Lee, Hoseoup	3	M	6 2 0 00		6 2 0 00	31 3 4 0 00			0 00	6 2 0 00
6	Swaney, Linda	2	S	6 0 0 00	2 2 5 00	8 2 5 00	30 5 0 0 00			0 00	8 2 5 00
7	Tucci, Paul	3	M	6 1 0 00		6 1 0 00	30 1 0 0 00			0 00	6 1 0 00
8	Wiles, Harry	1	S	3 6 0 00		3 6 0 00	6 3 0 0 00			3 6 0 00	3 6 0 00
9				6 1 5 0 00	7 4 7 00	6 8 9 7 00	337 0 6 5 00			3 6 0 00	5 8 9 7 00
10											

Time cards, pay rates

Prior period total + current period earnings

Current below $7,000 cumul. total

Current below $128,400 cumul. total

Discussed in Chapter 9

Social Security Taxable Earnings	×	Tax Rate	=	Tax
$5,897		0.062		$365.61

The Medicare tax applies to the total earnings of $6,897. The employer's Medicare tax on these earnings is computed as follows:

Total Earnings	×	Tax Rate	=	Tax
$6,897		0.0145		$100.01

These amounts plus the employees' Social Security and Medicare taxes withheld must be paid by the employer to the Internal Revenue Service (IRS).

LEARNING KEY

Use the information in the payroll register to compute employer payroll taxes.

Self-Employment Tax

Individuals who own and run their own business are considered self-employed. These individuals can be viewed as both employer and employee. They do not receive salary or wages from the business, but they do have earnings in the form of the business net income. Self-employment income is the net income of a trade or business run by an individual. The **Self-Employment Contributions Act (SECA)** requires self-employed individuals earning net self-employment income of $400 or more to pay a self-employment tax. Self-employment tax is a contribution to the FICA program. The tax rates are double the Social Security and Medicare rates (12.4% + 2.9% = 15.3% total). They are applied to the same income bases as those used for the Social Security and Medicare taxes. *Publication 334, Tax Guide for Small Business*, contains helpful information for self-employed persons.

The self-employment tax rate is double the employee and employer Social Security and Medicare rates because the self-employed person is considered both the employer and employee.

FIGURE 9-1 Payroll Register (right side)

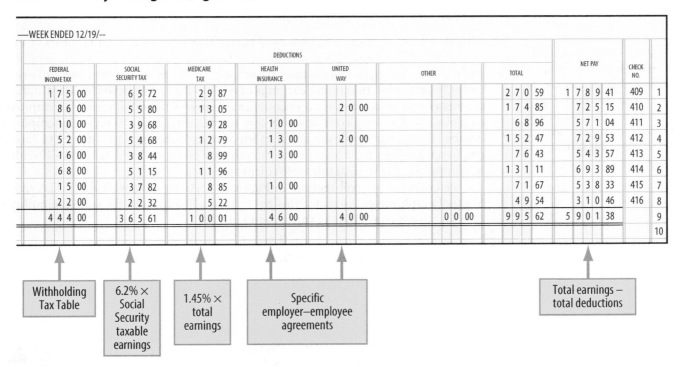

Employer FUTA Tax

The **FUTA (Federal Unemployment Tax Act)** tax is levied only on employers. It is not deducted from employees' earnings. The purpose of this tax is to raise funds to administer the combined federal/state unemployment compensation program. The maximum amount of earnings subject to the FUTA tax and the tax rate can be changed by Congress. The current rate is 6.0% applied to maximum earnings of $7,000 for each employee, but employers are allowed a credit of up to 5.4% for participation in state unemployment programs. Thus, the effective federal rate is commonly 0.6%.

Gross FUTA rate	6.0%
Credit for state unemployment taxes	5.4%
Net FUTA rate	0.6%

To illustrate the computation of the FUTA tax, refer to Figure 9-1. The Taxable Earnings Unemployment Compensation column shows that only $360 of employee earnings were subject to the FUTA tax. This amount is low because the payroll period is late in the calendar year (December 19, 20--). It is common for most employees to exceed the $7,000 earnings limit by this time. The FUTA tax is computed as shown in Figure 9-2.

FIGURE 9-2 Computation of FUTA Tax

SUTA Tax

State unemployment tax rates and maximum earnings amounts vary greatly. Current rates range from 5.4% to 14.3%. Maximum earnings amounts are $7,000 to $45,000.

The **SUTA (state unemployment tax)** tax is also levied only on employers in most states. The purpose of this tax is to raise funds to pay unemployment benefits. Tax rates and unemployment benefits vary among the states. In this text, we will use a rate of 5.4% applied to maximum earnings of $7,000 for each employee. Most states have an **experience-rating system** to encourage employers to provide regular employment to workers. If an employer has very few former employees receiving unemployment compensation, the employer qualifies for a lower state unemployment tax rate. If an employer qualifies for a lower state rate, the full credit of 5.4% would still be allowed in computing the federal unemployment tax due.

Refer to the payroll register in Figure 9-1. As we saw with the FUTA tax, only $360 of employee earnings for this pay period are subject to the state unemployment tax. The tax is computed as shown in Figure 9-3.

FIGURE 9-3 Computation of SUTA Tax

CHECKPOINT ✔
Complete Checkpoint-1 on page 340 to test your basic understanding of LO1.

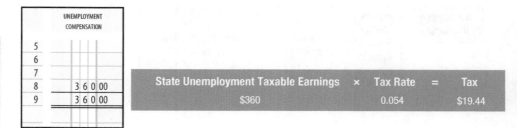

LO2	Accounting for Employer Payroll Taxes

Account for employer payroll taxes expense.

Now that we have computed the employer payroll taxes, we need to journalize them. It is common to debit all employer payroll taxes to a single account—Payroll Taxes Expense. However, we usually credit separate liability accounts for Social Security, Medicare, FUTA, and SUTA taxes payable.

Journalizing Employer Payroll Taxes

The employer payroll taxes computed in the previous section can be summarized as follows:

Employer's Social Security tax	$365.61
Employer's Medicare tax	100.01
FUTA tax	2.16
SUTA tax	19.44
Total employer payroll taxes	$487.22

These amounts provide the basis for the following journal entry:

5	Dec.	19	Payroll Taxes Expense	4	8	7	22					5
6			Social Security Tax Payable					3	6	5	61	6
7			Medicare Tax Payable					1	0	0	01	7
8			FUTA Tax Payable							2	16	8
9			SUTA Tax Payable						1	9	44	9
10			Employer payroll taxes for week ended Dec. 19									10

The steps needed to prepare this journal entry for employer payroll taxes are as follows:

STEP 1   Obtain the total earnings and taxable earnings amounts from the Earnings—Total and Taxable Earnings columns of the payroll register. In this case, total earnings were $6,897; Social Security taxable earnings were $5,897; and Unemployment Compensation taxable earnings were $360.

STEP 2   Compute the amount of employer Social Security tax by multiplying the Social Security taxable earnings by 6.2%.

STEP 3   Compute the amount of employer Medicare tax by multiplying total earnings by 1.45%.

STEP 4   Compute the amount of FUTA tax by multiplying the Unemployment Taxable earnings by 0.6%.

STEP 5   Compute the amount of SUTA tax by multiplying the Unemployment Taxable earnings by 5.4%.

STEP 6   Prepare the appropriate journal entry using the amounts computed in steps 2–5.

To understand the journal entry for employer payroll taxes, let's use the accounting equation to examine the accounts involved. The five accounts affected by the payroll taxes entry above are shown in the accounting equation in Figure 9-4.

FIGURE 9-4 Accounting for Payroll Taxes

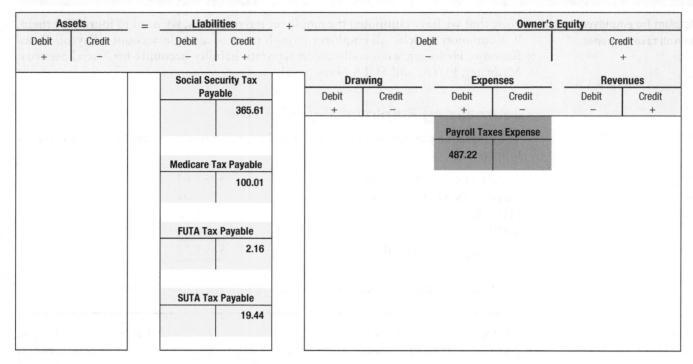

Payroll Taxes Expense

The Social Security, Medicare, FUTA, and SUTA taxes imposed on the employer are expenses of doing business. Each of the employer taxes is debited to Payroll Taxes Expense.

Payroll Taxes Expense

Debit	Credit
Social Security, Medicare, FUTA, and SUTA taxes imposed on the employer	

Social Security and Medicare Taxes Payable

These are the same liability accounts used in Chapter 8 to record the Social Security and Medicare taxes withheld from employees' earnings. The accounts are credited to enter the Social Security and Medicare taxes imposed on the employer. They are debited when the taxes are paid to the IRS. When all of the Social Security and Medicare taxes have been paid, the accounts will have zero balances.

Social Security Tax Payable

Debit	Credit
Payment of Social Security tax	Social Security taxes (1) withheld from employees' earnings and (2) imposed on the employer

Medicare Tax Payable

Debit	Credit
Payment of Medicare tax	Medicare taxes (1) withheld from employees' earnings and (2) imposed on the employer

LEARNING KEY 🔑

Employer and employee Social Security and Medicare taxes are credited to the same liability accounts because both of these taxes are due and will be paid to the IRS.

FUTA Tax Payable

A separate liability account entitled FUTA Tax Payable is kept for the employer's FUTA tax. This account is credited for the tax imposed on employers under the Federal Unemployment Tax Act. The account is debited when this tax is paid. When all of the FUTA taxes have been paid, the account will have a zero balance.

FUTA Tax Payable

Debit	Credit
Payment of FUTA tax	FUTA tax imposed on the employer

SUTA Tax Payable

A separate liability account entitled SUTA Tax Payable is kept for the state unemployment tax. This account is credited for the tax imposed on employers under the state unemployment compensation laws. The account is debited when this tax is paid. When all of the state unemployment taxes have been paid, the account will have a zero balance.

SUTA Tax Payable

Debit	Credit
Payment of SUTA tax	SUTA tax imposed on the employer

Total Payroll Cost of an Employee

It is interesting to note what it really costs to employ a person. The employer must, of course, pay the gross wages of an employee. In addition, the employer must pay payroll taxes on employee earnings up to certain dollar limits.

To illustrate, assume that an employee earns $26,000 a year. The total cost of this employee to the employer is calculated as follows:

Gross wages	$26,000
Employer Social Security tax, 6.2% of $26,000	1,612
Employer Medicare tax, 1.45% of $26,000	377
State unemployment tax, 5.4% of $7,000	378
FUTA tax, 0.6% of $7,000	42
	$28,409

> **CHECKPOINT ✔**
>
> Complete Checkpoint-2 on page 340 to test your basic understanding of LO2.

Thus, the total payroll cost of employing a person whose stated compensation is $26,000 is $28,409. Employer payroll taxes clearly are a significant cost of doing business. Employer-paid medical insurance and pension plans can further increase total payroll costs.

LO3 — Reporting and Payment Responsibilities

Describe employer reporting and payment responsibilities.

Employer payroll reporting and payment responsibilities fall into six areas:

1. Federal income tax withholding and Social Security and Medicare taxes
2. FUTA taxes
3. SUTA taxes
4. Employee Wage and Tax Statement (Form W-2)
5. Summary of employee wages and taxes (Form W-3)
6. Employment eligibility verification (Form I-9)

Federal Income Tax Withholding and Social Security and Medicare Taxes

Three important aspects of employer reporting and payment responsibilities for federal income tax withholding and Social Security and Medicare taxes are as follows:

1. Determining when payments are due
2. Use of electronic funds transfer to make federal tax deposits
3. Use of Form 941, Employer's Quarterly Federal Tax Return

When Payments Are Due

The date by which federal income tax withholding and Social Security and Medicare taxes must be paid depends on the amount of these taxes. Figure 9-5 summarizes the deposit rules stated in *Circular E—Employer's Tax Guide*. In general, the larger the amount that needs to be deposited, the more frequently payments must be made. For simplicity, we will assume that deposits must be made 15 days after the end of each month.

FIGURE 9-5 **Summary of Deposit Rules**

ACCUMULATED TAX LIABILITY	DEPOSIT DUE
1. Less than $2,500 at the end of the current quarter	1. Pay with Form 941 at end of the month following end of the quarter
2. $2,500 or more at the end of the current quarter and $50,000 or less in total during the lookback period	2. Deposit 15 days after end of the month
3. $2,500 or more at the end of the current quarter and more than $50,000 in total during the lookback period	3. Deposit every Wednesday or Friday, depending on day of the week payroll payments are made
4. $100,000 or more on any day during the current quarter	4. Deposit by the end of the next banking day

The "lookback period" identified in Figure 9-5 is the four quarters beginning July 1, two years ago, and ending June 30, one year ago. For example, the lookback period for calendar year 2019 is illustrated in Figure 9-6. The four-quarter lookback period begins July 1, 2017 ("two years ago") and ends June 30, 2018 ("one year ago").

FIGURE 9-6 **Lookback Period for 2019**

	JAN. 1, 2018			**JAN. 1, 2019**	
July 1, 2017 through Sept. 30, 2017	Oct. 1, 2017 through Dec. 31, 2017	Jan. 1, 2018 through Mar. 31, 2018	Apr. 1, 2018 through June 30, 2018	July 1, 2018 through Sept. 30, 2018	Oct. 1, 2018 through Dec. 31, 2018
Quarter 1	Quarter 2	Quarter 3	Quarter 4		

Making Federal Tax Deposits

Deposits of employee federal income tax withheld, and Social Security and Medicare taxes must be made using electronic funds transfer. Generally, the Electronic Federal Tax Payment System (EFTPS) is used. The EFTPS is an electronic funds transfer system designed for making federal tax deposits.

The IRS strongly encourages businesses to both file and pay electronically. To file: go to www.IRS.gov /EmploymentEFile for additional information. To pay: go to www.EFTPS.gov.

On February 15, Westly, Inc., used the EFTPS to deposit $6,325.70 for the following taxes on wages paid in January:

Employees' income tax withheld from wages		$2,042.00
Social Security tax:		
Withheld from employees' wages	$1,681.80	
Imposed on employer	1,681.80	3,363.60
Medicare tax:		
Withheld from employees' wages	$ 460.05	
Imposed on employer	460.05	920.10
Amount of check		$6,325.70

The journal entry for this deposit would be as follows:

5	Feb.	15	Employee Federal Income Tax Payable	2 0 4 2 00		5
6			Social Security Tax Payable	3 3 6 3 60		6
7			Medicare Tax Payable	9 2 0 10		7
8			Cash		6 3 2 5 70	8
9			Deposit of employee federal income tax and			9
10			Social Security and Medicare taxes			10

Form 941

If the total tax liability for federal income taxes, Social Security, and Medicare taxes is less than $1,000, Form 944, Employer's Annual Federal Tax Return, may be used. Permission to do so must be obtained from the IRS, and the form must be filed by January 31.

Form 941, Employer's Quarterly Federal Tax Return, must be filed with the IRS at the end of the month following each calendar quarter. This form reports the following taxes for the quarter:

1. Employee federal income tax withheld
2. Employee Social Security and Medicare taxes withheld
3. Employer Social Security and Medicare taxes

If the total amount of taxes due is less than $2,500, payment may be made with Form 941, using Form 941-V.

A completed Form 941 for Westly, Inc., for the first quarter of the calendar year is shown in Figure 9-7. Westly had made its monthly tax deposits using EFTPS. Instructions for completing the form are provided with the form and in *Circular E*.

FUTA Taxes

Federal unemployment taxes must be calculated on a quarterly basis. If the accumulated liability exceeds $500, the total must be deposited by the end of the month following the close of the quarter. If the liability is $500 or less, no deposit is necessary. The amount is simply added to the amount to be deposited for the next quarter. FUTA taxes are deposited using an electronic funds transfer, usually EFTPS.

Assume that an employer's accumulated FUTA tax liability for the first quarter of the calendar year is $508. The employer would deposit this amount on April 30. The journal entry for this transaction would be as follows:

15	Apr.	30	FUTA Tax Payable	5 0 8 00		15
16			Cash		5 0 8 00	16
17			Deposit of federal unemployment tax			17

FIGURE 9-7 Employer's Quarterly Federal Tax Return (Form 941)

Form **941 for 20--:** **Employer's QUARTERLY Federal Tax Return**   950117
(Rev. January 2018)   Department of the Treasury — Internal Revenue Service   OMB No. 1545-0029

Employer identification number (EIN) [4] [3] – [0] [2] [1] [1] [6] [3] [0]

Name *(not your trade name)*

Trade name *(if any)*   Westly, Inc.

Address   5221 Natural Bridge
          Number   Street   Suite or room number

          St. Louis   MO   63115-8230
          City   State ZIP code

          Foreign country name   Foreign province/county   Foreign postal code

Report for this Quarter of 2018
(Check one.)

[X] **1:** January, February, March

[ ] **2:** April, May, June

[ ] **3:** July, August, September

[ ] **4:** October, November, December

Go to *www.irs.gov/Form941* for
instructions and the latest information.

Read the separate instructions before you complete Form 941. Type or print within the boxes.

Part 1: **Answer these questions for this quarter.**

1 Number of employees who received wages, tips, or other compensation for the pay period
   including: *Mar. 12* (Quarter 1), *June 12* (Quarter 2), *Sept. 12* (Quarter 3), or *Dec. 12* (Quarter 4) **1** | 8

2 Wages, tips, and other compensation . . . . **2** | 81,900.00

3 Federal income tax withheld from wages, tips, and other compensation . . . . . . **3** | 6,552.00 ◄ Employee federal income tax withheld

4 If no wages, tips, and other compensation are subject to social security or Medicare tax [ ] Check and go to line 6.

                                          Column 1   Column 2

5a Taxable social security wages . . | 81,900.00 | × 0.124 = | 10,155.60 | ◄ Employee and employer Social Security taxes

5b Taxable social security tips . . . | . | × 0.124 = | . |

5c Taxable Medicare wages & tips. . | 81,900.00 | × 0.029 = | 2,375.10 | ◄ Employee and employer Medicare taxes

5d Taxable wages & tips subject to
    Additional Medicare Tax withholding | . | × 0.009 = | . |

5e Add Column 2 from lines 5a, 5b, 5c, and 5d . . . . **5e** | 12,530.70

5f Section 3121(q) Notice and Demand—Tax due on unreported tips (see instructions) . . **5f** | .

6 Total taxes before adjustments. Add lines 3, 5e, and 5f . . . . **6** | 19,082.70

7 Current quarter's adjustment for fractions of cents . . . . **7** | .

8 Current quarter's adjustment for sick pay . . . . **8** | .

9 Current quarter's adjustments for tips and group-term life insurance . . . . . **9** | .

10 Total taxes after adjustments. Combine lines 6 through 9 . . . . **10** | 19,082.70

11 Qualified small business payroll tax credit for increasing research activities. Attach Form 8974 **11** | 19,082.70

12 Total taxes after adjustments and credits. Subtract line 11 from line 10 . . . . . **12** | .

13 Total deposits for this quarter, including overpayment applied from a prior quarter and
    overpayments applied from Form 941-X, 941-X (PR), 944-X, or 944-X (SP) filed in the current quarter **13** | .

14 Balance due. If line 12 is more than line 13, enter the difference and see instructions . . . **14** | .

15 Overpayment. If line 13 is more than line 12, enter the difference | . | Check one: [ ] Apply to next return.   [ ] Send a refund.

   ► You MUST complete both pages of Form 941 and SIGN it.   Next ►
For Privacy Act and Paperwork Reduction Act Notice, see the back of the Payment Voucher.   Cat. No. 17001Z   Form **941** (Rev. 1-20--)

FIGURE 9-7 Employer's Quarterly Federal Tax Return (Form 941) (concluded)

950217

Name *(not your trade name)*	Employer identification number (EIN)

Part 2: Tell us about your deposit schedule and tax liability for this quarter.

If you are unsure about whether you are a monthly schedule depositor or a semiweekly schedule depositor, see section 11 of Pub. 15.

16 Check one: ☐ **Line 12 on this return is less than $2,500 or line 12 on the return for the prior quarter was less than $2,500, and you didn't incur a $100,000 next-day deposit obligation during the current quarter.** If line 12 for the prior quarter was less than $2,500 but line 12 on this return is $100,000 or more, you must provide a record of your federal tax liability. If you are a monthly schedule depositor, complete the deposit schedule below; if you are a semiweekly schedule depositor, attach Schedule B (Form 941). Go to Part 3.

☒ **You were a monthly schedule depositor for the entire quarter.** Enter your tax liability for each month and total liability for the quarter, then go to Part 3.

Tax liability:	Month 1	6,325.70
	Month 2	5,900.20
	Month 3	6,856.80
Total liability for quarter		19,082.70	Total must equal line 12.

☐ **You were a semiweekly schedule depositor for any part of this quarter.** Complete Schedule B (Form 941), Report of Tax Liability for Semiweekly Schedule Depositors, and attach it to Form 941.

Part 3: Tell us about your business. If a question does NOT apply to your business, leave it blank.

17 If your business has closed or you stopped paying wages . . . . ☐ Check here, and

enter the final date you paid wages   /   /   .

18 If you are a seasonal employer and you don't have to file a return for every quarter of the year . . . ☐ Check here.

Part 4: May we speak with your third-party designee?

Do you want to allow an employee, a paid tax preparer, or another person to discuss this return with the IRS? See the instructions for details.

☐ Yes. Designee's name and phone number

Select a 5-digit Personal Identification Number (PIN) to use when talking to the IRS. ☐ ☐ ☐ ☐ ☐

☒ No.

Part 5: Sign here. You MUST complete both pages of Form 941 and SIGN it.

Under penalties of perjury, I declare that I have examined this return, including accompanying schedules and statements, and to the best of my knowledge and belief, it is true, correct, and complete. Declaration of preparer (other than taxpayer) is based on all information of which preparer has any knowledge.

X **Sign your name here**   *William P. Jones*

Print your name here *William P Jones*
Print your title here *Treasurer*

Date *4 / 301 --*   Best daytime phone

Paid Preparer Use Only   Check if you are self-employed . . . ☐

Preparer's name		PTIN	
Preparer's signature		Date	/ /
Firm's name (or yours if self-employed)		EIN	
Address		Phone	
City		State		ZIP code	

Page **2**   Form **941** (Rev. 1-20--)

Form 940

In addition to making quarterly deposits, employers are required to file an annual report of federal unemployment tax using Form 940 (Figure 9-8). If all quarterly deposits have been made, this form must be filed with the IRS by the beginning of the second week of February. Otherwise, it must be filed by January 31. Figure 9-8 shows a completed

FIGURE 9-8 Employer's Annual Federal Unemployment (FUTA) Tax Return (Form 940)

Form **940 for 20--:** Employer's Annual Federal Unemployment (FUTA) Tax Return

850113

Department of the Treasury — Internal Revenue Service

OMB No. 1545-0028

Employer identification number (EIN) 4 3 – 0 2 1 1 6 3 0

Name (not your trade name)

Trade name (if any) Westly, Inc.

Address 5221 Natural Bridge

Number | Street | | Suite or room number

St. Louis | MO | 63115-8230

City | State | ZIP code

Foreign country name | Foreign province/county | Foreign postal code

Type of Return
(Check all that apply.)

☐ **a.** Amended

☐ **b.** Successor employer

☐ **c.** No payments to employees in 2014

☐ **d.** Final: Business closed or stopped paying wages

Instructions and prior-year forms are available at *www.irs.gov/form940.*

Read the separate instructions before you complete this form. Please type or print within the boxes.

Part 1: Tell us about your return. If any line does NOT apply, leave it blank.

1a If you had to pay state unemployment tax in one state only, enter the state abbreviation . **1a** M O

1b If you had to pay state unemployment tax in more than one state, you are a multi-state employer . . . . **1b** ☐ Check here. Complete Schedule A (Form 940).

2 If you paid wages in a state that is subject to CREDIT REDUCTION . . . . **2** ☐ Check here. Complete Schedule A (Form 940).

Part 2: Determine your FUTA tax before adjustments for 2014. If any line does NOT apply, leave it blank.

3 Total payments to all employees **3** 343,400.00

4 Payments exempt from FUTA tax **4**

Check all that apply: **4a** ☐ Fringe benefits **4c** ☐ Retirement/Pension **4e** ☐ Other
4b ☐ Group-term life insurance **4d** ☐ Dependent care

5 Total of payments made to each employee in excess of $7,000 . . . . **5** 280,820.00

6 Subtotal (line 4 + line 5 = line 6) **6** 280,820.00

7 Total taxable FUTA wages (line 3 – line 6 = line 7) (see instructions) . . . . **7** 62,580.00 ← FUTA taxable wages

8 FUTA tax before adjustments (line 7 x .006 = line 8) **8** 375.48

Part 3: Determine your adjustments. If any line does NOT apply, leave it blank.

9 If ALL of the taxable FUTA wages you paid were excluded from state unemployment tax, multiply line 7 by .054 (line 7 x .054 = line 9). Go to line 12 . . . . **9** .

10 If SOME of the taxable FUTA wages you paid were excluded from state unemployment tax, OR you paid ANY state unemployment tax late (after the due date for filing Form 940), complete the worksheet in the instructions. Enter the amount from line 7 of the worksheet . . **10** .

11 If credit reduction applies, enter the total from Schedule A (Form 940) . . . . . . **11** .

Part 4: Determine your FUTA tax and balance due or overpayment for 2014. If any line does NOT apply, leave it blank.

12 Total FUTA tax after adjustments (lines 8 + 9 + 10 + 11 = line 12) . . . . **12** 375.48 ← FUTA tax

13 FUTA tax deposited for the year, including any overpayment applied from a prior year . **13** . ← FUTA tax paid

14 Balance due (If line 12 is more than line 13, enter the excess on line 14.)
• If line 14 is more than $500, you must deposit your tax.
• If line 14 is $500 or less, you may pay with this return. (see instructions) . . . . . **14** 375.48 ← FUTA tax due

15 Overpayment (If line 13 is more than line 12, enter the excess on line 15 and check a box below.) . . . . **15** .

▶ You **MUST** complete both pages of this form and **SIGN** it. Check one: ☐ Apply to next return. ☐ Send a refund.

Next ▶

For Privacy Act and Paperwork Reduction Act Notice, see the back of Form 940-V, Payment Voucher. Cat. No. 112340 Form **940** (20--)

Form 940 for Westly, Inc. Instructions for completing the form are provided with the form and in *Circular E.* If a balance is due, it may be paid using EFTPS, or Form 940-V if the amount due is $500 or less. Figure 9-9 shows a completed Form 940-V for Westly.

SUTA Taxes

Deposit rules and forms for state unemployment taxes vary among the states. Deposits usually are required on a quarterly basis. Assume that Westly's accumulated state

FIGURE 9-8 Employer's Annual Federal Unemployment (FUTA) Tax Return (Form 940) (*concluded*)

FIGURE 9-9 Payment Voucher (Form 940-V)

Form **940-V**		**Payment Voucher**		OMB No. 1545-0028
Department of the Treasury Internal Revenue Service		► Do not staple or attach this voucher to your payment.		20--

1 Enter your employer identification number (EIN).	2 **Enter the amount of your payment.** ► Make your check or money order payable to "**United States Treasury**"	Dollars	Cents
43 0211630		375	48

3 Enter your business name (individual name if sole proprietor).
Westly, Inc.
Enter your address.
5221 Natural Bridge
Enter your city, state, and ZIP code or your city, foreign country name, foreign province/county, and foreign postal code.
St. Louis, MO 63115-8230

unemployment liability for the first quarter of the calendar year is $3,240. The journal entry for the deposit of this amount with the state on April 30 would be as follows:

19	Apr.	30	SUTA Tax Payable	3 2 4 0 00		19
20			Cash		3 2 4 0 00	20
21			Deposit of state unemployment tax			21

Employee Wage and Tax Statement

By January 31 of each year, employers must furnish each employee with a Wage and Tax Statement, Form W-2 (Figure 9-10). This form shows the total amount of wages

FIGURE 9-10 Wage and Tax Statement (Form W-2)

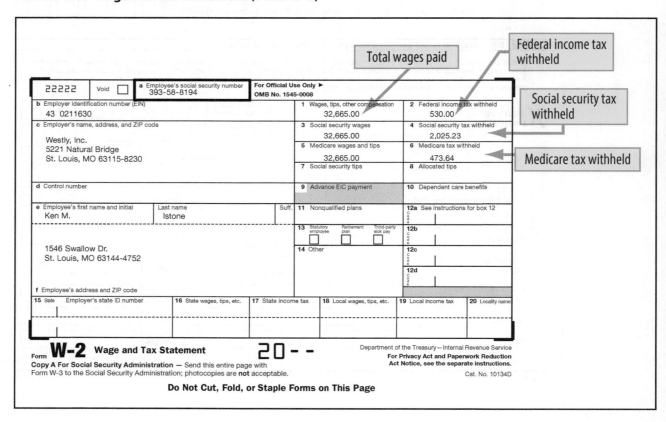

paid to the employee and the amounts of taxes withheld during the preceding taxable year. The employee earnings record contains the information needed to complete this form.

Multiple copies of Form W-2 are needed for the following purposes:

- Copy A—Employer sends to Social Security Administration
- Copy B—Employee files with federal income tax return
- Copy C—Employee retains for his or her own records
- Copy D—Employer retains for business records
- Copy 1—Employer sends to state, city, or local tax department
- Copy 2—Employee files with state, city, or local income tax return

> The Social Security Administration is encouraging employers to file Form W-3 and Forms W-2 electronically instead of on paper.

Summary of Employee Wages and Taxes

Employers send Form W-3, Transmittal of Wage and Tax Statements (Figure 9-11), with Copy A of Forms W-2 to the Social Security Administration. Form W-3 must be filed by January 31 following the end of each taxable year. This form summarizes

FIGURE 9-11 Transmittal of Wage and Tax Statements (Form W-3)

the employee earnings and tax information presented on Forms W-2 for the year. Information needed to complete Form W-3 is contained in the employee earnings records.

Employment Eligibility Verification

Every employee hired after November 6, 1986, must complete Form I-9, Employment Eligibility Verification. The purpose of this form is to document that each employee is authorized to work in the United States. The employee completes Section 1 of the form and provides the employer with evidence of the employee's identity and authorization to work. The employer completes Section 2 of the form indicating what evidence the employer examined.

Form I-9 is not filed with any government agency. Instead, it must be retained by the employer and made available for inspection if requested by the Department of Homeland Security or the Department of Labor.

Summary of Taxes, Reports, and Payments

Keeping track of the many payroll taxes can be a challenge for an employer. Figure 9-12 summarizes the various employee and employer taxes we have discussed in Chapters 8 and 9. Figure 9-13 shows a calendar that highlights the due dates for the various reports and deposits. The calendar assumes the following for an employer:

1. Undeposited FIT (federal income tax) and Social Security and Medicare taxes of $2,500 at the end of each quarter and less than $50,000 during the lookback period

2. Undeposited FUTA taxes of more than $500 at the end of each quarter

3. SUTA taxes deposited quarterly

The combination of payroll taxes, reports, deposit rules, and due dates can make payroll accounting rather complex. In fact, this is a major reason why small businesses often hire an accountant or an outside company to handle payroll.

FIGURE 9-12 **Summary of Employee and Employer Taxes**

TAX	TAX APPLIES TO	
	EMPLOYEE	EMPLOYER
Federal income tax	X	
State income tax	X	
Social Security	X	X
Medicare	X	X
FUTA		X
SUTA		X*

*Also applies to employees in some states.

CHECKPOINT ✔
Complete Checkpoint-3 on page 341 to test your basic understanding of LO3.

FIGURE 9-13 Payroll Calendar

File Forms 940, 941, W-3, and state unemployment tax report, and send W-2 to employees.	File Form 940	File Form 941 and make FUTA and SUTA tax deposits.	Deposit FIT and Social Security and Medicare taxes from previous month.

January

S	M	T	W	T	F	S
			1	2	3	4
5	6	7	8	9	10	11
12	13	14	15	16	17	18
19	20	21	22	23	24	25
26	27	28	29	30	31	

February

S	M	T	W	T	F	S
						1
2	3	4	5	6	7	8
9	10	11	12	13	14	15
16	17	18	19	20	21	22
23	24	25	26	27	28	29

March

S	M	T	W	T	F	S
1	2	3	4	5	6	7
8	9	10	11	12	13	14
15	16	17	18	19	20	21
22	23	24	25	26	27	28
29	30	31				

April

S	M	T	W	T	F	S
			1	2	3	4
5	6	7	8	9	10	11
12	13	14	15	16	17	18
19	20	21	22	23	24	25
26	27	28	29	30		

May

S	M	T	W	T	F	S
					1	2
3	4	5	6	7	8	9
10	11	12	13	14	15	16
17	18	19	20	21	22	23
24	25	26	27	28	29	30
31						

June

S	M	T	W	T	F	S
	1	2	3	4	5	6
7	8	9	10	11	12	13
14	15	16	17	18	19	20
21	22	23	24	25	26	27
28	29	30				

July

S	M	T	W	T	F	S
			1	2	3	4
5	6	7	8	9	10	11
12	13	14	15	16	17	18
19	20	21	22	23	24	25
26	27	28	29	30	31	

August

S	M	T	W	T	F	S
						1
2	3	4	5	6	7	8
9	10	11	12	13	14	15
16	17	18	19	20	21	22
23	24	25	26	27	28	29
30	31					

September

S	M	T	W	T	F	S
		1	2	3	4	5
6	7	8	9	10	11	12
13	14	15	16	17	18	19
20	21	22	23	24	25	26
27	28	29	30			

October

S	M	T	W	T	F	S
				1	2	3
4	5	6	7	8	9	10
11	12	13	14	15	16	17
18	19	20	21	22	23	24
25	26	27	28	29	30	31

November

S	M	T	W	T	F	S
1	2	3	4	5	6	7
8	9	10	11	12	13	14
15	16	17	18	19	20	21
22	23	24	25	26	27	28
29	30					

December

S	M	T	W	T	F	S
		1	2	3	4	5
6	7	8	9	10	11	12
13	14	15	16	17	18	19
20	21	22	23	24	25	26
27	28	29	30	31		

LO4 | Workers' Compensation Insurance

Describe and account for workers' compensation insurance.

Most states require employers to carry workers' compensation insurance. Workers' compensation insurance provides insurance for employees who suffer a work-related illness or injury.

The employer usually pays the entire cost of workers' compensation insurance. The cost of the insurance depends on the number of employees, riskiness of the job, and the company's accident history. For example, the insurance premium for workers in a chemical plant could be higher than for office workers. Employers generally obtain the insurance either from the state in which they operate or from a private insurance company.

The employer usually pays the premium at the beginning of the year, based on the estimated payroll for the year. At the end of the year, after the actual amount of payroll is known, an adjustment is made. If the employer has overpaid, a credit is received from the state or insurance company. If the employer has underpaid, an additional premium is paid.

A BROADER VIEW

Dealing with Payroll Complexity—Let Someone Else Do It

A common way for both small and large businesses to deal with the complexity of payroll reports, deposit rules, and due dates is to hire an outside company to handle the payroll. Payroll processing companies have combined payroll expertise with the power of computers to create a major business enterprise based on the efficient and effective provision of payroll services.

The extent to which businesses use outside companies to handle payroll can be seen in two of the largest payroll processing companies: Automatic Data Processing, Inc. (ADP) and Paychex, Inc. ADP has operations in the United States, Canada, Europe, South America, Africa, the Mid-East, Australia, and Asia; provides payroll services to 650,000 clients; and has revenues of over $12.5 billion. Paychex has more than 100 locations nationwide, provides services to 605,000 clients, and has revenues of $3.2 billion. These companies prepare employee paychecks, journals, and summary reports; collect and remit funds for federal, and local payroll taxes; and file all required forms with government taxing authorities.

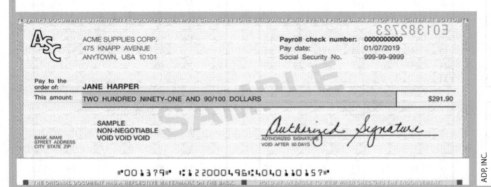

To illustrate the accounting for workers' compensation insurance, assume that Lockwood Co. expects its payroll for the year to be $210,000. If Lockwood's insurance premium rate is 0.2%, its payment for workers' compensation insurance at the beginning of the year would be $420.

Estimated Payroll	×	Rate	=	Estimated Insurance Premium
$210,000		0.002		$420.00

The journal entry for the payment of this $420 premium would be as follows:

7	Jan.	2	Workers' Compensation Insurance Expense		4 2 0 00					7
8			Cash				4 2 0 00			8
9			Paid insurance premium							9

If Lockwood's actual payroll for the year is $220,000, Lockwood would owe an additional premium of $20 at year-end.

Actual Payroll	×	Rate	=	Insurance Premium
$220,000		0.002		$440.00
Less premium paid				420.00
Additional premium due				$ 20.00

The adjusting entry at year-end for this additional expense would be as follows:

11	Dec.	31	Workers' Compensation Insurance Expense			2	0	00						11
12			Workers' Compensation Insurance Payable							2	0	00		12
13			Adjustment for insurance premium											13

In T account form, the total Workers' Compensation Insurance Expense of $440.00 would look like this:

Workers' Compensation Insurance Expense

Debit	Credit
420.00	
20.00	
440.00	

If Lockwood's actual payroll for the year is only $205,000, Lockwood would be due a refund of $10.

Payroll	×	Rate	=	Insurance Premium
$205,000		0.002		$410.00
Less premium paid				420.00
Refund due				$ (10.00)

The adjusting entry at year-end for this refund due would be as follows:

16	Dec.	31	Insurance Refund Receivable			1	0	00						16
17			Workers' Compensation Insurance Expense							1	0	00		17
18			Adjustment for insurance premium											18

In T account form, the total Workers' Compensation Insurance Expense of $410 would look like this:

Workers' Compensation Insurance Expense

Debit	Credit
420.00	10.00
410.00	

CHECKPOINT ✔

Complete Checkpoint-4 on page 341 to test your basic understanding of LO4.

| LEARNING OBJECTIVES | Key Points to Remember |

LO1 Describe and calculate employer payroll taxes.

LO2 Account for employer payroll taxes expense.

Employer payroll taxes include FICA, FUTA, and SUTA taxes. These taxes represent additional payroll expenses of the employer. The journal entry for payroll taxes is as follows:

8	Payroll Taxes Expense					x	x	x	xx							8
9	Social Security Tax Payable									x	x	x	xx			9
10	Medicare Tax Payable									x	x	x	xx			10
11	FUTA Tax Payable									x	x	x	xx			11
12	SUTA Tax Payable									x	x	x	xx			12

The steps to be followed in preparing this journal entry are as follows:

1. Obtain the total earnings and taxable earnings amounts from the Earnings—Total and Taxable Earnings columns of the payroll register.
2. Compute the amount of employer Social Security tax by multiplying the Social Security taxable earnings by 6.2%.
3. Compute the amount of employer Medicare tax by multiplying total earnings by 1.45%.
4. Compute the amount of FUTA tax by multiplying the Unemployment Taxable earnings by 0.6%.
5. Compute the amount of SUTA tax by multiplying the Unemployment Taxable earnings by 5.4%.
6. Prepare the appropriate journal entry using the amounts computed in steps 2–5.

LO3 Describe employer reporting and payment responsibilities.

Employer payroll reporting and payment responsibilities fall into six areas:

1. Federal income tax withholding and Social Security and Medicare taxes
2. FUTA taxes
3. SUTA taxes
4. Employee Wage and Tax Statement (Form W-2)
5. Summary of employee wages and taxes (Form W-3)
6. Employment eligibility verification (Form I-9)

Most federal tax deposits are made using the EFTPS. In addition, two forms are needed in reporting and paying employer payroll taxes:

1. Form 941, Employer's Quarterly Federal Tax Return
2. Form 940, Employer's Annual Federal Unemployment Tax Return

By January 31 of each year, employers must provide each employee with a Wage and Tax Statement, Form W-2.

By January 31 of each year, employers must file Form W-3 and Copy A of Forms W-2 with the Social Security Administration.

LEARNING OBJECTIVES	**Key Points to Remember**
LO4 **Describe and account for workers' compensation insurance.**	Workers' compensation insurance provides insurance for employees who suffer a work-related illness or injury. Employers generally are required to carry and pay the entire cost of this insurance.

DEMONSTRATION PROBLEM

The Totals line from Hart Company's payroll register for the week ended December 31, 20--, is as follows:

(left side)   PAYROLL REGISTER

	NAME	EMPLOYEE NUMBER	ALLOWANCES	MARITAL STATUS	EARNINGS			CUMULATIVE TOTAL	TAXABLE EARNINGS	
					REGULAR	OVERTIME	TOTAL		UNEMPLOYMENT COMPENSATION	SOCIAL SECURITY
21	Totals				3 5 0 0 00	3 0 0 00	3 8 0 0 00	197 6 0 0 00	4 0 0 00	3 8 0 0 00

—PERIOD ENDED December 31, 20--   (right side)

FEDERAL INCOME TAX	SOCIAL SECURITY TAX	MEDICARE TAX	HEALTH INSURANCE	UNITED WAY	OTHER	TOTAL	NET PAY	CHECK NO.
3 8 0 00	2 3 5 60	5 5 10	5 0 00	1 0 0 00		8 2 0 70	2 9 7 9 30	21

Payroll taxes are imposed as follows: Social Security, 6.2%; Medicare, 1.45%; FUTA, 0.6%; and SUTA, 5.4%.

REQUIRED

1. a. Prepare the journal entry for payment of this payroll on December 31, 20--.
   b. Prepare the journal entry for the employer's payroll taxes for the period ended December 31, 20--.
2. Hart Company had the following balances in its general ledger *after* the entries for requirement (1) were made:

Employee Federal Income Tax Payable	$1,620.00
Social Security Tax Payable	1,847.00
Medicare Tax Payable	433.00
FUTA Tax Payable	27.20
SUTA Tax Payable	183.60

   a. Prepare the journal entry for payment of the liabilities for employee federal income taxes and Social Security and Medicare taxes on January 15, 20--.
   b. Prepare the journal entry for payment of the liability for FUTA tax on January 31, 20--.
   c. Prepare the journal entry for payment of the liability for SUTA tax on January 31, 20--.

3. Hart Company paid a premium of $280 for workers' compensation insurance based on estimated payroll as of the beginning of the year. Based on actual payroll as of the end of the year, the premium is $298. Prepare the adjusting entry on December 31 for the additional workers' compensation insurance premium.

SOLUTION 1.

	DATE		DESCRIPTION	POST. REF.	DEBIT	CREDIT	
1	20-- Dec.	31	Wages and Salaries Expense		3 8 0 0 00		1
2			Employee Federal Income Tax Payable			3 8 0 00	2
3			Social Security Tax Payable			2 3 5 60	3
4			Medicare Tax Payable			5 5 10	4
5			Health Insurance Premiums Payable			5 0 00	5
6			United Way Contributions Payable			1 0 0 00	6
7			Cash			2 9 7 9 30	7
8			To record Dec. 31 payroll				8
9							9
10		31	Payroll Taxes Expense		3 1 4 70		10
11			Social Security Tax Payable			2 3 5 60	11
12			Medicare Tax Payable			5 5 10	12
13			FUTA Tax Payable			2 40	13
14			SUTA Tax Payable			2 1 60	14
15			Employer payroll taxes for week ended Dec. 31				15

GENERAL JOURNAL — PAGE 1

SOLUTION 2. and 3.

	DATE		DESCRIPTION	POST. REF.	DEBIT	CREDIT	
18	Jan.	15	Employee Federal Income Tax Payable		1 6 2 0 00		18
19			Social Security Tax Payable		1 8 4 7 00		19
20			Medicare Tax Payable		4 3 3 00		20
21			Cash			3 9 0 0 00	21
22			Deposit of employee federal income tax and				22
23			Social Security and Medicare taxes				23
24							24
25		31	FUTA Tax Payable		2 7 20		25
26			Cash			2 7 20	26
27			Paid FUTA tax				27
28							28
29		31	SUTA Tax Payable		1 8 3 60		29
30			Cash			1 8 3 60	30
31			Paid SUTA tax				31
32							32
33	Dec.	31	Workers' Compensation Insurance Expense		1 8 00		33
34			Workers' Compensation Insurance Payable			1 8 00	34
35			Adjustment for insurance premium				35

KEY TERMS

Electronic Federal Tax Payment System (EFTPS) (324)   An electronic funds transfer system for making federal tax deposits.

employer FICA taxes (318)   Taxes levied on employers at the same rates and on the same earnings bases as the employee FICA taxes.

experience-rating system (320)   A system to encourage employers to provide regular employment to workers.

FUTA (Federal Unemployment Tax Act) tax (320)   A tax levied on employers to raise funds to administer the federal/state unemployment compensation program.

Self-Employment Contributions Act (SECA) (319)   A government Act that requires self-employed individuals to pay tax on net self-employment income.

self-employment income (319)   The net income of a trade or business run by an individual.

self-employment tax (319)   A tax on the earnings of a self-employed person at double the Social Security and Medicare rates.

SUTA (state unemployment tax) tax (320)   A tax levied on employers to raise funds to pay unemployment benefits.

workers' compensation insurance (333)   Insurance carried by employers for employees who suffer a work-related illness or injury.

SELF-STUDY TEST QUESTIONS

True/False

1. **LO1**   Employer payroll taxes are deducted from the employee's pay.

2. **LO1**   The payroll register is a key source of information for computing employer payroll taxes.

3. **LO1**   Self-employment income is the net income of a trade or business owned and run by an individual.

4. **LO1**   The FUTA tax is levied only on the employees.

5. **LO3**   The W-4, which shows total annual earnings and deductions for federal and state income taxes, must be completed by the employer and given to the employee by January 31.

Multiple Choice

1. **LO2**   The general ledger accounts commonly used to record the employer's Social Security, Medicare, FUTA, and SUTA taxes are classified as
   (a) assets.   (c) expenses.
   (b) liabilities.   (d) owner's equity.

2. **LO2**   Joyce Lee earns $30,000 a year. Her employer pays a matching Social Security tax of 6.2% on the first $128,400 in earnings, a Medicare tax of 1.45% on gross earnings, and a FUTA tax of 0.6% and a SUTA tax of 5.4%, both on the first $7,000 in earnings. What is the total cost of Joyce Lee to her employer?

   (a) $32,295   (c) $30,420
   (b) $30,000   (d) $32,715

3. **LO3**   The Form 941 tax deposit includes which of the following types of taxes withheld from the employee and paid by the employer?

   (a) Federal income tax and FUTA tax
   (b) Federal income tax and Social Security and Medicare taxes
   (c) Social Security and Medicare taxes and SUTA tax
   (d) FUTA tax and SUTA tax

4. **LO4**   Workers' compensation provides insurance for employees who

   (a) are unemployed due to a layoff.
   (b) are unemployed due to a plant closing.
   (c) are underemployed and need additional compensation.
   (d) suffer a work-related illness or injury.

5. **LO4**   The journal entry at the end of the year that recognizes an additional premium owed under workers' compensation insurance will include a

   (a) debit to Workers' Compensation Insurance Expense.
   (b) debit to Cash.
   (c) debit to Workers' Compensation Insurance Payable.
   (d) credit to Workers' Compensation Insurance Expense.

CHECKPOINT

Checkpoint Exercises

1. **LO1**   Total earnings for the employees of Gary's Grill for the week ended January 14, 20--, were $6,400. The following payroll taxes were levied on these earnings:

Social Security	6.2%
Medicare	1.45%
FUTA	0.6%
SUTA	5.4%

   Calculate Gary's payroll taxes expense for the week ended January 14, 20--.

2. **LO2**   Liu's Lounge had the following payroll taxes expense for the week ended February 10, 20--:

Social Security	$595.20
Medicare	139.20
FUTA	76.80
SUTA	518.40

   Prepare the journal entry for these payroll taxes.

3. **LO3**   ARC Co. owes the following amounts for payroll taxes and employees' withholding of Social Security, Medicare, and federal income tax as of April 15:

Social Security Tax Payable	$6,750.00
Medicare Tax Payable	1,575.00
FUTA Tax Payable	360.00
SUTA Tax Payable	2,646.00
Employee Federal Income Tax Payable	4,095.00

Prepare the journal entries for:

(a)   Deposit of the employees' federal income taxes and the Social Security and Medicare taxes on April 15.

(b)   Deposits of the FUTA and SUTA taxes on April 30.

4. **LO4**   LC Co. estimates that its total payroll for the year will be $260,000. LC's workers' compensation insurance premium rate is 0.22%. Calculate LC's estimated workers' compensation insurance premium and prepare the journal entry for the payment of this amount.

The answers to the Self-Study Test Questions are at the end of the chapter (pages 351–352).

APPLYING YOUR KNOWLEDGE

CengageNowv2 provides "Show Me How" videos for selected exercises and problems. Additional resources, such as Excel templates for completing selected exercises and problems, are available for download from the companion website at Cengage.com.

REVIEW QUESTIONS

LO1   1.   Why do employer payroll taxes represent an additional expense to the employer, whereas the various employee payroll taxes do not?

LO1   2.   At what rate and on what earnings base is the employer's Social Security tax levied?

LO1   3.   What is the purpose of the FUTA tax, and who must pay it?

LO1   4.   What is the purpose of the state unemployment tax, and who must pay it?

LO2   5.   What accounts are affected when employer payroll tax expenses are properly recorded?

LO2   6.   Identify all items that are debited or credited to Social Security Tax Payable and to Medicare Tax Payable.

LO2   7.   Explain why an employee whose gross salary is $20,000 costs an employer more than $20,000 to employ.

LO3   8.   What is the purpose of the EFTPS?

LO3   9.   What is the purpose of Form 941, Employer's Quarterly Federal Tax Return?

LO3   10. What is the purpose of Form 940, Employer's Annual Federal Unemployment Tax Return?

LO3   11. What information appears on Form W-2, the employee's Wage and Tax Statement?

LO3   12. What is the purpose of Form I-9, Employment Eligibility Verification?

LO4   13. What is the purpose of workers' compensation insurance, and who must pay for it?

SERIES A EXERCISES

E 9-1A   (LO1/2)
✓ SUTA tax: $567

CALCULATION AND JOURNAL ENTRY FOR EMPLOYER PAYROLL TAXES Portions of the payroll register for Barney's Bagels for the week ended July 15 are shown below. The SUTA tax rate is 5.4%, and the FUTA tax rate is 0.6%, both of which are levied on the first $7,000 of earnings. The Social Security tax rate is 6.2% on the first $128,400 of earnings. The Medicare rate is 1.45% on gross earnings.

Barney's Bagels
Payroll Register

Total Earnings	Total Taxable Earnings of All Employees	
	Unemployment Compensation	Social Security
$12,200	$10,500	$12,200

Calculate the employer's payroll taxes expense and prepare the journal entry to record the employer's payroll taxes expense for the week ended July 15 of the current year.

E 9-2A   (LO1/2)
✓ Medicare tax: $58

CALCULATION AND JOURNAL ENTRY FOR EMPLOYER PAYROLL TAXES Earnings for several employees for the week ended March 12, 20--, are as follows:

Employee Name	Current Earnings	Unemployment Compensation	Social Security
Aus, Glenn E.	$ 700	$200	$ 700
Diaz, Charles K.	350	350	350
Knapp, Carol S.	1,200	—	1,200
Mueller, Deborah F.	830	125	830
Yeager, Jackie R.	920	35	920

Calculate the employer's payroll taxes expense and prepare the journal entry as of March 12, 20--, assuming that FUTA tax is 0.6%, SUTA tax is 5.4%, Social Security tax is 6.2%, and Medicare tax is 1.45%.

E 9-3A   (LO1/2)
✓ Soc. Sec. tax: $672.70

CALCULATION OF TAXABLE EARNINGS AND EMPLOYER PAYROLL TAXES AND PREPARATION OF JOURNAL ENTRY Selected information from the payroll register of Joanie's Boutique for the week ended September 14, 20--, is as follows: Social Security tax is 6.2% on the first $128,400 of earnings for each employee. Medicare tax is 1.45% of gross earnings. FUTA tax is 0.6% and SUTA tax is 5.4% on the first $7,000 of earnings.

	Cumulative Pay Before Current Earnings	Current Gross Pay	Taxable Earnings	
Employee Name			Unemployment Compensation	Social Security
Jordahl, Stephanie	$ 6,600	$1,190		
Keesling, Emily	6,150	1,070		
Palmer, Stefan	55,200	2,410		
Soltis, Robin	54,300	2,280		
Stout, Hannah	29,050	2,030		
Xia, Xu	126,530	2,850		

Calculate the amount of taxable earnings for unemployment, Social Security, and Medicare taxes, and prepare the journal entry to record the employer's payroll taxes as of September 14, 20--.

E 9-4A   (LO1/2)
✓ Soc. Sec. Tax: $2,170

TOTAL COST OF EMPLOYEE Mandy Feng employs Jay Johnson at a salary of $35,000 a year. Feng is subject to employer Social Security taxes at a rate of 6.2% and Medicare taxes at a rate of 1.45% on Johnson's salary. In addition, Feng must pay SUTA tax at a rate of 5.4% and FUTA tax at a rate of 0.6% on the first $7,000 of Johnson's salary.

Compute the total cost to Feng of employing Johnson for the year.

E 9-5A   (LO3)
✓ 941 deposit: $19,735

JOURNAL ENTRIES FOR PAYMENT OF EMPLOYER PAYROLL TAXES Angel Ruiz owns a business called Ruiz Construction Co. He does his banking at Citizens National Bank in Portland, Oregon. The amounts in his general ledger for payroll taxes and the employees' withholding of Social Security, Medicare, and federal income tax payable as of April 15 of the current year are as follows:

Social Security tax payable (includes both employer and employee)	$11,250
Medicare tax payable (includes both employer and employee)	2,625
FUTA tax payable	600
SUTA tax payable	4,050
Employee income tax payable	5,860

Journalize the quarterly payment of the employee federal income taxes and Social Security and Medicare taxes on April 15, 20--, and the payments of the FUTA and SUTA taxes on April 30, 20--.

E 9-6A   (LO4)
✓ 2. Additional premium due: $12

WORKERS' COMPENSATION INSURANCE AND ADJUSTMENT Specialty Manufacturing estimated that its total payroll for the coming year would be $450,000. The workers' compensation insurance premium rate is 0.2%.

REQUIRED

1. Calculate the estimated workers' compensation insurance premium and prepare the journal entry for the payment as of January 2, 20--.

2. Assume that Specialty Manufacturing's actual payroll for the year is $456,000. Calculate the total insurance premium owed and prepare a journal entry as of December 31, 20--, to record the adjustment for the underpayment. The actual payment of the additional premium will take place in January of the next year.

SERIES A PROBLEMS

P 9-7A   (LO1/2)
✓ Soc. Sec. tax: $455.08

CALCULATING PAYROLL TAXES EXPENSE AND PREPARING JOURNAL ENTRY Selected information from the payroll register of Ebeling's Dairy for the week ended July 7, 20--, is shown below. The SUTA tax rate is 5.4%, and the FUTA tax rate is 0.6%, both on the first $7,000 of earnings. Social Security tax on the employer is 6.2% on the first $128,400 of earnings, and Medicare tax is 1.45% on gross earnings.

| | | | Taxable Earnings | |
| | Cumulative Pay Before Current | Current Weekly | Unemployment | Social |
Employee Name	Earnings	Earnings	Compensation	Security
Click, Katelyn	$ 6,650	$ 800		
Coombs, Michelle	6,370	720		
Fauss, Erin	33,460	1,200		
Lenihan, Marcus	6,930	900		
McMahon, Drew	127,050	4,440		
Newell, Marg	35,470	1,110		
Stevens, Matt	38,675	1,260		

REQUIRED

1. Calculate the total employer payroll taxes for these employees.

2. Prepare the journal entry to record the employer payroll taxes as of July 7, 20--.

P 9-8A   (LO2/3)
✓ Payroll taxes expense: $3,864

JOURNALIZING AND POSTING PAYROLL ENTRIES Cascade Company has four employees. All are paid on a monthly basis. The fiscal year of the business is June 1 to May 31.

The accounts kept by Cascade include the following:

Account Number	Title	Balance on June 1
101	Cash	$70,200
211	Employee Federal Income Tax Payable	3,553
212	Social Security Tax Payable	5,103
213	Medicare Tax Payable	1,197
218	Savings Bond Deductions Payable	1,225
221	FUTA Tax Payable	574
222	SUTA Tax Payable	2,835
511	Wages and Salaries Expense	0
530	Payroll Taxes Expense	0

The following transactions relating to payrolls and payroll taxes occurred during June and July:

June 15   Paid $9,853 covering the following May taxes:

Social Security tax	$5,103
Medicare tax	1,197
Employee federal income tax withheld	3,553
Total	$9,853

    30   June payroll:

Total wages and salaries expense		$42,000
Less amounts withheld:		
Social Security tax	$2,604	
Medicare tax	609	
Employee federal income tax	3,570	
Savings bond deductions	1,225	8,008
Net amount paid		$33,992

    30   Purchased savings bonds for employees, $2,450

    30   Employer payroll taxes expenses for June were:

Social Security	$2,604
Medicare	609
FUTA	84
SUTA	567
Total	$3,864

July 15   Paid $9,996 covering the following June taxes:

Social Security tax	$5,208
Medicare tax	1,218
Employee federal income tax withheld	3,570
Total	$9,996

    31   Paid SUTA tax for the quarter, $3,402

    31   Paid FUTA tax, $658

REQUIRED

1. Journalize the preceding transactions using a general journal.

2. Open T accounts for the payroll expenses and liabilities. Enter the beginning balances and post the transactions recorded in the journal.

P 9-9A   (LO4)
✓ 3. Refund due: $48

WORKERS' COMPENSATION INSURANCE AND ADJUSTMENT   Willamette Manufacturing estimated that its total payroll for the coming year would be $650,000. The workers' compensation insurance premium rate is 0.3%.

REQUIRED

1. Calculate the estimated workers' compensation insurance premium and prepare the journal entry for the payment as of January 2, 20--.

2. Assume that Willamette Manufacturing's actual payroll for the year was $672,000. Calculate the total insurance premium owed and prepare a journal entry as of December 31, 20--, to record the adjustment for the underpayment. The actual payment of the additional premium will take place in January of the next year.

3. Assume instead that Willamette Manufacturing's actual payroll for the year was $634,000. Prepare a journal entry as of December 31, 20--, for the total amount that should be refunded. The refund will not be received until the next year.

SERIES B EXERCISES

E 9-1B   (LO1/2)
✓ SUTA tax: $664.74

CALCULATION AND JOURNAL ENTRY FOR EMPLOYER PAYROLL TAXES Portions of the payroll register for Kathy's Cupcakes for the week ended June 21 are shown below. The SUTA tax rate is 5.4%, and the FUTA tax rate is 0.6%, both on the first $7,000 of earnings. The Social Security tax rate is 6.2% on the first $128,400 of earnings. The Medicare rate is 1.45% on gross earnings.

Kathy's Cupcakes
Payroll Register

| | Total Taxable Earnings of All Employees | |
Total Earnings	Unemployment Compensation	Social Security
$15,680	$12,310	$15,680

Calculate the employer's payroll taxes expense and prepare the journal entry to record the employer's payroll taxes expense for the week ended June 21 of the current year.

E 9-2B   (LO1/2)
✓ Medicare tax: $79.24

CALCULATION AND JOURNAL ENTRY FOR EMPLOYER PAYROLL TAXES Earnings for several employees for the week ended April 7, 20--, are as follows:

| | | Taxable Earnings | |
Employee Name	Current Earnings	Unemployment Compensation	Social Security
Boyd, Glenda L.	$ 850	$300	$ 850
Evans, Sheryl N.	970	225	970
Fox, Howard J.	830	830	830
Jacobs, Phyllis J.	1,825	—	1,825
Roh, William R.	990	25	990

Calculate the employer's payroll taxes expense and prepare the journal entry as of April 7, 20--, assuming that FUTA tax is 0.6%, SUTA tax is 5.4%, Social Security tax is 6.2%, and Medicare tax is 1.45%.

E 9-3B   (LO1/2)
✓ Soc. Sec. tax: $569.16

CALCULATION OF TAXABLE EARNINGS AND EMPLOYER PAYROLL TAXES, AND PREPARATION OF JOURNAL ENTRY Selected information from the payroll register of Howard's Cutlery for the week ended October 7, 20--, is presented below. Social Security tax is 6.2% on the first $128,400 of earnings for each employee. Medicare tax is 1.45% on gross earnings. FUTA tax is 0.6% and SUTA tax is 5.4% on the first $7,000 of earnings.

| | Cumulative Pay Before Current Earnings | Current Gross Pay | Taxable Earnings | |
Employee Name			Unemployment Compensation	Social Security
Carlson, David J.	$ 6,635	$ 950		
Delgado, Luisa	6,150	1,215		
Lewis, Arlene S.	54,375	2,415		
Nixon, Robert R.	53,870	1,750		
Shippe, Lance W.	24,830	1,450		
Watts, Brandon Q.	127,000	3,120		

Calculate the amount of taxable earnings for unemployment, Social Security, and Medicare taxes, and prepare the journal entry to record the employer's payroll taxes as of October 7, 20--.

E 9-4B   (LO1/2)
✓ Soc. Sec. tax: $2,852

TOTAL COST OF EMPLOYEE B. F. Goodson employs Eduardo Gonzales at a salary of $46,000 a year. Goodson is subject to employer Social Security taxes at a rate of 6.2% and Medicare taxes at a rate of 1.45% on Gonzales's salary. In addition, Goodson must pay SUTA tax at a rate of 5.4% and FUTA tax at a rate of 0.6% on the first $7,000 of Gonzales's salary.

Compute the total cost to Goodson of employing Gonzales for the year.

E 9-5B   (LO3)
✓ 941 deposit: $17,073

JOURNAL ENTRIES FOR PAYMENT OF EMPLOYER PAYROLL TAXES Francis Baker owns a business called Baker Construction Co. She does her banking at the American National Bank in Seattle, Washington. The amounts in her general ledger for payroll taxes and employees' withholding of Social Security, Medicare, and federal income tax payable as of July 15 of the current year are as follows:

Social Security tax payable (includes both employer and employee)	$9,563
Medicare tax payable (includes both employer and employee)	2,250
FUTA tax payable	504
SUTA tax payable	3,402
Employee federal income tax payable	5,260

Journalize the quarterly payment of the employee federal income taxes and Social Security and Medicare taxes on July 15, 20--, and the payments of the FUTA and SUTA taxes on July 31, 20--.

E 9-6B   (LO4)
✓ 2. Additional premium due: $22

WORKERS' COMPENSATION INSURANCE AND ADJUSTMENT Columbia Industries estimated that its total payroll for the coming year would be $385,000. The workers' compensation insurance premium rate is 0.2%.

REQUIRED

1. Calculate the estimated workers' compensation insurance premium and prepare the journal entry for the payment as of January 2, 20--.

2. Assume that Columbia Industries' actual payroll for the year is $396,000. Calculate the total insurance premium owed and prepare a journal entry as of December 31, 20--, to record the adjustment for the underpayment. The actual payment of the additional premium will take place in January of the next year.

SERIES B PROBLEMS

P 9-7B   (LO1/2)
✓ Soc. Sec. tax: $543.74

CALCULATING PAYROLL TAXES EXPENSE AND PREPARING JOURNAL ENTRY Selected information from the payroll register of Wray's Drug Store for the week ended July 14, 20--, is shown below. The SUTA tax rate is 5.4% and the FUTA tax rate is 0.6%, both on the first $7,000 of earnings. Social Security tax on the employer is 6.2% on the first $128,400 of earnings, and Medicare tax is 1.45% on gross earnings.

(*continued*)

| Employee Name | Cumulative Pay Before Current Earnings | Current Weekly Earnings | Taxable Earnings | |
			Unemployment Compensation	Social Security
Ackers, Alice	$ 6,460	$ 645		
Conley, Dorothy	27,560	1,025		
Davis, James	6,850	565		
Lawrence, Kevin	62,850	2,875		
Rawlings, Judy	26,350	985		
Tanaka, Sumio	22,320	835		
Vadillo, Raynette	126,560	3,540		

REQUIRED

1. Calculate the total employer payroll taxes for these employees.

2. Prepare the journal entry to record the employer payroll taxes as of July 14, 20--.

P 9-8B   (LO2/3)

✓ Payroll taxes expense: $2,105.33

JOURNALIZING AND POSTING PAYROLL ENTRIES Oxford Company has five employees. All are paid on a monthly basis. The fiscal year of the business is June 1 to May 31.

The accounts kept by Oxford Company include the following:

Account Number	Title	Balance on June 1
101	Cash	$69,500.00
211	Employee Federal Income Tax Payable	2,018.00
212	Social Security Tax Payable	2,735.00
213	Medicare Tax Payable	641.00
218	Savings Bond Deductions Payable	787.50
221	FUTA Tax Payable	540.00
222	SUTA Tax Payable	1,380.00
511	Wages and Salaries Expense	0.00
530	Payroll Taxes Expense	0.00

The following transactions relating to payrolls and payroll taxes occurred during June and July:

June 15   Paid $5,394.00 covering the following May taxes:

Social Security tax		$2,735.00
Medicare tax		641.00
Employee federal income tax withheld		2,018.00
Total		$5,394.00

30   June payroll:

Total wages and salaries expense		$22,050.00
Less amounts withheld:		
Social Security tax	$1,367.10	
Medicare tax	319.73	
Employee federal income tax	1,920.00	
Savings bond deductions	787.50	4,394.33
Net amount paid		$17,655.67

30   Purchased savings bonds for employees, $1,575.00

30	Employer payroll taxes expenses for June were:		
	Social Security	$1,367.10	
	Medicare	319.73	
	FUTA	54.00	
	SUTA	364.50	
	Total	$2,105.33	

July 15   Paid $5,293.66 covering the following June taxes:

Social Security tax	$2,734.20
Medicare tax	639.46
Employee federal income tax withheld	1,920.00
Total	$5,293.66

31   Paid SUTA tax for the quarter, $1,744.50

31   Paid FUTA tax, $594.00

REQUIRED

1. Journalize the preceding transactions using a general journal.

2. Open T accounts for the payroll expenses and liabilities. Enter the beginning balances and post the transactions recorded in the journal.

P 9-9B   (LO4)
✓ 3. Refund due: $16

WORKERS' COMPENSATION INSURANCE AND ADJUSTMENT   Multnomah Manufacturing estimated that its total payroll for the coming year would be $540,000. The workers' compensation insurance premium rate is 0.2%.

REQUIRED

1. Calculate the estimated workers' compensation insurance premium and prepare the journal entry for the payment as of January 2, 20--.

2. Assume that Multnomah Manufacturing's actual payroll for the year was $562,000. Calculate the total insurance premium owed and prepare a journal entry as of December 31, 20--, to record the adjustment for the underpayment. The actual payment of the additional premium will take place in January of the next year.

3. Assume instead that Multnomah Manufacturing's actual payroll for the year was $532,000. Prepare a journal entry as of December 31, 20--, for the total amount that should be refunded. The refund will not be received until the next year.

CHECK LIST
- [ ] **Managing**
- [ ] **Planning**
- [ ] **Drafting**
- [ ] **Break**
- [ ] **Revising**
- [ ] **Managing**

MANAGING YOUR WRITING

The director of the art department at an advertising company, Wilson Watson, wants to hire new office staff. His boss tells him that to do so he must find in his budget not only the base salary for this position but an additional 30% for "fringe benefits." Wilson explodes: "How in the world can there be 30% in fringe benefits?" Write a memo to Wilson Watson explaining the costs that probably make up these fringe benefits.

ETHICS

ETHICS CASE

Bob Estes works at Cliffrock Company in the central receiving department. He unpacks incoming shipments and verifies quantities of goods received. Over the weekend, Bob pulled a muscle in his back while playing basketball. When he came to work on Monday and started unpacking shipments, his back started to hurt again. Bob called the human resources department and told them he hurt his back lifting a package at work. He was told to fill out an accident report and sent to an orthopedic clinic with a workers' compensation form. The doctor at the clinic told Bob not to lift anything heavy for two weeks and to stay home from work for at least one week.

1. Is Bob entitled to workers' compensation? Why or why not?
2. What effect will Bob's claim have on Cliffrock Company's workers' compensation insurance premium?
3. Write a short memo from the human resources department to Cliffrock Company's employees explaining the purpose of workers' compensation.
4. In small groups, discuss the job-related illness or injury risks of a computer input operator and measures an employer might take to minimize these risks.

MASTERY PROBLEM

✓ Payroll taxes expense: $720.75

The totals line from Nix Company's payroll register for the week ended March 31, 20--, is as follows:

(left side)   PAYROLL REGISTER

| | NAME | EMPLOYEE NUMBER | ALLOWANCES | MARITAL STATUS | EARNINGS | | | CUMULATIVE TOTAL | TAXABLE EARNINGS | |
					REGULAR	OVERTIME	TOTAL		UNEMPLOYMENT COMPENSATION	SOCIAL SECURITY
21	Totals				5 4 0 0 00	1 0 0 00	5 5 0 0 00	71 5 0 0 00	5 0 0 0 00	5 5 0 0 00

—PERIOD ENDED March 31, 20--   (right side)

| | DEDUCTIONS | | | | | | NET PAY | CHECK NO. |
FEDERAL INCOME TAX	SOCIAL SECURITY TAX	MEDICARE TAX	HEALTH INSURANCE	LIFE INSURANCE	OTHER	TOTAL		
5 0 0 00	3 4 1 00	7 9 75	1 6 5 00	2 0 0 00		1 2 8 5 75	4 2 1 4 25	21

Payroll taxes are imposed as follows: Social Security tax, 6.2%; Medicare tax, 1.45%; FUTA tax, 0.6%; and SUTA tax, 5.4%.

REQUIRED

1. a. Prepare the journal entry for payment of this payroll on March 31, 20--.
   b. Prepare the journal entry for the employer's payroll taxes for the period ended March 31, 20--.
2. Nix Company had the following balances in its general ledger before the entries for requirement (1) were made:

Employee federal income tax payable	$2,500
Social Security tax payable	2,008
Medicare tax payable	470
FUTA tax payable	520
SUTA tax payable	4,510

a. Prepare the journal entry for payment of the liabilities for federal income taxes and Social Security and Medicare taxes on April 15, 20--.
b. Prepare the journal entry for payment of the liability for FUTA tax on April 30, 20--.
c. Prepare the journal entry for payment of the liability for SUTA tax on April 30, 20--.

3. Nix Company paid a premium of $420 for workers' compensation insurance based on the estimated payroll as of the beginning of the year. Based on actual payroll as of the end of the year, the premium is only $400. Prepare the adjusting entry to reflect the overpayment of the insurance premium at the end of the year (December 31, 20--).

CHALLENGE PROBLEM

This problem challenges you to apply your cumulative accounting knowledge to move a step beyond the material in the chapter.

✓ Payroll taxes expense: $1,281.25

Payrex Co. has six employees. All are paid on a weekly basis. For the payroll period ending January 7, total employee earnings were $12,500, all of which were subject to SUTA, FUTA, Social Security, and Medicare taxes. The SUTA tax rate in Payrex's state is 5.4%, but Payrex qualifies for a rate of 2.0% because of its good record of providing regular employment to its employees. Other employer payroll taxes are at the rates described in the chapter.

REQUIRED

1. Calculate Payrex's FUTA, SUTA, Social Security, and Medicare taxes for the week ended January 7.
2. Prepare the journal entry for Payrex's payroll taxes for the week ended January 7.
3. What amount of payroll taxes did Payrex save because of its good employment record?

ANSWERS TO SELF-STUDY TEST QUESTIONS

True/False

1. F (these taxes are paid by the employer)
2. T
3. T
4. F (FUTA tax is levied on employers)
5. F (this Form is W-2)

Multiple Choice

1. b   2. d   3. b   4. d   5. a

Checkpoint Exercises

1. Social Security $396.80
   Medicare   92.80
   FUTA   38.40
   SUTA   345.60
   Total $873.60

2. Payroll Taxes Expense   1,329.60

     Social Security Tax Payable   595.20

     Medicare Tax Payable   139.20

     FUTA Tax Payable   76.80

     SUTA Tax Payable   518.40

        Employer payroll taxes for week ended Feb. 10

3. (a) Social Security Tax Payable   6,750.00

       Medicare Tax Payable   1,575.00

       Employee Federal Income Tax Payable   4,095.00

       Cash   12,420.00

          Deposit of employee federal income tax
          and Social Security and Medicare taxes

  (b) FUTA Tax Payable

       Cash   360.00

         Paid FUTA tax   360.00

       SUTA Tax Payable

       Cash   2,646.00

         Paid SUTA tax   2,646.00

4. Workers' Compensation Insurance Expense

     Cash   572.00

       Paid insurance premium   572.00

3 Accounting for a Merchandising Business

Add some color to your learning!

Throughout the text, you will be introduced to many important terms and types of accounts. To help you learn the different terms and types of accounts, we have coded many of them using the following color key in Part 3:

Assets   Contra-Assets   Liabilities   Capital   Drawing   Revenues   Contra-Revenues   Expenses   Contra-Costs (Contra-Purchases)   Income Summary (Net Income/Net Loss)

SHOP ONLINE   EARTH BRANDS   ABOUT EARTH   SHOP LOCALLY

🔍 Search

SHOP ALL

You are viewing: Women ✕

1 2 3 4 5 6 ▶

Sort by

CATEGORY

Athleisure
Sandals
Casual Shoes
Flats
Boots
Heels
Negative Heel
Vegan
Wedges
Outlet
View All

BRANDS

Earth
Earth
Kalso
Earth

Chapter 10 Accounting for Sales and Cash Receipts

In recent years, we have seen increasing concern about how our actions affect the environment. Kalso Earth Shoes is an example of a company whose business reflects this concern. Kalso Earth Shoes is a storefront and online shoe retailer specializing in eco-friendly shoes. Its shoes use less-toxic, water-based rather than solvent- or oil-based, adhesives. All leathers are tanned using a vegetable-tanning process, which uses tannic acids found in plants. Even its shoe boxes are glue-free.

Kalso Earth Shoes began as one small store in Copenhagen, Denmark, in 1960. By the late 1960's, it expanded beyond Denmark, and to the United States in 1970. It surged in popularity, experiencing growth so strong that it was unable to keep up with demand. At one point, franchise owners sued the United States distributor for lack of product. Today Kalso Earth Shoes has operations in many countries, selling both from storefronts and online. The company has learned that it needs a good system to manage and account for its high volume of sales, including cash, on account, and by credit card. In this chapter, you will learn how to account for these different kinds of sales transactions.

LEARNING OBJECTIVES

Careful study of this chapter should enable you to:

LO1 Describe merchandise sales transactions.

LO2 Describe and use merchandise sales accounts.

LO3 Describe and use the accounts receivable ledger.

LO4 Prepare a schedule of accounts receivable.

Over the last nine chapters, we have learned how to account for a service business. We are now ready to consider accounting for a different kind of business—merchandising. A merchandising business purchases merchandise such as clothing, furniture, or computers, and sells that merchandise to customers. For example, some large shoe and department stores buy shoes from Kalso Earth Shoes and sell them to their customers.

This chapter examines how to account for the sale of merchandise using the accrual basis of accounting. We will learn how to use five new accounts and a subsidiary ledger.

LO1	Merchandise Sales Transactions

Describe merchandise sales transactions.

A company such as Kalso Earth Shoes makes some sales online. For Web-based transactions, companies use electronic forms that are similar to the paper documents described in this chapter.

A sale is a transfer of merchandise from one business or individual to another in exchange for cash or a promise to pay cash. Sales procedures and documents vary greatly, depending on the nature and size of the business.

Retailer

Retail businesses generally sell to customers who enter the store, select the merchandise they want, and bring it to a salesclerk. The salesclerk enters the sale in some type of electronic cash register that generates a receipt for the customer. A copy of the receipt is retained in the register. Most registers can print a summary of the day's sales activity, like the one in Figure 10-1. This summary can be sent to accounting and used to journalize sales in the accounting records.

FIGURE 10-1 Cash Register Tape Summary

```
              (1)
CASH SALES         327.79  *
              (3)
MCARD/VISA         550.62  *
              (6)
LAYAWAY             79.50  *
TOTAL CASH         957.91  *
              (2)
CHARGE SALES       543.84  *
              (5)
APPROVAL           126.58  *
TOTAL CHARGE       670.42  *

TOTAL SALES      1,628.33  G*
SALES TAX           81.42  *
                    81.42  *

REC'D ON ACCT.     324.51  *
                   324.51  *

PAID OUT            76.51  *
                    76.51  *

NO SALE              0.00  *
                     0.00  *

  *     SUB-TOTAL
  G*    GRAND TOTAL
```

An additional document often created as evidence of a sale in a retail business is a sales ticket (Figure 10-2). One copy of the sales ticket is given to the customer and the other copy is sent to accounting.

FIGURE 10-2 Sales Ticket

134C   *Sunflower* **CYCLE**   804 Massachusetts St.
Lawrence, KS 66044

Account No.	Sold By	Date
		4/10/--

Sold To Brenda Myers
Address 1613 Stone Meadows
City Lawrence   State KS   Zip 66049

Send To Same
Address
City   State   Zip

Rec'd on Acct. ☐   Charge Sale ☒   Sales Ret/Allow ☐

Quantity	Articles	Amount
1	Shimano #3438	$440.00
	Tax	22.00
		$462.00

Brenda Myers
Customers Signature

All Claims & Returned Goods MUST Be Accompanied By This Bill.

Wholesaler

Figure 10-3 shows how the wholesaler plays a different role than the retailer in the marketing chain. Retailers usually sell to final consumers, whereas wholesalers tend to sell to retailers. This causes the wholesale sales transaction process to differ, as shown in Figure 10-4.

FIGURE 10-3 Marketing Chain

Manufacturer → Wholesaler → Retailer → Consumer

> In a computerized system, customer orders can be submitted electronically. Even the credit approval can be processed electronically.

Customers commonly mail, fax, or send electronic orders to buy merchandise from wholesalers. When the customer purchase order arrives, the customer name and items being ordered are determined. Since wholesalers typically make sales on account, credit approval is needed. Three copies of a sales invoice are then generated.

FIGURE 10-4 **Wholesale Sales Transaction Process**

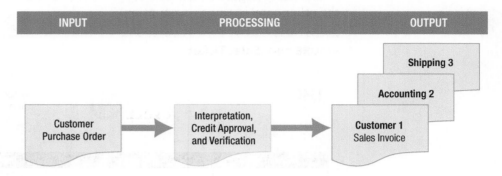

One is sent to the customer as a bill for the merchandise, one is sent to accounting to record the sale, and one is shipped with the merchandise. Figure 10-5 shows the customer copy of a sales invoice for Gragg's Paint Company.

FIGURE 10-5 **Sales Invoice**

Sales Invoice		No. 453

Gragg's Paint Co.
1520 Wakarusa Dr., Lawrence, KS 66047

CUSTOMER:	DATE:	
Picasso Painting	May 5, 20--	
1108 SW Chetopa Trl.	TERMS:	
Topeka, KS 66615	2/10, n/30	

QUANTITY	DESCRIPTION	UNIT PRICE	AMOUNT
6	Behr Gr Gloss-Gal	$30	$180.00
5	Behr W Flat-5 Gal	$80	$400.00
TOTAL			$580.00

Credit Memorandum

Both retailers and wholesalers sometimes have customers return goods or seek price reductions for damaged goods. Merchandise returned by a customer for a refund is called a sales return. Price reductions granted by the seller because of defects or other problems with the merchandise are called sales allowances. When credit is given for merchandise returned or for an allowance, a credit memo is issued for the amount involved. This document gets its name from the same debit and credit concepts you learned in Chapter 3. It is called a credit memo because the customer's account receivable is *credited* to reduce the amount the customer owes. One copy of the credit memo is given to the customer and one copy is sent to accounting. Figure 10-6 shows a credit memo issued by Sunflower Cycle for merchandise returned by a customer.

FIGURE 10-6 **Credit Memo**

| LO2 | **Merchandise Sales Accounts** |

Describe and use merchandise sales accounts.

To account for merchandise sales transactions, we will use five new accounts:

1. Sales
2. Sales Tax Payable
3. Sales Returns and Allowances
4. Customer Refunds Payable
5. Sales Discounts

The position of these accounts in the accounting equation and their normal balances are shown in Figure 10-7.

Sales Account

The sales account is a revenue account used to record sales of merchandise. The account is credited for the selling price of merchandise sold during the period.

Sales

Debit	Credit
	to enter the selling price of merchandise sold

FIGURE 10-7 Accounting for Merchandise Sales Transactions

If a $100 sale is made for cash, the following entry is made:

5	Cash	1	0	0	00					5
6	Sales					1	0	0	00	6
7	Made cash sale									7

If the same sale is made on account, the entry is as follows:

The customer's name is placed after Accounts Receivable

5	Accounts Receivable/Customer	1	0	0	00					5
6	Sales					1	0	0	00	6
7	Made credit sale									7

Accounts Receivable is followed by a slash (/) and the name of the specific customer who owes the money. Accounts Receivable is the same account we first saw in Chapter 2. It is a general ledger account. The "Customer" name is for the customer's account in the accounts receivable ledger. This ledger is explained later in this chapter.

Sales Tax Payable Account

Most states require retailers to collect sales tax on sales to final consumers. When sales tax is imposed on merchandise sold, a separate account for Sales Tax Payable is kept. This is a liability account that is credited for the taxes imposed on sales. The account is debited for sales taxes paid to the proper taxing authority or for sales taxes on merchandise returned by customers. A credit balance in the account indicates the amount owed to the taxing authority for taxes collected.

Sales Tax Payable

Debit	Credit
to enter payment of tax to taxing authority or adjustment of tax on merchandise returned by customers	to enter tax imposed on sales

If a cash sale for $100 plus 5% sales tax (5% × $100 = $5) occurs, the following entry is made:

10		Cash			1	0	5	00					10
11		Sales							1	0	0	00	11
12		Sales Tax Payable									5	00	12
13		Made cash sale											13

If the same sale is made on account, the entry is as follows:

10		Accounts Receivable/Customer			1	0	5	00					10
11		Sales							1	0	0	00	11
12		Sales Tax Payable									5	00	12
13		Made credit sale											13

The debit to Accounts Receivable indicates that the amount owed by customers to the business has increased. Since the buyer has accepted the merchandise and promised to pay for it, revenue is recognized by crediting Sales. Sales Tax Payable is credited because the amount of sales tax owed to the taxing authority has increased.

Sales Returns and Allowances Account

Sales Returns and Allowances is a contra-revenue account, which has a debit balance and is deducted from the related revenue account. Sales returns and sales allowances are debited to this account. As shown in Figure 10-8, this account is reported as a deduction from Sales on the income statement. Returns and allowances are debited to a separate account rather than directly to Sales so that the business can more readily keep track of this activity.

Sales Returns and Allowances

Debit	Credit
to enter returns and allowances	

Look at the credit memo in Figure 10-6 on page 359. The entry for the return of the riding helmet by Wilma Cutz would be as follows:

19		Sales Returns and Allowances			4	6	00						19
20		Sales Tax Payable			2	30							20
21		Accounts Receivable/Wilma Cutz							4	8	30		21
22		Returned merchandise—Credit Memo #72											22

FIGURE 10-8 Sales Returns and Allowances on the Income Statement

Sales	$38,500	
Less sales returns and allowances	200	
Net sales		$38,300

Note carefully the parts of this entry. Sales Returns and Allowances is debited for the amount of the sale, *excluding* the sales tax. Sales Tax Payable is debited separately for the sales tax on the original sale amount. Accounts Receivable is credited for the total amount originally billed to Cutz.

End-of-Period Adjustment

In addition to the sales returns and allowances that occurred during the current year, other returns and allowances will happen in the following year on sales that occurred in the current year. To account for these later returns and allowances in the correct time period, an adjusting entry is needed as follows:

23		Sales Returns and Allowances		x x x			23
24		Customer Refunds Payable			x x x		24
25		Estimated returns and allowances					25

> **LEARNING KEY** 🔑
>
> To record returns and allowances, debit Sales Returns and Allowances for the amount of the sale excluding the sales tax.

First, Sales Returns and Allowances is debited for the estimated amount of current year sales that will be returned in the following year. Then, Customer Refunds Payable is credited for the estimated amount of current year sales that will be refunded in the following year. Customer Refunds Payable is a current liability reported with liabilities on the balance sheet, as shown in Figure 10-9.

FIGURE 10-9 Customer Refunds Payable on the Balance Sheet

Current Liabilities	
Accounts payable	xxxx
Customer Refunds Payable	xxxx

Sales Discounts Account

> Another type of discount sometimes offered between businesses is a trade discount. This discount is explained in Chapter 11.

Some businesses offer cash discounts to encourage prompt payment by customers who buy merchandise on account. When credit is tight and businesses are short of cash, it is particularly important to convert accounts receivable into cash as soon as possible. Prompt collection of accounts receivable also reduces the risk that those receivables will become uncollectible. Some possible credit terms are shown in Figure 10-10.

FIGURE 10-10 Credit Terms

TERMS	MEANING
2/10, n/30*	2% discount off sales price if paid within 10 days Total amount due within 30 days
1/10, n/30	Same as 2/10, n/30, except 1% discount instead of 2%
2/eom, n/60	2% discount if paid before end of month Total amount due within 60 days
3/10 eom, n/60	3% discount if paid within 10 days after end of month Total amount due within 60 days

*See Figure 10-5. A discount of $11.60 (2% × $580) is allowed if this invoice is paid by May 15 (invoice date of May 5 + 10 days).

To the seller, cash discounts are considered sales discounts. Sales Discounts is a contra-revenue account to which cash discounts allowed are debited. Like Sales Returns and Allowances, this account is reported as a deduction from Sales on the income statement, as shown in Figure 10-11.

Sales Discounts

Debit	Credit
to enter cash discounts	

FIGURE 10-11 Sales Discounts on the Income Statement

Sales		$38,500
Less: Sales returns and allowances	$200	
Sales discounts	140	340
Net sales		$38,160

If merchandise is sold for $100 with credit terms of 2/10, n/30, and cash is received within the discount period, two entries are made.

At time of sale:

26		Accounts Receivable/Customer	1 0 0 00		26
27		Sales		1 0 0 00	27
28		Made sale on account			28

At time of collection:

30		Cash	9 8 00		30
31		Sales Discounts	2 00		31
32		Accounts Receivable/Customer		1 0 0 00	32
33		Received cash on account			33

Figure 10-12 shows how (1) a sale on account followed by (2) collection with a cash discount affects the accounts receivable, sales, cash, and sales discounts accounts.

FIGURE 10-12 Sales on Account → Collection with Cash Discount

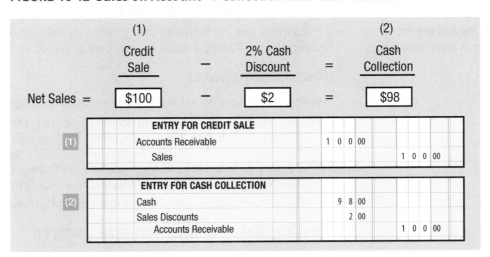

If any merchandise has been returned, the sales discount is calculated on the sale amount after deducting the return. For the above sale for $100, if $30 of merchandise is returned, the following entry is made:

5		Sales Returns and Allowances	3 0 00		5
6		Accounts Receivable		3 0 00	6
7		Returned merchandise			7

The discount on the remaining $70 collection then would be 2% × $70 = $1.40. The journal entry for the collection is:

9		Cash		6	8	60					9
10		Sales Discount			1	40					10
11		Accounts Receivable						7	0	00	11
12		Received cash on account									12

If there is a sales tax, the discount is calculated on the sale amount excluding the sales tax. Assume merchandise is sold for $100 plus 5% sales tax (5% × $100 = $5), with credit terms of 2/10, n/30. At the time of the sale, the following entry is made:

1		Accounts Receivable		1	0	5	00				1
2		Sales						1	0	0	00	2
3		Sales Tax Payable							5	00	3
4		Made sale on account									4

If cash is received within the discount period, the discount is 2% × $100 = $2, and the entry is:

6		Cash		1	0	3	00				6
7		Sales Discounts				2	00				7
8		Accounts Receivable						1	0	5	00	8
9		Received cash on account									9

Note that this entry does not affect Sales Tax Payable. The sales tax is based on the amount of the sale, which is not affected by the timing of the collection on account.

> **CHECKPOINT ✓**
>
> Complete Checkpoint-2 on page 383 to test your basic understanding of LO2.

LO3 Journalizing and Posting Sales and Cash Receipts Transactions

Describe and use the accounts receivable ledger.

To illustrate the journalizing and posting of sales and cash receipts transactions, we use Sunflower Cycle, a retail bicycle and accessories business.

Journalizing Sales

Assume the following sales transactions occurred during April 20--:

Apr. 4 Made Sale No. 133C on account to Enrico Lorenzo, $1,520 plus $76 sales tax.
　　10 Made Sale No. 134C on account to Brenda Myers, $440 plus $22 sales tax.
　　18 Made Sale No. 105D on account to Edith Walton, $980 plus $49 sales tax.
　　21 Made Sale No. 202B on account to Wilma Cutz, $620 plus $31 sales tax.
　　24 Made Sale No. 162A on account to Heidi Schwitzer, $1,600 plus $80 sales tax.

These transactions are entered in a general journal, as shown in Figure 10-13.

Posting Sales to the General Ledger

Sales transactions are posted from the general journal to the general ledger in the same manner as was illustrated in Chapter 4. Several steps are used, as indicated in Figure 10-14, for Sunflower Cycle's April 4 and 10 sales transactions.

In the general ledger account:

STEP 1 Enter the date of the transaction in the Date column.

STEP 2 Enter the amount of the debit or credit in the Debit or Credit column.

STEP 3 Enter the new balance in the Balance columns under Debit or Credit.

STEP 4 Enter the journal page number from which each transaction is posted in the Posting Reference column.

FIGURE 10-13 Sales Entered in General Journal

	Date		Account	Debit	Credit	
4	Apr.	4	Accounts Receivable/E. Lorenzo	1 5 9 6 00		4
5			Sales		1 5 2 0 00	5
6			Sales Tax Payable		7 6 00	6
7			Sale No. 133C			7
8						8
9		10	Accounts Receivable/B. Myers	4 6 2 00		9
10			Sales		4 4 0 00	10
11			Sales Tax Payable		2 2 00	11
12			Sale No. 134C			12
13						13
14		18	Accounts Receivable/E. Walton	1 0 2 9 00		14
15			Sales		9 8 0 00	15
16			Sales Tax Payable		4 9 00	16
17			Sale No. 105D			17
18						18
19		21	Accounts Receivable/W. Cutz	6 5 1 00		19
20			Sales		6 2 0 00	20
21			Sales Tax Payable		3 1 00	21
22			Sale No. 202B			22
23						23
24		24	Accounts Receivable/H. Schwitzer	1 6 8 0 00		24
25			Sales		1 6 0 0 00	25
26			Sales Tax Payable		8 0 00	26
27			Sale No. 162A			27

In the journal:

STEP 5 Enter the ledger account number in the Posting Reference column of the journal for each transaction that is posted.

Other sales transactions would be posted in the same manner.

Posting Sales to the Accounts Receivable Ledger

After all posting to the general ledger is completed, the accounts receivable, sales tax payable, and sales accounts in the general ledger are up to date. But at this point, Sunflower Cycle has no complete record of the account receivable from *individual customers*. To run the business properly, Sunflower Cycle needs this information.

A common approach to keeping a record of each customer's account receivable is to use an accounts receivable ledger. This is a separate ledger containing an individual account receivable for each customer. It is called a subsidiary ledger. A summary accounts receivable account called a controlling account is still maintained in the general ledger. The accounts receivable ledger is "subsidiary" to this account. If there are many customer accounts, it is good practice to assign each customer an account number. The subsidiary ledger accounts are kept in either alphabetical or numerical order, depending on whether customer accounts are identified by number. Figure 10-15 shows part of the accounts receivable ledger for Sunflower Cycle.

Figure 10-15 illustrates the use of the accounts receivable ledger for Sunflower Cycle's April 4 and 10 sales transactions. The accounts receivable ledger is posted from the journal *daily* so that current information is available for each customer at

FIGURE 10-14 Posting Sales to the General Ledger

GENERAL JOURNAL (Partial)				Page 8	
Date	Description	Post. Ref.	Debit	Credit	
20-- Apr. 4	Accounts Receivable/E. Lorenzo	122	1,596.00		
	Sales	401		1,520.00	
	Sales Tax Payable	231		76.00	
	Sale No.133C				
10	Accounts Receivable/B. Myers	122	462.00		
	Sales	401		440.00	
	Sales Tax Payable	231		22.00	
	Sale No.134C				

GENERAL LEDGER (Partial)

ACCOUNT Accounts Receivable   ACCOUNT NO.122

			Post.			Balance	
Date		Item	Ref.	Debit	Credit	Debit	Credit
20-- Apr.	1	Bal.	✓			12,000.00	
	4		J8	1,596.00		13,596.00	
	10		J8	462.00		14,058.00	

ACCOUNT Sales Tax Payable   ACCOUNT NO.231

			Post.			Balance	
Date		Item	Ref.	Debit	Credit	Debit	Credit
20-- Apr.	4		J8		76.00		76.00
	10		J8		22.00		98.00

ACCOUNT Sales   ACCOUNT NO. 401

			Post.			Balance	
Date		Item	Ref.	Debit	Credit	Debit	Credit
20-- Apr.	1	Bal.	✓				67,000.00
	4		J8		1,520.00		68,520.00
	10		J8		440.00		68,960.00

all times. Note that including the individual customer name after Accounts Receivable in each journal entry helps in the posting process. Several steps are used to post from the general journal to the accounts receivable ledger, as shown in Figure 10-15.

In the accounts receivable ledger account:

STEP 1 Enter the date of the transaction in the Date column.

STEP 2 Enter the amount of the debit or credit in the Debit or Credit column.

STEP 3 Enter the new balance in the Balance column.

STEP 4 Enter the journal page number from which each transaction is posted in the Posting Reference column.

In the journal:

STEP 5 Enter a slash (/) followed by a check mark (✓) in the Posting Reference column of the journal for each transaction that is posted.

FIGURE 10-15 Posting Sales to the Accounts Receivable Ledger

A three-column account form is commonly used for customer accounts. Only one balance column is needed because the normal balance is a debit. If a credit balance occurs, the amount may be bracketed.

The accounts receivable ledger also can be posted from the source document used to make the general journal entry. For example, Sales Ticket No. 134C (see Figure 10-2) could be used to post that sale to Brenda Myers' account in the accounts receivable ledger. In this case, 134C would be inserted in the Posting Reference column of her account. In addition, a slash and check mark would be entered in the Posting Reference column of the journal.

Note the relationship between the general journal, accounts receivable ledger, and general ledger. Entries in the general journal are posted to the general ledger and accounts receivable ledger. After the posting of the accounts receivable ledger and the general ledger is completed, the total of the accounts receivable ledger balances should equal the Accounts Receivable balance in the general ledger. Remember, the accounts receivable ledger is simply a detailed listing of the same information that is summarized in Accounts Receivable in the general ledger.

LEARNING KEY 🔑
The total of the accounts receivable ledger balances must equal the Accounts Receivable balance in the general ledger.

Sales Returns and Allowances

If a customer returns merchandise or is given an allowance for damaged merchandise, a general journal entry is required. On May 5, Wilma Cutz returned a riding helmet costing $46 plus $2.30 sales tax (Figure 10-6, page 359). Figure 10-16 shows the general journal entry, general ledger posting, and accounts receivable ledger posting for this transaction.

The general journal entry is made in the usual manner. The general ledger is posted using the same five steps as were illustrated for sales transactions in Figure 10-14. The accounts receivable ledger is posted using the five steps below, as illustrated in Figure 10-16.

In the accounts receivable ledger account:

STEP 1   Enter the date of the transaction in the Date column.

STEP 2   Enter the amount of the debit or credit in the Debit or Credit column.

STEP 3   Enter the new balance in the Balance column.

STEP 4   Enter the journal page number from which each transaction is posted in the Posting Reference column.

In the journal:

STEP 5   Enter a slash (/) followed by a check mark (✓) in the Posting Reference column of the journal for each transaction that is posted.

Cash Receipts

Like sales transactions, cash receipt transactions occur frequently in most businesses. Three common types of cash receipts from sales are collections on account, cash sales, and bank credit card sales.

Collections on Account

Sales on account lead to cash receipts, which are entered in the general journal. For example, assume that Sunflower Cycle receives cash from Enrico Lorenzo for Sale No. 133C on April 14. The transaction is recorded in the general journal as follows:

25	Apr.	14	Cash		1	5	9	6	00							25
26			Accounts Receivable/E. Lorenzo								1	5	9	6	00	26
27			Received cash on account													27

YOUR PERSPECTIVE

Financial Clerk

Financial clerks are found in many organizations including retail businesses, medical offices, banks, and government agencies. Some financial clerks, such as *billing* and *posting clerks*, prepare and send invoices to customers after reviewing documents such as purchase orders, sales tickets, and charge slips. These clerks also interact with customers to get or give account information. Some financial clerks specialize as *credit authorizers and checkers*, reviewing a business's or individual customer's credit history to aid in determining creditworthiness. Other types of financial clerks include *brokerage clerks, loan interviewers, new account clerks*, and *insurance claims and policy-processing clerks*.

FIGURE 10-16 Accounting for Sales Returns and Allowances

Cash Sales

Most businesses also regularly make cash sales. The following entry shows a cash sale of $500 plus sales tax of $25 (5% × $500) recorded in the general journal on May 5:

					Debit			Credit			
3	May	5	Cash		5	2	5	00			3
4			Sales						5 0 0 00		4
5			Sales Tax Payable						2 5 00		5
6			Made cash sale								6

Bank Credit Card Sales

An increasing amount of sales today are made using bank credit cards. In fact, consider Kalso Earth Shoes, the company in the chapter introduction. Many of its sales are online, so all of these sales would be by bank credit card. Most of Sunflower Cycle's sales also are by bank credit card. Bank credit card sales are similar to cash sales because the cash is available to the business as soon as an electronic deposit is made at the end of the day. The credit card company makes the electronic deposit to the merchandiser's bank account for the gross amount of credit card sales less a processing fee. The fee is based on the gross amount of the sale, including the sales tax. Thus, on a sale of $100 plus sales tax of $5, the credit card fee at 4% would be $4.20 (4% × $105). The following entry shows this credit card sale recorded on May 6:

8	May	6	Cash		1	0	0	80						8
9			Bank Credit Card Expense				4	20						9
10			Sales							1	0	0	00	10
11			Sales Tax Payable									5	00	11
12			Made credit card sale											12

A BROADER VIEW

Is This Sale for Real?

U.S. businesses lose billions of dollars annually because of credit card fraud and bad checks. To reduce credit card fraud, cashiers should do two things: (1) Watch the customer sign the credit card slip and match it to the signature on the card. (2) Obtain an approval code on all credit card transactions. To reduce bad check losses, cashiers should accept only a driver's license as identification. They should compare the picture with the customer, watch the check being signed, and match the check signature with that on the driver's license.

AASTOCK/SHUTTERSTOCK.COM

Journalizing Cash Receipts

To illustrate the journalizing and posting of cash receipts transactions, we continue to use Sunflower Cycle. Assume the following cash receipts transactions related to sales occurred during April 20--. (To simplify the illustration, cash sales and bank credit card sales for the month are summarized as single transactions at the end of the month.)

Apr. 14 Received cash on account from Enrico Lorenzo for Sale No. 133C, $1,596.

20 Received cash on account from Brenda Myers for Sale No. 134C, $462.

28 Received cash on account from Edith Walton for Sale No. 105D, $1,029.

30 Cash sales for the month are $3,600 plus tax of $180.

30 Bank credit card sales for the month are $22,500 plus tax of $1,125. Bank credit card expenses on these sales are $900.

These transactions are entered in a general journal as shown in Figure 10-17.

FIGURE 10-17 Cash Receipts Entered in General Journal

4	Apr.	14	Cash		1	5	9	6	00							4
5			Accounts Receivable/E. Lorenzo								1	5	9	6	00	5
6			Received cash on account													6
7																7
8		20	Cash			4	6	2	00							8
9			Accounts Receivable/B. Myers									4	6	2	00	9
10			Received cash on account													10
11																11
12		28	Cash		1	0	2	9	00							12
13			Accounts Receivable/E. Walton								1	0	2	9	00	13
14			Received cash on account													14
15																15
16		30	Cash		3	7	8	0	00							16
17			Sales								3	6	0	0	00	17
18			Sales Tax Payable									1	8	0	00	18
19			Made cash sales													19
20																20
21		30	Cash	22	7	2	5	00								21
22			Bank Credit Card Expense		9	0	0	00								22
23			Sales							22	5	0	0	0	00	23
24			Sales Tax Payable								1	1	2	5	00	24
25			Made credit card sales													25

Posting Cash Receipts to the General Ledger and Accounts Receivable Ledger

Cash receipts transactions are posted to the general ledger in the same manner as was illustrated for sales transactions in Figure 10-14. To post cash receipts to the accounts receivable ledger, the steps below are used, as illustrated in Figure 10-18 for Sunflower Cycle's April 14 and 20 cash receipts transactions.

In the accounts receivable ledger account:

STEP 1 Enter the date of the transaction in the Date column.

STEP 2 Enter the amount of the debit or credit in the Debit or Credit column.

STEP 3 Enter the new balance in the Balance column.

STEP 4 Enter the journal page number from which each transaction is posted in the Posting Reference column.

In the journal:

STEP 5 Enter a slash (/) followed by a check mark (✓) in the Posting Reference column of the journal for each transaction that is posted.

CHECKPOINT ✔

Complete Checkpoint-3 on page 383 to test your basic understanding of LO3.

FIGURE 10-18 Posting Cash Receipts to the General Ledger and Accounts Receivable Ledger

---

Schedule of Accounts Receivable

Prepare a schedule of accounts receivable.

At the end of the month, all postings to Accounts Receivable in the general ledger and to the accounts receivable ledger should be complete, as shown in Figure 10-19. At this point, the Accounts Receivable balance in the general ledger should equal the sum of the customer balances in the accounts receivable ledger.

To verify that the sum of the accounts receivable ledger balances equals the Accounts Receivable balance, a schedule of accounts receivable is prepared. This is an alphabetical or numerical listing of customer accounts and balances, usually prepared at the end of the month. Note that customers whose account balance is zero are not included. The schedule of accounts receivable for Sunflower Cycle as of April 30 is illustrated in Figure 10-20.

This schedule is prepared from the list of customer accounts in the accounts receivable ledger. The total calculated in the schedule is compared with the balance in Accounts Receivable in the general ledger. Note that the $14,331 total listed in the schedule equals the Accounts Receivable balance shown in Figure 10-19. If the schedule total and the Accounts Receivable balance do not agree, the error must be located and corrected. To find the error, use the following procedures:

STEP 1 Verify the total of the schedule.

STEP 2 Verify the postings to the accounts receivable ledger.

STEP 3 Verify the postings to Accounts Receivable in the general ledger.

FIGURE 10-19 General Ledger and Accounts Receivable Ledger after Posting

ACCOUNTS RECEIVABLE LEDGER

NAME   Helen Avery
ADDRESS   308 Devon Ave, Overbrook, KS 66524

Date	Item	Post. Ref.	Debit	Credit	Balance
20-- Apr. 1	Bal.	✓			2,302.00

NAME   Wilma Cutz
ADDRESS   1116 Williamsburg Place, Lawrence, KS 66049

Date	Item	Post. Ref.	Debit	Credit	Balance
20-- Apr. 21		J9	651.00		651.00

NAME   Enrico Lorenzo
ADDRESS   1827 N. 100 Rd., Baldwin City, KS 66006

Date	Item	Post. Ref.	Debit	Credit	Balance
20-- Apr. 4		J8	1,596.00		1,596.00
14		J8		1,596.00	0

NAME   Brenda Myers
ADDRESS   1613 Stone Meadows, Lawrence, KS 66049

Date	Item	Post. Ref.	Debit	Credit	Balance
20-- Apr. 10		J8	462.00		462.00
20		J8		462.00	0

NAME   Heidi Schwitzer
ADDRESS   13913 Nicklaus Dr., Overland Park, KS 66223

Date	Item	Post. Ref.	Debit	Credit	Balance
20-- Apr. 1	Bal.	✓			1,883.00
24		J9	1,680.00		3,563.00

ACCOUNTS RECEIVABLE LEDGER (Continued)

NAME   Ken Ulmet
ADDRESS   2616 Sawgrass Dr., Lawrence, KS 66047

Date	Item	Post. Ref.	Debit	Credit	Balance
20-- Apr. 1	Bal.	✓			3,315.00

NAME   Edith Walton
ADDRESS   1418 N. 600 Rd., Baldwin, KS 66006

Date	Item	Post. Ref.	Debit	Credit	Balance
20-- Apr. 18		J8	1,029.00		1,029.00
28		J9		1,029.00	0

NAME   Vivian Winston
ADDRESS   1613 Alvamar Dr., Lawrence, KS 66047

Date	Item	Post. Ref.	Debit	Credit	Balance
20-- Apr. 1	Bal.	✓			4,500.00

GENERAL LEDGER (Partial)

ACCOUNT   Accounts Receivable   ACCOUNT NO. 122

Date	Item	Post. Ref.	Debit	Credit	Balance Debit	Balance Credit
20-- Apr. 1	Bal.	✓			12,000.00	
4		J8	1,596.00		13,596.00	
10		J8	462.00		14,058.00	
14		J8		1,596.00	12,462.00	
18		J8	1,029.00		13,491.00	
20		J8		462.00	13,029.00	
21		J9	651.00		13,680.00	
24		J9	1,680.00		15,360.00	
28		J9		1,029.00	14,331.00	

FIGURE 10-20 Schedule of Accounts Receivable

Sunflower Cycle
Schedule of Accounts Receivable
April 30, 20--

Helen Avery	$ 2,302.00
Wilma Cutz	651.00
Heidi Schwitzer	3,563.00
Ken Ulmet	3,315.00
Vivian Winston	4,500.00
Total	$14,331.00

CHECKPOINT ✓

Complete Checkpoint-4 on pages 383–384 to test your basic understanding of LO4.

SELF-STUDY

LEARNING OBJECTIVES	Key Points to Remember
LO1 **Describe merchandise sales transactions.**	A merchandising business buys and sells merchandise. Retailers generally make sales in the store. Important accounting documents are cash register tapes and sales tickets. Wholesalers generally ship merchandise to retailers. A key accounting document is the sales invoice. When customers return merchandise or obtain price adjustments, a credit memo is issued.
LO2 **Describe and use merchandise sales accounts.**	Five accounts are used in accounting for merchandise sales transactions. 1. Sales 2. Sales Tax Payable 3. Sales Returns and Allowances 4. Customer Refunds Payable 5. Sales Discounts
LO3 **Describe and use the accounts receivable ledger.**	To post sales transactions to the general ledger, use these five steps. **In the general ledger account:** **STEP 1** Enter the date of the transaction in the Date column. **STEP 2** Enter the amount of the debit or credit in the Debit or Credit column. **STEP 3** Enter the new balance in the Balance columns under Debit or Credit. **STEP 4** Enter the journal page number from which each transaction is posted in the Posting Reference column. **In the journal:** **STEP 5** Enter the ledger account number in the Posting Reference column of the journal for each transaction that is posted. An accounts receivable ledger is a separate ledger containing an individual account receivable for each customer. To post sales transactions to the accounts receivable ledger, use these five steps. **In the accounts receivable ledger account:** **STEP 1** Enter the date of the transaction in the Date column. **STEP 2** Enter the amount of the debit or credit in the Debit or Credit column. **STEP 3** Enter the new balance in the Balance column. **STEP 4** Enter the journal page number from which each transaction is posted in the Posting Reference column. **In the journal:** **STEP 5** Enter a slash (/) followed by a check mark (✓) in the Posting Reference column of the journal for each transaction that is posted. To post cash receipts transactions to the general ledger, use these five steps. **In the general ledger account:** **STEP 1** Enter the date of the transaction in the Date column. **STEP 2** Enter the amount of the debit or credit in the Debit or Credit column.

LEARNING OBJECTIVES	**Key Points to Remember**
LO3 (concluded)	**STEP 3** Enter the new balance in the Balance columns under Debit or Credit.
	STEP 4 Enter the journal page number from which each transaction is posted in the Posting Reference column.
	In the journal:
	STEP 5 Enter the ledger account number in the Posting Reference column of the journal for each transaction that is posted.
	To post cash receipts transactions to the accounts receivable ledger, use these five steps.
	In the accounts receivable ledger account:
	STEP 1 Enter the date of the transaction in the Date column.
	STEP 2 Enter the amount of the debit or credit in the Debit or Credit column.
	STEP 3 Enter the new balance in the Balance column.
	STEP 4 Enter the journal page number from which each transaction is posted in the Posting Reference column.
	In the journal:
	STEP 5 Enter a slash (/) followed by a check mark (✓) in the Posting Reference column of the journal for each transaction that is posted.
LO4 **Prepare a schedule of accounts receivable.**	The schedule of accounts receivable is used to verify that the sum of the accounts receivable ledger balances equals the Accounts Receivable balance.

DEMONSTRATION PROBLEM

Karen Hunt operates Hunt's Audio-Video Store. The books include a general journal, general ledger, and accounts receivable ledger. The following transactions related to sales on account and cash receipts occurred during April 20--:

Apr. 3 Sold merchandise on account to Susan Haberman, $159.50 plus tax of $11.17. Sale No. 41.

4 Sold merchandise on account to Goro Kimura, $299.95 plus tax of $21. Sale No. 42.

6 Received payment from Tera Scherrer on account, $69.50.

7 Issued Credit Memo No. 48 to Kenneth Watt for merchandise returned that had been sold on account, $42.75 including tax of $2.80.

10 Received payment from Kellie Cokley on account, $99.95.

11 Sold merchandise on account to Victor Cardona, $499.95 plus tax of $35. Sale No. 43.

14 Received payment from Kenneth Watt in full settlement of account, $157.

17 Sold merchandise on account to Susan Haberman, $379.95 plus tax of $26.60. Sale No. 44.

(continued)

Apr. 19   Sold merchandise on account to Tera Scherrer, $59.95 plus tax of $4.20. Sale No. 45.

21   Issued Credit Memo No. 49 to Goro Kimura for merchandise returned that had been sold on account, $53.45 including tax of $3.50.

24   Received payment from Victor Cardona on account, $299.95.

25   Sold merchandise on account to Kellie Cokley, $179.50 plus tax of $12.57. Sale No. 46.

26   Received payment from Susan Haberman on account, $250.65.

28   Sold merchandise on account to Kenneth Watt, $49.95 plus tax of $3.50. Sale No. 47.

30   Bank credit card sales for the month were $1,220 plus tax of $85.40. Bank credit card expense on these sales was $65.27.

30   Cash sales for the month were $2,000 plus tax of $140.

Hunt had the following general ledger account balances as of April 1:

Account Title	Account No.	General Ledger Balance on April 1
Cash	101	$5,000.00
Accounts Receivable	122	1,208.63
Sales Tax Payable	231	72.52
Sales	401	8,421.49
Sales Returns and Allowances	401.1	168.43
Bank Credit Card Expense	513	215.00

Hunt also had the following accounts receivable ledger account balances as of April 1:

Customer	Accounts Receivable Balance
Victor Cardona 6300 Washington Blvd. St. Louis, MO 63130-9523	$299.95
Kellie Cokley 4220 Kingsbury Blvd. St. Louis, MO 63130-1645	$99.95
Susan Haberman 9421 Garden Ct. Kirkwood, MO 63122-1878	$79.98
Goro Kimura 6612 Arundel Pl. Clayton, MO 63150-9266	$379.50
Tera Scherrer 315 W. Linden St. Webster Groves, MO 63119-9881	$149.50
Kenneth Watt 11742 Fawnridge Dr. St. Louis, MO 63131-1726	$199.75

REQUIRED

1. Open general ledger accounts and three-column accounts receivable ledger accounts for Hunt's Audio-Video Store as of April 1, 20--. Enter the April 1 balance in each of the accounts.

2. Enter each transaction in a general journal (beginning on page 7).

3. Post directly from the journal to the proper customers' accounts in the accounts receivable ledger. Each subsidiary ledger account should show the initial "J," followed by the appropriate journal page number as a posting reference for each transaction.

4. Post from the journal to the proper general ledger accounts. Each general ledger account should show the initial "J," followed by the appropriate journal page number as a posting reference for each transaction.

5. Prove the balance of the summary accounts receivable account by preparing a schedule of accounts receivable as of April 30, based on the accounts receivable ledger.

SOLUTION 1. and 3.

ACCOUNTS RECEIVABLE LEDGER

NAME: Victor Cardona

DATE		ITEM	POST. REF.	DEBIT	CREDIT	BALANCE
20-- Apr.	1	Balance	✓			2 9 9 95
	11		J7	5 3 4 95		8 3 4 90
	24		J8		2 9 9 95	5 3 4 95

NAME: Kellie Cokley

DATE		ITEM	POST. REF.	DEBIT	CREDIT	BALANCE
20-- Apr.	1	Balance	✓			9 9 95
	10		J7		9 9 95	—
	25		J8	1 9 2 07		1 9 2 07

NAME: Susan Haberman

DATE		ITEM	POST. REF.	DEBIT	CREDIT	BALANCE
20-- Apr.	1	Balance	✓			7 9 98
	3		J7	1 7 0 67		2 5 0 65
	17		J7	4 0 6 55		6 5 7 20
	26		J8		2 5 0 65	4 0 6 55

NAME: Goro Kimura

DATE		ITEM	POST REF.	DEBIT	CREDIT	BALANCE
20-- Apr.	1	Balance	✓			3 7 9 50
	4		J7	3 2 0 95		7 0 0 45
	21		J8		5 3 45	6 4 7 00

(continued)

NAME: Tera Scherrer						
DATE	ITEM	POST. REF.	DEBIT	CREDIT	BALANCE	
20-- Apr. 1	Balance	✓			1 4 9 50	
6		J7		6 9 50	8 0 00	
19		J8	6 4 15		1 4 4 15	

NAME: Kenneth Watt						
DATE	ITEM	POST. REF.	DEBIT	CREDIT	BALANCE	
20-- Apr. 1	Balance	✓			1 9 9 75	
7		J7		4 2 75	1 5 7 00	
14		J7	1 5 7 00		—	
28		J8	5 3 45		5 3 45	

SOLUTION 2., 3., and 4.

		GENERAL JOURNAL				PAGE 7	
	DATE	DESCRIPTION	POST. REF.	DEBIT	CREDIT		
1	20-- Apr. 3	Accounts Receivable/Susan Haberman	122/✓	1 7 0 67			1
2		Sales	401		1 5 9 50		2
3		Sales Tax Payable	231		1 1 17		3
4		Sale No. 41					4
5							5
6	4	Accounts Receivable/Goro Kimura	122/✓	3 2 0 95			6
7		Sales	401		2 9 9 95		7
8		Sales Tax Payable	231		2 1 00		8
9		Sale No. 42					9
10							10
11	6	Cash	101	6 9 50			11
12		Accounts Receivable/Tera Scherrer	122/✓		6 9 50		12
13		Received cash on account					13
14							14
15	7	Sales Returns and Allowances	401.1	3 9 95			15
16		Sales Tax Payable	231	2 80			16
17		Accounts Receivable/Kenneth Watt	122/✓		4 2 75		17
18		Returned merchandise					18
19							19
20	10	Cash	101	9 9 95			20
21		Accounts Receivable/Kellie Cokley	122/✓		9 9 95		21
22		Received cash on account					22
23							23
24	11	Accounts Receivable/Victor Cardona	122/✓	5 3 4 95			24
25		Sales	401		4 9 9 95		25
26		Sales Tax Payable	231		3 5 00		26
27		Sale No. 43					27
28							28
29	14	Cash	101	1 5 7 00			29
30		Accounts Receivable/Kenneth Watt	122/✓		1 5 7 00		30
31		Received cash on account					31
32							32
33	17	Accounts Receivable/Susan Haberman	122/✓	4 0 6 55			33
34		Sales	401		3 7 9 95		34
35		Sales Tax Payable	231		2 6 60		35
36		Sale No. 44					36

SOLUTION 2., 3., and 4.

	DATE		DESCRIPTION	POST. REF.	DEBIT	CREDIT	
1	20-- Apr.	19	Accounts Receivable/Tera Scherrer	122/✔	6 4 15		1
2			Sales	401		5 9 95	2
3			Sales Tax Payable	231		4 20	3
4			Sale No. 45				4
5							5
6		21	Sales Returns and Allowances	401.1	4 9 95		6
7			Sales Tax Payable	231	3 50		7
8			Accounts Receivable/Goro Kimura	122/✔		5 3 45	8
9			Returned merchandise—Credit Memo #49				9
10							10
11		24	Cash	101	2 9 9 95		11
12			Accounts Receivable/Victor Cardona	122/✔		2 9 9 95	12
13			Received cash on account				13
14							14
15		25	Accounts Receivable/Kellie Cokley	122/✔	1 9 2 07		15
16			Sales	401		1 7 9 50	16
17			Sales Tax Payable	231		1 2 57	17
18			Sale No. 46				18
19							19
20		26	Cash	101	2 5 0 65		20
21			Accounts Receivable/Susan Haberman	122/✔		2 5 0 65	21
22			Received cash on account				22
23							23
24		28	Accounts Receivable/Kenneth Watt	122/✔	5 3 45		24
25			Sales	401		4 9 95	25
26			Sales Tax Payable	231		3 50	26
27			Sale No. 47				27
28							28
29		30	Cash	101	1 2 4 0 13		29
30			Bank Credit Card Expense	513	6 5 27		30
31			Sales	401		1 2 2 0 00	31
32			Sales Tax Payable	231		8 5 40	32
33			Credit card sales				33
34							34
35		30	Cash	101	2 1 4 0 00		35
36			Sales	401		2 0 0 0 00	36
37			Sales Tax Payable	231		1 4 0 00	37
38			Made cash sales				38

GENERAL JOURNAL — PAGE 8

SOLUTION 1. and 4.

GENERAL LEDGER (PARTIAL)

ACCOUNT: Cash   ACCOUNT NO. 101

DATE		ITEM	POST. REF.	DEBIT	CREDIT	BALANCE DEBIT	BALANCE CREDIT
20-- Apr.	1	Balance	✔			5 0 0 0 00	
	6		J7	6 9 50		5 0 6 9 50	
	10		J7	9 9 95		5 1 6 9 45	
	14		J7	1 5 7 00		5 3 2 6 45	
	24		J8	2 9 9 95		5 6 2 6 40	
	26		J8	2 5 0 65		5 8 7 7 05	
	30		J8	1 2 4 0 13		7 1 1 7 18	
	30		J8	2 1 4 0 00		9 2 5 7 18	

(*continued*)

SOLUTION 1. and 4.

ACCOUNT: Accounts Receivable   ACCOUNT NO. 122

DATE		ITEM	POST. REF.	DEBIT	CREDIT	BALANCE DEBIT	BALANCE CREDIT
20-- Apr.	1	Balance	✓			1 2 0 8 63	
	3		J7	1 7 0 67		1 3 7 9 30	
	4		J7	3 2 0 95		1 7 0 0 25	
	6		J7		6 9 50	1 6 3 0 75	
	7		J7		4 2 75	1 5 8 8 00	
	10		J7		9 9 95	1 4 8 8 05	
	11		J7	5 3 4 95		2 0 2 3 00	
	14		J7		1 5 7 00	1 8 6 6 00	
	17		J7	4 0 6 55		2 2 7 2 55	
	19		J8	6 4 15		2 3 3 6 70	
	21		J8		5 3 45	2 2 8 3 25	
	24		J8		2 9 9 95	1 9 8 3 30	
	25		J8	1 9 2 07		2 1 7 5 37	
	26		J8		2 5 0 65	1 9 2 4 72	
	28		J8	5 3 45		1 9 7 8 17	

ACCOUNT: Sales Tax Payable   ACCOUNT NO. 231

DATE		ITEM	POST. REF.	DEBIT	CREDIT	BALANCE DEBIT	BALANCE CREDIT
20-- Apr.	1	Balance	✓				7 2 52
	3		J7		1 1 17		8 3 69
	4		J7		2 1 00		1 0 4 69
	7		J7	2 80			1 0 1 89
	11		J7		3 5 00		1 3 6 89
	17		J7		2 6 60		1 6 3 49
	19		J8		4 20		1 6 7 69
	21		J8	3 50			1 6 4 19
	25		J8		1 2 57		1 7 6 76
	28		J8		3 50		1 8 0 26
	30		J8		8 5 40		2 6 5 66
	30		J8		1 4 0 00		4 0 5 66

ACCOUNT: Sales   ACCOUNT NO. 401

DATE		ITEM	POST. REF.	DEBIT	CREDIT	BALANCE DEBIT	BALANCE CREDIT
20-- Apr.	1	Balance	✓				8 4 2 1 49
	3		J7		1 5 9 50		8 5 8 0 99
	4		J7		2 9 9 95		8 8 8 0 94
	11		J7		4 9 9 95		9 3 8 0 89
	17		J7		3 7 9 95		9 7 6 0 84
	19		J8		5 9 95		9 8 2 0 79
	25		J8		1 7 9 50		10 0 0 0 29
	28		J8		4 9 95		10 0 5 0 24
	30		J8	1 2 2 0 00			11 2 7 0 24
	30		J8	2 0 0 0 00			13 2 7 0 24

SOLUTION 1. and 4.

ACCOUNT: Sales Returns and Allowances										ACCOUNT NO. 401.1	
DATE	ITEM	POST. REF.	DEBIT		CREDIT		BALANCE				
							DEBIT			CREDIT	
20-- Apr. 1	Balance	✓					1 6 8	43			
7		J7	3 9	95			2 0 8	38			
21		J8	4 9	95			2 5 8	33			

ACCOUNT: Bank Credit Card Expense										ACCOUNT NO. 513	
DATE	ITEM	POST. REF.	DEBIT		CREDIT		BALANCE				
							DEBIT			CREDIT	
20-- Apr. 1	Balance	✓					2 1 5	00			
30		J8	6 5	27			2 8 0	27			

SOLUTION 5.

Hunt's Audio-Video Store Schedule of Accounts Receivable April 30, 20--				
Victor Cardona	5	3	4	95
Kellie Cokley	1	9	2	07
Susan Haberman	4	0	6	55
Goro Kimura	6	4	7	00
Tera Scherrer	1	4	4	15
Kenneth Watt		5	3	45
Total	1 9	7	8	17

KEY TERMS

accounts receivable ledger (365)   A separate ledger containing an individual account receivable for each customer, kept in either alphabetical or numerical order.

cash discounts (362)   Discounts to encourage prompt payment by customers who buy merchandise on account.

contra-revenue account (361)   An account with a debit balance that is deducted from the related revenue account.

controlling account (365)   A summary account maintained in the general ledger with a subsidiary ledger (for example, the accounts receivable ledger).

credit memo (358)   A document issued when credit is given for merchandise returned or for an allowance.

merchandising business (356)   A business that purchases merchandise such as clothing, furniture, or computers, and sells that merchandise to its customers.

sale (356)   A transfer of merchandise from one business or individual to another in exchange for cash or a promise to pay cash.

sales allowances (358)   Reductions in the price of merchandise granted by the seller because of defects or other problems with the merchandise.

sales discounts (362)   To the seller, cash discounts are considered sales discounts.

sales invoice (357)   A document that is generated to bill the customer to whom the sale was made.

sales return (358)   Merchandise returned by a customer for a refund.

sales ticket (357)   A document created as evidence of a sale in a retail business.

schedule of accounts receivable (372)   An alphabetical or numerical listing of customer accounts and balances, usually prepared at the end of the month.

subsidiary ledger (365)   A separate ledger made up of individual accounts that contain the detail for a controlling account.

SELF-STUDY TEST QUESTIONS

True/False

1. **LO1**   Reductions in the price of merchandise granted by the seller because of defects or other problems with the merchandise are called sales allowances.

2. **LO2**   All sales, for cash or on credit, can be recorded in the general journal.

3. **LO2**   Sales Tax Payable is a liability account that is credited for the amount of tax imposed on sales.

4. **LO2**   Sales Returns and Allowances is debited for the amount of the sale, including the sales tax on that amount.

5. **LO2**   Cash discounts are offered to encourage prompt payment by customers who buy on account.

Multiple Choice

1. **LO2**   A credit sale of $250 plus a 6% sales tax would require a debit to Accounts Receivable of
   (a) $15.   (c) $30.
   (b) $280.   (d) $265.

2. **LO2**   When $25 of merchandise is returned for a credit on account, what is the amount of the credit to Accounts Receivable, assuming a 6% sales tax rate?
   (a) $1.50   (c) $26.50
   (b) $25.00   (d) $31.00

3. **LO3**   When $300 plus sales tax of 6% is received for an amount previously owed, Cash is debited for what amount?
   (a) $18   (c) $300
   (b) $318   (d) $282

4. **LO3**   When credit sales are $325 plus sales tax of 5%, and there is a bank credit card fee of 3%, what is the debit to Bank Credit Card Expense?
   (a) $16.25   (c) $341.25
   (b) $10.24   (d) $331.01

5. **LO3**   Cash receipts should
   (a) be posted to customer accounts daily.
   (b) be posted to customer accounts weekly.
   (c) be posted to customer accounts at the end of the month.
   (d) not be posted.

CHECKPOINT ✔

Checkpoint Exercises

1. **LO1** The sales transaction process for a wholesale business is shown below.

INPUT	PROCESSING	OUTPUT

Customer Purchase Order

Complete the illustration by providing the missing information in the blank symbols.

2. **LO2** Prepare journal entries for the following sales and cash receipts transactions.

   (a) Merchandise is sold on account for $300 plus 3% sales tax, with 2/10, n/30 cash discount terms.

   (b) Part of the merchandise sold in transaction (a) for $70 plus sales tax is returned for credit.

   (c) The balance on account for the merchandise sold in transaction (a) is paid in cash within the discount period.

3. **LO3** The following journal entries are for current sales and cash receipts transactions. Using T accounts, post these transactions to Cash, Accounts Receivable, Sales, Sales Returns and Allowances, and Sales Tax Payable in the general ledger, and to the customer account in the accounts receivable ledger.

(a)													
		Accounts Receivable/M. Schapiro			2	8	8	40					
		Sales							2	8	0	00	
		Sales Tax Payable									8	40	
		Made sale on account											

(b)													
		Sales Returns and Allowances				6	0	00					
		Sales Tax Payable					1	80					
		Accounts Receivable/M. Shapiro								6	1	80	
		Returned merchandise											

(c)													
		Cash			2	2	6	60					
		Accounts Receivable/M. Shapiro							2	2	6	60	
		Received on account											

4. **LO4** On March 24, MS Company's Accounts Receivable consisted of the following customer balances:

S. Burton	$310
A. Tangier	240
J. Holmes	504
F. Fullman	110
P. Molty	90

(*continued*)

During the following week, MS made a sale of $104 to Molty and collected cash on account of $207 from Burton and $360 from Holmes. Prepare a schedule of accounts receivable for MS at March 31, 20--.

The answers to the Self-Study Test Questions are at the end of the chapter (pages 397–398).

APPLYING YOUR KNOWLEDGE

REVIEW QUESTIONS

LO1   1. Identify the sales documents commonly used in retail and wholesale businesses.

LO1   2. What is the purpose of a credit memo?

LO2   3. Describe how each of the following accounts is used: (1) Sales, (2) Sales Tax Payable, (3) Sales Returns and Allowances, (4) Customer Refunds Payable, and (5) Sales Discounts.

LO3   4. What steps are followed in posting sales from the general journal to the general ledger?

LO3   5. What steps are followed in posting sales from the general journal to the accounts receivable ledger?

LO3   6. What steps are followed in posting sales returns and allowances from the general journal to the general ledger and accounts receivable ledger?

LO3   7. What steps are followed in posting cash receipts from the general journal to the general ledger?

LO3   8. What steps are followed in posting cash receipts from the general journal to the accounts receivable ledger?

LO4   9. If the total of the schedule of accounts receivable does not agree with the Accounts Receivable balance, what procedures should be used to search for the error?

SERIES A EXERCISES

E 10-1A   (LO1)   SALES DOCUMENTS For each document or procedure listed below, indicate whether it would be used for a retail business or a wholesale business, as described in the chapter.

1. sales ticket
2. sales invoice
3. credit approval
4. cash register tape summary
5. credit memo
6. customer purchase order

E 10-2A   (LO2)

✓ 3(d):

Sales Ret. & Allow.	25	
Accts. Rec.		25

SALES TRANSACTIONS AND T ACCOUNTS Using T accounts for Cash, Accounts Receivable, Sales Tax Payable, Sales, Sales Returns and Allowances, and Sales Discounts, enter the following sales transactions. Use a new set of accounts for each part, 1–5.

1. No sales tax.
   (a) Merchandise is sold for $320 cash.
   (b) Merchandise is sold on account for $385.
   (c) Payment is received for merchandise sold on account.
2. 5% sales tax.
   (a) Merchandise is sold for $320 cash plus sales tax.
   (b) Merchandise is sold on account for $385 plus sales tax.
   (c) Payment is received for merchandise sold on account.
3. Cash and credit sales, with returned merchandise.
   (a) Merchandise is sold for $340 cash.
   (b) $30 of merchandise sold for $340 is returned for refund.
   (c) Merchandise is sold on account for $280.
   (d) $25 of merchandise sold for $280 is returned for a credit.
   (e) Payment is received for balance owed on merchandise sold on account.
4. 5% sales tax, with returned merchandise.
   (a) Merchandise is sold on account for $400 plus sales tax.
   (b) Merchandise sold on account for $60 plus sales tax is returned for a credit.
   (c) Balance on account is received in cash.
   (d) Merchandise is sold for $260 cash plus sales tax.
   (e) $40 of merchandise sold for $260 cash plus sales tax is returned for a refund.
5. Sales on account, with 2/10, n/30 cash discount terms.
   (a) Merchandise is sold on account for $450.
   (b) The balance is paid within the discount period.
   (c) Merchandise is sold on account for $280.
   (d) The balance is paid after the discount period.

E 10-3A   (LO2)

✓ Net sales: $3,370

COMPUTING NET SALES Based on the following information, compute net sales.

Gross sales	$3,860
Sales returns and allowances	410
Sales discounts	80

E 10-4A   (LO2)

SALES RETURNS AND ALLOWANCES ADJUSTMENT At the end of year 1, JC's estimates that $2,000 of the current year's sales will be returned in year 2. Prepare the adjusting entry at the end of year 1 to record the estimated sales returns and allowances and customer refunds payable for this $2,000. Use accounts as illustrated in the chapter.

E 10-5A   (LO2)

✓ Aug 20:

Cash	176.80	
Accts Rec/K. Krtek		176.80

JOURNALIZING SALES, SALES RETURNS AND ALLOWANCES, AND CASH RECEIPTS Prepare journal entries for the following transactions.

Aug.   4   Sold merchandise on account to S. Miller for $320 plus sales tax of 4%, with 2/10, n/30 cash discount terms.

6   Sold merchandise on account to K. Krtek for $210 plus sales tax of 4%.

10   S. Miller returned merchandise purchased on August 4 for $20 plus sales tax for credit.

(continued)

Aug. 13   S. Miller paid the balance due on her account.

15   K. Krtek returned merchandise purchased on August 6 for $40 plus sales tax for credit.

20   K. Krtek paid the balance due on his account.

E 10-6A   (LO3)

✓ May 1:

A/R–J. Adams	2,120	
Sales		2,000
Sales Tax Payable		120

JOURNALIZING SALES TRANSACTIONS Enter the following transactions in a general journal. Use a 6% sales tax rate.

May   1   Sold merchandise on account to J. Adams, $2,000 plus sales tax. Sale No. 488.

4   Sold merchandise on account to B. Clark, $1,800 plus sales tax. Sale No. 489.

8   Sold merchandise on account to A. Duck, $1,500 plus sales tax. Sale No. 490.

11   Sold merchandise on account to E. Hill, $1,950 plus sales tax. Sale No. 491.

E 10-7A   (LO3)

✓ Ending Accts. Rec. balance: $4,059

JOURNALIZING SALES RETURNS AND ALLOWANCES Enter the following transactions starting on page 60 of a general journal and post them to the appropriate general ledger and accounts receivable ledger accounts. Use account numbers as shown in the chapter. Beginning balance in Accounts Receivable is $4,200. Beginning balances in selected customer accounts are Abramowitz, $850; Gruder, $428; and Perez, $1,018.

June   1   John B. Abramowitz returned merchandise previously purchased on account (Sale No. 329), $73.

6   Marie L. Perez returned merchandise previously purchased on account (Sale No. 321), $44.

8   L. B. Gruder returned merchandise previously purchased on account (Sale No. 299), $24.

E 10-8A   (LO3)

✓ July 6:

| Cash | 643 | |
| A/R–J. Adler | | 643 |

JOURNALIZING CASH RECEIPTS Enter the following transactions in a general journal:

July   6   James Adler made payment on account, $643.

10   Cash sales for the week were $2,320.

14   Betty Havel made payment on account, $430.

15   J. L. Borg made payment on account, $117.

17   Cash sales for the week were $2,237.

E 10-9A   (LO4)

✓ Accts. Rec. balance: $4,586

SCHEDULE OF ACCOUNTS RECEIVABLE From the accounts receivable ledger shown, prepare a schedule of accounts receivable for Pheng Co. as of August 31, 20--.

ACCOUNTS RECEIVABLE LEDGER															
NAME	B & G Distributors														
ADDRESS	2628 Burlington Avenue, Chicago, IL 60604-1329														
DATE		ITEM	POST. REF.	DEBIT					CREDIT				BALANCE		
20-- Aug.	3		J1	1	3	8	0	00					1	3	8	0	00
	8		J1						1	4	0	00	1	2	4	0	00

NAME	M. Chang					
ADDRESS	1422 SW Pacific, Chicago, IL 60603-8596					
DATE	ITEM	POST. REF.	DEBIT	CREDIT	BALANCE	
20-- Aug. 5		J1	2 1 3 6 00		2 1 3 6 00	
11		J2		2 1 3 6 00		

NAME	B. J. Hinschliff & Co.					
ADDRESS	133 College Blvd., Des Plaines, IL 60611-4431					
DATE	ITEM	POST. REF.	DEBIT	CREDIT	BALANCE	
20-- Aug. 15		J2	1 1 0 6 00		1 1 0 6 00	
21		J3	3 8 4 00		1 4 9 0 00	

NAME	Sally M. Pitts					
ADDRESS	213 East 29th Place, Chicago, IL 60601-6287					
DATE	ITEM	POST. REF.	DEBIT	CREDIT	BALANCE	
20-- Aug. 21		J3	8 3 8 00		8 3 8 00	

NAME	Trendsetters, Inc.					
ADDRESS	29 Industrial Way, Chicago, IL 60600-5918					
DATE	ITEM	POST. REF.	DEBIT	CREDIT	BALANCE	
20-- Aug. 28		J4	1 0 1 8 00		1 0 1 8 00	

SERIES A PROBLEMS

P 10-10A   **(LO2/3)**
✓ Accts. Rec. balance: $16,345.20

SALES TRANSACTIONS J. K. Bijan owns a retail business and made the following sales on account during the month of August 20--. There is a 6% sales tax on all sales.

Aug. 1   Sale No. 213 to Jung Manufacturing Co., $1,200 plus sales tax.

3   Sale No. 214 to Hassad Co., $3,600 plus sales tax.

7   Sale No. 215 to Helsinki, Inc., $1,400 plus sales tax. (Open a new account for this customer. Address is 125 Fishers Dr., Noblesville, IN 47870-8867.)

11   Sale No. 216 to Ardis Myler, $1,280 plus sales tax.

18   Sale No. 217 to Hassad Co., $4,330 plus sales tax.

22   Sale No. 218 to Jung Manufacturing Co., $2,000 plus sales tax.

30   Sale No. 219 to Ardis Myler, $1,610 plus sales tax.

REQUIRED

1. Record the transactions starting on page 15 of a general journal.

2. Post from the journal to the general ledger and accounts receivable ledger accounts. Use account numbers as shown in the chapter.

P 10-11A   (LO2/3)
✓ Accts. Rec. balance: $3,533.08

CASH RECEIPTS TRANSACTIONS Zebra Imaginarium, a retail business, had the following cash receipts during December 20--. The sales tax is 6%.

Dec.   1   Received payment on account from Michael Anderson, $1,360.

2   Received payment on account from Ansel Manufacturing, $382.

7   Cash sales for the week were $3,160 plus tax. Bank credit card sales for the week were $1,000 plus tax. Bank credit card fee is 3%.

8   Received payment on account from J. Gorbea, $880.

11   Michael Anderson returned merchandise for a credit, $60 plus tax.

14   Cash sales for the week were $2,800 plus tax. Bank credit card sales for the week were $800 plus tax. Bank credit card fee is 3%.

20   Received payment on account from Tom Wilson, $1,110.

21   Ansel Manufacturing returned merchandise for a credit, $22 plus tax.

21   Cash sales for the week were $3,200 plus tax.

24   Received payment on account from Rachel Carson, $2,000.

Beginning general ledger account balances were:

Cash	$9,862
Accounts Receivable	9,352

Beginning customer account balances were:

M. Anderson	$2,480
Ansel Manufacturing	982
J. Gorbea	880
R. Carson	3,200
T. Wilson	1,810

REQUIRED

1. Record the transactions starting on page 20 of a general journal.

2. Post from the journal to the general ledger and accounts receivable ledger accounts. Use account numbers as shown in the chapter.

P 10-12A   (LO2/3)
✓ Accts. Rec. balance: $8,208.80

SALES AND CASH RECEIPTS TRANSACTIONS Sourk Distributors is a retail business. The following sales, returns, and cash receipts occurred during March 20--. There is an 8% sales tax. Beginning general ledger account balances were Cash, $9,586; and Accounts Receivable, $1,016. Beginning customer account balances included Whitaker Group, $1,016.

Mar.   1   Sale on account No. 33C to Donachie & Co., $1,700 plus sales tax.

3   Sale on account No. 33D to R. J. Kibubu, Inc., $2,190 plus sales tax.

5   Donachie & Co. returned merchandise from Sale No. 33C for a credit (Credit Memo No. 66), $40 plus sales tax.

7   Cash sales for the week were $3,140 plus sales tax.

10   Received payment from Donachie & Co. for Sale No. 33C less Credit Memo No. 66.

11   Sale on account No. 33E to Eck Bakery, $1,230 plus sales tax.

13   Received payment from R. J. Kibubu for Sale No. 33D.

14   Cash sales for the week were $4,100 plus sales tax.

Mar. 16   Eck Bakery returned merchandise from Sale No. 33E for a credit (Credit Memo No. 67), $34 plus sales tax.

18   Sale on account No. 33F to R. J. Kibubu, Inc., $2,580 plus sales tax.

20   Received payment from Eck Bakery for Sale No. 33E less Credit Memo No. 67.

21   Cash sales for the week were $2,510 plus sales tax.

25   Sale on account No. 33G to Eck Bakery, $2,010 plus sales tax.

27   Sale on account No. 33H to Whitaker Group, $2,070 plus sales tax.

28   Cash sales for the week were $3,420 plus sales tax.

REQUIRED

1. Record the transactions starting on page 7 of a general journal.
2. Post from the journal to the general ledger and accounts receivable ledger accounts. Use account numbers as shown in the chapter.

P 10-13A (LO4)
✓ Accts. Rec. balance, Whitaker Group:
$3,251.60

SCHEDULE OF ACCOUNTS RECEIVABLE Based on the information provided in Problem 10-12A, prepare a schedule of accounts receivable for Sourk Distributors as of March 31, 20--. Verify that the accounts receivable account balance in the general ledger agrees with the schedule of accounts receivable total.

SERIES B EXERCISES

E 10-1B (LO1)

SALES DOCUMENTS Indicate whether each of the following documents or procedures is for a retail business or for a wholesale business, as described in the chapter.

1. A cash register receipt is given to the customer.
2. Credit approval is required since sales are almost always "on account."
3. Three copies of the sales invoice are prepared: one for shipping, one for the customer (as a bill), and one for accounting.
4. A sales ticket is given to a customer and another copy is sent to accounting.
5. The sales process begins with a customer purchase order.
6. The sales invoice itemizes what is sold, its cost, and the total amount owed.

E 10-2B (LO2)
✓ 3(d):
Sales Ret. & Allow.   24
   Accts. Rec.   24

SALES TRANSACTIONS AND T ACCOUNTS Using T accounts for Cash, Accounts Receivable, Sales Tax Payable, Sales, Sales Returns and Allowances, and Sales Discounts, enter the following sales transactions. Use a new set of accounts for each part, 1–5.

1. No sales tax.
   (a) Merchandise is sold for $250 cash.
   (b) Merchandise is sold on account for $225.
   (c) Payment is received for merchandise sold on account.
2. 6% sales tax.
   (a) Merchandise is sold for $250 cash plus sales tax.
   (b) Merchandise is sold on account for $225 plus sales tax.
   (c) Payment is received for merchandise sold on account.

(continued)

3. Cash and credit sales, with returned merchandise.
   (a) Merchandise is sold for $481 cash.
   (b) $18 of merchandise sold for $481 is returned for a refund.
   (c) Merchandise is sold on account for $388.
   (d) $24 of merchandise sold for $388 is returned for a credit.
   (e) Payment is received for balance owed on merchandise sold on account.

4. 6% sales tax, with returned merchandise.
   (a) Merchandise is sold on account for $480 plus sales tax.
   (b) Merchandise sold on account for $30 plus sales tax is returned.
   (c) The balance on the account is received in cash.
   (d) Merchandise is sold for $300 cash plus sales tax.
   (e) $30 of merchandise sold for $300 cash plus sales tax is returned for a refund.

5. Sales on account, with 2/10, n/30 cash discount terms.
   (a) Merchandise is sold on account for $280.
   (b) The balance is paid within the discount period.
   (c) Merchandise is sold on account for $203.
   (d) The balance is paid after the discount period.

E 10-3B   (LO2)
✓ Net sales: $2,502

COMPUTING NET SALES Based on the following information, compute net sales:

Gross sales	$2,880
Sales returns and allowances	322
Sales discounts	56

E 10-4B   (LO2)

SALES RETURNS AND ALLOWANCES ADJUSTMENT At the end of year 1, MC's estimates that $2,400 of the current year's sales will be returned in year 2. Prepare the adjusting entry at the end of year 1 to record the estimated sales returns and allowances and customer refunds payable for this $2,400. Use accounts as illustrated in the chapter.

E 10-5B   (LO2)
✓ Oct. 20:

Cash	228.80	
Accts Rec/B. Farnsby		228.80

JOURNALIZING SALES, SALES RETURNS AND ALLOWANCES, AND CASH RECEIPTS Prepare journal entries for the following transactions.

Oct. 5 Sold merchandise on account to B. Farnsby for $280 plus sales tax of 4%.
      8 Sold merchandise on account to F. Preetee for $240 plus sales tax of 4%, with 2/10, n/30 cash discount terms.
     11 F. Preetee returned merchandise purchased on October 8 for $50 plus sales tax for credit.
     17 F. Preetee paid the balance due on her account.
     18 B. Farnsby returned merchandise purchased on October 5 for $60 plus sales tax for credit.
     20 B. Farnsby paid the balance due on his account.

E 10-6B   (LO3)
✓ Sept. 1:

A/R–K. Smith	1,890	
Sales		1800
Sales Tax Payable		90

JOURNALIZING SALES TRANSACTIONS Enter the following transactions in a general journal. Use a 5% sales tax rate.

Sept. 1 Sold merchandise on account to K. Smith, $1,800 plus sales tax. Sale No. 228.
       3 Sold merchandise on account to J. Arnes, $3,100 plus sales tax. Sale No. 229.
       5 Sold merchandise on account to M. Denison, $2,800 plus sales tax. Sale No. 230.
       7 Sold merchandise on account to B. Marshall, $1,900 plus sales tax. Sale No. 231.

E 10-7B (LO3)

✓ Ending Accts. Rec. balance: $3,777

JOURNALIZING SALES RETURNS AND ALLOWANCES Enter the following transactions starting on page 60 of a general journal and post them to the appropriate general ledger and accounts receivable ledger accounts. Use account numbers as shown in the chapter. Beginning balance in Accounts Receivable is $3,900. Beginning balances in selected customer accounts are Adams, $850; Greene, $428; and Phillips, $1,018.

June 1 Marie L. Phillips returned merchandise previously purchased on account (Sale No. 33), $43.

11 John B. Adams returned merchandise previously purchased on account (Sale No. 34), $59.

15 L. B. Greene returned merchandise previously purchased on account (Sale No. 35), $21.

E 10-8B (LO3)

✓ Nov. 1:

Cash 750
　A/R–J. Haghighat 750

JOURNALIZING CASH RECEIPTS Enter the following transactions in a general journal:

Nov. 1 Jean Haghighat made payment on account, $750.

12 Marc Antonoff made payment on account, $464.

15 Cash sales were $3,763.

18 Will Mossein made payment on account, $241.

25 Cash sales were $2,648.

E 10-9B (LO4)

✓ Accts. Rec. balance: $6,402

SCHEDULE OF ACCOUNTS RECEIVABLE From the accounts receivable ledger shown, prepare a schedule of accounts receivable for Gelph Co. as of November 30, 20--.

ACCOUNTS RECEIVABLE LEDGER						
NAME	James L. Adams Co.					
ADDRESS	24481 McAdams Road, Dallas, TX 77001-3465					
DATE	ITEM	POST. REF.	DEBIT	CREDIT	BALANCE	
20-- Nov. 1		J1	3 1 8 0 00		3 1 8 0 00	
5		J1		1 8 0 00	3 0 0 0 00	
7		J2	2 0 0 00		3 2 0 0 00	

NAME	Trish Berens					
ADDRESS	34 West 55th Avenue, Fort Worth, TX 76310-8182					
DATE	ITEM	POST. REF.	DEBIT	CREDIT	BALANCE	
20-- Nov. 3		J1	1 3 6 0 00		1 3 6 0 00	

NAME	M and T Jenkins, Inc.					
ADDRESS	100 NW Richfield, Austin, TX 78481-3791					
DATE	ITEM	POST. REF.	DEBIT	CREDIT	BALANCE	
20-- Nov. 5		J1	2 6 2 8 00		2 6 2 8 00	
12		J2		2 6 2 8 00		

(continued)

NAME	R & J Travis																					
ADDRESS	288 Beacon Street, Dallas, TX 79301-6642																					
DATE	ITEM	POST. REF.		DEBIT						CREDIT						BALANCE						
20-- Nov. 22		J3	1	8	4	2	00							1	8	4	2	00				

SERIES B PROBLEMS

P 10-10B (LO2/3)

✓ Accts. Rec. balance: $13,072.50

SALES TRANSACTIONS T. M. Maxwell owns a retail business and made the following sales on account during the month of July 20--. There is a 5% sales tax on all sales.

July 1 Sale No. 101 to Saga, Inc., $1,200 plus sales tax.

8 Sale No. 102 to Vinnie Ward, $2,100 plus sales tax.

15 Sale No. 103 to Dvorak Manufacturing, $4,300 plus sales tax.

21 Sale No. 104 to Vinnie Ward, $1,800 plus sales tax.

24 Sale No. 105 to Zapata Co., $1,600 plus sales tax. (Open a new account for this customer. Address is 789 N. Stafford Dr., Bloomington, IN 47401-6201.)

29 Sale No. 106 to Saga, Inc., $1,450 plus sales tax.

REQUIRED

1. Record the transactions starting on page 15 of a general journal.
2. Post from the journal to the general ledger and accounts receivable ledger accounts. Use account numbers as shown in the chapter.

P 10-11B (LO2/3)

✓ Accts. Rec. balance: $2,744.45

CASH RECEIPTS TRANSACTIONS Color Florists, a retail business, had the following cash receipts during January 20--. The sales tax is 5%.

Jan. 1 Received payment on account from Ray Boyd, $880.

3 Received payment on account from Clint Hassell, $271.

5 Cash sales for the week were $2,800 plus tax. Bank credit card sales for the week were $1,200 plus tax. Bank credit card fee is 3%.

8 Received payment on account from Jan Sowada, $912.

11 Ray Boyd returned merchandise for a credit, $40 plus tax.

12 Cash sales for the week were $3,100 plus tax. Bank credit card sales for the week were $1,900 plus tax. Bank credit card fee is 3%.

15 Received payment on account from Robert Zehnle, $1,100.

18 Robert Zehnle returned merchandise for a credit, $31 plus tax.

19 Cash sales for the week were $2,230 plus tax.

25 Received payment on account from Dazai Manufacturing, $318.

Beginning general ledger account balances were:

Cash $2,890.75

Accounts Receivable 6,300.00

Beginning customer account balances were:

R. Boyd	$1,400
Dazai Manufacturing	318
C. Hassell	815
J. Sowada	1,481
R. Zehnle	2,286

REQUIRED

1. Record the transactions starting on page 20 of a general journal.
2. Post from the journal to the general ledger and accounts receivable ledger accounts. Use account numbers as shown in the chapter.

P 10-12B   (LO2/3)
✓ Accts. Rec. balance: $6,104.25

SALES AND CASH RECEIPTS TRANSACTIONS Paul Jackson owns a retail business. The following sales, returns, and cash receipts are for April 20--. There is a 7% sales tax.

Apr.	1	Sale on account No. 111 to O. L. Meyers, $2,100 plus sales tax.
	3	Sale on account No. 112 to Andrew Plaa, $1,000 plus sales tax.
	6	O. L. Meyers returned merchandise from Sale No. 111 for a credit (Credit Memo No. 42), $50 plus sales tax.
	7	Cash sales for the week were $3,240 plus sales tax.
	9	Received payment from O. L. Meyers for Sale No. 111 less Credit Memo No. 42.
	12	Sale on account No. 113 to Melissa Richfield, $980 plus sales tax.
	14	Cash sales for the week were $2,180 plus sales tax.
	17	Melissa Richfield returned merchandise from Sale No. 113 for a credit (Credit Memo No. 43), $40 plus sales tax.
	19	Sale on account No. 114 to Kelsay Munkres, $1,020 plus sales tax.
	21	Cash sales for the week were $2,600 plus sales tax.
	24	Sale on account No. 115 to O. L. Meyers, $920 plus sales tax.
	27	Sale on account No. 116 to Andrew Plaa, $1,320 plus sales tax.
	28	Cash sales for the week were $2,800 plus sales tax.
	29	Received payment from Melissa Richfield for $2,186.

Beginning general ledger account balances were:

Cash	$2,864.54
Accounts Receivable	2,726.25

Beginning customer account balances were:

K. Munkres	$ 482.00
M. Richfield	2,244.25

REQUIRED

1. Record the transactions starting on page 7 of a general journal.
2. Post from the journal to the general ledger and accounts receivable ledger accounts. Use account numbers as shown in the chapter.

P 10-13B   (LO4)
✓ Accts. Rec. balance,
  Melissa Richfield: $1,064.05

SCHEDULE OF ACCOUNTS RECEIVABLE   Based on the information provided in Problem 10-12B, prepare a schedule of accounts receivable for Paul Jackson as of April 30, 20--. Verify that the accounts receivable account balance in the general ledger agrees with the schedule of accounts receivable total.

CHECK LIST
- ☐ Managing
- ☐ Planning
- ☐ Drafting
- ☐ Break
- ☐ Revising
- ☐ Managing

MANAGING YOUR WRITING

You and your spouse have separate charge accounts at a local department store. When you tried to use your card last week, you were told that you were over your credit limit. This puzzled you because you had paid the entire account balance several weeks ago. When the monthly statements arrived yesterday, the error was clear. The store had credited your payment to your spouse's account.

Your account was treated as over the limit, and the store charged you interest on the unpaid balance. You suspect that part of the problem is that you and your spouse use the same last name (Morales) and have similar first names (Carmen and Carmelo).

Write a letter to the store requesting correction of your accounts and suggesting a way to identify your accounts so that this error does not happen again.

ETHICS

ETHICS CASE

Wholesale Health Supply sells a variety of medical equipment and supplies to retailers. When a new retailer is approved for credit, one of the criteria is that the retailer must have been in business for at least six months. Good Earth Foods placed a large order with Wholesale Health Supply and requested credit terms. Wholesale Health Supply faxed a credit request form to Good Earth Foods, and the buyer at Good Earth Foods faxed the completed form back to Wholesale Health Supply. Robin Sylvester, the sales manager at Wholesale Health Supply, saw the credit application and noticed Good Earth Foods had only been in business for two months. Thinking she might lose the order if Good Earth Foods wasn't extended credit, Robin authorized the shipment. She figured by the time the credit department rejected the application, Good Earth Foods would have received the order and the vice president would override the rejection to keep a new customer. Robin was sure that everything would turn out alright.

1. Do you think Robin's decision to ship the order was unethical? Why or why not?
2. What would you have done if you were in Robin's position?
3. Write a memo from the credit department manager to Robin Sylvester explaining the reasoning behind requiring a new credit customer to be in business for at least six months.
4. In small groups, discuss ways to prevent a situation like this from happening.

MASTERY PROBLEM

✓ Accts. Rec. balance: $1,900.54

Geoff and Sandy Harland own and operate Wayward Kennel and Pet Supply. Their motto is, "If your pet is not becoming to you, he should be coming to us." The Harlands maintain a sales tax payable account throughout the month to account for the 6% sales tax. They use a general journal, general ledger, and accounts receivable ledger. The following sales and cash collections took place during the month of September:

Sept. 2 Sold a fish aquarium on account to Ken Shank, $125 plus tax of $7.50, terms n/30. Sale No. 101.

3 Sold dog food on account to Nancy Truelove, $68.25 plus tax of $4.10, terms n/30. Sale No. 102.

5 Sold a bird cage on account to Jean Warkentin, $43.95 plus tax of $2.64, terms n/30. Sale No. 103.

8 Cash sales for the week were $2,332.45 plus tax of $139.95.

10 Received cash for boarding and grooming services, $625 plus tax of $37.50.

11 Jean Warkentin stopped by the store to point out a minor defect in the bird cage purchased in Sale No. 103. The Harlands offered a sales allowance of $10 plus tax on the price of the cage which satisfied Warkentin.

12 Sold a cockatoo on account to Tully Shaw, $1,200 plus tax of $72, terms n/30. Sale No. 104.

14 Received cash on account from Rosa Alanso, $256.

15 Rosa Alanso returned merchandise, $93.28 including tax of $5.28.

15 Cash sales for the week were $2,656.85 plus tax of $159.41.

16 Received cash on account from Nancy Truelove, $58.25.

18 Received cash for boarding and grooming services, $535 plus tax of $32.10.

19 Received cash on account from Ed Cochran, $63.25.

20 Sold pet supplies on account to Susan Hays, $83.33 plus tax of $5, terms n/30. Sale No. 105.

21 Sold three Labrador Retriever puppies to All American Day Camp, $375 plus tax of $22.50, terms n/30. Sale No. 106.

22 Cash sales for the week were $3,122.45 plus tax of $187.35.

23 Received cash for boarding and grooming services, $515 plus tax of $30.90.

25 Received cash on account from Ken Shank, $132.50.

26 Received cash on account from Nancy Truelove, $72.35.

27 Received cash on account from Joe Gloy, $273.25.

28 Borrowed cash to purchase a pet limousine, $11,000.

29 Cash sales for the week were $2,835.45 plus tax of $170.13.

30 Received cash for boarding and grooming services, $488 plus tax of $29.28.

(continued)

Wayward had the following general ledger account balances as of September 1:

Account Title	Account No.	General Ledger Balance on Sept. 1
Cash	101	$23,500.25
Accounts Receivable	122	850.75
Notes Payable	201	2,500.00
Sales Tax Payable	231	909.90
Sales	401	13,050.48
Sales Returns and Allowances	401.1	86.00
Boarding and Grooming Revenue	402	2,115.00

Wayward also had the following accounts receivable ledger balances as of September 1:

Customer	Accounts Receivable Balance
Rosa Alanso 2541 East 2nd Street Bloomington, IN 47401-5356	$456.00
Ed Cochran 2669 Windcrest Drive Bloomington, IN 47401-5446	$ 63.25
Joe Gloy 1458 Parnell Avenue Muncie, IN 47304-2682	$273.25
Nancy Truelove 2300 E. National Road Cumberland, IN 46229-4824	$ 58.25

New customers opening accounts during September were as follows:

All American Day Camp
3025 Old Mill Run
Bloomington, IN 47408-1080

Tully Shaw
3315 Longview Avenue
Bloomington, IN 47401-7223

Susan Hays
1424 Jackson Creek Road
Nashville, IN 47448-2245

Jean Warkentin
1813 Deep Well Court
Bloomington, IN 47401-5124

Ken Shank
6422 E. Bender Road
Bloomington, IN 47401-7756

REQUIRED

1. Enter the transactions for the month of September in a general journal. (Begin with page 7.)
2. Post the entries to the general and subsidiary ledgers. Open new accounts for any customers who did not have a balance as of September 1.
3. Prepare a schedule of accounts receivable.
4. Compute the net sales for the month of September.

> This problem challenges you to apply your cumulative accounting knowledge to move a step beyond the material in the chapter.

✓ June 14: Dr. Sales Discount, $12

CHALLENGE PROBLEM

Enter the following transactions in a general journal:

June 4 Sold merchandise on account to T. Allen, $1,500 plus 6% sales tax, with 1/10, n/30 cash discount terms.

   7 Sold merchandise on account to K. Bryant, $1,800 plus 6% sales tax, with 1/10, n/30 cash discount terms.

   11 T. Allen returned merchandise totaling $300 from the June 4 sale, for credit.

   14 T. Allen paid the balance due from the June 4 sale, less discount.

   17 K. Bryant paid the balance due from the June 7 sale, less discount.

ANSWERS TO SELF-STUDY TEST QUESTIONS

True/False

1. T
2. T
3. T
4. F (the debit *excludes* the sales tax)
5. T

Multiple Choice

1. d   2. c   3. b   4. b   5. a

Checkpoint Exercises

1.

2.

(a)									3	0	9	00						
		Accounts Receivable							3	0	9	00						
		Sales												3	0	0	00	
		Sales Tax Payable														9	00	
		Made credit sale																

(b)																		
		Sales Returns and Allowances							7	0	00							
		Sales Tax Payable								2	10							
		Accounts Receivable												7	2	10		
		Returned merchandise																

(c)																		
		Cash						2	3	2	30							
		Sales Discounts							4	60								
		Accounts Receivable											2	3	6	90		
		Received cash on account																

3.

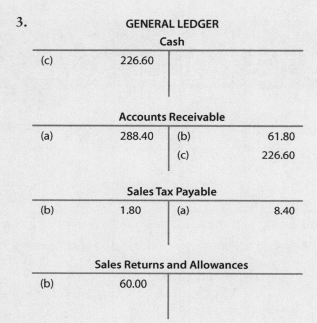

GENERAL LEDGER

Cash

(c)	226.60		

Accounts Receivable

(a)	288.40	(b)	61.80
		(c)	226.60

Sales Tax Payable

(b)	1.80	(a)	8.40

Sales Returns and Allowances

(b)	60.00		

Sales

		(a)	280.00

Accounts Receivable Ledger
M. Schapiro

(a)	288.40	(b)	61.80
		(c)	226.60

4. Schedule of Accounts Receivable
March 31, 20--

S. Burton	$103
A. Tangier	240
J. Holmes	144
F. Fullman	110
P. Molty	194
Total	$791

Chapter 11

Accounting for Purchases and Cash Payments

In Chapter 10, we heard about Kalso Earth Shoes, the company whose eco-friendly shoes reflect a concern about the environment. Innovar Environmental is a different kind of company that addresses environmental issues in a totally different way. Innovar provides services to enable government and businesses to become green through environmental consulting, construction, and renovation. Its projects include lead paint, asbestos, and mold abatement; facilities demolition; site enhancements; green construction; natural disaster recovery; storage tank removal; and more.

Innovar was founded in 2000 and is based in Denver, Colorado. It has benefited from the nationwide interest in going green, increasing its revenues in one three-year period by 200%, to $12.2 million. You might recall that one of Kalso Earth Shoes' biggest challenges was accounting for its high volume of sales activity. In contrast, Innovar has far fewer but larger sales transactions. Its challenge is accounting for the many purchases of items used in its major construction and renovation projects. In this chapter, you will learn how to account for purchases transactions, including various discounts, freight charges, and the return of items to the manufacturer.

LEARNING OBJECTIVES

Careful study of this chapter should enable you to:

LO1 Describe merchandise purchases transactions.

LO2 Describe and use merchandise purchases accounts and compute gross profit.

LO3 Describe and use the accounts payable ledger.

LO4 Prepare a schedule of accounts payable.

Chapter 10 demonstrated how to account for sales in a merchandising business. This chapter continues the study of the merchandising business by examining how to account for merchandise purchases. We will learn how to use four new accounts and another subsidiary ledger.

| LO1 | **Merchandise Purchases Transactions** |

Describe merchandise purchases transactions.

In everyday language, purchases can refer to almost anything we have bought. For a merchandising business, however, purchases refer to merchandise acquired for resale. These are goods a business buys for the sole purpose of selling them to its customers.

Purchasing procedures and documents vary, depending on the nature and size of a business. For example, in a small business, the owner or an employee might do the buying on a part-time basis. In a large business, there might be a separate purchasing department with a full-time manager and staff. In addition, the procedures and documents used can be affected by whether purchases are made on account or for cash.

Figure 11-1 shows some of the major documents used in the purchasing process of a merchandising business. In discussing the purchasing process, we will assume that the business makes purchases on account and has a purchasing department.

FIGURE 11-1 Purchasing Process Documents (Flowchart)

Purchase Requisition

Electronic forms used in a computerized system are similar to the paper documents described in this chapter.

A purchase requisition is an internal form sent to the purchasing department to request the purchase of merchandise or other property. Any authorized person or department can prepare this form and submit it to the purchasing department. Figure 11-2 shows a purchase requisition used by Sunflower Cycle. One copy of this form is sent to the purchasing department, one goes to the accounting department, and one is kept by the department that prepared the requisition.

Purchase Order

When electronic purchase orders are used, the information is sent to the vendor and the accounting and purchasing departments at the same time.

The purchasing department reviews and approves the purchase requisition and prepares a purchase order. A purchase order is a written order to buy goods from a specific vendor (supplier). Figure 11-3 shows a purchase order prepared by Sunflower Cycle based on the purchase requisition in Figure 11-2. One copy of the purchase order is sent to the vendor to order the goods, one goes to the accounting department, and one copy is kept in the purchasing department. Other copies may be sent to the department that prepared the purchase requisition and to the receiving area.

Receiving Report and Purchase Invoice

When the merchandise is received, a receiving report indicating what has been received is prepared. The receiving report can be a separate form, such as a copy of the purchase order received from the purchasing department, or one can be created from

FIGURE 11-2 Purchase Requisition

PURCHASE REQUISITION NO. A-106

Sunflower CYCLE
804 Massachusetts St., Lawrence, KS 66044

Date Issued February 24, 20--	Order From
Date Required March 12, 20--	Quality Bike Products
Required For Department Parts	6400 W. 105th St.
Deliver To Sam Tangari	Bloomington, MN 55438

Quantity	Description
3	SRAM Apex Double Tap Right Lever
3	SRAM PG-1070 10-speed 11-28
2	Campagnolo Big Corkscrew

Purchasing Department Memorandum

Placed By *Emily Green*	Date February 26, 20--
Approved By *Dan Hughes*	Issued To
Purchase Order No. 312	Quality Bike Products 6400 W. 105th St. Bloomington, MN 55438

FIGURE 11-3 Purchase Order

PURCHASE ORDER NO. 312

Sunflower CYCLE
804 Massachusetts St., Lawrence, KS 66044

Date February 26, 20--	Order From
Deliver By March 12, 20--	Quality Bike Products
Ship By UPS Ground	6400 W. 105th St.
FOB Bloomington	Bloomington, MN 55438

Quantity	Description	Unit Price	Total
3	SRAM Apex Double Tap Right Lever	$ 78.00	$234.00
3	SRAM PG-1070 10-speed 11-28	62.00	186.00
2	Campagnolo Big Corkscrew	170.00	340.00
	Total		$760.00

Dan Hughes

YOUR PERSPECTIVE

Procurement Clerk

In many large businesses the task of keeping track of purchases and supplies is done by a *procurement clerk*. Procurement clerks compile requests for materials and prepare purchase orders. They also handle questions concerning orders as well as order changes or cancelations.

They make sure the purchases arrive on time and that the items meet the required specifications. Upon receiving an order, procurement clerks prepare a receiving report or stamp the vendor's invoice to show that the item has been received. As this chapter explains, the receiving report is an important part of good internal control over purchases and payments.

the vendor's purchase invoice. Figure 11-4 shows a vendor invoice on which a rubber stamp has been used to imprint a type of receiving report. The receiving clerk has indicated on the form the date and condition of the goods received.

An **invoice** is a document prepared by the seller (vendor) as a bill for the merchandise shipped. To the seller, this is a sales invoice, as explained in Chapter 10. To the buyer, this is a **purchase invoice**. Figure 11-4 shows an invoice sent by Quality Bike Products to Sunflower Cycle for the goods ordered with the purchase order in Figure 11-3.

The accounting department compares the purchase invoice with the purchase requisition, purchase order, and receiving report. If the invoice is for the goods ordered and received and the correct price, the invoice is paid by the due date.

This is an example of good internal control. The procedure helps ensure that the business pays only for goods it ordered and received, and at the correct price.

FIGURE 11-4 Purchase Invoice

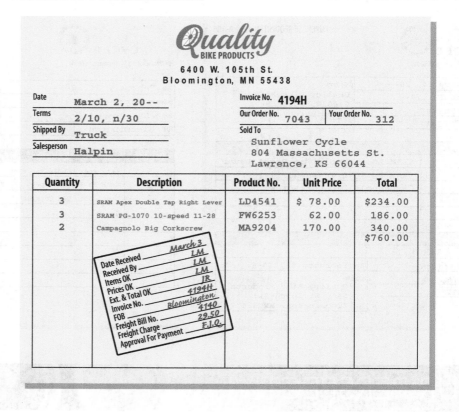

Voucher System

Internal control over purchases and cash payments can be strengthened further by using a voucher system, as described in the Appendix to Chapter 7. Recall that a voucher is a document which shows that an acquisition is proper and that payment is authorized. A voucher system is a control technique that requires every acquisition and subsequent payment to be supported by an approved voucher.

Figure 11-5 is a copy of Figure 7A-5, a voucher used by Sunflower Cycle. The voucher is prepared in the accounting department based on the purchase requisition, purchase order, receiving report, and purchase invoice. The completed and signed voucher provides the support for paying the purchase invoice. The voucher in Figure 11-5 represents the basis on which a payment of $3,621.42 would be made to King Creek Corporation. The voucher system is a key internal control to see that all purchases and payments are properly authorized.

Cash and Trade Discounts

Notice that the invoice in Figure 11-5 shows terms of 1/15, n/30. These are the same credit terms discussed in Chapter 10. A discount is available if the bill is paid within the discount period. The only difference is that we are now looking from the buyer's point of view rather than the seller's. We will see how to account for these discounts later in this chapter.

Another type of discount, called a trade discount, is often offered by manufacturers and wholesalers. This discount is a reduction from the list or catalog price offered to different classes of customers. By simply adjusting the trade discount percentages,

FIGURE 11-5 Voucher

Front

Back

LEARNING KEY 🔑

Purchases and sales subject to trade discounts should be recorded in the accounting records at the *net amount* after deducting the trade discounts.

CHECKPOINT ✔

Complete Checkpoint-1 on page 423 to test your basic understanding of LO1.

companies can avoid the cost of reprinting catalogs every time there is a change in prices. Trade discounts are usually shown as a deduction from the total amount of the invoice. For example, the invoice in Figure 11-6 includes a trade discount of 10%. The amount to be entered in the accounting records for this invoice is $684, the net amount after deducting the trade discount of $76. Trade discounts represent a reduction in the price of the merchandise and should not be entered in the accounts of either the seller or the buyer.

We need to be careful in computing the cash discount when an invoice has both cash and trade discounts. The cash discount applies to the *net amount* after deducting the trade discount. For example, the cash discount and amount to be paid on the invoice in Figure 11-6 would be calculated as follows:

Gross amount	$760.00
Less 10% trade discount	76.00
Net amount	$684.00
Less 2% cash discount	13.68
Amount to be paid	$670.32

FIGURE 11-6 Purchase Invoice with Trade Discount

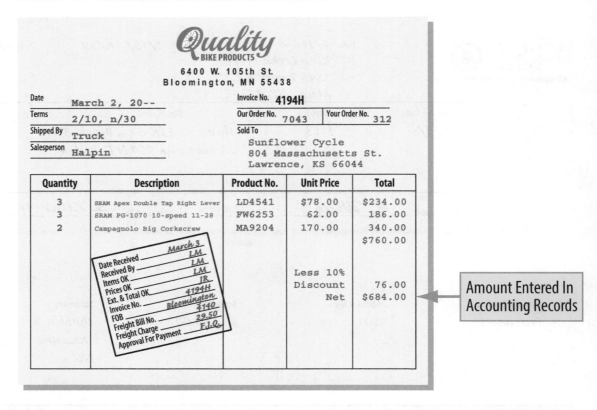

Merchandise Purchases Accounts

LO2

Describe and use merchandise purchases accounts and compute gross profit.

To account for merchandise purchases transactions, we will use four new accounts.

1. Purchases
2. Purchases Returns and Allowances
3. Purchases Discounts
4. Freight-In

The position of these accounts in the accounting equation and their normal balances are shown in Figure 11-7.

Purchases Account

The approach to accounting for merchandise purchases shown in this chapter is known as the periodic method. Other inventory methods are covered in Chapter 13.

The purchases account is used to record the cost of merchandise purchased.

Purchases

Debit	Credit
to enter the cost of merchandise purchased	

If a $100 purchase is made for cash, the following entry is made:

5		Purchases		1 0 0 00			5
6		Cash			1 0 0 00		6
7		Made cash purchase					7

FIGURE 11-7 Accounting for Merchandise Purchases Transactions

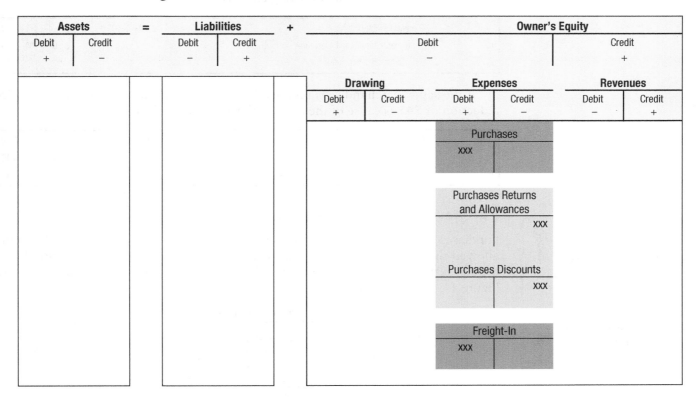

If the same purchase is made on account, the entry is as follows:

The vendor's name is placed after Accounts Payable.

5		Purchases			1	0	0	00						5
6		Accounts Payable/Vendor								1	0	0	00	6
7		Made purchase on account												7

Accounts Payable is followed by a slash (/) and the name of the specific vendor to whom the purchaser owes money. The vendor name is for the vendor's account in the accounts payable ledger. This ledger is explained later in this chapter.

Purchases Returns and Allowances Account

LEARNING KEY 🔑
Purchases returns and allowances on the income statement:
Purchases   xxx
Less: Purch.
ret. & all.   xx
Net purchases   xxx

Purchases Returns and Allowances is a contra-cost (or contra-purchases) account, which has a credit balance and is deducted from the related cost account. Purchases returns and purchases allowances are credited to this account. It is reported as a deduction from Purchases on the income statement to compute net purchases (see Figure 11-8 on page 409).

Purchases returns and allowances are similar to the sales returns and allowances we discussed in Chapter 10. We are simply looking at returns and allowances from the buyer's point of view. If merchandise is returned to a supplier, or the supplier grants a price reduction because of defects or other problems with merchandise purchased, Purchases Returns and Allowances is credited.

Purchases Returns and Allowances

Debit	Credit
	to enter returns and allowances

If merchandise that was purchased on account for $200 is defective and is returned to the supplier, the following entry is made:

9	Accounts Payable/Vendor	2 0 0 00		9
10	Purchases Returns and Allowances		2 0 0 00	10
11	Returned merchandise			11

If the same merchandise is retained by the buyer but the supplier grants a price reduction of $45 because of the defects, the entry is as follows:

9	Accounts Payable/Vendor	4 5 00		9
10	Purchases Returns and Allowances		4 5 00	10
11	Allowance for defective merchandise			11

Purchases Discounts Account

Purchases Discounts is a contra-purchases account used to record cash discounts allowed on purchases. Like Purchases Returns and Allowances, it is reported as a deduction from Purchases on the income statement to compute net purchases (see Figure 11-8 on page 409).

LEARNING KEY 🔑

Purchases discounts on the income statement:

Purchases   xxx
Less: Purchases
      discounts   xx
Net purchases   xxx

Purchases Discounts

Debit	Credit
	to enter cash discounts taken

If merchandise is purchased for $100 on account, with credit terms of 2/10, n/30, the following entry is made:

14	Purchases	1 0 0 00		14
15	Accounts Payable/Vendor		1 0 0 00	15
16	Made purchase on account			16

If payment for the merchandise is then made within the discount period, the entry is as follows:

18	Accounts Payable/Vendor	1 0 0 00		18
19	Cash		9 8 00	19
20	Purchases Discounts		2 00	20
21	Made payment on account			21

This approach to accounting for purchases discounts is known as the "gross-price method." The "net-price method" is described in the appendix.

Note the parts of this entry. Accounts Payable is debited for $100, the full amount of the invoice, because the entire debt has been satisfied. Cash is credited for only $98 because that is all that was required to pay the debt. The difference of $2 ($100 − $98) is credited to Purchases Discounts, which represents a reduction in the purchase price of the merchandise. That is why Purchases Discounts is deducted from Purchases on the income statement.

Freight-In Account

Freight-In is an adjunct-purchases account used to record transportation charges on merchandise purchases. Transportation costs are part of the total cost of the merchandise, so they are added to net purchases on the income statement to compute cost of goods purchased (see Figure 11-8 on page 409).

A BROADER VIEW

Cash Management—Those Discounts Matter

If a business makes a $2,000 purchase on account, with terms of 2/10, n/30, the available discount is only $40 ($2,000 × 0.02). On the surface, this seems unimportant, like "small change." But take a closer look. If the business does not pay $1,960 ($2,000 – $40) within 10 days, it must pay $2,000 within 30 days. This means that the business would pay $40 for the use of $1,960 for 20 more days. If we assume a 360-day year, the approximate annual interest rate for using the $1,960 for 20 days is 36%. (In Chapter 17 you will learn to compute the exact interest rate.)

The innocent looking 2% cash discount represents a very high rate of interest. If a business regularly misses cash discount opportunities, the annual dollar cost can be substantial. For sound cash management, take advantage of discounts.

MARMADUKE ST. JOHN/ALAMY STOCK PHOTO

<table>
<tr><th colspan="2">Freight-In</th></tr>
<tr><th>Debit</th><th>Credit</th></tr>
<tr><td>to enter transportation charges
on merchandise purchases</td><td></td></tr>
</table>

LEARNING KEY

Freight-in on the income statement:

Net purchases	xxx
Add freight-in	
Cost of goods purchased	xx
	xxx

Transportation charges are expressed in FOB (free on board) terms that indicate who is responsible for paying the freight costs. **FOB shipping point** means that transportation charges are paid by the buyer. The buyer records these costs in a freight-in account. **FOB destination** means that transportation charges are paid by the seller. The seller records these costs in a freight-out or delivery expense account. FOB terms also tell us who owns the inventory and who should count it in their inventory account. Under FOB shipping point, the buyer owns the inventory as soon as it is shipped and should count it in inventory. Under FOB destination, the seller owns the inventory until it is delivered to the buyer and the seller should count it in inventory.

When the terms are FOB shipping point, either the freight charges will be listed separately on the purchase invoice or a separate freight bill will be sent. Assume Sunflower Cycle receives an invoice for $400 plus freight charges of $38. The entry for this purchase is as follows:

25		Purchases		4	0	0	00						25
26		Freight-In			3	8	00						26
27		Accounts Payable/Vendor						4	3	8	00		27
28		Made purchase on account											28

Assume instead that Sunflower Cycle receives an invoice for $400 for the same merchandise, shipped FOB shipping point. Sunflower Cycle then receives a separate bill from the transportation company for $38. These two transactions are entered as follows:

30		Purchases			4	0	0	00							30
31		Accounts Payable/Vendor							4	0	0	00			31
32		Made purchase on account													32
33															33
34		Freight-In				3	8	00							34
35		Accounts Payable/Vendor								3	8	00			35
36		Freight charges on merchandise purchase													36

When the terms are FOB destination, generally no freight charges appear on the purchase invoice. The buyer simply records the purchase at the amount of the invoice. The freight-in account is not used in recording this purchase.

Computation of Gross Profit

An important step in determining net income for a merchandising business is the calculation of its gross profit. Gross profit (also called gross margin) is the difference between net sales and cost of goods sold. Cost of goods sold (also called cost of merchandise sold) is the difference between the goods available for sale and the ending inventory. It indicates the cost of the goods sold during the period. Gross profit provides very important information. It tells management the amount of sales dollars available to cover expenses, after covering the cost of the goods sold.

As a simple example, gross profit is computed as follows:

Net sales	$8,400
Cost of goods sold	5,300
Gross profit	$3,100

In a more realistic situation, we must compute net sales and cost of goods sold, in order to compute gross profit. Multiple steps are involved. To illustrate, we use three of the four new accounts described in Chapter 10, the four new accounts described in this chapter, and the merchandise inventory balances. Assume that a company has the following sales, purchases, and merchandise inventory balances for the year ended December 31, 20--:

From Chapter 10 →

Sales	$201,500
Sales returns and allowances	1,200
Sales discounts	1,000

From Chapter 11 →

Purchases	105,000
Purchases returns and allowances	800
Purchases discounts	1,000
Freight-in	300
Merchandise inventory, January 1, 20--	26,000
Merchandise inventory, December 31, 20--	18,000

Figure 11-8 uses these balances to compute net sales, net purchases, cost of goods sold, and gross profit. The following four steps in computing gross profit are labeled in the figure:

STEP 1 Compute net sales.
(Sales – Sales Returns and Allowances – Sales Discounts)

STEP 2 Compute goods available for sale.
(Beginning Inventory + Cost of Goods Purchased)

STEP 3   Compute cost of goods sold.
(Goods Available for Sale – Ending Inventory)

Merchandise inventory is discussed more fully in Chapters 14-15, including explanation of an additional component of inventory.

STEP 4   Compute gross profit.
(Net Sales – Cost of Goods Sold)

FIGURE 11-8 Computation of Gross Profit on a Partial Income Statement

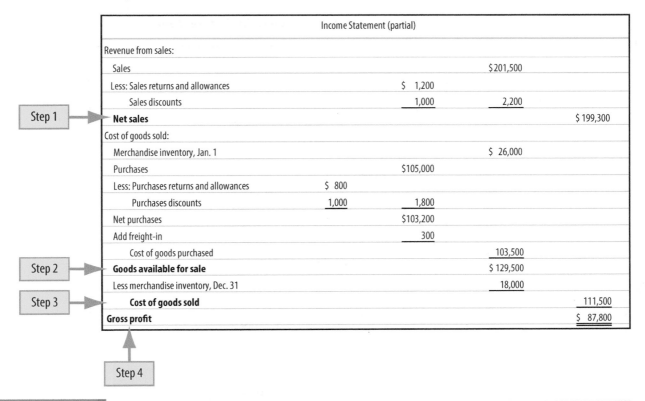

Income Statement (partial)			
Revenue from sales:			
Sales		$201,500	
Less: Sales returns and allowances	$ 1,200		
Sales discounts	1,000	2,200	
Net sales			$ 199,300
Cost of goods sold:			
Merchandise inventory, Jan. 1		$ 26,000	
Purchases	$105,000		
Less: Purchases returns and allowances	$ 800		
Purchases discounts	1,000	1,800	
Net purchases		$103,200	
Add freight-in		300	
Cost of goods purchased		103,500	
Goods available for sale		$ 129,500	
Less merchandise inventory, Dec. 31		18,000	
Cost of goods sold			111,500
Gross profit			$ 87,800

Step 1 → Net sales
Step 2 → Goods available for sale
Step 3 → Cost of goods sold
Step 4 → Gross profit

CHECKPOINT ✔

Complete Checkpoint-2 on page 424 to test your basic understanding of LO2.

LEARNING KEY 🔑

Cost of Goods Sold = Beginning Inventory + Net Purchases + Freight-In − Ending Inventory

Gross Profit = Net Sales − Cost of Goods Sold

LO3

Journalizing and Posting Purchases and Cash Payments Transactions

Describe and use the accounts payable ledger.

To illustrate the journalizing and posting of purchases transactions, we will continue with the transactions of Sunflower Cycle.

Purchases

Assume the following purchases on account occurred during the month of April:

Apr.   4   Purchased merchandise from Bilenky Cycle Works, $3,300. Invoice No. 631, dated April 2, terms, n/30.

8   Purchased merchandise from Ellsworth, $2,500. Invoice No. 927D, dated April 6, terms, n/30.

(*continued*)

Apr. 11 Purchased merchandise from Gunnar Cycles, $8,700.
Invoice No. 804, dated April 9, terms, 1/15, n/30.

17 Purchased merchandise from Milwaukee Cycle Co., $800.
Invoice No. 611, dated April 16, terms, n/30.

23 Purchased merchandise from Rans Designs, Inc., $5,300.
Invoice No. 1465, dated April 22, terms, 1/10, n/30.

These transactions are entered in a general journal as shown in Figure 11-9.

FIGURE 11-9 Purchases Entered in General Journal

	DATE		DESCRIPTION	POST. REF.	DEBIT	CREDIT	
1	20-- Apr.	4	Purchases		3 3 0 0 00		1
2			Accounts Payable/Bilenky Cycle Works			3 3 0 0 00	2
3			Invoice No. 631				3
4							4
5		8	Purchases		2 5 0 0 00		5
6			Accounts Payable/Ellsworth			2 5 0 0 00	6
7			Invoice No. 927D				7
8							8
9		11	Purchases		8 7 0 0 00		9
10			Accounts Payable/Gunnar Cycles			8 7 0 0 00	10
11			Invoice No. 804				11
12							12
13		17	Purchases		8 0 0 00		13
14			Accounts Payable/Milwaukee Cycle Co.			8 0 0 00	14
15			Invoice No. 611				15
16							16
17		23	Purchases		5 3 0 0 00		17
18			Accounts Payable/Rans Designs, Inc.			5 3 0 0 00	18
19			Invoice No. 1465				19

GENERAL JOURNAL — PAGE 6

Posting Purchases to the General Ledger

Purchases transactions are posted from the general journal to the general ledger in the same manner as was illustrated for sales in Chapter 10. The following steps are used, as indicated in Figure 11-10 for Sunflower Cycle's April 4 and 8 purchases transactions:

In the general ledger account:

STEP 1 Enter the date of the transaction in the Date column.

STEP 2 Enter the amount of the debit or credit in the Debit or Credit column.

STEP 3 Enter the new balance in the Balance columns under Debit or Credit.

STEP 4 Enter the journal page number from which each transaction is posted in the Posting Reference column.

In the journal:

STEP 5 Enter the ledger account number in the Posting Reference column of the journal for each transaction that is posted.

Other purchases transactions would be posted in the same manner.

FIGURE 11-10 Posting Purchases to the General Ledger

A three-column account form is commonly used for supplier accounts. Only one balance column is needed because the normal balance is a credit. If a debit balance occurs, the amount may be bracketed.

When an accounts payable ledger is used, the Posting Reference column in the general journal serves two purposes. (1) The account number is inserted to indicate the general ledger account has been posted. (2) A slash (/) and a check mark (✔) are inserted to indicate the accounts payable ledger account has been posted.

Posting Purchases to the Accounts Payable Ledger

The Purchases and Accounts Payable resulting from merchandise purchases on account are now up to date in the general ledger. A record can be kept of the amount owed to each supplier by using an accounts payable ledger. This is a separate ledger containing an individual account payable for each supplier. It is similar to the accounts receivable ledger we saw in Chapter 10. A summary accounts payable account called a controlling account is maintained in the general ledger. The accounts payable ledger is "subsidiary" to this account. If there are many supplier accounts, it is a good practice to assign each supplier an account number. The subsidiary ledger accounts are kept in either alphabetical or numerical order, depending on whether the supplier accounts are identified by number.

Figure 11-11 illustrates the use of the accounts payable ledger for Sunflower Cycle's April 4 and 8 purchases transactions. Note that the individual vendor name follows accounts payable in each journal entry affecting Accounts Payable. The following steps are used to post from the general journal to the accounts payable ledger, as shown in Figure 11-11:

In the accounts payable ledger account:

STEP 1　Enter the date of the transaction in the Date column.

STEP 2　Enter the amount of the debit or credit in the Debit or Credit column.

FIGURE 11-11 Posting Purchases to the Accounts Payable Ledger

	GENERAL JOURNAL (Partial)				Page 6
Date	Description	Post. Ref.	Debit	Credit	
20-- Apr. 4	Purchases	501	3,300.00		
	Accounts Payable/Bilenky Cycle Works	202/ ✔		3,300.00	
	Invoice No. 631				
8	Purchases	501	2,500.00		
	Accounts Payable/Ellsworth	202/ ✔		2,500.00	
	Invoice No. 927D				

ACCOUNTS PAYABLE LEDGER (Partial)

NAME Bilenky Cycle Works
ADDRESS 5319 N. 2nd. St., Philadelphia, PA 19120

Date	Item	Post. Ref.	Debit	Credit	Balance
20-- Apr. 4		J6		3,300.00	3,300.00

NAME Ellsworth
ADDRESS 16275 Technology Dr., San Diego, CA 92127

Date	Item	Post. Ref.	Debit	Credit	Balance
20-- Apr. 8		J6		2,500.00	2,500.00

GENERAL LEDGER (Partial)

ACCOUNT Accounts Payable ACCOUNT NO. 202

Date	Item	Post. Ref.	Debit	Credit	Balance Debit	Balance Credit
20-- Apr. 1	Bal.	✔				4,800.00
4		J6		3,300.00		8,100.00
8		J6		2,500.00		10,600.00

ACCOUNT Purchases ACCOUNT NO. 501

Date	Item	Post. Ref.	Debit	Credit	Balance Debit	Balance Credit
20-- Apr. 1	Bal.	✔			37,400	
4		J6	3,300.00		40,700	
8		J6	2,500.00		43,200	

STEP 3 Enter the new balance in the Balance column.

STEP 4 Enter the journal page number from which each transaction is posted in the Posting Reference column.

In the journal:

STEP 5 Enter a slash (/) followed by a check mark (✔) in the Posting Reference column of the journal for each transaction that is posted.

Note the relationship between the general journal, accounts payable ledger, and general ledger. All general journal entries are posted to both the general ledger and the accounts payable ledger. After the posting of the accounts payable ledger and general ledger is completed, the total of the accounts payable ledger balances should equal the Accounts Payable balance in the general ledger.

> **LEARNING KEY** 🔑
>
> The total of the accounts payable ledger balances must equal the Accounts Payable balance in the general ledger.

Purchases Returns and Allowances

If a buyer returns merchandise or is given an allowance for damaged merchandise, a general journal entry is required. Assume that on May 4, Sunflower Cycle returns $200 of merchandise to Rans Designs, Inc. These goods were part of a purchase made on April 23. Figure 11-12 shows the general journal entry, general ledger posting, and accounts payable ledger posting for this transaction.

The general journal entry is made in the usual manner. The general ledger is posted using the same five steps as were illustrated for purchases transactions in Figure 11-10. The accounts payable ledger is posted using the following five steps, as illustrated in Figure 11-12:

In the accounts payable ledger account:

STEP 1 Enter the date of the transaction in the Date column.

STEP 2 Enter the amount of the debit or credit in the Debit or Credit column.

FIGURE 11-12 Accounting for Purchases Returns and Allowances

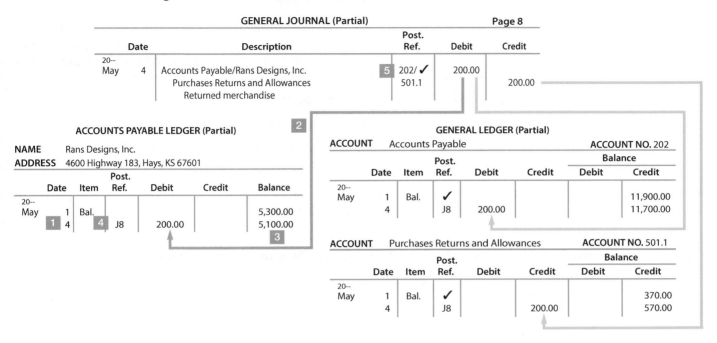

STEP 3   Enter the new balance in the Balance column.

STEP 4   Enter the journal page number from which each transaction is posted in the Posting Reference column.

In the journal:

STEP 5   Enter a slash (/) followed by a check mark (✓) in the Posting Reference column of the journal for each transaction that is posted.

Cash Payments

To illustrate the journalizing and posting of cash payments, we will use Sunflower Cycle's cash payment transactions. Assume Sunflower Cycle made the following two payments on account during the month of April:

Apr. 10   Paid Ace Wheelworks $4,800 for purchases made on account.

  24   Paid Gunnar Cycles $8,700 less discount of 1% for purchases made on account.

These transactions are entered in a general journal as shown in Figure 11-13.

FIGURE 11-13 Cash Payments Entered in a General Journal

30	Apr.	10	Accounts Payable/Ace Wheelworks		4	8	0	0	00									30
31			Cash								4	8	0	0	00			31
32			Made payment on account															32
33																		33
34		24	Accounts Payable/Gunnar Cycles		8	7	0	0	00									34
35			Cash								8	6	1	3	00			35
36			Purchases Discounts										8	7	00			36
37			Made payment less discount on account															37

Posting Cash Payments to the General Ledger and Accounts Payable Ledger

Cash payment transactions are posted to the general ledger in the same manner as was illustrated for purchases transactions in Figure 11-10. To post cash payments to the accounts payable ledger, the following steps are used, as indicated in Figure 11-14 for Sunflower Cycle's April 10 and 24 cash payment transactions:

In the accounts payable ledger account:

STEP 1 Enter the date of the transaction in the Date column.

STEP 2 Enter the amount of the debit or credit in the Debit or Credit column.

STEP 3 Enter the new balance in the Balance column.

STEP 4 Enter the journal page number from which each transaction is posted in the Posting Reference column.

FIGURE 11-14 Posting Cash Payments to the General Ledger and Accounts Payable Ledger

CHECKPOINT ✔

Complete Checkpoint-3 on page 424 to test your basic understanding of LO3.

In the journal:

STEP 5   Enter a slash (/) followed by a check mark (✓) in the Posting Reference column of the journal for each transaction that is posted.

LO4	Schedule of Accounts Payable

Prepare a schedule of accounts payable.

At the end of the month, all postings to Accounts Payable in the general ledger and to the accounts payable ledger should be complete, as shown in Figure 11-15. At this point, the Accounts Payable balance in the general ledger should equal the sum of the supplier balances in the accounts payable ledger.

To verify that the sum of the accounts payable ledger balances equals the Accounts Payable balance, a schedule of accounts payable is prepared. This is an alphabetical or numerical listing of supplier accounts and balances, usually prepared at the end of the month. Figure 11-16 shows the schedule of accounts payable for Sunflower Cycle as of April 30. Note that suppliers whose account balance is zero are not included.

FIGURE 11-15 General Ledger and Accounts Payable Ledger after Posting

ACCOUNTS PAYABLE LEDGER

NAME   Ace Wheelworks
ADDRESS   145 Elm St., Somerville, MA 02144

Date		Item	Post. Ref.	Debit	Credit	Balance
20--						
Apr.	1	Bal.	✓			4,800.00
	10		J6	4,800.00		—

NAME   Bilenky Cycle Works
ADDRESS   5319 N. 2nd. St., Philadelphia, PA 19120

Date		Item	Post. Ref.	Debit	Credit	Balance
20--						
Apr.	4		J6		3,300.00	3,300.00

NAME   Ellsworth
ADDRESS   16275 Technology Dr., San Diego, CA 92127

Date		Item	Post. Ref.	Debit	Credit	Balance
20--						
Apr.	8		J6		2,500.00	2,500.00

NAME   Gunnar Cycles
ADDRESS   816 W. Bakke Ave, Waterford, WI 53185

Date		Item	Post. Ref.	Debit	Credit	Balance
20--						
Apr.	11		J6		8,700.00	8,700.00
	24		J6	8,700.00		—

NAME   Milwaukee Cycle Co.
ADDRESS   1018 W. Lincoln Ave, Milwaukee, WI 53215

Date		Item	Post. Ref.	Debit	Credit	Balance
20--						
Apr.	17		J6		800.00	800.00

NAME   Rans Designs, Inc.
ADDRESS   4600 Highway 183, Hays, KS 67601

Date		Item	Post. Ref.	Debit	Credit	Balance
20--						
Apr.	23		J6		5,300.00	5,300.00

GENERAL LEDGER (Partial)

ACCOUNT   Accounts Payable   **ACCOUNT NO.** 202

Date		Item	Post. Ref.	Debit	Credit	Balance Debit	Balance Credit
20--							
Apr.	1	Bal.	✓				4,800.00
	4		J6		3,300.00		8,100.00
	8		J6		2,500.00		10,600.00
	10		J6	4,800.00			5,800.00
	11		J6		8,700.00		14,500.00
	17		J6		800.00		15,300.00
	23		J6		5,300.00		20,600.00
	24		J6	8,700.00			11,900.00

FIGURE 11-16 **Schedule of Accounts Payable**

Sunflower Cycle Schedule of Accounts Payable April 30, 20--						
Bilenky Cycle Works	$	3	3	0	0	00
Ellsworth		2	5	0	0	00
Milwaukee Cycle Co.			8	0	0	00
Rans Designs, Inc.		5	3	0	0	00
	$11	9	0	0	00	

This schedule is prepared from the supplier accounts in the accounts payable ledger. The total calculated in the schedule is compared with the balance in Accounts Payable in the general ledger. Note that the $11,900 total listed in the schedule equals the Accounts Payable balance shown in Figure 11-15. If the schedule total and the Accounts Payable balance do not agree, the error must be located and corrected. To find the error, use the following procedures:

STEP 1 Verify the total of the schedule.

STEP 2 Verify the postings to the accounts payable ledger.

STEP 3 Verify the postings to Accounts Payable in the general ledger.

CHECKPOINT ✔

Complete Checkpoint-4 on page 424 to test your basic understanding of LO4.

SELF-STUDY

LEARNING OBJECTIVES	**Key Points to Remember**
LO1 Describe merchandise purchases transactions.	For a merchandising business, purchases refers to merchandise acquired for resale. Major documents used in the purchasing process are the purchase requisition, purchase order, receiving report, and purchase invoice.
LO2 Describe and use merchandise purchases accounts and compute gross profit.	Four accounts are used in accounting for merchandise purchases transactions. 1. Purchases 2. Purchases Returns and Allowances 3. Purchases Discounts 4. Freight-In Cost of Goods Sold = Beginning Inventory + Net Purchases + Freight-In − Ending Inventory Gross Profit = Net Sales − Cost of Goods Sold
LO3 Describe and use the accounts payable ledger.	To post purchases transactions to the general ledger: **In the general ledger account:** **STEP 1** Enter the date of the transaction in the Date column. **STEP 2** Enter the amount of the debit or credit in the Debit or Credit column. **STEP 3** Enter the new balance in the Balance columns under Debit or Credit. **STEP 4** Enter the journal page number from which each transaction is posted in the Posting Reference column.

LEARNING OBJECTIVES	**Key Points to Remember**
LO3 (concluded)	**In the journal:**

In the journal:

STEP 5   Enter the ledger account number in the Posting Reference column of the journal for each transaction that is posted.

An accounts payable ledger is a separate ledger containing an individual account payable for each supplier. To post from the general journal to the accounts payable ledger:

In the accounts payable ledger account:

STEP 1   Enter the date of the transaction in the Date column.

STEP 2   Enter the amount of the debit or credit in the Debit or Credit column.

STEP 3   Enter the new balance in the Balance column.

STEP 4   Enter the journal page number from which each transaction is posted in the Posting Reference column.

In the journal:

STEP 5   Enter a slash (/) followed by a check mark (✓) in the Posting Reference column of the journal for each transaction that is posted.

To post cash payments transactions to the general ledger:

In the general ledger account:

STEP 1   Enter the date of the transaction in the Date column.

STEP 2   Enter the amount of the debit or credit in the Debit or Credit column.

STEP 3   Enter the new balance in the Balance columns under Debit or Credit.

STEP 4   Enter the journal page number from which each transaction is posted in the Posting Reference column.

In the journal:

STEP 5   Enter the ledger account number in the Posting Reference column of the journal for each transaction that is posted.

To post cash payments transactions to the accounts payable ledger:

In the accounts payable ledger account:

STEP 1   Enter the date of the transaction in the Date column.

STEP 2   Enter the amount of the debit or credit in the Debit or Credit column.

STEP 3   Enter the new balance in the Balance column.

STEP 4   Enter the journal page number from which each transaction is posted in the Posting Reference column.

In the journal:

STEP 5   Enter a slash (/) followed by a check mark (✓) in the Posting Reference column of the journal for each transaction that is posted.

| **LO4** **Prepare a schedule of accounts payable.** | The schedule of accounts payable is used to verify that the sum of the accounts payable ledger balances equals the Accounts Payable balance. |

DEMONSTRATION PROBLEM

Jodi Rutman operates a retail pharmacy called Rutman Pharmacy. The books include a general journal, a general ledger, and an accounts payable ledger. The following transactions are related to purchases and cash payments for the month of June 20--:

June 1 Purchased merchandise from Sullivan Co. on account, $234.20. Invoice No. 71, dated June 1, terms 2/10, n/30.

2 Issued Check No. 536 for payment of June rent (Rent Expense), $1,000.

5 Purchased merchandise from Amfac Drug Supply on account, $562.40. Invoice No. 196, dated June 2, terms 1/15, n/30.

7 Purchased merchandise from University Drug Co. on account, $367.35. Invoice No. 914A, dated June 5, terms 3/10 eom, n/30.

9 Issued Check No. 537 to Sullivan Co. in payment of Invoice No. 71 less 2% discount.

12 Received a credit memo from Amfac Drug Supply for merchandise returned that was purchased on June 5, $46.20.

14 Purchased merchandise from Mutual Drug Co. on account, $479.40. Invoice No. 745, dated June 14, terms 2/10, n/30.

15 Received a credit memo from University Drug Co. for merchandise returned that was purchased on June 7, $53.70.

16 Issued Check No. 538 to Amfac Drug Supply in payment of Invoice No. 196 less the credit memo of June 12 and less 1% discount.

23 Issued Check No. 539 to Mutual Drug Co. in payment of Invoice No. 745 less 2% discount.

27 Purchased merchandise from Flites Pharmaceuticals on account, $638.47. Invoice No. 675, dated June 27, terms 2/10 eom, n/30.

29 Issued Check No. 540 to Dolgin Candy Co. for a cash purchase of merchandise, $270.20.

30 Issued Check No. 541 to Vashon Medical Supply in payment of Invoice No. 416, $1,217.69. No discount allowed.

REQUIRED

1. Enter the transactions in a general journal (start with page 7).

2. Post from the journal to the general ledger accounts and the accounts payable ledger. Account numbers and June 1 balances are as indicated in the accounts presented below. Then, update the account balances.

3. Prepare a schedule of accounts payable from the accounts payable ledger in the problem. Verify that the total of accounts payable in the schedule equals the June 30 balance of Accounts Payable in the general ledger.

SOLUTION 1.

	DATE		DESCRIPTION	POST. REF.	DEBIT	CREDIT	
1	20-- June	1	Purchases	501	2 3 4 20		1
2			Accounts Payable/Sullivan Co.	202/✔		2 3 4 20	2
3			Invoice No. 71				3
4							4
5		2	Rent Expense	521	1 0 0 0 00		5
6			Cash	101		1 0 0 0 00	6
7			Check No. 536				7
8							8
9		5	Purchases	501	5 6 2 40		9
10			Accounts Payable/Amfac Drug Supply	202/✔		5 6 2 40	10
11			Invoice No. 196				11
12							12
13		7	Purchases	501	3 6 7 35		13
14			Accounts Payable/University Drug Co.	202/✔		3 6 7 35	14
15			Invoice No. 914A				15
16							16
17		9	Accounts Payable/Sullivan Co.	202/✔	2 3 4 20		17
18			Cash	101		2 2 9 52	18
19			Purchases Discounts	501.2		4 68	19
20			Check No. 537				20
21							21
22		12	Accounts Payable/Amfac Drug Supply	202/✔	4 6 20		22
23			Purchases Returns and Allowances	501.1		4 6 20	23
24			Returned merchandise				24
25							25
26		14	Purchases	501	4 7 9 40		26
27			Accounts Payable/Mutual Drug Co.	202/✔		4 7 9 40	27
28			Invoice No. 745				28

GENERAL JOURNAL — Page 7

	DATE		DESCRIPTION	POST. REF.	DEBIT	CREDIT	
1	20-- June	15	Accounts Payable/University Drug Co.	202/✔	5 3 70		1
2			Purchases Returns and Allowances	501.1		5 3 70	2
3			Returned merchandise				3
4							4
5		16	Accounts Payable/Amfac Drug Supply	202/✔	5 1 6 20		5
6			Cash	101		5 1 1 04	6
7			Purchases Discounts	501.2		5 16	7
8			Check No. 538				8
9							9
10		23	Accounts Payable/Mutual Drug Co.	202/✔	4 7 9 40		10
11			Cash	101		4 6 9 81	11
12			Purchases Discounts	501.2		9 59	12
13			Check No. 539				13
14							14
15		27	Purchases	501	6 3 8 47		15
16			Accounts Payable/Flites Pharmaceuticals	202/✔		6 3 8 47	16
17			Invoice No. 675				17
18							18
19		29	Purchases	501	2 7 0 20		19
20			Cash	101		2 7 0 20	20
21			Check No. 540				21
22							22
23		30	Accounts Payable/Vashon Medical Supply	202/✔	1 2 1 7 69		23
24			Cash	101		1 2 1 7 69	24
25			Check No. 541				25

GENERAL JOURNAL — Page 8

(continued)

SOLUTION 2.

ACCOUNT: Cash																ACCOUNT NO. 101					

DATE		ITEM	POST. REF.	DEBIT					CREDIT					BALANCE								
														DEBIT					CREDIT			
20-- June	1	Balance	✓												9	1	8	0	00			
	2		J7						1	0	0	0	00		8	1	8	0	00			
	9		J7							2	2	9	52		7	9	5	0	48			
	16		J8							5	1	1	04		7	4	3	9	44			
	23		J8							4	6	9	81		6	9	6	9	63			
	29		J8							2	7	0	20		6	6	9	9	43			
	30		J8						1	2	1	7	69		5	4	8	1	74			

ACCOUNT: Accounts Payable																ACCOUNT NO. 202					

DATE		ITEM	POST. REF.	DEBIT					CREDIT					BALANCE								
														DEBIT					CREDIT			
20-- June	1	Balance	✓																	1	2	1	7	69
	1		J7							2	3	4	20							1	4	5	1	89
	5		J7							5	6	2	40							2	0	1	4	29
	7		J7							3	6	7	35							2	3	8	1	64
	9		J7		2	3	4	20												2	1	4	7	44
	12		J7			4	6	20												2	1	0	1	24
	14		J7							4	7	9	40							2	5	8	0	64
	15		J8			5	3	70												2	5	2	6	94
	16		J8		5	1	6	20												2	0	1	0	74
	23		J8		4	7	9	40												1	5	3	1	34
	27		J8							6	3	8	47							2	1	6	9	81
	30		J8	1	2	1	7	69													9	5	2	12

ACCOUNT: Purchases																ACCOUNT NO. 501					

DATE		ITEM	POST. REF.	DEBIT					CREDIT					BALANCE								
														DEBIT					CREDIT			
20-- June	1	Balance	✓											13	8	2	6	25					
	1		J7		2	3	4	20						14	0	6	0	45					
	5		J7		5	6	2	40						14	6	2	2	85					
	7		J7		3	6	7	35						14	9	9	0	20					
	14		J7		4	7	9	40						15	4	6	9	60					
	27		J8		6	3	8	47						16	1	0	8	07					
	29		J8		2	7	0	20						16	3	7	8	27					

ACCOUNT: Purchases Returns and Allowances																ACCOUNT NO. 501.1					

DATE		ITEM	POST. REF.	DEBIT					CREDIT					BALANCE								
														DEBIT					CREDIT			
20-- June	1	Balance	✓																		3	1	2	63
	12		J7								4	6	20								3	5	8	83
	15		J8								5	3	70								4	1	2	53

ACCOUNT: Purchases Discounts   **ACCOUNT NO.** 501.2

DATE	ITEM	POST. REF.	DEBIT	CREDIT	BALANCE DEBIT	BALANCE CREDIT
20-- June 1	Balance	✔				2 1 1 45
9		J7		4 68		2 1 6 13
16		J8		5 16		2 2 1 29
23		J8		9 59		2 3 0 88

ACCOUNT: Rent Expense   **ACCOUNT NO.** 521

DATE	ITEM	POST. REF.	DEBIT	CREDIT	BALANCE DEBIT	BALANCE CREDIT
20-- June 1	Balance	✔			5 0 0 0 00	
2		J7	1 0 0 0 00		6 0 0 0 00	

ACCOUNTS PAYABLE LEDGER

NAME: Amfac Drug Supply

DATE	ITEM	POST. REF.	DEBIT	CREDIT	BALANCE
20-- June 5		J7		5 6 2 40	5 6 2 40
12		J7	4 6 20		5 1 6 20
16		J8	5 1 6 20		

NAME: Flites Pharmaceuticals

DATE	ITEM	POST. REF.	DEBIT	CREDIT	BALANCE
20-- June 27		J8		6 3 8 47	6 3 8 47

NAME: Mutual Drug Co.

DATE	ITEM	POST. REF.	DEBIT	CREDIT	BALANCE
20-- June 14		J7		4 7 9 40	4 7 9 40
23		J8	4 7 9 40		

NAME: Sullivan Co.

DATE	ITEM	POST. REF.	DEBIT	CREDIT	BALANCE
20-- June 1		J7		2 3 4 20	2 3 4 20
9		J7	2 3 4 20		

NAME: University Drug Co.

DATE	ITEM	POST. REF.	DEBIT	CREDIT	BALANCE
20-- June 7		J7		3 6 7 35	3 6 7 35
15		J8	5 3 70		3 1 3 65

NAME: Vashon Medical Supply

DATE	ITEM	POST. REF.	DEBIT	CREDIT	BALANCE
20-- June 1	Balance	✔			1 2 1 7 69
30		J8	1 2 1 7 69		

(continued)

SOLUTION 3.

Rutman Pharmacy Schedule of Accounts Payable June 30, 20--					
Flites Pharmaceuticals	$	6	3	8	47
University Drug Co.		3	1	3	65
	$	9	5	2	12
Proof					
Balance of Accounts Payable, June 30	$	9	5	2	12

KEY TERMS

accounts payable ledger (411)   A separate ledger containing an individual account payable for each supplier.

contra-cost account (405)   An account with a credit balance that is deducted from the related cost account.

contra-purchases account (405)   See contra-cost account.

cost of goods sold (408)   The difference between the goods available for sale and the ending inventory.

cost of merchandise sold (408)   See cost of goods sold.

FOB destination (407)   Shipping terms indicating that transportation charges are paid by the seller.

FOB shipping point (407)   Shipping terms indicating that transportation charges are paid by the buyer.

gross margin (408)   See gross profit.

gross profit (408)   The difference between net sales and cost of goods sold.

invoice (401)   A document prepared by the seller as a bill for the merchandise shipped. To the seller, this is a sales invoice. To the buyer, this is a purchase invoice.

purchase invoice (401)   A document prepared by the seller as a bill for the merchandise shipped. To the buyer, this is a purchase invoice.

purchase order (400)   A written order to buy goods from a specific vendor (supplier).

purchase requisition (400)   An internal form sent to the purchasing department to request the purchase of merchandise or other property.

purchases (400)   Merchandise acquired for resale to customers.

receiving report (400)   A report indicating what has been received.

schedule of accounts payable (415)   An alphabetical or numerical listing of supplier accounts and balances, usually prepared at the end of the month.

trade discount (402)   A reduction from the list or catalog price offered to different classes of customers.

voucher (402)   A document which shows that an acquisition is proper and that payment is authorized.

voucher system (402)   A control technique that requires every acquisition and subsequent payment to be supported by an approved voucher.

SELF-STUDY TEST QUESTIONS

True/False

1. **LO1**   In the purchasing process, the purchase invoice is the first document prepared.

2. **LO1**   A sales invoice prepared by the seller is called a purchase invoice by the buyer.

3. **LO1**   A trade discount is a reduction from the list or catalog price offered to different classes of customers.

4. **LO2**   Purchases Returns and Allowances is debited when merchandise is returned for credit.

5. **LO2**   FOB shipping point means that transportation charges are paid by the seller.

Multiple Choice

1. **LO1**   A purchase of merchandise for $300 with a trade discount of 10% would require a debit to Purchases of
   - (a) $330.
   - (b) $300.
   - (c) $297.
   - (d) $270.

2. **LO2**   In the income statement, Freight-In is
   - (a) added to purchases.
   - (b) subtracted from purchases.
   - (c) added to sales.
   - (d) subtracted from cost of goods sold.

3. **LO2**   The difference between net sales and cost of goods sold is called
   - (a) gross profit.
   - (b) net purchases.
   - (c) goods available for sale.
   - (d) the bottom line.

4. **LO2**   The difference between merchandise available for sale and the end-of-period merchandise inventory is called
   - (a) gross profit.
   - (b) net purchases.
   - (c) net sales.
   - (d) cost of goods sold.

5. **LO2**   A purchase invoice for $1,200 with credit terms 2/10, n/30, and a return of $300 received by the seller prior to payment, is paid within the discount period. A check should be sent for
   - (a) $1,200.
   - (b) $882.
   - (c) $900.
   - (d) $810.

Checkpoint Exercises

1. **LO1**   Deering Housewares purchased merchandise for $1,200 less a 10% trade discount with credit terms of 1/10, n/30.
   - a. Compute the trade discount.
   - b. Compute the amount at which to record this purchase.
   - c. Compute the cash discount if the payment for the merchandise is made within the discount period.

2. **LO2** Based on the following data for Dave's Supply House, determine the gross profit.

Net sales	$92,000
Merchandise inventory, January 1, 20--	27,000
Purchases during the year	60,800
Purchases returns and allowances during the year	3,100
Purchases discounts during the year	1,300
Merchandise inventory, December 31, 20--	24,000

3. **LO3** The following journal entries are for current purchases and cash payments transactions. Using T accounts, post these transactions to Cash, Accounts Payable, Purchases, Purchases Returns and Allowances, and Purchases Discounts in the general ledger, and the vendor account in the accounts payable ledger.

a. Purchases	350.00	
Accounts Payable/J. Bedas		350.00
b. Accounts Payable/J. Bedas	70.00	
Purchases Returns and Allowances		70.00
c. Accounts Payable/J. Bedas	280.00	
Cash		274.40
Purchases Discounts		5.60

4. **LO4** On June 23, Felini Plumbing's accounts payable consisted of the following vendor balances:

B. Sutton	$245
A. Gagne	703
L. Mohler	410
P. Luffman	190
Z. Quary	263

During the following week, Felini Plumbing made a purchase of $180 from Mohler and made cash payments on account of $375 to Gagne and $110 to Quary. Prepare a schedule of accounts payable for Felini Plumbing at June 30, 20--.

The answers to the Self-Study Test Questions are at the end of the chapter (pages 436–437).

APPLYING YOUR KNOWLEDGE

REVIEW QUESTIONS

LO1   1. Identify the major documents commonly used in the purchasing process.

LO1   2. Distinguish between a cash discount and a trade discount.

LO1   3. What is a voucher system?

LO1   4. In a voucher system, a payment is supported by what five documents?

LO2   5. Describe how each of the following accounts is used: (1) Purchases, (2) Purchases Returns and Allowances, (3) Purchases Discounts, and (4) Freight-In.

LO2   6. How are cost of goods sold and gross profit computed?

LO3   7. What steps are followed in posting purchases from the general journal to the general ledger?

LO3   8. What steps are followed in posting purchases from the general journal to the accounts payable ledger?

LO3   9. What steps are followed in posting purchases returns and allowances from the general journal to the general ledger and accounts payable ledger?

LO3   10. What steps are followed in posting cash payments from the general journal to the general ledger?

LO3   11. What steps are followed in posting cash payments from the general journal to the accounts payable ledger?

LO4   12. If the total of the schedule of accounts payable does not agree with the Accounts Payable balance, what procedures should be used to search for the error?

SERIES A EXERCISES

E 11-1A   (LO1)

PURCHASING DOCUMENTS AND FLOWCHART LABELING A partially completed flowchart showing some of the major documents commonly used in the purchasing function of a merchandise business is presented below. Identify documents 1, 3, and 4.

E 11-2A   (LO1/2)
✓ 2: $1,764

TRADE DISCOUNT AND CASH DISCOUNTS Merchandise was purchased on account from Jacob's Distributors on May 17. The purchase price was $2,000, less a 10% trade discount and credit terms of 2/10, n/30.

1. Calculate the net amount to record the invoice, less the 10% trade discount.

2. Calculate the amount to be paid on this invoice within the discount period.

3. Journalize the purchase of the merchandise on May 17 in a general journal. Journalize the payment on May 27 (within the discount period).

E 11-3A   (LO2)
✓ 3(c): Purchases Discounts: $70

PURCHASE TRANSACTIONS AND T ACCOUNTS Using T accounts for Cash, Accounts Payable, Purchases, Purchases Returns and Allowances, Purchases Discounts, and Freight-In, enter the following purchase transactions. Identify each transaction with its corresponding letter. Use a new set of T accounts for each set of transactions, 1–4.

1. Purchase of merchandise with cash.

   (a) Merchandise is purchased for cash, $1,500.

   (b) Merchandise listed at $3,500, less a trade discount of 15%, is purchased for cash.

(continued)

2. Purchase of merchandise on account with credit terms.

    (a) Merchandise is purchased on account, credit terms 2/10, n/30, $2,000.

    (b) Merchandise is purchased on account, credit terms 3/10, n/30, $1,200.

    (c) Payment is made on invoice (a) within the discount period.

    (d) Payment is made on invoice (b) too late to receive the cash discount.

3. Purchase of merchandise on account with return of merchandise.

    (a) Merchandise is purchased on account, credit terms 2/10, n/30, $4,000.

    (b) Merchandise is returned for credit before payment is made, $500.

    (c) Payment is made within the discount period.

4. Purchase of merchandise with freight-in.

    (a) Merchandise is purchased on account, $2,500 plus freight charges of $100. Terms of the sale were FOB shipping point.

    (b) Payment is made for the cost of merchandise and the freight charge.

E 11-4A (LO2)
✓ Cost of goods sold: $43,000

COMPUTING GROSS PROFIT The following data were taken from the accounts of Fluter Hardware, a small retail business. Determine the gross profit.

Sales	$120,000
Sales returns and allowances	900
Sales discounts	650
Merchandise inventory, January 1	35,000
Purchases during the period	77,600
Purchases returns and allowances during the period	4,100
Purchases discounts taken during the period	2,300
Freight-in on merchandise purchased during the period	1,250
Merchandise inventory, December 31	32,000

E 11-5A (LO3)
✓ May 9: Dr. Purchases, $2,500

JOURNALIZING PURCHASES TRANSACTIONS Journalize the following transactions in a general journal:

May 3 Purchased merchandise from Reed, $6,100. Invoice No. 321, dated May 1, terms n/30.

       9 Purchased merchandise from Omana, $2,500. Invoice No. 614, dated May 8, terms 2/10, n/30.

    18 Purchased merchandise from Yao Distributors, $2,200. Invoice No. 180, dated May 15, terms 1/15, n/30.

    23 Purchased merchandise from Brown, $5,300. Invoice No. 913, dated May 22, terms 1/10, n/30.

E 11-6A (LO3)
✓ Ending Accounts Payable balance: $8,600

JOURNALIZING PURCHASES RETURNS AND ALLOWANCES AND POSTING TO GENERAL LEDGER AND ACCOUNTS PAYABLE LEDGER Using page 3 of a general journal and the following general ledger and accounts payable ledger accounts, journalize and post the following transactions:

July 7 Returned merchandise to Starcraft Industries, $700.

    15 Returned merchandise to XYZ, Inc., $450.

    27 Returned merchandise to Datamagic, $900.

General Ledger

Account No.	Account	Balance July 1, 20--
202	Accounts Payable	$10,650
501.1	Purchases Returns and Allowances	---

Accounts Payable Ledger

Name	Balance July 1, 20--
Datamagic	$2,600
Starcraft Industries	4,300
XYZ, Inc.	3,750

E 11-7A (LO3)
✓ Sept. 12: Cr. Cash, $8,019

JOURNALIZING CASH PAYMENTS TRANSACTIONS Enter the following cash payments transactions in a general journal:

Sept. 5 Issued Check No. 318 to Whittle Corp. for merchandise purchased August 28, $5,000, terms 2/10, n/30. Payment is made within the discount period.

12 Issued Check No. 319 to Martin Company for merchandise purchased September 2, $8,500, terms 1/10, n/30. A credit memo had been received on September 8 from Martin Company for merchandise returned, $400. Payment is made within the discount period after deduction for the return dated September 8.

19 Issued Check No. 320 to Cloud Systems for merchandise purchased August 20, $6,100, terms n/30.

27 Issued Check No. 321 to Dynamic Data for merchandise purchased September 17, $7,000, terms 2/10, n/30. Payment is made within the discount period.

E 11-8A (LO4)
✓ Total Accounts Payable: $14,370

SCHEDULE OF ACCOUNTS PAYABLE Ryan's Express, a retail business, had the following beginning balances and purchases and payments activity in its accounts payable ledger during October. Prepare a schedule of accounts payable for Ryan's Express as of October 31, 20--.

Accounts Payable Ledger

Name	Balance Oct. 1, 20--	Purchases	Payments
Columbia Products	$4,350	$3,060	$2,060
Favorite Fashions	4,910	1,970	2,600
Rustic Legends	5,130	2,625	3,015

SERIES A PROBLEMS

P 11-9A (LO2/3)
✓ Purchases balance: $20,790

PURCHASES TRANSACTIONS J. B. Speck, owner of Speck's Galleria, made the following purchases of merchandise on account during the month of September:

Sept. 3 Purchase Invoice No. 415, $2,650, from Smith Distributors.

8 Purchase Invoice No. 132, $3,830, from Michaels Wholesaler.

11 Purchase Invoice No. 614, $3,140, from J. B. Sanders & Co.

18 Purchase Invoice No. 329, $2,250, from Bateman & Jones, Inc.

(*continued*)

Sept. 23 Purchase Invoice No. 767, $4,160, from Smith Distributors.

    27 Purchase Invoice No. 744, $1,980, from Anderson Company.

    30 Purchase Invoice No. 652, $2,780, from Michaels Wholesaler.

REQUIRED

1. Record the transactions starting with page 16 of a general journal.

2. Post from the general journal to the general ledger accounts and to the accounts payable ledger accounts. Use general ledger account numbers as shown in the chapter.

P 11-10A (LO2/3)
✓ Accounts Payable balance: $1,900

CASH PAYMENTS TRANSACTIONS Sam Santiago operates a retail variety store. The books include a general journal and an accounts payable ledger.

Selected account balances on May 1 are as follows:

General Ledger	
Cash	$40,000
Accounts Payable	20,000

Accounts Payable Ledger	
Fantastic Toys	$ 5,200
Goya Outlet	3,800
Mueller's Distributors	3,600
Van Kooning	7,400

The following are the transactions related to cash payments for the month of May:

May 1 Issued Check No. 426 in payment of May rent (Rent Expense), $2,400.

    3 Issued Check No. 427 to Mueller's Distributors in payment of merchandise purchased on account, $3,600, less a 3% discount. Check was written for $3,492.

    7 Issued Check No. 428 to Van Kooning in partial payment of merchandise purchased on account, $5,500. A cash discount was not allowed.

    12 Issued Check No. 429 to Fantastic Toys for merchandise purchased on account, $5,200, less a 1% discount. Check was written for $5,148.

    15 Issued Check No. 430 to City Power and Light (Utilities Expense), $1,720.

    18 Issued Check No. 431 to A-1 Warehouse for a cash purchase of merchandise, $4,800.

    26 Issued Check No. 432 to Goya Outlet for merchandise purchased on account, $3,800, less a 2% discount. Check was written for $3,724.

    30 Issued Check No. 433 to Mercury Transit Company for freight charges on merchandise purchased (Freight-In), $1,200.

    31 Issued Check No. 434 to Town Merchants for a cash purchase of merchandise, $3,000.

REQUIRED

1. Enter the transactions starting with page 9 of a general journal.

2. Post from the general journal to the general ledger and the accounts payable ledger. Use general ledger account numbers as shown in the chapter.

P 11-11A   (LO2/3)
✓ Cash balance: $10,284

PURCHASES AND CASH PAYMENTS TRANSACTIONS Emily Frank owns a small retail business called Frank's Fantasy. The cash account has a balance of $21,000 on July 1. The following transactions occurred during July:

July   1   Issued Check No. 414 in payment of July rent, $2,500.

1   Purchased merchandise on account from Tilly's Toys, Invoice No. 311, $2,800, terms 2/10, n/30.

3   Purchased merchandise on account from Scheer & Company, Invoice No. 812, $3,300, terms 1/10, n/30.

5   Returned merchandise purchased from Tilly's Toys, receiving a credit memo on the amount owed, $300.

8   Purchased merchandise on account from Donna's Dolls, Invoice No. 139, $2,900, terms 2/10, n/30.

11   Issued Check No. 415 to Tilly's Toys for merchandise purchased on account, less return of July 5 and less 2% discount.

13   Issued Check No. 416 to Scheer & Company for merchandise purchased on account, less 1% discount.

15   Returned merchandise purchased from Donna's Dolls, receiving a credit memo on the amount owed, $350.

18   Issued Check No. 417 to Donna's Dolls for merchandise purchased on account, less return of July 15 and less 2% discount.

25   Purchased merchandise on account from Applied Business, Invoice No. 489, $2,650, terms n/30.

26   Purchased merchandise on account from Tilly's Toys, Invoice No. 375, $2,180, terms 2/10, n/30.

29   Purchased merchandise on account from Scheer & Company, Invoice No. 883, $3,560, terms 1/10, n/30.

REQUIRED

1. Enter the transactions starting with page 16 of a general journal.

2. Post from the journal to the general ledger and accounts payable ledger accounts. Use general ledger account numbers as shown in the chapter.

P 11-12A   (LO4)
✓ Accounts Payable balance, Tilly's Toys: $2,180

SCHEDULE OF ACCOUNTS PAYABLE Based on the information provided in Problem 11-11A, prepare a schedule of accounts payable for Frank's Fantasy as of July 31, 20--. Verify that the accounts payable account balance in the general ledger agrees with the schedule of accounts payable total.

SERIES B EXERCISES

E 11-1B   (LO1)

PURCHASING DOCUMENTS AND FLOWCHART LABELING A flowchart showing some of the major documents commonly used in the purchasing function of a merchandise business is presented below. Briefly describe each document.

E 11-2B   (LO1/2)
✓ 2: $4,365

TRADE DISCOUNT AND CASH DISCOUNTS Merchandise was purchased on account from Grant's Distributors on June 12. The purchase price was $5,000, less a 10% trade discount and credit terms of 3/10, n/30.

1. Calculate the net amount to record the invoice, less the 10% trade discount.
2. Calculate the amount to be paid on this invoice within the discount period.
3. Journalize the purchase of the merchandise on June 12 and the payment on June 22 (within the discount period) in a general journal.

E 11-3B   (LO2)
✓ 3(c): Purchases Discounts, $100

PURCHASE TRANSACTIONS AND T ACCOUNTS Using T accounts for Cash, Accounts Payable, Purchases, Purchases Returns and Allowances, Purchases Discounts, and Freight-In, enter the following purchase transactions. Identify each transaction with its corresponding letter. Use a new set of T accounts for each set of transactions, 1–4.

1. Purchase of merchandise with cash.
   (a) Merchandise is purchased for cash, $2,300.
   (b) Merchandise listed at $4,000, less a trade discount of 10%, is purchased for cash.
2. Purchase of merchandise on account with credit terms.
   (a) Merchandise is purchased on account, credit terms 2/10, n/30, $4,000.
   (b) Merchandise is purchased on account, credit terms 3/10, n/30, $2,800.
   (c) Payment is made on invoice (a) within the discount period.
   (d) Payment is made on invoice (b) too late to receive the cash discount.
3. Purchase of merchandise on account with return of merchandise.
   (a) Merchandise is purchased on account, credit terms 2/10, n/30, $5,600.
   (b) Merchandise is returned for credit before payment is made, $600.
   (c) Payment is made within the discount period.
4. Purchase of merchandise with freight-in.
   (a) Merchandise is purchased on account, $3,800 plus freight charges of $200. Terms of the sale were FOB shipping point.
   (b) Payment is made for the cost of merchandise and the freight charge.

E 11-4B   (LO2)
✓ Cost of goods sold: $76,700

COMPUTING GROSS PROFIT The following data were taken from the accounts of Burnside Bedknobs, a retail business. Determine the gross profit.

Sales	$116,900
Sales returns and allowances	1,100
Sales discounts	400
Merchandise inventory, January 1	30,000
Purchases during the period	100,000
Purchases returns and allowances during the period	2,000
Purchases discounts taken during the period	2,800
Freight-in on merchandise purchased during the period	1,500
Merchandise inventory, December 31	50,000

E 11-5B   (LO3)
✓ Jan. 12: Dr. Purchases, $9,000

JOURNALIZING PURCHASES TRANSACTIONS Journalize the following transactions in a general journal:

Jan. 3 Purchased merchandise from Feng, $6,000. Invoice No. 416, dated January 1, terms 2/10, n/30.

     12 Purchased merchandise from Miranda, $9,000. Invoice No. 624, dated January 10, terms n/30.

Jan. 19   Purchased merchandise from J. B. Barba, $6,400. Invoice No. 190, dated January 18, terms 1/10, n/30.

26   Purchased merchandise from Ramirez, $3,700. Invoice No. 923, dated January 25, terms 1/15, n/30.

E 11-6B   (LO3)
✓ **Ending Accounts Payable balance: $6,950**

JOURNALIZING PURCHASES RETURNS AND ALLOWANCES AND POSTING TO GENERAL LEDGER AND ACCOUNTS PAYABLE LEDGER Using page 3 of a general journal and the following general ledger accounts and accounts payable ledger accounts, journalize and post the following transactions:

Mar. 5   Returned merchandise to Tower Industries, $500.
11   Returned merchandise to A & D Arms, $625.
23   Returned merchandise to Mighty Mansion, $275.

General Ledger

Account No.	Account	Balance Mar. 1, 20--
202	Accounts Payable	$8,350
501.1	Purchases Returns and Allowances	---

Accounts Payable Ledger

Name	Balance Mar. 1, 20--
A & D Arms	$2,300
Mighty Mansion	1,450
Tower Industries	4,600

E 11-7B   (LO3)
✓ **Apr. 19: Cr. Cash, $4,950**

JOURNALIZING CASH PAYMENTS TRANSACTIONS Enter the following cash payments transactions in a general journal:

Apr. 5   Issued Check No. 429 to Standard Industries for merchandise purchased March 27, $8,000, terms 2/10, n/30. Payment is made within the discount period.

19   Issued Check No. 430 to Finest Company for merchandise purchased April 10, $5,300, terms 1/10, n/30. A credit memo had been received on April 12 from Finest Company for merchandise returned, $300. Payment is made within the discount period after deduction for the return dated April 12.

21   Issued Check No. 431 to Funny Follies for merchandise purchased March 22, $3,250, terms n/30.

29   Issued Check No. 432 to Classic Data for merchandise purchased April 20, $7,000, terms 2/10, n/30. Payment is made within the discount period.

E 11-8B   (LO4)
✓ **Total accounts payable: $10,565**

SCHEDULE OF ACCOUNTS PAYABLE Crystal's Candles, a retail business, had the following balances and purchases and payments activity in its accounts payable ledger during November. Prepare a schedule of accounts payable for Crystal's Candles as of November 30, 20--.

Accounts Payable Ledger

Name	Balance Nov. 1, 20--	Purchases	Payments
Carl's Candle Wax	$4,135	$ 955	$1,610
Handy Supplies	3,490	1,320	1,850
Wishy Wicks	3,300	1,905	1,080

SERIES B PROBLEMS

P 11-9B   (LO2/3)
✓ Purchases balance: $18,515

PURCHASES TRANSACTIONS Ann Benton, owner of Benton's Galleria, made the following purchases of merchandise on account during the month of October:

Oct. 2 Purchase Invoice No. 321, $1,950, from Boggs Distributors.
      7 Purchase Invoice No. 152, $2,915, from Wolfs Wholesaler.
     10 Purchase Invoice No. 634, $3,565, from Komuro & Co.
     16 Purchase Invoice No. 349, $2,845, from Fritz & McCord, Inc.
     24 Purchase Invoice No. 587, $3,370, from Boggs Distributors.
     26 Purchase Invoice No. 764, $2,240, from Sanderson Company.
     31 Purchase Invoice No. 672, $1,630, from Wolfs Wholesaler.

REQUIRED

1. Record the transactions starting with page 16 of a general journal.
2. Post from the general journal to the general ledger accounts and to the accounts payable ledger accounts. Use general ledger account numbers as shown in the chapter.

P 11-10B   (LO2/3)
✓ Accounts Payable balance: $600

CASH PAYMENTS TRANSACTIONS Kay Zembrowski operates a retail variety store. The books include a general journal and an accounts payable ledger. Selected account balances on May 1 are as follows:

General Ledger

Cash	$40,000
Accounts Payable	20,000

Accounts Payable Ledger

Cortez Distributors	$ 4,200
Indra & Velga	6,800
Toy Corner	4,600
Troutman Outlet	4,400

The following transactions are related to cash payments for the month of May:

May 1 Issued Check No. 326 in payment of May rent (Rent Expense), $2,600.
      4 Issued Check No. 327 to Cortez Distributors in payment of merchandise purchased on account, $4,200, less a 3% discount. Check was written for $4,074.
      7 Issued Check No. 328 to Indra & Velga in partial payment of merchandise purchased on account, $6,200. A cash discount was not allowed.
     11 Issued Check No. 329 to Toy Corner for merchandise purchased on account, $4,600, less a 1% discount. Check was written for $4,554.
     15 Issued Check No. 330 to County Power and Light (Utilities Expense), $1,500.
     19 Issued Check No. 331 to Builders Warehouse for a cash purchase of merchandise, $3,500.
     25 Issued Check No. 332 to Troutman Outlet for merchandise purchased on account, $4,400, less a 2% discount. Check was written for $4,312.

May 30   Issued Check No. 333 to Rapid Transit Company for freight charges on merchandise purchased (Freight-In), $800.

31   Issued Check No. 334 to City Merchants for a cash purchase of merchandise, $2,350.

REQUIRED

1. Enter the transactions starting with page 9 of a general journal.
2. Post from the general journal to the general ledger and the accounts payable ledger. Use general ledger account numbers as shown in the chapter.

P 11-11B   (LO2/3)
✓ Cash balance: $12,790

PURCHASES AND CASH PAYMENTS TRANSACTIONS Debbie Mueller owns a small retail business called Debbie's Doll House. The cash account has a balance of $20,000 on July 1. The following transactions occurred during July:

July   1   Issued Check No. 314 for July rent, $1,400.

1   Purchased merchandise on account from Topper's Toys, Invoice No. 211, $2,500, terms 2/10, n/30.

3   Purchased merchandise on account from Jones & Company, Invoice No. 812, $2,800, terms 1/10, n/30.

5   Returned merchandise purchased from Topper's Toys receiving a credit memo on the amount owed, $400.

8   Purchased merchandise on account from Downtown Merchants, Invoice No. 159, $1,600, terms 2/10, n/30.

11   Issued Check No. 315 to Topper's Toys for merchandise purchased on account, less return of July 5 and less 2% discount.

13   Issued Check No. 316 to Jones & Company for merchandise purchased on account, less 1% discount.

15   Returned merchandise purchased from Downtown Merchants receiving a credit memo on the amount owed, $600.

18   Issued Check No. 317 to Downtown Merchants for merchandise purchased on account, less return of July 15 and less 2% discount.

25   Purchased merchandise on account from Columbia Products, Invoice No. 468, $3,200, terms n/30.

26   Purchased merchandise on account from Topper's Toys, Invoice No. 395, $1,430, terms 2/10, n/30.

29   Purchased merchandise on account from Jones & Company, Invoice No. 853, $2,970, terms 1/10, n/30.

REQUIRED

1. Enter the transactions starting with page 16 of a general journal.
2. Post from the journal to the general ledger and accounts payable ledger accounts. Use general ledger account numbers as shown in the chapter.

P 11-12B   (LO4)
✓ Accounts Payable balance, Topper's Toys: $1,430

SCHEDULE OF ACCOUNTS PAYABLE Based on the information provided in Problem 11-11B, prepare a schedule of accounts payable for Debbie's Doll House as of July 31, 20--. Verify that the accounts payable account balance in the general ledger agrees with the schedule of accounts payable total.

CHECK LIST

☐ **Managing**
☐ **Planning**
☐ **Drafting**
☐ **Break**
☐ **Revising**
☐ **Managing**

MANAGING YOUR WRITING

You are working as a summer intern at a rapidly growing organic food distributor. Part of your responsibility is to assist in the accounts payable department. You notice that most bills from suppliers are not paid within the discount period. The manager of accounts payable says the bills are organized by vendor, like the accounts payable ledger, and she is too busy to keep track of the discount periods. Besides, the owner has told her that the 1% and 2% discounts available are not worth worrying about.

Write a memo to the owner explaining why it is expensive not to take advantage of cash discounts on credit purchases. In addition, suggest a way to file (organize) supplier invoices so that they are paid within the discount period.

ETHICS

ETHICS CASE

Bob's Discount Auto Parts receives a cash discount of 2% from Auto Warehouse if it pays an invoice within 10 days. Bob, the owner, consistently sends payments 15 to 20 days after receiving the invoice and still deducts the amount of the discount. Last week, Bob received a call from Auto Warehouse reminding him that in order to get the discount, an invoice must be paid within 10 days. When Bob received the next invoice, he dated the check exactly 10 days from the date of the invoice but didn't mail the check for another week. The receivables manager from Auto Warehouse called Bob and again reminded him that the check should be mailed by the 10th day in order to receive the 2% discount. When Bob received the next invoice, he mailed it on time but post-dated the check for the following week.

1. Are Bob's attempts to extend the discount period unethical?
2. What alternatives can Auto Warehouse take to prevent Bob's Discount Auto Parts from stretching the discount period?
3. Write a short note from Auto Warehouse to Bob's Discount Auto Parts explaining cash discounts and credit terms.
4. In small groups, make a list of the advantages and disadvantages of offering cash discounts.

MASTERY PROBLEM

✓ Accounts Payable balance: $10,000

Michelle French owns and operates Books and More, a retail book store. Selected account balances on June 1 are as follows:

General Ledger

Cash	$32,200.00
Accounts Payable	2,000.00
M. French, Drawing	18,000.00
Purchases	67,021.66
Purchases Returns and Allowances	2,315.23
Purchases Discounts	905.00
Freight-In	522.60
Rent Expense	3,125.00
Utilities Expense	1,522.87

Accounts Payable Ledger

Northeastern Publishing Co.	$ 2,000.00

The following purchases and cash payments transactions took place during the month of June:

June 1   Purchased books on account from Irving Publishing Company, $2,100. Invoice No. 101, terms 2/10, n/30, FOB destination.

        2   Issued Check No. 300 to Northeastern Publishing Co. for goods purchased on May 23, terms 2/10, n/30, $1,960 (the $2,000 invoice amount less the 2% discount).

        3   Purchased books on account from Broadway Publishing, Inc., $2,880. Invoice No. 711, less a 20% trade discount, and invoice terms of 3/10, n/30, FOB shipping point.

        3   Issued Check No. 301 to Mayday Shipping for delivery from Broadway Publishing, Inc., $250.

        4   Issued Check No. 302 for June rent, $625.

        8   Purchased books on account from Northeastern Publishing Co., $5,825. Invoice No. 268, terms 2/eom, n/60, FOB destination.

     10   Received a credit memo from Irving Publishing Company, $550. Books had been returned because the covers were on upside down.

     13   Issued Check No. 304 to Broadway Publishing, Inc., for the purchase made on June 3. (Check No. 303 was voided because an error was made in preparing it.)

     28   Made the following purchases:

Invoice No.	Company	Amount	Terms
579	Broadway Publishing, Inc.	$2,350	2/10, n/30, FOB destination
406	Northeastern Publishing Co.	4,200	2/eom, n/60, FOB destination
964	Riley Publishing Co.	3,450	3/10, n/30, FOB destination

     30   Issued Check No. 305 to Taylor County Utility Co. for June utilities, $325.

     30   French withdrew cash for personal use, $4,500. Issued Check No. 306.

     30   Issued Check No. 307 to Irving Publishing Company for purchase made on June 1 less returns made on June 10.

     30   Issued Check No. 308 to Northeastern Publishing Co. for purchase made on June 8.

     30   Issued Check No. 309 for books purchased at an auction, $1,328.

REQUIRED

1. Enter the transactions in a general journal (start with page 16).
2. Post from the journal to the general ledger accounts and the accounts payable ledger. Use general ledger account numbers as indicated in the chapter.
3. Prepare a schedule of accounts payable.
4. If merchandise inventory was $35,523 on January 1 and $42,100 as of June 30, prepare the cost of goods sold section of the income statement for the six months ended June 30, 20--.

CHALLENGE PROBLEM

This problem challenges you to apply your cumulative accounting knowledge to move a step beyond the material in the chapter.

✓ May 14: Cr. Purchases Discounts, $9

Record the following transactions in a general journal:

May   4   Merchandise listed at $2,900, less a trade discount of 10%, is purchased on account, credit terms of 1/10, n/30, shipping terms FOB destination.

        8   Merchandise purchased on May 4, listed at $520, is returned for credit.

       14   Partial payment is made for the merchandise purchased on May 4, listed at $1,000, less 1% discount.

June   3   Payment is made of the balance due on the May 4 purchase.

ANSWERS TO SELF-STUDY TEST QUESTIONS

True/False

1. F (purchase requisition)

2. T

3. T

4. F (credited)

5. F (buyer)

Multiple Choice

1. d   2. a   3. a   4. d   5. b

Checkpoint Exercises

1. a. $1,200 × 10% = $120
   b. $1,200 − $120 = $1,080
   c. $1,200 − $120 = $1,080 × 1% = $10.80

2. Net sales $92,000
   Cost of goods sold:
      Merchandise inventory, Jan. 1 $27,000
      Purchases $60,800
      Less: Purchases returns and allowances $3,100
         Purchases discounts   1,300   4,400
         Cost of goods purchased   56,400
      Goods available for sale $83,400
      Less merchandise inventory, Dec. 31   24,000
         Cost of goods sold   59,400
   Gross profit $32,600

3.

GENERAL LEDGER

Cash

		(c)	274.40

Accounts Payable

(b)	70.00	(a)	350.00
(c)	280.00		

Purchases

(a)	350.00		

Purchases Returns and Allowances

		(b)	70.00

Purchases Discounts

		(c)	5.60

Accounts Payable Ledger
J. Bedas

(b)	70.00	(a)	350.00
(c)	280.00		

4.

Felini Plumbing
Schedule of Accounts Payable
June 30, 20--

B. Sutton	$ 245
A. Gagne	328
L. Mohler	590
P. Luffman	190
Z. Quary	153
Total	$1,506

The Net-Price Method of Recording Purchases

LO1 — Net-Price Method

Describe the net-price method of recording purchases.

In this chapter, purchases were recorded using the gross-price method. Under this method, purchases are recorded at the gross amount, regardless of available cash discounts. An alternative approach to accounting for purchases is the net-price method. Under this method, purchases are recorded at the net amount, assuming that all available cash discounts will be taken.

LO2 — Recording with the Net-Price Method

Record purchases and cash payments using the net-price method.

To compare the gross-price and net-price methods, reconsider the purchase for $100 on account, with credit terms of 2/10, n/30, on page 405. At the time of the purchase, the following entries are made under the two methods:

Gross-Price			Net-Price		
Purchases	100.00		Purchases	98.00*	
Accounts Payable		100.00	Accounts Payable		98.00

*$100—$2 (2% cash discount)

If the payment for the merchandise is made within the discount period, the entries are as follows:

Gross-Price			Net-Price		
Accounts Payable	100.00		Accounts Payable	98.00	
Cash		98.00	Cash		98.00
Purchases Discounts		2.00			

If payment for the merchandise is not made until after the discount period, the entries are as follows:

Gross-Price			Net-Price		
Accounts Payable	100.00		Accounts Payable	98.00	
Cash		100.00	Purchases Discounts Lost	2.00	
			Cash		100.00

Note that under the net-price method a new account, Purchases Discounts Lost, is used. Purchases Discounts Lost is a temporary owner's equity account used to record cash discounts lost on purchases. It is reported as an expense on the income statement.

Purchases Discounts Lost

Debit	Credit
to enter discounts lost because of late payment of invoices	

Purchases Discounts Lost represents a finance charge for postponing the payment for merchandise. If the balance in this account is large relative to the amount of gross purchases, management should review its cash payment procedures.

LEARNING OBJECTIVES	Key Points to Remember
LO1 Describe the net-price method of recording purchases.	Under the net-price method, purchases are recorded at the net amount, assuming all available cash discounts will be taken.
LO2 Record purchases and cash payments using the net-price method.	Assume a purchase is made for $100 on account, with credit terms of 2/10, n/30. Under the net-price method, the entry at the time of purchase is as follows:

Purchases   98
    Accounts Payable   98

If payment is made within the discount period, the entry is as follows:

Accounts Payable   98
    Cash   98

If payment is not made until after the discount period, the entry is as follows:

Accounts Payable   98
Purchases Discounts Lost   2
    Cash   100

KEY TERMS

gross-price method (438)   Under this method, purchases are recorded at the gross amount.

net-price method (438)   Under this method, purchases are recorded at the net amount, assuming all available cash discounts are taken.

REVIEW QUESTIONS

LO1 1. At what amount are purchases recorded under the net-price method?

LO2 2. Under the net-price method, if payment for merchandise is not made within the discount period, what accounts are debited when the payment is made?

LO2 3. (a) What kind of an account is Purchases Discounts Lost?
(b) How is this item reported on the income statement?

SERIES A EXERCISE

E 11Apx-1A (LO2)
✓ 1. Apr. 11: Cr. Purchases Discounts, $20

PURCHASES TRANSACTIONS—GROSS-PRICE AND NET-PRICE METHODS
Romero's Heating and Cooling had the following transactions during April:

Apr. 2 Purchased merchandise on account from Alanon Valve for $1,000, terms 2/10, n/30.
5 Purchased merchandise on account from Leon's Garage for $1,400, terms 1/10, n/30.
11 Paid the amount due to Alanon Valve for the purchase on April 2.
25 Paid the amount due to Leon's Garage for the purchase on April 5.

1. Prepare general journal entries for these transactions using the gross-price method.

2. Prepare general journal entries for these transactions using the net-price method.

SERIES B EXERCISE

E 11Apx-1B (LO2)
✓ 2. May 27: Dr. Purchases Discounts Lost, $12

PURCHASES TRANSACTIONS—GROSS-PRICE AND NET-PRICE METHODS
Gloria's Repair Shop had the following transactions during May:

May 2 Purchased merchandise on account from Delgado's Supply for $900, terms 2/10, n/30.
6 Purchased merchandise on account from Goro's Auto Care for $1,200, terms 1/10, n/30.
11 Paid the amount due to Delgado's Supply for the purchase on May 2.
27 Paid the amount due to Goro's Auto Care for the purchase on May 6.

1. Prepare general journal entries for these transactions using the gross-price method.
2. Prepare general journal entries for these transactions using the net-price method.

Chapter **12** Special Journals

If you are an active health and fitness enthusiast, you might already know of NutraPlanet, perhaps through its nutraplanet. com Web sites. NutraPlanet was founded in 2004 and is head-quartered in Graham, North Carolina. After a slow start, it has grown into one of the world's top Web sites for sports and nutrition supplements.

NutraPlanet sells a wide array of health supplements. Many are targeted at bodybuilding, but its product categories include amino acids, carbohydrates, cardiovascular support, fat burners, herbs, joint support, and many others. Its products tend to be priced in the $13–$70 range. Most of the sales for a company like this probably would be for relatively small dollar amounts. This means the volume of transactions to generate annual sales in the millions would be huge. NutraPlanet would need a way to record all of this activity that is more efficient than the methods we have seen in Chapters 10 and 11. In Chapter 12, you will learn about a more efficient way to record transactions. In the "A Broader View" feature, you will see how computer software can add even greater efficiency.

LEARNING OBJECTIVES

Careful study of this chapter should enable you to:

LO1 Describe, explain the purpose of, and identify transactions recorded in special journals.

LO2 Describe and use the sales journal.

LO3 Describe and use the cash receipts journal.

LO4 Describe and use the purchases journal.

LO5 Describe and use the cash payments journal.

Chapters 10 and 11 demonstrated how to account for sales, cash receipts, purchases, and cash payments in a merchandising business. We also saw how to use accounts receivable and accounts payable ledgers to keep track of individual customer and supplier accounts. In this chapter, we continue to study how to account for sales, cash receipts, purchases, and cash payments, but our objective is to find a way to be more efficient. We will learn how to use four special journals that enable us to achieve this objective.

LO1	Special Journals

Describe, explain the purpose of, and identify transactions recorded in special journals.

A special journal is a journal designed for recording only certain kinds of transactions. A special journal can be created for almost any kind of transaction. The types of special journals a business uses should depend on the types of transactions that occur most frequently for a business. The more transactions of a specific type that occur, the more likely a special journal of that type would be useful for the business.

The primary purpose of using special journals is to save time journalizing and posting transactions. In a general journal, we recorded transactions by writing the account names, debit and credit amounts, and an explanation for each transaction on several lines in the journal. In contrast, most transactions are entered in a special journal on a single line, with the debit and credit amounts indicated in special columns provided for each account. This enables substantial time saving. The posting process also is more efficient. Using the general journal, each transaction is posted separately to the appropriate general ledger accounts. With a special journal, summary postings of column totals are made to appropriate accounts on a periodic basis.

Of course, even if a business uses special journals, there still is a need for a general journal. For example, transactions that occur infrequently, and adjusting and closing entries, usually are recorded in the general journal.

The following four special journals are commonly used by businesses:

> **LEARNING KEY** 🔑
>
> The special journals and general journal are books of original entry. Each transaction is recorded in only <u>one</u> of these journals.

- Sales journal
- Cash receipts journal
- Purchases journal
- Cash payments journal

Figure 12-1 identifies the types of transactions recorded in each of the four special journals and the general journal. You might find it helpful to refer back to Figure 12-1 as the four special journals are introduced in this chapter.

FIGURE 12-1 Types of Journals and Transactions

TYPE OF JOURNAL	TYPE OF TRANSACTIONS RECORDED
Sales journal	All sales of merchandise on account
Cash receipts journal	All cash receipts
Purchases journal	All purchases of merchandise on account
Cash payments journal	All cash payments
General journal	All other transactions

In the following sections, we will examine the journalizing and posting process using each of the four special journals.

LO2	Sales Journal

Describe and use the sales journal.

A sales journal is a special journal used to record only sales of merchandise on account. To illustrate the journalizing and posting of sales transactions in the sales journal, we use the following five sales transactions for Sunflower Cycle from Chapter 10.

Apr. 4 Made Sale No. 133C on account to Enrico Lorenzo, $1,520, plus $76 sales tax.

> [!NOTE]
> **LEARNING KEY** 🔑
> Use a sales journal only for recording sales of merchandise on account.

10 Made Sale No. 134C on account to Brenda Myers, $440, plus $22 sales tax.

18 Made Sale No. 105D on account to Edith Walton, $980, plus $49 sales tax.

21 Made Sale No. 202B on account to Wilma Cutz, $620, plus $31 sales tax.

24 Made Sale No. 162A on account to Heidi Schwitzer, $1,600, plus $80 sales tax.

The general journal entries for these five transactions are shown in Figure 12-2.

FIGURE 12-2 Sales Entered in General Journal

4	Apr.	4	Accounts Receivable/E. Lorenzo		1	5	9	6	00								4
5			Sales							1	5	2	0	00			5
6			Sales Tax Payable									7	6	00			6
7			Sale No. 133C														7
8																	8
9		10	Accounts Receivable/B. Myers			4	6	2	00								9
10			Sales								4	4	0	00			10
11			Sales Tax Payable									2	2	00			11
12			Sale No. 134C														12
13																	13
14		18	Accounts Receivable/E. Walton		1	0	2	9	00								14
15			Sales								9	8	0	00			15
16			Sales Tax Payable									4	9	00			16
17			Sale No. 105D														17
18																	18
19		21	Accounts Receivable/W. Cutz			6	5	1	00								19
20			Sales								6	2	0	00			20
21			Sales Tax Payable									3	1	00			21
22			Sale No. 202B														22
23																	23
24		24	Accounts Receivable/H. Schwitzer		1	6	8	0	00								24
25			Sales							1	6	0	0	00			25
26			Sales Tax Payable									8	0	00			26
27			Sale No. 162A														27

Notice that each of these five entries involved the same three accounts. The same account titles were recorded five times. Similarly, to post these entries to the general ledger, five separate postings would be made to each of the three accounts, a total of 15 postings.

These transactions can be recorded more efficiently by using a sales journal. To illustrate, reconsider the five sales made on account by Sunflower Cycle. They are entered in the sales journal in Figure 12-3. The sales journal provides separate columns for Accounts Receivable Debit, Sales Credit, and Sales Tax Payable Credit, the

Remember that sales returns and allowances are recorded in the general journal, as illustrated in Chapter 10, <u>not</u> in the sales journal.

three accounts used repeatedly in the general journal in Figure 12-2. A sale is recorded in the sales journal by entering the following information:

1. Date
2. Sale number
3. Customer (to whom sold)
4. Dollar amounts

There is no need to enter any general ledger account titles, since they appear in the column headings.

FIGURE 12-3 Sunflower Cycle Sales Journal

	DATE		SALE NO.	TO WHOM SOLD	POST. REF.	ACCOUNTS RECEIVABLE DEBIT					SALES CREDIT					SALES TAX PAYABLE CREDIT				
	20--																			
1	Apr.	4	133C	Enrico Lorenzo		1	5	9	6	00	1	5	2	0	00		7	6	00	1
2		10	134C	Brenda Myers			4	6	2	00		4	4	0	00		2	2	00	2
3		18	105D	Edith Walton		1	0	2	9	00		9	8	0	00		4	9	00	3
4		21	202B	Wilma Cutz			6	5	1	00		6	2	0	00		3	1	00	4
5		24	162A	Heidi Schwitzer		1	6	8	0	00	1	6	0	0	00		8	0	00	5

SALES JOURNAL — PAGE 6

This chapter illustrates a manual accounting system. With a computerized system, journals/ledgers are updated simultaneously when a transaction is entered, and there is no need for special journals (see A Broader View on page 452).

The sales journal in Figure 12-3 is designed for a company, like Sunflower Cycle, that charges sales tax. For a wholesaler or any other company that does not charge sales tax, a sales journal like that in Figure 12-4 would be sufficient. In this case, there is only a single amount column headed Accounts Receivable Debit/Sales Credit. With no sales tax, the Accounts Receivable Debit and Sales Credit amounts are identical for each sale. Thus, only a single column is needed.

FIGURE 12-4 Sales Journal Without Sales Tax

DATE	SALE NO.	TO WHOM SOLD	POST. REF.	ACCOUNTS RECEIVABLE DEBIT/ SALES CREDIT			

SALES JOURNAL — PAGE 1

Posting from the Sales Journal

Posting from the sales journal also is very efficient. Each general ledger account used in the sales journal requires only one posting each period. Figure 12-5 illustrates the general ledger posting process for Sunflower Cycle's sales journal for the month of April.

The following steps are used to post from the sales journal to the general ledger at the end of each month, as indicated in Figure 12-5:

In the sales journal:

Step 1 is the main difference in posting the sales journal to the general ledger. Steps 2–6 are essentially the same as steps 1–5 used to post from the general journal.

STEP 1 Total the amount columns, verify that the total of the debit column equals the total of the credit columns, and rule the columns.

In the ledger account:

STEP 2 Enter the date of the transaction in the Date column.

STEP 3 Enter the amount of the debit or credit in the Debit or Credit column.

FIGURE 12-5 Posting the Sales Journal to the General Ledger

	Date	Sale No.	To Whom Sold	Post. Ref.	Accounts Receivable Debit	Sales Credit	Sales Tax Payable Credit
20--							
Apr.	4	133C	Enrico Lorenzo		1,596.00	1,520.00	76.00
	10	134C	Brenda Myers		462.00	440.00	22.00
	18	105D	Edith Walton		1,029.00	980.00	49.00
	21	202B	Wilma Cutz		651.00	620.00	31.00
	24	162A	Heidi Schwitzer		1,680.00	1,600.00	80.00
					5,418.00	5,160.00	258.00 **1**
					(122)	(401)	(231) **6**

SALES JOURNAL — Page 6

GENERAL LEDGER (Partial)

1 Debit total: $5,418

Credit total: $5,160
                   258
                $5,418

STEP 4 Enter the new balance in the Balance columns under Debit or Credit.

STEP 5 Enter the initial "S" and the journal page number in the Posting Reference column.

In the sales journal:

STEP 6 Enter the ledger account number immediately below the column totals for each account that is posted.

As we saw in Chapter 10, Sunflower Cycle also needs a record of the accounts receivable from *individual customers*. Figure 12-6 illustrates the use of the accounts receivable ledger. The accounts receivable ledger is posted *daily* so that current information is available for each customer at all times. The following steps are used to post the sales journal to the accounts receivable ledger, as shown in Figure 12-6:

LEARNING KEY 🔑

All special journal entries are posted to the general and subsidiary ledger accounts, *not* to the general journal.

If the accounts receivable ledger is posted daily and the general ledger is posted at the end of the month, the accounts receivable ledger total will equal the general ledger Accounts Receivable total only at the end of the month.

FIGURE 12-6 Posting from the Sales Journal to the Accounts Receivable Ledger

SALES JOURNAL — Page 6

Date	Sale No.	To Whom Sold	Post. Ref.	Accounts Receivable Debit	Sales Credit	Sales Tax Payable Credit
20--						
Apr. 4	133C	Enrico Lorenzo	✔	1,596.00	1,520.00	76.00
10	134C	Brenda Myers	✔	462.00	440.00	22.00
18	105D	Edith Walton	✔	1,029.00	980.00	49.00
21	202B	Wilma Cutz	✔	651.00	620.00	31.00
24	162A	Heidi Schwitzer	✔	1,680.00	1,600.00	80.00
				5,418.00	5,160.00	258.00
				(122)	(401)	(231)

ACCOUNTS RECEIVABLE LEDGER

NAME Helen Avery
ADDRESS 308 Devon Ave., Overbrook, KS 66524

Date	Item	Post. Ref.	Debit	Credit	Balance
20--					
Apr. 1	Bal.	✔			2,302.00

NAME Wilma Cutz
ADDRESS 1116 Williamsburg Place, Lawrence, KS 66049

Date	Item	Post. Ref.	Debit	Credit	Balance
20--					
Apr. 21		S6	651.00		651.00

NAME Enrico Lorenzo
ADDRESS 1827 N. 100 Rd., Baldwin City, KS 66006

Date	Item	Post. Ref.	Debit	Credit	Balance
20--					
Apr. 4		S6	1,596.00		1,596.00

NAME Brenda Myers
ADDRESS 1613 Stone Meadows, Lawrence, KS 66049

Date	Item	Post. Ref.	Debit	Credit	Balance
20--					
Apr. 10		S6	462.00		462.00

NAME Heidi Schwitzer
ADDRESS 13913 Nicklaus Dr., Overland Park, KS 66223

Date	Item	Post. Ref.	Debit	Credit	Balance
20--					
Apr. 1	Bal.	✔			1,883.00
24		S6	1,680.00		3,563.00

NAME Ken Ulmet
ADDRESS 2616 Sawgrass Dr., Lawrence, KS 66047

Date	Item	Post. Ref.	Debit	Credit	Balance
20--					
Apr. 1	Bal.	✔			3,315.00

NAME Edith Walton
ADDRESS 1418 N. 600 Rd., Baldwin, KS 66006

Date	Item	Post. Ref.	Debit	Credit	Balance
20--					
Apr. 18		S6	1,029.00		1,029.00

NAME Vivian Winston
ADDRESS 1613 Alvamar Dr., Lawrence, KS 66047

Date	Item	Post. Ref.	Debit	Credit	Balance
20--					
Apr. 1	Bal.	✔			4,500.00

GENERAL LEDGER (Partial)

ACCOUNT Accounts Receivable   ACCOUNT NO. 122

Date	Item	Post. Ref.	Debit	Credit	Balance Debit	Balance Credit
20--						
Apr. 1	Bal.	✔			12,000.00	
30		S6	5,418.00		17,418.00	

ACCOUNT Sales Tax Payable   ACCOUNT NO. 231

Date	Item	Post. Ref.	Debit	Credit	Balance Debit	Balance Credit
20--						
Apr. 30		S6		258.00		258.00

ACCOUNT Sales   ACCOUNT NO. 401

Date	Item	Post. Ref.	Debit	Credit	Balance Debit	Balance Credit
20--						
Apr. 1	Bal.	✔				67,000.00
30		S6		5,160.00		72,160.00

In the accounts receivable ledger account:

STEP 1   Enter the date of the transaction in the Date column.

STEP 2   Enter the amount of the debit or credit in the Debit or Credit column.

STEP 3   Enter the new balance in the Balance column.

STEP 4   Enter the initial "S" and the journal page number in the Posting Reference column.

In the sales journal:

STEP 5   Enter a check mark (✓) in the Posting Reference column of the journal for each transaction that is posted.

LEARNING KEY 🔑

The total of the accounts receivable ledger balances must equal the Accounts Receivable balance in the general ledger.

The accounts receivable ledger also can be posted from the source document used to make the sales journal entry. For example, sales ticket #134C (see Figure 10-2) could be used to post that sale to Brenda Myers' account in the accounts receivable ledger. In this case, 134C would be inserted in the Posting Reference column of her account.

Note the relationship between the sales journal, accounts receivable ledger, and general ledger. All individual entries in the sales journal are posted to the accounts receivable ledger. The totals of all entries in the sales journal are posted to the general ledger accounts. After the posting of the accounts receivable ledger and the general ledger is completed, the total of the accounts receivable ledger balances should equal the Accounts Receivable balance in the general ledger.

CHECKPOINT ✔

Complete Checkpoint-1 on page 470 to test your basic understanding of LO2.

Complete Checkpoint-1 on page 470 to test your basic understanding of LO2.

LO3

Cash Receipts Journal

Describe and use the cash receipts journal.

A cash receipts journal is a special journal used to record only cash receipts transactions. To illustrate its use, we continue with the transactions of Sunflower Cycle. Sunflower Cycle's cash receipts journal for the month of April is shown in Figure 12-7, with the following transactions:

LEARNING KEY 🔑

Use a cash receipts journal to streamline journalizing and posting of cash receipts.

Apr. 14   Received cash on account from Enrico Lorenzo for Sale No. 133C, $1,596.

20   Received cash on account from Brenda Myers for Sale No. 134C, $462.

28   Received cash on account from Edith Walton for Sale No. 105D, $1,029.

30   Made cash sales for the month of $3,600 plus tax of $180.

30   Made bank credit card sales for the month of $22,500 plus tax of $1,125. Bank credit card expenses on these sales are $900.

30   Received cash for rent revenue, $600.

30   Borrowed cash from the bank by signing a note, $3,000.

Sunflower Cycle's cash receipts journal provides separate columns for Accounts Receivable Credit, Sales Credit, Sales Tax Payable Credit, Bank Credit Card Expense Debit, and Cash Debit. These are the accounts most frequently affected by Sunflower Cycle's cash receipts transactions. In addition, a General Credit column is provided for credits to any other accounts affected by cash receipts transactions.

FIGURE 12-7 Sunflower Cycle Cash Receipts Journal

	DATE	ACCOUNT CREDITED	POST. REF.	GENERAL CREDIT	ACCOUNTS RECEIVABLE CREDIT	SALES CREDIT	SALES TAX PAYABLE CREDIT	BANK CREDIT CARD EXPENSE DEBIT	CASH DEBIT	
				CASH RECEIPTS JOURNAL					PAGE 7	
1	20-- Apr. 14	Enrico Lorenzo			1 5 9 6 00				1 5 9 6 00	1
2	20	Brenda Myers			4 6 2 00				4 6 2 00	2
3	28	Edith Walton			1 0 2 9 00				1 0 2 9 00	3
4	30					3 6 0 0 00	1 8 0 00		3 7 8 0 00	4
5	30					22 5 0 0 00	1 1 2 5 00	9 0 0 00	22 7 2 5 00	5
6	30	Rent Revenue		6 0 0 0 00					6 0 0 0 00	6
7	30	Notes Payable		3 0 0 0 00					3 0 0 0 00	7
8										8

A cash receipt is recorded in the cash receipts journal by entering the following information:

1. Date
2. Account credited (if applicable)
3. Dollar amounts

The Account Credited column is used for two purposes.

1. To identify the customer name for any collection on account. This column is used whenever the Accounts Receivable Credit column is used.
2. To enter the appropriate account name whenever the General Credit column is used.

The Account Credited column is left blank if the entry is for cash sales or bank credit card sales.

The cash receipts journal in Figure 12-7 is designed for a company like Sunflower Cycle, which charges sales tax, makes bank credit card sales, and offers no cash discounts. For a wholesaler that does not charge sales tax, makes no bank credit card sales, and offers cash discounts, a cash receipts journal like the one in Figure 12-8 would be used. Recall that a special journal should be designed with column headings for frequently used accounts. Thus, the cash receipts journal in Figure 12-8 has no Sales Tax Payable Credit or Bank Credit Card Expense Debit column. Instead, a Sales Discounts Debit column is provided. In this way, the common cash receipts transactions of the wholesaler can be easily and efficiently recorded.

FIGURE 12-8 Cash Receipts Journal Without Sales Tax

	DATE	ACCOUNT CREDITED	POST. REF.	GENERAL CREDIT	ACCOUNTS RECEIVABLE CREDIT	SALES CREDIT	SALES DISCOUNTS DEBIT	CASH DEBIT	
				CASH RECEIPTS JOURNAL				PAGE 1	
1									1

Posting from the Cash Receipts Journal

The cash receipts journal is posted to the general ledger in two stages, as illustrated in Figure 12-9. First, on a daily basis, the individual amounts in the General Credit column are posted. Second, at the end of the month, the totals of each of the other amount columns are posted.

FIGURE 12-9 Posting from the Cash Receipts Journal to the General Ledger

CASH RECEIPTS JOURNAL   Page 7

Date	Account Credited	Post. Ref.	General Credit	Accounts Receivable Credit	Sales Credit	Sales Tax Payable Credit	Bank Credit Card Expense Debit	Cash Debit
20--								
Apr. 14	Enrico Lorenzo			1,596.00				1,596.00
20	Brenda Myers			462.00				462.00
28	Edith Walton			1,029.00				1,029.00
30		✔			3,600.00	180.00		3,780.00
30		✔			22,500.00	1,125.00	900.00	22,725.00
30	Rent Revenue	412	600.00					600.00
30	Notes Payable	201	3,000.00					3,000.00
			3,600.00	3,087.00	26,100.00	1,305.00	900.00	33,192.00
			(✔)	(122)	(401)	(231)	(513)	(101)

Debit total: $ 900
              33,192
           $34,092

Credit total: $ 3,600
                    3,087
                26,100.00
                 1,305.00
              $34,092.00

GENERAL LEDGER (Partial)

ACCOUNT   Cash   ACCOUNT NO. 101

Date	Item	Post. Ref.	Debit	Credit	Balance Debit	Balance Credit
20--						
Apr. 1	Bal.	✔			20,000.00	
30		CR7	33,192.00		53,192.00	

ACCOUNT   Accounts Receivable   ACCOUNT NO. 122

Date	Item	Post. Ref.	Debit	Credit	Balance Debit	Balance Credit
20--						
Apr. 1	Bal.	✔			12,000.00	
30		S6	5,418.00		17,418.00	
30		CR7		3,087.00	14,331.00	

ACCOUNT   Notes Payable   ACCOUNT NO. 201

Date	Item	Post. Ref.	Debit	Credit	Balance Debit	Balance Credit
20--						
Apr. 1	Bal.	✔				6,000.00
30		CR7		3,000.00		9,000.00

ACCOUNT   Sales Tax Payable   ACCOUNT NO. 231

Date	Item	Post. Ref.	Debit	Credit	Balance Debit	Balance Credit
20--						
Apr. 30		S6		258.00		258.00
30		CR7		1,305.00		1,563.00

ACCOUNT   Sales   ACCOUNT NO. 401

Date	Item	Post. Ref.	Debit	Credit	Balance Debit	Balance Credit
20--						
Apr. 1	Bal.	✔				67,000.00
30		S6		5,160.00		72,160.00
30		CR7		26,100.00		98,260.00

ACCOUNT   Rent Revenue   ACCOUNT NO. 412

Date	Item	Post. Ref.	Debit	Credit	Balance Debit	Balance Credit
20--						
Apr. 1	Bal.	✔				1,800.00
30		CR7		600.00		2,400.00

ACCOUNT   Bank Credit Card Expense   ACCOUNT NO. 513

Date	Item	Post. Ref.	Debit	Credit	Balance Debit	Balance Credit
20--						
Apr. 1	Bal.	✔			1,590.00	
30		CR7	900.00		2,490.00	

To post the General Credit column, on a daily basis, use the following steps:

In the general ledger account:

STEP 1   Enter the date of the transaction in the Date column.

STEP 2   Enter the amount of the debit or credit in the Debit or Credit column.

STEP 3   Enter the new balance in the Balance columns under Debit or Credit.

STEP 4   Enter the initials "CR" and the journal page number in the Posting Reference column.

In the cash receipts journal:

STEP 5   Enter the ledger account number in the Posting Reference column for each account that is posted.

To post the other amount columns, at the end of the month, use the following steps:

In the cash receipts journal:

STEP 6   Total the amount columns, verify that the total of the debit columns equals the total of the credit columns, and rule the columns.

In the general ledger account:

STEP 7   Enter the date in the Date column.

STEP 8   Enter the amount of the debit or credit in the Debit or Credit column.

STEP 9   Enter the new balance in the Balance columns under Debit or Credit.

STEP 10   Enter the initials "CR" and the journal page number in the Posting Reference column.

In the cash receipts journal:

STEP 11   Enter the ledger account number immediately below the column totals for each account that is posted.

STEP 12   Enter a check mark (✓) in the Posting Reference column for the cash sales and bank credit card sales, and immediately below the General Credit column.

The general ledger accounts affected by the cash receipts transactions are now up to date. Postings to the accounts receivable ledger also must be made. These postings are made daily. Figure 12-10 illustrates the posting procedures, as follows:

In the accounts receivable ledger account:

STEP 1   Enter the date of the transaction in the Date column.

STEP 2   Enter the amount of the debit or credit in the Debit or Credit column.

STEP 3   Enter the new balance in the Balance column.

STEP 4   Enter the initials "CR" and the journal page number in the Posting Reference column.

In the cash receipts journal:

STEP 5   Enter a check mark (✓) in the Posting Reference column of the journal for each transaction that is posted.

FIGURE 12-10 Posting from the Cash Receipts Journal to the Accounts Receivable Ledger

CASH RECEIPTS JOURNAL — Page 7

Date	Account Credited	Post. Ref.	General Credit	Accounts Receivable Credit	Sales Credit	Sales Tax Payable Credit	Bank Credit Card Expense Debit	Cash Debit
20--								
Apr. 14	Enrico Lorenzo	✔		1,596.00				1,596.00
20	Brenda Myers	✔		462.00				462.00
28	Edith Walton	✔		1,029.00				1,029.00
30		✔			3,600.00	180.00		3,780.00
30		✔			22,500.00	1,125.00	900.00	22,725.00
30	Rent Revenue	412	600.00					600.00
30	Notes Payable	201	3,000.00					3,000.00
			3,600.00	3,087.00	26,100.00	1,305.00	900.00	33,192.00
			(✔)	(122)	(401)	(231)	(513)	(101)

5

ACCOUNTS RECEIVABLE LEDGER

NAME Helen Avery
ADDRESS 308 Devon Ave., Overbrook, KS 66524

Date	Item	Post. Ref.	Debit	Credit	Balance
20--					
Apr. 1	Bal.	✔			2,302.00

NAME Wilma Cutz
ADDRESS 1116 Williamsburg Place, Lawrence, KS 66049

Date	Item	Post. Ref.	Debit	Credit	Balance
20--					
Apr. 21		S6	651.00		651.00

NAME Enrico Lorenzo
ADDRESS 1827 N. 100 Rd., Baldwin City, KS 66006

Date	Item	Post. Ref.	Debit	Credit	Balance
20--					
Apr. 4		S6	1,596.00		1,596.00
14		CR7		1,596.00	—

1 4 3

NAME Brenda Myers
ADDRESS 1613 Stone Meadows, Lawrence, KS 66049

Date	Item	Post. Ref.	Debit	Credit	Balance
20--					
Apr. 10		S6	462.00		462.00
20		CR7		462.00	—

1 4 3

NAME Heidi Schwitzer
ADDRESS 13913 Nicklaus Dr., Overland Park, KS 66223

Date	Item	Post. Ref.	Debit	Credit	Balance
20--					
Apr. 1	Bal.	✔			1,883.00
24		S6	1,680.00		3,563.00

NAME Ken Ulmet
ADDRESS 2616 Sawgrass Dr., Lawrence, KS 66047

Date	Item	Post. Ref.	Debit	Credit	Balance
20--					
Apr. 1	Bal.	✔			3,315.00

NAME Edith Walton
ADDRESS 1418 N. 600 Rd., Baldwin, KS 66006

Date	Item	Post. Ref.	Debit	Credit	Balance
20--					
Apr. 18		S6	1,029.00		1,029.00
28		CR7		1,029.00	—

1 4 3

NAME Vivian Winston
ADDRESS 1613 Alvamar Dr., Lawrence, KS 66047

Date	Item	Post. Ref.	Debit	Credit	Balance
20--					
Apr. 1	Bal.	✔			4,500.00

2

GENERAL LEDGER (Partial)

ACCOUNT Cash   ACCOUNT NO. 101

Date	Item	Post. Ref.	Debit	Credit	Balance Debit	Balance Credit
20--						
Apr. 1	Bal.	✔			20,000.00	
30		CR7	33,192.00		53,192.00	

ACCOUNT Accounts Receivable   ACCOUNT NO. 122

Date	Item	Post. Ref.	Debit	Credit	Balance Debit	Balance Credit
20--						
Apr. 1	Bal.	✔			12,000.00	
30		S6	5,418.00		17,418.00	
30		CR7		3,087.00	14,331.00	

ACCOUNT Notes Payable   ACCOUNT NO. 201

Date	Item	Post. Ref.	Debit	Credit	Balance Debit	Balance Credit
20--						
Apr. 1	Bal.	✔				6,000.00
30		CR7		3,000.00		9,000.00

ACCOUNT Sales Tax Payable   ACCOUNT NO. 231

Date	Item	Post. Ref.	Debit	Credit	Balance Debit	Balance Credit
20--						
Apr. 30		S6		258.00		258.00
30		CR7		1,305.00		1,563.00

ACCOUNT Sales   ACCOUNT NO. 401

Date	Item	Post. Ref.	Debit	Credit	Balance Debit	Balance Credit
20--						
Apr. 1	Bal.	✔				67,000.00
30		S6		5,160.00		72,160.00
30		CR7		26,100.00		98,260.00

ACCOUNT Rent Revenue   ACCOUNT NO. 412

Date	Item	Post. Ref.	Debit	Credit	Balance Debit	Balance Credit
20--						
Apr. 1	Bal.	✔				1,800.00
30		CR7		600.00		2,400.00

ACCOUNT Bank Credit Card Expense   ACCOUNT NO. 513

Date	Item	Post. Ref.	Debit	Credit	Balance Debit	Balance Credit
20--						
Apr. 1	Bal.	✔			1,590.00	
30		CR7	900.00		2,490.00	

A BROADER VIEW

KURHAN/SHUTTERSTOCK.COM

Improving Efficiency—The Power of Computerized Bookkeeping

In this chapter, we see many examples of the ways in which special journals can make the bookkeeping process more efficient. Yet, these efficiency gains pale by comparison with the power of computerized bookkeeping. By means of a single keyboard entry, journals, general and subsidiary ledgers, customer and supplier accounts, periodic financial reports, and more can be updated, and there is no need to maintain special journals. You can even pay bills when due electronically as part of the system.

Some good examples of computerized bookkeeping software are QuickBooks® and Sage 50 Accounting. Both of these software packages utilize the one entry-many reports feature. The user makes entries using the keyboard; then the system tracks the effects on the financial status of the business. The software can analyze accounts receivable and accounts payable, process payroll, print checks, and track expenses by vendor and revenues by customer. It can also produce income statements and balance sheets. It is even possible to customize the programs to match different business types.

CHECKPOINT ✔

Complete Checkpoint-2 on page 470 to test your basic understanding of LO3.

LO4

Purchases Journal

Describe and use the purchases journal.

A **purchases journal** is a special journal used to record only purchases of merchandise on account. To illustrate the journalizing and posting of purchases transactions in the purchases journal, we continue with the transactions of Sunflower Cycle. The following five purchases on account are from Chapter 11:

Apr.   4   Purchased merchandise from Bilenky Cycle Works, $3,300.
          Invoice No. 631, dated April 2, terms n/30.

     8   Purchased merchandise from Ellsworth, $2,500.
          Invoice No. 927D, dated April 6, terms n/30.

   11   Purchased merchandise from Gunnar Cycles, $8,700.
          Invoice No. 804, dated April 9, terms 1/15, n/30.

   17   Purchased merchandise from Milwaukee Cycle Co., $800.
          Invoice No. 611, dated April 16, terms n/30.

   23   Purchased merchandise from Rans Designs, Inc., $5,300.
          Invoice No. 1465, dated April 22, terms 1/10, n/30.

LEARNING KEY 🔑

Use a purchases journal only for recording purchases of merchandise on account.

In some accounting systems, a purchases journal can be used to record all purchases on account. For example, see Figure 12-13.

As we saw with sales transactions, these purchases transactions can be recorded efficiently in a special journal, in this case a purchases journal. To illustrate, the five merchandise purchases on account of Sunflower Cycle are entered in the purchases journal in Figure 12-11. Sunflower Cycle's purchases journal has a single column for Purchases Debit/Accounts Payable Credit, the two accounts used repeatedly when these transactions are recorded in a general journal. A purchase is recorded in the purchases journal by entering the following information:

FIGURE 12-11 **Sunflower Cycle Purchases Journal**

	DATE	INVOICE NO.	FROM WHOM PURCHASED	POST. REF.	PURCHASES DEBIT/ ACCOUNTS PAYABLE CREDIT	
1	20-- Apr. 4	631	Bilenky Cycle Works		3 3 0 0 00	1
2	8	927D	Ellsworth		2 5 0 0 00	2
3	11	804	Gunnar Cycles		8 7 0 0 00	3
4	17	611	Milwaukee Cycle Co.		8 0 0 00	4
5	23	1465	Rans Designs, Inc.		5 3 0 0 00	5
6					20 6 0 0 00	6

PURCHASES JOURNAL — PAGE 8

> Remember that purchases returns and allowances are recorded in the general journal, as illustrated in Chapter 11, not in the purchases journal.

1. Date
2. Invoice number
3. Supplier (from whom purchased)
4. Dollar amount

There is no need to enter any general ledger account titles, since they appear in the column heading.

The purchases journal in Figure 12-11 is designed for a company like Sunflower Cycle, whose suppliers generally pay freight charges. For a company that frequently pays freight charges as part of the purchase price of merchandise, a purchases journal like the one in Figure 12-12 would be used. In this case, there are three columns: (1) Purchases Debit, (2) Freight-In Debit, and (3) Accounts Payable Credit.

FIGURE 12-12 **Purchases Journal with Freight-In Column**

DATE	INVOICE NO.	FROM WHOM PURCHASED	POST. REF.	PURCHASES DEBIT	FREIGHT-IN DEBIT	ACCOUNTS PAYABLE CREDIT

PURCHASES JOURNAL

If a company uses a purchases journal to record all purchases on account, including merchandise purchases, a purchases journal like the one in Figure 12-13 could be used.

FIGURE 12-13 **Purchases Journal for All Purchases on Account**

DATE	INVOICE NO.	FROM WHOM PURCHASED	POST. REF.	MERCH. PURCHASES DEBIT	SUPPLIES DEBIT	COMPUTER EQUIP. DEBIT	OTHER ACCOUNTS DEBIT	ACCOUNTS PAYABLE CREDIT

PURCHASES JOURNAL

Posting from the Purchases Journal

Each general ledger account used in the purchases journal requires only one posting each period. Figure 12-14 illustrates the general ledger posting process for Sunflower Cycle's purchases journal for the month of April.

The following steps are used to post from the purchases journal to the general ledger at the end of each month, as indicated in Figure 12-14:

In the purchases journal:

STEP 1   Total and rule the amount column.

> Step 1 is the main difference in posting the purchases journal to the general ledger. Steps 2–6 are essentially the same as steps 1–5 used to post the general journal.

FIGURE 12-14 Posting from the Purchases Journal to the General Ledger

				PURCHASES JOURNAL		Page 8

Date		Invoice No.	From Whom Purchased	Post. Ref.	Purchases Debit/ Accounts Payable Credit
20--					
Apr.	4	631	Bilenky Cycle Works		3,300.00
	8	927D	Ellsworth		2,500.00
	11	804	Gunnar Cycles		8,700.00
	17	611	Milwaukee Cycle Co.		800.00
	23	1465	Rans Designs, Inc.		5,300.00
					20,600.00 **1**
					(501) (202) **6** **3**

GENERAL LEDGER (Partial)

ACCOUNT	Accounts Payable					ACCOUNT NO. 202	
			Post.			Balance	
	Date	Item	Ref.	Debit	Credit	Debit	Credit
20--							
Apr.	1	Bal	✔				4,800.00
2	30	**5**	P8		20,600.00		25,400.00
							4

ACCOUNT	Purchases					ACCOUNT NO.501	
			Post.			Balance	
	Date	Item	Ref.	Debit	Credit	Debit	Credit
20--							
Apr.	1	Bal	✔			37,400.00	
2	30	**5**	P8	20,600.00		58,000.00	
						4	

In the general ledger account:

STEP 2 Enter the date in the Date column.

STEP 3 Enter the amount of the debit or credit in the Debit or Credit column.

STEP 4 Enter the new balance in the Balance columns under Debit or Credit.

STEP 5 Enter the initial "P" and the journal page number in the Posting Reference column.

In the purchases journal:

STEP 6 Enter the Purchases and Accounts Payable account numbers immediately below the column total.

To maintain a record of the amount owed to each supplier, an accounts payable ledger is used. Figure 12-15 illustrates the use of the accounts payable ledger. The following steps are used to post from the purchases journal to the accounts payable ledger daily, as shown in Figure 12-15:

In the accounts payable ledger account:

STEP 1 Enter the date of the transaction in the Date column.

STEP 2 Enter the amount of the debit or credit in the Debit or Credit column.

> If the accounts payable ledger is posted daily and the general ledger is posted at the end of the month, the accounts payable ledger total will equal the general ledger Accounts Payable total only at the end of the month.

STEP 3   Enter the new balance in the Balance column.

STEP 4   Enter the initial "P" and the journal page number in the Posting Reference column.

In the purchases journal:

STEP 5   Enter a check mark (✔) in the Posting Reference column of the journal for each transaction that is posted.

After the posting of the accounts payable ledger and general ledger is completed, the total of the accounts payable ledger balances should equal the Accounts Payable balance in the general ledger.

CHECKPOINT ✔

Complete Checkpoint-3 on page 471 to test your basic understanding of LO4.

FIGURE 12-15 Posting from the Purchases Journal to the Accounts Payable Ledger

Cash Payments Journal

LO5

Describe and use the cash payments journal.

A **cash payments journal** is a special journal used to record only cash payments transactions. To illustrate its use, we will record the cash payments transactions of Sunflower Cycle. Sunflower Cycle's cash payments journal for the month of April is shown in Figure 12-16. Five types of cash payments transactions are shown as follows:

1. Payment of an expense (April 2)
2. Cash purchase (April 4)
3. Payment of an account payable (April 10 and 24)
4. Payment of a note payable (April 14)
5. Withdrawal by the owner (April 22)

FIGURE 12-16 Sunflower Cycle Cash Payments Journal

	DATE	CK. NO.	ACCOUNT DEBITED	POST. REF.	GENERAL DEBIT	ACCOUNTS PAYABLE DEBIT	PURCHASES DEBIT	PURCHASES DISCOUNTS CREDIT	CASH CREDIT	
1	Apr. 2	307	Rent Expense		1 2 0 0 00				1 2 0 0 00	1
2	4	308					1 4 0 0 00		1 4 0 0 00	2
3	10	309	Ace Wheelworks			4 8 0 0 00			4 8 0 0 00	3
4	14	310	Notes Payable		2 0 0 0 00				2 0 0 0 00	4
5	22	311	Sam Tangari, Drawing		1 6 0 0 00				1 6 0 0 00	5
6	24	312	Gunnar Cycles			8 7 0 0 00		8 7 00	8 6 1 3 00	6
7					4 8 0 0 00	13 5 0 0 00	1 4 0 0 00	8 7 00	19 6 1 3 00	7

Sunflower Cycle's cash payments journal provides separate columns for Accounts Payable Debit, Purchases Debit, Purchases Discounts Credit, and Cash Credit. These are the accounts most frequently affected by Sunflower Cycle's cash payments transactions. In addition, a General Debit column is provided for debits to any other accounts affected by cash payments transactions. For good internal control over cash payments, all payments (except out of petty cash) should be made by check. Therefore, the cash payments journal also includes a Check No. column.

A cash payment is recorded in the cash payments journal by entering the following information:

1. Date
2. Check number
3. Account debited (if applicable)
4. Dollar amounts

The Account Debited column is used for two purposes:

1. To identify the supplier name for any payment on account. This column is used whenever the Accounts Payable Debit column is used.
2. To enter the appropriate account name whenever the General Debit column is used.

The Account Debited column is left blank if the entry is for cash purchases.

Posting from the Cash Payments Journal

The cash payments journal is posted to the general ledger in two stages, as illustrated in Figure 12-17. First, on a daily basis, the individual amounts in the General Debit column are posted. Second, at the end of the month, the totals of each of the other amount columns are posted.

To post the General Debit column, on a daily basis, the following steps are used:

In the general ledger account:

STEP 1   Enter the date of the transaction in the Date column.

STEP 2   Enter the amount of the debit or credit in the Debit or Credit column.

STEP 3   Enter the new balance in the Balance columns under Debit or Credit.

STEP 4   Enter the initials "CP" and the journal page number in the Posting Reference column.

In the cash payments journal:

STEP 5   Enter the ledger account number in the Posting Reference column for each account that is posted.

To post the other amount columns, at the end of the month, the following steps are used:

In the cash payments journal:

STEP 6   Total the amount columns, verify that the total of the debit columns equals the total of the credit columns, and rule the columns.

In the general ledger account:

STEP 7   Enter the date in the Date column.

STEP 8   Enter the amount of the debit or credit in the Debit or Credit column.

STEP 9   Enter the new balance in the Balance columns under Debit or Credit.

STEP 10   Enter the initials "CP" and the journal page number in the Posting Reference column.

In the cash payments journal:

STEP 11   Enter the ledger account number immediately below the column totals for each account that is posted.

STEP 12   Enter a check mark (✓) in the Posting Reference column for the cash purchases, and immediately below the General Debit column.

Postings from the cash payments journal to the accounts payable ledger also must be made. These postings are made daily. Posting procedures are as follows, as shown in Figure 12-18:

In the accounts payable ledger account:

STEP 1   Enter the date of the transaction in the Date column.

STEP 2   Enter the amount of the debit or credit in the Debit or Credit column.

STEP 3   Enter the new balance in the Balance column.

STEP 4   Enter the initials "CP" and the journal page number in the Posting Reference column.

In the cash payments journal:

STEP 5   Enter a check mark (✓) in the Posting Reference column of the journal for each transaction that is posted.

FIGURE 12-17 Posting from the Cash Payments Journal to the General Ledger

CASH PAYMENTS JOURNAL Page 12

Date	Check No.	Account Debited	Post. Ref.	General Debit	Accounts Payable Debit	Purchases Debit	Purchases Discounts Credit	Cash Credit
20--								
Apr. 2	307	Rent Expense	521	1,200.00				1,200.00
4	308		✔			1,400.00		1,400.00
10	309	Ace Wheelworks			4,800.00			4,800.00
14	310	Notes Payable	201	2,000.00				2,000.00
22	311	Sam Tangari, Drawing	312	1,600.00				1,600.00
24	312	Gunnar Cycles			8,700.00		87.00	8,613.00
				4,800.00	13,500.00	1,400.00	87.00	19,613.00
				(✔)	(202)	(501)	(501.2)	(101)

6 Debit total:

$ 4,800.00
13,500
1,400
$19,700.00

Credit total:

$ 87
19,613.00
$19,700.00

GENERAL LEDGER (Partial)

ACCOUNT Cash   ACCOUNT NO. 101

Date	Item	Post. Ref.	Debit	Credit	Balance Debit	Balance Credit
20--						
Apr. 1	Bal.	✔			20,000.00	
30		CR7	12,992.00		32,992.00	
30		CP12		19,613.00	13,379.00	

ACCOUNT Notes Payable   ACCOUNT NO. 201

Date	Item	Post. Ref.	Debit	Credit	Balance Debit	Balance Credit
20--						
Apr. 1	Bal.	✔				6,000.00
14		CP12	2,000.00			4,000.00

ACCOUNT Accounts Payable   ACCOUNT NO. 202

Date	Item	Post. Ref.	Debit	Credit	Balance Debit	Balance Credit
20--						
Apr. 1	Bal.	✔				4,800.00
30		P8		20,600.00		25,400.00
30		CP12	13,500.00			11,900.00

ACCOUNT Sam Tangari, Drawing   ACCOUNT NO. 312

Date	Item	Post. Ref.	Debit	Credit	Balance Debit	Balance Credit
20--						
Apr. 1	Bal.	✔			1,500.00	
22		CP12	1,600.00		3,100.00	

ACCOUNT Purchases   ACCOUNT NO. 501

Date	Item	Post. Ref.	Debit	Credit	Balance Debit	Balance Credit
20--						
Apr. 1	Bal.	✔			37,400.00	
30		P8	20,600.00		58,000.00	
30		CP12	1,400.00		59,400.00	

ACCOUNT Purchases Discounts   ACCOUNT NO. 501.2

Date	Item	Post. Ref.	Debit	Credit	Balance Debit	Balance Credit
20--						
Apr. 1	Bal.	✔				330.00
30		CP12		87.00		417.00

ACCOUNT Rent Expense   ACCOUNT NO. 521

Date	Item	Post. Ref.	Debit	Credit	Balance Debit	Balance Credit
20--						
Apr. 1	Bal.	✔			3,600.00	
2		CP12	1,200.00		4,800.00	

FIGURE 12-18 Posting from the Cash Payments Journal to the Accounts Payable Ledger

CASH PAYMENTS JOURNAL   Page 12

Date	Check No.	Account Debited	Post. Ref.	General Debit	Accounts Payable Debit	Purchases Debit	Purchases Discounts Credit	Cash Credit
20--								
Apr. 2	307	Rent Expense	521	1,200.00				1,200.00
4	308		✔			1,400.00		1,400.00
10	309	Ace Wheelworks	✔		4,800.00			4,800.00
14	310	Notes Payable	201	2,000.00				2,000.00
22	311	Sam Tangari, Drawing	312	1,600.00				1,600.00
24	312	Gunnar Cycles	✔		8,700.00		87.00	8,613.00
				4,800.00	13,500.00	1,400.00	87.00	19,613.00
				(✔)	(202)	(501)	(501.2)	(101)

ACCOUNTS PAYABLE LEDGER (Partial)

NAME   Ace Wheelworks
ADDRESS   145 Elm St., Somerville, MA 02144

Date	Item	Post. Ref.	Debit	Credit	Balance
20--					
Apr. 1	Bal.	✔			4,800.00
10		CP12	4,800.00		—

NAME   Bilenky Cycle Works
ADDRESS   5319 N. 2nd. St., Philadelphia, PA 19120

Date	Item	Post. Ref.	Debit	Credit	Balance
20--					
Apr. 4		P8		3,300.00	3,300.00

NAME   Ellsworth
ADDRESS   16275 Technology Dr., San Diego, CA 92127

Date	Item	Post. Ref.	Debit	Credit	Balance
20--					
Apr. 8		P8		2,500.00	2,500.00

NAME   Gunnar Cycles
ADDRESS   816 W. Bakke Ave, Waterford, WI 53185

Date	Item	Post. Ref.	Debit	Credit	Balance
20--					
Apr. 11		P8		8,700.00	8,700.00
24		CP12	8,700.00		—

NAME   Milwaukee Cycle Co.
ADDRESS   1018 W. Lincoln Ave, Milwaukee, WI 53215

Date	Item	Post. Ref.	Debit	Credit	Balance
20--					
Apr. 17		P8		800.00	800.00

NAME   Rans Designs, Inc.
ADDRESS   4600 Highway 183, Hays, KS 67601

Date	Item	Post. Ref.	Debit	Credit	Balance
20--					
Apr. 23		P8		5,300.00	5,300.00

GENERAL LEDGER (Partial)

ACCOUNT   Cash   ACCOUNT NO. 101

Date	Item	Post. Ref.	Debit	Credit	Balance Debit	Balance Credit
20--						
Apr. 1	Bal.	✔			20,000.00	
30		CR7	12,992.00		32,992.00	
30		CP12		19,613.00	13,379.00	

ACCOUNT   Notes Payable   ACCOUNT NO. 201

Date	Item	Post. Ref.	Debit	Credit	Balance Debit	Balance Credit
20--						
Apr. 1	Bal.	✔				6,000.00
14		CP12	2,000.00			4,000.00

ACCOUNT   Accounts Payable   ACCOUNT NO. 202

Date	Item	Post. Ref.	Debit	Credit	Balance Debit	Balance Credit
20--						
Apr. 1	Bal.	✔				4,800.00
30		P8		20,600.00		25,400.00
30		CP12	13,500.00			11,900.00

ACCOUNT   Sam Tangari, Drawing   ACCOUNT NO. 312

Date	Item	Post. Ref.	Debit	Credit	Balance Debit	Balance Credit
20--						
Apr. 1	Bal.	✔			1,500.00	
22		CP12	1,600.00		3,100.00	

ACCOUNT   Purchases   ACCOUNT NO. 501

Date	Item	Post. Ref.	Debit	Credit	Balance Debit	Balance Credit
20--						
Apr. 1	Bal.	✔			37,400.00	
30		P8	20,600.00		58,000.00	
30		CP12	1,400.00		59,400.00	

ACCOUNT   Purchases Discounts   ACCOUNT NO. 501.2

Date	Item	Post. Ref.	Debit	Credit	Balance Debit	Balance Credit
20--						
Apr. 1	Bal.	✔				330.00
30		CP12		87.00		417.00

ACCOUNT   Rent Expense   ACCOUNT NO. 521

Date	Item	Post. Ref.	Debit	Credit	Balance Debit	Balance Credit
20--						
Apr. 1	Bal.	✔			3,600.00	
2		CP12	1,200.00		4,800.00	

CHECKPOINT ✔

Complete Checkpoint-4 on page 471 to test your basic understanding of LO5.

SELF-STUDY

LEARNING OBJECTIVES	Key Points to Remember
LO1 Describe, explain the purpose of, and identify transactions recorded in special journals.	A special journal is a journal designed for recording only certain kinds of transactions. The primary purpose of using special journals is to save time journalizing and posting transactions.
LO2 Describe and use the sales journal.	A sales journal is a special journal for recording sales of merchandise on account. A sale is recorded by entering the following: 1. Date 2. Sale number 3. Customer (to whom sold) 4. Dollar amounts

To post from the sales journal to the general ledger, use the following steps:

In the sales journal:

STEP 1 Total the amount columns, verify that the total of the debit column equals the total of the credit columns, and rule the columns.

In the general ledger account:

STEP 2 Enter the date of the transaction in the Date column.

STEP 3 Enter the amount of the debit or credit in the Debit or Credit column.

STEP 4 Enter the new balance in the Balance columns under Debit or Credit.

STEP 5 Enter the initial "S" and the journal page number in the Posting Reference column.

In the sales journal:

STEP 6 Enter the ledger account number immediately below the column totals for each account that is posted.

To post from the sales journal to the accounts receivable ledger:

In the accounts receivable ledger account:

STEP 1 Enter the date of the transaction in the Date column.

STEP 2 Enter the amount of the debit or credit in the Debit or Credit column.

STEP 3 Enter the new balance in the Balance column.

STEP 4 Enter the initial "S" and the journal page number in the Posting Reference column.

In the sales journal:

STEP 5 Enter a check mark (✓) in the Posting Reference column of the journal for each transaction that is posted.

| **LO3** Describe and use the cash receipts journal. | A cash receipts journal is a special journal for recording cash receipts. A cash receipt is recorded by entering the following: 1. Date 2. Account credited (if applicable) 3. Dollar amounts |

LEARNING OBJECTIVES	**Key Points to Remember**

LO3 (continued)

To post from the cash receipts journal to the general ledger:

    To post the General Credit column, on a daily basis, use the following steps:

In the general ledger account:

STEP 1   Enter the date of the transaction in the Date column.

STEP 2   Enter the amount of the debit or credit in the Debit or Credit column.

STEP 3   Enter the new balance in the Balance columns under Debit or Credit.

STEP 4   Enter the initials "CR" and the journal page number in the Posting Reference column.

In the cash receipts journal:

STEP 5   Enter the ledger account number in the Posting Reference column for each account that is posted.

    To post the other amount columns, at the end of the month, use the following steps:

In the cash receipts journal:

STEP 6   Total the amount columns, verify that the total of the debit columns equals the total of the credit columns, and rule the columns.

In the general ledger account:

STEP 7   Enter the date in the Date column.

STEP 8   Enter the amount of the debit or credit in the Debit or Credit column.

STEP 9   Enter the new balance in the Balance columns under Debit or Credit.

STEP 10   Enter the initials "CR" and the journal page number in the Posting Reference column.

In the cash receipts journal:

STEP 11   Enter the ledger account number immediately below the column totals for each account that is posted.

STEP 12   Enter a check mark (✓) in the Posting Reference column for the cash sales and bank credit card sales, and immediately below the General Credit column.

To post from the cash receipts journal to the accounts receivable ledger, use the following steps:

In the accounts receivable ledger account:

STEP 1   Enter the date of the transaction in the Date column.

STEP 2   Enter the amount of the debit or credit in the Debit or Credit column.

STEP 3   Enter the new balance in the Balance column.

STEP 4   Enter the initials "CR" and the journal page number in the Posting Reference column.

In the cash receipts journal:

STEP 5   Enter a check mark (✓) in the Posting Reference column of the journal for each transaction that is posted.

(continued)

LEARNING OBJECTIVES	**Key Points to Remember**
LO4 Describe and use the purchases journal.	A purchases journal is a special journal for recording purchases of merchandise on account. A purchase is recorded by entering the following: 1. Date 2. Invoice number 3. Supplier (from whom purchased) 4. Dollar amount To post from the purchases journal to the general ledger, use the following steps: **In the purchases journal:** **STEP 1** Total and rule the amount column. **In the general ledger account:** **STEP 2** Enter the date in the Date column. **STEP 3** Enter the amount of the debit or credit in the Debit or Credit column. **STEP 4** Enter the new balance in the Balance columns under Debit or Credit. **STEP 5** Enter the initial "P" and the journal page number in the Posting Reference column. **In the purchases journal:** **STEP 6** Enter the Purchases and Accounts Payable account numbers immediately below the column total. To post from the purchases journal to the accounts payable ledger, use the following steps: **In the accounts payable ledger account:** **STEP 1** Enter the date of the transaction in the Date column. **STEP 2** Enter the amount of the debit or credit in the Debit or Credit column. **STEP 3** Enter the new balance in the Balance column. **STEP 4** Enter the initial "P" and the journal page number in the Posting Reference column. **In the purchases journal:** **STEP 5** Enter a check mark (✓) in the Posting Reference column of the journal for each transaction that is posted.
LO5 Describe and use the cash payments journal.	A cash payments journal is a special journal for recording cash payments. A cash payment is recorded by entering the following: 1. Date 2. Check number 3. Account debited (if applicable) 4. Dollar amounts

LEARNING OBJECTIVES	**Key Points to Remember**

LO5 (concluded)

To post from the cash payments journal to the general ledger:

To post the General Debit column, on a daily basis, use the following steps:

In the general ledger account:

STEP 1 Enter the date of the transaction in the Date column.

STEP 2 Enter the amount of the debit or credit in the Debit or Credit column.

STEP 3 Enter the new balance in the Balance columns under Debit or Credit.

STEP 4 Enter the initials "CP" and the journal page number in the Posting Reference column.

In the cash payments journal:

STEP 5 Enter the ledger account number in the Posting Reference column for each account that is posted.

To post the other amount columns, at the end of the month, use the following steps:

In the cash payments journal:

STEP 6 Total the amount columns, verify that the total of the debit columns equals the total of the credit columns, and rule the columns.

In the general ledger account:

STEP 7 Enter the date in the Date column.

STEP 8 Enter the amount of the debit or credit in the Debit or Credit column.

STEP 9 Enter the new balance in the Balance columns under Debit or Credit.

STEP 10 Enter the initials "CP" and the journal page number in the Posting Reference column.

In the cash payments journal:

STEP 11 Enter the ledger account number immediately below the column totals for each account that is posted.

STEP 12 Enter a check mark (✓) in the Posting Reference column for the cash purchases, and immediately below the General Debit column.

To post from the cash payments journal to the accounts payable ledger, use the following steps:

In the accounts payable ledger account:

STEP 1 Enter the date of the transaction in the Date column.

STEP 2 Enter the amount of the debit or credit in the Debit or Credit column.

STEP 3 Enter the new balance in the Balance column.

STEP 4 Enter the initials "CP" and the journal page number in the Posting Reference column.

In the cash payments journal:

STEP 5 Enter a check mark (✓) in the Posting Reference column of the journal for each transaction that is posted.

DEMONSTRATION PROBLEM

During the month of May 20--, David's Specialty Shop engaged in the following transactions:

May 1 Sold merchandise on account to Molly Mac, $2,000, plus tax of $100. Sale No. 533.

2 Issued Check No. 750 to Kari Co. in partial payment of May 1 balance, $800, less 2% discount.

3 Purchased merchandise on account from Scanlan Wholesalers, $2,000. Invoice No. 621, dated May 3, terms 2/10, n/30.

4 Purchased merchandise on account from Simpson Enterprises, $1,500. Invoice No. 767, dated May 4, terms 2/15, n/30.

4 Issued Check No. 751 in payment of phone expense for the month of April, $200.

8 Sold merchandise for cash, $3,600, plus tax of $180.

9 Received payment from Cody Slaton in full settlement of account, $2,500.

10 Issued Check No. 752 to Scanlan Wholesalers in payment of May 1 balance of $1,200.

12 Sold merchandise on account to Cody Slaton, $3,000, plus tax of $150. Sale No. 534.

12 Received payment from Kori Reynolds on account, $2,100.

13 Issued Check No. 753 to Simpson Enterprises in payment of May 4 purchase. Invoice No. 767, less 2% discount.

13 Cody Slaton returned merchandise for a credit, $1,000, plus sales tax of $50.

17 Returned merchandise to Johnson Essentials for credit, $500.

22 Received payment from Natalie Gabbert on account, $1,555.

27 Sold merchandise on account to Natalie Gabbert, $2,000, plus tax of $100. Sale No. 535.

29 Issued Check No. 754 in payment of wages (Wages Expense) for the four-week period ending May 30, $1,100.

Selected account balances as of May 1 were as follows:

Account	Account No.	Debit	Credit
Cash	101	$10,050	
Accounts Receivable	122	6,900	
Accounts Payable	202		$4,550

David's also had the following subsidiary ledger balances as of May 1:

Accounts Receivable:

Customer	Accounts Receivable Balance
Natalie Gabbert 12 Jude Lane Hartford, CT 06117	$1,821
Molly Mac 52 Juniper Road Hartford, CT 06118	279
Kori Reynolds 700 Hobbes Dr. Avon, CT 06108	2,300
Cody Slaton 5200 Hamilton Ave. Hartford, CT 06111	2,500

Accounts Payable:

Vendor	Accounts Payable Balance
Johnson Essentials 34 Harry Ave. East Hartford, CT 05234	$2,350
Kari Co. 1009 Drake Rd. Farmington, CT 06082	1,000
Scanlan Wholesalers 43 Lucky Lane Bristol, CT 06007	1,200
Simpson Enterprises 888 Anders Street Newington, CT 06789	—

> When the general journal and multiple special journals are used, post to the ledger in the following sequence:
> General Journal
> Sales Journal
> Cash Receipts Journal
> Purchases Journal
> Cash Payments Journal

REQUIRED

1. Record the transactions in the sales journal, cash receipts journal, purchases journal, cash payments journal, and general journal. Total, verify, and rule the columns where appropriate at the end of the month.

2. Post from the journals to the general ledger, accounts receivable ledger, and accounts payable ledger accounts. Use account numbers as shown in the chapter.

SOLUTION 1.

	DATE		SALE NO.	TO WHOM SOLD	POST. REF.	ACCOUNTS RECEIVABLE DEBIT	SALES CREDIT	SALES TAX PAYABLE CREDIT	
	20–								
1	May	1	533	Molly Mac	✔	2 1 0 0 00	2 0 0 0 00	1 0 0 00	1
2		12	534	Cody Slaton	✔	3 1 5 0 00	3 0 0 0 00	1 5 0 00	2
3		27	535	Natalie Gabbert	✔	2 1 0 0 00	2 0 0 0 00	1 0 0 00	3
4						7 3 5 0 00	7 0 0 0 00	3 5 0 00	4
5						(1 2 2)	(4 0 1)	(2 3 1)	5

SALES JOURNAL — PAGE 7

(continued)

PURCHASES JOURNAL
PAGE 6

	DATE		INVOICE NO.	FROM WHOM PURCHASED	POST. REF.	PURCHASES DEBIT/ ACCOUNTS PAYABLE CREDIT	
1	20-- May	3	621	Scanlan Wholesalers	✔	2 0 0 0 00	1
2		4	767	Simpson Enterprises	✔	1 5 0 0 00	2
3						3 5 0 0 00	3
4						(50 1) (2 02)	4

GENERAL JOURNAL
PAGE 5

	DATE		DESCRIPTION	POST. REF.	DEBIT	CREDIT	
1	20-- May	13	Sales Returns and Allowances	401.1	1 0 0 0 00		1
2			Sales Tax Payable	231	5 0 00		2
3			Accounts Receivable/Cody Slaton	122/✔		1 0 5 0 00	3
4			Accepted returned merchandise				4
5							5
6		17	Accounts Payable/Johnson Essentials	202/✔	5 0 0 00		6
7			Purchases Returns and Allowances	501.1		5 0 0 00	7
8			Returned merchandise				8
9							9

CASH PAYMENTS JOURNAL
PAGE 11

	DATE		CK. NO.	ACCOUNT DEBITED	POST. REF.	GENERAL DEBIT	ACCOUNTS PAYABLE DEBIT	PURCHASES DEBIT	PURCHASES DISCOUNTS CREDIT	CASH CREDIT	
1	20-- May	2	750	Kari Co.	✔		8 0 0 00		1 6 00	7 8 4 00	1
2		4	751	Phone Expense	525	2 0 0 00				2 0 0 00	2
3		10	752	Scanlan Wholesalers	✔		1 2 0 0 00			1 2 0 0 00	3
4		13	753	Simpson Enterprises	✔		1 5 0 0 00		3 0 00	1 4 7 0 00	4
5		29	754	Wages Expense	511	1 1 0 0 00				1 1 0 0 00	5
6						1 3 0 0 00	3 5 0 0 00		4 6 00	4 7 5 4 00	6
7						(✔)	(2 0 2)		(5 0 1 .2)	(1 0 1)	7

CASH RECEIPTS JOURNAL
PAGE 10

	DATE		ACCOUNT CREDITED	POST. REF.	GENERAL CREDIT	ACCOUNTS RECEIVABLE CREDIT	SALES CREDIT	SALES TAX PAYABLE CREDIT	CASH DEBIT	
1	20-- May	8		✔			3 6 0 0 00	1 8 0 00	3 7 8 0 00	1
2		9	C. Slaton	✔		2 5 0 0 00			2 5 0 0 00	2
3		12	K. Reynolds	✔		2 1 0 0 00			2 1 0 0 00	3
4		22	N. Gabbert	✔		1 5 5 5 00			1 5 5 5 00	4
5						6 1 5 5 00	3 6 0 0 00	1 8 0 00	9 9 3 5 00	5
6						(1 2 2)	(4 0 1)	(2 3 1)	(1 0 1)	6

SOLUTION 2.

GENERAL LEDGER

ACCOUNT: Cash   ACCOUNT NO. 101

DATE	ITEM	POST. REF.	DEBIT	CREDIT	BALANCE DEBIT	BALANCE CREDIT
20-- May 1	Balance	✔			10 0 5 0 00	
31		CR10	9 9 3 5 00		19 9 8 5 00	
31		CP11		4 7 5 4 00	15 2 3 1 00	

ACCOUNT: Accounts Receivable   ACCOUNT NO. 122

DATE	ITEM	POST. REF.	DEBIT	CREDIT	BALANCE DEBIT	BALANCE CREDIT
20-- May 1	Balance	✔			6 9 0 0 00	
13		J5		1 0 5 0 00	5 8 5 0 00	
31		S7	7 3 5 0 00		13 2 0 0 00	
31		CR10		6 1 5 5 00	7 0 4 5 00	

ACCOUNT: Accounts Payable   ACCOUNT NO. 202

DATE	ITEM	POST. REF.	DEBIT	CREDIT	BALANCE DEBIT	BALANCE CREDIT
20-- May 1	Balance	✔				4 5 5 0 00
17		J5	5 0 0 00			4 0 5 0 00
31		P6		3 5 0 0 00		7 5 5 0 00
31		CP11	3 5 0 0 00			4 0 5 0 00

ACCOUNT: Sales Tax Payable   ACCOUNT NO. 231

DATE	ITEM	POST. REF.	DEBIT	CREDIT	BALANCE DEBIT	BALANCE CREDIT
20-- May 13		J5	5 0 00		5 0 00	
31		S7		3 5 0 00		3 0 0 00
31		CR10		1 8 0 00		4 8 0 00

ACCOUNT: Sales   ACCOUNT NO. 401

DATE	ITEM	POST. REF.	DEBIT	CREDIT	BALANCE DEBIT	BALANCE CREDIT
20-- May 31		S7		7 0 0 0 00		7 0 0 0 00
31		CR10		3 6 0 0 00		10 6 0 0 00

ACCOUNT: Sales Returns and Allowances   ACCOUNT NO. 401.1

DATE	ITEM	POST. REF.	DEBIT	CREDIT	BALANCE DEBIT	BALANCE CREDIT
20-- May 13		J5	1 0 0 0 00		1 0 0 0 00	

ACCOUNT: Purchases   ACCOUNT NO. 501

DATE	ITEM	POST. REF.	DEBIT	CREDIT	BALANCE DEBIT	BALANCE CREDIT
20-- May 31		P6	3 5 0 0 00		3 5 0 0 00	

ACCOUNT: Purchases Returns and Allowances   ACCOUNT NO. 501.1

DATE	ITEM	POST. REF.	DEBIT	CREDIT	BALANCE DEBIT	BALANCE CREDIT
20-- May 17		J5		5 0 0 00		5 0 0 00

(*continued*)

ACCOUNT: Purchases Discounts   ACCOUNT NO. 501.2

DATE	ITEM	POST. REF.	DEBIT	CREDIT	BALANCE DEBIT	BALANCE CREDIT
20-- May 31		CP11		4 6 00		4 6 00

ACCOUNT: Wages Expense   ACCOUNT NO. 511

DATE	ITEM	POST. REF.	DEBIT	CREDIT	BALANCE DEBIT	BALANCE CREDIT
20-- May 29		CP11	1 1 0 0 00		1 1 0 0 00	

ACCOUNT: Phone Expense   ACCOUNT NO. 525

DATE	ITEM	POST. REF.	DEBIT	CREDIT	BALANCE DEBIT	BALANCE CREDIT
20-- May 4		CP11	2 0 0 00		2 0 0 00	

ACCOUNTS RECEIVABLE LEDGER

NAME: Natalie Gabbert
ADDRESS: 12 Jude Lane, Hartford, CT 06117

DATE	ITEM	POST. REF.	DEBIT	CREDIT	BALANCE
20-- May 1	Balance	✔			1 8 2 1 00
22		CR10		1 5 5 5 00	2 6 6 00
27		S7	2 1 0 0 00		2 3 6 6 00

NAME: Molly Mac
ADDRESS: 52 Juniper Road, Hartford, CT 06118

DATE	ITEM	POST. REF.	DEBIT	CREDIT	BALANCE
20-- May 1	Balance	✔			2 7 9 00
1		S7	2 1 0 0 00		2 3 7 9 00

NAME: Kori Reynolds
ADDRESS: 700 Hobbes Dr., Avon, CT 06108

DATE	ITEM	POST. REF.	DEBIT	CREDIT	BALANCE
20-- May 1	Balance	✔			2 3 0 0 00
12		CR10		2 1 0 0 00	2 0 0 00

NAME: Cody Slaton
ADDRESS: 5200 Hamilton Ave., Hartford, CT 06111

DATE	ITEM	POST. REF.	DEBIT	CREDIT	BALANCE
20-- May 1	Balance	✔			2 5 0 0 00
9		CR10		2 5 0 0 00	—
12		S7	3 1 5 0 00		3 1 5 0 00
13		J5		1 0 5 0 00	2 1 0 0 00

ACCOUNTS PAYABLE LEDGER

NAME: Johnson Essentials

ADDRESS: 34 Harry Ave., East Hartford, CT 05234

DATE		ITEM	POST. REF.	DEBIT	CREDIT	BALANCE
20-- May	1	Balance	✔			2 3 5 0 00
	17		J5	5 0 0 00		1 8 5 0 00

NAME: Kari Co.

ADDRESS: 1009 Drake Rd., Farmington, CT 06082

DATE		ITEM	POST. REF.	DEBIT	CREDIT	BALANCE
20-- May	1	Balance	✔			1 0 0 0 00
	2		CP11	8 0 0 00		2 0 0 00

NAME: Scanlan Wholesalers

ADDRESS: 43 Lucky Lane, Bristol, CT 06007

DATE		ITEM	POST. REF.	DEBIT	CREDIT	BALANCE
20-- May	1	Balance	✔			1 2 0 0 00
	3		P6		2 0 0 0 00	3 2 0 0 00
	10		CP11	1 2 0 0 00		2 0 0 0 00

NAME: Simpson Enterprises

ADDRESS: 888 Anders Street, Newington, CT 06789

DATE		ITEM	POST. REF.	DEBIT	CREDIT	BALANCE
20-- May	1	Balance	✔			
	4		P6		1 5 0 0 00	1 5 0 0 00
	13		CP11	1 5 0 0 00		

KEY TERMS

cash payments journal (456)   A special journal used to record only cash payments transactions.

cash receipts journal (447)   A special journal used to record only cash receipts transactions.

purchases journal (452)   A special journal used to record only purchases of merchandise on account. (Or in some systems, to record all purchases on account.)

sales journal (443)   A special journal used to record only sales of merchandise on account.

special journal (442)   A journal designed for recording only certain kinds of transactions.

SELF-STUDY TEST QUESTIONS

True/False

1. **LO1**   The types of special journals a business uses should depend on the types of transactions it has most frequently.

2. **LO1**   If a business uses special journals, it generally will not need a general journal.

3. **LO2**   All sales, for cash or on credit, are recorded in the sales journal.

4. **LO3**   A cash receipts journal is used to record all cash receipts transactions.

5. **LO4**   Purchases returns and allowances are recorded in the general journal.

Multiple Choice

1. **LO2**   The first step in posting the sales journal to the general ledger is to
   (a) total and verify the equality of the amount columns.
   (b) enter the date in the Date column of the ledger account.
   (c) enter the new balance in the Balance columns of the ledger account.
   (d) enter the ledger account number below the column totals in the journal.

2. **LO3**   In the cash receipts journal, each amount in the General Credit column is posted
   (a) daily.   (c) at the end of the month.
   (b) weekly.   (d) at the end of the year.

3. **LO4**   The journal that should be used to record the return of merchandise for credit is the
   (a) purchases journal.   (c) general journal.
   (b) cash payments journal.   (d) accounts payable journal.

4. **LO4**   A purchases journal usually is used to record all
   (a) purchases.   (c) purchases of merchandise on account.
   (b) cash purchases.   (d) purchases returns and allowances.

5. **LO5**   In the cash payments journal, each amount in the General Debit column is posted
   (a) daily.   (c) at the end of the month.
   (b) weekly.   (d) at the end of the year.

CHECKPOINT

Checkpoint Exercises

1. **LO2**   Enter the following transaction in a sales journal like the one illustrated in the chapter:

   June   1   Made Sale No. 214 on account to Erin Lucas, $840, plus $42 sales tax.

2. **LO3**   Enter the following transactions in a cash receipts journal like the one illustrated in the chapter:

   June   7   Received cash on account from Erin Lucas, $882.
          30   Made cash sales for the month of $2,150, plus sales tax of $107.50.
          30   Received cash for rent revenue, $750.

3. **LO4**   Enter the following transaction in a purchases journal like the one illustrated in the chapter:

   Apr.   6   Purchased merchandise from Clever, $1,680. Invoice No. 131, dated April 6, terms n/30.

4. **LO5**   Enter the following transactions in a cash payments journal like the one illustrated in the chapter:

   Aug.   2   Issued Check No. 193 in payment of August rent (Rent Expense), $2,200.

   6   Issued Check No. 194 to Mason Hardware in payment of merchandise purchased on account, $1,700, less 2% discount. The check was written for $1,666.

   10   Issued Check No. 195 to Augie's Wholesale for cash purchase of merchandise, $2,730.

The answers to the Self-Study Test Questions are at the end of the chapter (pages 486–487).

APPLYING YOUR KNOWLEDGE

REVIEW QUESTIONS

LO1   1.   What is the primary purpose of using special journals?

LO2   2.   List four items of information about each sale entered in the sales journal.

LO2   3.   What steps are followed in posting from the sales journal to the general ledger?

LO2   4.   What steps are followed in posting from the sales journal to the accounts receivable ledger?

LO3   5.   List three items of information about each cash receipt entered in the cash receipts journal.

LO3   6.   What steps are followed in posting from the cash receipts journal to the general ledger?

LO3   7.   What steps are followed in posting from the cash receipts journal to the accounts receivable ledger?

LO4   8.   List four items of information about each purchase entered in the purchases journal.

LO4   9.   What steps are followed in posting from the purchases journal to the general ledger?

LO4   10.   What steps are followed in posting from the purchases journal to the accounts payable ledger?

LO5   11.   List four items of information about each cash payment entered in the cash payments journal.

LO5   12. What steps are followed in posting from the cash payments journal to the general ledger?

LO5   13. What steps are followed in posting from the cash payments journal to the accounts payable ledger?

SERIES A EXERCISES

E 12-1A   (LO1)

RECORDING TRANSACTIONS IN THE PROPER JOURNAL Identify the journal (sales, cash receipts, purchases, cash payments, or general) in which each of the following transactions should be recorded:

(a) Sold merchandise on account.

(b) Purchased delivery truck on account for use in the business.

(c) Received payment from customer on account.

(d) Purchased merchandise on account.

(e) Issued check in payment of electric bill.

(f) Recorded depreciation on factory building.

E 12-2A   (LO2)
✓ May 1: Dr. Accounts Receivable/ J. Adams, $2,120

JOURNALIZING SALES TRANSACTIONS Enter the following transactions in a sales journal. Use a 6% sales tax rate.

May   1   Sold merchandise on account to J. Adams, $2,000, plus sales tax. Sale No. 488.

      4   Sold merchandise on account to B. Clark, $1,800, plus sales tax. Sale No. 489.

      8   Sold merchandise on account to A. Duck, $1,500, plus sales tax. Sale No. 490.

     11   Sold merchandise on account to E. Hill, $1,950, plus sales tax. Sale No. 491.

E 12-3A   (LO3)
✓ July 6: Cr. Accounts Receivable/ Daren Chesbrough, $527

JOURNALIZING CASH RECEIPTS Enter the following transactions in a cash receipts journal:

July   6   Daren Chesbrough made payment on account, $527.

      10   Made cash sales for the week, $2,470.

      14   Adam Casady made payment on account, $394.

      15   Yue Zou made payment on account, $203.

      17   Made cash sales for the week, $2,360.

E 12-4A   (LO4)
✓ May 9: Purchases Dr./Accounts Payable Cr., $3,100

JOURNALIZING PURCHASES TRANSACTIONS Enter the following transactions in a purchases journal like the one below:

May   3   Purchased merchandise from Climen, $7,200. Invoice No. 321, dated May 1, terms n/30.

      9   Purchased merchandise from Misho, $3,100. Invoice No. 614, dated May 8, terms 2/10, n/30.

     18   Purchased merchandise from Alelu Distributors, $4,700. Invoice No. 180, dated May 15, terms 1/15, n/30.

     23   Purchased merchandise from Saltex, $5,900. Invoice No. 913, dated May 22, terms 1/10, n/30.

PURCHASES JOURNAL					PAGE	
DATE	INVOICE NO.	FROM WHOM PURCHASED	POST. REF.	PURCHASES DEBIT/ ACCOUNTS PAYABLE CREDIT		

E 12-5A (LO5)
✓ Sept. 12: Cash Cr., $7,920

JOURNALIZING CASH PAYMENTS Lakeview Industries uses a cash payments journal. Prepare a cash payments journal using the same format and account titles as illustrated in the chapter. Record the following payments for merchandise purchased:

Sept. 5 Issued Check No. 318 to Clausen Corp. for merchandise purchased August 28, $5,000, terms 2/10, n/30. Payment is made within the discount period.

   12 Issued Check No. 319 to McGonigle Co. for merchandise purchased September 2, $8,400, terms 1/10, n/30. A credit memo had previously been received from McGonigle Co. for merchandise returned, $400. Payment is made within the discount period after deduction for the return dated September 8.

   19 Issued Check No. 320 to Elite Systems for merchandise purchased August 19, $4,600, terms n/30.

   27 Issued Check No. 321 to Glenn Falls for merchandise purchased September 17, $7,000, terms 2/10, n/30. Payment is made within the discount period.

SERIES A PROBLEMS

P 12-6A (LO2)
✓ Total Accounts Receivable Dr.: $16,599.60

SALES JOURNAL Futi Ishanyan owns a retail business and made the following sales during the month of August 20--. There is a 6% sales tax on all sales.

Aug. 1 Sale No. 213 to Jeter Manufacturing Co., $1,300, plus sales tax.

   3 Sale No. 214 to Hassan Co., $2,600, plus sales tax.

   7 Sale No. 215 to Habrock, Inc., $1,700, plus sales tax. (Open a new account for this customer. Address is 125 Fishers Dr., Noblesville, IN 47870–8867.)

   11 Sale No. 216 to Seth Mowbray, $1,400, plus sales tax.

   18 Sale No. 217 to Hassan Co., $3,960, plus sales tax.

   22 Sale No. 218 to Jeter Manufacturing Co., $2,800, plus sales tax.

   30 Sale No. 219 to Seth Mowbray, $1,900, plus sales tax.

REQUIRED

1. Record the transactions in the sales journal starting with page 8. Total and verify the column totals and rule the columns.

2. Post from the sales journal to the general ledger and accounts receivable ledger accounts. Use account numbers as shown in the chapter.

P 12-7A (LO3)
✓ Total Accounts Receivable Cr.: $5,732

CASH RECEIPTS JOURNAL Zebra Imaginarium, a retail business, had the following cash receipts during December 20--. The sales tax is 6%.

Dec. 1 Received payment on account from Michael Anderson, $1,360.

   2 Received payment on account from Ansel Manufacturing, $382.

   7 Made cash sales for the week, $3,160, plus tax. Bank credit card sales for the week, $1,000, plus tax. Bank credit card fee is 3%.

(continued)

Dec. 8 Received payment on account from J. Gorbea, $880.

11 Michael Anderson returned merchandise for a credit, $60, plus tax.

14 Made cash sales for the week, $2,800, plus tax. Bank credit card sales for the week, $800, plus tax. Bank credit card fee is 3%.

20 Received payment on account from Tom Wilson, $1,110.

21 Ansel Manufacturing returned merchandise for a credit, $22, plus tax.

21 Made cash sales for the week, $3,200, plus tax.

24 Received payment on account from Rachel Carson, $2,000.

Beginning general ledger account balances were as follows:

Cash	$9,862
Accounts Receivable	9,352

Beginning customer account balances were as follows:

M. Anderson	$2,480
Ansel Manufacturing	982
J. Gorbea	880
R. Carson	3,200
T. Wilson	1,810

REQUIRED

1. Record the transactions in the cash receipts journal. Total and verify column totals and rule the columns. Use the general journal to record sales returns and allowances.

2. Post from the journals to the general ledger and accounts receivable ledger accounts. Use account numbers as shown in the chapter.

P 12-8A **(LO2/3)**
✓ Total Accounts Receivable
Dr.: $12,745.08

SALES JOURNAL, CASH RECEIPTS JOURNAL, AND GENERAL JOURNAL Owens Distributors is a retail business. The following sales, returns, and cash receipts occurred during March 20--. There is an 8% sales tax. Beginning general ledger account balances were Cash, $9,741; and Accounts Receivable, $1,058.25. Beginning customer account balances were Thompson Group, $1,058.25.

Mar. 1 Sold merchandise to Able & Co., $1,800, plus sales tax. Sale No. 33C.

3 Sold merchandise to R. J. Kalas, Inc., $2,240, plus sales tax. Sale No. 33D.

5 Able & Co. returned merchandise from Sale No. 33C for a credit (Credit Memo No. 66), $30, plus sales tax.

7 Made cash sales for the week, $3,160, plus sales tax.

10 Received payment from Able & Co. for Sale No. 33C less Credit Memo No. 66.

11 Sold merchandise to Blevins Bakery, $1,210, plus sales tax. Sale No. 33E.

13 Received payment from R. J. Kalas for Sale No. 33D.

14 Made cash sales for the week, $4,200, plus sales tax.

16 Blevins Bakery returned merchandise from Sale No. 33E for a credit (Credit Memo No. 67), $44, plus sales tax.

18 Sold merchandise to R. J. Kalas, Inc., $2,620, plus sales tax. Sale No. 33F.

20 Received payment from Blevins Bakery for Sale No. 33E less Credit Memo No. 67.

Mar. 21   Made cash sales for the week, $2,400, plus sales tax.

25   Sold merchandise to Blevins Bakery, $1,915, plus sales tax.
Sale No. 33G.

27   Sold merchandise to Thompson Group, $2,016, plus sales tax.
Sale No. 33H.

28   Made cash sales for the week, $3,500, plus sales tax.

REQUIRED

1. Record the transactions in the sales journal, cash receipts journal, and general journal. Total, verify, and rule the columns where appropriate at the end of the month.

2. Post from the journals to the general ledger and accounts receivable ledger accounts. Use account numbers as shown in the chapter.

P 12-9A   (LO4)
✓ Total Purchases Dr.: $20,790

PURCHASES JOURNAL   J. B. Speck, owner of Speck's Galleria, made the following purchases of merchandise on account during the month of September:

Sept.   3   Purchase Invoice No. 415, $2,650, from Smith Distributors.

8   Purchase Invoice No. 132, $3,830, from Michaels Wholesaler.

11   Purchase Invoice No. 614, $3,140, from J. B. Sanders & Co.

18   Purchase Invoice No. 329, $2,250, from Bateman & Jones, Inc.

23   Purchase Invoice No. 867, $4,160, from Smith Distributors.

27   Purchase Invoice No. 744, $1,980, from Anderson Company.

30   Purchase Invoice No. 652, $2,780, from Michaels Wholesaler.

REQUIRED

1. Record the transactions in the purchases journal. Total and rule the journal.

2. Post from the purchases journal to the general ledger and accounts payable ledger accounts. Use account numbers as shown in the chapter.

P 12-10A   (LO4)
✓ Helmut's Hair Supply account balance: $4,240

PURCHASES JOURNAL, GENERAL LEDGER, AND ACCOUNTS PAYABLE LEDGER
The purchases journal of Kevin's Kettle, a small retail business, is as follows:

							PURCHASES JOURNAL							PAGE 1	
	DATE		INVOICE NO.	FROM WHOM PURCHASED					POST. REF.		PURCHASES DEBIT/ ACCOUNTS PAYABLE CREDIT				
1	20-- Jan.	2	101	Ruiz Imports						3	0	0	0	00	1
2		3	621	Helmut's Hair Supply						2	4	8	0	00	2
3		7	195	Viola's Boutique						4	3	6	0	00	3
4		12	267	Royal Flush						1	9	5	0	00	4
5		18	903	Maria's Melodies						4	7	0	0	00	5
6		25	680	Helmut's Hair Supply						1	7	6	0	00	6
7										18	2	5	0	00	7

REQUIRED

1. Post the total of the purchases journal to the appropriate general ledger accounts. Use account numbers as shown in the chapter.

2. Post the individual purchase amounts to the accounts payable ledger.

P 12-11A (LO5)
✓ Total Cash Cr.: $30,984

CASH PAYMENTS JOURNAL Sam Santiago operates a retail variety store. The books include a cash payments journal and an accounts payable ledger. All cash payments (except petty cash) are entered in the cash payments journal.

Selected account balances on May 1 are as follows:

General Ledger

Cash	$40,000
Accounts Payable	20,000

Accounts Payable Ledger

Fantastic Toys	$5,200
Goya Outlet	3,800
Mueller's Distributors	3,600
Van Kooning	7,400

The following are the transactions related to cash payments for the month of May:

May 1 Issued Check No. 426 in payment of May rent (Rent Expense), $2,400.

3 Issued Check No. 427 to Mueller's Distributors in payment of merchandise purchased on account, $3,600, less a 3% discount. Check was written for $3,492.

7 Issued Check No. 428 to Van Kooning in partial payment of merchandise purchased on account, $5,500. A cash discount was not allowed.

12 Issued Check No. 429 to Fantastic Toys for merchandise purchased on account, $5,200, less a 1% discount. Check was written for $5,148.

15 Issued Check No. 430 to City Power and Light (Utilities Expense), $1,720.

18 Issued Check No. 431 to A-1 Warehouse for a cash purchase of merchandise, $4,800.

26 Issued Check No. 432 to Goya Outlet for merchandise purchased on account, $3,800, less a 2% discount. Check was written for $3,724.

30 Issued Check No. 433 to Mercury Transit Company for freight charges on merchandise purchased (Freight-In), $1,200.

31 Issued Check No. 434 to Town Merchants for a cash purchase of merchandise, $3,000.

REQUIRED

1. Enter the transactions in a cash payments journal. Total, rule, and prove the cash payments journal.

2. Post from the cash payments journal to the general ledger and accounts payable ledger. Use general ledger account numbers as shown in the chapter.

P 12-12A (LO4/5)
✓ Total Cash Cr.: $11,170

PURCHASES JOURNAL, CASH PAYMENTS JOURNAL, AND GENERAL JOURNAL Freddy Flint owns a small retail business called Flint's Fantasy. The cash account has a balance of $20,000 on July 1. The following transactions occurred during July:

July 1 Issued Check No. 414 in payment of July rent, $1,500.

1 Purchased merchandise on account from Tang's Toys, Invoice No. 311, $2,700, terms 2/10, n/30.

July   3   Purchased merchandise on account from Sillas & Company, Invoice No. 812, $3,100, terms 1/10, n/30.

5   Returned merchandise purchased from Tang's Toys, receiving a credit memo on the amount owed, $500.

8   Purchased merchandise on account from Daisy's Dolls, Invoice No. 139, $1,900, terms 2/10, n/30.

11   Issued Check No. 415 to Tang's Toys for merchandise purchased on account, less return of July 5 and less 2% discount.

13   Issued Check No. 416 to Sillas & Company for merchandise purchased on account, less 1% discount.

15   Returned merchandise purchased from Daisy's Dolls, receiving a credit memo on the amount owed, $400.

18   Issued Check No. 417 to Daisy's Dolls for merchandise purchased on account, less return of July 15 and less 2% discount.

25   Purchased merchandise on account from Allied Business, Invoice No. 489, $2,450, terms n/30.

26   Purchased merchandise on account from Tang's Toys, Invoice No. 375, $1,980, terms 2/10, n/30.

29   Purchased merchandise on account from Sillas & Company, Invoice No. 883, $3,460, terms 1/10, n/30.

31   Freddy Flint withdrew cash for personal use, $2,000. Issued Check No. 418.

31   Issued Check No. 419 to Glisan Distributors for a cash purchase of merchandise, $975.

REQUIRED

1. Record the transactions in the purchases journal, cash payments journal, and general journal. Total and rule the purchases and cash payments journals. Prove the cash payments journal.

2. Post from the journals to the general ledger and accounts payable ledger accounts. Use general ledger account numbers as shown in the chapter.

SERIES B EXERCISES

E 12-1B   (LO1)

RECORDING TRANSACTIONS IN THE PROPER JOURNAL Identify the journal (sales, cash receipts, purchases, cash payments, or general) in which each of the following transactions should be recorded:

(a) Issued credit memo to customer for merchandise returned.

(b) Sold merchandise for cash.

(c) Purchased merchandise on account.

(d) Issued checks to employees in payment of wages.

(e) Purchased factory supplies on account.

(f) Sold merchandise on account.

E 12-2B   (LO2)
✓ Sept. 1: Dr. Accounts Receivable/
    K. Smith, $1,890

JOURNALIZING SALES TRANSACTIONS Enter the following transactions in a sales journal. Use a 5% sales tax rate.

(continued)

Sept. 1 Sold merchandise on account to K. Smith, $1,800, plus sales tax. Sale No. 228.

3 Sold merchandise on account to J. Arnes, $3,100, plus sales tax. Sale No. 229.

5 Sold merchandise on account to M. Denison, $2,800, plus sales tax. Sale No. 230.

7 Sold merchandise on account to B. Marshall, $1,900, plus sales tax. Sale No. 231.

E 12-3B (LO3)
✓ Nov. 1: Cr. Accounts Receivable/ Jean Haghighat, $750

JOURNALIZING CASH RECEIPTS Enter the following transactions in a cash receipts journal:

Nov. 1 Jean Haghighat made payment on account, $750.

12 Marc Antonoff made payment on account, $464.

15 Made cash sales, $3,763.

18 Will Mossein made payment on account, $241.

25 Made cash sales, $2,648.

E 12-4B (LO4)
✓ Jan. 3: Purchases Dr./Accounts Payable Cr., $6,000

JOURNALIZING PURCHASES TRANSACTIONS Enter the following transactions in a purchases journal like the one below:

Jan. 3 Purchased merchandise from Feng, $6,000. Invoice No. 416, dated January 1, terms 2/10, n/30.

12 Purchased merchandise from Miranda, $9,000. Invoice No. 624, dated January 10, terms n/30.

19 Purchased merchandise from J. B. Barba, $6,400. Invoice No. 190, dated January 18, terms 1/10, n/30.

26 Purchased merchandise from Ramirez, $3,700. Invoice No. 923, dated January 25, terms 1/15, n/30.

PURCHASES JOURNAL					PAGE
DATE	INVOICE NO.	FROM WHOM PURCHASED		POST. REF.	PURCHASES DEBIT/ ACCOUNTS PAYABLE CREDIT

E 12-5B (LO5)
✓ Apr. 19: Cash Cr., $4,950

JOURNALIZING CASH PAYMENTS Sandcastles Northwest uses a cash payments journal. Prepare a cash payments journal using the same format and account titles as illustrated in the chapter. Record the following payments for merchandise purchased:

Apr. 5 Issued Check No. 429 to Standard Industries for merchandise purchased April 3, $8,000, terms 2/10, n/30. Payment is made within the discount period.

19 Issued Check No. 430 to Finest Company for merchandise purchased April 10, $5,300, terms 1/10, n/30. A credit memo had previously been received from Finest Company for merchandise returned, $300. Payment is made within the discount period after deduction for the return dated April 12.

21 Issued Check No. 431 to Funny Follies for merchandise purchased March 21, $3,250, terms n/30.

29 Issued Check No. 432 to Classic Data for merchandise purchased April 20, $7,000, terms 2/10, n/30. Payment is made within the discount period.

SERIES B PROBLEMS

P 12-6B **(LO2)**
✓ Total Accounts Receivable
Dr.: $13,072.50

SALES JOURNAL T. M. Maxwell owns a retail business and made the following sales during the month of July 20--. There is a 5% sales tax on all sales.

July 1 Sale No. 101 to Saga, Inc., $1,200, plus sales tax.
   8 Sale No. 102 to Vinnie Ward, $2,100, plus sales tax.
  15 Sale No. 103 to Dvorak Manufacturing, $4,300, plus sales tax.
  21 Sale No. 104 to Vinnie Ward, $1,800, plus sales tax.
  24 Sale No. 105 to Zapata Co., $1,600, plus sales tax. (Open a new account for this customer. Address is 789 N. Stafford Dr., Bloomington, IN 47401–6201.)
  29 Sale No. 106 to Saga, Inc., $1,450, plus sales tax.

REQUIRED

1. Record the transactions in the sales journal. Total and verify the column totals and rule the columns.
2. Post the sales journal to the general ledger and accounts receivable ledger accounts. Use account numbers as shown in the chapter.

P 12-7B **(LO3)**
✓ Total Accounts Receivable Cr.: $3,481

CASH RECEIPTS JOURNAL Color Florists, a retail business, had the following cash receipts during January 20--. The sales tax is 5%.

Jan. 1 Received payment on account from Ray Boyd, $880.
   3 Received payment on account from Clint Hassell, $271.
   5 Made cash sales for the week, $2,800, plus tax. Bank credit card sales for the week, $1,200, plus tax. Bank credit card fee is 3%.
   8 Received payment on account from Jan Sowada, $912.
  11 Ray Boyd returned merchandise for a credit, $40, plus tax.
  12 Made cash sales for the week, $3,100, plus tax. Bank credit card sales for the week, $1,900, plus tax. Bank credit card fee is 3%.
  15 Received payment on account from Robert Zehnle, $1,100.
  18 Robert Zehnle returned merchandise for a credit, $31, plus tax.
  19 Made cash sales for the week, $2,230, plus tax.
  25 Received payment on account from Dazai Manufacturing, $318.

Beginning general ledger account balances were as follows:

Cash	$2,890.75
Accounts Receivable	6,300.00

Beginning customer account balances were as follows:

R. Boyd	$1,400
Dazai Manufacturing	318
C. Hassell	815
J. Sowada	1,481
R. Zehnle	2,286

(*continued*)

REQUIRED

1. Record the transactions in the cash receipts journal. Total and verify the column totals and rule the columns. Use the general journal to record sales returns and allowances.

2. Post from the journals to the general ledger and accounts receivable ledger accounts. Use account numbers as shown in the chapter.

P 12-8B **(LO2/3)**
✓ Total Accounts Receivable
Dr.: $7,853.80

SALES JOURNAL, CASH RECEIPTS JOURNAL, AND GENERAL JOURNAL Paul Jackson owns a retail business. The following sales, returns, and cash receipts are for April 20--. There is a 7% sales tax.

Apr.	1	Sold merchandise to O. L. Meyers, $2,100, plus sales tax. Sale No. 111.
	3	Sold merchandise to Andrew Plaa, $1,000, plus sales tax. Sale No. 112.
	6	O. L. Meyers returned merchandise from Sale No. 111 for a credit (Credit Memo No. 42), $50, plus sales tax.
	7	Made cash sales for the week, $3,240, plus sales tax.
	9	Received payment from O. L. Meyers for Sale No. 111, less Credit Memo No. 42.
	12	Sold merchandise to Melissa Richfield, $980, plus sales tax. Sale No. 113.
	14	Made cash sales for the week, $2,180, plus sales tax.
	17	Melissa Richfield returned merchandise from Sale No. 113 for a credit (Credit Memo No. 43), $40, plus sales tax.
	19	Sold merchandise to Kelsay Munkres, $1,020, plus sales tax. Sale No. 114.
	21	Made cash sales for the week, $2,600, plus sales tax.
	24	Sold merchandise to O. L. Meyers, $920, plus sales tax. Sale No. 115.
	27	Sold merchandise to Andrew Plaa, $1,320, plus sales tax. Sale No. 116.
	28	Made cash sales for the week, $2,800, plus sales tax.

Beginning general ledger account balances were as follows:

Cash	$2,864.54
Accounts Receivable	2,726.25

Beginning customer account balances were as follows:

O. L. Meyers	$2,186.00
K. Munkres	482.00
M. Richfield	58.25

REQUIRED

1. Record the transactions in the sales journal, cash receipts journal, and general journal. Total, verify, and rule the columns where appropriate at the end of the month.

2. Post from the journals to the general ledger and accounts receivable ledger accounts. Use account numbers as shown in the chapter.

P 12-9B **(LO4)**
✓ Total Purchases Dr.: $18,515

PURCHASES JOURNAL Ann Benton, owner of Benton's Galleria, made the following purchases of merchandise on account during the month of October:

Oct. 2 Purchase Invoice No. 321, $1,950, from Boggs Distributors.
    7 Purchase Invoice No. 152, $2,915, from Wolfs Wholesaler.
   10 Purchase Invoice No. 634, $3,565, from Komuro & Co.
   16 Purchase Invoice No. 349, $2,845, from Fritz & McCord, Inc.
   24 Purchase Invoice No. 587, $3,370, from Boggs Distributors.
   26 Purchase Invoice No. 764, $2,240, from Sanderson Company.
   31 Purchase Invoice No. 672, $1,630, from Wolfs Wholesaler.

REQUIRED

1. Record the transactions in the purchases journal. Total and rule the journal.
2. Post from the purchases journal to the general ledger and accounts payable ledger accounts. Use account numbers as shown in the chapter.

P 12-10B **(LO4)**
✓ Amelia & Vincente account
  balance: $7,810

PURCHASES JOURNAL, GENERAL LEDGER, AND ACCOUNTS PAYABLE LEDGER The purchases journal of Ryan's Rats Nest, a small retail business, is as follows:

	DATE		INVOICE NO.	FROM WHOM PURCHASED	POST. REF.	PURCHASES DEBIT/ ACCOUNTS PAYABLE CREDIT					
1	20-- Jan.	3	121	Sandra's Sweets		4	4	9	0	00	1
2		5	641	Amelia & Vincente		5	9	2	0	00	2
3		9	215	Nobuko's Nature Store		2	6	8	0	00	3
4		15	227	Smith and Johnson Company		6	5	6	0	00	4
5		21	933	Hidemi, Inc.		1	3	0	0	00	5
6		30	650	Amelia & Vincente		1	8	9	0	00	6
7						22	8	4	0	00	7

PURCHASES JOURNAL — PAGE 1

REQUIRED

1. Post the total of the purchases journal to the appropriate general ledger accounts. Use account numbers as shown in the chapter.
2. Post the individual purchase amounts to the accounts payable ledger.

P 12-11B **(LO5)**
✓ Total Cash Cr.: $29,890

CASH PAYMENTS JOURNAL Kay Zembrowski operates a retail variety store. The books include a cash payments journal and an accounts payable ledger. All cash payments (except petty cash) are entered in the cash payments journal. Selected account balances on May 1 are as follows:

General Ledger

Cash	$40,000
Accounts Payable	20,000

Accounts Payable Ledger

Cortez Distributors	$4,200
Indra & Velga	6,800
Toy Corner	4,600
Troutman Outlet	4,400

(*continued*)

The following transactions are related to cash payments for the month of May:

May 1 Issued Check No. 326 in payment of May rent (Rent Expense), $2,600.

    4 Issued Check No. 327 to Cortez Distributors in payment of merchandise purchased on account, $4,200, less a 3% discount. Check was written for $4,074.

    7 Issued Check No. 328 to Indra & Velga in partial payment of merchandise purchased on account, $6,200. A cash discount was not allowed.

   11 Issued Check No. 329 to Toy Corner for merchandise purchased on account, $4,600, less a 1% discount. Check was written for $4,554.

   15 Issued Check No. 330 to County Power and Light (Utilities Expense), $1,500.

   19 Issued Check No. 331 to Builders Warehouse for a cash purchase of merchandise, $3,500.

   25 Issued Check No. 332 to Troutman Outlet for merchandise purchased on account, $4,400, less a 2% discount. Check was written for $4,312.

   30 Issued Check No. 333 to Rapid Transit Company for freight charges on merchandise purchased (Freight-In), $800.

   31 Issued Check No. 334 to City Merchants for a cash purchase of merchandise, $2,350.

REQUIRED

1. Enter the transactions in a cash payments journal. Total, rule, and prove the cash payments journal.

2. Post from the cash payments journal to the general ledger and accounts payable ledger. Use general ledger account numbers as shown in the chapter.

P 12-12B   (LO4/5)
✓ Total Cash Cr.: $10,760

PURCHASES JOURNAL, CASH PAYMENTS JOURNAL, AND GENERAL JOURNAL Debbie Mueller owns a small retail business called Debbie's Doll House. The cash account has a balance of $20,000 on July 1. The following transactions occurred during July:

July 1 Issued Check No. 314 for July rent, $1,400.

    1 Purchased merchandise on account from Topper's Toys, Invoice No. 211, $2,500, terms 2/10, n/30.

    3 Purchased merchandise on account from Jones & Company, Invoice No. 812, $2,800, terms 1/10, n/30.

    5 Returned merchandise purchased from Topper's Toys receiving a credit memo on the amount owed, $400.

    8 Purchased merchandise on account from Downtown Merchants, Invoice No. 159, $1,600, terms 2/10, n/30.

   11 Issued Check No. 315 to Topper's Toys for merchandise purchased on account, less return of July 5 and less 2% discount.

   13 Issued Check No. 316 to Jones & Company for merchandise purchased on account, less 1% discount.

   15 Returned merchandise purchased from Downtown Merchants receiving a credit memo on the amount owed, $600.

July 18   Issued Check No. 317 to Downtown Merchants for merchandise purchased on account, less return of July 15 and less 2% discount.

     25   Purchased merchandise on account from Columbia Products, Invoice No. 468, $3,200, terms n/30.

     26   Purchased merchandise on account from Topper's Toys, Invoice No. 395, $1,430, terms 2/10, n/30.

     29   Purchased merchandise on account from Jones & Company, Invoice No. 853, $2,970, terms 1/10, n/30.

     31   Mueller withdrew cash for personal use, $2,500. Issued Check No. 318.

     31   Issued Check No. 319 to Burnside Warehouse for a cash purchase of merchandise, $1,050.

REQUIRED

1. Record the transactions in the purchases journal, cash payments journal, and general journal. Total and rule the purchases and cash payments journals. Prove the cash payments journal.

2. Post from the journals to the general ledger and accounts payable ledger accounts. Use general ledger account numbers as shown in the chapter.

CHECK LIST
- ☐ **Managing**
- ☐ **Planning**
- ☐ **Drafting**
- ☐ **Break**
- ☐ **Revising**
- ☐ **Managing**

MANAGING YOUR WRITING

You have a part-time job as a bookkeeper at a local office supply store. The accounting records consist of a general journal and general ledger. The manager is concerned about efficiency and feels that too much time is spent recording transactions. In addition, there sometimes is difficulty determining the amount owed to specific suppliers. The manager knows you are an accounting student and asks for your suggestions to improve the accounting function.

Write a memo to the manager describing how to increase efficiency and accuracy by using different accounting records.

 ETHICS

ETHICS CASE

Judy Baresford, the store manager of Comfort Futons, noticed that the amount of time the two bookkeepers were spending on accounts receivable, accounts payable, and cash receipts was increasing due to the store's increase in sales. A friend of Judy's who is also a store manager suggested that she might want to have some special journals designed that would reduce the amount of work involved in the day-to-day bookkeeping at her store. Judy approached Jon Fortner and Sue Stavio, the bookkeepers, and asked them to come up with a proposal for special journals. During lunch, Jon told Sue he thought designing special journals would be a lot of work and it was not in his job description. Sue told him not to worry because she would just copy pages of special journals from her accounting textbook and they could submit these journals as their own design. Jon liked the idea and they agreed to meet the next night, scan the journals into Word, and submit them to Judy the following morning.

1. Do you think Sue's suggestion is unethical? Why or why not?

2. In using the generic special journals from Sue's accounting textbook, what possible problems can you foresee?

3. If you were Judy, how would you respond to Sue and Jon's "plan"?

MASTERY PROBLEM

✓ Total Accounts Receivable Cr.: $7,235

During the month of October 20--, The Pink Petal flower shop engaged in the following transactions:

Oct. 1 Sold merchandise on account to Elizabeth Shoemaker, $1,000, plus tax of $50. Sale No. 222.

2 Issued Check No. 190 to Jill Hand in payment of October 1 balance of $500, less 2% discount.

2 Purchased merchandise on account from Flower Wholesalers, $4,000. Invoice No. 500, dated October 2, terms 2/10, n/30.

4 Purchased merchandise on account from Seidl Enterprises, $700. Invoice No. 527, dated October 4, terms 2/15, n/30.

5 Issued Check No. 191 in payment of phone expense for the month of September, $150.

7 Sold merchandise for cash, $3,500, plus tax of $175.

9 Received payment from Leigh Summers in full settlement of account, $2,000.

11 Issued Check No. 192 to Flower Wholesalers in payment of October 1 balance of $1,500.

12 Sold merchandise on account to Leigh Summers, $2,000, plus tax of $100. Sale No. 223.

12 Received payment from Meg Johnson on account, $3,100.

13 Issued Check No. 193 to Seidl Enterprises in payment of October 4 purchase. Invoice No. 527, less 2% discount.

14 Meg Johnson returned merchandise for a credit, $300, plus sales tax of $15.

17 Returned merchandise to Vases Etc. for credit, $900.

24 Received payment from David's Decorating on account, $2,135.

27 Sold merchandise on account to David's Decorating, $3,000, plus tax of $150. Sale No. 224.

29 Issued Check No. 194 in payment of wages (Wages Expense) for the four-week period ending October 30, $900.

Selected account balances as of October 1 were as follows:

Account	Account No.	Debit	Credit
Cash	101	$18,225	
Accounts Receivable	122	9,619	
Accounts Payable	202		$5,120

The Pink Petal also had the following subsidiary ledger balances as of October 1:

Accounts Receivable:

Customer	Accounts Receivable Balance
David's Decorating 12 Jude Lane Hartford, CT 06117	$3,340

Elizabeth Shoemaker
52 Juniper Road
Hartford, CT 06118 $ 279

Meg Johnson
700 Hobbes Dr.
Avon, CT 06108   4,000

Leigh Summers
5200 Hamilton Ave.
Hartford, CT 06111   2,000

Accounts Payable:

Vendor	Accounts Payable Balance
Vases Etc. 34 Harry Ave. East Hartford, CT 05234	$3,120
Jill Hand 1009 Drake Rd. Farmington, CT 06082	500
Flower Wholesalers 43 Lucky Lane Bristol, CT 06007	1,500
Seidl Enterprises 888 Anders Street Newington, CT 06789	—

REQUIRED

1. Record the transactions in a sales journal (page 7), cash receipts journal (page 10), purchases journal (page 6), cash payments journal (page 11), and general journal (page 5). Total, verify, and rule the columns where appropriate at the end of the month.
2. Post from the journals to the general ledger, accounts receivable ledger, and accounts payable ledger accounts. Use account numbers as shown in the chapter.

CHALLENGE PROBLEM

> This problem challenges you to apply your cumulative accounting knowledge to move a step beyond the material in the chapter.
>
> ✓ June 3: Cr. City Sales Tax Payable, $4.22

Screpcap Co. had the following transactions during the first week of June:

June   1   Purchased merchandise on account from Acme Supply, $2,700, plus freight charges of $160.

  1   Issued Check No. 219 to Denver Wholesalers for merchandise purchased on account, $720, less 1% discount.

  1   Sold merchandise on account to F. Colby, $246, plus 5% state sales tax plus 2% city sales tax.

(continued)

June 2 Received cash on account from N. Dunlop, $315.

2 Made cash sale of $413 plus 5% state sales tax plus 2% city sales tax.

2 Purchased merchandise on account from Permon Co., $3,200, plus freight charges of $190.

3 Sold merchandise on account to F. Ayres, $211, plus 5% state sales tax plus 2% city sales tax.

3 Issued Check No. 220 to Ellis Co. for merchandise purchased on account, $847, less 1% discount.

3 Received cash on account from F. Graves, $463.

4 Issued Check No. 221 to Penguin Warehouse for merchandise purchased on account, $950, less 1% discount.

4 Sold merchandise on account to K. Stanga, $318, plus 5% state sales tax plus 2% city sales tax.

4 Purchased merchandise on account from Mason Milling, $1,630, plus freight charges of $90.

4 Received cash on account from O. Alston, $381.

5 Made cash sale of $319 plus 5% state sales tax plus 2% city sales tax.

5 Issued Check No. 222 to Acme Supply for merchandise purchased on account, $980, less 1% discount.

REQUIRED

1. Record the transactions in a general journal.

2. Assuming these are the types of transactions Screpcap Co. experiences on a regular basis, design the following special journals for Screpcap:

   (a) Sales journal

   (b) Cash receipts journal

   (c) Purchases journal

   (d) Cash payments journal

ANSWERS TO SELF-STUDY TEST QUESTIONS

True/False

1. T
2. F (general journal is still needed)
3. F (only credit sales)
4. T
5. T

Multiple Choice

1. a 2. a 3. c 4. c 5. a

Checkpoint Exercises

1.

			SALES JOURNAL											PAGE 7	
	DATE	SALE NO.	TO WHOM SOLD	POST. REF.	ACCOUNT RECEIVABLE DEBIT			SALES CREDIT			SALES TAX PAYABLE CREDIT				
1	June 1	214	Erin Lucas		8 8 2	00		8 4 0	00		4 2	00			1

2.

			CASH RECEIPTS JOURNAL																	PAGE	
	DATE		ACCOUNT CREDITED	POST. REF.	GENERAL CREDIT			ACCOUNTS RECEIVABLE CREDIT			SALES CREDIT			SALES TAX PAYABLE CREDIT			CASH DEBIT				
1	June	7	Erin Lucas					8 8 2	00								8 8 2	00			1
2		30									2 1 5 0	00		1 0 7	50		2 2 5 7	50			2
3		30	Rent Revenue		7 5 0	00											7 5 0	00			3
4																					4

3.

			PURCHASES JOURNAL				PAGE			
	DATE	INVOICE NO.	FROM WHOM PURCHASED	POST. REF.	PURCHASES DEBIT/ ACCOUNTS PAYABLE CREDIT					
1	Apr. 6	131	Clever		1 6 8 0	00				1
2										2

4.

			CASH PAYMENTS JOURNAL														PAGE	
	DATE	CK NO.	ACCOUNT DEBITED	POST. REF.	GENERAL DEBIT			ACCOUNTS PAYABLE DEBIT			PURCHASES DEBIT			PURCHASES DISCOUNTS CREDIT		CASH CREDIT		
1	Aug. 2	193	Rent Expense		2 2 0 0	00										2 2 0 0	00	1
2	6	194	Mason Hardware					1 7 0 0	00					3 4	00	1 6 6 6	00	2
3	10	195									2 7 3 0	00				2 7 3 0	00	3
4																		4

Chapter 13 Accounting for Merchandise Inventory

LEARNING OBJECTIVES

Careful study of this chapter should enable you to:

LO1 Explain the impact of merchandise inventory on the financial statements.

LO2 Describe the two principal systems of accounting for merchandise inventory—the periodic system and the perpetual system.

LO3 Compute the costs allocated to the ending inventory and cost of goods sold using different inventory methods.

LO4 Estimate the ending inventory and cost of goods sold by using the gross profit and retail inventory methods.

"**B**e particular. Never sell anything you would not want yourself." That was Barney Kroger's motto in 1883 when he invested his life savings of $372 to open a grocery store at 66 Pearl Street in downtown Cincinnati. With nearly 2,800 stores in 35 states and annual sales of more than $115.3 billion, Kroger today ranks as one of the world's largest retailers. In addition, they operate over 700 convenience stores, 300 jewelry stores, just under 1,500 supermarket fuel centers and about 2,000 pharmacies.

As you walk through a grocery store, have you ever wondered what the store paid for each item? It would be nice to know which items are "good buys" and which are "overpriced." What happens when management pays different amounts for identical products on the shelf? In this chapter, you will learn how merchandising firms determine which items were sold and which remain. That is, how they determine the cost of the goods sold and the cost of the goods remaining on the shelves at the end of the year.

In Chapters 10 and 11, you learned how to account for the purchase and sale of merchandise. One of the major reasons for keeping accounting records is to determine the net income (or net loss) of a business. A major component of net income is the gross profit. In Chapter 11, you learned how to compute gross profit. An abbreviated form of this calculation is shown below.

Calculation of Gross Profit		
Net sales		$110
Cost of goods sold		
Merchandise inventory, Jan. 1	$ 20	
Purchases	80	
Cost of goods available for sale	$100	
Less merchandise inventory, Dec. 31	30	
Cost of goods sold		70
Gross profit		$ 40

> The terms *goods* and *merchandise* mean the same thing and are used interchangeably.

For a merchandising business, the cost of goods available for sale ($100) during the accounting period must be divided between cost of goods sold ($70) and ending merchandise inventory ($30). In Chapter 11, the costs assigned to these accounts were provided. In this chapter, you will learn how to determine the dollar amounts assigned to cost of goods sold and ending merchandise inventory. In Chapter 14, we will illustrate the end-of-period adjustments required to bring the cost of goods sold and merchandise inventory accounts up to date to reflect their proper balances.

The Impact of Merchandise Inventory on Financial Statements

LO1

Explain the impact of merchandise inventory on the financial statements.

> This year's ending inventory becomes next year's beginning inventory.

> LEARNING KEY 🔑
>
> If the ending inventory for 20-1 is understated, net income for 20-1 is understated and net income for 20-2 is overstated.

> LEARNING KEY 🔑
>
> If the ending inventory for 20-1 is overstated, net income for 20-1 is overstated and net income for 20-2 is understated.

A company's ending inventory must be reported accurately. An error in the reported inventory will cause errors on the income statement, statement of owner's equity, and balance sheet. In addition, since this year's ending inventory becomes next year's beginning inventory, financial statements for the following year will also contain errors.

Figure 13-1 illustrates the impact of an error in the *ending inventory*. The first pair of columns presents partial financial statements when the ending inventory is correct. For this illustration, sales, cost of goods sold, and operating expenses are assumed to be the same for 20-1 and 20-2. Thus, the same net income of $30 and beginning and ending merchandise inventories of $20 are reported for both years.

The second pair of columns in Figure 13-1 illustrates the effects of understating the ending inventory. Understating the ending inventory for 20-1 by $5 causes the cost of goods sold to be overstated by $5 and net income to be understated by $5. Since net income is reported on the statement of owner's equity, Erv Bultman's capital on December 31 is understated by $5. The understated capital also appears in the owner's equity section of the balance sheet. The understated ending inventory is reported in the current assets section of the balance sheet.

Even if the ending inventory for 20-2 is accurately reported, we still have a problem with the income statement. Since the ending inventory for 20-1 was understated, the beginning inventory for 20-2 is understated also ($15 instead of $20). This error causes cost of goods sold to be understated by $5 and net income to be overstated by $5.

At this point, we can see that this inventory error "washes out" over the two-year period. The understated net income for 20-1 is offset by overstated net income in 20-2. Thus, Bultman's capital account as of December 31, 20-2, is reported accurately on the statement of owner's equity and balance sheet at $160. Assuming no future inventory errors, the financial statements for 20-3 and thereafter will be correct.

FIGURE 13-1 Effect of Inventory Errors on Net Income

FINANCIAL STATEMENTS	ENDING INVENTORY FOR 20-1 IS CORRECT		ENDING INVENTORY FOR 20-1 IS UNDERSTATED		ENDING INVENTORY FOR 20-1 IS OVERSTATED	
	20-1	20-2	20-1	20-2	20-1	20-2
Income Statement						
Sales	80	80	80	80	80	80
Cost of goods sold:						
Beginning merchandise inventory	20	**20**	20	**15**	20	**25**
Add purchases (net)	40	40	40	40	40	40
Cost of goods available for sale	60	60	60	55	60	65
Less ending merchandise inventory	**(20)**	(20)	**(15)**	(20)	**(25)**	(20)
Cost of goods sold		(40)		(45)		(45)
	(40)		(45)	(35)	(35)	
Gross profit	40	40	35	45	45	35
Operating expenses	(10)	(10)	(10)	(10)	(10)	(10)
Net income	30	30	25	35	35	25
Statement of Owner's Equity						
Erv Bultman, capital, January 1	100	130	100	125	100	135
Net income	30	30	25	35	35	25
Erv Bultman, capital, December 31		130	160	125	160	135	160
Balance Sheet (Partial)						
Current assets:						
Merchandise inventory	20	20	15	20	25	20
Owner's equity:						
Erv Bultman, capital	130	160	125	160	135	160

The third pair of columns in Figure 13-1 illustrates the effects of overstating the ending inventory in 20-1. This causes net income to be overstated in 20-1 and understated in 20-2. As previously discussed, these errors "wash out" by the end of 20-2. Thus, Bultman's capital account is correct in the 20-2 financial statements.

It is very important to have an accurate count and valuation for the ending inventory. Since errors in the ending inventory have a direct effect on net income for the period, managers may be tempted to manipulate this amount to achieve a desired result: to either increase net income to make the company look good, or decrease net income to reduce taxes or smooth earnings. For this reason, observing and verifying the ending inventory is an important aspect of an external auditor's job.

CHECKPOINT ✓

Complete Checkpoint-1 on page 508 to test your basic understanding of LO1.

YOUR PERSPECTIVE

Material Recording Clerk – Part 1

Material recording clerks track the shipment, receipt, or movement of items within a business. They use computers, tablets, or other electronic devices to keep an accurate record of the organization's inventory and compile reports on the organization's inventory. Sensors and tags allow the devices to detect movement of the inventory items, which enables the clerks to update reports without having to count the items manually. Information material recording clerks collect helps managers to know the cost of goods sold to date and the inventory on hand. Managers use this information to make important operating decisions.

LO2 — Types of Inventory Systems: Periodic and Perpetual

Describe the two principal systems of accounting for merchandise inventory—the periodic system and the perpetual system.

LEARNING KEY
Under the periodic inventory system, the ending inventory and cost of goods sold are determined at the end of the accounting period, when a physical inventory is taken.

LEARNING KEY
Under the perpetual inventory system, cost of goods sold and the amount of merchandise inventory on hand are continually updated as merchandise is bought and sold.

CHECKPOINT ✔
Complete Checkpoint-2 on page 508 to test your basic understanding of LO2.

The two principal systems of accounting for merchandise inventory are the periodic and the perpetual systems. Entries made for inventory transactions under these systems are illustrated in Figure 13-2. Chapter 11 illustrated the periodic inventory system. As shown in Figure 13-2, under the periodic inventory system, no entries are made to the merchandise inventory or cost of goods sold account during the year. Thus, the balance in the merchandise inventory account is based on the physical count of inventory taken at the end of the last accounting period. The merchandise inventory and the cost of goods sold for the current period are not determined until the end of the current accounting period, when a physical inventory is taken. At that time, the following formula is applied to calculate cost of goods sold:

Beginning Inventory (based on last year's ending physical count)
+ Net Purchases (account balance at end of this year)
= Cost of Goods Available for Sale
− Ending Inventory (based on this year's ending physical count)
= Cost of Goods Sold (for this year)

Adjusting entries are needed at the end of the fiscal year to update the merchandise inventory account and cost of goods sold. These entries are illustrated in Chapter 14.

As shown in Figure 13-2, under the perpetual inventory system, entries are made to the merchandise inventory and cost of goods sold accounts as transactions take place during the accounting period. The merchandise inventory account is debited for the cost of all goods purchased, including freight charges, and credited for the cost of all goods sold. In addition, this account is debited when customers return merchandise and is credited when suppliers grant returns, allowances, and discounts. Thus, the balance of the account represents the cost of goods on hand at all times. The cost of goods sold account is debited when merchandise is sold and credited when customers return merchandise. Thus, the balance of the account reflects the cost of goods sold at any point during the accounting period. No year-end adjusting entry is necessary as long as the physical inventory agrees with the amount reported in the merchandise inventory account. In Chapter 14, we will illustrate the proper adjustments if this is not true and an additional adjustment for inventory expected to be returned in the next accounting period.

FIGURE 13-2 Entries for Periodic and Perpetual Inventory Systems

TRANSACTION	PERIODIC SYSTEM		PERPETUAL SYSTEM	

1. Purchased merchandise on account, $100.	Purchases 100
	  Accounts Payable
		100	Merchandise Inventory 100
			  Accounts Payable
				100

2. Paid freight charge, $30.	Freight-In 30
	  Cash
		30	Merchandise Inventory 30
			  Cash
				30

3. Sold merchandise on account, $80.
The cost of the merchandise was $50.
	Accounts Receivable 80
	  Sales
		80	Accounts Receivable 80
			  Sales
			Cost of Goods Sold 50
			  Merchandise Inventory
				80
				
				50

4. Merchandise costing $10 was returned to the supplier.	Accounts Payable 10
	  Purchases Ret. & Allow.
		10	Accounts Payable 10
			  Merchandise Inventory
				10

5. Customers returned merchandise sold for $20.
The cost of the merchandise was $15.
	Sales Ret. and Allow. 20
	  Accounts Receivable
		20	Sales Ret. and Allow. 20
			  Accounts Receivable
			Merchandise Inventory 15
			  Cost of Goods Sold
				20
				
				15

6. Paid for merchandise costing $100. The supplier granted a 2% discount for prompt payment.	Accounts Payable 100
	  Purchases Discounts
	  Cash
		2
		98
			Accounts Payable 100
			  Merchandise Inventory
			  Cash
				2
				98

| LO3 | Assigning Costs to Inventory and Cost of Goods Sold |

Compute the costs allocated to the ending inventory and cost of goods sold using different inventory methods.

To determine the cost of goods sold and ending inventory, it is important to understand:

1. the purpose of a physical inventory,
2. the specific calculations used under the periodic and perpetual systems, and
3. the role of the lower-of-cost-or-market rule.

Taking a Physical Inventory

Even under the perpetual inventory system, there will be differences between the actual inventory on the floor and the amount on the books. These differences are the result of breakage, spoilage, and theft. Thieves rarely yell "Debit Loss Due to Theft and credit Merchandise Inventory" as they attempt to leave the store with merchandise under their coats.

Under the periodic system, the goods on hand at the end of the period are counted to allocate merchandise costs between sold and unsold goods. This process is called taking a **physical inventory**. A physical inventory is also important under the perpetual system. It verifies that the amount of merchandise actually held agrees with what is reported in the accounting records.

Taking a physical inventory can be a sizable task. Frequently, it is done after regular business hours. Some companies even close for a few days to take inventory. The ideal time to count the goods is when the quantity on hand is at its lowest level. A fiscal year that starts and ends at the time the stock of goods is normally at its lowest level is known as a **natural business year**. Such a year is used by many businesses for accounting purposes.

Various procedures are followed in taking an inventory to be sure that no items are missed and that no items are included more than once. Frequently, persons taking inventory work in pairs: one counts the items and the other records the information. Usually, this information is entered on a special form called an **inventory sheet**, like the one illustrated in Figure 13-3. The inventory sheet has columns for recording the description of each item, the quantity on hand, the cost per unit, and the extension.

FIGURE 13-3 Inventory Sheet

INVENTORY Aug. 31 20-- Page 1

Sheet No. 1
Called by L.M.M.
Entered by K.N.
Department A
Location Storeroom
Costed by C.M.H.
Extended by C.M.H.
Examined by C.J.C.

Description	Quantity	Unit	Unit Cost	Extensions	
Table Lamp	20	ea.	62.80	1,256.00	
Wall Rack	18	ea.	19.70	354.60	
Bookcase	7	ea.	88.10	616.70	
End Table	13	ea.	53.20	691.60	
Desk	6	ea.	158.30	949.80	
Total					6,465.10

A BROADER VIEW

All Kinds of Businesses Need Accounting Systems

At any given time, a typical Wal-Mart discount store has more than 120,000 standard items in stock. Every item must be inventoried and replenished in a timely way to avoid having too much or too little stock. Wal-Mart associates have the aid of RFDI (radio frequency identification) tags to track pallets of products through their supply chain. These tags can be read by a handheld computer, linked by a radio-frequency network to in-store terminals. These high-tech devices provide up-to-the-minute information on inventory on hand, upcoming deliveries, and stock at Wal-Mart distribution centers.

MARC F. HENNING/ALAMY STOCK PHOTO

Only goods that are the property of the company should be included in a physical inventory. Two special situations that require care to determine ownership are (1) goods held for sale on consignment and (2) goods in transit. Sometimes one business will try to sell merchandise for another business or individual on a commission basis. This is called selling goods on consignment. Goods held on consignment remain the property of the shipper (consignor). They should not be included in the inventory of the company holding the goods (consignee).

To determine whether goods in transit at year-end should be included in inventory, we must know the FOB (free on board) terms. If goods are shipped FOB shipping point, the buyer pays for shipping and the goods belong to the buyer as soon as they are shipped. If goods are shipped FOB destination, the seller pays for shipping and the goods belong to the seller until they are received by the buyer.

After calculating the quantities of goods owned at the end of the period, the proper cost must be assigned to the inventory. In addition to the purchase price, we include delivery costs (freight-in), insurance, and, occasionally, storage fees. Therefore, cost means all necessary and reasonable costs incurred to get the goods to the buyer's place of business.

If all purchases of the same item were made at the same price per unit, computing the cost of the ending inventory would be simple. We would multiply the number of units by the cost per unit. In a world of changing prices, however, identical items are purchased at different times and at different costs per unit. Of the goods available for sale, how do we decide which units were sold and which units remain on the shelf? As shown in Figure 13-4, this decision affects the income statement and balance sheet. The following four inventory methods have become generally accepted for answering this question:

1. Specific identification
2. First-in, first-out (FIFO)
3. Weighted-average
4. Last-in, first-out (LIFO)

These methods may be applied under the periodic or perpetual inventory systems.

Use of Inventory Methods

- Other 3%
- Avg. Cost 22%
- FIFO 49%
- LIFO 26%

Pie chart is based on a recent survey of 500 companies listed with the SEC published in the AICPA's *Accounting Trends and Techniques.*

FIGURE 13-4 Allocation of Goods Available for Sale to Cost of Goods Sold and Ending Inventory

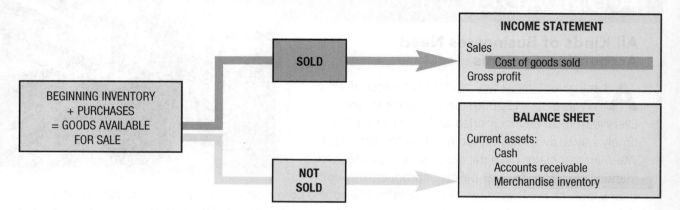

The Periodic Inventory System

Specific Identification Method

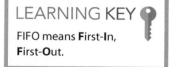
When each unit of inventory can be specifically identified, the specific identification method can be used. To use this method, inventory items must be physically different from each other, or they must have serial numbers. Examples include cars, motorcycles, furniture, appliances, and fine jewelry. When a unit is sold, its cost is determined from the supplier's invoice. Unless computerized, this method is practical only for businesses in which sales volume is relatively low and inventory unit value is relatively high. Otherwise, record keeping becomes expensive and time consuming.

To illustrate how specific identification costing works, assume the following data for an inventory of one specific model of color printers:

Color Printers (Model AP 4500)

	Units	Unit Price	Total Cost
On hand at start of period	40	$62	$ 2,480
Purchased during period:			
1st purchase	60	65	3,900
2nd purchase	80	67	5,360
3rd purchase	70	68	4,760
Number of units available for sale	250		$16,500
On hand at end of period	50		
Number of units sold during period	200		

Of the 200 units sold during the period, the printer serial numbers show that 30 were from the beginning inventory, 50 were from the first purchase, 60 were from the second purchase, and 60 were from the last purchase. The cost of goods sold and the cost of inventory at the end of the period are determined as shown in Figure 13-5.

First-In, First-Out (FIFO) Method

LEARNING KEY

FIFO means First-In, First-Out.

Another widely used method of allocating merchandise cost is called the first-in, first-out, or FIFO, method. This costing method assumes that the first goods purchased were the first goods sold. Therefore, the latest goods purchased remain in inventory.

Whenever possible, a business will attempt to sell the older goods first. This is particularly true of businesses that sell perishable items or merchandise that may become obsolete. Grocery stores, fresh fruit stands, and computer software businesses

FIGURE 13-5 Specific Identification Inventory Method

BEGINNING INVENTORY AND PURCHASES	COST OF GOODS SOLD			COST OF ENDING INVENTORY		
	Units	Unit Price	Total	Units	Unit Price	Total
Beginning inventory	30	$62	$ 1,860	10	$62	$ 620
1st purchase	50	65	3,250	10	65	650
2nd purchase	60	67	4,020	20	67	1,340
3rd purchase	60	68	4,080	10	68	680
Total	200		$13,210	50		$ 3,290
Alternative calculation if given goods available for sale and cost of goods sold or ending inventory.	Cost of goods available for sale $16,500 Less cost of ending inventory (3,290) Cost of goods sold $13,210			Cost of goods available for sale $16,500 Less cost of goods sold (13,210) Cost of ending inventory $ 3,290		

are good examples. These businesses must rotate their stock forward. They pull the oldest bread, milk, fruit, and vegetables to the front of the shelves and try to sell all copies of the current software before a new version arrives. FIFO costing is, therefore, widely used because it often follows the actual movement of goods. It assumes that the oldest units have been sold and the newest or freshest units are in the ending inventory.

Applying FIFO to the printer inventory data, the cost of goods sold and the cost of inventory at the end of the period are determined as shown in Figure 13-6.

FIGURE 13-6 FIFO Inventory Method

BEGINNING INVENTORY AND PURCHASES	COST OF GOODS SOLD			COST OF ENDING INVENTORY		
	Units	Unit Price	Total	Units	Unit Price	Total
Beginning inventory	40	$62	$ 2,480		$62	$ 0
1st purchase	60	65	3,900		65	0
2nd purchase	80	67	5,360		67	0
3rd purchase	20	68	1,360	50	68	3,400
Total	200		$13,100	50		$ 3,400
Alternative calculation if given goods available for sale and cost of goods sold or ending inventory.	Cost of goods available for sale $16,500 Less cost of ending inventory (3,400) Cost of goods sold $13,100			Cost of goods available for sale $16,500 Less cost of goods sold (13,100) Cost of ending inventory $ 3,400		

Note that the 50 items on hand at the end of the period are considered to be those most recently purchased.

FIFO costing is widely used because businesses have used this method for a long time. Accountants are reluctant to change a long-followed method of accounting when such a change would affect the comparability of their income calculations over a period of years. **Consistency** based on comparability is an important accounting principle.

Weighted-Average Method

Another method of allocating merchandise cost is called the weighted-average method, or average cost method. This costing method is based on the average cost of identical units.

LEARNING KEY 🔑

The consistency principle of accounting suggests that a business should use the same accounting techniques from year to year.

Consider the printer inventory data again. The average cost of identical units is determined by dividing the total cost of units available for sale ($16,500) by the total number of units available for sale (250).

$$\frac{\$16,500 \text{ (cost of units available for sale)}}{250 \text{ (units available for sale)}} = \$66 \text{ weighted-average cost per unit}$$

The cost of goods sold and the cost of the end-of-period inventory are calculated as follows:

Cost of goods sold	200 units @ $66	=	$13,200
Cost of ending inventory	50 units @ $66	=	3,300
Total	250 units		$16,500

There is a logical appeal to the weighted-average method of allocating cost between goods sold and goods on hand. In this example, one-fifth (50) of the total units available (250) were unsold. The weighted-average method assigns one-fifth ($3,300) of the total cost ($16,500) to these goods.

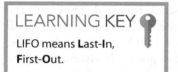

LEARNING KEY

LIFO means **Last-In, First-Out.**

Last-In, First-Out (LIFO) Method

A fourth method of allocating merchandise cost is called the last-in, first-out, or LIFO, method. It assumes that the sales in the period were made from the most recently purchased goods. Therefore, the earliest goods purchased remain in inventory.

This physical flow is associated with businesses selling products that are not perishable or likely to become obsolete, and may be difficult to handle. Imagine a large barrel of nails at a lumberyard. Customers take nails from the top of the barrel. When the supply gets low, new nails are simply piled on top of the old ones. There is no need to rotate the nails from the bottom to the top of the barrel.

Applying LIFO to the printer inventory data, the cost of goods sold and the cost of inventory at the end of the period are determined as shown in Figure 13-7.

FIGURE 13-7 LIFO Inventory Method

BEGINNING INVENTORY AND PURCHASES	COST OF GOODS SOLD			COST OF ENDING INVENTORY		
	Units	Unit Price	Total	Units	Unit Price	Total
Beginning inventory		$62	$ 0	40	$62	$ 2,480
1st purchase	50	65	3,250	10	65	650
2nd purchase	80	67	5,360		67	0
3rd purchase	70	68	4,760		68	0
Total	200		$13,370	50		$ 3,130
Alternative calculation if given goods available for sale and cost of goods sold or ending inventory.	Cost of goods available for sale		$16,500	Cost of goods available for sale		$ 16,500
	Less cost of ending inventory		(3,130)	Less cost of goods sold		(13,370)
	Cost of goods sold		$13,370	Cost of ending inventory		$ 3,130

Note that the 50 units on hand at the end of the period are considered to be the 40 units in the beginning inventory plus 10 of the units from the first purchase.

The LIFO method has been justified on the grounds that the physical movement of goods in some businesses is actually last-in, first-out. This is rarely the case, but the method has become popular for other reasons. One persuasive argument for the use of the LIFO method is that it matches the most current cost of items purchased

Although LIFO is acceptable under U.S. GAAP and many U.S. companies use this method for financial reporting and tax purposes, it is not permitted under International Financial Reporting Standards (IFRS).

against the current sales revenue. When the most current costs of purchases are subtracted from sales revenue, the impact of changing prices on the resulting gross profit figure is minimized. In the opinion of many accountants, this is proper and desirable.

Another reason for the popularity of the LIFO method is its effect on income taxes. When prices are rising, net income calculated under the LIFO method is less than net income calculated under either the FIFO or the weighted-average method. Since the net income amount under LIFO is less, the related income tax will be less. The reverse would be true if prices were falling. However, periods of falling prices over the past two centuries have been few and brief.

Opponents of the LIFO method contend that its use causes old, out-of-date inventory costs to be shown on the balance sheet. The theoretical and practical merits of FIFO versus LIFO are the subject of much professional debate.

Physical Flows and Cost Flows

LEARNING KEY

The inventory method used does not have to match the physical flow of goods.

Of the four inventory costing methods described, only the specific identification costing method will necessarily reflect cost flows that match physical flows of goods. Each of the other three methods—FIFO, weighted-average, and LIFO—is based on assumed cost flows. The assumed cost flows *are not required to reflect the actual physical movement of goods* within the company. Any one of the three assumed cost flow methods could be used under any set of physical flow conditions. For example, a fresh fruit stand with an actual FIFO flow of inventory may use LIFO for accounting purposes. Similarly, a supplier of building materials that sells nails, lumber, and sand off the top of the pile may use FIFO even though the physical flow of goods is LIFO.

Comparison of Methods

To compare the results of the four inventory methods, let's assume that the 200 printers in our example were sold for $18,000. Figure 13-8 contrasts the ending inventory, cost of goods sold, and gross profit under each of the four methods.

FIGURE 13-8 **Comparison of Inventory Methods**

PARTIAL INCOME STATEMENT	SPECIFIC IDENTIFICATION		FIFO		WEIGHTED AVERAGE		LIFO	
Sales		$18,000		$18,000		$18,000		$18,000
Cost of goods sold:								
Beginning inventory	$ 2,480		$ 2,480		$ 2,480		$ 2,480	
Purchases	14,020		14,020		14,020		14,020	
Goods available for sale	$16,500		$16,500		$16,500		$16,500	
Less ending inventory	3,290		3,400		3,300		3,130	
Cost of goods sold		13,210		13,100		13,200		13,370
Gross profit		$ 4,790		$ 4,900		$ 4,800		$ 4,630

LIFO is sometimes referred to as FISH: First In, Still Here.

During periods of rising prices, we can observe the following: LIFO generally produces the highest cost of goods sold, lowest gross profit, and lowest ending inventory. Since the most recent units purchased are assumed to have been sold, the most recent costs are matched against revenues and this provides the best measure of gross profit and net income. After all, the units sold must be replaced at current prices. However, under LIFO, the first units purchased are assumed to remain in inventory. This means that units purchased many years ago may remain in the ending inventory. These dollar amounts are likely to have little meaning when measuring the firm's assets, performance, or financial health.

FIFO generally produces the lowest cost of goods sold, highest gross profit, and highest ending inventory. Since the last units purchased are assumed to be in ending inventory, these most recent costs provide the best inventory measure on the balance sheet. However, under FIFO, the first units purchased are assumed to have been sold. This means that somewhat older prices are used to compute cost of goods sold and gross profit than under LIFO. Thus, these measures are somewhat less useful than those computed under LIFO.

The weighted-average inventory method produces measures between LIFO and FIFO. The specific identification method will produce measures based on the actual units sold.

The Internal Revenue Service requires the use of the same inventory method for tax and financial reporting purposes. Since LIFO generally produces the highest cost of goods sold, lowest gross profit, and lowest tax liability, many firms use the LIFO inventory method to minimize federal income taxes. The tax dollars saved are then available for other purposes.

As discussed earlier, keep the following in mind when selecting the inventory method to be used by a business:

1. The physical flow of the inventory does not need to match the flow assumed by the inventory method.
2. The consistency principle requires that the same accounting methods be followed from period to period. Although it is acceptable to make changes, it is not appropriate to switch back and forth from FIFO to LIFO based on the desire to maximize or minimize earnings for a given year.

The Perpetual Inventory System

Under the perpetual inventory system, a continuous record is maintained for the quantities and costs of goods on hand at all times. The general ledger account for Merchandise Inventory under such a system is somewhat like the account for Cash. It provides a day-by-day record of each addition (purchase) and subtraction (sale). The balance of the account at any time shows the cost of goods that should be on hand.

When perpetual inventory records are kept, the merchandise inventory account in the general ledger is usually a controlling account. A subsidiary ledger is maintained with an account for each type of merchandise. These accounts are often recorded on cards or, more likely, in computer files. As shown in Figure 13-9, the subsidiary accounts are designed to handle additions and subtractions and determine the new balance after each change. Goods sold usually are assigned cost on either a FIFO, moving-average, or LIFO basis. Procedures for applying the FIFO method in a perpetual inventory system are similar to those illustrated for a periodic system. The first units purchased are treated as the first units sold. The illustration in Figure 13-9 is based on the FIFO method. The specific techniques used to apply the moving-average and LIFO methods in a perpetual system are more complicated. They are illustrated in the chapter appendix.

Lower-of-Cost-or-Market Method of Inventory Valuation

If the value of inventory declines while it is being held, the loss should be recognized in the period of the decline. The purpose of the lower-of-cost-or-market method is to recognize such losses on the income statement and to report the lower inventory valuation on the balance sheet.

FIGURE 13-9 Perpetual Inventory Record: FIFO Method

DATE	PURCHASES			COST OF GOODS SOLD				INVENTORY ON HAND				
	Units	Cost/Unit	Total	Units	Cost/Unit	CGS	Cumulative CGS	Layer	Units	Cost/Unit	Layer Cost	Total
Jan. 1 (BI)								(1)	40	$62	$2,480	$2,480
Feb. 15				30	$62	$1,860	$1,860	(1)	10	$62	$620	$620
Mar. 1	60	$65	$3,900					(1)	10	$62	$620	
								(2)	60	65	3,900	$4,520
Apr. 1				10	$62	$620		(2)	30	$65	$1,950	
				30	$65	1,950	$4,430					$1,950
May 15	80	$67	$5,360					(2)	30	$65	$1,950	
								(3)	80	67	5,360	$7,310
June 30				30	$65	$1,950		(3)	20	$67	$1,340	
				60	67	4,020	$10,400					$1,340
Aug. 28	70	$68	$4,760					(3)	20	$67	$1,340	
								(4)	70	68	4,760	$6,100
Oct. 30				20	$67	$1,340		(4)	50	$68	$3,400	
				20	68	1,360	$13,100					$3,400
Cost of Goods Sold during 20--							$13,100					

BI: Beginning Inventory

In applying the lower-of-cost-or-market method, "cost" means the dollar amount calculated using one of the four inventory costing methods. "Market" means the cost to replace the inventory. It is the price in the market in which goods are purchased by the business—not the price in the market in which they are normally sold by the business. The lower-of-cost-or-market method assumes that a decline in the purchase (replacement) price of inventory is accompanied by a decline in the selling price. In this sense, a decline in the purchase (replacement) price signals a decline in the value of the inventory.

To illustrate the lower-of-cost-or-market method, assume the following end-of-period inventory data for three items:

LEARNING KEY 🔑

Under lower-of-cost-or-market, market represents the cost to replace the inventory item, not the selling price.

Item	Recorded Purchase Cost	End-of-Period Market Value	Lower-of-Cost-or-Market
1	$8,000	$7,000	$7,000
2	9,000	10,000	9,000
3	7,000	6,500	6,500
	$24,000	$23,500	$22,500

The illustration shows two ways to calculate the lower-of-cost-or-market. First, the lower-of-cost-or-market method can be applied to the total inventory. This involves comparing the $24,000 total cost with the $23,500 *total end-of-period market value*. Under the second approach, the method is applied to each item in inventory. This involves comparing the $24,000 total cost with the

$22,500 lower-of-cost-or-market value determined by comparing cost with market value for *each item*. Either approach is acceptable, but the one chosen should be applied consistently across periods.

The difference between the cost and market value is considered a loss due to holding inventory. Normally, it is charged to an account such as **Loss on Write-Down of Inventory**. For example, based on application of the method to the total inventory in the previous illustration, a $500 loss ($24,000 – $23,500) is recognized as follows:

14		Loss on Write-Down of Inventory	5	0	0	00						14
15		Merchandise Inventory					5	0	0	00		15
16		To recognize loss in value of inventory held										16

CHECKPOINT ✔

Complete Checkpoint-3 on page 508 to test your basic understanding of LO3.

The loss due to write-down of inventory should be reported on the income statement as an expense. Although not a preferred treatment, some businesses include it in cost of goods sold if the amounts are small.

LO4 Estimating Ending Inventory and Cost of Goods Sold

Estimate the ending inventory and cost of goods sold by using the gross profit and retail inventory methods.

Many businesses prepare monthly or quarterly financial statements. To do this, the business must estimate the inventory at the end of the month or quarter and the cost of goods sold for the period. This is not a problem for businesses using the perpetual inventory method. Although these amounts need to be verified by a physical inventory at the end of the year, the unverified amounts are generally reliable estimates and can be used for these "interim" statements.

Businesses using the periodic inventory method must use other methods to estimate the ending inventory and cost of goods sold. Two generally accepted methods are the gross profit method and the retail inventory method.

Gross Profit Method of Estimating Inventory

Under the **gross profit method**, a business's normal gross profit (net sales – cost of goods sold) is used to estimate the cost of goods sold and ending inventory. To illustrate the gross profit method, assume the following data with respect to Groomer Company:

Inventory, start of period	$ 80,000
Net purchases, first month	$ 70,000
Net sales, first month	$110,000
Normal gross profit as a percentage of sales	40%

The estimated cost of goods sold for the month and the estimated merchandise inventory at the end of the month would be determined as shown in Figure 13-10.

This calculation is appropriate only if the firm's normal gross profit as a percentage of net sales has been relatively stable over time. This type of calculation also can be used to test the reasonableness of the amount of inventory that was computed on the basis of a physical count. A large difference between the two amounts might indicate a mistake in the count, a mistake in the costing of the items, or a marked change in the gross profit rate. The gross profit procedure also can be used to estimate the cost of an inventory that was destroyed by fire or other casualty.

FIGURE 13-10 Steps for the Gross Profit Method

STEP 1	Compute the cost of goods available for sale.	Cost of goods available for sale:		
		Inventory, start of period	$ 80,000	
		Net purchases, first month	70,000	
		Cost of goods available for sale:		$150,000
STEP 2	Estimate cost of goods sold by deducting the normal gross profit from net sales.	Estimated cost of goods sold:		
		Net sales	$110,000	
		Normal gross profit ($110,000 × 40%)	44,000	
		Estimated cost of goods sold		66,000
STEP 3	Estimate the ending inventory by deducting cost of goods sold from the cost of goods available for sale.	Estimated end-of-month inventory		$ 84,000

Retail Method of Estimating Inventory

Many retail businesses, such as department and clothing stores, use a variation of the gross profit method to calculate cost of goods sold and ending inventory. The procedure used, called the retail method of inventory, requires keeping records of both the cost and selling (retail) prices of all goods purchased. This information can be used to estimate cost of goods sold and ending inventory, as shown in Figure 13-11.

FIGURE 13-11 Steps in the Retail Inventory Method

			COST	RETAIL
STEP 1	Compute the cost of goods available for sale at cost and retail.	Inventory, start of period	$ 60,000	$ 85,000
		Net purchases during period	126,000	163,000
		Goods available for sale	$186,000	$248,000
STEP 2	Compute the ending inventory at retail by subtracting sales at retail from goods available for sale at retail.	Less net sales for period		180,000
		Inventory, end of period, at retail		$ 68,000
STEP 3	Compute the cost-to-retail ratio by dividing the cost of goods available for sale by the retail value of the goods available for sale.	Ratio of cost-to-retail prices of goods available for sale ($186,000 ÷ $248,000)		75%
STEP 4	Estimate the cost of the ending inventory by multiplying the ending inventory at retail (step 2) by the cost-to-retail ratio.	Inventory, end of period, at estimated cost (75% of $68,000)	(51,000)	
STEP 5	Estimate cost of goods sold by a. Subtracting the estimated ending inventory from the cost of goods available for sale, or b. Multiplying sales at retail by the cost-to-retail ratio.	Estimated cost of goods sold	$135,000	
		Sales of $180,000 × 75% = $135,000		

CHECKPOINT ✔

Complete Checkpoint-4 on page 508 to test your basic understanding of LO4.

LEARNING OBJECTIVES	**Key Points to Remember**

LO1   **Explain the impact of merchandise inventory on the financial statements.**

The cost of goods available for sale during the accounting period must be divided between the cost of goods sold and the ending merchandise inventory. Cost of goods sold is reported on the income statement and used to determine the gross profit for the period. The ending merchandise inventory is reported as a current asset on the balance sheet. Figure 13-12 illustrates the allocation of cost of goods available for sale into cost of goods sold and ending inventory.

FIGURE 13-12   Allocation of Goods Available for Sale to Cost of Goods Sold and Ending Inventory

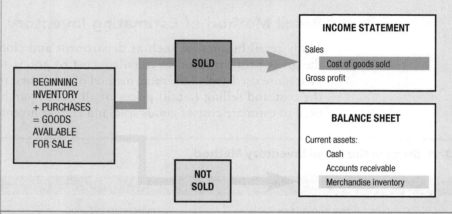

LO2   **Describe the two principal systems of accounting for merchandise inventory— the periodic system and the perpetual system.**

There are two systems of accounting for merchandise.

Periodic Inventory System

1. The purchases account is debited for the cost of all goods purchased.
2. The sales account is credited for the selling prices of all goods sold.
3. At the end of the accounting period, a physical inventory is taken, and the following formula is applied to calculate cost of goods sold:

> Beginning Inventory (last year's ending physical count)
> +   Net Purchases (account balance at end of this year)
> =   Cost of Goods Available for Sale
> −   Ending Inventory (this year's ending physical count)
> =   Cost of Goods Sold (for this year)

Perpetual Inventory System

1. The merchandise inventory account is debited for all purchases.
2. The cost of goods sold account is debited, and the merchandise inventory account is credited for all sales.
3. Thus, the merchandise inventory account provides a running balance of the goods on hand.

LEARNING OBJECTIVES	**Key Points to Remember**
LO3 **Compute the costs allocated to the ending inventory and cost of goods sold using different inventory methods.**	One of the following four inventory methods is generally used to determine the costs assigned to the goods sold and ending inventory: • Specific identification • FIFO: first-in, first-out • Weighted-average • LIFO: last-in, first-out The actual physical flow of inventory does not have to match the method used. During periods of rising prices, LIFO produces the lowest net income, and FIFO produces the highest net income.

LO4 **Estimate the ending inventory and cost of goods sold by using the gross profit and retail inventory methods.**	Firms using the periodic inventory method often need to estimate their inventory. Two methods are used for this purpose.
	
	• **Gross Profit Method**—The firm's normal gross profit as a percentage of net sales is used to estimate cost of goods sold and ending inventory in three steps:
	 1. Compute the cost of goods available for sale.
	 2. Estimate cost of goods sold by deducting the normal gross profit (net sales × normal gross profit as percentage of net sales) from net sales.
	 3. Estimate the ending inventory by deducting cost of goods sold from the cost of goods available for sale.
	
	• **Retail Inventory Method**—The firm's ratio of cost-to-retail prices of goods available for sale is used to estimate ending inventory and cost of goods sold in five basic steps:
	 1. Compute the cost of goods available for sale at cost and retail.
	 2. Compute the ending inventory at retail by subtracting sales at retail from goods available for sale at retail.
	 3. Compute the cost-to-retail ratio by dividing the cost of goods available for sale by the retail value of the goods available for sale.
	 4. Estimate the cost of ending inventory by multiplying the ending inventory at retail (step 2) by the cost-to-retail ratio.
	 5. Estimate cost of goods sold by:
	  a. subtracting the estimated ending inventory from the cost of goods available for sale, or
	  b. multiplying sales at retail by the cost-to-retail ratio.

DEMONSTRATION PROBLEM

Fialka Company's beginning inventory and purchases during the fiscal year ended October 31, 20-2, were as follows:

		Units	Unit Price	Total Cost
November 1, 20-1	Beginning inventory	500	$25.00	$ 12,500
November 12, 20-1	1st purchase	600	26.25	15,750
December 28, 20-1	2nd purchase	400	27.50	11,000

(continued)

		Units	Unit Price	Total Cost
March 29, 20-2	3rd purchase	1,000	28.00	28,000
May 31, 20-2	4th purchase	750	28.50	21,375
July 29, 20-2	5th purchase	350	29.00	10,150
August 30, 20-2	6th purchase	675	30.00	20,250
October 21, 20-2	7th purchase	225	31.00	6,975
		4,500		$126,000

There are 1,600 units of inventory on hand on October 31, 20-2.

REQUIRED

1. Calculate the total amount to be assigned to cost of goods sold for the fiscal year and ending inventory on October 31, 20-2, under each of the following periodic inventory methods:
   (a) FIFO
   (b) LIFO
   (c) Weighted-average cost (round calculations to two decimal places)

2. Assume that the market price per unit (cost to replace) of Fialka's inventory on October 31, 20-2, was $29. Calculate the total amount to be assigned to the ending inventory on October 31, 20-2, under each of the following methods:
   (a) FIFO lower-of-cost-or-market
   (b) Weighted-average lower-of-cost-or-market

3. Prepare required entries to apply:
   (a) FIFO lower-of-cost-or-market
   (b) Weighted-average lower-of-cost-or-market

4. Assume that a fire destroyed Fialka's store and all inventory on October 31, just prior to taking a physical inventory. Thus, Fialka must estimate the ending inventory and cost of goods sold. During the fiscal year ended October 31, 20-2, net sales of $134,000 were made. The normal gross profit rate is 40%. Use the gross profit method to estimate the cost of goods sold for the fiscal year ended October 31, 20-2, and the inventory on October 31, 20-2.

SOLUTION 1a.

DATE		FIFO INVENTORY METHOD Cost of Goods Sold			COST OF ENDING INVENTORY		
20-1/-2		Units	Unit Price	Total	Units	Unit Price	Total
Nov. 1	Beginning inventory	500	$25.00	$ 12,500		$25.00	$ 0
Nov. 12	1st purchase	600	26.25	15,750		26.25	0
Dec. 28	2nd purchase	400	27.50	11,000		27.50	0
Mar. 29	3rd purchase	1,000	28.00	28,000		28.00	0
May 31	4th purchase	400	28.50	11,400	350	28.50	9,975
July 29	5th purchase		29.00	0	350	29.00	10,150
Aug. 30	6th purchase		30.00	0	675	30.00	20,250
Oct. 21	7th purchase		31.00	0	225	31.00	6,975
	Total	2,900		$ 78,650	1,600		$ 47,350
Alternative calculation if given goods available for sale and cost of goods sold or ending inventory.		Cost of goods available for sale	$126,000		Cost of goods available for sale		$126,000
		Less cost of ending inventory	(47,350)		Less cost of goods sold		(78,650)
		Cost of goods sold	$ 78,650		Cost of ending inventory		$ 47,350

SOLUTION 1b.

DATE		LIFO INVENTORY METHOD Cost of Goods Sold			COST OF ENDING INVENTORY		
20-1/-2		Units	Unit Price	Total	Units	Unit Price	Total
Nov. 1	Beginning inventory		$25.00	$ 0	500	$25.00	$ 12,500
Nov. 12	1st purchase		26.25	0	600	26.25	15,750
Dec. 28	2nd purchase		27.50	0	400	27.50	11,000
Mar. 29	3rd purchase	900	28.00	25,200	100	28.00	2,800
May 31	4th purchase	750	28.50	21,375		28.50	0
July 29	5th purchase	350	29.00	10,150		29.00	0
Aug. 30	6th purchase	675	30.00	20,250		30.00	0
Oct. 21	7th purchase	225	31.00	6,975		31.00	0
	Total	2,900		$ 83,950	1,600		$ 42,050
Alternative calculation if given goods available for sale and cost of goods sold or ending inventory.		Cost of goods available for sale $126,000 Less cost of ending inventory (42,050) Cost of goods sold $ 83,950			Cost of goods available for sale $126,000 Less cost of goods sold (83,950) Cost of ending inventory $ 42,050		

SOLUTION 1c. Weighted-average method:

Average cost per unit: $126,000 ÷ 4,500 units = $28

Inventory, October 31, 20-2:

  1,600 units @ $28 = $ 44,800

Cost of goods sold for 20-1/-2:

  2,900 units @ $28 = $ 81,200

SOLUTION 2a. FIFO lower-of-cost-or-market:

FIFO cost $ 47,350

Market 1,600 units @ $29   46,400

Choose market   46,400

SOLUTION 2b. Weighted-average lower-of-cost-or-market:

Weighted-average cost $ 44,800

Market 1,600 units @ $29   46,400

Choose weighted-average cost   44,800

SOLUTION 3a. Loss on Write-Down of Inventory   950

    Merchandise Inventory   950

SOLUTION 3b. No entry required.

SOLUTION 4. Estimated inventory on October 31, 20-2:

Inventory, November 1, 20-1 $ 12,500

Net purchases, November 1, 20-1

  through October 31, 20-2   113,500

Cost of goods available for sale $126,000

Estimated cost of goods sold:

  Net sales $134,000

  Normal gross profit ($134,000 × 40%)   53,600

Estimated cost of goods sold   80,400

Estimated inventory on October 31, 20-2 $ 45,600

KEY TERMS

average cost method (495)   See weighted-average method.

consignee (493)   The company holding the merchandise of another business to be sold.

consignment (493)   Goods that are held by one business for sale but that are owned by another business.

consignor (493)   The owner of the merchandise that is held by another business.

consistency (495)   The principle that states that a business should use the same accounting methods from period to period. This improves the comparability of the financial statements over time.

cost (499)   In applying the lower-of-cost-or-market method, cost means the dollar amount calculated using one of the four inventory costing methods.

first-in, first-out (FIFO) method (494)   A method of allocating merchandise cost which assumes that the first goods purchased were the first goods sold and, therefore, that the latest goods purchased remain in inventory.

gross profit method (500)   A method of estimating inventory in which a business's normal gross profit percentage is used to estimate the cost of goods sold and ending inventory.

in transit (493)   Goods that are in the process of being shipped between the seller and the buyer.

inventory sheet (492)   A form used for recording inventory items. It has columns for recording the description of each item, the quantity on hand, the cost per unit, and the extension.

last-in, first-out (LIFO) method (496)   A method of allocating merchandise cost which assumes that the sales in the period were made from the most recently purchased goods. Therefore, the earliest goods purchased remain in inventory.

Loss on Write-Down of Inventory (500)   This account is debited when the market value (replacement cost) of the inventory is below cost when applying the lower-of-cost-or-market method of inventory valuation. It is reported on the income statement as an expense.

lower-of-cost-or-market method (498)   An inventory valuation method under which inventory is valued at the lower-of-cost-or-market value (replacement cost).

market (499)   In applying the lower-of-cost-or-market method, market means the cost to replace the inventory. It is the prevailing price in the market in which goods are purchased—not the prevailing price in the market in which they are normally sold.

natural business year (492)   A fiscal year that starts and ends at the time the stock of goods is normally at its lowest level.

periodic inventory system (491)   Under this system, the ending inventory and cost of goods sold are determined at the end of the accounting period, when a physical inventory is taken.

perpetual inventory system (491)   Under this system, the merchandise inventory and cost of goods sold accounts are updated when merchandise is bought and sold.

physical inventory (492)   A physical count of the goods on hand.

retail method (501)   A variation of the gross profit method that is used by many retail businesses, such as department and clothing stores, to estimate the cost of goods sold and ending inventory.

specific identification method (494)   A method of allocating merchandise cost in which each unit of inventory is specifically identified.

weighted-average method (495)   A method of allocating merchandise cost based on the average cost of identical units. The average cost of identical units is determined by dividing the total cost of units available for sale by the total number of units available for sale.

SELF-STUDY TEST QUESTIONS

True/False

1. **LO1**   An overstatement of ending inventory in the year 20-1 will cause net income to be overstated in the year 20-1.

2. **LO1**   An understatement of ending inventory in the year 20-1 will cause net income to be overstated in the year 20-2, assuming no other errors.

3. **LO2**   Under the perpetual system of accounting for inventory, the current merchandise inventory and the cost of goods sold are not determined until the end of the accounting period when a physical inventory is taken.

4. **LO3**   A fiscal year that starts and ends at the time the stock of goods is normally at its lowest level is known as a natural business year.

5. **LO3**   If goods are shipped FOB shipping point, the seller pays for the shipping costs.

Multiple Choice

1. **LO1**   An understatement of ending inventory in the year 20-1 will cause the owner's equity account at the end of the year 20-2, assuming no other errors, to be
   (a) understated.   (c) overstated.
   (b) correctly stated.   (d) none of the above.

2. **LO3**   Goods held on consignment remain the property of the
   (a) consignee.   (c) buyer.
   (b) consignor.   (d) seller.

3. **LO3**   In times of rising prices, the inventory cost method that will yield the lowest net income is
   (a) FIFO.   (c) LIFO.
   (b) weighted-average.   (d) none of the above.

4. **LO3**   In times of rising prices, the inventory cost method that will yield the highest cost of goods sold is

(a) LIFO. (c) FIFO.

(b) weighted-average. (d) none of the above.

5. **LO3**   In the application of "lower-of-cost-or-market," market is the

(a) lowest sales price. (c) replacement cost.

(b) highest sales price. (d) average sales price.

CHECKPOINT

Checkpoint Exercises

1. **LO1**   If the ending inventory is overstated by $10,000, indicate what, if anything, is incorrect about the following:

Cost of goods sold   _____

Gross profit   _____

Net income   _____

Ending owner's capital   _____

2. **LO2**   Using the following information, compute the ending balance of the merchandise inventory account under the perpetual inventory system.

a. Merchandise inventory, beginning balance	$ 20,000
b. Purchased merchandise on account	200,000
c. Sold merchandise on account	240,000
d. Cost of merchandise sold in (c)	120,000
e. Freight charges paid on inventory delivered to showroom	1,000
f. Refund provided to customers for merchandise returned	800
g. Cost of merchandise returned by customers	500

3. **LO3**   Use the following information to compute cost of goods sold under the FIFO and LIFO inventory methods. The firm sold 200 units.

	Units	Unit Price	Total
Beginning inventory	50	$ 5	$ 250
1st purchase	100	8	800
2nd purchase	150	10	1,500

4. **LO4**   Kulsrud Company would like to estimate the current inventory level. Using the gross profit method and the following information, estimate the current inventory level for Kulsrud Company.

Goods available for sale	$100,000
Net sales	150,000
Normal gross profit as a percent of sales	40%

The answers to the Self-Study Test Questions are at the end of the chapter (pages 518–519).

REVIEW QUESTIONS

LO1   1. What financial statements are affected by an error in the ending inventory?

LO2   2. What is the main difference between the periodic system of accounting for inventory and the perpetual system of accounting for inventory?

LO3   3. Is a physical inventory necessary under the periodic system? Why or why not?

LO3   4. Is a physical inventory necessary under the perpetual system? Why or why not?

LO3   5. In a period of rising prices, which inventory method will result in:

(a) the highest cost of goods sold?
(b) the lowest cost of goods sold?
(c) the highest ending inventory?
(d) the lowest ending inventory?
(e) the highest gross profit?
(f) the lowest gross profit?

LO3   6. What two factors are taken into account by the weighted-average method of merchandise cost allocation?

LO3   7. Which inventory method always follows the actual physical flow of merchandise?

LO3   8. When lower-of-cost-or-market is assigned to the items that comprise the ending merchandise inventory, what does "cost" mean? What does "market" mean?

LO4   9. List the three steps followed under the gross profit method of estimating inventory.

LO4 10. List the five steps followed under the retail method of estimating inventory.

SERIES A EXERCISES

E 13-1A   (LO1)

INVENTORY ERRORS Assume that in year 1, the ending merchandise inventory is overstated by $50,000. If this is the only error in years 1 and 2, indicate which items will be understated, overstated, or correctly stated for years 1 and 2.

	Year 1	Year 2
Ending merchandise inventory	_____	_____
Beginning merchandise inventory	_____	_____
Cost of goods sold	_____	_____
Gross profit	_____	_____
Net income	_____	_____
Ending owner's capital	_____	_____

E 13-2A (LO2)

JOURNAL ENTRIES—PERIODIC INVENTORY Paul Nasipak owns a business called Diamond Distributors. The following transactions took place during January of the current year. Journalize the transactions in a general journal using the periodic inventory method.

Jan. 5   Purchased merchandise on account from Prestigious Jewelers, $3,300.
      8   Paid freight charge on merchandise purchased, $300.
      12   Sold merchandise on account to Diamonds Unlimited, $4,500.
      15   Received a credit memo from Prestigious Jewelers for merchandise returned, $700.
      22   Issued a credit memo to Diamonds Unlimited for merchandise returned, $900.

E 13-3A (LO2)

JOURNAL ENTRIES—PERPETUAL INVENTORY Joan Ziemba owns a small variety store. The following transactions took place during March of the current year. Journalize the transactions in a general journal using the perpetual inventory method.

Mar. 3   Purchased merchandise on account from City Galleria, $2,900.
      7   Paid freight charge on merchandise purchased, $225.
      13   Sold merchandise on account to Amber Specialties, $3,400. The cost of the merchandise was $2,200.
      18   Received a credit memo from City Galleria for merchandise returned, $650.
      22   Issued a credit memo to Amber Specialties for merchandise returned, $600. The cost of the merchandise was $320.

E 13-4A (LO3)
✓ End. inv.: $52,000

ENDING INVENTORY COSTS Sandy Chen owns a small specialty store, named Chen's Chattel, whose year-end is June 30. Determine the total amount that should be included in Chen's Chattel's year-end inventory. A physical inventory taken on June 30 reveals the following:

Cost of merchandise on the showroom floor and in the warehouse	$43,600
Goods held on consignment (consignor is National Manufacturer)	6,400
Goods that Chen's Chattel, as the consignor, has for sale at the location of the Grand Avenue Vista	4,400
Sales invoices indicate that merchandise was shipped on June 29, terms FOB shipping point, delivered at buyer's receiving dock on July 3	3,800
Sales invoices indicate that merchandise was shipped on June 25, terms FOB destination, delivered at buyer's receiving dock on July 5	4,000

E 13-5A   (LO3)
✓ 1. End. inv., FIFO: $300.00
✓ Weighted-avg.: $242.50

LOWER-OF-COST-OR-MARKET Stalberg Company's beginning inventory and purchases during the fiscal year ended December 31, 20--, were as follows:

		Units	Unit Price	Total Cost
Jan. 1	Beginning inventory	10	$20	$200
Mar. 5	1st purchase	10	22	220
Sept. 9	2nd purchase	10	25	250
Dec. 8	3rd purchase	10	30	300
		40		$970

There are 10 units of inventory on hand on December 31.

1. Calculate the total amount to be assigned to the ending inventory under each of the following periodic inventory methods:
   (a) FIFO
   (b) Weighted-average (round calculations to two decimal places)
2. Assume that the market price per unit (cost to replace) of Stalberg's inventory on December 31, 20--, was $26. Calculate the total amount to be assigned to the ending inventory on December 31 under each of the following methods:
   (a) FIFO lower-of-cost-or-market
   (b) Weighted-average lower-of-cost-or-market
3. What journal entry would be made under lower-of-cost-or-market for parts 2(a) and (b) above?

SERIES A PROBLEMS

P 13-6A   (LO3)
✓ Cost of goods sold, FIFO: 61,500
✓ LIFO: 68,450
✓ Weighted-avg.: 64,530
✓ Specific I.D.: 63,200

SPECIFIC IDENTIFICATION, FIFO, LIFO, AND WEIGHTED-AVERAGE Swing Company's beginning inventory and purchases during the fiscal year ended September 30, 20-2, were as follows:

		Units	Unit Price	Total Cost
October 1, 20-1	Beginning inventory	400	$20.00	$ 8,000
October 18	1st purchase	500	20.50	10,250
November 25	2nd purchase	200	21.50	4,300
January 12, 20-2	3rd purchase	300	23.00	6,900
March 17	4th purchase	900	24.50	22,050
June 2	5th purchase	800	25.00	20,000
August 21	6th purchase	200	26.00	5,200
September 27	7th purchase	700	27.00	18,900
		4,000		$95,600

Use the following information for the specific identification method.

There are 1,300 units of inventory on hand on September 30, 20-2. Of these 1,300 units:

100 are from October 18, 20-1	1st purchase
200 are from January 12, 20-2	3rd purchase
100 are from March 17	4th purchase
400 are from June 2	5th purchase
200 are from August 21	6th purchase
300 are from September 27	7th purchase

(continued)

REQUIRED

Calculate the total amount to be assigned to cost of goods sold for the fiscal year ended September 30, 20-2, and ending inventory on September 30, 20-2, under each of the following periodic inventory methods:

1. FIFO
2. LIFO
3. Weighted-average (round calculations to two decimal places)
4. Specific identification

P 13-7A   (LO3)

✓ 1. Ending inv., FIFO: $13,825
✓ LIFO: $8,000
✓ Weighted-avg.: $10,500

COST ALLOCATION AND LOWER-OF-COST-OR-MARKET Douglas Company's beginning inventory and purchases during the fiscal year ended December 31, 20--, were as follows:

		Units	Unit Price	Total Cost
January 1, 20--	Beginning inventory	1,100	$ 8.00	$ 8,800
March 5	1st purchase	900	9.00	8,100
April 16	2nd purchase	400	9.50	3,800
June 3	3rd purchase	700	10.25	7,175
August 18	4th purchase	600	11.00	6,600
September 13	5th purchase	800	12.00	9,600
November 14	6th purchase	400	14.00	5,600
December 3	7th purchase	500	14.05	7,025
		5,400		$56,700

There are 1,000 units of inventory on hand on December 31.

REQUIRED

1. Calculate the total amount to be assigned to the ending inventory and cost of goods sold on December 31 under each of the following methods:
   (a) FIFO
   (b) LIFO
   (c) Weighted-average (round calculations to two decimal places)

2. Assume that the market price per unit (cost to replace) of Douglas's inventory on December 31 was $13. Calculate the total amount to be assigned to the ending inventory on December 31 under each of the following methods:
   (a) FIFO lower-of-cost-or-market
   (b) Weighted-average lower-of-cost-or-market

3. Prepare required entries to apply:
   (a) FIFO lower-of-cost-or-market
   (b) Weighted-average lower-of-cost-or-market

P 13-8A   (LO4)

✓ Est. ending inv.: $80,800

GROSS PROFIT METHOD A fire completely destroyed all the inventory of Glisan Lumber Yard on August 5, 20--. Fortunately, the accounting records were not destroyed in the fire. The following information is provided by Glisan Lumber Yard for the time period January 1 through August 5:

Beginning inventory, January 1, 20--	$100,000
Net purchases, January 1 through August 5	420,000
Net sales, January 1 through August 5	732,000
Normal gross profit as a percentage of sales	40%

REQUIRED

Estimate the amount of merchandise inventory destroyed in the fire on August 5 using the gross profit method.

P 13-9A   (LO4)
✓ Est. ending inv.: $39,000

RETAIL INVENTORY METHOD The following information is provided by Raynette's Pharmacy for the last quarter of its fiscal year ending on March 31, 20--:

	Cost	Retail
Inventory, start of period, January 1, 20--	$ 32,000	$ 52,000
Net purchases during the period	176,000	268,000
Net sales for the period		260,000

REQUIRED

1. Estimate the ending inventory as of March 31 using the retail inventory method.

2. Estimate the cost of goods sold for the time period January 1 through March 31 using the retail inventory method.

SERIES B EXERCISES

E 13-1B   (LO1)

INVENTORY ERRORS Assume that in year 1, the ending merchandise inventory is understated by $40,000. If this is the only error in years 1 and 2, indicate which items will be understated, overstated, or correctly stated for years 1 and 2.

	Year 1	Year 2
Ending merchandise inventory	_____	_____
Beginning merchandise inventory	_____	_____
Cost of goods sold	_____	_____
Gross profit	_____	_____
Net income	_____	_____
Ending owner's capital	_____	_____

E 13-2B   (LO2)

JOURNAL ENTRIES—PERIODIC INVENTORY Amy Douglas owns a business called Douglas Distributors. The following transactions took place during January of the current year. Journalize the transactions in a general journal using the periodic inventory method.

Jan.   5   Purchased merchandise on account from Elite Warehouse, $4,100.

    8   Paid freight charge on merchandise purchased, $300.

    12   Sold merchandise on account to Memories Unlimited, $5,200.

    15   Received a credit memo from Elite Warehouse for merchandise returned, $700.

    22   Issued a credit memo to Memories Unlimited for merchandise returned, $400.

(*continued*)

E 13-3B   (LO2)

JOURNAL ENTRIES—PERPETUAL INVENTORY Doreen Woods owns a small variety store. The following transactions took place during March of the current year. Journalize the transactions in a general journal using the perpetual inventory method.

Mar. 3   Purchased merchandise on account from Corner Galleria, $3,500.

7   Paid freight charge on merchandise purchased, $200.

13   Sold merchandise on account to Sonya Specialties, $4,250. The cost of the merchandise was $2,550.

18   Received a credit memo from Corner Galleria for merchandise returned, $900.

22   Issued a credit memo to Sonya Specialties for merchandise returned, $500. The cost of the merchandise was $300.

E 13-4B   (LO3)
✓ Ending inv.: $53,700

ENDING INVENTORY COSTS Danny Steele owns a small specialty store, named Steele's Storeroom, whose year-end is June 30. Determine the total amount that should be included in Steele's Storeroom's year-end inventory. A physical inventory taken on June 30 reveals the following:

Cost of merchandise on the showroom floor and in the warehouse	$42,600
Goods held on consignment (consignor is Quality Manufacturer)	7,600
Goods that Steele's Storeroom, as the consignor, has for sale at the location of Midtown Galleria	8,300
Sales invoices indicate that merchandise was shipped on June 28, terms FOB shipping point, delivered at buyer's receiving dock on July 6	4,350
Sales invoices indicate that merchandise was shipped on June 26, terms FOB destination, delivered at buyer's receiving dock on July 1	2,800

E 13-5B   (LO3)
✓ 1. Ending inv., FIFO: $800
✓ Weighted-avg.: $697.20

LOWER-OF-COST-OR-MARKET Bouie Company's beginning inventory and purchases during the fiscal year ended December 31, 20--, were as follows:

		Units	Unit Price	Total Cost
Jan. 1	Beginning inventory	20	$30	$ 600
Mar. 5	1st purchase	22	34	748
Sept. 9	2nd purchase	24	35	840
Dec. 8	3rd purchase	22	40	880
		88		$3,068

There are 20 units of inventory on hand on December 31.

1. Calculate the total amount to be assigned to the ending inventory under each of the following periodic inventory methods:
   (a) FIFO
   (b) Weighted-average (round calculations to two decimal places)

2. Assume that the market price per unit (cost to replace) of Bouie's inventory on December 31, 20--, was $39. Calculate the total amount to be assigned to the ending inventory on December 31 under each of the following methods:
   (a) FIFO lower-of-cost-or-market
   (b) Weighted-average lower-of-cost-or-market

3. What journal entry would be made under lower-of-cost-or-market for parts 2(a) and (b) above?

SERIES B PROBLEMS

P 13-6B   (LO3)
✓ Ending inv., FIFO: $19,075
✓ LIFO: $14,350
✓ Weighted-avg.: $16,290
✓ Specific I.D.: $17,000

SPECIFIC IDENTIFICATION, FIFO, LIFO, AND WEIGHTED-AVERAGE Boyce Company's beginning inventory and purchases during the fiscal year ended September 30, 20-2, were as follows:

		Units	Unit Price	Total Cost
October 1, 20-1	Beginning inventory	400	$15.00	$ 6,000
October 18	1st purchase	300	16.50	4,950
November 25	2nd purchase	600	17.00	10,200
January 12, 20-2	3rd purchase	700	17.25	12,075
March 17	4th purchase	800	18.00	14,400
June 2	5th purchase	400	19.00	7,600
August 21	6th purchase	300	21.00	6,300
September 27	7th purchase	500	21.75	10,875
		4,000		$72,400

Use the following information for the specific identification method.

There are 900 units of inventory on hand on September 30, 20-2. Of these 900 units:

50 are from October 18, 20-1	1st purchase
300 are from January 12, 20-2	3rd purchase
100 are from March 17	4th purchase
200 are from June 2	5th purchase
50 are from August 21	6th purchase
200 are from September 27	7th purchase

REQUIRED

Calculate the total amount to be assigned to the cost of goods sold for the fiscal year ended September 30, 20-2, and ending inventory on September 30, 20-2, under each of the following periodic inventory methods:

1. FIFO
2. LIFO
3. Weighted-average (round calculations to two decimal places)
4. Specific identification

P 13-7B   (LO3)
✓ 1. Cost of goods sold, FIFO: $55,950
✓ LIFO: $64,300
✓ Weighted avg.: $60,475

COST ALLOCATION AND LOWER-OF-COST-OR-MARKET Hall Company's beginning inventory and purchases during the fiscal year ended December 31, 20--, were as follows:

		Units	Unit Price	Total Cost
January 1	Beginning inventory	800	$11.00	$ 8,800
March 5	1st purchase	600	12.00	7,200
April 16	2nd purchase	500	12.50	6,250
June 3	3rd purchase	700	14.00	9,800
August 18	4th purchase	800	15.00	12,000
September 13	5th purchase	900	17.00	15,300
November 14	6th purchase	400	18.00	7,200
December 3	7th purchase	500	20.30	10,150
		5,200		$76,700

There are 1,100 units of inventory on hand on December 31.

(continued)

REQUIRED

1. Calculate the total amount to be assigned to the ending inventory and cost of goods sold on December 31 under each of the following methods:
   (a) FIFO
   (b) LIFO
   (c) Weighted-average (round calculations to two decimal places)

2. Assume that the market price per unit (cost to replace) of Hall's inventory on December 31 was $16. Calculate the total amount to be assigned to the ending inventory on December 31 under each of the following methods:
   (a) FIFO lower-of-cost-or-market
   (b) Weighted-average lower-of-cost-or-market

3. Prepare required entries to apply:
   (a) FIFO lower-of-cost-or-market
   (b) Weighted-average lower-of-cost-or-market

P 13-8B   (LO4)
✓ Est. inv.: $82,500

GROSS PROFIT METHOD A flood completely destroyed all the inventory of Bayside Waterworks Company on July 1, 20--. Fortunately, the accounting records were not destroyed in the flood. The following information is provided by Bayside Waterworks for the time period January 1 through July 1, 20--:

Beginning inventory, January 1, 20--	$ 60,000
Net purchases, January 1 through July 1	380,000
Net sales, January 1 through July 1	650,000
Normal gross profit as a percentage of sales	45%

REQUIRED

Estimate the amount of merchandise inventory destroyed in the flood on July 1 using the gross profit method.

P 13-9B   (LO4)
✓ Est. cost of goods sold: $193,750

RETAIL INVENTORY METHOD The following information is provided by Beverly's Basket Corner for the last quarter of its fiscal year ending on March 31, 20--:

	Cost	Retail
Inventory, start of period, January 1, 20--	$ 50,000	$ 80,000
Net purchases during the period	220,000	352,000
Net sales for the period		310,000

REQUIRED

1. Estimate the ending inventory as of March 31 using the retail inventory method.

2. Estimate the cost of goods sold for the time period January 1 through March 31 using the retail inventory method.

CHECK LIST
☐ **Managing**
☐ **Planning**
☐ **Drafting**
☐ **Break**
☐ **Revising**
☐ **Managing**

MANAGING YOUR WRITING

Most major grocery chains have optical scanning devices at the checkout stands and they certainly reduce the time required to check out. What benefits do they provide to the business? Next time you go to the grocery store, take a few minutes to chat with the manager. Ask the manager to describe the benefits of the scanning devices over the old machines that required the clerk to key in each purchase. Pay particular attention to the linkage between the scanning devices and the inventory systems. Be sure to ask whether the grocery store is on a periodic or perpetual system.

After your visit, write a memo to your instructor describing the benefits of the scanning devices and how they are linked with the inventory system.

ETHICS

ETHICS CASE

Electronics, Inc. is a high-volume, wholesale merchandising company. Most of its inventory turns over four or five times a year. The company has had 50 units of a particular brand of computers on hand for over a year. These computers have not sold and probably will not sell unless they are discounted 60 to 70%. The accountant is carrying them on the books at cost and intends to recognize the loss when they are sold. This way, she can avoid a significant write-down in inventory on the current year's financial statements.

1. Is the accountant correct in her treatment of the inventory? Why or why not?

2. If the computers cost $1,000 each and their market value is 40% of their cost, journalize the entry necessary for the write-down.

3. In groups of three or four, make a list of reasons why inventories of electronic equipment might have to be written down.

MASTERY PROBLEM

✓ 1. Cost of goods sold, FIFO: $64,250
✓ LIFO: $75,000
✓ Weighted-avg.: $69,600
✓ 2. Ending inv., FIFO LCM: $21,600
✓ Weighted-avg. LCM: $17,400
✓ 3. Estimated inv.: $22,000

Hurst Company's beginning inventory and purchases during the fiscal year ended December 31, 20-2, were as follows:

		Units	Unit Price	Total Cost
January 1, 20-2	Beginning inventory	1,500	$10.00	$15,000
January 12	1st purchase	500	11.50	5,750
February 28	2nd purchase	600	14.50	8,700
June 29	3rd purchase	1,200	15.00	18,000
August 31	4th purchase	800	16.50	13,200
October 29	5th purchase	300	18.00	5,400
November 30	6th purchase	700	18.50	12,950
December 21	7th purchase	400	20.00	8,000
		6,000		$87,000

There are 1,200 units of inventory on hand on December 31, 20-2.

REQUIRED

1. Calculate the total amount to be assigned to the cost of goods sold for 20-2 and ending inventory on December 31 under each of the following periodic inventory methods:
   (a) FIFO
   (b) LIFO
   (c) Weighted-average (round calculations to two decimal places)

(*continued*)

2. Assume that the market price per unit (cost to replace) of Hurst's inventory on December 31 was $18. Calculate the total amount to be assigned to the ending inventory on December 31 under each of the following methods:
   (a) FIFO lower-of-cost-or-market
   (b) Weighted-average lower-of-cost-or-market

3. In addition to taking a physical inventory on December 31, Hurst decides to estimate the ending inventory and cost of goods sold. During the fiscal year ended December 31, 20-2, net sales of $100,000 were made at a normal gross profit rate of 35%. Use the gross profit method to estimate the cost of goods sold for the fiscal year ended December 31 and the inventory on December 31.

> This problem challenges you to apply your cumulative accounting knowledge to move a step beyond the material in the chapter.

> ✓ FIFO CGS 20-2: $4,250
> ✓ LIFO CGS 20-2: $4,200

CHALLENGE PROBLEM

Bhushan Company has been using LIFO for inventory purposes because it would prefer to keep gross profits low for tax purposes. In its second year of operation (20-2), the controller pointed out that this strategy did not appear to work and suggested that FIFO cost of goods sold would have been higher than LIFO cost of goods sold for 20-2. Is this possible?

20-1	Units	Cost/Unit
Purchase 1	100	$1.00
Purchase 2	200	2.00
Purchase 3	300	3.00
Ending inventory	200	

20-2	Units	Cost/Unit
Beginning inventory	200	
Purchase 4	150	$4.00
Purchase 5	250	5.00
Purchase 6	350	6.00
Ending inventory	50	

REQUIRED

Using the information provided, compute the cost of goods sold for 20-1 and 20-2 comparing the LIFO and FIFO methods.

ANSWERS TO SELF-STUDY TEST QUESTIONS

True/False

1. T
2. T
3. F (this is true for the periodic method)
4. T
5. F (the buyer pays)

Multiple Choice

1. b   2. b   3. c   4. a   5. c

Checkpoint Exercises

1. Cost of goods sold   Understated by $10,000
   Gross profit   Overstated by $10,000
   Net income   Overstated by $10,000
   Ending owner's capital Overstated by $10,000

2. Beginning inventory

   Merchandise inventory, beginning
   balance...$ 20,000

   Purchased merchandise on
   account.. 200,000

   Cost of merchandise sold................... (120,000)

   Freight charges paid on inventory
   delivered to showroom......................   1,000

   Cost of merchandise returned by
   customers...   500

   Ending inventory............................... $101,500

3. FIFO cost of goods sold:

50 units @ $ 5 =	$ 250
100 units @ $ 8 =	800
50 units @ $10 =	500
FIFO cost of goods sold	$1,550

   LIFO cost of goods sold:

150 units @ $10 =	$1,500
50 units @ $ 8 =	400
LIFO cost of goods sold	$1,900

4. Estimated inventory using the gross profit method:

   Cost of goods available for sale.............. $100,000

   Net sales $150,000
   Normal gross profit   60,000
      ($150,000 × 40% = $60,000)

   Estimated cost of goods sold.................   90,000

   Estimated inventory.............................. $ 10,000

Perpetual Inventory Method: LIFO and Moving-Average Methods

In Chapter 13, you learned how to apply the LIFO and weighted-average inventory methods under the periodic inventory system. Recall that all calculations under the periodic system are done at the end of the accounting period. Under the perpetual system, costs are computed every time merchandise is purchased and sold. These costs are used to maintain a running record of the cost of goods sold to date and the balance of inventory on hand.

LO1

Perpetual LIFO

Compute the costs allocated to the ending inventory and cost of goods sold using the perpetual LIFO inventory method.

When using the **perpetual LIFO inventory method**, every time inventory is purchased a new layer is formed. When inventory is sold, we assume that the most recently purchased layer is sold first. As those units are used up, units are taken from the next most recently purchased layer. To illustrate, let's assume that Phaler's Fishing Supplies has the following beginning inventory, purchases, and sales of one type of bobber during the month of June. Note that the beginning inventory also has layers based on the prices paid in earlier periods.

Date	Beginning Inventory and Purchases		Sales
	Units	Cost/Unit	Units
June 1 (BI)	20	$0.80	
	160	1.00	
	20	1.20	
June 4	300	1.50	
June 20			400
June 30	100	1.80	

BI: Beginning Inventory

As shown in Figure 13A-1, the beginning inventory of 200 units forms Phaler's first three layers of inventory. The purchase on June 4 forms a fourth layer (300 units @ $1.50 = $450). At this point, Phaler has a total of 500 units at a total cost of $650. On June 20, Phaler sells 400 units. Under perpetual LIFO, we assume that the 300 units purchased on June 4 are sold first, followed by 20 that cost $1.20 each and 80 units that cost $1.00 each from the beginning inventory. The cost of goods sold on June 20 is $554. The cost of the inventory on hand is $96. At this point, Phaler has 100 units remaining from the beginning inventory.

FIGURE 13A-1 Perpetual LIFO Inventory System

DATE	PURCHASES			COST OF GOODS SOLD				INVENTORY ON HAND				
	Units	Cost/ Unit	Total	Units	Cost/ Unit	CGS	Cumulative CGS	Layer	Units	Cost/ Unit	Layer Cost	Total
June 1 (BI)								(1)	20	$0.80	$ 16.00	
								(2)	160	1.00	160.00	
								(3)	20	1.20	24.00	$200.00
June 4								(1)	20	$0.80	$ 16.00	
								(2)	160	1.00	160.00	
								(3)	20	1.20	24.00	
	300	$1.50	$450.00					(4)	300	1.50	450.00	$650.00
June. 20				300	$1.50	$450.00		(1)	20	$0.80	$ 16.00	
				20	1.20	24.00		(2)	80	1.00	80.00	$ 96.00
				80	1.00	80.00	$554.00					
June 30								(1)	20	$0.80	$ 16.00	
								(2)	80	1.00	80.00	
	100	$1.80	$180.00					(5)	100	1.80	180.00	$276.00
Cost of Goods Sold for June							$554.00					
BI: Beginning Inventory												

On June 30, Phaler purchases 100 units at $1.80 each. This forms a new fifth layer (100 @ $1.80 = $180). This layer is added to the two layers remaining from the beginning inventory for a total of 200 units at a total cost of $276 of inventory on hand on June 30. Note that the third ($1.20 layer) and fourth ($1.50 layer) layers of inventory are gone. They will never reappear. If Phaler makes additional sales before buying more inventory, they will come from the fifth layer at $1.80 each, followed by units from the second ($1.00) and then the first ($0.80) layers.

LO2   Perpetual Moving-Average

Compute the costs allocated to the ending inventory and cost of goods sold using the perpetual moving-average inventory method.

When using the perpetual moving-average inventory method, every time inventory is purchased a new average cost per unit is calculated. When inventory is sold, the most recent average cost is used to measure cost of goods sold and the remaining inventory on hand. To illustrate, let's look again at the purchases and sales of Phaler's Fishing Supplies for the month of June.

Date	Beginning Inventory and Purchases		Sales
	Units	Cost/Unit	Units
June 1 (BI)	20	$0.80	
	160	1.00	
	20	1.20	
June 4	300	1.50	
June 20			400
June 30	100	1.80	

BI: Beginning Inventory

When using the moving average inventory method, it is best to do the calculations on a calculator or computer spreadsheet. Carry each calculation out to the number of decimal places allowed by the technology used. This will reduce rounding errors.

As shown in Figure 13A-2, a new average cost is calculated each time a purchase is made. The average cost of the June 1 beginning inventory is shown as $1 ($200 cost/ 200 units). To compute the average cost after buying more inventory on June 4, we take the cost of the inventory on hand ($200 + $450 = $650) and divide by the number of units on hand (200 + 300 = 500). Thus, the average cost of the inventory on hand on June 4 is $1.30 per unit. To compute the cost of the 400 units sold on June 20, multiply the 400 units by $1.30 to get the cost of goods sold of $520. The remaining cost of the inventory on hand is $130 ($650 − $520). The number of units on hand is reduced to 100 (500 − 400).

On June 30, 100 additional units are purchased. This increases the units on hand to 200 (100 + 100) and the cost of the inventory on hand to $310 ($130 + $180). Dividing the cost of the inventory on hand by the number of units on hand provides a new moving-average cost of $1.55 ($310 ÷ 200). If Phaler makes another sale before buying additional units, this average cost will be used to compute the cost of goods sold and determine the cost of the inventory remaining on hand. Note that selling inventory does not change the moving-average cost. This is because the units are being removed at the most recent average cost.

FIGURE 13A-2 Perpetual Moving-Average Inventory System

DATE	PURCHASES			COST OF GOODS SOLD				INVENTORY ON HAND AND AVG. COST/UNIT			
	Units	Cost/ Unit	Total	Units	Cost/ Unit	CGS	Cumulative CGS	Cost of Purchase or (Sale)	Cost of Inventory on Hand	Units on Hand	AVG. Cost/Unit
June 1 (BI)									$200.00	200.00	$1.0000
June 4	300.00	$1.50	$450.00					$450.00	650.00	500.00	1.3000
June 20				400.00	$1.30	$520.00	$520.00	(520.00)	130.00	100.00	1.3000
June 30	100.00	$1.80	$180.00					180.00	310.00	200.00	1.5500
Cost of Goods Sold during June							$520.00				

BI: Beginning Inventory

LEARNING OBJECTIVES — Key Points to Remember

LO1	Compute the costs allocated to the ending inventory and cost of goods sold using the perpetual LIFO inventory method.	When using the perpetual LIFO inventory method, every time inventory is purchased, a new layer is formed. When inventory is sold, we assume the units were sold out of the most recent layer. As those units are used up, additional sales are taken from the next most recently purchased layer.
LO2	Compute the costs allocated to the ending inventory and cost of goods sold using the perpetual moving-average inventory method.	When using the perpetual moving-average inventory method, every time inventory is purchased, a new average cost per unit is calculated. When inventory is sold, the most recent average cost is used to measure cost of goods sold and the remaining inventory on hand.

KEY TERMS

perpetual LIFO inventory method (520)   A method of allocating merchandise cost which assumes that every time inventory is purchased, a new layer is formed. When inventory is sold, units are sold out of the most recent layer. As those units are used up, additional sales are taken from the next most recently purchased layer.

perpetual moving-average inventory method (521)   A method of allocating merchandise cost which assumes that every time inventory is purchased, a new average cost per unit is calculated. When inventory is sold, the most recent average cost is used to measure cost of goods sold and the remaining inventory on hand.

LO1

REVIEW QUESTION

1. Explain the primary difference between the periodic and perpetual inventory systems when calculating cost of goods sold and merchandise inventory.

SERIES A EXERCISE

E 13Apx-1A   (LO1/2)
✓ CGS under perpetual LIFO: $3,345
✓ CGS under perpetual moving-average: $3,250

PERPETUAL: LIFO AND MOVING-AVERAGE The beginning inventory, purchases, and sales for Myrl Sign Company for the month of April follow.

Date	Beginning Inventory and Purchases		Sales
	Units	**Cost/Unit**	**Units**
April 1 (BI)	100	$4.30	
	100	4.50	
	200	4.60	
April 20	400	5.50	
April 30			650

BI: Beginning Inventory

REQUIRED

Calculate the total amount to be assigned to cost of goods sold for April and the ending inventory on April 30, under each of the following methods:

1. Perpetual LIFO inventory method.
2. Perpetual moving-average inventory method.

SERIES A PROBLEM

P 13Apx-2A   (LO1/2)
✓ CGS under perpetual LIFO: $1,900
✓ CGS under perpetual moving-average: $1,856.64

PERPETUAL: LIFO AND MOVING-AVERAGE Kelley Company began business on January 1, 20-1. Purchases and sales during the month of January follow.

Date	Purchases		Sales
	Units	**Cost/Unit**	**Units**
Jan. 1	100	$1.00	
Jan. 4	400	1.10	
Jan. 5			300
Jan. 10	300	1.30	
Jan. 12			200
Jan. 15	200	1.35	
Jan. 18	500	1.60	
Jan. 22			800
Jan. 27			100
Jan. 31	300	1.80	

(continued)

REQUIRED

Calculate the total amount to be assigned to cost of goods sold for January and the ending inventory on January 31, under each of the following methods:

1. Perpetual LIFO inventory method.
2. Perpetual moving-average inventory method.

SERIES B EXERCISE

E 13Apx-1B   (LO1/2)

✓ CGS under perpetual LIFO: $5,435

✓ CGS under perpetual moving-average: $5,395

PERPETUAL: LIFO AND MOVING-AVERAGE The beginning inventory, purchases, and sales for Harrington Equipment Company for the month of August follow.

Date	Beginning Inventory and Purchases		Sales
	Units	Cost/Unit	Units
Aug. 1 (BI)	100	$8.00	
	150	8.10	
	250	8.30	
Aug. 15	300	8.50	
Aug. 31			650

BI: Beginning Inventory

REQUIRED

Calculate the total amount to be assigned to cost of goods sold for August and the ending inventory on August 31, under each of the following methods:

1. Perpetual LIFO inventory method.

2. Perpetual moving-average inventory method.

SERIES B PROBLEM

P 13Apx-2B   (LO1/2)

✓ CGS under perpetual LIFO: $3,720

✓ CGS under perpetual moving-average: $3,665.25

PERPETUAL: LIFO AND MOVING-AVERAGE Vozniak Company began business on January 1, 20-1. Purchases and sales during the month of January follow.

Date	Purchases		Sales
	Units	Cost/Unit	Units
Jan. 1	100	$2.00	
Jan. 5	500	2.30	
Jan. 7			300
Jan. 12	300	2.40	
Jan. 15			300
Jan. 17	200	2.50	
Jan. 19	500	2.70	
Jan. 24			800
Jan. 28			100
Jan. 31	200	2.90	

REQUIRED

Calculate the total amount to be assigned to cost of goods sold for January and the ending inventory on January 31, under each of the following methods:

1. Perpetual LIFO inventory method.
2. Perpetual moving-average inventory method.

Chapter 14 Adjustments for a Merchandising Business

The Scranton/Wilkes-Barre (PA) RailRiders are the Class AAA affiliate of the New York Yankees. They play in the North Division of the International League with the Buffalo Bisons, Lehigh Valley IronPigs, Pawtucket Red Sox, Rochester Red Wings, and Syracuse Chiefs. The franchise was founded in 1989 when the Maine Guides moved to Pennsylvania. From 1989 to 2006, the team was the Class AAA International League affiliate of the Philadelphia Phillies known as the Red Barons.

The RailRiders play at PNC Field, which was built on Montage Mountain between Scranton and Wilkes-Barre and has a capacity of 10,300, including luxury suites with indoor and outdoor seating. It opened in 1989 and was completely rebuilt for the 2013 season.

Often, we are expected to pay in advance for goods and services. This is true for season tickets for sporting events like the Scranton/Wilkes-Barre RailRiders, magazine subscriptions, or tickets for popular operas or rock concerts. In return, we expect to receive the goods or services. In this chapter, you will learn proper accounting for cash receipts received in advance, which are known as unearned revenues.

LEARNING OBJECTIVES

Careful study of this chapter should enable you to:

LO1 Prepare adjustments for merchandise inventory using the periodic inventory system.

LO2 Prepare an adjustment for unearned revenue.

LO3 Prepare adjustments for a merchandising business.

LO4 Journalize adjusting entries for a merchandising business.

LO5 Prepare adjustments for merchandise inventory using the perpetual inventory system.

In Chapters 10 through 13, we learned how to account for the day-to-day transactions of a merchandising business. In this chapter, we focus on end-of-period adjustments. Finally, in Chapter 15, we will complete the accounting cycle by preparing financial statements and closing entries.

In Chapter 5 we illustrated the preparation of a traditional 10-column work sheet that was used to prepare adjusting entries and the financial statements in Chapter 6. With the use of computers and accounting software, traditional work sheets are not as prevalent as in the past. The updating of accounts (posting) and the preparation of financial statements are often computer driven. Nevertheless, we believe spreadsheets that capture the adjusting process and organize the accounts for the preparation of the financial statements are beneficial when learning about the flow of accounting information. Thus, we will use an abbreviated, six column, work sheet (spreadsheet) in this chapter to help illustrate this flow of information.

This spreadsheet is used to prepare adjustments for supplies, prepaid insurance, wages earned but not paid, depreciation, and other necessary year-end adjustments. A merchandising business must also make adjustments to properly report the amount of merchandise inventory held at the end of the accounting period, sales returns and allowances, and expected customer refunds. We will also introduce a new adjustment for unearned revenue.

Adjustments for Merchandise Inventory: Periodic Inventory System

LO1

Prepare adjustments for merchandise inventory using the periodic inventory system.

As discussed in Chapter 13, under the periodic inventory system when merchandise inventory is purchased, the purchases account is debited and Cash or Accounts Payable is credited. When inventory is sold, Cash or Accounts Receivable is debited and Sales is credited. Figure 14-1 provides a review of these entries.

FIGURE 14-1 Review of Entries for Purchase and Sale of Merchandise

TRANSACTION	ENTRY		
Purchase of merchandise	Purchases	xxx	
	Accounts Payable or Cash		xxx
Sale of merchandise	Accounts Receivable or Cash	xxx	
	Sales		xxx

Note that the merchandise inventory account is not debited or credited in either of these entries. Since sales, purchases, sales returns, and purchases returns have taken place during the year and have not been entered in the merchandise inventory account, the beginning balance of the merchandise inventory account no longer provides an accurate measure of the inventory held at the end of the year. Thus, adjustments must be made. For other assets, like prepaid insurance, we would simply make an adjustment for the change in the asset account. *We do not follow this procedure for merchandise inventory.*

The adjustment for merchandise inventory is done in two steps.

1. Remove the beginning inventory from the merchandise inventory account by making the following entry:

Income Summary	old	
Merchandise Inventory		old

Periodic Inventory
Adjustments:
1. Take out the old.
2. Bring in the new.

2. Enter the ending inventory in the merchandise inventory account by making the following entry:

Merchandise Inventory   new
   Income Summary   new

As discussed in Chapter 13, the quantity of inventory on hand at the end of the accounting period is determined by taking a physical count of the goods on hand. The cost of these goods is determined by using FIFO, LIFO, or another inventory method. Of course, this year's ending inventory becomes next year's beginning inventory.

To illustrate the adjustment for merchandise inventory, let's assume that Andy's Auto Parts had a beginning merchandise inventory of $23,000. During the year, the entries shown in Figure 14-1 were made as merchandise was purchased and sold. At the end of the accounting period, a physical inventory of the merchandise determined that merchandise costing $27,000 was still on hand.

To appreciate the reason for the different adjustment process, recall the discussion in Chapter 13 of how the beginning and ending inventories are used when computing cost of goods sold. As shown in the bottom portion of Figure 14-2, the beginning

FIGURE 14-2 Calculation of Cost of Goods Sold

YOUR PERSPECTIVE

Store Merchandiser

Some *material recording clerks*—such as shipping clerks, stock clerks, expediting clerks, and material and product inspecting clerks—have specialized responsibilities. *Shipping clerks* process shipment orders, compute freight costs, and prepare invoices. *Stock clerks* receive shipments and put products on shelves. *Expediting clerks* work with vendors to ensure that supplies are shipped on time. *Material and product inspecting clerks* both record the quantity of products that come into a store or warehouse and inspect for damaged goods. Because the perpetual inventory system is continuously updated, inventory must be verified to determine shrinkage due to theft, breakage, or spoilage. Material recording clerks take physical inventory counts on a regular basis enabling journal entries to be adjusted.

---

inventory is added to purchases to compute cost of goods available for sale. The ending inventory is subtracted from cost of goods available for sale to compute cost of goods sold.

Many firms use a spreadsheet to prepare financial statements. Thus, all of the information needed to compute cost of goods sold should be readily available in the Adjusted Trial Balance columns of the spreadsheet. To provide this information, we need an adjustment technique that results in the beginning inventory being extended into the Adjusted Trial Balance *Debit* column so it can be *added* to purchases. Further, we need the ending inventory extended into the Adjusted Trial Balance *Credit* column so it will be *subtracted* when computing cost of goods sold. As shown in Figure 14-2, this can be accomplished in two steps by using the income summary account.

STEP 1 The beginning inventory ($23,000) is removed by crediting Merchandise Inventory. Income Summary is debited because this amount is used in the calculation of cost of goods sold and net income.

STEP 2 The ending inventory ($27,000) is entered by debiting Merchandise Inventory. Income Summary is credited because this amount is also used in the calculation of cost of goods sold and net income.

> **LEARNING KEY** 🔑
>
> Both the debit and credit amounts on the income summary line are extended to the Adjusted Trial Balance columns.

Note that the debit *and* credit adjustments made to Income Summary are extended into the Adjusted Trial Balance columns. This is done because the individual amounts are needed for the calculation of cost of goods sold on the income statement (beginning inventory + purchases − ending inventory = cost of goods sold).

STEPS 3–5 Steps 3–5 in the inventory adjustment process address issues related to customers returning inventory. Recall from Chapters 10 and 13, that in a merchandising business, it is likely that customers will return some of the merchandise that was purchased. The entry made when merchandise is returned during the current period is as follows:

> Merchandise Returns
> Throughout the Year

Sales Returns and Allowances	xxx	
Accounts Receivable (or Cash)		xxx

Under the periodic method, the returned inventory is not debited to the merchandise inventory account. Instead, it will be captured in the physical count of the ending inventory, if not sold by the end of the year.

It is also important to recognize that some of the inventory sold this year is likely to be returned <u>next</u> year. To properly measure assets, liabilities, and related revenues and expenses, we must make adjusting entries at the end of the period. Let's assume Andy's estimates that customers will be granted $4,000 in refunds of this year's sales next year and the merchandise expected to be returned will have a cost of $3,000. Thus, as discussed in Chapter 10, **Customer Refunds Payable** must be adjusted to equal the estimated $4,000 liability. As shown in Figures 14-2 and 14-3, the Trial Balance reflects a balance of $2,600 before adjustment. Therefore, we must make the following adjusting entry.

Year-End Adjusting Entry →	STEP 3	Sales Returns and Allowances	1,400	
		Customer Refunds Payable		1,400

As shown in Figure 14-3, Sales Returns and Allowances is a contra-revenue account subtracted from the Sales account on the income statement when computing net sales. Customer Refunds Payable is a current liability account. It will be adjusted at the end of each accounting period to properly reflect the amount of refunds expected to be paid next period as a result of sales in the current period.

FIGURE 14-3 Adjustments for Sales Returns and Allowances

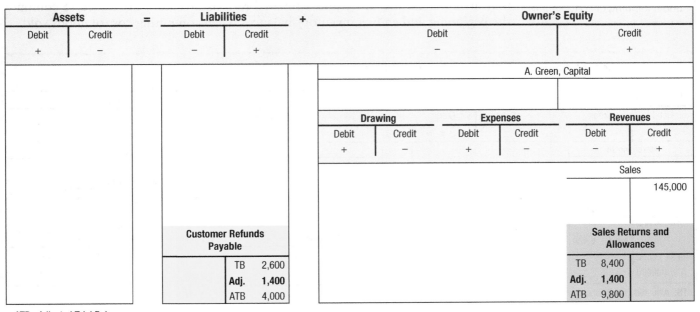

ATB: Adjusted Trial Balance

When customers return merchandise purchased this year, or last year, we assume Sales Returns and Allowances is debited and Accounts Receivable (or Cash) is credited. As with Merchandise Inventory under the periodic method, no entries are made to Customer Refunds Payable during the year. At the end of each year, Customer Refunds Payable is adjusted to reflect estimated refunds to be paid next year as a result of this year's sales. This adjustment may increase or decrease the balance in Customer Refunds Payable and, as a result, Sales Returns and Allowances.

In **STEPS 4 AND 5**, we adjust for the estimated inventory to be returned next year. **Estimated Returns Inventory** is an asset account that represents the estimated cost of merchandise inventory sold this year, but expected to be returned next year. This account is reported as a current asset on the Balance Sheet and is often combined with Merchandise Inventory. Since it is a new account, we will report it separately here and in Chapter 15. Keep in mind, however, both accounts are used to measure the beginning and ending inventory on the balance sheet and when calculating cost of goods sold on the income statement. As with the Merchandise Inventory account, under the periodic inventory system, no entries will be made to this account during the year. This account will be adjusted at the end of each period to properly reflect the cost of merchandise sold this period, but expected to be returned next period.

As shown in Figures 14-2 and 14-4, Estimated Returns Inventory has a trial balance of $2,000 before adjustment. The adjustment to properly reflect the required $3,000 balance, the cost of the expected returns, will be done in two steps. This approach is the same as that used for merchandise inventory.

Year End Adjusting Entries →	**STEP 4**	Income Summary	2,000	
		Estimated Returns Inventory		2,000
	STEP 5	Estimated Returns Inventory	3,000	
		Income Summary		3,000

CHECKPOINT ✔

Complete Checkpoint-1 on page 546 to test your basic understanding of LO1.

Note in Figure 14-2, the adjustment and extensions of the Estimated Returns Inventory account are treated the same as Merchandise Inventory. The adjustments are done in two steps and the debits and credits to Income Summary are extended to the Adjusted Trial Balance columns. Note also in the lower portion of Figure 14-2 that merchandise inventory and estimated returns inventory are added to compute the beginning and ending inventory balances when computing cost of goods sold.

FIGURE 14-4 Adjustments for Estimated Returns Inventory

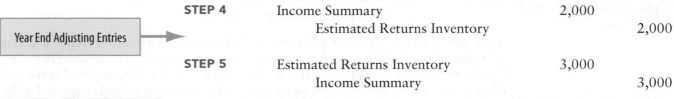

ATB: Adjusted Trial Balance

LO2   Adjustment for Unearned Revenue

Prepare an adjustment for unearned revenue.

Unearned revenue and customer refunds payable are similar liabilities. In both cases, the customer has paid for a product or service with the promise of a refund if not satisfied.

Some businesses require payment before delivering a product or performing a service. Examples include insurance companies, magazine publishers, apartment complexes, college food services, and professional sports and theater companies that sell season tickets. The cash received in advance is called unearned revenue. Since the cash has been received in advance, the company owes the customers the product or service, or must refund their money. Thus, unearned revenue is reported as a *liability* on the balance sheet.

To illustrate, let's assume that Brown County Playhouse sells season tickets for five plays produced throughout the year. Tickets sell for $10 for each play ($50 for a season ticket) and a maximum of 1,000 seats can be sold for each play. For simplicity, let's assume that all shows sell out during the first week that season tickets are available for sale. As shown below and in Figure 14-5, the sale of the tickets would be recorded as follows:

8		(1)	Cash		50	0	0	0	00							8
9			Unearned Ticket Revenue							50	0	0	0	00		9
10			Season ticket sales													10
11			($10 × 1,000 seats × 5 shows)													11

To prepare financial statements following production of the third show, an adjusting entry is needed to recognize that $30,000 ($10 × 1,000 seats × 3 shows) in ticket revenue has been earned. To do this, the following adjusting entry is made:

13		Adjusting Entries													13
14		Unearned Ticket Revenue		30	0	0	0	00							14
15		Ticket Revenue								30	0	0	0	00	15

The remaining balance of $20,000 in Unearned Ticket Revenue is reported as a current liability on the balance sheet.

FIGURE 14-5 Entries for Unearned Revenue

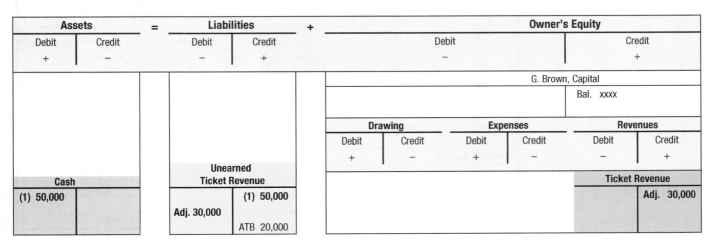

Expanded Chart of Accounts

Let's take a look at where the new accounts for a merchandising business fit into a chart of accounts. Recall that the chart of accounts follows the form of the accounting equation (assets = liabilities + owner's equity + revenues − expenses). A chart of accounts for Sunflower Cycle is provided in Figure 14-6. Note the classification of the new accounts introduced in Chapters 10 and 11 for a merchandising firm.

Merchandise Inventory and Estimated Returns Inventory are listed as current assets. Since Sunflower Cycle sells subscriptions to a computer magazine that it produces, Unearned Subscriptions Revenue is listed as a current liability, and Subscriptions Revenue is listed as a revenue. Customer Refunds Payable is also listed as a current liability. Sales Returns and Allowances and Sales Discounts are contra-revenue accounts. Recall, however, that Sunflower Cycle does not offer sales discounts.

FIGURE 14-6 **Chart of Accounts for Sunflower Cycle**

SUNFLOWER CYCLE CHART OF ACCOUNTS			
Assets		**Revenue**	
Current Assets		401	Sales
101	Cash	401.1	Sales Returns and
122	Accounts Receivable		Allowances
131	Merchandise Inventory	**Other Revenue**	
135	Estimated Returns Inventory	411	Interest Revenue
141	Supplies	412	Rent Revenue
145	Prepaid Insurance	413	Subscriptions Revenue
Property, Plant, and Equipment		**Expenses**	
161	Land	**Cost of Goods Sold**	
171	Building	501	Purchases
171.1	Accumulated Depreciation—	501.1	Purchases Returns and
	Building		Allowances
181	Equipment	501.2	Purchases Discounts
181.1	Accumulated Depreciation—	502	Freight-In
	Equipment	**Operating Expenses**	
Liabilities		511	Wages Expense
Current Liabilities		512	Advertising Expense
201	Notes Payable	513	Bank Credit Card
202	Accounts Payable		Expense
203	Customer Refunds Payable	521	Rent Expense
219	Wages Payable	523	Supplies Expense
231	Sales Tax Payable	525	Phone Expense
241	Unearned Subscriptions	533	Utilities Expense
	Revenue	535	Insurance Expense
Long-Term Liabilities		540	Depreciation Expense—
251	Mortgage Payable		Building
		541	Depreciation Expense—
Owner's Equity			Equipment
311	Sam Tangari, Capital	549	Miscellaneous Expense
312	Sam Tangari, Drawing		
313	Income Summary	**Other Expenses**	
		551	Interest Expense

CHECKPOINT ✓

Complete Checkpoint-2 on page 546 to test your basic understanding of LO2.

Purchases, Purchases Returns and Allowances, Purchases Discounts, and Freight-In are used to compute cost of goods sold. Thus, they are listed under this heading. Purchases Returns and Allowances and Purchases Discounts are often called contra-cost accounts or contra-purchases accounts.

Interest Expense is classified as "Other Expenses" instead of being listed under Operating Expenses. This is because it represents the expense of obtaining money to do business, rather than an expense directly associated with operating the business.

A BROADER VIEW

The Importance of Inventory

Note the important role of the ending inventory in the calculation of cost of goods sold in Figure 14-2. If the ending inventory is overstated for any reason, net income will also be overstated. Given this important relationship, auditors observe and verify the accuracy of the physical inventory. However, unethical managers, desperate to improve profits, have on occasion found ways to mislead auditors.

In one case, managers overstated inventory counts for items that the auditors had not physically verified. In another case, auditors found a barrel whose contents had been valued by management at thousands of dollars. It actually contained floor sweepings. Finally, there was a case where management called the auditor, the day after the inventory audit, to report that additional inventory had arrived and should be included in the inventory count. The auditor never verified that the inventory was real. It turned out to be a scam that helped the company double its reported profits for the year. These unfortunate events highlight the reason auditors must exercise great care when conducting an inventory audit.

LO3

Adjustments for a Merchandising Business

Prepare adjustments for a merchandising business.

Let's first look at the preparation of adjustments for a merchandising business using T accounts. Figure 14-7 provides year-end adjustment information for Sunflower Cycle. Figure 14-8 shows adjusting entries based on this information. The unadjusted balances for these accounts were taken from Sunflower Cycle's trial balance.

FIGURE 14-7 Year-End Adjustment Data for Sunflower Cycle

YEAR-END ADJUSTMENT DATA FOR SUNFLOWER CYCLE	
(a, b)	A physical count showed that merchandise inventory costing $45,600 is on hand as of December 31.
(c, d, e)	It is estimated that $3,000 in this year's sales will be returned by customers next year. The cost of the merchandise expected to be returned is estimated to be $2,100.
(f)	Supplies remaining at the end of the year, $800.
(g)	Unexpired insurance on December 31, $400.
(h)	Depreciation expense on the building for the year, $4,000.
(i)	Depreciation expense on the equipment for the year, $3,000.
(j)	Wages earned but not paid as of December 31, $700.
(k)	Sunflower Cycle publishes a cycling magazine. Subscribers pay in advance. Unearned subscriptions revenue as of December 31, $1,000.

FIGURE 14-8 Adjusting Entries for Sunflower Cycle

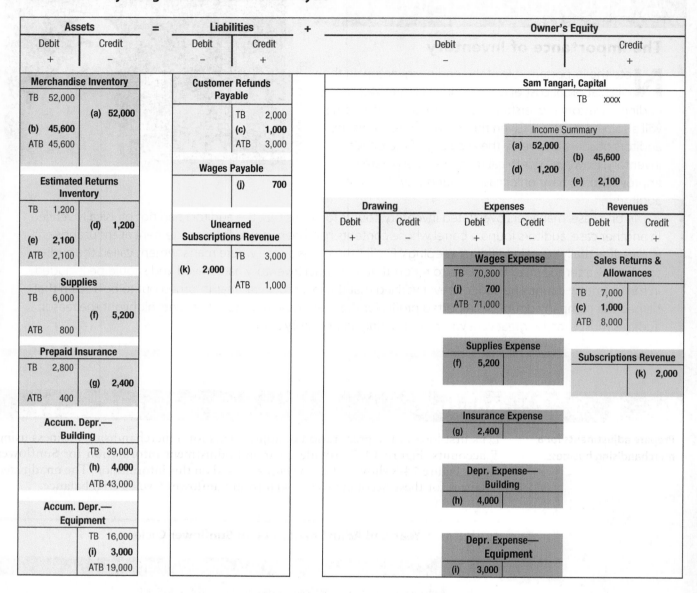

Adjustments may also be planned using an end-of-period spreadsheet. A spreadsheet for Sunflower Cycle is provided in Figure 14-9. It is prepared in four basic steps.

STEP 1 The Trial Balance columns are completed by copying the balances of all accounts from the general ledger (not shown).

STEP 2 Adjustments are entered. These entries are exactly the same as those made in T account form in Figure 14-8.

STEP 3 Extensions are made to the Adjusted Trial Balance columns. Note that all debit and credit amounts for Income Summary are extended.

STEP 4   By using a spreadsheet it is easy to compute net income for the period. Simply add all of the income statement accounts listed in the Adjusted Trial Balance columns. The income statement accounts are grouped together and include all accounts from Income Summary to the bottom of the columns. Those with credit balances total $533,000 and represent revenues and other accounts that increase net income. Those with debit balances total $432,600 and represent expenses and other accounts that reduce net income. Since the credits are greater than the debits, the difference of $100,400 equals net income for the period. If the debits exceed the credits, we would have a net loss.

FIGURE 14-9 Year End Spreadsheet for Sunflower Cycle

	A	B	C	D	E	F	G	H	I
1		Sunflower Cycle							
2		End-of-Period Spreadsheet							
3		For the Year Ended December 31, 20--							
4	ACCOUNT TITLE	TRIAL BALANCE			ADJUSTMENTS			ADJUSTED TRIAL BALANCE	
5		DEBIT	CREDIT		DEBIT		CREDIT	DEBIT	CREDIT
6	Cash	26,000.00						26,000.00	
7	Accounts Receivable	13,000.00						13,000.00	
8	Merchandise Inventory	52,000.00		(b)	45,600.00	(a)	52,000.00	45,600.00	
9	Estimated Returns Inventory	1,200.00		(e)	2,100.00	(d)	1,200.00	2,100.00	
10	Supplies	6,000.00				(f)	5,200.00	800.00	
11	Prepaid Insurance	2,800.00				(g)	2,400.00	400.00	
12	Land	115,000.00						115,000.00	
13	Building	390,000.00						390,000.00	
14	Accum. Depr.—Building		39,000.00			(h)	4,000.00		43,000.00
15	Equipment	48,000.00						48,000.00	
16	Accum. Depr.—Equipment		16,000.00			(i)	3,000.00		19,000.00
17	Notes Payable		5,000.00						5,000.00
18	Accounts Payable		24,000.00						24,000.00
19	Customer Refunds Payable		2,000.00			(c)	1,000.00		3,000.00
20	Wages Payable					(j)	700.00		700.00
21	Sales Tax Payable		1,600.00						1,600.00
22	Unearned Subscriptions Revenue		3,000.00	(k)	2,000.00				1,000.00
23	Mortgage Payable		30,000.00						30,000.00
24	Sam Tangari, Capital		417,200.00						417,200.00
25	Sam Tangari, Drawing	4,000.00						4,000.00	
26	Income Summary			(a)	52,000.00	(b)	45,600.00	52,000.00	45,600.00
27				(d)	1,200.00	(e)	2,100.00	1,200.00	2,100.00
28	Sales		473,000.00						473,000.00
29	Sales Returns and Allowances	7,000.00		(c)	1,000.00			8,000.00	
30	Interest Revenue		800.00						800.00
31	Rent Revenue		7,500.00						7,500.00
32	Subscriptions Revenue					(k)	2,000.00		2,000.00
33	Purchases	239,600.00						239,600.00	
34	Purchases Returns and Allowances		1,100.00						1,100.00
35	Purchases Discounts		900.00						900.00
36	Freight-In	1,300.00						1,300.00	
37	Wages Expense	70,300.00		(j)	700.00			71,000.00	
38	Advertising Expense	10,200.00						10,200.00	
39	Bank Credit Card Expense	8,100.00						8,100.00	
40	Rent Expense	14,000.00						14,000.00	
41	Supplies Expense			(f)	5,200.00			5,200.00	
42	Phone Expense	1,800.00						1,800.00	
43	Utilities Expense	7,500.00						7,500.00	
44	Insurance Expense			(g)	2,400.00			2,400.00	
45	Depr. Expense—Building			(h)	4,000.00			4,000.00	
46	Depr. Expense—Equipment			(i)	3,000.00			3,000.00	
47	Miscellaneous Expense	1,700.00						1,700.00	
48	Interest Expense	1,600.00						1,600.00	
49		1,021,100.00	1,021,100.00		119,200.00		119,200.00	1,077,500.00	1,077,500.00
50		STEP 1			STEP 2			STEP 3	
51	STEP 4							$ 432,600.00	$ 533,000.00
52	Net Income							100,400.00	

LO4   Adjusting Entries

Journalize adjusting entries for a merchandising business.

Adjustments on a spreadsheet have no effect on the actual accounts in the general ledger. Journal entries must be made to enter the adjustments into the accounting system. Figure 14-10 shows the adjusting entries for Sunflower Cycle.

LEARNING KEY 🔑

Recall that the spreadsheet is just a planning tool. The adjusting entries must be entered in the general journal.

FIGURE 14-10 Adjusting Entries for Sunflower Cycle

	DATE		DESCRIPTION	POST. REF.	DEBIT	CREDIT	
1			Adjusting Entries				1
2	20-- Dec.	31	Income Summary		52 0 0 0 00		2
3			Merchandise Inventory			52 0 0 0 00	3
4							4
5		31	Merchandise Inventory		45 6 0 0 00		5
6			Income Summary			45 6 0 0 00	6
7							7
8		31	Sales Returns and Allowances		1 0 0 0 00		8
9			Customer Refunds Payable			1 0 0 0 00	9
10							10
11		31	Income Summary		1 2 0 0 00		11
12			Estimated Returns Inventory			1 2 0 0 00	12
13							13
14		31	Estimated Returns Inventory		2 1 0 0 00		14
15			Income Summary			2 1 0 0 00	15
16							16
17		31	Supplies Expense		5 2 0 0 00		17
18			Supplies			5 2 0 0 00	18
19							19
20		31	Insurance Expense		2 4 0 0 00		20
21			Prepaid Insurance			2 4 0 0 00	21
22							22
23		31	Depr. Expense—Building		4 0 0 0 00		23
24			Accumulated Depr.—Building			4 0 0 0 00	24
25							25
26		31	Depr. Expense—Equipment		3 0 0 0 00		26
27			Accumulated Depr.—Equipment			3 0 0 0 00	27
28							28
29		31	Wages Expense		7 0 0 00		29
30			Wages Payable			7 0 0 00	30
31							31
32		31	Unearned Subscriptions Revenue		2 0 0 0 00		32
33			Subscriptions Revenue			2 0 0 0 00	33
34							34

GENERAL JOURNAL   PAGE 3

CHECKPOINT ✔

Complete Checkpoint-4 on page 547 to test your basic understanding of LO4.

LO5	**Adjusting Entries Under the Perpetual Inventory System**

Prepare adjustments for merchandise inventory using the perpetual inventory system.

Under the perpetual inventory system, the merchandise inventory, estimated returns inventory, cost of goods sold, and customer refunds payable accounts are continually updated throughout the year to reflect inventory purchases, sales, returns by customers, and returns to suppliers. Figure 14-11 illustrates the entries made for these transactions under the periodic and perpetual inventory systems. In addition, it illustrates year-end adjusting entries under both systems. Many of these entries are provided as review. Complete discussions of new entries for expected sales returns and allowances and inventory shrinkage under the perpetual inventory system follow the figure.

FIGURE 14-11 Entries for Periodic and Perpetual Inventory Systems

TRANSACTION	PERIODIC SYSTEM		PERPETUAL SYSTEM	

Purchased merchandise on account, $800	Purchases
	    Accounts Payable
		800
		
		800
			Merchandise Inventory
			    Accounts Payable
				800
				
				800

Sold merchandise on account, $400. The cost of the merchandise sold was $300	Accounts Receivable
	    Sales
		400
		
		400
			Accounts Receivable
			    Sales
			
			Cost of Goods Sold
			    Merchandise Inventory
				400
				
				400
				
				300
				
				300

Returned merchandise to supplier. Cost was $100.	Accounts Payable
	    Purchases Returns and Allowances
		100
		
		100
			Accounts Payable
			    Merchandise Inventory
				100
				
				100

Customer returns merchandise sold in the <u>current</u> period for a refund of $50, cost was $40.	Sales Returns and Allowances
	    Accounts Receivable or Cash
		50
		
		50
			Sales Returns and Allowances
			    Accounts Receivable or Cash
			
			Merchandise Inventory
			    Cost of Goods Sold
				50
				
				50
				
				40
				
				40

Customer returns merchandise sold in the <u>prior</u> period for a refund of $60, cost was $48.	Sales Returns and Allowances
	    Accounts Receivable or Cash
		60
		
		60
			Customer Refunds Payable
			    Accounts Receivable or Cash
			
			Merchandise Inventory
			    Estimated Returns Inventory
				60
				
				60
				
				48
				
				48

YEAR-END ADJUSTMENTS	PERIODIC SYSTEM		PERPETUAL SYSTEM	

Adjustment for Merchandise Inventory	Income Summary
	    Merchandise Inventory
	
	Merchandise Inventory
	    Income Summary
		XX
		
		XX
		
		XX
		
		XX
			Inventory Short and Over
			    Merchandise Inventory
				XX
				
				XX

Adjustment for Estimated Returns Inventory: Sales made this year, but expected to be returned next year.	Income Summary
	    Estimated Returns Inventory
	
	Estimated Returns Inventory
	    Income Summary
		XX
		
		XX
		
		XX
		
		XX
			Estimated Returns Inventory
			    Cost of Goods Sold
				XX
				
				XX

Adjustment for Sales Returns and Allowances: Sales made this year, but expected to be returned next year.	Sales Returns and Allowances
	    Customer Refunds Payable
		XX
		
		XX
			Sales Returns and Allowances
			    Customer Refunds Payable
				XX
				
				XX

Adjustments for Expected Sales Returns and Allowances

At the end of each period, it is important to adjust for merchandise sold this accounting period, but expected to be returned in the next period. As shown below, the adjusting entries for the perpetual inventory system are similar to the periodic system. But there are important differences.

Sales Returns and Allowances	xxx	
Customer Refunds Payable		xxx
Estimated Returns Inventory	xxx	
Cost of Goods Sold		xxx

Year End Adjusting Entries →

Since the business has the ability to track the details of inventory transactions, Merchandise Inventory, Estimated Returns Inventory, Cost of Goods Sold, and Customer Refunds Payable are updated throughout the year, <u>and</u> adjusted at year-end for next year's estimates.

To illustrate the underlying accounting let's assume facts similar to those used in Figure 14-2 for Andy's Auto Parts. Andy's estimates that customers will be granted $4,000 in refunds of this year's sales next year and the merchandise expected to be returned will have a cost of $3,000. Thus, Customer Refunds Payable and Estimated Returns Inventory must be adjusted to equal these amounts. This is the same process as followed under the periodic system. However, the dollar amounts for these adjustments will be different under the perpetual inventory system. This is because of the entries made <u>during the year</u>. As shown in Figure 14-11, when a customer returns merchandise purchased in the prior year, the following entries are made under the perpetual system.

Customer Refunds Payable	xxx	
Accounts Receivable or Cash		xxx
Merchandise Inventory	xxx	
Estimated Returns Inventory		xxx

Merchandise Sold Last Year, Returned This Year. →

> It is preferable to debit Returned Merchandise Inventory instead of Merchandise Inventory to maintain a distinction between inventory that is brand new and inventory that has been returned and may need to be discounted. We will leave this distinction to more advanced texts.

Thus, if last year's estimates for refunds and returns inventory were accurate, the ending balances of these accounts should approach zero. Let's assume these unadjusted balances are as follows:

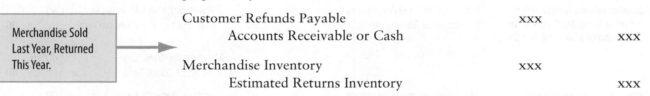

	A	B	C
1		TRIAL BALANCE	
2		DEBIT	CREDIT
3	Estimated Returns Inventory	300.00	
4	Customer Refunds Payable		400.00
5			

Therefore, under the perpetual inventory system, we must make the following adjusting entries at year-end:

Year-End Adjusting Entries (See Fig. 14-11.)

Sales Returns and Allowances	3,600	
Customer Refunds Payable		3,600
(4,000 − 400 = 3,600)		
Estimated Returns Inventory	2,700	
Cost of Goods Sold		2,700
(3,000 − 300 = 2,700)		

Adjustments for Inventory Shrinkage

As discussed in Chapter 13, the perpetual inventory system does not eliminate the need for taking physical inventories. The perpetual records must be compared with the physical inventory to discover and correct any errors or losses of merchandise from theft, breakage, or spoilage. This is known as inventory shrinkage. If a difference is found between the physical count and the amount in the perpetual inventory records, the records must be corrected by an adjusting entry. Some firms use Cost of Goods Sold to make this adjustment. A preferable approach is to use an account called Inventory Short and Over. For example, if the book balance is $3,840 and the physical count shows $3,710 worth of merchandise, the $130 shortage would be entered as follows:

3	Adjusting Entries			3
4	Inventory Short and Over	1 3 0 00		4
5	Merchandise Inventory		1 3 0 00	5
6	To adjust inventory per physical count			6

Similarly, if the book balance is $3,840 and the physical count shows $3,900 worth of merchandise, this $60 overage would be entered as follows:

3	Adjusting Entries			3
4	Merchandise Inventory	6 0 00		4
5	Inventory Short and Over		6 0 00	5
6	To adjust inventory per physical count			6

LEARNING KEY

A physical inventory is still important under the perpetual inventory system. It is used to verify the accuracy of the inventory records.

If Inventory Short and Over has a debit balance, the account is listed with other expenses on the income statement. If it has a credit balance, the account is listed with other revenues on the income statement.

Using a separate account, Inventory Short and Over, makes it easier for management to track inventory problems associated with errors, theft, breakage, and spoilage. Further, it removes these items from the calculation of cost of goods sold and provides a better measure of the gross profit on sales.

A business that sells a wide selection of low-cost goods may not find it practical to keep a perpetual inventory. In contrast, a business that sells a few high-cost items (cars, fine jewelry, stereo equipment) can maintain such a record without incurring excessive processing costs. The increasing use of computers and optical scanning devices at the point of sale has enabled more and more businesses to switch from the periodic to the perpetual inventory system.

CHECKPOINT

Complete Checkpoint-5 on page 547 to test your basic understanding of LO5.

LEARNING OBJECTIVES	**Key Points to Remember**

LO1 Prepare adjustments for merchandise inventory using the periodic inventory system.

Extra care is required for the end-of-period adjustment for merchandise inventory and the related extensions on a spreadsheet. The five-step adjustment process used on a spreadsheet is shown below. This technique is used so that all of the information required to compute cost of goods sold on the income statement is provided in the Adjusted Trial Balance columns of the spreadsheet.

	A	B	C	D	E	F	G
1	ACCOUNT TITLE	TRIAL BALANCE		ADJUSTMENTS		ADJUSTED TRIAL BALANCE	
2		DEBIT	CREDIT	DEBIT	CREDIT	DEBIT	CREDIT
3							
4							
5	Merchandise Inventory	23,000.00		27,000.00	23,000.00	27,000.00	
6	Estimated Returns Inventory	2,000.00		3,000.00	2,000.00	3,000.00	
7	Customer Refunds Payable		2,600.00		1,400.00		4,000.00
8	Income Summary			23,000.00	27,000.00	23,000.00	27,000.00
9				2,000.00	3,000.00	2,000.00	3,000.00
10	Sales		145,000.00				145,000.00
11	Sales Returns and Allowances	8,400.00		1,400.00		9,800.00	
12	Purchases	80,000.00				80,000.00	
13							

Step 1: Remove Beginning Inventory	Income Summary	23,000.00
	Merchandise Inventory		23,000.00
Step 2: Enter Ending Inventory	Merchandise Inventory	27,000.00
	Income Summary		27,000.00
Step 3: Update for New Estimate of Customer Refunds Payable	Sales Returns and Allowances	1,400.00
	Customer Refunds Payable		1,400.00
Step 4: Remove Beginning Estimated Returns Inventory	Income Summary	2,000.00
	Estimated Returns Inventory		2,000.00
Step 5: Enter Ending Estimated Returns Inventory	Estimated Returns Inventory	3,000.00
	Income Summary		3,000.00

Cost of goods sold:			
Merchandise Inventory, January 1	$ 23,000.00		
Estimated returns inventory, January 1	2,000.00	$ 25,000.00	
Purchases		80,000.00	
Goods available for sale		$ 105,000.00	
Less: Merchandise inventory, December 31	$ 27,000.00		
Estimated returns inventory, December 31	3,000.00	30,000.00	
Cost of goods sold		75,000.00	

LO2 Prepare an adjustment for unearned revenue.

Some firms receive cash before providing a service or selling a product. The cash received in advance is considered a liability, unearned revenue, until earned. The adjusting entry to recognize that unearned revenue has become earned is as follows:

Unearned Revenue	xxx
Revenue	xxx

LO3 Prepare adjustments for a merchandising business.

Adjustments can be prepared electronically using accounting software, with T accounts, or on a spreadsheet. Steps to follow when using a spreadsheet are as follows:

1. Prepare the trial balance.
2. Prepare the adjustments.
3. Prepare the adjusted trial balance.
4. Compute net income using the income statement accounts in the adjusted trial balance columns.

LEARNING OBJECTIVES	**Key Points to Remember**
LO4 Journalize adjusting entries for a merchandising business.	A spreadsheet is a useful tool when preparing end-of-period adjustments and financial statements. Adjustments made on a spreadsheet must be entered in a journal and posted to the ledger.
LO5 Prepare adjustments for merchandise inventory using the perpetual inventory system.	At the end of each period, it is important to adjust for merchandise sold this accounting period, but expected to be returned in the next period. As shown below, the adjusting entries for the perpetual inventory system are similar to the periodic system. However, since these accounts are updated throughout the year, the dollar amounts for the adjustment will be quite different.

Sales Returns and Allowances	xxx	
Customer Refunds Payable		xxx
Estimated Returns Inventory	xxx	
Cost of Goods Sold		xxx

Since the business has the ability to track the details of inventory transactions, Merchandise Inventory, is updated throughout the year for all transactions affecting this account. Thus, the firm knows how much inventory should be on hand at any given point in time. However, the balance of the merchandise inventory account must be verified with an actual physical count of the inventory before issuing financial statements. If there is a difference, an adjusting entry is made. If the balance in the inventory account is greater than the physical count, the following entry is made:

Inventory Short and Over	xxx	
Merchandise Inventory		xxx

If the balance in the inventory account is less than the physical count, the following entry is made:

Merchandise Inventory	xxx	
Inventory Short and Over		xxx

DEMONSTRATION PROBLEM

Aaron Patton owns and operates Patton's Bait Shop. A year-end trial balance is shown on page 542.

Patton uses the periodic inventory system. Year-end adjustment data are as follows:

(a, b)   A physical count shows that merchandise inventory costing $53,000 is on hand as of December 31, 20--.

(c, d, e)   Patton estimates that customers will be granted $5,000 in refunds of this year's sales next year and the merchandise expected to be returned will have a cost of $2,800.

(f)   Supplies remaining at the end of the year, $200.

(continued)

(g)   Unexpired insurance on December 31, $300.
(h)   Depreciation expense on the building for 20--, $2,000.
(i)   Depreciation expense on the equipment for 20--, $1,500.
(j)   Wages earned but not paid as of December 31, $1,200.
(k)   Patton also offers guided tours which clients pay for in advance.
        Unearned tour guide revenue as of December 31, $5,000.

REQUIRED

1. Prepare a year-end spreadsheet.
2. Journalize the adjusting entries.
3. Compute cost of goods sold using the spreadsheet prepared for part (1).

	A	B	C
1	Patton's Bait Shop		
2	Trial Balance		
3	For the Year Ended December 31, 20--		
4	ACCOUNT TITLE	DEBIT BALANCE	CREDIT BALANCE
5			
6	Cash	40,400.00	
7	Accounts Receivable	7,500.00	
8	Merchandise Inventory	47,400.00	
9	Estimated Returns Inventory	2,500.00	
10	Supplies	900.00	
11	Prepaid Insurance	1,200.00	
12	Land	85,000.00	
13	Building	45,000.00	
14	Accumulated Depreciation—Building		8,000.00
15	Equipment	25,000.00	
16	Accumulated Depreciation—Equipment		7,500.00
17	Accounts Payable		5,000.00
18	Customer Refunds Payable		3,000.00
19	Wages Payable		
20	Unearned Tour Guide Revenue		30,000.00
21	Aaron Patton, Capital		174,900.00
22	Aaron Patton, Drawing	10,000.00	
23	Income Summary		
24			
25	Sales		222,750.00
26	Sales Returns and Allowances	12,000.00	
27	Tour Guide Revenue		
28	Purchases	102,500.00	
29	Purchases Returns and Allowances		400.00
30	Purchases Discounts		500.00
31	Freight-In	150.00	
32	Wages Expense	61,000.00	
33	Advertising Expense	3,750.00	
34	Supplies Expense		
35	Phone Expense	1,750.00	
36	Utilities Expense	6,000.00	
37	Insurance Expense		
38	Depreciation Expense—Building		
39	Depreciation Expense—Equipment		
40		452,050.00	452,050.00
41			

SOLUTION 1.

	A	B	C	D	E	F	G	H	I
1			Patton's Bait Shop						
2			End-of-Period Spreadsheet						
3			For the Year Ended December 31, 20--						
4	ACCOUNT TITLE	TRIAL BALANCE			ADJUSTMENTS			ADJUSTED TRIAL BALANCE	
5		DEBIT	CREDIT		DEBIT		CREDIT	DEBIT	CREDIT
6	Cash	40,400.00						40,400.00	
7	Accounts Receivable	7,500.00						7,500.00	
8	Merchandise Inventory	47,400.00		(b)	53,000.00	(a)	47,400.00	53,000.00	
9	Estimated Returns Inventory	2,500.00		(e)	2,800.00	(d)	2,500.00	2,800.00	
10	Supplies	900.00				(f)	700.00	200.00	
11	Prepaid Insurance	1,200.00				(g)	900.00	300.00	
12	Land	85,000.00						85,000.00	
13	Building	45,000.00						45,000.00	
14	Accum. Depr.—Building		8,000.00			(h)	2,000.00		10,000.00
15	Equipment	25,000.00						25,000.00	
16	Accum. Depr.—Equipment		7,500.00			(i)	1,500.00		9,000.00
17	Accounts Payable		5,000.00						5,000.00
18	Customer Refunds Payable		3,000.00			(c)	2,000.00		5,000.00
19	Wages Payable					(j)	1,200.00		1,200.00
20	Unearned Tour Guide Revenue		30,000.00	(k)	25,000.00				5,000.00
21	Aaron Patton, Capital		174,900.00						174,900.00
22	Aaron Patton, Drawing	10,000.00						10,000.00	
23	Income Summary			(a)	47,400.00	(b)	53,000.00	47,400.00	53,000.00
24				(d)	2,500.00	(e)	2,800.00	2,500.00	2,800.00
25	Sales		222,750.00						222,750.00
26	Sales Returns and Allowances	12,000.00		(c)	2,000.00			14,000.00	
27	Tour Guide Revenue					(k)	25,000.00		25,000.00
28	Purchases	102,500.00						102,500.00	
29	Purchases Returns and Allowances		400.00						400.00
30	Purchases Discounts		500.00						500.00
31	Freight-In	150.00						150.00	
32	Wages Expense	61,000.00		(j)	1,200.00			62,200.00	
33	Advertising Expense	3,750.00						3,750.00	
34	Supplies Expense			(f)	700.00			700.00	
35	Phone Expense	1,750.00						1,750.00	
36	Utilities Expense	6,000.00						6,000.00	
37	Insurance Expense			(g)	900.00			900.00	
38	Depr. Expense—Building			(h)	2,000.00			2,000.00	
39	Depr. Expense—Equipment			(i)	1,500.00			1,500.00	
40		452,050.00	452,050.00		139,000.00		139,000.00	514,550.00	514,550.00
41								245,350.00	304,450.00
42	Net Income							59,100.00	
43									

SOLUTION 2.

	DATE		DESCRIPTION	POST REF.	DEBIT	CREDIT	
1			Adjusting Entries				1
2	20-- Dec.	31	Income Summary		47 4 0 0 00		2
3			Merchandise Inventory			47 4 0 0 00	3
4							4
5		31	Merchandise Inventory		53 0 0 0 00		5
6			Income Summary			53 0 0 0 00	6
7							7
8		31	Sales Returns and Allowances		2 0 0 0 00		8
9			Customer Refunds Payable			2 0 0 0 00	9
10							10
11		31	Income Summary		2 5 0 0 00		11
12			Estimated Returns Inventory			2 5 0 0 00	12
13							13
14		31	Estimated Returns Inventory		2 8 0 0 00		14
15			Income Summary			2 8 0 0 00	15
16							16
17		31	Supplies Expense		7 0 0 00		17
18			Supplies			7 0 0 00	18
19							19
20		31	Insurance Expense		9 0 0 00		20
21			Prepaid Insurance			9 0 0 00	21
22							22
23		31	Depreciation Expense—Building		2 0 0 0 00		23
24			Accumulated Depreciation—Building			2 0 0 0 00	24
25							25
23		31	Depreciation Expense—Equipment		1 5 0 0 00		23
24			Accumulated Depreciation—Equipment			1 5 0 0 00	24
25							25
26		31	Wages Expense		1 2 0 0 00		26
27			Wages Payable			1 2 0 0 00	27
28							28
29		31	Unearned Tour Guide Revenue		25 0 0 0 00		29
30			Tour Guide Revenue			25 0 0 0 00	30

GENERAL JOURNAL PAGE 3

SOLUTION 3.

Cost of goods sold:			
Merchandise inventory, January 1		$ 47,400	
Estimated returns inventory, January 1		2,500	$ 49,900
Purchases		$102,500	
Less: Purchases returns and allowances	$400		
Purchases discounts	500	900	
Net purchases		$101,600	
Add freight-in		150	
Cost of goods purchased			101,750
Goods available for sale			$151,650
Less: Merchandise inventory, December 31		$ 53,000	
Estimated returns inventory, December 31		2,800	55,800
Cost of goods sold			95,850

KEY TERMS

Customer Refunds Payable (529)   A liability account used to report the estimated refunds to be paid to customers next year as a result of returning merchandise sold this year.

Estimated Returns Inventory (529)   An asset-account that represents the estimated cost of merchandise inventory sold this year, but expected to be returned next year.

inventory shrinkage (539)   Losses of merchandise from theft, breakage, or spoilage.

Inventory Short and Over (539)   An account used to adjust the perpetual inventory records when a difference exists between the physical count and the amount in the perpetual inventory records.

unearned revenue (530)   Cash received in advance of delivering a product or performing a service.

SELF-STUDY TEST QUESTIONS

True/False

1. **LO1**   Under the periodic inventory system, the beginning inventory is removed from the merchandise inventory account with a credit to Merchandise Inventory and a debit to Income Summary.

2. **LO1**   Under the periodic inventory system, the ending inventory is entered by debiting Merchandise Inventory and crediting Income Summary.

3. **LO2**   The cash received in advance before delivering a product or performing a service is called unearned revenue.

4. **LO2**   Unearned revenue is adjusted into an expense account at the end of the accounting period.

5. **LO1/2**   Sales Returns and Allowances is classified as a contra-cost account on the income statement.

Multiple Choice

1. **LO1**   Under the periodic inventory system, what account is credited when an estimate is made for sales made this year, but expected to be returned next year?
   (a) Merchandise Inventory
   (b) Customer Refunds Payable
   (c) Sales
   (d) Sales Returns and Allowances

2. **LO1**   Under the periodic inventory system, what account is debited when an estimate is made for sales made this year, but expected to be returned next year?
   (a) Sales Returns and Allowances
   (b) Merchandise Inventory
   (c) Customer Refunds Payable
   (d) Sales

3. **LO1**   Under the periodic inventory system, what account is debited when an estimate is made for the cost of merchandise inventory sold this year, but expected to be returned next year?
(a) Estimated Returns Inventory
(b) Sales Returns and Allowances
(c) Merchandise Inventory
(d) Customer Refunds Payable

4. **LO2**   Unearned revenue is classified as what type of account?
(a) Asset
(b) Liability
(c) Owner's Equity
(d) Revenue
(e) Expense

5. **LO5**   Under the perpetual inventory method, what account is credited when adjusting for the estimated cost of the merchandise sold this period, but expected to be returned next period?
(a) Merchandise Inventory
(b) Cost of Goods Sold
(c) Customer Refunds Payable
(d) Sales Returns and Allowances

Checkpoint Exercises

CHECKPOINT ✔

1. **LO1**   Prepare the cost of goods sold section for Joseph's Gift Shop. The following amounts are known:

Beginning merchandise inventory	$ 20,000
Ending merchandise inventory	15,000
Purchases	171,000

2. **LO2**   The Venice Theatre sold and collected cash of $45,000 for season tickets. Upon collection of cash, Unearned Ticket Revenue was credited. At the end of the accounting period, $15,000 had been earned. Make the appropriate adjusting entry.

3. **LO3**   Information relating to inventory for Janie Par Gifts is provided below.

Beginning merchandise inventory	$120,000
Ending merchandise inventory	90,000
Purchases	250,000

1. Set up a spreadsheet similar to the one provided below.

2. Enter the appropriate information from above into the Trial Balance columns.

3. Prepare appropriate adjustments and extensions to the Adjusted Trial Balance columns.

	A	B	C	D	E	F	G
1	ACCOUNT TITLE	TRIAL BALANCE		ADJUSTMENTS		ADJUSTED TRIAL BALANCE	
2		DEBIT	CREDIT	DEBIT	CREDIT	DEBIT	CREDIT
3	Merchandise Inventory						
4	Income Summary						
5	Purchases						
6							

4. **LO4**   Using the spreadsheet provided below, prepare the adjusting entries for merchandise inventory.

▲	A	B	C	D	E	F	G
1	ACCOUNT TITLE	TRIAL BALANCE			ADJUSTMENTS		
2		DEBIT	CREDIT		DEBIT		CREDIT
3	Merchandise Inventory	50,000.00		(b)	60,000.00	(a)	50,000.00
4	Income Summary			(a)	50,000.00	(b)	60,000.00
5	Purchases	80,000.00					
6							

5. **LO5**   The following information is provided by Koffi Products:

Ending balance of merchandise inventory account	$50,000
Physical count of ending merchandise inventory	48,000

Prepare the appropriate adjusting entry under the perpetual inventory system.

The answers to the Self-Study Test Questions are at the end of the chapter (page 562).

APPLYING YOUR KNOWLEDGE

REVIEW QUESTIONS

CengageNowv2 provides "Show Me How" videos for selected exercises and problems. Additional resources, such as Excel templates for completing selected exercises and problems, are available for download from the companion website at Cengage.com.

LO1   1.   A firm is preparing to make adjusting entries at the end of the accounting period. The balance of the merchandise inventory account is $200,000. If the firm is using the periodic inventory system, what does this balance represent?

LO1   2.   What spreadsheet amounts are used to compute cost of goods sold?

LO1   3.   Why are both the debit and credit amounts in the Adjustments columns on the Income Summary line of the spreadsheet extended to the Adjusted Trial Balance columns?

LO2   4.   What is an unearned revenue?

LO2   5.   Give three examples of unearned revenue.

LO3   6.   List the four steps taken to prepare an end-of-period spreadsheet.

LO1/5   7.   Why is it important to make end-of-period adjustments for merchandise sold this year, but expected to be returned next period?

LO5   8.   A firm is preparing to make adjusting entries at the end of the accounting period. The balance of the merchandise inventory account is $100,000. If the firm is using the perpetual inventory system, what does this balance represent?

SERIES A EXERCISES

E 14-1A **(LO1)**

ADJUSTMENT FOR MERCHANDISE INVENTORY USING T ACCOUNTS: PERIODIC INVENTORY SYSTEM Ibby Smith owns and operates Ibby's Ice Cream Cones. Her beginning inventory as of January 1, 20--, was $45,000, and her ending inventory as of December 31, 20--, was $57,000. Set up T accounts for Merchandise Inventory and Income Summary and perform the year-end adjustment for Merchandise Inventory.

E 14-2A **(LO1)**
✓ Sales R&A end bal.: $21,000

ADJUSTMENT FOR MERCHANDISE INVENTORY USING T ACCOUNTS: PERIODIC INVENTORY SYSTEM WITH SALES RETURNS AND ALLOWANCES Sam Edwards owns a business called Sam's Stuff. A physical count determined his ending inventory as of December 31, 20-- was $72,000. Based on past experience, Sam estimates that $5,000 of sales from this year will be returned next year. The cost of the merchandise expected to be returned is $3,000. Using the partial Trial Balance provided below, set up T accounts for Merchandise Inventory, Estimated Returns Inventory, Customer Refunds Payable, Sales Returns and Allowances, and Income Summary and prepare the year-end adjustments for Merchandise Inventory and related accounts.

	A	B	C
1		TRIAL BALANCE	
2		(PARTIAL)	
3	Merchandise Inventory	60,000.00	
4	Estimated Returns Inventory	2,500.00	
6	Customer Refunds Payable		4,000.00
7	Sales Returns and Allowances	20,000.00	
8	Income Summary		
9			

E-14-3A **(LO1)**
✓ Cost of goods sold: $73,450

CALCULATION OF COST OF GOODS SOLD: PERIODIC INVENTORY SYSTEM Prepare the cost of goods sold section for Adams Gift Shop. The following amounts are known:

Beginning merchandise inventory	$27,000
Ending merchandise inventory	22,000
Purchases	78,000
Purchases returns and allowances	3,900
Purchases discounts	6,000
Freight-in	350

E 14-4A **(LO1)**
✓ Cost of goods sold: $73,850

CALCULATION OF COST OF GOODS SOLD: PERIODIC INVENTORY SYSTEM WITH SALES RETURNS AND ALLOWANCES Use the same information as provided in Exercise 14-3A, but assume the business makes estimates for sales returns and allowances at year-end. The balances for estimated returns inventory are provided below. Prepare the cost of goods sold section of the income statement.

Beginning estimated returns inventory	$2,000
Ending estimated returns inventory	1,600

CHAPTER 14   Applying Your Knowledge   **549**

E 14-5A   (LO2)

ADJUSTMENT FOR UNEARNED REVENUES USING T ACCOUNTS Set up T accounts for Cash, Unearned Ticket Revenue, and Ticket Revenue. Post the following two transactions to the appropriate accounts, indicating each transaction by letter:

(a) Sold 1,200 season tickets at $400 each, receiving cash of $480,000.

(b) An end-of-period adjustment is needed to recognize that $120,000 in ticket revenue has been earned.

E 14-6A   (LO3)
✓ Cost of goods sold: $188, 900

MERCHANDISE INVENTORY ADJUSTMENTS: PERIODIC INVENTORY SYSTEM WITH SALES RETURNS AND ALLOWANCES Use the information provided below to prepare a partial end-of-period spreadsheet for Karen's Gift Shop for the year ended December 31, 20--. The ending merchandise inventory is $60,000. Karen estimates that customers will be granted $15,000 in refunds next year for merchandise sold this year. The estimated cost of the returned inventory is $10,000.

	A	B	C
1	Karen's Gift Shop		
2	Partial Trial Balance		
3	For Year Ended December 31, 20--		
4	ACCOUNT TITLE	DEBIT BALANCE	CREDIT BALANCE
5			
6	Merchandise Inventory	55,000.00	
7	Estimated Returns Inventory	8,000.00	
8	Customer Refunds Payable		12,000.00
9	Income Summary		
10			
11	Sales		280,000.00
12	Sales Returns and Allowances	18,000.00	
13	Purchases	200,000.00	
14	Purchases Returns and Allowances		3,000.00
15	Purchases Discounts		2,500.00
16	Freight-In	1,400.00	
17			

1. Complete the Adjustments columns for Merchandise Inventory and related accounts.

2. Extend all accounts to the Adjusted Trial Balance columns.

3. Prepare the cost of goods sold section from the spreadsheet.

E 14-7A   (LO3)
✓ Beg. inv.: $60,500

DETERMINING THE BEGINNING AND ENDING INVENTORY FROM A PARTIAL SPREADSHEET: PERIODIC INVENTORY SYSTEM From the following partial spreadsheet, indicate the dollar amount of beginning and ending merchandise inventory to be used to compute cost of goods sold.

	A	B	C	D	E
1	ACCOUNT TITLE	ADJUSTMENTS		ADJUSTED TRIAL BALANCE	
2		DEBIT	CREDIT	DEBIT	CREDIT
3	Merchandise Inventory	60,000.00	55,000.00	60,000.00	
4	Estimated Returns Inventory	6,000.00	5,500.00	6,000.00	
5	Supplies		4,700.00	3,300.00	
6	Prepaid Insurance		1,600.00	3,800.00	
7	Customer Refunds Payable		2,200.00		7,200.00
8	Income Summary	55,000.00	60,000.00	55,000.00	60,000.00
9		5,500.00	6,000.00	5,500.00	6,000.00
10	Sales				525,140.00
11	Sales Returns and Allowances	2,200.00		16,700.00	
12					

E 14-8A   (LO4)

✓ (a)

  Inc. Sum.   45,000

    Mdse. Inv.   45,000

JOURNALIZE ADJUSTING ENTRIES FOR A MERCHANDISING BUSINESS The following partial spreadsheet is taken from the books of Vinnie's Vegetable Market, for the year ended December 31, 20--. Journalize the adjustments in a general journal.

◢	A	B	C	D	E	F	G
1	Vinnie's Vegetable Market						
2	End-of-Period Spreadsheet (Partial)						
3	For Year Ended December 31, 20--						
4	ACCOUNT TITLE	TRIAL BALANCE			ADJUSTMENTS		
5		DEBIT	CREDIT		DEBIT		CREDIT
6	Merchandise Inventory	45,000.00		(b)	50,000.00	(a)	45,000.00
7	Supplies	10,000.00				(d)	7,000.00
8	Building	60,000.00					
9	Accum. Depr.—Building		15,000.00			(e)	5,000.00
10	Wages Payable					(f)	1,200.00
11	Unearned Membership Fees		3,000.00	(c)	2,000.00		
12	Income Summary			(a)	45,000.00	(b)	50,000.00
13	Membership Fees		20,000.00			(c)	2,000.00
14	Wages Expense	37,000.00		(f)	1,200.00		
15	Supplies Expense			(d)	7,000.00		
16	Depr. Expense—Building			(e)	5,000.00		
17					110,200.00		110,200.00
18							

E 14-9A   (LO5)

JOURNAL ENTRIES UNDER THE PERPETUAL INVENTORY SYSTEM Bhushan Building Supplies entered into the following transactions. Prepare journal entries under the perpetual inventory system.

June 1   Purchased merchandise on account from Brij Builder's Materials, $500,000.

     3   Purchased merchandise for cash, $400,000.

     5   Sold merchandise on account to Champa Construction for $20,000. The merchandise cost $15,000.

E 14-10A   (LO5)

✓ Cost of goods sold: $282,600

ADJUSTMENTS FOR A MERCHANDISING BUSINESS: PERPETUAL INVENTORY SYSTEM WITH SALES RETURNS AND ALLOWANCES A partial Trial Balance for Curless Company as of December 31, 20-- is provided below.

◢	A	B	C
1	Curless Company		
2	Partial Trial Balance		
3	For Year Ended December 31, 20--		
4	ACCOUNT TITLE	DEBIT BALANCE	CREDIT BALANCE
5			
6	Merchandise Inventory	150,000.00	
7	Estimated Returns Inventory	500.00	
8	Customer Refunds Payable		650.00
9	Sales		425,000.00
10	Sales Returns and Allowances	18,000.00	
11	Cost of Goods Sold	288,000.00	
12			

Curless has made the following estimates for next year:

1. Sales made this year of $7,800 will be returned next year and customers will be granted full refunds.

2. The estimated cost of the inventory sold this year and expected to be returned by customers next year is $5,900.

Open T accounts and enter the balances for the above accounts. Make appropriate adjustments to the T accounts.

E 14-11A   (LO5)   JOURNALIZE ADJUSTING ENTRY FOR INVENTORY SHRINKAGE: PERPETUAL INVENTORY SYSTEM On December 31, Anup Enterprises completed a physical count of its inventory. Although the merchandise inventory account shows a balance of $350,000, the physical count comes to $325,000. Prepare the appropriate adjusting entry under the perpetual inventory system.

SERIES A PROBLEMS

P 14-12A   (LO1/2/3/4)
✓ Adj. col. total: $201,400
✓ Adj. Trial Bal. total: $1,093,050

PREPARATION OF ADJUSTMENTS ON A SPREADSHEET FOR A MERCHANDIS-ING BUSINESS: PERIODIC METHOD The trial balance for the Venice Beach Kite Shop, a business owned by Molly Young is shown on page 552. Year-end adjustment information is as follows:

(a, b)   A physical count shows that merchandise inventory costing $85,000 is on hand as of December 31, 20--.

(c, d, e)   Young estimates that customers will be granted $5,700 in refunds of this year's sales next year and the merchandise expected to be returned will have a cost of $4,300.

(f)   Supplies remaining at the end of the year, $3,300.

(g)   Unexpired insurance on December 31, $3,800.

(h)   Depreciation expense on the building for 20--, $12,500.

(i)   Depreciation expense on the store equipment for 20--, $5,000.

(j)   Unearned rent revenue as of December 31, $4,500.

(k)   Wages earned but not paid as of December 31, $3,500.

REQUIRED

1. Complete the Adjustments columns, identifying each adjustment with its corresponding letter.

2. Complete the spreadsheet.

3. Enter the adjustments in a general journal.

(*continued*)

◢	A	B	C
1	**Venice Beach Kite Shop**		
2	**Trial Balance**		
3	**For the Year Ended December 31, 20--**		
4	ACCOUNT TITLE	DEBIT BALANCE	CREDIT BALANCE
5			
6	Cash	20,000.00	
7	Accounts Receivable	14,000.00	
8	Merchandise Inventory	75,000.00	
9	Estimated Returns Inventory	3,200.00	
10	Supplies	8,000.00	
11	Prepaid Insurance	5,400.00	
12	Land	130,000.00	
13	Building	250,000.00	
14	Accumulated Depreciation—Building		100,000.00
15	Store Equipment	100,000.00	
16	Accumulated Depreciation—Equipment		40,000.00
17	Accounts Payable		9,600.00
18	Customer Refunds Payable		3,500.00
19	Wages Payable		
20	Sales Tax Payable		5,900.00
21	Unearned Rent Revenue		8,900.00
22	M. Young, Capital		284,310.00
23	M. Young, Drawing	26,000.00	
24	Income Summary		
25			
26	Sales		525,140.00
27	Sales Returns and Allowances	14,500.00	
28	Rent Revenue		
29	Purchases	125,000.00	
30	Purchases Returns and Allowances		1,400.00
31	Purchases Discounts		1,800.00
32	Freight-In	2,100.00	
33	Wages Expense	125,000.00	
34	Advertising Expense	13,000.00	
35	Supplies Expense		
36	Phone Expense	1,350.00	
37	Utilities Expense	8,000.00	
38	Insurance Expense		
39	Depreciation Expense—Building		
40	Depreciation Expense—Equipment		
41	Rent Expense	60,000.00	
42		980,550.00	980,550.00
43			

P 14-13A   (LO1/2/4)
✓ Adj. col. total: $221,540

WORKING BACKWARD FROM ADJUSTED TRIAL BALANCE TO DETERMINE ADJUSTING ENTRIES The partial spreadsheet shown below is taken from the books of Sunstate Computer Supply, a business owned by Michelle Thibeault, for the year ended December 31, 20--. Sunstate is on the periodic inventory system.

REQUIRED

1. Determine the adjusting entries by analyzing the difference between the adjusted trial balance and the trial balance.
2. Journalize the adjusting entries in a general journal.

	A	B	C	D	E	F	G
1		Sunstate Computer Supply					
2		End-of-Period Spreadsheet					
3		For the Year Ended December 31, 20--					
4	ACCOUNT TITLE	TRIAL BALANCE		ADJUSTMENTS		ADJUSTED TRIAL BALANCE	
5		DEBIT	CREDIT	DEBIT	CREDIT	DEBIT	CREDIT
6	Cash	22,000.00				22,000.00	
7	Accounts Receivable	15,400.00				15,400.00	
8	Merchandise Inventory	82,500.00				93,500.00	
9	Estimated Returns Inventory	3,520.00				4,730.00	
10	Supplies	8,800.00				3,630.00	
11	Prepaid Insurance	5,940.00				4,180.00	
12	Land	143,000.00				143,000.00	
13	Building	275,000.00				275,000.00	
14	Accum. Depr.—Building		110,000.00				123,750.00
15	Store Equipment	110,000.00				110,000.00	
16	Accum. Depr.—Store Equipment		44,000.00				49,500.00
17	Accounts Payable		10,560.00				10,560.00
18	Customer Refunds Payable		3,850.00				6,270.00
19	Wages Payable						3,850.00
20	Sales Tax Payable		6,490.00				6,490.00
21	Unearned Rent Revenue		9,790.00				4,950.00
22	M. Thibeault, Capital		312,741.00				312,741.00
23	M. Thibeault, Drawing	28,600.00				28,600.00	
24	Income Summary					82,500.00	93,500.00
25						3,520.00	4,730.00
26	Sales		577,654.00				577,654.00
27	Sales Returns and Allowances	15,950.00				18,370.00	
28	Rent Revenue						4,840.00
29	Purchases	137,500.00				137,500.00	
30	Purchases Returns and Allowances		1,540.00				1,540.00
31	Purchases Discounts		1,980.00				1,980.00
32	Freight-In	2,310.00				2,310.00	
33	Wages Expense	137,500.00				141,350.00	
34	Advertising Expense	14,300.00				14,300.00	
35	Supplies Expense					5,170.00	
36	Phone Expense	1,485.00				1,485.00	
37	Utilities Expense	8,800.00				8,800.00	
38	Insurance Expense					1,760.00	
39	Depr. Expense—Building					13,750.00	
40	Depr. Expense—Store Equipment					5,500.00	
41	Rent Expense	66,000.00				66,000.00	
42		1078,605.00	1078,605.00			1202,355.00	1202,355.00
43		STEP 1		STEP 2		STEP 3	
44	STEP 4					502,315.00	684,244.00
45	Net Income					181,929.00	
46							

SERIES B EXERCISES

E 14-1B (LO1)

ADJUSTMENT FOR MERCHANDISE INVENTORY USING T ACCOUNTS: PERIODIC INVENTORY SYSTEM Doran May owns and operates the Chocolate Moose Ice Cream stand. His beginning inventory as of January 1, 20--, was $33,000, and his ending inventory as of December 31, 20--, was $36,000. Set up T accounts for Merchandise Inventory and Income Summary and perform the year-end adjustment for Merchandise Inventory.

E 14-2B (LO1)
✓ Sales R&A end bal.: $16,500

ADJUSTMENT FOR MERCHANDISE INVENTORY USING T ACCOUNTS: PERIODIC INVENTORY SYSTEM WITH SALES RETURNS AND ALLOWANCES Ronica Kluge owns a business called Roni's Rummage. A physical count determined the ending inventory as of December 31, 20-- was $80,000. Based on past experience, Roni estimates that $6,000 of sales from this year will be refunded next year. The cost of the merchandise expected to be returned is $4,000. Using the partial Trial Balance provided below, set up T accounts for Merchandise Inventory, Estimated Returns Inventory, Customer Refunds Payable, Sales Returns and Allowances, and Income Summary and prepare the year-end adjustments for Merchandise Inventory and related accounts.

	A	B	C
1			
2		TRIAL BALANCE	
3	Merchandise Inventory	75,000.00	
4	Estimated Returns Inventory	3,000.00	
5	Customer Refunds Payable		4,500.00
6	Sales Returns and Allowances	15,000.00	
7	Income Summary		
8			

E 14-3B (LO1)
✓ Cost of goods sold: $58,100

CALCULATION OF COST OF GOODS SOLD: PERIODIC INVENTORY SYSTEM Prepare the cost of goods sold section for Havens Gift Shop. The following amounts are known:

Beginning merchandise inventory	$29,000
Ending merchandise inventory	27,000
Purchases	62,000
Purchases returns and allowances	2,800
Purchases discounts	3,400
Freight-in	300

E 14-4B (LO1)
✓ Cost of goods sold: $57,200

CALCULATION OF COST OF GOODS SOLD: PERIODIC INVENTORY SYSTEM WITH SALES RETURNS AND ALLOWANCES Use the same information as provided in Exercise 14-3B, but assume the business makes estimates for sales returns and allowances at year end. The balances for estimated returns inventory are provided below. Prepare the cost of goods sold section of the income statement.

Beginning estimated returns inventory	$2,600
Ending estimated returns inventory	3,500

E 14-5B   (LO2)

ADJUSTMENT FOR UNEARNED REVENUES USING T ACCOUNTS Set up T accounts for Cash, Unearned Ticket Revenue, and Ticket Revenue. Post the following two transactions to the appropriate accounts, indicating each transaction by letter:

(a) Sold 1,200 season tickets at $20 each, receiving cash of $24,000.

(b) An end-of-period adjustment is needed to recognize that $19,000 in ticket revenue has been earned.

E 14-6B   (LO3)
✓ Cost of goods sold: $112,400

MERCHANDISE INVENTORY ADJUSTMENTS: PERIODIC INVENTORY SYSTEM WITH SALES RETURNS AND ALLOWANCES Use the information provided below to prepare a partial end-of-period spreadsheet for Nick's Gift Shop for the year ended December 31, 20--. The ending merchandise inventory is $45,000. Nick estimates that customers will be granted $5,500, in refunds next year for merchandise sold this year. The estimated cost of the returned inventory is $3,500.

	A	B	C
1	Nick's Gift Shop		
2	Partial Trial Balance		
3	For Year Ended December 31, 20--		
4	ACCOUNT TITLE	DEBIT BALANCE	CREDIT BALANCE
5			
6	Merchandise Inventory	40,000.00	
7	Estimated Returns Inventory	2,500.00	
8	Customer Refunds Payable		5,000.00
9	Income Summary		
10			
11	Sales		175,000.00
12	Sales Returns and Allowances	13,000.00	
13	Purchases	120,000.00	
14	Purchases Returns and Allowances		1,400.00
15	Purchases Discounts		1,000.00
16	Freight-In	800.00	
17			

1. Complete the Adjustments columns for Merchandise Inventory and related accounts.
2. Extend all accounts to the Adjusted Trial Balance columns.
3. Prepare the cost of goods sold section from the spreadsheet.

E 14-7B   (LO3)
✓ Beg.inv.: $49,000

DETERMINING THE BEGINNING AND ENDING INVENTORY FROM A PARTIAL SPREADSHEET: PERIODIC INVENTORY SYSTEM From the following partial spreadsheet, indicate the dollar amount of beginning and ending merchandise inventory to be used to compute cost of goods sold.

	A	B	C	D	E
1	ACCOUNT TITLE	ADJUSTMENTS		ADJUSTED TRIAL BALANCE	
2		DEBIT	CREDIT	DEBIT	CREDIT
3	Merchandise Inventory	40,000.00	45,000.00	40,000.00	
4	Estimated Returns Inventory	5,000.00	4,000.00	5,000.00	
5	Supplies		4,700.00	3,300.00	
6	Prepaid Insurance		1,600.00	3,800.00	
7	Customer Refunds Payable		2,200.00		6,000.00
8	Income Summary	45,000.00	40,000.00	45,000.00	40,000.00
9		4,000.00	5,000.00	4,000.00	5,000.00
10	Sales				525,140.00
11	Sales Returns and Allowances	2,200.00		16,700.00	
12					

E 14-8B **(LO4)**

✓ (b)

Mdse. Inv.	30,000	
Inc. Sum.		30,000

JOURNALIZE ADJUSTING ENTRIES FOR A MERCHANDISING BUSINESS The following partial spreadsheet is taken from the books of the Venice Vegetable Market, for the year ended December 31, 20--. Journalize the adjustments in a general journal.

	A	B	C	D	E	F	G
1	Venice Vegetable Market						
2	Spreadsheet (Partial)						
3	For Year Ended December 31, 20--						
4	ACCOUNT TITLE	TRIAL BALANCE			ADJUSTMENTS		
5		DEBIT	CREDIT		DEBIT		CREDIT
6	Merchandise Inventory	35,000.00		(b)	30,000.00	(a)	35,000.00
7	Supplies	4,500.00				(d)	3,100.00
8	Building	50,000.00					
9	Accum. Depr.—Building		23,000.00			(e)	6,000.00
10	Wages Payable					(f)	1,300.00
11	Unearned Membership Revenue		7,000.00	(c)	5,500.00		
12	Income Summary			(a)	35,000.00	(b)	30,000.00
13	Membership Revenue		24,000.00			(c)	5,500.00
14	Wages Expense	41,000.00		(f)	1,300.00		
15	Supplies Expense			(d)	3,100.00		
16	Depr. Expense—Building			(e)	6,000.00		
17					80,900.00		80,900.00
18							

E 14-9B **(LO5)**

JOURNAL ENTRIES UNDER THE PERPETUAL INVENTORY SYSTEM Sunita Computer Supplies entered into the following transactions. Prepare journal entries under the perpetual inventory system.

May 1 Purchased merchandise on account from Anju Enterprises, $200,000.

8 Purchased merchandise for cash, $100,000.

15 Sold merchandise on account to Salil's Pharmacy for $8,000. The merchandise cost $5,000.

E 14-10B **(LO5)**

✓ Sales R&A end. bal.: $24,400

ADJUSTMENTS FOR A MERCHANDISING BUSINESS: PERPETUAL INVENTORY SYSTEM WITH SALES RETURNS AND ALLOWANCES A partial Trial Balance for Coleman Company as of December 31, 20-- is provided below.

	A	B	C
1	Coleman Company		
2	Partial Trial Balance		
3	For Year Ended December 31, 20--		
4	ACCOUNT TITLE	DEBIT BALANCE	CREDIT BALANCE
5			
6	Merchandise Inventory	165,000.00	
7	Estimated Returns Inventory	600.00	
8	Customer Refunds Payable		825.00
9	Sales		450,000.00
10	Sales Returns and Allowances	16,000.00	
11	Cost of Goods Sold	255,000.00	
12			

Coleman has made the following estimates for next year:

1. Sales made this year of $8,800 will be returned next year and customers will be granted full refunds.

2. The estimated cost of the inventory sold this year and expected to be returned by customers next year is $6,400.

Open T accounts and enter the balances for the above accounts. Make appropriate adjustments to the T accounts.

E 14-11B   (LO5)   JOURNALIZE ADJUSTING ENTRY FOR INVENTORY SHRINKAGE: PERPETUAL INVENTORY SYSTEM On December 31, Anup Enterprises completed a physical count of its inventory. Although the merchandise inventory account shows a balance of $200,000, the physical count comes to $210,000. Prepare the appropriate adjusting entry under the perpetual inventory system.

SERIES B PROBLEMS

P 14-12B   (LO1/2/3/4)
✓ Adj. col. total: $241,680
✓ Adj. Trial Bal. total: $1,311,660

PREPARATION OF ADJUSTMENTS ON A SPREADSHEET FOR A MERCHANDISING BUSINESS: PERIODIC METHOD The trial balance for the Basket Corner, a business owned by Linda Palermo is shown on page 558. Year-end adjustment information is as follows:

(a, b)   A physical count shows that merchandise inventory costing $102,000 is on hand as of December 31, 20--.

(c, d, e)   Palermo estimates that customers will be granted $6,840 in refunds of this year's sales next year and the merchandise expected to be returned will have a cost of $5,160.

(f)   Supplies remaining at the end of the year, $3,960.

(g)   Unexpired insurance on December 31, $4,560.

(h)   Depreciation expense on the building for 20--, $15,000.

(i)   Depreciation expense on the store equipment for 20--, $6,000.

(j)   Unearned rent revenue as of December 31, $5,400.

(k)   Wages earned but not paid as of December 31, $4,200.

REQUIRED

1. Complete the Adjustments columns, identifying each adjustment with its corresponding letter.

2. Complete the spreadsheet.

3. Enter the adjustments in a general journal.

(continued)

◢	A	B	C
1	**Basket Corner**		
2	**Trial Balance**		
3	**For the Year Ended December 31, 20--**		
4	ACCOUNT TITLE	DEBIT BALANCE	CREDIT BALANCE
5			
6	Cash	24,000.00	
7	Accounts Receivable	16,800.00	
8	Merchandise Inventory	90,000.00	
9	Estimated Returns Inventory	3,840.00	
10	Supplies	9,600.00	
11	Prepaid Insurance	6,480.00	
12	Land	156,000.00	
13	Building	300,000.00	
14	Accumulated Depreciation—Building		120,000.00
15	Store Equipment	120,000.00	
16	Accumulated Depreciation—Store Equipment		48,000.00
17	Accounts Payable		11,520.00
18	Customer Refunds Payable		4,200.00
19	Wages Payable		
20	Sales Tax Payable		7,080.00
21	Unearned Rent Revenue		10,680.00
22	L. Palermo, Capital		341,172.00
23	L. Palermo, Drawing	31,200.00	
24	Income Summary		
25			
26	Sales		630,168.00
27	Sales Returns and Allowances	17,400.00	
28	Rent Revenue		
29	Purchases	150,000.00	
30	Purchases Returns and Allowances		1,680.00
31	Purchases Discounts		2,160.00
32	Freight-In	2,520.00	
33	Wages Expense	150,000.00	
34	Advertising Expense	15,600.00	
35	Supplies Expense		
36	Phone Expense	1,620.00	
37	Utilities Expense	9,600.00	
38	Insurance Expense		
39	Depreciation Expense—Building		
40	Depreciation Expense—Store Equipment		
41	Rent Expense	72,000.00	
42		1,176,660.00	1,176,660.00
43			

P 14-13B (LO1/2/4)
✓ Adj. col. total: $261,820

WORKING BACKWARD FROM ADJUSTED TRIAL BALANCE TO DETERMINE ADJUSTING ENTRIES The partial spreadsheet shown below is taken from the books of Albers Pet Supply, a business owned by Carm Albers, for the year ended December 31, 20--. Albers is on the periodic inventory system.

REQUIRED

1. Determine the adjusting entries by analyzing the difference between the adjusted trial balance and the trial balance.
2. Journalize the adjusting entries in a general journal.

	A	B	C	D	E	F	G
1		Albers Pet Supply					
2		End-of-Period Spreadsheet					
3		For the Year Ended December 31, 20--					
4	ACCOUNT TITLE	TRIAL BALANCE		ADJUSTMENTS		ADJUSTED TRIAL BALANCE	
5		DEBIT	CREDIT	DEBIT	CREDIT	DEBIT	CREDIT
6	Cash	26,000.00				26,000.00	
7	Accounts Receivable	18,200.00				18,200.00	
8	Merchandise Inventory	97,500.00				110,500.00	
9	Estimated Returns Inventory	4,160.00				5,590.00	
10	Supplies	10,400.00				4,290.00	
11	Prepaid Insurance	7,020.00				4,940.00	
12	Land	169,000.00				169,000.00	
13	Building	325,000.00				325,000.00	
14	Accum. Depr.—Building		130,000.00				146,250.00
15	Store Equipment	130,000.00				130,000.00	
16	Accum. Depr.—Store Equipment		52,000.00				58,500.00
17	Accounts Payable		12,480.00				12,480.00
18	Customer Refunds Payable		4,550.00				7,410.00
19	Wages Payable						4,550.00
20	Sales Tax Payable		7,670.00				7,670.00
21	Unearned Rent Revenue		11,570.00				5,850.00
22	C. Albers, Capital		369,603.00				369,603.00
23	C. Albers, Drawing	33,800.00				33,800.00	
24	Income Summary					97,500.00	110,500.00
25						4,160.00	5,590.00
26	Sales		682,682.00				682,682.00
27	Sales Returns and Allowances	18,850.00				21,710.00	
28	Rent Revenue						5,720.00
29	Purchases	162,500.00				162,500.00	
30	Purchases Returns and Allowances		1,820.00				1,820.00
31	Purchases Discounts		2,340.00				2,340.00
32	Freight-In	2,730.00				2,730.00	
33	Wages Expense	162,500.00				167,050.00	
34	Advertising Expense	16,900.00				16,900.00	
35	Supplies Expense					6,110.00	
36	Phone Expense	1,755.00				1,755.00	
37	Utilities Expense	10,400.00				10,400.00	
38	Insurance Expense					2,080.00	
39	Depr. Expense—Building					16,250.00	
40	Depr. Expense—Store Equipment					6,500.00	
41	Rent Expense	78,000.00				78,000.00	
42		1,274,715.00	1,274,715.00			1,420,965.00	1,420,965.00
43						593,645.00	808,652.00
44	Net Income					215,007.00	
45							

MANAGING YOUR WRITING

A friend of yours recently opened Abracadabra, a sportswear shop specializing in mono-grammed athletic gear. Most merchandise is special ordered for customers. However, a small inventory is on hand. Your friend does not understand why a physical inventory is necessary before preparing the financial statements. She knows how much she paid for all merchandise purchased. Why not simply use this amount for cost of goods sold? After all, it has been paid for. Write a brief memo explaining the purpose of the physical inventory and why she should not use the cost of purchases as cost of goods sold.

ETHICS

ETHICS CASE

Jason Tierro, an inventory clerk at Lexmar Company, is responsible for taking a physical count of the goods on hand at the end of the year. He has been performing this duty for several years. This year, Jason was very busy due to a shortage of personnel at the company, so he decided to just estimate the amount of ending inventory instead of doing an accurate count. He reasoned that he could come very close to the true amount because of his past experience working with inventory. Besides, he was sure that the sophisticated computer program that Lexmar had just invested in kept an accurate record of inventory on hand.

1. What is your opinion of Jason's reasoning?
2. If Jason underestimates the dollar amount of ending inventory, what effect will it have on net income for the current accounting period?
3. Write a short paragraph explaining why a physical inventory should be taken at least once a year.
4. In groups of three or four, make a list of possible reasons that the actual ending inventory might not agree with the ending inventory according to a computer system.

MASTERY PROBLEM

✓ Adj. Trial Bal. total: $153,800
✓ Cost of goods sold: $159,475

John Neff owns and operates Waikiki Surf Shop. A year-end trial balance is provided on page 561. Year-end adjustment data for the Waikiki Surf Shop are shown below. Neff uses the periodic inventory system. Year-end adjustment data are as follows:

(a, b)   A physical count shows that merchandise inventory costing $51,800 is on hand as of December 31, 20--.
(c, d, e)   Neff estimates that customers will be granted $2,000 in refunds of this year's sales next year and the merchandise expected to be returned will have a cost of $1,200.
(f)   Supplies remaining at the end of the year, $600.
(g)   Unexpired insurance on December 31, $2,600.
(h)   Depreciation expense on the building for 20--, $5,000.
(i)   Depreciation expense on the store equipment for 20--, $3,000.
(j)   Wages earned but not paid as of December 31, $1,800.
(k)   Neff also offers boat rentals which clients pay for in advance. Unearned boat rental revenue as of December 31 is $3,000.

REQUIRED

1. Prepare a year-end spreadsheet.
2. Journalize the adjusting entries.
3. Compute cost of goods sold using the spreadsheet prepared for part (1).

	A	B	C
1	**Waikiki Surf Shop**		
2	**Trial Balance**		
3	**For the Year Ended December 31, 20--**		
4	ACCOUNT TITLE	DEBIT BALANCE	CREDIT BALANCE
5			
6	Cash	30,000.00	
7	Accounts Receivable	22,500.00	
8	Merchandise Inventory	56,200.00	
9	Estimated Returns Inventory	800.00	
10	Supplies	2,700.00	
11	Prepaid Insurance	3,600.00	
12	Land	115,000.00	
13	Building	135,000.00	
14	Accumulated Depreciation—Building		24,000.00
15	Store Equipment	75,000.00	
16	Accumulated Depreciation—Store Equipment		22,500.00
17	Accounts Payable		15,000.00
18	Customer Refunds Payable		1,100.00
19	Wages Payable		
20	Unearned Boat Rent Revenue		33,000.00
21	J. Neff, Capital		240,100.00
22	J. Neff, Drawing	40,875.00	
23	Income Summary		
24			
25	Sales		404,950.00
26	Sales Returns and Allowances	6,000.00	
27	Boat Rental Revenue		
28	Purchases	157,500.00	
29	Purchases Returns and Allowances		1,200.00
30	Purchases Discounts		1,500.00
31	Freight-In	675.00	
32	Wages Expense	63,000.00	
33	Advertising Expense	11,250.00	
34	Supplies Expense		
35	Phone Expense	5,250.00	
36	Utilities Expense	18,000.00	
37	Insurance Expense		
38	Depreciation Expense—Building		
39	Depreciation Expense—Equipment		
40		743,350.00	743,350.00
41			

CHALLENGE PROBLEM

> This problem challenges you to apply your cumulative accounting knowledge to move a step beyond the material in the chapter.

Block Foods, a retail grocery store, has agreed to purchase all of its merchandise from Square Wholesalers. In return, Block receives a special discount on purchases. Over recent months, Square noticed that purchases by Block had been falling off. At first, Square simply thought that business might be down for Block and was hopeful that their purchases would pick up. When business with Block did not return to a normal level, Square requested financial statements from Block. Square's records indicate that Block purchased $300,000 worth of merchandise during 20-1, the most recent year.

✓ Net purchases in 20-1: $410,000

(*continued*)

Selected information taken from Block's financial statements is as follows:

Balance Sheet	12/31/-1	12/31/-0
Inventory	$30,000	$20,000

Income Statement		
Cost of goods sold	$400,000	

REQUIRED

Compute net purchases made by Block during 20-1. Does it appear that Block violated the agreement?

ANSWERS TO SELF-STUDY TEST QUESTIONS

True/False

1. T   **2.** T   **3.** T   **4.** F (revenue is recognized)   **5.** F (contra-revenue account)

Multiple Choice

1. b   **2.** a   **3.** a   **4.** b   **5.** b

Checkpoint Exercises

1.
Beginning merchandise inventory	$ 20,000
Purchases	171,000
Goods available for sale	$191,000
Less ending inventory	15,000
Cost of goods sold	$176,000

2.
Unearned Ticket Revenue	15,000	
Ticket Revenue		15,000

3.

	A	B	C	D	E	F	G
1	ACCOUNT TITLE	TRIAL BALANCE		ADJUSTMENTS		ADJUSTED TRIAL BALANCE	
2		DEBIT	CREDIT	DEBIT	CREDIT	DEBIT	CREDIT
3	Merchandise Inventory	120,000.00		(b) 90,000.00	(a) 120,000.00	90,000.00	
4	Income Summary			(a) 120,000.00	(b) 90,000.00	120,000.00	90,000.00
5	Purchases	250,000.00				250,000.00	
6							
7							
8							

4.

10	Income Summary	50 0 0 0 00			10
11	Merchandise Inventory		50 0 0 0 00		11
12	Merchandise Inventory	60 0 0 0 00			12
13	Income Summary		60 0 0 0 00		13

5.

8	Inventory Short and Over	2 0 0 0 00			8
9	Merchandise Inventory		2 0 0 0 00		9
10					10

Expense Method of Accounting for Prepaid Expenses

LO1 The Expense Method

Use the expense method of accounting for prepaid expenses.

Under the expense method of accounting for prepaid expenses, supplies and other prepaid items are entered as expenses when purchased. Under this method, we must adjust the accounts at the end of each accounting period to record the unused portions as assets. To illustrate, let's assume that the following entry was made when office supplies were purchased:

4		Office Supplies Expense			4	2	5	00				4
5		Cash							4	2	5	00	5
6		Purchased office supplies											6

In the next section, we will illustrate the proper adjusting entry when using the expense method.

LO2 Adjusting Entries Under the Expense Method

Make the appropriate adjusting entries when the expense method is used for prepaid expenses.

Office Supplies Expense was debited for a total of $425 during the period. An inventory taken at the end of the period shows that supplies on hand amounted to $150. The following adjusting entry is made for supplies on hand:

8		Office Supplies			1	5	0	00				8
9		Office Supplies Expense							1	5	0	00	9
10													10

As shown in the T accounts below, after this entry is posted, the office supplies expense account has a debit balance of $275. This amount is reported on the income statement as an operating expense. The office supplies account has a debit balance of $150. It is reported on the balance sheet as a current asset.

Office Supplies		Office Supplies Expense	
Adj. 150		425	Adj. 150
		Bal. 275	

Let's consider another example of the use of the expense method. The following entry was made for the payment of $6,000 for a three-year insurance policy:

11		Insurance Expense		6	0	0	0	00							11
12		Cash								6	0	0	0	00	12
13		Paid insurance premium													13

At the end of the first year, one-third of the premium has expired and two-thirds remains. Thus, $2,000 for insurance expense should be reported on the income statement and $4,000 in prepaid insurance should be reported on the balance sheet. The following adjusting entry is made:

15		Prepaid Insurance		4	0	0	0	00							15
16		Insurance Expense								4	0	0	0	00	16
17															17

As shown in the T accounts below, after this entry is posted, the prepaid insurance account has a debit balance of $4,000. The insurance expense account has a debit balance of $2,000.

Prepaid Insurance			Insurance Expense	
Adj. 4,000			6,000	
		Bal. 2,000	Adj. 4,000

The asset and expense methods of accounting for prepaid expenses give the same final result. In the asset method, the prepaid item is first debited to an asset account. At the end of each period, the amount consumed is debited to an expense account. In the expense method, the original amount is debited to an expense account. At the end of each accounting period, the portion not consumed is debited to an asset account.

LEARNING OBJECTIVES	**Key Points to Remember**
LO1 Use the expense method of accounting for prepaid expenses.	Under the expense method, an expense account is debited when prepaid items are acquired.
LO2 Make the appropriate adjusting entries when the expense method is used for prepaid expenses.	At the end of the accounting period, an asset must be recognized for the amount of the prepaid item remaining. The expense account must be credited so that the ending balance represents the amount of the item consumed.

KEY TERMS

asset method (564)   Under this method, the acquisition of a prepaid item is debited to an asset account.

expense method (563)   Under this method, the acquisition of a prepaid item is debited to an expense account.

SERIES A EXERCISE

E 14Apx-1A   (LO1/2)   EXPENSE METHOD OF ACCOUNTING FOR PREPAID EXPENSES Davidson's Food Mart paid $1,200 in advance to the local newspaper for advertisements that will appear monthly. The following entry was made:

4	Advertising Expense	1	2	0	0	00						4
5	Cash						1	2	0	0	00	5
6	Paid prepaid advertising											6

At the end of the year, December 31, 20--, Davidson received notification that advertisements costing $800 had been run. Prepare the adjusting entry.

SERIES B EXERCISE

E 14Apx-1B   (LO1/2)   EXPENSE METHOD OF ACCOUNTING FOR PREPAID EXPENSES Ryan's Fish House purchased supplies costing $3,000 for cash. This amount was debited to the supplies expense account. At the end of the year, December 31, 20--, an inventory showed that supplies costing $500 remained. Prepare the adjusting entry.

Chapter **15**
Financial Statements and Year-End Accounting for a Merchandising Business

LEARNING OBJECTIVES

Careful study of this chapter should enable you to:

LO1 Prepare a single-step and multiple-step income statement for a merchandising business.

LO2 Prepare a statement of owner's equity.

LO3 Prepare a classified balance sheet.

LO4 Compute standard financial ratios.

LO5 Prepare closing entries for a merchandising business.

LO6 Prepare reversing entries.

"**W**oot" was originally a truncated expression commonly used by players of Dungeons and Dragons for "Wow, loot!" Woot, Inc. is an online store, founded in 2004, that focuses on "selling cool stuff cheap." The company is known for its honest item descriptions and limited customer service. For example, the website explains that the company doesn't take calls because its employees are busy finding new products and shipping orders. Further, don't try to return something until all other options have been exhausted. If you want cheap prices, don't expect great service. This candor is refreshing, but we suspect they will help you out if you need it. Early on, the company claimed profitability was anticipated by 2043. "By then we should be retired; someone smarter might take over and jack up the prices." Clever, but they must have been doing something right. Woot was acquired by Amazon for $110 million, though it does not appear that prices have increased. Originally, the most unique characteristic of this merchandiser was that it sold only one product each day. It was available from 12:00 A.M. until sold out, or 11:59 P.M., when a different product was posted. Missed a cool product? Too bad. You couldn't buy yesterday's item. More recently, Woot has been offering multiple products including electronics **woot!**, computers **woot!**, home **woot!**, **woot!** Tools & Gardens, sport **woot!**, **woot!** Accessories & Watches, kids **woot!**, shirt **woot!**, wine **woot!**, and sellout **woot!**. And, of course, there is Today's Woot, the featured deal of the day. This is the best deal Woot has to offer, at the lowest price you will find on the Web. But if you miss it, you are out of luck.

Though clearly unique, this business must perform year-end accounting in the same manner as other retailers. In this chapter, you will learn how Woot and other merchandising firms prepare financial statements, compute financial ratios to evaluate performance, and prepare closing and reversing entries. No matter how unique, businesses must follow similar accounting procedures so that profitability and financial health can be compared across years and with other companies.

The first six chapters of this text illustrated the accounting cycle for a service business. In this chapter, we complete the accounting cycle for a merchandising business.

In Chapter 14, we prepared the end-of-period spreadsheet and adjusting entries for Sunflower Cycle. In this chapter, we will prepare financial statements, look briefly at financial statement analysis, and demonstrate closing and reversing entries.

LO1	The Income Statement

Prepare a single-step and multiple-step income statement for a merchandising business.

As you know, a primary purpose of the spreadsheet is to serve as an aid in preparing the financial statements. Figure 15-1 shows the completed spreadsheet for Sunflower Cycle. We will use it to prepare financial statements.

The purpose of an income statement is to summarize the results of operations during an accounting period. The income statement shows the sources of revenue, types of expenses, and the amount of the net income or net loss for the period. Two forms of the income statement commonly used are the single step and the multiple step. The single-step income statement lists all revenue items and their total first, followed by all expense items and their total. The difference, which is either net income or net loss, is then calculated. A single-step income statement for Sunflower Cycle is illustrated in Figure 15-2.

The use of the spreadsheet to prepare a multiple-step income statement is illustrated in Figure 15-3. This type of income statement is commonly used for merchandising businesses. The term "multiple-step" is used because the final net income is calculated on a step-by-step basis. Gross sales is shown first, less sales returns and allowances and sales discounts. This difference is called net sales. (Many published income statements begin with the amount of net sales.) Cost of goods sold is subtracted next to arrive at gross profit (sometimes called gross margin).

Operating expenses are then listed and subtracted from the gross profit to compute income from operations (sometimes called operating income). Operating expenses are directly associated with providing the primary goods and services of the business. Some companies divide operating expenses into the following subcategories:

Selling expenses. These expenses are directly associated with selling activities. Examples include:

• Sales Salaries Expense
• Sales Commissions Expense
• Advertising Expense
• Bank Credit Card Expense
• Delivery Expense
• Depreciation Expense—Store Equipment and Fixtures

FIGURE 15-1 Sunflower Cycle Spreadsheet

Sunflower Cycle
End-of-Period Spreadsheet
For the Year Ended December 31, 20--

	A	B	C	D	E	F	G	H	I
	ACCOUNT TITLE	TRIAL BALANCE		ADJUSTMENTS				ADJUSTED TRIAL BALANCE	
		DEBIT	CREDIT		DEBIT		CREDIT	DEBIT	CREDIT
6	Cash	26,000.00						26,000.00	
7	Accounts Receivable	13,000.00						13,000.00	
8	Merchandise Inventory	52,000.00		(b)	45,600.00	(a)	52,000.00	45,600.00	
9	Estimated Returns Inventory	1,200.00		(e)	2,100.00	(d)	1,200.00	2,100.00	
10	Supplies	6,000.00				(f)	5,200.00	800.00	
11	Prepaid Insurance	2,800.00				(g)	2,400.00	400.00	
12	Land	115,000.00						115,000.00	
13	Building	390,000.00						390,000.00	
14	Accum. Depr.—Building		39,000.00			(h)	4,000.00		43,000.00
15	Equipment	48,000.00						48,000.00	
16	Accum. Depr.—Equipment		16,000.00			(i)	3,000.00		19,000.00
17	Notes Payable		5,000.00						5,000.00
18	Accounts Payable		24,000.00						24,000.00
19	Customer Refunds Payable		2,000.00			(c)	1,000.00		3,000.00
20	Wages Payable					(j)	700.00		700.00
21	Sales Tax Payable		1,600.00						1,600.00
22	Unearned Subscriptions Revenue		3,000.00						1,000.00
23	Mortgage Payable		30,000.00	(k)	2,000.00				30,000.00
24	Sam Tangari, Capital		417,200.00						417,200.00
25	Sam Tangari, Drawing	4,000.00						4,000.00	
26	Income Summary			(a)	52,000.00	(b)	45,600.00	52,000.00	45,600.00
27				(d)	1,200.00	(e)	2,100.00	1,200.00	2,100.00
28	Sales		473,000.00						473,000.00
29	Sales Returns and Allowances	7,000.00		(c)	1,000.00			8,000.00	
30	Interest Revenue		800.00						800.00
31	Rent Revenue		7,500.00						7,500.00
32	Subscriptions Revenue					(k)	2,000.00		2,000.00
33	Purchases	239,600.00						239,600.00	
34	Purchases Returns and Allowances		1,100.00						1,100.00
35	Purchases Discounts		900.00						900,00
36	Freight-in	1,300.00						1,300.00	
37	Wages Expense	70,300.00		(j)	700.00			71,000.00	
38	Advertising Expense	10,200.00						10,200.00	
39	Bank Credit Card Expense	8,100.00						8,100.00	
40	Rent Expense	14,000.00						14,000.00	
41	Supplies Expense			(f)	5,200.00			5,200.00	
42	Phone Expense	1,800.00						1,800.00	
43	Utilities Expense	7,500.00						7,500.00	
44	Insurance Expense			(g)	2,400.00			2,400.00	
45	Depr. Expense—Building			(h)	4,000.00			4,000.00	
46	Depr. Expense—Equipment			(i)	3,000.00			3,000.00	
47	Miscellaneous Expense	1,700.00						1,700.00	
48	Interest Expense	1,600.00						1,600.00	
49		1,021,100.00	1,021,100.00		119,200.00		119,200.00	1,077,500.00	1,077,500.00
50								432,600.00	533,000.00
51	Net Income							100,400.00	
52									

FIGURE 15-2 Single-Step Income Statement

Sunflower Cycle		
Income Statement		
For Year Ended December 31, 20--		
Revenues:		
Net sales	$465,000	
Interest revenue	800	
Rent revenue	7,500	
Subscriptions revenue	2,000	
Total revenues		$475,300
Expenses:		
Cost of goods sold	$244,400	
Wages expense	71,000	
Advertising expense	10,200	
Bank credit card expense	8,100	
Rent expense	14,000	
Supplies expense	5,200	
Phone expense	1,800	
Utilities expense	7,500	
Insurance expense	2,400	
Depreciation expense—building	4,000	
Depreciation expense—equipment	3,000	
Miscellaneous expense	1,700	
Interest expense	1,600	
Total expenses		374,900
Net income		$100,400

General expenses. These expenses are associated with administrative, office, or general operating activities. Examples include:

- Rent Expense
- Office Salaries Expense
- Office Supplies Expense
- Phone Expense
- Utilities Expense
- Insurance Expense
- Depreciation Expense—Office Equipment

Finally, other revenues are added and other expenses are subtracted to arrive at net income (or net loss). Note that the operating expenses are arranged according to the order given in the chart of accounts. They could also be listed by descending amount, with Miscellaneous Expense last.

FIGURE 15-3 Using a Spreadsheet to Prepare a Multiple-Step Income Statement

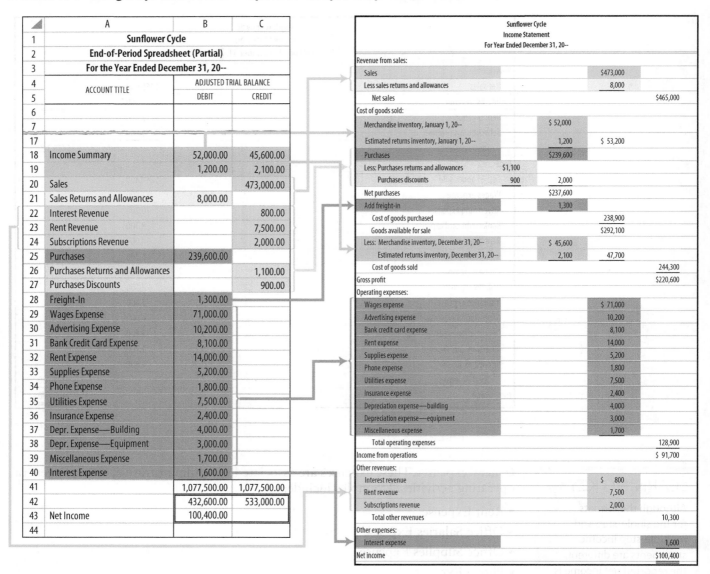

CHECKPOINT ✔

Complete Checkpoint-1 on page 592 to test your basic understanding of LO1.

LO2

The Statement of Owner's Equity

Prepare a statement of owner's equity.

The statement of owner's equity summarizes all changes in the owner's equity during the period. It includes the net income or loss and any additional investments or withdrawals by the owner. These changes result in the end-of-period balance shown on this statement and the balance sheet.

To prepare the statement of owner's equity for Sunflower Cycle, two sources of information are needed: (1) the spreadsheet and (2) Sam Tangari's capital account (no. 311) in the general ledger. The spreadsheet (Figure 15-1) shows net income of $100,400 and withdrawals of $4,000 during the year. Tangari's capital account (Figure 15-4) shows a beginning balance of $407,200. An additional $10,000 was invested in the business in February of the current year. The statement of owner's equity for Sunflower Cycle for the year ended December 31, 20--, is shown in Figure 15-5.

FIGURE 15-4 Capital Account for Sam Tangari

ACCOUNT: Sam Tangari, Capital							ACCOUNT NO. 311	
						BALANCE		
DATE	ITEM	POST. REF.	DEBIT	CREDIT		DEBIT	CREDIT	
20-- Jan. 1	Balance	✓					407 2 0 0 00	
Feb. 12		CR7		10 0 0 0 00			417 2 0 0 00	

The statement of owner's equity is the same for a service business and a merchandising business.

FIGURE 15-5 Statement of Owner's Equity

Sunflower Cycle Statement of Owner's Equity For Year Ended December 31, 20--		
Sam Tangari, capital, January 1, 20 --		$407,200
Add additional investments		10,000
Total investment		$417,200
Net income for the year	$100,400	
Less withdrawals for the year	4,000	
Increase in capital		96,400
Sam Tangari, capital, December 31, 20--		$513,600

CHECKPOINT ✔

Complete Checkpoint-2 on page 592 to test your basic understanding of LO2.

LO3

Balance Sheet

Prepare a classified balance sheet.

The use of the spreadsheet to prepare a report form classified balance sheet is illustrated in Figure 15-6. The balance sheet classifications used by Sunflower Cycle are explained below.

LEARNING KEY 🔑

Note the use of the ending balance for merchandise inventory. It is reported on the income statement as part of the calculation of cost of goods sold. It also is reported on the balance sheet as a current asset.

Current Assets

Current assets include cash and all other assets expected to be converted into cash or consumed within one year or the normal operating cycle of the business, whichever is longer. The operating cycle is the length of time generally required for a business to buy inventory, sell it, and collect the cash. This time period is generally less than a year. Thus, most firms use one year for classifying current assets. In a merchandising business, the current assets usually include cash, receivables (such as accounts receivable and notes receivable), merchandise inventory, and estimated returns inventory. Since prepaid expenses, such as unused supplies and unexpired insurance, are likely to be consumed within a year, and they also are reported as current assets.

FIGURE 15-6 Using a Spreadsheet to Prepare a Report Form Classified Balance Sheet

	A	B	C
1	Sunflower Cycle		
2	End-of-Period Spreadsheet (Partial)		
3	For the Year Ended December 31, 20--		
4	ACCOUNT TITLE	ADJUSTED TRIAL BALANCE	
5		DEBIT	CREDIT
6	Cash	26,000.00	
7	Accounts Receivable	13,000.00	
8	Merchandise Inventory	45,600.00	
9	Estimated Returns Inventory	2,100.00	
10	Supplies	800.00	
11	Prepaid Insurance	400.00	
12	Land	115,000.00	
13	Building	390,000.00	
14	Accum. Depr.—Building		43,000.00
15	Equipment	48,000.00	
16	Accum. Depr.—Equipment		19,000.00
17	Notes Payable		5,000.00
18	Accounts Payable		24,000.00
19	Customer Refunds Payable		3,000.00
20	Wages Payable		700.00
21	Sales Tax Payable		1,600.00
22	Unearned Subscriptions Revenue		1,000.00
23	Mortgage Payable		30,000.00
24	Sam Tangari, Capital		417,200.00
25	Sam Tangari, Drawing	4,000.00	
26			
43			

Sunflower Cycle
Balance Sheet
December 31, 20--

Assets			
Current assets:			
Cash		$ 26,000	
Accounts receivable		13,000	
Merchandise inventory		45,600	
Estimated returns inventory		2,100	
Supplies		800	
Prepaid insurance		400	
Total current assets			$ 87,900
Property, plant, and equipment:			
Land		$115,000	
Building	$ 390,000		
Less accum. depr.—building	43,000	347,000	
Equipment	$ 48,000		
Less accum. depr.—equip.	19,000	29,000	491,900
Total assets			$578,900
Liabilities			
Current liabilities:			
Notes payable	$ 5,000		
Accounts payable	24,000		
Customer refunds payable	3,000		
Wages payable	700		
Sales tax payable	1,600		
Unearned subscriptions revenue	1,000		
Mortgage payable (current portion)	500		
Total current liabilities		$ 35,800	
Long-term liabilities:			
Mortgage payable (current portion)	$ 30,000		
Less current portion	500	29,500	
Total liabilities			$ 65,300
Owner's Equity			
Sam Tangari, capital			513,600
Total liabilities and owner's equity			$578,900

*From statement of owner's equity.

Current assets are listed on the balance sheet from the most liquid to least liquid. **Liquidity** refers to the speed with which the company can convert the asset to cash. Cash is the most liquid asset and is always listed first. Notes Receivable, Accounts Receivable, Merchandise Inventory, and Estimated Returns Inventory often follow it on the balance sheet.

Property, Plant, and Equipment

Assets that are expected to be used for more than one year in the operation of a business are called **property, plant, and equipment**. Examples include land, buildings, office equipment, store equipment, and delivery equipment. Of these assets, only land is permanent; however, all of these assets have useful lives that are comparatively long. Typically, assets with longer useful lives are listed first.

The balance sheet of Sunflower Cycle shows Land, Building, and Equipment. Land is not depreciated. Accumulated depreciation amounts are shown as deductions from the costs of the building and equipment. The difference represents the undepreciated cost, or book value, of the assets. This amount less any salvage value will be written off as depreciation expense in future periods.

Current Liabilities

> The current portion of long-term debt, the amount due within one year, is reported as a current liability. The remainder, the amount not due for more than one year, is reported under long-term liabilities.

Current liabilities include those obligations that are due within one year or the normal operating cycle of the business, whichever is longer, and will require the use of current assets. As of December 31, the current liabilities of Sunflower Cycle consist of Notes Payable, Accounts Payable, Customer Refunds Payable, Wages Payable, Sales Tax Payable, Unearned Subscriptions Revenue, and the portion of Mortgage Payable that is due within the next year.

Long-Term Liabilities

Long-term liabilities include those obligations that will extend beyond one year or the normal operating cycle, whichever is longer. A common long-term liability is a mortgage payable.

A mortgage is a written agreement specifying that if the borrower does not repay a debt, the lender has the right to take over specific property to satisfy the debt. When the debt is paid, the mortgage becomes void. Mortgage Payable is an account that is used to reflect an obligation that is secured by a mortgage on certain property.

Owner's Equity

CHECKPOINT ✔

Complete Checkpoint-3 on page 592 to test your basic understanding of LO3.

The permanent owner's equity accounts reported on the balance sheet are determined by the type of organization. The accounts for a sole proprietorship, a partnership, and a corporation differ. Sunflower Cycle is a sole proprietorship and reports one owner's equity account, Sam Tangari, Capital. The balance of this account is taken from the statement of owner's equity. Partnerships are illustrated in Chapter 19 and corporations are discussed in Chapters 20 and 21.

LO4   Financial Statement Analysis

Compute standard financial ratios.

Both management and creditors are interested in using the financial statements to evaluate the financial condition and profitability of the firm. This can be done by making a few simple calculations.

Balance Sheet Analysis

Recall the following:

1. Current assets include cash, items that will be converted to cash, and items that will be consumed within one year.
2. Current liabilities are obligations that will require the use of current assets.

Thus, the difference between current assets and current liabilities represents the amount of capital the business has available for current operations. This is called working capital.

Working Capital = Current Assets − Current Liabilities

The balance sheet in Figure 15-6 shows that Sunflower Cycle has current assets of $87,900 and current liabilities of $35,800. Thus, the working capital at year end is $52,100 ($87,900 − $35,800). This amount should be more than adequate to satisfy current operating requirements.

Two measures of the firm's ability to pay its current liabilities are the **current ratio** and **quick ratio**. The formulas for calculating these ratios are as follows:

Sunflower Cycle

$$\text{Current Ratio} = \frac{\text{Current Assets}}{\text{Current Liabilities}} = \frac{\$87,900}{\$35,800} = 2.5 \text{ to } 1$$

$$\text{Quick Ratio} = \frac{\text{Quick Assets}}{\text{Current Liabilities}} = \frac{\$39,000}{\$35,800} = 1.1 \text{ to } 1$$

Sunflower Cycle's current ratio of 2.5 to 1 is a little high which indicates a favorable financial position. The traditional "rule of thumb" has been that a current ratio should be about 2 to 1, but many businesses operate successfully on a current ratio of 1.5 to 1. Although a rule of thumb is helpful, it is better to compare an individual company to industry averages, which are available on the Internet.

Quick assets include cash and all other current assets that can be converted into cash quickly, such as accounts receivable and temporary investments. Temporary investments are discussed in more advanced textbooks. The balance sheet in Figure 15-6 shows total quick assets of $39,000 ($26,000 in cash + $13,000 in accounts receivable). This produces a quick ratio of 1.1 to 1. Quick assets appear to be more than adequate to meet current obligations. The traditional rule of thumb has been that a quick ratio should be about 1 to 1, but many businesses operate successfully on a quick ratio of 0.6 to 1.

Interstatement Analysis

Interstatement analysis provides a comparison of the relationships between selected income statement and balance sheet amounts. A good example of interstatement analysis is the ratio of net income to owner's equity in the business. This ratio is known as **return on owner's equity**.

Sunflower Cycle

$$\text{Return on Owner's Equity} = \frac{\text{Net Income}}{\text{Average Owner's Equity}} = \frac{\$100,400}{(\$407,200 + \$513,600) \div 2}$$

$$= \frac{\$100,400}{\$460,400}$$

$$= 21.8\%$$

The statement of owner's equity in Figure 15-5 shows that the owner's equity of Sunflower Cycle was $407,200 on January 1 and $513,600 on December 31. The net income for the year of $100,400 is 21.8% of the average owner's equity. A comparison of this ratio with the return on owner's equity in prior years should be of interest to the owner. It may also be of interest to compare the return on owner's equity of Sunflower Cycle with the same ratio for other businesses of comparable nature and size. In general, however, this is considered an excellent rate of return.

A second ratio involving both income statement and balance sheet accounts is a measure of the time required to collect cash from credit customers. This financial measure is often computed in two ways. The **accounts receivable turnover** is the number of times the accounts receivable "turned over," or were collected, during the

Net credit sales is generally not reported in the financial statements. Use net sales, instead. As long as the proportion of cash and credit sales is reasonably stable over time, this ratio will provide a reasonable measure of the business's ability to collect receivables in a timely manner from year to year.

accounting period. Of course, a higher number indicates that cash is collected more quickly. This ratio is calculated as follows:

$$\text{Accounts Receivable Turnover} = \frac{\text{Net Credit Sales for the Period}}{\text{Average Accounts Receivable}}$$

The accounts receivable turnover for Sunflower Cycle for the year ended December 31 is computed as follows:

Net credit sales for the year (determined from the accounting records)	$110,000
Accounts receivable balance, January 1, 20-- (taken from last year's balance sheet)	10,000
Accounts receivable balance, December 31, 20--	13,000

$$\text{Average Accounts Receivable} = \frac{\text{Beginning Balance} + \text{Ending Balance}}{2} = \frac{\$10,000 + \$13,000}{2}$$

Sunflower Cycle

$$= \$11,500$$

$$\text{Accounts Receivable Turnover} = \frac{\text{Net Credit Sales for the Period}}{\text{Average Accounts Receivable}} = \frac{\$110,000}{\$11,500}$$

$$= 9.6$$

The **average collection period** is calculated by dividing the number of days in the year (365) by the rate of turnover to determine the number of days credit customers take to pay for their purchases. Sunflower Cycle's customers are taking about 38 days.

$$365 \text{ days} \div 9.6 = 38.2 \text{ days}$$

Comparing the average collection period with a business's credit terms offers an indication of whether customers are paying within the terms. If Sunflower Cycle allows credit terms of n/45, an average collection period of 38 days would suggest that customers are paying on a timely basis.

A third ratio involving both income statement and balance sheet accounts is the rate of **inventory turnover**. This is the number of times the merchandise inventory turned over, or was sold, during the accounting period. This ratio is calculated as follows:

$$\text{Inventory Turnover} = \frac{\text{Cost of Goods Sold for the Period}}{\text{Average Inventory}}$$

If inventory is taken only at the end of each accounting period, the average inventory for the period can be calculated by adding the beginning and ending inventories (including estimated returns inventory) and dividing their sum by two. Sunflower Cycle's turnover for the year ended December 31 is computed as follows:

Cost of goods sold for the period	$244,400
Beginning inventory	53,200
Ending inventory	47,700

$$\text{Average Inventory} = \frac{\text{Beginning Inventory} + \text{Ending Inventory}}{2} = \frac{\$53,200 + \$47,700}{2}$$

Sunflower Cycle

$$= \$50,450$$

$$\text{Inventory Turnover} = \frac{\text{Cost of Goods Sold for the Period}}{\text{Average Inventory}} = \frac{\$244,400}{\$50,450}$$

$$= 4.8$$

The **average days to sell inventory** can be computed by dividing the number of days in the year (365) by the inventory turnover. For Sunflower Cycle, it takes about two and one half months.

$$365 \text{ days} \div 4.8 = 76 \text{ days}$$

The higher the rate of inventory turnover, the smaller the profit required on each dollar of sales to produce a satisfactory gross profit. This is because the increase in the number of units sold offsets the smaller amount of gross profit earned per unit. For example, grocery stores have a very small gross profit on each item sold, but make up for this with a rapid inventory turnover. Other types of businesses, jewelers for example, need a high gross profit on each item because their inventory turnover is quite slow. Evaluations of Sunflower Cycle's rate of inventory turnover would require comparison with prior years, other companies, or its industry.

> **CHECKPOINT** ✔
>
> Complete Checkpoint-4 on pages 592–593 to test your basic understanding of LO4.

LO5	Closing Entries

Prepare closing entries for a merchandising business.

Closing entries for a service business were illustrated in Chapter 6. The process is essentially the same for a merchandising business. All revenues and expenses reported on the income statement must be closed to Income Summary. Then, the income summary and drawing accounts are closed to the owner's capital account. Keep in mind, however, that a few new accounts were needed for a merchandising business. These include Sales Returns and Allowances, Sales Discounts, Purchases Returns and Allowances, and Purchases Discounts. Since these are temporary accounts reported on the income statement, they also must be closed. The easiest way to complete the closing process is by using the spreadsheet to prepare the closing entries in four basic steps, as illustrated in Figures 15-7 and 15-8.

FIGURE 15-7 The Closing Process

THE CLOSING PROCESS FOR A MERCHANDISING BUSINESS

STEP 1   All income statement accounts with credit balances are debited, with an offsetting credit to Income Summary.

STEP 2   All income statement accounts with debit balances are credited, with an offsetting debit to Income Summary.

STEP 3   The resulting balance in Income Summary, which is the net income or loss for the period, is transferred to the owner's capital account.

ACCOUNT: Income Summary   ACCOUNT NO. 331

DATE		ITEM	POST. REF.	DEBIT	CREDIT	BALANCE DEBIT	BALANCE CREDIT	Adjustments to:
20-- Dec.	31	Adjusting	J5	52 0 0 0 00		52 0 0 0 00		Remove Beg. Inventory
	31	Adjusting	J5		45 6 0 0 00	6 4 0 0 00		Enter End. Inventory
	31	Adjusting	J5	1 2 0 0 00		7 6 0 0 00		Remove Beg. Est. Ret. Inv.
	31	Adjusting	J5		2 1 0 0 00	5 5 0 0 00		Enter End. Est. Ret. Inv.
	31	Closing	J6		485 3 0 0 00		479 8 0 0 00	Closing step 1
	31	Closing	J6	379 4 0 0 00			100 4 0 0 00	Closing step 2
	31	Closing	J6	100 4 0 0 00				Closing step 3

STEP 4   The balance in the owner's drawing account is transferred to the owner's capital account.

FIGURE 15-8 Closing Entries for a Merchandising Business

	A	B	C
1	Sunflower Cycle		
2	End-of-Period Spreadsheet (Partial)		
3	For Year Ended December 31, 20--		
4	ACCOUNT TITLE	ADJUSTED TRIAL BALANCE	
5		DEBIT	CREDIT
6	Sam Tangari, Capital		417,200.00
7	Sam Tangari, Drawing	4,000.00	
8	Income Summary	52,000.00	45,600.00
9		1,200.00	2,100.00
10	Sales		473,000.00
11	Sales Returns and Allowances	8,000.00	
12	Interest Revenue		800.00
13	Rent Revenue		7,500.00
14	Subscriptions Revenue		2,000.00
15	Purchases	239,600.00	
16	Purchases Returns and Allow.		1,100.00
17	Purchases Discounts		900.00
18	Freight-In	1,300.00	
19	Wages Expense	71,000.00	
20	Advertising Expense	10,200.00	
21	Bank Credit Card Expense	8,100.00	
22	Rent Expense	14,000.00	
23	Supplies Expense	5,200.00	
24	Phone Expense	1,800.00	
25	Utilities Expense	7,500.00	
26	Insurance Expense	2,400.00	
27	Depr. Expense—Building	4,000.00	
28	Depr. Expense—Equipment	3,000.00	
29	Miscellaneous Expense	1,700.00	
30	Interest Expense	1,600.00	
31			

	GENERAL JOURNAL			PAGE 6	
	DATE	DESCRIPTION	POST. REF.	DEBIT	CREDIT
1	20--	Closing Entries			1
2	Dec. 31	Sales		473 0 0 0 00	2
3		Interest Revenue		8 0 0 00	3
4		Rent Revenue		7 5 0 0 00	4
5		Subscriptions Revenue		2 0 0 0 00	5
6		Purchases Returns and Allowances		1 1 0 0 00	6
7		Purchases Discounts		9 0 0 00	7
8		Income Summary		485 3 0 0 00	8
9					9
10	31	Income Summary		379 4 0 0 00	10
11		Sales Returns and Allowances		8 0 0 0 00	11
12		Purchases		239 6 0 0 00	12
13		Freight-In		1 3 0 0 00	13
14		Wages Expense		71 0 0 0 00	14
15		Advertising Expense		10 2 0 0 00	15
16		Bank Credit Card Expense		8 1 0 0 00	16
17		Rent Expense		14 0 0 0 00	17
18		Supplies Expense		5 2 0 0 00	18
19		Phone Expense		1 8 0 0 00	19
20		Utilities Expense		7 5 0 0 00	20
21		Insurance Expense		2 4 0 0 00	21
22		Depreciation Exp.—Building		4 0 0 0 00	22
23		Depreciation Exp.—Equip.		3 0 0 0 00	23
24		Miscellaneous Expense		1 7 0 0 00	24
25		Interest Expense		1 6 0 0 00	25
26					26
27	31	Income Summary		100 4 0 0 00	27
28		Sam Tangari, Capital		100 4 0 0 00	28
29					29
30	31	Sam Tangari, Capital		4 0 0 0 00	30
31		Sam Tangari, Drawing		4 0 0 0 00	31
32					32

Post-Closing Trial Balance

A trial balance of the general ledger accounts taken after the temporary owner's equity accounts have been closed is called a post-closing trial balance. The purpose of the post-closing trial balance is to prove that the general ledger is in balance at the beginning of a new accounting period, before any transactions for the new accounting period are entered. It should also confirm that all temporary accounts have zero balances. Figure 15-9 shows a post-closing trial balance for Sunflower Cycle.

The post-closing trial balance must be prepared by taking the balances from the general ledger accounts. It should not be prepared from the balances on the spreadsheet. Using the general ledger accounts helps ensure that all temporary accounts have been closed properly.

CHECKPOINT ✔

Complete Checkpoint-5 on page 594 to test your basic understanding of LO5.

FIGURE 15-9 Post-Closing Trial Balance

	A	B	C	D
1	Sunflower Cycle			
2	Post-Closing Trial Balance			
3	For the Year Ended December 31, 20--			
4–5	ACCOUNT TITLE	ACCOUNT NO.	DEBIT BALANCE	CREDIT BALANCE
6	Cash	101	26,000.00	
7	Accounts Receivable	122	13,000.00	
8	Merchandise Inventory	131	45,600.00	
9	Estimated Returns Inventory	135	2,100.00	
10	Supplies	141	800.00	
11	Prepaid Insurance	145	400.00	
12	Land	161	115,000.00	
13	Building	171	390,000.00	
14	Accumulated Depreciation—Building	171.1		43,000.00
15	Equipment	181	48,000.00	
16	Accumulated Depreciation—Equipment	181.1		19,000.00
17	Notes Payable	201		5,000.00
18	Accounts Payable	202		24,000.00
19	Customer Refunds Payable	203		3,000.00
20	Wages Payable	219		700.00
21	Sales Tax Payable	231		1,600.00
22	Unearned Subscriptions Revenue	241		1,000.00
23	Mortgage Payable	251		30,000.00
24	Sam Tangari, Capital	311		513,600.00
25			640,900.00	640,900.00
26				

VOLODYMYR KRASYUK/SHUTTERSTOCK.COM

A BROADER VIEW

Who Cares About Tracking Financial Ratios?

Tracking a business's average collection period for receivables can help investors avoid making poor investments. Take the case of Kendall Square, a supercomputer maker. In an effort to increase sales and profits, Kendall Square recognized large amounts of revenues that had not actually been earned. Since no cash was received for these sales, accounts receivable increased dramatically (by 57%). Similarly, the average collection period increased to 157 days. Large increases in the average collection period should warn potential investors that something might be wrong. What happened at Kendall Square? Over $10 million of sales on account was never collected. This was equal to almost half of the revenues reported for the year. When eventually discovered, Kendall Square's stock price fell from $24.25 to $2.28 a share.

LO6	**Reversing Entries**

Prepare reversing entries.

Numerous adjusting entries are needed at the end of the accounting period to bring the account balances up to date for presentation in the financial statements. Although not required, some of these adjusting entries should be reversed at the beginning of the next accounting period. This is done to simplify the recording of transactions in the new accounting period. As its name implies, a reversing entry is the reverse or opposite of the adjusting entry.

ADJUSTING ENTRY

4	Dec.	31	Wages Expense		7	0	0	00						4
5			Wages Payable							7	0	0	00		5

REVERSING ENTRY
(OPPOSITE)

7	Jan.	1	Wages Payable		7	0	0	00						7
8			Wages Expense							7	0	0	00		8

To see the advantage of using reversing entries, let's consider the effect of reversing Sunflower Cycle's adjusting entry for wages earned, but not paid, at the end of the year. Figure 15-10 shows that accrued wages on December 31 were $700. These wages are for work performed by the employees on the last three days of the accounting period ($200 + $200 + $300 = $700). The employees will be paid on Friday, January 2, the normal payday.

Note that the adjusting and closing entries are the same, regardless of whether a reversing entry is made. However, the reversing entry on January 1 has an impact on the entry made when the employees are paid. **Without** a reversing entry, the payment on January 2, 20-2, must be split between reduction of the wages payable account for wages earned in 20-1 and Wages Expense for wages earned in 20-2. **With** a reversing entry, the bookkeeper simply debits Wages Expense and credits Cash, as is done on every other payday. Thus, the likelihood of error is reduced. Reversing entries are particularly important in large businesses where the individual recording the entry for wages may not even know what adjusting entries were made.

Not all adjusting entries should be reversed. To determine which adjusting entries to reverse, follow this rule: *Except for the first year of operations, reverse all adjusting entries that increase an asset or liability account from a zero balance.*

Except for the first year of operation, merchandise inventory, and contra-assets like accumulated depreciation, will have existing balances. Thus, they should never be reversed. The adjusting entries for Sunflower Cycle are shown in Figure 15-11. Note that only the adjustment for accrued wages is reversed in Figure 15-12.

> **LEARNING KEY** 🔑
> Reverse all adjusting entries that increase an asset or liability account from a zero balance.

FIGURE 15-10 Adjusting, Closing, and Reversing Entries for Wages

| | 20-1 | | | 20-2 | |
	12/29/-1 Monday	12/30/-1 Tuesday	12/31/-1 Wednesday	1/1/-2 Thursday	1/2/-2 Friday
Wages Earned	200	200	300	200	200
Wages Paid	0	0	0	0	1,100
Total Earned			700		400
Total Paid			0		1,100
Accrued Wages on 12/31/-1			700		

Date	Without Reversing Entry		With Reversing Entry	

12/31/-1 Adj. Entry	Wages Expense 700
	    Wages Payable 700
			Wages Expense 700
			    Wages Payable 700	

12/31/-1 Closing Entry	Income Summary 71,000
	    Wages Expense 71,000
			Income Summary 71,000
			    Wages Expense 71,000	

1/1/-2 Rev. Entry	No Entry		Wages Payable 700 Wages Expense 700	

1/2/-2 Payment of Payroll	Wages Expense 400
	Wages Payable 700
	    Cash 1,100
			Wages Expense 1,100
			    Cash 1,100	

Without Reversing Entry

Description	Wages Expense		Description
Bal.	70,300		
12/31/-1 Adj.	700		
		71,000	12/31/-1 Close
1/2/-2 Payroll	400		

	Wages Payable		
		700	12/31/-1 Adj.
1/2/-2 Payroll	700		

	Cash		
		1,100	1/2/-2 Payroll

With Reversing Entry

Description	Wages Expense		Description
Bal.	70,300		
12/31/-1 Adj.	700		
		71,000	12/31/-1 Close
		700	1/1/-2 Reversing
1/2/-2 Payroll	1,100		
Bal.	400		

	Wages Payable		
		700	12/31/-1 Adj.
1/1/-2 Reverse	700		

	Cash		
		1,100	1/2/-2 Payroll

FIGURE 15-11 Which Adjusting Entries to Reverse?

	DATE		DESCRIPTION	POST. REF.	DEBIT	CREDIT	
1			Adjusting Entries				1
2	20-- Dec.	31	Income Summary		52 0 0 0 00		2
3			Merchandise Inventory			52 0 0 0 00	3
4							4
5		31	Merchandise Inventory		45 6 0 0 00		5
6			Income Summary			45 6 0 0 00	6
7							7
8		31	Sales Returns and Allowances		1 0 0 0 00		8
9			Customer Refunds Payable			1 0 0 0 00	9
10							10
11		31	Income Summary		1 2 0 0 00		11
12			Estimated Returns Inventory			1 2 0 0 00	12
13							13
14		31	Estimated Returns Inventory		2 1 0 0 00		14
15			Income Summary			2 1 0 0 00	15
16							16
17		31	Supplies Expense		5 2 0 0 00		17
18			Supplies			5 2 0 0 00	18
19							19
20		31	Insurance Expense		2 4 0 0 00		20
21			Prepaid Insurance			2 4 0 0 00	21
22							22
23		31	Depr. Expense—Building		4 0 0 0 00		23
24			Accum. Depr.—Building			4 0 0 0 00	24
25							25
26		31	Depr. Expense—Equipment		3 0 0 0 00		26
27			Accum. Depr.—Equipment			3 0 0 0 00	27
28							28
29		31	Wages Expense		7 0 0 00		29
30			Wages Payable			7 0 0 00	30
31							31
32		31	Unearned Subscriptions Revenue		2 0 0 0 00		32
33			Subscriptions Revenue			2 0 0 0 00	33
34							34

GENERAL JOURNAL PAGE 5

SHOULD THE ADJUSTMENT BE REVERSED?

Never reverse adjustments for merchandise inventory.

Never reverse adjustments for merchandise inventory.

No. No asset or liability with a zero balance has been increased.

Never reverse adjustments for merchandise inventory.

Never reverse adjustments for merchandise inventory.

No. No asset or liability with a zero balance has been increased.

No. No asset or liability with a zero balance has been increased.

Never reverse adjustments for depreciation.

Never reverse adjustments for depreciation.

Yes. A liability account with a zero balance has been increased.

No. No asset or liability with a zero balance has been increased.

FIGURE 15-12 Reversing Entry for Sunflower Cycle

GENERAL JOURNAL PAGE 7

	DATE		DESCRIPTION	POST. REF.	DEBIT	CREDIT	
1			Reversing Entries				1
2	20-- Jan.	1	Wages Payable		7 0 0 00		2
3			Wages Expense			7 0 0 00	3
4							4
5							5

CHECKPOINT ✔

Complete Checkpoint-6 on page 594 to test your basic understanding of LO6.

LEARNING OBJECTIVES	Key Points to Remember

LO1 Prepare a single-step and multiple-step income statement for a merchandising business.

The general formats for a single-step and multiple-step income statement are shown below.

Single-Step
Income Statement
For Year Ended December 31, 20--

Revenues:		
List all revenues	$xxx	
Total revenues		$xxx
Expenses:		
Cost of goods sold	$xxx	
List all other expenses	xxx	
Total expenses		xxx
Net income		$xxx

Multiple-Step
Income Statement
For Year Ended December 31, 20--

Revenue from sales:		
Sales	$xxx	
Less sales returns and allowances	xxx	
Net sales		$xxx
Cost of goods sold		xxx
Gross profit		$xxx
Operating expenses:		
List all operating expenses	$xxx	
Total operating expenses		xxx
Income from operations		$xxx
Other revenue:		
List all other revenue	$xxx	
Total other revenue		xxx
Other expenses:		
List all other expenses	$xxx	
Total other expenses		xxx
Net income		$xxx

LO2 Prepare a statement of owner's equity.

A statement of owner's equity has the following format:

Business Name
Statement of Owner's Equity
For Year Ended December 31, 20--

Capital, January 1, 20--		$xxx
Add additional investments		xxx
Total investment		$xxx
Net income for the year	$xxx	
Less withdrawals	xxx	
Increase in capital		xxx
Capital, December 31, 20--		$xxx

LEARNING OBJECTIVES	**Key Points to Remember**

LO3 Prepare a classified balance sheet.

A classified balance sheet has the following major headings:

Business Name
Balance Sheet
December 31, 20--

Assets

Current assets:

List all current assets	$xxx	
Total current assets		$xxx

Property, plant, and equipment:

List all property, plant, and equipment	$xxx	
Less accumulated depreciation (if appropriate)	xxx	$xxx
Total property, plant, and equipment		xxx
Total assets		$xxx

Liabilities

Current liabilities:

List all current liabilities	$xxx	
Total current liabilities		$xxx

Long-term liabilities:

List all long-term liabilities	$xxx	
Total long-term liabilities		xxx
Total liabilities		$xxx

Owner's Equity

Owner's capital	xxx
Total liabilities and owner's equity	$xxx

LO4 Compute standard financial ratios.

The following measures of financial condition may be computed from financial statement information:

Working Capital	=	Current Assets – Current Liabilities
Current Ratio	=	Current Assets ÷ Current Liabilities
Quick Ratio	=	Quick Assets ÷ Current Liabilities
Return on Owner's Equity	=	Net Income ÷ Average Owner's Equity
Accounts Receivable Turnover	=	$\dfrac{\text{Net Credit Sales for the Period}}{\text{Average Accounts Receivable}}$
Average Collection Period	=	$\dfrac{365}{\text{Accounts Receivable Turnover}}$
Inventory Turnover	=	$\dfrac{\text{Cost of Goods Sold for the Period}}{\text{Average Inventory}}$
Average Days to Sell Inventory	=	$\dfrac{365}{\text{Inventory Turnover}}$

(*continued*)

LEARNING OBJECTIVES	Key Points to Remember
LO5 **Prepare closing entries for a merchandising business.**	The four steps in the closing process for a merchandising business are as follows:
	STEP 1 All income statement accounts with credit balances are debited, with an offsetting credit to Income Summary.
	STEP 2 All income statement accounts with debit balances are credited, with an offsetting debit to Income Summary.
	STEP 3 The resulting balance in Income Summary, which is the net income or loss for the period, is transferred to the owner's capital account.
	STEP 4 The balance in the owner's drawing account is transferred to the owner's capital account.
LO6 **Prepare reversing entries.**	Use the following rule to determine which adjusting entries to reverse: Except for the first year of operations, reverse all adjusting entries that increase an asset or liability account from a zero balance.

DEMONSTRATION PROBLEM

Sara Wilson owns and operates Home Electronics. She has a store where she sells and repairs televisions and stereo equipment. A completed spreadsheet for 20-1 is provided on page 585. Sara made a $20,000 additional investment during 20-1. The current portion of Mortgage Payable is $1,000. Net credit sales for 20-1 were $200,000, and the balance of Accounts Receivable on January 1 was $26,000.

REQUIRED

1. Prepare a multiple-step income statement.
2. Prepare a statement of owner's equity.
3. Prepare a balance sheet.
4. Compute the following measures of performance and financial condition for 20-1:
   (a) Current ratio
   (b) Quick ratio
   (c) Working capital
   (d) Return on owner's equity
   (e) Accounts receivable turnover and the average number of days required to collect receivables
   (f) Inventory turnover and the average number of days required to sell inventory
5. Prepare adjusting entries and indicate which should be reversed and why.
6. Prepare closing entries.
7. Prepare reversing entries for the adjustments where appropriate.

	A	B	C	D	E	F	G	H	I
1		Home Electronics							
2		End-of-Period Spreadsheet							
3		For the Year Ended December 31, 20--							
4	ACCOUNT TITLE	TRIAL BALANCE			ADJUSTMENTS			ADJUSTED TRIAL BALANCE	
5		DEBIT	CREDIT		DEBIT		CREDIT	DEBIT	CREDIT
6	Cash	10,000.00						10,000.00	
7	Accounts Receivable	22,500.00						22,500.00	
8	Merchandise Inventory	37,400.00		(b)	44,400.00	(a)	37,400.00	44,400.00	
9	Estimated Returns Inventory	1,600.00		(e)	1,200.00	(d)	1,600.00	1,200.00	
10	Supplies	2,700.00				(f)	2,100.00	600.00	
11	Prepaid Insurance	3,600.00				(g)	2,700.00	900.00	
12	Land	15,000.00						15,000.00	
13	Building	135,000.00						135,000.00	
14	Accum. Depr.—Building		24,000.00			(h)	6,000.00		30,000.00
15	Store Equipment	75,000.00						75,000.00	
16	Accum. Depr.—Store Equipment		22,500.00			(i)	4,500.00		27,000.00
17	Notes Payable		7,500.00						7,500.00
18	Accounts Payable		15,000.00						15,000.00
19	Customer Refunds Payable		1,000.00			(c)	500.00		1,500.00
20	Wages Payable					(j)	675.00		675.00
21	Sales Tax Payable		2,250.00						2,250.00
22	Unearned Repair Revenue		18,000.00	(k)	15,000.00				3,000.00
23	Mortgage Payable		45,000.00						45,000.00
24	Sara Wilson, Capital		158,600.00						158,600.00
25	Sara Wilson, Drawing	30,000.00						30,000.00	
26	Income Summary			(a)	37,400.00	(b)	44,400.00	37,400.00	44,400.00
27				(d)	1,600.00	(e)	1,200.00	1,600.00	1,200.00
28	Sales		300,750.00						300,750.00
29	Sales Returns and Allowances	9,000.00		(c)	500.00			9,500.00	
30	Sales discounts	800.00						800.00	
31	Repair Fees						15,000.00		15,000.00
32	Interest Revenue		1,350.00						1,350.00
33	Purchases	157,500.00						157,500.00	
34	Purchases Returns and Allowances		1,200.00						1,200.00
35	Purchases Discounts		1,500.00						1,500.00
36	Freight-In	450.00						450.00	
37	Wages Expense	63,500.00		(j)	675.00			63,675.00	
38	Advertising Expense	3,750.00						3,750.00	
39	Supplies Expense			(f)	2,100.00			2,100.00	
40	Phone Expense	5,250.00						5,250.00	
41	Utilities Expense	18,000.00						18,000.00	
42	Insurance Expense			(g)	2,700.00			2,700.00	
43	Depr. Expense—Building			(h)	6,000.00			6,000.00	
44	Depr. Expense—Store Equipment			(i)	4,500.00			4,500.00	
45	Miscellaneous Expense	3,375.00						3,375.00	
46	Interest Expense	4,725.00						4,725.00	
47		598,650.00	598,650.00		116,075.00		116,075.00	655,925.00	655,925.00
48								321,325.00	365,400.00
49	Net Income							44,075.00	
50									

(continued)

SOLUTION 1.

Home Electronics
Income Statement
For Year Ended December 31, 20-1

Revenue from sales:			
Sales		$300,750	
Less: Sales returns and allowances	$ 9,500		
Sales discounts	800	10,300	
Net sales			$290,450
Cost of goods sold:			
Merchandise inventory, January 1, 20--	$ 37,400		
Estimated returns inventory	1,600	$ 39,000	
Purchases	$157,500		
Less: Purchases returns and allowances	$1,200		
Purchases discounts	1,500	2,700	
Net purchases		$154,800	
Add freight-in		450	
Cost of goods purchased		155,250	
Goods available for sale		$194,250	
Less: Merchandise inventory, December 31, 20--	$ 44,400		
Estimated returns inventory	1,200	45,600	
Cost of goods sold			148,650
Gross profit			$141,800
Operating expenses:			
Wages expense		$ 63,675	
Advertising expense		3,750	
Supplies expense		2,100	
Phone expense		5,250	
Utilities expense		18,000	
Insurance expense		2,700	
Depreciation expense—building		6,000	
Depreciation expense—store equipment		4,500	
Miscellaneous expense		3,375	
Total operating expenses			109,350
Income from operations			$ 32,450
Other revenues:			
Interest revenue		$ 1,350	
Repair fees		15,000	
Total other revenues			16,350
Other expenses:			
Interest expense			4,725
Net income			$ 44,075

SOLUTION 2.

Home Electronics
Statement of Owner's Equity
For Year Ended December 31, 20-1

S. Wilson, capital, January 1, 20--		$138,600
Add additional investments		20,000
Total investment		$158,600
Net income for the year	$44,075	
Less withdrawals for the year	30,000	
Increase in capital		14,075
S. Wilson, capital, December 31, 20--		$172,675

SOLUTION 3.

Home Electronics Balance Sheet December 31, 20-1			
Assets			
Current assets:			
Cash		$ 10,000	
Accounts receivable		22,500	
Merchandise inventory		44,400	
Estimated returns inventory		1,200	
Supplies		600	
Prepaid insurance		900	
Total current assets			$ 79,600
Property, plant, and equipment:			
Land		$ 15,000	
Building	$ 135,000		
Less accumulated depreciation	30,000	105,000	
Equipment	$ 75,000		
Less accumulated depreciation	27,000	48,000	168,000
Total assets			$247,600
Liabilities			
Current liabilities:			
Notes payable	$ 7,500		
Accounts payable	15,000		
Customer refunds payable	1,500		
Wages payable	675		
Sales tax payable	2,250		
Unearned repair fees	3,000		
Mortgage payable (current portion)	1,000		
Total current liabilities		$ 30,925	
Long-term liabilities:			
Mortgage payable	$ 45,000		
Less current portion	1,000	44,000	
Total liabilities			$ 74,925
Owner's Equity			
Sara Wilson, capital			172,675
Total liabilities and owner's equity			$247,600

SOLUTION 4.   (a) **Current Ratio**

$$\frac{\text{Current Assets}}{\text{Current Liabilities}} = \frac{\$79,600}{\$30,925} = 2.6 \text{ to } 1$$

(b) **Quick Ratio**

$$\frac{\text{Quick Assets}}{\text{Current Liabilities}} = \frac{\$32,500}{\$30,925} = 1.1 \text{ to } 1$$

Cash	$10,000
Accts. Rec.	22,500
	$32,500

(c) **Working Capital** = Current Assets − Current Liabilities

$79,600 − $30,925 = $48,675

(d) **Return on Owner's Equity**

$$\frac{\text{Net Income}}{\text{Average Owner's Equity}} = \frac{\$44,075}{\$155,638} = 28.3\%$$

(*continued*)

Jan. 1	$138,600
Dec. 31	$172,675
Average	$155,638

(e) **Accounts Receivable Turnover**

$$\frac{\text{Net Credit Sales for the Period}}{\text{Average Accounts Receivable}} = \frac{\$200,000}{\$24,250} = 8.25 \quad \frac{365}{8.25} = 44.3 \text{ days to collect}$$

A/R 1-1	$26,000
A/R 12-31	$25,500
Average	$24,250

(f) **Inventory Turnover**

$$\frac{\text{CGS}}{\text{Average Inventory}} = \frac{\$148,650}{42,300} = 3.51 \quad \frac{365}{3.51} = 103.9 \text{ days to sell}$$

Inv. 1-1	$39,000
Inv. 12-31	$45,600
Average	$42,300

SOLUTION 5.

GENERAL JOURNAL PAGE 3

#	DATE		DESCRIPTION	POST. REF.	DEBIT	CREDIT	#
1			Adjusting Entries				1
2	20-1 Dec.	31	Income Summary		37 4 0 0 00		2
3			Merchandise Inventory			37 4 0 0 00	3
4							4
5		31	Merchandise Inventory		44 4 0 0 00		5
6			Income Summary			44 4 0 0 00	6
7							7
8		31	Sales Returns and Allowances		5 0 0 00		8
9			Customer Refunds Payable			5 0 0 00	9
10							10
11		31	Income Summary		1 6 0 0 00		11
12			Estimated Returns Inventory			1 6 0 0 00	12
13							13
14		31	Estimated Returns Inventory		1 2 0 0 00		14
15			Income Summary			1 2 0 0 00	15
16							16
17		31	Supplies Expense		2 1 0 0 00		17
18			Supplies			2 1 0 0 00	18
19							19
20		31	Insurance Expense		2 7 0 0 00		20
21			Prepaid Insurance			2 7 0 0 00	21
22							22
23		31	Depr. Expense—Building		6 0 0 0 00		23
24			Accum. Depr.—Building			6 0 0 0 00	24
25							25
26		31	Depr. Expense—Store Equipment		4 5 0 0 00		26
27			Accum. Depr.—Store Equipment			4 5 0 0 00	27
28							28
29		31	Wages Expense		6 7 5 00		29
30			Wages Payable			6 7 5 00	30
31							31
32		31	Unearned Repair Fees		15 0 0 0 00		32
33			Repair Fees			15 0 0 0 00	33
34							34

SHOULD THE ADJUSTMENT BE REVERSED?

Never reverse adjustments for merchandise inventory.

Never reverse adjustments for merchandise inventory.

No. No asset or liability with a zero balance has been increased.

Never reverse adjustments for merchandise inventory.

Never reverse adjustments for merchandise inventory.

No. No asset or liability with a zero balance has been increased.

No. No asset or liability with a zero balance has been increased.

Never reverse adjustments for depreciation.

Never reverse adjustments for depreciation.

Yes. A liability account with a zero balance has been increased.

No. No asset or liability with a zero balance has been increased.

SOLUTION 6.

	DATE		DESCRIPTION	POST. REF.	DEBIT					CREDIT					
			GENERAL JOURNAL										PAGE 4		
1			Closing Entries												1
2	20-1 Dec.	31	Repair Fees		15	0	0	0	00						2
3			Sales		300	7	5	0	00						3
4			Interest Revenue		1	3	5	0	00						4
5			Purchases Returns and Allowances		1	2	0	0	00						5
6			Purchases Discounts		1	5	0	0	00						6
7			Income Summary							319	8	0	0	00	7
8															8
9		31	Income Summary		282	3	2	5	00						9
10			Sales Returns and Allowances							9	5	0	0	00	10
11			Sales Discounts							8	0	0	00		11
12			Purchases							157	5	0	0	00	12
13			Freight-In							4	5	0	00		13
14			Wages Expense							63	6	7	5	00	14
15			Advertising Expense							3	7	5	0	00	15
16			Supplies Expense							2	1	0	0	00	16
17			Phone Expense							5	2	5	0	00	17
18			Utilities Expense							18	0	0	0	00	18
19			Insurance Expense							2	7	0	0	00	19
20			Depr. Expense—Building							6	0	0	0	00	20
21			Depr. Expense—Store Equipment							4	5	0	0	00	21
22			Miscellaneous Expense							3	3	7	5	00	22
23			Interest Expense							4	7	2	5	00	23
24															24
25		31	Income Summary		44	0	7	5	00						25
26			Sara Wilson, Capital							44	0	7	5	00	26
27															27
28		31	Sara Wilson, Capital		30	0	0	0	00						28
29			Sara Wilson, Drawing							30	0	0	0	00	29
30															30

> Recall, four adjusting entries have already been made to Income Summary.

ACCOUNT: Income Summary   ACCOUNT NO. 331

DATE	ITEM	POST. REF.	DEBIT	CREDIT	BALANCE DEBIT	BALANCE CREDIT	
20— Dec. 31	Adjusting		37 4 0 0 00		37 4 0 0 00		← Remove Beg. Inv.
31	Adjusting			44 4 0 0 00		7 0 0 0 00	← Enter End. Inv.
31	Adjusting		1 6 0 0 00			5 4 0 0 00	← Remove Beg. Est. Ret. Inv.
31	Adjusting			1 2 0 0 00		6 6 0 0 00	← Enter End. Est. Ret. Inv.
31	Closing			319 8 0 0 00		326 4 0 0 00	← Closing step 1
31	Closing		282 3 2 5 00			44 0 7 5 00	← Closing step 2
31	Closing		44 0 7 5 00				← Closing step 3

SOLUTION 7.

	DATE		DESCRIPTION	POST. REF.	DEBIT	CREDIT	
1			Reversing Entries				1
2	20-2 Jan.	1	Wages Payable		6 7 5 00		2
3			Wages Expense			6 7 5 00	3
4							4

GENERAL JOURNAL PAGE 5

KEY TERMS

accounts receivable turnover (574) The number of times the accounts receivable turned over, or were collected, during the accounting period. When 365 is divided by the turnover, this measure can be expressed in terms of the average number of days required to collect receivables.

average collection period (575) The number of days in the year (365) divided by the accounts receivable turnover. Provides an indication of the number of days credit customers take to pay for their purchases.

average days to sell inventory (576) The number of days in the year (365) divided by the inventory turnover. Provides an indication of the average number of days required to sell inventory.

book value (573) See undepreciated cost.

current assets (571) Cash and all other assets expected to be converted into cash or consumed within one year or the normal operating cycle of the business, whichever is longer.

current liabilities (573) Those obligations that are due within one year or the normal operating cycle of the business, whichever is longer, and will require the use of current assets.

current ratio (574) Current assets divided by current liabilities.

general expenses (569) Those expenses associated with administrative, office, or general operating activities.

gross margin (567) See gross profit.

gross profit (567) Net sales minus cost of goods sold.

income from operations (567) Gross profit minus operating expenses on a multiple-step income statement.

interstatement analysis (574) Compares the relationship between certain amounts in the income statement and balance sheet.

inventory turnover (575) The number of times the merchandise inventory turned over, or was sold, during the accounting period. When 365 is divided by the turnover, this measure can be expressed in terms of the average number of days required to sell inventory.

liquidity (572) Refers to the speed with which an asset can be converted to cash.

long-term liabilities (573) Those obligations that will extend beyond one year or the normal operating cycle, whichever is longer.

mortgage (573) A written agreement specifying that if the borrower does not repay a debt, the lender has the right to take over specific property to satisfy the debt.

Mortgage Payable (573) An account that is used to reflect an obligation that is secured by a mortgage on certain property.

multiple-step income statement (567)   This statement shows a step-by-step calculation of net sales, cost of goods sold, gross profit, operating expenses, income from operations, other revenues and expenses, and net income.

net sales (567)   Gross sales less sales returns and allowances and less sales discounts.

operating cycle (571)   The length of time generally required for a business to buy inventory, sell it, and collect the cash.

operating income (567)   See income from operations.

post-closing trial balance (577)   A trial balance taken after the temporary owner's equity accounts have been closed.

property, plant, and equipment (572)   Assets that are expected to be used for more than one year in the operation of a business.

quick assets (574)   Cash and all other current assets that can be converted into cash quickly, such as accounts receivable and temporary investments.

quick ratio (574)   Quick assets divided by current liabilities.

return on owner's equity (574)   Net income divided by average owner's equity.

reversing entry (579)   The opposite of the adjusting entry. It is made on the first day of the next accounting period and simplifies recording transactions in the new period.

selling expenses (567)   Those expenses directly associated with selling activities.

single-step income statement (567)   This statement lists all revenue items and their total first, followed by all expense items and their total.

undepreciated cost (573)   Cost of plant and equipment less the accumulated depreciation amounts. Also called book value.

working capital (573)   The difference between current assets and current liabilities, which represents the amount of capital the business has available for current operations.

SELF-STUDY TEST QUESTIONS

True/False

1. **LO1**   A multiple-step form of income statement calculates gross profit, before subtracting operating expenses.

2. **LO3**   Current assets include cash, items expected to convert into cash, and items that will be consumed during a year or the normal operating cycle, whichever is shorter.

3. **LO3**   Current assets are listed on the balance sheet in order of liquidity.

4. **LO4**   Working capital is the difference between current assets and current liabilities.

5. **LO4**   Accounts receivable turnover is the number of times merchandise inventory turned over or was sold during the accounting period.

Multiple Choice

1. **LO3**   Which of these assets is *not* a current asset?
   - (a) Cash
   - (b) Accounts Receivable
   - (c) Office Equipment
   - (d) Merchandise Inventory

2. **LO3**   Which of these would be listed *first* on a balance sheet?
   - (a) Accounts Receivable
   - (b) Delivery Equipment
   - (c) Accounts Payable
   - (d) Prepaid Insurance

3. **LO4**   Which of these is considered a *quick asset*?
   (a) Merchandise Inventory   (c) Office Equipment
   (b) Accounts Receivable   (d) Prepaid Insurance

4. **LO4**   To calculate the accounts receivable turnover ratio, _____ is divided by average accounts receivable.
   (a) Net sales   (c) Total sales
   (b) Cost of goods sold   (d) Net credit sales

5. **LO4**   Inventory turnover is calculated by dividing cost of goods sold by
   (a) average accounts receivable.   (c) average inventory.
   (b) average owner's equity.   (d) accounts receivable turnover.

CHECKPOINT ✔

Checkpoint Exercises

Use the following spreadsheet for Yoder's Cool Stuff for Checkpoint Exercises 1, 2, and 3.

	A	B	C	D	E	F	G	H	I
1					Yoder's Cool Stuff				
2					End-of-Period Spreadsheet				
3					For the Year Ended December 31, 20--				
4	ACCOUNT TITLE	TRIAL BALANCE		ADJUSTMENTS				ADJUSTED TRIAL BALANCE	
5		DEBIT	CREDIT	DEBIT			CREDIT	DEBIT	CREDIT
6	Cash	7,400.00						7,400.00	
7	Accounts Receivable	13,000.00						13,000.00	
8	Merchandise Inventory	36,000.00		(b) 75,000.00		(a)	36,000.00	75,000.00	
9	Estimated Returns Inventory	4,000.00		(e) 5,000.00			4,000.00	5,000.00	
10	Supplies	1,600.00				(f)	1,200.00	400.00	
11	Prepaid Insurance	4,000.00				(g)	500.00	3,500.00	
12	Delivery Equipment	160,000.00						160,000.00	
13	Accum. Depr.—Delivery Equipment		40,000.00			(i)	20,000.00		60,000.00
14	Accounts Payable		30,000.00						30,000.00
15	Customer Refunds Payable		6,000.00			(c)	3,000.00		9,000.00
16	Wages Payable					(j)	1,000.00		1,000.00
17	Pete Yoder, Capital		88,000.00						88,000.00
18	Pete Yoder, Drawing	3,000.00						3,000.00	
19	Income Summary			(a) 36,000.00		(b)	75,000.00	36,000.00	75,000.00
20				(d) 4,000.00		(e)	5,000.00	4,000.00	5,000.00
21	Sales		261,000.00						261,000.00
22	Sales Returns and Allowances	18,000.00		(c) 3,000.00				21,000.00	
23	Purchases	160,000.00						160,000.00	
24	Wages Expense	13,000.00		(j) 1,000.00				14,000.00	
25	Rent Expense	4,000.00						4,000.00	
26	Supplies Expense			(f) 1,200.00				1,200.00	
27	Phone Expense	1,000.00						1,000.00	
28	Insurance Expense			(g) 500.00				500.00	
29	Depr. Expense—Delivery Equipment			(i) 20,000.00				20,000.00	
30		425,000.00	425,000.00	145,700.00			145,700.00	529,000.00	529,000.00
31								261,700.00	341,000.00
32	Net Income							79,300.00	
33									

1. **LO1**   Prepare a multiple-step income statement for Yoder's Cool Stuff.

2. **LO2**   Prepare a statement of owner's equity for Yoder's Cool Stuff. Assume the beginning balance of Yoder's capital account was $88,000.

3. **LO3**   Prepare a balance sheet for Yoder's Cool Stuff.

4. **LO4**   Using the financial statements for Herman's Parts provided on page 593, compute the following ratios:
   (a) Working capital   (c) Return on owner's equity
   (b) Current ratio   (d) Inventory turnover

Herman's Parts
Income Statement
For Month Ended May 31, 20--

Revenue from sales:			
Sales		$28,000	
Less sales returns and allowances		500	
Net sales			$27,500
Cost of goods sold:			
Merchandise inventory, May 1, 20--	$3,800		
Estimated returns inventory, May 1, 20--	200	$ 4,000	
Purchases		18,000	
Goods available for sale		$22,000	
Less: Merchandise inventory May 31, 20--	$5,700		
Estimated returns inventory, May 31, 20--	300	6,000	
Cost of goods sold			16,000
Gross profit			$11,500
Operating expenses:			
Wages expense		$ 7,800	
Rent Expense		300	
Supplies expense		100	
Phone expense		80	
Insurance expense		50	
Depreciation expense—delivery equipment		1,000	
Total operating expenses			9,330
Net income			$ 2,170

Herman's Parts
Statement of Owner's Equity
For Month Ended May 31, 20--

Herman Gillespie, capital, May 1, 20--		$5,000
Add additional investment		1,000
Total investment		$6,000
Net income for the month	$2,170	
Less withdrawals for the month	1,000	
Increase in capital		1,170
Herman Gillespie, capital, May 31, 20--		$7,170

Herman's Parts
Balance Sheet
May 31, 20--

Assets			
Current assets:			
Cash		$ 500	
Accounts receivable		1,920	
Merchandise inventory		5,700	
Estimated returns inventory		300	
Supplies		200	
Prepaid insurance		400	
Total current assets			$ 9,020
Property, plant, and equipment:			
Delivery equipment		$6,000	
Less accumulated depreciation		3,000	3,000
Total assets			$12,020
Liabilities			
Current liabilities:			
Accounts payable		$3,300	
Customer refunds payable		500	
Wages payable		1,050	
Total current liabilities			$ 4,850
Owner's Equity			
Herman Gillespie, capital			7,170
Total liabilities and owner's equity			$12,020

5. **LO5**   Using the spreadsheet provided on page 594 for Yoder's Cool Stuff, prepare the closing entries.

6. **LO6**   Pinto Company made the following adjusting entries at the end of the year. It is Pinto's fifth year in operation. Prepare the appropriate reversing entry(ies).

Depreciation Expense—Delivery Equipment	500.00	
Accumulated Depreciation—Delivery Equipment		500.00
Interest Expense	1,000.00	
Interest Payable		1,000.00

The answers to the Self-Study Test Questions are at the end of the chapter (pages 611–613).

APPLYING YOUR KNOWLEDGE

REVIEW QUESTIONS

LO1   1. Describe the nature of the two forms of an income statement.

LO4   2. Name and describe the calculation of two measures that provide an indication of a business's ability to pay current obligations.

LO4   3. Describe how to calculate the following ratios:
   (a) Return on owner's equity
   (b) Accounts receivable turnover
   (c) Inventory turnover

LO5   4. Where is the information obtained that is needed in journalizing the closing entries?

LO5   5. Explain the function of each of the four closing entries made by Sunflower Cycle.

LO5   6. What is the purpose of a post-closing trial balance?

LO6   7. What is the primary purpose of reversing entries?

LO6   8. What is the customary date for reversing entries?

LO6   9. What adjusting entries should be reversed?

SERIES A EXERCISES

E 15-1A   (LO1)
✓ Net sales: $140,600

REVENUE SECTION, MULTIPLE-STEP INCOME STATEMENT Based on the information that follows, prepare the revenue section of a multiple-step income statement.

Sales	$150,000
Sales Returns and Allowances	6,000
Sales Discounts	3,400

E 15-2A   (LO1)
✓ Cost of goods sold: $103,670

COST OF GOODS SOLD SECTION, MULTIPLE-STEP INCOME STATEMENT Based on the information that follows, prepare the cost of goods sold section of a multiple-step income statement.

Merchandise Inventory, January 1, 20--	$ 35,000
Estimated Returns Inventory, January 1,20--	2,000
Purchases	106,000
Purchases Returns and Allowances	5,800
Purchases Discounts	3,230
Freight-In	700
Merchandise Inventory, December 31, 20--	29,500
Estimated Returns Inventory, December 31, 20--	1,500

E 15-3A   (LO1)
✓ Cost of goods sold: $101,145
✓ Net income: $1,463

MULTIPLE-STEP INCOME STATEMENT Use the following information to prepare a multiple-step income statement, including the revenue section and the cost of goods sold section, for Sauter Office Supplies for the year ended December 31, 20--.

Sales	$156,300
Sales Returns and Allowances	2,360
Sales Discounts	4,167
Interest Revenue	425
Merchandise Inventory, January 1, 20--	29,000
Estimated Returns Inventory, January 1, 20--	600
Purchases	112,000
Purchases Returns and Allowances	5,640
Purchases Discounts	2,690
Freight-In	875
Merchandise Inventory, December 31, 20--	32,000
Estimated Returns Inventory, December 31, 20--	1,000
Wages Expense	27,600
Supplies Expense	700
Phone Expense	900
Utilities Expense	8,000
Insurance Expense	1,300
Depreciation Expense—Equipment	3,800
Miscellaneous Expense	590
Interest Expense	4,700

E 15-4A   (LO4)
✓ Current ratio: 4.64 to 1
✓ Return on owner's equity: 28.9%
✓ Inventory turnover: 3.13

FINANCIAL RATIOS Based on the financial statements for Jackson Enterprises (income statement, statement of owner's equity, and balance sheet) shown on pages 596–597, prepare the following financial ratios. All sales are credit sales. The Accounts Receivable balance on January 1, 20--, was $21,600.

1. Working capital
2. Current ratio
3. Quick ratio
4. Return on owner's equity
5. Accounts receivable turnover and average number of days required to collect receivables
6. Inventory turnover and average number of days required to sell inventory

(continued)

Jackson Enterprises
Income Statement
For Year Ended December 31, 20--

Revenue from sales:			
Sales		$184,200	
Less sales returns and allowances		2,100	
Net sales			$182,100
Cost of goods sold:			
Merchandise Inventory, January 1, 20--	$30,000		
Estimated Returns Inventory, January 1, 20--	1,300	$ 31,300	
Purchases	$92,800		
Less: Purchases returns and allowances			
$1,800			
Purchases discounts 1,856	3,656		
Net purchases	$89,144		
Add freight-in	933		
Cost of goods purchased		90,077	
Goods available for sale		$121,377	
Less: Merchandise inventory, Dec. 31, 20--	$27,000		
Estimated returns inventory, Dec. 31, 20--	1,177	28,177	
Cost of goods sold			93,200
Gross profit			$ 88,900
Operating expenses:			
Wages expense		$ 38,000	
Advertising expense		1,180	
Supplies expense		380	
Phone expense		2,210	
Utilities expense		11,000	
Insurance expense		900	
Depreciation expense—building		4,000	
Depreciation expense—equipment		3,800	
Miscellaneous expense		530	
Total operating expenses			62,000
Income from operations			$ 26,900
Other revenues:			
Interest revenue		$ 1,800	
Other expenses:			
Interest expense		900	900
Net income			$ 27,800

Jackson Enterprises
Statement of Owner's Equity
For Year Ended December 31, 20--

J. B. Gray, capital, January 1, 20--		$ 88,000
Net income for the year	$27,800	
Less withdrawals for the year	11,600	
Increase in capital		16,200
J. B. Gray, capital, December 31, 20--		$104,200

Jackson Enterprises Balance Sheet December 31, 20--			
Assets			
Current assets:			
Cash		$20,800	
Accounts receivable		18,900	
Merchandise inventory, Dec. 31, 20--	$27,000		
Estimated returns inventory, Dec. 31, 20--	1,177	28,177	
Supplies		1,323	
Prepaid insurance		900	
Total current assets			$ 70,100
Property, plant, and equipment:			
Building	$90,000		
Less accumulated depreciation—building	28,000	$62,000	
Equipment	$33,000		
Less accumulated depreciation—equipment	7,500	25,500	
Total property, plant, and equipment			87,500
Total assets			$157,600
Liabilities			
Current liabilities:			
Accounts payable	$11,100		
Customer refunds payable	1,500		
Wages payable	500		
Sales tax payable	1,200		
Mortgage payable (current portion)	800		
Total current liabilities		$15,100	
Long-term liabilities:			
Mortgage payable	$39,100		
Less current portion	800	38,300	
Total liabilities			$ 53,400
Owner's Equity			
J. B. Gray, capital			104,200
Total liabilities and owner's equity			$157,600

E 15-5A (LO5) CLOSING ENTRIES Using the spreadsheet and partially completed Income Summary Account on page 598, prepare the following:

1. Closing entries for Gimbel's Gifts and Gadgets in a general journal.
2. A post-closing trial balance.

E 15-6A (LO6) REVERSING ENTRIES From the spreadsheet used in Exercise 15-5A, identify the adjusting entry(ies) that should be reversed and prepare the reversing entry(ies).

E 15-7A (LO5/6) ADJUSTING, CLOSING, AND REVERSING ENTRIES Prepare entries for (a), (b), and (c) listed below using two methods. First, prepare the entries without making a reversing entry. Second, prepare the entries with the use of a reversing entry. Use T-accounts to assist your analysis.

(a) Wages paid during 20-1 are $20,800.
(b) Wages earned but not paid (accrued) as of December 31, 20-1, are $300.
(c) On January 3, 20-2, payroll of $800 is paid, which includes the $300 of wages earned but not paid in December.

EXERCISE 15-5A

	A	B	C	D	E	F	G	H	I
1		Gimbles Gifts and Gadgets							
2		End-of-Period Spreadsheet							
3		For the Year Ended December 31, 20-1							
4	ACCOUNT TITLE	TRIAL BALANCE			ADJUSTMENTS			ADJUSTED TRIAL BALANCE	
5		DEBIT	CREDIT		DEBIT		CREDIT	DEBIT	CREDIT
6	Cash	16,000.00						16,000.00	
7	Accounts Receivable	11,200.00						11,200.00	
8	Merchandise Inventory	60,000.00		(b)	68,000.00	(a)	60,000.00	68,000.00	
9	Estimated Returns Inventory	2,560.00		(e)	3,440.00	(d)	2,560.00	3,440.00	
10	Supplies	6,400.00				(f)	3,760.00	2,640.00	
11	Prepaid Insurance	4,320.00				(g)	1,280.00	3,040.00	
12	Land	104,000.00						104,000.00	
13	Building	200,000.00						200,000.00	
14	Accum. Depr.—Building		80,000.00			(h)	10,000.00		90,000.00
15	Store Equipment	80,000.00						80,000.00	
16	Accum. Depr.—Store Equipment		32,000.00			(i)	4,000.00		36,000.00
17	Accounts Payable		7,680.00						7,680.00
18	Customer Refunds Payable		2,800.00			(c)	1,760.00		4,560.00
19	Wages Payable					(j)	2,800.00		2,800.00
20	Sales Tax Payable		4,720.00						4,720.00
21	Unearned Subscriptions Revenue		7,120.00	(k)	3,520.00				3,600.00
22	J.M. Gimble, Capital		227,448.00						227,448.00
23	J.M. Gimble, Drawing	20,800.00						20,800.00	
24	Income Summary			(a)	60,000.00	(b)	68,000.00	60,000.00	68,000.00
25				(d)	2,560.00	(e)	3,440.00	2,560.00	3,440.00
26	Sales		420,112.00						420,112.00
27	Sales Returns and Allowances	11,600.00		(c)	1,760.00			13,360.00	
28	Rent Revenue					(k)	3,520.00		3,520.00
29	Purchases	100,000.00						100,000.00	
30	Purchases Returns and Allowances		1,120.00						1,120.00
31	Purchases Discounts		1,440.00						1,440.00
32	Freight-In	1,680.00						1,680.00	
33	Wages Expense	100,000.00		(j)	2,800.00			102,800.00	
34	Advertising Expense	10,400.00						10,400.00	
35	Supplies Expense			(f)	3,760.00			3,760.00	
36	Phone Expense	1,080.00						1,080.00	
37	Utilities Expense	6,400.00						6,400.00	
38	Insurance Expense			(g)	1,280.00			1,280.00	
39	Depr. Expense—Building			(h)	10,000.00			10,000.00	
40	Depr. Expense—Store Equipment			(f)	4,000.00			4,000.00	
41	Rent Expense	48,000.00						48,000.00	
42		784,440.00	784,440.00		161,120.00		161,120.00	874,440.00	874,440.00
43								365,320.00	497,632.00
44	Net Income							132,312.00	
45									

ACCOUNT: Income Summary   ACCOUNT NO. 331

DATE		ITEM	POST. REF.	DEBIT	CREDIT	BALANCE	
						DEBIT	CREDIT
20-1 Dec.	31	Adjusting		60 0 0 0 00		60 0 0 0 00	
	31	Adjusting			68 0 0 0 00		8 0 0 0 00
	31	Adjusting		2 5 6 0 00			5 4 4 0 00
	31	Adjusting			3 4 4 0 00		8 8 8 0 00

SERIES A PROBLEMS

P 15-8A   **(LO1/2/3)**
✓ Cost of goods sold: $150,960
✓ Total assets: $639,400

INCOME STATEMENT, STATEMENT OF OWNER'S EQUITY, AND BALANCE SHEET Paulson's Pet Store completed the Adjusted Trial Balance on page 600 for the year ended December 31, 20--. Owner's equity as of January 1, 20--, was $504,320. The current portion of Note Payable is $2,000.

REQUIRED

1. Prepare a multiple-step income statement.

2. Prepare a statement of owner's equity.

3. Prepare a balance sheet.

P 15-9A   **(LO4)**
✓ Working capital: $85,200
✓ Quick ratio: 1.8 to 1
✓ Accts. receivable turnover: 32.8

FINANCIAL RATIOS Use the spreadsheet and financial statements prepared in Problem 15-8A. All sales are credit sales. The Accounts Receivable balance on January 1, 20--, was $10,200.

REQUIRED

Prepare the following financial ratios:

(a) Current ratio

(b) Quick ratio

(c) Working capital

(d) Return on owner's equity

(e) Accounts receivable turnover and average number of days required to collect receivables

(f) Inventory turnover and average number of days required to sell inventory

P 15-10A   **(LO5/6)**
✓ Net income: $123,300
✓ Post-closing trial bal. col. totals: $687,150

END-OF-PERIOD SPREADSHEET, ADJUSTING, CLOSING, AND REVERSING ENTRIES Vicki's Fabric Store shows the trial balance on page 601 as of December 31, 20-1.

At the end of the year, the following adjustments need to be made:

(a, b)   Merchandise inventory as of December 31, $31,600.

(c, d, e)   Vicki estimates that customers will be granted $2,500 in refunds of this year's sales next year and the merchandise expected to be returned will have a cost of $1,800.

(f)   Unused supplies on hand, $350.

(g)   Insurance expired, $2,400.

(h)   Depreciation expense for the year on building, $20,000.

(i)   Depreciation expense for the year on equipment, $4,000.

(j)   Wages earned but not paid (Wages Payable), $520.

(k)   Unearned revenue on December 31, 20-1, $1,200.

(*continued*)

PROBLEM 15-8A

	A	B	C
		ADJUSTED TRIAL BALANCE	
1	**Paulson's Pet Store**		
2	**End-of-Period Spreadsheet (Partial)**		
3	**December 31, 20--**		
4	ACCOUNT TITLE	DEBIT	CREDIT
5			
6	Cash	23,440.00	
7	Accounts Receivable	9,360.00	
8	Merchandise Inventory	64,800.00	
9	Estimated Returns Inventory	1,200.00	
10	Supplies	2,400.00	
11	Prepaid Insurance	1,800.00	
12	Land	90,000.00	
13	Building	350,000.00	
14	Accum. Depr.—Building		20,000.00
15	Store Equipment	120,000.00	
16	Accum. Depr.—Store Equipment		3,600.00
17	Accounts Payable		9,560.00
18	Customer Refunds Payable		1,600.00
19	Wages Payable		1,200.00
20	Sales Tax Payable		3,440.00
21	Note Payable		16,000.00
22	B. Paulson, Capital		534,320.00
23	B. Paulson, Drawing	4,800.00	
24	Income Summary	59,200.00	64,800.00
25		800.00	1,200.00
26	Sales		326,040.00
27	Sales Returns and Allowances	5,360.00	
28	Purchases	162,640.00	
29	Purchases Returns and Allowances		4,080.00
30	Purchases Discounts		3,200.00
31	Freight-In	1,600.00	
32	Wages Expense	69,400.00	
33	Advertising Expense	1,200.00	
34	Supplies Expense	800.00	
35	Phone Expense	2,736.00	
36	Utilities Expense	2,864.00	
37	Insurance Expense	1,600.00	
38	Depr. Expense—Building	10,000.00	
39	Depr. Expense—Equipment	1,800.00	
40	Miscellaneous Expense	600.00	
41	Interest Expense	640.00	
42		989,040.00	989,040.00
43		321,240.00	399,320.00
44	Net Income	78,080.00	
45			

PROBLEM 15-10A CONT.

	A	B	C
1	**Vicki's Fabric Store**		
2	**Trial Balance**		
3	**For the Year Ended December 31, 20-1**		
4 5	ACCOUNT TITLE	DEBIT	CREDIT
6	Cash	28,000.00	
7	Accounts Receivable	14,200.00	
8	Merchandise Inventory	30,000.00	
9	Estimated Returns Inventory	3,000.00	
10	Supplies	1,600.00	
11	Prepaid Insurance	3,600.00	
12	Land	120,000.00	
13	Building	400,000.00	
14	Accum. Depr.—Building		60,000.00
15	Equipment	90,000.00	
16	Accumulated Depr.—Equipment		12,000.00
17	Accounts Payable		11,420.00
18	Customer Refunds Payable		4,200.00
19	Wages Payable		
20	Sales Tax Payable		2,000.00
21	Unearned Costume Design Revenue		5,000.00
22	Note Payable		80,000.00
23	Vicki Roberts, Capital		387,620.00
24	Vicki Roberts, Drawing	21,610.00	
25	Income Summary		
26			
27	Sales		374,500.00
28	Sales Returns and Allowances	12,800.00	
29	Costume Design Revenue		1,200.00
30	Purchases	141,500.00	
31	Purchases Returns and Allowances		1,800.00
32	Purchases Discounts		830.00
33	Freight-In	800.00	
34	Wages Expense	65,000.00	
35	Advertising Expense	810.00	
36	Supplies Expense		
37	Phone Expense	1,210.00	
38	Utilities Expense	3,240.00	
39	Insurance Expense		
40	Depreciation Expense—Building		
41	Depreciation Expense—Equip.		
42	Interest Expense	3,200.00	
43		940,570.00	940,570.00
44			

(continued)

REQUIRED

1. Prepare an end-of-period spreadsheet.
2. Prepare adjusting entries and post adjusting entries to an Income Summary T account.
3. Prepare closing entries and post to a Capital T account. There were no additional investments this year.
4. Prepare a post-closing trial balance.
5. Prepare reversing entry(ies).

SERIES B EXERCISES

E 15-1B   (LO1)
✓ Net sales: $82,196

REVENUE SECTION, MULTIPLE-STEP INCOME STATEMENT Based on the information that follows, prepare the revenue section of a multiple-step income statement.

Sales	$86,200
Sales Returns and Allowances	2,280
Sales Discounts	1,724

E 15-2B   (LO1)
✓ Cost of goods sold: $59,442

COST OF GOODS SOLD SECTION, MULTIPLE-STEP INCOME STATEMENT Based on the information that follows, prepare the cost of goods sold section of a multiple-step income statement.

Merchandise Inventory, January 1, 20--	$13,000
Estimated Returns Inventory, January 1, 20--	800
Purchases	71,300
Purchases Returns and Allowances	3,188
Purchases Discounts	1,460
Freight-In	390
Merchandise Inventory, December 31, 20--	20,000
Estimated Returns Inventory, December 31, 20--	1,400

E 15-3B   (LO1)
✓ Cost of goods sold: $109,714
✓ Net income: $12,040

MULTIPLE-STEP INCOME STATEMENT Use the following information to prepare a multiple-step income statement, including the revenue section and the cost of goods sold section, for Aeito's Plumbing Supplies for the year ended December 31, 20--.

Sales	$166,000
Sales Returns and Allowances	1,620
Sales Discounts	3,320
Interest Revenue	3,184
Merchandise Inventory, January 1, 20--	32,600
Estimated Returns Inventory, January 1, 20--	600
Purchases	111,300
Purchases Returns and Allowances	3,600
Purchases Discounts	2,226
Freight-In	640
Merchandise Inventory, December 31, 20--	29,200
Estimated Returns Inventory, December 31, 20--	400
Wages Expense	22,000
Supplies Expense	650
Phone Expense	1,100
Utilities Expense	9,000
Insurance Expense	1,000
Depreciation Expense—Building	4,600
Depreciation Expense—Equipment	2,800
Miscellaneous Expense	214
Interest Expense	1,126

E 15-4B   (LO4)

✓ Current ratio: 3.68 to 1
✓ Return on owner's equity: 42.6%
✓ Inventory turnover: 3.42

FINANCIAL RATIOS Based on the financial statements, shown on pages 603–604, for McDonald Carpeting Co. (income statement, statement of owner's equity, and balance sheet), prepare the following financial ratios. All sales are credit sales. The balance of Accounts Receivable on January 1, 20--, was $6,800.

1. Working capital
2. Current ratio
3. Quick ratio
4. Return on owner's equity
5. Accounts receivable turnover and the average number of days required to collect receivables
6. Inventory turnover and the average number of days required to sell inventory

McDonald Carpeting Co. Income Statement For Year Ended December 31, 20--			
Revenue from sales:			
Sales		$122,800	
Less sales returns and allowances		1,100	
Net sales			$121,700
Cost of goods sold:			
Merchandise Inventory, January 1, 20--		$18,000	
Estimated Returns Inventory, January 1, 20--		1,300	$ 19,300
Purchases		$62,800	
Less: Purchases returns and allowances	$2,800		
Purchases discounts	1,944	4,744	
Net purchases		$58,056	
Add freight-in		944	
Cost of goods purchased		59,000	
Goods available for sale		$ 78,300	
Less: Merchandise inventory, December 31, 20--		$16,000	
Estimated returns inventory, December 31, 20--		700	16,700
Cost of goods sold			61,600
Gross profit			$ 60,100
Operating expenses:			
Wages expense		$ 18,000	
Advertising expense		980	
Supplies expense		320	
Phone expense		1,200	
Utilities expense		8,000	
Insurance expense		800	
Depreciation expense—building		3,500	
Depreciation expense—equipment		2,500	
Miscellaneous expense		200	
Total operating expenses			35,500
Income from operations			$ 24,600
Other revenues:			
Interest revenue		$ 2,800	
Other expenses:			
Interest expense		2,100	700
Net income			$ 25,300

(continued)

McDonald Carpeting Co. Statement of Owner's Equity For Year Ended December 31, 20--		
C. S. McDonald, capital, January 1, 20--		$52,000
Net income for the year	$25,300	
Less withdrawals for the year	10,400	
Increase in capital		14,900
C. S. McDonald, capital, December 31, 20--		$66,900

McDonald Carpeting Co. Balance Sheet December 31, 20--			
Assets			
Current assets:			
Cash		$10,400	
Accounts receivable		8,900	
Merchandise inventory, December 31, 20--	$16,000		
Estimated returns inventory, December 31, 20--	700	16,700	
Supplies		1,200	
Prepaid insurance		700	
Total current assets			$37,900
Property, plant, and equipment:			
Building	$60,000		
Less accumulated depreciation—building	18,000	$42,000	
Equipment	$22,000		
Less accumulated depreciation—equipment	6,200	15,800	
Total property, plant, and equipment			57,800
Total assets			$95,700
Liabilities			
Current liabilities:			
Accounts payable	$ 7,500		
Customer refunds payable	900		
Wages payable	300		
Sales tax payable	1,000		
Mortgage payable (current portion)	600		
Total current liabilities		$10,300	
Long-term liabilities:			
Mortgage payable	$19,100		
Less current portion	600	18,500	
Total liabilities			$28,800
Owner's Equity			
C. S. McDonald, capital			66,900
Total liabilities and owner's equity			$95,700

E 15-5B   (LO5)   CLOSING ENTRIES Using the spreadsheet and partially completed Income Summary Account on page 605 prepare the following:

1. Closing entries for Balloons and Baubbles in a general journal.
2. A post-closing trial balance.

E 15-6B   (LO6)   REVERSING ENTRIES From the spreadsheet in Exercise 15-5B, identify the adjusting entry(ies) that should be reversed and prepare the reversing entry(ies).

E 15-7B   (LO5/6)   ADJUSTING, CLOSING, AND REVERSING ENTRIES Prepare entries for (a), (b), and (c) listed below using two methods. First, prepare the entries without making a reversing entry. Second, prepare the entries with the use of a reversing entry. Use T-accounts to assist your analysis.

(a) Wages paid during 20-1 are $20,080.

(b) Wages earned but not paid (accrued) as of December 31, 20-1, are $280.

(c) On January 3, 20-2, payroll of $840 is paid, which includes the $280 of wages earned but not paid in December.

EXERCISE 15-5B

	A	B	C	D	E	F	G	H	I
1		Balloons and Baubbles							
2		End-of-Period Spreadsheet							
3		For the Year Ended December 31, 20-1							
4	ACCOUNT TITLE	TRIAL BALANCE		ADJUSTMENTS				ADJUSTED TRIAL BALANCE	
5		DEBIT	CREDIT		DEBIT		CREDIT	DEBIT	CREDIT
6	Cash	18,000.00						18,000.00	
7	Accounts Receivable	12,600.00						12,600.00	
8	Merchandise Inventory	67,500.00		(b)	76,500.00	(a)	67,500.00	76,500.00	
9	Estimated Returns Inventory	2,880.00		(e)	3,870.00	(d)	2,880.00	3,870.00	
10	Supplies	7,200.00				(f)	4,230.00	2,970.00	
11	Prepaid Insurance	4,860.00				(g)	1,440.00	3,420.00	
12	Land	117,000.00						117,000.00	
13	Building	225,000.00						225,000.00	
14	Accum. Depr.—Building		90,000.00			(h)	11,250.00		101,250.00
15	Store Equipment	90,000.00						90,000.00	
16	Accum. Depr.—Store Equipment		36,000.00			(i)	4,500.00		40,500.00
17	Accounts Payable		8,640.00						8,640.00
18	Customer Refunds Payable		3,150.00			(c)	1,980.00		5,130.00
19	Wages Payable					(j)	3,150.00		3,150.00
20	Sales Tax Payable		5,310.00						5,310.00
21	Unearned Repair Revenue		8,010.00	(k)	3,960.00				4,050.00
22	L. Marlow, Capital		255,879.00						255,879.00
23	L. Marlow, Drawing	23,400.00						23,400.00	
24	Income Summary			(a)	67,500.00	(b)	76,500.00	67,500.00	76,500.00
25				(d)	2,880.00	(e)	3,870.00	2,880.00	3,870.00
26	Sales		472,626.00						427,626.00
27	Sales Returns and Allowances	13,050.00		(c)	1,980.00			15,030.00	
28	Rent Revenue					(k)	3,960.00		3,960.00
29	Purchases	112,500.00						112,500.00	
30	Purchases Returns and Allowances		1,260.00						1,260.00
31	Purchases Discounts		1,620.00						1,620.00
32	Freight-In	1,890.00						1,890.00	
33	Wages Expense	112,500.00		(j)	3,150.00			115,650.00	
34	Advertising Expense	11,700.00						11,700.00	
35	Supplies Expense			(f)	4,230.00			4,230.00	
36	Phone Expense	1,215.00						1,215.00	
37	Utilities Expense	7,200.00						7,200.00	
38	Insurance Expense			(g)	1,440.00			1,440.00	
39	Depr. Expense—Building			(h)	11,250.00			11,250.00	
40	Depr. Expense—Store Equipment			(i)	4,500.00			4,500.00	
41	Rent Expense	54,000.00						54,000.00	
42		882,495.00	882,495.00		181,260.00		181,260.00	983,745.00	983,745.00
43								410,985.00	559,836.00
44	Net Income							148,851.00	
45									

(*continued*)

EXERCISE 15-5B (Concluded)

ACCOUNT: Income Summary								ACCOUNT NO. 331		
DATE	ITEM	POST. REF.	DEBIT		CREDIT		BALANCE			
							DEBIT		CREDIT	
20-1 Dec. 31	Adjusting		67 5 0 0 00				67 5 0 0 00			
31	Adjusting				76 5 0 0 00				9 0 0 0 00	
31	Adjusting		2 8 8 0 00						6 1 2 0 00	
31	Adjusting				3 8 7 0 00				9 9 9 0 00	

SERIES B PROBLEMS

P 15-8B   (LO1/2/3)
✓ Cost of goods sold: $166,056
✓ Total assets: $703,340

INCOME STATEMENT, STATEMENT OF OWNER'S EQUITY, AND BALANCE SHEET Backlund Farm Supply completed the Adjusted Trial Balance on page 607 for the year ended December 31, 20--. Owner's equity as of January 1, 20--, was $507,752. The current portion of Note Payable is $3,000.

REQUIRED

1. Prepare a multiple-step income statement.
2. Prepare a statement of owner's equity.
3. Prepare a balance sheet.

P 15-9B   (LO4)
✓ Working capital: $92,920
✓ Quick ratio: 1.8 to 1
✓ Accts. receivable turnover: 20.9

FINANCIAL RATIOS Use the spreadsheet and financial statements prepared in Problem 15-8B. Net credit sales were $210,000. The Accounts Receivable balance on January 1 was $9,800.

REQUIRED
Prepare the following financial ratios:

(a) Current ratio
(b) Quick ratio
(c) Working capital
(d) Return on owner's equity
(e) Accounts receivable turnover and the average number of days required to collect receivables
(f) Inventory turnover and the average number of days required to sell inventory

P 15-10B   (LO5/6)
✓ Net income: $147,960
✓ Post-closing trial bal. columns: $824,580

END-OF-PERIOD SPREADSHEET, ADJUSTING, CLOSING, AND REVERSING ENTRIES The trial balance for Danbury Kite Shop as of December 31, 20-1, is shown on page 608.

At the end of the year, the following adjustments need to be made:

(a, b)   Merchandise inventory as of December 31, $37,920.
(c, d, e) Bill Danbury estimates that customers will be granted $3,000 in refunds of this year's sales next year and the merchandise expected to be returned will have a cost of $2,160.
(f)   Unused supplies on hand, $420.
(g)   Insurance expired, $2,880.
(h)   Depreciation expense for the year on building, $24,000.
(i)   Depreciation expense for the year on equipment, $4,800.
(j)   Wages earned but not paid (Wages Payable), $624.
(k)   Unearned repair revenue on December 31, 20-1, $1,440.

REQUIRED

1. Prepare an end-of-period spreadsheet.
2. Prepare adjusting entries and post adjusting entries to an Income Summary T account.
3. Prepare closing entries and post to a Capital T account. There were no additional investments this year.
4. Prepare a post-closing trial balance.
5. Prepare reversing entry(ies).

PROBLEM 15-8B

	A	B	C
1	**Backlund Farm Supply**		
2	**End-of-Period Spreadsheet (Partial)**		
3	**December 31, 20--**		
4	ACCOUNT TITLE	ADJUSTED TRIAL BALANCE	
5		DEBIT	CREDIT
6	Cash	25,784.00	
7	Accounts Receivable	10,296.00	
8	Merchandise Inventory	71,280.00	
9	Estimated Returns Inventory	1,320.00	
10	Supplies	2,640.00	
11	Prepaid Insurance	1,980.00	
12	Land	99,000.00	
13	Building	385,000.00	
14	Accum. Depr.—Building		22,000.00
15	Store Equipment	132,000.00	
16	Accum. Depr.—Store Equipment		3,960.00
17	Accounts Payable		10,516.00
18	Customer Refunds Payable		1,760.00
19	Wages Payable		1,320.00
20	Sales Tax Payable		3,784.00
21	Note Payable		17,600.00
22	J. Buckland, Capital		587,752.00
23	J. Buckland, Drawing	5,280.00	
24	Income Summary	65,120.00	71,280.00
25		880.00	1,320.00
26	Sales		358,644.00
27	Sales Returns and Allowances	5,896.00	
28	Purchases	178,904.00	
29	Purchases Returns and Allowances		4,488.00
30	Purchases Discounts		3,520.00
31	Freight-In	1,760.00	
32	Wages Expense	76,340.00	
33	Advertising Expense	1,320.00	
34	Supplies Expense	880.00	
35	Phone Expense	3,010.00	
36	Utilities Expense	3,150.00	
37	Insurance Expense	1,760.00	
38	Depr. Expense—Building	11,000.00	
39	Depr. Expense—Store Equipment	1,980.00	
40	Miscellaneous Expense	660.00	
41	Interest Expense	704.00	
42		1,087,944.00	1,087,944.00
43		353,364.00	439,252.00
44	Net Income	85,888.00	
45			

PROBLEM 15-10B

	A	B	C
1	Danbury Kite Shop		
2	Trial Balance		
3	For the Year Ended December 31, 20-1		
4	ACCOUNT TITLE	DEBIT	CREDIT
5			
6	Cash	33,600.00	
7	Accounts Receivable	17,040.00	
8	Merchandise Inventory	36,000.00	
9	Estimated Returns Inventory	3,600.00	
10	Supplies	1,920.00	
11	Prepaid Insurance	4,320.00	
12	Land	144,000.00	
13	Building	480,000.00	
14	Accum. Depr.—Building		72,000.00
15	Equipment	108,000.00	
16	Accumulated Depr.—Equipment		14,400.00
17	Accounts Payable		13,744.00
18	Customer Refunds Payable		5,000.00
19	Wages Payable		
20	Sales Tax Payable		2,400.00
21	Unearned Repair Revenue		6,000.00
22	Note Payable		96,000.00
23	W. Danbury, Capital		465,144.00
24	W. Danbury, Drawing	25,932.00	
25	Income Summary		
26			
27	Sales		449,400.00
28	Sales Returns and Allowances	15,360.00	
29	Repair Revenue		1,440.00
30	Purchases	169,800.00	
31	Purchases Returns and Allowances		2,160.00
32	Purchases Discounts		996.00
33	Freight-In	960.00	
34	Wages Expense	78,000.00	
35	Advertising Expense	972.00	
36	Supplies Expense		
37	Phone Expense	1,452.00	
38	Utilities Expense	3,888.00	
39	Insurance Expense		
40	Depreciation Expense—Building		
41	Depreciation Expense—Equip.		
42	Interest Expense	3,840.00	
43		1,128,684.00	1,128,684.00
44			

MANAGING YOUR WRITING

A friend of yours has the opportunity to invest in a small business. She has come to you for advice on how she might determine whether this would be a good investment. In particular, she is concerned about how long it takes to sell the merchandise and collect receivables. Draft a memo suggesting various ratios that should be computed to evaluate the business's profitability, ability to pay its current obligations, and time required to sell inventory and collect receivables.

ETHICS ⭐

ETHICS CASE

Brian Marlow recently was hired to prepare Louise Michener Consulting's year-end financial statements. Brian just earned his CPA certificate, and Louise Michener was one of his first clients. Louise employs a bookkeeper, Martha Halling, who does the daily journal entries and prepares a year-to-date trial balance at the end of each month. Martha gives the December 31 trial balance to a CPA to make the adjustments and generate the financial statements. As Brian was looking through Louise Michener's books, he noticed two things. First, in each of the last three years, a different CPA had prepared the financial statements. Second, the amount shown on the December 31 trial balance for miscellaneous expense was quite high this year compared to prior years. Brian called Martha to find out if she knew why miscellaneous expense had such a high balance. Martha's response was "I just do what Louise tells me to do. If she wants to charge personal expenses to the company, it's none of my business."

1. What should Brian do?

2. How might Brian's decision affect Martha? Has Martha done anything unethical?

3. Write a short letter from Brian to Louise explaining why personal items should not be charged to a business.

4. In small groups, discuss the ethical responsibilities of an accountant relating to a client's books.

MASTERY PROBLEM

✓ Net income: $25,650
✓ Total assets: $125,000
✓ Current ratio: 3.4 to 1
✓ Return on owner's equity: 26.1%

Dominique Fouque owns and operates Dominique's Doll House. She has a small shop in which she sells new and antique dolls. She is particularly well known for her collection of antique Ken and Barbie dolls. A completed spreadsheet for 20-3 is shown on page 610. Fouque made no additional investments during the year and the long-term note payable is due in 20-9. No portion of the long-term note is due within the next year. Net credit sales for 20-3 were $38,000, and receivables on January 1 were $3,000.

REQUIRED

1. Prepare a multiple-step income statement.

2. Prepare a statement of owner's equity.

3. Prepare a balance sheet.

4. Compute the following measures of performance and financial condition for 20-3:
   (a) Current ratio
   (b) Quick ratio
   (c) Working capital
   (d) Return on owner's equity
   (e) Accounts receivable turnover and average number of days required to collect receivables
   (f) Inventory turnover and the average number of days required to sell inventory

5. Prepare adjusting entries and indicate which should be reversed and why.

6. Open an Income Summary account. Post adjusting and closing entries (prepared in 7) to this account.

7. Prepare closing entries.

8. Prepare reversing entries for the adjustments where appropriate.

(continued)

MASTERY PROBLEM

	A	B	C	D	E	F	G	H	I
1		Dominique's Doll House							
2		End-of-Period Spreadsheet							
3		For the Year Ended December 31, 20-3							
4	ACCOUNT TITLE	TRIAL BALANCE			ADJUSTMENTS			ADJUSTED TRIAL BALANCE	
5		DEBIT	CREDIT		DEBIT		CREDIT	DEBIT	CREDIT
6	Cash	16,700.00						16,700.00	
7	Accounts Receivable	3,200.00						3,200.00	
8	Merchandise Inventory	31,300.00		(b)	28,000.00	(a)	31,300.00	28,000.00	
9	Estimated Returns Inventory	1,000.00		(e)	1,100.00	(d)	1,000.00	1,100.00	
10	Office Supplies	800.00				(f)	600.00	200.00	
11	Prepaid Insurance	1,200.00				(g)	400.00	800.00	
12	Store Equipment	95,000.00						95,000.00	
13	Accum. Depr.—Store Equipment		15,000.00			(h)	5,000.00		20,000.00
14	Notes Payable		6,000.00						6,000.00
15	Accounts Payable		5,500.00						5,500.00
16	Customer Refunds Payable		1,500.00			(c)	200.00		1,700.00
17	Wages Payable					(i)	200.00		200.00
18	Sales Tax Payable		850.00						850.00
19	Unearned Show Revenue		1,000.00	(j)	700.00				300.00
20	Long-term Note Payable		10,000.00						10,000.00
21	Dominique Fouque, Capital		95,800.00						95,800.00
22	Dominique Fouque, Drawing	21,000.00						21,000.00	
23	Income Summary			(a)	31,300.00	(b)	28,000.00	31,300.00	28,000.00
24				(d)	1,000.00	(e)	1,100.00	1,000.00	1,100.00
25	Sales		201,500.00						201,500.00
26	Sales Returns and Allowances	5,900.00		(c)	200.00			6,100.00	
27	Show Revenue		5,000.00			(j)	700.00		5,700.00
28	Purchases	72,000.00						72,000.00	
29	Purchases Returns and Allowances		750.00						750.00
30	Freight-In	1,200.00						1,200.00	
31	Wages Expense	42,000.00		(i)	200.00			42,200.00	
32	Rent Expense	42,000.00						42,000.00	
33	Office Supplies Expense			(f)	600.00			600.00	
34	Phone Expense	1,500.00						1,500.00	
35	Utilities Expense	7,600.00						7,600.00	
36	Insurance Expense			(g)	400.00			400.00	
37	Depr. Expense—Store Equipment			(h)	5,000.00			5,000.00	
38	Interest Expense	500.00						500.00	
39		342,900.00	342,900.00		68,500.00		68,500.00	377,400.00	377,400.00
40								211,400.00	237,050.00
41	Net Income							25,650.00	
42									

CHALLENGE PROBLEM

This problem challenges you to apply your cumulative accounting knowledge to move a step beyond the material in the chapter.

✓ Average days to convert inventory to cash: 45.0 days

John Byers owns and operates Byers Building Supplies. The following information was taken from his financial statements:

Balance Sheet	12/31/-2	12/31/-1
Accounts Receivable	$700	$500
Inventory	300	100

Income Statement	
Net Credit Sales	$7,200
Cost of Goods Sold	5,000

All sales are made on account.

REQUIRED

Based on the above information, on average, approximately how many days pass from the time Byers purchases inventory until he receives cash from customers?

ANSWERS TO SELF-STUDY TEST QUESTIONS

True/False

1. T
2. F (whichever is longer)
3. T
4. T
5. F (number of times accounts receivable turned over)

Multiple Choice

1. c
2. a
3. b
4. d
5. c

Checkpoint Exercises

1.

Yoder's Cool Stuff Income Statement For Year Ended December 31, 20--			
Revenue from sales:			
Sales		$261,000	
Less: sales returns and allowances		21,000	
Net sales			$240,000
Cost of goods sold:			
Merchandise inventory, January 1, 20--	$36,000		
Estimated returns inventory, January 1, 20--	4,000	$ 40,000	
Purchases		160,000	
Goods available for sale		$200,000	
Less: Merchandise inventory, December 31, 20--	$75,000		
Estimated returns inventory, December 31, 20--	5,000	80,000	
Cost of goods sold			120,000
Gross profit			$120,000
Operating expenses:			
Wages expense		$ 14,000	
Rent expense		4,000	
Supplies expense		1,200	
Phone expense		1,000	
Insurance expense		500	
Depr. expense—delivery equipment		20,000	
Total operating expenses			40,700
Net income			$ 79,300

2.

Yoder's Cool Stuff Statement of Owner's Equity For Year Ended December 31, 20--		
P. Yoder, capital, January 1, 20--		$ 88,000
Net income for the year	$79,300	
Less withdrawals for the year	3,000	
Increase in capital		76,300
P. Yoder, capital, December 31, 20--		$164,300

3.

Yoder's Cool Stuff Balance Sheet December 31, 20--		
Assets		
Current assets:		
Cash	$ 7,400	
Accounts receivable	13,000	
Merchandise inventory	75,000	
Estimated returns inventory	5,000	
Supplies	400	
Prepaid insurance	3,500	
Total current assets		$104,300
Property, plant, and equipment:		
Delivery equipment	$160,000	
Less accumulated depreciation—delivery equipment	60,000	100,000
Total assets		$204,300
Liabilities		
Current liabilities:		
Accounts payable	$ 30,000	
Customer refunds payable	9,000	
Wages payable	1,000	
Total current liabilities		$ 40,000
Owner's Equity		
Pete Yoder, capital		164,300
Total liabilities and owner's equity		$204,300

4. a. Working capital:

Current assets	$9,020
– Current liabilities	4,850
	$4,170

b. Current ratio:

$$\frac{\text{Current Assets}}{\text{Current Liabilities}} = \frac{\$9,020}{\$4,850} = 1.86 \text{ to } 1$$

c. Return on owner's equity:

$$\frac{\text{Net Income}}{\text{Average Owner's Equity}} = \frac{\$2,170}{(\$5,000 + \$7,170)/2} = \frac{\$2,170}{\$6,085} = 35.7\%$$

d. Inventory turnover:

$$\frac{\text{Cost of Goods Sold}}{\text{Average Inventory}} = \frac{\$16,000}{(\$4,000 + \$6,000)/2} = \frac{\$16,000}{\$5,000} = 3.2$$

5.

	DATE		DESCRIPTION	POST. REF.	DEBIT	CREDIT	
1	20--		Closing Entries				1
2	Dec.	31	Sales		261 0 0 0 00		2
3			Income Summary			261 0 0 0 00	3
4							4
5		31	Income Summary		221 7 0 0 00		5
6			Sales Returns and Allowances			21 0 0 0 00	6
7			Purchases			160 0 0 0 00	7
8			Wages Expense			14 0 0 0 00	8
9			Rent Expense			4 0 0 0 00	9
10			Supplies Expense			1 2 0 0 00	10
11			Phone Expense			1 0 0 0 00	11
12			Insurance Expense			5 0 0 00	12
13			Depr. Expense—Delivery Equipment			20 0 0 0 00	13
14							14
15		31	Income Summary		79 3 0 0 00		15
16			Pete Yoder, Capital			79 3 0 0 00	16
17							17
18		31	Pete Yoder, Capital		3 0 0 0 00		18
19			Pete Yoder, Drawing			3 0 0 0 00	19
20							20

Income Summary

BI	36,000.00	75,000.00	EI
B-ERI	4,000.00	5,000.00	E-ERI
		261,000.00	Rev.
Exp	221,700.00		
NI	79,300.00		

ERI: Estimated Returns Inventory

Pete Yoder, Capital

		88,000.00	ATB
Drawing	3,000.00	79,300.00	Net Income
		164,300.00	Bal.

6.

Interest Payable	1,000.00	
Interest Expense		1,000.00

Do not reverse the adjustment for depreciation expense. The adjusting entry does not increase an asset or liability from a zero balance and does not make the subsequent entry easier.

COMPREHENSIVE PROBLEM 2:
Accounting Cycle with Subsidiary Ledgers, Part 1

During the second half of December 20-1, TJ's Specialty Shop engaged in the following transactions:

Dec. 16   Received payment from Lucy Greene on account, $1,960.

16   Sold merchandise on account to Kim Fields, $160, plus sales tax of $8. Sale No. 640.

17   Returned merchandise to Evans Essentials for credit, $150.

18   Issued Check No. 813 to Evans Essentials in payment of December 1 balance of $1,250, less the credit received on December 17.

19   Sold merchandise on account to Lucy Greene, $620, plus tax of $31. Sale No. 641.

22   Received payment from John Dempsey on account, $1,560.

23   Issued Check No. 814 for the purchase of supplies, $120. (Debit Supplies)

24   Purchased merchandise on account from West Wholesalers, $1,200. Invoice No. 465, dated December 24, terms n/30.

26   Purchased merchandise on account from Nathen Co., $800. Invoice No. 817, dated December 26, terms 2/10, n/30.

27   Issued Check No. 815 to KC Power & Light (Utilities Expense) for the month of December, $630.

27   Sold merchandise on account to John Dempsey, $2,020, plus tax of $101. Sale No. 642.

29   Received payment from Martha Boyle on account, $2,473.

29   Issued Check No. 816 in payment of wages (Wages Expense) for the two-week period ending December 28, $1,100.

30   Issued Check No. 817 to Meyers Trophy Shop for a cash purchase of merchandise, $200.

As of December 16, TJ's account balances were as follows:

Account	Account No.	Debit	Credit
Cash	101	$ 9,705	
Accounts Receivable	122	10,256	
Merchandise Inventory	131	21,800	
Estimated Returns Inventory	135	250	
Supplies	141	1,035	
Prepaid Insurance	145	1,380	
Land	161	8,750	
Building	171	52,000	
Accum. Depr.—Building	171.1		$ 9,200
Store Equipment	181	28,750	
Accum. Depr.—Store Equipment	181.1		9,300
Accounts Payable	202		3,600
Customer Refunds Payable	203		300

Wages Payable	219		
Sales Tax Payable	231		1,378
Mortgage Payable	251		12,525
Tom Jones, Capital	311		90,000
Tom Jones, Drawing	312	8,500	
Income Summary	313		
Sales	401		124,900
Sales Returns and Allowances	401.1	1,430	
Purchases	501	64,400	
Purchases Returns and Allowances	501.1		460
Purchases Discounts	501.2		698
Freight-In	502	175	
Wages Expense	511	26,100	
Advertising Expense	512	4,700	
Supplies Expense	524		
Phone Expense	525	2,180	
Utilities Expense	533	6,900	
Insurance Expense	535		
Depr. Expense—Building	540		
Depr. Expense—Store Equipment	541		
Miscellaneous Expense	549	2,700	
Interest Expense	551	1,350	
		$252,361	$252,361

TJ's also had the following subsidiary ledger balances as of December 16:

Accounts Receivable Ledger			*Accounts Payable Ledger*	
Customer	**Balance**		**Vendor**	**Balance**
Martha Boyle 12 Jude Lane Hartford, CT 06117	$3,796		Evans Essentials 34 Harry Ave. East Hartford, CT 05234	$3,600
Anne Clark 52 Juniper Road Hartford, CT 06118	2,100		Nathen Co. 1009 Drake Rd. Farmington, CT 06082	—
John Dempsey 700 Hobbes Dr. Avon, CT 06108	1,560		Owen Enterprises 43 Lucky Lane Bristol, CT 06007	—
Kim Fields 5200 Hamilton Ave. Hartford, CT 06117	—		West Wholesalers 888 Anders Street Newington, CT 06789	—
Lucy Greene 236 Bally Lane Simsbury, CT 06123	2,800			

(*continued*)

At the end of the year, the following adjustments (a)–(j) need to be made:

(a, b) Merchandise inventory as of December 31, $19,700.

(c, d, e) Jones estimates that customers will be granted $400 in refunds of this year's sales next year, and the merchandise expected to be returned will have a cost of $300.

(f) Unused supplies on hand, $525.

(g) Unexpired insurance on December 31, $1,000.

(h) Depreciation expense on the building for the year, $800.

(i) Depreciation expense on the store equipment for the year, $450.

(j) Wages earned but not paid as of December 31, $330.

REQUIRED

For those not using working papers:

1. If you are not using the working papers, open a general ledger, an accounts receivable ledger, and an accounts payable ledger as of December 16. Enter the December 16 balance of each of the accounts, with a check mark in the Posting Reference column.

For working paper users and nonusers:

2. Enter transactions for the second half of December in the general journal. Post immediately to the accounts receivable and accounts payable ledgers.

3. Post from the journal to the general ledger.

4. Prepare schedules of accounts receivable and accounts payable.

5. Prepare a year-end spreadsheet, an income statement, a statement of owner's equity, and a balance sheet. The mortgage payable includes $600 that is due within one year.

6. Journalize and post adjusting entries.

7. Journalize and post closing entries. (*Hint*: Close all expense and revenue account balances. Then, close Income Summary and Tom Jones, Drawing to Tom Jones, Capital.)

8. Prepare a post-closing trial balance.

9. Journalize and post reversing entries for the adjustments where appropriate, as of January 1, 20-2.

COMPREHENSIVE PROBLEM 2:

Accounting Cycle with Subsidiary Ledgers, Part 2

During the month of January 20-2, TJ's Specialty Shop engaged in the following transactions:

Jan. 1 Sold merchandise on account to Anne Clark, $3,000, plus tax of $150. Sale No. 643.

2 Issued Check No. 818 to Nathen Co. in payment of January 1 balance of $800, less 2% discount.

(*continued*)

Jan. 3   Purchased merchandise on account from West Wholesalers, $1,500. Invoice No. 678, dated January 3, terms 2/15, n/30.

4   Purchased merchandise on account from Owen Enterprises, $2,000. Invoice No. 767, dated January 4, terms 2/10, n/30.

4   Issued Check No. 819 in payment of phone expense for the month of January, $180.

8   Sold merchandise for cash, $3,600, plus tax of $180.

9   Received payment from Lucy Greene in full settlement of account, $1,491.

10   Issued Check No. 820 to West Wholesalers in payment of January 1 balance of $1,200.

12   Sold merchandise on account to Martha Boyle, $1,000, plus tax of $50. Sale No. 644.

12   Received payment from Anne Clark on account, $2,100.

12   Issued Check No. 821 in payment of wages (Wages Expense) for the two-week period ending January 11, $1,100.

13   Issued Check No. 822 to Owen Enterprises in payment of January 4 purchase. Invoice No. 767, less 2% discount.

13   Martha Boyle returned merchandise for a credit, $800, plus sales tax of $40.

17   Returned merchandise to Evans Essentials for credit, $300.

22   Received payment from John Dempsey on account, $2,121.

26   Issued Check No. 823 in payment of wages (Wages Expense) for the two-week period ending January 25, $1,100.

27   Issued Check No. 824 to KC Power & Light (Utilities Expense) for the month of January, $630.

27   Sold merchandise on account to John Dempsey, $2,000, plus tax of $100. Sale No. 645.

Late in January, TJ's agreed to sell the business to a competitor. To agree on a selling price, financial statements are needed as of January 31 and for the month of January 20-2. To prepare these financial statements, TJ's must perform the same procedures it normally does at year-end.

At the end of January, the following adjustments (a)–(j) need to be made:

(a, b)   Merchandise inventory as of January 31, $19,000.

(c, d, e)   Jones estimates that customers will be granted $500 in refunds of this month's sales in subsequent months, and the merchandise expected to be returned will have a cost of $360.

(f)   Unused supplies on hand, $115.

(g)   Unexpired insurance on January 31, $968.

(h)   Depreciation expense on the building for the month, $67.

(i)   Depreciation expense on the store equipment for the month, $38.

(j)   Wages earned but not paid as of January 31, $330.

REQUIRED

For those not using working papers:

1. If you are not using the working papers, open a general ledger, an accounts receivable ledger, and an accounts payable ledger as of January 1. Enter the January 1 balance of each of the accounts, with a check mark in the Posting Reference column. The beginning balances for Part 2 are the same as the balances from your solution to Part 1 of Comprehensive Problem 2.

For working paper users and nonusers:

2. Enter transactions for the month of January in the general journal. Post immediately to the accounts receivable and accounts payable ledgers.

3. Post from the journal to the general ledger.

4. Prepare schedules of accounts receivable and accounts payable.

5. Prepare a month-end spreadsheet income statement, statement of owner's equity, and balance sheet. The mortgage payable includes $600 that is due within one year.

6. Journalize and post adjusting entries.

7. Journalize and post closing entries. (*Hint*: Close all expense and revenue account balances. Then close Income Summary and Tom Jones, Drawing to Tom Jones, Capital.)

8. Prepare a post-closing trial balance.

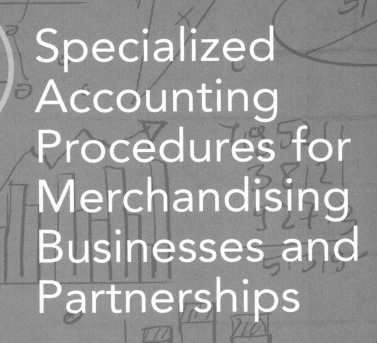

4

Specialized Accounting Procedures for Merchandising Businesses and Partnerships

Add some color to your learning!

Throughout the text, you will be introduced to many important terms and types of accounts. To help you learn the different terms and types of accounts, we have coded many of them using the following color key in Part 4:

Assets

Contra-Assets

Liabilities

Capital

Drawing

Revenues

Contra-Revenues

Expenses

Contra-Costs (Contra-Purchases)

Income Summary (Net Income/Net Loss)

Chapter 16 Accounting for Accounts Receivable

Consumers are so accustomed to buying on account today that it is difficult for most businesses to function without making credit sales. Of course, this means businesses must manage their accounts receivable. To whom should credit sales be made? How much credit should be allowed? How much time should customers be allowed to pay their accounts? What should be done if a customer fails to make timely payments? What strategies can be used to encourage payment? Remember: Sales on account can be a good thing, but to succeed, the business must collect the cash. As you can see, the management of credit sales and accounts receivable can be challenging and complex.

You might recall from Chapter 9 that businesses can hire outside companies to manage payroll because of its complexity. Well, the same kind of outside service is available for managing accounts receivable. Receivables Performance Management (RPM) is a company that offers such services. RPM was founded in 2002, and its revenues in a recent six-year period grew by almost 500%, from $3.9 million to $19 million. From its headquarters in Lynnwood, Washington, the company specializes in receivables management and collection services. It analyzes and manages the entire receivables process, including the challenging collection stage and handling delinquent and disputed accounts. Its clients include large utilities, telecommunication companies, banks, and many small businesses. In this chapter, you will learn how to account for accounts receivable, including accounting for accounts that cannot be collected.

LEARNING OBJECTIVES

Careful study of this chapter should enable you to:

LO1 Apply the allowance method of accounting for uncollectible accounts.

LO2 Apply the percentage of sales and percentage of receivables methods of estimating uncollectible accounts.

LO3 Apply the direct write-off method of accounting for uncollectible accounts.

Accounts receivable are an integral part of operating a business. We first learned about them way back in Chapter 2, as an example of the assets accounting element, and as part of a common business transaction. Businesses generally are willing to sell goods and services on account and to carry accounts receivable because they want to increase sales. Most of us simply tend to buy more if we can "charge it" rather than pay cash. In fact, one way a business can increase sales is to have easy credit policies and sell on account to virtually anyone. Unfortunately, some businesses and individuals who "charge it" then are unwilling or unable to "pay for it." Thus, a cost to a business of selling goods and services on account is that some of the accounts receivable will be uncollectible or bad debts. The more willing a business is to make sales on account, the more uncollectible accounts it is likely to have.

There are two methods of accounting for uncollectible accounts: (1) the allowance method and (2) the direct write-off method. The purpose of this chapter is to learn how to use these methods.

LO1 Allowance Method

Apply the allowance method of accounting for uncollectible accounts.

Bad debt expense is an expense from failure to collect an account receivable. The allowance method is a technique that attempts to recognize bad debt expense in the same period that the related credit sales are made. This method is consistent with the matching principle, which states that expenses should be matched with the revenues they helped to produce.

Under the accrual basis of accounting, the allowance method is generally required for financial reporting purposes. To use the allowance method, three steps are followed:

> **LEARNING KEY** 🔑
>
> Under the allowance method, bad debt expense is recorded as a *year-end adjustment*.

STEP 1 At the end of each accounting period, the amount of bad debt expense or uncollectible accounts is estimated.

STEP 2 An adjusting entry is made to recognize the bad debt expense and reduce reported receivables for the amount of estimated uncollectible accounts. For example, if the estimated amount at December 31 is $900, the entry is as shown below and in Figure 16-1.

4	Dec.	31	Bad Debt Expense		9 0 0 00		4
5			Allowance for Doubtful Accounts			9 0 0 00	5
6							6

FIGURE 16-1 Adjusting Entry for Bad Debt Expense

Assets		=	Liabilities		+	Owner's Equity						
Debit +	Credit −		Debit −	Credit +				Debit −			Credit +	
						Drawing		Expenses		Revenues		
						Debit +	Credit −	Debit +	Credit −	Debit −	Credit +	
Accounts Receivable								Bad Debt Expense				
Bal. 30,000								900				
Allowance for Doubtful Accounts												
	900											

Note that the credit is not to Accounts Receivable. This is because at this time we do not know which specific customers will fail to pay. Instead, a contra-asset account, Allowance for Doubtful Accounts (also known as Allowance for Uncollectible Accounts or Allowance for Bad Debts), is credited. The balance of this account is deducted from Accounts Receivable on the balance sheet. The remaining amount is known as the net receivables or net realizable value of accounts receivable because it is the amount the business expects to collect. Accounts receivable of $30,000 with an allowance of $900 would appear as follows:

Current assets:
Accounts receivable $30,000
Less allowance for doubtful accounts   900 $29,100   ◄—— Net receivables (Net realizable value)

STEP 3   In a subsequent period, when a specific account is identified as uncollectible, an entry is made to write off the account and reduce the balance in Allowance for Doubtful Accounts. For example, if the uncollectible account is $250, the entry is as follows:

8	Allowance for Doubtful Accounts			2 5 0 00			8
9	Accounts Receivable/Customer Name				2 5 0 00		9
10	Wrote off uncollectible account						10

LO2   Estimating and Writing Off Uncollectibles

Apply the percentage of sales and percentage of receivables methods of estimating uncollectible accounts.

To use the allowance method, we need a way to estimate the amount of bad debt expense or uncollectible accounts. Two basic methods are used: the percentage of sales method and the percentage of receivables method. A company chooses one method or the other and uses it consistently over time.

Percentage of Sales Method

The percentage of sales method is based on the idea that some portion of the credit sales will not lead to collections. This way of viewing uncollectible accounts is illustrated in Figure 16-2 on page 624 for total credit sales of $10,000. In this case, 1% ($100) of the credit sales for the year are estimated to be uncollectible. In other words, there is a $100 (1%) leak in the collection pipeline. Because of its focus on sales and the related bad debt expense, this method is often called the "income statement approach."

To apply this method, we focus on the relationship between the amount of credit sales during the year and the amount of uncollectible accounts. We ask the question: "What portion of this year's credit sales will not be collected?" Assume that during 20-1 and 20-2, Chris Co. had total credit sales of $200,000 and that $2,000 of those credit sales had become uncollectible. Based on this experience, Chris could estimate its bad debt expense at 1% of credit sales.

$$\frac{\text{Uncollectible Accounts}}{\text{Credit Sales}} = \frac{\$2,000}{\$200,000} = 1\%$$

FIGURE 16-2 Percentage of Sales Method

If during 20-3 Chris had credit sales of $120,000, the estimate of bad debt expense would be made as follows:

Credit sales	$ 120,000
Estimated % uncollectible	× 1%
Estimated bad debt expense	$ 1,200

Thus, the following adjusting entry would be made on December 31, 20-3:

4	Dec.	31	Bad Debt Expense	1 2 0 0 00		4
5			Allowance for Doubtful Accounts		1 2 0 0 00	5
6						6

In T account form at the end of 20-3, Allowance for Doubtful Accounts would appear as follows:

Allowance for Doubtful Accounts

	20-3
	12/31 1,200

Assume that during the following year, 20-4, uncollectible accounts totaling $1,100 were written off as follows:

8		Allowance for Doubtful Accounts	1 1 0 0 00		8
9		Accounts Receivable/Customer Names		1 1 0 0 00	9
10		Wrote off uncollectible accounts			10

After posting this entry, Allowance for Doubtful Accounts would have a credit balance of $100.

Allowance for Doubtful Accounts

20-4	1,100	20-3		
		12/31		1,200
		20-4	Bal.	100

Accounts written off during 20-4

Assume that during 20-4, Chris had credit sales of $130,000. Based on experience, Chris would still estimate its bad debt expense at 1% of credit sales. Thus, the following adjusting entry for $1,300 (1% × $130,000) would be made on December 31, 20-4:

4	Dec.	31	Bad Debt Expense			1	3	0	0	00								4
5			Allowance for Doubtful Accounts										1	3	0	0	00	5
6																		6

This would increase the Allowance for Doubtful Accounts balance to $1,400.

Allowance for Doubtful Accounts

		20-3		
		12/31		1,200
20-4	1,100			
		20-4	Bal.	100
		12/31	Adj.	1,300
		12/31	Bal.	1,400

LEARNING KEY 🔑

Percentage of sales method: When making the adjusting entry, ignore the balance in Allowance for Doubtful Accounts prior to adjustment.

This demonstrates an important feature of the percentage of sales method. Allowance for Doubtful Accounts may have a debit or credit balance prior to adjustment. This is a normal result of underestimating or overestimating uncollectible accounts. Under the percentage of sales method, any balance in Allowance for Doubtful Accounts prior to adjustment is generally *ignored* in making the current period's adjusting entry.

This is because the percentage of sales method focuses on the *current year's* credit sales. Any previous balance in the allowance account relates to credit sales and uncollectible accounts from *prior years*. In the above illustration, the balance was a credit of $100. This balance could have been a credit of $300 or a debit of $200, and it would not have mattered. The adjusting entry for bad debt expense would have been the same—$1,300.

There is one exception to ignoring the balance in Allowance for Doubtful Accounts in making the adjustment. When a large debit or credit balance accumulates in the allowance account, the percentage of credit sales used to estimate bad debt expense should be increased or decreased. This provides a better estimate based on recent experience.

If a business is new and has no prior credit experience, companies may use industry averages of percentages in initial years of operation.

Percentage of Receivables Method

The percentage of receivables method is based on the idea that some portion of the existing accounts receivable will not be collected. This way of viewing uncollectible accounts is illustrated in Figure 16-3 on page 626 for accounts receivable of $20,000. In this case, 4% ($800) of the accounts receivable at the end of the year are estimated to be uncollectible. In other words, there is an $800 (4%) leak in the collection pipeline. Because of its focus on accounts receivable and the related uncollectible accounts, this method is often called the "balance sheet approach."

To apply this method, we focus on the relationship between the amount of accounts receivable at the end of the year and the amount that will be uncollectible. We ask the question: "What portion of the accounts receivable at year-end will not be collected?" The simplest form of this method involves computing uncollectible accounts as a percentage of the Accounts Receivable balance. Assume that Craft Co. had an average Accounts Receivable balance at the end of the past two years of $110,000, and average uncollectible accounts of $4,400 per year. Craft would estimate its percentage of uncollectible accounts as follows:

$$\frac{\text{Average Uncollectible Accounts}}{\text{Average Accounts Receivable}} = \frac{\$4,400}{\$110,000} = 4\%$$

FIGURE 16-3 Percentage of Receivables Method

If the Accounts Receivable balance at the end of the current year was $120,000, the estimate of uncollectible accounts would be made as follows:

Accounts receivable	$120,000
Estimated % uncollectible	× 4%
Estimated uncollectible accounts	$ 4,800

Assuming Allowance for Doubtful Accounts has a zero balance prior to adjustment, the following adjusting entry would be made at year-end:

4	Dec.	31	Bad Debt Expense		4 8 0 0 00		4
5			Allowance for Doubtful Accounts			4 8 0 0 00	5
6							6

Although the above approach is simple, the estimate of uncollectible accounts is not very precise. This is because with this approach each dollar of receivables is treated as having the same chance of being uncollectible. In fact, we know from experience that the older an amount is, the greater the chance it will be uncollectible.

Therefore, the percentage of receivables method usually is applied in a way that yields a better estimate of uncollectible accounts. In general, the longer an account receivable has been outstanding, the less likely it is to be collected. So, instead of using the total accounts receivable in making the estimate, each customer's account is analyzed to determine how long the amounts have been outstanding. Different percentages are then applied to amounts that have been outstanding for different lengths of time. Because of the emphasis on the length of time the accounts have been outstanding, this process is called aging the receivables.

An aging schedule similar to the one in Figure 16-4 is often used to analyze the receivables and estimate the uncollectible amount. As indicated in Figure 16-4, the following steps are used in preparing the aging schedule:

STEP 1 Categorize each account receivable according to the length of time the amounts have been outstanding.

STEP 2 Multiply the amount of receivables in each category by an estimate of the percent that will be uncollectible. This percentage is based on past experience and increases as the number of days past due increases.

STEP 3 Total the estimates for each category to determine the amount that is not expected to be collected.

FIGURE 16-4 Aging Schedule

	CUSTOMER	TOTAL	NOT YET DUE	1–30	31–60	61–90	91–180	181–365	OVER 365	
1	AGING SCHEDULE OF ACCOUNTS RECEIVABLE — December 31, 20-1									1
2				NUMBER OF DAYS PAST DUE						2
4	W. Billiard	$ 3,000.00	$ 2,500.00	$ 500.00						4
5	K. Campbell	950.00			$ 650.00		$ 300.00			5
6	J. Farley	4,325.00	3,800.00			$ 525.00				6
7	L. Gilbert	1,900.00	1,500.00		400.00					7
8	E. Rome	3,950.00	3,170.00					$ 780.00		8
20	B. Zimmerman	200.00					200.00			20
21	Total	$100,500.00	$65,000.00	$18,000.00	$8,250.00	$6,310.00	$1,810.00	$780.00	$350.00	21
22	Estimated percent									22
23	uncollectible		× 2 %	× 5 %	× 10 %	× 20 %	× 30 %	× 50 %	× 80 %	23
24	Total est. uncollectible									24
25	accounts	$ 5,500.00	$ 1,300.00	$ 900.00	$ 825.00	$1,262.00	$ 543.00	$ 390.00	$ 280.00	25
27		($ 5,500.00 = 1,300.00 + 900.00 + 825.00 + 1,262.00 + 543.00 + 390.00 + 280.00)									27

(1), (2), (3) bracket markings on left side of table.

Based on the aging schedule in Figure 16-4, uncollectible accounts would be estimated as $5,500 as indicated in the Total column. In other words, it is estimated that $5,500 of the $100,500 of accounts receivable at December 31, 20-1, will not be collected. Thus, assuming Allowance for Doubtful Accounts has a zero balance prior to adjustment, the following adjusting entry would be made at December 31, 20-1:

4	Dec.	31	Bad Debt Expense	5,500.00		4
5			Allowance for Doubtful Accounts		5,500.00	5
6						6

In T account form, Allowance for Doubtful Accounts would appear as follows:

Allowance for Doubtful Accounts

	20-1
	12/31 Adj. 5,500

Assume that during the following year, 20-2, uncollectible accounts totaling $5,200 were written off as follows:

8			Allowance for Doubtful Accounts	5,200.00		8
9			Accounts Receivable/Customer Names		5,200.00	9
10			Wrote off uncollectible accounts			10

Allowance for Doubtful Accounts now would have a credit balance of $300.

Allowance for Doubtful Accounts

	20-1
	12/31 Adj. 5,500
20-2 5,200	
Accounts written off during 20-2	20-2 Bal. 300

Assume that at the end of 20-2 another aging schedule like the one in Figure 16-4 is prepared, and that the estimated uncollectible amount is $5,700. To bring the credit balance in the allowance account to $5,700, an adjustment of $5,400 is needed.

Estimated uncollectible amount	$5,700
Current credit balance in account	− 300
Adjustment needed	$5,400

Thus, the following adjusting entry would be made on December 31, 20-2:

4	Dec.	31	Bad Debt Expense		5 4 0 0 00			4
5			Allowance for Doubtful Accounts			5 4 0 0 00		5
6								6

This would increase the Allowance for Doubtful Accounts balance to $5,700.

Allowance for Doubtful Accounts

			20-1			
			12/31	Adj.	5,500	Adjustment to increase the balance to $5,700
20-2		5,200				
			20-2	Bal.	300	
			12/31	Adj.	5,400	
			12/31	Bal.	5,700	

This demonstrates an important feature of the percentage of receivables method. Allowance for Doubtful Accounts may have a debit or credit balance prior to adjustment. Under the percentage of receivables method, this balance must be considered in making the current period's adjusting entry.

This is because the percentage of receivables method focuses on the Accounts Receivable balance at the end of the year. That balance contains receivables from the current year and any remaining from prior years. The total Accounts Receivable balance consisting of current and prior year receivables is analyzed to determine the proper allowance account balance. The adjusting entry is then made to achieve that balance in the allowance account. In the above illustration, the balance prior to adjustment was a credit of $300. Therefore, the adjustment to bring the balance to $5,700 was $5,400 ($5,700 − $300). If the balance prior to adjustment had been a debit of $200, the necessary adjusting entry would have been $5,900.

> **LEARNING KEY** 🔑
>
> Percentage of receivables method: Unlike the percentage of sales method, when making the adjusting entry, consider the balance in Allowance for Doubtful Accounts prior to adjustment.

Estimated uncollectible amount	$5,700
Current debit balance in account	+ 200
Adjustment needed	$5,900

Notice that the resulting credit balance in Allowance for Doubtful Accounts after adjustment would once again be $5,700.

Allowance for Doubtful Accounts

20-2	Bal.	200	20-2			
			12/31	Adj.	5,900	Adjustment to increase the balance to $5,700
			12/31	Bal.	5,700	

Comparison of Methods

Let's summarize the differences between the percentage of sales and percentage of receivables methods of estimating uncollectibles. Figure 16-5 identifies the key features of the two methods.

FIGURE 16-5 Key Features of Allowance Methods

FEATURE	PERCENTAGE OF SALES	PERCENTAGE OF RECEIVABLES
1. Basis for estimate	% of credit sales	Aging (%) of accounts receivable
2. Amount of year-end adjustment	% of credit sales	Amount calculated by aging accounts receivable **Plus** debit balance in allowance account before adjustment or **Minus** credit balance in allowance account before adjustment
3. Balance in allowance account after adjustment	% of credit sales **Plus** credit balance in allowance account before adjustment or **Minus** debit balance in allowance account before adjustment	Amount calculated by aging accounts receivable

Effects of Write-Offs on Financial Statements

Recall that under the allowance method, to write off a $250 uncollectible account, the following entry is made:

4	Allowance for Doubtful Accounts	2 5 0 00		4
5	Accounts Receivable/Customer Name		2 5 0 00	5
6	Wrote off uncollectible account			6

This entry is the same under both the percentage of sales and percentage of receivables methods.

Note the effect of this entry on the income statement and balance sheet. No income statement accounts are used in the entry, so clearly there is no effect on the income statement. Not so obviously, the net assets on the balance sheet are not affected either. Since Allowance for Doubtful Accounts is a contra-asset and Accounts Receivable is an asset, the effects offset each other. Let's look more closely at this perhaps surprising situation.

Effect of Entry on the Income Statement

First, how can we write off an account as uncollectible and have no income statement effect? The answer lies in the adjusting entry we made at year-end for the estimated uncollectibles. Assume the entry was for $900.

9	Bad Debt Expense	9 0 0 00		9
10	Allowance for Doubtful Accounts		9 0 0 00	10
11				11

A BROADER VIEW

Accounts Receivable and Management of Cash Flows

It is important to be aware of the difference between sales on account and cash inflows, particularly in running a small business. Green Co., a construction and metal recycling contractor in Connecticut, learned this distinction the hard way.

During a period of rapid growth, Green bid successfully on several municipal contracts. This led to major increases in revenue. Unfortunately, accounts receivable also increased dramatically because municipalities tend to be slow in paying their bills, particularly on construction contracts. Thus, Green found itself facing payroll expenses and major bills from its suppliers that required prompt payment, but its cash was tied up in the accounts receivable.

Fortunately, with help from the Small Business Development Center, Green was able to obtain financing to make it through this "cash crunch." But it will long remember that accounts receivable are not the same as cash inflows.

The bad debt expense was already recognized with this adjusting entry in the year the expense was estimated and recorded. It would be double counting to recognize the expense again in the following year when the specific account is written off.

Effect of Entry on the Balance Sheet

Second, why are net assets on the balance sheet not affected? The best way to answer is with an example. Assume that on December 31, 20-1, the balance sheet showed the following information concerning Accounts Receivable:

Current assets:
Accounts receivable $100,500
Less allowance for doubtful accounts   5,500 $95,000 ← Net receivables

On January 15, 20-2, Bill McDonald's account for $500 is written off by making the following entry:

14	Jan.	15	Allowance for Doubtful Accounts		5 0 0 00			14
15			Accounts Receivable/B. McDonald			5 0 0 00		15
16			Wrote off uncollectible account					16

If a new balance sheet was prepared immediately after posting the above transaction, the following information would be reported for Accounts Receivable:

Current assets:
Accounts receivable $100,000
Less allowance for doubtful accounts   5,000 $95,000 ← Net receivables

Note that both Accounts Receivable and Allowance for Doubtful Accounts have been reduced by $500. Thus, the reported net receivables are not changed. The business expected to collect $95,000 before writing off McDonald's account and still expects to collect $95,000 after writing off his account. Management knew that there would be some uncollectible accounts. Now they know that McDonald is one of them.

Recovery of Accounts Previously Written Off—Allowance Method

Occasionally, an account that was written off is collected. For example, assume that a check for $500 was received on February 1 from Bill McDonald, whose account was written off on January 15. McDonald's account would be written off on January 15 as follows:

5	Jan.	15	Allowance for Doubtful Accounts		5	0	0	00						5
6			Accounts Receivable/B. McDonald							5	0	0	00	6
7			Wrote off uncollectible account											7

To record the recovery on February 1, two entries are required:

1. Reinstate the account.
2. Record the collection.

To reinstate an account, simply reverse the entry made to write off the account, as follows:

5	Feb.	1	Accounts Receivable/B. McDonald		5	0	0	00						5
6			Allowance for Doubtful Accounts							5	0	0	00	6
7			Reinstated account receivable											7

To record the collection, the following entry is made:

9	Feb.	1	Cash		5	0	0	00						9
10			Accounts Receivable/B. McDonald							5	0	0	00	10
11			Collection on account											11

CHECKPOINT ✔

Complete Checkpoint-2 on page 638 to test your basic understanding of LO2.

Instead of making these entries, it might be simpler to debit Cash and credit Allowance for Doubtful Accounts. However, this shortcut should not be taken. Without the reinstatement, the subsidiary ledger will report only that McDonald's account was written off as uncollectible. With the reinstatement, the subsidiary ledger will reflect the fact that McDonald has paid his account. This information will be important to McDonald and the business should he desire credit in the future.

LO3	## Direct Write-Off Method

Apply the direct write-off method of accounting for uncollectible accounts.

Under the direct write-off method, the bad debt expense is not recognized until it has been determined that an account is uncollectible. For example, assume that on August 15, John Lafollette's account for $500 is judged to be uncollectible. The following entry would be made:

5	Aug.	15	Bad Debt Expense			5	0	0	00							5
6			Accounts Receivable/J. Lafollette								5	0	0	00		6
7			Wrote off uncollectible account													7

Advantage and Disadvantages of Direct Method

The direct write-off method has one advantage. It is very simple to apply. However, there are three disadvantages of using this method. First, efforts to collect the account often extend over many months. Thus, the revenue from the sale might be recognized in one period and the bad debt expense recognized in another. This violates the matching principle.

Second, the amount of bad debt expense recognized in a given period can be manipulated by management. This occurs because there is no general rule for deciding when an account becomes uncollectible. Thus, management can use its subjective judgment in deciding when to recognize bad debt expense.

Third, the amount of accounts receivable reported on the balance sheet does not represent the net realizable value of the receivables, the amount of cash actually expected to be collected. Thus, the assets are overstated by the amount of uncollectible accounts included in accounts receivable. For these reasons, the direct write-off method is generally not acceptable for financial reporting purposes. It is acceptable only if the amount of uncollectible accounts cannot be reasonably estimated and if the estimated amount is very small. This method is required, however, for income tax purposes.

> To deduct bad debt expense for income tax purposes, the taxpayer must first attempt but fail to collect the account.

Recovery of Accounts Previously Written Off—Direct Write-Off Method

Occasionally, an account that was written off is collected. The proper entries for the recovery depend on the period in which the cash is collected.

Write-Off and Recovery in Same Accounting Period

Assume the write-off and recovery are made in the same accounting period, the write-off on August 15 and the recovery on December 20.

Lafollette's account would be written off on August 15 as follows:

5	Aug.	15	Bad Debt Expense			5	0	0	00							5
6			Accounts Receivable/J. Lafollette								5	0	0	00		6
7			Wrote off uncollectible account													7

To record the recovery on December 20, two entries are required:

1. Reinstate the account.
2. Record the collection.

To reinstate the account, reverse the entry for the write-off, as follows:

35	Dec.	20	Accounts Receivable/J. Lafollette			5	0	0	00							35
36			Bad Debt Expense								5	0	0	00		36
37			Reinstated account receivable													37

YOUR PERSPECTIVE

Bill and Account Collector

One thing is clear from business experience—no matter how carefully a business screens its customers, it will have some uncollectible accounts. This is a normal part of doing business, and when it happens, the business often refers the problem to *bill* and *account collectors* in a third-party collection agency. Organization skills and attention to detail are important for bill and account collectors. Their duties may include learning the reasons for the overdue bill, offering credit advice, explaining the terms of the sale or contract with the debtor, and trying to negotiate payment. It may not be the most enjoyable job for some, but uncollectible accounts are a vital part of a business, and so are the individuals working for the debt collection company.

To record the collection, the following entry is made:

39	Dec.	20	Cash			5	0	0	00						39
40			Accounts Receivable/J. Lafollette								5	0	0	00	40
41			Collection on account												41

Write-Off and Recovery in Different Accounting Periods

What if the write-off is made in one period and the recovery in a following accounting period?

Lafollette's account would be written off in the same way we saw previously, as follows:

5	Aug.	15	Bad Debt Expense			5	0	0	00						5
6			Accounts Receivable/J. Lafollette								5	0	0	00	6
7			Wrote off uncollectible account												7

But Lafollette's account is reinstated by debiting Accounts Receivable and crediting Uncollectible Accounts Recovered, as follows:

35	Jan.	20	Accounts Receivable/J. Lafollette			5	0	0	00						35
36			Uncollectible Accounts Recovered								5	0	0	00	36
37			Reinstated account receivable												37

This revenue account is credited instead of Bad Debt Expense because a credit to the expense account would understate bad debt expense for the current year. Uncollectible Accounts Recovered is reported on the income statement as other revenue.

To record the collection, the following entry is made:

CHECKPOINT ✔

Complete Checkpoint-3 on page 638 to test your basic understanding of LO3.

39	Jan.	20	Cash			5	0	0	00						39
40			Accounts Receivable/J. Lafollette								5	0	0	00	40
41			Collection on account												41

SELF-STUDY

LEARNING OBJECTIVES	Key Points to Remember
LO1 **Apply the allowance method of accounting for uncollectible accounts.**	To use the allowance method, apply three steps. **STEP 1** At the end of the period, estimate the uncollectible amount. **STEP 2** Make the following adjusting entry:

4	Bad Debt Expense	x x x xx		4
5	Allowance for Doubtful Accounts		x x x xx	5

STEP 3 When a specific account is identified as uncollectible, make the following entry:

8	Allowance for Doubtful Accounts	x x x xx		8
9	Accounts Receivable/Customer Name		x x x xx	9
10	Wrote off uncollectible account			10

LEARNING OBJECTIVES	Key Points to Remember
LO2 **Apply the percentage of sales and percentage of receivables methods of estimating uncollectible accounts.**	The *percentage of sales method* is based on the relationship between the amount of credit sales and the amount of sales that will be uncollectible. Any balance in Allowance for Doubtful Accounts prior to adjustment is ignored in making the current period's adjusting entry. The *percentage of receivables method* is based on the relationship between the amount of accounts receivable and the amount of uncollectible accounts. The estimate of uncollectibles is usually based on an aging of receivables. Any balance in Allowance for Doubtful Accounts prior to adjustment is considered in making the current period's adjusting entry. Under the allowance method, the actual write-off of an uncollectible account does not affect either the income statement or the net assets on the balance sheet. When an account is collected that has been written off, the account is reinstated and then the collection is recorded.
LO3 **Apply the direct write-off method of accounting for uncollectible accounts.**	Under the direct write-off method, bad debt expense is not recognized until an account is written off as uncollectible. The entries for collection of an account previously written off depend on when the collection occurs. If the collection is in the same period as the write-off, the credit is to Bad Debt Expense. If the collection is in a following period, the credit is to Uncollectible Accounts Recovered.

DEMONSTRATION PROBLEM

Budke and Budke, a landscaping service, uses the allowance method to record the following transactions related to accounts receivable. Adjusting and closing entries completed during the current year ended December 31, 20--, are also described below.

Mar. 6   Received 50% of the $12,000 balance owed by Columbia Gardens, a bankrupt business, and wrote off the remainder as uncollectible.

June 12   Reinstated the account of Ramon Burgos, which had been written off in the previous year, and received $2,250 cash in full settlement.

Sept. 19   Wrote off the $13,800 balance owed by Kelly Richeson, who has no assets.

Nov. 9   Reinstated the account of Jackie Kwas, which had been written off in the preceding year, and received $2,175 cash in full settlement.

Dec. 27   Wrote off the following accounts as uncollectible, in compound entry form: Blair & Smith, $10,480; Landscapes Unlimited, $8,570; Beekman Brothers, $22,500; B. J. McKay, $9,300.

31   Based on an aging analysis of $1,460,000 of accounts receivable, it was estimated that $73,500 will be uncollectible. Made the adjusting entry.

31   Made the entry to close the appropriate account to Income Summary.

Selected accounts and beginning balances on January 1, 20--, are as follows:

122.1	Allowance for Doubtful Accounts	$95,000 credit
313	Income Summary	—
532	Bad Debt Expense	—

REQUIRED

1. Open the three selected accounts.

2. Enter the transactions and the adjusting and closing entries in general journal form (page 12 for the first 2 entries; page 13 for all others). After each entry, post to the three accounts named.

3. Determine the net realizable value of the accounts receivable as of December 31, 20--.

SOLUTION 1. and 2.

GENERAL LEDGER

ACCOUNT: Allowance for Doubtful Accounts   ACCOUNT NO. 122.1

DATE		ITEM	POST. REF.	DEBIT	CREDIT	BALANCE DEBIT	BALANCE CREDIT
20-- Jan.	1	Balance	✓				95 0 0 0 00
Mar.	6		J12	6 0 0 0 00			89 0 0 0 00
June	12		J13		2 2 5 0 00		91 2 5 0 00
Sept.	19		J13	13 8 0 0 00			77 4 5 0 00
Nov.	9		J13		2 1 7 5 00		79 6 2 5 00
Dec.	27		J13	50 8 5 0 00			28 7 7 5 00
	31	Adjusting	J13		44 7 2 5 00		73 5 0 0 00

ACCOUNT: Income Summary   ACCOUNT NO. 313

DATE		ITEM	POST. REF.	DEBIT	CREDIT	BALANCE DEBIT	BALANCE CREDIT
20-- Dec.	31	Closing	J13	44 7 2 5 00		44 7 2 5 00	

ACCOUNT: Bad Debt Expense   ACCOUNT NO. 532

DATE		ITEM	POST. REF.	DEBIT	CREDIT	BALANCE DEBIT	BALANCE CREDIT
20-- Dec.	31	Adjusting	J13	44 7 2 5 00		44 7 2 5 00	
	31	Closing	J13		44 7 2 5 00		

GENERAL JOURNAL PAGE 12

	DATE		DESCRIPTION	POST. REF.	DEBIT	CREDIT	
1	20-- Mar.	6	Cash		6 0 0 0 00		1
2			Accounts Receivable/Columbia Gardens			6 0 0 0 00	2
3			Collection on account				3
4							4
5		6	Allowance for Doubtful Accounts	122.1	6 0 0 0 00		5
6			Accounts Receivable/Columbia Gardens			6 0 0 0 00	6
7			Wrote off uncollectible account				7
8							8

GENERAL JOURNAL PAGE 13

	DATE		DESCRIPTION	POST. REF.	DEBIT	CREDIT	
1	20-- June	12	Accounts Receivable/R. Burgos		2 2 5 0 00		1
2			Allowance for Doubtful Accounts	122.1		2 2 5 0 00	2
3			Reinstated account receivable				3
4							4
5		12	Cash		2 2 5 0 00		5
6			Accounts Receivable/R. Burgos			2 2 5 0 00	6
7			Collection on account				7
8							8
9	Sept.	19	Allowance for Doubtful Accounts	122.1	13 8 0 0 00		9
10			Accounts Receivable/K. Richeson			13 8 0 0 00	10
11			Wrote off uncollectible account				11
12							12
13	Nov.	9	Accounts Receivable/J. Kwas		2 1 7 5 00		13
14			Allowance for Doubtful Accounts	122.1		2 1 7 5 00	14
15			Reinstated account receivable				15
16							16
17		9	Cash		2 1 7 5 00		17
18			Accounts Receivable/J. Kwas			2 1 7 5 00	18
19			Collection on account				19
20							20
21	Dec.	27	Allowance for Doubtful Accounts	122.1	50 8 5 0 00		21
22			Accounts Receivable/Blair & Smith			10 4 8 0 00	22
23			Accounts Receivable/Landscapes Unlimited			8 5 7 0 00	23
24			Accounts Receivable/Beekman Brothers			22 5 0 0 00	24
25			Accounts Receivable/B. J. McKay			9 3 0 0 00	25
26			Wrote off uncollectible accounts				26
27							27
28			Adjusting Entry				28
29		31	Bad Debt Expense	532	44 7 2 5 00		29
30			Allowance for Doubtful Accounts	122.1		44 7 2 5 00	30
31							31
32			Closing Entry				32
33		31	Income Summary	313	44 7 2 5 00		33
34			Bad Debt Expense	532		44 7 2 5 00	34
35							35

3. Accounts receivable, December 31, 20-- $1,460,000
   Less allowance for doubtful accounts   73,500
   Net realizable value $1,386,500

KEY TERMS

aging the receivables (626)   The process of estimating the uncollectible amount by analyzing account balances according to the length of time the accounts have been outstanding.

allowance method (622)   A technique that attempts to recognize bad debt expense in the same period that the related credit sales are made.

bad debt expense (622)   An expense from failure to collect an account receivable.

direct write-off method (631)   A method in which the bad debt expense is not recognized until it has been determined that an account is uncollectible.

matching principle (622)   A concept that requires expenses to be matched with the revenues they helped to produce.

net realizable value (623)   The amount a business expects to collect from its accounts receivable; calculated as Accounts Receivable less Allowance for Doubtful Accounts. Also called net receivables.

net receivables (623)   See net realizable value.

percentage of receivables method (625)   A method in which the current year's uncollectible accounts are estimated based on the relationship between the amount of accounts receivable and the amount of uncollectible accounts experienced in prior years.

percentage of sales method (623)   A method in which the current year's bad debt expense is estimated based on the relationship between the amount of credit sales and the amount of uncollectible accounts experienced in prior years.

SELF-STUDY TEST QUESTIONS

True/False

1. **LO1**   There are two methods of accounting for uncollectible accounts: the allowance method and the direct write-off method.

2. **LO1**   The matching principle states that debits should be matched with credits.

3. **LO2**   Using the percentage of sales method, the balance in Allowance for Doubtful Accounts must be taken into consideration before making the adjusting entry.

4. **LO2**   When an account is written off under the allowance method, there should be a debit to Bad Debt Expense.

5. **LO3**   Each time an account is written off under the direct write-off method, Bad Debt Expense is debited.

Multiple Choice

1. **LO1**   The dollar difference between Accounts Receivable and Allowance for Doubtful Accounts is called
   - (a) book value.
   - (b) interest value.
   - (c) carrying value.
   - (d) net realizable value.

2. **LO2** A business has an ending balance in Accounts Receivable of $35,000; credit sales for the year of $300,000; and a credit balance in Allowance for Doubtful Accounts of $800. If the percentage of sales method is used and the percentage is estimated at 1% of credit sales, what is the amount to be entered for the adjusting entry?

(a) $3,000   (c) $2,200
(b) $3,800   (d) $1,150

3. **LO2** A business has an ending balance in Accounts Receivable of $35,000; credit sales for the year of $300,000; and a credit balance in Allowance for Doubtful Accounts of $800. If the percentage of sales method is used and the percentage is estimated at 1% of credit sales, what is the ending balance in Allowance for Doubtful Accounts *after* the adjusting entry?

(a) $3,000   (c) $2,200
(b) $3,800   (d) $1,150

4. **LO2** A business has an ending balance in Accounts Receivable of $40,000; credit sales for the year of $500,000; and a debit balance in Allowance for Doubtful Accounts of $300. If an aging analysis indicates that $4,800 should be the balance in Allowance for Doubtful Accounts, the amount to be entered for the adjusting entry is

(a) $4,800.   (c) $5,000.
(b) $4,500.   (d) $5,100.

5. **LO2** Under the allowance method, when an account is determined to be worthless, the journal entry to write off the account will include a

(a) debit to Allowance for Doubtful Accounts.
(b) debit to Bad Debt Expense.
(c) credit to Allowance for Doubtful Accounts.
(d) debit to Accounts Receivable.

CHECKPOINT ✔

Checkpoint Exercises

1. **LO1** Beamon Department Store has an Accounts Receivable balance of $32,500 and an Allowance for Doubtful Accounts balance of $1,100. Determine the net realizable value of Beamon's accounts receivable.

2. **LO2** (a) Toni's Tech Shop has total credit sales for the year of $170,000 and estimates that 3% of its credit sales will be uncollectible. Allowance for Doubtful Accounts has a credit balance of $275.

Prepare the adjusting entry at year-end for the estimated bad debt expense.

(b) Based on an aging of its accounts receivable, Kyle's Cyclery estimates that $3,200 of its year-end accounts receivable will be uncollectible. Allowance for Doubtful Accounts has a debit balance of $280 at year-end.

Prepare the adjusting entry at year-end for the estimated uncollectible accounts.

3. **LO3** Fiona's Pharmacy uses the direct write-off method of accounting for bad debt expense. Prepare the journal entry on July 25 to write off $1,320 owed by P. Wahdia.

The answers to the Self-Study Test Questions are at the end of the chapter (pages 649–650).

APPLYING YOUR KNOWLEDGE

REVIEW QUESTIONS

LO1 1. What method of accounting for uncollectible accounts is generally required for financial reporting purposes?

LO1 2. Describe the steps to follow when using the allowance method to account for uncollectible accounts.

LO1 3. Explain how to compute net realizable value.

LO2 4. Describe the process followed when estimating bad debt expense under the percentage of sales method.

LO2 5. Describe the process followed when estimating uncollectible accounts under the percentage (aging) of receivables method.

LO2 6. How does the balance in Allowance for Doubtful Accounts before adjustment affect the amount of the year-end adjustment under the percentage of sales method? Under the percentage of receivables method?

LO2 7. Under the allowance method, what impact does the write-off of a customer's account have on the financial statements?

LO2 8. Under the allowance method, what journal entries are made if an account is collected that was previously written off?

LO3 9. Describe the accounting procedures when using the direct write-off method to account for uncollectible accounts.

LO3 10. What are three disadvantages of using the direct write-off method?

SERIES A EXERCISES

E 16-1A (LO1)
✓ 1. Net realizable value: $47,500

CALCULATION OF NET REALIZABLE VALUE L. R. Updike owns a department store that has a $50,000 balance in Accounts Receivable and a $2,500 credit balance in Allowance for Doubtful Accounts.

1. Determine the net realizable value of the accounts receivable.

2. Assume that an account receivable in the amount of $500 was written off using the allowance method. Determine the net realizable value of the accounts receivable after the write-off.

E 16-2A (LO2)
✓ 1. Dr. Bad Debt Exp.: $8,400

UNCOLLECTIBLE ACCOUNTS—PERCENTAGE OF SALES Rossin's Racers has total credit sales for the year of $280,000 and estimates that 3% of its credit sales will be uncollectible. Record the end-of-period adjusting entry on December 31, in general journal form, for the estimated bad debt expense. Assume the following independent conditions existed prior to the adjustment:

1. Allowance for Doubtful Accounts has a credit balance of $570.

2. Allowance for Doubtful Accounts has a debit balance of $360.

E 16-3A   (LO2)
✓ 2. Dr. Bad Debt Exp.: $4,805

UNCOLLECTIBLE ACCOUNTS—PERCENTAGE OF RECEIVABLES Brito's Hundai Sales and Service estimates the amount of uncollectible accounts using the percentage of receivables method. Based on aging the accounts, it is estimated that $4,500 will not be collected. Record the end-of-period adjusting entry on December 31, in general journal form, for the estimated uncollectible accounts. Assume the following independent conditions existed prior to the adjustment:

1. Allowance for Doubtful Accounts has a credit balance of $710.

2. Allowance for Doubtful Accounts has a debit balance of $305.

E 16-4A   (LO2)
✓ Sept. 27, Cr. Allow. for Doubtful Accounts: $5,350

COLLECTION OF ACCOUNTS WRITTEN OFF—ALLOWANCE METHOD Julia Alvarez, owner of Alvarez Rentals, uses the allowance method in accounting for uncollectible accounts. Record the following transactions in general journal form:

July   7   Wrote off $5,350 owed by Randy Dalzell, who has no assets.

Aug. 12   Wrote off $2,870 owed by Jason Flint, who declared bankruptcy.

Sept. 27   Reinstated the account of Randy Dalzell, which had been written off on July 7, and received $5,350 cash in full settlement.

E 16-5A   (LO2)
✓ 1(b). Dr. Bad Debt Exp.: $28,570

UNCOLLECTIBLE ACCOUNTS—PERCENTAGE OF SALES AND PERCENTAGE OF RECEIVABLES At the end of the current year, the accounts receivable account of Glenn's Nursery Supplies has a debit balance of $390,000. Credit sales are $2,800,000. Record the end-of-period adjusting entry on December 31, in general journal form, for the estimated uncollectible accounts. Assume the following independent conditions existed prior to the adjustment:

1. Allowance for Doubtful Accounts has a credit balance of $1,760.

  (a) The percentage of sales method is used and bad debt expense is estimated to be 1% of credit sales.

  (b) The percentage of receivables method is used and an analysis of the accounts produces an estimate of $30,330 in uncollectible accounts.

2. Allowance for Doubtful Accounts has a debit balance of $1,900.

  (a) The percentage of sales method is used and bad debt expense is estimated to be ¾ of 1% of credit sales.

  (b) The percentage of receivables method is used and an analysis of the accounts produces an estimate of $29,890 in uncollectible accounts.

E 16-6A   (LO3)
✓ July 20, Dr. Bad Debt Exp.: $2,325

DIRECT WRITE-OFF METHOD Maria Rivera, owner of Rivera Pharmacy, uses the direct write-off method in accounting for uncollectible accounts. Record the following transactions in general journal form:

July 20   Wrote off $2,325 owed by Joe Balouka, who has no assets.

Oct. 15   Wrote off $1,675 owed by Alice Rose, who declared bankruptcy.

E 16-7A   (LO3)
✓ Sept. 2, Cr. Bad Debt Exp.: $1,745

COLLECTION OF ACCOUNT WRITTEN OFF—DIRECT WRITE-OFF METHOD
Como's Music Store uses the direct write-off method in accounting for uncollectible accounts. Record the following transactions in general journal form:

20-1

May   8   Wrote off $1,745 owed by Vickie Lawrence, who has no assets.

July 15   Wrote off $1,300 owed by Dan Utter, who has made no payments in more than a year.

Sept. 2   Reinstated the account of Vickie Lawrence, which had been written off on May 8, and received $1,745 cash in full settlement.

20-2

May   5   Reinstated the account of Dan Utter, which had been written off in the previous year, and received $1,300 cash in full settlement.

SERIES A PROBLEMS

P 16-8A   (LO1/2)
✓ 3. $914,200

UNCOLLECTIBLE ACCOUNTS—ALLOWANCE METHOD Pyle Nurseries used the allowance method to record the following transactions, adjusting entries, and closing entries during the year ended December 31, 20--:

Feb.   9   Received 60% of the $4,000 balance owed by Wiley's Waterworks, a bankrupt business, and wrote off the remainder as uncollectible.

May 28   Reinstated the account of Amanda Akin, which had been written off in the preceding year, and received $2,100 cash in full settlement.

Aug. 16   Wrote off the $5,700 balance owed by JoJo Xu as uncollectible.

Oct.   5   Reinstated the account of Tomi Kennedy which had been written off in the preceding year, and received $3,100 cash in full settlement.

Dec. 28   Wrote off the following accounts as uncollectible, in compound entry form: Jacobs & Wilson, $10,900; Specialty Landscapes, $15,360; Kiana Hoyer, $13,170.

31   Based on an aging analysis of the $965,000 of accounts receivable, it was estimated that $50,800 will be uncollectible. Made the adjusting entry.

31   Made the entry to close the appropriate account to Income Summary.

Selected accounts and beginning balances on January 1, 20--, are as follows:

122.1	Allowance for Doubtful Accounts	$43,000 credit
313	Income Summary	—
532	Bad Debt Expense	—

REQUIRED

1. Open the three selected general ledger accounts.
2. Enter the transactions and the adjusting and closing entries in a general journal (page 6). After each entry, post to the appropriate selected accounts.
3. Determine the net realizable value as of December 31.

P 16-9A **(LO2)**

✓ 1(b). Dr. Bad Debt Exp.: $6,620

UNCOLLECTIBLE ACCOUNTS—PERCENTAGE OF SALES AND PERCENTAGE OF RECEIVABLES At the completion of the current fiscal year ending December 31, the balance of Accounts Receivable for Yang's Gift Shop was $30,000. Credit sales for the year were $355,200.

REQUIRED

Make the necessary adjusting entry in general journal form under each of the following assumptions. Show calculations for the amount of each adjustment and the resulting net realizable value.

1. Allowance for Doubtful Accounts has a credit balance of $330.

   (a) The percentage of sales method is used and bad debt expense is estimated to be 2% of credit sales.

   (b) The percentage of receivables method is used and an analysis of the accounts produces an estimate of $6,950 in uncollectible accounts.

2. Allowance for Doubtful Accounts has a debit balance of $400.

   (a) The percentage of sales method is used and bad debt expense is estimated to be 1.5% of credit sales.

   (b) The percentage of receivables method is used and an analysis of the accounts produces an estimate of $5,685 in uncollectible accounts.

P 16-10A **(LO2)**

✓ 2. Dr. Bad Debt Exp.: $2,790

AGING ACCOUNTS RECEIVABLE An analysis of the accounts receivable of Johnson Company as of December 31, 20--, reveals the following:

Age Interval	Balance	Estimated Percent Uncollectible
Not yet due	$65,000	2%
1–30 days past due	4,500	5
31–60 days past due	3,550	10
61–90 days past due	1,650	25
91–180 days past due	1,200	35
181–365 days past due	650	55
Over 365 days past due	400	85
Total	$76,950	

REQUIRED

1. Prepare an aging schedule as of December 31, 20--, by adding the following column to the three columns shown above: Estimated Amount Uncollectible.

2. Assuming that Allowance for Doubtful Accounts had a credit balance of $620 before adjustment, record the end-of-period adjusting entry in general journal form to enter the estimate for uncollectible accounts.

P 16-11A **(LO3)**

✓ 20-2, Jan. 17, Cr. Uncoll. Accounts Recovered: $6,300

DIRECT WRITE-OFF METHOD Williams & Hendricks Distributors uses the direct write-off method in accounting for uncollectible accounts.

20-1

Feb. 18 Sold merchandise on account to Merry Merchants, $17,500.

Mar. 22 Sold merchandise on account to Utter Unicorns, $14,300.

June 3   Received $10,000 from Merry Merchants and wrote off the remainder owed on the sale of February 18 as uncollectible.

Sept. 9   Received $8,000 from Utter Unicorns and wrote off the remainder owed on the sale of March 22 as uncollectible.

Nov. 13   Reinstated the account of Merry Merchants, which had been written off on June 3, and received $7,500 cash in full settlement.

20-2

Jan. 17   Reinstated the account of Utter Unicorns, which had been written off on September 9 of the previous year, and received $6,300 cash in full settlement.

REQUIRED

Record these transactions in general journal form.

SERIES B EXERCISES

E 16-1B   (LO1)
✓ 1. Net realizable value: $60,025

CALCULATION OF NET REALIZABLE VALUE Mary Martin owns a department store that has a $65,200 balance in Accounts Receivable and a $5,175 credit balance in Allowance for Doubtful Accounts.

1. Determine the net realizable value of the accounts receivable.

2. Assume that an account receivable in the amount of $900 was written off using the allowance method. Determine the net realizable value of the accounts receivable after the write-off.

E 16-2B   (LO2)
✓ 1. Dr. Bad Debt Exp.: $7,600

UNCOLLECTIBLE ACCOUNTS—PERCENTAGE OF SALES Nicole's Neckties has total credit sales for the year of $380,000 and estimates that 2% of its credit sales will be uncollectible. Record the end-of-period adjusting entry on December 31, in general journal form, for the estimated bad debt expense. Assume the following independent conditions existed prior to the adjustment:

1. Allowance for Doubtful Accounts has a credit balance of $430.

2. Allowance for Doubtful Accounts has a debit balance of $295.

E 16-3B   (LO2)
✓ 2. Dr. Bad Debt Exp.: $4,495

UNCOLLECTIBLE ACCOUNTS—PERCENTAGE OF RECEIVABLES Charlie's Chevy Sales and Service estimates the amount of uncollectible accounts using the percentage of receivables method. Based on aging the accounts, it is estimated that $3,935 will not be collected. Record the end-of-period adjusting entry on December 31, in general journal form, for the estimated uncollectible accounts. Assume the following independent conditions existed prior to the adjustment:

1. Allowance for Doubtful Accounts has a credit balance of $245.

2. Allowance for Doubtful Accounts has a debit balance of $560.

E 16-4B   (LO2)
✓ Sept. 23, Cr. Allow. for Doubtful Accounts: $6,040

COLLECTION OF ACCOUNT WRITTEN OFF—ALLOWANCE METHOD Raynette Ramos, owner of Ramos Rentals, uses the allowance method in accounting for uncollectible accounts. Record the following transactions in general journal form:

July 9   Wrote off $6,040 owed by Sue Sanchez, who has no assets.

Aug. 15   Wrote off $4,790 owed by Lonnie Jones, who declared bankruptcy.

Sept. 23   Reinstated the account of Sue Sanchez, which had been written off on July 9, and received $6,040 cash in full settlement.

E 16-5B   (LO2)
✓ 1(b). Dr. Bad Debt Exp.: $22,640

UNCOLLECTIBLE ACCOUNTS—PERCENTAGE OF SALES AND PERCENTAGE OF RECEIVABLES   At the end of the current year, the accounts receivable account of Parker's Nursery Supplies has a debit balance of $350,000. Credit sales are $2,300,000. Record the end-of-period adjusting entry on December 31, in general journal form, for the estimated uncollectible accounts. Assume the following independent conditions existed prior to the adjustment:

1. Allowance for Doubtful Accounts has a credit balance of $1,920.

   (a) The percentage of sales method is used and bad debt expense is estimated to be 1% of credit sales.

   (b) The percentage of receivables method is used and an analysis of the accounts produces an estimate of $24,560 in uncollectible accounts.

2. Allowance for Doubtful Accounts has a debit balance of $1,280.

   (a) The percentage of sales method is used and bad debt expense is estimated to be ¾ of 1% of credit sales.

   (b) The percentage of receivables method is used and an analysis of the accounts produces an estimate of $22,440 in uncollectible accounts.

E 16-6B   (LO3)
✓ July 19, Dr. Bad Debt Exp.: $1,935

DIRECT WRITE-OFF METHOD   Brent Mussellman, owner of Brent's Barbells, uses the direct write-off method in accounting for uncollectible accounts. Record the following transactions in general journal form:

July 19   Wrote off $1,935 owed by Arnold Swartz, who has no assets.

Oct. 12   Wrote off $2,125 owed by Janice Strong, who declared bankruptcy.

E 16-7B   (LO3)
✓ Sept. 20, Cr. Bad Debt Exp.: $2,360

COLLECTION OF ACCOUNT WRITTEN OFF—DIRECT WRITE-OFF METHOD   Madonna's Music Store uses the direct write-off method in accounting for uncollectible accounts. Record the following transactions in general journal form:

20-1

May 5   Wrote off $2,360 owed by Neal Dammond, who has no assets.

July 18   Wrote off $1,255 owed by Maxine Mouse, who has made no payments in more than a year.

Sept. 20   Reinstated the account of Neal Dammond, which had been written off on May 5, and received $2,360 cash in full settlement.

20-2

May 11   Reinstated the account of Maxine Mouse, which had been written off in the previous year, and received $1,255 cash in full settlement.

SERIES B PROBLEMS

P 16-8B   (LO1/2)
✓ 3. $1,107,850

UNCOLLECTIBLE ACCOUNTS—ALLOWANCE METHOD Lewis Warehouse used the allowance method to record the following transactions, adjusting entries, and closing entries during the year ended December 31, 20--:

Feb.   7   Received 70% of the $8,000 balance owed by Luxury Sofas, a bankrupt business, and wrote off the remainder as uncollectible.

May 26   Reinstated the account of Sandy Johnson, which had been written off in the preceding year, and received $3,725 cash in full settlement.

Aug. 15   Wrote off the $9,350 balance owed by Izumi Goto as uncollectible.

Oct.   6   Reinstated the account of Doreen Woods, which had been written off in the preceding year, and received $4,320 cash in full settlement.

Dec. 29   Wrote off the following accounts as uncollectible, in compound entry form: Schmidt & Yeager, $13,945; Economy Homes, $15,830; Davis Industries, $11,865.

31   Based on an aging analysis of the $1,175,000 of accounts receivable, it was estimated that $67,150 will be uncollectible. Made the adjusting entry.

31   Made the entry to close the appropriate account to Income Summary.

Selected accounts and beginning balances on January 1, 20--, are as follows:

122.1	Allowance for Doubtful Accounts	$49,850 credit
313	Income Summary	—
532	Bad Debt Expense	—

REQUIRED

1. Open the three selected general ledger accounts.
2. Enter the transactions and the adjusting and closing entries in a general journal (page 6). After each entry, post to the appropriate selected accounts.
3. Determine the net realizable value as of December 31, 20--.

P 16-9B   (LO2)
✓ 1(b). Dr. Bad Debt Exp.: $27,650

UNCOLLECTIBLE ACCOUNTS—PERCENTAGE OF SALES AND PERCENTAGE OF RECEIVABLES At the completion of the current fiscal year ending December 31, the balance of Accounts Receivable for Anderson's Greeting Cards was $180,000. Credit sales for the year were $1,950,000.

REQUIRED

Make the necessary adjusting entry in general journal form under each of the following assumptions. Show calculations for the amount of each adjustment and the resulting net realizable value.

1. Allowance for Doubtful Accounts has a credit balance of $2,600.

   (a) The percentage of sales method is used and bad debt expense is estimated to be 1.5% of credit sales.

   (b) The percentage of receivables method is used and an analysis of the accounts produces an estimate of $30,250 in uncollectible accounts.

(continued)

2. Allowance for Doubtful Accounts has a debit balance of $1,900.

   (a) The percentage of sales method is used and bad debt expense is estimated to be 1.0% of credit sales.

   (b) The percentage of receivables method is used and an analysis of the accounts produces an estimate of $20,500 in uncollectible accounts.

P 16-10B   (LO2)
✓ 2. Dr. Bad Debt Exp.: $9,792

AGING ACCOUNTS RECEIVABLE An analysis of the accounts receivable of Matsushita Company as of December 31, 20--, reveals the following:

Age Interval	Balance	Estimated Percent Uncollectible
Not yet due	$250,000	1.5%
1–30 days past due	17,000	4
31–60 days past due	12,800	9
61–90 days past due	8,200	20
91–180 days past due	4,600	30
181–365 days past due	4,200	45
Over 365 days past due	1,400	75
Total	$298,200	

REQUIRED

1. Prepare an aging schedule as of December 31, 20--, by adding the following column to the three columns shown above: Estimated Amount Uncollectible.

2. Assuming that Allowance for Doubtful Accounts had a credit balance of $1,750 before adjustment, record the end-of-period adjusting entry in general journal form to enter the estimate for uncollectible accounts.

P 16-11B   (LO3)
✓ 20-2, Jan. 11, Cr. Uncoll. Accounts Recovered: $5,800

DIRECT WRITE-OFF METHOD Lee and Chen Distributors uses the direct write-off method in accounting for uncollectible accounts.

20-1

Feb. 16	Sold merchandise on account to Biggs and Daughters, $16,000.
Mar. 23	Sold merchandise on account to Lloyd Place, $12,800.
June 8	Received $12,000 from Biggs and Daughters and wrote off the remainder owed on the sale of February 16 as uncollectible.
Sept. 27	Received $7,000 from Lloyd Place and wrote off the remainder owed on the sale of March 23 as uncollectible.
Nov. 18	Reinstated the account of Biggs and Daughters, which had been written off on June 8, and received $4,000 cash in full settlement.

20-2

Jan. 11	Reinstated the account of Lloyd Place, which had been written off on September 27 of the previous year, and received $5,800 cash in full settlement.

REQUIRED

Record these transactions in general journal form.

MANAGING YOUR WRITING

The heads of the marketing and finance areas at your business are arguing about tight versus easy credit policies. One feels the policy should be tightened, and the other feels it should be eased. The division manager is concerned about which approach to use and asks for your advice. Prepare a memo to the division manager stating arguments for and against tight and easy credit policies. The manager will use this information to decide on which policy to establish.

ETHICS ★

ETHICS CASE

Preston Enterprises uses the direct write-off method of accounting for uncollectible accounts. On October 12, a very large account was written off. The amount was subsequently recovered on December 15. Ray Preston, the owner of the company, instructed the accountant to not make a journal entry for the recovery and to hold the check in his desk until after the first of the year "for tax purposes."

1. If you were the accountant, what would you think of Preston's request?
2. If the December 15 entry is not made, how will it affect Preston's current year financial statements?
3. Assume the amount of the charge-off and the subsequent recovery was $10,000. Prepare the proper journal entries for October 12 and December 15.
4. In groups of two or three, discuss the possible consequences for the accountant holding the check in his desk drawer for a couple of weeks.

MASTERY PROBLEM

✓ 5. Net realizable value: $59,000

Sam and Robert are identical twins. They opened identical businesses and experienced identical transactions. However, they decided to estimate uncollectible accounts in different ways. Sam elected to use the percentage of sales method, and Robert elected to use the percentage of receivables method. Listed below are the beginning balances of Cash, Accounts Receivable, and Allowance for Doubtful Accounts [items (a)–(c)], and summary transactions that occurred during the year [items (d)–(g)] for both businesses. Remember, both businesses experienced the same events: credit sales, collections of receivables, and write-offs. The only difference between the businesses is the method of estimating uncollectible accounts.

	Sam	Robert
(a) Balance of Cash, January 1, 20--	$300,000	$300,000
(b) Balance of Accounts Receivable, January 1	50,000	50,000
(c) Balance of Allowance for Doubtful Accounts, January 1	5,000	5,000
(d) Sales on account during 20--	550,000	550,000
(e) Collections on account during 20--	530,000	530,000
(f) Uncollectible accounts written off during 20--	4,500	4,500
(g) Collections made on accounts written off during 20--	500	500

(*continued*)

REQUIRED

1. Enter items (a) through (c) in two sets of general ledger accounts: one for Sam and one for Robert.

For Sam:

2. Prepare entries in a general journal (page 4) for summary transactions (d) through (g) for Sam.

3. Post the entries to a general ledger for Sam, using the following accounts and numbers.

Cash	101
Accounts Receivable	122
Allowance for Doubtful Accounts	122.1
Sales	401
Bad Debt Expense	532

4. Sam estimates that 1% of all sales on account will be uncollectible. Calculate the estimated bad debt expense and make the appropriate adjusting entry in a general journal. Post the entry to the general ledger accounts on December 31, 20--.

5. Compute the net realizable value of Sam's accounts receivable on December 31, 20--.

For Robert:

6. Prepare entries in a general journal (page 4) for summary transactions (d) through (g) for Robert.

7. Post the entries to a general ledger for Robert, using the same accounts and numbers as were used for Sam.

8. Robert bases the estimate of uncollectible accounts on an aging schedule of accounts receivable. Using the following information, compute the estimated uncollectible amounts and make the appropriate adjusting entry in a general journal. Post the entry to the general ledger accounts on December 31, 20--.

Customers	Invoice Dates and Amounts for Unpaid Invoices					
Beets, D.	10/7	$2,300	11/15	$1,200	12/18	$8,500
Cook, L.	6/1	1,200	8/15	2,500		
Hylton, D.	9/23	4,300	10/22	2,500	12/23	2,800
Martin, D.	10/15	5,400	11/12	3,200	12/15	1,500
Stokes, D.	9/9	200	12/15	9,500		
Taylor, T.	11/20	400	12/10	1,400		
Thomas, O.	12/2	5,500				
Tower, R.	12/15	2,300				
Williams, G.	11/18	2,800	12/8	8,000		

All sales are billed n/30. The following aging chart is used to estimate the uncollectibles using the percentage of receivables method:

Age Interval	Estimated Percent Uncollectible
Not yet due	2%
1–30 days	5
31–60 days	10
61–90 days	25
91–120 days	50
Over 120 days	80

9. Compute the net realizable value of Robert's accounts receivable on December 31, 20--.

CHALLENGE PROBLEM

> This problem challenges you to apply your cumulative accounting knowledge to move a step beyond the material in the chapter.

✓ 2. Dr. Bad Debt Exp.: $25,000

1. Martel Co. has $320,000 in Accounts Receivable on December 31, 20-1, the end of its first year of operations. The business is new, so it has no prior experience with uncollectible accounts. In Martel's overall industry, the percentage of uncollectible accounts receivable is about 3%. For companies similar to Martel in size and operations, the percentage is about 5%. Martel decides to use the overall industry experience as the basis for its estimate of uncollectible accounts.

REQUIRED

Prepare the adjusting entry on December 31, 20-1 for Martel Co.'s uncollectible accounts.

2. At the end of 20-2, Martel Co. had $380,000 in Accounts Receivable and a debit balance of $6,000 in Allowance for Doubtful Accounts. Because it has been operating for only two years, Martel once again wants to base its estimate of uncollectible accounts on the industry average or the experience of similar companies. The industry and similar company percentages for the year were the same as in 20-1.

REQUIRED

Based on Martel Co.'s experience in 20-2, select the most appropriate basis (industry or similar company) for estimating its uncollectible accounts for 20-2. Prepare the adjusting entry on December 31, 20-2 for Martel Co.'s uncollectible accounts.

3. At the end of 20-3, Martel Co. had $410,000 in Accounts Receivable and a credit balance of $300 in Allowance for Doubtful Accounts. Martel has now been in business for three years and wants to base its estimate of uncollectible accounts on its own experience.

REQUIRED

Assume that Martel Co.'s adjusting entry for uncollectible accounts on December 31, 20-2, was a debit to Bad Debt Expense and a credit to Allowance for Doubtful Accounts of $25,000.

(a) Estimate Martel's uncollectible accounts percentage based on its actual bad debt experience during the past two years.

(b) Prepare the adjusting entry on December 31, 20-3, for Martel Co.'s uncollectible accounts.

ANSWERS TO SELF-STUDY TEST QUESTIONS

True/False

1. T
2. F (expenses matched with revenues)

3. F (balance in Allowance for Doubtful Accounts is ignored)
4. F (debit to Allowance for Doubtful Accounts)
5. T

Multiple Choice

1. d

2. a

3. b

4. d (note the debit balance in the allowance account)

5. a

Checkpoint Exercises

1.

Accounts receivable	$32,500
Less allowance for doubtful accounts	1,100
Net realizable value	$31,400

2.

1			(a) Bad Debt Expense				5	1	0	0	00*						1
2			Allowance for Doubtful Accounts									5	1	0	0	00	2
3			*($170,000 total sales × 3% = $5,100														3
4			bad debt expense needed)														4
5																	5
6			(b) Bad Debt Expense				3	4	8	0	00*						6
7			Allowance for Doubtful Accounts									3	4	8	0	00	7
8			*($3,200 desired credit balance + $280														8
9			debit balance = $3,480 adjustment needed)														9

3.

1			Bad Debt Expense				1	3	2	0	00						1
2			Accounts Receivable/P. Wahdia									1	3	2	0	00	2
3			Wrote off uncollectible account														3

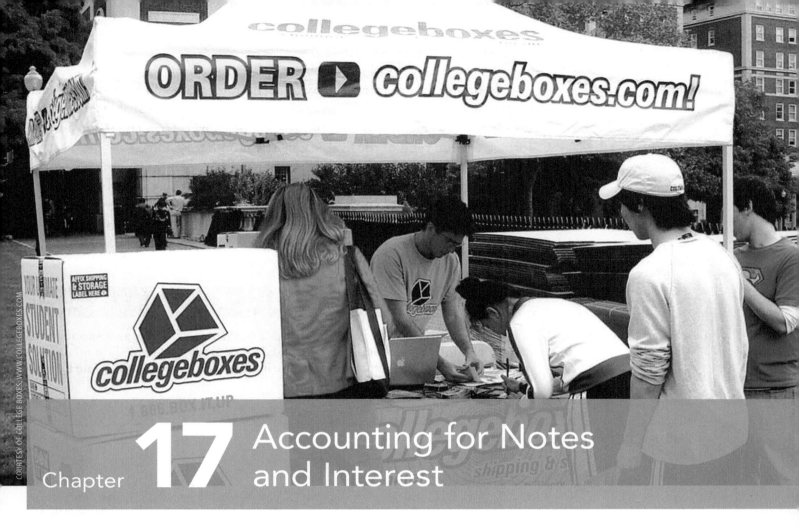

COURTESY OF COLLEGE BOXES; WWW.COLLEGEBOXES.COM

Chapter 17 Accounting for Notes and Interest

In 1999, two Duke and Washington University students noticed many of their colleagues struggling with the same questions. How do we transport our stuff to and from the university? And where do we store our stuff in the summer? In response, each of them started a small business that provided transport and storage services for students at their schools. After graduation, they merged their efforts in 2000 to form Collegeboxes, Inc.

Collegeboxes is now part of the U-Haul Company, serves hundreds of schools nationally, and is the number one student storage and shipping provider in the country. The company provides packing materials, picks up packed goods, and either ships them to the intended destination or stores them in secure facilities until the end of summer or whenever needed. Students can store furniture, refrigerators, computers, bicycles, books, etc. In addition, the students can select the exact move out and move in dates. The convenience for the students and parents is very appealing.

For a business like Collegeboxes, there no doubt are times of the year when activity and revenues are substantial, and other times when hardly anything is happening. During the periods when cash inflow is slow, the company might need a short-term loan to meet its bills. A common way of meeting this need is by signing a promissory note at a bank. In this chapter, you will learn about these notes, how to calculate interest on the amount borrowed, and how to account for both notes receivable and notes payable.

LEARNING OBJECTIVES

Careful study of this chapter should enable you to:

LO1 Describe a promissory note.

LO2 Calculate interest on and determine the due date of promissory notes.

LO3 Account for notes receivable transactions and accrued interest.

LO4 Account for notes payable transactions and accrued interest.

In Chapter 16, we learned how to account for accounts receivable. Recall that an account receivable is an unwritten promise by a customer to pay for goods or services. In this chapter, we will learn how to account for a more formal, written type of receivable called a promissory note.

After completing our study of notes receivable, we will learn to account for notes payable. You will see that a note payable is very similar to a note receivable. Both are promissory notes. We simply look at the note from two different points of view. A note receivable is someone's promise to pay you. A note payable is your promise to pay someone else.

LO1	The Promissory Note

Describe a promissory note.

A **promissory note** (usually called a note) is a written promise to pay a specific sum at a definite future date. Notes are often used when credit is extended for 60 days or more, or when large amounts of money are involved. Figure 17-1 shows one form of promissory note.

FIGURE 17-1 Promissory Note

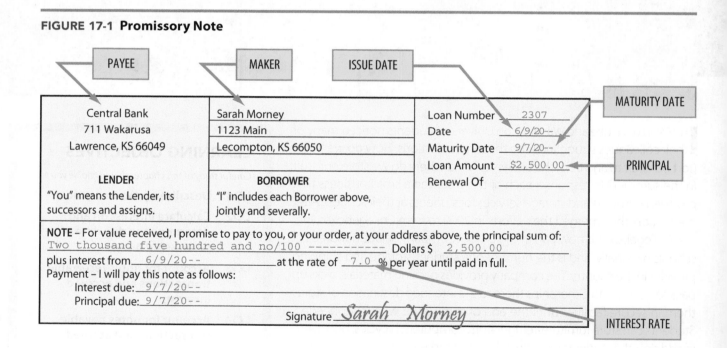

> To the payee of a note, the note is a note receivable. To the maker of a note, the note is a note payable.

- The **maker** of the note is Sarah Morney, the person or business who borrows the money and promises to pay the amount of the note plus interest when it comes due.
- The **payee** of the note is Central Bank, the person or business to whom the amount of the note plus interest will be paid.
- The **principal of the note** is $2,500, the amount the maker promises to pay when the note comes due.
- The **issue date** of the note is June 9, the date when the money is borrowed.

- The maturity date of the note is September 7, the date when the note will come due.

- The rate of interest, or interest rate, on the note is 7%, the rate at which interest is charged on the note.

Notice that to Morney it is a note payable while to Central Bank it is a note receivable.

Notes may be interest bearing or non-interest bearing. An interest-bearing note is one with an explicit interest rate stated on the face of the note. The note in Figure 17-1 is a 7% interest-bearing note. A non-interest-bearing note is one on which no rate of interest is specified, although the note does include an interest component. Notes signed when borrowing from a bank often are of this type. This type of transaction is illustrated later in the chapter.

<table>
<tr><td>**LO2**</td><td>## Calculating Interest and Determining Due Date</td></tr>
</table>

Calculate interest on and determine the due date of promissory notes.

To calculate interest on notes, three factors are used.

1. Principal of the note
2. Rate of interest
3. Term of the note

The principal of the note is the amount the maker promises to pay at maturity. In Figure 17-1, the principal is $2,500. This is the amount on which the interest is calculated.

The rate of interest usually is expressed as a percentage, such as 6% or 8%. Ordinarily, an annual rate is used, but in some cases a monthly rate is quoted, such as ¾% a month. A rate of ¾% a month is equivalent to a rate of 9% a year payable monthly (¾% × 12 = 9%). The rate of interest on the note in Figure 17-1 is 7% per year.

The term of the note is the months or days from the issue date to the maturity date. The term of the note is used to calculate time, which is the term of the note stated as a fraction of a year. When the term of the note is specified in months, time is calculated on the basis of months. For example, a three-month note issued on June 1 is payable on September 1, and time is calculated as follows:

Time
3 mos./12 mos. = 3/12 = ¼ year

When the term of a note is specified in days or when the due date is specified in a note, time is computed using the exact number of days from the issue date of the note to the maturity date. In making this computation, the maturity date is counted but the issue date is not. For example, the issue date of the note in Figure 17-1 is June 9 and the due date is specified as September 7. The term of the note is 90 days, calculated as follows:

Days in June	30	
Less issue date of note, June 9	9	
Days remaining in June		21
Add: Days in July		31
Days in August	31	
Maturity date, September 7	7	
Total term in days		90

LEARNING KEY

To calculate the time of a note, count the maturity date; do *not* count the issue date.

The time of this note is expressed as follows:

Time 90 days / 360 days = 90/360 year

Notice the use of 360 in the denominator in the above calculation. We do this for simplicity here. Most banks and business firms and all federal government agencies use 365 days as the base in computing daily interest.

Calculating Interest

The principal, interest rate, and time of the note are used in the following formula to calculate interest:

$$\text{Interest} = \text{Principal} \times \text{Rate} \times \text{Time}$$

For the note in Figure 17-1, interest is calculated as follows:

I	=	P	×	R	×	T
	=	$2,500	×	0.07	×	90/360
	=	$43.75				

For a $2,000, 6% note due in three months, interest is calculated as follows:

I	=	P	×	R	×	T
	=	$2,000	×	0.06	×	3/12
	=	$30				

The principal of the note plus interest equals the maturity value of the note. For example, the maturity value of the $2,500 note in Figure 17-1 is $2,543.75. Similarly, the maturity value of the $2,000 note is $2,030. Figure 17-2 uses a time line to illustrate the gradual accumulation of interest on the $2,500 note to its $2,543.75 maturity value.

FIGURE 17-2 Accumulation of Interest Time Line

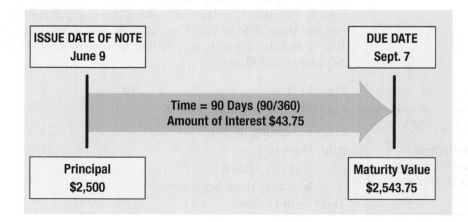

ISSUE DATE OF NOTE June 9		DUE DATE Sept. 7
	Time = 90 Days (90/360) Amount of Interest $43.75	
Principal $2,500		Maturity Value $2,543.75

Most of the examples in this chapter are for notes of 90 days or less. Notes can be for much longer periods of time—two to five years is common with auto loans.

Determining the Due Date

As previously explained, the period of time between the issue date and the maturity date of a note may be stated in either months or days. If the term of the note is stated in months, the due date is determined by counting the number of months from the date the note was issued. The note is due on the date in the month of maturity that corresponds with the date the note was issued. For example, a three-month note dated August 10 would be due November 10. If there is no date in the month of maturity corresponding to the issue date, the due date is the last day of the month. For example, a three-month note dated January 31 would be due April 30.

If the term of the note is stated in days, the due date is the specified number of days after the issue date. To determine the due date, apply these three steps:

STEP 1 Subtract the issue date from the number of days in the month of issuance.

STEP 2 Add to the result of step 1 the number of days in as many months as possible without exceeding the time of the note.

STEP 3 Subtract the result of step 2 from the time of the note. The result is the date of the month the note is due.

To calculate the due date of the note in Figure 17-1, a 90-day note dated June 9, apply the three steps as follows:

STEP 1	Days in June		30
	Less issue date of note: June		9
	Result of step 1		**21**
STEP 2	Result of step 1		21
	Plus days in July		31
	Plus days in August		31
	Result of step 2		**83**
STEP 3	Time of note		90 days
	Less result of step 2		83
	Due date:	September	7

CHECKPOINT ✔

Complete Checkpoint-1 on page 673 to test your basic understanding of LO2.

LO3 — Accounting for Notes Receivable Transactions

Account for notes receivable transactions and accrued interest.

In this section of the chapter, we examine promissory note transactions from the perspective of the payee of the note, for whom it is a note receivable. Businesses other than banks and savings and loans generally encounter seven types of transactions involving notes receivable.

1. Note received from a customer in exchange for assets sold
2. Note received from a customer to extend time for payment of an account
3. Note collected at maturity
4. Note renewed at maturity
5. Note discounted before maturity
6. Note dishonored
7. Collection of dishonored note

Note Received from a Customer in Exchange for Assets Sold

When a business makes a large sale, it may accept a note for the amount of the sale. A business may be willing to accept the note for two reasons. First, the note is a formal, written promise to pay. This note can be converted to cash at a bank if necessary. Second, the note is likely to bear interest.

Assume that on June 1 Linesch Hardware Co. sells an industrial mower to Williams Manufacturing for $8,500. Williams gives Linesch a 180-day, 8% note for $8,500 in exchange for the mower. This transaction is entered by Linesch as follows:

1	June	1	Notes Receivable	8 5 0 0 00		1
2			Sales		8 5 0 0 00	2
3			Received note for merchandise sale			3

Note Received from a Customer to Extend Time for Payment

When a customer's account is due, the customer may issue a note for all or part of the amount. Assume that Michael Putter owes Linesch Hardware Co. $2,000 on account. To settle the account, Putter gives Linesch a 90-day, 7.5% note dated June 8. This transaction is entered by Linesch as follows:

15	June	8	Notes Receivable	2 0 0 0 00		15
16			Accounts Receivable/M. Putter		2 0 0 0 00	16
17			Received note to settle account			17

If instead Putter gives a check for $250 and a note for $1,750 to settle the account, Linesch makes the following entry:

15	June	8	Cash	2 5 0 00		15
16			Notes Receivable	1 7 5 0 00		16
17			Accounts Receivable/M. Putter		2 0 0 0 00	17
18			Received cash and note to settle account			18

Note Collected at Maturity

When a note receivable matures, it may be collected by one of the following:

1. The payee (in Figure 17-1, Central Bank; in the above example, Linesch Hardware Co.)
2. The bank named in the note
3. A bank where it was left for collection

Assume that on September 6, Putter pays Linesch the $2,000 principal plus $37.50 interest on the note described above. Linesch makes the following entry:

$$I = P \times R \times T$$
$$= \$2,000 \times .075 \times 90/360$$
$$= \$37.50$$

31	Sept.	6	Cash	2 0 3 7 50		31
32			Notes Receivable		2 0 0 0 00	32
33			Interest Revenue		3 7 50	33
34			Received payment of note with interest			34

When a bank makes the collection, because it is named in the note or the note is left with the bank for collection, it notifies the payee that the net amount has been added to the payee's account. The bank uses a credit advice like the one in Figure 17-3 for this purpose.

FIGURE 17-3 Credit Advice

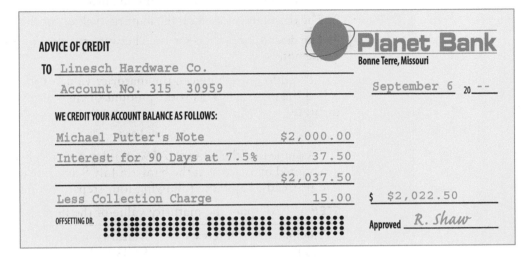

For example, assume that Linesch left Putter's 90-day, 7.5% note for $2,000 at Planet Bank for collection. On September 6, the bank notifies Linesch that the note plus $37.50 interest have been collected. The bank fee for collecting the note was $15. Linesch enters this transaction as follows:

37	Sept.	6	Cash			2	0	2	2	50							37
38			Collection Expense					1	5	00							38
39			Notes Receivable									2	0	0	0	00	39
40			Interest Revenue										3	7	50	40
41			Received payment of note with interest													41
42			less collection fee													42

Note Renewed at Maturity

If the maker of a note is unable to pay the amount due at maturity, the payee may allow the maker to renew all or part of the note. Assume that at maturity of the $2,000 note, Putter pays only the $37.50 interest and gives a new 60-day, 8% note. Linesch enters this transaction as follows:

31	Sept.	6	Cash				3	7	50						31
32			Notes Receivable (new note)		2	0	0	0	00						32
33			Notes Receivable (old note)							2	0	0	0	00	33
34			Interest Revenue								3	7	50	34
35			Received new note plus interest on old note											35

If Putter pays $37.50 interest plus $500 on the principal and gives a new 90-day, 8% note for $1,500, Linesch makes the following entry:

31	Sept.	6	Cash			5	3	7	50						31
32			Notes Receivable (new note)		1	5	0	0	00						32
33			Notes Receivable (old note)							2	0	0	0	00	33
34			Interest Revenue								3	7	50	34
35			Received new note plus partial payment											35
36			and interest on old note											36

Note Discounted Before Maturity

If a business needs cash before the due date of a note, it can endorse the note and transfer it to a bank. This process is called discounting a note receivable. The bank charges an interest fee called a bank discount.

The bank discount is similar to interest except for the following:

1. The discount is paid to the bank in advance.
2. The discount is based on the maturity value, not the principal of the note.
3. The discount period is the time between the date of discounting and the due date of the note.

The difference between the maturity value of the note and the bank discount is called the proceeds. This is the amount of cash received by the business discounting the note.

$$\text{Maturity Value} - \text{Discount} = \text{Proceeds}$$

Assume that the $2,000, 7.5%, 90-day note receivable from Putter dated June 8 is discounted by Linesch at the bank on July 8 at a rate of 8%. To calculate the discount and proceeds, apply the following four steps:

STEP 1   Compute the maturity value of the note.

Principal	+	Interest	=	Maturity Value
$2,000	+	$37.50	=	$2,037.50

STEP 2   Compute the number of days in the discount period—from the discount date to the due date.

Discount date	July 8	
Days in July		31
Less discount date	July	8
Remaining days in July		23
Plus days in August		31
Plus due date	September	6
Days in discount period		60

STEP 3   Compute the discount amount.

The formula for computing the discount amount is similar to the basic $I = P \times R \times T$ formula we used for calculating interest on page 654. In the case of the discount,

I = Discount Amount
P = Maturity Value
R = Discount Rate
T = Discount Period

Discount Amount	=	Maturity Value*	×	Discount Rate	×	Discount Period
$27.17	=	$2,037.50	×	8%	×	60/360

*Note that in calculating the discount amount, the *maturity value* of the note is used, not the principal.

STEP 4   Compute the proceeds.

Maturity Value	−	Discount Amount	=	Proceeds
$2,037.50	−	$27.17	=	$2,010.33

Figure 17-4 shows a time line illustration of this transaction.

FIGURE 17-4 Discounted $2,000, 7.5% Note Receivable at 8% for 60 days: Time Line

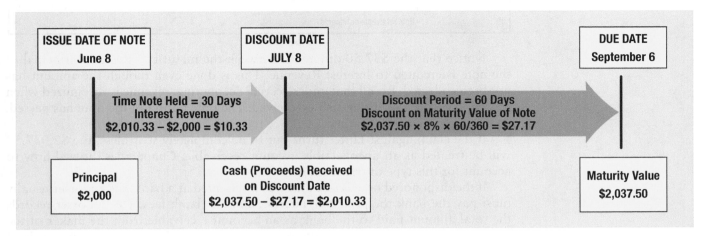

The excess of the $2,010.33 proceeds over the $2,000 principal value of the note represents interest revenue of $10.33. Linesch enters this transaction as follows:

26	July	8	Cash		2	0	1	0	33							26
27			Notes Receivable								2	0	0	0	00	27
28			Interest Revenue										1	0	33	28
29			Discounted note receivable													29

If the proceeds from discounting a note are less than the principal value of the note, the difference represents interest expense. For example, if the proceeds from discounting Putter's $2,000 note were only $1,992, Linesch would make the following entry:

26	July	8	Cash		1	9	9	2	00							26
27			Interest Expense					8	00							27
28			Notes Receivable								2	0	0	0	00	28
29			Discounted note receivable													29

When a note receivable is discounted, the business that endorses the note becomes potentially liable to the bank. If the maker of the note does not pay it at maturity, the business that discounted the note must pay the maturity value and any bank fees to the bank. This kind of potential liability that may become a real liability, depending on future events, is called a **contingent liability**. A contingent liability does not affect the accounting records. It is disclosed in the notes to the financial statements.

Note Dishonored

If the maker of a note does not pay or renew it at maturity, the note is said to be **dishonored**. The maker of the note is still liable to the payee for the principal amount plus interest. But a dishonored note loses its legal status as a note receivable. Therefore, the payee transfers the amount due from Notes Receivable to Accounts Receivable. For example, if the $2,000, 7.5%, 90-day note from Putter is dishonored, Linesch makes the following entry:

16	Sept.	6	Accounts Receivable/M. Putter		2	0	3	7	50							16
17			Notes Receivable								2	0	0	0	00	17
18			Interest Revenue										3	7	50	18
19			Note receivable dishonored													19

Notice that the $37.50 difference between the maturity value and principal of the note is credited to Interest Revenue. This is done even though the amount has not been collected. Recall that under accrual accounting, revenue is recognized when earned, regardless of when cash is received. The time period of the note has passed, so the interest has been earned.

If the claim against Putter turns out to be completely worthless, the $2,037.50 will be treated as an uncollectible account receivable. Chapter 16 showed how to account for this type of transaction.

If the dishonored note is one that was discounted at a bank, the endorser usually must pay the bank the principal, interest, and any bank fees. The endorser records the total amount paid to the bank as an account receivable from the maker of the note. Assume that the $2,000 note receivable discounted on July 8 for proceeds of $2,010.33 was dishonored by Putter at maturity. The bank bills Linesch for the $2,000 principal of the note, $37.50 interest, and a $25 bank fee, a total of $2,062.50. Linesch pays the bank and makes the following journal entry:

23	Sept.	6	Accounts Receivable/M. Putter		2	0	6	2	50							23
24			Cash								2	0	6	2	50	24
25			Paid bank for dishonored note													25

Note that the $25 bank fee is included in the amount receivable from Putter. This is because the fee was incurred as a result of Putter's dishonoring of the note, and this is not Linesch's expense.

Collection of Dishonored Note

What if a note that has been dishonored eventually is collected? When that occurs, the payee records collection of the account receivable. In addition, interest often is charged for the period from the due date of the original note to the final collection date. Interest is based on the maturity value of the note plus the bank fee, if any, incurred when the note was dishonored. Let's look again at Putter's $2,000 note that Linesch discounted at the bank on July 8. When this note was dishonored on September 6, the $2,000 principal of the note, $37.50 interest, and $25 bank fee were transferred to Accounts Receivable. Assume that on October 16, Putter pays the original maturity value of the note plus the bank fee ($2,062.50) and interest for the period from September 6 to October 16. Interest would be computed as follows:

Original Maturity Value Plus Bank Fee	×	Rate	×	Time		
$2,062.50	×	7.5%	×	40*/360	=	$17.19

*Days in September	30
Less original maturity date of note	6
Days remaining in September	24
Plus collection date in October	16
Total days	40

A BROADER VIEW

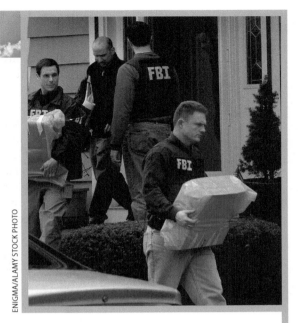

ENIGMA/ALAMY STOCK PHOTO

These Notes Were No Longer *Receivable*

The former chief financial officer (CFO) of Intermountain Mortgage Company, Inc. (IMC), in Billings, Montana, pleaded guilty to defrauding the company's mortgage loan lender. IMC's main line of business was originating, brokering, and servicing first and second mortgage loans. To fund these loans, the company obtained a line of credit from First Citizens Bank of Billings and then sold the loans in a secondary market. This is a common practice with mortgage notes receivable.

Like all lenders, First Citizens Bank relied on IMC's financial reports in order to continue to fund the line of credit. When IMC started to have financial difficulties that could cause it to lose the line of credit, the CFO began including fraudulent "notes receivable" on its financial reports. The reports claimed that IMC had sold these notes but had not yet received payment. In fact, these were no longer actual notes receivable because IMC had already been paid. After two years, 26 fraudulent notes receivable were listed in the financial reports provided to First Citizens Bank. The fraud was uncovered during an investigation by the FBI. The former CFO was sentenced to a short time in prison, six months of house arrest, and five years of supervision.

Linesch would make the following journal entry:

16	Oct.	16	Cash		2	0	7	9	69								16
17			Accounts Receivable								2	0	6	2	50		17
18			Interest Revenue										1	7	19		18
19			Collected dishonored note with interest														19

Notes Receivable Register

When a business receives many notes, it may keep a notes receivable register. This is a detailed auxiliary record of notes receivable. Figure 17-5 shows an abbreviated version of a notes receivable register. A more complete register might also include the number of each note and where the note is payable. The information contained in the register is obtained directly from the notes.

FIGURE 17-5 Notes Receivable Register

NOTES RECEIVABLE REGISTER												PAGE 1
DATE RECEIVED	MAKER	TIME	DUE DATE	AMOUNT	INTEREST RATE	INTEREST AMOUNT	DISCOUNTED BANK	DISCOUNTED DATE	DATE COLLECTED	REMARKS
20-- Apr. 4	L. Peters	60 days	June 3	4 0 0 00	8%	5 33			June 3	
21	J. Slaw	60 days	June 20	6 0 0 00	9%	9 00			June 20	Renewal for $500
May 2	S. Alpart	30 days	June 1	7 0 0 00	7%	4 08			June 1	Sent for collection 5/30
19	L. Shein	90 days	Aug. 17	8 0 0 00	8%	1 6 00				
June 20	J. Slaw	60 days	Aug. 19	5 0 0 00	8%	6 67				Renewal of 4/21 note

Accrued Interest Receivable

Under accrual accounting, revenue is recognized when it is earned. For notes receivable, interest literally is earned day by day. It would be impractical, however, to record the interest revenue each day. Instead, for notes that are received and due within a single accounting period, no entry is made for interest revenue until the note is due.

For notes that are received in one period and due in the following period, however, accrued interest must be recorded at the end of the period. Accrued interest on notes receivable is interest revenue that has been earned but not yet received. The amount of accrued interest can be computed from the notes themselves or from the notes receivable register. The notes receivable register in Figure 17-5 can be used as an example. At June 30, the end of this company's fiscal year, two notes are outstanding. Accrued interest on these notes is calculated as follows:

Principal	Issue Date	Rate of Interest	Days from Issue Date to June 30	Accrued Interest June 30
$800.00	May 19	8%	42	$7.47
500.00	June 20	8%	10	1.11
Total accrued interest on notes				$8.58

The following adjusting entry is made on June 30 for the accrued interest:

16	June	30	Accrued Interest Receivable			8	58						16
17			Interest Revenue							8	58		17
18			Interest accrued on notes receivable										18

Accrued interest receivable is reported as a current asset on the balance sheet. Interest revenue is reported as other revenue on the income statement.

CHECKPOINT ✔

Complete Checkpoint-2 on page 673 to test your basic understanding of LO3.

LO4

Account for notes payable transactions and accrued interest.

Accounting for Notes Payable Transactions

In this section of the chapter, we examine promissory note transactions from the perspective of the maker of the note, for whom it is a note payable. Businesses generally encounter five types of transactions involving notes payable.

1. Note issued to a supplier in exchange for assets purchased
2. Note issued to a supplier to extend time for payment of an account
3. Note issued as security for cash loan
4. Note paid at maturity
5. Note renewed at maturity

Note Issued to a Supplier in Exchange for Assets Purchased

When a business makes a large purchase, it may give a note for the amount of the purchase. Assume that on June 1 Linesch Hardware Co. purchases a truckload of trees and shrubs from Evergreen Enterprises for $4,000. Linesch gives Evergreen a 90-day, 7% note for $4,000 in exchange for the trees and shrubs. This transaction is entered by Linesch as follows:

5	June	1	Purchases		4	0	0	0	00							5
6			Notes Payable								4	0	0	0	00	6
7			Issued note for inventory purchase													7

If another purchase is made of a fork lift for the warehouse, using a 90-day, 7% note for $12,000, this transaction is entered as follows:

5	June	1	Equipment		12	0	0	0	00							5
6			Notes Payable								12	0	0	0	00	6
7			Issued note for fork lift purchase													7

Note Issued to a Supplier to Extend Time for Payment

When a firm's account with a supplier is due, the supplier may be willing to accept a note for all or part of the amount due. Assume that Linesch Hardware Co. owes Bella & Co. $700 on June 11. If Linesch issues Bella a 90-day, 6% note for $700, Linesch makes the following entry:

26	June	11	Accounts Payable/Bella & Co.		7	0	0	00						26
27			Notes Payable							7	0	0	00	27
28			Issued note to settle account											28

If instead, Linesch gives Bella a check for $200 and a 90-day, 6% note for $500, the entry by Linesch is as follows:

26	June	11	Accounts Payable/Bella & Co.		7	0	0	00						26
27			Cash							2	0	0	00	27
28			Notes Payable							5	0	0	00	28
29			Made partial payment and issued note											29
30			to settle account											30

Note Issued as Security for Cash Loan

Businesses sometimes have brief periods during which receipts from customers are not adequate to finance operations. During such periods, businesses commonly borrow money from banks on short-term notes.

Interest-Bearing Notes

Assume that on June 16, Linesch borrows $6,000 from Planet Bank on a 60-day, 7% note. This transaction is entered as follows:

38	June	16	Cash		6	0	0	0	00							38
39			Notes Payable								6	0	0	0	00	39
40			Issued note for bank loan													40

Non-Interest-Bearing Notes

When making a loan, banks often deduct interest in advance, using a procedure known as discounting. The nature of this transaction and the procedures for handling it are very similar to those for discounting notes receivable (see pages 662–663). To illustrate, suppose that Linesch borrowed $6,000 on a 60-day, non-interest-bearing note that the bank discounted at 7%. No interest rate is stated on the face of a non-interest-bearing note, but clearly there is an interest component. In this case, it is the 7% discount rate. The bank calculates the bank discount at 7% and deducts this amount from the $6,000 principal of the note. The principal of the note less the discount is the proceeds, the amount of cash the borrower receives from the bank. The amount of the discount and the proceeds to Linesch are calculated using three steps.

LEARNING KEY

As with discounting notes receivable, to calculate the discount amount, use the maturity value of the note.

STEP 1   Compute the maturity value of the note.

Principal	+	Interest	=	**Maturity Value**
$6,000	+	0	=	$6,000

STEP 2   Compute the discount amount.

As we saw with notes receivable, the formula for computing the discount amount on a note payable is similar to the basic $I = P \times R \times T$ formula, where

I = Discount Amount
P = Maturity Value
R = Discount Rate
T = Discount Period

Discount Amount	=	Maturity Value*	×	Discount Rate	×	Discount Period
$70	=	$6,000	×	7%	×	60/360

*Note that in calculating the discount amount, the *maturity value* of the note is used.

STEP 3   Compute the proceeds.

Maturity Value	−	Discount Amount	=	**Proceeds**
$6,000	−	$70	=	$5,930

Figure 17-6 shows a time line illustration of this transaction.

Linesch records receipt of the $5,930 proceeds ($6,000 − $70) from the loan as shown below and in Figure 17-7.

14	June	16	Cash						5	9	3	0	00						14
15			Discount on Notes Payable								7	0	00						15
16			Notes Payable											6	0	0	0	00	16
17			Issued note for bank loan																17

FIGURE 17-6 Discounted $6,000, 7% Note Payable: Time Line

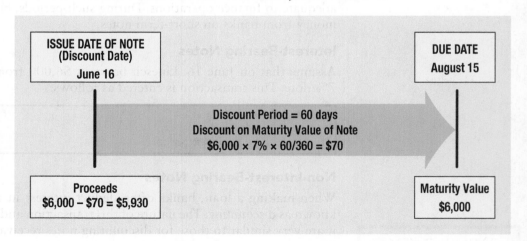

The $70 debit to Discount on Notes Payable is an offset to the $6,000 note payable. Linesch's liability at this time is only $5,930, which is the net amount or proceeds received from the bank. Discount on Notes Payable is a contra-liability account. As shown in Figure 17-8, it is reported as a deduction from Notes Payable on the balance sheet.

FIGURE 17-7 Journal Entry for Discounted Note Payable

Assets		=	Liabilities		+	Owner's Equity					
Debit +	Credit −		Debit −	Credit +		Debit −				Credit +	
							Drawing		Expenses		Revenues
						Debit +	Credit −	Debit +	Credit −	Debit −	Credit +

Cash			Notes Payable	
5,930				6,000
			Discount on Notes Payable	
			70	

FIGURE 17-8 Notes Payable and Related Discount on the Balance Sheet

Current liabilities:									
Notes payable			$6	0	0	0	00		
Less discount on notes payable					7	0	00	$5 9 3 0	00

Stated versus Effective Interest Rate

The stated rate of interest was 7% on both the interest-bearing and discounted notes. Notice, however, that the real interest rates on the two notes are not the same. With the interest-bearing note, Linesch obtained $6,000 for 60 days at a cost of $70—exactly 7%.

$$\$70 \div \$6,000 = 1.167\% \text{ for } 60 \text{ days}$$
$$\underline{\times 6} \quad (360 \div 60)$$
$$= \quad 7\% \text{ for } 360 \text{ days}$$

With the discounted note, Linesch paid $70 for the use of only $5,930 for 60 days—a rate of nearly 7.1%. This rate is known as the effective rate of interest.

$$\$70 \div \$5,930 = 1.18\% \text{ for } 60 \text{ days}$$
$$\underline{\times 6} \quad (360 \div 60)$$
$$= \quad 7.083\% \text{ for } 360 \text{ days}$$

Note Paid at Maturity

The proper entry to make when a note is paid at maturity depends on whether the note is interest bearing or non-interest bearing. For an interest-bearing note, the same entry is made for payment to a supplier or to a bank. For example, let's reconsider Linesch's $6,000, 60-day, 7% note due August 15. When the note is paid on August 15, Linesch will make the following entry:

21	Aug.	15	Notes Payable		6 0 0 0	00			21
22			Interest Expense		7 0	00			22
23			Cash				6 0 7 0	00	23
24			Paid note with interest at maturity						24

For a non-interest-bearing note from a bank, the entry to record the payment of the note is different. This is because Discount on Notes Payable was debited when the money was borrowed. For example, recall Linesch's $6,000, 60-day, non-interest-bearing note discounted by the bank at 7%. When the money was borrowed, the following entry was made:

14	June	16	Cash	5 9 3 0 00		14
15			Discount on Notes Payable	7 0 00		15
16			Notes Payable		6 0 0 0 00	16
17			Issued note for bank loan			17

The $70 discount gradually becomes interest expense. This expense is recognized when the $6,000 principal amount of the note is repaid on August 15, the due date. Linesch will enter the payment of the note at maturity as follows:

22	Aug.	15	Notes Payable	6 0 0 0 00		22
23			Interest Expense	7 0 00		23
24			Cash		6 0 0 0 00	24
25			Discount on Notes Payable		7 0 00	25
26			Paid note at maturity			26

Note Renewed at Maturity

The payee of a note may allow the maker to renew all or a part of the note at maturity. For example, let's reconsider the $6,000 interest-bearing note that Linesch issued to Planet Bank on June 16. Assume that on August 15 Linesch pays $70 interest and $1,000 on the principal of this note and gives a new 60-day, 7% note for $5,000. Linesch enters this transaction as follows:

27	Aug.	15	Notes Payable (old note)	6 0 0 0 00		27
28			Interest Expense	7 0 00		28
29			Cash		1 0 7 0 00	29
30			Notes Payable (new note)		5 0 0 0 00	30
31			Paid interest and part of principal on			31
32			old note and issued new note			32

Notes Payable Register

When a business issues many notes, it may keep a notes payable register. This is a detailed auxiliary record of notes payable. An abbreviated version of a notes payable register is shown in Figure 17-9. A more complete register might also include the number of each note and where the note is payable. The information contained in the register is obtained directly from the notes.

FIGURE 17-9 Notes Payable Register

									NOTES PAYABLE REGISTER							PAGE 1
DATE ISSUED		PAYEE	TIME	DUE DATE		AMOUNT			INTEREST			DATE PAID		REMARKS
									RATE	AMOUNT				
20— Apr.	14	L. Knoop	60 days	June	13	2 0 0 0 00	7%			2 3 33	June	13	Settled 2/14 invoice
May	13	Apex Bank	90 days	Aug.	11	8 0 0 0 00	8%			1 6 0 00			
June	2	S. Bront	30 days	July	2	1 5 0 0 00	7%			8 75			Settled 4/2 invoice

Accrued Interest Payable

As with notes receivable, it also is necessary to record accrued interest on notes payable at the end of the period. For notes payable issued in one period and due in the following period, accrued interest payable must be recorded. Accrued interest on notes payable is interest expense that has been incurred but not paid. The amount of accrued interest can be computed from the notes themselves or from the notes payable register.

The proper entry for accrued interest on notes payable depends on whether the note is interest bearing or non-interest bearing. Assume that a $900, 60-day, 8% note was issued on May 31. On June 30, this company's fiscal year-end, an adjusting entry for accrued interest of $6.00 ($900 × 8% × 30/360) is recorded as follows:

19	June	30	Interest Expense			6	00					19
20			Accrued Interest Payable						6	00		20
21			Interest accrued on note payable									21

Assume instead that the $900, 60-day note was non-interest bearing and discounted at the bank at 8%. When the money was borrowed, the following entry was made:

23	May	31	Cash	8	8	8	00					23
24			Discount on Notes Payable*	1	2	00						24
25			Notes Payable					9	0	0	00	25
26			Issued note for bank loan									26
27												27

*$900 × 8% × 60/360 = $12

On June 30, part of the discount must be transferred from Discount on Notes Payable to Interest Expense. The note was issued on May 31, so 30 days of the 60-day life of the note have passed. Thus, half of the balance in Discount on Notes Payable should be recognized as interest expense. The following adjusting entry is made on June 30:

29	June	30	Interest Expense			6	00					29
30			Discount on Notes Payable						6	00		30
31			Interest accrued on note payable									31

Note that the credit is to Discount on Notes Payable rather than Accrued Interest Payable. This is because the bank already deducted the interest at the time the money was borrowed. Thus, there is no additional interest payable to recognize. There is an increase in a liability, but that liability is notes payable instead of accrued interest payable. As shown below, the credit to Discount on Notes Payable increases the carrying value of the notes payable from $888 to $894.

Balance Sheet:	May 31	June 30
Notes payable	$900.00	$900.00
Less discount on notes payable	(12.00)	(6.00)
	$888.00	$894.00

Interest expense is reported as other expense on the income statement. Accrued interest payable is reported as a current liability on the balance sheet. As previously illustrated in Figure 17-8 (page 665), discount on notes payable is reported as a contra-liability to notes payable on the balance sheet.

SELF-STUDY

LEARNING OBJECTIVES	Key Points to Remember
LO1 **Describe a promissory note.**	A promissory note is a written promise to pay a specific sum at a future date. Notes are used when credit is extended for periods of 60 days or more, or when large amounts of money are involved. To the maker of a note, the note is a note payable. To the payee of a note, the note is a note receivable.
LO2 **Calculate interest on and determine the due date of promissory notes.**	The following formula is used to calculate interest on notes receivable and payable: $$\begin{array}{ccccccc} \text{I} & = & \text{P} & \times & \text{R} & \times & \text{T} \\ \text{Interest} & = & \text{Principal} & \times & \text{Rate} & \times & \text{Time} \end{array}$$ To determine the due date of a note with a term stated in months, count the number of months from the issue date of the note. To determine the due date of a note with a term stated in days, follow these steps: **STEP 1** Subtract the issue date from the number of days in the month of issuance. **STEP 2** Add to the result of step 1 the number of days in as many months as possible without exceeding the time of the note. **STEP 3** Subtract the result of step 2 from the time of the note.

LO3 **Account for notes receivable transactions and accrued interest.**	Businesses generally encounter seven types of transactions involving notes receivable.
	
	1. Note received from a customer in exchange for assets sold
	2. Note received from a customer to extend time for payment of an account
	3. Note collected at maturity
	4. Note renewed at maturity
	5. Note discounted before maturity
	6. Note dishonored
	7. Collection of dishonored note
	
	    When a note receivable is discounted at a bank, four steps are applied to calculate the discount and proceeds as follows:
	
	STEP 1 Compute the maturity value of the note.
	
	STEP 2 Compute the number of days in the discount period.
	
	STEP 3 Compute the discount amount.
	
	STEP 4 Compute the proceeds.
	
	    If a note receivable that was discounted at a bank is dishonored, the endorser of the note is liable to the bank for the maturity value of the note and any bank fees.
	
	    Notes that are received in one period and due in the following period require an adjustment for accrued interest at the end of the period.

LO4 **Account for notes payable transactions and accrued interest.**	Businesses generally encounter five types of transactions involving notes payable. 1. Note issued to a supplier in exchange for assets purchased 2. Note issued to a supplier to extend time for payment of an account

LEARNING OBJECTIVES	**Key Points to Remember**
LO4 **(concluded)**	3. Note issued as security for cash loan
	4. Note paid at maturity
	5. Note renewed at maturity

When money is borrowed at a bank on a non-interest-bearing note that is discounted by the bank, three steps are used to calculate the discount and proceeds.

STEP 1 Compute the maturity value of the note.

STEP 2 Compute the discount amount.

STEP 3 Compute the proceeds.

Notes payable that are issued in one period and due in the following period require an adjustment for accrued interest at the end of the period. The proper entry depends on whether or not the note is interest bearing.

DEMONSTRATION PROBLEM

Barbar Brothers, partners in a wholesale hardware business, completed the following transactions involving notes and interest during the first half of 20--:

Jan. 11 Received a $900, 60-day, 7% note from Paul Heinsius in payment for sale of merchandise.

18 Borrowed $10,000 from Landmark Bank issuing a 90-day, 8% note.

Feb. 6 Received an $875, 30-day, 6% note from Ana Fuentes in payment of an account receivable.

21 Issued a $650, 60-day, 7% note to Swanson & Johnson, a supplier, in payment of an account payable.

Mar. 1 Received a $1,000, 90-day, 7.5% note from Steve Roberts, a customer, in payment of an account receivable.

8 Received a check for $879.38 from Ana Fuentes in payment of note due March 8, including interest.

12 Paul Heinsius dishonored his $900 note due March 12.

31 Discounted the $1,000 note from Steve Roberts at Manchester Bank at a discount rate of 8%.

Apr. 11 Paul Heinsius paid the original maturity value of his note due March 12, plus interest at 7% on the maturity value for the 30 days from March 12 to April 11.

18 Paid Landmark Bank for $10,000 note due today, including interest. (See January 18 transaction.)

22 Paid Swanson & Johnson $57.58 on the note due today (interest of $7.58 plus $50 toward the principal), and issued a new $600, 60-day, 7% note.

(*continued*)

May 31   Steve Roberts dishonored his $1,000 note due at the Manchester Bank yesterday. Paid Manchester Bank $1,000, plus interest, plus a $25 bank fee, for the dishonored note.

June 20   Issued a $750, 90-day, 7% note to Greene Acres, a supplier, for purchase of merchandise.

REQUIRED

Record each transaction in a general journal.

	DATE		DESCRIPTION	POST. REF.	DEBIT	CREDIT	
1	20-- Jan.	11	Notes Receivable		9 0 0 00		1
2			Sales			9 0 0 00	2
3			Received note for merchandise sale				3
4							4
5		18	Cash		10 0 0 0 00		5
6			Notes Payable			10 0 0 0 00	6
7			Issued note for bank loan				7
8							8
9	Feb.	6	Notes Receivable		8 7 5 00		9
10			Accounts Receivable/A. Fuentes			8 7 5 00	10
11			Received note to settle account				11
12							12
13		21	Accounts Payable/Swanson & Johnson		6 5 0 00		13
14			Notes Payable			6 5 0 00	14
15			Issued note to settle account				15
16							16
17	Mar.	1	Notes Receivable		1 0 0 0 00		17
18			Accounts Receivable/S. Roberts			1 0 0 0 00	18
19			Received note to settle account				19
20							20
21		8	Cash		8 7 9 38		21
22			Notes Receivable			8 7 5 00	22
23			Interest Revenue			4 38	23
24			Received payment of note with interest				24
25							25
26		12	Accounts Receivable/P. Heinsius		9 1 0 50		26
27			Notes Receivable			9 0 0 00	27
28			Interest Revenue			1 0 50	28
29			Note receivable dishonored				29
30							30
31		31	Cash		1 0 0 5 17		31
32			Notes Receivable			1 0 0 0 00	32
33			Interest Revenue			5 17	33
34			Discounted note receivable				34
35							35
36			Principal $1,000.00				36
37			Interest to maturity 18.75				37
38			Maturity value $1,018.75				38
39			Less discount				39
40			($1,018.75 × 8% × 60/360) 13.58				40
41			Cash proceeds $1,005.17				41
42							42
43	Apr.	11	Cash		9 1 5 81		43
44			Accounts Receivable/P. Heinsius			9 1 0 50	44
45			Interest Revenue			5 31	45
46			Collected dishonored note with interest				46

GENERAL JOURNAL   PAGE 5

SOLUTION

	DATE		DESCRIPTION	POST REF.	DEBIT						CREDIT					
1	20-- Apr.	18	Notes Payable		10	0	0	0	00							1
2			Interest Expense			2	0	0	00							2
3			Cash							10	2	0	0	00		3
4			Paid note with interest at maturity													4
5																5
6		22	Notes Payable (old note)			6	5	0	00							6
7			Interest Expense					7	58							7
8			Cash									5	7	58		8
9			Notes Payable (new note)									6	0	0	00	9
10			Paid interest and part of principal on old note													10
11			and issued new note													11
12																12
13	May	31	Accounts Receivable/S. Roberts		1	0	4	3	75							13
14			Cash							1	0	4	3	75		14
15			Paid bank for dishonored note													15
16																16
17			Principal $1,000.00													17
18			Interest 18.75													18
19			Bank fee 25.00													19
20			$1,043.75													20
21																21
22	June	20	Purchases			7	5	0	00							22
23			Notes Payable									7	5	0	00	23
24			Issued note for inventory purchase													24
25																25

GENERAL JOURNAL   PAGE 6

KEY TERMS

accrued interest on notes payable (667)   Interest expense that has been incurred but not paid.

accrued interest on notes receivable (662)   Interest revenue that has been earned but not yet received.

bank discount (note payable) (663)   The interest that the bank deducts in advance from the principal of a note.

bank discount (note receivable) (658)   An interest fee that the bank charges for the time between the date of discounting and the due date of the note.

contingent liability (659)   A potential liability that may become a real liability depending on future events. In the case of a note discounted at a bank, the business that discounted the note must pay the maturity value and any bank fees if the maker of the note does not pay it at maturity.

contra-liability account (664)   An account with a debit balance that is deducted from the related liability account.

credit advice (657)   A notification to the payee that the bank has collected a note plus interest and added the amount to the payee's account.

discount period (658) The time between the date of discounting and the due date of the note.

discounting (note payable) (663) The procedure, which banks often use, of deducting interest in advance when making a loan.

discounting a note receivable (658) Endorsing a note receivable and transferring it to a bank for cash.

dishonored (659) A note which the maker does not pay or renew at maturity.

effective rate (665) The interest amount paid divided by the proceeds received on a discounted note.

interest rate (653) See rate of interest.

interest-bearing note (653) A note with an explicit interest rate stated on the face of the note.

issue date (652) The date when money is borrowed on a note.

maker (652) The person or business agreeing to pay the amount of a note plus interest on the due date.

maturity date (653) The date when a note will come due.

maturity value (654) The principal of the note plus interest equals the maturity value of the note.

non-interest-bearing note (653) A note on which no rate of interest is specified, although the note does include an interest component.

notes payable register (666) A detailed auxiliary record of notes payable.

notes receivable register (661) A detailed auxiliary record of notes receivable.

payee (652) The specific person or business to whom a note plus interest are payable.

principal of the note (652) The amount of the note that the maker promises to pay at maturity.

proceeds (note payable) (663) The difference between the principal of the note and the discount. The amount of cash received from the bank.

proceeds (note receivable) (658) The difference between the maturity value of the note and the bank discount. This is the amount of cash received by the business discounting the note.

promissory note (652) A written promise to pay a specific sum at a definite future date.

rate of interest (653) The rate at which interest is charged on a note, usually expressed as an annual rate, but in some cases a monthly rate is quoted.

term of the note (653) The months or days from the date of issue to the date of maturity.

time (653) The term of the note stated as a fraction of a year.

SELF-STUDY TEST QUESTIONS

True/False

1. **LO2** The maturity value of a note includes both principal and interest.

2. **LO3** When a note is renewed at maturity, the old note is cancelled and a new note is issued.

3. **LO3**   The difference between the maturity value of a note and the net proceeds is called discounting.

4. **LO3**   When a note is dishonored, the interest is not credited to Interest Revenue because it is not earned.

5. **LO3**   When a dishonored note is collected, interest is collected for the time between date of maturity and date of collection.

Multiple Choice

1. **LO2**   Principal plus interest equals _____ of a note.
   (a) discount
   (b) net proceeds
   (c) interest rate
   (d) maturity value

2. **LO3**   Which account is debited for interest earned but not yet received?
   (a) Interest Revenue
   (b) Accrued Interest Receivable
   (c) Accrued Interest Payable
   (d) Interest Expense

3. **LO3**   The discount amount is calculated by multiplying the maturity value times the _____ times the discount period.
   (a) discount rate
   (b) interest rate
   (c) term of note
   (d) net proceeds

4. **LO4**   When a note payable is paid at maturity, what account is debited for the amount of the interest?
   (a) Interest Revenue
   (b) Notes Payable
   (c) Interest Expense
   (d) Discount on Notes Payable

5. **LO4**   Accrued interest payable is reported as a _____ on the balance sheet.
   (a) current asset
   (b) long-term asset
   (c) current liability
   (d) long-term liability

CHECKPOINT

Checkpoint Exercises

1. **LO2**   On September 5, Y. Haun borrowed $4,000 from the bank, giving a 90-day, interest-bearing 7% note.
   (a) Calculate the interest on this note.
   (b) Determine the due date for this note.

2. **LO3**   Prepare general journal entries for the following transactions:
   (a) Received $250 plus a 60-day, 7% note for $1,000 in payment for an account receivable balance of $1,250.
   (b) Received $90 interest plus $500 principal on an old $3,000 note; the old note is renewed for 60 days at 8%.
   (c) Discounted at a rate of 8% a 120-day, 7% note issued 30 days ago for $6,000.

3. **LO4**   Prepare general journal entries for the following transactions:
   (a) Issued a $2,500, 30-day, 6% note in payment of an account payable.
   (b) Borrowed $3,000 cash from the bank, giving a 60-day, non-interest-bearing note discounted at 7% by the bank.
   (c) Paid the note in transaction (b) in full at maturity.

The answers to the Self-Study Test Questions are at the end of the chapter (pages 685–686).

REVIEW QUESTIONS

LO1	1.	How does a note receivable differ from an account receivable?
LO1	2.	Who is the maker of a note?
LO1	3.	Who is the payee of a note?
LO2	4.	What is the formula for calculating interest on notes?
LO2	5.	In the formula for calculating interest, how is time computed?
LO2	6.	What number of days in a year is used by most banks and businesses and all federal government agencies as the base in computing interest?
LO3	7.	What seven types of transactions involving notes receivable do businesses generally encounter?
LO3	8.	If a note receivable is discounted at a bank, on what amount and for what time period does the bank compute the discount?
LO3	9.	If a note receivable that was discounted at a bank is dishonored by its maker, what is the responsibility of the person or business discounting the note?
LO3/4	10.	On which notes receivable and notes payable is it necessary to record accrued interest at the end of the period?
LO4	11.	What five types of transactions involving notes payable do businesses generally encounter?
LO4	12.	When a business borrows money from a bank on a non-interest-bearing note, how are the bank discount and proceeds calculated?
LO4	13.	What kind of account is Discount on Notes Payable, and how is it reported on the balance sheet?
LO4	14.	What is the appropriate entry for accrued interest on notes payable for an interest-bearing note? For a non-interest-bearing note from a bank?
LO3/4	15.	How are accrued interest receivable and accrued interest payable reported on the balance sheet?

SERIES A EXERCISES

E 17-1A (LO2)
✓ May 4 note: 74 days

TERM OF A NOTE Calculate total time in days for the following notes. (Assume there are 28 days in February.)

Date of Note	Due Date	Time in Days
May 4	July 17	_____
August 17	October 1	_____
July 5	September 5	_____
December 11	February 5	_____
March 24	May 16	_____
January 6	March 18	_____

E 17-2A   (LO2)
✓ $5,000 note: $25

CALCULATING INTEREST Using 360 days as the denominator, calculate interest for the following notes using the formula $I = P \times R \times T$.

Principal	Rate	Time	Interest
$5,000	6.00%	30 days	_____
1,000	7.50	60	_____
4,500	8.00	120	_____
950	6.80	95	_____
1,250	7.25	102	_____
2,900	7.00	90	_____

E 17-3A   (LO2)
✓ Aug. 12 note: Nov. 10

DETERMINING DUE DATE Determine the due date for the following notes. (Assume there are 28 days in February.)

Date of Note	Term of Note	Due Date
August 12	90 days	_____
September 1	60	_____
January 3	120	_____
March 18	88	_____
June 11	200	_____
May 17	38	_____

E 17-4A   (LO3)
✓ Feb. 15, Cr. Interest Rev.: $100

JOURNAL ENTRIES (NOTE RECEIVED, RENEWED, AND COLLECTED) Prepare general journal entries for the following transactions:

Jan. 16   Received a 30-day, 6% note in payment for merchandise sale of $20,000.

Feb. 15   Received $100 (interest) on the old (January 16) note; the old note is renewed for 30 days at 7%.

Mar. 17   Received principal and interest on the new (February 15) note.

    19   Received a 60-day, 6% note in payment for accounts receivable balance of $8,000.

May 18   Received $80 (interest) plus $1,000 principal on the old (March 19) note; the old note is renewed for 60 days (from May 18) at 6%.

July 17   Received principal and interest on the new (May 18) note.

E 17-5A   (LO3)
✓ June 2, Cr. Interest Rev.: $5.25

JOURNAL ENTRIES (NOTE RECEIVED, DISCOUNTED, DISHONORED, AND COLLECTED) Prepare general journal entries for the following transactions:

Apr. 6   Received a 120-day, 6% note in payment for accounts receivable balance of $3,000.

    26   Discounted the note at a rate of 7%.

May 3   Received a 30-day, 7% note in payment for accounts receivable balance of $900.

June 2   The $900, 30-day, 7% note is dishonored.

    5   The dishonored note is paid, plus interest at 7% on the maturity value.

E 17-6A **(LO3)**

✓ Cr. Interest Rev.: $32.67

JOURNAL ENTRIES (ACCRUED INTEREST RECEIVABLE) At the end of the year, the following interest is earned, but not yet received. Record the adjusting entry in a general journal.

Interest on $4,000, 90-day, 7% note (for 15 days)	$11.67
Interest on $7,000, 60-day, 6% note (for 18 days)	21.00
	$32.67

E 17-7A **(LO4)**

✓ July 1, Dr. Interest Exp.: $25.00

JOURNAL ENTRIES (NOTE ISSUED, RENEWED, AND PAID) Prepare general journal entries for the following transactions:

May 1   Purchased $5,000 worth of equipment from a supplier on account.

June 1   Issued a $5,000, 30-day, 6% note in payment of the account payable.

July 1   Paid $500 cash plus interest to the supplier, extending the note for 30 days from July 1.

31   Paid the note in full.

Aug. 10   Issued a $3,500, 60-day, 7% note to a supplier for purchase of merchandise.

E 17-8A **(LO4)**

✓ Discount: $66.67

JOURNAL ENTRIES (NOTE ISSUED FOR BANK LOAN) Prepare general journal entries for the following transactions:

July 15   Borrowed $5,000 cash from the bank, giving a 60-day non-interest-bearing note. The note is discounted 8% by the bank.

Sept. 13   Paid the $5,000 note, recognizing the discount as interest expense.

E 17-9A **(LO4)**

✓ Dr. Interest Exp.: $16.67

JOURNAL ENTRIES (ACCRUED INTEREST PAYABLE) At the end of the year, the following interest is payable, but not yet paid. Record the adjusting entry in the general journal.

Interest on $5,000, 60-day, 7% note (for 12 days)	$11.67
Interest on $2,500, 30-day, 8% note (for 9 days)	5.00
	$16.67

SERIES A PROBLEMS

P 17-10A **(LO2/3)**

✓ Feb. 13, Cr. Interest Rev.: $7.92

NOTES RECEIVABLE ENTRIES J. K. Pratt Co. had the following transactions:

20-1

July 20   Received a $750, 30-day, 5% note from J. Akita in payment for sale of merchandise.

Aug. 19   J. Akita paid note issued July 20 plus interest.

25   Sold merchandise on account to L. Beene, $1,100.

Sept. 5   L. Beene paid $100 and gave a $1,000, 30-day, 6% note to extend time for payment.

Oct. 5   L. Beene paid note issued September 5, plus interest.

10   Sold merchandise to R. Harris for $750: $50 plus a $700, 30-day, 6% note.

Nov. 9 R. Harris paid $200 plus interest on note issued October 10 and extended the note ($500) for 30 days.

Dec. 9 R. Harris paid note extended on November 9, plus interest.

10 Sold merchandise on account to B. Kraus, $1,500.

15 B. Kraus paid $150 on merchandise purchased on account, and gave a $1,350, 30-day, 7% note to extend time for payment.

20-2

Jan. 14 B. Kraus's note of December 15 is dishonored.

Feb. 13 Collected B. Kraus's dishonored note, plus interest at 7% on the maturity value.

REQUIRED

Record the transactions in a general journal.

P 17-11A   (LO2/3)
✓ May 5, Cr. Interest Rev.: $3.49

NOTES RECEIVABLE DISCOUNTING Marienau Suppliers had the following transactions:

Mar. 1 Sold merchandise on account to G. Perez, $5,000.

20 G. Perez gave a $5,000, 90-day, 6% note to extend time for payment.

30 G. Perez's note is discounted at Commerce Bank at a discount rate of 8%.

Apr. 20 Received a $3,000, 60-day, 6% note from D. Larson in payment for sale of merchandise.

May 5 D. Larson's note is discounted at Commerce Bank at a discount rate of 7%.

June 19 D. Larson's note is dishonored. The bank bills Marienau for the maturity value of the note plus a $40 bank fee.

July 31 D. Larson's dishonored note is collected; Larson pays Marienau the maturity value of the note, the $40 bank fee, and interest at 6% on the maturity value plus the bank fee.

Aug. 1 Sold merchandise on account to A. Bauer, $5,600.

12 A. Bauer paid $400 and gave a $5,200, 30-day, 5% note to extend time for payment.

Sept. 11 A. Bauer paid $400, plus interest, and gave a new $4,800, 60-day, 6% note to extend time for payment.

26 A. Bauer's note is discounted at Commerce Bank at a discount rate of 7.5%.

Nov. 10 A. Bauer's note is dishonored. The bank bills Marienau for the maturity value of the note plus a $40 bank fee.

Dec. 15 A. Bauer's dishonored note is collected. Bauer pays Marienau the maturity value of the note, the $40 bank fee, and interest at 6% on the maturity value plus the bank fee.

REQUIRED

Record the transactions in a general journal.

P 17-12A (LO3)
✓ Accrued interest: $107.55

ACCRUED INTEREST RECEIVABLE The following is a list of outstanding notes receivable as of December 31, 20--:

Maker	Date of Note	Principal	Interest	Term	No. of Days
K. Savelin	12/15/--	$1,000	5%	60 days	16
R. Hillier	12/3/--	5,000	6	90	28
B. Miranda	11/30/--	2,800	8	90	31
R. Hansen	11/18/--	7,500	7	120	43

REQUIRED

1. Compute the accrued interest at the end of the year.
2. Prepare the adjusting entry in the general journal.

P 17-13A (LO4)
✓ June 4, Dr. Interest Exp.: $23.33

NOTES PAYABLE ENTRIES Milo Radio Shop had the following notes payable transactions:

Apr. 1 Borrowed $5,000 from Builder's Bank, signing a 90-day, 8% note.

  5 Gave a $2,000, 60-day, 7% note to Breaker Parts Co. for purchase of merchandise.

  10 Paid $500 cash and gave a $1,500, 30-day, 6% note to M. K. Reynolds in payment of an account payable.

May 10 Paid $500 cash, plus interest, and issued a new $1,000, 30-day, 7% note to M. K. Reynolds.

  20 Borrowed $3,500 for 60 days from Builder's Bank on a non-interest-bearing note. The discount rate is 7%.

June 4 Paid $500 cash, plus interest, to Breaker Parts Co. (see April 5) and gave a new $1,500, 30-day, 7% note to extend time for payment.

  9 Paid the principal and interest due on the $1,000 note to M. K. Reynolds. (See May 10.)

  30 Paid the principal and interest due on the $5,000 note to Builder's Bank. (See April 1.)

July 4 Paid the principal and interest due on the $1,500 note to Breaker Parts Co. (See June 4.)

  19 Paid the $3,500 non-interest-bearing note to Builder's Bank. (See May 20.)

REQUIRED

Record the transactions in a general journal.

P 17-14A (LO4)
✓ Accrued interest: $50.29

ACCRUED INTEREST PAYABLE The following is a list of outstanding notes payable as of December 31, 20--:

Maker	Date of Note	Principal	Interest	Term	No. of Days
B. Jones	12/1/--	$1,000	6%	90 days	30
M. Aguilar	11/25/--	2,500	6	80	36
T. Plant	12/14/--	3,800	7	120	17
W. Brand	11/19/--	1,900	8	180	42

REQUIRED

1. Compute the accrued interest at the end of the year.
2. Prepare the adjusting entry in the general journal.

SERIES B EXERCISES

E 17-1B   (LO2)
✓ Aug. 17 note: 54 days

TERM OF A NOTE Calculate total time in days for the following notes. (Assume there are 28 days in February.)

Date of Note	Due Date	Time in Days
August 17	October 10	_____
January 12	March 10	_____
July 15	September 13	_____
December 3	February 1	_____
April 11	July 6	_____
October 6	December 18	_____

E 17-2B   (LO2)
✓ $4,000 note: $46.67

CALCULATING INTEREST Using 360 days as the denominator, calculate interest for the following notes using the formula $I = P \times R \times T$.

Principal	Rate	Time	Interest
$4,000	7.00%	60 days	_____
3,000	6.50	30	_____
7,500	8.00	150	_____
850	7.90	99	_____
2,250	7.55	122	_____
1,900	6.80	82	_____

E 17-3B   (LO2)
✓ July 11 note: Aug. 25

DETERMINING DUE DATE Determine the due date for the following notes. (Assume there are 28 days in February.)

Date of Note	Term of Note	Due Date
July 11	45 days	_____
December 23	90	_____
April 18	120	_____
October 3	77	_____
January 1	180	_____
August 13	65	_____

E 17-4B   (LO3)
✓ July 21, Cr. Interest Rev.: $128.33

JOURNAL ENTRIES (NOTE RECEIVED, RENEWED, AND COLLECTED) Prepare general journal entries for the following transactions:

May 22   Received a 30-day, 6% note in payment for merchandise sale of $22,000.

June 21   Received $110.00 cash (interest) on the old (May 22) note; the old note is renewed for 30 days at 7%.

July 21   Received principal and interest on the new (June 21) note.

28   Received a 45-day, 7% note in payment for accounts receivable balance of $11,600.

(*continued*)

Sept. 11 Received $101.50 cash (interest) plus $1,600 principal on the old (July 28) note; the old note is renewed for 60 days (from September 11) at 7.5%.

Nov. 10 Received principal and interest on the new (September 11) note.

E 17-5B   (LO3)
✓ Oct. 5, Cr. Interest Rev.: $6

JOURNAL ENTRIES (NOTE RECEIVED, DISCOUNTED, DISHONORED, AND COLLECTED) Prepare general journal entries for the following transactions:

Aug.   4 Received a 120-day, 7% note in payment for accounts receivable balance of $4,000.

14 Discounted the note at a rate of 8%.

Sept. 5 Received a 30-day, 6% note in payment for accounts receivable balance of $1,200.

Oct.   5 The $1,200, 30-day, 6% note is dishonored.

Nov.   4 The dishonored note is paid, plus interest at 6% on the maturity value.

E 17-6B   (LO3)
✓ Cr. Interest Rev.: $40

JOURNAL ENTRIES (ACCRUED INTEREST RECEIVABLE) At the end of the year, the following interest is earned, but not yet received. Record the adjusting entry in a general journal.

Interest on $6,000, 60-day, 5.5% note (for 24 days) $22.00

Interest on $9,000, 90-day, 6% note (for 12 days)   18.00

$40.00

E 17-7B   (LO4)
✓ Aug. 14, Dr. Interest Exp.: $35

JOURNAL ENTRIES (NOTE ISSUED, RENEWED, AND PAID) Prepare general journal entries for the following transactions:

June 15 Purchased $6,000 worth of equipment from a supplier on account.

July 15 Issued a $6,000, 30-day, 7% note in payment of the account payable.

Aug. 14 Paid $600 cash plus interest to the supplier, extending the note for 30 days from August 14.

Sept. 13 Paid the note in full.

27 Issued a $5,000, 60-day, 6% note to a supplier for purchase of merchandise.

E 17-8B   (LO4)
✓ Discount: $93.33

JOURNAL ENTRIES (NOTE ISSUED FOR BANK LOAN) Prepare general journal entries for the following transactions:

Sept. 15 Borrowed $7,000 cash from the bank, giving a 60-day non-interest-bearing note. The note is discounted 8% by the bank.

Nov. 14 Paid the $7,000 note, recognizing the discount as interest expense.

E 17-9B   (LO4)
✓ Dr. Interest Exp.: $38.13

JOURNAL ENTRIES (ACCRUED INTEREST PAYABLE) At the end of the year, the following interest is payable, but not yet paid. Record the adjusting entry in the general journal.

Interest on $8,000, 90-day, 8% note (for 18 days) $32.00

Interest on $4,500, 60-day, 7% note (for 7 days)   6.13

$38.13

SERIES B PROBLEMS

P 17-10B   (LO2/3)
✓ Jan. 13, Cr. Interest Rev.: $13.80

NOTES RECEIVABLE ENTRIES M. L. DiMaurizio had the following notes receivable transactions:

20-3

June 20   Received a $2,400, 30-day, 6% note from K. Lorenzo in payment for sale of merchandise.

July 20   K. Lorenzo paid the note plus interest.

     25   Sold merchandise on account to R. Boone, $5,600.

Aug. 4   R. Boone paid $600 and gave a $5,000, 30-day, 7% note to extend time for payment.

Sept. 3   R. Boone paid the note plus interest.

     10   Sold merchandise to T. Akins for $3,000: $400 plus a $2,600, 30-day, 6% note.

Oct. 10   T. Akins paid $600, plus interest, and extended the note ($2,000) for 30 days.

Nov. 9   T. Akins paid the note plus interest.

     10   Sold merchandise on account to J. Brown, $5,000.

     25   J. Brown paid $1,000 and gave a $4,000, 30-day, 6.5% note to extend time for payment.

Dec. 25   J. Brown's note is dishonored.

20-4

Jan. 13   J. Brown's dishonored note is collected, plus interest at 6.5% on the maturity value.

REQUIRED
Record the transactions in a general journal.

P 17-11B   (LO2/3)
✓ July 25, Cr. Interest Rev.: $11.37

NOTES RECEIVABLE DISCOUNTING Madison Graphics had the following notes receivable transactions:

May 1   Sold merchandise on account to L. Carney, $5,600.

     20   L. Carney gave a $5,600, 90-day, 6% note to extend time for payment.

     30   L. Carney's note is discounted at Commercial Bank at a discount rate of 7.5%.

June 20   Received a $2,400, 60-day, 6% note from P. Arnst in payment for sale of merchandise.

July 25   P. Arnst's note is discounted at Commercial Bank at a discount rate of 7.5%.

Aug. 19   P. Arnst's note is dishonored. The bank bills Madison Graphics for the maturity value of the note plus a $30 bank fee.

     31   P. Arnst's dishonored note is collected; Arnst pays Madison the maturity value of the note, the $30 bank fee, and interest at 6% on the maturity value plus the bank fee.

Sept. 1   Sold merchandise on account to B. Faust, $6,400.

(continued)

Sept. 12 B. Faust paid $400 and gave a $6,000, 30-day, 6.5% note to extend time for payment.

Oct. 12 B. Faust paid $400, plus interest, and gave a new $5,600, 60-day, 7% note to extend time for payment.

26 B. Faust's note is discounted at Commercial Bank at a discount rate of 8%.

Dec. 11 B. Faust's note is dishonored. The bank bills Madison Graphics for the maturity value of the note plus a $30 bank fee.

Dec. 27 B. Faust's dishonored note is collected. Faust pays Madison Graphics the maturity value of the note, the $30 bank fee, and interest at 7% on the maturity value plus the bank fee.

REQUIRED

Record the transactions in a general journal.

P 17-12B **(LO3)**
✓ Accrued interest: $70.41

ACCRUED INTEREST RECEIVABLE The following is a list of outstanding notes receivable as of December 31, 20--:

Maker	Date of Note	Principal	Interest	Term	No. of Days
P. Harrison	12/17/--	$1,200	6%	60 days	14
T. Rieber	12/3/--	4,000	7	90	28
K. Burke	12/1/--	2,200	7	90	30
A. Pai	11/28/--	4,500	8	120	33

REQUIRED

1. Compute the accrued interest at the end of the year.
2. Prepare the adjusting entry in the general journal.

P 17-13B **(LO4)**
✓ June 4, Dr. Interest Exp.: $35

NOTES PAYABLE Mary's Travel Agency had the following notes payable transactions:

Apr. 1 Borrowed $4,000 from Finance Bank, signing a 90-day, 8% note.

5 Gave a $3,000, 60-day, 7% note to Krenshaw Airline for purchase of merchandise.

10 Paid $400 cash and issued a $1,600, 30-day, 6% note to Andrew Adams in payment of an account payable.

May 10 Paid $400, plus interest, and gave a new $1,200, 30-day, 7% note to Andrew Adams.

20 Borrowed $4,500 for 60 days from Finance Bank on a non-interest-bearing note. The discount rate is 8%.

June 4 Paid $500, plus interest, to Krenshaw Airline (see April 5) and gave a new $2,500, 30-day, 7% note to extend time for payment.

9 Paid the principal and interest due on the $1,200 note to Andrew Adams. (See May 10.)

30 Paid the principal and interest due on the $4,000 note to Finance Bank. (See April 1.)

July 4 Paid the principal and interest due on the $2,500 note to Krenshaw Airline. (See June 4.)

19 Paid the $4,500 non-interest-bearing note to Finance Bank. (See May 20.)

REQUIRED

Record the transactions in a general journal.

P 17-14B   (LO4)
✓ Accrued interest: $57.92

ACCRUED INTEREST PAYABLE The following is a list of outstanding notes payable as of December 31, 20--:

Payee	Date of Note	Principal	Interest	Term	No. of Days
X. Rayal	12/1/--	$1,200	6.0%	90 days	30
G. Richards	11/28/--	2,300	8.0	80	33
A. Gray	12/16/--	3,400	7.0	120	15
O. Hankins	11/13/--	2,900	6.5	180	48

REQUIRED

1. Compute the accrued interest at the end of the year.
2. Prepare the adjusting entry in the general journal.

CHECK LIST
- [ ] **Managing**
- [ ] **Planning**
- [ ] **Drafting**
- [ ] **Break**
- [ ] **Revising**
- [ ] **Managing**

MANAGING YOUR WRITING

You are purchasing a new car and plan to finance it through your employee credit union. The credit union has offered you two different promissory note plans, as follows:

Option 1: Three years at 6%, with interest payable annually.
Option 2: One year at 5%, renewable each year for up to three more years, at the then-current interest rate. Interest is payable at the end of each year.

Prepare a written report summarizing the advantages and disadvantages of each of these options.

ETHICS

ETHICS CASE

Rochelle needed to borrow $3,000 for three months in order to pay for college expenses while waiting for her scholarship to arrive. After Rochelle filled out the loan application, the loan officer at the bank asked her if she would like to pay the interest up front or at the maturity of the note. He went on to explain that it didn't make a difference, but he preferred that she pay it up front because it would make his paperwork easier. He also told Rochelle that the interest rate and amount would be the same. Rochelle agreed, signed the three-month, 8%, discounted note and left with a check for $2,940.

1. Did the loan officer offer Rochelle an acceptable explanation of the interest rate? Justify your answer.
2. What is the effective rate of interest on Rochelle's loan? Round to the nearest tenth of a percent.
3. In a short paragraph, explain the difference between an "interest-bearing" note and a "discounted" note.
4. In groups of two or three, discuss some common situations where the average person might misunderstand interest rate quotations.

MASTERY PROBLEM

✓ Nov. 1, Cr. Interest Rev.: $3.11

Eddie Edwards and Phil Bell own and operate The Second Hand Equipment Shop. The following transactions involving notes and interest were completed during the last three months of 20--:

Oct.   1   Issued a $6,800, 60-day, 5% note to Mac Farm Equipment for purchase of merchandise.

       15   Received a $2,000, 60-day, 6% note from R. Chambers in payment for sale of merchandise.

Nov.   1   Discounted the note received from R. Chambers on October 15 at Merchants National Bank. The discount rate is 7%.

       1   Borrowed $5,000 from First National Bank on a three-month, non-interest-bearing note that was discounted at 6%.

       20   Received a $4,000, 90-day, 6.5% note from L. Revsine in payment of an account receivable.

       30   Issued a check to Mac Farm Equipment in payment of the note issued on October 1, including interest.

Dec. 10   Issued a $3,000, 90-day, 6% note to Remak Tractors to extend time for payment of an account payable.

       16   Received notification from Merchants National Bank that R. Chambers has dishonored his note. A check is issued to cover the note plus a $20 bank fee that must be paid to the bank.

REQUIRED

1. Prepare general journal entries for the transactions.
2. Prepare necessary adjusting entries for the notes outstanding on December 31.

CHALLENGE PROBLEM

This problem challenges you to apply your cumulative accounting knowledge to move a step beyond the material in the chapter.

✓ July 1, Lawrence Bank, Dr. Interest Rec.: $9.47

REQUIRED

Prepare general journal entries on the books of both Mirror Co. and the other party (either Rosman Co., Kaw County Bank, or Lawrence Bank) for each of the following transactions:

June   1   Rosman Co. gave Mirror Co. a $3,000, 90-day, 6% note to extend the time for payment of its account.

       20   Mirror Co. borrowed $2,000 for 60 days from Kaw County Bank on a non-interest-bearing note. The discount rate was 7%.

July   1   Mirror Co. discounted Rosman Co.'s note at Lawrence Bank at a discount rate of 7%.

Aug. 19   Mirror Co. paid the $2,000 non-interest-bearing note to Kaw County Bank.

       30   Rosman Co.'s $3,000 note (see June 1 transaction) was collected by Lawrence Bank. (Treat Lawrence Bank as the other party.)

True/False

1. T

2. T

3. F (Difference is called the discount.)

4. F (Interest is credited to Interest Revenue; time has passed and interest has been earned.)

5. T

Multiple Choice

1. d   **2.** b   **3.** a   **4.** c   **5.** c

Checkpoint Exercises

1. (a) $\$4,000 \times 7\% \times 90/360 = \$70$

    (b) Sept. 25
           Oct.   31
           Nov. $\underline{30}$
                   86
           Dec. $\underline{4}$
                   90

Due date = Dec. 4

2.

1	(a)	Cash			2	5	0	00				
2		Notes Receivable		1	0	0	0	00				
3		Accounts Receivable							1	2	5	0	00
4		Received cash and note to settle account										
5	(b)	Cash			5	9	0	00				
6		Notes Receivable (new note)		2	5	0	0	00				
7		Notes Receivable (old note)							3	0	0	0	00
8		Interest Revenue									9	0	00
9		Received new note plus partial payment and										
10		interest on old note										
11	(c)	Cash		6	0	1	7	20*				
12		Notes Receivable							6	0	0	0	00
13		Interest Revenue									1	7	20
14		Discounted note receivable										
15		*Maturity value = $\$6,000 + (\$6,000 \times 7\% \times 120/360) = \$6,140$										
16		Discount amount = $\$6,140 \times 8\% \times 90/360 = \$122.80$										
17		Proceeds = $\$6,140 - \$122.80 = \$6,017.20$										

3.

1		(a)	Accounts Payable				2	5	0	0	00						
2			Notes Payable										2	5	0	0	00
3			Issued note to settle account														
4		(b)	Cash				2	9	6	5	00						
5			Discount on Notes Payable						3	5	00*						
6			Notes Payable										3	0	0	0	00
7			Issued note for bank loan														
8			* Discount = $3,000 × 7% × 60/360 = $35														
9		(c)	Notes Payable				3	0	0	0	00						
10			Interest Expense						3	5	00						
11			Cash										3	0	0	0	00
12			Discount on Notes Payable												3	5	00
13			Paid note at maturity														

Chapter 18 Accounting for Long-Term Assets

IMI, Irving Materials, Inc., is a privately held, employee-owned corporation with company headquarters in Greenfield, Indiana. It has four regional operation centers located in Greenfield, Indiana; Evansville, Indiana; Louisville, Kentucky; and Nashville, Tennessee. Skunk Irving founded IMI in 1946 as a building materials supplier. The company serves six states through the four regional operation centers. Over the years, IMI has not only delivered quality concrete and aggregates, but has also become a leader in the development of new technologies. IMI led the way in the design of the front discharge mixer that is now a staple of the concrete industry. IMI has also developed a number of concrete batch mixes and specialty admixtures that have revolutionized construction processes.

IMI must make substantial investments in heavy equipment, like the truck shown above. In this chapter, you will learn how to account for long-term assets, such as equipment, from the time they are acquired until they are retired.

LEARNING OBJECTIVES

Careful study of this chapter should enable you to:

LO1 Determine the cost of property, plant, and equipment.

LO2 Explain the nature and purpose of depreciation.

LO3 Compute depreciation using the straight-line, declining-balance, sum-of-the-years'-digits, units-of-production, and MACRS depreciation methods.

LO4 Account for repairs, maintenance, additions, improvements, and replacements to plant and equipment.

LO5 Account for the disposition of property, plant, and equipment.

LO6 Explain the nature of, purpose of, and accounting for depletion.

LO7 Explain the nature of and accounting for intangible assets.

Assets that are expected to provide benefits for a number of accounting periods are called long-term assets. Long-term assets that are tangible (have physical substance) and that are used in the operations of the business are called property, plant, and equipment; plant assets; or fixed assets. Examples include land, buildings, furniture, and equipment. Assets whose physical substance consists of natural resources that are consumed in the operation of the business are often called wasting assets. Examples include mines (coal, salt, and gold), stands of timber, and oil and gas wells. Long-term assets that have no physical substance are called intangible assets. Common examples include patents, copyrights, trademarks, franchises, and goodwill.

Most long-term assets gradually wear out or are used up as time passes. As an asset's useful life expires, a portion of the asset's cost is recognized as an expense. This is often referred to as "writing off" the asset. A different term is used to describe this expense for the different types of long-term assets. For plant assets, the expense is called depreciation; for natural resources, it is called depletion; and for intangible assets, it is called amortization. In this chapter, proper accounting for property, plant, and equipment; natural resources; and intangible assets is described and illustrated.

> Land and some intangibles are not depreciated or amortized.

| LO1 | Acquisition Cost of Property, Plant, and Equipment |

Determine the cost of property, plant, and equipment.

The cost of a long-term asset includes all amounts spent to acquire the asset and prepare it for its intended use. Purchases of long-term assets are entered by debiting the proper asset account and crediting either the cash or the proper liability account.

Land

> **LEARNING KEY 🔑**
> Since land does not wear out, no depreciation is recognized.

All costs incurred to purchase land and prepare it for its intended use are debited to the land account. These costs include legal and real estate fees as well as the cost of removing old buildings and grading the land to prepare it for its intended use. Special tax assessments for streets, sewers, or parks also are debited to the land account, because these items are viewed as permanent.

Land Improvements

Costs related to land that are not permanent in nature are normally debited to the land improvements account. Common examples include the costs of planting trees and shrubs, installing fences, and paving parking areas. Items debited to the land improvements account are depreciated over their expected useful lives.

Buildings

The cost of buildings that are purchased includes the purchase price, realtor and legal fees, and related taxes on the purchase. If the purchase price includes land, the cost of the land and building must be determined and accounted for separately. If the building is constructed, costs include all normal construction costs for material and labor and architectural and engineering fees. In addition, insurance premiums and interest on loans *while the building is being constructed* are considered part of the cost of the asset.

Equipment

The cost of equipment includes the purchase price, transportation charges, insurance while in transit, installation costs, and any other costs that are incurred up to the point of placing the asset in service.

Treatment of Interest When Acquiring or Constructing Assets

The proper treatment of interest depends on whether the asset is being purchased or constructed. Often, businesses must borrow money to buy major long-term assets. The method used to finance the *acquisition* of an asset should not affect its cost. For example, interest on a mortgage to purchase a building should not be included in the cost of the asset. We always use the cash equivalent price, which is the amount of cash that could have been paid for the asset on the date of purchase.

Interest costs are treated differently for assets being constructed. Interest incurred *while an asset is being constructed* should be included as part of the cost of the asset. Since the asset is not operational during the construction period, it is not generating revenues against which the interest could be matched. Thus, the interest is included in the cost of the asset and recognized as part of depreciation expense when the asset is placed in operation and begins generating revenues.

CHECKPOINT ✔

Complete Checkpoint-1 on page 713 to test your basic understanding of LO1.

LO2	**Depreciation**

Explain the nature and purpose of depreciation.

The purpose of depreciation is to match a plant asset's cost with the revenues it helps to produce. As discussed in earlier chapters, the following is a typical adjusting entry made at the end of each accounting period:

LEARNING KEY 🔑

Depreciation matches an asset's cost with the revenues it helps generate.

4			Adjusting Entry												4
5	Dec.	31	Depr. Expense—Delivery Equipment	541	1	0	0	00							5
6			Accum. Depr.—Delivery Equipment	185.1						1	0	0	00		6
7															7

Recall that Depreciation Expense is reported on the income statement and Accumulated Depreciation is reported on the balance sheet as a contra-asset. Accumulated Depreciation is deducted from the asset account to report the book value, or undepreciated cost, of the asset. For example, a machine with a cost of $3,000 and accumulated depreciation of $600 would be reported on the balance sheet as follows:

Property, Plant, and Equipment
Equipment	$3,000	
Less accumulated depreciation	600	$2,400

Keep in mind that depreciation is a process of *cost allocation*, not a process of valuation. Many factors cause the market values of plant assets to change over time. The recognition of depreciation is not intended to make the assets reflect their market values on the balance sheet. The net amounts reported on the balance sheet (book values) are merely the portions of the original costs that have not yet been allocated to expense.

LEARNING KEY 🔑

Market Value = Amount Asset Can Be Sold for
Book Value = Cost − Accumulated Depreciation
The recognition of depreciation is not intended to represent market values on the balance sheet.

The two major types of depreciation are physical and functional. **Physical depreciation** is the loss of usefulness because of deterioration from age and wear. **Functional depreciation** is the loss of usefulness because of inadequacy or obsolescence. As a business grows, some of its plant assets may become inadequate to handle the increased workload. As new manufacturing methods are developed, assets may become obsolete because there are faster, more efficient, or more effective assets that may be used to perform this work.

LO3   Depreciation Methods

Compute depreciation using the straight-line, declining-balance, sum-of-the-years'-digits, units-of-production, and MACRS depreciation methods.

Before we discuss the methods of calculating depreciation, there are several terms to be defined.

- **Cost:** The sum of all amounts spent to acquire an asset and prepare it for its intended use.
- **Useful Life:** The amount of service expected to be obtained from an asset. It can be expressed in years, hours of operation, units of production, or miles driven. There is no way of knowing exactly how long an asset will last or exactly what its output will be. Therefore, estimates must be made based on past experience and information from trade associations and engineers.
- **Salvage Value:** The estimated **scrap value**, or market value, for the asset on its expected disposal date. This amount can be difficult to predict. Often, a zero salvage value is used if the asset is expected to have little or no value at the end of its useful life.
- **Depreciable Cost (Base):** The original cost less salvage (or scrap) value.

    Depreciable Cost = Original Cost − Salvage Value

Since the salvage value is expected to be recovered, it should not be included in depreciation expense recognized over the life of the asset.

- **Book Value:** The undepreciated cost of the asset.

    Book Value = Cost − Accumulated Depreciation

There are several different ways of calculating the amount of depreciation for each period. The most commonly used methods for financial reporting purposes are the following:

1. Straight-line method
2. Declining-balance method
3. Sum-of-the-years'-digits method
4. Units-of-production method

Straight-Line Method

As shown in the chart in Figure 18-1, the straight-line method is by far the most popular method used for financial reporting. Under the **straight-line method**, the depreciable cost of an asset is allocated equally over the years of the asset's useful life according to the following formula:

Straight-Line Method

$$\text{Annual Depreciation} = \frac{(\text{Cost} - \text{Salvage Value})}{\text{Estimated Useful Life}}$$

To illustrate, assume that a new asset costs $10,000, has an expected life of four years, and has a $1,000 estimated salvage value. Using the straight-line method, the amount of depreciation allocated to each year would be $2,250, computed as follows:

Original Cost	–	Salvage Value	=	Depreciable Cost
$10,000	–	$1,000	=	$9,000

$$\frac{\text{Depreciable Cost}}{\text{Estimated Useful Life}} = \frac{\$9,000}{4 \text{ years}} = \$2,250 \text{ annual depreciation}$$

LEARNING KEY 🔑

Under the straight-line method, the same amount of depreciation is recorded each period.

The annual *rate* of depreciation is 25% (100% ÷ years) of the depreciable cost.

A month is usually the shortest period that is used in depreciation accounting. An asset purchased on or before the fifteenth of the month is considered to have been owned for the full month. An asset purchased after the fifteenth of the month is considered to have been acquired the first of the next month.

FIGURE 18-1 Use of Depreciation Methods

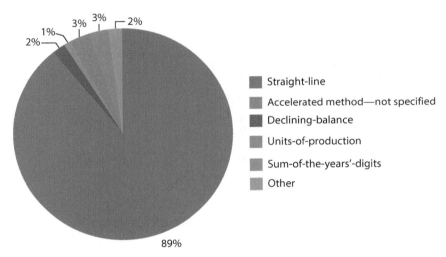

Pie chart is based on a survey of 500 companies listed with the SEC published in the AICPA's *Accounting Trends and Techniques*.

With the straight-line method, the book value of the asset decreases uniformly period by period. As shown in Figure 18-2, the book value over several periods is a downward-sloping, perfectly straight line. That is how the method got its name.

Declining-Balance Method

Many plant assets require repairs and replacement of parts to keep them in service. Such expenses usually increase as the assets get older. Some accountants believe that depreciation expense, therefore, should be higher in the early years to offset the higher repair and maintenance expenses of the later years. Others suggest that assets contribute more to the business when they are comparatively new. For these reasons, it may be desirable to calculate depreciation in a way that will give larger write-offs in the early years of the asset's life. Depreciation methods that provide for a higher depreciation charge in the first year of an asset's life and gradually decreasing charges in subsequent years are called accelerated depreciation methods.

One popular accelerated method is the declining-balance method. As shown in the following formula, under this method, the book value is multiplied by a fixed rate.

Declining-Balance Method

$$\text{Annual Depreciation} = \text{Depreciation Rate} \times \text{Book Value at Beginning of Year}$$

FIGURE 18-2 Comparison of Depreciation Methods Used for Financial Reporting

Straight-Line Method

Year	Depr. Exp.	Accum. Depr.	Book Value
			10,000
1	2,250	2,250	7,750
2	2,250	4,500	5,500
3	2,250	6,750	3,250
4	2,250	9,000	1,000

Double-Declining-Balance Method

Year	Depr. Exp.	Accum. Depr.	Book Value
			10,000
1	5,000	5,000	5,000
2	2,500	7,500	2,500
3	1,250	8,750	1,250
4	250	9,000	1,000

Sum-of-the-Years'-Digits Method

Year	Depr. Exp.	Accum. Depr.	Book Value
			10,000
1	3,600	3,600	6,400
2	2,700	6,300	3,700
3	1,800	8,100	1,900
4	900	9,000	1,000

Units-of-Production Method

Year	Depr. Exp.	Accum. Depr.	Book Value
			10,000
1	2,400	2,400	7,600
2	4,000	6,400	3,600
3	2,000	8,400	1,600
4	600	9,000	1,000

This method results in successively smaller depreciation charges as the book value declines year by year. The rate is expressed as a multiple of the straight-line rate (200%, 150%, etc.). The most common rate used is double the straight-line rate. For this reason, this technique is sometimes referred to as the **double-declining-balance method**.

To illustrate, let's use the same asset as for the straight-line method. The asset costs $10,000, has an expected life of four years, and has a $1,000 estimated salvage value. Using the double-declining-balance method, the depreciation rate to be applied to the book value of the asset each year is 50%, computed as follows:

$$\text{Straight-Line Rate} = 25\% \ (100\% \div 4 \text{ years})$$
$$\text{Double-Declining-Balance Rate} = 50\% \ (2 \times 25\%)$$

The annual depreciation and the book value at the end of each year are as follows:

Year	Book Value Beginning of Year	Rate	Annual Depreciation	Accumulated Depreciation End of Year	Book Value End of Year
1	$10,000	50%	$5,000	$5,000	$5,000
2	5,000	50	2,500	7,500	2,500
3	2,500	50	1,250	8,750	1,250
4	1,250	—	250*	9,000	1,000

*$250 = $1,250 (book value at beginning of year) − $1,000 (salvage value)

The salvage value is not considered in determining the annual depreciation. *However, the asset's book value should not be allowed to fall below its estimated salvage value.* Thus, the amount of depreciation actually recorded in the final year (year 4) is limited to $250 ($1,250 − $1,000). If the book value is still greater than the salvage value at the end of year 4, the process continues until the book value is reduced to the salvage value in subsequent years. As shown in Figure 18-2, with the declining-balance method, the book value declines rapidly in the early years and more slowly in the later years of an asset's life.

Declining-Balance Method for Partial Periods

If the asset was acquired at some time other than the beginning of the year, a change would be necessary in the computation of depreciation for the year. For example, if the asset was acquired on April 1, the depreciation for year 1 would be calculated as follows:

$$\text{Year 1: } \$10,000 \times 50\% = \$5,000 \times 9/12 = \$3,750$$

Depreciation for years 2 through 4 would then be calculated by applying the 50% depreciation rate to the book value of the asset at the beginning of each year, as follows:

Year	Book Value Beginning of Year	Rate	Annual Depreciation	Accumulated Depreciation End of Year	Book Value End of Year
2	$6,250*	50%	$3,125	$6,875	$3,125
3	3,125	50	1,563	8,438	1,562
4	1,562	—	562**	9,000	1,000

*$6,250 = $10,000 (cost) − $3,750 (depreciation for year 1)

**$562 = $1,562 (book value at beginning of year) − $1,000 (salvage value)

Depreciation in year 4 is limited to $562 because the asset should not be depreciated below its estimated salvage value. If the asset continued to be used in year 5, no depreciation would be recorded.

Sum-of-the-Years'-Digits Method

As shown in the following formula, under the **sum-of-the-years'-digits method**, the depreciation each year is determined by multiplying the depreciable cost by a schedule of fractions.

Sum-of-the-Years'-Digits Method

$$\text{Annual Depreciation} = (\text{Cost} - \text{Salvage Value}) \times \frac{\text{Remaining Useful Life from Beginning of Current Year}}{\text{Sum-of-the-Years'-Digits}}$$

The numerator in any year is the number of years of remaining life for the asset, measured from the beginning of the year. The denominator for all fractions is determined by listing the digits that represent the years of the estimated life of the asset and adding these digits. For example, suppose that the estimated life of an asset is four years. The sum of the digits $(4 + 3 + 2 + 1)$ equals 10 (the denominator). The following formula can also be used to determine the denominator.

Calculating the Sum-of-the-Years'-Digits

$$S = \frac{N \times (N + 1)}{2}$$

S = sum of the digits
N = number of years of estimated life

If the life of the asset is four years:

$$S = \frac{4 \times (4 + 1)}{2} = \frac{4 \times 5}{2} = 10$$

The denominator equals 10. Therefore, the fractions used for an asset with a four-year life would be 4/10, 3/10, 2/10, and 1/10. Applying these fractions to the asset in our illustration, the results are as follows:

Year	Depreciable Cost	Rate	Annual Depreciation	Accumulated Depreciation End of Year	Book Value End of Year
1	$9,000	4/10	$3,600	$3,600	$6,400
2	9,000	3/10	2,700	6,300	3,700
3	9,000	2/10	1,800	8,100	1,900
4	9,000	1/10	900	9,000	1,000

As shown in Figure 18-2, the pattern of decline in the book value using the sum-of-the-years'-digits method is accelerated. However, the write-off is not as rapid as it is with the double-declining-balance method.

Sum-of-the-Years'-Digits Method for Partial Periods

If the asset is acquired at some time other than the beginning of the year, a modification is necessary in the calculation. For example, if the asset is acquired on April 1, the depreciation for years 1 through 5 is calculated as follows:

Year	Depreciable Cost	Rate	Annual Depreciation	Portion of Year	Depreciation for Year	Accumulated Depreciation End of Year	Book Value End of Year
1	$9,000	4/10	$3,600	9/12	<u>$2,700</u>	$2,700	$7,300
2	$9,000	4/10	$3,600	3/12	$ 900		
	9,000	3/10	2,700	9/12	2,025		
					<u>$2,925</u>	$5,625	$4,375
3	$9,000	3/10	$2,700	3/12	$ 675		
		2/10	1,800	9/12	1,350		
					<u>$2,025</u>	$7,650	$2,350
4	$9,000	2/10	$1,800	3/12	$ 450		
		1/10	900	9/12	675		
					<u>$1,125</u>	$8,775	$1,225
5	$9,000	1/10	$ 900	3/12	<u>$ 225</u>	$9,000	$1,000

Units-of-Production Method

Under the units-of-production method, depreciation is based on the extent to which the asset was used during the year. As shown below, annual depreciation is computed in two steps. First, a depreciation charge per unit produced or consumed is computed. Second, this unit rate is multiplied by the number of units produced or consumed during the year.

Units-of-Production Method

Step 1:   Depreciation per Unit $=\dfrac{\text{(Cost − Salvage Value)}}{\text{Estimated Useful Life in Units}}$

Step 2:   Annual Depreciation = Depreciation per Unit $\times$ Number of Units Produced or Consumed this Year

This method can be used for certain types of machinery, equipment, and vehicles. It is most appropriate for assets that receive varying amounts of use over time. For example, assume that a company purchases a used truck at a cost of $10,000 and expects that it can be sold for $1,000 after 90,000 miles of service. The calculation of depreciation for the first year when the truck was driven 24,000 miles follows:

Depreciable Cost = $10,000 Original Cost − $1,000 Salvage Value = $9,000

Depreciation per Mile $=\dfrac{\$9,000 \text{ Depreciable Cost}}{90,000 \text{ Total Miles}}$ = $0.10

First-Year Depreciation = 24,000 miles $\times$ $0.10/mile = $2,400

As shown in Figure 18-2, the depreciation expense and book value for each year do not follow a particular pattern. They are a function of the miles driven each year (24,000; 40,000; 20,000; and 6,000 in this illustration).

Depreciation for Federal Income Tax Purposes

A business is allowed to deduct depreciation expense when calculating taxable income on the tax return. Several depreciation methods are permitted under the tax law. Most recently, tax reforms enacted in 2017 allow businesses to expense 100% of the cost of most assets (not buildings) acquired and placed into service after September 27, 2017. Thus, the entire cost of an asset may be expensed in the first year, rather than over the life of the asset. Since a tax dollar saved now is more valuable than a tax dollar saved later, this legislation is likely to encourage businesses to make capital investments.

For plant assets acquired earlier, but after 1986, either the straight-line method or the **Modified Accelerated Cost Recovery System (MACRS)** may be used. MACRS identifies eight categories of useful life for plant assets, ranging from 3 to 39 years. Most business assets, other than real estate, fall into one of two categories: five-year or seven-year property. Rates set by the IRS for selected asset classes are provided in Figure 18-3.

FIGURE 18-3 **MACRS Depreciation Rates for Selected Asset Classes**

MACRS PROPERTY CLASS	3-YEAR	5-YEAR	7-YEAR	15-YEAR	27.5-YEAR	39-YEAR
METHOD	200% DB	200% DB	200% DB	150% DB	Straight-Line	Straight-Line
Examples of Assets/Year	Small tools, race horses, tractors.	Automobiles, trucks, computers and peripheral equipment, copiers, and office machines.	Office furniture, fixtures, most machinery.	Land improvements including sidewalks, roads, parking lots, irrigation systems, sewers, fences, and landscaping.	Residential rental real estate, including apartment buildings, duplexes, etc.	Nonresidential real estate, including factories, warehouses, office buildings, and farm buildings.
1	33.33%	20.00%	14.29%	5.00%	3.64%	2.56%
2	44.45%	32.00%	24.49%	9.50%	3.64%	2.56%
3	14.81%	19.20%	17.49%	8.55%	3.64%	2.56%
4	7.41%	11.52%*	12.49%	7.70%	3.64%	2.56%
5		11.52%	8.93%*	6.93%	3.64%	2.56%
6		5.76%	8.92%	6.23%	3.64%	2.56%
7			8.93%	5.90%*	3.64%	2.56%
8			4.46%	5.90%	3.64%	2.56%
9				5.91%	3.64%	2.56%
10				5.90%	3.64%	2.56%
11				5.91%	3.64%	2.56%
12				5.90%	3.64%	2.56%
13				5.91%	3.64%	2.56%
14				5.90%	3.64%	2.56%
15				5.91%	3.64%	2.56%
16				2.95%	3.64%	2.56%
17					3.64%	2.56%
28					1.82%	2.56%
39						2.56%

DB: Declining Balance
*At this point in the schedule, the IRS switches to straight-line depreciation taken as early as possible.

When using these rates, salvage value is ignored when determining the depreciable cost. This permits a 100% write-off of the original cost. Note that depreciation under MACRS for a five-year asset must be spread over six years. This is because, regardless of when the asset is purchased, the MACRS depreciation rates assume one-half year's depreciation in year 1 and one-half year's depreciation in year 6. The same is true for the other asset classes using MACRS.

To compute MACRS depreciation for a five-year asset, let's assume the following: cost of $50,000 and salvage value of $10,000. Using the rates from the MACRS depreciation rates schedule for a 5-year class of property shown in Figure 18-3, depreciation expense for years 1 through 6 may be computed as follows:

Year	Original Cost	MACRS Depreciation Rates: 5-Year Class of Property	Depreciation Expense
1	$50,000	20.00%	$10,000
2	50,000	32.00%	16,000
3	50,000	19.20%	9,600
4	50,000	11.52%	5,760
5	50,000	11.52%	5,760
6	50,000	5.76%	2,880
Total			$50,000

As shown above, the salvage value is not deducted from the original cost to determine the depreciable cost. This permits a 100% write-off.

LO4 — Repairs, Maintenance, Additions, Improvements, and Replacements to Plant and Equipment

Account for repairs, maintenance, additions, improvements, and replacements to plant and equipment.

Plant and equipment require normal repairs and maintenance for proper operating efficiency and quality. Replacement of minor parts, lubrication, and cleaning are typical examples of normal repairs and maintenance. These expenditures are debited to Repairs Expense, as follows:

5	Repairs Expense	x x x xx		5
6	Cash (or Supplies Inventory)		x x x xx	6
7	Made repairs			7

Additions or improvements to plant and equipment are accounted for in the same way. As the word implies, an addition indicates the company has added a new asset. For example, the addition of a wing to a building or the installation of partitions, shelving, sprinkler systems, or air conditioning systems would be additions. When making an improvement, sometimes called a betterment, the company substitutes a better component of a major asset for the one currently used. For example, a concrete floor might be substituted for a wooden one. Both additions and improvements enhance the quality and efficiency of the building or equipment. These expenditures are debited to the building or equipment account and credited to either the cash or a liability account, as follows:

9	Building or Equipment					x	x	x	xx					9
10	Cash (or Liability)									x	x	x	xx	10
11	Made addition (or improvement)													11

Since these improvements will benefit future periods, depreciation will be recognized in future periods.

Sometimes, component parts of assets are replaced with similar components. For example, a business may replace the engine in a truck with a similar engine, or replace a wooden floor with a new wooden floor. These replacements extend the lives of the truck or building beyond the original estimate, but do not improve their usefulness or efficiency. This expenditure is debited to Accumulated Depreciation and credited to either the cash or a liability account, as follows:

14	Accum. Depr.—Building or Equipment					x	x	x	xx					14
15	Cash (or Liability)									x	x	x	xx	15
16	Made replacement													16

Accumulated Depreciation is debited because the depreciation taken on the original engine or floor has been recaptured by replacing it with a new one. The debit to Accumulated Depreciation increases the book value of the asset. Since the new engine or floor will benefit future periods, additional depreciation will be taken in future periods.

Notice that the book value of the asset is increased regardless of whether we debit the asset account or the accumulated depreciation account. This increase in book value leads to an increase in the amount of depreciation recognized in future periods. To illustrate, assume that a business owns the following two computers that were purchased on January 1, 20-1:

	Computer A	Computer B
Cost	$6,500	$6,500
Salvage value	500	500
Depreciable base	$6,000	$6,000
Estimated life	3 years	3 years
Depreciation method	Straight-line	Straight-line
Depreciation expense 20-1	$2,000	$2,000

At the beginning of 20-2, a failing disk drive is replaced on Computer A and a new graphics card that will enable the use of new programs is added to Computer B. Let's assume that the disk drive and graphics card cost $400 each. The entries for the replacement of the disk drive to Computer A, which extends its life by an additional two years beyond the original estimate but does not increase its usefulness, and the addition of a new graphics card to Computer B are shown in T account form, as follows:

Computer A			Computer B		
6,500				6,500	
			Jan. 1, 20-2	400	
			Bal.	6,900	

Accum. Depr.—Computer A			Accum. Depr.—Computer B		
		Dec. 31, 20-1 2,000			Dec. 31, 20-1 2,000
Jan. 1, 20-2	400				
		Bal. 1,600			

Note that after recording the expenditures on January 1, 20-2, Computers A and B both have book values of $4,900, as follows:

	Computer A	Computer B
Asset account balance	$ 6,500	$ 6,900
Accumulated depreciation	(1,600)	(2,000)
Book value	$ 4,900	$ 4,900

Compute depreciation expense for 20-2 as follows:

1. Compute the new depreciable base by deducting the salvage value from the book value of the computers after recording the expenditures.

2. Divide the new depreciable base by the remaining useful life, four years for Computer A and two years for Computer B.

	Computer A	Computer B
Book value	$4,900	$4,900
Salvage value	(500)	(500)
New depreciable base	$4,400	$4,400
Remaining useful life	4 years	2 years
Depreciation expense	$1,100	$2,200

Thus, depreciation expense is $1,100 for Computer A in 20-2 through 20-5 and $2,200 for Computer B in 20-2 and 20-3.

LEARNING KEY 🔑

Expenditures on plant and equipment are accounted for in the following ways:

- If the expenditures simply maintain the asset's operating condition, debit the Repairs Expense account.
- If the expenditures increase the asset's usefulness or efficiency, debit the asset account.
- If the expenditures extend the asset's useful life beyond the original estimate, but do not increase its usefulness or efficiency, debit the accumulated depreciation account.

CHECKPOINT ✔

Complete Checkpoint-4 on page 714 to test your basic understanding of LO4.

Disposal of Plant Assets

Account for the disposition of property, plant, and equipment.

A plant asset can be disposed of in several ways.

1. It may be discarded or retired.

2. It may be sold.

3. It may be exchanged or traded in for another asset.

Regardless of the method of disposal, any gain or loss that occurred on the disposal must be determined. This is done by comparing the market and book values of the asset on the date of disposal. *To determine the book value on the date of disposal, an adjusting entry must be made to record depreciation from the end of the previous period to the disposal date.* Gains and losses are determined, as follows:

Determining Gains and Losses on Disposal of Assets

Gain = Market Value Greater than Book Value

Loss = Market Value Less than Book Value

Gains are similar to revenue and increase net income. Losses are similar to expenses and reduce net income. They are reported on the income statement under Other Revenues and Other Expenses.

Discarding or Retiring Plant Assets

A plant asset may be discarded or retired at any time. If its book value on the disposal date is zero, no gain or loss will be realized. If it is greater than zero, the book value of the discarded asset will represent a loss.

To illustrate, assume that a printer with a cost of $800 and accumulated depreciation of $800 is discarded. Because the printer is fully depreciated, its book value is zero and no gain or loss results from this transaction. The removal of the asset and related accumulated depreciation is recorded as follows:

5		Accum. Depr.—Office Equipment			8	0	0	00				5
6		Office Equipment							8	0	0	00	6
7		Discarded printer											7

However, if at the time the printer is discarded, the accumulated depreciation is $720, the book value is $80 and a loss results. In this case, the discard of the asset and recognition of the loss are recorded as follows:

9		Accum. Depr.—Office Equipment			7	2	0	00				9
10		Loss on Discarded Office Equipment				8	0	00				10
11		Office Equipment							8	0	0	00	11
12		Discarded printer											12

Selling Plant Assets

Now let's assume that this same printer is sold for $80 at the time its book value is $80. This transaction is entered as follows:

5		Cash				8	0	00				5
6		Accum. Depr.—Office Equipment			7	2	0	00				6
7		Office Equipment							8	0	0	00	7
8		Sold printer											8

No gain or loss results from this transaction because the printer's selling price, or market value, is equal to its book value.

If the printer is sold for $120 at the time its book value is $80, there is a gain of $40. In this case, the journal entry is as follows:

5	Cash	1 2 0 00		5
6	Accum. Depr.—Office Equipment	7 2 0 00		6
7	Office Equipment		8 0 0 00	7
8	Gain on Sale of Printer		4 0 00	8
9	Sold printer			9

If, instead, the printer is sold for $50, there is a loss of $30. This transaction is recorded as follows:

5	Cash	5 0 00		5
6	Accum. Depr.—Office Equipment	7 2 0 00		6
7	Loss on Sale of Printer	3 0 00		7
8	Office Equipment		8 0 0 00	8
9	Sold printer			9

Exchange or Trade-In of Plant Assets

When one plant asset is exchanged for another, a gain or loss is recognized if the exchange is considered to have "commercial substance." The gain or loss is computed by comparing the difference between the market and book values of the asset given up. A transaction is considered to *lack* commercial substance if significant changes in cash flows are *not* expected. In our discussions, we will assume all exchanges have commercial substance.

If one asset is traded in on the purchase of another asset, a trade-in allowance may be granted. This trade-in allowance may be greater than, less than, or equal to the book value of the asset traded. If you have ever traded in a car for a newer model, you know that the trade-in allowance frequently is not equal to the fair market value. Therefore, the fair market value of the asset traded in must be determined to calculate the gain or loss on the exchange. For simplicity, however, we will assume in our illustrations that the trade-in allowance is equal to the market value of the old asset being traded.

To illustrate accounting for the exchange of plant assets, let's assume that an old delivery truck is traded for a new one. Relevant information for this transaction is as follows:

Old Delivery Truck		New Delivery Truck	
Cost	$8,000	Market value (new truck)	$30,000
Accumulated depreciation	6,900	Trade-in allowance (old truck)	1,000
Book value	$1,100	Cash required	$29,000

Gain or Loss on Exchange

$ 1,100	Book value
(1,000)	Market value (trade-in allowance)
$ 100	Loss

If the new truck has a fair market value of $30,000 and the trade-in value of the old truck is $1,000, then $29,000 is due in cash ($30,000 − $1,000). As discussed earlier, the gain or loss on the exchange is determined by comparing the market value of the old asset ($1,000) with its book value ($1,100). In this case, there is a $100 loss. The transaction is entered as follows:

5		Delivery Equipment (new truck)	30	0	0	0	00						5
6		Accum. Depr.—Delivery Equipment	6	9	0	0	00						6
7		Loss on Exchange of Delivery Equipment		1	0	0	00						7
8		Delivery Equipment (old truck)						8	0	0	0	00	8
9		Cash						29	0	0	0	00	9
10		Purchased a new truck											10

This entry has the following effects on the accounting records:

1. The original cost ($8,000) and accumulated depreciation ($6,900) for the old truck are removed from the books.
2. Cash is credited to show the amount paid ($29,000).
3. The new delivery equipment is entered on the books at its market value ($30,000).
4. The loss on the exchange is recognized ($100).

Now let's assume the same event, except that the market value and trade-in allowance for the old truck is $1,500. As shown below, this means that only $28,500 in cash is required and there is a $400 gain on the exchange ($1,500 − $1,100 = $400).

Old Delivery Truck		New Delivery Truck	
Cost	$8,000	Market value (new truck)	$30,000
Accumulated depreciation	6,900	Trade-in allowance (old truck)	1,500
Book value	$1,100	Cash required	$28,500

Gain or Loss on Exchange	
$ 1,500	Market value (trade-in allowance)
(1,000)	Book value
$ 400	Gain

The proper entry is as follows:

5		Delivery Equipment (new truck)	30	0	0	0	00						5
6		Accum. Depr.—Delivery Equipment	6	9	0	0	00						6
7		Delivery Equipment (old truck)						8	0	0	0	00	7
8		Cash						28	5	0	0	00	8
9		Gain on Exchange of Delivery Equipment							4	0	0	00	9
10		Purchased a new truck											10

This entry has the following effects on the accounting records:

1. The original cost ($8,000) and accumulated depreciation ($6,900) for the old truck are removed from the books.
2. Cash is credited to show the amount paid ($28,500).
3. The new delivery equipment is entered on the books at its market value ($30,000).
4. The gain on the exchange is recognized ($400).

For tax purposes, gains and losses are not recognized on the exchange of similar assets ("like-kind" exchanges).

A BROADER VIEW

Value? Which Value?

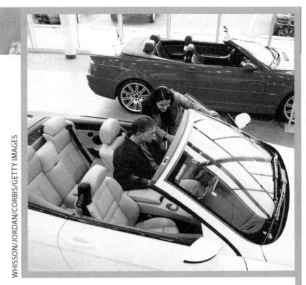

WHISSON/JORDAN/CORBIS/GETTY IMAGES

Determining the market value of an asset is not always easy. For example, if you have ever traded your car for a newer one, you probably learned that the trade-in allowance is often different from what the dealer would "pay" for the car and different from what you might sell it for by advertising in the newspaper and online. To test this concept, try it. Next time you are shopping for a car, ask the dealer two questions. First, ask the dealer what trade-in allowance he or she would offer on your car. Then, ask what he or she would accept for the new car if you paid cash. The difference between the "cash price" and the cash that you must pay with a trade-in offers a measure of what the dealer is paying you for your old car. (See illustration below.) This amount probably is not the same as the trade-in allowance offered by the dealer and may not be the same as the amount you could sell the car for on your own. Of course, you need this information to make a good decision on whether to trade your car or sell it yourself.

Sticker price of new car	$20,000	
Trade-in allowance	5,000	Cash price for new
Cash that must be paid	$15,000	car $18,000

The value of your old car to the dealer is $3,000. Compare this with what you might sell it for by advertising in the newspaper and online.

The accounting described above is also applied when a business exchanges one type of plant asset for another. For example, a pizza business may exchange a delivery truck for a pizza oven from another pizza business. Gains and losses are recognized on this type of exchange in the same manner as described above.

Property, Plant, and Equipment Records

If a business has many depreciable assets, a summary general ledger account will be kept for each major class of assets. For example, separate accounts might be kept for buildings, equipment, and furniture. Each summary account has a related accumulated depreciation account. Subsidiary records in the form of cards or computer files support these summary accounts. A typical property, plant, and equipment record is shown in Figure 18-4.

FIGURE 18-4 Property, Plant, and Equipment Record

PROPERTY, PLANT, AND EQUIPMENT RECORD

Description	Computer	Account	Office Equipment
Age when acquired	New	Estimated salvage value	$500
Estimated life	5 years	Rate of annual depreciation based on cost less salvage value	20%

COST				DEPRECIATION RECORD			
Date Purchased	Description	Amount		Year	Rate	Amount	Total To Date
20-2 Jan. 9	ABC DE/3 MODEL50	5,000	00	20-2	20%	900 00	900 00
	Serial No. 8403637			20-3	20%	900 00	1,800 00
	American Micro			20-4	20%	450 00	2,250 00
	Less estimated salvage value	500	00	20			
	Depreciable cost	4,500	00	20			
				20			
				20			
				20			
				20			
SOLD, EXCHANGED, OR DISCARDED				20			
Date	Explanation	Amount Realized	Book Value on Disposal Date	Gain (Loss)	20		
20-4 July 1	Sold	3,000 00	2,750 00	250 00	20		
					20		
					20		
					20		

Fully Depreciated Plant Assets

CHECKPOINT ✔

Complete Checkpoint-5 on page 714 to test your basic understanding of LO5.

A plant asset is fully depreciated when the book value is equal to the salvage value. When an asset is fully depreciated, no further depreciation should be entered. Since the rate of depreciation is based on its *estimated* useful life, an asset may still be used after it is fully depreciated. In this case, the cost of the asset and the accumulated depreciation are left in the accounts. When the asset eventually is disposed of, the cost and accumulated depreciation should be removed from the accounts, as illustrated in previous sections.

LO6   Natural Resources

Explain the nature of, purpose of, and accounting for depletion.

The consumption or exhaustion of *natural resources* is called *depletion*. The purpose of depletion is to allocate the cost of these assets to the periods in which they are consumed. Computing *depletion* is similar to computing depreciation using the units-of-production method. The cost of the property, less the estimated salvage or residual value, is divided by the estimated number of units that the property contains. The result is the depletion expense per unit. This amount times the number of units removed and sold during the period is the depletion expense for the period.

To illustrate, assume a coal mine is acquired at a cost of $1,000,000. No salvage value is expected. The estimated recoverable amount of coal in the mine is 1,000,000 tons. During the current year, 180,000 tons of coal are mined and sold. The computation of the amount of depletion expense is as follows:

$$\frac{\$1,000,000}{1,000,000 \text{ tons}} = \$1 \text{ per ton}$$

180,000 tons × $1 per ton = $180,000 depletion expense

An adjusting entry is made at the end of the accounting period to recognize the depletion expense. For the coal mine, this entry is as follows:

11		Depletion Expense—Coal Mine	180	0	0	0	00						11
12		Accum. Depletion—Coal Mine						180	0	0	0	00	12
13													13

The difference between the cost of the mine and the amount of the accumulated depletion is the undepleted cost of the property.

Cost of coal mine	$1,000,000
Less accumulated depletion	180,000
Undepleted cost of mine	$ 820,000

Depletion Expense is reported as an operating expense on the income statement. Accumulated Depletion is reported on the balance sheet as a deduction from the related asset account, with the difference identified as undepleted cost of the asset. As was explained for depreciation, this undepleted cost of the wasting asset simply represents the cost not yet charged to operations. It is not intended to reflect the market value of the asset.

CHECKPOINT ✔

Complete Checkpoint-6 on page 714 to test your basic understanding of LO6.

LO7

Intangible Assets

Explain the nature of and accounting for intangible assets.

In an accounting sense, the term "intangible" has come to have a very restricted meaning. Intangible assets refers to a limited group of valuable legal or economic rights that a firm may acquire. All items classified as intangibles are considered to be long-term assets. Major examples of intangibles include patents, copyrights, franchises, trademarks, and goodwill.

Patents

A patent is a grant by the federal government to an inventor giving the exclusive right to produce, use, and sell an invention for a period of 20 years. A firm may purchase a patent from a prior patent owner or may develop its own and acquire an original patent from the government. If purchased, the amount paid represents the cost of the patent.

If a company carries on regular research and development activities to develop its own patents, the costs of such activities are treated as current expenses. If the government grants a patent on an invention the company develops, the cost of this patent includes only the fees paid to the government and to patent attorneys for their services. This amount is debited to an asset account and amortized over the patent's useful life.

Since the life of a patent is specifically limited, any cost assigned to it is allocated over no more than the number of years that the patent right will exist. The greatest number of years would be 20 if the firm developed and applied for the patent. If the expected useful or economic life of a patent is less than its legal life, the cost should be allocated over the shorter period.

With the straight-line method, the amortization each year is determined by dividing the cost of the patent by its expected life. Let's assume that a patent with 13 years to run is purchased at a cost of $12,000, and that the buyer expects the useful life of the patent to be only 10 years. In that event, $1,200 ($12,000 ÷ 10 years) would be amortized as expense for each of the 10 years. The adjusting entry for the amortization at the end of each year is as follows:

7		Patent Amortization	1	2	0	0	00						7
8		Patents						1	2	0	0	00	8

Patent amortization is usually treated as an operating expense. Since patents are assets, their unamortized cost is reported on the balance sheet as an intangible long-term asset.

Copyrights

A copyright is similar in many respects to a patent. It consists of a federal grant of the exclusive right to the reproduction and sale of a literary, artistic, or musical composition. A copyright is granted for life plus 70 years after the death of the holder. The cost of obtaining the initial copyright on a composition is nominal. It is treated as an ordinary expense. However, if an existing copyright is purchased, the cost may be large enough and the expected future value sufficient to warrant charging the cost to an asset account entitled Copyrights.

It is a rare case in which a copyright would have an economic life as long as its legal life. In most cases, the cost of a copyright is written off in a very few years. The write-off can be on a straight-line basis or in the proportion of the actual sales of the copyrighted item during the period to the total expected sales of the item. The amount of the write-off for each period is debited to Copyright Amortization (or Copyright Expense) and credited to Copyrights. Copyright amortization is treated as an operating expense. Any unamortized portion of the cost of copyrights is reported on the balance sheet as an intangible long-term asset.

Trademark or Trade Name

A trademark or trade name is a symbol, word, phrase, or jingle identified with a particular product or company. Examples include the Nike swoosh, Adidas stripes, McDonald's arches, or simply names like BMW, Coke, and Big Mac. Though registration is not required for the trademark or trade name to be enforced, such designations can be legally protected by registering them with the United States Patent and Trademark Office. As long as the trademark or trade name is continuously used, legal protection can be renewed for an indefinite number of 10-year periods.

Research and development costs incurred to develop a trademark or trade name are expensed as incurred. However, costs incurred to register a trademark or trade name are debited to an asset account. These costs include attorney and registration fees. Since the asset has an indefinite life, the costs are not amortized. The balance of the account is reported on the balance sheet as an intangible long-term asset.

If a trademark or trade name is acquired by purchase, its cost is debited to an asset account. Again, since the life expectancy is indefinite, this asset is not amortized. The balance of the account is reported on the balance sheet as an intangible long-term asset.

Franchises and Licenses

A franchise or license is a contract under which a franchisor grants the franchisee the rights to sell products or services and to use trademarks or trade names under specified conditions. Examples include Dairy Queen, Papa John's, Steak 'n Shake, Rent-a-Wreck, RE/MAX, and Motel 6. Franchises and licenses may be for a definite or indefinite period of time, or perpetual. Costs associated with securing the franchise or license, typically legal fees or an upfront payment to the franchisor, are reported as an intangible asset on the balance sheet. A company should amortize these costs as an operating expense if the franchise or license is for a definite period of time. If the franchise or license is for an indefinite period of time, or perpetual, these costs should not be amortized.

Goodwill

Goodwill may only be recognized when one company buys another. It is measured as follows:

Market Value (acquisition price) of the Company
− Market Value of the Company's Net Assets (Assets − Liabilities)
= Goodwill

Clearly, excellent management, a skilled workforce, superior use of technology, loyal customers, reliable suppliers, quality products and services at a competitive price, and other competitive advantages contribute to the overall market value of a company. As you know, none of these factors are captured by the accounting system. Thus, it is not surprising that goodwill must be recognized when a successful business is acquired. Goodwill is considered to have an indefinite life and is not amortized by the acquiring company.

Impairment of Property, Plant, Equipment, and Intangible Assets

Land has an unlimited life and is not depreciated. Plant and equipment have definite useful lives and are depreciated. Some intangible assets have definite lives (patents and copyrights) and are amortized. Other intangible assets have indefinite lives (trademarks, trade names, and goodwill) and are not amortized. All of these assets are tested for impairment. Impairment occurs when an asset's fair market value falls below the book value reported on the balance sheet. If impaired, the asset must be written down and a loss recognized. The exact process for these tests is addressed in more advanced courses.

> CHECKPOINT ✔
>
> Complete Checkpoint-7 on page 714 to test your basic understanding of LO7.

SELF-STUDY

LEARNING OBJECTIVES	Key Points to Remember
LO1 Determine the cost of property, plant, and equipment.	The cost to acquire an asset includes the purchase price and all costs incurred to prepare the asset for its intended use.
LO2 Explain the nature and purpose of depreciation.	The purpose of depreciation is to match a plant asset's cost with the revenues it helps to produce.
LO3 Compute depreciation using the straight-line, declining-balance, sum-of-the-years'-digits, units-of-production, and MACRS depreciation methods.	Depreciation methods for financial reporting purposes are as follows: *Straight-Line Method* $$\text{Annual Depreciation} = \frac{(\text{Cost} - \text{Salvage Value})}{\text{Estimated Useful Life}}$$ *Declining-Balance Method* $$\text{Annual Depreciation} = \text{Depreciation Rate} \times \text{Book Value at Beginning of Year}$$ *Sum-of-the-Years'-Digits Method* $$\text{Annual Depreciation} = (\text{Cost} - \text{Salvage Value}) \times \frac{\text{Remaining Useful Life from Beginning of Current Year}}{\text{Sum-of-the-Years'-Digits}}$$

(continued)

LEARNING OBJECTIVES	**Key Points to Remember**

LO3 (concluded)	*Units-of-Production Method*
	
	$$\text{Depreciation per Unit} = \frac{(\text{Cost} - \text{Salvage Value})}{\text{Estimated Useful Life in Units}}$$
	
	$$\text{Annual Depreciation} = \text{Depreciation per Unit} \times \frac{\text{Number of Units Produced or}}{\text{Consumed this Year}}$$
	
	Depreciation Methods for Federal Taxes
	   For plant assets acquired and placed into service after 1986:
	     MACRS Depreciation Method
	
	$$\text{Annual Depreciation} = \text{Original Cost} \times \frac{\text{Rate from MACRS Rate Schedule for}}{\text{Appropriate Class of Property}}$$
	
	     Straight-Line Method—Same as above.
	
	For qualified assets acquired and placed into service after September 27, 2017, businesses may also choose to immediately expense 100% of the cost. This does not include buildings.

LO4 Account for repairs, maintenance, additions, improvements, and replacements to plant and equipment.	The entry for additions and improvements that increase the usefulness of equipment would be as follows:
	
	    Building or Equipment xxx
	        Cash or Liability account xxx
	
	The entry for replacements that extend the life of the asset, but do not improve usefulness or efficiency, would be as follows:
	
	    Accumulated Depreciation—Building or Equipment xxx
	        Cash or Liability account xxx
	
	To compute straight-line depreciation expense for the year following an addition, an improvement, or a replacement, use the following steps:
	
	1. Compute the new depreciable base by deducting the salvage value from the book value of the asset following the expenditures.
	2. Divide the new depreciable base by the remaining useful life.

LO5 Account for the disposition of property, plant, and equipment.	Disposal of Plant Assets
	When an asset is discarded:
	
	  1. Remove cost and accumulated depreciation from accounting records.
	  2. If book value is greater than zero, recognize loss.
	
	When an asset is sold:
	
	  1. Remove cost and accumulated depreciation from accounting records.
	  2. Debit Cash for amount received.
	  3. Recognize gain or loss (market value − book value of asset sold).
	
	When an asset is traded in for another similar asset:
	
	  1. Debit new asset for its market value.
	  2. Remove cost and accumulated depreciation for asset traded in from accounting records.
	  3. Credit Cash for amount paid.
	  4. Record gain or loss on exchange (market value − book value of asset traded in).

(continued)

LEARNING OBJECTIVES	Key Points to Remember
LO6 Explain the nature of, purpose of, and accounting for depletion.	The consumption or exhaustion of natural resources is called *depletion*. The purpose of accounting for depletion is to allocate the cost of these assets to the periods in which they are consumed.
LO7 Explain the nature of and accounting for intangible assets.	The term *intangible assets* is used to refer to a limited group of valuable legal or economic rights (patent, copyright, trademark, franchise, and goodwill) that a firm may acquire. Intangible assets with a definite life are amortized. Those with indefinite lives are not amortized. All are tested for impairment.

DEMONSTRATION PROBLEM

Stillman Company purchased a new machine at the start of its current year at a cost of $37,500. The machine is expected to serve for five years and to have a salvage value of $3,000. Ronald L. Stillman, the chief executive officer, has asked for information as to the effects of alternative depreciation methods.

REQUIRED

1. Calculate the annual depreciation expense for each of the five years of expected life of the machine, the accumulated depreciation at the end of each year, and the book value at the end of each year using the following methods:
   (a) Straight-line
   (b) Double-declining-balance
   (c) Sum-of-the-years'-digits

2. Assume this asset is placed in the five-year asset class for federal income tax purposes. Compute depreciation expense for each year of the asset's life using the MACRS depreciation method and the rates shown in Figure 18-3, page 696.

3. Assume that in years 2 and 4 of the five-year life of this machine, revenues are $45,000 and costs and expenses other than depreciation are $25,000. Calculate the net income for years 2 and 4 using the same three depreciation methods used in part (1).

4. Assume that Stillman chose the double-declining-balance method of depreciation for this machine. Then, in the first week of year 5, the machine was exchanged (traded in) for similar equipment costing $45,000. The market value and trade-in allowance on the old machine was $4,000 and cash was paid for the balance. Prepare the necessary journal entry to record this exchange.

SOLUTION 1.

	Year	Annual Depreciation Expense	Accumulated Depreciation End of Year	Book Value End of Year
a.	1	$6,900	$ 6,900	$30,600
	2	6,900	13,800	23,700
	3	6,900	20,700	16,800
	4	6,900	27,600	9,900
	5	6,900	34,500	3,000

(*continued*)

b.	1	$15,000	$15,000	$22,500
	2	9,000	24,000	13,500
	3	5,400	29,400	8,100
	4	3,240	32,640	4,860
	5	1,860*	34,500	3,000
c.	1	$11,500	$11,500	$26,000
	2	9,200	20,700	16,800
	3	6,900	27,600	9,900
	4	4,600	32,200	5,300
	5	2,300	34,500	3,000

*The machine is not depreciated below its estimated salvage value of $3,000.

SOLUTION 2.

Year	Original Cost	MACRS Depreciation Rates	Depreciation Expense
1	$37,500	20.00%	$ 7,500
2	37,500	32.00%	12,000
3	37,500	19.20%	7,200
4	37,500	11.52%	4,320
5	37,500	11.52%	4,320
6	37,500	5.76%	2,160
Total			$37,500

SOLUTION 3.

Year 2	(a) Straight-Line Method	(b) Double-Declining-Balance Method	(c) Sum-of-the-Years'-Digits Method
Revenue	$45,000	$45,000	$45,000
Costs and expenses other than depreciation	25,000	25,000	25,000
Depreciation	6,900	9,000	9,200
Net income	$13,100	$11,000	$10,800
Year 4			
Revenue	$45,000	$45,000	$45,000
Costs and expenses other than depreciation	25,000	25,000	25,000
Depreciation	6,900	3,240	4,600
Net income	$13,100	$16,760	$15,400

SOLUTION 4.

5		Equipment (new machine)		45 0 0 0 00		5
6		Accum. Depr.—Equipment		32 6 4 0 00		6
7		Loss on Exchange of Equipment		8 6 0 00		7
8		Equipment (old machine)			37 5 0 0 00	8
9		Cash			41 0 0 0 00	9
10		Purchased a new machine				10

Old Equipment		New Equipment	
Cost of old equipment	$37,500	Market value (new)	$45,000
Accumulated depreciation	32,640	Trade-in allowance (old)	4,000
Book value	$ 4,860	Cash required	$41,000
Book value	$ 4,860		
Trade-in (market value)	(4,000)		
Loss	$ 860		

KEY TERMS

accelerated depreciation methods (692)   Depreciation methods that provide for a higher depreciation charge in the first year of an asset's life and gradually decreasing charges in subsequent years.

additions (697)   The company has added a new asset. Examples include the addition of a wing to a building and the installation of shelving, sprinklers, and air conditioning.

amortization (688)   The portion of an intangible asset's cost that is recognized as expense.

betterment (697)   See improvements.

book value (690)   The undepreciated cost of the asset (cost − accumulated depreciation).

cash equivalent price (689)   The amount of cash that could have been paid for the asset on the date of purchase.

copyright (706)   A grant by the federal government of the exclusive right to the reproduction and sale of a literary, artistic, or musical composition.

cost (690)   The sum of all amounts spent to acquire an asset and prepare it for its intended use.

declining-balance method (692)   An accelerated depreciation method in which the book value is multiplied by a fixed rate. A common rate is double the straight-line rate (the double-declining-balance method).

depletion (688)   The consumption or exhaustion of natural resources.

depreciable cost (base) (690)   The original cost less salvage (or scrap) value.

depreciation (688)   The portion of a plant asset's cost that is recognized as expense.

double-declining-balance method (693)   An accelerated depreciation method in which the book value is multiplied by double the straight-line rate.

fixed assets (688)   See property, plant, and equipment.

franchise (706)   A franchise is a contract under which a franchisor grants the franchisee the rights to sell products or services and to use trademarks or trade names under specified conditions.

functional depreciation (690)   The loss of usefulness because of inadequacy or obsolescence.

goodwill (706)   Goodwill is the excess of the market value of the company over the market value of the company's net assets (assets − liabilities). Goodwill is only recognized when one company buys another.

impairment (707)   If the fair market value of any property, plant, equipment, or intangible asset falls below the book value reported on the balance sheet, the asset is considered impaired and must be written down and a loss recognized.

improvements (697)   The company substitutes a better component of a plant asset for the existing one, such as a marble floor for a wooden floor. Also known as betterments.

intangible assets (688) Long-term assets that have no physical substance (patents, copyrights, trademarks, franchises, and goodwill).

license (706) A license is a contract under which a licensor grants the licensee the rights to sell products or services and to use trademarks or trade names under specified conditions.

long-term assets (688) Assets that are expected to provide benefits for a number of accounting periods.

Modified Accelerated Cost Recovery System (MACRS) (696) A method of depreciation used for federal income tax purposes for plant assets acquired after 1986.

patent (705) A grant by the federal government to an inventor giving the exclusive right to produce, use, and sell an invention for a period of 20 years.

physical depreciation (690) The loss of usefulness because of deterioration from age and wear.

plant assets (688) See property, plant, and equipment.

property, plant, and equipment (688) Long-term tangible assets that are used in the operations of the business. Also called plant assets or fixed assets.

replacements (698) A component of a plant asset is replaced with a similar component. That is, a wooden floor is replaced with a new wooden floor. These replacements extend the lives of the assets beyond the original estimates, but do not improve their usefulness or efficiency.

salvage value (690) The estimated market value of an asset on its expected disposal date.

scrap value (690) See salvage value.

straight-line method (690) A depreciation method in which the depreciable cost of an asset is allocated equally over the years of the asset's useful life.

sum-of-the-years'-digits method (694) A depreciation method in which the annual depreciation is determined by multiplying the depreciable cost by a schedule of fractions.

tangible assets (688) Long-term assets that have physical substance.

trade name (706) A name that is identified with a particular product or company.

trade-in allowance (701) An allowance granted when one asset is traded in on the purchase of another similar asset.

trade-in value (701) See trade-in allowance.

trademark (706) A symbol or jingle identified with a particular product or company.

units-of-production method (695) A depreciation method in which depreciation is based on the extent to which the asset was used during the year.

useful life (690) The amount of service expected to be obtained from an asset.

wasting assets (688) Assets whose physical substance consists of natural resources that are consumed in the operation of the business.

SELF-STUDY TEST QUESTIONS

True/False

1. **LO1** All long-term assets wear out gradually or are gradually used up entirely.

2. **LO1** Intangible assets are depreciated; plant assets are amortized.

3. **LO2** Depreciation is a process of asset valuation; that is, book value is the same as true asset value.

4. **LO3** The straight-line method of depreciation allocates the cost of an asset more rapidly than the sum-of-the-years'-digits method.

5. **LO3** The units-of-production method of depreciation allocates the cost of an asset equally over each year of the useful life.

Multiple Choice

1. **LO3** Using the sum-of-the-years'-digits method, the denominator for a five-year useful life would be
   (a) 5.   (c) 12.
   (b) 7.   (d) 15.

2. **LO5** A machine that cost $100 and had accumulated depreciation of $80 was sold for $20.
   (a) There was a $20 gain.   (c) There was no gain or loss.
   (b) There was a $20 loss.   (d) There was a $60 loss.

3. **LO5** A computer was sold on April 1, 20-2, for $575. Its cost was $3,000, and accumulated depreciation as of December 31, 20-1, was $2,100 ($700 a year).
   (a) There was a gain of $150.   (c) There was a gain of $325.
   (b) There was a loss of $150.   (d) There was a loss of $325.

4. **LO6** Cost depletion of natural resources is most like which of these depreciation methods?
   (a) straight-line   (c) declining-balance
   (b) units-of-production   (d) sum-of-the-years'-digits

5. **LO7** Which of these is granted for life plus 70 years after the death of the holder?
   (a) patent   (c) copyright
   (b) mineral rights   (d) trademark

Checkpoint Exercises

1. **LO1** The following costs were incurred to purchase a machine:

Purchase price	$50,000
Transportation costs	800
Insurance during transportation	100
Interest on loan during first month of asset's use	250

   Determine the acquisition cost.

2. **LO2** The following information is provided for a building:

Cost	$500,000
Depreciation expense per year	25,000
Accumulated depreciation	100,000
Current market value	600,000

   How would information about the above building be reported on the balance sheet?

3. **LO3** A machine costing $350,000 has a salvage value of $15,000 and an estimated life of three years. Prepare depreciation schedules reporting the depreciation expense, accumulated depreciation, and book value of the machine for each year under the double-declining-balance and sum-of-the-years'-digits methods. For the double-declining-balance method, round the depreciation rate to two decimal places.

4. **LO4**   Grandorf Company replaced the engine in a truck for $8,000 and expects the new engine will extend the life of the truck two years beyond the original estimated life. Related information is provided below.

Cost of truck	$65,000
Salvage value	5,000
Original estimated life	6 years

The truck was purchased on January 1, 20-1. The engine was replaced on January 1, 20-6. Using straight-line depreciation, compute depreciation expense for 20-6.

5. **LO5**   Prepare journal entries for the following transactions:
   a. A machine with a cost of $10,000 and accumulated depreciation of $8,000 was sold for $2,500.
   b. A machine with a cost of $10,000 and accumulated depreciation of $8,000 was traded for a new machine with a market value of $12,000. Cash of $9,500 was also paid.

6. **LO6**   Popilarz Mining acquired a coal mine at a cost of $4,000,000 with the expectation that 1,250,000 tons of coal would be mined over its lifetime. The estimated salvage value of the land is $250,000, and 100,000 tons of coal are mined in the first year. Compute the depletion expense for the first year.

7. **LO7**   Todd Company purchased a patent with a remaining life of 10 years for $100,000 cash. Prepare the journal entry for the acquisition and the first year's amortization. Assume straight-line amortization.

The answers to the Self-Study Test Questions are at the end of the chapter (pages 726–727).

APPLYING YOUR KNOWLEDGE

CengageNowv2 provides "Show Me How" videos for selected exercises and problems. Additional resources, such as Excel templates for completing selected exercises and problems, are available for download from the companion website at Cengage.com.

REVIEW QUESTIONS

LO1   1. What costs should be included when measuring the total cost to acquire a long-term asset?

LO1   2. How should the cost of such activities as planting trees and shrubs be entered?

LO2   3. What are the two major types of depreciation?

LO3   4. What is meant by the "depreciable cost" of a plant asset?

LO3   5. What are the four most commonly used methods of calculating depreciation for financial reporting purposes? How do they differ in their application?

LO3   6. Which depreciation method provides the fastest write-off of an asset?

LO3   7. Explain how the depreciation method selected affects the balance sheet and income statement.

LO3	8.	For assets acquired after 1986, but before September 27, 2017, what depreciation methods are allowed for federal income tax purposes?
LO3	9.	For assets acquired after September 27, 2017, what depreciation methods are allowed for federal income tax purposes?
LO4	10.	How should additions or improvements representing an increase in the usefulness of plant assets be entered?
LO4	11.	Explain what is meant by the "replacement" of a component of a plant asset.
LO5	12.	What are the three major ways of disposing of a plant asset?
LO5	13.	For what time interval should depreciation expense be entered on the date of an asset's disposal?
LO5	14.	When a plant asset is sold, what must be known about the asset in order to determine the proper amount of gain or loss on the sale?
LO5	15.	What details about a particular asset are provided by a property, plant, and equipment record?
LO6	16.	What is the purpose of depletion?
LO3/6	17.	Which depreciation method is similar to the method used to compute depletion expense?
LO7	18.	Over what period of time should the cost of a patent be allocated if its economic life is expected to be less than its legal life?
LO7	19.	How should the unamortized portion of the cost of a copyright be reported on the balance sheet?
LO7	20.	What is a trademark?
LO7	21.	What is a franchise? Name a franchise you have visited.
LO7	22.	What is goodwill? When is it recognized?
LO7	23.	What is impairment?

SERIES A EXERCISES

E 18-1A   (LO1)   COST OF PROPERTY, PLANT, AND EQUIPMENT Consider the following list of expenditures and indicate whether each would be debited to Land, Building, or Equipment as part of the cost to purchase these assets. Place a check mark in the appropriate column.

	Yes	No
Debit Land?		
Real estate fees	_____	_____
Cost to remove old buildings	_____	_____
Cost to pave parking areas	_____	_____
Tax assessment for streets	_____	_____
Debit Building?		
Cost of land on which the building is located	_____	_____
Legal fees related to purchase	_____	_____

(*continued*)

Taxes related to purchase	_____	_____
Realtor fees	_____	_____
Interest on construction loan while building was under construction	_____	_____
Debit Equipment?		
Transportation charges	_____	_____
Insurance while in transit	_____	_____
Installation costs	_____	_____
Interest on loan to buy equipment	_____	_____

E 18-2A   (LO3)
✓ Year 1: SL, $3,750
✓ DDB, $8,750
✓ SYD, $6,666.67

STRAIGHT-LINE, DECLINING-BALANCE, AND SUM-OF-THE-YEARS'-DIGITS METHODS A light truck is purchased on January 1 at a cost of $35,000. It is expected to serve for eight years and have a salvage value of $5,000. Calculate the depreciation expense for the first and third years of the truck's life using the following methods:

1. Straight-line

2. Double-declining-balance (round to two decimal places)

3. Sum-of-the-years'-digits (round to two decimal places)

E 18-3A   (LO3)
✓ Depr. exp. for year 1: $6,000

UNITS-OF-PRODUCTION METHOD The truck purchased in Exercise 18-2A is expected to be used for 100,000 miles over its eight-year useful life. Using the units-of-production method, calculate the depreciation expense for the first and third years of use if the truck is driven 20,000 miles in year 1 and 24,000 miles in year 3.

E 18-4A   (LO4)

JOURNAL ENTRIES: REPAIRS, MAINTENANCE, ADDITIONS, IMPROVEMENTS, AND REPLACEMENTS Prepare the entries for the following transactions for Stepanski's Food Mart using a general journal:

1. Replaced the checkout computer in Checkout Stand A for $3,500 cash. The computer is part of the checkout stand. The replacement is expected to extend the life of the checkout stand.

2. Added a laser scanner to Checkout Stand B for $1,000 cash to decrease checkout time.

3. Cleaned scanner window on Checkout Stand A for $30 cash (normal maintenance).

E 18-5A   (LO5)
✓ 1(a): Loss, $500
✓ 1(b): No gain/loss
✓ 1(c): Gain, $50
✓ 2(a): Loss, $2,000
✓ 2(b): Gain, $3,000

JOURNAL ENTRIES: DISPOSITION OF PLANT ASSETS Prepare the entries for the following transactions using a general journal:

1. Discarding an asset.
   (a) On January 4, shelving units, which had a cost of $6,400 and had accumulated depreciation of $5,900, were discarded.
   (b) On June 15, a hand cart, which had a cost of $1,500 and had accumulated depreciation of $1,350, was sold for $150.
   (c) On October 1, a copy machine, which had a cost of $7,200 and had accumulated depreciation of $6,800, was sold for $450.

2. Exchange or trade-in of assets.
   (a) On December 31, a drill press, which had a cost of $60,000 and had accumulated depreciation of $48,000, was traded in for a new drill press with a fair market value of $75,000. The old drill press and $65,000 in cash were given for the new drill press.
   (b) On December 31, the old drill press in (a) and $60,000 in cash were given for the new drill press.

E 18-6A   (LO6)
✓ 1. Depletion Exp.: $25,000
✓ 2. Depletion Exp.: $500,000

DEPLETION Prepare the following entries using a general journal:

1. A coal mine was acquired at a cost of $1,500,000 and estimated to contain 6,000,000 tons of ore. No salvage value is expected. During the year, 100,000 tons were mined and sold. Prepare the journal entry for the year's depletion expense.

2. A silver mine was acquired at a cost of $3,000,000 and estimated to contain 750,000 tons of ore. No salvage value is expected. During the year, 125,000 tons were mined and sold. Prepare the journal entry for the year's depletion expense.

SERIES A PROBLEMS

P 18-7A   (LO3)
✓ Depr. exp. for year 8:
✓ 1(a) $7,000.00
✓ 1(b) $1,968.89
✓ 1(c) $1,555.56
✓ 2 $2,631.40

STRAIGHT-LINE, DECLINING-BALANCE, SUM-OF-THE-YEARS'-DIGITS, AND MACRS METHODS A machine is purchased January 1 at a cost of $59,000. It is expected to serve for eight years and have a salvage value of $3,000.

REQUIRED

1. Prepare a schedule showing depreciation for each of the eight years and the book value at the end of each year using the following methods:
   (a) Straight-line
   (b) Double-declining-balance (round to two decimal places)
   (c) Sum-of-the-years'-digits (round to two decimal places)

2. Assuming a seven-year class of property, compute MACRS depreciation expense for each year of the asset's life.

P 18-8A   (LO3)
✓ Depr. exp. year 1: $4,300

UNITS-OF-PRODUCTION METHOD A machine is purchased January 1 at a cost of $59,000. It is expected to produce 130,000 units and have a salvage value of $3,000 at the end of its useful life.

Units produced are as follows:

Year 1	10,000
Year 2	8,000
Year 3	12,000
Year 4	16,000
Year 5	11,000

REQUIRED

Prepare a schedule showing depreciation for each year and the book value at the end of each year using the units-of-production method (round calculations to two decimal places).

P 18-9A   (LO3)
✓ 1. Depr. exp.: $8,075

CALCULATING AND JOURNALIZING DEPRECIATION Equipment records for Johnson Machine Co. for the year follow. Johnson Machine uses the straight-line method of depreciation. In the case of assets acquired by the fifteenth day of the month, depreciation should be computed for the entire month. In the case of assets acquired after the fifteenth day of the month, no depreciation should be considered for the month in which the asset was acquired.

(continued)

Asset	Purchase Price	Useful Life	Salvage Value	Date Purchased
Truck #1	$20,000	8 years	$4,000	January 1
Truck #2	24,000	8	4,000	April 10
Tractor #1	18,000	5	3,000	May 1
Tractor #2	14,000	6	2,000	June 18
Forklift	40,000	10	4,000	September 1

REQUIRED

1. Calculate the depreciation expense for Johnson Machine as of December 31, 20--.

2. Prepare the entry for depreciation expense using a general journal.

P 18-10A (LO4)

✓ 1: Depr. exp. is $9,000 for each
✓ 2: Sim. A—Dr. Accum. Depr., $6,000
✓ 3: Sim. A—$6,900 per year

IMPACT OF IMPROVEMENTS AND REPLACEMENTS ON THE CALCULATION OF DEPRECIATION On January 1, 20-1, two flight simulators were purchased by a space camp for $77,000 each with a salvage value of $5,000 each and estimated useful lives of eight years. On January 1, 20-2, the hydraulic system for Simulator A was replaced for $6,000 cash and an updated computer for more advanced students was installed in Simulator B for $9,000 cash. The hydraulic system is expected to extend the life of Simulator A three years beyond the original estimate.

REQUIRED

1. Using the straight-line method, prepare general journal entries for depreciation on December 31, 20-1, for Simulators A and B.

2. Enter the transactions for January 20-2 in a general journal.

3. Assuming no other additions, improvements, or replacements, calculate the depreciation expense for each simulator for 20-2 through 20-8.

P 18-11A (LO5)

✓ Jan. 8, Loss: $200
✓ Feb. 1, Gain, $200

DISPOSITION OF ASSETS: JOURNALIZING Mitchell Parts Co. had the following plant asset transactions during the year:

1. Assets discarded or sold:

Jan. 1 Motor #12, which had a cost of $2,800 and accumulated depreciation of $2,800, was discarded.

8 Motor #8, which had a cost of $4,400 and accumulated depreciation of $4,000, was sold for $200.

14 Motor #16, which had a cost of $5,600 and accumulated depreciation of $5,400, was sold for $450.

2. Assets exchanged or traded in:

Feb. 1 Motor #6, which had a cost of $6,000 and accumulated depreciation of $4,800, was traded in for a new motor (#22) with a fair market value of $7,000. The old motor and $5,600 in cash were given for the new motor.

9 Motor #9, which had a cost of $5,500 and accumulated depreciation of $5,000, was traded in for a new motor (#23) with a fair market value of $6,500. The old motor and $6,200 in cash were given for the new motor.

REQUIRED

Prepare general journal entries for the transactions.

P 18-12A   (LO6)

✓ 1. Depletion exp. for year 1:
    $100,000

DEPLETION: CALCULATING AND JOURNALIZING Mineral Works Co. acquired a salt mine at a cost of $1,700,000, with no expected salvage value. The estimated number of units available for production from the mine is 3,400,000 tons.

(a) During the first year, 200,000 tons are mined and sold.
(b) During the second year, 600,000 tons are mined and sold.

REQUIRED

1. Calculate the amount of depletion expense for both years.

2. Prepare general journal entries for depletion expense.

P 18-13A   (LO7)

✓ 1. Patent amortization: $1,000

INTANGIBLE LONG-TERM ASSETS Track Town Co. had the following transactions involving intangible assets:

Jan.   1   Purchased a patent for leather soles for $10,000 and estimated its useful life to be 10 years.

Apr.   1   Purchased a copyright for a design for $15,000 with a life left on the copyright of 25 years. The estimated remaining (economic) life of the copyright is five years.

July   1   Signed a five-year franchise agreement and opened a Starting Line high-tech running shoe store. Paid $50,000 to the franchisor.

REQUIRED

1. Using the straight-line method, calculate the amortization of the patent, copyright, and franchise.

2. Prepare general journal entries to record the end-of-year amortizations.

SERIES B EXERCISES

E 18-1B   (LO1)

✓ Cost of asset: (a) $61,400
✓ (b) $41,900
✓ (c) $108,400

COST OF PROPERTY, PLANT, AND EQUIPMENT Lam Company purchased the following long-term assets. Determine the purchase cost of each asset.

(a) Ten computers:

Purchase price	$60,000
Transportation costs	500
Insurance during transportation	100
Installation	800
Interest on loan to purchase computers	3,000

(b) Three acres of land:

Purchase price	$30,000
Grading of land in preparation to build	10,000
Planting of trees around border	5,000
Fence on southern border	3,000
Tax assessment for sewer	1,000
Legal fees related to purchase	900

(*continued*)

(c) Five-thousand-square-foot building:

Purchase price	$102,000
Real estate fees	5,000
Land on which building is located	10,000
Legal fees related to purchase	600
Taxes related to purchase	800
Interest on mortgage to buy building	300

E 18-2B   (LO3)

✓ Year 1: SL: $3,600

✓ DDB: $7,600

✓ SYD: $6,000

STRAIGHT-LINE, DECLINING-BALANCE, AND SUM-OF-THE-YEARS'-DIGITS METHODS A light truck is purchased on January 1 at a cost of $19,000. It is expected to serve for five years and have a salvage value of $1,000. Calculate the depreciation expense for the first and third years of the truck's life using the following methods:

1. Straight-line
2. Double-declining-balance
3. Sum-of-the-years'-digits

E 18-3B   (LO3)

✓ Depr. exp. for year 1: $3,240

UNITS-OF-PRODUCTION METHOD The truck purchased in Exercise 18-2B is expected to be used for 100,000 miles over its five-year useful life. Using the units-of-production method, calculate the depreciation expense for the first and third years of use if the truck is driven 18,000 miles in year 1 and 22,000 miles in year 3.

E 18-4B   (LO4)

JOURNAL ENTRIES: REPAIRS, MAINTENANCE, ADDITIONS, IMPROVEMENTS, AND REPLACEMENTS Enter the following transactions for Larry's Lawn Service in a general journal:

1. Added a second mower deck to Tractor A for $550 cash to decrease mowing time.
2. Replaced the engine in Mower D for $200 cash. The replacement is expected to extend the life of the mower.
3. Lubricated engine of Tractor A for $25 cash (normal maintenance).

E 18-5B   (LO5)

✓ 1(a): Loss, $300

✓ 1(b): No gain/loss

✓ 1(c): Gain, $100

✓ 2(a): Gain, $2,500

✓ 2(b): Loss, $2,500

JOURNAL ENTRIES: DISPOSITION OF PLANT ASSETS Prepare the entries for the following transactions using a general journal:

1. Discarding an asset.
   (a) On January 4, shelving units, which had a cost of $7,200 and accumulated depreciation of $6,900, were discarded.
   (b) On June 15, a hand cart, which had a cost of $2,500 and accumulated depreciation of $2,250, was sold for $250.
   (c) On October 1, a copy machine, which had a cost of $5,200 and accumulated depreciation of $4,800, was sold for $500.
2. Exchange or trade-in of assets.
   (a) On December 31, a drill press, which had a cost of $50,000 and accumulated depreciation of $37,500, was traded in for a new drill press with a fair market value of $55,000. The old drill press and $40,000 in cash were given for the new drill press.
   (b) On December 31, the old drill press in (a) and $45,000 in cash were given for the new drill press.

E 18-6B (LO6)

✓ 1. Depletion Exp.: $77,000
✓ 2. Depletion Exp.: $300,000

DEPLETION Prepare the following entries using a general journal:

1. A coal mine was acquired at a cost of $1,750,000 and estimated to contain 2,500,000 tons of ore. No salvage value is expected. During the year, 110,000 tons were mined and sold. Prepare the journal entry for the year's depletion expense.

2. A silver mine was acquired at a cost of $2,000,000 and estimated to contain 500,000 tons of ore. No salvage value is expected. During the year, 75,000 tons were mined and sold. Prepare the journal entry for the year's depletion expense.

SERIES B PROBLEMS

P 18-7B (LO3)

✓ Depr. exp. for year 1:
✓ 1(a) $9,000.00
✓ 1(b) $19,250.00
✓ 1(c) $16,000.00
✓ 2 $11,003.30

STRAIGHT-LINE, DECLINING-BALANCE, SUM-OF-THE-YEARS'-DIGITS, AND MACRS METHODS A machine is purchased January 1 at a cost of $77,000. It is expected to serve for eight years and have a salvage value of $5,000.

REQUIRED

1. Prepare a schedule showing depreciation for each of the eight years and the book value at the end of each year using the following methods:

   (a) Straight-line
   (b) Double-declining-balance (round to two decimal places)
   (c) Sum-of-the-years'-digits (round to two decimal places)

2. Assuming a seven-year class of property, compute MACRS depreciation expense for each year of the asset's life.

P 18-8B (LO3)

✓ Depr. exp. for year 1: $9,000

UNITS-OF-PRODUCTION METHOD A machine is purchased January 1 at a cost of $58,000. It is expected to produce 110,000 units and have a salvage value of $3,000 at the end of its useful life.

Units produced are as follows:

Year 1	18,000
Year 2	16,000
Year 3	20,000
Year 4	16,000
Year 5	12,000

REQUIRED

Prepare a schedule showing depreciation for each year and the book value at the end of each year using the units-of-production method.

P 18-9B (LO3)

✓ Depr. exp.: $10,250

CALCULATING AND JOURNALIZING DEPRECIATION Equipment records for Byerly Construction Co. for the year follow. Byerly Construction uses the straight-line method of depreciation. In the case of assets acquired by the fifteenth day of the month, depreciation should be computed for the entire month. In the case of assets acquired after the fifteenth day of the month, no depreciation should be considered for the month in which the asset was acquired.

(continued)

Asset	Purchase Price	Useful Life	Salvage Value	Date Purchased
Truck #1	$22,000	7 years	$1,000	January 17
Truck #2	24,000	5	4,000	March 23
Molding #1	18,000	5	3,000	May 14
Molding #2	24,000	6	6,000	July 1
Forklift	35,000	8	3,000	September 19

REQUIRED

1. Calculate the depreciation expense for Byerly Construction as of December 31, 20--.

2. Prepare the entry for depreciation expense using a general journal.

P 18-10B (LO4)

✓ 1: Depr. exp. is $600 each
✓ 2: J–H A—Dr. Asset for $800
✓ 3: J–H A—$866.67 per year

IMPACT OF IMPROVEMENTS AND REPLACEMENTS ON THE CALCULATION OF DEPRECIATION On January 1, 20-1, Dan's Demolition purchased two jackhammers for $2,500 each with a salvage value of $100 each and estimated useful lives of four years. On January 1, 20-2, a stronger blade to improve performance was installed in Jackhammer A for $800 cash and the compressor was replaced in Jackhammer B for $200 cash. The compressor is expected to extend the life of Jackhammer B one year beyond the original estimate.

REQUIRED

1. Using the straight-line method, prepare general journal entries for depreciation on December 31, 20-1, for Jackhammers A and B.

2. Enter the transactions for January 20-2 in a general journal.

3. Assuming no other additions, improvements, or replacements, calculate the depreciation expense for each jackhammer for 20-2 through 20-4.

P 18-11B (LO5)

✓ Jan. 8, Loss: $200
✓ Feb. 1, Gain: $300

DISPOSITION OF ASSETS: JOURNALIZING Mayer Delivery Co. had the following plant asset transactions during the year:

1. Assets discarded or sold:

Jan. 1 Van #11, which had a cost of $8,800 and accumulated depreciation of $8,800, was discarded.

8 Van #7, which had a cost of $9,400 and accumulated depreciation of $9,000, was sold for $200.

14 Van #13, which had a cost of $7,600 and accumulated depreciation of $7,400, was sold for $250.

2. Assets exchanged or traded in:

Feb. 1 Van #8, which had a cost of $11,000 and accumulated depreciation of $8,800, was traded in for a new van (#20) with a fair market value of $13,000. The old van and $10,500 in cash were given for the new van.

9 Van #3, which had a cost of $7,500 and accumulated depreciation of $7,000, was traded in for a new van (#21) with a fair market value of $9,500. The old van and $9,200 in cash were given for the new van.

REQUIRED

Prepare general journal entries for the transactions.

P 18-12B   (LO6)

✓ 1. Depletion exp. for year 1: $160,000

DEPLETION: CALCULATING AND JOURNALIZING Mining Works Co. acquired a copper mine at a cost of $1,200,000, with no expected salvage value. The estimated number of units available for production from the mine is 3,000,000 tons.

(a) During the first year, 400,000 tons are mined and sold.

(b) During the second year, 700,000 tons are mined and sold.

REQUIRED

1. Calculate the amount of depletion expense for both years.

2. Prepare general journal entries for depletion expense.

P 18-13B   (LO7)

✓ 1. Patent amortization: $1,000

INTANGIBLE LONG-TERM ASSETS B. J. Bakery had the following transactions involving intangible assets:

Jan. 1   Purchased a patent for a new pastry for $10,000 and estimated its useful life to be 10 years.

Apr. 1   Purchased a copyright for a cookie cutter design for $5,000 with a life left on the copyright of 15 years. Estimated that the future remaining (economic) life of the copyright is five years.

July 1   Signed a five-year franchise agreement and opened a Raisabon Bakery. Paid $40,000 to the franchisor.

REQUIRED

1. Using the straight-line method, calculate the amortization of the patent, copyright, and franchise.

2. Prepare journal entries to record the end-of-year amortizations using a general journal.

CHECK LIST
☐ **Managing**
☐ **Planning**
☐ **Drafting**
☐ **Break**
☐ **Revising**
☐ **Managing**

MANAGING YOUR WRITING

A friend owns and operates her own business and is concerned about completing her tax return. She owns several assets purchased prior to September 27, 2017, and uses straight-line depreciation for business purposes. She intended to use straight-line depreciation for tax purposes also, but recently heard about another method called MACRS. She has asked for your advice on which method to use on her tax return. Write a brief memo recommending a depreciation method and explaining why you believe it should be used. Would your memo change if the assets (not buildings) were purchased after September 27, 2017?

ETHICS

ETHICS CASE

Creative Solutions purchased a patent from Russell Lazarus, an inventor. At the time of the purchase, the patent had two years remaining. The president of Creative Solutions decided to have the accountant amortize the cost of the patent, $200,000, over 10 years rather than two years. His reasoning was that the $200,000 has already been spent and stockholders might ask a lot of questions about a $100,000 expense showing up on the income statement but probably wouldn't pay much attention to a $20,000 expense.

(continued)

1. What is Creative Solutions' ethical responsibility to the company's stockholders?
2. According to GAAP, how should the amortization of patents be treated?
3. Write a short paragraph explaining similarities and differences between plant assets and intangible assets.
4. In groups of two or three, determine an appropriate method of depreciation, depletion, or amortization of the following assets for financial reporting purposes:

   (a) a car used as a taxi, (b) a parcel of land that will be resold in a few years, (c) a computer that has a very short life and loses most of its value in the first year or two, (d) an ore mine, and (e) research and development costs incurred to develop a trademark.

MASTERY PROBLEM

✓ 1(c). Loss on exchange: $4,750
✓ 2(c). Gain on exchange: $3,500

On April 1, 20-3, Kwik Kopy Printing purchased a copy machine for $50,000. The estimated life of the machine is five years, and it has an estimated salvage value of $5,000. The machine was used until July 1, 20-6.

REQUIRED

1. Assume that Kwik Kopy uses straight-line depreciation and prepare the following entries:
   (a) Adjusting entries for depreciation on December 31 of 20-3 through 20-5.
   (b) Adjusting entry for depreciation on June 30, 20-6, just prior to trading in the asset.
   (c) On July 1, 20-6, the copy machine was traded in for a new copy machine. The market value of the new machine is $38,000. Kwik Kopy must trade in the old copy machine and pay $22,000 for the new machine.
2. Assume that Kwik Kopy uses sum-of-the-years'-digits depreciation and prepare the following entries:
   (a) Adjusting entries for depreciation on December 31, 20-3 through 20-5.
   (b) Adjusting entry for depreciation on June 30, 20-6, just prior to trading in the asset.
   (c) On July 1, 20-6, the copy machine was traded in for a new copy machine. The market value of the new machine is $38,000. Kwik Kopy must trade in the old copy machine and pay $22,000 for the new machine.

CHALLENGE PROBLEM

This problem challenges you to apply your cumulative accounting knowledge to move a step beyond the material in the chapter.

✓ 4. Cumulative tax savings over eight years: $841.20

Don Burnette is starting a new home planning business. For years, people have asked Don to draw up the blueprints for their homes and he has done so in his spare time. Don has decided to go into business full time and believes that he will need to add one new draftsman each year for the next five years as his business grows. Don believes that the best way to design homes is by using home designing software on a computer. Thus, he plans to buy himself a new computer and a computer for each new associate who joins the company.

Don has heard that using MACRS for tax purposes will save him taxes and has asked you to develop a schedule illustrating the depreciation expense that would be recognized using straight-line depreciation for his income statement and

MACRS depreciation for his tax return over the next eight years under the following assumptions:

1. Don will start his business on July 1, 20-1, and will purchase a new computer on that date.
2. Don will hire four new associates, one on July 1 of each year for the next four years, 20-2 through 20-5. He will also buy each associate a computer.
3. The computers cost $4,000, have useful lives of five years, and have no salvage value. Don will take a half-year's depreciation in the first and last year of each computer's life when computing straight-line depreciation. He will use the MACRS rates, which also assume a half-year's depreciation in the first and last years of the asset's life.
4. As each computer completes its five-year life, Don will buy a new one to replace it.
5. Don's tax rate is 30%.

REQUIRED

1. Prepare a depreciation schedule showing the straight-line depreciation expense for years 20-1 through 20-8.
2. Prepare a depreciation schedule showing the MACRS depreciation for years 20-1 through 20-8. Use the MACRS rates shown below.

Depreciation Rates for Five-Year Assets
MACRS Depreciation

Year	MACRS
1	20.0%
2	32.0
3	19.2
4	11.5
5	11.5
6	5.8
	100.0%

3. Compute the difference between straight-line depreciation and MACRS depreciation for each year, 20-1 through 20-8.
4. The differences in part (3) represent the differences in Don's taxable income each year. By using MACRS, how much does Don save in taxes each year, and in total?
5. Under what conditions would Don lose the accumulated tax savings?

ANSWERS TO SELF-STUDY TEST QUESTIONS

True/False

1. F (land is not used up)

2. F (reverse is true)

3. F (depreciation is a method of cost allocation)

4. F (the opposite is true)

5. F (the units-of-production method is based on the usage or output of the asset)

Multiple Choice

1. d   **2.** c   **3.** b   **4.** b   **5.** c

Checkpoint Exercises

1.

Purchase price	$50,000
Transportation costs	800
Insurance during transportation	100
Total	$50,900

2.

Property, Plant, and Equipment: Building	$500,000	
Less accumulated depreciation, building	100,000	$400,000

3.

Double-Declining-Balance Method

Year	Beginning Book Value	Rate	Annual Depreciation	Accumulated Depreciation End of year	Book Value End of Year
1	$350,000	0.67	$234,500	$234,500	$115,500
2	115,500	0.67	77,385	311,885	38,115
3	38,115	0.67	23,115*	335,000	15,000

*$23,115 = $38,115 (book value at beginning of year) − $15,000 (salvage value)

Sum-of-the-Years'-Digits Method

Year	Depreciable Base	Rate	Annual Depreciation	Accumulated Depreciation End of year	Book Value End of Year
1	$335,000	3/6	$167,500	$167,500	$182,500
2	335,000	2/6	111,667	279,167	70,833
3	335,000	1/6	55,833	335,000	15,000

4.

Cost	$65,000
Salvage value	5,000
Depreciable base	$60,000

Depreciation during years 20-1 through 20-5:

$60,000/6-year life = $10,000 per year × 5 = $50,000 (See also T accounts below)

Truck		Accum. Depr.—Truck	
65,000		10,000	12/31/20-1
		10,000	12/31/20-2
		10,000	12/31/20-3
		10,000	12/31/20-4
		10,000	12/31/20-5
	1/1/20-6 8,000		
		42,000	Bal.

New Depreciable Base 1/1/20-6:

Cost	$65,000
Accumulated depreciation	42,000 (See T account)
Book value	$23,000
Less salvage value	5,000
New depreciable base	$18,000

$$\frac{\text{New Depreciable Base}}{\text{Remaining Expected Life}} = \text{Depreciation Expense per Year}$$

$$\frac{\$18,000}{3} = \$6,000 \quad \text{Per year for remaining three years}$$

The depreciation expense for 20-6 is $6,000.

5. a

1	Cash	2 5 0 0 00		1
2	Accumulated Depreciation—Machine	8 0 0 0 00		2
3	Machine		10 0 0 0 00	3
4	Gain on Sale of Machine		5 0 0 00	4
5	Sold machine			5

b

6	Machine (new)	12 0 0 0 00		6
7	Accumulated Depreciation—Machine	8 0 0 0 00		7
8	Machine (old)		10 0 0 0 00	8
9	Cash		9 5 0 0 00	9
10	Gain on Exchange of Machine		5 0 0 00	10
11	Purchased new machine			11

6.

Cost of mine	$4,000,000
Salvage value	250,000
Depletable cost	$3,750,000

$$\frac{\text{Depletable cost}}{\text{Estimated recoverable amount}} = \frac{\$3,750,000}{1,250,000 \text{ tons}} = \$3 \text{ depletion per ton}$$

Depletion for first year = 100,000 tons × $3 per ton = $300,000 depletion

7.

1	Patents	100 0 0 0 00		1
2	Cash		100 0 0 0 00	2
3	Purchased a patent			3
4				4
5	Adjusting Entry			5
6	Patents Amortization	10 0 0 0 00		6
7	Patents		10 0 0 0 00	7

Alwin C Ernst
1881–1948

Arthur Young
1863–1948

Chapter **19** Accounting for Partnerships

LEARNING OBJECTIVES

Careful study of this chapter should enable you to:

LO1 Describe the various types of partnerships, their characteristics, the partnership agreement, and the advantages and disadvantages of a partnership.

LO2 Prepare entries for the initial investments in a partnership.

LO3 Explain how partners are compensated and account for the allocation of net income.

LO4 Prepare financial statements reporting the allocation of net income and partnership equity.

LO5 Describe the actions that result in the dissolution of a partnership and account for the dissolution.

LO6 Describe how a partnership is liquidated and prepare associated entries and a statement of partnership liquidation.

Born in Cleveland, Ohio, Alwin C. Ernst worked as a bookkeeper after leaving school. In 1903, he and his brother, Theodore, started Ernst & Ernst, a small public accounting firm.

Born in Glasgow, Scotland, Arthur Young graduated in law but became interested in investments and banking. In 1890, he moved to the United States to pursue his career in accounting. In 1906, he and his brother, Stanley, formed an accounting firm, Arthur Young & Company.

Although A. C. Ernst and Arthur Young were contemporaries and died within days of each other, they never met. In 1989, their names were joined when the accounting partnerships they started combined to create Ernst & Young, one of the "Big Four" accounting firms.

Many service businesses, like accounting and law firms, use the partnership form of business. In this chapter, you will learn to account for the formation, operation, dissolution, and liquidation of partnerships.

When two or more individuals engage in an enterprise as co-owners, the organization is known as a **partnership**. This form of organization is common to practically all types of enterprises. However, it is more popular among personal service enterprises than among merchandising businesses. For example, the partnership form of organization is quite common in the legal and public accounting professions. In this chapter, the important features of and accounting procedures for partnerships will be discussed and illustrated.

LO1	Types of Partnerships and How They are Formed

Describe the various types of partnerships, their characteristics, the partnership agreement, and the advantages and disadvantages of a partnership.

The Uniform Partnership Act states that "a partnership is an association of two or more persons who carry on, as co-owners, a business for profit." Partnerships are formed for many reasons. Primarily, however, they are formed on the belief that individuals with complementary resources and abilities can operate more profitably together than as individuals.

In the United States, there are three primary forms of a partnership: general, limited, and limited liability partnerships. Although state laws vary, the basic characteristics of these forms of partnerships are provided below.

General Partnership (or simply a partnership)

- All partners are general partners who actively participate in the operation and management of the partnership.
- General partners are subject to unlimited personal liability for any legal actions and debts of the firm.

Limited Partnership (LP)

- A limited partnership must have at least one general partner with the rights and responsibilities of partners in a general partnership.
- A limited partnership also has limited partners. Limited partners do not participate in the management of the business. They provide capital and are paid a return on their investment, and their liability is limited to the amount of their investment.

Limited Liability Partnership (LLP)

- All partners may actively participate in the operation and management of the firm.
- In general, LLP partners are personally liable for their own actions and the actions of those they supervise. They are not, however, personally liable for inappropriate actions by others in the firm. The LLP is a popular form of ownership for accounting and law firms.

Characteristics of Partnerships

The characteristics of a partnership are different from those of the sole proprietorships we have accounted for in previous chapters. Some of the more important of these characteristics are listed as follows:

Co-Ownership of Assets

All assets held by a partnership are co-owned by all partners. If one partner contributes an asset to the business, the asset is jointly owned by all partners.

Mutual Agency

Any partner can bind the other partners to a contract if he or she is acting within the general scope of the business. Thus, if one partner signs a contract to purchase merchandise for the business, other partners are bound by that contract. On the other hand, if one partner contracts to buy a personal automobile, this is not part of normal business operations, and other partners would not be bound by it.

Limited Life

A partnership has a limited life. It may be dissolved as the result of any change in the ownership. These include death, bankruptcy, incapacity, withdrawal of a partner, addition of a new partner, or expiration of the time specified in the partnership agreement.

Unlimited Liability

In a general partnership, each partner is personally liable for all debts incurred by the partnership. If the partnership cannot pay a bill, creditors will expect payment from the personal assets of the partners. As discussed earlier, the liability can be limited for some or all of the partners by adopting other forms of a partnership.

Federal Income Taxes

Partnerships are not subject to federal income taxes. However, partnerships file federal income tax returns for informational purposes and to notify partners of the amount of partnership income that must be reported on their individual federal (and state if appropriate) income tax returns. Note that partners are taxed on their share of net income, not the amount withdrawn.

The Partnership Agreement

A written agreement containing the various provisions for operating a partnership is known as a partnership agreement. There is no standard form of partnership agreement, but the following provisions are essential:

1. Date of agreement
2. Names of the partners
3. Kind of business to be conducted
4. Length of time the partnership is to run
5. Name and location of the business
6. Investment of each partner
7. Basis on which profits or losses are to be shared by the partners
8. Limitation of partners' rights and activities
9. Salary allowances to partners
10. Division of assets upon dissolution of the partnership
11. Signatures of the partners

Figure 19-1 is an example of a partnership agreement.

LEARNING KEY 🔑

There must be a clear understanding of the key elements of the partnership: expectations for each partner, payments to partners, sharing of profits and losses, and dissolution of the partnership. The best way to do so is to put everything in writing.

FIGURE 19-1 Partnership Agreement

PARTNERSHIP AGREEMENT

THIS CONTRACT, made and entered into on the first day of January 20--, by and between Sam Mitchell of Indianapolis, Indiana, and Lisa Jenkins of the same city and state.

WITNESSETH: That the said parties have this day formed a partnership for the purpose of engaging in and conducting a wholesale and retail business in the city of Indianapolis under the following stipulations which are a part of this contract:

FIRST: The said partnership is to continue for a term of twenty-five years from January 1, 20--.

SECOND: The business is to be conducted under the firm name of Mitchell & Jenkins, at 2200 East Washington Street, Indianapolis, Indiana.

THIRD: The investments are as follows: Sam Mitchell, cash, $350,000; Lisa Jenkins, cash, $200,000. These invested assets are partnership property.

FOURTH: Each partner is to devote his/her entire time and attention to the business and to engage in no other business enterprise without the written consent of the other partner.

FIFTH: During the operation of the partnership, neither partner is to become surety or bonding agent for anyone without the written consent of the other partner.

SIXTH: Sam Mitchell is to receive a salary allowance of $36,000 a year, payable $1,500 in cash on the fifteenth day and last business day of each month. Lisa Jenkins is to receive a salary allowance of $48,000 a year, payable $2,000 in cash on the fifteenth day and last business day of each month. At the end of each annual fiscal period, the net income or the net loss shown by the income statement after the salaries of the two partners have been allowed is to be shared as follows: Sam Mitchell, 60 percent; Lisa Jenkins, 40 percent.

SEVENTH: Neither partner is to withdraw assets in excess of his/her salary, any part of the assets invested, or assets in anticipation of net income to be earned, without the written consent of the other partner.

EIGHTH: In the case of the death or the legal disability of either partner, the other partner is to continue the operations of the business until the close of the annual fiscal period on the following December 31. At that time, the continuing partner is to be given an option to buy the interest of the deceased or incapacitated partner at not more than 10 percent above the value of the deceased or incapacitated partner's proprietary interest as shown by the balance of his/her capital account after the books are closed on December 31. It is agreed that this purchase price is to be paid one-half in cash and the balance in four equal installments payable quarterly.

NINTH: At the conclusion of this contract, unless it is mutually agreed to continue the operation of the business under a new contract, the assets of the partnership, after the liabilities are paid, are to be divided in proportion to the net credit of each partner's capital account on that date.

IN WITNESS WHEREOF, the parties aforesaid have hereunto set their hands and affixed their seals on the day and year above written.

Sam Mitchell　　(Seal)
Sam Mitchell

Lisa Jenkins　　(Seal)
Lisa Jenkins

A BROADER VIEW

Partnerships: How Large Can They Go?

When we think of partnerships, we often picture small businesses with a few partners. This is often the case. However, some partnerships are quite large. Take PwC (formerly PricewaterhouseCoopers), an international accounting firm, as an example. This partnership has over 11,000 partners worldwide guiding the efforts of over 235,000 personnel in 743 locations across 158 countries. Worldwide revenues exceed $37 billion. This is not what you might call a "mom and pop" operation.

ASHOK SAXENA/ALAMY STOCK PHOTO

Advantages and Disadvantages

In comparison with the sole proprietorship, the partnership form of business offers certain advantages.

1. The ability and experience of the partners are combined in one enterprise.

2. More capital may be raised because the resources of the partners are combined.

3. Credit may be improved because each general partner is personally liable for partnership debts.

There also are some disadvantages of the partnership form of organization.

1. Unlimited liability is a major disadvantage of the general partnership form of ownership. This means that a partner could lose not only the amount invested, but also personal assets. Although this is also true for a sole proprietorship, it is not true for the corporate form of ownership, which will be introduced in Chapters 20 and 21. As discussed earlier, this disadvantage may be avoided for most partners by forming limited partnerships or limited liability partnerships.

2. Mutual agency can lead to serious problems if all partners do not act responsibly and consult each other before signing contracts. Yes, unwitting partners could be liable for swamp land purchased by another partner.

3. The interest of a partner in the partnership cannot be transferred without the consent of the other partners.

4. Termination of the partnership agreement, bankruptcy of the firm, death of one of the partners, or any change in partner membership dissolves the partnership.

LO2

Accounting for Initial Investments

Prepare entries for the initial investments in a partnership.

Accounting for the various forms of a partnership is similar to accounting for a sole proprietorship. The main difference is that separate capital and drawing accounts are maintained for each partner. Care should be used when preparing the opening entry and entering any transactions that affect the respective interests of the partners.

Cash Investments

A partnership may be formed by the investment of cash by the partners. In opening the books for a partnership, a separate journal entry is made for each partner's investment. The opening entries for Mitchell & Jenkins based on the partnership agreement shown in Figure 19-1 are as follows:

5	Cash		350 0 0 0 00		5
6	Sam Mitchell, Capital			350 0 0 0 00	6
7	S. Mitchell invested $350,000 in cash				7
8					8
9	Cash		200 0 0 0 00		9
10	Lisa Jenkins, Capital			200 0 0 0 00	10
11	L. Jenkins invested $200,000 in cash				11

Investment of Cash and Other Assets

When forming a partnership, market values are used to measure the investment of each partner. This is reasonable. Investing $1,000 in cash is equivalent to investing an asset that could be sold for $1,000.

A partnership may also be formed by the investment of cash and other assets by the partners. Certain liabilities also may be assumed by the partnership. Each partner's capital account should be credited for the difference between the market value of the assets invested and liabilities assumed.

Instead of investing $200,000 in cash, assume that Jenkins invested:

1 inventory valued at $47,500 on which $10,500 was owed,

2 office equipment valued at $40,000,

3 delivery equipment valued at $92,000, on which $19,000 was owed on a note, and

4 $50,000 in cash.

The following opening entry would be made:

5	Cash	4	50 0 0 0 00		5
6	Inventory	1	47 5 0 0 00		6
7	Office Equipment	2	40 0 0 0 00		7
8	Delivery Equipment	3	92 0 0 0 00		8
9	Notes Payable	3		19 0 0 0 00	9
10	Accounts Payable	1		10 5 0 0 00	10
11	Lisa Jenkins, Capital			200 0 0 0 00	11
12	L. Jenkins' investment in partnership				12

Partnerships Formed from Existing Businesses

Two or more sole proprietors may combine their businesses to form a partnership. Their respective balance sheets serve as the basis for the opening entries for the investments of such partners. For example, assume that on April 1, Donna Morning and Larry Knight form a partnership under the firm name of Morning & Knight

FIGURE 19-2 Balance Sheets for Morning Sports and Knight Athletics Prior to the Formation of the Partnership

Morning Sports **Balance Sheet** **March 31, 20--**					
Assets			Liabilities		
Cash		$ 6,344	Notes payable	$ 4,600	
Accounts receivable	$5,524		Accounts payable	9,082	
Less allowance for bad debts	430	5,094	Total liabilities		$13,682
Merchandise inventory		24,574			
Store equipment	$3,840		Owner's Equity		
Less accumulated depreciation	1,000	2,840	Donna Morning, capital		25,170
Total assets		$38,852	Total liabilities and owner's equity		$38,852

Knight Athletics **Balance Sheet** **March 31, 20--**					
Assets			Liabilities		
Cash		$ 3,544	Notes payable	$ 6,000	
Accounts receivable	$5,280		Accounts payable	13,238	
Less allowance for bad debts	720	4,560	Total liabilities		$19,238
Merchandise inventory		29,692			
Supplies		286			
Office equipment	$4,320				
Less accumulated depreciation	1,100	3,220			
Store equipment	$4,800		Owner's Equity		
Less accumulated depreciation	1,200	3,600	Larry Knight, capital		25,664
Total assets		$44,902	Total liabilities and owner's equity		$44,902

Sports. The balance sheets shown in Figure 19-2 are made a part of the partnership agreement. They agree to invest their assets and that the partnership will assume the liabilities shown in their respective balance sheets. Each partner's investment is measured by the difference between the assets invested and the liabilities assumed. The profits and losses are to be shared on a 50-50 basis. In case of dissolution, the assets are to be distributed between the partners in the ratio of their capital interests at the time of dissolution.

When two sole proprietors decide to combine their businesses, assets should be recorded at their fair market values as of the date of formation of the partnership. For Morning and Knight, any accounts receivable known to be uncollectible as of March 31, 20--, should be written off. None were considered uncollectible in this case. The balance in Accounts Receivable is debited, and the amount of the Allowance for Bad Debts is credited in the books of the partnership. In this way, the accounts receivable are entered at their approximate fair market value.

Both Morning and Knight had been using the first-in, first-out (FIFO) method of inventory costing. Recall that under FIFO, the most recently purchased inventory is considered to be on hand. Thus, the values shown for merchandise inventories on their respective balance sheets are close to their fair market values as of March 31, 20--. If Morning or Knight had been using some other inventory costing method, the merchandise inventory amounts might have required restatement to reflect fair market value.

The fair market value of Morning's store equipment as of March 31, 20--, is $3,600. This amount should be entered on the books of the new partnership rather than the book value of $2,840 shown on Morning's balance sheet in Figure 19-2. In like manner, the fair market values of Knight's office equipment and store equipment as of March 31, 20--, are $3,850 and $4,200, respectively. These amounts should be entered on the books of the new partnership, rather than the respective book values of $3,220 and $3,600 shown on Knight's balance sheet. Once again, the difference between assets invested and liabilities assumed is credited to each partner's capital account. The opening entries for Morning & Knight Sports are as follows:

GENERAL JOURNAL — PAGE 1

	DATE		DESCRIPTION	POST. REF.	DEBIT	CREDIT	
1	20-- Apr.	1	Cash		6 3 4 4 00		1
2			Accounts Receivable		5 5 2 4 00		2
3			Merchandise Inventory		24 5 7 4 00		3
4			Store Equipment		3 6 0 0 00		4
5			Allowance for Bad Debts			4 3 0 00	5
6			Notes Payable			4 6 0 0 00	6
7			Accounts Payable			9 0 8 2 00	7
8			Donna Morning, Capital			25 9 3 0 00	8
9			D. Morning's investment in partnership				9
10							10
11		1	Cash		3 5 4 4 00		11
12			Accounts Receivable		5 2 8 0 00		12
13			Merchandise Inventory		29 6 9 2 00		13
14			Supplies		2 8 6 00		14
15			Office Equipment		3 8 5 0 00		15
16			Store Equipment		4 2 0 0 00		16
17			Allowance for Bad Debts			7 2 0 00	17
18			Notes Payable			6 0 0 0 00	18
19			Accounts Payable			13 2 3 8 00	19
20			Larry Knight, Capital			26 8 9 4 00	20
21			L. Knight's investment in partnership				21

CHECKPOINT ✔
Complete Checkpoint-1 on page 757 to test your basic understanding of LO2.

LO3   Partner Compensation and the Allocation of Net Income

Explain how partners are compensated and account for the allocation of net income.

In the absence of any agreement between the partners, profits and losses must be shared equally regardless of the partners' investments. Generally, however, the basis on which reported profits and losses are shared is a matter of agreement between the partners. If both partners invest similar amounts of assets in the business and devote the same amount of time to the operation of the business, they may elect to allocate profits and losses equally. However, if the contributions to the success of the business are not similar, they may agree to allocate profits and losses based on each partner's contribution. For example, one partner may contribute most of the assets but render no services, while the other partner may contribute less in assets but devote full time to operating the business. In this case, the partners may agree to allocate the net income or loss based on salary and interest allowances. One partner would have a higher salary allowance to reflect the greater number of hours devoted to running the business. The other partner would have a higher interest allowance to reflect the larger financial investment in the partnership.

Partner compensation is reported on the income statement but is not used to compute net income. *Salary and interest are not listed on the income statement as expenses. Instead, these allowances indicate how net income is allocated to each partner's capital account.* The salary allowance is generally based on the services provided by each partner to the operations of the business. The interest allowance is based on the balance of each partner's capital account.

Withdrawals in a partnership are essentially the same as discussed earlier for a sole proprietorship. In a partnership, however, the agreement often sets limits on the amount a partner may withdraw. For example, the Mitchell & Jenkins partnership agreement limits withdrawals to the amount of the salary allowance. To make an additional withdrawal, the written consent of the other partner is required. These agreements vary across partnerships. Since partners must pay federal income taxes on their share of net income, many partnership agreements permit the withdrawal of a partner's entire share of net income.

Profits and Losses Shared Equally

If the Mitchell & Jenkins partnership agreement shown in Figure 19-1 did not specify how the partners would be compensated, the profits and losses would be shared equally. If net income for the year was $190,800, the allocation would be reported on the income statement as shown in Figure 19-3.

Let's assume Mitchell and Jenkins withdrew $36,000 and $48,000, respectively, during the year. Mitchell withdrew $36,000 cash. Jenkins withdrew $40,000 in cash and $8,000 in inventory, as is often done by partners. The entries to record the withdrawals are the same as they would be for a sole proprietorship.

FIGURE 19-3 Allocation of Profit and Loss (Equal Division)

	Mitchell & Jenkins Income Statement (Partial) For Year Ended December 31, 20--		
Net income			$190,800
	S. MITCHELL	L. JENKINS	TOTAL
Allocation of net income	$95,400	$95,400	$190,800

For Mitchell, we would make the following entry:

1		S. Mitchell, Drawing	36	0	0	0	00				1
2		Cash						36	0	0	0	00	2
3											3

We need to be a little more careful with the withdrawal by Jenkins because the entry depends on the inventory method used, as shown below.

Periodic inventory method								Perpetual inventory method								
1	L. Jenkins, Drawing	48	0	0	0	00		L. Jenkins, Drawing	48	0	0	0	00			1
2	Cash			40	0	0	0	00	Cash			40	0	0	0	00	2
3	Purchases			8	0	0	0	00	Merchandise Inventory			8	0	0	0	00	3
4																	4

Maintaining a record of each partner's share of net income and the amount of drawing each year requires a minor change in the way closing entries are made. Recall that four closing entries are made for sole proprietorships at the end of the accounting period. For a partnership, separate capital and drawing accounts are maintained for each partner. Thus, entries three and four must be changed as shown in Figure 19-4.

FIGURE 19-4 Closing Entries

CLOSING ENTRIES—SOLE PROPRIETOR	CLOSING ENTRIES—PARTNERSHIP
Entry 1. Close all revenues to Income Summary.	Entry 1. Close all revenues to Income Summary.
Entry 2. Close all expenses to Income Summary.	Entry 2. Close all expenses to Income Summary.
Entry 3. Close Income Summary to the owner's capital account.	Entry 3. Close Income Summary *by allocating each partner's share of net income or loss to the individual capital accounts.*
Entry 4. Close Drawing to the owner's capital account.	Entry 4. Close *each partner's drawing account to the individual capital accounts.*

Based on the income allocation shown in Figure 19-3, the third closing entry is as follows:

3rd Closing Entry →

4	Closing Entry											4
5	Income Summary	190	8	0	0	00						5
6	S. Mitchell, Capital						95	4	0	0	00	6
7	L. Jenkins, Capital						95	4	0	0	00	7

If Mitchell and Jenkins withdrew $36,000 and $48,000, the fourth closing entry would actually require two entries as shown below.

4th Closing Entries →

8	Closing Entries											8
9	S. Mitchell, Capital	36	0	0	0	00						9
10	S. Mitchell, Drawing						36	0	0	0	00	10
11												11
12	L. Jenkins, Capital	48	0	0	0	00						12
13	L. Jenkins, Drawing						48	0	0	0	00	13

The four closing entries for a partnership are summarized in T account form in Figure 19-5.

FIGURE 19-5 Closing Process for a Partnership

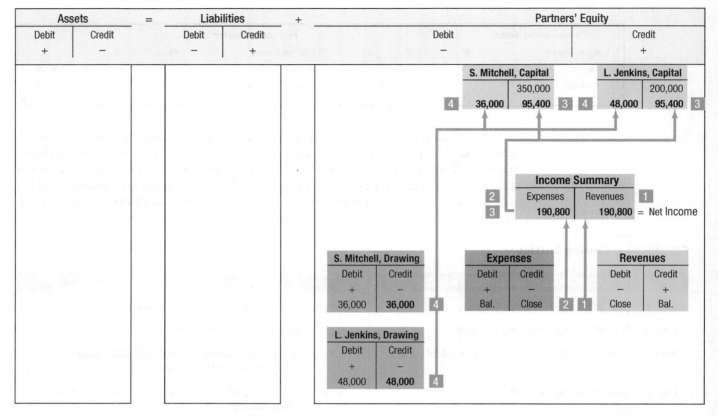

Allocation of Profits and Losses with Salary Allowances

Net Income Exceeds Salary Allowances

The partnership agreement in Figure 19-1 specifies that after providing for salary allowances of $36,000 for Mitchell and $48,000 for Jenkins, the remaining net income or loss is divided on a 60-40 basis. Recall that payments made to partners for salaries or other reasons are debited to the partners' drawing accounts. They are not considered an expense and are not included in the calculation of net income. Under these conditions, the allocation of net income would be reported on the income statement as shown in Figure 19-6.

Based on the net income allocation shown above, the closing entry is as follows:

4			Closing Entry											4
5	Dec.	31	Income Summary	190	8	0	0	00						5
6			S. Mitchell, Capital						100	0	8	0	00	6
7			L. Jenkins, Capital						90	7	2	0	00	7

3rd Closing Entry (points to rows 6–7)

Assuming that Mitchell and Jenkins withdrew their salaries as described in the partnership agreement, the balances in the drawing accounts at year-end would be $36,000 and $48,000, respectively. The drawing accounts would be closed to the partners' capital accounts at year-end in the same manner as illustrated earlier.

8			Closing Entries											8
9	Dec.	31	S. Mitchell, Capital	36	0	0	0	00						9
10			S. Mitchell, Drawing						36	0	0	0	00	10
11														11
12			L. Jenkins, Capital	48	0	0	0	00						12
13			L. Jenkins, Drawing						48	0	0	0	00	13

4th Closing Entries (points to rows 9–13)

FIGURE 19-6 Allocation of Profit and Loss when Net Income Exceeds Salary Allowances

If net income is greater than the salary allowances, the remaining income is allocated according to the ratio specified in the partnership agreement.

Net income		$190,800
Less salary allowances		(84,000)
Remaining income		$106,800
60% of $106,800	=	$64,080
40% of $106,800	=	$42,720

Mitchell & Jenkins
Income Statement (Partial)
For Year Ended December 31, 20--

	S. MITCHELL	L. JENKINS	TOTAL
Net income			$190,800
Allocation of net income:			
Salary allowances	$ 36,000	$48,000	$ 84,000
Remaining income	64,080	42,720	106,800
Allocation of net income	$100,080	$90,720	$190,800

Net Income Is Less than Salary Allowances

If the salary allowances are greater than net income, the earnings shortfall or deficiency is allocated to the partners according to the ratio specified in the partnership agreement. If net income for Mitchell and Jenkins is $44,000, the allocation is made as shown in Figure 19-7.

Think of the excess of salary allowances over net income as an economic loss to the partnership. Although net income of $44,000 is reported, the partnership did not generate enough revenues to cover expenses **and** the partners' salary allowances. This loss ($40,000) is allocated per the profit/loss sharing ratio to determine the proper allocation of the reported net income.

Note that the debits to the capital accounts ($30,000 + $40,000 = $70,000) exceed the credits ($12,000 + $32,000 = $44,000). Thus, the partners' capital accounts are decreasing. This is consistent with the concept of an earnings shortfall.

FIGURE 19-7 Allocation of Profit and Loss when Net Income is Less than Salary Allowances

Net income		$ 44,000
Less salary allowances		(84,000)
Earnings shortfall		$(40,000)
60% of ($40,000)	=	$(24,000)
40% of ($40,000)	=	$(16,000)

Mitchell & Jenkins
Income Statement (Partial)
For Year Ended December 31, 20--

	S. MITCHELL	L. JENKINS	TOTAL
Net income			$ 44,000
Allocation of net income:			
Salary allowances	$36,000	$48,000	$ 84,000
Earnings shortfall	(24,000)	(16,000)	(40,000)
Allocation of net income	$12,000	$ 32,000	$ 44,000

Given the lower profits of the partnership, let's assume in this case that Mitchell and Jenkins withdrew only $30,000 and $40,000, respectively, during this period. Based on the net income allocation in Figure 19-7, the closing entries are as follows:

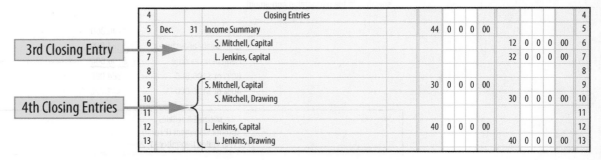

Allocation of Profits and Losses with Salary and Interest Allowances

Net Income Exceeds Allowances

Partners may agree that the best method of allocating profits and losses is to base salaries on the services rendered by each partner and to provide interest on capital investments. The remainder is then shared equally, or according to a predefined ratio. Assume that B. K. Kelly and S. B. Arthur form a partnership on January 1 of the current year. Kelly will devote full time to operating the business, invest $50,000, and draw a salary of $35,000 per year. Arthur will devote about 10 hours per week, invest $150,000, and draw a salary of $10,000 per year. The partners will be allowed interest of 10% *on capital balances on January 1 of each year* and the balance of earnings will be divided equally. Net income of $80,000 in the first year of operation would be allocated as reported in Figure 19-8.

> Remember: These allocations are simply a method of assigning net income/loss to the partners' capital accounts. There are no cash flows here. Withdrawals by the partners are generally defined in the partnership agreement and are debited to the partners' drawing accounts.

FIGURE 19-8 Allocation of Profit and Loss when Net Income Exceeds Salary and Interest Allowances

Salary allowances:	Kelly:		$ 35,000	
	Arthur:		10,000	$45,000
Interest allowances:	Kelly:	$50,000 × 10% =	$ 5,000	
	Arthur:	$150,000 × 10% =	15,000	20,000
				$65,000
Salary and interest allowances:				
Net income			$ 80,000	
Less salary and interest allowances			(65,000)	
Remaining income			$ 15,000	

$15,000 ÷ 2 = $7,500 allocated to each partner

Kelly and Arthur
Income Statement (Partial)
For Year Ended December 31, 20--

	B. K. KELLY	S. B. ARTHUR	TOTAL
Net income			$80,000
Allocation of net income:			
Salary allowances	$35,000	$10,000	$45,000
Interest allowances	5,000	15,000	20,000
Remaining income	7,500	7,500	15,000
Allocation of net income	$47,500	$32,500	$80,000

Based on the net income allocation shown in Figure 19-8, the closing entry is as follows:

			Closing Entry												
4			Closing Entry												4
5	Dec.	31	Income Summary		80	0	0	0	00						5
6			B. K. Kelly, Capital							47	5	0	0	00	6
7			S. B. Arthur, Capital							32	5	0	0	00	7

3rd Closing Entry →

Net Income Is Less than Total Allowances

If Kelly and Arthur incurred a net loss of $20,000 in year 1, the allocation would be made as shown in Figure 19-9.

FIGURE 19-9 Allocation of Net Loss with Salary and Interest Allowances

> Note that subtracting the allowances from a net loss makes the earnings shortfall larger.

Net Loss	$(20,000)
Less salary and interest allowances	(65,000)
Earnings shortfall	$(85,000)

($85,000) ÷ 2 = ($42,500) allocated to each partner

Kelly and Arthur
Income Statement (Partial)
For Year Ended December 31, 20--

	B. K. KELLY	S. B. ARTHUR	TOTAL
Net loss			$ (20,000)
Allocation of net loss:			
Salary allowances	$ 35,000	$ 10,000	$ 45,000
Interest allowances	5,000	15,000	20,000
Earnings shortfall	(42,500)	(42,500)	(85,000)
Allocation of net loss	$ (2,500)	$(17,500)	$ (20,000)

> **CHECKPOINT ✔**
> Complete Checkpoint-2 on page 757 to test your basic understanding of LO3.

The following closing entry would be made to allocate the loss of $20,000:

			Closing Entry												
4			Closing Entry												4
5	Dec.	31	B. K. Kelly, Capital		2	5	0	0	00						5
6			S. B. Arthur, Capital		17	5	0	0	00						6
7			Income Summary							20	0	0	0	00	7

3rd Closing Entry →

LO4   ## Statements for Partnerships

Prepare financial statements reporting the allocation of net income and partnership equity.

The allocation of net income and its impact on the partners' capital balances should be disclosed in the financial statements. All three financial statements are affected: the income statement, statement of partners' (owners') equity, and balance sheet. As illustrated in the preceding section, the allocation is often reported in the lower portion of the income statement. In addition, the statement of partners' equity reflects the equity of each partner and summarizes the allocation of net income for the year.

Recall that the capital balances for Kelly and Arthur on January 1, 20--, were $50,000 and $150,000, respectively. Let's assume that Arthur invested an additional

$10,000, net income was $80,000 and allocated as reported in Figure 19-8. Further, let's assume the partners withdrew only the salary portion of their compensation ($35,000 and $10,000, respectively) during the first year of operation. As shown in Figure 19-10, the statement of partners' equity reports this information and the income allocations reported on the income statement.

FIGURE 19-10 Statement of Partners' Equity

<table>
<tr><td colspan="4">Kelly and Arthur
Statement of Partners' Equity
For Year Ended December 31, 20--</td></tr>
<tr><td></td><td>B. K. KELLY</td><td>S. B. ARTHUR</td><td>TOTAL</td></tr>
<tr><td>Capital, January 1, 20--</td><td>$50,000</td><td>$150,000</td><td>$200,000</td></tr>
<tr><td>Additional investments during the year</td><td>———</td><td>10,000</td><td>10,000</td></tr>
<tr><td></td><td>$50,000</td><td>$160,000</td><td>$210,000</td></tr>
<tr><td>Net income for the year (see Figure 19-8)</td><td>47,500</td><td>32,500</td><td>80,000</td></tr>
<tr><td></td><td>$97,500</td><td>$192,500</td><td>$290,000</td></tr>
<tr><td>Withdrawals</td><td>35,000</td><td>10,000</td><td>45,000</td></tr>
<tr><td>Capital, December 31, 20--</td><td>$62,500</td><td>$182,500</td><td>$245,000</td></tr>
</table>

Interest allowances for next year would be computed as follows:
Kelly: $62,500 × 10% = $6,250
Arthur: $182,500 × 10% = $18,250
The additional investment is reported in the same manner as for a sole proprietorship.

Finally, the partners' equity section of the balance sheet reports the equity of each partner. This is illustrated as follows:

<table>
<tr><td colspan="3">Kelly and Arthur
Balance Sheet (Partial)
December 31, 20--</td></tr>
<tr><td colspan="3">Partners' Equity</td></tr>
<tr><td>B. K. Kelly, capital</td><td>$ 62,500</td><td></td></tr>
<tr><td>S. B. Arthur, capital</td><td>182,500</td><td></td></tr>
<tr><td>Total partners' equity</td><td></td><td>$245,000</td></tr>
</table>

CHECKPOINT ✔

Complete Checkpoint-3 on page 757 to test your basic understanding of LO4.

LO5   Dissolution of a Partnership

Describe the actions that result in the dissolution of a partnership and account for the dissolution.

LEARNING KEY 🔑

The partnership is dissolved if there is any change in the members of the partnership.

One of the primary characteristics of the partnership form of organization is its limited life. Any change in the members of the partnership results in dissolution. Dissolution of a partnership may occur because of the addition of a new partner, the death or withdrawal of one of the partners, or bankruptcy.

Dissolution of the partnership does not necessarily imply that business operations will halt. It simply means that the partnership is dissolved. The business may continue with a new group of partners, or a different form of ownership. Any time the original partnership agreement is altered, a new partnership agreement must be prepared to replace the original agreement.

Admitting a New Partner

A new partner may be admitted by agreement among the existing partners. When this happens, the old partnership is dissolved and a new one is created. A new partner may buy into the business in three ways: (1) by purchasing an interest directly from existing partners, (2) by making a cash investment in the partnership, or (3) by contributing assets and liabilities from an existing business.

Purchasing an Interest Directly from Existing Partners

Assume that Morning and Knight admit Sunny Noon as a new partner as of July 1, 20--, when Morning and Knight have capital interests of $30,000 and $20,000, respectively. Noon pays $12,000 to Morning for one-third of her interest and $12,000 to Knight for one-half of his interest. These cash payments go to the partners directly, not to the business. Thus, the following entry is made by the partnership:

	20--														
1	July	1	Donna Morning, Capital		10	0	0	0	00*						1
2			Larry Knight, Capital		10	0	0	0	00**						2
3			Sunny Noon, Capital							20	0	0	0	00	3
4			S. Noon admitted to partnership												4
5			*$30,000 × 1/3 = $10,000												5
6			**$20,000 × 1/2 = $10,000												6

The extra $2,000 ($12,000 − $10,000) paid to both Morning and Knight represents profit to them, but it has no effect on the *partnership's* financial statements. Total capital for the partnership remains at $50,000. Noon holds a 40% interest ($20,000/$50,000).

Making a Cash Investment in the Partnership

Now, assume instead that Noon invested $25,000 cash in the new partnership. Total capital in the partnership increases to $75,000 and Noon is granted a 33% interest ($25,000/$75,000). In this case, the following entry would be made to admit Noon:

	20--														
1	July	1	Cash		25	0	0	0	00						1
2			Sunny Noon, Capital							25	0	0	0	00	2
3			S. Noon admitted to partnership												3
4															4

In some cases, a new partner agrees to pay a bonus to the existing partners. This might be done because the book value of the partnership's net assets (assets − liabilities) is understated relative to market value. Or, the partnership may have unrecognized goodwill. If Noon agrees to pay $30,000 for a $25,000 capital interest in the partnership, the $5,000 bonus is treated like profit. Thus, it is allocated to the original partners based on their profit and loss sharing agreement. If we assume Morning and Knight agreed to share profits and losses equally, the following entry would be made to admit Noon:

	20--														
1	July	1	Cash		30	0	0	0	00						1
2			Sunny Noon, Capital							25	0	0	0	00	2
3			Donna Morning, Capital							2	5	0	0	00*	3
4			Larry Knight, Capital							2	5	0	0	00*	4
5			S. Noon admitted to partnership												5
6			*$5,000 × 1/2 = $2,500												6
7															7

Alternatively, Noon may have skills and expertise urgently needed by the partnership. In this case the original partners may grant a bonus to Noon to encourage her to join the partnership. This bonus would be treated as a loss to the original partners and shared equally according to their profit and loss sharing agreement. If we assume Noon agrees to pay $20,000 for a $25,000 capital interest in the partnership, the following entry would be made to admit Noon:

	20--														
1	July	1	Cash		20	0	0	0	00						1
2			Donna Morning, Capital			2	5	0	0	00*					2
3			Larry Knight, Capital			2	5	0	0	00*					3
4			Sunny Noon, Capital								25	0	0	0	00	4
5			S. Noon admitted to partnership													5
6			*$5,000 × 1/2 = $2,500													6
7																7

Contributing Assets and Liabilities from an Existing Business

Finally, let's assume that Noon had been operating her own business, which was then taken over by the new partnership. In this case, the balance sheet for Sunny Noon's Golf, shown in Figure 19-11, would serve as a basis for preparing the opening entry. The assets listed in the balance sheet are taken over, the liabilities are assumed, and a capital account for Noon is established.

FIGURE 19-11 Balance Sheet for Sunny Noon's Golf

Sunny Noon's Golf Balance Sheet June 30, 20--				
Assets			**Liabilities**	
Cash		$ 5,000	Notes payable	$9,048
Accounts receivable	$14,290		Accounts payable	7,550
Less allowance for bad debts	1,078	13,212	Total liabilities	$16,598
Merchandise inventory		27,290	**Owner's Equity**	
			Sunny Noon, capital	28,904
Total assets		$45,502	Total liabilities and owner's equity	$45,502

> All contributed assets should be recorded at market value when admitting a new partner.

Noon has no knowledge of any uncollectible accounts receivable as of June 30, 20--. If she did, the receivables would need to be written off. Also, she has been using the FIFO method of inventory costing. Thus, the amounts reported on the balance sheet are reasonable approximations of market values. If we assume no bonus is to be granted to the original partners, or to Noon, the entry to admit Noon as a partner would be as follows:

	20--														
1	July	1	Cash		5	0	0	0	00						1
2			Accounts Receivable		14	2	9	0	00						2
3			Merchandise Inventory		27	2	9	0	00						3
4			Allowance for Bad Debts							1	0	7	8	00	4
5			Notes Payable							9	0	4	8	00	5
6			Accounts Payable							7	5	5	0	00	6
7			Sunny Noon, Capital							28	9	0	4	00	7
8			S. Noon admitted to partnership													8
9																9

As discussed earlier, if a bonus is paid by Noon, the credit to her capital account would be reduced by the amount of the bonus and it would be shared equally, according to their profit and loss sharing agreement, by crediting the original partners' capital accounts. If Noon received a bonus, the credit to her capital account would be increased by the amount of the bonus and it would be shared equally by debiting the other original owners' capital accounts.

Withdrawal of Partner

By agreement, a partner may retire and be permitted to withdraw assets equal to, less than, or greater than the amount of his or her interest in the partnership. The book value of a partner's interest is shown by the credit balance of the partner's capital account. The balance is computed after all profits or losses have been allocated in accordance with the partnership agreement and the books closed. If a retiring partner withdraws cash or other assets equal to the credit balance of his or her capital account, the transaction will have no effect on the capital of the remaining partners.

To illustrate, assume that several years after the formation of Morning, Noon, and Knight Sports, Sunny Noon decided to retire. The partners agreed to the withdrawal of cash equal to the amount of Noon's equity in the assets of the partnership. After bringing all accounts up to date, assume that the partners' capital accounts had credit balances as follows:

Donna Morning	$55,000
Sunny Noon	40,000
Larry Knight	45,000

If Noon withdraws $40,000 in cash, the entry on the books of the partnership is as follows:

12		Sunny Noon, Capital	40	0	0	0	00						12
13		Cash						40	0	0	0	00	13
14		S. Noon retired, withdrawing											14
15		$40,000 in equity settlement											15

Note that this transaction decreases cash and decreases the total capital of the partnership, but it does not affect the equity of the remaining partners. Morning still has an equity of $55,000 and Knight an equity of $45,000 in the partnership assets.

If a retiring partner agrees to withdraw less than the amount in his or her capital account, the transaction will increase the capital accounts of the remaining partners. For example, if Noon withdraws only $30,000 in settlement of the interest, the entry in the books of the partnership is as follows:

12		Sunny Noon, Capital	40	0	0	0	00						12
13		Cash						30	0	0	0	00	13
14		Donna Morning, Capital							5	0	0	00	14
15		Larry Knight, Capital							4	5	0	0	00	15
16		S. Noon retired, withdrawing											16
17		$30,000 in equity settlement											17

The difference between Noon's equity in the assets of the partnership and the amount of cash withdrawn is $10,000 ($40,000 − $30,000). This difference is divided between the remaining partners on the basis stated in the partnership agreement. In this case, it is divided according to the ratio of their capital interests after allocating net income and closing their drawing accounts. On this basis, Morning's capital account is credited for $5,500 and Knight's is credited for $4,500. The calculations are as follows:

Remaining Equity in Partnership

Morning	$ 55,000
Knight	45,000
Total	$100,000

Allocation to Morning: ($55,000 ÷ $100,000) × $10,000 = $5,500
Allocation to Knight: ($45,000 ÷ $100,000) × $10,000 = $4,500

If a retiring partner withdraws more than the amount in his or her capital account, the transaction will decrease the capital accounts of the remaining partners. Thus, if Morning and Knight allow Noon to withdraw $45,000 in settlement of Noon's interest, the entry in the books of the partnership is as follows:

12	Sunny Noon, Capital	40	0	0	0	00						12
13	Donna Morning, Capital	2	7	5	0	00						13
14	Larry Knight, Capital	2	2	5	0	00						14
15	Cash						45	0	0	0	00	15
16	S. Noon retired, withdrawing											16
17	$45,000 in equity settlement											17

The excess of the amount of cash withdrawn over Noon's equity in the partnership ($5,000) is divided between the remaining partners on the basis stated in the partnership agreement. Thus, Donna Morning, Capital is debited for $2,750 ($55,000/$100,000 × $5,000), while Larry Knight, Capital is debited for $2,250 ($45,000/$100,000 × $5,000).

When a partner retires from the business, the partner's interest may be purchased directly by one or more of the remaining partners or by an outside party. If the retiring partner's interest is sold to one of the remaining partners, the retiring partner's equity is merely transferred to the other partner. For example, assume that Noon's equity is sold to Morning. The entry for the transaction on the books of the partnership is as follows:

12	Sunny Noon, Capital	40	0	0	0	00						12
13	Donna Morning, Capital						40	0	0	0	00	13
14	D. Morning purchased S. Noon's											14
15	interest in partnership											15

The amount paid to Noon by Morning is a personal transaction and has no effect on the above entry. Any gain or loss resulting from the transaction is a personal gain or loss of the withdrawing partner and not of the business. Thus, whatever amount is involved, the credit in Noon's account is transferred to Morning's account.

Death of a Partner

The death of a partner dissolves the partnership. On the date of death, the accounts are closed and the net income for the year to date is allocated to the partners' capital accounts. Most agreements call for an audit and revaluation of the assets at this time. The balance of the deceased partner's capital account is then transferred to a liability account with the deceased's estate. The surviving partners may continue the business or liquidate. If the business continues, the procedures for settling with the estate are the same as those described earlier for the withdrawal of a partner. Liquidation procedures are described in the following section.

CHECKPOINT ✔

Complete Checkpoint-4 on page 758 to test your basic understanding of LO5.

LO6

Liquidation of a Partnership

Describe how a partnership is liquidated and prepare associated entries and a statement of partnership liquidation.

When normal operations are discontinued in preparation for liquidation, adjusting and closing entries are made in the same manner as done at the end of each year. Thus, only the assets, liabilities, and partners' equity accounts remain open. Liquidation of a partnership is generally completed in four basic steps:

STEP 1 The assets are sold.

STEP 2 Gains and losses are allocated to the partners.

STEP 3 Liabilities are paid.

STEP 4 The remaining cash or other assets are distributed to the partners.

As the assets are sold, the cash realized is applied first to the claims of creditors. Once all liabilities are paid, the remaining cash and other assets are distributed to the partners according to their ownership interests as indicated by their capital accounts.

To illustrate, assume that after several years of operations, the partnership of Morning, Noon, and Knight Sports is to be liquidated. After making closing entries on May 31, 20--, the following accounts remain open. For simplicity, "Other Assets" and "Liabilities" are used as account titles. In actual practice, several asset, contra-asset, and liability accounts would be involved.

LEARNING KEY 🔑

When a partnership is liquidated, the assets are sold, liabilities are paid, and the remaining cash or other assets are distributed to the partners.

	Account Balance	
Account Title	Debit	Credit
Cash	$ 10,000	
Inventory	120,000	
Other Assets	220,000	
Liabilities		$ 80,000
Donna Morning, Capital		95,000
Larry Knight, Capital		120,000
Sunny Noon, Capital		55,000

Using these account balances, accounting for the liquidation of the partnership is illustrated in Figure 19-12. For convenience, let's assume that all assets are sold in one transaction on June 1, 20--, and all liabilities are paid at once on June 15, 20--. On June 18, cash settlements are made with the partners who share equally in all profits and losses.

Gain on Sale of Assets

Assume that the noncash assets are sold for $370,000. Since these assets have a book value of $340,000, a gain of $30,000 on the sale is recognized. The gain is allocated to the partners' capital accounts according to the profit-and-loss sharing ratio. In this case, the gain is shared equally. Next, the liabilities are paid and the remaining cash is distributed to the partners according to their capital account balances. A statement of partnership liquidation summarizing these transactions is provided in Figure 19-12.

FIGURE 19-12 Statement of Partnership Liquidation Reporting a Gain on Sale of Assets

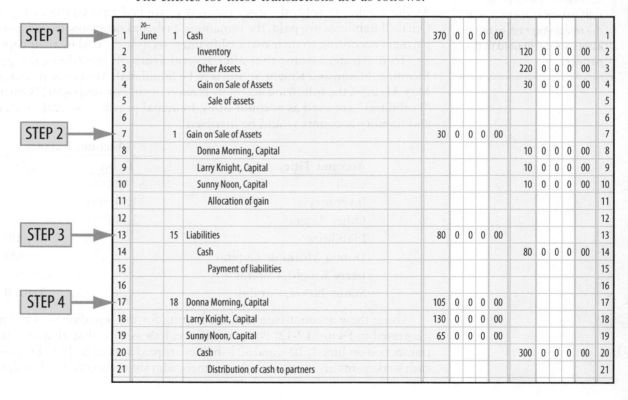

Morning, Noon, and Knight Sports
Statement of Partnership Liquidation
For Period June 1–18, 20--

	CASH	INVENTORY	OTHER ASSETS	LIABILITIES	CAPITAL D. MORNING	L. KNIGHT	S. NOON
Balance before sale of assets	$ 10,000	$120,000	$ 220,000	$ 80,000	$ 95,000	$ 120,000	$ 55,000
Sale of noncash assets and allocation of gain	370,000	(120,000)	(220,000)		10,000	10,000	10,000
Balance after sale	$ 380,000	0	0	$ 80,000	$ 105,000	$ 130,000	$ 65,000
Payment of liabilities	(80,000)			(80,000)			
Balance after payment of liabilities	$ 300,000	0	0	0	$ 105,000	$ 130,000	$ 65,000
Distribution of cash to partners	(300,000)				(105,000)	(130,000)	(65,000)
Final balance	0	0	0	0	0	0	0

STEPS 1 & 2
STEP 3
STEP 4

The entries for these transactions are as follows:

STEP 1

	20--														
1	June	1	Cash	370	0	0	0	00							1
2			Inventory						120	0	0	0	00	2
3			Other Assets						220	0	0	0	00	3
4			Gain on Sale of Assets						30	0	0	0	00	4
5			Sale of assets											5
6														6
7		1	Gain on Sale of Assets	30	0	0	0	00							7
8			Donna Morning, Capital						10	0	0	0	00	8
9			Larry Knight, Capital						10	0	0	0	00	9
10			Sunny Noon, Capital						10	0	0	0	00	10
11			Allocation of gain											11
12														12
13		15	Liabilities	80	0	0	0	00							13
14			Cash						80	0	0	0	00	14
15			Payment of liabilities											15
16														16
17		18	Donna Morning, Capital	105	0	0	0	00							17
18			Larry Knight, Capital	130	0	0	0	00							18
19			Sunny Noon, Capital	65	0	0	0	00							19
20			Cash						300	0	0	0	00	20
21			Distribution of cash to partners											21

STEP 2
STEP 3
STEP 4

Loss on Sale of Assets

Using the same information for Morning, Noon, and Knight as given on page 747, assume that the noncash assets are sold for $295,000, resulting in a loss of $45,000.

A statement of partnership liquidation reflecting the equal allocation of the loss on the sale of assets, payment of the liabilities, and distribution of the cash to the partners is illustrated in Figure 19-13.

FIGURE 19-13 Statement of Partnership Liquidation Reporting a Loss on Sale of Assets

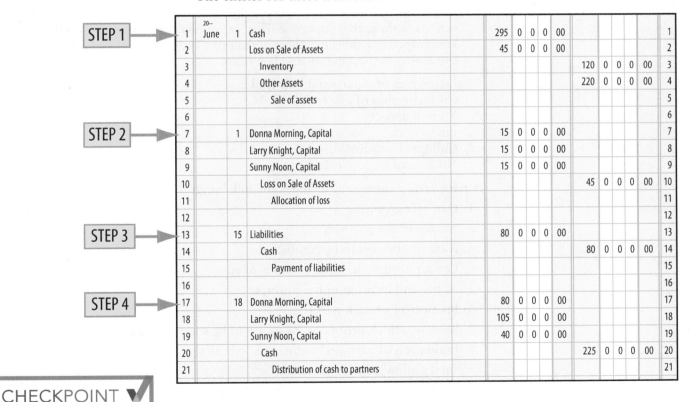

	CASH	INVENTORY	OTHER ASSETS	LIABILITIES	CAPITAL D. MORNING	CAPITAL L. KNIGHT	CAPITAL S. NOON
STEPS 1 & 2 → Balance before sale of assets	$ 10,000	$120,000	$220,000	$ 80,000	$ 95,000	$ 120,000	$ 55,000
Sale of noncash assets and allocation of loss	295,000	(120,000)	(220,000)		(15,000)	(15,000)	(15,000)
Balance after sale	$305,000	0	0	$ 80,000	$ 80,000	$ 105,000	$ 40,000
STEP 3 → Payment of liabilities	(80,000)			(80,000)			
Balance after payment of liabilities	$225,000	0	0	0	$ 80,000	$ 105,000	$ 40,000
STEP 4 → Distribution of cash to partners	(225,000)				(80,000)	(105,000)	(40,000)
Final balance	0	0	0	0	0	0	0

Morning, Noon, and Knight Sports
Statement of Partnership Liquidation
For Period June 1–18, 20--

The entries for these transactions are as follows:

STEP 1 → 1	20-- June	1	Cash	295 0 0 0 00				1
2			Loss on Sale of Assets	45 0 0 0 00				2
3			Inventory		120 0 0 0 00			3
4			Other Assets		220 0 0 0 00			4
5			Sale of assets					5
6								6
STEP 2 → 7		1	Donna Morning, Capital	15 0 0 0 00				7
8			Larry Knight, Capital	15 0 0 0 00				8
9			Sunny Noon, Capital	15 0 0 0 00				9
10			Loss on Sale of Assets		45 0 0 0 00			10
11			Allocation of loss					11
12								12
STEP 3 → 13		15	Liabilities	80 0 0 0 00				13
14			Cash		80 0 0 0 00			14
15			Payment of liabilities					15
16								16
STEP 4 → 17		18	Donna Morning, Capital	80 0 0 0 00				17
18			Larry Knight, Capital	105 0 0 0 00				18
19			Sunny Noon, Capital	40 0 0 0 00				19
20			Cash		225 0 0 0 00			20
21			Distribution of cash to partners					21

CHECKPOINT ✔

Complete Checkpoint-5 on page 758 to test your basic understanding of LO6.

LEARNING OBJECTIVES	**Key Points to Remember**

LO1   **Describe the various types of partnerships, their characteristics, the partnership agreement, and the advantages and disadvantages of a partnership.**

The partnership form of business includes the following three types:

General Partnership (or simply a partnership)

- All partners actively participate in the operation and management of the partnership.
- All partners are "general" partners and are subject to unlimited personal liability for any legal actions and debts of the firm.

Limited Partnership (LP)

- A limited partnership must have at least one general partner with the rights and responsibilities of partners in a general partnership.
- A limited partnership also has "limited" partners. Limited partners do not participate in the management of the business. They provide capital and are paid a return on their investment, and their liability is limited to the amount of their investment.

Limited Liability Partnership (LLP)

- All partners may actively participate in the operation and management of the firm.
- In general, LLP partners are personally liable for their own actions and the actions of those they supervise. They are not, however, personally liable for inappropriate actions by others in the firm. The LLP is a popular form of ownership for accounting and law firms.

Characteristics of a partnership include:
    Co-ownership of assets
    Mutual agency
    Limited life
    Unlimited liability
    No federal income taxes

A partnership agreement includes the following:

1. Date of agreement
2. Names of the partners
3. Kind of business to be conducted
4. Length of time the partnership is to run
5. Name and location of the business
6. Investment of each partner
7. Basis on which profits or losses are to be shared by the partners
8. Limitation of partners' rights and activities
9. Salary allowances to partners
10. Division of assets upon dissolution of the partnership
11. Signatures of the partners

| LEARNING OBJECTIVES | Key Points to Remember |

LO1 (concluded)

Advantages:
Combined experience of partners
Increased ability to raise capital
Improved credit standing

Disadvantages:
Unlimited liability of general partners
Mutual agency
Difficulty transferring the interests of partners to others
Various events can cause the partnership to be dissolved

LO2 Prepare entries for the initial investments in a partnership.

The proper accounting for the formation of a partnership depends on the type of investment made by each partner. Cash investments are recorded by recognizing the cash and an equal amount of partnership capital as follows:

5		Cash		50	0	0	0	00						5
6		Katherine Meisenheimer, Capital							50	0	0	0	00	6
7		K. Meisenheimer invested												7
8		$50,000 in cash												8

If a partner invests cash and other assets, the assets are entered at their market values. The partner's capital account is credited for the sum of the cash and the market value of assets contributed as follows:

5		Cash	10	0	0	0	00						5
6		Inventory (market value)	20	0	0	0	00						6
7		Office Equipment (market value)	8	0	0	0	00						7
8		Delivery Equipment (market value)	15	0	0	0	00						8
9		Sara Bates, Capital						53	0	0	0	00	9
10		S. Bates' investment in											10
11		partnership											11

If existing sole proprietorships are combined, the balance sheets of the proprietorships are used to prepare the entry for the formation of the partnership. Each partner's investment is measured by the difference between the market value of the assets invested and the liabilities assumed by the partnership as shown below. Before transferring receivables to the partnership, any known uncollectible accounts must be written off by the proprietorship.

1		Cash	5	0	0	0	00						1
2		Accounts Receivable	20	0	0	0	00						2
3		Merchandise Inventory (market value)	50	0	0	0	00						3
4		Store Equipment (market value)	30	0	0	0	00						4
5		Allowance for Bad Debts							2	0	0	00	5
6		Notes Payable						10	0	0	0	00	6
7		Accounts Payable						12	0	0	0	00	7
8		Alex Von Rosenberger, Capital						82	8	0	0	00	8
9		A. Von Rosenberger's investment											9
10		in partnership											10

(continued)

LEARNING OBJECTIVES	**Key Points to Remember**

LO3 Explain how partners are compensated and account for the allocation of net income.

Partner compensation may be based on salary and interest allowances as well as an allocation of remaining profits as stated in the partnership agreement.

LO4 Prepare financial statements reporting the allocation of net income and partnership equity.

Partnership financial statements report the allocation of net income and partnership equity as shown in the statements below.

Kelly and Arthur
Income Statement (Partial)
For Year Ended December 31, 20--

	B. K. KELLY	S. B. ARTHUR	TOTAL
Net income			$80,000
Allocation of net income:			
Salary allowances	$35,000	$10,000	$45,000
Interest allowances	5,000	15,000	20,000
Remaining income	7,500	7,500	15,000
	$47,500	$32,500	$80,000

Kelly and Arthur
Statement of Partners' Equity
For Year Ended December 31, 20--

	B. K. KELLY	S. B. ARTHUR	TOTAL
Capital, January 1, 20--	$50,000	$150,000	$200,000
Additional investments during the year	——	10,000	10,000
	$50,000	$160,000	$210,000
Net income for the year	47,500	32,500	80,000
	$97,500	$192,500	$290,000
Withdrawals (salaries during the year)	35,000	10,000	45,000
Capital, December 31, 20--	$62,500	$182,500	$245,000

Kelly and Arthur
Balance Sheet (Partial)
December 31, 20--

Partners' Equity		
B. K. Kelly, capital	$ 62,500	
S. B. Arthur, capital	182,500	
Total partners' equity		$245,000

LEARNING OBJECTIVES	Key Points to Remember
LO5 Describe the actions that result in the dissolution of a partnership and account for the dissolution.	Any change in the members of the partnership results in its dissolution. Accounting for the dissolution varies depending on whether a new partner is admitted or a partner withdraws, and whether an additional investment is made in the partnership or payments are made directly to existing partners.
LO6 Describe how a partnership is liquidated and prepare associated entries and a statement of partnership liquidation.	The steps in the liquidation process are as follows: 1. Assets are sold. 2. Gains or losses are allocated to the partners. 3. Liabilities are paid. 4. Remaining cash and other assets are distributed to the partners according to their capital accounts.

DEMONSTRATION PROBLEM

Molly Young, Gary Hurst, and Rob Carey are partners in Gulf Horizons Law. They share profits and losses in a 50-30-20 ratio. The partnership agreement calls for annual salaries of $120,000, $105,000, and $90,000, respectively, and interest of 12% on their January 1 capital balances.* Any remaining net income (or net loss) is to be divided in accordance with the ratios used for sharing profits and losses.

The partners' capital balances as of January 1, 20-1, were Young, $360,000; Hurst, $225,000; and Carey, $150,000. No additional investments were made during the year. The net income of the partnership for the year 20-1 was $480,000. Partners' withdrawals for the year were Young, $150,000; Hurst, $120,000; and Carey, $105,000.

On March 4, 20-2, the partners decide to liquidate their law firm. On that date, the firm has a cash balance of $138,000, noncash assets of $822,000, and liabilities of $120,000. No additional investments or withdrawals were made in 20-2. Between March 5 and March 31, the noncash assets are sold for $870,000, the gain is divided according to the profit and loss sharing ratio, and the liabilities are paid. The remaining cash is then distributed to the partners.

*Salaries and interest are not recognized as expenses in the determination of net income.

REQUIRED

1. Prepare the lower portion of the income statement of Gulf Horizons Law for the year ended December 31, 20-1, showing the division of the partnership net income for the year.

2. Prepare the general journal entry to close Income Summary to the partners' capital accounts as of December 31, 20-1.

3. Prepare a statement of partners' equity for Gulf Horizons Law for the year ended December 31, 20-1.

4. Prepare a statement of partnership liquidation for Gulf Horizons Law for the period March 5 through March 31, 20-2.

5. Prepare the general journal entries as of March 31, 20-2, for:

   (a) The sale of the noncash assets of the partnership

   (b) The division of any loss or gain on the sale of assets

   (c) The payment of partnership liabilities

   (d) The distribution of remaining cash to the partners

SOLUTION 1.

Gulf Horizons Law
Income Statement (Partial)
For Year Ended December 31, 20 -1

	M. YOUNG	G. HURST	R. CAREY	TOTAL
Net income				$480,000
Allocation of net income:				
Salary allowances	$120,000	$105,000	$ 90,000	$315,000
Interest allowances	43,200	27,000	18,000	88,200
Remaining income	38,400	23,040	15,360	76,800
	$201,600	$155,040	$123,360	$480,000

SOLUTION 2.

4						4
5	Dec.	31	Income Summary	480 0 0 0 00		5
6			Molly Young, Capital		201 6 0 0 00	6
7			Gary Hurst, Capital		155 0 4 0 00	7
8			Rob Carey, Capital		123 3 6 0 00	8
9						9

SOLUTION 3.

Gulf Horizons Law
Statement of Partners' Equity
For Year Ended December 31, 20 -1

	M. YOUNG	G. HURST	R. CAREY	TOTAL
Capital, January 1, 20-1	$360,000	$225,000	$150,000	$ 735,000
Net income for the year	201,600	155,040	123,360	480,000
	$561,600	$380,040	$273,360	$1,215,000
Withdrawals	150,000	120,000	105,000	375,000
Capital, December 31, 20-1	$411,600	$260,040	$168,360	$ 840,000

SOLUTION 4.

Gulf Horizons Law
Statement of Partnership Liquidation
For Period March 5–31, 20 -2

	CASH	NONCASH ASSETS	LIABILITIES	CAPITAL M. YOUNG	CAPITAL G. HURST	CAPITAL R. CAREY
Balance before sale of assets	$ 138,000	$ 822,000	$ 120,000	$ 411,600	$ 260,040	$ 168,360
Sale of noncash assets and allocation of gain	870,000	(822,000)		24,000	14,400	9,600
Balance after sale	$ 1,008,000	0	$ 120,000	$ 435,600	$ 274,440	$ 177,960
Payment of liabilities	(120,000)		(120,000)			
Balance after payment of liabilities	$ 888,000	0	0	$ 435,600	$ 274,440	$ 177,960
Distribution of cash to partners	(888,000)			(435,600)	(274,440)	(177,960)
Final balance	0	0	0	0	0	0

SOLUTION 5.

GENERAL JOURNAL   PAGE 1

	DATE		DESCRIPTION	POST. REF.	DEBIT	CREDIT	
	20- 2						
a. 1	Mar.	31	Cash		870 0 0 0 00		1
2			Noncash Assets			822 0 0 0 00	2
3			Gain on Sale of Assets			48 0 0 0 00	3
4			Sale of assets				4
b. 5							5
6		31	Gain on Sale of Assets		48 0 0 0 00		6
7			Molly Young, Capital			24 0 0 0 00	7
8			Gary Hurst, Capital			14 4 0 0 00	8
9			Rob Carey, Capital			9 6 0 0 00	9
10			Allocation of gain				10
c. 11							11
12		31	Liabilities		120 0 0 0 00		12
13			Cash			120 0 0 0 00	13
14			Payment of liabilities				14
d. 15							15
16		31	Molly Young, Capital		435 6 0 0 00		16
17			Gary Hurst, Capital		274 4 4 0 00		17
18			Rob Carey, Capital		177 9 6 0 00		18
19			Cash			888 0 0 0 00	19
20			Distribution of cash to partners				20

KEY TERMS

dissolution (742)   Dissolving of the partnership resulting from any change in the members of the partnership.

general partners (729)   A partner who participates in the management of the business and is personally responsible for any legal actions and debts of the firm.

general partnership (729)   A partnership made up of general partners who actively participate in the management of the business and are personally liable for all debts of the partnership.

interest allowance (736)   An allocation of partnership net income based on the balance of each partner's capital account.

limited liability partnership (LLP) (729)   A partnership in which all partners may actively participate in the management of the firm, but whose personal liability is limited to their own actions and the actions of those they supervise.

limited partners (729)   A partner who does not participate in the management of the business and whose liability is limited to the amount invested.

limited partnership (LP) (729)   A partnership with at least one general partner and limited partners.

liquidation (747)   The process of selling the assets, paying the liabilities, and distributing the remaining cash or other assets to the partners.

mutual agency (730)   One partner can bind other partners to a contract if he or she is acting within the general scope of the business.

partnership (729)   The form of organization in which two or more individuals engage in an enterprise as co-owners.

partnership agreement (730)   A written agreement containing the various provisions for operating a partnership.

salary allowance (736)   An allocation of partnership net income based on the services provided by each partner to the operations of the business.

unlimited liability (730)   The concept that a general partner's personal assets may be claimed by a creditor to satisfy partnership debts.

SELF-STUDY TEST QUESTIONS

True/False

1. **LO1**   When two or more individuals engage in an enterprise as co-owners, the organization is known as a proprietorship.

2. **LO1**   Mutual agency is a characteristic of a partnership in which any partner can bind the other partners to a contract if he/she is acting within the general scope of the business.

3. **LO1**   Limited life is a characteristic of a partnership in which each partner is personally liable for all debts incurred by the partners.

4. **LO1**   One advantage of a partnership is that the interest of a partner cannot be transferred without the consent of the other partners.

5. **LO2**   When two or more sole proprietors form a partnership, their respective balance sheets serve as the basis for the opening entries for the investments of such partners.

Multiple Choice

1. **LO1**   The basis on which profits and losses are to be shared among partners is
   (a) a matter of agreement among the partners.
   (b) the same as their withdrawal ratio.

(c) the same as their investment ratio.

(d) always equal among all partners.

2. **LO1**   In the absence of any agreement among partners, profits and losses must be shared

(a) equally among all partners.

(b) on the basis of their withdrawals.

(c) on the basis of their investment ratio.

(d) in accordance with the Uniform Partnership Act.

3. **LO3**   If the partnership agreement specifies how profits are to be shared but does not specify how losses are to be shared, the losses must be shared

(a) equally among all partners.

(b) on the basis of their withdrawals.

(c) on the basis of their investment ratio.

(d) none of the above.

4. **LO5**   After closing the temporary owner's equity accounts into Income Summary and after allocating the net income and closing the partners' drawing accounts, assume the partners' capital accounts had credit balances as follows: Abbott, $20,000; Barnes, $30,000; Costello, $45,000.

   If Abbott retired and withdrew $25,000 in settlement of her equity, the debit to her capital account would be in the amount of

(a) $25,000.   (c) $20,000.

(b) $55,000.   (d) $45,000.

5. **LO5**   After closing the temporary owner's equity accounts into Income Summary and after allocating the net income and closing the partners' drawing accounts, assume the partners' capital accounts had credit balances as follows: Abbott, $20,000; Barnes, $30,000; Costello, $45,000. The difference between the withdrawing partner's equity and amount of cash withdrawn is divided according to the ratio of the remaining partners' capital interests.

   If Costello retired and withdrew $40,000 in settlement of his equity, the amount entered in Abbott's capital account would be a

(a) $2,000 credit.   (c) $3,000 credit.

(b) $2,000 debit.   (d) $3,000 debit.

CHECKPOINT

Checkpoint Exercises

1. **LO2**   On January 1, 20-1, Paul Dimmitt and Mike Stiglitz decided to form The Bogey Men, a partnership to offer golf instruction and equipment to beginning golfers. They promise to have you shooting bogey golf by next Thursday. Prepare the journal entry for the investment of $100,000 by each partner.

2. **LO3**   Dimmitt and Stiglitz are to receive salary allowances of $40,000 and $50,000, respectively. The remaining income is to be divided on a 60-40 basis. Net income for the year ended December 31, 20-1, was $200,000. Determine the amount of net income allocated to each partner.

3. **LO4**   Using the information in Checkpoint-2, prepare the lower portion of the income statement showing the allocation of net income between Dimmitt and Stiglitz.

4. **LO5**   On January 1, 20-5, the capital balances of Dimmitt and Stiglitz are $200,000 and $250,000, respectively. On that date, James Mantz paid Stiglitz $60,000 for one-fifth of Stiglitz's capital interest in The Bogey Men. In addition, Jack Sacks contributed $50,000 to the business for a $50,000 capital interest. Prepare journal entries for the transactions admitting Mantz and Sacks to the partnership.

5. **LO6**   On December 31, 20-8, the partners decided to liquidate The Bogey Men. The balance sheet reported the following information:

	Account Balance	
Account Title	Debit	Credit
Cash	$500,000	
Inventory	400,000	
Paul Dimmitt, Capital		$400,000
James Mantz, Capital		300,000
Jack Sacks, Capital		100,000
Mike Stiglitz, Capital		100,000

From January 1 through 18, 20-9, partners sold off the inventory for $600,000 and then distributed the cash in proportion to their capital balances. At this time, the partners' shares in profits and losses are as follows:

Dimmitt	30%
Mantz	30%
Sacks	20%
Stiglitz	20%

Prepare the journal entries to record the sale of inventory for $600,000 and the allocation of the gain or loss.

The answers to the Self-Study Test Questions are at the end of the chapter (pages 770–771).

APPLYING YOUR KNOWLEDGE

REVIEW QUESTIONS

LO1   1.   Identify 11 essential provisions of a partnership agreement.

LO1   2.   Identify three advantages of a partnership as compared with a sole proprietorship.

LO1   3.   Identify four disadvantages of a partnership form of business organization.

LO2   4.   When two sole proprietors decide to combine their businesses, at what values should the noncash assets be taken over by the partnership?

LO3   5.   In the absence of any agreement between the partners, how must profits and losses be shared? If the partnership agreement specifies how profits are to be shared, but there is no agreement as to how losses are to be shared, what must be true with respect to losses?

LO3   6.   What factors generally are considered in determining the allocation of profits and losses?

LO5   7.   Identify three ways in which a partnership may be dissolved.

LO5   8.   When a new partner who has been the sole owner of a business is admitted to a partnership by having the partnership take over the old business, what usually serves as the basis for preparing the opening entry?

LO6   9.   Describe the four accounting entries for the liquidation of a partnership.

SERIES A EXERCISES

E 19-1A   (LO2)

PARTNERSHIP OPENING ENTRIES Patty McShane and Betty Lou Blixt agreed on September 1 to go into business as partners. According to the agreement, McShane is to contribute $55,000 cash and Blixt is to contribute $80,000 cash. Provide a separate journal entry for the investment of each partner.

E 19-2A   (LO3)
✓ 4. Wilson: $29,375

ENTRIES FOR ALLOCATION OF NET INCOME Danny Spurlock and Tracy Wilson decided to form a partnership on July 1, 20-1. Spurlock invested $100,000 and Wilson invested $25,000. For the fiscal year ended June 30, 20-2, a net income of $80,000 was earned. Determine the amount of net income that Spurlock and Wilson would receive under each of the following independent assumptions:

1. There is no agreement concerning the distribution of net income.
2. Each partner is to receive 10% interest on their original investment. The remaining net income is to be divided equally.
3. Spurlock and Wilson are to receive a salary allowance of $35,000 and $25,000, respectively. The remaining net income is to be divided equally.
4. Each partner is to receive 10% interest on their original investment. Spurlock and Wilson are to receive a salary allowance of $35,000 and $25,000, respectively. The remaining net income is to be divided as follows: Spurlock, 75% and Wilson, 25%.

E 19-3A   (LO3/4)
✓ 1. Allocation of net income: Kluge, $75,000
✓ 2. Capital: Kluge, $210,000

PARTIAL FINANCIAL STATEMENTS Ronica Kluge and Sam Edwards formed a partnership on May 1, 20-1. Kluge contributed $120,000 and Edwards contributed $50,000. During the year, Kluge contributed an additional $30,000. The partnership agreement states that Kluge is to receive $35,000 and Edwards is to receive $65,000 as a salary allowance. Any remaining net income is to be divided as follows: Kluge, 40% and Edwards, 60%. The partnership earned net income of $200,000 for the fiscal year ending April 30, 20-2. During the first year of operation, Kluge and Edwards withdrew $15,000 and $20,000, respectively.

1. Prepare the lower portion of the income statement showing the allocation of net income between Kluge and Edwards for the fiscal year ended April 30, 20-2.
2. Prepare a statement of partners' equity showing each individual partner's equity for the fiscal year ended April 30, 20-2.

E 19-4A   (LO5)

✓ 2. Ending capital bal.: Bowman, $80,000; Emery, $45,000

ADMITTING NEW PARTNERS Jeff Bowman and Kristi Emery, who have ending capital balances of $100,000 and $60,000, respectively, agree to admit two new partners to their business on August 18, 20--. Dan Bridges will buy one-fifth of Bowman's capital interest for $30,000 and one-fourth of Emery's capital interest for $20,000. Payments will be made directly to the partners. Anna Terrell will invest $50,000 in the business, for which she will receive a $50,000 capital interest.

1. Prepare general journal entries showing the transactions admitting Bridges and Terrell to the partnership.
2. Calculate the ending capital balances of all four partners after the transactions.

E 19-5A   (LO6)

✓ Gain: $50,000

ENTRIES: PARTNERSHIP LIQUIDATION On liquidation of the partnership of J. Hui and K. Cline, as of November 1, 20--, inventory with a book value of $180,000 is sold for $230,000. Given that Hui and Cline share profits and losses equally, prepare the entries for the sale and the allocation of gain.

SERIES A PROBLEMS

P 19-6A   (LO2)

✓ Cr. to Woodworth, Capital: $29,010

PARTNERSHIP OPENING ENTRIES On July 1, 20--, Susan Woodworth and Barbara Holly combined their two businesses to form a partnership under the firm name of Woodworth and Holly. The balance sheets of the two sole proprietorships are shown below and on the next page.

The balance sheets reflect fair market values except for the following:

(a) The fair market value of Woodworth's store equipment is $7,500.

(b) The fair market values of Holly's office equipment and store equipment are $6,100 and $6,800, respectively.

REQUIRED

Prepare the opening entry for the formation of the Woodworth and Holly partnership as of July 1, 20--, using fair market values. The difference between assets invested and liabilities assumed should be credited to each partner's capital account. Neither partner has knowledge of any uncollectible accounts receivable.

		Woodworth's Antiques Balance Sheet June 30, 20--			
Assets			Liabilities		
Cash		$ 7,100	Notes payable	$2,500	
Accounts receivable	$4,500		Accounts payable	8,400	
Less allowance for bad debts	620	3,880	Total liabilities		$10,900
Merchandise inventory		21,430			
Store equipment	$8,200		Owner's Equity		
Less accumulated depreciation	1,300	6,900	Susan Woodworth, capital		28,410
Total assets		$39,310	Total liabilities and owner's equity		$39,310

		Holly's Unfinished Furniture			
		Balance Sheet			
		June 30, 20--			
Assets			**Liabilities**		
Cash		$ 4,520	Notes payable	$8,000	
Accounts receivable	$3,275		Accounts payable	6,300	
Less allowance for bad debts	475	2,800	Total liabilities		$14,300
Merchandise inventory		28,190			
Supplies		960			
Office equipment	$7,400				
Less accumulated depreciation	1,800	5,600			
Store equipment	$7,700		**Owner's Equity**		
Less accumulated depreciation	1,500	6,200	Barbara Holly, capital		33,970
Total assets		$48,270	Total liabilities and owner's equity		$48,270

P 19-7A   (LO4)

✓ 1. Allocation of net income:
   Robo, $81,750
✓ 2. Capital: Robo, $66,250

PREPARING PARTIAL FINANCIAL STATEMENTS AND CLOSING ENTRIES The partnership of Robo and Swing, CPAs, reported revenues of $215,000 and expenses of $80,000 on their year-end work sheet. Their capital balances as of January 1, 20--, were $55,000 for I. Robo and $45,000 for B. Swing. No additional investments were made during the year. As stated in their partnership agreement, after withdrawing salary allowances of $65,000 for Robo and $35,000 for Swing, the partners each withdrew their full 10% interest allowances on their January 1 capital balances. No additional withdrawals were made. Any remaining net income is to be divided on a 45–55 basis.

REQUIRED

1. Prepare the lower portion of the income statement of the partnership for the year ended December 31, 20--, showing the division of the partnership net income for the year.

2. Prepare a statement of partners' equity for the year ended December 31, 20--, and the partners' equity section of the balance sheet on that date.

3. Prepare closing entries for the partnership as of December 31, 20--. (For simplicity, use the account titles "Revenues" for all revenues and "Expenses" for all expenses.)

P 19-8A   (LO5)

✓ 1. Cr. to Mike Kelly, Capital: $5,000
✓ 2. Dr. to Mike Kelly, Capital: $7,500

ENTRIES FOR DISSOLUTION OF PARTNERSHIP The Kelly and Kelly Wrecking Company, a partnership, operates a general demolition business. Ownership of the company is divided among the partners, Mike Kelly, Kim Kelly, Larry Dennis, and Jim Wheeles. Profits and losses are shared equally. The books are kept on a calendar-year basis.

On September 15, after the business had been in operation for several years, Dennis passed away. Mrs. Dennis wished to sell her husband's interest in the partnership for $25,000. After the books were closed, the partners' capital accounts had credit balances as follows:

Mike Kelly	$50,000
Kim Kelly	25,000
Larry Dennis	35,000
Jim Wheeles	25,000

(continued)

REQUIRED

1. Prepare the general journal entry required to enter the check issued to Mrs. Dennis in payment of her deceased husband's interest in the partnership. According to the partnership agreement, the difference between the amount paid to Mrs. Dennis and the book value of Larry Dennis's capital account is allocated to the remaining partners based on their ending capital account balances.

2. Assume instead that Mrs. Dennis is paid $50,000 for the book value of Larry Dennis's capital account. Prepare the necessary journal entry.

3. Assume instead that Jim Wheeles (with the consent of the remaining partners) purchased Dennis's interest for $40,000 and gave Mrs. Dennis a personal check for that amount. Prepare the general journal entry for the partnership only.

P 19-9A **(LO6)**

✓ 1. Distribution of cash to partners: Baldwin, $55,000

STATEMENT OF PARTNERSHIP LIQUIDATION WITH GAIN After several years of operations, the partnership of Baldwin, Cowan, and Stewart is to be liquidated. After making closing entries on June 30, 20--, the following accounts remain open:

	Account Balance	
Account Title	Debit	Credit
Cash	$ 5,000	
Inventory	55,000	
Other Assets	180,000	
Liabilities		$40,000
R. J. Baldwin, Capital		50,000
N. R. Cowan, Capital		90,000
K. M. Stewart, Capital		60,000

The noncash assets are sold for $250,000. Profits and losses are shared equally.

REQUIRED

1. Prepare a statement of partnership liquidation for the period July 1–20, 20--, showing the following:
   (a) The sale of noncash assets on July 1
   (b) The allocation of any gain or loss to the partners on July 1
   (c) The payment of the liabilities on July 15
   (d) The distribution of cash to the partners on July 20
2. Journalize these four transactions in a general journal.

P 19-10A **(LO6)**

✓ 1. Distribution of cash to partners: Nelson, $30,000

STATEMENT OF PARTNERSHIP LIQUIDATION WITH LOSS After several years of operations, the partnership of Nelson, Pope, and Williams is to be liquidated. After making closing entries on March 31, 20--, the following accounts remain open:

	Account Balance	
Account Title	Debit	Credit
Cash	$ 15,000	
Inventory	40,000	
Other Assets	220,000	
Liabilities		$ 75,000
C. W. Nelson, Capital		40,000
J. R. Pope, Capital		60,000
M. L. Williams, Capital		100,000

The noncash assets are sold for $230,000. Profits and losses are shared equally.

REQUIRED

1. Prepare a statement of partnership liquidation for the period April 1–15, 20--, showing the following:

   (a) The sale of the noncash assets on April 1

   (b) The allocation of any gain or loss to the partners on April 1

   (c) The payment of the liabilities on April 12

   (d) The distribution of cash to the partners on April 15

2. Journalize these four transactions in a general journal.

SERIES B EXERCISES

E 19-1B   (LO2)

PARTNERSHIP OPENING ENTRIES Sharon Usher and Leann Gomez agreed on September 1 to go into business as partners. According to the agreement, Usher is to contribute $30,000 cash and Gomez is to contribute $50,000 cash. Provide a separate journal entry for the investment of each partner.

E 19-2B   (LO3)
✓ 4. Clark: $35,500

ENTRIES FOR ALLOCATION OF NET INCOME John Clark and David Haase decided to form a partnership on July 1, 20-6. Clark invested $60,000 and Haase invested $40,000. For the fiscal year ended June 30, 20-7, a net income of $80,000 was earned. Determine the amount of net income that Clark and Haase would receive under each of the following independent assumptions:

1. There is no agreement concerning the distribution of net income.

2. Each partner is to receive 10% interest on their original investment. The remaining net income is to be divided equally.

3. Clark and Haase are to receive a salary allowance of $25,000 and $30,000, respectively. The remaining net income is to be divided equally.

4. Each partner is to receive 10% interest on their original investment. Clark and Haase are to receive a salary allowance of $25,000 and $30,000, respectively. The remaining net income is to be divided as follows: Clark, 30% and Haase, 70%.

E 19-3B   (LO4)
✓ 1. Allocation of net income:
     Nolan, $33,000
✓ 2 Capital: Nolan, $78,000

PARTIAL FINANCIAL STATEMENTS Randy Nolan and Jill Brenton formed a partnership on May 1, 20-1. Nolan contributed $50,000 and Brenton contributed $25,000. During the year, Nolan contributed an additional $10,000. The partnership agreement states that Nolan is to receive $15,000 and Brenton is to receive $50,000 as a salary allowance. Any remaining net income is to be divided as follows: Nolan, 40% and Brenton, 60%. The partnership earned net income of $110,000 for the fiscal year ending April 30, 20-2. During the first year of operation, Nolan and Brenton withdrew $15,000 and $40,000, respectively.

1. Prepare the lower portion of the income statement showing the allocation of net income between Nolan and Brenton for the fiscal year ended April 30, 20-2.

2. Prepare a statement of partners' equity, showing each individual partner's equity for the fiscal year ended April 30, 20-2.

E 19-4B (LO5)
✓ 2. Capital bal.: Rhodes, $60,000;
✓ Blair, $32,000

ADMITTING NEW PARTNERS Maria Rhodes and Craig Blair, who have ending capital balances of $90,000 and $40,000, respectively, agree to admit two new partners to their business on September 1, 20--. Lori Kinder will buy one-third of Rhodes's capital interest for $40,000 and one-fifth of Blair's capital interest for $12,000. Payments will be made directly to the partners. Todd Gilbert will invest $30,000 in the business for which he will receive a $30,000 capital interest.

1. Prepare general journal entries showing the transactions admitting Kinder and Gilbert to the partnership.
2. Calculate the ending capital balances of all four partners after the transactions.

E 19-5B (LO6)
✓ Loss: $16,000

ENTRIES: PARTNERSHIP LIQUIDATION On liquidation of the partnership of L. Straw and M. Maury, as of February 9, 20--, assets with a book value of $156,000 are sold for $140,000. Given that the profit-and-loss ratio is 60% for Straw and 40% for Maury, prepare the entries for the sale and the allocation of loss.

SERIES B PROBLEMS

P 19-6B (LO2)
✓ Cr. to Bush, Capital: $32,960

PARTNERSHIP OPENING ENTRIES On July 1, 20--, Lisa Bush and Wally Dodge combined their two businesses to form a partnership under the firm name of Bush and Dodge. The balance sheets of the two sole proprietorships are shown below.

Bush's Grooming & Pet Supplies
Balance Sheet
June 30, 20--

Assets			Liabilities		
Cash		$ 4,600	Notes payable	$3,600	
Accounts receivable	$4,200		Accounts payable	7,690	
Less allowance for bad debts	480	3,720	Total liabilities		$11,290
Merchandise inventory		28,580			
Store equipment	$9,260		Owner's Equity		
Less accumulated depreciation	2,400	6,860	Lisa Bush, capital		32,470
Total assets		$43,760	Total liabilities and owner's equity		$43,760

Wally's Pet World
Balance Sheet
June 30, 20--

Assets			Liabilities		
Cash		$ 3,350	Notes payable	$6,000	
Accounts receivable	$4,150		Accounts payable	5,500	
Less allowance for bad debts	250	3,900	Total liabilities		$11,500
Merchandise inventory		27,240			
Supplies		845			
Office equipment	$8,830				
Less accumulated depreciation	3,400	5,430			
Store equipment	$9,175		Owner's Equity		
Less accumulated depreciation	4,250	4,925	Wally Dodge, capital		34,190
Total assets		$45,690	Total liabilities and owner's equity		$45,690

The balance sheets reflect fair market values except for the following:

(a) The fair market value of Bush's store equipment is $7,350.

(b) The fair market values of Dodge's office equipment and store equipment are $5,875 and $6,100, respectively.

REQUIRED

Prepare the opening entry for the formation of the Bush and Dodge partnership as of July 1, 20--, using fair market values. The difference between assets invested and liabilities assumed should be credited to each partner's capital account. Neither partner has knowledge of any uncollectible accounts receivable.

P 19-7B   (LO4)

✓ 1. Allocation of net income: Rummel, $52,140

✓ 2. Capital: Rummel, $46,040

PREPARING PARTIAL FINANCIAL STATEMENTS AND CLOSING ENTRIES The partnership of Rummel and Kang, Stonecutters, reported revenues of $133,000 and expenses of $41,000 on the year-end work sheet. The capital balances as of January 1, 20--, were $41,000 for C. Rummel and $25,000 for V. Kang. No additional investments were made during the year. As stated in their partnership agreement, after withdrawing salary allowances of $43,000 for Rummel and $34,000 for Kang, the partners each withdrew their full 10% interest allowances on their January 1 capital balances. No additional withdrawals were made. Any remaining net income is to be divided on a 60–40 basis.

REQUIRED

1. Prepare the lower portion of the income statement of the partnership for the year ended December 31, 20--, showing the division of the partnership net income for the year.

2. Prepare a statement of partners' equity for the year ended December 31, 20--, and the partners' equity section of the balance sheet on that date.

3. Prepare closing entries for the partnership as of December 31, 20--. (For simplicity, use the account titles "Revenues" for all revenues and "Expenses" for all expenses.)

P 19-8B   (LO5)

✓ 1. Cr. to Cummings, Capital: $4,500

✓ 2. Dr. to Cummings, Capital: $9,000

ENTRIES FOR DISSOLUTION OF PARTNERSHIP Cummings and Stickel Construction Company, a partnership, is operating a general contracting business. Ownership of the company is divided among the partners, Katie Cummings, Julie Stickel, Roy Hewson, and Patricia Weber. Profits and losses are shared equally. The books are kept on the calendar-year basis.

On August 10, after the business had been in operation for several years, Patricia Weber passed away. Mr. Weber wished to sell his wife's interest for $30,000. After the books were closed, the partners' capital accounts had credit balances as follows:

Katie Cummings	$90,000
Julie Stickel	60,000
Roy Hewson	50,000
Patricia Weber	40,000

REQUIRED

1. Prepare the general journal entry required to enter the check issued to Mr. Weber in payment of his deceased wife's interest in the partnership. According to the partnership agreement, the difference between the amount paid to Mr. Weber and the book value of Patricia Weber's capital account is allocated to the remaining partners based on their ending capital account balances.

(continued)

2. Assume instead that Mr. Weber is paid $60,000 for the book value of Patricia Weber's capital account. Prepare the necessary journal entry.

3. Assume instead that Julie Stickel (with the consent of the remaining partners) purchased Weber's interest for $70,000 and gave Mr. Weber a personal check for that amount. Prepare the general journal entry for the partnership only.

P 19-9B   (LO6)
✓ 1. Distribution of cash to partners:
Leonard, $67,000

STATEMENT OF PARTNERSHIP LIQUIDATION WITH GAIN After several years of operations, the partnership of Leonard, Mitchell, and Swanson is to be liquidated. After making closing entries on June 30, 20--, the following accounts remain open:

Account Title	Account Balance Debit	Credit
Cash	$ 4,000	
Inventory	40,000	
Other Assets	150,000	
Liabilities		$44,000
B. J. Leonard, Capital		60,000
W. T. Mitchell, Capital		15,000
J. C. Swanson, Capital		75,000

The noncash assets are sold for $211,000. Profits and losses are shared equally.

REQUIRED

1. Prepare a statement of partnership liquidation for the period July 1–20, 20--, showing the following:

(a) The sale of noncash assets on July 1

(b) The allocation of any gain or loss to the partners on July 1

(c) The payment of the liabilities on July 15

(d) The distribution of cash to the partners on July 20

2. Journalize these four transactions in a general journal.

P 19-10B   (LO6)
✓ 1. Distribution of cash to partners:
Delco, $15,000

STATEMENT OF PARTNERSHIP LIQUIDATION WITH LOSS After several years of operations, the partnership of Delco, Smith, and Walker is to be liquidated. After making closing entries on March 31, 20--, the following accounts remain open.

Account Title	Account Balance Debit	Credit
Cash	$ 7,000	
Inventory	25,000	
Other Assets	185,000	
Liabilities		$17,000
D. W. Delco, Capital		30,000
C. S. Smith, Capital		90,000
T. R. Walker, Capital		80,000

The noncash assets are sold for $165,000. Profits and losses are shared equally.

REQUIRED

1. Prepare a statement of partnership liquidation for the period April 1–15, 20--, showing the following:
   (a) The sale of noncash assets on April 1
   (b) The allocation of any gain or loss to the partners on April 1
   (c) The payment of the liabilities on April 12
   (d) The distribution of cash to the partners on April 15
2. Journalize these four transactions in a general journal.

CHECK LIST
☐ **Managing**
☐ **Planning**
☐ **Drafting**
☐ **Break**
☐ **Revising**
☐ **Managing**

MANAGING YOUR WRITING

A friend, Joan Mellencamp, has mentioned that she is thinking about forming a partnership with a small group of colleagues. She is interested in learning about the advantages and disadvantages of the partnership form of ownership. In addition, she has asked for your advice on the kinds of issues that should be agreed upon in advance of the formation of the partnership. Write a memo to your friend explaining the advantages and disadvantages of a partnership and offer your advice on the issues that should be settled in advance.

ETHICS ⭐

ETHICS CASE

Kathy Lentz, Rob Snyder, and Tom Rohm were all general partners in a consulting business. Each partner owned one-third of the business. The partnership agreement stated that all three partners must approve vouchers for payments in amounts exceeding $5,000. While Tom was on vacation, Kathy and Rob decided to purchase a new computer system costing $6,800. A voucher was prepared and Rob signed both his and Tom's name. Kathy signed her name and gave the voucher to the accounts payable clerk who wrote the check for $6,800.

1. Why would a partnership agreement specify that all purchases over a certain amount be approved by all partners? Are there any circumstances that would warrant deviation from this policy?
2. What are the disadvantages of the partnership form of business ownership?
3. Write a short memo from Tom Rohm to Kathy Lentz and Rob Snyder expressing disapproval of the situation.
4. In groups of three or four, discuss some of the possible outcomes of this situation.

MASTERY PROBLEM

✓ 4. Distribution of cash to partners:
   I. Fleming, $71,500

Jim Bond, a plumber, has been working for Fleming's Plumbing Supplies for several years. Based on his hard work and the fact that he recently married Ivan Fleming's daughter, Jim has been invited to enter into a partnership with Fleming. The new partnership will be called Fleming and Bond's Plumbing Supplies. The terms of the partnership are as follows:

(continued)

(a) Fleming will invest the assets of Fleming's Plumbing Supplies, and the partnership will assume all liabilities. The market values of the office and store equipment are estimated to be $18,000 and $8,000, respectively. All other values reported on the balance sheet (shown below) are reasonable approximations of market values. Fleming has no knowledge of any uncollectible accounts receivable.

(b) Bond will invest $50,000 cash.

(c) Fleming will draw a salary allowance of $50,000 per year, and Bond will receive $30,000.

(d) Each partner will receive 10% interest on the January 1 balance of his capital account.

(e) Profits or losses remaining after allocating salaries and interest will be distributed as follows: Fleming, 60% and Bond, 40%.

Fleming's Plumbing Supplies Balance Sheet December 31, 20-1						
Assets			Liabilities			
Cash		$ 13,544	Notes payable	$36,000		
Accounts receivable	$15,280		Accounts payable	18,082		
Less allowance for bad debts	1,720	13,560	Total liabilities			$ 54,082
Merchandise inventory		89,692				
Supplies		1,286				
Office equipment	$14,320					
Less accumulated depreciation	1,100	13,220				
Store equipment	$ 8,800		Owner's Equity			
Less accumulated depreciation	2,200	6,600	Ivan Fleming, capital			83,820
Total assets		$137,902	Total liabilities and owner's equity			$137,902

REQUIRED

1. Prepare the entries on January 1, 20-2, for the formation of the partnership.

2. Net income for the partnership for 20-2 was $150,000. Prepare the lower portion of the income statement reporting the allocation of the profits to each partner.

3. In December 20-4, Fleming's daughter, Penny, graduated from business college and asked to join the business as a partner. She has $30,000 to invest and it is agreed, given Penny's expertise in accounting, she will be given a capital interest of $36,000. Profits and losses will be shared as follows: I. Fleming, 50%; J. Bond, 30%; P. Fleming, 20%. Prepare the entry for Penny's investment on January 1, 20-5. Recall from (e) above, the original partnership called for profit sharing, after allocating interest and salaries, of 60% to I. Fleming and 40% to J. Bond.

4. After several years of operations, it is decided to liquidate the partnership. After making closing entries on July 31, 20-9, the following accounts remain open:

Cash	$ 20,000	
Inventory	150,000	
Office Equipment	30,000	
Accum. Depreciation—Office Equipment		$18,000
Store Equipment	22,000	
Accum. Depreciation—Store Equipment		15,000
Notes Payable		20,000
Ivan Fleming, Capital		80,000
Jim Bond, Capital		50,000
Penny Fleming, Capital		39,000

(a) On August 1, 20-9, the inventory is sold for $130,000.

(b) On August 3, the office equipment is sold for $10,000.

(c) On August 5, the store equipment is sold for $12,000.

(d) On August 10, the notes payable are paid.

(e) On August 15, the remaining cash is distributed to the partners according to the balances in their capital accounts.

Prepare a statement of partnership liquidation and related journal entries for the period August 1–15, 20-9.

CHALLENGE PROBLEM

> This problem challenges you to apply your cumulative accounting knowledge to move a step beyond the material in the chapter.

> ✓ **Allocation of net income:**
> **Dewi, $122,500**

The partnership agreement for the law firm of Dewi, Cheetem, and Howe states that net income should be allocated in the following manner:

1. Salaries are to be paid as follows:
   - Dewi, $50,000 per year
   - Cheetem, $40,000 per year
   - Howe, $20,000 per year

2. Each partner is to be paid a bonus of 25% of all revenues he or she generated. During 20-1, each partner generated the following revenues:
   - Dewi, $250,000
   - Cheetem, $150,000
   - Howe, $100,000

3. Each partner receives 10% interest on the beginning balance of his or her capital account. Beginning balances of the capital accounts are as follows:
   - Dewi, $200,000
   - Cheetem, $100,000
   - Howe, $50,000

Net income for the year ended December 31, 20-1, was $240,000.

REQUIRED

Prepare the lower portion of the income statement showing the allocation of net income to Dewi, Cheetem, and Howe.

True/False

1. F (partnership)

2. T

3. F (limited life is a characteristic of a partnership because the partnership is dissolved with any change in the partners)

4. F (this is a disadvantage)

5. T

Multiple Choice

1. a   **2.** a   **3.** d   **4.** c   **5.** a

Checkpoint Exercises

1.

	20-1														
1	Jan.	1	Cash				100	0	0	0	00				1
2			Paul Dimmitt, Capital									100	0	0	0	00	2
3			Investment in partnership													3
4		1	Cash				100	0	0	0	00				4
5			Mike Stiglitz, Capital									100	0	0	0	00	5
6			Investment in partnership													6

2.

	Net income	$200,000
	Total allowances	(90,000)
	Remaining income	$110,000

	Allocation of Remaining Income		Salary Allowances		Total
Dimmitt	60% of $110,000 = $66,000	+	$40,000	=	$106,000
Stiglitz	40% of $110,000 = 44,000	+	50,000	=	94,000
					$200,000

3.

The Bogey Men
Income Statement (Partial)
For Year Ended December 31, 20-1

	P. Dimmitt	M. Stiglitz	TOTAL
Net income			$200,000
Allocation of net income:			
Salary allowances	$ 40,000	$50,000	$ 90,000
Remaining income	66,000	44,000	110,000
Allocation of net income	$106,000	$94,000	$200,000

4.

1	20-5 Jan.	1	Mike Stiglitz, Capital		50	0	0	0	00						1
2			James Mantz, Capital							50	0	0	0	00	2
3			Mantz admitted to partnership												3
4		1	Cash		50	0	0	0	00						4
5			Jack Sacks, Capital							50	0	0	0	00	5
6			Sacks' investment in partnership												6

5.

1	20-9 Jan.	1-18	Cash		600	0	0	0	00						1
2			Inventory							400	0	0	0	00	2
3			Gain on Sale of inventory							200	0	0	0	00	3
4			Sale of inventory												4
5			Gain on Sale of Inventory		200	0	0	0	00						5
6			Paul Dimmitt, Capital							60	0	0	0	00	6
7			James Mantz, Capital							60	0	0	0	00	7
8			Jack Sacks, Capital							40	0	0	0	00	8
9			Mike Stiglitz, Capital							40	0	0	0	00	9
10			Allocation of gain												10
11															11

COMPREHENSIVE PROBLEM 3:

Specialized Accounting Procedures

Siblings Jordan and Morgan Hartley are partners in a trendy toy store called ToyMania! Jordan, as senior partner, receives an annual salary allowance of $20,000 and 60 percent of all income/losses after salary and interest allowances are paid. Junior partner Morgan receives an annual salary allowance of $15,000 and 40 percent of all income/losses after salary and interest allowances are paid. The partners receive a 10 percent interest allowance at the end of the accounting period based on their respective January 1 capital account balances. Capital balances as of January 1 are $60,000 for Jordan Hartley and $40,000 for Morgan Hartley.

ToyMania! uses the allowance method for uncollectible accounts. Credit terms are 2/10, n/30. Longer payment terms are available by accepting interest-bearing notes receivable. Terms will vary depending on individual circumstances and will be provided in the related transactions. Notes under $1,000 are collected by ToyMania! while notes greater than $1,000 are collected by either Dean Bank or Marshall Bank. Interest is based on a 360-day year. Estimated uncollectibles are based on 3 percent of accounts receivable. Accounts are written off as they are deemed uncollectible; however, efforts to collect all receivables continue for a two-year period.

ToyMania! occasionally writes notes to finance larger purchases and to extend time on accounts payable. Terms will be specified in the related transactions. Again, interest is based on a 360-day year.

Plant assets are depreciated using one of the various GAAP methods for depreciation. Fully depreciated assets that are useful remain in service until a sale, trade, or disposal is necessary. ToyMania! holds a patent on a toy which is amortized during year-end adjustments. The $25,000 patent's economic life is 10 years although the legal life is 20 years.

A periodic inventory system is maintained valuing inventory using the First-In, First-Out (FIFO) method. The lower-of-cost-or-market rule is applied by recognizing a loss on write-down of inventory when necessary. Beginning balances for Merchandise Inventory and Estimated Returns Inventory were $91,250 and $3,000, respectively, on January 1. The January 1 balance of Customer Refunds Payable was $4,000.

Selected transactions for 20-1 are provided below.

Jan. 5   Reinstated the account of Christine Roby, which had been written off in the preceding year, and received $500 cash in full settlement.

     14   Issued a $3,000, 3-month, 6% note to Zekir Computer Systems to purchase a new computer system (*Computer System*). The system, with an expected life of four years and no salvage value, will be depreciated using the double-declining-balance method.

Feb. 15   Received a $2,500, 6-month, 7% note from Carol Reynolds for sale of merchandise.

Mar. 11   Morgan Hartley invested an additional $5,000 into the business.

Apr. 1   Disposed of a cash register (*Store Equipment*) originally costing $675 with a $75 salvage value. Depreciation is computed on a monthly basis with adjusting entries made at the end of each year. Depreciation after eight years of use was $480 as of December 31. The cash register had an estimated life of 10 years.

Apr. 12 Borrowed $5,000 from Dean Bank, signing a 75-day, 10% note.

14 Paid $500, plus interest, to Zekir Computer Systems (see January 14) and gave a new $2,500, 30-day, 8% note to extend time for payment.

May 1 Wrote off the $1,200 balance owed by Brenda Husband as uncollectible.

14 Paid the principal and interest due on the $2,500 note to Zekir Computer Systems. (See April 14.)

25 Paid $75 cash to Snowden's Service Station for an oil change and tire rotation on the company van.

June 1 Received a $1,700, 120-day, 8% note from Heidi Kruczkiewicz to settle an account receivable.

20 Reinstated the account of Brenda Husband, which had been written off last month, and received $1,200 cash in full settlement. (See May 1.)

22 Paid $30,000 cash to Klippi Construction for an addition (*Addition*) to the store so that more merchandise could be displayed. The addition has an estimated salvage value of $2,000 and an estimated life of 20 years. Depreciation is to be calculated using the straight-line method.

26 Paid the principal and interest due on the $5,000 note to Dean Bank. (See April 12.)

30 Upon opening the store, it was apparent that someone had entered the store illegally. Jordan and Morgan need to determine whether anything had been stolen. A physical inventory was taken and it was determined that $67,500 in inventory was on hand, but they need to know how much inventory should have been on hand. Estimate the cost using the retail method based on the following information. Figures at cost: beginning inventory, $91,250; and net purchases, $70,000. Figures at retail: beginning inventory, $120,000; net purchases, $95,000; and net sales, $125,000. Compare your estimate with the balance of $67,500. Does it appear that any inventory was stolen? *Space is provided for your calculations following the journal pages for the problem in your working papers.*

July 1 Heidi Kruczkiewicz's note (see June 1) is discounted at Marshall Bank at a discount rate of 12%.

8 Sold $4,250 in merchandise to Kim Sackett, terms 2/10, n/30.

10 Purchased merchandise on account for $15,000 from Dionis Distributing. Credit terms are 3/20, n/30.

18 Received payment in full from Kim Sackett, less discount, for merchandise sold on July 8.

30 Paid Dionis Distributing for merchandise purchased on account on July 10.

Aug. 1 Paid $500 to Snowden's Service Station to replace the exhaust system on the company van.

15 Received notification from Dean Bank that the principal and interest were collected on the note from Carol Reynolds. (See February 15.) The bank fee for collecting the note was $10.

22 Wrote off the $750 balance owed by Shelley Kozub as uncollectible.

(*continued*)

Sept. 1 Traded the company car (*Automobile*) for a newer one at Plume Motors. The old car originally cost $23,000 and is depreciated up-to-date in the amount of $19,000. A trade-in allowance of $5,500 was given. The new car had a market value of $40,000 and the balance was paid in cash. The new car should last at least 100,000 miles and will be depreciated at $0.375 per mile.

9 Received a $2,000, 60-day, 7.5% note from Tammy Jones in payment of an account receivable.

15 Purchased $3,500 worth of toys from Dennis Designs, terms n/30.

29 Received notification from Marshall Bank that Heidi Kruczkiewicz's note was dishonored. (See June 1 and July 1.) A check is issued to cover the maturity value plus a $50 bank fee that must be paid to the bank.

Oct. 15 Issued a $3,500, 90-day, 8% note to Dennis Designs to extend time for payment on an account payable.

20 Borrowed $10,000 for 180 days from Ohler-Cupplo Savings Association on a non-interest-bearing note. The discount rate is 7.5%.

31 Sold $125 of merchandise for cash to Melinda Miller.

Nov. 1 Received a $500, 30-day, 5% note from Laura Nottingham in payment of an account receivable.

8 Received notification from Marshall Bank that Tammy Jones dishonored her note. (See September 9.) No fee was charged.

30 Heidi Kruczkiewicz's dishonored note is collected; Kruczkiewicz pays ToyMania! the maturity value of the note, the $50 bank fee, and interest at 9% on the maturity value plus bank fee. (See September 29.)

Dec. 1 Laura Nottingham paid the interest due on her note (see November 1), and gave a new note ($500) for 45 days at 8%.

14 Paid $2,000 to landscape and improve a grassy area on the lot. There will be no salvage value after 5 years and the landscaping will be depreciated using the sum-of-the-years'-digits method.

31 Sold building fixtures for $100. The original cost of the fixtures was $500 with an estimated 5-year life and no salvage value. Depreciation up-to-date is $300.

REQUIRED

1. Journalize the above transactions as needed.

2. Prepare selected adjusting entries using the following information:

   (a) Accrued interest receivable. (See December 1.)

   (b) Accrued interest payable. *Separate entries should be made for discounted and non-discounted notes.* (See October 15 and October 20.)

   (c) Depreciation for the year on the computer system put into service on January 14.

   (d) Depreciation for the year on the new car. Seven thousand miles were traveled this period. (See September 1.)

   (e) Depreciation for the year on the addition completed June 22.

   (f) Depreciation for the year on the landscaping recorded December 14.

(g) Annual amortization on the patent.

(h) Estimated uncollectibles are based on accounts receivable of $48,940. Current Allowance for Doubtful Accounts balance is $375 credit.

(i, j) A physical count shows that merchandise inventory costing $102,000 is on hand as of December 31.

(k, l, m) ToyJoy! estimates that customers will be granted $2,600 in refunds of this year's sales next year and the merchandise expected to be returned will have a cost of $2,000.

(n) Ending inventory valued at market prices on December 31 is $100,500.

3. Prepare the following financial statements:

(a) Partial Income Statement showing the allocation of net income. ToyMania! had a net income of $84,000 for the year. Each partner made withdrawals equal to his/her salary and interest allowances as stated in the partnership agreement.

(b) Statement of Partners' Equity. No additional withdrawals were made after salary and interest allowances were allocated.

4. Prepare selected closing entries, referring to the financial statements as needed.

(a) Close Income Summary to the capital accounts.

(b) Close drawing accounts to the capital accounts.

5. Prepare reversing entries when appropriate.

6. Journalize the following transactions that occurred in the subsequent year:

Jan. 13   Paid the principal and interest due on the $3,500 note to Dennis Designs. (See October 15.)

15   Laura Nottingham paid her note plus interest. (See December 1.)

Apr. 18   Paid the principal on the $10,000 non-interest-bearing note to Ohler-Cupplo Savings Association. (See October 20.)

5

Accounting for Corporations and Manufacturing Businesses

Add some color to your learning!

Throughout the text, you will be introduced to many important terms and types of accounts. To help you learn the different terms and types of accounts, we have coded many of them using the following color key in Part 5:

Assets
Contra-Assets
Liabilities
Capital
Drawing
Revenues
Contra-Revenues
Expenses
Contra-Costs (Contra-Purchases)
Income Summary (Net Income/Net Loss)

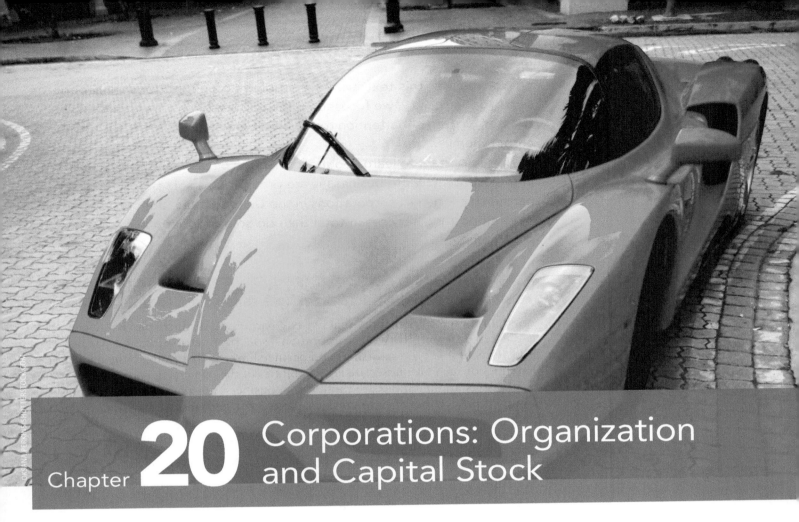

Chapter 20 Corporations: Organization and Capital Stock

If you have watched a James Bond movie, have you ever dreamed of zooming down the road in an exotic car like a Ferrari or Lamborghini? Based on the growth of Gotham Dream Cars, that's not an unusual dream. Gotham Dream Cars rents out extremely high-end cars, like Ferraris, Lamborghinis, Bentleys, Porsches, Aston Martins, and Rolls Royces, for as little as one day or as much as a month. The company also runs a Dream Car Tour in which participants drive six different exotic sports cars for 3 hours over the area's best roads; and a Dream Car Sprint in which drivers can race cars on a specially designed autocross course.

Gotham Dream Cars was founded in New York in 2004 and is headquartered in Englewood, New Jersey. Its main operations are in New York, Miami, and Los Angeles, and it has rental offices in Las Vegas, San Diego, San Francisco, Boston, and Philadelphia. In 2008, it was named to the Inc. 500 list of America's fastest growing private companies, with a three-year growth rate of 980%. The basis for Gotham Dream Cars' rental business is a fleet of 25 cars costing more than $5 million. A question that naturally comes to mind is how can you generate the money to begin and operate a business of this kind? One possibility is by incorporating. As you will learn in this chapter, one of the advantages of the corporate form of organization is that it makes it easier to raise capital. You will also learn about other advantages and some disadvantages of a corporation, types of ownership in a corporation, dividends, and how to account for some key transactions.

LEARNING OBJECTIVES

Careful study of this chapter should enable you to:

LO1 Describe the characteristics, formation, and organization of a corporation.

LO2 Describe stockholders' equity and the types of capital stock, and compute dividends on preferred and common stock.

LO3 Account for capital stock transactions.

LO4 Prepare the stockholders' equity section of a corporation balance sheet.

For most of this text, we have studied accounting for sole proprietorships. In Chapter 19, we focused on the partnership form of business. In this chapter, we turn our attention to the third type of business organization—the corporation.

It is important to learn about corporations because they play a major role in the economy. More businesses are organized as sole proprietorships and partnerships than as corporations in the United States. But corporations sell more goods and services in total than do sole proprietorships and partnerships combined.

LO1   **The Corporation**

Describe the characteristics, formation, and organization of a corporation.

A corporation is a legal entity that exists separate and distinct from its owners. This is the key difference between corporations, sole proprietorships, and partnerships. The assets of sole proprietorships and partnerships legally belong to the owners. The liabilities of such businesses are legal liabilities of the owners. In contrast, a corporation's assets and liabilities are those of the business, not the owners. A corporation can own property, enter into contracts, and incur debt in its own name. It can sue and be sued.

Advantages and Disadvantages

In comparison with sole proprietorships and partnerships, the corporate form of organization offers five advantages.

1. *Limited liability of owners*. The owners of a corporation generally have no personal liability for the debts of the corporation. Their financial responsibility is limited to the amount they have invested. The limited liability feature is a major reason for the popularity of the corporate form of organization.

2. *Transferable ownership units*. The owners' equity in a corporation is called capital stock. The capital stock is divided into shares representing ownership rights in the corporation. These shares can be transferred from one person to another without the consent of the other owners and without disturbing the corporation's normal activities.

3. *Ease of raising capital*. The limited liability and transferable ownership characteristics make the corporation an attractive investment for many people. Therefore, a corporation generally can obtain capital by selling additional shares of stock.

4. *No mutual agency*. Mutual agency means that each owner has the power to act as an agent and engage in contracts for a business. In a corporation, individual owners do *not* have such power, unless the other owners have granted it to them.

5. *Unlimited life*. A corporation's life is specified in its charter. The charter either states the life as perpetual or provides for renewal if a limit is indicated. Changes of ownership through transfer of shares or death of owners have no effect on the life of a corporation.

Two disadvantages of the corporate form of organization are:

1. *Taxation of earnings*. A major disadvantage is that corporations must pay income taxes. In contrast, sole proprietorships and partnerships do not pay income taxes. The earnings of sole proprietorships and partnerships are taxed only as the personal income of the owners.

In addition to the corporate income tax, the corporation's owners pay personal income tax on dividends they receive. Dividends are distributions of corporate income to the owners. Taxing corporate income both to the company that earns it and to the owners who receive it is called double taxation.

2. *Government regulation.* The corporation's activities may be regulated by federal, state, and local laws. These laws may restrict the corporation's ownership of real property, the purchase of its own stock, and the retention of its earnings. If a corporation does business in several states, each state may impose its own financial and tax reporting requirements.

Forming a Corporation

In the United States, the power to create corporations rests largely with the states. To form a corporation, the incorporators file an application with the state in which the company is to be incorporated. After the application is approved, a legal document called a charter, or articles of incorporation, is prepared. The contents of the charter may vary, but it typically includes the following:

1. Name of the corporation
2. Location of the principal office
3. Purpose of the business
4. Description of the capital stock
5. Names and addresses of the incorporators

After the state approves the charter, the incorporators meet to elect a temporary board of directors and to prepare the corporation bylaws. The charter and bylaws provide the general guidelines for conducting the business.

Next, the corporation issues capital stock. Those who buy the stock become owners and are known as stockholders. Each stockholder receives a form called a stock certificate that shows the name of the stockholder and the number of shares owned.

Organization of a Corporation

Major officers in large corporations today typically include:

- Chief Executive Officer (CEO), usually the president
- Chief Operating Officer (COO)
- Chief Financial Officer (CFO)
- Chief Information Officer (CIO)

The stockholders elect a board of directors. The board of directors determines corporate policies and selects the corporate officers. The officers generally manage the corporation and are responsible to the board. The officers usually consist of the president, one or more vice presidents, a secretary, and a treasurer. Figure 20-1 illustrates a common corporate organization, from the owners/stockholders through the employees.

FIGURE 20-1 Corporate Organization

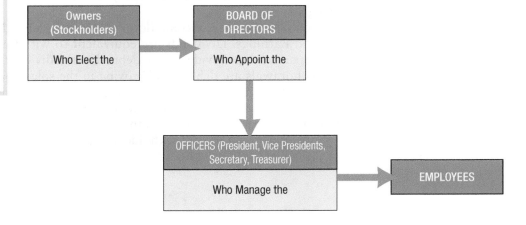

Organization Costs

The costs of organizing a corporation, such as incorporation fees, attorneys' fees, and promotion expenses, are called organization costs. Organization costs may be viewed as benefiting the entire life of a corporation, but accepted practice is to record them as expenses as they are incurred.

Assume that Neo Company was billed $8,000 for incorporation and attorney's fees. The journal entry for this transaction is as follows:

4	Organization Expenses	8 0 0 0 00			4
5	Accounts Payable		8 0 0 0 00		5
6	Corporate organization costs				6
7					7

CHECKPOINT ✔
Complete Checkpoint-1 on page 800 to test your basic understanding of LO1.

Organization expenses are reported under Other Expenses on the income statement.

LO2

Stockholders' Equity and Types of Capital Stock

Describe stockholders' equity and the types of capital stock, and compute dividends on preferred and common stock.

A corporation's asset, liability, revenue, and expense accounts are generally the same as those for a sole proprietorship or partnership. The owners' equity accounts, however, are quite different, as shown in T account form in Figure 20-2.

In sole proprietorships and partnerships, the owners' capital accounts are affected by three types of events, identified by number in Figure 20-2.

1. Initial and subsequent investments in the business
2. Net income or losses during the life of the business
3. Withdrawals by the owners

The only difference between the sole proprietorship and partnership accounts is that the partnership has multiple capital and drawing accounts. The drawing accounts represent the amount withdrawn from the business by an owner during a given accounting period. Recall that each partner's drawing account is closed to his or her capital account at the end of the period. This closing process is shown as item 4 in the T accounts.

In a corporation, owners' equity is called stockholders' equity. More importantly, a distinction is made between capital invested by the owners and earnings retained in the business. As shown in Figure 20-2, the amount paid by the stockholders for their shares of stock is called paid-in capital and is generally recorded in two new types of accounts: Capital Stock and Additional Paid-In Capital. Both accounts are reported as part of stockholders' equity. These accounts will be explained in the following sections.

A corporation's net income (loss) is credited (debited) to another new account, Retained Earnings. Dividends are equivalent to withdrawals in a sole proprietorship or partnership. Dividends are debited to the dividends account in the same way that withdrawals are debited to Drawing in the sole proprietorship or partnership. Similarly, the dividends account is closed to Retained Earnings in the same way that Drawing is closed to the capital accounts in a sole proprietorship or partnership. Thus, retained earnings represents the accumulated earnings of the corporation that have not been paid out to stockholders as dividends.

FIGURE 20-2 Owners' Equity Accounts

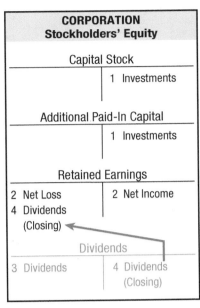

We will look at a complete illustration of the stockholders' equity section of the corporate balance sheet near the end of the chapter. But to help you picture the paid-in capital and retained earnings accounts described here, Figure 20-3 illustrates the general format of the stockholders' equity section.

FIGURE 20-3 Stockholders' Equity Section Format

Paid-in capital:		
Capital stock	$xxx	
Additional paid-in capital:		
Paid-in capital in excess of par	xxx	
Total paid-in capital		$xxx
Retained earnings		xxx
Total stockholders' equity		$xxx

Capital Stock

Ownership rights in a corporation are represented by shares of capital stock issued by the corporation to the owners. As shown in Figure 20-4, the total number of shares the corporate charter authorizes a corporation to issue is called **1** authorized stock. Capital stock that has been sold and issued is called **2** issued stock. This typically is only a small portion of the authorized stock. A corporation may buy back some of its own stock. This stock is known as **3** treasury stock. The issued stock less treasury stock equals **4** outstanding stock, which is the number of shares in the hands of stockholders.

Shares of stock commonly have a dollar amount per share printed on the stock certificate. This dollar amount is known as the **par value** of the stock. Par value is strictly a legal matter and has no direct relationship to the market value per share. **Market value** is the amount for which the stock can be bought and sold on the open market.

FIGURE 20-4 Capital Stock

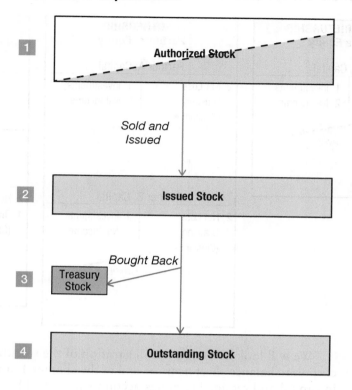

The par value has accounting importance, however, because that amount must be recorded in the capital stock account when stock is issued. If stock is issued for more than its par value, the excess is credited to Paid-In Capital in Excess of Par.

Stock that has no dollar amount printed on it is called no-par stock. No-par stock sometimes is assigned a value per share by the board of directors. This amount is known as the stated value of the stock. From an accounting standpoint, par value and stated value stock are virtually the same.

Common Stock

If a corporation issues only one class or type of stock, each share usually gives its owner the right to:

1. Vote at stockholders' meetings
2. Share in earnings distributions
3. Purchase additional shares in proportion to the owner's present holding, if more shares are issued by the corporation (This is called a preemptive right.)
4. Share in the assets if the corporation liquidates

Such stock is called common stock.

Preferred Stock

Corporations sometimes issue two classes of stock—common stock and preferred stock. Preferred stock is stock that gives its owner certain preferences or rights superior to those of common stock. Usually, these preferences pertain to dividends or to

> A corporation must maintain a listing or subsidiary ledger of who owns all shares of its stock. Larger corporations use independent registrars and transfer agents to maintain these records.

> As a way of enabling original owners or key executives to maintain control, some companies issue multiple classes of common stock. One class might have one vote per share; another, "power" class might have ten votes per share.

distribution of assets at liquidation. To obtain these preferences, owners of preferred stock usually do not have one or more of the four rights stated previously. Most commonly, preferred stock owners have no voting rights.

The owners of preferred stock usually have the right to dividends of a certain amount before owners of common stock can receive any dividends. The dividend preference is usually stated as a dollar amount per share or as a percentage of par value. For example, preferred stock might be described as "$50 par, $4 preferred stock," or "$50 par, 8% preferred stock."

To illustrate the dividend preference, assume that Pref Company has 2,000 shares of $50 par, $4 preferred stock, and 2,000 shares of $10 par common stock outstanding. The amount available for dividends for the year is $14,000. This $14,000 would be allocated between the preferred and common shares as follows:

1.	Total amount available for dividends	$14,000
2.	Dividend to preferred stock (2,000 shares × $4)	8,000
3.	Amount available for common stock	$ 6,000
	Dividends per share:	
	Preferred stock	$4
	Common stock ($6,000 ÷ 2,000 shares)	$3

Cumulative and Noncumulative Preferred Stock

Preferred stock on which any unpaid dividends accumulate from year to year is called **cumulative preferred stock**. The accumulated amounts and the current year preferred dividends must be paid to the preferred stockholders before the common stockholders can receive any dividends.

Preferred stock on which dividend claims do not accumulate from year to year is called **noncumulative preferred stock**. If dividends are not declared in one year, there is no carryover of dividends to the following years.

Assume that the Pref Company described in the previous illustration had no dividends available in year 1 of operation and $22,000 in year 2. Neither the preferred stock nor the common stock owners would receive any dividends in year 1. The dividends in year 2 for the cumulative and noncumulative preferred stock situations would be as follows:

	Year 2			
	Cumulative		Noncumulative	
Total amount available for dividends		$22,000		$22,000
Cumulative preferred dividend from prior year (2,000 shares × $4)	$8,000		$ 0	
Preferred dividend—current year (2,000 shares × $4)	8,000	16,000	8,000	8,000
Amount available for common stock		$ 6,000		$14,000
Dividends per share:				
Preferred		$8		$4
Common ($6,000 ÷ 2,000 shares)		$3		
($14,000 ÷ 2,000 shares)				$7

The cumulative feature of preferred stock is an important preference. Most preferred stock issued today is cumulative.

Participating and Nonparticipating Preferred Stock

Participating preferred stock gives its owners the right to share with common stock owners in dividends in excess of a stated dividend rate. If preferred dividends are limited to the stated dividend rate, the stock is called nonparticipating. It is unusual to find the participation feature in preferred stock today.

Convertible Preferred Stock

Convertible preferred stock gives its owner the right to convert that stock to common stock of the corporation. The number of shares of common stock that will be issued for each share of preferred stock is indicated on the preferred stock certificate. The purpose of the convertible feature is to make the preferred stock more attractive to potential investors. Common stock is riskier but normally has a better chance of increasing in market value.

> **CHECKPOINT ✔**
>
> Complete Checkpoint-2 on page 800 to test your basic understanding of LO2.

SERGEY YECHIKOV/SHUTTERSTOCK.COM

A BROADER VIEW

Did You Say Company or Country?

This chapter introduces the corporate form of business. Corporations tend to be the largest business enterprises. In fact, the size of some corporations can be difficult to imagine. One way to appreciate the magnitude of some of the largest corporations is to compare them with countries.

In economic terms, the gross domestic product of a country is comparable to the sales of a corporation. Based on these yardsticks, consider the following:

1. Based on sales, Walmart is the largest corporation in the world. Its sales are larger than the gross domestic product of Belgium.
2. Toyota ranks fifth. Its sales are larger than the gross domestic product of Chile or Finland.
3. Apple, which ranks 9th, has sales larger than the gross domestic product of Portugal or New Zealand.

These comparisons give real meaning to the expression "big business."

LO3	Capital Stock Transactions

Account for capital stock transactions.

Corporations issue capital stock in exchange for cash and noncash assets. Issuance for cash is the most common transaction.

Issuing Par Value Stock at Par

If capital stock is issued at par for cash, Cash is debited and Common Stock or Preferred Stock is credited for the amount received. Assume that Linc Corp. issues 10,000 shares of $5 par common stock at par for $50,000 cash. The journal entry for this transaction is as follows:

5	Cash		50	0	0	0	00								5
6	Common Stock								50	0	0	0	00		6
7	Issued common stock at par														7

Issuing Par Value Stock at a Premium

If stock is issued at a price above par, the amount received above par is known as a premium. Enter this transaction as follows:

1. Debit Cash for the amount received.
2. Credit Common Stock or Preferred Stock for the par amount.
3. Credit Paid-In Capital in Excess of Par for the amount above par.

Assume that Linc Corp. issues 10,000 shares of $5 par common stock for $60,000 cash. The journal entry for this transaction is as follows:

5	Cash		60	0	0	0	00								5
6	Common Stock*								50	0	0	0	00		6
7	Paid-In Capital in Excess of Par—														7
8	Common Stock**								10	0	0	0	00		8
9	Issued common stock at a premium														9
10															10
11	*10,000 shares × $5 par														11
12	**$60,000 cash received − $50,000 par value of stock														12

Callouts:
- 1. Amount received → Cash (line 5)
- 2. Par amount → Common Stock* (line 6)
- 3. Amount above par → Paid-In Capital in Excess of Par— (line 7)

As shown in Figure 20-3 on page 783, Paid-In Capital in Excess of Par is reported as an addition to paid-in capital on the balance sheet.

Issuing Stock with a Stated Value

If no-par stock has a stated value, this value is treated virtually the same as par value in the accounts. Only a slight change in account titles is needed.

Assume that Stat Company issues 5,000 shares of no-par common stock with a stated value of $10 per share for $70,000 cash. The journal entry for this transaction is as follows:

5	Cash		70	0	0	0	00								5
6	Common Stock*								50	0	0	0	00		6
7	Paid-In Capital in Excess of Stated Value—														7
8	Common Stock**								20	0	0	0	00		8
9	Issued common stock at a premium														9
10															10
11	*5,000 shares × $10 stated value														11
12	**$70,000 cash received − $50,000 stated														12
13	value of stock														13

Like Paid-In Capital in Excess of Par, Paid-In Capital in Excess of Stated Value is reported as an addition to paid-in capital on the balance sheet.

Issuing No-Par Stock

Accounting for the issuance of no-par stock is generally simpler than for stock with a par or stated value. If no-par stock is issued, Cash is debited and Common Stock or Preferred Stock is credited for the amount received. No premium or discount is entered, regardless of the amount received.

Assume that Noll Company issues 5,000 shares of no-par common stock for $70,000 cash. The journal entry for this transaction is as follows:

5		Cash	70	0 0 0	00			5
6		Common Stock				70	0 0 0 00	6
7		Issued common stock						7

Similarly, if Noll issues 5,000 shares of no-par common stock for $40,000 cash, the journal entry is as follows:

5		Cash	40	0 0 0	00			5
6		Common Stock				40	0 0 0 00	6
7		Issued common stock						7

Issuing Stock for Noncash Assets

Each transaction illustrated thus far has involved issuance of stock for cash. Corporations also sometimes issue stock for noncash assets. The accounting for this transaction can be more complicated because the value of the noncash assets received may need to be determined.

If stock is issued for noncash assets, follow this guideline:

> The assets received are recorded at the fair market value of the assets or of the stock, whichever can be more clearly determined.

Once the value of the noncash assets or the stock is determined, the journal entry for the stock issuance is very similar to those involving cash. Assume that Linc Corp. issues 5,000 shares of $5 par common stock for a truck. Linc's stock is not actively traded, so its market value is difficult to determine, but the truck has a known fair market value of $30,000. Thus, the fair market value of the truck is used to record this transaction. The journal entry is as follows:

11		Truck	30	0 0 0	00			11
12		Common Stock*				25	0 0 0 00	12
13		Paid-In Capital in Excess of Par—						13
14		Common Stock**				5	0 0 0 00	14
15		Issued common stock at a premium						15
16								16
17		*5,000 shares × $5 par						17
18		**$30,000 fair market value of truck						18
19		received − $25,000 par value of stock						19

Assume instead that Linc Corp. issues 10,000 shares of $5 par common stock for a building with several different appraisal values. Linc's stock is actively traded and has a fair market value of $7 per share. In this case, the fair market value of the stock, $70,000 (10,000 shares × $7), is used to record this transaction. The journal entry is as follows:

15		Building	70	0	0	0	00						15
16		Common Stock*						50	0	0	0	00	16
17		Paid-In Capital in Excess of Par—											17
18		Common Stock**						20	0	0	0	00	18
19		Issued common stock at a premium											19
20													20
21		*10,000 shares × $5 par											21
22		**$70,000 fair market value of stock											22
23		− $50,000 par value of stock											23

Capital Stock Subscriptions

Corporations sometimes accept subscriptions for capital stock. A capital stock subscription is an agreement in which a buyer (subscriber) contracts to buy shares of stock from a corporation at a specific price. The subscriber generally agrees to pay the amount in full on a specified date or in installments. The corporation does not issue the stock until the subscriber makes the full payment.

Accounting for stock subscriptions requires the use of some new accounts. Assume that Linc Corp. received subscriptions for 10,000 shares of its $5 par common stock for $60,000. The journal entry for this transaction is as follows:

8		Common Stock Subscriptions Receivable	60	0	0	0	00						8
9		Common Stock Subscribed*						50	0	0	0	00	9
10		Paid-In Capital in Excess of Par—											10
11		Common Stock**						10	0	0	0	00	11
12		Received subscriptions for common stock											12
13													13
14		*10,000 shares × $5 par											14
15		**$60,000 subscription amount −											15
16		$50,000 par value of stock											16

The SEC generally requires the contra-owners' equity treatment of stock subscriptions receivable.

Common Stock Subscriptions Receivable looks like an asset, but current practice generally calls for treating it as a contra-equity account. It is reported as a deduction from the total of paid-in capital and retained earnings on the balance sheet. Common stock subscribed and paid-in capital in excess of par are reported as additions to paid-in capital on the balance sheet.

As the subscriber makes payments on the stock, the Common Stock Subscriptions Receivable balance is decreased. If the subscriber to Linc Corp.'s shares makes a payment of $40,000, the following journal entry is made:

25		Cash	40	0	0	0	00						25
26		Common Stock Subscriptions Receivable						40	0	0	0	00	26
27		Received subscription payment											27

When the stock subscription has been fully paid, the corporation issues the stock. At this point, Common Stock Subscribed is debited and Common Stock is credited for the par amount of $50,000. The $10,000 premium on the stock issuance was already credited to Paid-In Capital in Excess of Par—Common Stock at the time the subscription was recorded. Assume the subscriber to Linc Corp.'s shares makes the final payment of $20,000 and Linc issues the 10,000 shares. The following journal entries are made:

5	Cash	20	0	0	0	00							5
6	Common Stock Subscriptions Receivable						20	0	0	0	00		6
7	Received subscription payment												7
8													8
9	Common Stock Subscribed	50	0	0	0	00							9
10	Common Stock						50	0	0	0	00		10
11	Issued common stock												11

The (a) subscription, (b) payments, and (c) issuance of the stock are shown in T account form in Figure 20-5.

FIGURE 20-5 Stock Subscription, Payments, and Issuance

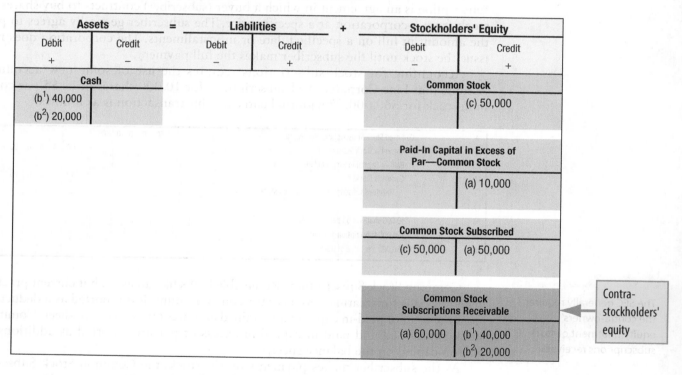

Subscriptions at par, for no-par stock, and for stated value stock are accounted for in a similar manner. The only new accounts that require special care are the same in each instance: Common (or Preferred) Stock Subscriptions Receivable and Common (or Preferred) Stock Subscribed.

LEARNING KEY 🔑

Record the purchase of treasury stock at cost, regardless of any par or stated value.

Treasury Stock

When a company buys back some of its own shares of stock, these shares are called treasury stock. When the purchase occurs, Treasury Stock is debited for the cost of the stock, regardless of any par or stated value. Assume Linc Corp. purchases

3,000 shares of its $5 par common stock for $6 per share, a total of $18,000. The journal entry for this transaction is as follows:

5		Common Treasury Stock	18	0	0	0	00							5
6		Cash						18	0	0	0	00		6
7		Purchased treasury stock												7

If treasury stock is subsequently sold, the transaction is handled as follows:

1. Cash is debited for the amount received.
2. Treasury Stock is credited for its cost.
3. Any difference between the amount received and the cost is debited or credited to Paid-In Capital from Sale of Treasury Stock.

Assume that Linc Corp. sells 2,000 of the 3,000 treasury shares for $7 per share, a total of $14,000. The journal entry is as follows:

15		Cash	14	0	0	0	00							15
16		Common Treasury Stock*						12	0	0	0	00		16
17		Paid-In Capital from Sale of Treasury Stock**						2	0	0	0	00		17
18		Sold treasury stock												18
19														19
20		*2,000 shares × $6 cost per share												20
21		**$14,000 cash received − $12,000 cost												21
22		of treasury shares												22

Assume that Linc Corp. subsequently sells the remaining 1,000 treasury shares for $5.50 per share, a total of $5,500. The journal entry for this transaction is as follows:

8		Cash	5	5	0	0	00							8
9		Paid-In Capital from Sale of Treasury Stock**	5	0	0	00								9
10		Common Treasury Stock*						6	0	0	0	00		10
11		Sold treasury stock												11
12														12
13		*1,000 shares × $6 cost per share												13
14		**$6,000 cost of treasury shares												14
15		− $5,500 cash received												15

If treasury stock is sold for less than its cost and Paid-In Capital from Sale of Treasury Stock has a zero balance, the difference is debited to Retained Earnings.

Note that no gain or loss is recognized on treasury stock transactions. A corporation cannot realize a gain or incur a loss by dealing in its own shares.

Be careful in presenting treasury stock on the balance sheet. Treasury stock is *not* an asset. It is a contra-stockholders' equity account and is reported as a deduction from the total of paid-in capital and retained earnings. Paid-In Capital from Sale of Treasury Stock is reported as an addition to paid-in capital on the balance sheet.

CHECKPOINT ✔
Complete Checkpoint-3 on
pages 800–801 to test your
basic understanding of LO3.

Summary of Capital Stock Transaction Accounts

In recording capital stock transactions, we have been introduced to many new accounts. Figure 20-6 summarizes these new accounts by type, purpose, and balance sheet presentation. Figure 20-7 shows each of these accounts in the accounting equation. Refer to these figures as you work the exercises and problems for this chapter.

FIGURE 20-6 Summary of Capital Stock Transaction Accounts

ACCOUNT	TYPE	PURPOSE	BALANCE SHEET TREATMENT
Common Stock and Preferred Stock	Stockholders' Equity	If stock has par or stated value: Credited for par or stated value of stock issued. If stock has no par or stated value: Credited for amount received for stock issued	Part of paid-in capital
Paid-In Capital in Excess of Par—Common and Preferred Stock Paid-In Capital in Excess of Stated Value—Common and Preferred Stock	Stockholders' Equity	Credited for amount by which issue price exceeds par or stated value of stock (Used only for stock with par or stated value)	Additional paid-in capital
Common and Preferred Stock Subscribed	Stockholders' Equity	If stock has par or stated value: Credited for par or stated value of stock subscribed. If stock has no par or stated value: Credited for amount of stock subscription	Additional paid-in capital from common or preferred stock
Common and Preferred Stock Subscriptions Receivable	Contra-Stockholders' Equity	Debited for subscription price of stock	Deduction from total of paid-in capital and retained earnings
Paid-In Capital from Sale of Treasury Stock	Stockholders' Equity	Credited for excess of selling price over cost of treasury stock or Debited for excess of cost over selling price of treasury stock (if a credit balance)	Additional paid-in capital
Treasury Stock—Common and Preferred	Contra-Stockholders' Equity	Debited for cost of stock purchased	Deduction from total of paid-in capital and retained earnings

FIGURE 20-7 Capital Stock Accounts in the Accounting Equation

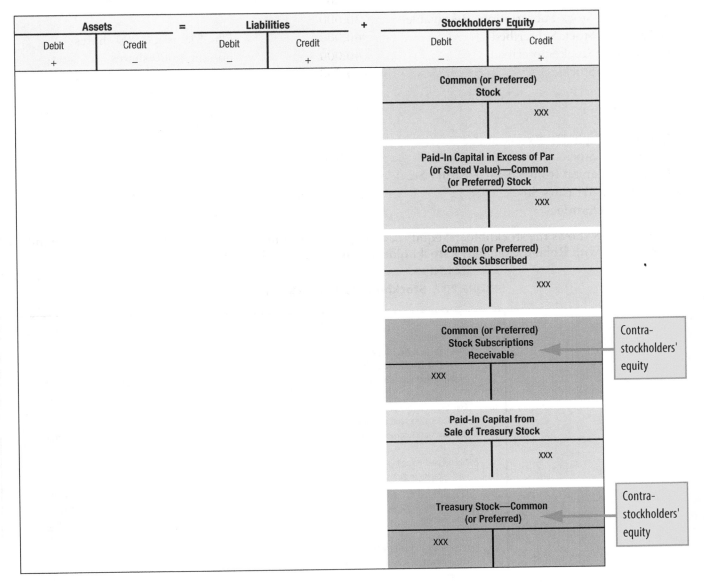

LO4

Stockholders' Equity Section

Prepare the stockholders' equity section of a corporation balance sheet.

The basic format of the stockholders' equity section was illustrated in Figure 20-3 on page 783. Now that we have seen the various accounts used in capital stock transactions, let's bring them together in a more complete stockholders' equity section of the balance sheet. We will use Roland Company for this purpose.

After closing its books on December 31, Roland Company's stockholders' equity accounts have balances as shown at the top of the next page.

Account	Balance	Additional Information
(1) Preferred Stock Subscriptions Receivable	$ 20,000	
(2) Common Stock Subscriptions Receivable	30,000	
(3) Preferred Stock Subscribed	60,000	7%, $10 par, 6,000 shares
(4) Common Stock Subscribed	40,000	no-par, 4,000 shares
(5) Preferred Stock	140,000	7%, $10 par, 20,000 shares authorized, 14,000 shares issued
(6) Common Stock	163,000	no-par, 40,000 shares authorized, 16,300 shares issued
(7) Paid-In Capital in Excess of Par—Preferred Stock	56,000	
(8) Paid-In Capital from Sale of Treasury Stock	600	
(9) Common Treasury Stock	22,000 (Dr.)	no par, 2,000 shares, at cost
(10) Retained Earnings	60,000	

Figure 20-8 shows the stockholders' equity section prepared from these accounts. The line items are numbered to correspond with Roland Company's stockholders' equity accounts in the list shown above.

FIGURE 20-8 Stockholders' Equity Section

	Stockholders' Equity		
	Paid-in capital:		
(5)	Preferred stock, 7%, $10 par		
	(20,000 shares authorized; 14,000 shares issued)	$140,000	
(3)	Preferred stock subscribed (6,000 shares)	60,000	$200,000
(6)	Common stock, no par		
	(40,000 shares authorized; 16,300 shares issued)	$163,000	
(4)	Common stock subscribed (4,000 shares)	40,000	203,000
	Additional paid-in capital:		
(7)	Paid-in capital in excess of par—preferred stock	$ 56,000	
(8)	Paid-in capital from sale of treasury stock	600	56,600
	Total paid-in capital		$459,600
(10)	Retained earnings		60,000
			$519,600
(1)	Less: Preferred stock subscriptions receivable	$ 20,000	
(2)	Common stock subscriptions receivable	30,000	
(9)	Common treasury stock (2,000 shares at cost)	22,000	72,000
	Total stockholders' equity		$447,600

Note the following characteristics of this stockholders' equity presentation:

1. Stockholders' equity is separated by source:
   Paid-in capital—amounts contributed by owners
   Retained earnings—accumulated, undistributed earnings

2. Paid-in capital is separated by source:
   Preferred stock
   Common stock
   Stock subscriptions
   Paid-in capital in excess of par
   Paid-in capital from sale of treasury stock

3. Stock characteristics are indicated:
   Dividend rate for preferred stock—7%
   Par or no-par value

4. Numbers of shares authorized, subscribed, issued, and held as treasury stock are indicated.

CHECKPOINT ✔

Complete Checkpoint-4 on page 801 to test your basic understanding of LO4.

5. Preferred stock is listed first. (This is because of its preferred claim on dividends and assets.)

6. Retained earnings is listed after all paid-in capital.

7. Preferred stock subscriptions receivable, common stock subscriptions receivable, and treasury stock are subtracted from the total of paid-in capital and retained earnings.

SELF-STUDY

LEARNING OBJECTIVES	Key Points to Remember
LO1 Describe the characteristics, formation, and organization of a corporation.	A corporation exists independently of its owners. Its assets and liabilities are those of the business. A corporation is formed according to the laws of the state in which it incorporates. It normally has a board of directors and at least four officers. Organization costs are expensed in the period they are incurred.
LO2 Describe stockholders' equity and the types of capital stock, and compute dividends on preferred and common stock.	A key characteristic of owners' equity in a corporation is the distinction between paid-in capital and retained earnings. Paid-in capital is the amount paid in by stockholders. Retained earnings is the accumulated earnings not paid out as dividends. Owners of capital stock generally have the right to: 1. Vote at stockholders' meetings 2. Share in earnings distributions 3. Purchase additional shares if more shares are issued by the corporation 4. Share in the assets if the corporation liquidates Owners of preferred stock generally give up the right to vote in order to have a preferential right to dividends and assets. Features such as cumulative and participating that may apply to preferred stock must be considered when calculating preferred stock and common stock dividends.
LO3 Account for capital stock transactions.	The accounting for par value and stated value stock is virtually the same. In each case, the difference between the par or stated value and the amount received at issuance is recorded as a premium. • There is no premium to account for when no-par stock is issued. • If stock is issued for noncash assets, the assets received are recorded at the fair market value of the assets or of the stock, whichever can be more clearly determined. • If capital stock subscriptions are received, the corporation does not issue the stock until the subscription is paid in full. • No gains or losses are recognized on treasury stock transactions.

(continued)

LEARNING OBJECTIVES	**Key Points to Remember**
LO4 **Prepare the stockholders' equity section of a corporation balance sheet.**	The stockholders' equity section of the corporate balance sheet has the following characteristics: 1. Stockholders' equity is separated into paid-in capital and retained earnings. 2. Paid-in capital is separated into preferred stock, common stock, stock subscriptions, paid-in capital in excess of par, and paid-in capital from sale of treasury stock. 3. The dividend rates for preferred stock and par or no-par value are indicated. 4. Numbers of shares authorized, subscribed, issued, and held as treasury stock are indicated. 5. Preferred stock is listed first. 6. Retained earnings is listed after all paid-in capital. 7. Preferred stock subscriptions receivable, common stock subscriptions receivable, and treasury stock are subtracted from the total of paid-in capital and retained earnings.

DEMONSTRATION PROBLEM

Stockholders' equity accounts and other related accounts of the JKL Manufacturing Corporation as of October 1, 20-1, the beginning of its fiscal year, follow.

Preferred Stock Subscriptions Receivable	$ 80,000
Preferred Stock, 8%, $10 par (200,000 shares authorized, 50,000 shares issued)	500,000
Preferred Stock Subscribed (10,000 shares)	100,000
Paid-In Capital in Excess of Par—Preferred Stock	50,000
Common Stock, $10 par (1,000,000 shares authorized, 200,000 shares issued)	2,000,000
Paid-In Capital in Excess of Par—Common Stock	500,000
Retained Earnings	2,250,000

During the fiscal year ended September 30, 20-2, JKL Manufacturing completed the following transactions affecting stockholders' equity:

(a) Received the balance due on preferred stock subscriptions and issued the necessary certificates.

(b) Purchased 10,000 shares of common treasury stock for $120,000.

(c) Received subscriptions for 8,000 shares of 8% preferred stock at $12 each, collecting one-fourth of the subscription price.

(d) Sold 6,000 shares of common treasury stock for $78,000.

(e) Issued 80,000 shares of common stock at $15, receiving cash.

(f) Sold 2,000 shares of common treasury stock for $22,000.

(g) Issued 100,000 shares of common stock with a market value of $15 per share in exchange for land for business expansion.

REQUIRED

1. Prepare general journal entries for the transactions, identifying each transaction by the appropriate letter.
2. Prepare the stockholders' equity section of the balance sheet as of September 30, 20-2. The beginning retained earnings balance must be increased by the net income for the year, $720,000. The preferred stock was paid dividends at 8% on $600,000 par value of stock, and the common stock was paid dividends of $0.80 per share on 378,000 outstanding shares.

SOLUTION 1.

		GENERAL JOURNAL				PAGE 1	
	DATE	DESCRIPTION	POST. REF.	DEBIT	CREDIT		
1	(a)	Cash		80 0 0 0 00			1
2		Preferred Stock Subscriptions Receivable			80 0 0 0 00		2
3		Received subscription payments					3
4							4
5		Preferred Stock Subscribed		100 0 0 0 00			5
6		Preferred Stock			100 0 0 0 00		6
7		Issued preferred stock					7
8							8
9	(b)	Common Treasury Stock		120 0 0 0 00			9
10		Cash			120 0 0 0 00		10
11		Purchased treasury stock					11
12							12
13	(c)	Cash		24 0 0 0 00			13
14		Preferred Stock Subscriptions Receivable		72 0 0 0 00			14
15		Preferred Stock Subscribed			80 0 0 0 00		15
16		Paid-In Capital in Excess of Par—					16
17		Preferred Stock			16 0 0 0 00		17
18		Received subscriptions for preferred stock					18
19							19
20	(d)	Cash		78 0 0 0 00			20
21		Common Treasury Stock			72 0 0 0 00		21
22		Paid-In Capital from Sale of Treasury Stock			6 0 0 0 00		22
23		Sold treasury stock					23
24							24
25	(e)	Cash		1,200 0 0 0 00			25
26		Common Stock			800 0 0 0 00		26
27		Paid-In Capital in Excess of Par—					27
28		Common Stock			400 0 0 0 00		28
29		Issued common stock at a premium					29
30							30
31	(f)	Cash		22 0 0 0 00			31
32		Paid-In Capital from Sale of Treasury Stock		2 0 0 0 00			32
33		Common Treasury Stock			24 0 0 0 00		33
34		Sold treasury stock					34
35							35
36	(g)	Land		1,500 0 0 0 00			36
37		Common Stock			1,000 0 0 0 00		37
38		Paid-In Capital in Excess of Par—					38
39		Common Stock			500 0 0 0 00		39
40		Issued common stock at a premium					40

(*continued*)

SOLUTION 2.

Stockholders' Equity		
Paid-in capital:		
Preferred stock, 8%, $10 par (200,000 shares authorized; 60,000 shares issued)	$ 600,000	
Preferred stock subscribed (8,000 shares)	80,000	$ 680,000
Common stock, $10 par (1,000,000 shares authorized; 380,000 shares issued)		3,800,000
Additional paid-in capital:		
Paid-in capital in excess of par—preferred stock	$ 66,000	
Paid-in capital in excess of par—common stock	1,400,000	
Paid-in capital from sale of treasury stock	4,000	1,470,000
Total paid-in capital		$5,950,000
Retained earnings*		2,619,600
		$8,569,600
Less: Preferred stock subscriptions receivable	$ 72,000	
Common treasury stock (2,000 shares at cost)	24,000	96,000
Total stockholders' equity		$8,473,600

* $2,250,000 + $720,000 − $48,000 − $302,400 = $2,619,600

KEY TERMS

articles of incorporation (781)   See charter.

authorized stock (783)   The total number of shares the corporate charter authorizes a corporation to issue.

board of directors (781)   A group elected by the stockholders to determine corporate policies and to select corporate officers.

bylaws (781)   Together with the charter, the bylaws provide the general guidelines for conducting the business.

capital stock (780)   Represents ownership rights in a corporation. Generally broken down into common and preferred stock.

capital stock subscription (789)   An agreement in which a buyer contracts to buy shares of a corporation at a specific price.

charter (781)   A legal document that includes the name of the corporation, the location of the principal office, the purpose of the business, the description of the capital stock, and the names and addresses of the incorporators.

common stock (784)   Stock that gives its owner the right to vote at stockholders' meetings, share in earnings distributions, purchase additional shares if more shares are issued by the corporation, and share in the assets if the corporation liquidates.

convertible preferred stock (786)   A type of preferred stock that gives its owners the right to convert the stock to common stock of the corporation.

cumulative preferred stock (785)   Preferred stock on which unpaid dividends accumulate from year to year.

dividends (781)   The distributions of corporate income to the owners.

double taxation (781)   The process of taxing corporate income both to the company that earns it and to the owners who receive it.

incorporators (781)   Those who form a corporation by filing an application with the state in which the company is to be incorporated.

issued stock (783)   Capital stock that has been sold and issued.

market value (783)   The amount for which the stock can be sold on the open market.

mutual agency (780)   The power of each owner to act as an agent and engage in contracts for a business.

noncumulative preferred stock (785)   Preferred stock on which dividend claims do not accumulate from year to year.

nonparticipating (786)   Preferred stock on which the dividends are limited to the stated dividend rate.

no-par stock (784)   Stock that has no dollar amount printed on it.

organization costs (782)   The costs of organizing a corporation, such as incorporation fees, attorneys' fees, and promotion expenses.

outstanding stock (783)   The number of shares in the hands of stockholders.

paid-in capital (782)   The amount paid by stockholders for their shares of stock.

par value (783)   The dollar amount printed on the share of stock.

participating (786)   Preferred stock that has a right to share with common stock in dividends in excess of a stated dividend rate.

preemptive right (784)   The right to purchase additional shares in proportion to the owner's present holding, if more shares are issued by the corporation.

preferred stock (784)   Stock that has certain preferences or rights superior to common stock.

premium (787)   The difference between the par value and the price of a stock when the stock is issued at a price above par.

retained earnings (782)   The accumulated earnings of the corporation that have not been paid out to stockholders as dividends.

shares (780)   Capital stock is divided into shares that represent ownership rights in the corporation.

stated value (784)   Value per share assigned to no-par stock by the board of directors.

stock certificate (781)   A form received by each stockholder that shows the name of the stockholder and the number of shares owned.

stockholders (781)   Owners of the corporation.

stockholders' equity (782)   Owners' equity within a corporation.

subscriber (789)   A buyer who contracts to purchase shares of stock from a corporation at a specific price.

treasury stock (783)   Shares of stock that have been bought back by the issuing company.

SELF-STUDY TEST QUESTIONS

True/False

1. **LO1** Corporations do more dollar volume of business than sole proprietorships and partnerships combined.

2. **LO1** Owners of corporations have no personal liability for debts of the corporation.

(*continued*)

3. **LO1**   Dividends are not taxable because these earnings have already been taxed to the corporation.

4. **LO1**   Organization costs are recorded as an intangible asset and are generally amortized over a period of five years.

5. **LO2**   Convertible preferred stock is a type of preferred stock that gives its owners the right to convert the stock to common stock of the corporation.

Multiple Choice

1. **LO3**   When par value stock is issued at a price above par, the amount above par is called a
   (a) discount.   (c) stated value.
   (b) market value.   (d) premium.

2. **LO2**   Preferred stock normally has a preference pertaining to
   (a) dividends.   (c) participation.
   (b) voting.   (d) market value.

3. **LO3**   Shares of stock reacquired by the issuing company are called
   (a) par value stock.   (c) treasury stock.
   (b) no-par value stock.   (d) stock subscription.

4. **LO3**   Stock subscriptions receivable are listed as _____ on the balance sheet.
   (a) current liabilities   (c) long-term assets
   (b) current assets   (d) contra-stockholders' equity

5. **LO3**   Treasury stock is listed as a(n) _____ on the balance sheet.
   (a) current liability   (c) deduction from stockholders' equity
   (b) current asset   (d) addition to stockholders' equity

 CHECKPOINT

Checkpoint Exercises

1. **LO1**   AB Company incurred the following costs in organizing the corporation:

   | Attorneys' fees | $6,200 |
   | State incorporation fees | 900 |

   Prepare the general journal entry to record payment of these costs on March 1.

2. **LO2**   Genous Company has 20,000 shares of common stock and 2,000 shares of cumulative, $20 par, $1 dividend, preferred stock outstanding. No dividends were declared in year 1 of operation. In year 2, $9,000 is available for dividends. Compute the dividends per share for common stock and preferred stock in year 2.

3. **LO3**   Prepare general journal entries for the following transactions of GOTE Company:
   (a) Received subscriptions for 10,000 shares of $2 par common stock for $80,000.
   (b) Received payment of $30,000 on the stock subscription in transaction (a).

   (c) Received the balance in full for the stock subscription in transaction (a) and issued the stock.

   (d) Purchased 1,000 shares of its own $2 par common stock for $7.50 a share.

   (e) Sold 500 shares of the stock on transaction (d) for $8.50 a share.

4. **LO4**   Prepare the stockholders' equity section of the balance sheet based on the following account balances:

Common stock, $2 par, 60,000 shares	$120,000
Preferred stock, $10 par, 5%, 4,000 shares	40,000
Common stock subscribed, $2 par, 3,000 shares	6,000
Retained earnings	17,000

The answers to the Self-Study Test Questions are at the end of the chapter (pages 811–812).

APPLYING YOUR KNOWLEDGE

CengageNowv2 provides "Show Me How" videos for selected exercises and problems. Additional resources, such as Excel templates for completing selected exercises and problems, are available for download from the companion website at Cengage.com.

REVIEW QUESTIONS

LO1   1. Briefly describe five advantages of the corporate form of business organization. Describe two disadvantages.

LO1   2. What information usually is included in the charter?

LO1   3. Who elects the permanent board of directors?

LO1   4. Describe how to account for organization costs.

LO2   5. How do owners' equity accounts in a corporation differ from those in a sole proprietorship or partnership?

LO2   6. If a corporation issues only one class of stock, what four rights does each stockholder have?

LO3/4   7. How is paid-in capital in excess of par usually reported on the balance sheet?

LO3   8. If stock is issued for noncash assets, at what amount should the assets be recorded?

LO3/4   9. How is common stock subscriptions receivable usually reported on the balance sheet?

LO3/4 10. How is treasury stock usually shown on the balance sheet?

LO3/4 11. How is paid-in capital from sale of treasury stock usually shown on the balance sheet?

SERIES A EXERCISES

E 20-1A   (LO1)
✓ Dr. Organization Expenses: $10,900

ORGANIZATION COSTS B&B Electric decided to incorporate and has incurred the following costs of organizing:

Incorporation fees	$ 400
Attorneys' fees	4,800
Promotion expenses	5,700

Prepare the entry for the payment of these organization costs for cash on January 31.

E 20-2A   (LO2)
✓ Situation 2. Div. per share, common: $0.40

DIVIDEND ALLOCATIONS

Situation 1   Nguyen Company has the following stock outstanding:

Common Stock	Preferred Stock
60,000 shares	5,000 shares
$1 par value	$60 par, $3 dividend

The amount available for dividends this year is $57,000. Prepare the dividend allocation between the preferred and common shares in total and per share.

Situation 2   Bell Company has the following stock outstanding:

Common Stock	Preferred Stock
60,000 shares	Cumulative: 2,000 shares
$1 par value	$50 par, $2 dividend
	Noncumulative: 3,000 shares
	$50 par, $2 dividend

No dividends were declared in year 1 of operation. In year 2, there is $38,000 available for dividends. Prepare the dividend allocation between the preferred and common shares in total and per share.

E 20-3A   (LO3)
✓ (b) Cr. Paid-In Capital in Excess of Par—Common Stock: $12,000

STOCK ISSUANCE (PAR, NO-PAR, AND STATED VALUE) The following independent stock transactions occurred during January 20-- for various corporations:

(a) Issued 6,000 shares of $10 par common stock for $60,000 cash.

(b) Issued 4,000 shares of $10 par common stock for $52,000 cash.

(c) Issued 5,000 shares of no-par common stock for $55,000 cash.

(d) Issued 4,000 shares of no-par common stock for $42,000 cash.

(e) Issued 6,000 shares of no-par common stock with a stated value of $8 per share for $48,000 cash.

(f) Issued 3,000 shares of no-par common stock with a stated value of $8 per share for $25,000 cash.

Prepare general journal entries for these transactions, identifying each by letter.

E 20-4A   (LO3)
✓ (b) Cr. Paid-In Capital in Excess of Par—Common Stock: $7,500

STOCK ISSUANCE (NONCASH ASSETS, SUBSCRIPTIONS, AND TREASURY STOCK) Smith & Cline had the following stock transactions during the year:

(a) Issued 5,000 shares of common stock with a $5 par value in exchange for real estate (land) with a fair market value of $27,500.

(b) Issued 7,500 shares of common stock with a $5 par value and $6 fair market value in exchange for a building with an uncertain fair market value.

(c) Received subscriptions for 10,000 shares of $5 par common stock for $65,000.

(d) Received a payment of $30,000 on the stock subscription in transaction (c).

(e) Received the balance in full for the stock subscription in transaction (c) and issued the stock.

(f) Purchased 1,000 shares of its own $5 par common stock for $7 a share.

(g) Sold 500 shares of the treasury stock in transaction (f) for $7.50 a share.

(h) Sold 500 shares of the treasury stock in transaction (f) for $6.75 a share.

Prepare general journal entries for these transactions, identifying each by letter.

E 20-5A (LO4)
✓ **Total paid-in capital: $119,000**

STOCKHOLDERS' EQUITY SECTION After closing its books on December 31, Pro Parts' stockholders' equity accounts had the following balances:

Common stock subscriptions receivable	$ 5,000
Common stock, $5 par, 12,000 shares	60,000
Preferred stock, $10 par, 4%, 4,000 shares	40,000
Common stock subscribed, $5 par, 3,000 shares	15,000
Paid-in capital in excess of par-common stock	4,000
Retained earnings	35,000

Prepare the stockholders' equity section of the balance sheet.

SERIES A PROBLEMS

P 20-6A (LO2/3)
✓ **(d) Cr. Paid-in Capital in Excess of Par—Preferred Stock: $1,500**

PAR AND NO-PAR, COMMON AND PREFERRED STOCK Hernandez Company had the following stock transactions during its first 5 years of operations:

(a) Issued 25,000 shares of $1 par common stock for $25,000 cash.

(b) Issued 20,000 shares of $1 par common stock for $22,000 cash.

(c) Issued 2,000 shares of $50 par, 8% preferred stock for $100,000 cash.

(d) Issued 1,000 shares of $50 par, 8% preferred stock for $51,500 cash.

(e) Issued 2,500 shares of no-par common stock for $11,875 cash.

(f) Issued 1,500 shares of no-par, $7 preferred stock for $72,000 cash.

REQUIRED

1. Prepare general journal entries for these transactions, identifying each by letter.

2. Assume that stock transactions a, b, and c occurred in year 1. The amount available for dividends at the end of year 1 is $26,000. Prepare the dividend allocation between the preferred and common shares in total and per share for year 1.

P 20-7A (LO3)
✓ **(e) Dr. Building: $140,000**

STATED VALUE, COMMON AND PREFERRED STOCK, AND NONCASH ASSETS Kris Kraft Stores had the following stock transactions during the year:

(a) Issued 8,000 shares of no-par common stock with a stated value of $5 per share for $40,000 cash.

(b) Issued 6,000 shares of no-par common stock with a stated value of $5 per share for $33,000 cash.

(continued)

(c) Issued 5,000 shares of no-par, 6% preferred stock with a stated value of $15 per share for $75,000 cash.

(d) Issued 10,000 shares of $5 par common stock for land with a fair market value of $50,000.

(e) Issued 20,000 shares of $5 par common stock with a $7 fair market value for a building with an uncertain fair market value.

(f) Issued 8,000 shares of $50 par, 8% preferred stock for land with a fair market value of $405,000.

REQUIRED

Prepare general journal entries for these transactions, identifying each by letter.

P 20-8A   (LO3)

✓ (a) Cr. Paid-In Capital in Excess of Par—Common Stock: $5,000

STOCK SUBSCRIPTIONS Juneau & Associates had the following stock transactions during the year:

(a) Received subscriptions for 100,000 shares of $1 par common stock for $105,000.

(b) Received subscriptions for 5,000 shares of $15 par, 8% preferred stock for $80,000.

(c) Received a payment of $55,000 on the common stock subscription.

(d) Received a payment of $40,000 on the preferred stock subscription.

(e) Issued 40,000 shares of $1 par common stock in exchange for a truck with a fair market value of $48,000.

(f) Received the balance in full for the common stock subscription and issued the stock.

(g) Received the balance in full for the preferred stock subscription and issued the stock.

REQUIRED

Prepare general journal entries for these transactions, identifying each by letter.

P 20-9A   (LO1/3)

✓ Sept. 18. Dr. Common Stock Subscribed: $80,000

STOCK SUBSCRIPTIONS AND TREASURY STOCK Nash & Roth formed a corporation and had the following organization costs and stock transactions during the year:

June 30	Incurred the following costs of incorporation:	
	Incorporation fees	$ 800
	Attorneys' fees	9,000
	Promotion fees	8,000

July 15   Issued 7,000 shares of $10 par common stock for $73,000 cash.

Aug. 1   Received subscriptions for 8,000 shares of $10 par common stock for $81,500.

     15   Issued 16,000 shares of $10 par common stock in exchange for a building and fixtures with a fair market value of $165,000.

     31   Received a payment of $51,500 for the common stock subscription.

Sept. 3   Purchased 2,000 shares of its own $10 par common stock for $11 a share.

     18   Received the balance in full for the common stock subscription and issued the stock.

     30   Sold 800 shares of its treasury stock for $11.50 a share.

Oct. 15   Issued 3,000 shares of $40 par, 5% preferred stock in exchange for land with a fair market value of $125,000.

   31   Sold 400 shares of its treasury stock for $10.75 a share.

REQUIRED
Prepare journal entries for these transactions.

P 20-10A   (LO4)
✓ Total paid-in capital: $491,000

STOCKHOLDERS' EQUITY SECTION After closing its books on December 31, 20--, Jackson Corporation's stockholders' equity accounts had the following balances:

Account	Balance	Additional Information
Preferred Stock Subscriptions Receivable	$ 15,000	
Common Stock Subscriptions Receivable	10,000	
Preferred Stock Subscribed	50,000	$4 dividend, $5 par, 10,000 shares
Common Stock Subscribed	30,000	$10 par, 3,000 shares
Preferred Stock	150,000	$4 dividend, $5 par, 30,000 shares
Common Stock	250,000	$10 par, 25,000 shares
Paid-In Capital in Excess of Par—Preferred Stock	10,000	
Paid-In Capital from Sale of Treasury Stock	1,000	
Common Treasury Stock	10,000	
Retained Earnings	75,000	

REQUIRED
Prepare the stockholders' equity section of the balance sheet for Jackson for the year ended December 31, 20--.

SERIES B EXERCISES

E 20-1B   (LO1)
✓ Dr. Organization Expenses: $12,000

ORGANIZATION COSTS T&R TrackTown has decided to incorporate and has incurred the following costs of organizing:

Incorporation fees	$ 500
Attorneys' fees	6,800
Promotion fees	4,700

Prepare the entry for the payment of these organization costs for cash on January 20.

E 20-2B   (LO2)
✓ Situation 2. Div. per share, common: $0.75

DIVIDEND ALLOCATIONS

Situation 1   Espino Company has the following stock outstanding:

Common Stock	Preferred Stock
100,000 shares	9,000 shares
$0.50 par value	$20 par, $2 dividend

(*continued*)

The amount available for dividends this year is $50,000. Prepare the dividend allocation between the preferred and common shares.

Situation 2   Chiola Corporation has the following stock outstanding:

Common Stock	Preferred Stock
40,000 shares	Cumulative: 4,000 shares
$1 par value	$40 par, $2 dividend
	Noncumulative: 5,000 shares
	$40 par, $2 dividend

No dividends were declared in year 1 of operation. In year 2, there is $56,000 available for dividends. Prepare the dividend allocation between the preferred and common shares.

E 20-3B   (LO3)
✓ (b) Cr. Paid-in Capital in Excess of Par—Common Stock: $3,500

STOCK ISSUANCE (PAR, NO-PAR, AND STATED VALUE) The following independent stock transactions occurred during January 20-- for various corporations:

(a) Issued 4,000 shares of $10 par common stock for $40,000 cash.
(b) Issued 5,000 shares of $10 par common stock for $53,500 cash.
(c) Issued 6,000 shares of no-par common stock for $60,000 cash.
(d) Issued 4,000 shares of no-par common stock for $40,000 cash.
(e) Issued 6,000 shares of no-par common stock with a stated value of $8 per share for $48,000 cash.
(f) Issued 3,000 shares of no-par common stock with a stated value of $8 per share for $25,000 cash.

Prepare general journal entries for these stock transactions, identifying each by letter.

E 20-4B   (LO3)
✓ (b) Cr. Paid-In Capital in Excess of Par—Common Stock: $11,000

STOCK ISSUANCE (NONCASH ASSETS, SUBSCRIPTIONS, AND TREASURY STOCK) Brant & Evans had the following stock transactions during the year:

(a) Issued 6,000 shares of common stock with a $5 par value in exchange for real estate (land) with a fair market value of $33,500.
(b) Issued 5,500 shares of common stock with a $5 par value and $7 fair market value in exchange for a building with an uncertain fair market value.
(c) Received subscriptions for 11,000 shares of $5 par common stock for $58,000.
(d) Received a payment of $29,000 on the stock subscription in transaction (c).
(e) Received the balance in full for the stock subscription in transaction (c) and issued the stock.
(f) Purchased 2,000 shares of its own $5 par common stock for $6 a share.
(g) Sold 1,000 shares of the treasury stock in transaction (f) for $6.50 a share.
(h) Sold 1,000 shares of the treasury stock in transaction (f) for $5.75 a share.

Prepare general journal entries for these transactions, identifying each by letter.

E 20-5B   (LO4)

✓ Total paid-in capital: $220,000

STOCKHOLDERS' EQUITY SECTION After closing its books on December 31, Mel Brothers' stockholders' equity accounts have the following balances:

Common stock subscriptions receivable	$ 6,000
Common stock, $6 par, 15,000 shares	90,000
Preferred stock, $10 par, 8%, 10,000 shares	100,000
Common stock subscribed, $6 par, 5,000 shares	30,000
Retained earnings	50,000

Prepare the stockholders' equity section of the balance sheet.

SERIES B PROBLEMS

P 20-6B   (LO2/3)

✓ (d) Cr. Paid-in Capital in Excess of Par—Preferred Stock: $1,500

PAR AND NO-PAR, COMMON AND PREFERRED STOCK Valdez Company had the following stock transactions during the first 5 years of operations:

(a) Issued 24,000 shares of $1 par common stock for $26,000 cash.

(b) Issued 18,000 shares of $1 par common stock for $18,000 cash.

(c) Issued 3,000 shares of $10 par, 7% preferred stock for $30,000 cash.

(d) Issued 4,500 shares of $10 par, 7% preferred stock for $46,500 cash.

(e) Issued 1,800 shares of no-par common stock for $10,475 cash.

(f) Issued 1,100 shares of no-par, $7 preferred stock for $32,000 cash.

REQUIRED

1. Prepare general journal entries for these transactions, identifying each by letter.

2. Assume that stock transactions a, b, and c occurred in year 1. The amount available for dividends at the end of year 1 is $12,600. Prepare the dividend allocation between the preferred and common shares in total and per share for year 1.

P 20-7B   (LO3)

✓ (e) Dr. Building: $121,000

STATED VALUE, COMMON AND PREFERRED STOCK, AND NONCASH ASSETS Dan's Hobby Stores had the following stock transactions during the year:

(a) Issued 5,000 shares of no-par common stock with a stated value of $10 per share for $50,000 cash.

(b) Issued 6,000 shares of no-par common stock with a stated value of $10 per share for $63,000 cash.

(c) Issued 3,500 shares of no-par, 6% preferred stock with a stated value of $22 per share for $77,000 cash.

(d) Issued 10,000 shares of $10 par common stock for land with a fair market value of $100,000.

(e) Issued 11,000 shares of $10 par common stock with an $11 fair market value for a building with an uncertain fair market value.

(f) Issued 8,000 shares of $30 par, 6% preferred stock for land with a fair market value of $243,000.

REQUIRED

Prepare general journal entries for these transactions, identifying each by letter.

P 20-8B   (LO3)

✓ (e) Cr. Paid-in Capital in Excess of Par—Common Stock: $6,000

STOCK SUBSCRIPTIONS Athletics West had the following stock transactions during the year:

(a) Received subscriptions for 100,000 shares of $1 par common stock for $118,000.

(b) Received subscriptions for 5,000 shares of $18 par, 7% preferred stock for $92,000.

(c) Received a payment of $59,000 on the common stock subscription.

(d) Received a payment of $46,000 on the preferred stock subscription.

(e) Issued 60,000 shares of $1 par common stock in exchange for a truck with a fair market value of $66,000.

(f) Received the balance in full for the common stock subscription and issued the stock.

(g) Received the balance in full for the preferred stock subscription and issued the stock.

REQUIRED
Prepare general journal entries for these transactions, identifying each by letter.

P 20-9B   (LO1/3)

✓ Sept. 18. Dr. Common Stock Subscribed: $100,000

STOCK SUBSCRIPTIONS AND TREASURY STOCK Rogers & Hart formed a corporation and had the following organization costs and stock transactions during the year:

June 30   Incurred the following costs of incorporation:

Incorporation fees	$ 900
Attorneys' fees	6,000
Promotion fees	8,000

July 15   Issued 8,000 shares of $10 par common stock for $82,000 cash.

Aug. 1   Received subscriptions for 10,000 shares of $10 par common stock for $101,500.

     15   Issued 10,000 shares of $10 par common stock in exchange for a building with a fair market value of $104,800.

     31   Received a payment of $51,500 for the common stock subscription.

Sept. 3   Purchased 1,000 shares of its own $10 par common stock for $11 a share.

     18   Received the balance in full for the common stock subscription and issued the stock.

     30   Sold 500 shares of its treasury stock for $11.70 a share.

Oct. 15   Issued 4,000 shares of $25 par, 8% preferred stock in exchange for land with a fair market value of $105,000.

     31   Sold 500 shares of its treasury stock for $10.50 a share.

REQUIRED
Prepare journal entries for these transactions.

P 20-10B   (LO4)

✓ Total paid-in capital: $533,150

STOCKHOLDERS' EQUITY SECTION After closing its books on December 31, 20--, Merrill Corporation's stockholders' equity accounts have the following balances:

Account	Balance	Additional Information
Preferred Stock Subscriptions Receivable	$ 12,000	
Common Stock Subscriptions Receivable	30,000	
Preferred Stock Subscribed	40,000	$4 dividend, $5 par, 8,000 shares
Common Stock Subscribed	80,000	$10 par, 8,000 shares
Preferred Stock	120,000	$4 dividend, $5 par, 24,000 shares
Common Stock	280,000	$10 par, 28,000 shares
Paid-In Capital in Excess of Par—Preferred Stock	12,000	
Paid-In Capital from Sale of Treasury Stock	1,150	
Common Treasury Stock	24,000	
Retained Earnings	88,000	

REQUIRED

Prepare the stockholders' equity section of the balance sheet for Merrill Corporation for the year ended December 31, 20--.

MANAGING YOUR WRITING

Your boss started a construction company as a partnership with several other contractors 20 years ago. Twelve years later, the partners incorporated to gain access to additional capital by issuing common stock. Forty percent of the shares were sold to the general public, and 60% were acquired by the partners. In this way, the partners kept voting control of the business.

Now the company has an opportunity for a major expansion. To obtain additional capital to fund the expansion, the company is considering another stock offering. But the original partners do not want to lose voting control of the business. Your boss knows you are taking college business courses and asks whether there is a way the company can sell additional stock without the partners losing control of the business. Prepare a report for him describing the kinds of capital stock the company could issue that would accomplish his purpose.

ETHICS

ETHICS CASE

Tyler Corporation started its operations in March. During the first year of operation, a significant amount of money was spent on attorneys' fees and promotional expenses connected with organizing the corporation. The amount of revenue Tyler Corporation earned for the year was much higher than expected. Because of this, the accountant

(continued)

decided to charge the attorneys' fees and promotional expenses to advertising expense in the current year.

1. If the accountant simply was not aware of the proper treatment of these expenditures, were any ethical principles violated? Why or why not?

2. How would you have treated these expenditures?

3. Write a short memo from the accountant to the board of directors of Tyler Corporation explaining how costs of organizing a corporation are treated for accounting purposes.

4. In groups of two or three, discuss the difference between making unethical decisions and making careless decisions.

MASTERY PROBLEM

✓ 3. Total paid-in capital: $1,792,000

Stockholders' equity accounts and other related accounts of Gonzales Company as of January 1, 20--, the beginning of its fiscal year, are shown below.

Preferred stock subscriptions receivable	$ 50,000
Preferred stock, $10 par, 9% (200,000 shares authorized; 20,000 shares issued)	200,000
Preferred stock subscribed (10,000 shares)	100,000
Paid-in capital in excess of par—preferred stock	40,000
Common stock, $10 par (100,000 shares authorized; 60,000 shares issued)	600,000
Paid-in capital in excess of par—common stock	250,000
Retained earnings	750,000

During 20--, Gonzales Company completed the following transactions affecting stockholders' equity:

(a) Received $20,000 for the balance due on subscriptions for 4,000 shares of preferred stock with a par value of $40,000 and issued the stock.

(b) Purchased 10,000 shares of common treasury stock for $18 per share.

(c) Received subscriptions for 10,000 shares of common stock at $19 per share, collecting down payments of $45,000.

(d) Issued 15,000 shares of common stock in exchange for land with a fair market value of $290,000.

(e) Sold 5,000 shares of common treasury stock for $100,000.

(f) Issued 10,000 shares of preferred stock at $11.50 per share, receiving cash.

(g) Sold 3,000 shares of common treasury stock for $17 per share.

REQUIRED

1. Prepare general journal entries for the transactions, identifying each transaction by letter.

2. Post the journal entries to appropriate T accounts. The cash account has a beginning balance of $300,000.

3. Prepare the stockholders' equity section of the balance sheet as of December 31, 20--. Net income for the year was $825,000 and dividends of $400,000 were paid.

CHALLENGE PROBLEM

This problem challenges you to apply your cumulative accounting knowledge to move a step beyond the material in the chapter.

✓ (e) Dr. Retained Earnings: $1,000

Prepare general journal entries for the following transactions, identifying each transaction by letter:

(a) Gnu Company issued 5,000 shares of $1 par common stock to the Prendergas law firm as partial payment of fees incurred to incorporate the business. Gnu was short of cash, so Prendergas agreed to accept $10,000 cash and the shares of common stock in full settlement of its bill for $55,000.

(b) Gnu issued 50,000 shares of $1 par common stock in exchange for a parcel of land for building a shopping plaza. (The list price for the land was $400,000; a similar parcel in the same area sold last week for $380,000. During the past month, the price at which Gnu's common stock has traded on the open market has ranged from $5 to $12 per share. Two trades occurred yesterday at $7 and $10 per share.)

(c) Gnu purchased 10,000 shares of $1 par value common treasury stock for $70,000. (This is the only treasury stock that Gnu holds.)

(d) Gnu sold 4,000 shares of common treasury stock for $32,000.

(e) Gnu sold 5,000 shares of common treasury stock for $30,000.

ANSWERS TO SELF-STUDY TEST QUESTIONS

True/False

1. T
2. T
3. F (Dividends are taxable to the recipients.)
4. F (They are expensed when incurred.)
5. T

Multiple Choice

1. d   2. a   3. c   4. d   5. c

Checkpoint Exercises

1.

Mar.	1	Organization Expenses	7 1 0 0 00	
		Cash		7 1 0 0 00
		Corporate organization costs		

2. Total available for dividends $9,000

Cumulative preferred dividend for year 1 (2,000 shares × $1) $2,000

Preferred dividend for year 2 (2,000 shares × $1)   2,000   4,000

Available for common stock $5,000

Dividends per share:

Preferred $2.00

Common ($5,000/20,000 shares) $0.25

3.

(a)	Common Stock Subscriptions Receivable	80 0 0 0 00		
	Common Stock Subscribed		20 0 0 0 00
	Paid-In Capital in Excess of Par—Common Stock		60 0 0 0 00
	Received subscriptions for common stock		

(b)	Cash	30 0 0 0 00	
	Common Stock Subscriptions Receivable		30 0 0 0 00
	Received subscription payment		

(c)	Cash	50 0 0 0 00	
	Common Stock Subscriptions Receivable		50 0 0 0 00
	Received subscription payment		
	Common Stock Subscribed	20 0 0 0 00	
	Common Stock		20 0 0 0 00

(d)	Common Treasury Stock	7 5 0 0 00	
	Cash		7 5 0 0 00
	Purchased treasury stock		

(e)	Cash	4 2 5 0 00	
	Common Treasury Stock		3 7 5 0 00
	Paid-In Capital from Sale of Treasury Stock		5 0 0 00
	Sold treasury stock		

4. Paid-in capital:

Preferred stock, $10 par, 5%, 4,000 shares $ 40,000

Common stock, $2 par, 60,000 shares $120,000

Common stock subscribed (3,000 shares)   6,000   126,000

Total paid-in capital $166,000

Retained earnings   17,000

Total stockholders' equity $183,000

Chapter 21

Corporations: Taxes, Earnings, Distributions, and the Statement of Retained Earnings

Chapter 20 opened with the story of Gotham Dream Cars. One way for the company to generate the capital it needed to begin and operate a business with those ultra-expensive cars was by incorporating. In this chapter, our study of corporations continues. We set the stage by looking at a very different kind of company—Bamko, Inc. Bamko designs, manufactures, and distributes a vast array of promotional products, including shirts, hats, watches, jackets, mugs, neck pillows, backpacks, and many others. Bamko has thousands of customizable stock items or it can create from scratch virtually anything a client needs.

Bamko started in a small apartment in Los Angeles in 1999 as a t-shirt company and experienced phenomenal growth. In its first ten years, it doubled in size every year, and in 2015 had revenues of $31.5 million. Now it has expanded into product sourcing and development, custom packaging, and supply chain consulting, with offices in the United States, Brazil, China, England, and India. The key question for a company like Bamko is not how to find the capital to start the business but how to fund this pace of growth. In this chapter, you will learn how the corporate form of organization can help. You will learn about cash dividends, stock dividends, and strategies for retaining earnings to help grow the business.

LEARNING OBJECTIVES

Careful study of this chapter should enable you to:

LO1 Account for corporate income taxes.

LO2 Explain the use of the retained earnings account.

LO3 Account for dividends and stock splits.

LO4 Account for restriction of retained earnings.

LO5 Prepare a statement of retained earnings.

In Chapter 20, we learned that stockholders' equity is separated into paid-in capital (amounts contributed by owners) and retained earnings (amounts of accumulated earnings not paid out to stockholders). The emphasis in Chapter 20 was on accounting for paid-in capital, primarily the issuance of capital stock. In this chapter, we focus on retained earnings.

LO1

Account for corporate income taxes.

Corporate Income Taxes

In accounting for sole proprietorships and partnerships, we did not need to deal with income taxes. Sole proprietorships and partnerships, as businesses, do not pay taxes. But, as noted in Chapter 20, a disadvantage of corporations is that they must pay income taxes. To comply with the law and to determine net income, it is essential that the corporation correctly account for and pay corporate income taxes.

Most corporations must estimate their annual income taxes and make quarterly payments. To illustrate, assume Boot Corp. estimates that its income taxes for 20-1 will be $160,000. Based on this estimate, Boot will have to pay $40,000 ($160,000 ÷ 4) on April 15, June 15, September 15, and December 15. The journal entry for each payment is as follows:

5		Income Tax Expense	40 0 0 0 00		5
6		Cash		40 0 0 0 00	6
7		Made quarterly estimated tax payment			7

The actual amount of income taxes for the year typically differs from the estimated amount. Thus, at year-end, an adjusting entry is necessary to recognize the correct amount of income taxes for the year. Assume that as part of the year-end adjusting and closing process at Boot Corp., actual income taxes for the year are calculated as $163,000. The following adjusting journal entry would be made at December 31, 20-1:

> Corporations are subject to a specific corporate tax rate different from those for individuals. Currently, the corporate federal income tax rate is 21%.

5	Dec.	31	Income Tax Expense	3 0 0 0 00*		5
6			Income Tax Payable		3 0 0 0 00	6
7						7
8			*$163,000 actual − $160,000 estimated = $3,000			8

Income Tax Expense is closed to Income Summary at the end of the year in the same manner as other expense accounts. The following closing entry would be made at December 31, 20-1:

| | Dec. | 31 | Income Summary | 163 0 0 0 00 | | |
| | | | Income Tax Expense | | 163 0 0 0 00 | |

On March 15, 20-2, Boot Corp. would file its income tax return for the year ended December 31, 20-1, and pay the $3,000 income taxes due. The following entry would be made:

15	Mar.	15	Income Tax Payable	3	0	0	0	00						15
16			Cash						3	0	0	0	00	16
17			Made final 20-1 tax payment											17

Income taxes normally are reported as a separate expense item on the income statement, and are subtracted from income before income taxes. Assuming that Boot Corp. had income of $780,000 before considering income taxes, the bottom portion of Boot's income statement would appear as shown in Figure 21-1:

FIGURE 21-1 Bottom Portion of the Income Statement

CHECKPOINT ✔

Complete Checkpoint-1 on page 828 to test your basic understanding of LO1.

Income before income taxes	$780,000
Income tax expense	163,000
Net income	$617,000

LO2 — The Retained Earnings Account

Explain the use of the retained earnings account.

Two major sources of capital for every type of business are:

1. Capital that results from investments by the owners
2. Capital that results from earnings retained in the business

In a corporation, as mentioned in Chapter 20, capital resulting from the retention of earnings is entered in the retained earnings account. A corporation usually distributes only a portion of its earnings to stockholders. The balance is retained as additional capital to help finance the growth of the business. This would be very important to Bamko, the company described in the chapter opener.

Generally, there are very few debits and credits to the retained earnings account. Typically, the only credit to the account is for the net income of a period. The only debits are for a net loss, closing the dividends account, and appropriations (special restrictions) of retained earnings. In this section, we will learn how to close the net income or net loss and the dividends for a period to the retained earnings account.

The Adjusting and Closing Process

The adjusting and closing process at the end of the period is virtually the same for corporations as for sole proprietorships and partnerships. The accounts are adjusted and all revenue and expense accounts are closed to Income Summary. A credit balance in Income Summary represents net income; a debit balance signifies a net loss. Beyond this point, however, the closing procedures for corporations differ from those for sole proprietorships and partnerships. The balance of the income summary account of a corporation is transferred to the retained earnings account. For example, if the corporation has net income of $617,000 for the period, the closing entry is as follows and as shown in Figure 21-2.

18	(a)	Income Summary		617	0	0	0	00						18
19		Retained Earnings							617	0	0	0	00	19

FIGURE 21-2 Closing the Income Summary and Dividends Accounts to Retained Earnings

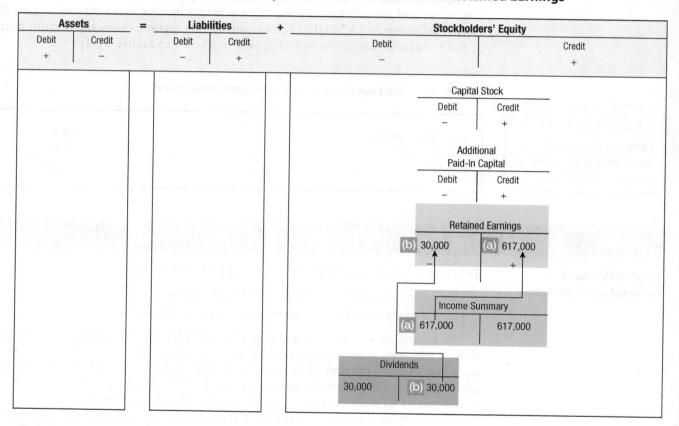

If the corporation has a net loss of $52,000 for the period, the closing entry is as follows:

18		Retained Earnings		52	0	0	0	00						18
19		Income Summary							52	0	0	0	00	19

As noted in Chapter 20, the dividends account also is closed to Retained Earnings. If the corporation declares $30,000 in dividends, the closing entry is as follows and as shown in Figure 21-2.

18	(b)	Retained Earnings		30	0	0	0	00						18
19		Dividends							30	0	0	0	00	19

A BROADER VIEW

DMITRY KALINOVSKY/SHUTTERSTOCK.COM

When Corporate Earnings Get Too Important

Earnings are important in virtually any business, but corporate managers sometimes become so focused on earnings growth that they "create" earnings that do not exist. This apparently is what happened at Kurzweil Applied Intelligence, Inc., a computerized speech recognition company based in Waltham, Massachusetts. Under pressure to produce consistently improving results, key executives at the company engaged in a scheme to regularly record fraudulent sales.

According to generally accepted accounting principles, a sale should be counted when goods are shipped from the company to the customer. Kurzweil took a different approach. Millions of dollars of sales were recorded based on shipments of goods to local warehouses for storage until "real" sales could occur. Most of these "real" sales never happened. The fraud was uncovered when Kurzweil's auditor investigated bills from the warehouses for storage of goods supposedly sold nine months previously.

LO3

Accounting for Dividends and Stock Splits

Account for dividends and stock splits.

A distribution of earnings by a corporation to its stockholders is known as a dividend. In this section, we consider two types of dividends: cash dividends and stock dividends.

Cash Dividends

A dividend payable in cash is known as a cash dividend. For a corporation to issue a cash dividend, three conditions are necessary.

1. Unrestricted retained earnings. In general, corporations can legally declare cash dividends only if the retained earnings balance is sufficient to cover the dividends.
2. Adequate cash balance. The retained earnings balance indicates whether a corporation can legally declare a dividend. But a corporation can pay a cash dividend only if an adequate amount of cash is available. Remember: Retained earnings is not the same as cash.
3. Declaration of dividend. Only the board of directors can declare a dividend. Regardless of the amount of cash or other assets accumulated by a corporation, no dividend can be paid unless the board of directors declares one.

Three dates are involved in the declaration and payment of dividends.

1. Date of declaration—the date on which the board of directors decides (declares) that a dividend is to be paid. This is the most important dividend date—when the corporation commits to paying the dividend.
2. Date of record—the date on which the names of stockholders entitled to receive the dividend are determined.
3. Date of payment—the date on which the dividend is actually paid by the corporation.

For example, assume that on February 1 the board of directors declares a dividend of $2 a share on common stock, payable on February 20 to stockholders of record on February 10. In this case, the date of declaration, date of record, and date of payment are as shown in Figure 21-3. To be eligible to receive the dividend, a stockholder's ownership of stock must be entered in the records of the corporation not later than February 10.

FIGURE 21-3 Dividend Dates

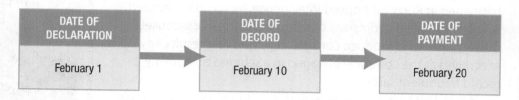

Dividends on different classes of capital stock should be accounted for separately. To illustrate, assume that on February 1 the board of directors declares the $2 per share dividend described above on 10,000 shares of common stock and a dividend of $4 per share on 4,000 shares of preferred stock. Both dividends are payable on February 20 to stockholders of record on February 10. These dividends are accounted for as follows:

Feb. 1   Date of Declaration:

4	Feb.	1	Cash Dividends	16 0 0 0 00		4
5			Preferred Dividends Payable		16 0 0 0 00	5
6			Declared preferred stock cash dividend			6
7						7
8		1	Cash Dividends	20 0 0 0 00		8
9			Common Dividends Payable		20 0 0 0 00	9
10			Declared common stock cash dividend			10

Feb. 10   Date of Record:

No journal entry is made. The date of record has no effect on the corporation accounts. This date simply determines which stockholders receive the dividends.

Feb. 20   Date of Payment:

18	Feb.	20	Preferred Dividends Payable	16 0 0 0 00		18
19			Cash		16 0 0 0 00	19
20			Paid preferred stock cash dividend			20
21						21
22		20	Common Dividends Payable	20 0 0 0 00		22
23			Cash		20 0 0 0 00	23
24			Paid common stock cash dividend			24

If a balance sheet is prepared between the date of declaration and date of payment, dividends payable accounts are reported as current liabilities.

As explained in Chapter 20 and shown in Figure 21-2, the dividends account is closed to Retained Earnings. If the two cash dividends described above were the only dividends declared for the year, the following closing entry would be made at December 31:

| 6 | Dec. | 31 | Retained Earnings | | 36 | 0 | 0 | 0 | 00 | | | | | | 6 |
| 7 | | | Cash Dividends | | | | | | | | 36 | 0 | 0 | 0 | 00 | 7 |

Note that cash dividends reduce the stockholders' equity in the corporation, as shown in Figure 21-4. A cash dividend is a distribution of corporate assets to the stockholders. After Cash Dividends is closed to Retained Earnings, the retained earnings portion of stockholders' equity is reduced accordingly.

FIGURE 21-4 Effect of Cash Dividend

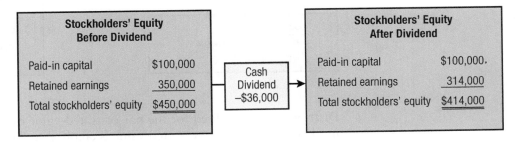

Stock Dividends

A stock dividend is a proportionate distribution of shares of a corporation's own stock to its stockholders. Corporations may distribute this type of dividend for several reasons.

1. The company may be short of cash but still want to make a distribution to the stockholders.
2. The company may want to increase the marketability of its shares by lowering the price per share. A greater number of shares outstanding decreases the price per share and makes wider ownership possible.
3. The corporation may want to transfer a portion of retained earnings to a paid-in capital category to indicate that it is unavailable for dividends.

Stock dividends usually involve issuing additional common shares to current common stockholders. Stock dividends typically are stated as a percentage of common stock outstanding. For example, a 10% stock dividend means that a stockholder receives one additional share for each 10 shares owned. Thus, the owner of 100 shares of common stock receives an additional 10 shares (10% × 100 shares = 10 shares).

An illustration of the effect of this 10% stock dividend is provided in Figure 21-5. Note that a 10% stock dividend does not give the stockholder any increased ownership in the corporation. As shown in Figure 21-5, *all* stockholders receive the 10% dividend, so everyone still owns the same portion of the corporation. Each stockholder owns 10% more shares, but each individual share is worth less.

When a stock dividend is declared, the proper journal entry depends on the dividend percentage. If the stock dividend is for less than 20%–25% of the outstanding shares, Stock Dividends is debited for the *market value* of the stock to be distributed. If the stock has neither par nor stated value, Stock Dividends Distributable is credited for the market value of the shares. If the stock has a par or stated value, Stock Dividends

---

LEARNING KEY 🔑

To record a stock dividend of less than 20%–25%, debit Stock Dividends for the *market value* of the shares distributed.

FIGURE 21-5 Effect of Stock Dividend

Ownership before Stock Dividend		Ownership after Stock Dividend

Total stockholders' equity $450,000
Total shares outstanding   10,000

→ 10% Stock Dividend →

Total stockholders' equity $450,000
Total shares outstanding   11,000

Ownership

9,900 shares
= 99% of 10,000 shares
= 99% owners

100 shares
= 1% of 10,000 shares
= 1% owner

10,000 shares
= 100% of 10,000 shares
= 100% owners

Ownership

10,890 shares
= 99% of 11,000 shares
= 99% owners

110 shares
= 1% of 11,000 shares
= 1% owner

11,000 shares
= 100% of 11,000 shares
= 100% owners

Distributable is credited for the par or stated value of the shares. The excess of the market value over par or stated value is credited to Paid-In Capital in Excess of Par (or Stated) Value—Common Stock.

To illustrate, assume that Diven Corp. has 4,000 shares of $5 par common stock outstanding. Diven declares a 10% stock dividend on March 5, payable on March 27 to stockholders of record on March 14. The market value of Diven's common stock on the date of declaration is $12 per share. This means that Diven will issue a total of 400 shares of common stock (4,000 shares × 10% = 400 shares) with a market value of $4,800 (400 shares × $12 = $4,800).

We account for this stock dividend as follows:

Mar. 5 Date of Declaration:

	Mar.	5	Stock Dividends	4 8 0 0 00		
23			Stock Dividends Distributable*		2 0 0 0 00	
24			Paid-In Capital in Excess of Par—			
25			Common Stock**		2 8 0 0 00	
26			Declared stock dividend			
27			*400 shares × $5 par			
28			**$4,800 market value − $2,000 par value			

Mar. 14 Date of Record:

No journal entry. As with cash dividends, the date of record has no effect on the corporation accounts.

Mar. 27 Date of Distribution:

14	Mar.	27	Stock Dividends Distributable	2 0 0 0 00		
15			Common Stock		2 0 0 0 00	
16			Distributed stock dividend			

If a balance sheet is prepared between the date of declaration and the date of distribution, Stock Dividends Distributable is reported as an addition to common stock in the stockholders' equity section of the balance sheet. Stock Dividends Distributable is not a liability since no assets or services are owed.

As shown in Figure 21-2, the stock dividends account is closed to Retained Earnings. If the stock dividend described above was the only dividend declared for the year, the following entry would be made on December 31:

6	Dec.	31	Retained Earnings		4	8	0	0	00				6
7			Stock Dividends							4	8	0	0	00	7

Note that stock dividends do not affect the assets, liabilities, or total stockholders' equity of the corporation. The stock dividends account is closed to Retained Earnings. However, there is no distribution of corporate assets. Stock dividends merely transfer part of the balance of the retained earnings account to one or more paid-in capital accounts.

If a stock dividend is more than 20%–25% of the outstanding shares, Stock Dividends is debited for the *par or stated value* rather than the market value of the shares to be distributed. Stock Dividends Distributable is credited for the same amount. The accounting on the date of distribution and the closing process at year end are the same as that illustrated for stock dividends of less than 20%–25%.

Stock Splits

A stock split is an exchange of one share of an old issue of stock for multiple shares of a new issue with a reduced par or stated value. The usual purpose of a stock split is to improve the marketability of the shares by reducing the market price per share. Having a greater number of shares outstanding also makes it possible to have a wider ownership of the stock.

Accounting for a stock split differs from accounting for a stock dividend. A stock split requires no formal journal entry and may be recognized simply by a memorandum notation in the general journal and in the appropriate capital stock accounts. Thus, stock splits do not affect the assets, liabilities, or any component of stockholders' equity of a corporation.

To illustrate, assume that Splice Corp. has 10,000 shares of $10 par common stock outstanding. Splice declares a two-for-one stock split. This means that Splice will issue a total of 20,000 shares of $5 par common stock in exchange for the 10,000 shares of $10 par common stock currently outstanding. Each stockholder will receive two shares of the new $5 par stock in exchange for one share of the old $10 par stock. The memorandum entry in the journal is as follows:

22		Declared two-for-one stock split. Issued									22
23		20,000 shares of $5 par common stock in exchange for									23
24		10,000 shares of $10 par common stock.									24

Summary of Dividend and Stock Split Transactions

We have seen that cash dividends, stock dividends, and stock splits affect stockholders' equity differently. Figure 21-6 briefly describes and summarizes the effects of these three transactions on the assets, paid-in capital, and retained earnings of the corporation. Refer to this figure as you work the exercises and problems for this chapter.

FIGURE 21-6 Summary of Dividend and Split Transactions

TRANS-ACTION	DESCRIPTION	JOURNAL ENTRIES	ASSETS	PAID-IN CAPITAL	RETAINED EARNINGS

Cash Dividend	Distribution of cash to stockholders	At declaration:
		Cash Dividends xxx
		  Dividends Payable xxx
		At payment:
		  Dividends Payable xxx
		    Cash xxx
			Decrease by amount of dividend distributed	No effect	Decrease by amount of cash dividend*

Stock Dividend Less than 20%–25%	Distribution of corporation's stock to stockholders	At declaration:
		Stock Dividends xxx
		  Stock Div. Distributable xxx
		  Paid-In Capital in
		  Excess of Par xxx
		At distribution:
		  Stock Div. Distributable xxx
		    Common Stock xxx
			No effect	Increase by market value of stock distributed	Decrease by market value of stock dividend*

More than 20%–25%	Distribution of corporation's stock to stockholders	At declaration:
		Stock Dividends xxx
		  Stock Div. Distributable xxx
		At distribution:
		  Stock Div. Distributable xxx
		    Common Stock xxx
			No effect	Increase by par value of stock distributed	Decrease by par value of stock dividend*

Stock Split	Exchange of old stock for multiple shares of new stock	Memo notation	No effect	No effect	No effect

*Recall that Cash Dividends and Stock Dividends are closed to Retained Earnings at the end of the period.

| **LO4** | **Restriction of Retained Earnings** |

Account for restriction of retained earnings.

Thus far, we have examined how net income, net loss, cash dividends, and stock dividends affect retained earnings. One other event that affects retained earnings is an appropriation. A retained earnings appropriation is a restriction of retained earnings by the board of directors for a specific purpose. Recall that corporations may pay dividends only if the retained earnings balance is sufficient to do so. A retained earnings appropriation is used primarily to limit the availability of retained earnings for paying dividends.

To illustrate, assume that Chem Corp. decides to appropriate $200,000 of retained earnings to help finance a new treatment plant. The following journal entry would be made:

1		Retained Earnings	200 0 0 0 00		1
2		Retained Earnings Appropriated			2
3		for Treatment Plant		200 0 0 0 00	3
4		Appropriated retained earnings for			4
5		treatment plant			5
6					6

In Chem's balance sheet and retained earnings statement, total retained earnings would be separated into appropriated and unappropriated amounts. When the appropriation is no longer needed, the above journal entry simply would be reversed.

The practice of appropriating retained earnings is unusual today. Stockholders generally do not regard the retained earnings balance as the total amount likely to be distributed as dividends. Thus, it generally is unnecessary to make appropriations to advise balance sheet readers that retained earnings is not all available for dividends.

In addition, restrictions of retained earnings often can be described more clearly in a footnote to the financial statements. For example, Chem Corp.'s financial statements in the year of the appropriation could include a footnote like the following:

> To help finance a new treatment plant, the board of directors has appropriated $200,000 of retained earnings this year.

CHECKPOINT ✓

Complete Checkpoint-4 on page 828 to test your basic understanding of LO4.

LO5   Statement of Retained Earnings

Prepare a statement of retained earnings.

A statement of retained earnings explains the change in the amount of retained earnings during the year. All of the information necessary to prepare the statement of retained earnings is contained in the dividends accounts and the unappropriated and appropriated retained earnings accounts in the general ledger. If there are no appropriated retained earnings, the statement begins with the beginning of the year retained earnings balance. Net income for the year is added (or net loss is subtracted). Any cash and stock dividends are then subtracted to yield the end of the year retained earnings balance. This balance is the same amount that appears in the stockholders' equity section of the year-end balance sheet. Figure 21-7 shows the format for a statement of retained earnings with no appropriated retained earnings.

FIGURE 21-7 Statement of Retained Earnings without Appropriated Retained Earnings

Sample Corporation		
Statement of Retained Earnings		
For Year Ended December 31, 20--		
Retained earnings, January 1		$1,100,000
Add net income for the year		280,000
		$1,380,000
Less: Cash dividends	$30,000	
Stock dividends	20,000	50,000
Retained earnings, December 31		$1,330,000

CHECKPOINT ✓

Complete Checkpoint-5 on page 828 to test your basic understanding of LO5.

If there are both appropriated and unappropriated retained earnings, each is shown separately in the statement of retained earnings. The appropriated portion is presented first.

LEARNING OBJECTIVES	Key Points to Remember
LO1 Account for corporate income taxes.	Corporations must pay income taxes. Most corporations must estimate their annual income taxes and make quarterly payments.
LO2 Explain the use of the retained earnings account.	Earnings retained in a corporation are recorded by closing the income summary account to the retained earnings account at the end of the period.
LO3 Account for dividends and stock splits.	Three important dates in the declaration and payment of dividends are as follows: 1. Date of declaration 2. Date of record 3. Date of payment Journal entries are necessary on the date of declaration and date of payment. For stock dividends of less than 20%–25%, Stock Dividends is debited for the market value of the shares to be distributed. For stock dividends of more than 20%–25%, Stock Dividends is debited for the par or stated value of the shares. A stock split requires no formal journal entry. A memorandum notation in the general journal and capital stock accounts is all that is necessary.
LO4 Account for restriction of retained earnings.	An appropriation of retained earnings restricts the corporation's ability to pay out its assets as dividends. Restriction of retained earnings also can be described in a footnote to the financial statements.
LO5 Prepare a statement of retained earnings.	A statement of retained earnings explains the change in the amount of retained earnings during the year. If there are both appropriated and unappropriated retained earnings, each is shown separately on the statement of retained earnings.

DEMONSTRATION PROBLEM

On January 1, 20-1, Grant Company's retained earnings account had the following balances:

Appropriated for warehouse	$ 50,000
Unappropriated retained earnings	675,000
	$725,000

During the year ended December 31, 20-1, Grant completed the following selected transactions:

Apr. 15   Estimated that its 20-1 income tax will be $40,000. Based on this estimate, it will make four quarterly payments of $10,000 each on April 15, June 15, September 15, and December 15.

     20   Declared semiannual dividend of $0.30 per share on common stock to shareholders of record on May 5, payable May 15. Currently, 50,000 shares of $3 par stock are outstanding.

May 15   Paid the cash dividend.

June 15   Made estimated tax payment of $10,000.

Sept. 15   Made estimated tax payment of $10,000.

Oct. 20   Declared a semiannual dividend of $0.30 per share on common stock to shareholders of record on November 5, payable on November 15.

Nov. 15   Paid the cash dividend.

16   Declared a 10% stock dividend to shareholders of record on December 2, distributable on December 10. Market value of the common stock was estimated at $7 per share.

Dec. 10   Issued certificates for common stock dividend.

15   Made estimated tax payment of $10,000.

On December 31, the following adjusting and closing entries were made:

31   Grant's actual 20-1 income tax is $44,000. The $4,000 ($44,000 − $40,000) additional amount owed will be paid by March 15, 20-2. Made adjustment for the additional amount owed.

31   Net income for 20-1 was $166,000. Closed the income summary account.

31   Closed the cash dividends and stock dividends accounts.

REQUIRED

1. Prepare journal entries for the above transactions and for the adjusting and closing process.

2. Post all entries affecting the appropriated and unappropriated retained earnings accounts to T accounts.

3. Prepare a statement of retained earnings for the year ended December 31, 20-1.

SOLUTION 1.

			GENERAL JOURNAL					PAGE 1	
	DATE		DESCRIPTION	POST. REF.	DEBIT		CREDIT		
1	20-1 Apr.	15	Income Tax Expense		10 0 0 0 00				1
2			Cash				10 0 0 0 00		2
3			Made quarterly estimated tax payment						3
4									4
5		20	Cash Dividends		15 0 0 0 00				5
6			Common Dividends Payable				15 0 0 0 00		6
7			Declared common stock cash dividend						7
8									8
9	May	15	Common Dividends Payable		15 0 0 0 00				9
10			Cash				15 0 0 0 00		10
11			Paid common stock cash dividend						11
12									12
13	June	15	Income Tax Expense		10 0 0 0 00				13
14			Cash				10 0 0 0 00		14
15			Made quarterly estimated tax payment						15
16									16
17	Sept.	15	Income Tax Expense		10 0 0 0 00				17
18			Cash				10 0 0 0 00		18
19			Made quarterly estimated tax payment						19
20									20
21	Oct.	20	Cash Dividends		15 0 0 0 00				21
22			Common Dividends Payable				15 0 0 0 00		22
23			Declared common stock cash dividend						23
24									24
25	Nov.	15	Common Dividends Payable		15 0 0 0 00				25
26			Cash				15 0 0 0 00		26
27			Paid common stock cash dividend						27

(*continued*)

	DATE		DESCRIPTION	POST. REF.	DEBIT		CREDIT		
			GENERAL JOURNAL				PAGE 2		
1	20-1 Nov.	16	Stock Dividends		35 0 0 0 00				1
2			Stock Dividends Distributable ($3 × 5,000)				15 0 0 0 00		2
3			Paid-In Capital in Excess of Par—						3
4			Common Stock ($4 × 5,000)				20 0 0 0 00		4
5			Declared stock dividend						5
6									6
7	Dec.	10	Stock Dividends Distributable		15 0 0 0 00				7
8			Common Stock				15 0 0 0 00		8
9			Distributed stock dividend						9
10									10
11		15	Income Tax Expense		10 0 0 0 00				11
12			Cash				10 0 0 0 00		12
13			Made quarterly estimated tax payment						13
14									14
15			Adjusting Entry						15
16		31	Income Tax Expense		4 0 0 0 00				16
17			Income Tax Payable				4 0 0 0 00		17
18									18
19			Closing Entries						19
20		31	Income Summary		166 0 0 0 00				20
21			Retained Earnings				166 0 0 0 00		21
22									22
23		31	Retained Earnings		30 0 0 0 00				23
24			Cash Dividends				30 0 0 0 00		24
25									25
26		31	Retained Earnings		35 0 0 0 00				26
27			Stock Dividends				35 0 0 0 00		27
28									28
29									29

SOLUTION 2.

Retained Earnings—Appropriated			Retained Earnings—Unappropriated			
	Bal.	50,000	Dec. 31	30,000	Bal.	675,000
			31	35,000	Dec. 31	166,000
				65,000		841,000
					Bal.	776,000

SOLUTION 3.

Grant Company Statement of Retained Earnings For Year Ended December 31, 20-1			
Appropriated:			
Appropriated for warehouse			$ 50,000
Unappropriated:			
Balance, January 1	$675,000		
Add net income for the year	166,000	$841,000	
Less: Cash dividends	$ 30,000		
Stock dividends	35,000	$ 65,000	
Retained earnings unappropriated, December 31			776,000
Total retained earnings, December 31			$826,000

KEY TERMS

cash dividend (817) A dividend payable in cash.

date of declaration (817) The date on which the board of directors declares that a dividend is to be paid.

date of payment (817) The date on which the dividend is actually paid by the corporation.

date of record (817) The date on which the names of stockholders entitled to receive the dividend are determined.

dividend (817) A distribution of earnings by a corporation to its stockholders.

retained earnings appropriation (822) A restriction of retained earnings by the board of directors for a specific purpose.

statement of retained earnings (823) A statement that explains the change in the amount of retained earnings during the year.

stock dividend (819) A proportionate distribution of shares of a corporation's own stock to its stockholders.

stock split (821) An exchange of one share of an old issue of stock for multiple shares of a new issue with a reduced par or stated value.

SELF-STUDY TEST QUESTIONS

True/False

1. **LO1** Income taxes are a unique expense of the corporate form of business.

2. **LO2** The adjusting and closing process at the end of the period is virtually the same for corporations as for sole proprietorships and partnerships.

3. **LO3** A distribution of earnings by a corporation to its stockholders is known as a dividend.

4. **LO3** A dividend payable in cash is known as a stock dividend.

5. **LO3** When accounting for the declaration and payment of dividends, the date of record requires a journal entry.

Multiple Choice

1. **LO3** A proportionate distribution of shares of a corporation's own stock to its stockholders is called a(n)
   (a) stock dividend.
   (b) cash dividend.
   (c) stock split.
   (d) appropriation.

2. **LO3** When a stock dividend is declared, the journal entry will include a credit to
   (a) Retained Earnings.
   (b) Stock Dividends Distributable.
   (c) Stock Dividends Payable.
   (d) Stock Dividends Declared.

3. **LO3** Stock Dividends Distributable is classified on the balance sheet as a(n)
   (a) asset.
   (b) liability.
   (c) expense.
   (d) stockholders' equity.

4. **LO3**   The payment of a cash dividend will include a
(a) debit to Dividends Declared.   (c) credit to Cash.
(b) credit to Dividends Payable.   (d) debit to Retained Earnings.

5. **LO4**   When retained earnings is appropriated, total retained earnings
(a) remains the same.   (c) decreases.
(b) increases.   (d) increases or decreases, depending
                                               on the amount.

CHECKPOINT

Checkpoint Exercises

1. **LO1**   Ozit Company made four quarterly income tax payments of $25,000 each during the year. On December 31, Ozit's actual income tax totals $103,000. Prepare the journal entry on December 31 to record the additional income tax owed.

2. **LO2**   DWP Company had net income of $183,000 and paid cash dividends totaling $16,000 throughout the year. Prepare the journal entries at December 31 to close Income Summary and Cash Dividends to Retained Earnings.

3. **LO3**   Teway Company declared and paid dividends in the current year as follows:

(a) On May 31, declared cash dividend of $12,000 on common stock.

(b) On June 20, paid the cash dividend declared in transaction (a).

(c) On November 30, declared a 10% stock dividend on 50,000 shares of $2 par common stock with a market value of $7 per share.

(d) On December 18, distributed the stock dividend declared in transaction (c).

Prepare the journal entries for these transactions.

4. **LO4**   On September 30, Polmax Power Company's board of directors appropriated $300,000 of retained earnings for emission reduction plant modifications. Prepare the journal entry for this appropriation.

5. **LO5**   On January 1, 20--, MC Company had a retained earnings balance of $720,500. During the year, it paid cash dividends of $24,000 and stock dividends of $47,000, and had net income of $88,000. Prepare the statement of retained earnings for MC Company for the year ended December 31, 20--.

The answers to the Self-Study Test Questions are at the end of the chapter (pages 838–839).

APPLYING YOUR KNOWLEDGE

REVIEW QUESTIONS

LO1   1. What expense do corporations incur that sole proprietorships and partnerships do not?

LO2   2. What are the two major sources of capital for every type of business?

LO2   3.   For what reason do corporations retain earnings in the business?

LO2   4.   How do the procedures for closing Income Summary of a corporation differ from those of a sole proprietorship or partnership?

LO3   5.   What are the three dates involved in the declaration and payment of dividends? What is the meaning of each date?

LO3   6.   What is the effect of a cash dividend on the corporation accounts?

LO3   7.   Give three reasons why a corporation may distribute a stock dividend.

LO3   8.   Where should stock dividends distributable be reported on the balance sheet? Why?

LO3   9.   What effect does a stock dividend have on the accounts of the corporation? A stock split?

LO4   10.   What is the primary reason for appropriating retained earnings?

LO5   11.   How are appropriated and unappropriated retained earnings shown on the statement of retained earnings?

SERIES A EXERCISES

E 21-1A   (LO1)
✓ Dec. 31. Dr. Income Tax Expense: $6,000

CORPORATE INCOME TAX Stanton Company estimates that its 20-1 income tax will be $80,000. Based on this estimate, it will make four quarterly payments of $20,000 each on April 15, June 15, September 15, and December 15.

1. Prepare the journal entry for April 15.
2. Assume that all four quarterly payments have been entered in the general journal. On December 31, Stanton's actual income tax amounts to $86,000. This amount will be paid by March 15, 20-2. Prepare the journal entry to record the additional income tax owed.

E 21-2A   (LO2/3)
✓ 2. Cr. Stock Dividends: $15,000

CLOSING INCOME SUMMARY AND DIVIDENDS TO RETAINED EARNINGS Adriana Company had a net income of $130,000 and paid cash dividends of $26,000 for 20--. Overman Company had a net loss of $25,000 and distributed a 10% stock dividend with a market value of $15,000.

1. Prepare the journal entries for Adriana as of December 31, 20--, to close Income Summary and Cash Dividends into Retained Earnings.
2. Prepare the journal entries for Overman as of December 31, 20--, to close Income Summary and Stock Dividends into Retained Earnings.

E 21-3A   (LO3)
✓ July 10. Dr. Cash Dividends: $60,000

COMMON AND PREFERRED CASH DIVIDENDS Wang Company currently has 200,000 shares of $1 par common stock outstanding and 3,000 shares of $50 par preferred stock outstanding. On July 10, the board of directors declared a semiannual dividend of $0.30 per share on common stock to shareholders of record on August 1, payable on August 5.

On July 15, the board of directors declared a semiannual dividend of $3 per share on preferred stock to shareholders of record on August 5, payable on August 10.

Prepare journal entries for the declaration and payment of the common and preferred stock cash dividends.

E 21-4A   (LO3)

✓ 1. Mar. 15. Dr. Stock Dividends: $100,000

STOCK DIVIDENDS Kaufman Company currently has 200,000 shares of $1 par common stock outstanding. On March 15, a 10% stock dividend was declared to shareholders of record on April 2, distributable on April 14. Market value of the common stock was estimated at $5 per share.

1. Prepare journal entries for the declaration and distribution of the 10% common stock dividend.

2. Assume Kaufman Company declared a stock dividend of 30% rather than 10%. Prepare journal entries for the declaration and distribution of the 30% common stock dividend.

E 21-5A   (LO3)

✓ Memo entry only

STOCK SPLIT Goldstein Company has 100,000 shares of $10 par common stock outstanding. On July 1, the board of directors declared a two-for-one stock split.

Prepare a memorandum entry in the general journal indicating the new par value and the total number of outstanding shares of common stock.

E 21-6A   (LO4)

✓ Oct. 2. Dr. Retained Earnings: $80,000

RETAINED EARNINGS APPROPRIATION On October 2, 20-1, the board of directors of Foxworth Company appropriated $80,000 of retained earnings for the purpose of buying a new sailboat (used for entertaining clients). On July 15, 20-2, the sailboat was purchased and the board of directors decided that the appropriation was no longer needed.

Prepare journal entries for the appropriation on October 2, 20-1, and the subsequent return on July 15, 20-2.

E 21-7A   (LO5)

✓ Retained Earnings: Dec. 31: $75,000

STATEMENT OF RETAINED EARNINGS McGregor Company had the following balances and results for the current calendar year:

Retained earnings, January 1	$60,000
Cash dividends declared	5,000
Net income for the year	20,000

Prepare a statement of retained earnings for the year ended December 31, 20--.

SERIES A PROBLEMS

P 21-8A   (LO1/3)

✓ 1st Dec. 31 entry. Dr. Income Tax Expense: $5,000

CASH DIVIDENDS AND INCOME TAXES During the year ended December 31, 20-2, Bebeto Company completed the following selected transactions:

Apr. 15   Estimated that its 20-2 income tax will be $30,000. Based on this estimate, it will make four quarterly payments of $7,500 each on April 15, June 15, September 15, and December 15. Made the first payment.

25   Declared a semiannual dividend of $0.45 per share on common stock to shareholders of record on May 10, payable May 20. Currently, 80,000 shares of $1 par common stock are outstanding.

May 20   Paid the cash dividends.

June 15   Made estimated tax payment of $7,500.

Sept. 15   Made estimated tax payment of $7,500.

Oct. 25   Declared semiannual dividend of $0.45 per share on common stock to shareholders of record on November 10, payable on November 20.

Nov. 20   Paid the cash dividends.

Dec. 15   Made estimated tax payment of $7,500.

31   Bebeto's actual 20-2 income tax is $35,000. This amount will be paid by March 15, 20-3. Made adjustment for the additional amount owed.

31   Net income for 20-2 was $134,000. Closed the income summary account.

31   Closed the cash dividends account.

REQUIRED
Prepare journal entries for the transactions.

P 21-9A   (LO3)
✓ Nov. 22. Dr. Stock Dividends: $56,000

CASH DIVIDENDS, STOCK DIVIDEND, AND STOCK SPLIT During the year ended December 31, 20--, Choi Company completed the following transactions:

Apr. 15   Declared a semiannual dividend of $1.50 per share on preferred stock and $0.40 per share on common stock to shareholders of record on May 5, payable on May 10. Currently, 6,000 shares of $50 par preferred stock and 80,000 shares of $1 par common stock are outstanding.

May 10   Paid the cash dividends.

Oct. 15   Declared semiannual dividend of $1.50 per share on preferred stock and $0.40 per share on common stock to shareholders of record on November 5, payable on November 20.

Nov. 20   Paid the cash dividends.

22   Declared a 10% stock dividend to common shareholders of record on December 8, distributable on December 16. Market value of the common stock was estimated at $7 per share.

Dec. 16   Issued certificates for common stock dividend.

20   Board of directors declared a two-for-one common stock split.

REQUIRED
Prepare journal entries for the transactions.

P 21-10A   (LO3/4)
✓ Nov. 12. Dr. Cash Dividends: $19,500

CASH DIVIDEND AND APPROPRIATION OF RETAINED EARNINGS On January 1, 20--, MacMillan Company's retained earnings accounts had the following balances:

Appropriated for warehouse	$ 80,000
Unappropriated retained earnings	600,000
	$680,000

During the year ended December 31, 20--, MacMillan completed the following selected transactions:

Mar. 16   MacMillan's board of directors appropriated $75,000 for acquisition of new computers.

Nov. 5   Purchased a new warehouse for $80,000, paying cash for the total amount.

5   The board of directors returned the amount of retained earnings set aside for the warehouse to unappropriated retained earnings.

12   Declared a cash dividend of $0.65 per share on common stock to shareholders of record on December 8, payable on December 19. Currently, 30,000 shares of common stock are outstanding.

Dec. 19   Paid the cash dividends.

REQUIRED
Prepare journal entries for the transactions.

P 21-11A (LO3/4/5)
✓ 3. Retained Earnings, Dec. 31: $1,094,000

RETAINED EARNINGS ACCOUNTS AND STATEMENT On January 1, 20--, Glover Company's retained earnings accounts had the following balances:

Appropriated for land acquisition	$ 60,000
Unappropriated retained earnings	900,000
	$960,000

During the year ended December 31, 20--, Glover completed the following selected transactions:

Mar. 20 Declared a semiannual dividend of $0.80 per share on preferred stock and $0.25 per share on common stock to shareholders of record on April 10, payable on April 15. Currently, 10,000 shares of $50 par preferred stock and 100,000 shares of $5 par common stock are outstanding.

Apr. 15 Paid the cash dividends.

Oct. 10 Declared semiannual dividend of $0.80 per share on preferred stock and $0.25 per share on common stock to shareholders of record on November 5, payable on November 10.

Nov. 10 Paid the cash dividends.

17 Declared a 5% stock dividend to shareholders of record on December 8, distributable on December 15. Market value of the common stock was estimated at $18 per share.

Dec. 15 Issued certificates for common stock dividend.

31 Net income for 20-- was $290,000. Closed the income summary account.

31 Closed the cash dividends and stock dividends accounts.

REQUIRED

1. Prepare journal entries for the transactions.
2. Post all entries affecting the retained earnings accounts to T accounts.
3. Prepare a statement of retained earnings for the year ended December 31, 20--.

SERIES B EXERCISES

E 21-1B (LO1)
✓ Dec. 31. Dr. Income Tax Expense: $12,000

CORPORATE INCOME TAX Regis Company estimates that its 20-1 income tax will be $100,000. Based on this estimate, it will make four quarterly payments of $25,000 each on April 15, June 15, September 15, and December 15.

1. Prepare the journal entry for April 15.
2. Assume that all four quarterly payments have been entered in the general journal. On December 31, Regis's actual income tax amounts to $112,000. This amount will be paid by March 15, 20-2. Prepare the journal entry to record the additional income tax owed.

E 21-2B (LO2/3)
✓ 2. Cr. Stock Dividends: $15,000

CLOSING INCOME SUMMARY AND DIVIDENDS TO RETAINED EARNINGS Kennington Company had a net income of $90,000 and paid cash dividends of $18,000 for 20--. Mueller and Hanson Company had a net loss of $20,000 and distributed a 10% stock dividend with a market value of $15,000.

1. Prepare the journal entries for Kennington as of December 31, 20--, to close Income Summary and Cash Dividends into Retained Earnings.

2. Prepare the journal entries for Mueller and Hanson as of December 31, 20--, to close Income Summary and Stock Dividends into Retained Earnings.

E 21-3B   (LO3)

✓ July 10. Dr. Cash Dividends: $30,000

COMMON AND PREFERRED CASH DIVIDENDS Ramirez Company currently has 100,000 shares of $1 par common stock outstanding and 5,000 shares of $50 par preferred stock outstanding. On July 10, the board of directors declared a semiannual dividend of $0.30 per share on common stock to shareholders of record on August 1, payable on August 5.

On July 15, the board of directors declared a semiannual dividend of $5 per share on preferred stock to shareholders of record on August 5, payable on August 10.

Prepare journal entries for the declaration and payment of the common and preferred stock cash dividends.

E 21-4B   (LO3)

✓ 1. Mar. 15. Dr. Stock Dividends: $130,000

STOCK DIVIDENDS Martinez Company currently has 200,000 shares of $1 par common stock outstanding. On March 15, a 5% stock dividend was declared to shareholders of record on April 2, distributable on April 14. Market value of the common stock was estimated at $13 per share.

1. Prepare journal entries for the declaration and distribution of the 5% common stock dividend.

2. Assume Martinez Company declared a stock dividend of 30% rather than 5%. Prepare journal entries for the declaration and distribution of the 30% common stock dividend.

E 21-5B   (LO3)

✓ Memo entry only

STOCK SPLIT Rogerson Company has 40,000 shares of $2 par common stock outstanding. On July 1, the board of directors declared a two-for-one stock split.

Prepare a memorandum entry in the general journal indicating the new par value and the total number of outstanding shares of common stock.

E 21-6B   (LO4)

✓ Oct. 2. Dr. Retained Earnings: $400,000

RETAINED EARNINGS APPROPRIATION On October 2, 20-1, the board of directors of Carr Company appropriated $400,000 of retained earnings for the purpose of buying a new yacht (used for entertaining clients). On July 15, 20-2, the yacht was purchased and the board of directors decided that the appropriation was no longer needed.

Prepare journal entries for the appropriation on October 2, 20-1, and the subsequent return on July 15, 20-2.

E 21-7B   (LO5)

✓ Retained Earnings, Dec. 31: $105,000

STATEMENT OF RETAINED EARNINGS Womack Company had the following balances and results for the current calendar year:

Retained earnings, January 1	$80,000
Cash dividends declared	15,000
Net income for the year	40,000

Prepare a statement of retained earnings for the year ended December 31, 20--.

SERIES B PROBLEMS

P 21-8B   (LO1/3)

✓ 1st Dec. 31 entry. Dr. Income Tax Expense: $14,000

CASH DIVIDENDS AND INCOME TAXES During the year ended December 31, 20-2, Tatu Company completed the following selected transactions:

Apr. 15   Estimated that its 20-2 income tax will be $160,000. Based on this estimate, it will make four quarterly payments of $40,000 each on April 15, June 15, September 15, and December 15. Made the first payment.

25   Declared a semiannual dividend of $0.50 per share on common stock to shareholders of record on May 10, payable May 20. Currently, 90,000 shares of $1 par common stock are outstanding.

May 20   Paid the cash dividends.

June 15   Made estimated tax payment of $40,000.

Sept. 15   Made estimated tax payment of $40,000.

Oct. 25   Declared semiannual dividend of $0.50 per share on common stock to shareholders of record on November 10, payable on November 20.

Nov. 20   Paid the cash dividends.

Dec. 15   Made estimated tax payment of $40,000.

31   Tatu's actual 20-2 income tax amounts to $174,000. This amount will be paid by March 15, 20-3. Made adjustment for the additional amount owed.

31   Net income for 20-2 was $656,000. Closed the income summary account.

31   Closed the cash dividends account.

REQUIRED

Prepare journal entries for the transactions.

P 21-9B   (LO3)

✓ Nov. 22. Dr. Stock Dividends: $105,000

CASH DIVIDENDS, STOCK DIVIDEND, AND STOCK SPLIT During the year ended December 31, 20--, Baggio Company completed the following transactions:

Apr. 15   Declared a semiannual dividend of $0.65 per share on preferred stock and $0.45 per share on common stock to shareholders of record on May 5, payable on May 10. Currently, 6,000 shares of $50 par preferred stock and 70,000 shares of $1 par common stock are outstanding.

May 10   Paid the cash dividends.

Oct. 15   Declared semiannual dividend of $0.65 per share on preferred stock and $0.45 per share on common stock to shareholders of record on November 5, payable on November 20.

Nov. 20   Paid the cash dividends.

22   Declared a 10% stock dividend to shareholders of record on December 8, distributable on December 16. Market value of the common stock was estimated at $15 per share.

Dec. 16   Issued certificates for common stock dividend.

20   Board of directors declared a two-for-one common stock split.

REQUIRED

Prepare journal entries for the transactions.

P 21-10B   (LO3/4)

✓ Nov. 12. Dr. Cash Dividends: $36,000

CASH DIVIDEND AND APPROPRIATION OF RETAINED EARNINGS On January 1, 20--, Krausert Company's retained earnings accounts had the following balances:

Appropriated for warehouse	70,000
Unappropriated retained earnings	800,000
	$870,000

During the year ended December 31, 20--, Krausert completed the following selected transactions:

Mar. 16   Krausert's board of directors appropriated $50,000 for acquisition of new factory equipment.

Nov. 5   Purchased a warehouse for $70,000, paying cash for the total amount.

      5   The board of directors returned the amount of retained earnings set aside for the warehouse to unappropriated retained earnings.

     12   Declared a cash dividend of $0.90 per share on common stock to shareholders of record on December 8, payable on December 19. Currently, 40,000 shares of common stock are outstanding.

Dec. 19   Paid the cash dividends.

REQUIRED
Prepare journal entries for the transactions.

P 21-11B   (LO3/4/5)

✓ 3. Retained Earnings: Dec. 31: $989,000

RETAINED EARNINGS ACCOUNTS AND STATEMENT On January 1, 20--, Nguyen Company's retained earnings accounts had the following balances:

Appropriated for land acquisition	$ 75,000
Unappropriated retained earnings	825,000
	$900,000

During the year ended December 31, 20--, Nguyen completed the following selected transactions:

Mar. 20   Declared a semiannual dividend of $0.75 per share on preferred stock and $0.20 per share on common stock to shareholders of record on April 10, payable on April 15. Currently, 12,000 shares of $50 par preferred stock and 90,000 shares of $2 par common stock are outstanding.

Apr. 15 Paid the cash dividends.

Oct. 10 Declared semiannual dividend of $0.75 per share on preferred stock and $0.20 per share on common stock to shareholders of record on November 5, payable on November 10.

Nov. 10 Paid the cash dividends.

      17 Declared a 10% stock dividend to shareholders of record on December 8, distributable on December 15. Market value of the common stock was estimated at $13 per share.

Dec. 15 Issued certificates for common stock dividend.

      31 Net income for 20-- was $260,000. Closed the income summary account.

      31 Closed the cash dividends and stock dividends accounts.

REQUIRED
1. Prepare journal entries for the transactions.
2. Post all entries affecting the retained earnings accounts to T accounts.
3. Prepare a statement of retained earnings for the year ended December 31, 20--.

CHECK LIST
☐ **Managing**
☐ **Planning**
☐ **Drafting**
☐ **Break**
☐ **Revising**
☐ **Managing**

MANAGING YOUR WRITING

The investments committee of your church has come to you for advice. One of the stocks held by the church has paid cash dividends for years. This year, the company issued a 10% stock dividend, so that the church received additional shares rather than cash. The committee is concerned about whether this stock dividend is really worth anything. One committee member argues the stock dividend is as good as cash; another argues that the dividend is worthless.

Write a brief report to the committee explaining the difference between a cash dividend and a stock dividend. Evaluate the value of the stock dividend compared with the cash dividend the church has received in prior years.

ETHICS

ETHICS CASE

Richard Petri is the chief financial officer at Computer Electronics, Inc. In this capacity, he attends all monthly board of directors meetings. A special meeting of the board of directors was called to discuss substantially increasing the amount of cash dividends paid to stockholders this year. The board voted unanimously to increase the dividend. Later that night, Richard called his uncle and hinted around that Computer Electronics, Inc., was going to make its stockholders very happy. His uncle didn't own any stock in Computer Electronics but went out and purchased 500 shares the next day.

1. Did Richard do anything unethical? Would your answer be different if Richard specifically stated that the dividends on Computer Electronics, Inc., were being increased substantially?

2. What should Richard's boss do if he finds out what Richard said to his uncle?

3. Write a short paragraph explaining the difference between cash dividends and stock dividends.

4. In groups of two or three, discuss possible reasons why a corporation might want to pay a very low or high dividend in any given year.

MASTERY PROBLEM

✓ 3. Retained Earnings, Dec. 31: $958,000

On January 1, 20--, Dover Company's retained earnings accounts had the following balances:

Appropriated for printing press	$ 50,000
Unappropriated retained earnings	800,000
	$850,000

During the year ended December 31, 20--, Dover completed the following selected transactions:

Mar. 15   Declared a semiannual dividend of $0.30 per share on preferred stock and $0.40 per share on common stock to shareholders of record on April 5, payable on April 10. Currently, 5,000 shares of $10 par preferred stock and 30,000 shares of $2 par common stock are outstanding.

Apr. 10   Paid the cash dividend.

Sept. 15   Declared semiannual dividend of $0.30 per share on preferred stock and $0.40 per share on common stock to shareholders of record on October 5, payable on October 10.

Oct. 10   Paid the cash dividend.

Nov. 10   Board of directors declared a two-for-one common stock split.

Dec. 31   Net income for 20-- was $135,000. Closed the income summary account.

   31   Closed the cash dividends account.

REQUIRED

1. Prepare journal entries for the transactions.

2. Post all entries affecting the appropriated and unappropriated retained earnings accounts to T accounts.

3. Prepare a statement of retained earnings for the year ended December 31, 20--.

CHALLENGE PROBLEM

This problem challenges you to apply your cumulative accounting knowledge to move a step beyond the material in the chapter.

✓ 1. (d) Dr. Cash Dividends: $57,200

LeeJin Corp. started a two-year period with 200,000 shares of $2 par common stock outstanding. During the two years, LeeJin had the following capital stock transactions:

(a) Declared a 10% common stock dividend. The market value of the common stock was estimated at $8 per share.

(b) Declared a cash dividend of $0.20 per share on common stock.

(c) Declared a 30% common stock dividend. The market value of the common stock was estimated at $9 per share.

(d) Declared a cash dividend of $0.20 per share on common stock.

(e) Declared a two-for-one stock split.

(f) Declared a cash dividend of $0.16 per share on common stock.

REQUIRED

1. Prepare general journal entries for each of the transactions. Identify each transaction by the appropriate letter. (Assume that any cash or share distributions have been completed and are a matter of record before the next transaction occurs.)

2. Compute the following:

   (a) Number of shares of common stock outstanding after all the transactions have been completed.

   (b) The par value per share of LeeJin's common stock after all the transactions have been completed.

ANSWERS TO SELF-STUDY TEST QUESTIONS

True/False

1. T
2. T
3. T
4. F (It is known as a cash dividend.)
5. F (Dates of declaration and payment require journal entries.)

Multiple Choice

1. a   **2.** b   **3.** d   **4.** c   **5.** a

Checkpoint Exercises

1.

	Dec.	31	Income Tax Expense		3	0	0	0	00						
			Income Tax Payable							3	0	0	0	00	

2.

	Dec.	31	Income Summary		183	0	0	0	00						
			Retained Earnings							183	0	0	0	00	
			Retained Earnings		16	0	0	0	00						
			Cash Dividends							16	0	0	0	00	

3.

(a)	May	31	Cash Dividends		12	0	0	0	00						
			Cash Dividends Payable							12	0	0	0	00	
			Declared common stock cash dividend												
(b)	June	20	Cash Dividends Payable		12	0	0	0	00						
			Cash							12	0	0	0	00	
			Paid common stock cash dividend												
(c)	Nov.	30	Stock Dividends		35	0	0	0	00						
			Stock Dividends Distributable*							10	0	0	0	00	
			Paid-In Capital in Excess of Par—												
			Common Stock**							25	0	0	0	00	
			Declared stock dividend												
			*50,000 shares × 10% × $2 par												
			*5,000 shares × $7 = $35,000 market value												
			−$10,000 par value												
(d)	Dec.	18	Stock Dividends Distributable		10	0	0	0	00						
			Common Stock							10	0	0	0	00	
			Distributed stock dividend												

4.

Sep.	30	Retained Earnings	300 0 0 0 00		
		Retained Earnings Appropriated for			300 0 0 0 00
		Plant Modification			
		Appropriated retained earnings for			
		plant modification			

5.

MC Company		
Statement of Retained Earnings		
For Year Ended December 31, 20- -		
Retained earnings, January 1		$720,500
Add net income for the year		88,000
		$808,500
Less: Cash dividends	$24,000	
Stock dividends	47,000	71,000
Retained earnings, December 31		$737,500

Chapter **22** Corporations: Bonds

LEARNING OBJECTIVES

Careful study of this chapter should enable you to:

LO1 Describe the types of bonds, ways bonds differ from common stock, and how the sales price of bonds is determined.

LO2 Account for bonds issued at face value.

LO3 Account for bonds issued at a premium.

LO4 Account for bonds issued at a discount.

LO5 Account for bond redemption and bond sinking funds.

One of the greatest challenges facing the U.S. health care system is how to deliver quality health care at a reasonable cost. In addition to increasingly sophisticated and expensive medical treatments and technology, there is a shortage of doctors and other medical professionals. One way to address this problem is to enable doctors to be in more than one place at the same time. This might sound a little silly and "space-age," but this is what InTouch Health Company has done. Founded in 2002 and located in Santa Barbara, California, InTouch Health develops, manufactures, and markets the Remote Presence Telemedicine System. The system includes wireless, mobile robots with two-way video and audio computer systems. It allows physicians to monitor and interact with patients remotely. The system currently supports 11,000 doctors and clinicians at 1,250 patient access locations in 30 countries. The robots are commonly used by doctors who are performing rounds on post-operation surgery patients, or who are on call but live some distance from emergency rooms.

As we saw for Gotham Dream Cars and Bamko, Inc., in Chapters 20 and 21, it would require a large amount of capital to produce these robots and conduct research and development in this field. In Chapters 20 and 21, we learned how corporations can issue common stock and subsequently use accumulated earnings to provide capital. In Chapter 22, we will learn about a third major way to access a large amount of capital—corporate bonds.

In Chapters 20 and 21, we learned how to account for two major sources of funds for a corporation—capital stock and retained earnings. In this chapter, we turn our attention to a third major source of funds—bonds.

Bonds are similar to the promissory notes payable we saw in Chapter 17. Both are formal, written promises to pay an amount of money at a specified date. The main differences are that bonds are usually for larger sums of money and for longer time periods.

LO1	**Types of Bonds and Determination of Sales Price**

Describe the types of bonds, ways bonds differ from common stock, and how the sales price of bonds is determined.

A bond is a written promise to pay a specific sum of money at a specific future date plus interest each period. Bonds are a major source of funds for most large corporations.

Bonds usually are issued in denominations of $1,000 each. For example, if a corporation issues $300,000 of bonds, this usually means it issues 300 individual bonds, each worth $1,000. This enables the issuing corporation to obtain large amounts of money by selling the bonds to many investors.

Classification of Bonds

To appeal to different types of investors, bonds come with many different features. Based on some of these features, bonds can be classified by (1) security, (2) timing of payment of principal, and (3) identification of ownership.

Security

All bonds are either secured or unsecured. A secured bond is one that is backed by specific corporate assets. A common type of secured bond is a mortgage bond—a bond secured by a mortgage on corporate property such as real estate or equipment.

An unsecured bond is backed solely by the general credit of the corporation, rather than by any specific assets. These bonds are called debenture bonds.

Timing of Payment of Principal

The principal of a bond is the amount to be paid to the bondholder at maturity. Based on the provisions made for payment of the principal, four types of bonds can be identified.

1. Term bonds—bonds that all have the same maturity date.
2. Serial bonds—bonds issued in a series so that a specified amount of the bonds matures each year.
3. Convertible bonds—bonds that give the holder the option of exchanging the bonds for capital stock of the corporation.
4. Callable bonds—bonds that give the issuing corporation the option of calling the bonds for redemption before the maturity date.

Identification of Ownership

There are two types of bonds according to identification of ownership.

1. **Registered bonds**—bonds whose ownership is recorded (registered) in the corporate records. The corporation maintains a record of the name and address of each owner. Any change of ownership must be registered with the corporation.

2. **Coupon bonds (bearer bonds)**—bonds whose ownership generally is not recorded by the corporation. Change of ownership is accomplished simply by delivering the bond. A coupon bond has interest coupons attached, one for each interest period during the life of the bond. As each coupon comes due, the holder of the bond removes the coupon and presents it to a bank for payment. Today, corporations rarely issue coupon bonds, but old ones are still in circulation.

Comparison of Bonds with Common Stock

Bonds and stock often are mentioned in the same breath, but they are quite different. Figure 22-1 summarizes the following key ways in which bonds differ from common stock.

(a) Status. Bondholders are creditors of a corporation; stockholders are owners.

(b) Life. The life of a bond is defined and limited, frequently 10–25 years. Common stock has unlimited life, like the corporation. As long as the corporation is alive, so is the common stock.

(c) Financial Statement Presentation. A bond is a liability, a debt of the corporation; stock represents corporate ownership or equity.

(d) Payments. A bond is a promise to pay certain amounts of money—interest and principal. Common stock offers no promise to pay any definite amount of money. Payments on common stock depend on corporate income and policies.

(e) Risk. If bond payments are not made, the creditors can force the company into bankruptcy. If a company has low earnings and cannot pay dividends, the stock price might decrease, but the corporation can continue to operate.

FIGURE 22-1 Comparison of Bonds and Common Stock

	CHARACTERISTIC	BONDS	COMMON STOCK
(a)	Status	Creditor	Shareholder with voice in management
(b)	Life	Defined/limited	Unlimited—same as corporation
(c)	Financial statement presentation	Liabilities—long-term debt	Stockholders' equity
(d)	Payments	Interest and principal required	No guarantee—dividends depend on corporate income and policies
(e)	Risk	If interest/principal not paid, can cause bankruptcy	If weak performance, can lower stock price
(f)	Net income and taxes	Interest deductible for net income and taxes—reported on income statement	Dividends not deductible for net income and taxes—reported on statement of retained earnings
(g)	Leverage	If rate of return > interest rate, net income is enhanced	None

(f) Net Income and Taxes. Interest payments to bondholders are interest expenses that are deducted in determining corporate net income and income taxes. Dividend payments to stockholders are not deductible in determining corporate net income and income taxes. Dividends are distributions of profits and are deducted on the statement of retained earnings.

(g) Leverage. Bonds also provide the corporation with the possibility of benefiting from leverage. Leverage is using other people's money to enhance earnings by earning a greater rate of return with funds you have borrowed than the rate you paid for those funds. For example, if a corporation can issue bonds at 6% interest and use the funds to earn a rate of return of 15%, this would be strong positive leverage.

Determining Sales Price

At first glance, you would expect a $1,000 bond to sell for $1,000, its face value, the amount written on the face of the bond certificate. But, for various reasons, bonds often do not sell at their face value. Two of the more important factors in determining the price at which bonds will sell are:

1. the rate of interest (stated or coupon rate) on the bonds, and

2. the current market rate of interest on similar investments.

The stated or coupon rate is the interest rate specified on the face of the bond. The market rate can be defined from two points of view. For the bond buyer, this is the rate that can be earned on similar investments. For the bond issuer, this is the rate that other companies in similar financial condition have to pay to borrow money.

To illustrate, assume that Watkin Corp. wants to sell $400,000 of 8%, 10-year bonds. If the current market rate on similar investments is 8%, the bonds will sell at their face value of $400,000. But if the current market rate is 9%, Watkin's bonds will sell at a discount, or at a price less than their face value of $400,000. This is because the lower interest rate (8% vs. 9%) on Watkin's bonds makes them less valuable. In simple terms, investors will not pay full price for Watkin's bonds with an 8% interest rate if they can get a similar investment with a 9% interest rate.

What if the current market rate is 7%? In this case, Watkin's bonds will sell at a premium, or at a price in excess of their face value of $400,000. This is because the higher interest rate (8% vs. 7%) on the bonds makes them more valuable. Investors will pay more for Watkin's bonds with an 8% interest rate if a similar investment pays only a 7% interest rate.

Figure 22-2 summarizes the conditions in which bonds will sell at face value, premium, and discount.

Bond prices usually are stated using numbers such as 95, 99, or 102. These numbers are percentages of the face values of bond issues. Thus, a $100,000 bond issue sold at 95 has a market price of $95,000 ($100,000 × 0.95). A similar issue sold at 102 has a market price of $102,000. Numbers below 100 indicate discount issues. Numbers above 100 indicate premium issues.

LEARNING KEY 🔑

To determine whether a bond will sell at a price equal to, greater than, or less than face value, compare the stated and market interest rates.

CHECKPOINT ✔

Complete Checkpoint-1 on pages 860–861 to test your basic understanding of LO1.

FIGURE 22-2 Interest Rates and Bond Selling Prices

INTEREST RATES				SELLING PRICE
Stated rate	=	Market rate	=	Face value
Stated rate	>	Market rate	>	Face value (Premium)
Stated rate	<	Market rate	<	Face value (Discount)

A BROADER VIEW

JEFFERY STONE/SHUTTERSTOCK.COM

Debt Can Be Dangerous

Horizon Lines, Inc. was the largest Jones Act container shipping and logistics company in the United States. It had been in business for 60 years and in 2010, it had revenue of almost $1.2 billion and assets of $786 million. Yet, the auditors' report on this large, apparently strong company's 2010 financial statements included the following passage: "... there is uncertainty that Horizon Lines, Inc. will remain in compliance with certain debt covenants throughout 2011 and will be able to cure the acceleration clause contained in the convertible notes. These conditions and their impact on the Company's liquidity raise substantial doubt about Horizon Lines Inc.'s ability to continue as a going concern." In other words, the independent auditors doubted that Horizon Lines would be able to survive as a business, because the company might not be able to meet its debt obligations.

Under the burdens of debt and other challenges, Horizon did in fact struggle to avoid bankruptcy for several years. It was able to obtain $653 million of refinancing late in 2011. But its final chapter came in 2015 when it was acquired by Matson Navigation Co., and Horizon ceased to exist.

This is a good example of the risk dimension of debt. By issuing stock, a company gives up ownership interest in the business. But when bonds and other types of debt are issued, a company runs the risk of going bankrupt if it cannot make the payments on its debts. Careful analysis and planning are needed in deciding how to finance a business.

LO2	Accounting for Bonds Issued at Face Value

Account for bonds issued at face value.

To illustrate the accounting for bonds, we will use bonds issued by Watkin Corp. Assume the following facts regarding these bonds:

Date of issue and sale:	April 1, 2001
Principal amount:	$400,000
Denomination of each bond:	$1,000
Life of bonds:	10 years
Stated rate:	8%, payable semiannually each April 1 and October 1

Issuance

Assume that on April 1, 2001, the stated rate of 8% on Watkin's bonds is the same as the current market rate. In this case, the bonds will sell at their face value. The journal entry for the sale and issuance of Watkin's bonds at face value on April 1, 2001, is as follows:

5	Apr.	1	Cash		400	0	0	0	00							5
6			Bonds Payable								400	0	0	0	00	6
7			Issued bonds at face value													7

Bonds payable is reported as a long-term liability on the corporation balance sheet.

Interest Expense

The journal entry for the first semiannual interest payment of $16,000 (8% × $400,000 × ½ year) on October 1, 2001, is as follows:

18	Oct.	1	Bond Interest Expense	16	0	0	0	00						18
19			Cash						16	0	0	0	00	19
20			Paid semiannual interest on bonds											20

On December 31, an adjusting entry is needed for interest accrued on the bonds since the last interest payment date, October 1, 2001. Three months' interest has accrued (October 1–December 31), which amounts to $8,000 (8% × $400,000 × ¼ year). The adjusting entry therefore is as follows:

25	Dec.	31	Bond Interest Expense	8	0	0	0	00						25
26			Bond Interest Payable						8	0	0	0	00	26

After the October 1 and December 31 entries are posted, Bond Interest Expense and Bond Interest Payable appear in T account form as follows:

Bond Interest Expense		Bond Interest Payable	
2001			2001
Oct. 1 16,000			Dec. 31 8,000
Dec. 31 8,000			
24,000			

The balance in the bond interest expense account is the total interest expense incurred from April 1 to December 31. Bond Interest Expense is reported as other expense on the income statement. The balance in the bond interest payable account is the accrued liability on December 31. Bond Interest Payable is reported as a current liability on the balance sheet.

The December 31, 2001, adjusting entry normally is reversed as of January 1, 2002, as follows:

8	Jan.	1	Bond Interest Payable	8	0	0	0	00						8
9			Bond Interest Expense						8	0	0	0	00	9

The next semiannual interest payment on April 1, 2002, is made exactly like the entry on October 1, 2001. After posting the closing entry, reversing entry, and the April 1 interest payment entry, Bond Interest Expense and Bond Interest Payable appear in T account form as follows:

CHECKPOINT ✔

Complete Checkpoint-2 on page 861 to test your basic understanding of LO2.

Bond Interest Expense				Bond Interest Payable			
2001						2001	
Oct. 1 16,000						Dec. 31 8,000	
Dec. 31 8,000	Dec. 31 Close	24,000		2002			
2002	2002			Jan. 1 Rev. 8,000			
Apr. 1 16,000	Jan. 1 Rev.	8,000					

Accounting for Bonds Issued at a Premium

Account for bonds issued at a premium.

Recall that if the stated interest rate on bonds is greater than the current market rate, the bonds will sell at a premium. When bonds are issued at a premium, both bonds payable on the balance sheet and interest expense on the income statement are affected.

Issuance

Assume that on April 1, 2001, the stated rate of 8% on Watkin's bonds is greater than the current market rate, so that the bonds sell for 106. This means that the bonds sell for $424,000 ($400,000 × 106%), a premium of $24,000. The journal entry for the sale and issuance of Watkin's bonds at a premium on April 1, 2001, is as follows:

5	Apr.	1	Cash		424	0	0	0	00							5
6			Bonds Payable							400	0	0	0	00	6
7			Premium on Bonds Payable							24	0	0	0	00	7
8			Issued bonds at a premium												8

Premium on Bonds Payable is an adjunct-liability account. It is added to bonds payable on the corporate balance sheet. On Watkin's balance sheet immediately after issuing the $400,000 of bonds for $424,000, the bonds payable and premium would appear as follows:

Long-term liabilities:		
Bonds payable	$400,000	
Premium on bonds payable	24,000	$424,000

Bonds payable plus the premium on bonds payable is called the carrying value of the bonds.

Interest Expense and Premium Amortization

When bonds are issued at a premium, the amount of interest actually paid is not the true interest expense. This is because the premium received when the bonds are issued effectively reduces the cost of borrowing. For example, Watkin received $424,000 for its bonds but will have to pay back only $400,000, the face value of the bonds. This $24,000 reduction ($424,000 – $400,000) in the cost of borrowing is spread over the life of the bond issue by adjusting interest expense on a regular basis.

In a sense, Premium on Bonds Payable is a "gain." Watkin received $424,000 in exchange for a promise to pay only $400,000, a "gain" of $24,000. This gain is spread as an "interest expense reduction" over the life of the bonds. As the premium is waiting to be spread, it is stored as a credit balance in an adjunct-liability account.

Figure 22-3 shows the "gain" from selling the $400,000 of bonds at a premium and how this gain is spread as an interest reduction over the life of the bonds.

The process of adjusting the bond interest expense account for any premium or discount is called amortization of the premium or discount. Two commonly used methods of amortizing premium (or discount) over the life of a bond are (1) effective interest and (2) straight-line. The effective interest method is recommended, but the straight-line method is much simpler to apply and generally provides acceptable results. We will use the straight-line method. The effective interest method is covered in the appendix to this chapter.

FIGURE 22-3 Bonds Issued at a Premium

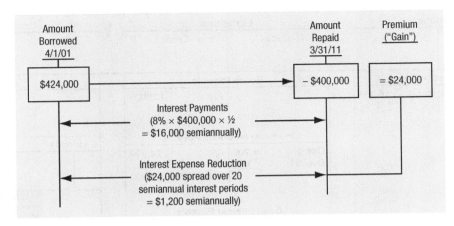

Using the straight-line method, $1,200 of the premium on Watkin's bonds is amortized each semiannual interest period, calculated as follows:

$$\frac{\text{Premium}}{\text{Life of Bonds}} \quad \times \quad \tfrac{1}{2}\text{Year} \quad = \quad \frac{\$24,000}{10\ \text{Years}} \quad \times \quad \tfrac{1}{2}\text{Year} \quad = \quad \$1,200$$

The entry for the first semiannual interest payment and amortization of bond premium on October 1, 2001, is as follows:

18	Oct.	1	Bond Interest Expense	14	8	0	0	00								18
19			Premium on Bonds Payable	1	2	0	0	00								19
20			Cash						16	0	0	0	00			20
21			Paid semiannual interest and													21
22			amortized premium on bonds													22

Note that the premium amortization does not affect the amount of cash paid. The amortization simply reduces the bond interest expense for the period and the carrying value of the bonds.

On December 31, an adjusting entry is needed both for accrued interest and for premium amortization for the period from October 1 through December 31. Three months' interest of $8,000 (8% × $400,000 × ¼ year) has accrued. Three months' premium of $600 ($24,000 ÷ 10 × ¼ year) should be amortized. The adjusting entry is as follows:

25	Dec.	31	Bond Interest Expense	7	4	0	0	00							25
26			Premium on Bonds Payable	6	0	0	00								26
27			Bond Interest Payable						8	0	0	0	00	27

After the April 1, October 1, and December 31 entries are posted, Cash, Bond Interest Expense, Bonds Payable, Premium on Bonds Payable, and Bond Interest Payable appear in the accounting equation as shown in Figure 22-4.

The December 31, 2001, adjusting entry normally is reversed as of January 1, 2002, as follows:

		Bond Interest Payable	8	0	0	0	00						
		Bond Interest Expense						7	4	0	0	00	
		Premium on Bonds Payable						6	0	0	00	

The next semiannual interest and premium amortization entry on April 1, 2002, is made exactly like the entry on October 1, 2001. Columns 2, 3, and 4 in Figure 22-5 summarize the semiannual interest and premium amortization entries for the life of the bonds.

FIGURE 22-4 Bonds Payable and Related Accounts after Interest Accrual and Premium Amortization

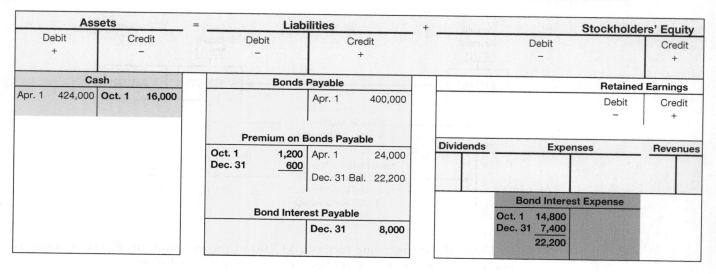

Consistent with the matching principle, note that the premium is spread over the period benefited—for Watkin, the 10-year life of the bonds.

Note that the effect of the premium amortization is to reduce both the interest expense for the period and the balance in the premium on bonds payable account. In fact, the premium on bonds payable account balance is gradually reduced to zero over the life of the bonds, as shown in column 6 of Figure 22-5. Recall that Premium on Bonds Payable is an adjunct-liability account. It is added to bonds payable on the balance sheet. The amount that Watkin will have to pay at maturity is $400,000. By amortizing the premium on bonds payable over the life of the bonds, the carrying value of the bonds decreases to $400,000 at maturity, as shown in column 7 of Figure 22-5.

FIGURE 22-5 Premium Amortization Schedule

			BOND PREMIUM AMORTIZATION SCHEDULE STRAIGHT-LINE METHOD			
(1)	(2)	(3)	(4)	(5)	(6)	(7)
Date	Interest Expense Debit	Premium on Bonds Payable Debit	Cash Credit	Bonds Payable Balance	Premium on Bonds Payable Balance	Carrying Value of Bonds [(5) + (6)]
4/1/01				$400,000	$24,000	$424,000
10/1/01	$14,800	$1,200	$16,000	400,000	22,800	422,800
4/1/02*	14,800	1,200	16,000	400,000	21,600	421,600
10/1/02	14,800	1,200	16,000	400,000	20,400	420,400
—	—	—	—	—	—	—
—	—	—	—	—	—	—
—	—	—	—	—	—	—
4/1/10	14,800	1,200	16,000	400,000	2,400	402,400
10/1/10	14,800	1,200	16,000	400,000	1,200	401,200
3/31/11	14,800	1,200	16,000	400,000	0	400,000

*The entry for the first interest payment each year assumes that the adjusting entry at December 31 of the preceding year was reversed.

CHECKPOINT ✔

Complete Checkpoint-3 on page 861 to test your basic understanding of LO3.

LO4	**Accounting for Bonds Issued at a Discount**

Account for bonds issued at a discount.

If the stated interest rate on bonds is less than the current market rate, the bonds will sell at a discount. When bonds are issued at a discount, both bonds payable on the balance sheet and interest expense on the income statement are affected.

Issuance

Assume that on April 1, 2001, the stated rate on Watkin's bonds is less than the current market rate, so that the bonds sell for 95. This means that the bonds sell for $380,000 ($400,000 × 95%), a discount of $20,000. The journal entry for the sale and issuance of Watkin's bonds at a discount on April 1, 2001, is as follows:

5	Apr.	1	Cash		380	0	0	0	00						5
6			Discount on Bonds Payable		20	0	0	0	00						6
7			Bonds Payable							400	0	0	0	00	7
8			Issued bonds at a discount												8

Discount on Bonds Payable is a contra-liability account. It is deducted from bonds payable on the corporate balance sheet. On Watkin's balance sheet immediately after issuing the $400,000 of bonds for $380,000, the bonds payable and discount would appear as follows:

Long-term liabilities:		
Bonds payable	$400,000	
Discount on bonds payable	(20,000)	$380,000

Bonds payable less the discount on bonds payable is called the carrying value of the bonds.

Interest Expense and Discount Amortization

When bonds are sold at a discount, we have a situation similar to what we saw in the case of bonds sold at a premium. The amount of interest actually paid is not the true interest expense. This is because the discount given when the bonds are issued effectively increases the cost of borrowing. For example, Watkin received only $380,000 for its bonds but will have to pay back $400,000, the face value of the bonds. This $20,000 increase ($400,000 − $380,000) in the cost of borrowing is amortized over the life of the bond issue by adjusting interest expense on a regular basis.

In a sense, Discount on Bonds Payable is a "loss." Watkin received only $380,000 in exchange for a promise to pay $400,000, a "loss" of $20,000. This loss is spread as an "interest expense increase" over the life of the bonds. As the discount is waiting to be spread, it is stored as a debit balance in a contra-liability account.

Figure 22-6 shows the "loss" from selling the $400,000 of bonds at a discount and how this loss is spread as an interest increase over the life of the bonds.

Using the straight-line method, $1,000 of the discount on Watkin's bonds is amortized each semiannual interest period, calculated as follows:

$$\frac{\text{Discount}}{\text{Life of Bonds}} \times \tfrac{1}{2}\text{Year} = \frac{\$20,000}{10\ \text{Years}} \times \tfrac{1}{2}\text{Year} = \$1,000$$

FIGURE 22-6 Bonds Issued at a Discount

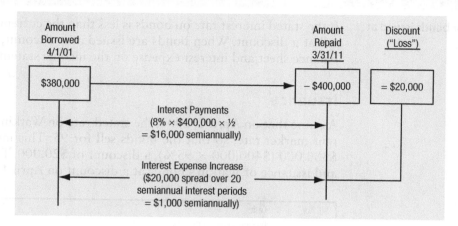

The entry for the first semiannual interest payment and amortization of bond discount on October 1, 2001, is as follows:

18	Oct.	1	Bond Interest Expense	17	0	0	0	00						18
19			Discount on Bonds Payable						1	0	0	0	00	19
20			Cash						16	0	0	0	00	20
21			Paid semiannual interest and											21
22			amortized discount on bonds											22

LEARNING KEY
Discount amortization increases the interest expense and carrying value of the bonds but has no effect on the amount of cash paid.

Note that the discount amortization does not affect the amount of cash paid. The amortization simply increases the bond interest expense for the period and the carrying value of the bonds.

On December 31, an adjusting entry is needed both for accrued interest and for discount amortization for the period from October 1 through December 31. Three months' interest of $8,000 (8% × $400,000 × ¼ year) has accrued. Three months' discount of $500 ($20,000 ÷ 10 × ¼ year) should be amortized. The adjusting entry is as follows:

25	Dec.	31	Bond Interest Expense	8	5	0	0	00						25
26			Bond Interest Payable						8	0	0	0	00	26
27			Discount on Bonds Payable							5	0	0	00	27

As with bonds sold at a premium, the discount is spread over the period benefited—for Watkin, the 10-year life of the bonds. This is consistent with the matching principle.

After the October 1 and December 31 entries are posted, Cash, Bond Interest Expense, Bonds Payable, Discount on Bonds Payable, and Bond Interest Payable appear in the accounting equation, as shown in Figure 22-7.

The December 31 adjusting entry normally is reversed as of January 1, 2002, as follows:

		Bond Interest Payable	8	0	0	0	00					
		Discount on Bonds Payable		5	0	0	00					
		Bond Interest Expense						8	5	0	0	00

The next semiannual interest and discount amortization entry on April 1, 2002, is made exactly like the entry on October 1, 2001. Columns 2, 3, and 4 in Figure 22-8 summarize the semiannual interest and discount amortization entries for the life of the bonds.

Note that the effect of the discount amortization is to increase the interest expense for the period and to decrease the balance in the discount on bonds payable account. In fact, the discount on bonds payable account balance is gradually reduced to zero over the life of the bonds, as shown in column 6 of Figure 22-8. Recall that Discount on

CHECKPOINT ✓
Complete Checkpoint-4 on page 861 to test your basic understanding of LO4.

Bonds Payable is a contra-liability account. It is subtracted from bonds payable on the balance sheet. The amount that Watkin will have to pay at maturity is $400,000. By amortizing the discount on bonds payable over the life of the bonds, the carrying value of the bonds increases to $400,000 at maturity, as shown in column 7 of Figure 22-8.

FIGURE 22-7 Bonds Payable and Related Accounts after Interest Accrual and Discount Amortization

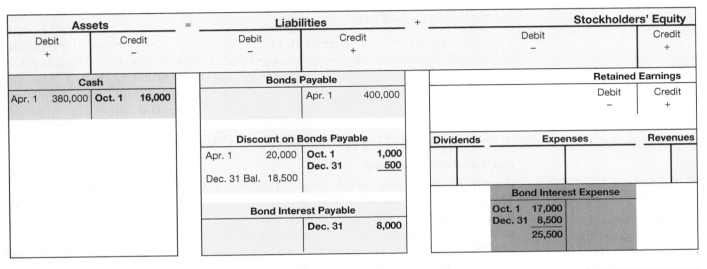

FIGURE 22-8 Discount Amortization Schedule

BOND DISCOUNT AMORTIZATION SCHEDULE STRAIGHT-LINE METHOD						
(1) Date	(2) Interest Expense Debit	(3) Discount on Bonds Payable Credit	(4) Cash Credit	(5) Bonds Payable Balance	(6) Discount on Bonds Payable Balance	(7) Carrying Value of Bonds [(5) − (6)]
4/1/01				$400,000	$20,000	$380,000
10/1/01	$17,000	$1,000	$16,000	400,000	19,000	381,000
4/1/02*	17,000	1,000	16,000	400,000	18,000	382,000
10/1/02	17,000	1,000	16,000	400,000	17,000	383,000
–	–	–	–	–	–	–
–	–	–	–	–	–	–
–	–	–	–	–	–	–
4/1/10	17,000	1,000	16,000	400,000	2,000	398,000
10/1/10	17,000	1,000	16,000	400,000	1,000	399,000
3/31/11	17,000	1,000	16,000	400,000	0	400,000

*The entry for the first interest payment each year assumes that the adjusting entry at December 31 of the preceding year was reversed.

LO5

Accounting for Bond Redemption and Sinking Funds

Account for bond redemption and bond sinking funds.

Proper accounting for bond redemption depends on whether the redemption is at maturity or before that date. Each of these conditions is explained in the following sections.

Redemption at Maturity

Usually, bonds issued by a corporation are redeemed at face value at their maturity. By that date, the entire amount of any premium or discount should have been amortized. To enter the redemption, Bonds Payable is debited and Cash is credited for the face value of the bonds. For example, if the $400,000 of Watkin bonds are redeemed at maturity, the following journal entry is made:

22		Bonds Payable	400	0	0	0	00						22
23		Cash						400	0	0	0	00	23
24		Redeemed bonds at face value											24

Redemption before Maturity

Corporations may redeem part or all of a bond issue before maturity. If the bonds are callable, a corporation may call in the bonds before they mature. The call price is defined in the original bond agreement. If the bonds are not callable, a corporation can purchase its bonds in the open market at the market price. When bonds are redeemed before maturity, any accrued interest must be paid and the premium or discount amortization must be brought up to date. Entries for doing so are the same as those illustrated in previous sections of this chapter.

Redemption at a Loss

Usually, there is a gain or loss involved when bonds are redeemed before maturity. The gain or loss is the difference between the amount paid to redeem the bonds and the carrying value of the bonds. When bonds are issued at face value, the carrying value equals the face value throughout the life of the bonds. When bonds are issued at a premium or discount, the carrying value changes over the life of the bonds, as the premium or discount is amortized.

To illustrate, consider the Watkin Corp. $400,000, 8% bonds that were sold at face value. If $40,000 of the bonds are redeemed at 103, there is a loss of $1,200 on redemption of the bonds, calculated as follows:

Cash paid ($40,000 × 103%)	$41,200
Less carrying value (= face value) of bonds	40,000
Loss on redemption	$ 1,200

The journal entry for this transaction is as follows:

31		Bonds Payable	40	0	0	0	00						31
32		Loss on Bonds Redeemed	1	2	0	0	00						32
33		Cash						41	2	0	0	00	33
34		Redeemed bonds at a loss											34

Loss on Bonds Redeemed generally is reported as other expense near the bottom of the income statement.

Now consider the Watkin Corp. bonds that were sold at a premium (106) for $424,000. Assume that eight years after the issuance, Watkin redeems $40,000 of this issue at 103. The carrying value of these bonds is calculated as follows:

Issue price ($40,000 × 106%)	$42,400	
Face value	40,000	
Premium received at issuance		$ 2,400
Premium amortized per year ($2,400 ÷ 10 yrs.)	$ 240	
Number of years since issuance	× 8	
Total premium amortized in 8 years		1,920
Unamortized premium		$ 480
Face value		40,000
Carrying value		$40,480

Thus, after the interest payment and premium amortization have been entered on April 1, 2009, the carrying value of the $40,000 of bonds is $40,480. There is a loss of $720 on redemption of the bonds, calculated as follows:

Cash paid ($40,000 × 103%)	$41,200
Less carrying value	40,480
Loss on redemption	$ 720

The journal entry for this transaction is as follows:

5	Apr.	1	Bonds Payable		40	0	0	0	00							5
6			Premium on Bonds Payable			4	8	0	00							6
7			Loss on Bonds Redeemed			7	2	0	00							7
8			Cash								41	2	0	0	00	8
9			Redeemed bonds at a loss													9

Redemption at a Gain

To illustrate the redemption of bonds at a gain, let's look again at two examples. Assume that $40,000 of Watkin's bonds that were issued at face value are redeemed at 97. In this case, Watkin has a gain of $1,200 on redemption of the bonds, calculated as follows:

Carrying value (= face value) of bonds	$40,000
Less cash paid ($40,000 × 97%)	38,800
Gain on bonds redeemed	$ 1,200

The journal entry for this transaction is as follows:

31		Bonds Payable		40	0	0	0	00							31
32		Gain on Bonds Redeemed								1	2	0	0	00	32
33		Cash								38	8	0	0	00	33
34		Redeemed bonds at a gain													34

Gain on Bonds Redeemed generally is reported as other income on the income statement.

Now consider the Watkin Corp. bonds that were sold at a discount (95) for $380,000. Assume that seven years after issuance, Watkin redeems $40,000 of this issue at 98. The carrying value of these bonds is calculated as follows:

Face value	$40,000	
Issue price ($40,000 × 95%)	38,000	
Discount at issuance		$ 2,000
Discount amortized per year ($2,000 ÷ 10 yrs.)	$ 200	
Number of years since issuance	× 7	
Total discount amortized in 7 years		1,400
Unamortized discount		$ 600
Face value		$40,000
Less unamortized discount		600
Carrying value		$39,400

Thus, after the interest payment and discount amortization have been entered on April 1, 2008, the carrying value of the $40,000 of bonds is $39,400. There is a gain of $200 on redemption of the bonds, calculated as follows:

Carrying value of bonds	$39,400
Less cash paid ($40,000 × 98%)	39,200
Gain on redemption	$ 200

The journal entry for this transaction is as follows:

5	Apr.	1	Bonds Payable	40 0 0 0 00		5
6			Discount on Bonds Payable		6 0 0 00	6
7			Gain on Bonds Redeemed		2 0 0 00	7
8			Cash		39 2 0 0 00	8
9			Redeemed bonds at a gain			9

Bond Sinking Funds

The formal written agreement for issuing bonds is called the bond indenture. Bond indentures for term bonds frequently require the accumulation and investment of money over a period of years. This is to provide the amount needed to redeem the bonds at maturity. Such accumulations are known as bond sinking funds. The sinking fund usually is administered by a trustee. The corporation makes periodic cash deposits with the trustee. The trustee is responsible for investing the cash and accumulating amounts necessary to redeem the bonds at maturity.

To illustrate, assume that the bond indenture for the Watkin bonds required Watkin to make deposits of $30,000 to a trustee each year. The entry for each deposit is as follows:

12			Bond Sinking Fund	30 0 0 0 00		12
13			Cash		30 0 0 0 00	13
14			Made sinking fund deposit			14

The bond sinking fund is a long-term asset and is reported under Investments on the corporation balance sheet.

The trustee invests the cash and adds any earnings on these investments to the sinking fund. Assume that Watkin's trustee reports sinking fund earnings of $2,800 for the year. The following entry is made:

26			Bond Sinking Fund	2 8 0 0 00		26
27			Sinking Fund Earnings		2 8 0 0 00	27
28			Annual sinking fund earnings			28

Sinking fund earnings are reported as other revenue on the corporation income statement.

When the bonds mature, the trustee sells all of the sinking fund investments. The corporation then deposits additional cash with the trustee so that the sum of the periodic deposits, the sinking fund earnings, and the additional cash is sufficient to redeem the bonds. When the Watkin bonds are redeemed at maturity by the trustee, the following entry is made:

5			Bonds Payable	400 0 0 0 00		5
6			Bond Sinking Fund		400 0 0 0 00	6
7			Redeemed bonds at face value			7

If any cash is left in the sinking fund after all of the bonds are redeemed, the cash is returned to the corporation. Assume that the sinking fund has a balance of $960 after all the bonds are redeemed. The following entry is made:

18			Cash	9 6 0 00		18
19			Bond Sinking Fund		9 6 0 00	19
20			Received sinking fund balance			20

CHECKPOINT ✔
Complete Checkpoint-5 on page 861 to test your basic understanding of LO5.

SELF-STUDY

LEARNING OBJECTIVES	Key Points to Remember
LO1 Describe the types of bonds, ways bonds differ from common stock, and how the sales price of bonds is determined.	Bonds can be classified by (1) security, (2) timing of payment of principal, and (3) identification of ownership. Bonds differ from common stock in many ways. Bonds are owned by creditors, are liabilities with limited lives, require interest and principal payments, have deductible interest expenses, and provide a leverage opportunity. If the bond and market interest rates are equal, bonds will sell at face value. If the bond interest rate is greater than the market rate, bonds will sell at a premium. If the bond interest rate is less than the market rate, bonds will sell at a discount.
LO2 Account for bonds issued at face value.	The journal entries for bond issuance, interest payments, premium or discount amortization, and redemption can be summarized as follows:
LO3 Account for bonds issued at a premium.	
LO4 Account for bonds issued at a discount.	

EVENT	BONDS ISSUED AT		
	FACE	**PREMIUM**	**DISCOUNT**

Issuance	Cash
	  Bonds Payable
		Cash
		  Bonds Payable
		  Premium on Bonds Payable
			Cash
			Discount on Bonds Payable
			  Bonds Payable

Interest Payment and Amortization	Interest Expense
	  Cash
		Interest Expense
		Premium on Bonds Payable
		  Cash
			Interest Expense
			  Discount on Bonds Payable
			  Cash

Redemption at:
Carrying Value
	Bonds Payable
	  Cash
		Bonds Payable
		Premium on Bonds Payable
		  Cash
			Bonds Payable
			  Discount on Bonds Payable
			  Cash

< Carrying Value	Bonds Payable
	  Gain on Redemption
	  Cash
		Bonds Payable
		Premium on Bonds Payable
		  Gain on Redemption
		  Cash
			Bonds Payable
			  Discount on Bonds Payable
			  Gain on Redemption
			  Cash

> Carrying Value	Bonds Payable
	Loss on Redemption
	  Cash
		Bonds Payable
		Premium on Bonds Payable
		Loss on Redemption
		  Cash
			Bonds Payable
			Loss on Redemption
			  Discount on Bonds Payable
			  Cash

(continued)

LEARNING OBJECTIVES	**Key Points to Remember**
LO5 Account for bond redemption and bond sinking funds.	The gain or loss on redemption of bonds is the difference between the amount paid to redeem the bonds and the carrying value of the bonds. Gains and losses on bonds redeemed are reported as other income or expense on the income statement. Bond sinking funds are used to accumulate the money needed for bond redemption. The sum of the amounts deposited in the sinking fund, sinking fund earnings, and any additional cash deposited in the sinking fund by the company when the bonds mature is used to redeem the bonds.

DEMONSTRATION PROBLEM

Brooks Inc.'s fiscal year ends December 31. Selected transactions for the period 20-1 through 20-8 involving bonds payable issued by Brooks are as follows:

20-1

Nov. 30   Issued $800,000 of 10-year, 9%, callable bonds dated November 30, 20-1, for $776,000. Interest is payable semiannually on November 30 and May 31. The bond indenture provides that Brooks is to pay to the trustee bank $30,000 by June 15 of each year (except the tenth year) as a sinking fund for the retirement of the bonds on call or at maturity.

Dec. 31   Made the adjusting entry for interest payable and amortized one month's discount on the bonds (straight-line method).

20-2

Jan. 2   Reversed the adjusting entry for interest payable and bond discount amortization.

May 31   Paid the semiannual interest on the bonds and amortized six months' discount.

June 15   Paid the sinking fund trustee $30,000.

Nov. 30   Paid the semiannual interest on the bonds and amortized six months' discount.

Dec. 31   Made the adjusting entry for interest payable and amortized one month's discount on the bonds.

31   Sinking fund earnings for the year were $1,100.

20-8

June 15   Paid the sinking fund trustee $30,000.

Nov. 30   Paid the semiannual interest on the bonds and amortized six months' discount.

30   Redeemed the bonds, which were called at 102.

The balance in the bond discount account is $7,200 after the payment of interest and amortization of discount have been entered. The cash balance in the sinking fund is $320,000. The sinking fund trustee is paid the additional cash needed to redeem the bonds. (*Hint:* First make the entry for payment to the sinking fund, then make the entry for redemption of the bonds.)

REQUIRED

1. Enter the transactions in general journal form.
2. Calculate the carrying value of the bonds as of December 31, 20-2.
3. Prepare the bonds payable section of a partial balance sheet as of December 31, 20-2.

SOLUTION 1.

	DATE		DESCRIPTION	POST. REF.	DEBIT	CREDIT	
			GENERAL JOURNAL			PAGE 1	
1	20-1 Nov.	30	Cash		776 0 0 0 00		1
2			Discount on Bonds Payable		24 0 0 0 00		2
3			Bonds Payable			800 0 0 0 00	3
4			Issued bonds at a discount				4
5							5
6			Adjusting Entry				6
7	Dec.	31	Bond Interest Expense		6 2 0 0 00		7
8			Bond Interest Payable			6 0 0 0 00	8
9			Discount on Bonds Payable*			2 0 0 00	9
10							10
11			Reversing Entry				11
12	20-2 Jan.	2	Bond Interest Payable		6 0 0 0 00		12
13			Discount on Bonds Payable		2 0 0 00		13
14			Bond Interest Expense			6 2 0 0 00	14
15							15
16	May	31	Bond Interest Expense		37 2 0 0 00		16
17			Discount on Bonds Payable			1 2 0 0 00	17
18			Cash			36 0 0 0 00	18
19			Paid semiannual interest and				19
20			amortized discount on bonds				20
21							21
22	June	15	Bond Sinking Fund		30 0 0 0 00		22
23			Cash			30 0 0 0 00	23
24			Made sinking fund deposit				24
25							25
26	Nov.	30	Bond Interest Expense		37 2 0 0 00		26
27			Discount on Bonds Payable			1 2 0 0 00	27
28			Cash			36 0 0 0 00	28
29			Paid semiannual interest and				29
30			amortized discount on bonds				30
31							31
32							32

*Amortization rate = $24,000 original discount ÷ 10 years = $2,400/year ÷ 12 months = $200/month

(*continued*)

	DATE		DESCRIPTION	POST. REF.	DEBIT					CREDIT					
			GENERAL JOURNAL										PAGE 2		
1			Adjusting Entry												1
2	20-2 Dec.	31	Bond Interest Expense		6	2	0	0	00						2
3			Bond Interest Payable							6	0	0	0	00	3
4			Discount on Bonds Payable								2	0	0	00	4
5															5
6		31	Bond Sinking Fund		1	1	0	0	00						6
7			Sinking Fund Earnings							1	1	0	0	00	7
8			Annual sinking fund earnings												8
9															9
10	20-8 June	15	Bond Sinking Fund		30	0	0	0	00						10
11			Cash							30	0	0	0	00	11
12			Made sinking fund deposit												12
13															13
14	Nov.	30	Bond Interest Expense		37	2	0	0	00						14
15			Discount on Bonds Payable							1	2	0	0	00	15
16			Cash							36	0	0	0	00	16
17			Paid semiannual interest and												17
18			amortized discount on bonds												18
19															19
20		30	Bond Sinking Fund		496	0	0	0	00						20
21			Cash							496	0	0	0	00	21
22			[($800,000 × 102%) − $320,000]												22
23			Made sinking fund deposit												23
24															24
25		30	Bonds Payable		800	0	0	0	00						25
26			Loss on Bonds Redeemed		23	2	0	0	00						26
27			Discount on Bonds Payable*							7	2	0	0	00	27
28			Bond Sinking Fund							816	0	0	0	00	28
29			Redeemed bonds at a loss												29

*Original discount on bonds payable $ 24,000
Amortization for 7 years at $2,400/year   (16,800)
Unamortized discount on November 30, 20-8 $ 7,200

SOLUTION 2.

Face value of bonds		$800,000
Original discount on bonds payable	$ 24,000	
Less:		
Discount amortized on December 31, 20-1	(200)	
Discount amortized during 20-2	(2,400)	
Balance of discount on bonds payable at December 31, 20-2		21,400
Carrying value of bonds, December 31, 20-2		$778,600

SOLUTION 3.

Long-term liabilities:		
Bonds payable	$800,000	
Discount on bonds payable	(21,400)	$778,600

KEY TERMS

amortization (846)   The process of adjusting the bond interest expense account for any premium or discount.

bearer bonds (842)   See coupon bonds.

bond (841)   A written promise to pay a specific sum of money at a specific future date.

bond indenture (854)   The formal written agreement for issuing bonds.

bond sinking funds (854)   The accumulation and investment of money over a period of years to provide the amount needed for the redemption of bonds.

callable bonds (841)   Bonds that give the issuing corporation the option of calling the bonds for redemption before the maturity date.

carrying value (846)   Bonds payable plus the premium or less the discount on bonds payable.

convertible bonds (841)   Bonds that give the holder the option of exchanging the bonds for capital stock of the corporation.

coupon bonds (842)   Bonds whose ownership generally is not recorded by the corporation. These bonds have interest coupons attached.

coupon rate (843)   See stated rate.

debenture bonds (841)   See unsecured bonds.

discount (843)   The difference between the face value and the price of a bond when the current market interest rate is greater than the stated rate of that bond.

face value (843)   The amount written on the face of the bond certificate.

leverage (843)   Using other people's money to enhance earnings. This can be done by earning a greater rate of return on funds you have borrowed than the rate you paid for those funds.

market rate (843)   The interest rate that can be earned on similar investments or the rate that other companies in similar financial condition have to pay to borrow money.

mortgage bonds (841)   Bonds secured by a mortgage on corporate property such as real estate or equipment.

premium (843)   The difference between the face value and the price of a bond when the current market interest rate is less than the stated rate of that bond.

principal (841)   The amount to be paid to the bondholder at maturity.

registered bonds (842)   Bonds whose ownership is recorded in the corporate records.

secured bonds (841)   Bonds that are backed by specific corporate assets.

serial bonds (841)   Bonds issued in a series so that a specified amount of the bonds matures each year.

stated rate (843)   The rate of interest specified on the face of the bond.

term bonds (841)   Bonds that all have the same maturity date.

unsecured bonds (841)   Bonds backed solely by the general credit of the corporation issuing the bonds.

SELF-STUDY TEST QUESTIONS

True/False

1. **LO1**   A secured bond is one that is backed by specific corporate assets.

2. **LO1**   If the stated rate of interest on a bond is 7% and the current market rate on similar investments is 8%, the bond will sell at a premium.

3. **LO2**   When bonds are issued at face value, the debit to Cash and credit to Bonds Payable are for the same amount.

4. **LO3**   Amortization of the premium on bonds payable increases the bond interest expense and the carrying value of the bonds.

5. **LO5**   To determine the amount of gain or loss on redemption of bonds, compare the redemption price with the carrying value of the bonds.

Multiple Choice

1. **LO1**   Bonds that give the holder the option of exchanging the bonds for capital stock in the corporation are called
   (a) debenture bonds.
   (b) serial bonds.
   (c) convertible bonds.
   (d) callable bonds.

2. **LO3**   If bonds with a face value of $200,000 are sold at 102, Cash is debited for
   (a) $200,000.
   (b) $202,000.
   (c) $204,000.
   (d) $196,000.

3. **LO3**   Ten-year bonds with a face value of $300,000 are sold at a premium of $6,000. If the premium is amortized using the straight-line method, each semi-annual interest payment and amortization of bond premium will include a
   (a) debit to Premium on Bonds Payable.
   (b) credit to Premium on Bonds Payable.
   (c) debit to Cash.
   (d) credit to Bond Interest Expense.

4. **LO4**   If bonds are issued at a discount, the amortization of the discount over the life of the bonds causes the
   (a) face value to decrease each period.
   (b) face value to increase each period.
   (c) carrying value of the bonds to decrease.
   (d) carrying value of the bonds to increase.

5. **LO5**   Bond sinking fund earnings are
   (a) subtracted from the bond sinking fund.
   (b) added to the bond sinking fund.
   (c) subtracted from the current year interest expense.
   (d) added to the current year interest expense.

Checkpoint Exercises

1. **LO1**   Jibble Company wants to sell $300,000 of 8%, 10-year bonds. If the current market rate on similar investments is 9%, at what price will these bonds sell?

(a) More than $300,000
(b) $300,000
(c) Less than $300,000

2. **LO2**   B&B Associates issued $300,000 of 8%, 10-year bonds at face value on April 1, 20-1. Interest is payable on September 30 and March 31. Prepare journal entries for the following:

(a) Interest payment on the bonds on September 30.
(b) Year-end adjustment for interest on the bonds.

3. **LO3**   Yingh Company issued $500,000 of 9%, 10-year bonds at 102 on July 1, 20-1. Interest is payable on December 31 and June 30. Prepare journal entries for the following:

(a) Issuance of the bonds.
(b) Interest payment and premium amortization on the bonds on December 31.

4. **LO4**   Mellis Company issued $300,000 of 8%, 10-year bonds at 97 on May 1, 20-1. Interest is payable on October 31 and April 30. Prepare journal entries for the following:

(a) Issuance of the bonds.
(b) Interest payment and discount amortization on the bonds on October 31.

5. **LO5**   FPD Company sold $300,000 of 9%, 10-year bonds at 97 six years ago. Prepare journal entries for each of the following possible redemptions of portions of these bonds:

(a) FPD redeems $30,000 of the issue at 99. The unamortized discount is $360.
(b) FPD redeems $40,000 of the bonds at 98. The unamortized discount is $480.

The answers to the Self-Study Test Questions are at the end of the chapter (page 873).

APPLYING YOUR KNOWLEDGE

REVIEW QUESTIONS

LO1   1. Describe the differences between corporate bonds and stock from the standpoint of the issuing corporation.

LO1   2. Describe leveraging and give an example of how a corporation can gain leverage by issuing bonds.

LO1   3. Will a bond sell at a discount or at a premium if the stated rate is greater than the market rate on the bond? If the stated rate is less than the market rate?

LO1	4.	Explain the meaning of a bond price quotation of 95. Of 102.
LO2	5.	What accounts are affected when bonds are issued at face value?
LO3/4	6.	How is Premium on Bonds Payable shown on the balance sheet? How is Discount on Bonds Payable shown?
LO3/4	7.	How is the amount of bond premium or discount to be amortized in a period determined using the straight-line method?
LO3/4	8.	How is the periodic interest expense affected by the amortization of the premium on bonds payable?
LO3/4	9.	How is the periodic interest expense affected by the amortization of the discount on bonds payable?
LO5	10.	When bonds are redeemed before maturity, how is the gain or loss on redemption determined? Why does the calculation differ for bonds issued at face value, at a premium, and at a discount?
LO5	11.	Who usually administers a bond sinking fund?
LO5	12.	How should sinking fund earnings be reported on the corporation income statement?
LO5	13.	How should the bond sinking fund be reported on the corporation balance sheet?

SERIES A EXERCISES

E 22-1A (LO2)

✓ Dec. 31. Dr. Bond Interest
Expense: $7,000

BONDS ISSUED AT FACE VALUE D&E Stamps issued the following bonds:

Date of issue and sale:	April 1, 20-1
Principal amount:	$400,000
Sale price of bonds:	100
Denomination of bonds:	$1,000
Life of bonds:	10 years
Stated rate:	7%, payable semiannually on September 30 and March 31

Prepare journal entries for:

(a) Issuance of the bonds.

(b) Interest payment on the bonds on September 30.

(c) Year-end adjustment on the bonds.

E 22-2A (LO3)

✓ Dec. 31. Dr. Bond Interest
Expense: $13,200

BONDS ISSUED AT A PREMIUM Ramos Travel Co. issued the following bonds at a premium:

Date of issue and sale:	April 1, 20-1
Principal amount:	$600,000
Sale price of bonds:	104
Denomination of bonds:	$1,000
Life of bonds:	20 years
Stated rate:	9%, payable semiannually on September 30 and March 31

Prepare journal entries for:

(a) Issuance of the bonds at a premium.

(b) Interest payment and premium amortization on the bonds on September 30.

(c) Year-end adjustment on the bonds.

E 22-3A   (LO4)

✓ Dec. 31. Dr. Bond Interest
   Expense: $9,000

BONDS ISSUED AT A DISCOUNT Brenner's Home Club issued the following bonds at a discount:

Date of issue and sale:	April 1, 20-1
Principal amount:	$500,000
Sale price of bonds:	98
Denomination of bonds:	$1,000
Life of bonds:	10 years
Stated rate:	7%, payable semiannually on September 30 and March 31

Prepare journal entries for:

(a) Issuance of the bonds at a discount.

(b) Interest payment and discount amortization on the bonds on September 30.

(c) Year-end adjustment on the bonds.

E 22-4A   (LO2/5)

✓ (b) Dr. Loss on Bonds
   Redeemed: $3,200

REDEMPTION OF BONDS ISSUED AT FACE VALUE Levesque Lumber Co. issued $800,000 in bonds at face value 10 years ago and has paid semiannual interest payments through the years.

(a)   Assume the bonds are redeemed at face value.

(b)   Assume that $80,000 of the bonds are redeemed at 104.

(c)   Assume that $80,000 of the bonds are redeemed at 96.

Prepare journal entries to record (a), (b), and (c).

E 22-5A   (LO3/5)

✓ (a) Cr. Gain on Bonds
   Redeemed: $1,800

REDEMPTION OF BONDS ISSUED AT A PREMIUM Brighton Unlimited sold bonds at a premium for $630,000 (premium of $30,000) eight years ago.

(a) The corporation redeems $60,000 of this issue at 98. The unamortized premium is $600.

(b) The corporation redeems $90,000 of this issue at 102. The unamortized premium is $900.

Prepare journal entries to record the redemption in (a) and (b).

E 22-6A   (LO4/5)

✓ (b) Dr. Loss on Bonds
   Redeemed: $150

REDEMPTION OF BONDS ISSUED AT A DISCOUNT Mutschelknaus Manufacturing sold bonds at a discount for $290,000 (discount of $10,000) seven years ago.

(a) The corporation redeems $25,000 of this issue at 97. The unamortized discount is $350.

(b) The corporation redeems $30,000 of this issue at 99. The unamortized discount is $450.

Prepare journal entries to record the redemption in (a) and (b).

E 22-7A   (LO5)

✓ (b) Cr. Sinking Fund
   Earnings: $3,200

BOND SINKING FUNDS M. J. Adams Corporation pays $40,000 into a bond sinking fund each year for the future redemption of bonds. At the end of the first year, earnings on the sinking fund are $3,200. When the bonds mature, there is a balance in the sinking fund of $301,800, of which $300,000 is used to redeem the bonds.

(*continued*)

Prepare journal entries to record:

(a) The initial sinking fund deposit.

(b) The first year's earnings.

(c) The redemption of the bonds.

(d) The return of excess cash to the corporation.

SERIES A PROBLEMS

P 22-8A   (LO2)
✓ Dec. 31 entry: Dr. Bond
   Interest Expense: $4,500

BONDS ISSUED AT FACE VALUE Ito Co. issued the following bonds:

Date of issue and sale:	April 1, 20-1
Principal amount:	$300,000
Sale price of bonds:	100
Denomination of bonds:	$5,000
Life of bonds:	5 years
Stated rate:	6%, payable semiannually on September 30 and March 31

REQUIRED

Prepare journal entries for:

(a) Issuance of the bonds.

(b) Interest payment on the bonds on September 30, 20-1.

(c) Year-end adjustment on the bonds for 20-1.

(d) Reversing entry for the beginning of 20-2.

(e) Interest payments on the bonds for 20-2 (March 31 and September 30).

(f) Redemption at maturity.

P 22-9A   (LO3)
✓ 2. Carrying value, Aug. 31,
   20-2: $820,400

BONDS ISSUED AT A PREMIUM Bunkichi Corporation issued the following bonds at a premium:

Date of issue and sale:	March 1, 20-1
Principal amount:	$800,000
Sale price of bonds:	103
Denomination of bonds:	$1,000
Life of bonds:	10 years
Stated rate:	8%, payable semiannually on August 31 and February 28

REQUIRED

1. Prepare journal entries for:

   (a) Issuance of the bonds at a premium.

   (b) Interest payment and premium amortization on the bonds on August 31, 20-1.

   (c) Year-end adjustment on the bonds for 20-1.

   (d) Reversing entry for the beginning of 20-2.

   (e) Interest payments and premium amortization on the bonds for 20-2 (February 28 and August 31).

2. Calculate the carrying value of the bonds on August 31, 20-2.

3. Prepare the bonds payable section of a partial balance sheet as of August 31, 20-2.

P 22-10A   (LO4)
✓ 2. Carrying value, Sept. 30, 20-2: $486,125

BONDS ISSUED AT A DISCOUNT Emerald, Inc. issued the following bonds at a discount:

Date of issue and sale:	April 1, 20-1
Principal amount:	$500,000
Sale price of bonds:	97
Denomination of bonds:	$1,000
Life of bonds:	20 years
Stated rate:	8%, payable semiannually on September 30 and March 31

REQUIRED

1. Prepare journal entries for:
   (a) Issuance of the bonds at a discount.
   (b) Interest payment and discount amortization on the bonds on September 30, 20-1.
   (c) Year-end adjustment on the bonds for 20-1.
   (d) Reversing entry for the beginning of 20-2.
   (e) Interest payments and discount amortization on the bonds for 20-2 (March 31 and September 30).
2. Calculate the carrying value of the bonds on September 30, 20-2.

P 22-11A   (LO3/5)
✓ Mar. 1, 20-6 entry: Dr. Loss on Bonds Redeemed, $2,250

BONDS ISSUED AT A PREMIUM, REDEEMED AT A LOSS Plantation Company issued the following bonds at a premium:

Date of issue and sale:	March 1, 20-1
Principal amount:	$700,000
Sale price of bonds:	103
Denomination of bonds:	$1,000
Life of bonds:	10 years
Stated rate:	9%, payable semiannually on August 31 and February 28

REQUIRED

Prepare journal entries for:
(a) Issuance of the bonds.
(b) Interest payment and premium amortization on the bonds on August 31, 20-1.
(c) Year-end adjustment on the bonds for 20-1.
(d) Reversing entry for the beginning of 20-2.
(e) Redemption of $50,000 of the bonds on March 1, 20-6, at 106.

P 22-12A   (LO4/5)
✓ Apr. 1, 20-4 entry: Cr. Gain on Bonds Redeemed, $1,150

BONDS ISSUED AT A DISCOUNT, REDEEMED AT A GAIN Cline & Co. issued the following bonds at a discount:

Date of issue and sale:	April 1, 20-1
Principal amount:	$500,000
Sale price of bonds:	98

(*continued*)

Denomination of bonds: $1,000
Life of bonds: 20 years
Stated rate: 7%, payable semiannually on
                                September 30 and March 31

REQUIRED

Prepare journal entries for:

(a) Issuance of the bonds.

(b) Interest payment and discount amortization on the bonds on September 30, 20-1.

(c) Year-end adjustment on the bonds for 20-1.

(d) Reversing entry for the beginning of 20-2.

(e) Redemption of $50,000 of the bonds on April 1, 20-4, at 96.

P 22-13A   (LO2/5)
✓ Dec. 31, 2002 entry: Dr. Bond
Interest Expense, $8,750

BONDS ISSUED AT FACE VALUE WITH SINKING FUND Martin Manufacturing issued the following bonds:

Date of issue and sale: April 1, 2001
Principal amount: $500,000
Sale price of bonds: 100
Denomination of bonds: $10,000
Life of bonds: 10 years
Stated rate: 7%, payable semiannually on
                                    September 30 and March 31
Annual sinking fund requirement: $34,000, payable June 1

REQUIRED

Prepare journal entries for:

(a) Issuance of the bonds.

(b) Deposit to sinking fund on June 1.

(c) Interest payment on the bonds on September 30, 2001.

(d) Earnings of $2,400 on the sinking fund in 2001.

(e) Year-end adjustment on the bonds for 2001.

(f) Reversing entry for the beginning of 2002.

(g) Interest payment on the bonds on March 31, 2002.

(h) Deposit to sinking fund on June 1, 2002.

(i) Redemption at maturity from the sinking fund.

(j) Return of excess cash of $1,050 from the sinking fund to the corporation.

SERIES B EXERCISES

E 22-1B   (LO2)
✓ Dec. 31. Dr. Bond Interest
Expense, $9,000

BONDS ISSUED AT FACE VALUE L & L Underwriters issued the following bonds:

Date of issue and sale: April 1, 20-1
Principal amount: $400,000
Sale price of bonds: 100
Denomination of bonds: $1,000
Life of bonds: 20 years
Stated rate: 9%, payable semiannually on
                              September 30 and March 31

Prepare journal entries for:

(a) Issuance of the bonds.

(b) Interest payment on the bonds on September 30.

(c) Year-end adjustment on the bonds.

E 22-2B (LO3)

✓ Dec. 31. Dr. Bond Interest
Expense, $6,416.67

BONDS ISSUED AT A PREMIUM Bryant and Nelson Company issued the following bonds at a premium:

Date of issue and sale:	May 1, 20-1
Principal amount:	$500,000
Sale price of bonds:	103
Denomination of bonds:	$1,000
Life of bonds:	10 years
Stated rate:	8%, payable semiannually on October 31 and April 30

Prepare journal entries for:

(a) Issuance of the bonds at a premium.

(b) Interest payment and premium amortization on the bonds on October 31.

(c) Year-end adjustment on the bonds.

E 22-3B (LO4)

✓ Dec. 31. Dr. Bond Interest
Expense, $8,150

BONDS ISSUED AT A DISCOUNT Beilke's Supply Stores issued the following bonds at a discount:

Date of issue and sale:	April 1, 20-1
Principal amount:	$400,000
Sale price of bonds:	97
Denomination of bonds:	$1,000
Life of bonds:	20 years
Stated rate:	8%, payable semiannually on September 30 and March 31

Prepare journal entries for:

(a) Issuance of the bonds at a discount.

(b) Interest payment and discount amortization on the bonds on September 30.

(c) Year-end adjustment on the bonds.

E 22-4B (LO2/5)

✓ (b) Dr. Loss on Bonds
Redeemed, $750

REDEMPTION OF BONDS ISSUED AT FACE VALUE Okano Medical Lab issued $300,000 in bonds at face value 10 years ago and has paid semiannual interest payments through the years.

(a) Assume the bonds are redeemed at face value.

(b) Assume that $25,000 of the bonds are redeemed at 103.

(c) Assume that $25,000 of the bonds are redeemed at 97.

Prepare the journal entries to record (a), (b), and (c).

E 22-5B (LO3/5)

✓ (a) Cr. Gain on Bonds
Redeemed, $3,000

REDEMPTION OF BONDS ISSUED AT A PREMIUM Miller & Miller sold bonds at a premium for $525,000 (premium of $25,000) eight years ago.

(a) The corporation redeems $50,000 of this issue at 95. The unamortized premium is $500.

(b) The corporation redeems $75,000 of this issue at 103. The unamortized premium is $750.

Prepare journal entries to record the redemption in (a) and (b).

E 22-6B   (LO4/5)
✓ (b) Dr. Loss on Bonds Redeemed, $600

REDEMPTION OF BONDS ISSUED AT A DISCOUNT Medina Optical Supply sold bonds at a discount for $420,000 (discount of $20,000) eight years ago.

(a) The corporation redeems $25,000 of this issue at 94. The unamortized discount is $250.

(b) The corporation redeems $30,000 of this issue at 101. The unamortized discount is $300.

Prepare journal entries to record the redemption in (a) and (b).

E 22-7B   (LO5)
✓ (b) Cr. Sinking Fund Earnings, $4,750

BOND SINKING FUNDS Sheng Corporation pays $50,000 into a bond sinking fund each year for the future redemption of bonds. At the end of the first year, earnings on the sinking fund are $4,750. When the bonds mature, there is a balance in the sinking fund of $502,125, of which $500,000 is used to redeem the bonds.

Prepare journal entries to record:

(a) The initial sinking fund deposit.

(b) The first year's earnings.

(c) The redemption of the bonds.

(d) The return of excess cash to the corporation.

SERIES B PROBLEMS

P 22-8B   (LO2)
✓ Dec. 31 entry: Dr. Bond Interest Expense, $5,625

BONDS ISSUED AT FACE VALUE Ramona Arroyo Co. issued the following bonds:

Date of issue and sale:	April 1, 20-1
Principal amount:	$250,000
Sale price of bonds:	100
Denomination of bonds:	$5,000
Life of bonds:	10 years
Stated rate:	9%, payable semiannually on September 30 and March 31

REQUIRED
Prepare journal entries for:

(a) Issuance of the bonds.

(b) Interest payment on the bonds on September 30, 20-1.

(c) Year-end adjustment on the bonds for 20-1.

(d) Reversing entry for the beginning of 20-2.

(e) Interest payments on the bonds for 20-2 (March 31 and September 30).

(f) Redemption at maturity.

P 22-9B   LO 3
✓ 2. Carrying value, Aug. 31, 20-2: $256,937.50

BONDS ISSUED AT A PREMIUM Wang Corporation issued the following bonds at a premium:

Date of issue and sale:	March 1, 20-1
Principal amount:	$250,000
Sale price of bonds:	103
Denomination of bonds:	$500
Life of bonds:	20 years
Stated rate:	8%, payable semiannually on August 31 and February 28

REQUIRED

1. Prepare journal entries for:

   (a) Issuance of the bonds at a premium.

   (b) Interest payment and premium amortization on the bonds on August 31, 20-1.

   (c) Year-end adjustment on the bonds for 20-1.

   (d) Reversing entry for the beginning of 20-2.

   (e) Interest payments and premium amortization on the bonds for 20-2 (February 28 and August 31).

2. Calculate the carrying value of the bonds on August 31, 20-2.

P 22-10B   (LO4)

✓ 2. Carrying value, Sept. 30, 20-2: $579,600

BONDS ISSUED AT A DISCOUNT Brandon, Inc., issued the following bonds at a discount:

Date of issue and sale:	April 1, 20-1
Principal amount:	$600,000
Sale price of bonds:	96
Denomination of bonds:	$1,000
Life of bonds:	10 years
Stated rate:	7%, payable semiannually on September 30 and March 31

REQUIRED

1. Prepare journal entries for:

   (a) Issuance of the bonds at a discount.

   (b) Interest payment and discount amortization on the bonds on September 30, 20-1.

   (c) Year-end adjustment on the bonds for 20-1.

   (d) Reversing entry for the beginning of 20-2.

   (e) Interest payments and discount amortization on the bonds for 20-2 (March 31 and September 30).

2. Calculate the carrying value of the bonds on September 30, 20-2.

3. Prepare the bonds payable section of a partial balance sheet as of September 30, 20-2.

P 22-11B   (LO3/5)

✓ Mar. 1, 20-6 entry: Dr. Loss on Bonds Redeemed, $1,875

BONDS ISSUED AT A PREMIUM, REDEEMED AT A LOSS Blackwell Company issued the following bonds at a premium:

Date of issue and sale:	March 1, 20-1
Principal amount:	$500,000
Sale price of bonds:	103
Denomination of bonds:	$1,000
Life of bonds:	20 years
Stated rate:	9%, payable semiannually on August 31 and February 28

REQUIRED

Prepare journal entries for:

(a) Issuance of the bonds.

(b) Interest payment and premium amortization on the bonds on August 31, 20-1.

(c) Year-end adjustment on the bonds for 20-1.

(continued)

(d) Reversing entry for the beginning of 20-2.

(e) Redemption of $50,000 of the bonds on March 1, 20-6, at 106.

P 22-12B   (LO4/5)

✓ Apr. 1, 20-4 entry: Cr. Gain on Bonds Redeemed, $950

BONDS ISSUED AT A DISCOUNT, REDEEMED AT A GAIN Ellis & Co. issued the following bonds at a discount:

Date of issue and sale:	April 1, 20-1
Principal amount:	$400,000
Sale price of bonds:	97
Denomination of bonds:	$1,000
Life of bonds:	10 years
Stated rate:	8%, payable semiannually on September 30 and March 31

REQUIRED

Prepare journal entries for:

(a) Issuance of the bonds.

(b) Interest payment and discount amortization on the bonds on September 30, 20-1.

(c) Year-end adjustment on the bonds for 20-1.

(d) Reversing entry for the beginning of 20-2.

(e) Redemption of $50,000 of the bonds on April 1, 20-4, at 96.

P 22-13B   (LO2/5)

✓ Dec. 31, 2002 entry: Dr. Bond Interest Expense, $12,000

BONDS ISSUED AT FACE VALUE WITH SINKING FUND Creswell Entertainment issued the following bonds:

Date of issue and sale:	April 1, 2001
Principal amount:	$600,000
Sale price of bonds:	100
Denomination of bonds:	$10,000
Life of bonds:	20 years
Stated rate:	8%, payable semiannually on September 30 and March 31
Annual sinking fund requirement:	$40,000, payable on June 1

REQUIRED

Prepare journal entries for:

(a) Issuance of the bonds.

(b) Deposit to sinking fund on June 1.

(c) Interest payment on the bonds on September 30, 2001.

(d) Earnings of $3,000 on the sinking fund in 2001.

(e) Year-end adjustment on the bonds for 2001.

(f) Reversing entry for the beginning of 2002.

(g) Interest payments on the bonds on March 31, 2002.

(h) Deposit to sinking fund on June 1, 2002.

(i) Redemption at maturity from the sinking fund.

(j) Return of excess cash of $1,900 from the sinking fund to the corporation.

MANAGING YOUR WRITING

The business where you work is considering issuing bonds to finance a major expansion. Your boss has just come from a lengthy meeting regarding the bonds, including the interest rate the bonds should carry. This has irritated your boss, who feels that the interest rate to use is obvious—the lowest one possible. This would yield the lowest interest expense to borrow the money. It seems stupid to pay big fees to financial advisors and lawyers when the question is so simple.

Write a report to your boss explaining how the issue price of the bonds (the net amount borrowed) is affected by the stated interest rate on the bonds. Include an explanation of how interest costs consist of more than just periodic interest payments.

ETHICS ♥

ETHICS CASE

Alva Reese is 65 years old and getting ready to retire. She called her investment broker to help her decide what to do with the $50,000 that she has in the stock market. Alva told him that she didn't want any risky investments but hoped for an investment that was relatively safe and offered steady income. She had heard that bonds were safer than stocks and asked the broker how he felt about bonds. Her broker said bonds were a good safe choice and the ones he had in mind would offer her a high yield. He recommended that she invest all $50,000 in corporate callable bonds. Alva asked him to explain what callable bonds were and he told her the explanation was too technical but they were a safe investment that would serve her needs.

1. What information should the investment broker have given Alva?
2. Are all bonds safe? Why or why not?
3. Write a short paragraph describing how to determine the sales (trading) price of a bond.
4. In groups of three or four, make a list of the factors that Alva and the investment broker should consider before deciding how to invest the $50,000.

MASTERY PROBLEM

✓ 2. Carrying value, Dec. 31, 20-2: $610,600

Jackson, Inc.'s fiscal year ends December 31. Selected transactions for the period 20-1 through 20-8 involving bonds payable issued by Jackson are as follows:

20-1

Oct. 31   Issued $600,000 of 10-year, 7%, callable bonds dated October 31, 20-1, for $612,000. Interest is payable semiannually on October 31 and April 30. The bond indenture provides that Jackson is to pay to the trustee bank $20,000 by May 15 of each year (except the tenth year) as a sinking fund for the retirement of the bonds on call or at maturity.

Dec. 31   Made the adjusting entry for interest payable and amortized two months' premium on the bonds (straight-line method).

(continued)

20-2

Jan. 2   Reversed the adjusting entry for interest payable and bond premium amortization.

Apr. 30   Paid the semiannual interest on the bonds and amortized six months' premium.

May 15   Paid the sinking fund trustee $20,000.

Oct. 31   Paid the semiannual interest on the bonds and amortized six months' premium.

Dec. 31   Made the adjusting entry for interest payable and amortized two months' premium on the bonds.

      31   Sinking fund earnings for the year were $900.

20-8

May 15   Paid the sinking fund trustee $20,000.

Oct. 31   Paid the semiannual interest on the bonds and amortized six months' premium.

      31   Redeemed the bonds, which were called at 97.

The balance in the bond premium account is $3,600 after the payment of interest and amortization of premium have been entered. The cash balance in the sinking fund is $200,000, which is applied to the redemption. Jackson paid the sinking fund trustee the additional cash needed to pay off the bonds. (*Hint:* First make the entry for payment to the sinking fund, then make the entry for redemption of the bonds.)

REQUIRED

1. Enter the preceding transactions in general journal form.
2. Calculate the carrying value of the bonds as of December 31, 20-2.

CHALLENGE PROBLEM

This problem challenges you to apply your cumulative accounting knowledge to move a step beyond the material in the chapter.

✓ 1. Net savings = $27,000

On April 1, 20-1, Rebound Co. issued $300,000 of 10%, 10-year bonds, callable at 105 after three years, at face value. On April 1, 20-4, after completing three years of interest payments on the bonds, Rebound is considering calling the bonds and issuing $300,000 of new 8%, 10-year bonds at face value. The current market interest rate is only 8%, so Rebound thinks it might save money by taking this action.

REQUIRED

1. Compute the net savings to Rebound over the life of the original bond issue if it calls the old bonds and issues the new bonds.
2. Assuming Rebound calls the original bond issue, prepare the journal entry for the bond redemption.

True/False

1. T   2. F (discount)   3. T   4. F (decreases)   5. T

Multiple Choice

1. c   2. c   3. a   4. d   5. b

Checkpoint Exercises

1. (c) Less than $300,000

2.

(a)	Sep.	30	Bond Interest Expense	12 0 0 0 00	
			Cash		12 0 0 0 00
			Paid semiannual interest on bonds		
(b)	Dec.	31	Bond Interest Expense	6 0 0 0 00	
			Bond Interest Payable		6 0 0 0 00

3.

(a)	July	1	Cash	510 0 0 0 00	
			Bonds Payable		500 0 0 0 00
			Premium on Bonds Payable		10 0 0 0 00
			Issued bonds at a premium		
(b)	Dec.	31	Bond Interest Expense	22 0 0 0 00	
			Premium on Bonds Payable	5 0 0 00	
			Cash		22 5 0 0 00
			Paid semiannual interest and amortized premium on bonds		

4.

(a)	May	1	Cash	291 0 0 0 00	
			Discount on Bonds Payable	9 0 0 0 00	
			Bonds Payable		300 0 0 0 00
			Issued bonds at a discount		
(b)	Oct.	31	Bond Interest Expense	12 4 5 0 00	
			Discount on Bonds Payable		4 5 0 00
			Cash		12 0 0 0 00
			Paid semiannual interest and amortized discount on bonds		

5.

(a)	Bonds Payable	30 0 0 0 00	
	Loss on Bonds Redeemed	6 0 00	
	Discount on Bonds Payable		3 6 0 00
	Cash		29 7 0 0 00
	Redeemed bonds at a loss		
(b)	Bonds Payable	40 0 0 0 00	
	Discount on Bonds Payable		4 8 0 00
	Gain on Bonds Redeemed		3 2 0 00
	Cash		39 2 0 0 00
	Redeemed bonds at a gain		

Effective Interest Method

In Chapter 22, you learned how to amortize premium and discount on bonds payable using the straight-line method. In this appendix, the effective interest method of amortization is explained and illustrated.

The key to applying the effective interest method is the effective interest rate at which the bonds are issued. The **effective interest rate** is the market rate of interest on the date the bonds are issued. This rate is used to determine both the interest expense and the premium or discount amortization for the period.

Under the **effective interest method**, the beginning-of-period carrying value of the bonds multiplied by the effective interest rate is the **effective interest expense**. The difference between the effective interest expense and the cash interest payment is the amount of premium or discount to be amortized for the period.

LO1

Amortization of Premium Using the Effective Interest Method

Amortize premium on bonds payable using the effective interest method.

To illustrate the effective interest method of amortizing bond premium, assume the following bond issue for Prime Co:

Date of issue and sale:	April 1, 2001
Principal amount:	$400,000
Denomination:	$1,000
Life:	10 years
Stated rate:	9%
Market rate at issue:	8%

Because the stated rate exceeds the market rate, these bonds will sell at a premium, for $427,181. The effective interest expense for the first semiannual interest period is $17,087, the carrying value of the bonds, $427,181, times the semiannual effective interest rate of 4%. The amount of bond premium to be amortized for the period is $913, the difference between the effective interest expense ($17,087) and the cash interest payment ($18,000). The bond premium amortization schedule for the Prime Co. bonds for the first three and the last three interest periods is shown in Figure 22A-1.

The amount in column 2 is the semiannual cash interest payment. Column 3 contains the semiannual effective interest expense. This amount is computed by multiplying the beginning-of-period carrying value of the bond, which appears in the previous row of column 6, by the semiannual effective interest rate (4%). The difference between columns 2 and 3 is shown in column 4, the semiannual premium amortization. The unamortized premium is shown in column 5. As with the straight-line method of amortization, over the life of the bond the unamortized premium decreases to zero and the carrying value of the bond decreases to its face value.

FIGURE 22A-1 Bond Premium Amortization Schedule

BOND PREMIUM AMORTIZATION SCHEDULE **EFFECTIVE INTEREST METHOD**					
(1)	**(2)**	**(3)**	**(4)**	**(5)**	**(6)**
Date	**Cash Payment**	**Interest Expense [(6) in previous row × 4%]**	**Premium Amortization [(2) − (3)]**	**Unamortized Premium**	**Carrying Value of Bonds**
4/1/01				$27,181	$427,181
10/1/01	$18,000	$17,087	$ 913	26,268	426,268
4/1/02	18,000	17,051	949	25,319	425,319
10/1/02	18,000	17,013	987	24,332	424,332
–	–	–	–	–	–
–	–	–	–	–	–
–	–	–	–	–	–
4/1/10	18,000	16,222	1,778	3,773	403,773
10/1/10	18,000	16,151	1,849	1,924	401,924
3/31/11	18,000	16,076*	1,924	0	400,000

*A $1 adjustment was subtracted to correct for rounding error.

Amortization of Discount Using the Effective Interest Method

LO2

Amortize discount on bonds payable using the effective interest method.

To illustrate the effective interest method of amortizing bond discount, assume the following bond issue for Disco Co.:

Date of issue and sale:	April 1, 2001
Principal amount:	$400,000
Denomination:	$1,000
Life:	10 years
Stated rate:	9%
Market rate at issue:	10%

Because the stated rate is less than the market rate, these bonds will sell at a discount, for $375,076. The effective interest expense for the first semiannual interest period is $18,754, the carrying value of the bonds, $375,076, times the semiannual effective interest rate of 5%. The amount of bond discount to be amortized for the period is $754, the difference between the effective interest expense ($18,754) and the cash interest payment ($18,000). The bond discount amortization schedule for the Disco Co. bonds for the first three and the last three interest periods is shown in Figure 22A-2.

The amount in column 2 is the semiannual cash interest payment. Column 3 contains the semiannual effective interest expense. This amount is computed by multiplying the beginning-of-period carrying value of the bond, which appears in the previous row of column 6, by the semiannual effective interest rate (5%). The difference between columns 2 and 3 is shown in column 4, the semiannual discount amortization. The unamortized discount is shown in column 5. As with the straight-line method of amortization, over the life of the bond the unamortized discount decreases to zero, and the carrying value of the bond increases to its face value.

FIGURE 22A-2 Bond Discount Amortization Schedule

		BOND DISCOUNT AMORTIZATION SCHEDULE EFFECTIVE INTEREST METHOD			
(1)	(2)	(3)	(4)	(5)	(6)
Date	Cash Payment	Interest Expense [(6) in previous row × 5%]	Discount Amortization [(3) − (2)]	Unamortized Discount	Carrying Value of Bonds
4/1/01				$24,924	$375,076
10/1/01	$18,000	$18,754	$ 754	24,170	375,830
4/1/02	18,000	18,792	792	23,378	376,622
10/1/02	18,000	18,831	831	22,547	377,453
–	–	–	–	–	–
–	–	–	–	–	–
–	–	–	–	–	–
4/1/10	18,000	19,728	1,728	3,717	396,283
10/1/10	18,000	19,814	1,814	1,903	398,097
3/31/11	18,000	19,903*	1,903	0	400,000

*A $2 adjustment was subtracted to correct for rounding error.

LEARNING OBJECTIVES   Key Points to Remember

LO1	**Amortize premium on bonds payable using the effective interest method.**	Under the effective interest method, the amount of premium to amortize for a period is the cash interest payment minus the effective interest expense on the bonds for the period.
LO2	**Amortize discount on bonds payable using the effective interest method.**	Under the effective interest method, the amount of discount to amortize for a period is the effective interest expense on the bonds for the period minus the cash interest payment.

KEY TERMS

effective interest expense (874)   The beginning-of-period carrying value of the bonds multiplied by the effective interest rate.

effective interest method (874)   A method of amortizing bond discount or premium that uses the effective interest rate on the bonds.

effective interest rate (874)   The market rate of interest on the date the bonds are issued.

In all exercises and problems, round amounts to the nearest whole dollar.

SERIES A EXERCISE

E 22Apx-1A   (LO1)
✓ Dr. Premium on Bonds Payable: $456

On May 1, Holiday Company issued $200,000, 9%, 10-year bonds for $213,591 when the market rate was 8%. Prepare the general journal entry for the first semiannual interest payment and bond premium amortization on November 1, using the effective interest method.

SERIES A PROBLEM

P 22Apx-2A   (LO1)

✓ Dec. 31 entry: Dr. Premium on Bonds Payable: $1,156

BOND PREMIUM AMORTIZATION Fields Company sold an issue of $800,000, 10%, 10-year bonds for $852,032 on March 1. The interest is payable semiannually on September 1 and March 1. The market rate of interest at the time the bonds were issued was 9%. Journalize the following transactions (round all amounts to the nearest dollar).

Sept. 1   Paid the first semiannual interest payment and amortized the bond premium, using the effective interest method.

Dec. 31   Made the adjusting entry for bond interest accrued and amortization of the bond premium from September 1. (*Hint:* Use the effective interest rate for the four-month period from September 1–December 31.)

Jan. 2   Reversed the adjusting entry for bond interest accrued and bond premium amortization as of December 31.

Mar. 1   Paid the second semiannual interest payment and amortized the bond premium.

SERIES B EXERCISE

E 22Apx-1B   (LO2)

✓ Cr. Discount on Bonds Payable: $565

On May 1, Saxophone Corp. issued $300,000, 9%, 10-year bonds for $281,307 when the market rate was 10%. Prepare the general journal entry for the first semiannual interest payment and bond discount amortization on November 1, using the effective interest method.

SERIES B PROBLEM

P 22Apx-2B   (LO2)

✓ Dec. 31 entry: Cr. Discount on Bonds Payable: $495

BOND DISCOUNT AMORTIZATION Zee Company sold an issue of $500,000, 9%, 10-year bonds for $468,845 on April 1. The interest is payable semiannually on October 1 and April 1. The market rate of interest at the time the bonds were issued was 10%. Journalize the following transactions (round all amounts to the nearest dollar).

Oct. 1   Paid the first semiannual interest payment and amortized the bond discount, using the effective interest method.

Dec. 31   Made the adjusting entry for bond interest accrued and amortization of the bond discount from October 1. (*Hint:* Use the effective interest rate for the three-month period from October 1–December 31.)

Jan. 2   Reversed the adjusting entry for bond interest accrued and bond discount amortization as of December 31.

Apr. 1   Paid the second semiannual interest payment and amortized the bond discount.

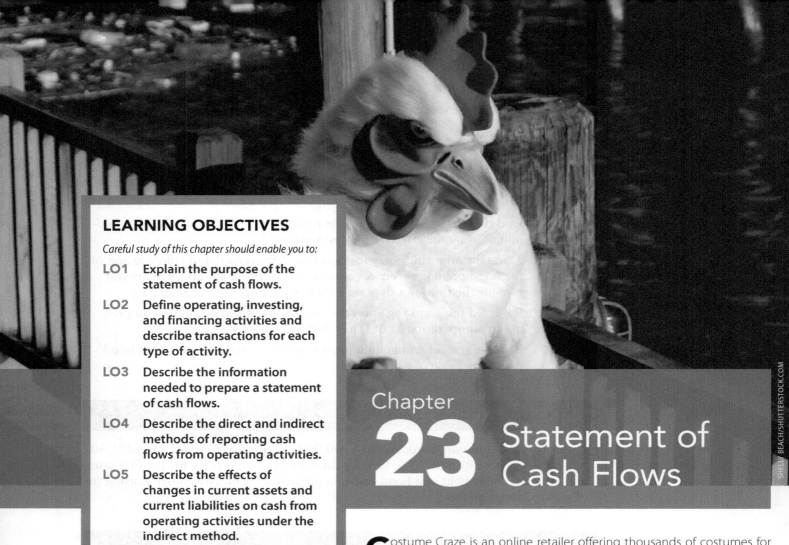

LEARNING OBJECTIVES

Careful study of this chapter should enable you to:

LO1 Explain the purpose of the statement of cash flows.

LO2 Define operating, investing, and financing activities and describe transactions for each type of activity.

LO3 Describe the information needed to prepare a statement of cash flows.

LO4 Describe the direct and indirect methods of reporting cash flows from operating activities.

LO5 Describe the effects of changes in current assets and current liabilities on cash from operating activities under the indirect method.

LO6 Prepare a statement of cash flows under the indirect method using T accounts and including adjustments for current assets and current liabilities related to operations.

LO7 Prepare a statement of cash flows under the indirect method, including adjustments when the company:
   a. defines cash as "cash and cash equivalents,"
   b. reports depreciation expense,
   c. reports gains or losses on transactions not related to operating activities,
   d. has noncash investing and financing activities, and
   e. provides supplemental disclosures of cash flows.

LO8 Interpret the statement of cash flows.

Chapter

23 Statement of Cash Flows

Costume Craze is an online retailer offering thousands of costumes for children, adults, and even pets that was founded by Kathleen, Matthew, and Kate Maloney. Kate serves as CEO. Matt and Kathleen oversee information technology and day-to-day operations, respectively. The company was started primarily to test a search engine optimization software program developed by Matthew. At that time, the company was known as Matthew's Robes, and only monk robes were offered for sale. Business was so good that the focus turned instead to expanding the costume product line. Today, clients include *The Early Show* on CBS, NFL cheerleading squads, World Wrestling Entertainment, and *The Tonight Show*. Odd as it may sound, the company once sold nearly 150 chicken costumes to a grocery store chain.

Headquartered in Pleasant Grove, Utah, the company operates year round, even though some costume businesses may be open just for the Halloween season. Costume Craze relies on Christmas, birthdays, theater productions, and other special events to keep cash coming in during the remainder of the year. So far, business is growing quite well. In just a few years, what started as a home-based business by Matthew is now one of the world's largest online costume retailers. As with all companies, but especially important for firms experiencing exceptional growth and large seasonal fluctuations, cash flows must be monitored carefully. In this chapter, you will learn that the statement of cash flows clarifies where cash came from and how it was used by classifying cash flows into three categories: operating, investing, and financing activities. This information is critical to the success of any business and to an understanding of the firm's financial health.

A business must have an adequate amount of cash to operate. Without sufficient cash, suppliers and employees cannot be paid, debt cannot be retired, and dividends cannot be paid to stockholders. Managers, creditors, stockholders, and others pay close attention to a company's cash position and the economic events and transactions leading to changes in that position. The statement of cash flows provides information about the events that affect the cash position of a company.

LO1	Nature and Purpose of the Statement of Cash Flows

Explain the purpose of the statement of cash flows.

> Recall, revenue is considered earned when a performance obligation has been satisfied.

The managers of a business must generate net income (profitability) and keep the enterprise solvent (liquidity). The income statement reports on the company's profitability by matching revenues and expenses on an accrual basis. Revenues are recognized when earned, regardless of when the cash is received. Expenses are recognized as incurred, regardless of when the cash is paid. Although the accrual basis of accounting is an excellent method for measuring profitability, it does not explain why a company's liquidity has improved or worsened. The income statement does not explain, for example, why a company reporting substantial profits can have difficulty paying bills on time.

It would seem logical that a profitable company would have plenty of cash. Net income brings in cash, either immediately or as soon as receivables are collected. However, the cash inflow resulting from profitable operations may be used to acquire long-term assets, to pay off long-term debt, or to pay stockholders in the form of dividends. Thus, an increase or decrease in cash results from a combination of operating, investing, and financing activities by management. The income statement alone does not adequately reflect all of these activities.

Management and outside users of the financial statements want to know how cash was generated and used during the period. The purpose of the statement of cash flows is to provide this information.

LO2	Operating, Investing, and Financing Activities

Define operating, investing, and financing activities and describe transactions for each type of activity.

> **LEARNING KEY** 🗝
>
> Cash flows from operating activities are primarily related to the revenues and expenses reported on the income statement.

The statement of cash flows categorizes all cash flows into three major types of activities: operating, investing, and financing.

Operating Activities

Operating activities are transactions and events associated with selling a product or providing a service and are related to the revenues and expenses reported on the income statement. Since interest revenue, interest expense, and dividend revenue are reported on the income statement, they are also considered cash flows from operating activities. Figure 23-1 shows cash inflows and outflows from operating activities.

Operating activities represent the company's primary source of cash over the life of the business. Ultimately, net cash inflows from operating activities must be used to purchase plant and equipment, repay loans, and pay dividends to stockholders. If a business is unable to generate positive cash flows from operating activities consistently over time, it will not remain in business.

The proper reporting of dividends and interest on the statement of cash flows can be confusing. Here's an easy way to keep it straight. If the item is reported on the income statement (interest <u>expense</u>, interest <u>revenue</u>, and dividend <u>revenue</u>), it is classified as an operating activity on the statement of cash flows. If not (dividends), it is classified as a financing activity.

Throughout this chapter, colors will be used to help you recognize the three types of business activities as follows:

Green	Operating Activities
Blue	Investing Activities
Orange	Financing Activities

FIGURE 23-1 Cash Flows from Operating Activities

OPERATING ACTIVITIES	
Cash Inflows	**Cash Outflows**
1. Cash receipts from the sale of goods or services.	1. Payments for the acquisition of inventory.
2. Interest received on loans made to outside entities.	2. Payments to employees and the government.
3. Dividends received on investments made in the stock of other corporations.	3. Payments for interest on loans.
	4. Payments to other suppliers and for other expenses.

Investing Activities

Investing activities include the following types of transactions:

1. The purchase and sale of long-term assets.
2. Buying and selling debt and equity securities.
3. Lending money and collecting the principal on the related loans.

Figure 23-2 shows typical transactions for cash inflows and outflows from investing activities.

FIGURE 23-2 Cash Flows from Investing Activities

INVESTING ACTIVITIES	
Cash Inflows	**Cash Outflows**
1. Proceeds from collection of principal amount of loans made to borrowers.*	1. Loans made by the company to other parties.
2. Proceeds from the sale of property, plant, and equipment; intangibles; and other productive assets.	2. Payments to acquire property, plant, and equipment; intangibles; and other productive assets.
3. Proceeds from the sale of investments in debt and equity securities.	3. Payments to acquire investments in debt and equity securities.
4. Proceeds from discounting notes receivable.	

*Note that interest received on loans is not included with investing activities. It is included with cash inflows from operating activities.

LEARNING KEY 🔑

Financing activities deal with the exchange of cash between the company and its stockholders and creditors.

Financing Activities

Financing activities are transactions dealing with the exchange of cash between the company and its owners (stockholders) and creditors. Cash inflows and outflows include the types of transactions listed in Figure 23-3.

FIGURE 23-3 Cash Flows from Financing Activities

FINANCING ACTIVITIES	
Cash Inflows	**Cash Outflows**
1. Proceeds from additional investments by the owners or the issuance of stock.	1. Payments of dividends to stockholders or withdrawals by the owners.
2. Proceeds from borrowing money through the signing of a mortgage, issuing a bond, or other long- or short-term loans.	2. Payments to purchase treasury stock.
	3. Repayment of the principal on loans.*

*Note that interest payments on loans are not reported under financing activities. They are reported as cash outflows under operating activities.

Note: Amounts owed to suppliers of goods and services are not considered financing activities. They are used in the calculation of cash from operating activities.

CHECKPOINT ✔

Complete Checkpoint-1 on page 916 to test your basic understanding of LO2.

Information Needed to Prepare a Statement of Cash Flows

LO3

Describe the information needed to prepare a statement of cash flows.

LEARNING KEY 🔑

The three major sections of the statement of cash flows focus on:
- operating activities
- investing activities
- financing activities

LEARNING KEY 🔑

Change in cash balance:

  Cash from operating activities

± Cash from investing activities

± Cash from financing activities

= Change in cash balance

To prepare a statement of cash flows, the following statements are needed:

1. Balance sheets for the beginning and end of the period.
2. Income statement for the period.
3. Statement of retained earnings for the period.

Additional information on major cash transactions is useful. This information and an analysis of *all noncash balance sheet accounts* are used to identify transactions involving cash flows during the year.

The statement of cash flows is divided into the following three sections:

1. cash flows from operating activities,
2. cash flows from investing activities, and
3. cash flows from financing activities.

The sum of the cash generated or used by each of the three activities should equal the difference between the beginning and ending balance of the cash account. For example, if $5,000 was generated from operations, $2,000 used for investing activities, and $3,000 provided by financing activities, the cash balance must have increased by $6,000 ($5,000 − $2,000 + $3,000) during the year. The accuracy of the statement can be verified by comparing the sum of the cash flows reported on the statement and the change in the balance of the cash account.

Statement of Cash Flows: Direct vs. Indirect Methods

LO4

Describe the direct and indirect methods of reporting cash flows from operating activities.

A sure sign of financial difficulty for a business is the continuing need to sell assets or issue long-term debt to pay operating expenses. Therefore, an important factor in evaluating a company's financial condition is the ability to generate positive cash flows from operating activities. Cash generated from operating activities may be computed and reported using one of two methods. Under the **direct method**, revenues and expenses reported on the income statement are adjusted to reflect the amount of cash received or paid for each item. These adjusted revenues and expenses are reported on the statement of cash flows.

Under the **indirect method**, net income is reported first on the statement of cash flows as the primary source of cash from operating activities. However, this amount must be adjusted for transactions that affect net income *and* cash flows from operating activities, but by different amounts.

To illustrate the difference in the two methods, let's consider a firm with the following events:

1. Sales during the year amounted to $100, but accounts receivable increased by $10.
2. Wages expense for the year amounted to $40, but wages payable increased by $5.

Summary entries for these two events are shown below and would be the same regardless of the method used for the statement of cash flows.

(1)	Cash	90	
	Accounts Receivable	10	
	Sales		100
(2)	Wages Expense	40	
	Wages Payable		5
	Cash		35

Net income would be computed as follows:

Sales	$100
Wages expense	40
Net income	$ 60

Cash from operating activities, reported under the direct and indirect methods, is shown below.

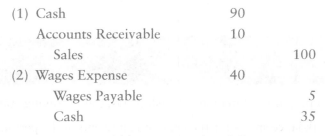

DIRECT METHOD		INDIRECT METHOD	
Cash from customers	$90	Net income	$60
Cash paid to employees	(35)	Increase in accounts receivable	(10)
		Increase in wages payable	5
Cash from operating activities	$55 =	Cash from operating activities	$55

Under the direct method, each line of the income statement is converted to cash paid or received: Sales ($100) to cash from customers ($90), and wages expense ($40) to cash paid to employees ($35). Summing these amounts yields cash from operating activities of $55.

Under the indirect method, net income is listed first. However, the increase in accounts receivable ($10) decreases cash from operating activities, and the increase in wages payable increases cash from operating activities ($5). Summing net income and these indirect adjustments yields the same result as under the direct method: cash from operating activities of $55.

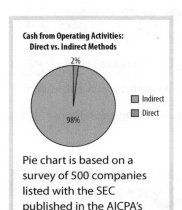

Cash from Operating Activities: Direct vs. Indirect Methods

Pie chart is based on a survey of 500 companies listed with the SEC published in the AICPA's *Accounting Trends and Techniques*.

Direct Method. The direct adjustment of each line item of the income statement to compute cash from operating activities provides the source for the name of this method.

When accounts receivables increase, cash has remained in the customer's pockets, rather than being paid to the business. This reduces cash from operating activities for the current period. When wages payable increase, cash remains with the business, rather than being paid to employees. This increases cash from operating activities for the current period.

Although the direct and indirect methods provide different formats for reporting cash flows from operating activities, the two methods report the same net amount of cash provided or used by operating activities. In addition, investing and financing activities are reported in the same manner under the direct and indirect methods. Thus, only the operating activities section is different. The vast majority of companies use the indirect method. Thus, the indirect method is illustrated in this chapter. The Financial Accounting Standards Board, however, has been encouraging firms to switch to the direct method. The direct method is illustrated in the appendix to this chapter.

CHECKPOINT ✔

Complete Checkpoint-2 on page 916 to test your basic understanding of LO4.

Cash Flows from Operating Activities: Indirect Method

LO5

Describe the effects of changes in current assets and current liabilities on cash from operating activities under the indirect method.

As you know, net income is measured using the accrual basis of accounting. Since increases and decreases in net income do not always increase or decrease cash from operating activities, the following adjustments must be made to net income to report cash flows from operating activities:

1. Changes in current assets related to operating activities.
2. Changes in current liabilities related to operating activities.
3. Noncash expenses.
4. Gains and losses on transactions not related to operating activities.

Adjustments for changes in current assets and current liabilities are discussed in this section of the chapter. Adjustments for noncash expenses and gains and losses not related to operating activities are discussed later.

LEARNING KEY 🔑

Under the indirect method, net income is considered the primary source of cash from operating activities. However, it must be adjusted for the following types of transactions:

1. transactions that impact net income and cash from operating activities, **but by different amounts** (items 1, 2, and 3 above); and

2. transactions that affect net income, **but are not related to cash from operating activities** (item 4 above).

Changes in Current Assets Related to Operating Activities

Accounts receivable, prepaid expenses, and inventories are examples of current assets related to operating activities. Increases in these assets reduce cash generated from operating activities; decreases have the opposite effect. If accounts receivable increased, cash received from customers was less than the sales revenue reported on the income statement. This increase is deducted from net income when computing cash generated from operating activities.

If current assets (A/R, Inventory, Prepaid Expenses) <u>increase</u>, we have more money tied up in these assets, and less cash generated from operating activities. The opposite is true if current assets <u>decrease</u>. Thus, the following adjustments are made:

Net Income	$xxx
Increase in A/R	(xx)
Decrease in	
Prepaid Items	xx
Net cash provided	
by operating	
activities	$xx

For example, if sales were $100,000 and accounts receivable increased by $5,000, think of the following entry:

Cash	95,000	
Accounts Receivable	5,000	
Sales		100,000

Since the revenue used to calculate net income ($100,000) is $5,000 greater than the cash received ($95,000), $5,000 must be subtracted from net income to compute cash from operating activities.

Similar adjustments are made for prepaid expenses. If prepaid expenses increased, cash paid during the period exceeded the expense reported on the income statement. This increase is deducted from net income. On the other hand, decreases in these assets increase cash from operating activities and must be added to net income when computing cash flows from operating activities.

For example, if rent expense was $30,000 and prepaid rent decreased by $2,000, think of the following entry:

Rent Expense	30,000	
Prepaid Rent		2,000
Cash		28,000

Since the rent expense used to calculate net income ($30,000) is $2,000 more than the cash paid ($28,000), $2,000 must be added to net income to compute cash from operating activities.

Changes in Current Liabilities Related to Operating Activities

Accounts payable, income tax payable, and salaries payable are examples of current liabilities related to operating activities. Not all current liabilities are related to operating activities. The declaration of dividends, for example, is not an operating activity and has no effect on net income. Therefore, changes in dividends payable do not require an adjustment to net income.

Changes in current liabilities require an adjustment opposite that of current assets. By increasing the amount owed to others, the company increases cash from operating activities in the current period. Thus, increases in current liabilities are added to net income to compute cash from operating activities. Decreases in current liabilities are deducted from net income to compute cash from operating activities.

An increase in salaries payable indicates that the expense recognized on the income statement for salaries is greater than the cash paid to employees. Thus, the increase in salaries payable must be added to net income to compute cash from operating activities. On the other hand, decreases in this account and other current liabilities reduce cash from operating activities and must be deducted from net income.

For example, if salaries expense was $5,000 and salaries payable increased by $500, think of the following entry:

If current liabilities (A/P, Salaries Payable, Interest Payable) <u>increase</u>, we have postponed payments to these "creditors," thus keeping more money in our pockets and increasing cash generated from operating activities. The opposite is true if current liabilities <u>decrease</u>. Thus, the following adjustments are made:

Net Income	$xxx
Increase in	
salaries payable	xx
Decrease in	
taxes payable	(xx)
Net cash provided	
by operating	
activities	$xx

Salaries Expense	5,000	
Salaries Payable		500
Cash		4,500

Since the expense ($5,000) is $500 greater than the cash paid ($4,500), $500 must be added to net income to compute cash from operating activities.

A decrease in income tax payable indicates that the expense recognized on the income statement for income taxes is less than the cash paid. Thus, the decrease in income tax payable must be subtracted from net income to compute cash from operating activities.

For example, if income tax expense was $40,000 and income tax payable decreased by $2,000, think of the following entry:

CHECKPOINT ✓

Complete Checkpoint-3 on page 916 to test your basic understanding of LO5.

Income Tax Expense	40,000	
Income Tax Payable	2,000	
Cash		42,000

Since the expense ($40,000) is $2,000 less than the cash paid ($42,000), $2,000 must be subtracted from net income to compute cash from operating activities.

LO6

Preparation of a Statement of Cash Flows under the Indirect Method: Simplex

Prepare a statement of cash flows under the indirect method using T accounts and including adjustments for current assets and current liabilities related to operations.

To prepare the statement of cash flows under the indirect method, the following steps are used for Simplex Company. These steps will be expanded later in the chapter as we consider more complex events.

STEP 1 Compute the change in cash.

STEP 2 Set up T accounts with the beginning and ending balances for all noncash balance sheet accounts.

STEP 3 Compute cash flows from operating activities by:

    (a) Reporting net income as the primary source of cash from operating activities.

    (b) Adjusting net income for changes in current assets and current liabilities related to operating activities.

STEP 4 Identify cash flows from investing activities.

STEP 5 Identify cash flows from financing activities.

STEP 6 Prepare a statement of cash flows and verify the accuracy of the statement.

Figure 23-4 shows the financial statements and additional information for Simplex. This illustration requires adjustments to net income for changes in current assets and current liabilities. Adjustments for noncash expenses and gains and losses on the sale of long-term assets will be illustrated later in the chapter. The statement of cash flows will be prepared using the six steps listed above.

FIGURE 23-4 Financial Statements and Additional Information for Simplex

Simplex Company Income Statement For Year Ended December 31, 20-2	
Net sales	$900,000
Cost of goods sold	600,000
Gross profit	$300,000
Operating expenses	177,000
Income before taxes	$123,000
Income tax expense	43,000
Net income	$ 80,000

FIGURE 23-4 Financial Statements and Additional Information for Simplex (*concluded*)

Simplex Company Statement of Retained Earnings For Year Ended December 31, 20-2		
Retained earnings, January 1, 20-2		$ 50,000
Net income	$80,000	
Less dividends	20,000	
Net increase in retained earnings		60,000
Retained earnings, December 31, 20-2		$110,000

Simplex Company Comparative Balance Sheet December 31, 20-2 and 20-1			
	20-2	20-1	INCREASE (DECREASE)
Assets			
Current assets:			
Cash	$ 90,000	$200,000	$(110,000)
Accounts receivable	160,000	190,000	(30,000)
Merchandise inventory	180,000	200,000	(20,000)
Total current assets	$430,000	$590,000	(160,000)
Property, plant, and equipment:			
Land	$ 40,000	$ 40,000	0
Building	140,000		140,000
Equipment	100,000		100,000
Total property, plant, and equipment	$280,000	$ 40,000	240,000
Total assets	$710,000	$630,000	80,000
Liabilities			
Current liabilities:			
Notes payable	$ 60,000	$ 50,000	10,000
Accounts payable	120,000	180,000	(60,000)
Total liabilities	$180,000	$230,000	(50,000)
Stockholders' Equity			
Common stock ($5 par, 100,000 shares authorized;			
Issued: 58,000 in 20-2, 50,000 in 20-1)	$290,000	$250,000	40,000
Paid-in capital in excess of par—common stock	130,000	100,000	30,000
Retained earnings	110,000	50,000	60,000
Total stockholders' equity	$530,000	$400,000	130,000
Total liabilities and stockholders' equity	$710,000	$630,000	80,000

Additional information for 20-2:

1. Building and equipment acquired for cash just before the year-end.

2. Issued 8,000 shares of common stock for $8.75 per share.

3. Declared and paid cash dividends of $20,000.

> Look at the financial statements for Simplex and find the change in cash. The decrease of $110,000 is what we are trying to explain with the statement of cash flows.

STEP 1   Compute the change in cash.

As shown on the balance sheet in Figure 23-4, cash decreased by $110,000. When completed, the net increase or decrease in cash reported on the statement of cash flows will be compared with this amount to verify the accuracy of the statement of cash flows.

STEP 2   Set up T accounts with the beginning and ending balances for all noncash balance sheet accounts.

The T accounts provided in Figure 23-5 must be reconciled as the cash flow effects are determined. That is, debits or credits are made to each account to explain why the account increased or decreased. The related debits or credits

FIGURE 23-5 T Accounts for Simplex

Operating, Investing, and Financing Activities Affecting Cash

Cash

Operating Activities:			
(1) Net income	80,000		
(2) Decrease in accounts receivable	30,000		
(3) Decrease in inventory	20,000		
		60,000	(4) Decrease in accounts payable
Net cash provided by operating activities	70,000		
Investing Activities:			
		140,000	(5) Cash paid for building
		100,000	(6) Cash paid for equipment
Total cash used by investing activities		240,000	
Financing Activities:			
(7) Issued common stock	70,000		
		20,000	(8) Paid dividends
(9) Issued note payable	10,000		
Net cash provided by financing activities	60,000		

T Accounts for Indirect Method Statement of Cash Flows
Simplex Company

Accounts Receivable

BB	190,000		
		30,000	(2)
EB	160,000		

Notes Payable

		50,000	BB
		10,000	(9)
		60,000	EB

Common Stock

		250,000	BB
		40,000	(7)
		290,000	EB

Merchandise Inventory

BB	200,000		
		20,000	(3)
EB	180,000		

Accounts Payable

		180,000	BB
(4)	60,000		
		120,000	EB

Paid-In Capital in Excess of Par—Common Stock

		100,000	BB
		30,000	(7)
		130,000	EB

Land

BB	40,000
EB	40,000

Retained Earnings

		50,000	BB
(8)	20,000	80,000	(1)
		110,000	EB

Building

BB	—
(5)	140,000
EB	140,000

Equipment

BB	—
(6)	100,000
EB	100,000

BB: Beginning Balance
EB: Ending Balance

are made to the cash account. This Cash T account represents a simple version of the statement of cash flows and is divided into three sections: operating, investing, and financing activities. Debits to the operating section represent additions to net income and credits represent deductions from net income. Debits to the investing and financing sections represent inflows of cash. Credits to these sections represent outflows of cash. As shown in Figure 23-6, this account will be very helpful in preparing the statement.

FIGURE 23-6 Statement of Cash Flows for Simplex

Simplex Company		
Statement of Cash Flows (Indirect Method)		
For Year Ended December 31, 20-2		
Cash flows from operating activities:		
Net income	$ 80,000	
Adjustments for changes in current assets and		
liabilities related to operating activities:		
Decrease in accounts receivable	30,000	
Decrease in inventory	20,000	
Decrease in accounts payable	(60,000)	
Net cash provided by operating activities		$ 70,000
Cash flows from investing activities:		
Purchased building	$(140,000)	
Purchased equipment	(100,000)	
Total cash used by investing activities		(240,000)
Cash flows from financing activities:		
Issued common stock	$ 70,000	
Paid dividends	(20,000)	
Issued note payable	10,000	
Net cash provided by financing activities		60,000
Net increase (decrease) in cash		$(110,000)
Cash balance, January 1, 20-2		200,000
Cash balance, December 31, 20-2		$ 90,000

STEP 3(a)   Compute cash flows from operating activities by reporting net income as the primary source of cash from operating activities.

As reported on the income statement, net income is $80,000. Net income is the primary source of cash from operating activities and should be debited to Cash. Since net income increases retained earnings, Retained Earnings should be credited for $80,000 (Entry 1, Figure 23-5).

STEP 3(b)   Compute cash flows from operating activities by adjusting net income for changes in current assets and current liabilities related to operating activities.

Increases in current assets related to operating activities require the use of cash and reduce cash from operating activities. On the other hand, decreases in current assets provide resources without using cash, thus increasing cash from operating activities. The opposite is true for current liabilities.

Accounts Receivable

Accounts receivable decreased by $30,000. If the amount that customers owe to the firm decreased, the amount of cash received by the firm has increased. This would represent an increase in cash from operating activities. A simple method of recording this event is to credit Accounts Receivable and debit Cash from operating activities (Entry 2) as shown in Figure 23-5. The credit to Accounts Receivable reconciles the account, and the debit to Cash is added to net income as one of the adjustments when calculating cash from operating activities.

We can also consider summary entries to reflect the decrease in accounts receivable. Simplex reports $900,000 in sales on the income statement (Figure 23-4). The balance sheet reports that accounts receivable decreased by $30,000. Thus, as shown in Figure 23-7, cash must have increased by $930,000.

FIGURE 23-7 Cash Received from Customers

Cash		Accounts Receivable				Sales	
		BB	190,000				
(2)	930,000	(1)	900,000	930,000	(2)	900,000	(1)
		EB	160,000				

↑——— Cash received from customers.

BB: Beginning Balance
EB: Ending Balance

(1) Entry to record sales (assume all on account).	Accounts Receivable	900,000	
	Sales		900,000

(2) Credit required to reconcile Accounts Receivable. This represents the amount of cash collected from customers.	Cash	930,000	
	Accounts Receivable		930,000

Net income represents the primary source of cash from operating activities. To compute net income, Simplex recognized $900,000 in sales. Since Simplex actually received $930,000 in cash from its customers, $30,000 is added to net income when adjusting to compute cash from operating activities.

Merchandise Inventory and Accounts Payable

The balance sheet for Simplex (Figure 23-4) reports that merchandise inventory decreased by $20,000 and accounts payable decreased by $60,000. The reduction in inventory increases cash from operating activities. Instead of buying additional inventory to cover the amount sold, Simplex sold inventory that was in stock from last year. Thus, less cash was spent on inventory and cash from operating activities increased.

Simplex reduced the amount owed to suppliers, thus decreasing accounts payable. Making additional payments to suppliers to reduce accounts payable reduces cash from operating activities this year.

These relationships are most easily captured using the entries reported in Figure 23-5. The credit to Merchandise Inventory for $20,000 is offset by a debit to Cash under operating activities (Entry 3). The debit to Cash represents an addition to net income when computing cash from operating activities. The debit to Accounts Payable for $60,000 is offset by a credit to Cash under operating activities (Entry 4) and represents a deduction from net income when computing cash from operating activities.

Let's see why these relationships are true. As shown on the income statement in Figure 23-4, when computing net income, Simplex subtracted cost of goods sold of $600,000 from sales. Is this the amount of cash paid for inventory this year? Summary entries made for the acquisition and sale of inventory are provided in Figure 23-8. Thus, even though Simplex reported cost of goods sold of $600,000, cash of $640,000 was actually paid for the merchandise inventory.

FIGURE 23-8 Cash Paid to Suppliers for Merchandise

Cash		Merchandise Inventory				Accounts Payable			Cost of Goods Sold	
		BB 200,000					180,000 BB			
640,000 (3)		(2) 580,000	600,000	(1)	(3) 640,000		580,000 (2)	(1) 600,000		
		EB 180,000					120,000 EB			

Purchases of merchandise.
Cash paid to suppliers for merchandise.

BB: Beginning Balance
EB: Ending Balance

(1)	Entry to record cost of goods sold.	Cost of Goods Sold	600,000
		Merchandise Inventory	600,000
(2)	Debit required to reconcile the inventory account. This represents purchases for the period. Assume that all purchases were made on account.	Merchandise Inventory	580,000
		Accounts Payable	580,000
(3)	Debit required to reconcile Accounts Payable. This represents the amount of cash paid to suppliers for merchandise.	Accounts Payable	640,000
		Cash	640,000

These facts fit nicely with the adjustments made to net income in Figure 23-5. By *adding* the decrease in inventory of $20,000 and *subtracting* the decrease of $60,000 in accounts payable, a net deduction of $40,000 was made to net income. This adjustment is consistent with the concept that Simplex subtracted $600,000 from sales to compute net income, but should subtract $640,000 to compute cash from operating activities, a net additional deduction of $40,000.

STEP 4 **Identify cash flows from investing activities.**

The balance sheet accounts related to investing activities are Land, Building, and Equipment. As reported under additional information on the balance sheet, a building and equipment were acquired for cash just before year-end. These acquisitions represent investing activities. As shown in Figure 23-4, the building account increased by $140,000. Thus, Building is debited for $140,000, and Cash is credited for $140,000 under investing activities (Entry 5). Similarly, equipment increased by $100,000. Thus, Equipment is debited for $100,000, and Cash is credited for $100,000 under investing activities (Entry 6). Both credits to the cash account represent outflows of cash from investing activities. There was no change in the land account. Thus, no reconciliation is required.

STEP 5 **Identify cash flows from financing activities.**

The balance sheet accounts related to financing activities are Notes Payable, Common Stock, Paid-In Capital in Excess of Par—Common Stock, and Retained Earnings. As reported in the additional information on the balance sheet in Figure 23-4, Simplex issued 8,000 shares of common stock for $8.75 per share, or a total of $70,000. This represents a financing activity and was recorded by making the following entry:

Cash	70,000	
Common Stock		40,000
Paid-In Capital in Excess of Par—		
Common Stock		30,000

To reconcile the accounts, credit Common Stock for $40,000 and Paid-In Capital in Excess of Par—Common Stock for $30,000, and debit Cash for $70,000 under financing activities (Entry 7). This debit to Cash represents an inflow of cash from financing activities. By making these entries to the T accounts, Common Stock and Paid-In Capital in Excess of Par—Common Stock have been reconciled. For example, the beginning balance of Common Stock was $250,000. By crediting this account for $40,000, the balance is increased to $290,000, the ending balance.

The additional information also indicates that Simplex declared and paid cash dividends of $20,000. The entry for this event is as follows:

Dividends	20,000	
Cash		20,000

Since the dividends account is closed to Retained Earnings, the debit to the balance sheet accounts is actually made to Retained Earnings, and Cash is credited under financing activities (Entry 8).

Finally, the balance sheet reports an increase in notes payable of $10,000. Thus, Simplex borrowed $10,000. To reconcile the accounts, credit Notes Payable and debit Cash for $10,000 under financing activities (Entry 9). This represents an inflow of cash from financing activities.

STEP 6 **Prepare a statement of cash flows and verify the accuracy of the statement.** After analyzing all additional information and confirming that all noncash balance sheet accounts have been reconciled, the cash account in Figure 23-5 may be used to prepare the statement of cash flows shown in Figure 23-6. Instead of using debits and credits, the statement of cash flows employs additions and subtractions in each section.

Cash Flows from Operating Activities

The first section is cash flows from operating activities. Net income of $80,000 is reported first, followed by additions for the decreases in accounts receivable, $30,000, and inventory, $20,000. Finally, a deduction is made for the decrease in accounts payable ($60,000). By summing net income and the related adjustments, cash from operating activities of $70,000 is reported.

Cash Flows from Investing Activities

As shown in the cash account, investing activities included the purchase of a building and equipment for $140,000 and $100,000, respectively. Thus, the statement of cash flows reports these events and net cash used by investing activities of $240,000.

Cash Flows from Financing Activities

Finally, the cash account indicates three financing activities. Inflows of cash resulted from issuing common stock for $70,000 and a note payable for $10,000. These inflows are offset by an outflow from paying dividends of $20,000. Thus, the statement of cash flows reports these events and net cash provided by financing activities of $60,000.

Verifying the Accuracy of the Statement

By summing the cash flows from operating, investing, and financing activities ($70,000 − $240,000 + $60,000), the statement of cash flows reports a net decrease in cash of $110,000. Simplex's balance sheet reports that cash decreased by $110,000 ($200,000 − $90,000) during the year. The fact that these numbers agree provides some assurance that all cash flow activities have been included in the statement. This reconciliation is reported at the bottom of the statement of cash flows as shown in Figure 23-6.

CHECKPOINT ✔

Complete Checkpoint-4 on page 916 to test your basic understanding of LO6.

Preparation of a Statement of Cash Flows Under the Indirect Method: Multiplex

Prepare a statement of cash flows under the indirect method, including adjustments when the company:

a. defines cash as "cash and cash equivalents."

LEARNING KEY 🔑

A cash equivalent is a short-term, highly liquid investment that can be readily converted to a known amount of cash.

CHECKPOINT ✔

Complete Checkpoint-5 on page 917 to test your basic understanding of LO7a.

LO7

Prepare a statement of cash flows under the indirect method, including adjustments when the company:

b. reports depreciation expense.

c. reports gains or losses on transactions not related to operating activities.

Recall from Chapter 22, corporations may redeem bonds before maturity at a gain or loss.

This section of the chapter illustrates how to prepare a statement of cash flows for a more complex business. Steps similar to those followed to prepare the statement of cash flows for Simplex will be followed for Multiplex. In addition, a few steps will be expanded, and different techniques will be illustrated to provide a more complete understanding of the methods used to prepare the statement of cash flows. Additional concepts to be discussed for Multiplex include the following:

• Cash equivalents
• Noncash expenses
• Gains and losses on the sale of long-term assets
• Noncash investing and financing activities
• Supplemental Disclosures

Cash Equivalents

To earn a return on idle cash, many companies invest in short-term, highly liquid investments known as **cash equivalents**. To qualify as cash equivalents, the investments must be readily convertible to a *known* amount of cash, so that when cash is needed, the investments can be easily liquidated. Examples of cash equivalents include short-term investments in government notes and money market funds. These investments are considered the same as cash when preparing the statement of cash flows. Thus, the statement should explain the change in the amount of cash *and* cash equivalents held at the beginning and at the end of an accounting period.

Noncash Expenses

Depreciation expense and the amortization of intangible assets are examples of **noncash expenses**. These expenses reduce net income, but do not require an outflow of cash during the period. Thus, they are added to net income to compute cash flows from operating activities.

Gains and Losses on Transactions Not Related to Operating Activities

Gains and losses on the sale of long-term assets or the retirement of liabilities are reported on the income statement and included in the calculation of net income. However, since these cash flows are not considered operating activities, the gains and losses should not be included in the calculation of cash from operating activities. Thus, net income must be adjusted on the statement of cash flows to compute cash from operating activities.

To illustrate, consider the financial statements for Stevie B's, shown in Figure 23-9. Let's assume no income tax and that all revenues and expenses for the period were for cash. Thus, the $300 of operating income reported on the income statement also represents cash from operating activities. During the accounting period, Stevie B's sold land that cost $200 for $250. Since this is not an operating activity, the gain of $50 is reported separately on the income statement.

FIGURE 23-9 Treatment of a Gain on the Statement of Cash Flows

Stevie B's
Income Statement
For Year Ended December 31, 20 -2

Sales (all cash)	$1,000
Wages expense (all cash)	700
Operating income	$ 300
Gain on sale of land	50
Net income	$ 350

Stevie B's
Balance Sheet
December 31, 20-2 and 20-1

Assets	20-2	20-1
Cash	$ 950	$ 400
Land	800	1,000
Total assets	$1,750	$1,400
Stockholders' Equity		
Common stock	$1,200	$1,200
Retained earnings	550	200
Total stockholders' equity	$1,750	$1,400

Additional information:
  Sold land that cost $200 for $250.

Stevie B's
Statement of Cash Flows
For Year Ended December 31, 20-2

Cash flows from operating activities:		
Net income	$350	
Less gain on sale of land	(50)	
Net cash provided by operating activities		$300
Investing activities:		
Sold land		250
Net increase in cash		$550

> If the land was sold for a loss, the loss would be added to net income to compute cash provided by operating activities.

CHECKPOINT ✔

Complete Checkpoint-6 on page 917 to test your basic understanding of LO7b and LO7c.

On the statement of cash flows, this gain must be deducted from net income to compute cash from operating activities, $300. The entire amount of cash received from the sale of the land, $250, is reported as a cash inflow under investing activities.

Noncash Investing and Financing Activities

LO7

Prepare a statement of cash flows under the indirect method, including adjustments when the company:

d. has noncash investing and financing activities.

Occasionally, firms will acquire assets by issuing debt. Acquiring assets is an investing activity and issuing debt is a financing activity, but no cash is involved in the transaction. Or, debt might be retired by issuing common stock. Similarly, retiring debt and issuing common stock are financing activities, but no cash is involved. As major events for the company, these transactions are of interest to users of the financial statements and should be included on the statement of cash flows. However, since no cash is involved, these transactions are *not* reported in the investing or financing sections of the statement. Instead, a separate section of the statement, noncash investing and financing activities, is used. For example, if a firm acquires a building by signing a mortgage for $500,000, the following entry would be made:

Building   500,000
      Mortgage Payable—Building   500,000

Since no cash is involved in this transaction, it is not reported in the investing or financing sections of the statement. Instead, it is reported in a separate section as follows:

Schedule of noncash investing and financing activities:

      Acquired a building by signing a mortgage $500,000

Figure 23-10 provides an income statement, statement of retained earnings, comparative balance sheet, and additional information about the cash flows for the period for Multiplex Corporation. We will use this information to prepare a statement of cash flows for Multiplex under the indirect method by following the steps listed on pages 896 to 904.

LEARNING KEY

Noncash investing and financing activities involve no cash flows. Thus, they are not included in the investing and financing sections of the statement. However, these transactions represent a significant change in the company's financial position. Therefore, they are reported in a separate section of the statement of cash flows: Noncash investing and financing activities.

FIGURE 23-10 Financial Statements and Additional Information for Multiplex

Multiplex Corporation
Income Statement
For Year Ended December 31, 20-2

Net sales		$460,100
Cost of goods sold		270,100
Gross profit		$190,000
Operating expenses		120,750
Operating income		$ 69,250
Other revenues and gains:		
Interest revenue	$ 155	
Gain on sale of equipment	3,000	3,155
Other expenses:		
Interest expense		650
Income before taxes		$ 71,755
Income tax expense		24,000
Net income		$ 47,755

Multiplex Corporation
Statement of Retained Earnings
For Year Ended December 31, 20-2

Retained earnings, January 1, 20-2		$23,660
Net income	$47,755	
Less dividends	22,800	
Net increase in retained earnings		24,955
Retained earnings, December 31, 20-2		$48,615

FIGURE 23-10 Financial Statements and Additional Information for Multiplex (*concluded*)

Multiplex Corporation
Comparative Balance Sheet
December 31, 20-2 and 20-1

	20-2		20-1		INCREASE (DECREASE)
Assets					
Current assets:					
Cash	$ 17,980		$20,000		$ (2,020)
Government notes	1,800		3,200		(1,400)
Accrued interest receivable	100		300		(200)
Accounts receivable (net)	60,215		51,510		8,705
Merchandise inventory	64,570		67,500		(2,930)
Supplies and prepayments	4,000		2,750		1,250
Total current assets		$148,665		$145,260	3,405
Property, plant, and equipment:					
Store equipment	$ 48,000		$38,800		9,200
Less accumulated depreciation—store equipment	18,000	30,000	14,000	24,800	4,000
Delivery equipment	$ 47,000		$32,000		15,000
Less accumulated depreciation—delivery equipment	6,500	40,500	8,000	24,000	(1,500)
Office equipment	$ 38,000		$34,000		4,000
Less accumulated depreciation—office equipment	8,000	30,000	6,100	27,900	1,900
Total property, plant, and equipment		$100,500		$ 76,700	23,800
Total assets		$249,165		$221,960	27,205
Liabilities					
Current liabilities:					
Notes payable	$ 10,000		$11,800		(1,800)
Accounts payable	33,500		45,900		(12,400)
Income tax payable	3,000		2,000		1,000
Accrued and withheld payroll taxes	950		1,520		(570)
Accrued interest payable	100		80		20
Total current liabilities		$ 47,550		$ 61,300	(13,750)
Long-term liabilities:					
Note payable (3-year)		13,000			13,000
Total liabilities		$ 60,550		$ 61,300	(750)
Stockholders' Equity					
Common stock ($10 par, 100,000 shares authorized;					
Issued: 10,000 in 20-2 and 9,800 in 20-1)	$100,000		$98,000		2,000
Paid-in capital in excess of par—common stock	40,000		39,000		1,000
Retained earnings	48,615		23,660		24,955
Total stockholders' equity		188,615		160,660	27,955
Total liabilities and stockholders' equity		$249,165		$221,960	27,205

Additional information:

1. Depreciation expense for the year was $10,400 as follows:

Store equipment	$ 4,000
Delivery equipment	4,500
Office equipment	1,900
	$10,400

2. The following cash purchases were made:

Store equipment	$ 9,200
Delivery equipment	12,000
Office equipment	4,000
	$25,200

3. Delivery equipment was sold for $7,000.

Cost	$10,000
Accumulated depreciation	6,000
Book value	$ 4,000
Market value	7,000
Gain on sale of delivery equipment	$ 3,000

4. A $13,000, three-year note was issued to acquire delivery equipment with a market value of $13,000.

5. Declared and paid cash dividends of $22,800.

6. Issued 200 shares of common stock for $15 per share.

STEP 1   Compute the change in cash and cash equivalents.

Multiplex has cash equivalents (government notes) of $1,800 and $3,200 on December 31, 20-2 and 20-1, respectively. Thus, the statement of cash flows must explain why cash and government notes decreased by $3,420 during the year.

	20-2 Dec. 31	20-1 Dec. 31	Increase (Decrease)
Cash	$17,980	$20,000	$(2,020)
Government notes	1,800	3,200	(1,400)
Cash and cash equivalents	$19,780	$23,200	$(3,420)

STEP 2   Set up T accounts with the beginning and ending balances for all non-cash (or cash equivalent) balance sheet accounts.

The purpose of the statement of cash flows is to report all transactions that resulted in cash receipts or payments. To provide a systematic method of searching for these transactions, all noncash (or cash equivalent) balance sheet accounts should be reconciled. The T accounts shown in Figure 23-11 (page 898) are helpful in completing this task. Figure 23-12 (page 899) shows the statement of cash flows for Multiplex. Instead of showing the cash effects in a cash T account as we did for Simplex, the cash flow effects are entered directly on the statement of cash flows. Thus, the T accounts and statement of cash flows are provided on facing pages to make it easier to follow the "entries." In addition, we will illustrate the use of the T accounts and the cash T account for selected adjustments throughout the chapter.

As with Simplex, the T accounts must be reconciled as the statement of cash flows is prepared. Each reconciling item has a debit and a credit. If a debit is made to a T account, an offsetting credit must be made either to another T account or on the statement of cash flows. Financial statements do not have debits and credits. However, we may use debits and credits to assist in the preparation of the statement as follows:

Debits—To enter cash receipts or additions to net income on the statement.

Credits—To enter cash payments or subtractions from net income on the statement.

Using this technique may help prevent errors when preparing the statement. Additions to net income and inflows of cash are shown on the statement of cash flows as positive numbers. Subtractions from net income and cash outflows are reported in parentheses ( ).

STEP 3(a)   Compute cash flows from operating activities by reporting net income as the primary source of cash from operating activities.

Under the indirect method, net income is considered the primary source of cash. Therefore, it is listed first on the statement of cash flows, followed by any necessary additions or subtractions.

Since net income increases retained earnings, $47,755 is credited to the Retained Earnings T account (see item number ▇). The credit to the T account (Figure 23-11) is offset by a debit (cash inflow or addition to net income) on the statement of cash flows (Figure 23-12).

The entry for net income ▮ would appear as follows:

Retained Earnings				Cash		
	23,660	BB		Operating		
	47,755	▮		▮ NI	47,755	
	48,615	EB		Investing		
				Financing		

BB: Beginning Balance
EB: Ending Balance

Retained Earnings is not completely reconciled. We will watch for other transactions that impact retained earnings.

STEP 3(b)   Compute cash flows from operating activities by adjusting net income for changes in current assets and current liabilities related to operating activities.
Multiplex has several current assets and current liabilities. Let's discuss changes in current assets first, followed by changes in current liabilities.

Changes in Current Assets Related to Operating Activities

Items ▮ and ▮ represent decreases in current assets related to operating activities. These decreases represent increases in cash from operating activities. They are reported as credits to each T account to reconcile each account and as additions to net income (debits) on the statement of cash flows.

The entry for the decrease in accrued interest receivable ▮ would appear as follows:

Accrued Interest Receivable				Cash		
BB	300			Operating		
				NI	47,755	
		200	▮	▮	200	
EB	100			Investing		
				Financing		

BB: Beginning Balance
EB: Ending Balance

Note that Accrued Interest Receivable has been reconciled and cash from operating activities has been increased by $200.

Items ▮ and ▮ represent increases in current assets related to operating activities. These increases represent reductions in cash from operating activities. They are reported as debits to the T accounts and as subtractions from net income (credits) on the statement of cash flows.

The entry for the increase in accounts receivable ▮ would appear as follows:

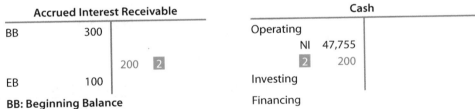

Accounts Receivable (net)				Cash		
BB	51,510			Operating		
				NI	47,755	
▮	8,705				8,705	▮
EB	60,215			Investing		
				Financing		

BB: Beginning Balance
EB: Ending Balance

FIGURE 23-11 T Accounts for Multiplex

T Accounts for Indirect Method Statement of Cash Flows
Multiplex Corporation

Accrued Interest Receivable			
BB	300		
		200	2
EB	100		

Notes Payable			
		11,800	BB
17	1,800		
		10,000	EB

Common Stock			
		98,000	BB
		2,000	15
		100,000	EB

Accounts Receivable			
BB	51,510		
3	8,705		
EB	60,215		

Accounts Payable			
		45,900	BB
6	12,400		
		33,500	EB

Paid-In Capital in Excess of Par—Common Stock			
		39,000	BB
		1,000	15
		40,000	EB

Merchandise Inventory			
BB	67,500		
		2,930	4
EB	64,570		

Income Tax Payable			
		2,000	BB
		1,000	7
		3,000	EB

Retained Earnings			
		23,660	BB
16	22,800	47,755	1
		48,615	EB

Supplies and Prepayments			
BB	2,750		
5	1,250		
EB	4,000		

Accrued and Withheld Payroll Taxes			
		1,520	BB
8	570		
		950	EB

Cash			
BB	20,000		
		2,020	19
EB	17,980		

Store Equipment			
BB	38,800		
13	9,200		
EB	48,000		

Accrued Interest Payable			
		80	BB
		20	9
		100	EB

Government Notes			
BB	3,200		
		1,400	19
EB	1,800		

Accumulated Depreciation— Store Equipment			
		14,000	BB
		4,000	10
		18,000	EB

Long-Term Notes Payable			
		—	BB
		13,000	18
		13,000	EB

Delivery Equipment			
BB	32,000		
12	12,000	10,000	11
18	13,000		
EB	47,000		

Major entries of interest:

Depreciation Expense	10	10,400	
Accum. Depr.—Store Equip.	10		4,000
Accum. Depr.—Delivery Equip.	10		4,500
Accum. Depr.—Office Equip.	10		1,900

Accumulated Depreciation— Delivery Equipment			
		8,000	BB
11	6,000	4,500	10
		6,500	EB

Cash	11	7,000	
Accum. Depr.—Delivery Equipment	11	6,000	
Delivery Equipment	11		10,000
Gain on Sale of Delivery Equip.	11		3,000

Office Equipment			
BB	34,000		
14	4,000		
EB	38,000		

Accumulated Depreciation— Office Equipment			
		6,100	BB
		1,900	10
		8,000	EB

BB: Beginning Balance
EB: Ending Balance

FIGURE 23-12 Statement of Cash Flows for Multiplex (Indirect Method)

Multiplex Corporation Statement of Cash Flows For Year Ended December 31, 20-2			
Cash flows from operating activities:			
Net income	$ 47,755	1*	
Adjustments for changes in current assets and liabilities			
related to operating activities:			
Decrease in accrued interest receivable	200	2	
Increase in accounts receivable	(8,705)	3	
Decrease in merchandise inventory	2,930	4	
Increase in supplies and prepayments	(1,250)	5	
Decrease in accounts payable	(12,400)	6	
Increase in income tax payable	1,000	7	
Decrease in accrued and withheld payroll taxes	(570)	8	
Increase in accrued interest payable	20	9	
Noncash expenses and other adjustments:			
Depreciation expense	10,400	10	
Gain on sale of delivery equipment	(3,000)	11	
Net cash provided by operating activities			$36,380
Cash flows from investing activities:			
Sold delivery equipment	$ 7,000	11	
Purchased delivery equipment	(12,000)	12	
Purchased store equipment	(9,200)	13	
Purchased office equipment	(4,000)	14	
Net cash used by investing activities			(18,200)
Cash flows from financing activities:			
Issued common stock	$ 3,000	15	
Paid cash dividends	(22,800)	16	
Retired notes payable	(1,800)	17	
Net cash used by financing activities			(21,600)
Net increase (decrease) in cash and cash equivalents		19	$ (3,420)
Cash and cash equivalents, January 1, 20-2			23,200
Cash and cash equivalents, December 31, 20-2			$19,780
Schedule of Noncash Investing and Financing Activities:			
Purchased delivery equipment by issuing a 3-year note		18	$13,000
Supplemental Disclosures of Cash Flow Information:			
Cash paid during the year for:			
Interest		20	$ 630
Income taxes		20	23,000
To compute cash paid for interest and taxes, prepare the following entries:			
Interest Expense (see income statement)	650		
Accrued Interest Payable (increase in Acc. Int. Pay.)			20
Cash (plug)		20	630
Income Tax Expense (see income statement)	24,000		
Income Tax Payable (increase in income tax payable)			1,000
Cash (plug)		20	23,000

*Note: Numbers show the relationship between the reconciling entries in the T Accounts and the items on the Statement of Cash Flows.

Note that Accounts Receivable has been reconciled and cash from operating activities has been decreased by $8,705.

Changes in Current Liabilities Related to Operating Activities

Items 6 and 8 represent decreases in current liabilities related to operating activities. These decreases reduce cash from operating activities. They are reported as debits to the T accounts and as subtractions from net income (credits) on the statement of cash flows.

The entry for the decrease in accounts payable 6 would appear as follows:

Accounts Payable				Cash				
		45,900	BB	Operating				
					NI	47,755		
6	12,400						12,400	6
		33,500	EB	Investing				

BB: Beginning Balance
EB: Ending Balance

Financing

Note that Accounts Payable has been reconciled and cash from operating activities has been reduced by $12,400.

Items 7 and 9, the increases in Income Tax Payable and Accrued Interest Payable, indicate that Multiplex did not pay all of the tax and interest expense incurred during the period. Thus, these increases are reported as additions to net income (debits) in the calculation of cash flows from operating activities and as credits to the T accounts.

The entry for the increase in income tax payable 7 would appear as follows:

Income Tax Payable				Cash				
		2,000	BB	Operating				
					NI	47,755		
		1,000	7	7		1,000		
		3,000	EB	Investing				

BB: Beginning Balance
EB: Ending Balance

Financing

Note that Income Tax Payable has been reconciled and cash from operating activities has been increased by $1,000.

STEP 3(c) Compute cash flows from operating activities by adjusting net income for noncash expenses.

Item 10 is for Depreciation Expense and represents noncash expenses. These expenses reduce net income on the income statement, but require no cash payments. Thus, they are added back to net income (debit) on the statement of cash flows. They are also entered as credits to the T accounts for Accumulated Depreciation—Store Equipment, Delivery Equipment, and Office Equipment.

The depreciation on the delivery equipment 10 would appear as follows:

Accumulated Depreciation—Delivery Equipment		Cash		
	8,000 BB	Operating		
		NI	47,755	
	4,500 10	10	4,500	
	6,500 EB	Investing		
		Financing		

BB: Beginning Balance
EB: Ending Balance

Note that accumulated depreciation requires additional adjustments to be reconciled and cash from operating activities has been increased by $4,500. Also note that $10,400 is added back to net income in Figure 23-12. Above, we illustrated the adjustment for the depreciation on the delivery equipment. When preparing the statement of cash flows, we must adjust for the depreciation on all equipment: $4,000 on store equipment, $4,500 on delivery equipment, and $1,900 on office equipment for a total of $10,400 as shown below.

Depreciation Expense	10,400	
Accumulated Depreciation—Store Equipment		4,000
Accumulated Depreciation—Delivery Equipment		4,500
Accumulated Depreciation—Office Equipment		1,900

STEP 3(d)   **Compute cash flows from operating activities by adjusting net income for gains and losses on transactions not related to operating activities.** The income statement reports a gain on the sale of equipment for $3,000. Further, the additional information indicates that the equipment was sold for $7,000. The cost of the equipment was $10,000, accumulated depreciation was $6,000, and the book value was $4,000. The entry for the sale of the equipment is shown below.

Cash	7,000	
Accum. Depr.—Delivery Equipment	6,000	
Delivery Equipment		10,000
Gain on Sale of Delivery Equipment		3,000

This transaction is related to investing activities, but increased net income by $3,000. Thus, the following adjustments are made to the statement of cash flows and T accounts. See entries marked 11.

1. Report the $7,000 cash inflow from investing activities. This represents a debit on the statement of cash flows under investing activities in Figure 23-12.

2. Debit Accumulated Depreciation—Delivery Equipment for $6,000. This helps reconcile the balance sheet account.

3. Credit Delivery Equipment for $10,000. This helps reconcile the balance sheet account.

4. Subtract the $3,000 gain from net income under cash from operating activities. Recall that a subtraction from net income is similar to a credit for analysis purposes. The $3,000 gain was included when computing net income of $47,755, but was not associated with operating activities; thus, subtract the $3,000 gain.

The entry for the sale of delivery equipment **11** would appear as follows:

BB: Beginning Balance
EB: Ending Balance

Delivery Equipment is credited for $10,000 to remove the cost of the equipment sold. Accumulated Depreciation—Delivery Equipment is debited to remove the accumulated depreciation on the equipment sold. The inflow of cash of $7,000 from investing activities is debited to the cash account, and the $3,000 gain is credited to the operating section of the cash account to remove the gain that was included in net income.

STEP 4 **Identify cash flows from investing activities.**

Items **12**, **13**, and **14** are for purchases of equipment. These amounts are entered as debits to the T accounts to reconcile the equipment accounts and as outflows of cash (credits) under investing activities on the statement of cash flows.

The entry for the purchase of delivery equipment **12** would appear as follows:

Delivery Equipment			Cash		
BB	32,000		Operating		
			NI	47,755	
12	12,000				
EB	47,000		Investing		
					12,000 **12**
			Financing		

BB: Beginning Balance
EB: Ending Balance

Delivery Equipment is debited to show the acquisition, and Cash is credited to report the outflow of cash for investing activities.

STEP 5 **Identify cash flows from financing activities.**

Item **15** is for the issuance of common stock. The T accounts for Common Stock and Paid-In Capital in Excess of Par—Common Stock are credited ($2,000 and $1,000, respectively), and the $3,000 is shown as an inflow of cash (debit) from financing activities on the statement of cash flows.

The entry for the issuance of common stock 15 would appear as follows:

Common Stock			Paid-In Capital in Excess of Par—Common Stock			Cash		
	98,000	BB		39,000	BB	Operating		
							NI 47,755	
	2,000	15						
	100,000	EB		1,000	15			
				40,000	EB	Investing		
						Financing		
						15	3,000	

BB: Beginning Balance
EB: Ending Balance

Note that Common Stock and Paid-In Capital in Excess of Par—Common Stock have been reconciled and an inflow of cash from financing activities has been recognized.

The statement of retained earnings in Figure 23-10 shows cash dividends of $22,800 were declared and paid during the year. Since dividends reduce retained earnings, $22,800 is debited to Retained Earnings. The outflow of cash (credit) is reported under financing activities as item 16.

The entry for the payment of dividends 16 would appear as follows:

Retained Earnings				Cash		
		23,660	BB	Operating		
16	22,800	47,755	(1)	(1) NI	47,755	
		48,615	EB	Investing		
				Financing		
					22,800	16

BB: Beginning Balance
EB: Ending Balance

Earlier, we credited Retained Earnings $47,755 (1) for net income. The above $22,800 debit to Retained Earnings for dividends 16 completes the reconciliation of the account. The dividends are credited to the cash account showing an outflow of cash from financing activities.

Item 17 represents the decrease of $1,800 in current notes payable. Therefore, Notes Payable is debited, and the $1,800 cash outflow (credit) is reported under financing activities on the statement of cash flows.

The entry for the reduction in notes payable 17 would appear as follows:

Notes Payable (current)				Cash		
		11,800	BB	Operating		
					NI 47,755	
17	1,800					
		10,000	EB	Investing		
				Financing		
					1,800	17

BB: Beginning Balance
EB: Ending Balance

STEP 6(a) **Prepare a statement of cash flows and disclose noncash investing and financing activities.**

A final review of all noncash balance sheet accounts reveals that Delivery Equipment and the long-term notes payable account have not yet been reconciled. This is consistent with the additional information (Figure 23-10)

Noncash investing and financing activities are listed in a separate section of the statement.

indicating that delivery equipment was acquired by issuing a three-year note for $13,000. Item **18** represents the issuance of the $13,000, three-year note for the acquisition of delivery equipment. Delivery Equipment is debited, and Long-Term Notes Payable is credited to reconcile these accounts. All debits and credits are made in the T accounts in Figure 23-11. Since there is no cash involved in this transaction, no entries are made in the investing or financing sections of the statement of cash flows. However, this event is noted in the schedule of noncash investing and financing activities on the statement of cash flows.

The entry for the purchase of delivery equipment by signing a three-year note **18** would appear as shown below. Note that when added to the previous adjustments (11 and 12), the accounts are reconciled.

Delivery Equipment				Long-Term Notes Payable		
BB	32,000				—	BB
		10,000	(11)			
(12)	12,000					
18	13,000				13,000	18
EB	47,000				13,000	EB

BB: Beginning Balance
EB: Ending Balance

STEP 6(b) **Prepare a statement of cash flows and verify the accuracy of the statement.** After accounting for the changes in all noncash balance sheet accounts, the net increase or decrease in cash as reported on the statement of cash flows is computed. This is done by taking the sum of net cash flows provided by operating activities ($36,380), cash used by investing activities ($18,200), and cash used by financing activities ($21,600). To verify the accuracy of the statement, sum the decrease in Cash (item **19**) and decrease in Government Notes (item **19**) ($2,020 + $1,400) reported in Figures 23-10 and 23-11. This amount is the same as the $3,420 decrease in cash and cash equivalents (item **19**) reported on the statement of cash flows, Figure 23-12.

This verification is reported at the bottom of the statement of cash flows. The $3,420 reduction in cash and cash equivalents is subtracted from the beginning balances of these accounts, $23,200, to compute the ending balance of cash and equivalents, $19,780.

CHECKPOINT ✔

Complete Checkpoint-7 on page 917 to test your basic understanding of LO7d.

LO7

Prepare a statement of cash flows under the indirect method, including adjustments when the company:

e. provides supplemental disclosures of cash flows.

STEP 6(c) **Prepare a statement of cash flows and provide supplemental disclosures of cash flows.**

Companies using the indirect method are required to provide separate disclosure of the following information:

1. The change in accounts receivable.
2. The change in inventory.
3. The change in accounts payable.
4. Cash paid for interest.
5. Cash paid for income taxes.

These items are required so users of the financial statements can compute cash received from customers and cash paid to suppliers. The first three items have already been reported in the statement of cash flows.

Cash Paid for Interest

Multiplex reports $650 of interest expense on the income statement. As reported on the balance sheet, Accrued Interest Payable increased by $20. This means that Multiplex did not pay for all of the $650 of interest expense incurred this period. The $20 increase in the liability is deducted from Interest Expense to compute cash paid for interest ($630). This relationship is easily seen if we consider the summary entry made by Multiplex.

Interest Expense	650	
Interest Payable		20
Cash		630

Cash Paid for Income Taxes

Income tax expense of $24,000 is reported on the income statement. The balance sheet reports that Income Tax Payable increased by $1,000. Postponing the payment for taxes reduces the cash paid for income taxes by $1,000. Thus, $1,000 is deducted from Income Tax Expense to compute the income taxes paid in cash ($24,000 − $1,000 = $23,000). This relationship is easily seen if we consider the summary entry made by Multiplex.

Income Tax Expense	24,000	
Income Tax Payable		1,000
Cash		23,000

Cash paid for interest and income taxes must be reported as supplemental disclosures on the face of the statement of cash flows, or in the notes to the financial statements. The items marked **20** represent the disclosure of this information on the face of the statement of cash flows for Multiplex.

LO8   **Interpreting the Statement of Cash Flows**

Interpret the statement of cash flows.

The purpose of the statement of cash flows is to provide information on the sources and uses of cash. To do this, all cash-related activities are grouped into three categories: operating, investing, and financing. *An important indicator of the financial health of a business is the net cash used or provided by operating activities.* Both Simplex and Multiplex had positive cash flows from operations. This is important because these funds are needed to purchase property, plant, and equipment to upgrade or expand operations. Expansion and renewal can be financed through borrowing or through the issuance of capital stock. However, loans must be repaid with interest, and dividends will be paid to stockholders in proportion to the amount invested. Ultimately, these funds must be generated from operations. A chronic inability to generate positive cash flows from operations is a sure sign of financial instability.

Information on investing and financing activities is also useful in evaluating the financial health of the company. For example, the statement of cash flows in Figure 23-12 shows that Multiplex generated $36,380 from operating activities. Net "spending" on investing and financing activities amounted to $39,800 ($18,200 + $21,600). Thus, cash and cash equivalents fell by $3,420. The major expenditures included a net outflow of $18,200 to purchase equipment and $22,800 paid for dividends. Approximately 63% ($22,800 ÷ $36,380) of the cash generated from operating activities went to the stockholders. If dividends begin to exceed the cash generated from operating activities, it could imply that the company is planning to go out of business.

Modest increases or decreases in cash balances are normal. Major fluctuations should be investigated and can generally be explained by current and expected future investment and financing activities.

A BROADER VIEW

Net Income versus Cash from Operating Activities: Eli Lilly Company

Since cash from operating activities (CFO) is related to revenues and expenses on the income statement, many financial statement users assume that CFO and net income (NI) are similar in value and move in the same direction. This relationship holds, except for a few considerations. For example, depreciation and amortization expenses reduce net income, but do not reduce cash. Thus, over the life of the firm, you should expect CFO to be greater than NI by the amount of depreciation and amortization expenses. This is basically true for Eli Lilly Company. However, for specific years, major differences between CFO and NI that go beyond depreciation are easy to observe.

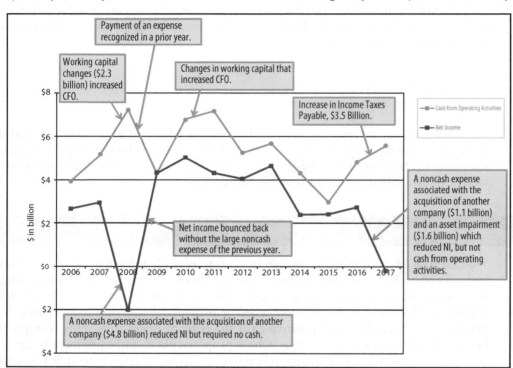

In 2008, we see a dramatic difference between CFO and NI. CFO is $7.3 billion while Lilly reported a net loss of $2.1 billion. This unusually large difference is driven by working capital changes ($2.3 billion) that increased CFO. In addition, depreciation ($1.1 billion), and a noncash expense associated with the acquisition of another company ($4.8 billion) reduced NI, but used no cash.

In 2009, NI and CFO were almost identical. This is because Lilly paid for $1.3 billion in expenses recognized in prior years. These payments reduced cash, but not net income and offset the effects of $1.3 billion in depreciation expense which reduced net income, but not cash.

In 2011, depreciation explains only half of the difference between NI and CFO. The other half is explained by decreases in inventory and other operating assets, and an increase in accounts payable and other operating liabilities. As you learned in this chapter, a company can increase CFO by reducing operating assets and increasing operating liabilities.

In 2017, there was another relatively large, $5.8 billion, difference between NI and CFO. As in 2008, Lilly had a large noncash expense associated with the acquisition of another company. There was also a $1.6 billion asset impairment (Chapter 18), which also reduced NI, but not CFO. In addition, there was a $3.5 billion increase in income taxes payable which increased CFO.

LEARNING OBJECTIVES	**Key Points to Remember**
LO1 Explain the purpose of the statement of cash flows.	The purpose of the statement of cash flows is to report how cash was generated and used throughout the accounting period.
LO2 Define operating, investing, and financing activities and describe transactions for each type of activity.	The statement has three major sections that report on cash flows from operating, investing, and financing activities. Operating activities include transactions and events associated with selling a product or providing a service and are related to the revenues and expenses reported on the income statement. Investing activities are those transactions involving the purchase and sale of long-term assets, investments in debt and equity securities, and lending money and collecting the principal on the related loans. Financing activities are those transactions dealing with the exchange of cash between the company and its stockholders and creditors. The inflows and outflows associated with these types of activities are as follows:

OPERATING ACTIVITIES

Cash Inflows	Cash Outflows
1. Cash receipts from the sale of goods or services.	1. Payments for the acquisition of inventory.
2. Interest received on loans made to outside entities.	2. Payments to employees and the government.
3. Dividends received on investments made in the stock of other corporations.	3. Payments for interest on loans.
	4. Payments to other suppliers and for other expenses.

INVESTING ACTIVITIES

Cash Inflows	Cash Outflows
1. Proceeds from collection of principal amount of loans made to borrowers.*	1. Loans made by the company to other parties.
2. Proceeds from the sale of property, plant, and equipment; intangibles; and other productive assets.	2. Payments to acquire property, plant, and equipment; intangibles; and other productive assets.
3. Proceeds from the sale of investments in debt and equity securities.	3. Payments to acquire investments in debt and equity securities.
4. Proceeds from discounting notes receivable.	

*Note that interest received on loans is not included with investing activities. It is included with cash inflows from operating activities.

(continued)

LEARNING OBJECTIVES	**Key Points to Remember**

LO2 (concluded)

FINANCING ACTIVITIES	
Cash Inflows	**Cash Outflows**
1. Proceeds from additional investments by the owners or the issuance of stock.	1. Payments of dividends to stockholders or withdrawals by the owners.
2. Proceeds from borrowing money through the signing of a mortgage, issuing a bond, or other long- or short-term loans.	2. Payments to purchase treasury stock.
	3. Repayment of the principal on loans.*

* Interest payments on loans are not reported under financing activities. They are reported as cash outflows under operating activities.

Note: Amounts owed to suppliers of goods and services are not considered financing activities. They are used in the calculation of cash from operating activities.

LO3 Describe the information needed to prepare a statement of cash flows.

To prepare a statement of cash flows, the following information is needed:

1. Balance sheets for the beginning and end of the period.
2. Income statement for the period.
3. Statement of retained earnings for the period.
4. Any additional information on major cash transactions.

LO4 Describe the direct and indirect methods of reporting cash flows from operating activities.

Under the direct method, cash from operating activities is determined by adjusting each revenue and expense on the income statement as shown below.

Income Statement	is converted to	Cash from operating activities.
Sales	is converted to	Cash received from customers.
Operating Expense	is converted to	Cash paid for operating expenses.

Under the indirect method, net income is considered the primary source of cash from operating activities. Thus, it is reported on the statement of cash flows under operating activities. However, net income must be adjusted for transactions that affect net income and cash flows from operating activities by different amounts.

LO5 Describe the effects of changes in current assets and current liabilities on cash from operating activities under the indirect method.

The effects of changes in current assets and liabilities on cash flows from operating activities are shown below.

Change in:		Impact on:
Current Asset	Current Liability	Cash from Operating Activities
Increase Decrease	Decrease Increase	Decrease Increase

LEARNING OBJECTIVES	**Key Points to Remember**

LO6 Prepare a statement of cash flows under the indirect method using T accounts and including adjustments for current assets and current liabilities related to operations.

Basic steps to prepare a statement of cash flows:

STEP 1 Compute the change in cash.

STEP 2 Set up T accounts with the beginning and ending balances for all non-cash balance sheet accounts.

STEP 3 Compute cash flows from operating activities by:

(a) Reporting net income as the primary source of cash from operating activities.

(b) Adjusting net income for changes in current assets and current liabilities related to operating activities.

STEP 4 Identify cash flows from investing activities.

STEP 5 Identify cash flows from financing activities.

STEP 6 Prepare a statement of cash flows and verify the accuracy of the statement.

T accounts may be used to prepare the statement of cash flows. All noncash or cash equivalent balance sheet accounts should be set up in T accounts. As these accounts are reconciled, debits or credits are made to the cash account. Debits to Cash reflect additions to net income or inflows from investing or financing activities. Credits to Cash reflect deductions from net income or cash outflows from investing or financing activities. Using T accounts, the adjustment for an increase in accounts receivable would appear as follows:

Accounts Receivable (net)				Cash			
BB	51,510			Operating			
				NI	47,755		
						8,705	(3)
(3)	8,705						
EB	60,215			Investing			
BB: Beginning Balance				Financing			
EB: Ending Balance							

LO7 Prepare a statement of cash flows under the indirect method, including adjustments when the company:

(a) defines cash as "cash and cash equivalents,"

(b) reports depreciation expense,

(c) reports gains or losses on transactions not related to operating activities,

Cash equivalents are short-term, highly liquid investments that are readily convertible to a *known* amount of cash, so that when cash is needed, the investments can be easily liquidated.

Depreciation expense reduces net income, but does not reduce cash. Thus, under the indirect method, depreciation expense should be added to net income when computing cash from operating activities.

Gains and losses on the sale of equipment or retirement of debt impact net income, but are not related to operating activities. Thus, gains should be deducted and losses added to net income when computing cash from operating activities.

(continued)

LEARNING OBJECTIVES	Key Points to Remember
LO7 (concluded) (d) has noncash investing and financing activities, and (e) provides supplemental disclosures of cash flows.	Some major investing and financing transactions do not involve cash. Though not reported in the investing or financing sections of the statement of cash flows, these noncash investing and financing activities are disclosed in a separate schedule on the statement. The following supplemental disclosures are required under the indirect method: • The change in accounts receivable. • The change in inventory. • The change in accounts payable. • Cash paid for interest. • Cash paid for income taxes. **Complete steps to prepare a statement of cash flows.** **STEP 1** Compute the change in cash and cash equivalents. **STEP 2** Set up T accounts with the beginning and ending balances for all non-cash (or cash equivalent) balance sheet accounts. **STEP 3** Compute cash flows from operating activities by: (a) Reporting net income as the primary source of cash from operating activities. (b) Adjusting net income for changes in current assets and current liabilities related to operating activities. (c) Adjusting net income for noncash expenses. (d) Adjusting net income for gains and losses on transactions not related to operating activities. **STEP 4** Identify cash flows from investing activities. **STEP 5** Identify cash flows from financing activities. **STEP 6** Prepare a statement of cash flows and: (a) Disclose noncash investing and financing activities. (b) Verify the accuracy of the statement. (c) Provide supplemental disclosures of cash flows.
LO8 Interpret the statement of cash flows.	An important indicator of the financial health of a company is the net cash used or provided by operating activities. These funds are needed to purchase property, plant, and equipment and pay dividends. Borrowing or issuing capital stock can be used to finance expansion, but these loans must be repaid with interest, and dividends must be paid to stockholders. These funds must ultimately be generated from operations.

DEMONSTRATION PROBLEM

Financial statements and additional information for Megaproducts, Inc. are provided below and on page 912.

Megaproducts, Inc. Income Statement For Year Ended December 31, 20-2		
Net sales		$4,601,000
Cost of goods sold		2,701,000
Gross profit		$1,900,000
Operating expenses		1,242,504
Operating income		$ 657,496
Other revenues and expenses:		
Interest revenue	$ 1,550	
Interest expense	(6,440)	
Loss on sale of delivery equipment	(5,000)	(9,890)
Income before taxes		$ 647,606
Income tax expense		240,000
Net income		$ 407,606

Megaproducts, Inc. Statement of Retained Earnings For Year Ended December 31, 20-2		
Retained earnings, January 1, 20-2		$236,622
Net income	$407,606	
Less dividends	128,000	
Net increase in retained earnings		279,606
Retained earnings, December 31, 20-2		$516,228

Additional information:

1. Delivery equipment was sold during the year for $10,000.

Cost	$ 50,000
Accumulated depreciation	(35,000)
Book value	$ 15,000
Market value	10,000
Loss	$ (5,000)

2. Depreciation expense for the year was $139,000 as follows:

Store equipment	$ 40,000
Delivery equipment	80,000
Office equipment	19,000
	$139,000

3. No other equipment was sold during the period. The following cash purchases were made:

Store equipment	$142,000
Delivery equipment	130,000
Office equipment	40,100
	$312,100

(*continued*)

4. Declared and paid cash dividends of $128,000.

5. Issued 2,000 shares of $10 par common stock for $15 per share.

6. Retired notes payable for $17,200 and acquired additional office equipment by issuing a note payable for $12,000.

Megaproducts, Inc.
Comparative Balance Sheet
December 31, 20-2 and 20-1

	20-2		20-1		INCREASE (DECREASE)
Assets					
Current assets:					
Cash	$ 171,786		$212,000		$(40,214)
Government notes	26,000		20,000		6,000
Accrued interest receivable	300		700		(400)
Accounts receivable (net)	544,000		506,000		38,000
Merchandise inventory	645,678		675,120		(29,442)
Supplies and prepayments	40,150		27,356		12,794
Total current assets		$1,427,914		$1,441,176	(13,262)
Property, plant, and equipment:					
Store equipment	$ 530,000		$388,000		142,000
Less accumulated depreciation—store equipment	180,000	350,000	140,000	248,000	40,000
Delivery equipment	$ 400,000		$320,000		80,000
Less accumulated depreciation—delivery equipment	125,000	275,000	80,000	240,000	45,000
Office equipment	$ 392,000		$339,900		52,100
Less accumulated depreciation—office equipment	80,000	312,000	61,000	278,900	19,000
Total property, plant, and equipment		$ 937,000		$ 766,900	170,100
Total assets		$2,364,914		$2,208,076	156,838
Liabilities					
Current liabilities:					
Notes payable	$ 112,800		$118,000		(5,200)
Accounts payable	200,150		367,454		(167,304)
Income tax payable	125,000		100,000		25,000
Accrued and withheld payroll taxes	9,896		15,200		(5,034)
Accrued interest payable	840		800		40
Total liabilities		$ 448,686		$ 601,454	(152,768)
Stockholders' Equity					
Common stock ($10 par, 1,000,000 shares authorized;					
Issued: 100,000 in 20-2 and 98,000 in 20-1)	$1,000,000		$980,000		20,000
Paid-in capital in excess of par—common stock	400,000		390,000		10,000
Retained earnings	516,228		236,622		279,606
Total stockholders' equity		1,916,228		1,606,622	309,606
Total liabilities and stockholders' equity		$2,364,914		$2,208,076	156,838

REQUIRED

1. Prepare a statement of cash flows explaining the change in cash and cash equivalents for the year ended December 31, 20-2.

2. Reconcile the cash and cash equivalents at the bottom of the statement of cash flows.

SOLUTION 1. and 2.

T Accounts for Indirect Method Statement of Cash Flows
Megaproducts, Inc.

Accrued Interest Receivable

BB	700		
		400	**2**
EB	300		

Accounts Receivable

BB	506,000	
3	38,000	
EB	544,000	

Merchandise Inventory

BB	675,120		
		29,442	**4**
EB	645,678		

Supplies and Prepayments

BB	27,356
5	12,794
EB	40,150

Store Equipment

BB	388,000
12	142,000
EB	530,000

Accumulated Depreciation—Store Equipment

	140,000	BB
	40,000	**11**
	180,000	EB

Delivery Equipment

BB	320,000			
13	130,000	50,000	**10**	
EB	400,000			

Accumulated Depreciation—Delivery Equipment

		80,000	BB
10	35,000	80,000	**11**
		125,000	EB

Office Equipment

BB	339,900
14	40,100
18	12,000
EB	392,000

Accumulated Depreciation—Office Equipment

	61,000	BB
	19,000	**11**
	80,000	EB

Notes Payable

		118,000	BB	
17	17,200	12,000	**18**	
		112,800	EB	

Accounts Payable

		367,454	BB
6	167,304		
		200,150	EB

Income Tax Payable

	100,000	BB
	25,000	**7**
	125,000	EB

Accrued and Withheld Payroll Taxes

		15,200	BB
8	5,304		
		9,896	EB

Accrued Interest Payable

	800	BB
	40	**9**
	840	EB

Common Stock

	980,000	BB
	20,000	**16**
	1,000,000	EB

Paid-In Capital in Excess of Par—Common Stock

	390,000	BB
	10,000	**16**
	400,000	EB

Retained Earnings

		236,622	BB
15	128,000	407,606	**1**
		516,228	EB

Cash

BB	212,000		
		40,214	**19**
EB	171,786		

Government Notes

BB	20,000
19	6,000
EB	26,000

Major entries of interest:

Cash	**10**	10,000	
Accum. Depr.—Delivery Equipment	**10**	35,000	
Loss on Sale of Del. Equip.	**10**	5,000	
Delivery Equipment	**10**		50,000

Depreciation Expense	**11**	139,000	
Accum. Depr.—Store Equip.	**11**		40,000
Accum. Depr.—Delivery Equip.	**11**		80,000
Accum. Depr.—Office Equip.	**11**		19,000

Note that the following accounts are affected by two transactions:
  Office Equipment
  Delivery Equipment
  Accumulated Depreciation—Delivery Equipment
  Notes Payable
  Retained Earnings

BB: Beginning Balance
EB: Ending Balance

(continued)

Megaproducts, Inc. Statement of Cash Flows For Year Ended December 31, 20-2			
Cash flows from operating activities:			
Net income	$ 407,606	1	
Adjustments for changes in current assets and liabilities			
related to operating activities:			
Decrease in accrued interest receivable	400	2	
Increase in accounts receivable	(38,000)	3	
Decrease in merchandise inventory	29,442	4	
Increase in supplies and prepayments	(12,794)	5	
Decrease in accounts payable	(167,304)	6	
Increase in income tax payable	25,000	7	
Decrease in accrued and withheld payroll taxes	(5,304)	8	
Increase in accrued interest payable	40	9	
Noncash expenses and other adjustments:			
Loss on sale of delivery equipment	5,000	10	
Depreciation expense	139,000	11	
Net cash provided by operating activities			$ 383,086
Cash flows from investing activities:			
Sold delivery equipment	$ 10,000	10	
Purchase of store equipment	(142,000)	12	
Purchase of delivery equipment	(130,000)	13	
Purchase of office equipment	(40,100)	14	
Net cash used by investing activities			(302,100)
Cash flows from financing activities:			
Paid cash dividends	$ (128,000)	15	
Issued common stock	30,000	16	
Retired notes payable	(17,200)	17	
Net cash used by financing activities			(115,200)
Net increase (decrease) in cash and cash equivalents		19	$ (34,214)
Cash and cash equivalents, January 1, 20-2			232,000
Cash and cash equivalents, December 31, 20-2			$ 197,786
Schedule of Noncash Investing and Financing Activities:			
Purchased office equipment by issuing a note payable		18	$ (12,000)
Supplemental Disclosures of Cash Flow Information:			
Cash paid during the year for:			
Interest		20	$ 6,400
Income taxes		20	215,000
To compute cash paid for interest and taxes, prepare the following entries:			
Interest Expense (see income statement)	6,440		
Accrued Interest Payable (increase in Acc. Int. Pay.)			40
Cash (plug)		20	6,400
Income Tax Expense (see income statement)	240,000		
Income Tax Payable (increase in income tax payable)			25,000
Cash (plug)		20	215,000

KEY TERMS

cash equivalents (892)   Short-term, highly liquid investments that are considered the same as cash when preparing the statement of cash flows.

direct method (882)   A method of preparing the statement of cash flows in which the revenues and expenses reported on the income statement are adjusted to reflect the amount of cash received or paid for each item.

financing activities (880)   Transactions dealing with the exchange of cash between the company and its owners (stockholders) and creditors.

indirect method (882)   A method of reporting cash from operating activities in which net income is adjusted for transactions that affect both net income and cash from operating activities, but in different ways.

investing activities (880)   Transactions involving the purchase and sale of long-term assets, buying and selling debt and equity securities, and lending money and collecting the principal on the related loans.

noncash expenses (892)   Expenses that reduce net income, but do not require an outflow of cash during the period.

noncash investing and financing activities (894)   Investing and financing activities that involve no cash flows, but represent a significant change in the company's financial position.

operating activities (879)   Transactions and events associated with selling a product or providing a service. They are related to the revenues and expenses reported on the income statement.

statement of cash flows (879)   Statement of the cash flows associated with the operating, investing, and financing activities of the company.

SELF-STUDY TEST QUESTIONS

True/False

1. **LO1**   The purpose of the statement of cash flows is to provide information about total revenue and expenses.

2. **LO2**   Investing activities are those transactions dealing with the exchange of cash between the company and its stockholders and creditors.

3. **LO5**   An increase in accounts receivable is deducted from net income to compute cash from operating activities.

4. **LO5**   A decrease in inventory is added to net income to compute cash from operating activities.

5. **LO8**   (A BROADER VIEW) Generally, cash from operating activities should be greater than net income.

Multiple Choice

1. **LO2**   The receipt of dividends on an investment is included on the statement of cash flows as a(n)
   - (a) operating activity.
   - (b) investing activity.
   - (c) financing activity.
   - (d) schedule of noncash investing and financing activities.

2. **LO2** The purchase of new equipment is included on the statement of cash flows as a(n)

(a) operating activity.
(b) investing activity.
(c) financing activity.
(d) schedule of noncash investing and financing activities.

3. **LO2** The payment of interest on a note payable is classified on the statement of cash flows as a(n)

(a) operating activity.
(b) investing activity.
(c) financing activity.
(d) schedule of noncash investing and financing activities.

4. **LO2** The payment of a cash dividend to stockholders is classified on the statement of cash flows as a(n)

(a) operating activity.
(b) investing activity.
(c) financing activity.
(d) schedule of noncash investing and financing activities.

5. **LO7** The acquisition of a building by signing a mortgage note payable is included on the statement of cash flows as a(n)

(a) operating activity.
(b) investing activity.
(c) financing activity.
(d) schedule of noncash investing and financing activities.

 CHECKPOINT

Checkpoint Exercises

1. **LO2** Please classify the following activities as operating, investing, or financing.

(a) Received cash from the sale of goods.
(b) Paid cash to employees.
(c) Received interest on an investment.
(d) Paid cash for equipment.
(e) Paid principal on a loan.

2. **LO4** The following events took place during the year.

(a) Sales during the year amounted to $500, and accounts receivable decreased by $30.
(b) Wage expense for the year amounted to $300 and wages payable decreased by $50.

Compute cash from operating activities under the direct and indirect methods.

3. **LO5** Indicate whether the following items increase or decrease cash from operating activities under the indirect method.

(a) Increase in accounts receivable.
(b) Increase in accounts payable.
(c) Increase in prepaid rent.
(d) Decrease in income taxes payable.

4. **LO6** Describe how the following activities would be reported on a statement of cash flows prepared under the indirect method.

(a) Paid cash for equipment.
(b) Received cash from signing a long-term loan.
(c) Received cash for interest on an investment.
(d) Paid cash dividends to stockholders.

5. **LO7(a)**   Kip Company has the following accounts on its balance sheet. Compute cash and cash equivalents.

Cash	$20,000
Government notes	5,000
Accounts receivable	30,000

6. **LO7(b) and 7(c)**   Simon's Used Furniture earned net income of $50,000 during the year. All revenues and expenses were for cash except the following:

(a) Depreciation of $1,000.
(b) Gain on the sale of a delivery truck, $3,000.

Compute cash from operating activities under the indirect method.

7. **LO7(d)**   Brown Company signed a $500,000 mortgage to acquire an office building. How is this event reported on the statement of cash flows?

8. **LO7(e)**   Brown Company also paid interest of $8,000 and income taxes of $40,000. How would this information be reported on the statement of cash flows?

Answers to the Self-Study Test Questions are at the end of the chapter (page 932).

APPLYING YOUR KNOWLEDGE

REVIEW QUESTIONS

LO1   1. What is the primary purpose of the statement of cash flows?

LO1   2. Name the four principal financial statements comprising a full set of financial statements.

LO2   3. What are the three categories of cash flows shown on a statement of cash flows?

LO2   4. Name the types of cash flows associated with financing activities.

LO2   5. Name the types of cash flows associated with investing activities.

LO2   6. Name the types of cash flows associated with operating activities.

LO2   7. If a company pays cash dividends, where on the statement of cash flows should the payment be reported?

LO2   8. Where is cash received for interest reported on the statement of cash flows?

LO3   9. What information is needed to prepare a statement of cash flows?

LO4   10. Describe the direct method of reporting cash flows from operating activities.

LO4 11. Describe the indirect method of reporting cash flows from operating activities.

LO5 12. Under the indirect method of preparing a statement of cash flows, what adjustment is made to net income if accounts payable increased from last year?

LO5 13. Under the indirect method of preparing a statement of cash flows, what adjustment is made to net income if accounts receivable increased from last year?

LO6/7 14. List the six steps to be followed when preparing a statement of cash flows. Be sure to include all aspects of the statement's preparation.

LO7 15. Explain the procedure for verifying the accuracy of the statement of cash flows.

LO7 16. What are cash equivalents?

LO7 17. Under the indirect method of preparing a statement of cash flows, what adjustment is made for depreciation expense?

LO7 18. Under the indirect method of preparing a statement of cash flows, what adjustment is made for gains and losses on the sale of equipment?

LO7 19. Provide an example of a noncash investing and financing activity.

LO7 20. List the two supplemental disclosures required under the indirect method.

LO8 21. What is the most important value reported on the statement of cash flows when evaluating the financial health of a company?

SERIES A EXERCISES

E 23-1A (LO2) IDENTIFICATION OF OPERATING, INVESTING, AND FINANCING ACTIVITIES The following activities took place during the current year. Indicate whether each activity is a cash inflow (+) or cash outflow (−), and whether it is an operating activity (O), an investing activity (I), or a financing activity (F).

(a) Proceeds from collection of principal amount of loans made to borrowers
(b) Cash receipts from the sale of goods
(c) Payments for interest on loans
(d) Payments of dividends to stockholders
(e) Payments to acquire investments in debt securities
(f) Dividends received on investments made in the stock of other corporations
(g) Repayment of the principal on loans
(h) Interest received on loans made to outside entities
(i) Salaries paid to employees
(j) Payments to acquire property, plant, and equipment and other productive assets
(k) Payments to purchase treasury stock
(l) Proceeds from the sale of common stock

E 23-2A   (LO7)

✓ Increase in cash and cash
equivalents: $25,500

CHANGE IN CASH AND CASH EQUIVALENTS Olsen Company's balance sheets as of December 31, 20-2 and 20-1, showed the following with regard to cash and cash equivalents:

	20-2	20-1
Cash	$75,000	$45,000
Government notes	2,000	6,500

Compute the amount of change in cash and cash equivalents and indicate whether it represented an increase or a decrease.

E 23-3A   (LO5)

✓ Net cash provided by operating
activities: $24,000

ADJUSTING NET INCOME FOR CHANGES IN CURRENT ASSETS AND CURRENT LIABILITIES Brady Company reported net income of $30,000 for 20-2. The December 31 balances of the current assets and current liabilities are shown below.

	20-2	20-1
Accounts Receivable	$ 6,000	$ 3,000
Merchandise Inventory	30,000	34,000
Accounts Payable	16,000	18,000
Wages Payable	5,000	10,000

Compute cash provided by operating activities.

E 23-4A   (LO7)

✓ Net cash provided by operating
activities: $57,500

ADJUSTING NET INCOME FOR NONCASH EXPENSES After adjusting net income for changes in current assets and current liabilities, Penguin Tuxedo's cash from operating activities is $45,000. However, Penguin reports $12,500 in depreciation expense for the year. Compute cash from operating activities after considering the impact of depreciation.

E 23-5A   (LO7)

✓ Net cash provided by operating
activities: $400

GAINS AND LOSSES ON THE SALE OF LONG-TERM ASSETS The income statement for Hubbard's Professional Edge Tennis Camp follows. Assume that all revenues and expenses were for cash and that land was sold for $500. There were no other investing or financing activities during the year. The Cash balances at the beginning and end of the year were $100 and $1,000, respectively. Prepare a statement of cash flows under the indirect method.

Hubbard's Professional Edge Tennis Camp Income Statement For Year Ended December 31, 20-2	
Sales (all cash)	$2,000
Wages expense (all cash)	1,600
Operating income	$ 400
Gain on sale of land	100
Net income	$ 500

E 23-6A   (LO6)

✓ Net cash provided by financing
activities: $60,000

CASH FLOWS FROM INVESTING AND FINANCING ACTIVITIES Rogerson Company's comparative balance sheet as of December 31, 20-2 and 20-1, showed the following with regard to investing and financing activities:

	20-2	20-1
Building	$130,000	$ 0
Equipment	90,000	0
Notes payable	30,000	20,000
Common stock at par	300,000	250,000
Paid-in capital in excess of par	80,000	50,000
Retained earnings	260,000	200,000

(continued)

Net income for 20-2 was $90,000, and cash dividends of $30,000 were declared and paid. Rogerson did not sell any buildings or equipment and did not retire any debt. Determine the amount of cash received and paid for financing and investing activities and the cash flows as they would appear on Rogerson's statement of cash flows for the year ended December 31, 20-2.

E 23-7A   (LO7)

NONCASH INVESTING AND FINANCING ACTIVITIES Norton's Sign Shop issued a $10,000, three-year note payable to acquire a new framing machine. Show how this transaction is reported on a statement of cash flows.

E 23-8A   (LO7)
✓ Cash paid for interest: $1,500

CASH PAID FOR INTEREST Ball Company's income statement for 20-2 reported interest expense of $1,540. The comparative balance sheet as of December 31, 20-2 and 20-1, reported the following:

	20-2	20-1
Accrued interest payable	$260	$220

Compute the amount of cash paid for interest in 20-2.

SERIES A PROBLEMS

P 23-9A   (LO6)
✓ Net cash provided by operating activities: $160,000

COMPUTE CASH PROVIDED BY OPERATING ACTIVITIES Zowine Company's condensed income statement for the year ended December 31, 20-2, was as follows:

Net sales	$765,000
Cost of goods sold	550,000
Gross profit	$215,000
Operating expenses	30,000
Income before taxes	$185,000
Income tax expense	65,000
Net income	$120,000

Additional information obtained from Zowine's comparative balance sheets as of December 31, 20-2 and 20-1, was as follows:

	20-2	20-1
Cash	$60,000	$ 20,000
Accounts receivable	70,000	100,000
Merchandise inventory	80,000	125,000
Accounts payable	55,000	90,000

REQUIRED
Prepare a partial statement of cash flows reporting cash provided by operating activities for the year ended December 31, 20-2.

P 23-10A   (LO6)
✓ Net increase in cash and cash equivalents: $40,000

STATEMENT OF CASH FLOWS Refer to Problem 23-9A. The following additional information was obtained from Zowine's financial statements and auxiliary records for the year ended December 31, 20-2:

Acquired a new warehouse	$120,000
Bought new warehouse equipment	80,000
Issued a note to the bank	40,000
Issued additional common stock:	
Par value	50,000
Paid-in capital in excess of par	20,000
Declared and paid cash dividends	30,000

REQUIRED

Prepare a statement of cash flows for Zowine for the year ended December 31, 20-2.

P 23-11A   (LO7)

✓ Net cash provided by operating activities: $206,070

COMPUTE CASH PROVIDED BY OPERATING ACTIVITIES Horn Company's condensed income statement for the year ended December 31, 20-2, was as follows:

Net sales		$1,220,000
Cost of goods sold		740,000
Gross profit		$ 480,000
Operating expenses		142,000
Operating income		$ 338,000
Other revenues and expenses:		
Interest revenue	$ 420	
Interest expense	(1,200)	(780)
Income before taxes		$ 337,220
Income tax expense		118,000
Net income		$ 219,220

Additional information obtained from Horn's comparative balance sheet and auxiliary records as of December 31, 20-2 and 20-1, was as follows:

	20-2	20-1
Accounts receivable	$135,000	$122,600
Merchandise inventory	145,300	158,900
Accounts payable	45,000	87,100
Income tax payable	2,000	1,000
Supplies and prepayments	11,300	6,800
Accrued and withheld payroll taxes	2,750	3,700
Accrued interest receivable	90	210
Accrued interest payable	240	160

Depreciation expense for 20-2, included in operating expenses on the income statement, was $32,000.

REQUIRED

Prepare a partial statement of cash flows reporting cash provided by operating activities for the year ended December 31, 20-2.

P 23-12A   (LO7)

✓ Operating activities: $152,840
✓ Investing activities: ($209,000)
✓ Financing activities: $80,000

EXPANDED STATEMENT OF CASH FLOWS Financial statements for McDowell Company as well as additional information relevant to cash flows during the period are given on pages 922–923.

(*continued*)

McDowell Company Income Statement For Year Ended December 31, 20-2		
Net sales		$1,890,000
Cost of goods sold		940,000
Gross profit		$ 950,000
Operating expenses		572,300
Operating income		$ 377,700
Other revenues and expenses:		
Interest revenue	$ 3,900	
Interest expense	(890)	
Loss on sale of store equipment	(15,000)	(11,990)
Income before taxes		$ 365,710
Income tax expense		133,000
Net income		$ 232,710

McDowell Company Statement of Retained Earnings For Year Ended December 31, 20-2		
Retained earnings, January 1, 20-2		$360,000
Net income	$232,710	
Less dividends	60,000	
Net increase in retained earnings		172,710
Retained earnings, December 31, 20-2		$532,710

Additional information:

1. Store equipment was sold in 20-2 for $25,000. Additional information on the store equipment sold is provided below.

Cost	$ 70,000
Accumulated depreciation	(30,000)
Book value	$ 40,000
Market value	25,000
Loss on sale	$ 15,000

2. Depreciation expense for the year was $112,000.
3. The following purchases were made for cash:

Store equipment	$ 64,000
Delivery equipment	140,000
Office equipment	30,000
	$234,000

4. Declared and paid cash dividends of $60,000.
5. Issued 10,000 shares of $10 par common stock for $14 per share.
6. Acquired additional store equipment by issuing a note payable for $16,000.

McDowell Company Comparative Balance Sheet December 31, 20-2 and 20-1					INCREASE (DECREASE)
	20-2		20-1		
Assets					
Current assets:					
Cash	$ 75,365		$ 40,325		$ 35,040
Government notes	6,800		18,000		(11,200)
Accrued interest receivable	720		610		110
Accounts receivable (net)	310,700		325,800		(15,100)
Merchandise inventory	685,400		540,200		145,200
Supplies and prepayments	27,000		39,000		(12,000)
Total current assets		$1,105,985		$ 963,935	142,050
Property, plant, and equipment:					
Store equipment	$470,000		$460,000		10,000
Less accumulated depreciation—store equipment	180,000	290,000	150,000	310,000	30,000
Delivery equipment	$530,000		$390,000		140,000
Less accumulated depreciation—delivery equipment	140,000	390,000	100,000	290,000	40,000
Office equipment	$430,000		$400,000		30,000
Less accumulated depreciation—office equipment	88,000	342,000	76,000	324,000	12,000
Total property, plant, and equipment		$1,022,000		$ 924,000	98,000
Total assets		$2,127,985		$1,887,935	240,050
Liabilities					
Current liabilities:					
Notes payable	$118,000		$102,000		16,000
Accounts payable	110,000		195,000		(85,000)
Income tax payable	20,000		25,000		(5,000)
Accrued and withheld payroll taxes	16,400		14,900		1,500
Accrued interest payable	875		1,035		(160)
Total current liabilities		$ 265,275		$ 337,935	(72,660)
Stockholders' Equity					
Common stock ($10 par, 300,000 shares authorized;					
Issued: 90,000 in 20-2 and 80,000 in 20-1)	$900,000		$800,000		100,000
Paid-in capital in excess of par—common stock	430,000		390,000		40,000
Retained earnings	532,710		360,000		172,710
Total stockholders' equity		1,862,710		1,550,000	312,710
Total liabilities and stockholders' equity		$2,127,985		$1,887,935	240,050

REQUIRED

Prepare a statement of cash flows explaining the change in cash and cash equivalents for the year ended December 31, 20-2.

SERIES B EXERCISES

E 23-1B   (LO2)   IDENTIFICATION OF OPERATING, INVESTING, AND FINANCING ACTIVITIES The following activities took place in Tomberlin Company during the most recent year. Indicate whether each activity is a cash inflow (+) or cash outflow (−), and whether it is an operating activity (O), investing activity (I), or financing activity (F).

(a) Payments to acquire productive assets

(b) Proceeds from the issuance of stock

(c) Interest received on loans made to outside entities

(d) Proceeds from the sale of productive assets

(continued)

(e) Dividends received on investments made in the stock of other corporations

(f) Payments to other suppliers and for other expenses

(g) Payments of dividends to stockholders

(h) Payments to acquire investments in debt securities

(i) Payments for interest on loans

(j) Cash receipts from the sale of services

(k) Repayment of the principal on loans

(l) Payments for the acquisition of inventory

E 23-2B   (LO7)

✓ Increase in cash and cash equivalents: $26,000

CHANGE IN CASH AND CASH EQUIVALENTS Pike Company's balance sheets as of December 31, 20-2 and 20-1, showed the following with regard to cash and cash equivalents:

	20-2	20-1
Cash	$90,000	$60,000
Government notes	4,000	8,000

Compute the amount of change in cash and cash equivalents and indicate whether it represented an increase or a decrease.

E 23-3B   (LO6)

✓ Net cash provided by operating activities: $48,000

ADJUSTING NET INCOME FOR CHANGES IN CURRENT ASSETS AND CURRENT LIABILITIES Roberts Company reported net income of $50,000 for 20-2. The December 31 balances of the current assets and current liabilities are shown below.

	20-2	20-1
Accounts Receivable	$ 6,000	$10,000
Merchandise Inventory	60,000	50,000
Accounts Payable	36,000	40,000
Wages Payable	24,000	16,000

Compute cash provided by operating activities.

E 23-4B   (LO7)

✓ Net cash provided by operating activities: $65,000

ADJUSTING NET INCOME FOR NONCASH EXPENSES After adjusting net income for changes in current assets and current liabilities, Cha Cha Dance Company's cash from operating activities is $60,000. However, Cha Cha reports $5,000 in patent amortization expense for the year. Compute cash from operating activities after considering the impact of amortization.

E 23-5B   (LO7)

✓ Total cash provided by operating activities: $2,000

GAINS AND LOSSES ON THE SALE OF LONG-TERM ASSETS The income statement for Leadbetter's Golf Camp follows. Assume that all revenues and expenses were for cash and that land was sold for $600. There were no other investing or financing activities during the year. The Cash balances at the beginning and end of the year were $1,000 and $3,600, respectively. Prepare a statement of cash flows under the indirect method.

Leadbetter's Golf Camp Income Statement For Year Ended December 31, 20-2	
Sales (all cash)	$5,000
Wages expense (all cash)	3,000
Operating income	$2,000
Loss on sale of land	200
Net income	$1,800

E 23-6B   (LO6)

✓ Total cash used by investing activities: ($230,000)

CASH FLOWS FROM INVESTING AND FINANCING ACTIVITIES Hansen Company's comparative balance sheets as of December 31, 20-2 and 20-1, showed the following with regard to investing and financing activities:

	20-2	20-1
Building	$160,000	$ 0
Equipment	70,000	0
Notes payable	20,000	30,000
Common stock at par	260,000	200,000
Paid-in capital in excess of par	60,000	40,000
Retained earnings	220,000	160,000

Net income for 20-2 was $80,000, and cash dividends of $20,000 were declared and paid. Hansen did not sell any buildings or equipment and did not retire any debt. Determine the amount of cash received and paid for financing and investing activities and the cash flows as they would appear on Hansen's statement of cash flows for the year ended December 31, 20-2.

E 23-7B   (LO7)

NONCASH INVESTING AND FINANCING ACTIVITIES Murry's consulting services issued a two-year, $5,000 note payable to acquire new office furniture. Show how this transaction is reported on the statement of cash flows.

E 23-8B   (LO7)

✓ Cash paid for interest: $2,260

CASH PAID FOR INTEREST Mulligan Company's income statement for 20-2 reported interest expense of $2,190. The comparative balance sheet as of December 31, 20-2 and 20-1, reported the following:

	20-2	20-1
Accrued interest payable	$340	$410

Compute the amount of cash paid for interest in 20-2.

SERIES B PROBLEMS

P 23-9B   (LO6)

✓ Net cash provided by operating activities: $155,000

COMPUTE CASH PROVIDED BY OPERATING ACTIVITIES Kennington Company's condensed income statement for the year ended December 31, 20-2, was as follows:

Net sales	$800,000
Cost of goods sold	475,000
Gross profit	$325,000
Operating expenses	148,000
Income before taxes	$177,000
Income tax expense	62,000
Net income	$115,000

Additional information obtained from Kennington's comparative balance sheet as of December 31, 20-2 and 20-1, was as follows:

	20-2	20-1
Cash	$75,000	$ 20,000
Accounts receivable	50,000	75,000
Merchandise inventory	70,000	110,000
Accounts payable	25,000	50,000

(*continued*)

REQUIRED

Prepare a partial statement of cash flows reporting cash provided by operating activities for the year ended December 31, 20-2.

P 23-10B   (LO6)
✓ Net increase in cash and cash
   equivalents: $55,000

STATEMENT OF CASH FLOWS Refer to Problem 23-9B. The following additional information was obtained from Kennington's financial statements and auxiliary records for the year ended December 31, 20-2.

Acquired a new warehouse	$90,000
Bought new warehouse equipment	60,000
Issued a note to the bank	30,000
Issued additional common stock:	
Par value	30,000
Paid-in capital in excess of par	10,000
Declared and paid cash dividends	20,000

REQUIRED

Prepare a statement of cash flows for Kennington for the year ended December 31, 20-2.

P 23-11B   (LO7)
✓ Net cash provided by operating
   activities: $179,395

COMPUTE CASH PROVIDED BY OPERATING ACTIVITIES Powell Company's condensed income statement for the year ended December 31, 20-2, was as follows:

Net sales		$1,160,000
Cost of goods sold		690,000
Gross profit		$ 470,000
Operating expenses		224,100
Operating income		$ 245,900
Other revenues and expenses:		
Interest revenue	$ 560	
Interest expense	(1,100)	(540)
Income before taxes		$ 245,360
Income tax expense		86,000
Net income		$ 159,360

Additional information obtained from Powell's comparative balance sheet and auxiliary records as of December 31, 20-2 and 20-1, was as follows:

	20-2	20-1
Accounts receivable	$122,700	$118,200
Merchandise inventory	116,800	139,300
Accounts payable	31,500	47,400
Income tax payable	10,000	15,000
Supplies and prepayments	10,900	5,200
Accrued and withheld payroll taxes	1,960	2,490
Accrued interest receivable	130	175
Accrued interest payable	230	110

Depreciation expense for 20-2, included in operating expenses on the income statement, was $29,000.

REQUIRED

Prepare a partial statement of cash flows reporting cash provided by operating activities for the year ended December 31, 20-2.

P 23-12B   (LO7)

✓ Operating activities: $99,300
✓ Investing activities: ($237,000)
✓ Financing activities: $180,000

EXPANDED STATEMENT OF CASH FLOWS Financial statements for McGinnis Company as well as additional information relevant to cash flows during the period are given below and on the next page.

McGinnis Company Income Statement For Year Ended December 31, 20-2		
Net sales		$1,750,000
Cost of goods sold		890,000
Gross profit		$ 860,000
Operating expenses		590,600
Operating income		$ 269,400
Other revenues and expenses:		
Interest revenue	$ 2,700	
Interest expense	(750)	
Gain on sale of office equipment	15,000	16,950
Income before taxes		$ 286,350
Income tax expense		95,000
Net income		$ 191,350

McGinnis Company Statement of Retained Earnings For Year Ended December 31, 20-2		
Retained earnings, January 1, 20-2		$320,000
Net income	$191,350	
Less dividends	40,000	
Net increase in retained earnings		151,350
Retained earnings, December 31, 20-2		$471,350

Additional information:

1. Office equipment was sold in 20-2 for $35,000. Additional information on the office equipment sold is provided below.

Cost	$100,000
Accumulated depreciation	(80,000)
Book value	$ 20,000
Market value	35,000
Gain on sale	$ 15,000

2. Depreciation expense for the year was $70,000.

3. The following purchases were made for cash:

Store equipment	$140,000
Delivery equipment	100,000
Office equipment	32,000
	$272,000

4. Declared and paid cash dividends of $40,000.

5. Issued 10,000 shares of $10 par common stock for $22 per share.

6. Acquired additional office equipment by issuing a note payable for $8,000.

(continued)

McGinnis Company Comparative Balance Sheet December 31, 20-2 and 20-1					
	20-2		20-1		INCREASE (DECREASE)
Assets					
Current assets:					
Cash	$103,420		$ 50,520		$ 52,900
Government notes	5,400		16,000		(10,600)
Accrued interest receivable	830		580		250
Accounts receivable (net)	300,600		309,200		(8,600)
Merchandise inventory	580,300		495,800		84,500
Supplies and prepayments	65,000		32,000		33,000
Total current assets		$1,055,550		$ 904,100	151,450
Property, plant, and equipment:					
Store equipment	$560,000		$420,000		140,000
Less accumulated depreciation—store equipment	120,000	440,000	90,000	330,000	30,000
Delivery equipment	$430,000		$330,000		100,000
Less accumulated depreciation—delivery equipment	150,000	280,000	120,000	210,000	30,000
Office equipment	$320,000		$380,000		(60,000)
Less accumulated depreciation—office equipment	30,500	289,500	100,500	279,500	(70,000)
Total property, plant, and equipment		$1,009,500		$ 819,500	190,000
Total assets		$2,065,050		$1,723,600	341,450
Liabilities					
Current liabilities:					
Notes payable	$117,000		$109,000		8,000
Accounts payable	135,000		185,000		(50,000)
Income tax payable	25,000		15,000		10,000
Accrued and withheld payroll taxes	15,800		13,400		2,400
Accrued interest payable	900		1,200		(300)
Total current liabilities		$ 293,700		$ 323,600	(29,900)
Stockholders' Equity					
Common stock ($10 par, 400,000 shares authorized;					
Issued: 80,000 in 20-2 and 70,000 in 20-1)	$800,000		$700,000		100,000
Paid-in capital in excess of par—common stock	500,000		380,000		120,000
Retained earnings	471,350		320,000		151,350
Total stockholders' equity		1,771,350		1,400,000	371,350
Total liabilities and stockholders' equity		$2,065,050		$1,723,600	341,450

REQUIRED

Prepare a statement of cash flows explaining the change in cash and cash equivalents for the year ended December 31, 20-2.

CHECK LIST
☐ Managing
☐ Planning
☐ Drafting
☐ Break
☐ Revising
☐ Managing

MANAGING YOUR WRITING

Direct Method

A friend of yours was looking at a schedule for the calculation of cash generated from operating activities prepared under the direct method and asked why depreciation expense is deducted from operating expenses. He is curious why depreciation is not considered an expense. Write a brief memo that explains why depreciation expense is deducted from operating expenses when preparing this schedule.

Indirect Method

A friend of yours was reading a statement of cash flows prepared under the indirect method and saw that depreciation expense was added when computing cash from operating activities. She is curious why depreciation is considered a source of cash. Write a brief memo that explains why depreciation expense is added to net income on the statement of cash flows and why it certainly is not a source of cash.

ETHICS CASE

Lyle McGee had been the chief accountant at L & B Corporation for well over 20 years. He routinely omitted noncash investing and financing activities from the statement of cash flows, even when they were significant events. When a junior accountant who had just been hired questioned this practice, Lyle told her that it doesn't make any difference how significant an item is "if it doesn't involve cash. Besides, we're a small company and our stockholders are only interested in the bottom line."

1. Is it possible that Lyle thinks he is treating the significant noncash investing and financing activities properly?

2. If you were the junior accountant, what would you do?

3. Suppose that Lyle wants the junior accountant to give him a refresher course on the statement of cash flows. Write a brief memo to Lyle explaining the purpose of the statement of cash flows. Include a description of both the direct and indirect methods. Also, explain the importance of including significant noncash investing and financing activities.

4. In groups of two or three, discuss which method of preparing the statement of cash flows is easier for you to understand, the direct or the indirect, and why.

MASTERY PROBLEM

✓ Operating activities: $40,032

Financial statements for Peachfield Corporation as well as additional information relevant to cash flows during the period follow.

Peachfield Corporation Income Statement For Year Ended December 31, 20-2		
Net sales		$985,000
Cost of goods sold		515,000
Gross profit		$470,000
Operating expenses		299,400
Operating income		$170,600
Other revenues and expenses:		
Gain on sale of office equipment	$5,000	
Interest revenue	2,100	
Interest expense	(436)	6,664
Income before taxes		$177,264
Income tax expense		60,500
Net income		$116,764

(continued)

Peachfield Corporation Statement of Retained Earnings For Year Ended December 31, 20-2		
Retained earnings, January 1, 20-2		$141,973
Net income	$116,764	
Less dividends	20,000	
Net increase in retained earnings		96,764
Retained earnings, December 31, 20-2		$238,737

Additional information:

1. Office equipment was sold during the year for $75,000.

Cost	$ 80,000
Accumulated depreciation	(10,000)
Book value	$ 70,000
Market value	75,000
Gain	$ 5,000

2. Depreciation expense for the year was $62,400 as follows:

Store equipment	$24,000
Delivery equipment	27,000
Office equipment	11,400
	$62,400

3. No other equipment was sold during the year. The following purchases were made for cash.

Store equipment	$ 55,200
Delivery equipment	78,000
Office equipment	24,060
	$157,260

4. Declared and paid cash dividends of $20,000.

5. Issued 11,200 shares of $10 par common stock for $118,000.

6. Issued a note payable for $10,700.

7. Additional store equipment was acquired by issuing a long-term note payable for $20,000.

REQUIRED

1. Prepare a statement of cash flows explaining the change in cash and cash equivalents.

2. Reconcile cash and cash equivalents at the bottom of the statement of cash flows.

	2002		2001		INCREASE (DECREASE)
Peachfield Corporation					
Comparative Balance Sheet					
December 31, 20-2 and 20-1					
Assets					
Current assets:					
Cash	$102,072		$ 27,200		$ 74,872
Government notes	3,600		12,000		(8,400)
Accrued interest receivable	320		250		70
Accounts receivable (net)	152,945		140,905		12,040
Merchandise inventory	355,490		295,400		60,090
Supplies and prepayments	14,500		21,500		(7,000)
Total current assets		$ 628,927		$497,255	131,672
Property, plant, and equipment:					
Store equipment	$308,000		$232,800		75,200
Less accumulated depreciation—store equipment	108,000	200,000	84,000	148,800	24,000
Delivery equipment	$270,000		$192,000		78,000
Less accumulated depreciation—delivery equipment	75,000	195,000	48,000	144,000	27,000
Office equipment	$148,000		$203,940		(55,940)
Less accumulated depreciation—office equipment	38,000	110,000	36,600	167,340	1,400
Total property, plant, and equipment		$ 505,000		$460,140	44,860
Total assets		$1,133,927		$957,395	176,532
Liabilities					
Current liabilities:					
Notes payable	$ 65,480		$ 54,780		10,700
Accounts payable	53,500		125,473		(71,973)
Income tax payable	7,000		5,000		2,000
Accrued and withheld payroll taxes	8,760		7,644		1,116
Accrued interest payable	450		525		(75)
Total current liabilities		$ 135,190		$193,422	(58,232)
Long-term liabilities:					
Notes payable		20,000			20,000
Total liabilities		$ 155,190		$193,422	(38,232)
Stockholders' Equity					
Common stock ($10 par, 1,000,000 shares authorized;					
Issued: 50,000 in 20-2 and 38,800 in 20-1)	$500,000		$388,000		112,000
Paid-in capital in excess of par—common stock	240,000		234,000		6,000
Retained earnings	238,737		141,973		96,764
Total stockholders' equity		978,737		763,973	214,764
Total liabilities and stockholders' equity		$1,133,927		$957,395	176,532

CHALLENGE PROBLEM

> This problem challenges you to apply your cumulative accounting knowledge to move a step beyond the material in the chapter.

> ✓ Cash received from bond issuance: $797,423

The long-term liabilities section of Guyton Enterprises follows. The bonds outstanding on January 1, 20-1, have an annual coupon rate of 4% and had been issued several years ago at a price to yield 5% per year. The discount is amortized using the effective interest method. On December 31, 20-1, $900,000, 5% bonds were issued at a price to yield 6%.

Long-Term Liabilities	December 31, 20-1	January 1, 20-1
Bonds payable	$1,900,000	$1,000,000
Discount on bonds payable	(202,461)	(104,651)
Total long-term liabilities	$1,697,539	$ 895,349

REQUIRED

Compute the cash received from issuing the bonds on December 31, 20-1. (*Hint*: If you have not covered the effective interest method, assume that bond interest expense for 20-1 was $44,767.)

True/False

1. F (Cash flows)

2. F (Investing is buying and selling long-term assets, debt and equity securities, and lending money and collecting principal on the related loans.)

3. T

4. T

5. T

Multiple Choice

1. a   2. b   3. a   4. c   5. d

Checkpoint Exercises

1. a.   Operating
   b.   Operating
   c.   Operating
   d.   Investing
   e.   Financing

2. Direct method statement of cash flows:

Cash received from customers	$ 530
Cash paid to employees	(350)
Cash from operating activities	$ 180

   Indirect method statement of cash flows:

Net income	$ 200
Decrease in accounts receivable	30
Decrease in wages payable	(50)
Cash from operating activities	$ 180

3. a.   Decrease
   b.   Increase
   c.   Decrease
   d.   Decrease

4. a.   Outflow from investing activities
   b.   Inflow from financing activities

c. It is included in net income under operating activities. This one is difficult. Recall that the receipt of interest is defined as an operating activity. The interest revenue is included on the income statement and, thus, included in net income on the statement of cash flows. If the interest revenue is equal to the cash received, there is no need to make any additional adjustment to the statement.

d. Cash outflow from financing activities.

5. Cash and cash equivalents:

Cash	$20,000
Government notes	5,000
Cash and cash equivalents	$25,000

6.

Net income	$50,000
Noncash expenses and other adjustments:	
Depreciation expense	1,000
Gain on sale of truck	(3,000)
Net cash provided by operating activities	$48,000

7. Noncash investing and financing activities:

Signed mortgage to acquire office building	$500,000

8. Interest and income tax expenses are included in net income under operating activities and adjusted for changes in interest and/or income taxes payable. Since the cash paid for these items is not readily recognizable, firms are required to report these amounts as supplemental disclosures as shown below.

   Supplemental disclosure of cash flow information:

Cash paid during the year for:	
Interest	$ 8,000
Income taxes	40,000

Statement of Cash Flows: The Direct Method

This appendix illustrates the direct method of reporting cash flows from operating activities. As discussed earlier, the method of preparing the statement of cash flows only affects the presentation of cash flows from operating activities. The reporting of cash flows from investing and financing activities is identical under the direct and indirect methods.

LO1   The Direct Method

Describe the direct method of reporting cash flows from operating activities.

Under the direct method, revenues and expenses reported on the income statement are adjusted to reflect the cash received or paid for each item. Since the investing and financing sections of the statement are identical under both methods, only the cash from operating activities section will be illustrated for Simplex.

LO2   Cash from Operating Activities Under the Direct Method: Simplex

Prepare a schedule for the calculation of cash generated from operating activities under the direct method by adjusting revenues and expenses for changes in current assets and current liabilities associated with operations.

Simplex Company was used to illustrate the indirect method in the chapter. The same company is used here to provide the opportunity to compare the two methods. Figure 23A-1 provides the financial statements and additional information for Simplex.

To compute cash generated from operating activities, a schedule like the one shown in Figure 23A-2 is prepared. Revenues and expenses reported on the income statement are converted to cash received or paid for operating purposes. Column 1 reports the revenue or expense as reported on the income statement. Columns 2 and 3 are used to make additions or subtractions necessary to reflect the associated cash flows in column 4.

FIGURE 23A-1 Financial Statements and Additional Information for Simplex

Simplex Company
Income Statement
For Year Ended December 31, 20-2

Net sales	$900,000
Cost of goods sold	600,000
Gross profit	$300,000
Operating expenses	177,000
Income before taxes	$123,000
Income tax expense	43,000
Net income	$ 80,000

Simplex Company
Statement of Retained Earnings
For Year Ended December 31, 20-2

Retained earnings, January 1, 20-2		$ 50,000
Net income	$80,000	
Less dividends	20,000	
Net increase in retained earnings		60,000
Retained earnings, December 31, 20-2		$110,000

Simplex Company
Comparative Balance Sheet
December 31, 20-2 and 20-1

	20-2	20-1	INCREASE (DECREASE)
Assets			
Current assets:			
Cash	$ 90,000	$200,000	$(110,000)
Accounts receivable	160,000	190,000	(30,000)
Merchandise inventory	180,000	200,000	(20,000)
Total current assets	$430,000	$590,000	(160,000)
Property, plant, and equipment:			
Land	$ 40,000	$ 40,000	0
Building	140,000		140,000
Equipment	100,000		100,000
Total property, plant, and equipment	$280,000	$ 40,000	240,000
Total assets	$710,000	$630,000	80,000
Liabilities			
Current liabilities:			
Notes payable	$ 60,000	$ 50,000	10,000
Accounts payable	120,000	180,000	(60,000)
Total liabilities	$180,000	$230,000	(50,000)
Stockholders' Equity			
Common stock ($5 par, 100,000 shares authorized;			
Issued: 58,000 in 20-2, 50,000 in 20-1)	$290,000	$250,000	40,000
Paid-in capital in excess of par—common stock	130,000	100,000	30,000
Retained earnings	110,000	50,000	60,000
Total stockholders' equity	$530,000	$400,000	130,000
Total liabilities and stockholders' equity	$710,000	$630,000	80,000

Additional information for 20-2:

1. Building and equipment acquired for cash just before the year-end.

2. Issued 8,000 shares of common stock for $8.75 per share.

3. Declared and paid cash dividends of $20,000.

FIGURE 23A-2 Schedule for the Calculation of Cash Generated from Operating Activities for Simplex: Direct Method

Simplex Company Schedule for the Calculation of Cash Generated from Operating Activities For Year Ended December 31, 20-2					
INCOME STATEMENT		ADDITIONS	DEDUCTIONS	CASH FLOWS	
Net sales	$900,000	**1** $30,000		$930,000	Cash received from customers
Cost of goods sold	600,000	**3** 60,000	**2** $(20,000)	640,000	Cash paid for merchandise
Gross profit	$300,000			$290,000	
Operating expenses	177,000			177,000	Cash paid for operating expenses
Income before taxes	$123,000			$113,000	
Income tax expense	43,000			43,000	Cash paid for income taxes
Net income	$ 80,000			$ 70,000	Cash generated from operating activities

1 The $30,000 reduction in receivables is added to sales to compute cash received from customers.

2 The $20,000 reduction in inventory is subtracted from cost of goods sold to compute the cost of merchandise purchased ($600,000 − $20,000 = $580,000).

3 Reducing the amount owed to suppliers (Accounts Payable) required the expenditure of additional cash. By adding the reduction in Accounts Payable to the cost of merchandise purchased, cash paid for merchandise is determined ($580,000 + $60,000 = $640,000).

Cash Received from Customers

The income statement for Simplex reports $900,000 in sales during the year. Remember that revenues are recognized when earned, regardless of the amount of cash actually received. To prepare the statement of cash flows, these revenues must be converted to the amount of *cash received from customers during the year*.

If all sales were made for cash, it would not be necessary to adjust sales reported on the income statement. However, the balance sheet reports that accounts receivable decreased by $30,000 ($190,000 − $160,000) this year. The decrease in receivables increases the cash received from customers. This relationship is most easily understood by observing the summary entry in Figure 23A-3.

FIGURE 23A-3 Cash Received from Customers

Cash		Accounts Receivable				Sales	
(2)	930,000	BB	190,000			900,000	(1)
		(1)	900,000	930,000	(2)		
		EB	160,000				

Cash received from customers.

BB: Beginning Balance
EB: Ending Balance

(1) Entry to record sales (assume all on account).	Accounts Receivable	900,000	
	Sales		900,000
(2) Credit required to reconcile Accounts Receivable. This represents the amount of cash collected from customers.	Cash	930,000	
	Accounts Receivable		930,000

The assumption that all sales were on account is not necessary. It just makes the analysis easier. Feel free to make your own assumption about cash sales and see if you get the same result. You should.

Thus, on the schedule in Figure 23A-2, $30,000 is added to the $900,000 in sales reported on the income statement to show that $930,000 was received from customers during the past year.

Cash Paid for Merchandise

Simplex reports cost of goods sold of $600,000 on the income statement. To determine cash generated from operating activities, cost of goods sold is adjusted to reflect *cash paid to suppliers for merchandise*. As under the indirect method, the impact of changes in merchandise inventory and accounts payable must be considered. This time, these changes will be used to adjust cost of goods sold.

Cost of goods sold, as reported on the income statement in Figure 23A-1, was $600,000. However, the balance sheet reports that inventory *decreased* by $20,000 ($200,000 − $180,000). The cost of merchandise purchased by Simplex, therefore, was $580,000 ($600,000 − $20,000). Thus, $20,000 is *deducted* from the cost of goods sold in column 3 of Figure 23A-2.

The balance sheet shows that Accounts Payable *decreased* by $60,000 ($180,000 − $120,000). This indicates that in addition to paying for the purchases made this period, Simplex paid $60,000 for merchandise purchased in prior periods. Thus, $60,000 must be *added* to the cost of goods sold in column 2 of Figure 23A-2 to compute the cash paid for merchandise of $640,000.

The impact of these two adjustments to cost of goods sold to compute cash paid to suppliers is summarized below.

Cost of Goods Sold	$600,000
Less the reduction in merchandise inventory ($200,000 − $180,000)	(20,000)
Cost of merchandise purchased	$580,000
Plus the reduction in accounts payable ($180,000 − $120,000)	60,000
Cash paid to suppliers	$640,000

As discussed earlier for the indirect method, T accounts are also helpful in computing cash paid to suppliers as shown in Figure 23A-4.

FIGURE 23A-4 Cash Paid to Suppliers for Merchandise

Cash		Merchandise Inventory			Accounts Payable			Cost of Goods Sold	
	640,000 (3)	BB 200,000				180,000 BB		(1) 600,000	
		(2) 580,000	600,000 (1)	(3) 640,000		580,000 (2)			
		EB 180,000				120,000 EB			

Purchases of merchandise.

Cash paid to suppliers for merchandise.

BB: Beginning Balance
EB: Ending Balance

(1)	Entry to record cost of goods sold.	Cost of Goods Sold	600,000
		Merchandise Inventory	600,000
(2)	Debit required to reconcile the merchandise inventory account. This represents purchases for the period. Assume that all purchases were made on account.	Merchandise Inventory	580,000
		Accounts Payable	580,000
(3)	Debit required to balance Accounts Payable. This represents the amount of cash paid to suppliers for merchandise.	Accounts Payable	640,000
		Cash	640,000

Cash Paid for Operating Expenses

Adjustments to operating expenses generally are necessary for items such as prepaid expenses, accrued liabilities, or depreciation on plant and equipment. Simplex does not have any of these items, so there is no need to adjust operating expenses. The entire $177,000 of operating expenses is reported as a cash outflow. It is assumed that all of these expenses required cash outflows.

Cash Paid for Income Taxes

The balance sheet reports no receivables, payables, or other items related to income tax expense. Thus, tax expense reported on the income statement represents the amount of cash paid for taxes.

The schedule in Figure 23A-2 demonstrates that net income was $80,000, but only $70,000 in cash was generated from operating activities. All of the information in column 4 is reported on the statement of cash flows illustrated in Figure 23A-5. Though not discussed in this appendix, note that cash flows from investing and financing activities are reported exactly as reported earlier under the indirect method.

FIGURE 23A-5 Statement of Cash Flows for Simplex—Direct Method

Simplex Company Statement of Cash Flows For Year Ended December 31, 20-2		
Cash flows from operating activities:		
Cash received from customers		$ 930,000
Cash paid for merchandise	$(640,000)	
Cash paid for operating expenses	(177,000)	
Cash paid for income taxes	(43,000)	
Total cash disbursed for operating activities		(860,000)
Net cash provided by operating activities		$ 70,000
Cash flows from investing activities:		
Purchased building	$(140,000)	
Purchased equipment	(100,000)	
Total cash used by investing activities		(240,000)
Cash flows from financing activities:		
Issued note payable	$ 10,000	
Issued common stock	70,000	
Paid cash dividends	(20,000)	
Net cash provided by financing activities		60,000
Net increase (decrease) in cash		$(110,000)
Cash balance, January 1, 20-2		200,000
Cash balance, December 31, 20-2		$ 90,000

Cash from Operating Activities Under the Direct Method: Multiplex

LO3

Prepare a schedule for the calculation of cash generated from operating activities under the direct method, including adjustments when the company reports:

a. changes in current assets and current liabilities associated with operations,

b. depreciation expense,

c. gains or losses on the sale of long-term assets,

d. receivables and payables associated with interest revenue, interest expense, and tax expense.

Simplex illustrated the basic adjustments needed for cash from operating activities under the direct method. Once again, Multiplex is used to illustrate additional concepts. The financial statements for Multiplex are provided in Figure 23A-6. The following additional concepts are addressed:

1. Adjustments to operating expenses for changes in current assets
2. Adjustments to operating expenses for changes in current liabilities
3. Adjustments to operating expenses for depreciation expense
4. Adjustments to interest revenue
5. Adjustments to interest expense
6. Adjustments to tax expense
7. Adjustments for gains or losses on the sale of long-term assets

FIGURE 23A-6 Financial Statements and Additional Information for Multiplex

Multiplex Corporation
Income Statement
For Year Ended December 31, 20-2

Net sales		$460,100
Cost of goods sold		270,100
Gross profit		$190,000
Operating expenses		120,750
Operating income		$ 69,250
Other revenues and gains:		
Interest revenue	$ 155	
Gain on sale of equipment	3,000	3,155
Other expenses:		
Interest expense		650
Income before taxes		$ 71,755
Income tax expense		24,000
Net income		$ 47,755

Multiplex Corporation
Statement of Retained Earnings
For Year Ended December 31, 20-2

Retained earnings, January 1, 20-2		$23,660
Net income	$47,755	
Less dividends	22,800	
Net increase in retained earnings		24,955
Retained earnings, December 31, 20-2		$48,615

Additional information:

1. Depreciation expense for the year was $10,400 as follows:

Store equipment	$ 4,000
Delivery equipment	4,500
Office equipment	1,900
	$10,400

2. The following cash purchases were made:

Store equipment	$ 9,200
Delivery equipment	12,000
Office equipment	4,000
	$25,200

3. Delivery equipment was sold for $7,000.

Cost	$ 10,000
Accumulated depreciation	6,000
Book value	$ 4,000
Market value	7,000
Gain on sale of delivery equipment	$ 3,000

4. A $13,000, three-year note was issued to acquire delivery equipment with a market value of $13,000.

5. Declared and paid cash dividends of $22,800.

6. Issued 200 shares of common stock for $15 per share

FIGURE 23A-6 Financial Statements and Additional Information for Multiplex (*concluded*)

Multiplex Corporation					
Comparative Balance Sheet					
December 31, 20-2 and 20-1					
	20-2		20-1		INCREASE (DECREASE)
Assets					
Current assets:					
Cash	$ 17,980		$20,000		$ (2,020)
Government notes	1,800		3,200		(1,400)
Accrued interest receivable	100		300		(200)
Accounts receivable (net)	60,215		51,510		8,705
Merchandise inventory	64,570		67,500		(2,930)
Supplies and prepayments	4,000		2,750		1,250
Total current assets		$148,665		$145,260	3,405
Property, plant, and equipment:					
Store equipment	$ 48,000		$38,800		9,200
Less accumulated depreciation—store equipment	18,000	30,000	14,000	24,800	4,000
Delivery equipment	$ 47,000		$32,000		15,000
Less accumulated depreciation—delivery equipment	6,500	40,500	8,000	24,000	(1,500)
Office equipment	$ 38,000		$34,000		4,000
Less accumulated depreciation—office equipment	8,000	30,000	6,100	27,900	1,900
Total property, plant, and equipment		$100,500		$ 76,700	23,800
Total assets		$249,165		$221,960	27,205
Liabilities					
Current liabilities:					
Notes payable	$ 10,000		$11,800		(1,800)
Accounts payable	33,500		45,900		(12,400)
Income tax payable	3,000		2,000		1,000
Accrued and withheld payroll taxes	950		1,520		(570)
Accrued interest payable	100		80		20
Total current liabilities		$ 47,550		$ 61,300	(13,750)
Long-term liabilities:					
Notes payable (3-year)		13,000			13,000
Total liabilities		$ 60,550		$ 61,300	(750)
Stockholders' Equity					
Common stock ($10 par, 100,000 shares authorized;					
Issued: 10,000 in 20-2 and 9,800 in 20-1)	$100,000		$98,000		2,000
Paid-in capital in excess of par—common stock	40,000		39,000		1,000
Retained earnings	48,615		23,660		24,955
Total stockholders' equity		188,615		160,660	27,955
Total liabilities and stockholders' equity		$249,165		$221,960	27,205

Cash Flows from Operating Activities:
The Direct Method

To compute cash flows from operating activities, prepare a schedule converting the accrual basis income statement to cash flows, as shown in Figure 23A-7. Following the same procedure used for Simplex, column 1 shows revenues and expenses as reported on the income statement. Columns 2 and 3 show additions and deductions to convert the accrual basis figures to the associated cash flows reported in column 4.

FIGURE 23A-7 Schedule for the Calculation of Cash Generated from Operating Activities (Direct Method)

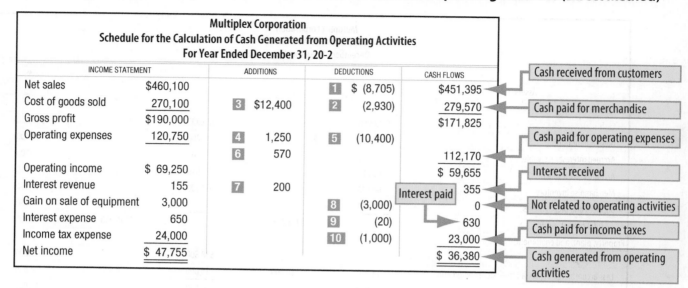

1   The increase in accounts receivable reduced the amount of cash received from sales. Subtract this $8,705 increase from sales to compute cash received from customers.

2   The $2,930 decrease in inventory indicates that Multiplex purchased less inventory than it sold. Subtract this decrease from cost of goods sold to compute the cost of merchandise purchased for the year ($270,100 − $2,930 = $267,170).

3   The $12,400 decrease in accounts payable means that Multiplex paid cash to suppliers in excess of amounts purchased. Add the decrease in the amount owed to suppliers to the cost of merchandise purchased to compute cash paid for merchandise ($267,170 + $12,400 = $279,570).

4   The increase in supplies and prepayments indicates that Multiplex not only replenished these items for the amounts used during the period, but also increased the supplies on hand and prepayments. Thus, the cash paid for these items is greater than the expense recognized for the period. Add the increase of $1,250 to compute cash paid for operating expenses.

5   Depreciation is an operating expense but requires no cash outflow. Subtract the $10,400 ($4,000 + $4,500 + $1,900) in depreciation expense from operating expenses to compute cash paid for operating expenses.

6   By making payments to the government and reducing accrued and withheld payroll taxes, the amount of cash paid to the government this period was increased. Add the reduction of $570 to operating expenses to compute cash paid for operating expenses.

7   Add the reduction in accrued interest receivable of $200 to interest revenue to compute the amount of interest received in cash.

8   The gain on the sale of equipment is not related to operating activities. Selling equipment is an investing activity. Therefore, the gain is eliminated from the calculation of cash from operating activities.

9   Deduct the increase in accrued interest payable of $20 from interest expense to compute the amount of interest paid in cash.

10 Deduct the increase in income tax payable of $1,000 to compute income taxes paid in cash.

Cash Received from Customers

The abbreviated income statement for Multiplex in Figure 23A-6 reports net sales of $460,100. The $8,705 increase in net receivables ($60,215 − $51,510) reported on the balance sheet means that cash was not received for all of the sales made during the year. Adjustment ▮ in Figure 23A-7 deducts the increase in net receivables ($8,705) from net sales to compute cash received from customers of $451,395.

Of course, as demonstrated earlier, cash received from customers may also be computed using T accounts as shown in Figure 23A-8.

FIGURE 23A-8 Cash Received from Customers

	Cash			Accounts Receivable					Sales	
(2)	451,395		BB	51,510					460,100	(1)
			(1)	460,100	451,395	(2)				
			EB	60,215						

⬆ ——— Cash received from customers.

BB: Beginning Balance
EB: Ending Balance

(1)	Entry to record sales (assume all on account).	Accounts Receivable	460,100
		Sales	460,100
(2)	Credit required to reconcile Accounts Receivable. This represents the amount of cash collected from customers.	Cash	451,395
		Accounts Receivable	451,395

Cash Paid for Merchandise

As discussed earlier, cost of goods sold must be adjusted for changes in merchandise inventory and accounts payable to compute cash paid for merchandise.

Merchandise Inventory

The balance sheet shows that inventory decreased by $2,930. This means that the cost of the goods *sold* exceeded the cost of the goods *purchased* during the year. Adjustment ❷ in Figure 23A-7 deducts the decrease in inventory ($2,930) from the cost of goods sold to compute net purchases.

Accounts Payable

Multiplex reports a decrease in accounts payable of $12,400 on the balance sheet. This means that Multiplex paid for merchandise purchased this period *and* for merchandise purchased on account in prior periods. Adjustment ❸ in Figure 23A-7 adds the $12,400 decrease in accounts payable to cost of goods sold. The combined adjustments for inventory and accounts payable result in $279,570 cash paid to suppliers for merchandise.

As illustrated earlier and in Figure 23A-9, T accounts are also helpful in determining cash paid to suppliers.

Cash Paid for Operating Expenses

The income statement shown in Figure 23A-6 reports $120,750 in operating expenses. The balance sheet and additional information provided in Figure 23A-6 are reviewed to identify necessary adjustments to compute cash paid for operating expenses.

Supplies and Prepayments

The balance sheet shows that supplies and prepayments increased by $1,250. The cash paid for these items was greater than the expense reported on the income statement. Adjustment ❹ in Figure 23A-7 adds the increase of $1,250 to operating expenses to compute cash paid for operating expenses.

FIGURE 23A-9 Cash Paid to Suppliers for Merchandise

Cash		Merchandise Inventory			Accounts Payable			Cost of Goods Sold	
		BB 67,500				45,900 BB			
279,570 (3)		(2) 267,170	270,100 (1)		(3) 279,570	267,170 (2)		(1) 270,100	
		EB 64,570				33,500 EB			

Purchases of merchandise.
Cash paid to suppliers for merchandise.

BB: Beginning Balance
EB: Ending Balance

(1)	Entry to record cost of goods sold.	Cost of Goods Sold	270,100	
		Merchandise Inventory		270,100
(2)	Debit required to reconcile the inventory account. This represents purchases for the period. Assume all purchases were made on account.	Merchandise Inventory	267,170	
		Accounts Payable		267,170
(3)	Debit required to reconcile Accounts Payable. This represents the amount of cash paid to suppliers for merchandise.	Accounts Payable	279,570	
		Cash		279,570

Depreciation Expense

As reported under additional information in Figure 23A-6 (page 938), depreciation expense on all equipment amounted to $10,400. To recognize depreciation expense, Multiplex made the following adjusting entries at the end of the year:

4	Dec.	31	Depreciation Expense—Store Equipment	4 0 0 0 00		4
5			Accumulated Depreciation—Store Equipment		4 0 0 0 00	5
6						6
7		31	Depreciation Expense—Delivery Equipment	4 5 0 0 00		7
8			Accumulated Depreciation—Delivery Equipment		4 5 0 0 00	8
9						9
10		31	Depreciation Expense—Office Equipment	1 9 0 0 00		10
11			Accumulated Depreciation—Office Equipment		1 9 0 0 00	11

> **LEARNING KEY**
>
> Depreciation expense increases operating expenses, but requires no cash outflow. Therefore, deduct this amount from operating expenses to compute cash paid.

These entries increase operating expenses and reduce net income, but do not require an outflow of cash. Therefore, adjustment **5** in Figure 23A-7 deducts depreciation expense from the operating expenses to determine the cash paid for operating expenses.

Accrued and Withheld Payroll Taxes

The balance sheet in Figure 23A-6 shows that accrued and withheld payroll taxes decreased by $570. This decrease means that payments made to the government by Multiplex exceeded the payroll tax expense by $570. Thus, adjustment **6** in Figure 23A-7 adds the $570 decrease in the accrued and withheld payroll taxes account to operating expenses to compute cash paid for operating expenses.

As reported in column 4 of Figure 23A-7, after completing the adjustments related to operating expenses, cash paid for operating expenses is $112,170. Since supplies expense, prepaid expenses, depreciation expense, and payroll tax expense are all included in operating expenses, cash paid for operating expenses may also be computed by making the following summary entry:

Operating Expenses	120,750	
Supplies and Prepayments	1,250	
Accrued and Withheld Payroll Taxes	570	
Accumulated Depreciation—Store Equipment		4,000
Accumulated Depreciation—Delivery Equipment		4,500
Accumulated Depreciation—Office Equipment		1,900
Cash (Cash paid for operating expenses) ⟶		112,170

Cash Received from Interest

As reported on the balance sheet in Figure 23A-6, accrued interest receivable decreased by $200. This means that Multiplex received $200 in cash for interest earned in prior periods in addition to the cash received for interest earned this period. Adjustment **7** in Figure 23A-7 adds this amount to interest revenue ($155) to compute cash received from interest ($355). The need for this adjustment may also be seen in the following summary entry for interest revenue:

Cash	355	
Accrued Interest Receivable		200
Interest Revenue		155

Gain on Sale of Equipment

As shown in Figure 23A-6, Multiplex reported a $3,000 gain on the sale of equipment on the income statement. Since this gain is not related to operating activities, adjustment **8** eliminates this gain when computing cash from operating activities.

Cash Paid for Interest

As reported on the balance sheet in Figure 23A-6, accrued interest payable increased by $20. This means that Multiplex did not pay all of the $650 of interest expense incurred this period. Adjustment **9** in Figure 23A-7 deducts the $20 increase in accrued interest payable from interest expense ($650) to compute cash paid for interest ($630). The need for this adjustment may also be seen in the following summary entry for interest expense:

Interest Expense	650	
Interest Payable		20
Cash		630

Cash Paid for Income Taxes

As shown in Figure 23A-6, income tax expense of $24,000 is reported on the income statement and an increase of $1,000 in income tax payable is reported on the balance sheet. Postponing the payment for taxes reduces cash paid for income taxes by $1,000. Thus, adjustment **10** in Figure 23A-7 deducts $1,000 from income tax expense ($24,000) to compute the income taxes paid in cash ($23,000). The need for this adjustment may also be seen in the following summary entry for income tax expense:

Income Tax Expense	24,000	
Income Tax Payable		1,000
Cash		23,000

| **Preparing a Statement of Cash Flows: The Direct Method**

Prepare a statement of cash flows under the direct method.

As shown in Figure 23A-7, once the accrual basis revenues and expenses are adjusted, cash from operating activities is determined to be $36,380. This amount is shown at the bottom of column 4. All of the information from column 4 is presented on the statement of cash flows, shown in Figure 23A-10, under cash flows from operating activities.

FIGURE 23A-10 Statement of Cash Flows for Multiplex (Direct Method)

Muliplex Corporation
Statement of Cash Flows (Direct Method)
For Year Ended December 31, 20-2

Cash flows from operating activities:		
Cash received from customers	$ 451,395	
Interest received	355	
Cash provided by operating activities		$ 451,750
Cash paid for merchandise	$(279,570)	
Cash paid for operating expenses	(112,170)	
Interest paid	(630)	
Income taxes paid	(23,000)	
Total cash disbursed for operating activities		(415,370)
Net cash provided by operating activities		$ 36,380
Cash flows from investing activities:		
Sold delivery equipment	$ 7,000	
Purchased delivery equipment	(12,000)	
Purchased store equipment	(9,200)	
Purchased office equipment	(4,000)	
Net cash used by investing activities		(18,200)
Cash flows from financing activities:		
Issued common stock	$ 3,000	
Paid cash dividends	(22,800)	
Retired note payable	(1,800)	
Net cash used by financing activities		(21,600)
Net increase (decrease) in cash and cash equivalents		$ (3,420)
Cash and cash equivalents, January 1, 20-2		23,200
Cash and cash equivalents, December 31, 20-2		$ 19,780
Schedule of Noncash Investing and Financing Activities:		
Acquired delivery equipment by issuing a 3-year note		$ 13,000

The cash flows from investing and financing activities sections are identical to the sections presented in Chapter 23 under the indirect method. Under the direct method, there is no need for supplementary disclosures of cash paid for interest or taxes. These amounts are already reported in the statement.

LEARNING OBJECTIVES	Key Points to Remember
LO1 Describe the direct method of reporting cash flows from operating activities.	Under the direct method, revenues and expenses reported on the income statement are adjusted to reflect the cash received or paid for each item.
LO2 Prepare a schedule for the calculation of cash generated from operating activities under the direct method by adjusting revenues and expenses for changes in current assets and current liabilities associated with operations.	A schedule for the calculation of cash generated from operating activities under the direct method is shown below. Current assets and current liabilities related to operating activities are used to adjust the revenues and expenses to cash receipts and cash payments. All of the adjustments below, except (5) and (9), illustrate adjustments for changes in current assets and current liabilities related to operating activities.

Sturm Corporation
Schedule for the Calculation of Cash Generated from Operating Activities
For Year Ended December 31, 20-2

INCOME STATEMENT		ADDITIONS		DEDUCTIONS		CASH FLOWS	
Net sales	$100			**1**	$ (5)	$95	← Cash received from customers
Cost of goods sold	40	**3**	$8	**2**	(10)	38	← Cash paid to suppliers
Gross profit	$ 60					$57	
Operating expenses	25	**4**	9	**5**	(6)		← Cash paid for operating expenses
		6	4			32	
Operating income	$ 35					$25	← Interest received
Interest revenue	5	**7**	1			6	
Interest expense	10			**8**	(7)	3	[Interest paid] → Gain not related to operating activities
Gain on sale of store equipment	2			**9**	(2)	0	← Cash paid for income taxes
Income tax expense	10	**10**	3			13	
Net income	$ 22					$15	← Cash generated from operating activities

1 Accounts receivable increased by $5. Subtract this amount from net sales.

2 Inventory decreased by $10. Subtract this amount from cost of goods sold.

3 Accounts payable decreased by $8. Add this amount to cost of goods sold.

4 Supplies increased by $9. Add this amount to operating expenses.

5 Depreciation was $6. Subtract this amount from operating expenses.

6 Accrued payroll taxes decreased by $4. Add this amount to operating expenses.

7 Accrued interest receivable decreased by $1. Add this amount to interest revenue.

8 Accrued interest payable increased by $7. Subtract this amount from interest expense.

9 The gain on the sale of store equipment is reduced to zero. It is not related to operating activities.

10 Income taxes payable decreased by $3. Add this amount to income tax expense.

(continued)

LEARNING OBJECTIVES	**Key Points to Remember**

LO3 Prepare a schedule for the calculation of cash generated from operating activities under the direct method, including adjustments when the company reports:

a. changes in current assets and current liabilities associated with operations,

b. depreciation expense,

c. gains or losses on the sale of long-term assets,

d. receivables and payables associated with interest revenue, interest expense, and tax expense.

Adjustments for receivables and payables associated with interest revenue, interest expense, and tax expense are treated the same as other current assets and current liabilities associated with operating activities. See adjustments 7, 8, and 10 on page 945.

Sturm reported $6 for depreciation expense. No cash is paid for depreciation. This amount is subtracted from operating expenses. See adjustment 5.

The gain on the sale of store equipment is related to an investing activity, not operating activities. Eliminate the gain of $2 as shown in adjustment 9.

LO4 Prepare a statement of cash flows under the direct method.

The investing and financing activities sections of the statement of cash flows are the same under the direct and indirect methods. Thus, only the operating activities section of the statement of cash flows under the direct method is shown below. The cash flows column from the illustration on page 945 is used to prepare this section.

Sturm Corporation
Statement of Cash Flows (Direct Method)
For Year Ended December 31, 20-2

Cash flows from operating activities:		
Cash received from customers	$ 95	
Interest received	6	
Cash provided by operating activities		$101
Cash paid to suppliers	$(38)	
Cash paid for operating expenses	(32)	
Cash paid for interest	(3)	
Cash paid for income taxes	(13)	
Total cash disbursed for operating activities		(86)
Net cash provided by operating activities		$ 15

REVIEW QUESTIONS

LO1 1. Describe the direct method of reporting cash flows from operating activities.

LO2 2. Under the direct method of preparing a statement of cash flows, what adjustment is made if accounts receivable increased from last year?

LO2 3. Under the direct method of preparing a statement of cash flows, what adjustments are made if merchandise inventory decreased and accounts payable increased from last year?

LO3 4. Under the direct method of preparing a statement of cash flows, what adjustment is made for depreciation expense?

LO3 5. Under the direct method of preparing a statement of cash flows, what adjustment is made for gains and losses on the sale of equipment?

SERIES A EXERCISES

E 23Apx-1A (LO2)
✓ Cash received from customers: $815,000

CASH RECEIVED FROM CUSTOMERS Potts Company's sales for 20-2 were $800,000. The Accounts Receivable balance as of December 31, 20-1, was $90,000. This same account had a balance of $75,000 as of December 31, 20-2. Compute the amount of cash received from customers in 20-2.

E 23Apx-2A (LO2)
✓ Cash paid for merchandise: $420,000

CASH PAID FOR MERCHANDISE Douglas Company's cost of goods sold for 20-2 was $400,000. Compute the amount of cash paid for merchandise in 20-2. The December 31, 20-2 and 20-1, balances of Merchandise Inventory and Accounts Payable were as follows:

	20-2	20-1
Merchandise Inventory	$60,000	$80,000
Accounts Payable	30,000	70,000

E 23Apx-3A (LO3)
✓ Cash paid for operating expenses: $332,200

CASH PAID FOR OPERATING EXPENSES The following information was obtained from Knox Company's income statement for 20-2, balance sheets as of December 31, 20-2 and 20-1, and auxiliary records:

Operating expenses for 20-2	$350,400
Depreciation expense for 20-2	22,000 (Included in operating expenses.)

	20-2	20-1
Supplies and prepayments	$9,600	$6,700
Accrued and withheld payroll taxes	2,900	3,800

Compute the amount of cash paid for operating expenses in 20-2.

E 23Apx-4A (LO3)
✓ Cash received for interest: $470

CASH RECEIVED FOR INTEREST Eary Company's income statement for 20-2 reported interest revenue of $430. The comparative balance sheet as of December 31, 20-2 and 20-1, reported the following:

	20-2	20-1
Accrued interest receivable	$150	$190

Compute the amount of cash received for interest in 20-2.

SERIES A PROBLEM

P 23Apx-5A   (LO2)
✓ Cash generated from operating
activities: $160,000

SCHEDULE FOR CALCULATION OF CASH GENERATED FROM OPERATING ACTIVITIES Using the information provided in Problem 23-9A for Zowine Company, prepare the following:

1. A schedule for the calculation of cash generated from operating activities for Zowine Company for the year ended December 31, 20-2.

2. A partial statement of cash flows for Zowine Company reporting cash from operating activities under the direct method for the year ended December 31, 20-2.

P 23Apx-6A   (LO3/4)
✓ Net cash provided by operating
activities: $206,070

SCHEDULE FOR CALCULATION OF CASH GENERATED FROM OPERATING ACTIVITIES Using the information provided in Problem 23-11A for Horn Company, prepare the following:

1. A schedule for the calculation of cash generated from operating activities for Horn Company for the year ended December 31, 20-2.

2. A partial statement of cash flows for Horn Company reporting cash from operating activities under the direct method for the year ended December 31, 20-2.

P 23Apx-7A   (LO3/4)
✓ Operating activities: $152,840
✓ Investing activities: ($209,000)
✓ Financing activities: $80,000

STATEMENT OF CASH FLOWS UNDER THE DIRECT METHOD Using the information provided in Problem 23-12A for McDowell Company, prepare the following:

1. A schedule for the calculation of cash generated from operating activities for McDowell Company for the year ended December 31, 20-2.

2. A statement of cash flows for McDowell Company prepared under the direct method for the year ended December 31, 20-2.

SERIES B EXERCISES

E 23Apx-1B   (LO2)
✓ Cash received from customers:
$735,000

CASH RECEIVED FROM CUSTOMERS Boyd Company's sales for 20-2 were $760,000. The Accounts Receivable balance as of December 31, 20-1, was $60,000. This same account had a balance of $85,000 as of December 31, 20-2. Compute the amount of cash received from customers in 20-2.

E 23Apx-2B   (LO2)
✓ Cash paid for merchandise: $550,000

CASH PAID FOR MERCHANDISE Guild Company's cost of goods sold for 20-2 was $500,000. Compute the amount of cash paid for merchandise in 20-2. The December 31, 20-2 and 20-1, balances of Merchandise Inventory and Accounts Payable were as follows:

	20-2	20-1
Merchandise Inventory	$70,000	$50,000
Accounts Payable	60,000	90,000

E 23Apx-3B   (LO3)
✓ Cash paid for operating expenses:
$258,200

CASH PAID FOR OPERATING EXPENSES The following information was obtained from Busby Company's income statement for 20-2, balance sheets as of December 31, 20-2 and 20-1, and auxiliary records:

Operating expenses for 20-2 $290,500
Depreciation expense for 20-2   30,000 (Included in operating expenses.)

	20-2	20-1
Supplies and prepayments	$7,100	$8,300
Accrued and withheld payroll taxes	3,800	2,700

Compute the amount of cash paid for operating expenses in 20-2.

E 23Apx-4B   (LO3)
✓ Cash received for interest: $590

CASH RECEIVED FOR INTEREST Dowling Company's income statement for 20-2 reported interest revenue of $670. The comparative balance sheet as of December 31, 20-2 and 20-1, reported the following:

	20-2	20-1
Accrued interest receivable	$320	$240

Compute the amount of cash received for interest in 20-2.

SERIES B PROBLEM

P 23Apx-5B   (LO2)
✓ Cash generated from operating activities: $155,000

SCHEDULE FOR CALCULATION OF CASH GENERATED FROM OPERATING ACTIVITIES Using the information provided in Problem 23-9B for Kennington Company, prepare the following:

1. A schedule for the calculation of cash generated from operating activities for Kennington Company for the year ended December 31, 20-2.

2. A partial statement of cash flows for Kennington Company reporting cash from operating activities under the direct method for the year ended December 31, 20-2.

P 23Apx-6B   (LO3/4)
✓ Net cash provided by operating activities: $179,395

SCHEDULE FOR CALCULATION OF CASH GENERATED FROM OPERATING ACTIVITIES Using the information provided in Problem 23-11B for Powell Company, prepare the following:

1. A schedule for the calculation of cash generated from operating activities for Powell Company for the year ended December 31, 20-2.

2. A partial statement of cash flows for Powell Company reporting cash from operating activities under the direct method for the year ended December 31, 20-2.

P 23Apx-7B   (LO3/4)
✓ Operating activities: $99,300
✓ Investing activities: ($237,000)
✓ Financing activities: $180,000

STATEMENT OF CASH FLOWS UNDER THE DIRECT METHOD Using the information provided in Problem 23-12B for McGinnis Company, prepare the following:

1. A schedule for the calculation of cash generated from operating activities for McGinnis Company for the year ended December 31, 20-2.

2. A statement of cash flows for McGinnis Company prepared under the direct method for the year ended December 31, 20-2.

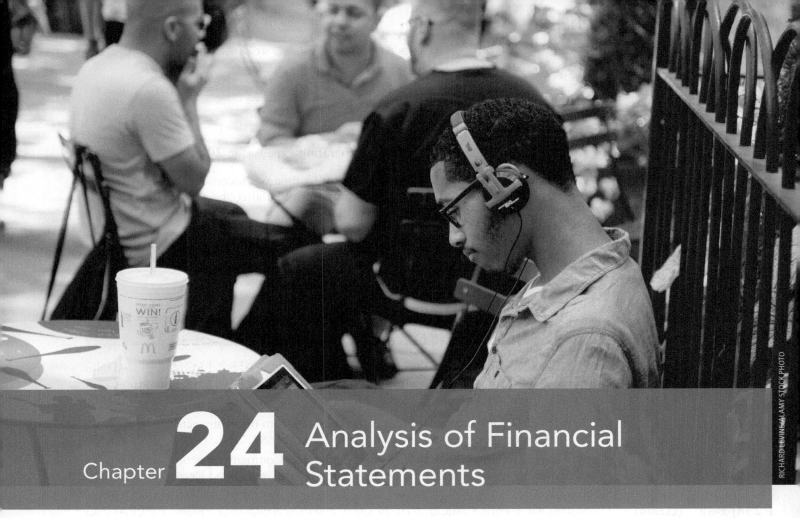

Chapter **24** Analysis of Financial Statements

LEARNING OBJECTIVES

Careful study of this chapter should enable you to:

LO1 Perform horizontal and vertical analyses of the income statement and balance sheet.

LO2 Compute and explain liquidity measures.

LO3 Compute and explain activity measures.

LO4 Compute and explain profitability measures.

LO5 Compute and explain leverage measures.

LO6 Explain the components of ROA and ROE.

LO7 Compute and explain market measures.

LO8 Explain the limitations of financial statement analysis.

Founded in 2003 by Rick Alden, Skullcandy designs, markets, and distributes audio and gaming headphones and other accessory-related products under the Skullcandy, Astro Gaming, and 2XL brands. Building on Alden's background in snowboarding and skateboarding, Skullcandy quickly became one of the world's most distinct audio brands by offering unique technology, color, character, and performance. As such, it tries to maintain a small-company, edgy feel. For example, its entire office in Park City, Utah, is designed to look like a skateboard park with steel coping and concrete curbing.

Managers, employees, investors, and creditors need to continually evaluate the financial health of a company. Skullcandy went public in 2011 and in 2016 was acquired by Incipio for $188.6 million. In this chapter, you will learn how to assess the financial health of a company by performing horizontal and vertical analyses, and computing standard financial ratios. In addition, you will learn to appreciate the limitations of these analyses.

This chapter demonstrates how to analyze financial statements to better understand the financial health of the company. Comparisons of financial statement variables over time and the calculation and interpretation of selected ratios will be presented.

Comparative Analysis

LO1

Perform horizontal and vertical analyses of the income statement and balance sheet.

A business's financial statements supply information to management, current and potential owners and creditors, employees and their unions, government agencies, and sometimes the general public. Normally, interest centers on five aspects of the business.

1. Liquidity measures—the ability to pay current debts when they come due. Liquidity measures focus primarily on current assets and current liabilities.
2. Activity measures—the efficiency with which assets are used to generate profits.
3. Profitability measures—the ability to earn a satisfactory return on the investments in the business.
4. Leverage—the proportion of debt used to operate.
5. Market measures—the use of the market value of common stock as evidence of how the company is viewed by investors.

Financial statements can be much more informative if they are analyzed on a comparative basis. The following are four possible types of comparisons:

1. with one or more previous periods
2. with data for the industry as a whole
3. with similar information for other businesses in the industry
4. with preset plans or goals (normally in the form of budgets)

We will use the financial statements of French Connection Importers (FCI) for the years ended December 31, 20-2 and 20-1, to illustrate the first type of analysis.

Horizontal Analysis

Comparing the amounts for the same item in the financial statements of two or more periods is called horizontal analysis. Figure 24-1 illustrates a horizontal analysis of the condensed comparative income statement of FCI for the two years under review, showing the amount and the percentage change in each item. In calculating the percentage change, the amount for the earlier year serves as the base. For example, to compute the percentage change in net sales, the increase or decrease in net sales for 20-2 is divided by net sales for 20-1.

Net sales in 20-2 were 17.9% greater than in 20-1. Cost of goods sold increased only 15.8%. Because of the smaller percentage increase in cost of goods sold, the percentage increase in the gross profit (23.9%) was greater than that for sales. Operating expenses increased only 12.7%, which was much less than the growth in sales. These events caused an increase of 36.6% in operating income. Although the percentage increase in other revenue was enormous (425.0%), the amount of this revenue was small. Because other expenses decreased 12.3%, income before income tax was 46.6% greater. The relative amount of income tax increased significantly (90.5%), and net income increased by 31.2%.

LEARNING KEY

In horizontal analysis, use the amount for the earlier year as the base when calculating the percentage change from year to year.

FIGURE 24-1 Comparative Income Statement—Horizontal Analysis

French Connection Importers Comparative Income Statement For Years Ended December 31, 20-2 and 20-1				
	20-2	20-1	INCREASE (DECREASE)	PERCENT
Net sales	$835,950	$708,800	$127,150	17.9
Cost of goods sold	602,380	520,260	82,120	15.8
Gross profit	$233,570	$188,540	$ 45,030	23.9
Operating expenses	113,000	100,250	12,750	12.7
Operating income	$120,570	$ 88,290	$ 32,280	36.6
Other revenue	525	100	425	425.0
Other expenses	12,650	14,420	(1,770)	−12.3
Income before income taxes	$108,445	$ 73,970	$ 34,475	46.6
Income tax expense	36,600	19,210	17,390	90.5
Net income	$ 71,845	$ 54,760	$ 17,085	31.2

This horizontal analysis of the income statement indicates a major improvement in FCI's operating results. A 17.9% increase in net sales accompanied by apparently successful cost control resulted in a 31.2% increase in net income.

The condensed comparative balance sheet as of December 31, 20-2 and 20-1, presented in Figure 24-2, illustrates horizontal analysis. The most noteworthy changes in the balance sheet follow (numbers correspond to those in the margin of Figure 24-2).

1 *Increase (18.4%) in current assets and decrease (38.3%) in current liabilities.*

The increase in current assets is due primarily to the increases in cash (30.4%) and receivables (23.5%). These increases probably were needed to support the higher level of operating activity indicated by the 17.9% increase in net sales noted previously.

The decrease in current liabilities is caused by the reduction in notes payable and accounts payable. FCI apparently used some of the funds from its successful operations during 20-2 to pay off a large portion of its current liabilities.

2 *Increase in building (12.0%) and store equipment (11.1%).*

Increases in building and store equipment are important because they are signs of growth. It is common for long-term asset accounts to *decrease* simply because of depreciation and amortization. The decreases in delivery and office equipment and organization costs are examples of this tendency. *Increases* in the building and store equipment accounts mean that new long-term assets were acquired during 20-2.

3 *Increases in common stock (25.0%) and paid-in capital in excess of par (60.0%).*

Increases in common stock and paid-in capital in excess of par also indicate growth. Common stock with a par value of $15,000 was issued for $22,500 ($15,000 par + $7,500 paid-in capital in excess of par). Financing growth by issuing additional common stock is often desirable, particularly for a company carrying as much debt as FCI.

4 *Substantial increase (53.6%) in retained earnings.*

The large increase in retained earnings results from a highly profitable year (net income of $71,845) combined with a moderate dividend policy ($7,500). Retention of large amounts of earnings is another desirable way to finance corporate growth.

FIGURE 24-2 Comparative Balance Sheet—Horizontal Analysis

<table>
<tr><td colspan="5" align="center">**French Connection Importers**
Comparative Balance Sheet
December 31, 20-2 and 20-1</td></tr>
<tr><td></td><td>20-2</td><td>20-1</td><td>INCREASE (DECREASE)</td><td>PERCENT</td></tr>
<tr><td align="center">Assets</td><td></td><td></td><td></td><td></td></tr>
<tr><td>Current assets:</td><td></td><td></td><td></td><td></td></tr>
<tr><td>Cash</td><td>$ 25,695</td><td>$ 19,700</td><td>$ 5,995</td><td>30.4</td></tr>
<tr><td>Government notes</td><td>5,000</td><td>1,000</td><td>4,000</td><td>400.0</td></tr>
<tr><td>Accounts receivable (net)</td><td>61,750</td><td>50,000</td><td>11,750</td><td>23.5</td></tr>
<tr><td>Merchandise inventory</td><td>55,500</td><td>54,250</td><td>1,250</td><td>2.3</td></tr>
<tr><td>Supplies and prepayments</td><td>2,400</td><td>2,000</td><td>400</td><td>20.0</td></tr>
<tr><td>Total current assets</td><td>$150,345</td><td>$126,950</td><td>$ 23,395</td><td>18.4 [1]</td></tr>
<tr><td>Property, plant, and equipment:</td><td></td><td></td><td></td><td></td></tr>
<tr><td>Land</td><td>$ 40,000</td><td>$ 40,000</td><td>$ 0</td><td>0.0</td></tr>
<tr><td>Building (net)</td><td>140,000</td><td>125,000</td><td>15,000</td><td>12.0 [2]</td></tr>
<tr><td>Store equipment (net)</td><td>100,000</td><td>90,000</td><td>10,000</td><td>11.1 [2]</td></tr>
<tr><td>Delivery and office equipment (net)</td><td>22,000</td><td>28,500</td><td>(6,500)</td><td>−22.8</td></tr>
<tr><td>Organization costs</td><td>1,200</td><td>2,400</td><td>(1,200)</td><td>−50.0</td></tr>
<tr><td>Total property, plant, and equipment</td><td>$303,200</td><td>$285,900</td><td>$ 17,300</td><td>6.1</td></tr>
<tr><td>Total assets</td><td>$453,545</td><td>$412,850</td><td>$ 40,695</td><td>9.9</td></tr>
<tr><td align="center">Liabilities</td><td></td><td></td><td></td><td></td></tr>
<tr><td>Current liabilities:</td><td></td><td></td><td></td><td></td></tr>
<tr><td>Accrued and withheld payroll taxes</td><td>$ 2,500</td><td>$ 2,750</td><td>$ (250)</td><td>−9.1</td></tr>
<tr><td>Notes payable</td><td>10,000</td><td>37,500</td><td>(27,500)</td><td>−73.3</td></tr>
<tr><td>Accounts payable</td><td>40,000</td><td>59,000</td><td>(19,000)</td><td>−32.2</td></tr>
<tr><td>Accrued interest payable</td><td>600</td><td>1,700</td><td>(1,100)</td><td>−64.7</td></tr>
<tr><td>Income tax payable</td><td>13,600</td><td>13,400</td><td>200</td><td>1.5</td></tr>
<tr><td>Dividends payable</td><td>7,500</td><td>6,000</td><td>1,500</td><td>25.0</td></tr>
<tr><td>Total current liabilities</td><td>$ 74,200</td><td>$120,350</td><td>$(46,150)</td><td>−38.3 [1]</td></tr>
<tr><td>Long-term liabilities:</td><td></td><td></td><td></td><td></td></tr>
<tr><td>Bonds payable</td><td>100,000</td><td>100,000</td><td>0</td><td>0.0</td></tr>
<tr><td>Total liabilities</td><td>$174,200</td><td>$220,350</td><td>$(46,150)</td><td>−20.9</td></tr>
<tr><td align="center">Stockholders' Equity</td><td></td><td></td><td></td><td></td></tr>
<tr><td>Common stock, $1 par</td><td>$ 75,000</td><td>$ 60,000</td><td>$ 15,000</td><td>25.0 [3]</td></tr>
<tr><td>Paid-in capital in excess of par</td><td>20,000</td><td>12,500</td><td>7,500</td><td>60.0 [3]</td></tr>
<tr><td>Retained earnings</td><td>184,345</td><td>120,000</td><td>64,345</td><td>53.6 [4]</td></tr>
<tr><td>Total stockholders' equity</td><td>$279,345</td><td>$192,500</td><td>$ 86,845</td><td>45.1</td></tr>
<tr><td>Total liabilities and stockholders' equity</td><td>$453,545</td><td>$412,850</td><td>$ 40,695</td><td>9.9</td></tr>
</table>

Vertical Analysis

Reporting the amount of each item in a statement as a percentage of some designated total is called vertical analysis. Vertical analysis is most helpful when statements relating to two or more periods are compared.

Figure 24-3 shows FCI's condensed comparative income statement for the years ended December 31, 20-2 and 20-1. Each item is shown as a percentage of net sales for the year. This statement reveals that several factors contributed to FCI's increased profitability from 20-1 to 20-2. Both cost of goods sold and operating expenses decreased as a percentage of net sales. This allowed operating income to increase from 12.5% to 14.4% of net sales. Other expenses decreased from 2.0% to 1.5% of net sales, so that income before income taxes jumped from 10.4% to 13.0% of net sales. These positive factors were offset somewhat by the increase in taxes from 2.7% to 4.4% of net sales. However, net income as a percentage of net sales still increased from 7.7% to 8.6%.

Vertical analysis of income statements automatically provides several important ratios. They include the following (numbers correspond to those in the margin of Figure 24-3):

1 Cost of goods sold ratio—ratio of cost of goods sold to net sales

2 Gross profit ratio—ratio of gross profit to net sales

3 Operating expense ratio—ratio of operating expenses to net sales

4 Operating income ratio—ratio of operating income to net sales

5 Profit margin ratio (also called net income ratio)—ratio of net income to net sales

> **LEARNING KEY**
>
> In vertical analysis of the income statement, each item is shown as a percentage of net sales for the year.

FIGURE 24-3 Comparative Income Statement—Vertical Analysis

French Connection Importers Comparative Income Statement For Years Ended December 31, 20-2 and 20-1					
	20-2	PERCENT*	20-1	PERCENT*	
Net sales	$835,950	100.0	$708,800	100.0	
Cost of goods sold	602,380	72.1	520,260	73.4	1
Gross profit	$233,570	27.9	$188,540	26.6	2
Operating expenses	113,000	13.5	100,250	14.1	3
Operating income	$120,570	14.4	$ 88,290	12.5	4
Other revenue	525	0.1	100	0.0	
Other expenses	12,650	1.5	14,420	2.0	
Income before income taxes	$108,445	13.0	$ 73,970	10.4	
Income tax expense	36,600	4.4	19,210	2.7	
Net income	$ 71,845	8.6	$ 54,760	7.7	5

*Percentages may not add due to rounding.

> **LEARNING KEY**
>
> In vertical analysis of the balance sheet, assets are shown as a percentage of total assets. Liabilities and stockholders' equity are shown as a percentage of total liabilities and stockholders' equity.

Vertical analysis is also performed on balance sheets. For assets, each item is shown as a percentage of the total assets. For liabilities and stockholders' equity, each item is shown as a percentage of the total equities (liabilities and stockholders' equity). Figure 24-4 shows a comparative balance sheet for FCI using vertical analysis. This statement reveals that current assets were a somewhat larger share (33.1% versus 30.7%) of total assets on December 31, 20-2, than on the same date in 20-1. In addition, current liabilities decreased dramatically (16.4% versus 29.2%) as a percentage of total equities. These two factors reflect a major improvement in FCI's current position. Retained earnings increased significantly in amount and as a percentage of total equities. Finally, the combination of favorable changes in current liabilities, common stock, paid-in capital in excess of par, and retained earnings resulted in total liabilities being a much smaller share (38.4% versus 53.4%) of total liabilities and stockholders' equity.

FIGURE 24-4 Comparative Balance Sheet—Vertical Analysis

French Connection Importers Comparative Balance Sheet December 31, 20-2 and 20-1				
	20-2	PERCENT*	20-1	PERCENT*
Assets				
Current assets:				
Cash	$ 25,695	5.7	$ 19,700	4.8
Government notes	5,000	1.1	1,000	0.2
Accounts receivable (net)	61,750	13.6	50,000	12.1
Merchandise inventory	55,500	12.2	54,250	13.1
Supplies and prepayments	2,400	0.5	2,000	0.5
Total current assets	$ 150,345	33.1	$ 126,950	30.7
Property, plant, and equipment:				
Land	$ 40,000	8.8	$ 40,000	9.7
Building (net)	140,000	30.9	125,000	30.3
Store equipment (net)	100,000	22.0	90,000	21.8
Delivery and office equipment (net)	22,000	4.9	28,500	6.9
Organization costs	1,200	0.3	2,400	0.6
Total property, plant, and equipment	$ 303,200	66.9	$285,900	69.3
Total assets	$ 453,545	100.0	$412,850	100.0
Liabilities				
Current liabilities:				
Accrued and withheld payroll taxes	$ 2,500	0.6	$ 2,750	0.7
Notes payable	10,000	2.2	37,500	9.1
Accounts payable	40,000	8.8	59,000	14.3
Accrued interest payable	600	0.1	1,700	0.4
Income tax payable	13,600	3.0	13,400	3.2
Dividends payable	7,500	1.7	6,000	1.5
Total current liabilities	$ 74,200	16.4	$120,350	29.2
Long-term liabilities:				
Bonds payable	100,000	22.0	100,000	24.2
Total liabilities	$ 174,200	38.4	$220,350	53.4
Stockholders' Equity				
Common stock, $1 par	$ 75,000	16.5	$ 60,000	14.5
Paid-in capital in excess of par	20,000	4.4	12,500	3.0
Retained earnings	184,345	40.6	120,000	29.1
Total stockholders' equity	$ 279,345	61.6	$192,500	46.6
Total liabilities and stockholders' equity	$ 453,545	100.0	$412,850	100.0

*Percentages may not add due to rounding.

LO2 Liquidity Measures

Compute and explain liquidity measures.

Liquidity measures indicate a company's ability to meet its current liabilities. These measures focus primarily on balance sheet amounts and on the company's ability to generate funds to liquidate current obligations.

Working Capital

Working capital is the excess of a company's current assets over current liabilities. This measures whether current assets are sufficient to pay off current liabilities. The calculation of working capital for FCI at the end of each year is shown in Figure 24-5.

FIGURE 24-5 Calculation of Working Capital

		20-2	20-1
Working Capital	Current Assets	$150,345	$126,950
	− Current Liabilities	(74,200)	(120,350)
	= Working Capital	$ 76,145	$ 6,600

FCI's working capital position improved dramatically between 20-1 and 20-2. Current assets were barely sufficient to cover current liabilities on December 31, 20-1, whereas there is a substantial margin of working capital at the end of 20-2.

Current Ratio

The current ratio, sometimes called working capital ratio because of its obvious linkage to working capital, is calculated by dividing current assets by current liabilities. The calculation of the current ratio for FCI at the end of each year is shown in Figure 24-6.

FIGURE 24-6 Calculation of Current Ratio

			20-2	20-1
Current Ratio	Current Assets / Current Liabilities	=	$150,345 / $74,200	$126,950 / $120,350
			2.0 to 1	1.1 to 1

The current position of FCI improved greatly during the year ended December 31, 20-2. The general rule is that a current ratio of 2 to 1 or better is satisfactory, although this rule can be modified for certain types of businesses or the makeup of the current assets. If the current assets consist primarily of cash and short-term investments, a lower ratio may be fine. However, if current assets include high amounts of risky receivables and inventory that is not selling well, a higher ratio may be necessary to satisfy investors and creditors. FCI's current ratio was not acceptable in 20-1, but it improved to an acceptable level in 20-2.

Quick or Acid-Test Ratio

Another frequently used measure of liquidity is the quick or acid-test ratio. This ratio is calculated by dividing "quick" assets—cash, temporary investments, and receivables—by current liabilities. The calculation of the quick ratio for FCI at the end of each year is shown in Figure 24-7.

FCI's quick ratio improved during 20-2. As a general rule, the ratio should not be less than 1 to 1. FCI was far below that standard in 20-1, but the company's quick ratio at the end of 20-2 is acceptable.

If the liquidity measures are too low, it can be a sign that the company will be unable to pay its bills. This could require the company to raise cash through additional borrowing, selling assets, or issuing stock. Thus, investors and creditors generally prefer higher liquidity measures. It is possible, however, for the measures to be

FIGURE 24-7 Calculation of Quick Ratio

			20-2	20-1
Quick or Acid-Test Ratio	Quick Assets / Current Liabilities	=	$92,445 / $74,200	$70,700 / $120,350
			1.2 to 1	0.6 to 1
Quick Assets	Cash		$25,695	$19,700
	Government notes		5,000	1,000
	Accounts receivable (net)		61,750	50,000
			$92,445	$70,700

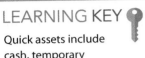
LEARNING KEY

Quick assets include cash, temporary investments, and receivables.

CHECKPOINT ✔

Complete Checkpoint-1 on pages 979–980 to test your basic understanding of LO2.

too high. Cash and most receivables are not "earning assets" (they do not produce goods or services to sell), and the return on most temporary investments is not large. Inventories are expensive to hold. They take up costly space, tie up money, and are subject to loss of value from various causes. Thus, management must try to maintain the optimal amount of each type of asset to maximize profits and pay bills on time.

LO3   Activity Measures

Compute and explain activity measures.

Activity measures focus primarily on the efficient use of assets. We discuss the speed with which receivables are collected and inventory is sold, as well as how efficiently assets are used to generate revenue.

Accounts Receivable Turnover

Since accounts receivable do not generally earn interest, and some receivables will never be collected, it is important to manage them carefully. The disadvantages of carrying receivables are accepted, however, because selling on account may generate greater sales and net income.

Accounts receivable turnover measures how promptly receivables are collected. It is calculated by dividing net sales on account by the average amount of net accounts receivable. It is preferable to calculate a monthly average of net receivables. However, if monthly figures are not available, averaging the beginning-of-year and end-of-year balances is acceptable if the receivables balance does not fluctuate widely. Only *accounts* receivable are considered. The calculations for FCI are shown in Figure 24-8.

FIGURE 24-8 Calculation of Accounts Receivable Turnover

			20-2	20-1
Accounts Receivable Turnover	Net Sales on Account / Average Accounts Receivable (Net)	=	$668,760 / $55,875	$567,040 / $45,000
			11.97	12.60
Average Accounts Receivable	Beginning Accounts Receivable + Ending Accounts Receivable / 2	=	$50,000 + $61,750 / 2	$40,000* + $50,000 / 2
			$55,875	$45,000
Average Collection Period	365 / Accounts Receivable Turnover	=	365 / 11.97	365 / 12.60
			30.5 days	29.0 days

*Beginning balances for 20-1 are taken from 20-0 financial statements, which are not shown here.

Note that beginning balances for 20-1 are not available on the current financial statements. These were taken from last year's financial statements.

Net sales *on account* is used in this ratio. However, this information is not generally available on the financial statements. Net sales may be used if net sales on account is not available. Using net sales will provide a useful measure across time periods as long as the proportion of cash and credit sales remains relatively stable.

Another way of examining accounts receivable turnover is to divide 365 days by the turnover figure to get the average collection period. This shows the number of days it takes a business to convert receivables into cash. Fluctuations in the average collection period over time should be investigated.

For FCI, Figure 24-8 shows that the average collection period is 30.5 days and 29.0 days, respectively, for the years ended December 31, 20-2 and 20-1. Although the accounts receivable turnover decreased slightly, both rates are quite good. The average number of days that receivables are on the books should not be greater than 1½ times the regular length of the credit period. FCI offered 30 days' credit to more customers in 20-2, which probably explains the slight decrease in turnover.

Faster collection of receivables is generally preferred. However, businesses are willing to wait for cash collections if extending credit increases sales. If the collection period increases substantially, however, it could be a sign that the firm's credit policy is too loose and too many customers may never pay. Or, worse yet, history has shown that some companies have attempted to pad revenues by booking bogus sales on account. Since these "sales" will never be collected, the collection period will increase substantially. Analysts have used this ratio to help identify unethical companies attempting to deceive investors and creditors.

Merchandise Inventory Turnover

Every seller of goods would like to have maximum sales and minimum inventory. Merchandise inventory turnover measures the relationship between sales and inventory and provides a measure of how long it takes to sell inventory. It is calculated by dividing cost of goods sold by average merchandise inventory. Again, calculating a monthly average of inventories is preferable. However, if monthly figures are not available, the average of the beginning-of-year and end-of-year inventories can be used. For FCI, the merchandise inventory turnover for each year is shown in Figure 24-9.

FIGURE 24-9 Calculation of Merchandise Inventory Turnover

			20-2	20-1
Merchandise Inventory Turnover	$\dfrac{\text{Cost of Goods Sold}}{\text{Average Merchandise Inventory}}$	=	$\dfrac{\$602,380}{\$54,875}$ 10.98	$\dfrac{\$520,260}{\$52,500}$ 9.91
Average Merchandise Inventory	$\dfrac{\text{Beginning Merchandise Inventory} + \text{Ending Merchandise Inventory}}{2}$	=	$\dfrac{\$54,250 + \$55,500}{2}$ $\$54,875$	$\dfrac{\$50,750^* + \$54,250}{2}$ $\$52,500$
Average Number of Days to Sell Inventory	$\dfrac{365}{\text{Merchandise Inventory Turnover}}$	=	$\dfrac{365}{10.98}$ 33.2 days	$\dfrac{365}{9.91}$ 36.8 days

*Beginning balances for 20-1 are taken from 20-0 financial statements, which are not shown here.

As with accounts receivable turnover, another way of examining merchandise inventory turnover is to divide 365 days by the turnover figure to get the average number of days required to sell the merchandise inventory. If all sales are made on account, this is the average number of days it takes FCI to convert merchandise inventory into accounts receivable. This number of days plus the number of days to collect accounts receivable indicates the number of days to convert inventory into cash. Figure 24-9 shows that merchandise remained in stock an average of 33 days and 37 days, respectively, for the years ended December 31, 20-2 and 20-1.

The turnover increased slightly from 20-1 to 20-2. Both years show acceptable inventory turnover rates. FCI maintained a reasonable inventory turnover while significantly increasing its sales volume.

Many factors impact the merchandise inventory turnover. In general, faster turnover is preferred. However, the actions required to speed up turnover may be harmful to the company. For example, one way to speed up turnover would be to reduce prices, increase the number of sales, and, thus, increase cost of goods sold. Of course, this would reduce profit margins. Similarly, the firm could reduce inventory levels. While this is desirable, it could mean that merchandise is not available when customers want it. Thus, the firm would lose sales. It is also worth noting that inventory turnover levels vary considerably across industries. As you might suspect, inventory turnover at a fruit stand should be considerably faster than at a car dealership. Yet, both businesses could be equally profitable.

Asset Turnover

The asset turnover, or ratio of net sales to assets, measures how efficiently a company used its assets to generate sales. The ratio is calculated by dividing net sales for the year by the average book value of the company's assets. The calculation for FCI is shown in Figure 24-10.

FIGURE 24-10 Calculation of Asset Turnover

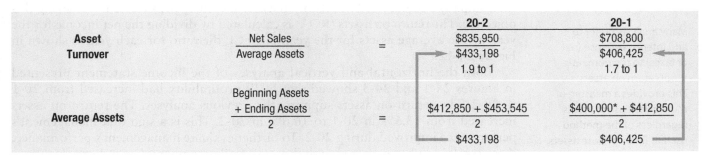

			20-2	20-1
Asset Turnover	$\dfrac{\text{Net Sales}}{\text{Average Assets}}$	=	$835,950 $433,198 1.9 to 1	$708,800 $406,425 1.7 to 1
Average Assets	$\dfrac{\text{Beginning Assets} + \text{Ending Assets}}{2}$	=	$\dfrac{\$412,850 + \$453,545}{2}$ $433,198	$\dfrac{\$400,000^* + \$412,850}{2}$ $406,425

*Beginning balances for 20-1 are taken from 20-0 financial statements, which are not shown here.

CHECKPOINT ✔

Complete Checkpoint-2 on pages 979–980 to test your basic understanding of LO3.

Asset turnover is heavily determined by the type of business. Those with little in the way of property, plant, and equipment, such as department stores, will have higher asset turnovers. Those in capital-intensive industries, like energy, transportation, and telecommunications, will have lower turnovers. Thus, it is important to compare turnover ratios with other companies in the same industry or with the historical performance of the company. FCI's asset turnover ratio increased modestly from 20-1 to 20-2.

LO4	**Profitability Measures**

Compute and explain profitability measures.

Profitability measures indicate a company's ability to earn income by operating efficiently. These measures focus primarily on the profit margin and the relationship between key income statement and balance sheet amounts.

Profit Margin

As discussed earlier, the profit margin measures the amount of profit for each dollar of sales. We want to reinforce these calculations here because of the important role they play in ratios to be discussed later in the chapter. The ratio is calculated by dividing net income by net sales for the year. The calculation for FCI is shown in Figure 24-11.

FIGURE 24-11 Calculation of Profit Margin Ratio

			20-2	20-1
Profit Margin Ratio	$\dfrac{\text{Net Income}}{\text{Net Sales}}$	=	$71,845	$54,760
			$835,950	$708,800
			8.6%	7.7%

Profit margins typically range from less than 1% to over 10%, depending on the industry. FCI earned 8.6% and 7.7% in 20-2 and 20-1, respectively. In other words, FCI earned 8.6 and 7.7 cents per dollar of sales, respectively, each year. This represents a strong and improving profit margin. This ratio should be compared over time and with other firms in the same industry.

Return on Assets

Owners or managers of most businesses strive to realize large earnings in relation to the company's resources. The return on assets measures the success in achieving this objective. The return on assets (ROA) is calculated by dividing the net income for the year by the average assets for the year. For FCI, the ratio for each year is shown in Figure 24-12.

> Many analysts prefer to add interest expense (net of taxes) to the numerator of return on assets. This provides a measure of the efficient use of assets regardless of the method used to finance those assets.

Both the horizontal and vertical analyses of the income statement presented in Figures 24-1 and 24-3 showed that FCI's profitability had increased from 20-1 to 20-2. The return on assets supports the previous analyses. The return on assets increased from 13.5% in 20-1 to 16.6% in 20-2. This is a sign that management's performance improved during 20-2. To further evaluate management's performance, these results can be compared with those of similar companies or industry results.

FIGURE 24-12 Calculation of Return on Assets

			20-2	20-1
Return on Assets	$\dfrac{\text{Net Income}}{\text{Average Assets}}$	=	$71,845	$54,760
			$433,198	$406,425
			16.6%	13.5%
Average Assets	$\dfrac{\text{Beginning Assets} + \text{Ending Assets}}{2}$	=	$\dfrac{\$412,850 + \$453,545}{2}$	$\dfrac{\$400,000^* + \$412,850}{2}$
			$433,198	$406,425

*Beginning balances for 20-1 are taken from 20-0 financial statements, which are not shown here.

Within reasonable constraints, management strives to maximize sales and net income and minimize the assets required to operate. However, some industries require higher investments in plant and equipment to generate similar sales and profits. Thus, it is difficult to compare these measures across industries. It is best to evaluate these measures for the same firm over time, or with other firms in the same industry. Also, since book values are used to measure the assets, it is difficult to compare an older company (with older assets and lower book values) with a newer company (with newer assets and higher book values).

> Stockholders' Equity includes Common Stock, Paid-in Capital in Excess of Par, and Retained Earnings. If FCI had preferred stock, the preferred dividends would be deducted from net income because these funds would not be available to common stockholders.

Return on Common Stockholders' Equity

Ultimately, the company must provide an adequate return to its common stockholders. Thus, **return on common stockholders' equity (ROE)** is a very important performance measure. It is calculated by dividing net income available to common stockholders (net income less preferred dividends) for the year by the average common stockholders' equity during the year. For FCI, the calculation of the ratio for each year is shown in Figure 24-13.

FIGURE 24-13 Calculation of Return on Common Stockholders' Equity

			20-2	20-1
Return on Common Stockholders' Equity	Net Income Available to Common Stockholders / Average Common Stockholders' Equity	=	$71,845 / $235,923 30.5%	$54,760 / $183,750 29.8%
Average Common Stockholders' Equity	Beginning Stockholders' Equity + Ending Stockholders' Equity / 2	=	$192,500 + $279,345 / 2 $235,923	$175,000* + $192,500 / 2 $183,750

*Beginning balances for 20-1 are taken from 20-0 financial statements, which are not shown here.

Net income increased from $54,760 in 20-1 to $71,845 in 20-2, leading to an increase in the return on common stockholders' equity from 29.8% to 30.5%. These rates of return are quite strong.

Earnings per Share of Common Stock

One of the most important measures of profitability of the company is earnings per share of common stock. If only common stock is outstanding, earnings per share is calculated by dividing net income for the year by the average number of shares of common stock outstanding during the year. FCI had only common stock outstanding—60,000 shares throughout 20-1, and 60,000 shares at the beginning and 75,000 shares at the end of 20-2. The 15,000 additional shares were issued in the middle of the year, so the average number of shares outstanding during 20-2 was 67,500 [(60,000 + 75,000) ÷ 2]. Therefore, FCI's earnings per share for each year is calculated as shown in Figure 24-14.

> **LEARNING KEY** 🔑
> Earnings per share means per *share of common stock.* Thus, we must focus on earnings available to common stockholders.

If preferred shares are outstanding, the earnings per share of common stock is calculated after deducting preferred dividend requirements. For example, if a corporation has 40,000 shares of $10 par, 8% preferred stock, $32,000 must be subtracted from net income before dividing by the average number of common shares outstanding. If net income is $310,000, and the average shares of common stock outstanding is 80,000, the earnings per share of common stock is computed as follows:

Net income	$310,000
Less preferred dividend requirements (40,000 × $10 × 8%)	32,000
Earnings available to common stockholders	$278,000
Average number of shares of common stock outstanding	80,000
Earnings per share of common stock	$3.48

FIGURE 24-14 Calculation of Earnings per Share of Common Stock

			20-2	20-1
Earnings per Share of Common Stock	$\dfrac{\text{Net Income Available to Common Stockholders}}{\text{Average Number of Common Shares Outstanding}}$	=	$\dfrac{\$71,845}{67,500}$ $\$1.06$	$\dfrac{\$54,760}{60,000}$ $\$0.91$
Average Number of Common Shares Outstanding	$\dfrac{\text{Beginning Shares Outstanding} + \text{Ending Shares Outstanding}}{2}$	=	$\dfrac{60,000 + 75,000}{2}$ 67,500	$\dfrac{60,000^{*} + 60,000}{2}$ 60,000

*Beginning balances for 20-1 are taken from 20-0 financial statements, which are not shown here.

CHECKPOINT ✔

Complete Checkpoint-3 on pages 979–980 to test your basic understanding of LO4.

Earnings per share is widely used as a measure of a company's performance. It is best tracked over time for the same company. Care must be taken to watch for major changes in the number of shares outstanding as these changes will have a significant impact on the measure.

LO5   Leverage Measures

Compute and explain leverage measures.

Leverage measures indicate the extent to which a company is being financed by debt and the ability of the company to meet its debt obligations. Two of these measures focus on balance sheet relationships, and another focuses on the income statement.

Debt-to-Equity Ratio

The debt-to-equity ratio, or ratio of liabilities to stockholders' equity, measures the extent of leverage, or proportion of borrowed capital, with which a business operates. This ratio is calculated by dividing total liabilities by total stockholders' equity. For FCI, the calculation of this ratio at the end of each year is shown in Figure 24-15.

FIGURE 24-15 Calculation of the Debt-to-Equity Ratio

			20-2	20-1
Debt-to-Equity Ratio	$\dfrac{\text{Total Liabilities}}{\text{Total Stockholders' Equity}}$	=	$\dfrac{\$174,200}{\$279,345}$	$\dfrac{\$220,350}{\$192,500}$
			0.6 to 1	1.1 to 1

This ratio was much lower on December 31, 20-2, than it was on December 31, 20-1. The reduction in the ratio appears to have been caused by three factors.

1. Stockholders' equity increased by issuance of common stock for $22,500.

2. Stockholders' equity increased by keeping a large portion of 20-2's earnings.

3. Both notes payable and accounts payable were significantly reduced during 20-2, so that total liabilities decreased.

On December 31, 20-1, the majority of the financing for FCI came from debt. Companies in low-risk industries with fairly stable earnings can operate with a high ratio of liabilities to stockholders' equity. Comparing FCI's ratio with the industry average would be helpful in evaluating the degree of leverage. If creditors view the debt-to-equity ratio as too high, it will be very difficult for the company to borrow additional funds.

Assets-to-Equity Ratio

Another way to view financial leverage is by comparing total assets with total stockholders' equity. This assets-to-equity ratio is calculated by dividing total assets by total stockholders' equity. For FCI, the calculation of this ratio at the end of each year is shown in Figure 24-16.

FIGURE 24-16 Calculation of Assets-to-Equity Ratio

			20-2	20-1
Assets-to-Equity Ratio	Total Assets	=	$453,545	$412,850
	Total Stockholders' Equity		$279,345	$192,500
			1.6	2.1

We know that assets = liabilities + stockholders' equity. So, if there are no liabilities, assets will equal stockholders' equity, there is no leverage, and the ratio will equal 1:1. When this ratio exceeds 1:1, it means the firm is using debt to acquire assets. Some firms are very conservative and try to use as little debt as possible. Others are more aggressive and try to use other people's money to acquire assets and increase profits.

Of course, leverage is risky whether viewed as debt-to-equity or assets-to-equity. While leverage can increase profits in good times, it can also lead to reduced profits or losses in bad times. The key is whether the firm's return on the additional assets is greater than the interest on the debt used to acquire the assets. Thus, it is important to monitor the firm's ability to pay interest. This is discussed in our next measure of leverage, the times interest earned ratio.

Times Interest Earned Ratio

When a business has long-term liabilities such as bonds payable or mortgage payable, creditors want to know the amount of earnings available to pay interest. The ratio of earnings before taxes and interest to the interest expense is called the times interest earned ratio.

FCI had bonds payable of $100,000 outstanding on December 31, 20-2 and 20-1. The interest rate on the bonds was 10.5%. Interest expense in each year was $10,500 ($100,000 × 10.5%). The calculation of the times interest earned ratio for each year is shown in Figure 24-17.

These times interest earned ratios would be very satisfactory to the bond holders of FCI and indicate that FCI is using leverage in a responsible manner. In many businesses, a ratio of 2 or 3 is considered adequate. Of course, if interest coverage is too low, it will be difficult to issue additional debt.

FIGURE 24-17 Calculation of Times Interest Earned Ratio

			20-2	20-1
Times Interest Earned	Income Before Taxes and Interest	=	$118,945	$84,470
	Interest Expense		$10,500	$10,500
			11.3	8.0
Income Before Taxes and Interest	Net income		$ 71,845	$54,760
	Add: Income tax		36,600	19,210
	Bond interest		10,500	10,500
			$118,945	$84,470

CHECKPOINT ▼

Complete Checkpoint-4 on pages 979–980 to test your basic understanding of LO5.

LO6

Explain the components of ROA and ROE.

Another Look at ROA and ROE

By employing three of the financial ratios that we have discussed, we are able to gain additional insight into how a company generates a return for its stockholders. First, we can break down the return on assets into two parts: profit margin and asset turnover as shown below in Figure 24-18 for FCI in 20-2.

FIGURE 24-18 Another Look at ROA

RETURN ON ASSETS

	Net Income			
	Average Assets			
Profit Margin	×	**Asset Turnover**		
Net Income	×	Net Sales		
Net Sales		Average Assets		
$71,845	×	$835,950		
$835,950		$433,198 ←		
		($412,850 + $453,545)/2		ROA
8.59%*	×	1.93*	=	16.6%

*Ratios carried out beyond one decimal place to void rounding error with ROA computed earlier.

Recall that some analysts prefer to add interest (net of tax) to the numerator to provide a measure of ROA that ignores how the assets were financed. We can see that FCI uses a relatively modest profit margin and moderately fast asset turnover to produce its return on assets.

By adding a measure of leverage (assets-to-equity ratio), we can see how FCI uses leverage to enhance its return on assets to generate a better return on common stockholders' equity. Note that when the assets-to-equity ratio is used to help compute ROE, we use average assets and average common stockholders' equity. Ultimately, we are computing the return on stockholders' equity. Whenever we use income statement and balance sheet measures in a ratio, we must use the average for the balance sheet measure. Since net income was earned throughout the year, we must use the average amount of stockholders' equity that was available during the year. This calculation is shown in Figure 24-19 for FCI in 20-2.

FIGURE 24-19 Another Look at ROE

RETURN ON COMMON STOCKHOLDERS' EQUITY				

$$\frac{\text{Net Income}}{\text{Average Common Stockholders' Equity}}$$

Profit Margin	×	**Asset Turnover**	×	**Leverage Ratio**
$\frac{\text{Net Income}}{\text{Net Sales}}$	×	$\frac{\text{Net Sales}}{\text{Average Assets}}$	×	$\frac{\text{Average Assets}}{\text{Average Common Stockholders' Equity}}$
$\frac{\$71,845}{\$835,950}$	×	$\frac{\$835,950}{\$433,198}$ $(\$412,850 + \$453,545)/2$	×	$\frac{\$433,198}{\$235,923}$ $(\$192,500 + \$279,345)/2$
				ROE
8.59%*	×	1.93*	×	1.84* = 30.5%
Or		16.6% (ROA)	×	1.84 = 30.5%

*Ratios carried out beyond one decimal place to avoid rounding error with ROE computed earlier.

A BROADER VIEW

Different Ways to Generate Return on Assets

Return on assets (ROA) may be broken down into two major ratios: profit margin and asset turnover. This view of ROA helps illustrate that there are different ways to be profitable. Some retail stores, like Walmart, minimize investments in plant and equipment and focus on low prices. Thus, profit margins are lower, but asset turnover is higher. For every dollar in net sales, net income is rather small, perhaps less than $0.02 (1.99%). However, retail businesses like Walmart are able to generate acceptable profits because they are not required to make major investments in plant and equipment to generate substantial revenues. As shown below, for every dollar invested in assets, Walmart generates $2.46 in net sales. In contrast, companies like IBM must make very large investments in plant and equipment, relative to net sales. For every dollar invested in assets, IBM is only able to generate $0.65 in revenues. Therefore, they must have higher profit margins to help pay for these large investments. IBM generates over $0.07 in net income for every dollar in net sales. As shown below, IBM and Walmart have a similar return on assets, but very different measures for profit margin and asset turnover.

$$\frac{\text{Net Income}}{\text{Average Assets}} = \frac{\text{Net Income}}{\text{Net Sales}} \times \frac{\text{Net Sales}}{\text{Average Assets}}$$

Return on Assets = Profit Margin × Asset Turnover

	Return on Assets	=	**Profit Margin**	×	**Asset Turnover**
IBM	$\frac{\$5,753}{\$121,413}$ 4.74%	=	$\frac{\$5,753}{\$79,139}$ 7.27%	×	$\frac{\$79,139}{\$121,413}$ 0.65
Walmart	$\frac{\$9,862}{\$201,674}$ 4.89%	=	$\frac{\$9,862}{\$496,785}$ 1.99%	×	$\frac{\$496,785}{\$201,674}$ 2.46

Source: Annual Reports for each company.   Dollars in millions.

CHECKPOINT ✔

Complete Checkpoint-5 on pages 979–980 to test your basic understanding of LO6.

Using this breakdown, we can see that FCI's use of leverage almost doubles (1.84) the return on assets when computing the return on common stockholders' equity. This appears to be a good use of leverage. Further, based on our earlier analysis of times interest earned, we know that FCI has no difficulty covering the interest payments.

LO7 | Market Measures

Compute and explain market measures.

Market measures use stock market prices to offer evidence of how the company is viewed by investors. Of course, we can compute these measures only if there is a ready market price for the stock. For these measures, we will assume FCI had market values of $9.00 and $7.00 per share of common stock in 20-2 and 20-1, respectively.

Price-Earnings Ratio (PE Ratio)

The price-earnings ratio (PE ratio) is often used by analysts and frequently cited on financial programs. It is computed by dividing the company's market price per share of common stock by the earnings per share of common stock. The calculations of the price earnings ratio for FCI are shown in Figure 24-20.

FIGURE 24-20 Calculation of Price-Earnings Ratio

			20-2	20-1
Price-Earnings Ratio	$\dfrac{\text{Market Price of Common Stock}}{\text{Earnings per Share of Common Stock}}$	=	$9.00	$7.00
			$1.06	$0.91
			8.5	7.7

In general, a higher PE ratio suggests that investors have more confidence in a company's future earnings and growth than for a company with a low PE ratio. PE ratios vary considerably across industries, so it is important to compare ratios with companies in the same industry or with the company's own historical performance.

Some investors will use earnings per share or an estimate of future earnings to attempt to estimate the market value of the stock. If, for example, an investor believes the "correct" PE ratio for FCI is 12, an estimated market price of $12.72 ($1.06 EPS × 12) could be computed. This would suggest that FCI is "undervalued" by the market. Of course, these estimates are highly subjective.

Book Value per Share of Common Stock

Book value per share of common stock is a measure of the ownership equity represented by each share. If a corporation has only common stock outstanding, book value per share is determined by dividing the total stockholders' equity as reported on the balance sheet by the number of shares outstanding at the end of the year. Book value per share means value per books, not the amount that stockholders would receive for their shares if sold or if the company liquidated.

FCI had 60,000 shares outstanding on December 31, 20-1, and 75,000 shares outstanding on December 31, 20-2. Therefore, the book value per share of common stock is calculated in Figure 24-21.

FIGURE 24-21 Calculation of Book Value per Share of Common Stock

			20-2	20-1
Book Value per Share of Common Stock	$\dfrac{\text{Common Stockholders' Equity}}{\text{Number of Common Shares Outstanding}}$	=	$279,345 / 75,000	$192,500 / 60,000
			$3.72	$3.21

When preferred shares are outstanding, the claims or equity of the preferred stock must be considered. These include liquidation values, dividends in arrears on cumulative preferred stock, and earnings available to participating preferred stock. For example, assume a corporation has 30,000 shares of $10 par, preferred stock with a liquidation value of $10.50 per share, and 60,000 shares of common stock outstanding. The total stockholders' equity in the company is $1,200,000. The book value per share of common stock is calculated as follows:

Total stockholders' equity	$1,200,000
Less liquidation claim of preferred stock ($10.50 × 30,000)	315,000
Balance applicable to common stock	$885,000
Number of shares outstanding	60,000
Book value per share of common stock	$14.75

As you probably noticed, market values are not used in these calculations. However, the market value of the common stock is often compared with its book value when attempting to determine whether the stock is valued properly. Since the market value of the company's assets generally exceeds their book values, the market value of the stock is generally well above its book value. Many investors watch for the market value of the stock to approach or fall below the book value and believe this is a good time to buy the stock. It's good to be cautious, however, since the price could be on its way to zero. Further analysis would be important.

> **CHECKPOINT ✔**
>
> Complete Checkpoint-6 on pages 979–980 to test your basic understanding of LO7.

LO8   Limitations of Financial Statement Analysis

Explain the limitations of financial statement analysis.

Financial statement analysis can be a valuable tool in evaluating management performance. However, the methods of analysis need to be used cautiously and with an awareness of their limitations. The accounting system does not measure all aspects of operating a business. For example, the accounting numbers do not reflect the level of customer satisfaction with the company's products, changing market conditions, the entry of new competitors, or current employee morale. Further, the reported data are based on many estimates and approximations.

The period of time covered by the financial statements is another consideration. In this chapter, the analysis is based on only two years. A period of two consecutive years is not sufficient to establish a long-term trend. Many companies provide five- and ten-year summaries of operating results in published annual reports.

Comparison of FCI's financial results with other companies and with its industry as a whole can be difficult because generally accepted accounting principles allow different methods of accounting for similar events. For example, the choice of different inventory and depreciation methods can significantly impact both the income statement and the balance sheet. At a minimum, the accounting methods used by the other companies must be identified, so that their possible effects on comparisons can be considered.

Finally, in using ratios, remember that the observed number is simply an expression of the relationship between two other numbers. Either the numerator or the denominator can cause a ratio to provide a distorted message. For example, a company with the same net income in two consecutive years could show a higher rate of return in the second year, simply because the total assets in the second year are lower due to depreciation.

SELF-STUDY

LEARNING OBJECTIVES	Key Points to Remember
LO1 Perform horizontal and vertical analyses of the income statement and balance sheet.	The financial statements can be much more informative and meaningful if they are analyzed on a comparative basis. The following are four possible types of comparisons: 1. with one or more previous periods 2. with data for the industry as a whole 3. with similar information for other businesses in the industry 4. with preset plans or goals (normally in the form of budgets) A comparison of the amounts for the same item in the financial statements of two or more periods is called *horizontal analysis*. Reporting the amount of each item in a statement as a percentage of some designated total is called *vertical analysis*.
LO2/3/4/5/7 Compute and explain liquidity, activity, profitability, leverage, and market measures of performance.	The following table summarizes the liquidity, activity, profitability, leverage, and market measures.

LIQUIDITY MEASURES	
Working Capital	Current Assets – Current Liabilities
Current Ratio	Current Assets / Current Liabilities
Quick (or Acid-Test) Ratio	Quick Assets / Current Liabilities

LEARNING OBJECTIVES   Key Points to Remember

ACTIVITY MEASURES

Accounts Receivable Turnover

$$\frac{\text{Net Sales on Account}}{\text{Average Accounts Receivable (net)}}$$

Also expressed in days

$365 \div$ Accounts Receivable Turnover

Merchandise Inventory Turnover

$$\frac{\text{Cost of Goods Sold}}{\text{Average Merchandise Inventory}}$$

Also expressed in days

$365 \div$ Merchandise Inventory Turnover

Asset Turnover

$$\frac{\text{Net Sales}}{\text{Average Assets}}$$

PROFITABILITY MEASURES

Profit Margin Ratio

$$\frac{\text{Net Income}}{\text{Net Sales}}$$

Return on Assets

$$\frac{\text{Net Income}}{\text{Average Assets}}$$

Return on Common
  Stockholders' Equity

$$\frac{\text{Net Income Available to Common Stockholders}}{\text{Average Common Stockholders' Equity}}$$

Earnings per Share
  of Common Stock

$$\frac{\text{Net Income Available to Common Stockholders}}{\text{Average Number of Common Shares Outstanding}}$$

LEVERAGE MEASURES

Debt-to-Equity Ratio

$$\frac{\text{Total Liabilities}}{\text{Total Stockholders' Equity}}$$

Assets-to-Equity Ratio

$$\frac{\text{Total Assets}}{\text{Total Stockholders' Equity}}$$

Times Interest Earned Ratio

$$\frac{\text{Income Before Taxes and Interest}}{\text{Interest Expense}}$$

MARKET MEASURES

Price-Earnings Ratio

$$\frac{\text{Market Price of Common Stock}}{\text{Earnings per Share of Common Stock}}$$

Book Value per
  Share of Common Stock

$$\frac{\text{Common Stockholders' Equity}}{\text{Number of Common Shares Outstanding at Year-End}}$$

(continued)

LEARNING OBJECTIVES   Key Points to Remember

LO6 Explain the components of ROA and ROE

The following table summarizes the components of return on assets (ROA) and return on equity (ROE).

COMPONENTS OF ROA AND ROE

Return on Assets

$$\frac{\text{Net Income}}{\text{Average Assets}}$$

$$\text{Profit Margin} \times \text{Asset Turnover}$$

$$\frac{\text{Net Income}}{\text{Net Sales}} \times \frac{\text{Net Sales}}{\text{Average Assets}}$$

Return on Common Stockholders' Equity

$$\frac{\text{Net Income}}{\text{Average Common Stockholders' Equity}}$$

$$\text{Profit Margin} \times \text{Asset Turnover} \times \text{Leverage Ratio}$$

$$\frac{\text{Net Income}}{\text{Net Sales}} \times \frac{\text{Net Sales}}{\text{Average Assets}} \times \frac{\text{Average Assets}}{\text{Average Common Stockholders' Equity}}$$

LO8 Explain the limitations of financial statement analysis.

Limitations of financial statement analysis include the following:

1. Factors not reported on the financial statements are also important in evaluating the financial health of a company.
2. Financial statement information is based on many estimates.
3. Statements from many years should be considered before drawing conclusions about long-term trends.
4. Comparisons across companies are difficult due to the possible use of different accounting techniques.
5. The cause of changes in key ratios must be investigated before drawing conclusions.

DEMONSTRATION PROBLEM

Garfinkle Inc.'s comparative financial statements for the years ending December 31, 20-2 and 20-1, are shown on page 972. The market value of Garfinkle Inc.'s common stock at the end of 20-2 was $15 per share.

REQUIRED

1. Prepare a horizontal analysis of Garfinkle's comparative income statement for 20-2 and 20-1.

2. Prepare a vertical analysis of Garfinkle's comparative income statement for 20-2 and 20-1.

3. Prepare a horizontal analysis of Garfinkle's comparative balance sheet for 20-2 and 20-1.

4. Prepare a vertical analysis of Garfinkle's comparative balance sheet for 20-2 and 20-1.

5. Determine the following measures for 20-2 (round all calculations to two decimal places):

   (a) working capital

   (b) current ratio

   (c) quick ratio

   (d) accounts receivable turnover

   (e) average collection period for accounts receivable

   (f) merchandise inventory turnover

   (g) average number of days required to sell merchandise inventory

   (h) asset turnover

   (i) profit margin ratio

   (j) return on assets

   (k) return on common stockholders' equity

   (l) earnings per share of common stock

   (m) debt-to-equity ratio

   (n) assets-to-equity ratio

   (o) times interest earned ratio

   (p) ROA showing two components

   (q) ROE showing three components

   (r) price-earnings ratio

   (s) book value per share of common stock

(*continued*)

Garfinkle Inc.
Comparative Income Statement
For Years Ended December 31, 20-2 and 20-1

	20-2	20-1
Sales (all on account)	$10,250,000	$6,515,200
Sales returns and allowances	250,000	115,200
Net sales	$10,000,000	$6,400,000
Cost of goods sold	6,800,000	4,160,000
Gross profit	$ 3,200,000	$2,240,000
Administrative expenses	$ 650,000	$ 448,000
Selling expenses	1,300,000	928,000
Total operating expenses	$ 1,950,000	$1,376,000
Operating income	$ 1,250,000	$ 864,000
Other expense (interest)	160,000	89,600
Income before income taxes	$ 1,090,000	$ 774,400
Income tax expense	390,000	234,400
Net income	$ 700,000	$ 540,000

Garfinkle Inc.
Comparative Balance Sheet
December 31, 20-2 and 20-1

	20-2	20-1
Assets		
Current assets:		
Cash	$ 350,000	$ 250,000
Accounts receivable (net)	1,150,000	750,000
Inventories	1,440,000	960,000
Supplies and prepayments	60,000	40,000
Total current assets	$3,000,000	$2,000,000
Plant assets (net)	4,686,000	4,346,000
Total assets	$7,686,000	$6,346,000
Liabilities		
Current liabilities	$1,500,000	$1,300,000
Stockholders' Equity		
Common stock, $10 par	$4,500,000	$4,000,000
Retained earnings	1,686,000	1,046,000
Total stockholders' equity	$6,186,000	$5,046,000
Total liabilities and stockholders' equity	$7,686,000	$6,346,000

SOLUTION 1. Horizontal analysis:

Garfinkle Inc. Comparative Income Statement For Years Ended December 31, 20-2 and 20-1				
	20-2	20-1	INCREASE (DECREASE)	PERCENT
Sales (all on account)	$10,250,000	$6,515,200	$3,734,800	57.3
Sales returns and allowances	250,000	115,200	134,800	117.0
Net sales	$10,000,000	$6,400,000	$3,600,000	56.3
Cost of goods sold	6,800,000	4,160,000	2,640,000	63.5
Gross profit	$ 3,200,000	$2,240,000	$ 960,000	42.9
Administrative expenses	$ 650,000	$ 448,000	$ 202,000	45.1
Selling expenses	1,300,000	928,000	372,000	40.1
Total operating expenses	$ 1,950,000	$1,376,000	$ 574,000	41.7
Operating income	$ 1,250,000	$ 864,000	$ 386,000	44.7
Other expense (interest)	160,000	89,600	70,400	78.6
Income before income taxes	$ 1,090,000	$ 774,400	$ 315,600	40.8
Income tax expense	390,000	234,400	155,600	66.4
Net income	$ 700,000	$ 540,000	$ 160,000	29.6

SOLUTION 2. Vertical analysis:

Garfinkle Inc. Comparative Income Statement For Years Ended December 31, 20-2 and 20-1				
	20-2	PERCENT	20-1	PERCENT
Sales (all on account)	$10,250,000	102.5	$6,515,200	101.8
Sales returns and allowances	250,000	2.5	115,200	1.8
Net sales	$10,000,000	100.0	$6,400,000	100.0
Cost of goods sold	6,800,000	68.0	4,160,000	65.0
Gross profit	$ 3,200,000	32.0	$2,240,000	35.0
Administrative expenses	$ 650,000	6.5	$ 448,000	7.0
Selling expenses	1,300,000	13.0	928,000	14.5
Total operating expenses	$ 1,950,000	19.5	$1,376,000	21.5
Operating income	$ 1,250,000	12.5	$ 864,000	13.5
Other expense (interest)	160,000	1.6	89,600	1.4
Income before income taxes	$ 1,090,000	10.9	$ 774,400	12.1
Income tax expense	390,000	3.9	234,400	3.7
Net income	$ 700,000	7.0	$ 540,000	8.4

(continued)

SOLUTION 3. Horizontal analysis:

Garfinkle Inc. **Comparative Balance Sheet** **December 31, 20-2 and 20-1**				
	20-2	20-1	INCREASE (DECREASE)	PERCENT
Assets				
Current assets:				
Cash	$ 350,000	$ 250,000	$ 100,000	40.0
Accounts receivable (net)	1,150,000	750,000	400,000	53.3
Inventories	1,440,000	960,000	480,000	50.0
Supplies and prepayments	60,000	40,000	20,000	50.0
Total current assets	$3,000,000	$2,000,000	$1,000,000	50.0
Plant assets (net)	4,686,000	4,346,000	340,000	7.8
Total assets	$7,686,000	$6,346,000	$1,340,000	21.1
Liabilities				
Current liabilities	$1,500,000	$1,300,000	$ 200,000	15.4
Stockholders' Equity				
Common stock, $10 par	$4,500,000	$4,000,000	$ 500,000	12.5
Retained earnings	1,686,000	1,046,000	640,000	61.2
Total stockholders' equity	$6,186,000	$5,046,000	$1,140,000	22.6
Total liabilities and stockholders' equity	$7,686,000	$6,346,000	$1,340,000	21.1

SOLUTION 4. Vertical analysis:

Garfinkle Inc. **Comparative Balance Sheet** **December 31, 20-2 and 20-1**				
	20-2	PERCENT*	20-1	PERCENT*
Assets				
Current assets:				
Cash	$ 350,000	4.6	$ 250,000	3.9
Accounts receivable (net)	1,150,000	15.0	750,000	11.8
Inventories	1,440,000	18.7	960,000	15.1
Supplies and prepayments	60,000	0.8	40,000	0.6
Total current assets	$3,000,000	39.0	$2,000,000	31.5
Plant assets (net)	4,686,000	61.0	4,346,000	68.5
Total assets	$7,686,000	100.0	$6,346,000	100.0
Liabilities				
Current liabilities	$1,500,000	19.5	$1,300,000	20.5
Stockholders' Equity				
Common stock, $10 par	$4,500,000	58.5	$4,000,000	63.0
Retained earnings	1,686,000	21.9	1,046,000	16.5
Total stockholders' equity	$6,186,000	80.5	$5,046,000	79.5
Total liabilities and stockholders' equity	$7,686,000	100.0	$6,346,000	100.0

*Percentages may not add due to rounding.

SOLUTION 5. (a) Working capital:

Current assets $ 3,000,000
− Current liabilities   (1,500,000)
                                   $ 1,500,000

(b) Current ratio:

$$\frac{\text{Current assets}}{\text{Current liabilities}} = \frac{\$3,000,000}{\$1,500,000} = 2.00 \text{ to } 1$$

(c) Quick ratio:

$$\frac{\text{Quick assets}}{\text{Current liabilities}} = \frac{\$1,500,000}{\$1,500,000} = 1.00 \text{ to } 1$$

(d) Accounts receivable turnover:

$$\frac{\text{Net sales on account}}{\text{Average accounts receivable}} = \frac{\$10,000,000}{(\$750,000 + \$1,150,000) \div 2} = 10.53$$

(e) Average collection period: $\dfrac{365}{10.53} = 34.66 \text{ days}$

(f) Merchandise inventory turnover:

$$\frac{\text{Cost of goods sold}}{\text{Avg. merchandise inventory}} = \frac{\$6,800,000}{(\$960,000 + \$1,440,000) \div 2} = 5.67$$

(g) Average number of days to sell inventory:

$(365 \div 5.67) = 64.37 \text{ days}$

(h) Asset turnover:

$$\frac{\text{Net sales}}{\text{Average assets}} = \frac{\$10,000,000}{(\$6,346,000 + \$7,686,000) \div 2} = 1.43 \text{ to } 1$$

(i) Profit margin ratio:

$$\frac{\text{Net income}}{\text{Net sales}} = \frac{\$700,000}{\$10,000,000} = 7.00\%$$

(j) Return on assets:

$$\frac{\text{Net income}}{\text{Average assets}} = \frac{\$700,000}{(\$6,346,000 + \$7,686,00) \div 2} = 9.98\%$$

(k) Return on common stockholders' equity:

$$\frac{\text{Net income}}{\text{Avg. common stockholders' equity}} = \frac{\$700,000}{(\$5,046,000 + \$6,186,000) \div 2} = 12.46\%$$

(l) Earnings per share of common stock:

$$\frac{\text{Net income}}{\substack{\text{Avg. no. of common}\\\text{shares outstanding}}} = \frac{\$700,000}{(400,000 \text{ shares} + 450,000 \text{ shares}) \div 2} = \$1.65$$

(m) Debt-to-equity ratio:

$$\frac{\text{Total liabilities}}{\text{Total stockholders' equity}} = \frac{\$1,500,000}{\$6,186,000} = 0.24 \text{ to } 1$$

(continued)

(n) Assets-to-equity ratio:

$$\frac{\text{Total assets}}{\text{Total stockholders' equity}} = \frac{\$7,686,000}{\$6,186,000} = \underline{\underline{1.24 \text{ to } 1}}$$

(o) Times interest earned ratio:

Net income	$ 700,000
Corporate income taxes	390,000
Interest expense	160,000
Income before taxes and interest	$1,250,000

$$\frac{\text{Income before taxes and interest}}{\text{Interest expense}} = \frac{\$1,250,000}{\$160,000} = \underline{\underline{7.81 \text{ times}}}$$

(p) ROA with 2 components: Profit margin ratio $\times$ Asset turnover

$$\frac{\text{Net income}}{\text{Average assets}} = \frac{\text{Net income}}{\text{Net sales}} \times \frac{\text{Net sales}}{\text{Average assets}}$$

$$\frac{\$700,000}{\$10,000,000} \times \frac{\$10,000,000}{\$7,016,000}$$

$$7.00\% \times 1.43 = \underline{\underline{10.01\%}}^*$$

*Difference with response to (j) is due to rounding.

(q) ROE with 3 components:

	Profit margin ratio	**Asset turnover**	**Leverage**

$$\frac{\text{Net income}}{\text{Average common stockholder' equity}} = \frac{\text{Net income}}{\text{Net sales}} \times \frac{\text{Net sales}}{\text{Average assets}} \times \frac{\text{Average assets}}{\text{Avg. common stockholders' equity}}$$

$$\frac{\$700,000}{\$10,000,000} \times \frac{\$10,000,000}{\$7,016,000} \times \frac{\$7,016,000}{\$5,616,000}$$

$$7.00\% \times 1.43^* \times 1.25^* = \underline{\underline{12.51\%}}^*$$

*Difference with response to (k) is due to rounding.

(r) Price-earnings ratio:

$$\frac{\text{Market price of stock}}{\text{Earnings per share}} \times \frac{\$15.00}{\$1.65} = 9.09$$

(s) Book value per share of common stock:

$$\frac{\text{Common stockholders' equity}}{\text{No. of common shares outstanding}} = \frac{\$6,186,000}{450,000 \text{ shares}} = \underline{\underline{\$13.75}}$$

KEY TERMS

accounts receivable turnover (957) The ratio of net sales on account to the average amount of net accounts receivable.

acid-test ratio (956) See quick ratio.

activity measures (951) Measure of the efficiency with which assets are used to generate a profit.

asset turnover ratio (959)   A measure of how efficiently a company used its assets to generate sales. Also called ratio of net sales to assets.

assets-to-equity ratio (963)   The ratio of total assets to total stockholders' equity.

book value per share of common stock (966)   The ratio of common stockholders' equity to the number of common shares outstanding at the end of the year.

cost of goods sold ratio (954)   The ratio of cost of goods sold to net sales.

current ratio (956)   The ratio of current assets to current liabilities. Also called working capital ratio.

debt-to-equity ratio (962)   The ratio of total liabilities to stockholders' equity. It is a measure of the extent of overall leverage or proportion of borrowed capital with which a business operates. Also called ratio of liabilities to stockholders' equity.

earnings per share of common stock (961)   The ratio of net income available to common stockholders to the average number of shares of common stock outstanding during the year.

gross profit ratio (954)   The ratio of gross profit to net sales.

horizontal analysis (951)   A comparison of the amounts for the same item in the financial statements of two periods.

leverage (951)   The proportion of debt to stockholders' equity.

leverage measures (962)   Measures that indicate the extent to which a company is being financed by debt, and the ability of the company to meet its debt obligations.

liquidity measures (951)   Measures that indicate a company's ability to meet its current debts as they come due.

market measures (951)   The use of the market value of common stock as evidence of how the company is viewed by investors.

merchandise inventory turnover (958)   The ratio of cost of goods sold to the average merchandise inventory.

net income ratio (954)   See profit margin ratio.

operating expense ratio (954)   The ratio of operating expenses to net sales.

operating income ratio (954)   The ratio of operating income to net sales.

price-earnings ratio (PE ratio) (966)   The price of the company's common stock divided by the earnings per share of common stock.

profit margin ratio (954)   The ratio of net income to net sales.

profitability measures (951)   Measures that indicate a company's ability to earn income by operating efficiently.

quick ratio (956)   The ratio of quick assets to current liabilities. Also called the acid-test ratio.

ratio of liabilities to stockholders' equity (962)   See debt-to-equity ratio.

ratio of net sales to assets (959)   See asset turnover ratio.

return on assets (ROA) (960)   The ratio of net income for the year to the average assets for the year.

return on common stockholders' equity (ROE) (961)   The ratio of net income available to common stockholders for the year to the average common stockholders' equity during the year.

times interest earned ratio (963) The ratio of earnings before interest and taxes to interest expense.

vertical analysis (953) Reporting the amount of each item in a statement as a percentage of some designated total.

working capital (956) The excess of a company's current assets over current liabilities.

working capital ratio (956) See current ratio.

SELF-STUDY TEST QUESTIONS

True/False

1. **LO1** A comparison of amounts for the same item in the financial statements of two or more periods is horizontal analysis.

2. **LO1** It is common for long-term asset accounts to show a decrease in the net balance from year to year.

3. **LO2** Working capital is calculated by dividing current assets by current liabilities.

4. **LO3** In calculating accounts receivable turnover, only accounts receivable are considered; others, such as accrued interest receivable, are not included.

5. **LO5** Leverage is the ability to pay debts when they come due.

Multiple Choice

1. **LO1** Financial statements are usually compared with
   (a) one or more previous periods.   (c) similar businesses in the industry.
   (b) data from the industry as a whole.   (d) all of the above.

2. **LO2** Which of these is not a measure of liquidity?
   (a) working capital   (c) quick ratio
   (b) current ratio   (d) return on assets

3. **LO2** Working capital is a measure of
   (a) liquidity.   (c) leverage.
   (b) profitability.

4. **LO4** The ability to earn a satisfactory return on investments is called
   (a) liquidity.   (c) leverage.
   (b) profitability.

5. **LO5** The times interest earned ratio is a measure of
   (a) liquidity.   (c) leverage.
   (b) profitability.

Checkpoint Exercises

Financial statements for Esplanade Enterprises are provided below. Use these financial statements to complete the Checkpoint Exercises. (Round final calculations to two decimal places.)

Esplanade Enterprises Income Statement For Year Ended December 31, 20-2	
	20-2
Net sales (all on account)	$900,000
Cost of goods sold	600,000
Gross profit	$300,000
Operating expenses	167,000
Operating income	$133,000
Interest expense	10,000
Income before taxes	$123,000
Income tax expense	43,000
Net income	$ 80,000

Esplanade Enterprises Balance Sheet December 31, 20-2 and 20-1		
	20-2	20-1
Assets		
Current assets:		
Cash	$ 90,000	$200,000
Accounts receivable	160,000	190,000
Merchandise inventory	180,000	200,000
Total current assets	$430,000	$590,000
Property, plant, and equipment:		
Land	$ 40,000	$ 40,000
Building	140,000	—
Equipment	100,000	—
Total property, plant, and equipment	$280,000	$ 40,000
Total assets	$710,000	$630,000
Liabilities		
Current liabilities:		
Notes payable	$ 20,000	$ 50,000
Accounts payable	40,000	60,000
Total current liabilities	$ 60,000	$110,000
Long-term liabilities:		
Bonds payable	120,000	120,000
Total liabilities	$180,000	$230,000
Stockholders' Equity		
Common stock ($5 par)	$290,000	$250,000
Paid-in capital in excess of par—common stock	130,000	100,000
Retained earnings	110,000	50,000
Total stockholders' equity	$530,000	$400,000
Total liabilities and stockholders' equity	$710,000	$630,000

(continued)

1. **LO2**   Compute the following liquidity measures for Esplanade Enterprises for 20-2:
   (a) Working capital   (c) Quick ratio
   (b) Current ratio

2. **LO3**   Compute the following activity measures for Esplanade Enterprises for 20-2:
   (a) Accounts receivable turnover and average collection period
   (b) Merchandise inventory turnover and average number of days to sell inventory
   (c) Asset turnover

3. **LO4**   Compute the following profitability measures for Esplanade Enterprises for 20-2:
   (a) Profit margin ratio
   (b) Return on assets (ROA)
   (c) Return on common stockholders' equity (ROE)
   (d) Earnings per share of common stock (EPS)

4. **LO5**   Compute the following leverage measures for Esplanade Enterprises for 20-2:
   (a) Debt-to-equity ratio   (c) Times interest earned ratio
   (b) Assets-to-equity ratio

5. **LO6**   Compute return on assets (ROA) using the two basic components and return on common stockholders' equity (ROE) using the three basic components for Esplanade Enterprises for 20-2.

6. **LO7**   Compute the following market measures for Esplanade Enterprises for 20-2:
   (a) Price-earnings ratio (PE ratio) (The market value of Esplanade's common stock is $12.00 per share.)
   (b) Book value per share of common stock

The answers to the Self-Study Test Questions are at the end of the chapter (pages 992–994).

APPLYING YOUR KNOWLEDGE

CengageNowv2 provides "Show Me How" videos for selected exercises and problems. Additional resources, such as Excel templates for completing selected exercises and problems, are available for download from the companion website at Cengage.com.

REVIEW QUESTIONS

LO1   1. Financial statement analysis generally focuses on five main aspects of the business's financial health. What are they?

LO1   2. Describe four possible types of comparisons that may be made in financial statement analysis.

LO1   3. Why was the increase in FCI's operating income so much greater than the increase in its net sales?

LO1   4. What were the main causes of the decrease in FCI's current liabilities?

LO1   5. List five ratios that are automatically provided by the vertical analysis of income statements.

LO2   6. Identify three measures of liquidity calculated by FCI.

LO3   7. Identify three activity measures calculated by FCI.

LO4   8. Identify four measures of profitability calculated by FCI.

LO5   9. Identify three measures of the extent of leverage calculated by FCI.

LO6   10. Identify the two primary components of return on assets.

LO6   11. Identify the three primary components of return on common stockholders' equity.

LO7   12. Identify the two market measures calculated by FCI.

LO8   13. Briefly describe five limitations of financial statement analysis.

SERIES A EXERCISES

E 24-1A   (LO2)
✓ (a) 2.00 to 1
✓ (c) $1,832,700

ANALYSIS OF LIQUIDITY Based on the comparative income statement and balance sheet of Cowan Kitchen Counters, Inc., that follow, compute the following liquidity measures for 20-2 (round all calculations to two decimal places):

(a) Quick or acid-test ratio

(b) Current ratio

(c) Working capital

Cowan Kitchen Counters, Inc. Comparative Income Statement For Years Ended December 31, 20-2 and 20-1		
	20-2	20-1
Net Sales (all on account)	$2,584,000	$2,163,000
Cost of goods sold	1,868,200	1,616,800
Gross profit	$ 715,800	$ 546,200
Operating expenses	315,200	221,800
Other expense (interest)	24,200	24,200
Income tax expense	176,800	106,300
Net income	$ 199,600	$ 193,900

(continued)

Cowan Kitchen Counters, Inc. Comparative Balance Sheet December 31, 20-2 and 20-1		
	20-2	20-1
Cash	$ 255,400	$ 243,200
Government notes	250,000	250,000
Accounts receivable (net)	903,500	797,500
Merchandise inventory	983,600	913,600
Supplies and prepayments	143,200	47,500
Land	108,200	108,200
Building (net)	330,000	390,600
Office equipment (net)	17,700	15,000
Total assets	$2,991,600	$2,765,600
Current liabilities (accounts payable)	$ 703,000	$ 532,000
Bonds payable	220,000	240,000
Total liabilities	$ 923,000	$ 772,000
Common stock ($10 par, 180,000 shares)	$1,800,000	$1,800,000
Retained earnings	268,600	193,600
Total stockholders' equity	$2,068,600	$1,993,600
Total liabilities and stockholders' equity	$2,991,600	$2,765,600

E 24-2A   (LO3)

✓ (a) 3.04 or 120.07 days
✓ (c) 0.90 to 1

ANALYSIS OF ACTIVITY MEASURES Based on the financial statement data in Exercise 24-1A, compute the following activity measures for 20-2 (round all calculations to two decimal places):

(a) Accounts receivable turnover and average collection period

(b) Merchandise inventory turnover and average number of days to sell inventory

(c) Asset turnover

E 24-3A   (LO4)

✓ (b) 6.93%
✓ (d) $1.11

ANALYSIS OF PROFITABILITY Based on the financial statement data in Exercise 24-1A, compute the following profitability measures for 20-2 (round all calculations to two decimal places):

(a) Profit margin ratio

(b) Return on assets

(c) Return on common stockholders' equity

(d) Earnings per share of common stock

E 24-4A   (LO5)

✓ (a) 0.45 to 1

ANALYSIS OF LEVERAGE Based on the financial statement data in Exercise 24-1A, compute the following leverage measures for 20-2 (round all calculations to two decimal places):

(a) Debt-to-equity ratio

(b) Times interest earned ratio (Bond interest is $24,200.)

(c) Assets-to-equity ratio

E 24-5A (LO6)
✓ asset turnover 0.90

ANALYSIS OF ROA COMPONENTS Based on the financial statement data in Exercise 24-1A, compute ROA for 20-2 using its two basic components (round all calculations to two decimal places).

E 24-6A (LO6)
✓ asset turnover 0.90

ANALYSIS OF ROE COMPONENTS Based on the financial statement data in Exercise 24-1A, compute ROE for 20-2 using its three basic components (round all calculations to two decimal places).

E 24-7A (LO7)
✓ (a) 25.23

CALCULATION OF MARKET MEASURES Based on the financial statement data in Exercise 24-1A, compute the following market measures for 20-2 (round all calculations to two decimal places).

(a) Price-earnings ratio (The market price of Cowan Kitchen Counters' common stock was $28.00 on December 31, 20-2.)

(b) Book value per share of common stock

SERIES A PROBLEMS

P 24-8A (LO1)

	(Inc.)	%
✓ NI	$32,139	52.8
✓ Cash	$20,894	94.9
✓ RE	$95,018	126.5

HORIZONTAL ANALYSIS OF COMPARATIVE FINANCIAL STATEMENTS Amounts from the comparative income statement and balance sheet of Miller Electronics Corporation for the last two years are as follows:

Miller Electronics Corporation Comparative Income Statement For Years Ended December 31, 20-2 and 20-1		
	20-2	20-1
Net sales (all on account)	$650,220	$420,600
Cost of goods sold	395,410	258,668
Gross profit	$254,810	$161,932
Administrative expenses	$ 63,518	$ 42,288
Selling expenses	65,992	43,936
Total operating expenses	$129,510	$ 86,224
Operating income	$125,300	$ 75,708
Interest expense	1,282	1,204
Income before income taxes	$124,018	$ 74,504
Income tax expense	31,005	13,630
Net income	$ 93,013	$ 60,874

(continued)

Miller Electronics Corporation
Comparative Balance Sheet
December 31, 20-2 and 20-1

	20-2	20-1
Assets		
Current assets:		
Cash	$ 42,900	$ 22,006
Receivables (net)	73,642	47,510
Merchandise inventory	92,060	50,396
Supplies and prepayments	3,788	1,158
Total current assets	$212,390	$121,070
Property, plant, and equipment:		
Office equipment (net)	$ 12,150	$ 8,490
Factory equipment (net)	105,360	71,190
Total property, plant, and equipment	$117,510	$ 79,680
Total assets	$329,900	$200,750
Liabilities		
Current liabilities		
Notes payable	$ 10,000	$ 6,000
Accounts payable	43,524	30,242
Accrued and withheld payroll taxes	6,250	5,400
Total current liabilities	$ 59,774	$ 41,642
Stockholders' Equity		
Common stock ($10 par)	$100,000	$ 84,000
Retained earnings	170,126	75,108
Total stockholders' equity	$270,126	$159,108
Total liabilities and stockholders' equity	$329,900	$200,750

REQUIRED

Prepare a horizontal analysis. Add columns to show the amount of increase (decrease) and the percentage change. Round percentages to one decimal place.

P 24-9A   (LO1)

	20-2	20-1
✓ CGS	60.8%	61.5%
✓ Cash	13.0%	11.0%

VERTICAL ANALYSIS OF COMPARATIVE FINANCIAL STATEMENTS Refer to the financial statements in Problem 24-8A.

REQUIRED

Prepare a vertical analysis of the income statement and balance sheet. Show each item on the income statement as a percentage of the net sales for each year. On the balance sheet, show each asset item as a percentage of the total assets and each liability and equity item as a percentage of the total liabilities and stockholders' equity. Round percentages to one decimal place.

P 24-10A   (LO2/3/4/5/7)

	20-1
✓ (a)	32.34%
✓ (c)	$7.25
✓ (e)	1.67 to 1
✓ (g)	$79,428
✓ (i)	5.21 or 70.06 days
✓ (k)	2.23 to 1
✓ (l)	62.88 times
✓ (n)	1.26

RATIO ANALYSIS OF COMPARATIVE FINANCIAL STATEMENTS Refer to the financial statements in Problem 24-8A.

REQUIRED

Calculate the following ratios and amounts for 20-1 and 20-2 (round all calculations to two decimal places):

(a) Return on assets (Total assets on January 1, 20-1, were $175,750.)

(b) Return on common stockholders' equity (Total common stockholders' equity on January 1, 20-1, was $106,944.)

(c) Earnings per share of common stock (The average numbers of shares outstanding were 8,400 shares in 20-1 and 9,200 in 20-2.)

(d) Book value per share of common stock

(e) Quick ratio

(f) Current ratio

(g) Working capital

(h) Receivables turnover and average collection period (Net receivables on January 1, 20-1, were $39,800.)

(i) Merchandise inventory turnover and average number of days to sell inventory (Merchandise inventory on January 1, 20-1, was $48,970.)

(j) Debt-to-equity ratio

(k) Asset turnover (Assets on January 1, 20-1, were $175,750.)

(l) Times interest earned ratio

(m) Profit margin ratio

(n) Assets-to-equity ratio

(o) Price-earnings ratio (The market price of the common stock was $100.00 and $85.00 on December 31, 20-2 and 20-1, respectively.)

SERIES B EXERCISES

E 24-1B   (LO2)
✓ (b) 3.87 to 1

ANALYSIS OF LIQUIDITY Based on the comparative income statement and balance sheet for Falcon Designers, Inc., given on the next page, compute the following liquidity measures for 20-2 (round all calculations to two decimal places):

(a) Quick or acid-test ratio

(b) Current ratio

(c) Working capital

E 24-2B   (LO3)
✓ (b) 1.81 or 201.66 days

ANALYSIS OF ACTIVITY MEASURES Based on the financial statement data in Exercise 24-1B, compute the following activity measures for 20-2 (round all calculations to two decimal places):

(a) Accounts receivable turnover and average collection period

(b) Merchandise inventory turnover and average number of days to sell inventory

(c) Asset turnover

(continued)

<table>
<tr><td colspan="3" align="center">**Falcon Designers, Inc.**
Comparative Income Statement
For Years Ended December 31, 20-2 and 20-1</td></tr>
<tr><td></td><td align="center">20-2</td><td align="center">20-1</td></tr>
<tr><td>Net sales (all on account)</td><td>$1,850,800</td><td>$ 1,532,600</td></tr>
<tr><td>Cost of goods sold</td><td>1,150,400</td><td>1,010,500</td></tr>
<tr><td>Gross profit</td><td>$ 700,400</td><td>$ 522,100</td></tr>
<tr><td>Operating expenses</td><td>180,300</td><td>156,600</td></tr>
<tr><td>Other expenses (interest)</td><td>18,200</td><td>18,200</td></tr>
<tr><td>Income tax expense</td><td>160,600</td><td>107,600</td></tr>
<tr><td>Net income</td><td>$ 341,300</td><td>$ 239,700</td></tr>
</table>

<table>
<tr><td colspan="3" align="center">**Falcon Designers, Inc.**
Comparative Balance Sheet
December 31, 20-2 and 20-1</td></tr>
<tr><td></td><td align="center">20-2</td><td align="center">20-1</td></tr>
<tr><td>Cash</td><td>$ 95,500</td><td>$ 79,700</td></tr>
<tr><td>Government notes</td><td>200,000</td><td>200,000</td></tr>
<tr><td>Accounts receivable (net)</td><td>639,300</td><td>570,600</td></tr>
<tr><td>Merchandise inventory</td><td>634,900</td><td>639,500</td></tr>
<tr><td>Supplies and prepayments</td><td>39,600</td><td>29,900</td></tr>
<tr><td>Land</td><td>81,900</td><td>78,400</td></tr>
<tr><td>Building (net)</td><td>227,500</td><td>289,300</td></tr>
<tr><td>Office equipment (net)</td><td>10,400</td><td>10,800</td></tr>
<tr><td>Total assets</td><td>$1,929,100</td><td>$1,898,200</td></tr>
<tr><td>Current liabilities (accounts payable)</td><td>$ 416,000</td><td>$ 394,500</td></tr>
<tr><td>Bonds payable</td><td>150,000</td><td>150,000</td></tr>
<tr><td>Total liabilities</td><td>$ 566,000</td><td>$ 544,500</td></tr>
<tr><td>Common stock ($10 par, 125,000 shares)</td><td>$1,250,000</td><td>$1,250,000</td></tr>
<tr><td>Retained earnings</td><td>113,100</td><td>103,700</td></tr>
<tr><td>Total stockholders' equity</td><td>$1,363,100</td><td>$1,353,700</td></tr>
<tr><td>Total liabilities and stockholders' equity</td><td>$1,929,100</td><td>$1,898,200</td></tr>
</table>

E 24-3B   (LO4)
✓ (a) 18.44%
✓ (c) 25.13%

ANALYSIS OF PROFITABILITY Based on the financial statement data in Exercise 24-1B, compute the following profitability measures for 20-2 (round all calculations to two decimal places):

(a) Profit margin ratio

(b) Return on assets

(c) Return on common stockholders' equity

(d) Earnings per share of common stock

E 24-4B   (LO5)
✓ (b) 28.58 times

ANALYSIS OF LEVERAGE Based on the financial statement data in Exercise 24-1B, compute the following leverage measures for 20-2 (round all calculations to two decimal places):

(a) Debt-to-equity ratio

(b) Times interest earned ratio (Bond interest is $18,200.)

(c) Assets-to-equity ratio

E 24-5B   (LO6)
✓ asset turnover 0.97

ANALYSIS OF ROA COMPONENTS Based on the financial statement data in Exercise 24-1B, compute ROA using its two basic components (round all calculations to two decimal places).

E 24-6B   (LO6)
✓ asset turnover 0.97

ANALYSIS OF ROE COMPONENTS Based on the financial statement data in Exercise 24-1B, compute ROE using its three basic components (round all calculations to two decimal places).

E 24-7B   (LO7)
✓ (a) 13.92

CALCULATION OF MARKET MEASURES Based on the financial statement data in Exercise 24-1B, compute the following market measures for 20-2 (round all calculations to two decimal places).

(a) Price-earnings ratio (The market price of Falcon Designers' common stock was $38.00 on December 31, 20-2.)

(b) Book value per share of common stock

SERIES B PROBLEMS

P 24-8B   (LO1)

	(Inc.)	%
✓ NI	$17,497	23.9
✓ Cash	$14,671	94.0
✓ RE	$39,148	70.2

HORIZONTAL ANALYSIS OF COMPARATIVE FINANCIAL STATEMENTS Amounts from the comparative income statement and balance sheet of Johnson Stores, Inc. for the last two years are as follows:

Johnson Stores, Inc. Comparative Income Statement For Years Ended December 31, 20-2 and 20-1		
	20-2	20-1
Net sales (all on account)	$467,865	$305,145
Cost of goods sold	256,955	149,005
Gross profit	$210,910	$156,140
Administrative expenses	$ 43,876	$ 30,617
Selling expenses	44,994	31,293
Total operating expenses	$ 88,870	$ 61,910
Operating income	$122,040	$ 94,230
Interest expense	916	903
Income before income taxes	$121,124	$ 93,327
Income tax expense	30,280	19,980
Net income	$ 90,844	$ 73,347

(continued)

Johnson Stores, Inc. Comparative Balance Sheet December 31, 20-2 and 20-1		
	20-2	20-1
Assets		
Current assets:		
Cash	$ 30,275	$ 15,604
Receivables (net)	42,441	33,565
Merchandise inventory	49,460	34,636
Supplies and prepayments	7,119	6,403
Total current assets	$129,295	$ 90,208
Property, plant, and equipment:		
Office equipment (net)	$ 9,025	$ 6,062
Factory equipment (net)	72,090	52,930
Total property, plant, and equipment	$ 81,115	$ 58,992
Total assets	$210,410	$149,200
Liabilities		
Current liabilities		
Notes payable	$ 4,000	$ 8,000
Accounts payable	30,233	14,821
Accrued and withheld payroll taxes	6,250	7,600
Total current liabilities	$ 40,483	$ 30,421
Stockholders' Equity		
Common stock ($10 par)	$ 75,000	$ 63,000
Retained earnings	94,927	55,779
Total stockholders' equity	$169,927	$118,779
Total liabilities and stockholders' equity	$210,410	$149,200

REQUIRED

Prepare a horizontal analysis of the statements. Add columns to show the amount of increase (decrease) and the percentage change. Round percentages to one decimal place.

P 24-9B   (LO1)

	20-2	20-1
✓ CGS	54.9%	48.8%
✓ Cash	14.4%	10.5%

VERTICAL ANALYSIS OF COMPARATIVE FINANCIAL STATEMENTS Refer to the financial statements in Problem 24-8B.

REQUIRED

Prepare a vertical analysis of the income statement and balance sheet. Show each item on the income statement as a percentage of the net sales for each year. On the balance sheet, show each asset item as a percentage of the total assets and each liability and equity item as a percentage of the total liabilities and stockholders' equity. Round percentages to one decimal place.

P 24-10B   (LO2/3/4/5/7)

	20-1
✓ (b)	73.06%
✓ (d)	$18.85
✓ (f)	2.97 to 1
✓ (h)	9.76 or 37.40 days
✓ (j)	0.26 to 1
✓ (l)	104.35 times
✓ (n)	1.26

RATIO ANALYSIS OF COMPARATIVE FINANCIAL STATEMENTS Refer to the financial statements in Problem 24-8B.

REQUIRED

Calculate the following ratios and amounts for 20-1 and 20-2 (round all calculations to two decimal places).

(a) Return on assets (Total assets on January 1, 20-1, were $111,325.)

(b) Return on common stockholders' equity (Total common stockholders' equity on January 1, 20-1, was $82,008.)

(c) Earnings per share of common stock (The average numbers of shares outstanding were 6,300 shares in 20-1 and 6,900 in 20-2.)

(d) Book value per share of common stock

(e) Quick ratio

(f) Current ratio

(g) Working capital

(h) Receivables turnover and average collection period (Net receivables on January 1, 20-1, were $28,995.)

(i) Merchandise inventory turnover and average number of days to sell inventory (Merchandise inventory on January 1, 20-1, was $32,425.)

(j) Debt-to-equity ratio

(k) Asset turnover (Assets on January 1, 20-1, were $111,325.)

(l) Times interest earned ratio

(m) Profit margin ratio

(n) Assets-to-equity ratio

(o) Price-earnings ratio (The market price of the common stock was $120.00 and $110.00 on December 31, 20-2 and 20-1, respectively.)

MANAGING YOUR WRITING

Many libraries have corporate annual reports and reports on the financial health of companies by financial analysts and rating agencies such as Standard and Poor's and Moody's. Go to the library and review financial information on two corporations in your favorite industry. Write a brief memo describing the information available and how it can be used to evaluate the financial health of a company.

ETHICS CASE

Jim Tennison, L & B Corporation's president, called the company's chief financial officer, Fred Harden, into his office late Friday afternoon. Jim had been reviewing the projected financial statements of L & B Corporation that would be issued as of year-end. Jim told Fred he was worried that the company's liquidity position had been declining over the past two years. Fred assured Jim that the company still had sufficient liquidity, and it had been steadily decreasing its debt. Jim said that there were three or four major stockholders who were very conservative and would raise lots of questions about the company's declining liquidity ratios. Jim and Fred then decided to take out a two-year loan secured by some land L & B Corporation owned, put the cash in the bank, and pay the loan off after January 1. Jim told Fred to account for the transaction as a long-term liability for financial reporting purposes. They agreed that this measure would solve the problem of liquidity at the annual stockholders' meeting because the company's ratios would be almost identical to last year. Jim was sure that most of the stockholders were only concerned with net income and ratios.

1. If you were a stockholder of L & B Corporation, how would you feel about Jim and Fred's idea? Have any ethical principles been violated?

2. If the transaction is booked as a debit to Cash and a credit to Long-Term Notes Payable, how will it affect the company's key current ratios and debt ratios?

(continued)

3. Suppose Jim and Fred decide not to take out the loan. Write a brief note to the stockholders justifying a decrease in liquidity measures. Assure them that the company is still in the "safe range."

4. In groups of two or three, list as many reasons as possible, both positive and negative, for a decrease in net working capital.

MASTERY PROBLEM

✓ 3(a)	$41,800
✓ 3(c)	0.58 to 1
✓ 4(b)	6.59 or 55.39 days
✓ 5(a)	7.60%
✓ 5(c)	14.96%
✓ 6(b)	45.76 times
✓ 7(a)	13.94

Comparative financial statements for Na Pali Coast Company for the years ending December 31, 20-1 and 20-2 are provided.

REQUIRED

1. Perform horizontal analysis of the comparative income statement and balance sheet. Round percentages to one decimal place.

2. Perform vertical analysis of the comparative income statement and balance sheet. Round percentages to one decimal place.

3. Compute the following liquidity measures for 20-2 (round all calculations to two decimal places):

    (a) Working capital

    (b) Current ratio

    (c) Quick or acid-test ratio

4. Compute the following activity measures for 20-2 (round all calculations to two decimal places):

    (a) Accounts receivable turnover and average number of days to collect receivables (Assume that sales on account for 20-2 were $120,000.)

    (b) Merchandise inventory turnover and average number of days to sell inventory

    (c) Asset turnover

5. Compute the following profitability measures for 20-2 (round all calculations to two decimal places):

    (a) Profit margin ratio

    (b) Return on assets

    (c) Return on common stockholders' equity

    (d) Earnings per share of common stock

6. Compute the following leverage measures for 20-2 (round all calculations to two decimal places):

    (a) Debt-to-equity ratio

    (b) Times interest earned ratio (Assume interest expense for 20-2 was $1,200.)

7. Compute the following market measures for 20-2 (round all calculations to two decimal places):

    (a) Price-earnings ratio (The market price of Na Pali Coast Company's common stock was $23.00 on December 31, 20-2.)

    (b) Book value per share of common stock

Na Pali Coast Company
Comparative Income Statement
For Years Ended December 31, 20-2 and 20-1

	20-2	20-1
Net sales	$466,451	$291,613
Cost of goods sold	285,889	188,626
Gross profit	$180,562	$102,987
Operating expenses	125,650	78,200
Operating income	$ 54,912	$ 24,787
Other expenses	1,200	500
Income before income taxes	$ 53,712	$ 24,287
Income tax expense	18,250	7,285
Net income	$ 35,462	$ 17,002

Na Pali Coast Company
Comparative Balance Sheet
December 31, 20-2 and 20-1

	20-2	20-1
Assets		
Current assets:		
Cash	$ 8,600	$ 7,500
Government notes	3,000	2,000
Accounts receivable (net)	10,500	8,600
Merchandise inventory	53,600	33,200
Supplies and prepayments	4,500	3,200
Total current assets	$ 80,200	$ 54,500
Property, plant, and equipment:		
Land	$ 40,000	$ 40,000
Building (net)	200,000	150,000
Delivery equipment (net)	13,000	15,000
Office equipment (net)	5,400	6,000
Patents	5,000	6,000
Total property, plant, and equipment	$263,400	$217,000
Total assets	$343,600	$271,500
Liabilities		
Current liabilities:		
Notes payable	$ 5,000	$ 3,000
Accounts payable	28,700	22,300
Accrued and withheld payroll taxes	4,200	5,600
Accrued interest payable	500	1,700
Total current liabilities	$ 38,400	$ 32,600
Long-term liabilities:		
Bonds payable	50,000	20,000
Total liabilities	$ 88,400	$ 52,600
Stockholders' Equity		
Common stock ($5 par)	$115,000	$100,000
Paid-in capital in excess of par	65,000	60,000
Retained earnings	75,200	58,900
Total stockholders' equity	$255,200	$218,900
Total liabilities and stockholders' equity	$343,600	$271,500

CHALLENGE PROBLEM

This problem challenges you to apply your cumulative accounting knowledge to move a step beyond the material in the chapter.

✓ Days cash is outstanding for merchandise: 54.04 days

Combining the information provided by various ratios can enhance your understanding of the financial condition of a business. Review the information provided for Na Pali Coast Company in the Mastery Problem. Using this information, respond to the following questions:

REQUIRED

1. Compute the average number of days required to sell inventory and collect cash from customers buying on account.

2. Note that Na Pali Coast Company also buys inventory on account. On average, how many days pass before Na Pali pays its creditors?

3. Using the information from your answers to parts (1) and (2), compute the number of days from the time Na Pali Coast pays for inventory until it receives cash from customers on account.

ANSWERS TO SELF-STUDY TEST QUESTIONS

True/False

1. T
2. T
3. F (WC = CA − CL)
4. T
5. F (Leverage is a measure of the extent to which debt is used to finance the business.)

Multiple Choice

1. d   2. d   3. a   4. b   5. c

Checkpoint Exercises

1. a. Working capital = $430,000 − $60,000 = $370,000
   b. Current ratio   = $430,000/$60,000   = 7.17 to 1
   c. Quick ratio   = $250,000/$60,000   = 4.17 to 1

2. a. Accounts receivable turnover:

$$\frac{\text{Net sales on account}}{\text{Average accounts receivable}} = \frac{\$900,000}{\$175,000} = \underline{5.14}$$
$$\text{(\$190,000 + \$160,000)/2}$$

   Average collection period $365/5.14 = \underline{71.01 \text{ days}}$

b. Merchandise inventory turnover:

$$\frac{\text{Cost of goods sold}}{\text{Average merchandise inventory}} = \frac{\$600,000}{\$190,000} = \underline{3.16}$$
$$(\$200,000 + \$180,000)/2$$

Average number of days to sell inventory $= 365/3.16 = \underline{115.51}$

c. Asset turnover:

$$\frac{\text{Net sales}}{\text{Average assets}} = \frac{\$900,000}{\$670,000} = \underline{1.34 \text{ to } 1}$$
$$(\$630,000 + \$710,000)/2$$

3. a. Profit margin ratio:

$$\frac{\text{Net income}}{\text{Net sales}} = \frac{\$80,000}{\$900,000} = \underline{8.89\%}$$

b. Return on assets (ROA):

$$\frac{\text{Net income}}{\text{Average assets}} = \frac{\$80,000}{\$670,000} = \underline{11.94\%}$$
$$(\$630,000 + \$710,000)/2$$

c. Return on common stockholders' equity (ROE):

$$\frac{\text{Net income}}{\text{Average common stockholders' equity}} = \frac{\$80,000}{\$465,000} = \underline{17.20\%}$$
$$(\$400,000 + \$530,000)/2$$

d. Earnings per share of common stock (EPS):

$$\frac{\text{Net income}}{\text{Average number of common shares outstanding}} = \frac{\$80,000}{54,000} = \underline{\$1.48}$$
$$(50,000 + 58,000)/2$$

4. a. Debt-to-equity ratio:

$$\frac{\text{Total liabilities}}{\text{Total stockholders' equity}} = \frac{\$180,000}{\$530,000} = \underline{0.34 \text{ to } 1}$$

b. Assets-to-equity ratio:

$$\frac{\text{Total assets}}{\text{Total stockholders' equity}} = \frac{\$710,000}{\$530,000} = \underline{1.34 \text{ to } 1}$$

c. Times interest earned ratio:

$$\frac{\text{Income before taxes and interest}}{\text{Interest expense}} = \frac{\$133,000}{\$10,000} = \underline{13.30 \text{ times}}$$

Net income	$ 80,000
Income tax expense	43,000
Interest expense	10,000
Income before taxes and interest	$133,000

5. ROA with 2 components:

		Profit margin ratio	×	**Asset turnover**

$$\frac{\text{Net income}}{\text{Average assets}} = \frac{\text{Net income}}{\text{Net sales}} \times \frac{\text{Net sales}}{\text{Average assets}}$$

$$\frac{\$80,000}{\$900,000} \times \frac{\$900,000}{\$670,000}$$

$$(\$630,000 + \$710,000)/2$$

$$8.89\% \quad \times \quad 1.34 \quad = \quad \underline{11.9\%}^*$$

*Variance from 11.94% in 3b. due to rounding.

ROE with 3 components:

	Profit margin ratio	×	**Asset turnover**	×	**Leverage**

$$\frac{\text{Net income}}{\text{Average stockholders' equity}} = \frac{\text{Net income}}{\text{Net sales}} \times \frac{\text{Net sales}}{\text{Average assets}} \times \frac{\text{Average assets}}{\text{Avg. stockholders' equity}}$$

$$\frac{\$80,000}{\$900,00} \times \frac{\$900,000}{\$670,000} \times \frac{\$670,000}{\$465,000}$$

$$(\$630,000 + \$710,000)/2 \qquad (\$400,000 + \$530,000)/2$$

$$8.89\% \quad \times \quad 1.34 \quad \times \quad 1.44 \quad = \quad \underline{17\%}^*$$

*Variance from 17.20% in 3c. due to rounding.

6. a. Price-earnings ratio (PE ratio):

$$\frac{\text{Market price of common stock}}{\text{Earnings per share of common stock}} = \frac{\$12.00}{\$1.48} = \underline{8.11}$$

b. Book value per share of common stock:

$$\frac{\text{Common stockholders' equity}}{\text{No. of common shares outstanding}} = \frac{\$530,000}{\$58,000} = \underline{\$9.14}$$

Chapter **25** Departmental Accounting

As you marvel at the clarity and crispness of the picture on your HDTV or the power of the sounds blasting from your sound system, you probably don't think much about tracking the costs and profitability of these products. Okay, as budding accountants, maybe you do, but most folks would not. VIZIO is a highly successful company that certainly would need to do this tracking. Founded in 2002, and headquartered in Irvine, California the company had a 4,000% revenue increase in one four-year period and has become a leading HDTV brand and the number one sound bar brand in the United States. VIZIO produces many models of HDTVs, plus multiple home theater systems, and a variety of accessories for such products. All of these are technology products, but HD screens, home theater systems, and various accessories would involve different production components and processes. How would VIZIO know the profitability of these different products? One possibility is to organize the business into departments: for example, HD screens, home theater equipment, and accessories. The activities of each department could then be separately accounted for and evaluated. In this chapter, we will learn how to account for departmental operations, including different measures of performance and how to interpret them.

LEARNING OBJECTIVES

Careful study of this chapter should enable you to:

LO1 Explain the nature and purpose of departmental accounting.

LO2 Describe and compute departmental gross profit.

LO3 Describe and compute departmental operating income.

LO4 Describe and compute departmental direct operating margin.

Companies often engage in different types of profit-making activities. For example, a merchandiser might sell different products, such as lawn mowers and bicycles. A service business might provide different services, such as auditing and management consulting. Such businesses are often organized into separate segments called departments. In this chapter, we will examine how to account for a business organized into departments.

LO1	**Departmental Accounting**

Explain the nature and purpose of departmental accounting.

When a business sells several products or services, it can be difficult to obtain useful and accurate information about the business. An income statement prepared for the business as a whole might show that the business is reasonably profitable. This statement would not show that one portion of the business is highly successful while another portion is operating at a loss. Departmental accounting overcomes this problem by providing separate financial information about each department.

Departmental reports are useful to management for three purposes: (1) planning, (2) control, and (3) performance evaluation.

1. Planning—Successful managers set goals and develop plans for achieving these goals. An important part of planning is identifying the strengths and weaknesses of the different parts of the firm. Departmental reports can be very helpful for this purpose.

2. Control—To properly control operations, managers must be able to identify revenues and expenses that are out of line. Departmental reports help management focus attention on problem areas or departments.

3. Performance evaluation—When a business is organized into departments, responsibility for each department can be assigned to a specific manager. Departmental reports can then be used to evaluate each manager's performance.

Departmental reports are usually not part of the basic financial statements. These reports are for internal management use only. This means the accounting rules for external reporting do not apply. Departmental reports can be prepared in whatever form and for whatever time period management finds useful.

A component of a business, such as a department or segment, for which a manager can be held responsible, is known as a **responsibility center**. There are three types of responsibility centers:

1. Cost center

2. Profit center

3. Investment center

If a department incurs costs but does not generate revenue, it is called a cost center. Some examples of cost centers are an accounting department, maintenance department, and research and development department. These departments provide important services for operating a business, but they do not directly generate revenue.

If a department incurs costs and generates revenue, it is called a profit center. For example, a bicycle shop might have a bicycle department and a clothing department. An automobile company might have a manufacturing segment and a financial services segment.

If a department incurs costs, generates revenue, and determines the assets invested in the department, it is called an **investment center**. Departmental reports are designed to fit the needs of management, and depend on whether the department is a cost center, profit center, or investment center.

In the following sections, we will look at departmental income statements of two profit centers for Annie's Sporting Goods, which sells golf and tennis equipment.

These income statements will be extended through three different levels: gross profit, operating income, and direct operating margin.

LO2	Departmental Gross Profit

Describe and compute departmental gross profit.

Departmental gross profit is the difference between a department's net sales and cost of goods sold. Each element used to compute gross profit must be determined for each department. Recall that the following elements are used to compute gross profit:

Sales
Sales returns and allowances
Sales discounts
Inventory
Purchases
Purchases returns and allowances
Purchases discounts
Freight-in

Two ways of accumulating this information are:

1. Maintain separate general ledger accounts by department for each element (account) making up gross profit.

2. Maintain a single general ledger account for each element. The total in each account is assigned to the appropriate departments at the end of the accounting period.

Computerized accounting systems have made it easy to record data by department and element.

Departmental Income Statement Showing Gross Profit

Figure 25-1 contains Annie's departmental income statement showing gross profit for the year 20--. The gross profit section is presented in condensed form. Gross profit is shown by department and in total.

FIGURE 25-1 Income Statement Showing Departmental Gross Profit

Annie's Sporting Goods Income Statement For Year Ended December 31, 20--			
	GOLF	TENNIS	TOTAL
Net sales	$1,075,000	$640,300	$1,715,300
Cost of goods sold	545,280	420,900	966,180
Gross profit	$ 529,720	$219,400	$ 749,120
Operating expenses:			
Store clerks' wages expense			$ 105,250
Truck drivers' wages expense			83,900
Advertising expense			79,500
Store rent expense			22,800
Bad debt expense			17,900
Depreciation expense—delivery equipment			24,000
Other operating expenses			325,430
Total operating expenses			$ 658,780
Operating income			$ 90,340

This report shows that the golf department provides the majority of Annie's sales and gross profit. The report also reveals a large difference in the gross profit percentages of the two departments.

For ease of presentation, many percentage calculations in this chapter are rounded to one or two decimal places.

Golf department gross profit percentage: ($529,720 ÷ $1,075,000)	**49.3%**
Tennis department gross profit percentage: ($219,400 ÷ $640,300)	**34.3%**

These gross profit percentages provide a good example of how departmental reports can be useful for control and performance evaluation. Management should determine the causes of the difference between the departments' results and take appropriate action. Perhaps the normal retail markup on golf equipment is higher than that on tennis equipment. If so, management might want to emphasize selling golf equipment. If the normal retail markup on the two products is similar, the pricing policies for tennis equipment should be evaluated. The tennis department may be using an inadequate markup percentage. Another possibility is that the purchase prices for tennis equipment are too high. If so, the purchasing department should try to obtain better prices from vendors.

Once the causes of the difference are determined, the departmental information can be used for planning. Management can set quantitative goals for the departments for the following period. Performance comparisons then could be made both between the departments, as in Figure 25-1, and with established goals.

Gross profit data can be useful, but they should be cautiously interpreted. A higher gross profit or gross profit percentage does not necessarily mean that a department is more profitable overall. To evaluate overall profitability, departmental operating expenses must also be considered.

LEARNING KEY 🔑

An income statement showing departmental gross profit enables management to see whether each department is earning an adequate gross profit.

CHECKPOINT ✔

Complete Checkpoint-1 on page 1012 to test your basic understanding of LO2.

LO3 Departmental Operating Income

Describe and compute departmental operating income.

Departmental operating income is the difference between a department's gross profit and its operating expenses. As with departmental gross profit, separate departmental accounts may be maintained for each operating expense. This approach is not common, however, because many operating expenses cannot be directly related to specific departments. Instead, a single general ledger account is maintained for each operating expense. The total of each expense is assigned or allocated to departments at the end of the period.

Departmental Gross Profit − Operating Expenses = Departmental Operating Income

Direct and Indirect Operating Expenses

Departmental operating expenses can be classified as direct and indirect. Direct expenses are incurred for the sole benefit of and are traceable directly to a specific department. Indirect expenses are incurred for the benefit of the business as a whole and cannot be traced directly to a specific department. Figure 25-2 provides examples of direct and indirect expenses for Annie's Sporting Goods.

FIGURE 25-2 Examples of Direct and Indirect Expenses

DIRECT EXPENSES	INDIRECT EXPENSES
Wages of golf department sales clerk	Cost of renting store space
Cost of advertising tennis equipment	Cost of advertising Annie's Sporting Goods store
Wages of driver who delivers golf equipment	Store manager's salary

To compute departmental operating income, direct expenses are *assigned* to departments based on the actual expenses incurred. If separate departmental accounts are used, the expenses are accumulated there. If separate departmental accounts are not used, the expenses are assigned to departments based on information contained in supporting records. For example, personnel records would show the departments in which employees work, and wages would be assigned accordingly.

Indirect expenses are *allocated* to departments on some reasonable basis, such as relative sales, cost of goods sold, floor space, or the estimated time spent serving a given department. There are no rules like generally accepted accounting principles. The key is to use a "reasonable basis."

Assigning and Allocating Departmental Expenses

To illustrate the computation of departmental operating income, we will assign and allocate the operating expenses of Annie's Sporting Goods. Annie's does not maintain separate general ledger departmental operating expense accounts.

Store Clerks' Wages Expense

Annie's employs five store clerks: two work solely in the golf department, one works in the tennis department, and two assist customers in both departments. Their wages are as follows:

EMPLOYEE NUMBER	DEPT.	WAGES	
1	Golf	$ 24,000	$46,000
2	Golf	22,000	
3	Tennis	20,250	
4	Both	18,000	$39,000
5	Both	21,000	
Total		$105,250	

Wages of $46,000 ($24,000 + $22,000) for the golf department clerks are assigned to golf. Wages of $20,250 for the tennis department clerk are assigned to tennis. Wages of $39,000 ($18,000 + $21,000) for the other two clerks are allocated between the departments based on the percentage of total net sales produced by each department.

Golf Net Sales	=	$1,075,000	=	62.67%
Total Net Sales		$1,715,300		
Tennis Net Sales	=	$640,300	=	37.33%
Total Net Sales		$1,715,300		

The total store clerks' wages expense is divided between the departments as follows:

	GOLF	TENNIS	TOTAL
Direct expense	$46,000	$20,250	$ 66,250
Indirect expense allocation:			
% Total Expense			
62.67% × $39,000	24,441		24,441
37.33% × $39,000		14,559	14,559
	$70,441	$34,809	$105,250

Another reasonable basis for allocating the clerks' wages might be the percentage of total cost of goods sold. This is a good example of the judgment that must be made any time expenses need to be allocated.

Truck Drivers' Wages Expense

Annie's employs three delivery truck drivers, one of whom delivers only golf equipment. Their wages are as follows:

DRIVER NUMBER	PRODUCT DELIVERED	WAGES	
1	Golf	$29,000	
2	Both	26,500	
3	Both	28,400	$54,900
Total		$83,900	

Other reasonable bases for allocating the drivers' wages might be the cost of the equipment delivered or the number of units delivered.

Wages of the driver who delivers only golf equipment ($29,000) are assigned to that department. Wages of the other two drivers ($54,900) are allocated based on the relative dollar amount of golf and tennis equipment delivered by the drivers. Shipping and delivery records are used to estimate the percentages as approximately 70% golf and 30% tennis. The total drivers' wages expense is divided between the departments as follows:

	GOLF	TENNIS	TOTAL
Direct expense	$29,000		$29,000
Indirect expense allocation:			
% **Total Expense**			
70% × $54,900	38,430		38,430
30% × $54,900		$16,470	16,470
	$67,430	$16,470	$83,900

Advertising Expense

Annie's total advertising expense is $79,500: $45,000 for newspaper advertising and $34,500 for radio. Newspaper advertising is classified as golf, tennis, or "mixed" based on the number of inches of copy space. The $45,000 of newspaper advertising is calculated to be $17,000 for golf, $12,000 for tennis, and $16,000 mixed. All radio advertising is classified as mixed. The total mixed expense for advertising of $50,500 ($16,000 + $34,500) is allocated between departments based on the percentage of total net sales produced by each department. These percentages are 62.67% golf and 37.33% tennis, as calculated for store clerks' wages expense. The total advertising expense is divided between the departments as follows:

	GOLF	TENNIS	TOTAL
Direct expense	$17,000	$12,000	$29,000
Indirect expense allocation:			
% **Total Expense**			
62.67% × $50,500	31,648		31,648
37.33% × $50,500		18,852	18,852
	$48,648	$30,852	$79,500

Store Rent Expense

Annie's rents 5,000 square feet of store space for $22,800 per year. This entire expense is an indirect expense, allocated on the basis of the relative number of square feet of floor space occupied by each department. The golf department occupies 3,200 square feet, or 64% of the floor space. The tennis department occupies the remaining 36% of floor space. The rent expense is divided between the departments as follows:

			GOLF	TENNIS	TOTAL
Indirect expense allocation:					
%	Total Expense				
64%	×	$22,800	$14,592		$14,592
36%	×	$22,800		$8,208	8,208
			$14,952	$8,208	$22,800

Bad Debt Expense

Annie's bad debt expense of $17,900 is treated as a direct expense. It is assigned to the departments based on experience with accounts written off. For the current year, $9,000 is assigned to golf and $8,900 to tennis.

Depreciation Expense—Delivery Equipment

Annie's has three delivery trucks, one of which is used to deliver only golf equipment. Total depreciation on the delivery equipment is $24,000 for the year, $9,000 of which relates to the golf delivery truck. The other $15,000 of depreciation is allocated on the basis of the relative dollar amount of golf and tennis equipment delivered with the other two trucks. These percentages are 70% golf and 30% tennis, as explained for the truck drivers' wages expense. The total depreciation expense on the delivery equipment is divided between the departments as follows:

			GOLF	TENNIS	TOTAL
Direct expense			$ 9,000		$ 9,000
Indirect expense allocation:					
%	Total Expense				
70%	×	$15,000	10,500		10,500
30%	×	$15,000		$4,500	4,500
			$19,500	$4,500	$24,000

Other Operating Expenses

Annie's other operating expenses totaled $325,430. This total includes a broad range of expenses, from managers' salaries to postage expense. These expenses are assigned and allocated using methods like those used for the various expenses previously described. A summary of the amounts assigned and allocated for other operating expenses is as follows:

	GOLF	TENNIS	TOTAL
Direct expense	$ 74,420	$26,980	$101,400
Indirect expense allocation	153,113	70,917	224,030
	$227,533	$97,897	$325,430

Departmental Operating Expense Summary

The assignment and allocation of departmental operating expenses can be summarized in a **departmental operating expense summary**. The summary in Figure 25-3 shows the following:

1. Classification of each operating expense as direct or indirect
2. Amount assigned (direct) or allocated (indirect) to each department
3. Total operating expenses for each department

FIGURE 25-3 Departmental Operating Expense Summary

Annie's Sporting Goods Departmental Operating Expense Summary For Year Ended December 31, 20--	TOTAL	GOLF DIRECT	GOLF INDIRECT	GOLF TOTAL	TENNIS DIRECT	TENNIS INDIRECT	TENNIS TOTAL
Store clerks' wages expense	$105 2 5 0 00	$ 46 0 0 0 00	$ 24 4 4 1 00	$ 70 4 4 1 00	$20 2 5 0 00	$ 14 5 5 9 00	$ 34 8 0 9 00
Truck drivers' wages expense	83 9 0 0 00	29 0 0 0 00	38 4 3 0 00	67 4 3 0 00		16 4 7 0 00	16 4 7 0 00
Advertising expense	79 5 0 0 00	17 0 0 0 00	31 6 4 8 00	48 6 4 8 00	12 0 0 0 00	18 8 5 2 00	30 8 5 2 00
Store rent expense	22 8 0 0 00		14 5 9 2 00	14 5 9 2 00		8 2 0 8 00	8 2 0 8 00
Bad debt expense	17 9 0 0 00	9 0 0 0 00		9 0 0 0 00	8 9 0 0 00		8 9 0 0 00
Depreciation expense—delivery equipment	24 0 0 0 00	9 0 0 0 00	10 5 0 0 00	19 5 0 0 00		4 5 0 0 00	4 5 0 0 00
Other operating expenses	325 4 3 0 00	74 4 2 0 00	153 1 1 3 00	227 5 3 3 00	26 9 8 0 00	70 9 1 7 00	97 8 9 7 00
Total	$658 7 8 0 00	$184 4 2 0 00	$272 7 2 4 00	$457 1 4 4 00	$68 1 3 0 00	$133 5 0 6 00	$201 6 3 6 00

Departmental Income Statement Showing Operating Income

Figure 25-4 contains Annie's departmental income statement showing operating income for the year 20--. Operating expense data on the statement were obtained from the departmental operating expense summary in Figure 25-3. Operating income is shown by department and in total.

Compare this income statement with the one in Figure 25-1. Notice that the departmental gross profit, total operating expenses, and total operating income are the same in both statements. The difference is that Figure 25-4 shows operating expenses and operating income for each department.

Management can use this income statement to evaluate the overall performance of the two departments. For example, the income statement shows that the operating income and operating income percentage of the golf department are much higher than those of the tennis department.

> **LEARNING KEY** 🔑
> An income statement showing departmental operating income enables management to evaluate the overall performance of each department.

Golf department operating income percentage: ($72,576 ÷ $1,075,000)	**6.8%**
Tennis department operating income percentage: ($17,764 ÷ $640,300)	**2.8%**

FIGURE 25-4 **Departmental Income Statement Showing Operating Income**

Annie's Sporting Goods Income Statement For Year Ended December 31, 20 --			
	GOLF	TENNIS	TOTAL
Net sales	$1,075,000	$640,300	$1,715,300
Cost of goods sold	545,280	420,900	966,180
Gross profit	$ 529,720	$219,400	$ 749,120
Operating expenses:			
Store clerks' wages expense	$ 70,441	$ 34,809	$ 105,250
Truck drivers' wages expense	67,430	16,470	83,900
Advertising expense	48,648	30,852	79,500
Store rent expense	14,592	8,208	22,800
Bad debt expense	9,000	8,900	17,900
Depreciation expense—delivery equipment	19,500	4,500	24,000
Other operating expenses	227,533	97,897	325,430
Total operating expenses	$ 457,144	$201,636	$ 658,780
Operating income	$ 72,576	$ 17,764	$ 90,340

Remember, however, that the golf department's gross profit and gross profit percentage are much higher than those of the tennis department. The golf department's operating income might be higher simply because the gross profit is higher. Further analysis shows that this is the case. As shown below, the operating expense percentage is lower for the tennis department (31.5%) than for the golf department (42.5%).

		Golf	Tennis
$\dfrac{\text{Operating Expenses}}{\text{Net Sales}}$	=	$\dfrac{\$457,144}{\$1,075,000}$	$\dfrac{\$201,636}{\$640,300}$
Operating expense percentage		42.5%	31.5%

As noted in the discussion of the difference in gross profit percentages, departmental reports showing operating income can be used for control and performance evaluation. Management can determine the causes of the difference in operating income and take corrective action.

The departmental operating income data also can be used for planning. Quantitative operating income goals can be set for the following year, and departmental operating income can be evaluated against those goals.

However, management must be cautious in interpreting departmental operating income results. Most of Annie's operating expenses for both departments are indirect. They therefore are allocated between departments based on estimates. Indirect expenses, by definition, are incurred for the benefit of the business as a whole and cannot be traced directly to any department. Thus, the departments have no control over such expenses. Further, it might be possible to reduce some indirect expenses by eliminating a department, but most of these expenses would continue to be incurred. Many accountants argue that to properly evaluate departmental performance, an income measure should be used that considers only the direct expenses of each department.

CHECKPOINT ✔

Complete Checkpoint-2 on page 1012 to test your basic understanding of LO3.

A BROADER VIEW

The Supply Chain—Reaching Beyond Your Department or Business

Businesses face increasing demands from their customers for higher quality, faster service, and lower costs. One way companies are responding to these demands is through supply-chain management. The supply chain includes all of the purchasing, production, storage, delivery, and sales functions across a set of businesses. Supply-chain management requires focusing on the entire supply chain across businesses instead of just on one's own department or business. By coordinating and participating with other companies, all partners in the chain can operate more efficiently. These arrangements can lead to some new challenges in measuring department performance.

ISTOCK.COM/WENDELL AND CAROLYN

LO4 Departmental Direct Operating Margin

Describe and compute departmental direct operating margin.

Departmental direct operating margin is the difference between a department's gross profit and its direct operating expenses. To compute departmental direct operating margin, the elements of gross profit and the direct operating expenses are needed for each department. For Annie's, this information was developed in the previous section. We can use it to prepare a departmental income statement showing departmental direct operating margin. The information in the departmental operating expense summary (Figure 25-3) and in the income statement (Figure 25-4) simply needs to be reorganized.

Annie's income statement for the year 20--, showing departmental direct operating margins, appears in Figure 25-5. To determine the departmental direct operating margins, the direct operating expenses listed in the departmental operating expense summary (Figure 25-3) are subtracted from the departmental gross profits.

Departmental Gross Profit − Direct Operating Expenses = Direct Operating Margin

YOUR PERSPECTIVE

Lodging Manager

Hotels and motels are run by *lodging managers.* In smaller establishments, *lodging general managers* ensure that guests on vacation or business have a pleasant experience. Their duties include setting room rates, authorizing spending, setting budgets for the establishment's various department, and tracking how much money the facility is making.

Larger hotels have assistant lodging managers such as convention service, front-office, and revenue managers. *Convention service managers*

plan services to offer guests. *Front-office managers* may be responsible for adjusting bills, while *revenue managers* oversee accounting and cash-flow matters at the hotel, projecting occupancy levels and setting special rates. Each of these managers may be required to prepare a report. Although these reports are not a part of basic financial statements, they are important for preparing the departmental income statement. The departmental income statement helps department managers set goals for the department and allows the general manager to make performance comparisons between departments.

Indirect expenses are then subtracted from the total direct operating margin to calculate total operating income. Note that the indirect expenses that are separated by department in the departmental operating expense summary (Figure 25-3) are combined in Figure 25-5. Indirect expenses are not allocated to specific departments in preparing this departmental income statement.

FIGURE 25-5 Departmental Income Statement Showing Direct Operating Margin

Annie's Sporting Goods Income Statement For Year Ended December 31, 20--			
	GOLF	TENNIS	TOTAL
Net sales	$1,075,000	$640,300	$1,715,300
Cost of goods sold	545,280	420,900	966,180
Gross profit	$ 529,720	$219,400	$ 749,120
Direct operating expenses:			
Store clerks' wages expense	$ 46,000	$ 20,250	$ 66,250
Truck drivers' wages expense	29,000		29,000
Advertising expense	17,000	12,000	29,000
Bad debt expense	9,000	8,900	17,900
Depreciation expense—delivery equipment	9,000		9,000
Other operating expenses	74,420	26,980	101,400
Total direct operating expenses	$ 184,420	$ 68,130	$ 252,550
Departmental direct operating margin	$ 345,300	$151,270	$ 496,570
Indirect operating expenses:			
Store clerks' wages expense			$ 39,000
Truck drivers' wages expense			54,900
Advertising expense			50,500
Store rent expense			22,800
Depreciation expense—delivery equipment			15,000
Other operating expenses			224,030
Total indirect operating expenses			$ 406,230
Operating income			$ 90,340

The total operating expenses of $658,780 in Figure 25-4 are separated into direct and indirect operating expenses in Figure 25-5:

Total direct operating expenses	$252,550
Total indirect operating expenses	406,230
Total operating expenses	$658,780

Compare this income statement with the one in Figure 25-4. Notice that the departmental gross profit ($529,720 and $219,400), total operating expenses ($252,550 + $406,230 = $658,780), and total operating income ($90,340) are the same in each statement. The key difference between the statements is that only direct operating expenses ($252,550) are split between departments in Figure 25-5. This permits calculation of the direct operating margin for each department.

Interpretation and Use of Direct Operating Margin

Management can use this form of income statement in several ways:

1. To evaluate departmental performance.
2. To determine the contribution a department makes to the overall operating income of the company.
3. To decide whether to discontinue a department.

Performance Evaluation

Recall that direct expenses are operating expenses that are traceable directly to a specific department. Departmental direct operating margin is calculated by subtracting only direct operating expenses from departmental gross profit. Thus, direct operating margin can be used to evaluate a department on the basis of only those expenses that it can control and for which it is directly responsible. The income statement in Figure 25-5 shows that the golf department's direct operating margin percentage is higher than that of the tennis department.

Golf department direct operating margin percentage:	**32.1%**
($345,300 ÷ $1,075,000)	
Tennis department direct operating margin percentage:	**23.6%**
($151,270 ÷ $640,300)	

Further analysis, however, shows that this is the case only because of the golf department's higher gross profit. In fact, the tennis department is controlling direct operating expenses more effectively than the golf department, as shown below. The tennis department's direct operating expenses are only 10.6% of net sales. The golf department's direct operating expenses are 17.2% of net sales.

		Golf	Tennis
Direct Operating Expenses	=	$184,420	$68,130
Net Sales		$1,075,000	$640,300
Direct operating expense percentage		17.2%	10.6%

Note once again that this evaluation is based on comparisons between departments. If management sets quantitative goals for the departments, performance can also be evaluated relative to those goals.

Contribution to Overall Operating Income

Departmental direct operating margin also shows a department's contribution to the company's overall operating income. The conventional departmental operating income in Figure 25-4 implies that the tennis department contributes only $17,764 to overall profits. In contrast, the departmental direct operating margin in Figure 25-5 shows that the tennis department contributes $151,270. This amount is available to cover the company's indirect operating expenses and provide operating income.

Decision to Discontinue

A third possible use of the departmental direct operating margin data is in deciding whether to discontinue a department. In making this decision, management must focus on the revenues and expenses that will be eliminated if a department is discontinued. This means focusing on departmental direct operating margin, not on operating income. Remember that the indirect expenses that are subtracted in calculating conventional operating income are expenses incurred for the business as a whole. Unless management can reduce these expenses by eliminating a department, such expenses will be incurred even if a department is discontinued.

To illustrate, assume that R & R Company is deciding whether to discontinue one of its three departments. Operating results for the current year for each department, for the business as a whole, and for departments A and B only are shown in Figure 25-6.

Operating income results show that department C is operating at a $5,000 loss. However, eliminating department C would actually reduce rather than increase R & R's total operating income, as shown in the last column for departments A and B only. This reduction in operating income would occur because department C's direct operating margin is $20,000. This $20,000 is available to cover the indirect operating expenses and add to the operating income of the firm. If department C is eliminated,

FIGURE 25-6 R & R Company

	DEPARTMENT A	DEPARTMENT B	DEPARTMENT C	TOTAL	DEPARTMENTS A & B ONLY
Net sales	$210 0 0 0 00	$185 0 0 0 00	$170 0 0 0 00	$565 0 0 0 00	$395 0 0 0 00
Cost of goods sold	115 0 0 0 00	110 0 0 0 00	96 0 0 0 00	321 0 0 0 00	225 0 0 0 00
Gross margin	$ 95 0 0 0 00	$ 75 0 0 0 00	$ 74 0 0 0 00	$244 0 0 0 00	$170 0 0 0 00
Direct operating expenses	55 0 0 0 00	45 0 0 0 00	54 0 0 0 00	154 0 0 0 00	100 0 0 0 00
Departmental direct operating margin	$ 40 0 0 0 00	$ 30 0 0 0 00	$ 20 0 0 0 00	$ 90 0 0 0 00	$ 70 0 0 0 00
Indirect operating expenses	27 0 0 0 00	22 0 0 0 00	25 0 0 0 00	74 0 0 0 00	74 0 0 0 00
Operating income (loss)	$ 13 0 0 0 00	$ 8 0 0 0 00	$ (5 0 0 0 00)	$ 16 0 0 0 00	$ (4 0 0 0 00)

Available to cover indirect operating expenses

Dept. C loss

$20,000 difference = benefit of retaining Dept. C

the remaining departments must absorb the indirect operating expenses of $25,000 allocated to department C. Thus, the schedule lists indirect operating expenses as $74,000 both in the Total column and in the Departments A and B Only column.

Note in Figure 25-6 that the difference between the total operating income of $16,000 and the operating loss of $4,000 for Departments A and B Only is $20,000. This $20,000 is department C's departmental direct operating margin. This amount would be lost if the department were eliminated. In general, if a department has a positive departmental direct operating margin, it should not be discontinued. An exception would be when management has a plan to reduce indirect expenses by at least the amount of that department's direct operating margin.

It can be difficult to determine which revenues and expenses will change if a department is discontinued. For example, if the products in Dept. A help draw customers for Dept. B, discontinuing Dept. A could harm the revenues of Dept. B and the business as a whole. Also, part of the plan to discontinue a department might be to use the space for other purposes or expand in some other area. The effects of other changes on departmental revenues and expenses must be considered in making a decision to discontinue.

CHECKPOINT ✔

Complete Checkpoint-3 on page 1012 to test your basic understanding of LO4.

SELF-STUDY

LEARNING OBJECTIVES	**Key Points to Remember**
LO1 **Explain the nature and purpose of departmental accounting.**	Departmental reports provide information about the revenues and expenses of each department. These reports are useful to management for planning, control, and performance evaluation.
LO2 **Describe and compute departmental gross profit.**	Departmental gross profit is the difference between a department's net sales and cost of goods sold. A departmental income statement showing gross profit can help management identify problems with both the sales prices and purchase prices of its products.

(continued)

LEARNING OBJECTIVES	Key Points to Remember
LO3 **Describe and compute departmental operating income.**	Departmental operating income is the difference between a department's gross profit and its operating expenses. Departmental operating expenses are either direct or indirect. Direct expenses are incurred for the sole benefit of a specific department. Indirect expenses are incurred for the benefit of the business as a whole. Direct expenses are assigned to departments based on actual expenses incurred. Indirect expenses are allocated to departments on various reasonable bases. A departmental income statement showing departmental operating income permits evaluation of both the gross profit and operating expense performance of a department.
LO4 **Describe and compute departmental direct operating margin.**	Departmental direct operating margin is the difference between a department's gross profit and its direct operating expenses. A departmental income statement showing departmental direct operating margin focuses attention on revenues and expenses under the control of a department manager. Such a statement can be very useful for performance evaluation, evaluating contribution to overall operating income, and deciding whether to discontinue a department.

DEMONSTRATION PROBLEM

Kristen Owen and Stephen Kaplan are partners who own OK Cycling. They sell outdoor bicycles and exercise bicycles. They keep accounts and prepare reports on a departmental basis. Direct expenses are assigned and indirect expenses are allocated to departments by various means. Selected operating information for the year ended December 31, 20--, is as follows:

	Outdoor Bicycles	Exercise Bicycles
Net sales	$1,612,500	$1,150,600
Cost of goods sold	935,420	791,800
Direct operating expenses:		
Store clerks' wages expense	45,000	19,500
Truck drivers' wages expense	26,000	10,000
Advertising expense	16,000	20,000
Depreciation expense—delivery equipment	12,000	0
Bad debt expense	12,000	11,700
Other operating expenses	92,080	44,840
Indirect operating expenses:		
Store clerks' wages expense	26,400	14,850
Truck drivers' wages expense	62,800	22,250
Advertising expense	48,200	20,500
Depreciation expense—delivery equipment	13,800	5,700
Store rent expense	21,600	14,400
Other operating expenses	197,360	111,190

REQUIRED

1. Prepare an income statement showing departmental operating income.

2. Prepare another income statement showing departmental and total direct operating margins.

3. For the first statement, determine which department has the higher operating income percentage.

4. For the second statement, determine which department has the higher direct operating margin percentage.

5. Which of the two measures is more meaningful for decision-making purposes? Why?

SOLUTION 1.

OK Cycling
Income Statement
For Year Ended December 31, 20 --

	OUTDOOR BICYCLES	EXERCISE BICYCLES	TOTAL
Net sales	$1,612,500	$1,150,600	$2,763,100
Cost of goods sold	935,420	791,800	1,727,220
Gross profit	$ 677,080	$ 358,800	$1,035,880
Operating expenses:			
Store clerks' wages expense	$ 71,400	$ 34,350	$ 105,750
Truck drivers' wages expense	88,800	32,250	121,050
Advertising expense	64,200	40,500	104,700
Depreciation expense—delivery equipment	25,800	5,700	31,500
Store rent expense	21,600	14,400	36,000
Bad debt expense	12,000	11,700	23,700
Other operating expenses	289,440	156,030	445,470
Total operating expenses	$ 573,240	$ 294,930	$ 868,170
Operating income	$ 103,840	$ 63,870	$ 167,710

SOLUTION 2.

OK Cycling
Income Statement
For Year Ended December 31, 20 --

	OUTDOOR BICYCLES	EXERCISE BICYCLES	TOTAL
Net sales	$1,612,500	$1,150,600	$2,763,100
Cost of goods sold	935,420	791,800	1,727,220
Gross profit	$ 677,080	$ 358,800	$1,035,880
Direct operating expenses:			
Store clerks' wages expense	$ 45,000	$ 19,500	$ 64,500
Truck drivers' wages expense	26,000	10,000	36,000
Advertising expense	16,000	20,000	36,000
Depreciation expense—delivery equipment	12,000	0	12,000
Bad debt expense	12,000	11,700	23,700
Other operating expenses	92,080	44,840	136,920
Total direct operating expenses	$ 203,080	$ 106,040	$ 309,120
Departmental direct operating margin	$ 474,000	$ 252,760	$ 726,760
Indirect operating expenses:			
Store clerks' wages expense			$ 41,250
Truck drivers' wages expense			85,050
Advertising expense			68,700
Depreciation expense—delivery equipment			19,500
Store rent expense			36,000
Other operating expenses			308,550
Total indirect operating expenses			$ 559,050
Operating income			$ 167,710

SOLUTION 3.   Operating income percentage:

For outdoor bicycles:

$$\frac{\text{Operating Income}}{\text{Net Sales}} = \frac{\$103,840}{\$1,612,500} = 6.4\%$$

For exercise bicycles:

$$\frac{\text{Operating Income}}{\text{Net Sales}} = \frac{\$63,870}{\$1,150,600} = 5.6\%$$

Outdoor bicycles has the higher operating income percentage.

SOLUTION 4.   Direct operating margin percentage:

For outdoor bicycles:

$$\frac{\text{Direct Operating Margin}}{\text{Net Sales}} = \frac{\$474,000}{\$1,612,500} = 29.4\%$$

For exercise bicycles:

$$\frac{\text{Direct Operating Margin}}{\text{Net Sales}} = \frac{\$252,760}{\$1,150,600} = 22.0\%$$

Outdoor bicycles has the higher direct operating margin percentage.

SOLUTION 5.   Most accountants believe that the departmental direct operating margin is more meaningful for decision-making purposes than departmental operating income. This is because the direct operating margin takes into account only the direct expenses of operating each department, while departmental operating income is affected by various allocations of indirect operating expenses.

OK Cycling's results demonstrate the importance of the direct operating margin. The answers to requirements 3 and 4 clearly show that the exercise bicycle department is less profitable than the outdoor bicycle department. Yet, the exercise bicycle department is still making a major contribution to the business. Its operating income is $63,870. More importantly, its direct operating margin is $252,760. Without the exercise bicycle department, OK Cycling would be operating at a loss of $85,050 ($167,710, the present total operating income, minus $252,760, the exercise bicycle department's direct operating margin).

KEY TERMS

cost center (996) A department that incurs costs but does not generate revenue.

departmental direct operating margin (1004) The difference between a department's gross profit and its direct operating expenses.

departmental gross profit (997) The difference between a department's net sales and cost of goods sold.

departmental operating expense summary (1002) A summary of the assignment and allocation of departmental operating expenses which shows the classification of each operating expense as direct or indirect, the amount assigned or allocated to each department, and total operating expenses for each department.

departmental operating income (998) The difference between a department's gross profit and its operating expenses.

direct expenses (998) Operating expenses that are incurred for the sole benefit of and are traceable directly to a specific department.

indirect expenses (998) Operating expenses that are incurred for the benefit of the business as a whole.

investment center (996) A department that incurs costs, generates revenue, and determines the assets invested in the department.

profit center (996) A department that incurs costs and generates revenue.

responsibility center (996) A component of a business, such as a department or segment, for which a manager can be held responsible.

SELF-STUDY TEST QUESTIONS

True/False

1. **LO1**   A department that incurs costs and generates revenue is called a profit center.

2. **LO2**   Departmental gross profit is the difference between a department's net sales and operating expenses.

3. **LO3**   Departmental operating income is the difference between a department's gross profit and its operating expenses.

4. **LO3**   Direct expenses are operating expenses incurred for the benefit of the business as a whole and untraceable directly to a specific department.

5. **LO4**   Departmental direct operating margin is the difference between a department's gross profit and its direct operating expenses.

Multiple Choice

1. **LO1**   A department that incurs costs but does not generate revenue is called a(n)
   (a) profit center.
   (b) cost center.
   (c) investment center.
   (d) limited center.

2. **LO2**   The difference between a department's net sales and cost of goods sold is called
   (a) departmental gross profit.
   (b) departmental direct operating income.
   (c) departmental operating income.
   (d) net income.

3. **LO3**   Operating expenses incurred for the sole benefit of and traceable directly to a specific department are called
   (a) budgeted expenses.
   (b) normal expenses.
   (c) indirect expenses.
   (d) direct expenses.

4. **LO3**   The difference between a department's gross profit and its operating expenses is called
   (a) departmental gross profit.
   (b) departmental direct operating margin.
   (c) departmental operating income.
   (d) net income.

5. **LO4**   The difference between a department's gross profit and its direct operating expenses is called
   (a) departmental gross profit.
   (b) departmental direct operating margin.
   (c) departmental operating income.
   (d) net income.

CHECKPOINT ✔

Checkpoint Exercises

1. **LO2**   JW Enterprises is organized into three departments: Department A, Department B, and Department C. At the end of the current year, the sales and cost of goods sold of the three departments are as follows:

	Dept. A	Dept. B	Dept. C
Sales	$46,000	$53,000	$21,000
Cost of goods sold	32,500	33,100	11,090

Compute the gross profit for each department and for the business in total.

2. **LO3**   The sales, gross profit, and condensed total operating expenses of departments A and B for YH Company for the current year are as follows:

	Dept. A	Dept. B
Sales	$120,000	$180,000
Gross profit	42,000	84,000
Total operating expenses	13,200	31,800

Compute the operating income and operating income percentage for each department.

3. **LO4**   The sales, gross profit, and condensed direct operating expenses of departments A and B of Beedles Distributors for the current year are as follows:

	Dept. A	Dept. B
Sales	$300,000	$400,000
Gross profit	140,000	210,000
Direct operating expenses	65,000	90,000

Compute the direct operating margin and direct operating margin percentage for each department.

The answers to the Self-Study Test Questions are at the end of the chapter (page 1022).

APPLYING YOUR KNOWLEDGE

CengageNowv2 provides "Show Me How" videos for selected exercises and problems. Additional resources, such as Excel templates for completing selected exercises and problems, are available for download from the companion website at Cengage.com.

REVIEW QUESTIONS

LO1   1.   For what purposes are departmental reports useful to management?

LO1   2.   What are the differences between a cost center, a profit center and an investment center?

LO2   3.   In what two ways can the information necessary to compute departmental gross profit be accumulated?

LO3   4.   What is the difference between direct and indirect operating expenses?

LO3   5.   On what basis are direct expenses assigned to departments?

LO3   6.   On what basis are indirect expenses allocated to departments?

LO3	7.	What information is contained in a departmental operating expense summary?
LO3	8.	Why must management be cautious in interpreting departmental operating income results?
LO4	9.	Distinguish between departmental gross profit, departmental operating income, and departmental direct operating margin.
LO4	10.	In what ways can an income statement showing departmental direct operating margin be used by management?

SERIES A EXERCISES

In solving all Exercises and Problems, round all percentages to one decimal place.

E 25-1A   (LO2)
✓ Gross profit, running shoes dept.: $12,600

GROSS PROFIT SECTION OF DEPARTMENTAL INCOME STATEMENT Bill Walters and Alice Jennings are partners in a business called Walters and Jennings Sportswear that sells athletic footwear. They have organized the business on a departmental basis as follows: running shoes, walking shoes, and specialty shoes. At the end of the first year of operation, the sales and cost of goods sold for the three departments are as follows:

	Running Shoes	Walking Shoes	Specialty Shoes
Sales	$36,000	$42,000	$12,000
Cost of goods sold	23,400	23,520	7,680

Prepare the gross profit section of a departmental income statement for the year ended December 31, 20--. Show the gross profit for each department and for the business in total.

E 25-2A   (LO3)
✓ Rent expense, dept. A: $9,360

ALLOCATING OPERATING EXPENSE—SQUARE FEET Weaverling Company rents 10,000 square feet of store space for $36,000 per year. The amount of square footage by department is as follows:

Department A:	2,600 sq. ft.
Department B:	2,400 sq. ft.
Department C:	1,800 sq. ft.
Department D:	3,200 sq. ft.

Allocate the annual rent expense among the four departments on the basis of relative square feet of floor space occupied.

E 25-3A   (LO3)
✓ Advertising expense, deluxe: $5,600

ALLOCATING OPERATING EXPENSE—RELATIVE NET SALES Hayley Doll owns a car stereo store. She has divided her store into three departments. Net sales for the month of July are as follows:

Deluxe:	$33,600
Standard:	38,400
Economy:	48,000

Advertising expense for July was $20,000.
Allocate the advertising expense among the three departments on the basis of relative net sales.

E 25-4A (LO3)
✓ Truck expense, dept. 1: $5,760

ALLOCATING OPERATING EXPENSE—MILES DRIVEN Mercado Lopez owns a furniture store that offers free delivery of merchandise delivered within the local area. Mileage records for the three sales departments are as follows:

Department 1:	36,000 miles
Department 2:	48,000 miles
Department 3:	16,000 miles

The cost of using the truck for the last year, including depreciation, was $16,000. Allocate the cost of the truck among the three departments on the basis of miles driven.

E 25-5A (LO3)
✓ Operating income, dept. A: $23,000

COMPUTING OPERATING INCOME The sales, cost of goods sold, and total operating expenses of departments A and B of Ash Company are as follows:

	Dept. A	Dept. B
Sales	$200,000	$160,000
Cost of goods sold	146,000	115,000
Total operating expenses	31,000	22,000

Compute the departmental operating income for each department.

E 25-6A (LO4)
✓ Direct operating margin, dept. A: $75,000

DEPARTMENTAL DIRECT OPERATING MARGIN AND DIRECT OPERATING MARGIN PERCENTAGE The sales, gross profit, and condensed direct and indirect operating expenses of departments A and B of Wei Zhao International are as follows:

	Dept. A	Dept. B	Total
Sales	$300,000	$400,000	$700,000
Gross profit	95,000	180,000	275,000
Direct operating expenses	20,000	72,000	92,000
Indirect operating expenses			81,000

Compute the departmental direct operating margin and direct operating margin percentage for each department.

SERIES A PROBLEMS

P 25-7A (LO2/3)
✓ 2. Gross profit %, commercial sales: 40%

INCOME STATEMENT WITH DEPARTMENTAL GROSS PROFIT AND OPERATING INCOME Thomas and Hill Distributors has divided its business into two departments: commercial sales and industrial sales. The following information is provided for the year ended December 31, 20--:

Net sales, commercial sales department	$630,000
Net sales, industrial sales department	470,000
Cost of goods sold, commercial sales department	378,000
Cost of goods sold, industrial sales department	188,000
Warehouse wages expense	99,400
Truck drivers' wages expense	88,200
Advertising expense	66,000
Warehouse lease expense	30,000
Depreciation expense—delivery equipment	11,000
Other operating expenses	115,000

REQUIRED

1. Prepare an income statement showing departmental gross profit and total operating income.
2. Calculate departmental gross profit percentages.

P 25-8A   (LO2/3)
✓ 2. Operating income %, breads: 10.2%

INCOME STATEMENT WITH DEPARTMENTAL OPERATING INCOME AND TOTAL OPERATING INCOME Alexa Cole owns a business called Alexa's Bakery. She has divided her business into two departments: breads and pastries. The following information is provided for the fiscal year ended June 30, 20--:

	Breads	Pastries
Net sales	$172,000	$119,000
Cost of goods sold	92,400	60,500
Wages expense	30,000	20,000
Advertising expense	11,000	8,000
Other operating expenses	21,000	14,000

REQUIRED

1. Prepare an income statement showing departmental operating income and total operating income.
2. Calculate departmental operating expense and operating income percentages.

P 25-9A   (LO2/3/4)
✓ 2. Direct operating margin %, commercial property: 15.4%

INCOME STATEMENT WITH DEPARTMENTAL DIRECT OPERATING MARGIN AND TOTAL OPERATING INCOME Durwood Thomas operates the business Thomas Security that sells security equipment for commercial property and residential homes. The following information is provided for the year ended December 31, 20--:

	Commercial Property	Residential Homes
Net sales	$465,000	$135,000
Cost of goods sold	279,250	54,000
Direct operating expenses:		
Advertising expense	35,000	20,000
Store clerks' wages expense	30,000	18,000
Truck drivers' wages expense	15,000	15,000
Bad debt expense	8,000	3,000
Depreciation expense—delivery equipment	6,000	4,000
Other operating expenses	20,000	10,000
Indirect operating expenses:		
Store clerks' wages expense		$10,000
Advertising expense		15,000
Store rent expense		20,000
Other operating expenses		10,000

REQUIRED

1. Prepare an income statement showing departmental direct operating margin and total operating income.
2. Calculate departmental direct operating margin percentages.

P 25-10A   (LO4)
✓ 1. Operating income, depts.
   A & C only: $5,000

WHETHER TO DISCONTINUE A DEPARTMENT Williams and Lloyd Company is trying to decide whether to discontinue department B. Operating results for the year just ended for each of the company's three departments and for the entire operation are as follows:

	Dept. A	Dept. B	Dept. C	Total
Net sales	$380,000	$260,000	$290,000	$930,000
Cost of goods sold	210,000	140,000	160,000	510,000
Gross profit	$170,000	$120,000	$130,000	$420,000
Direct operating expenses	100,000	90,000	80,000	270,000
Departmental direct operating margin	$ 70,000	$ 30,000	$ 50,000	$150,000
Indirect operating expenses	40,000	35,000	40,000	115,000
Operating income (loss)	$ 30,000	$ (5,000)	$ 10,000	$ 35,000

REQUIRED

1. Prepare an additional column that combines departments A and C only.
2. Review all data and decide if department B should be discontinued. Defend your decision.

SERIES B EXERCISES

E 25-1B   (LO2)
✓ Gross profit, letters dept.: $1,600

GROSS PROFIT SECTION OF DEPARTMENTAL INCOME STATEMENT Nicole Lawrence and Josh Doyle are partners in a business that sells cheerleading uniforms. They have organized the business, called L and D Uniforms, on a departmental basis as follows: letters, sweaters, and skirts. At the end of the first year of operation, the sales and cost of goods sold for the three departments are as follows:

	Letters	Sweaters	Skirts
Sales	$3,000	$12,000	$8,000
Cost of goods sold	1,400	5,900	4,750

Prepare the gross profit section of a departmental income statement for the year ended December 31, 20--. Show the gross profit for each department and for the business in total.

E 25-2B   (LO3)
✓ Rent expense, dept. A: $9,600

ALLOCATING OPERATING EXPENSE—SQUARE FEET Johnson Company rents 5,000 square feet of store space for $40,000 per year. The amount of square footage by department is as follows:

Department A: 1,200 sq. ft.
Department B: 1,400 sq. ft.
Department C: 1,500 sq. ft.
Department D: 900 sq. ft.

Allocate the annual rent expense among the four departments on the basis of relative square feet of floor space occupied.

E 25-3B **(LO3)**

✓ Advertising expense, football: $2,000

ALLOCATING OPERATING EXPENSE—RELATIVE NET SALES Amelia Diaz owns a sporting goods store. She has divided her store into three departments. Net sales for the month of July are as follows:

Football: $10,000
Basketball: 6,000
Baseball: 9,000

Advertising expense for July was $5,000.
Allocate the advertising expense among the three departments on the basis of relative net sales.

E 25-4B **(LO3)**

✓ Truck expense, dept. 1: $800

ALLOCATING OPERATING EXPENSE—MILES DRIVEN Herbert Quiong owns a furniture store that offers free delivery of merchandise delivered within the local area. Mileage records for the three sales departments are as follows:

Department 1:   4,000 miles
Department 2:   13,000 miles
Department 3:   8,000 miles

The cost of using the truck for the last year, including depreciation, was $5,000.
Allocate the cost of the truck among the three departments on the basis of miles driven.

E 25-5B **(LO3)**

✓ Operating income, dept. A: $15,000

COMPUTING OPERATING INCOME The sales, cost of goods sold, and total operating expenses of departments A and B of Barker Company are as follows:

	Dept. A	Dept. B
Sales	$180,000	$152,000
Cost of goods sold	138,000	118,000
Total operating expenses	27,000	16,000

Compute the departmental operating income for each department.

E 25-6B **(LO4)**

✓ Direct operating margin, dept. A: $75,000

DEPARTMENTAL DIRECT OPERATING MARGIN AND DIRECT OPERATING MARGIN PERCENTAGE The sales, gross profit, and condensed direct and indirect operating expenses of departments A and B of Robin Sun Enterprises are as follows:

	Dept. A	Dept. B	Total
Sales	$300,000	$400,000	$700,000
Gross profit	110,000	180,000	290,000
Direct operating expenses	35,000	72,000	107,000
Indirect operating expenses			78,000

Compute the departmental direct operating margin and direct operating margin percentage for each department.

SERIES B PROBLEMS

P 25-7B   (LO2/3)
✓ 2. Gross profit %, retail sales: 44%

INCOME STATEMENT WITH DEPARTMENTAL GROSS PROFIT AND OPERATING INCOME Bacon and Hand Distributors has divided its business into two departments: retail sales and wholesale sales. The following information is provided for the year ended December 31, 20--:

Net sales, retail sales department	$570,000
Net sales, wholesale sales department	830,000
Cost of goods sold, retail sales department	319,200
Cost of goods sold, wholesale sales department	398,400
Warehouse wages expense	110,000
Truck drivers' wages expense	90,500
Advertising expense	70,000
Warehouse lease expense	40,000
Depreciation expense—delivery equipment	12,000
Other operating expenses	130,000

REQUIRED

1. Prepare an income statement showing departmental gross profit and total operating income.

2. Calculate departmental gross profit percentages.

P 25-8B   (LO2/3)
✓ 2. Operating income %, domestic yarn: 10.5%

INCOME STATEMENT WITH DEPARTMENTAL OPERATING INCOME AND TOTAL OPERATING INCOME Sonya McDowell owns a business called The Knitting Chamber. She has divided her business into two departments: domestic yarn and international yarn. The following information is provided for the fiscal year ended June 30, 20--:

	Domestic Yarn	International Yarn
Net sales	$60,000	$40,000
Cost of goods sold	37,200	28,000
Wages expense	10,000	5,000
Advertising expense	2,500	1,500
Other operating expenses	4,000	1,000

REQUIRED

1. Prepare an income statement showing departmental operating income and total operating income.

2. Calculate departmental operating expense and operating income percentages.

P 25-9B   (LO2/3/4)
✓ 2. Direct operating margin %, furniture: 7.2%

INCOME STATEMENT WITH DEPARTMENTAL DIRECT OPERATING MARGIN AND TOTAL OPERATING INCOME Tom Peterson owns the business Peterson's Furniture and Appliances. The following information is provided for the year ended December 31, 20--:

	Furniture Department	Appliances Department
Net sales	$390,000	$810,000
Cost of goods sold	234,000	405,000
Direct operating expenses:		
Advertising expense	30,000	60,000
Store clerks' wages expense	40,000	90,000

	Furniture Department	Appliances Department
Truck drivers' wages expense	$35,000	$65,000
Bad debt expense	4,000	9,000
Depreciation expense—delivery equipment	4,000	8,000
Other operating expenses	15,000	50,000
Indirect operating expenses:		
Store clerks' wages expense	$20,000	
Advertising expense	15,000	
Store rent expense	50,000	
Other operating expenses	25,000	

REQUIRED

1. Prepare an income statement showing departmental direct operating margin and total operating income.

2. Calculate departmental direct operating margin percentages.

P 25-10B   (LO4)
✓ 1. Operating income, depts. B & C only: $20,000

WHETHER TO DISCONTINUE A DEPARTMENT Mueller and Kenington Company is trying to decide whether to discontinue department A. Operating results for the year just ended for each of the company's three departments and for the entire operation are as follows:

	Dept. A	Dept. B	Dept. C	Total
Net sales	$680,000	$730,000	$690,000	$2,100,000
Cost of goods sold	400,000	380,000	360,000	1,140,000
Gross profit	$280,000	$350,000	$330,000	$ 960,000
Direct operating expenses	230,000	240,000	210,000	680,000
Departmental direct operating margin	$ 50,000	$110,000	$120,000	$ 280,000
Indirect operating expenses	70,000	70,000	70,000	210,000
Operating income (loss)	$ (20,000)	$ 40,000	$ 50,000	$ 70,000

REQUIRED

1. Prepare an additional column that combines departments B and C only.

2. Review all data and decide if department A should be discontinued. Defend your decision.

CHECK LIST
☐ Managing
☐ Planning
☐ Drafting
☐ Break
☐ Revising
☐ Managing

MANAGING YOUR WRITING

Two department heads are engaging in an argument. The head of department A argues that department A makes a greater contribution to profits, having produced a higher operating income for three years. The business probably would be better off if department B were discontinued. In fact, department income statements from the last three years show department A had higher operating income than department B. Department B had an operating loss in two of the three years.

Write a memo addressing the following two issues:

1. What are the proper accounting measures to use to determine which department is making a greater contribution to the profits of the business?

2. What are the proper accounting measures to use to decide whether to discontinue one of the departments?

ETHICS

ETHICS CASE

Melanie Sanders and Joyce O'Dell were department heads at Hobgood's Toy and Hobby Store. They had been friends for a long time. Mr. Hobgood, the owner of the store, let the department heads make all decisions relating to the store's operations. During the summer the hobby department usually had a higher gross profit, but during the holidays the toy department usually caught up. This year the toy department wasn't doing well at all, mainly because a new discount toy store had opened less than a mile away. In early December, Melanie, the toy department manager, asked Joyce if she would mind charging all the remaining year's advertising and shipping expenses to the hobby department. Melanie went on to explain that she was afraid Mr. Hobgood would get upset if he found out the toy department wasn't doing well during the last quarter. She said she had a plan for next year to earn more revenue but was vague on what it involved. Joyce knew the hobby department's year-to-date earnings were above average but she felt uncomfortable with what Melanie had asked her to do.

1. What is your reaction to Melanie's idea?
2. If Joyce decides to let Melanie charge all advertising and shipping expenses to the hobby department in December, what impact will it have on the financial statements?
3. Write a short paragraph stating both the short- and long-run implications of Melanie's idea.
4. In groups of three or four, make a list of some suggestions to help Hobgood's Toy and Hobby Store earn more revenue.

MASTERY PROBLEM

✓ 2b. Direct operating margin %, grocery: 11.0%

Bob's Acme Supermarket has been in operation for many years, offering high-quality groceries, produce, and meat at reasonable prices. Accounting records are maintained on a departmental basis with assignment of direct expenses and allocation of indirect expenses through the use of various procedures. Selected operating information for the year ended December 31, 20--, is as follows:

	Grocery	Meat	Produce	Total
Net sales	$2,104,890	$660,500	$345,800	$3,111,190
Cost of goods sold	1,683,912	462,350	207,480	2,353,742
Direct operating expenses:				
Store clerks' wages expense	125,000	58,000	38,500	221,500
Advertising expense	25,000	38,500	18,400	81,900
Depreciation expense—store equipment	10,800	15,000	12,000	37,800
Other operating expenses	28,200	28,540	35,600	92,340
Indirect operating expenses:				
Store clerks' wages expense	12,000	5,000	4,000	21,000
Advertising expense	7,000	2,000	1,000	10,000
Depreciation expense—store equipment	35,000	10,000	5,000	50,000
Store rent	60,000	20,000	20,000	100,000
Other operating expenses	25,500	4,500	18,450	48,450

REQUIRED

1. (a) Prepare an income statement showing departmental operating income.
   (b) Compute the gross profit percentage and operating income percentage for each department (round to the nearest tenth of a percent).
2. (a) Prepare an income statement showing departmental and total direct operating margins.
   (b) Compute the departmental direct operating margin percentage for each department (round to the nearest tenth of a percent).
3. Should Bob be concerned about the profitability of the three departments? Should any of the departments be discontinued?

CHALLENGE PROBLEM

The results of the operating activities of Kobe Company for the current year are as follows:

	Dept. A	Dept. B	Dept. C	Total
Net sales	$590,000	$735,000	$450,000	$1,775,000
Cost of goods sold	365,000	545,750	267,000	1,177,750
Gross margin	$225,000	$189,250	$183,000	$ 597,250
Direct operating expenses	127,000	97,000	209,000	433,000
Direct operating margin	$ 98,000	$ 92,250	$ (26,000)	$ 164,250
Indirect operating expenses	61,000	52,000	20,000	133,000
Operating income (loss)	$ 37,000	$ 40,250	$ (46,000)	$ 31,250

Based on these results, Kobe is considering discontinuing department C and establishing a new department D. The estimated revenues and expenses of the new department are as follows:

	Dept. D
Net sales	$480,000
Cost of goods sold	270,000
Direct operating expenses	185,000

In addition, the proposed change will cause total indirect operating expenses to increase by $22,000.

REQUIRED

Determine whether Kobe should discontinue department C and establish department D.

ANSWERS TO SELF-STUDY TEST QUESTIONS

True/False

1. T   **2.** F (net sales − cost of goods sold)   **3.** T   **4.** F (traceable)   **5.** T

Multiple Choice

1. b   **2.** a   **3.** d   **4.** c   **5.** b

Checkpoint Exercises

1.

	Dept. A	Dept. B	Dept. C	Total
Sales	$46,000	$53,000	$21,000	$120,000
Cost of goods sold	32,500	33,100	11,090	76,690
Gross profit	$13,500	$19,900	$ 9,910	$ 43,310

2.

	Dept. A	Dept. B
Gross profit	$42,000	$84,000
Total operating expenses	13,200	31,800
Operating income	$28,800	$52,200

Operating income percentages:
  Dept. A: $28,800/$120,000 = 24%
  Dept. B: $52,200/$180,000 = 29%

3.

	Dept. A	Dept. B
Gross profit	$140,000	$210,000
Direct operating expenses	65,000	90,000
Direct operating margin	$ 75,000	$120,000

Direct operating margin percentages:
  Dept. A: $75,000/$300,000 = 25%
  Dept. B: $120,000/$400,000 = 30%

Chapter 26 Manufacturing Accounting: The Job Order Cost System

Have you ever been to an upscale restaurant or hotel, or perhaps seen one on television? How about a stroll through the lobbies of some Las Vegas hotels, or a visit to a Hard Rock hotel or restaurant? In each of these places, did you notice how the lighting provides much more than "light"—it is part of the design and image of these businesses. To obtain these fixtures, a hotel or restaurant might turn to Lusive Décor. Lusive, founded in 2002 and based in Los Angeles, is a leading designer and manufacturer of decorative, custom lighting for companies such as Ritz Carlton, Four Seasons, Hilton, Hyatt, Marriott, and many others throughout the United States. It sources materials locally and from places like Italy, Austria, Brazil, and India.

An interesting question for a company like Lusive Décor is how to cost and price the special orders it receives from customers for custom-designed lighting. A client might want a few unique pieces or 100, 1,000, or even 5,000 fixtures for a hotel or chain of hotels. What does it cost to design and produce these orders, and what should Lusive charge for them? In this chapter, you will learn about a job-order costing system that can help answer these questions. This system enables us to track production costs by (job) order and provides information to help determine what price to charge.

LEARNING OBJECTIVES

Careful study of this chapter should enable you to:

LO1 Describe the three manufacturing costs.

LO2 Describe the three inventories of a manufacturing business.

LO3 Describe and illustrate how manufacturing costs and inventories affect the financial statements of a manufacturing business.

LO4 Define and describe how to operate a job order cost accounting system.

LO5 Describe a process cost accounting system.

In the final two chapters of this book, we will study how to account for a manufacturing business. From an accounting standpoint, the key difference between a manufacturing and a merchandising business involves inventory. The manufacturer makes the items it sells; the merchandiser purchases inventory in final form for resale. This makes accounting for a manufacturer more complicated. Special cost accounting systems are needed to accumulate the costs of manufacturing the products. Multiple inventory accounts must be kept. Both the income statement and balance sheet are affected by these accounting changes.

LO1	Manufacturing Costs

Describe the three manufacturing costs.

The costs incurred to manufacture a product can be classified into three primary elements of manufacturing cost:

1. Materials
2. Labor
3. Factory overhead

As illustrated in Figure 26-1, these costs come together in a conversion process that produces completed products, commonly called finished goods.

FIGURE 26-1 The Manufacturing Process

Materials

Various materials are needed to manufacture a product. A manufacturer of automobiles requires items such as sheet metal, bar steel, plastic, fabric, and tires. A manufacturer of electric guitars requires wood, plastic, electrical wire, magnets, nuts, and screws. In many instances, the only distinction between materials and finished goods is their relationship to a particular manufacturer. The finished goods of one manufacturer may be the materials of another. For example, flour is finished goods to a miller but materials to a baker. Similarly, silver may be finished goods to a mining company but materials to a manufacturer of silverware. Materials used in manufacturing are classified as:

1. Direct materials
2. Indirect materials

Direct materials enter into and become a major part of the finished product. Thus, the leather and linings used in the manufacture of shoes are direct materials. Similarly, the sheet metal, bar steel, fabric, and many other materials used in the manufacture of an automobile are direct materials.

Indirect materials are used in the manufacturing process but do not become a major part of the finished product. Thus, oil and grease used in the operation of machinery are indirect materials. Such materials are often called factory supplies. Indirect materials also may include inexpensive items such as nails, screws, and washers. These items may become a part of the finished product, but their small cost is most easily accounted for as part of indirect materials.

Labor

Wages and salaries paid to factory workers and supervisors are part of the cost of manufacturing a product. These wages and salaries are classified as:

1. Direct labor
2. Indirect labor

Direct labor includes the wages of employees who are directly involved in converting materials into finished goods. Such workers may do assembly work or operate factory machinery. These wages are charged directly to the cost of the products being manufactured.

Indirect labor includes the wages and salaries of employees who devote their time to supervision or to work of a general nature. Such workers may include superintendents, inspectors, timekeepers, receiving clerks, and janitors. The costs of these employees cannot be charged directly to the cost of the products being manufactured. They must be included in the indirect costs of the factory operation.

Factory Overhead

All manufacturing costs other than direct materials and direct labor are classified as factory overhead. This group of costs is sometimes described as manufacturing overhead, indirect manufacturing cost, or factory burden. Factory overhead consists of:

1. Indirect materials
2. Indirect labor
3. Other factory overhead

Indirect materials and indirect labor have already been discussed. Other factory overhead includes a variety of items, such as:

- Depreciation of factory buildings and equipment
- Repairs to factory buildings and equipment
- Insurance on factory buildings and equipment
- Property taxes on factory buildings and equipment
- Heat, light, and power

LO2   Inventories

Describe the three inventories of a manufacturing business.

In accounting for a merchandising business, we used only a single inventory account, Merchandise Inventory. Because a manufacturing business acquires materials in one form and converts them into a different form for final sale, we need three inventory accounts:

1. Materials Inventory
2. Work in Process Inventory
3. Finished Goods Inventory

Materials Inventory consists of the materials acquired to be used in production. This account includes both direct and indirect materials.

Work in Process Inventory consists of products on which work has been started but is not yet finished at the end of the accounting period. Materials, labor, and overhead costs of producing a product are accumulated in this account until the product is completed.

Finished Goods Inventory contains products that have been completed and are ready for sale. All materials, labor, and overhead costs of completed products are accumulated in this account until the products are sold.

Flow of Manufacturing Costs

The flow of the three manufacturing costs through the three inventory accounts is illustrated in Figure 26-2. The figure shows how direct materials and direct labor flow directly into Work in Process. Indirect materials and indirect labor become part of Factory Overhead, which flows into Work in Process. All manufacturing costs then flow from Work in Process into Finished Goods when the manufacturing process is completed.

LEARNING KEY 🔑

Direct materials and direct labor go directly into Work in Process. Indirect materials and indirect labor go through Factory Overhead, and then into Work in Process.

CHECKPOINT ✓

Complete Checkpoint-1 on page 1046 to test your basic understanding of LO2.

FIGURE 26-2 Flow of Manufacturing Costs

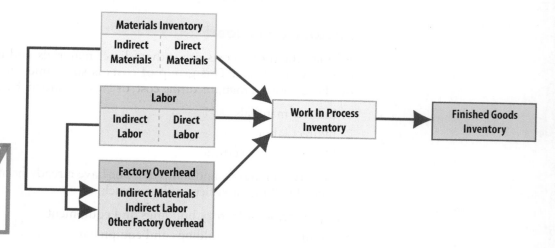

Financial Statement Effects

Describe and illustrate how manufacturing costs and inventories affect the financial statements of a manufacturing business.

The financial statements of a manufacturing business are very similar to those of a merchandiser. The main differences are in the cost of goods sold section of the income statement and the inventories on the balance sheet.

Income Statement

The key difference between the manufacturing and merchandising company income statements is highlighted in Figure 26-3. The purchases made by a merchandiser are the goods that eventually are sold. In contrast, the purchases made by a manufacturer are merely purchases of materials. As described in the first section of this chapter, the cost of manufacturing a product includes not only materials, but also labor and overhead. Thus, *cost of goods manufactured* on the manufacturer's income statement replaces *purchases* on the merchandiser's income statement.

LEARNING KEY 🔑

To determine cost of goods sold, purchases on the merchandiser's income statement are replaced by cost of goods manufactured on the manufacturer's income statement.

FIGURE 26-3 Cost of Goods Sold Sections

Merchandising Company Partial Income Statement	
Cost of goods sold:	
Merchandise inventory, January 1, 20--	$10,000
Purchases	42,000
Merchandise available for sale	$52,000
Merchandise inventory, December 31, 20--	8,000
Cost of goods sold	$44,000

Manufacturing Company Partial Income Statement	
Cost of goods sold:	
Finished goods inventory, January 1, 20--	$10,000
Cost of goods manufactured	42,000
Goods available for sale	$52,000
Finished goods inventory, December 31, 20--	8,000
Cost of goods sold	$44,000

The cost of goods sold section of the manufacturer's income statement is commonly supplemented by a schedule of cost of goods manufactured (see Figure 26-4). This schedule shows:

1. Beginning work in process.
2. Materials, labor, and overhead costs added to work in process during the period.
3. Ending work in process.
4. Cost of goods manufactured (cost of goods completed during the period). Note that this $42,000 is the same amount shown in Figure 26-3.

The *cost of direct materials used* of $15,500 is calculated in almost the same way the cost of goods sold is calculated in a merchandiser's income statement. Beginning inventory of materials plus purchases equals materials available. This amount less the

FIGURE 26-4 Schedule of Cost of Goods Manufactured

1 Work in process, January 1, 20--			$ 6,000
Direct materials:			
Materials inventory, January 1, 20--	$ 3,000		
Materials purchases	15,800		
Materials available	$18,800		
Materials inventory, December 31, 20--	2,500		
Cost of materials used	$16,300		
Less indirect materials included in overhead	800		
Cost of direct materials used		$15,500	
2 Direct labor		16,500	
Overhead		8,000	
Total manufacturing costs			40,000
Total work in process during the period			$46,000
3 Work in process, December 31, 20--			4,000
4 Cost of goods manufactured			$42,000

> If no indirect materials from the materials inventory are charged to overhead, it is not necessary to subtract the indirect materials cost in computing the cost of direct materials used.

ending inventory of materials equals cost of materials used. Some of these materials were indirect and charged to overhead. So the indirect materials cost is subtracted to compute the cost of direct materials used.

As shown in T account form below, the cost of goods manufactured of $42,000 represents:

(1) The amount *transferred out* of work in process during the period.

(2) The amount *added* to finished goods during the period.

Balance Sheet

A manufacturer's balance sheet has three inventory accounts rather than the single merchandise inventory account used by a merchandiser. The current assets sections of the merchandiser's and manufacturer's balance sheets might appear as shown in Figure 26-5. The three manufacturing company inventories are listed in decreasing order of liquidity, with finished goods first and materials last.

FIGURE 26-5 Current Assets Sections

Merchandising Company	
Current assets:	
Cash	$17,000
Accounts receivable (net)	12,000
Merchandise inventory	8,000
Supplies	2,300
Total current assets	$39,300

Manufacturing Company		
Current assets:		
Cash		$17,000
Accounts receivable (net)		12,000
Inventories:		
Finished goods	$8,000	
Work in process	4,000	
Materials	2,500	14,500
Supplies		2,300
Total current assets		$45,800

> **CHECKPOINT** ✔
>
> Complete Checkpoint-2 on page 1046 to test your basic understanding of LO3.

LO4	**Job Order Cost Accounting**

Define and describe how to operate a job order cost accounting system.

A cost accounting system is a system for accumulating detailed information about the cost of producing a product. Product cost information is needed for the following three purposes:

1. To assist in setting selling prices. A product's selling price must be sufficient to provide a gross profit and contribute to net income.
2. To assist in controlling production costs. If the actual costs of producing a product exceed the planned costs, management can take corrective action.
3. To assist in determining the net income or loss. When products are manufactured, the manufacturing costs must be accumulated to determine inventories, cost of goods sold, and net income or loss.

The two basic types of inventory cost accounting systems are:

1. Job order cost system.
2. Process cost system.

A job order cost system provides a separate record of the cost of producing each individual product or group of products. If products are made to customers' orders or in separately identifiable "lots" or "batches," a job order cost system is appropriate. A printing shop, consulting firm, or custom light fixture manufacturer like Lusive Décor in the chapter opener would use such a system.

A BROADER VIEW

Job Cost Systems—So Common You Find Them by Accident

Throughout this book, we have seen the accounting side of many items we regularly encounter in our everyday lives: managing our checking account, deductions for taxes on our paychecks, purchases we make with our credit cards, and use of promissory notes to borrow money. In this chapter, we see yet another accounting item that is far more common than we probably realize—the job order cost system.

Presented on the right is Job Order 75820 used by Warwick Garage to repair Samantha Moore's car. If you ever had your car repaired or serviced, even something as minor as an oil change, you probably were part of a job order. In fact, any repairs or servicing of any kind—on TVs, computers, lawn tractors, etc.—usually are based on a job order system. You can see accounting issues almost everywhere. It is indeed an important language to learn.

Warwick Garage
1187 Atwood Dr.
Cincinnati, OH 45211

Hours of Operation
Monday – Friday 7:30 a.m. to 6:00 p.m.
Saturday: 8:00 a.m. to 5:00 p.m.
Closed Sundays

Customer Name: Samantha Moore
Address: 2525 Broadwell Road, Cincinnati, OH 45826
Phone: (513) 555-1212

Color	Make/Model	Date dropped off	Date ready	Job Order #
Silver/Gray	Hyundai/Accent	09/12/2019	09/15/2019	75820

Details of work	AMOUNT
Install front brake pads	$ 79.99
Install rear brake pads	$ 79.99
Change oil	$ 25.99
Labor	$ 152.95
Subtotal	$338.92
Taxes	$ 11.16
Mechanic: Greg Anderson	
	$350.08

A **process cost system** accumulates manufacturing costs by process, such as cutting, painting, or finishing. Each unit of product passing through the process during a period of time is assigned a share of the costs. A business that manufactures cement, chemicals, or flour would use such a system.

Perpetual Inventories

A cost accounting system uses perpetual inventories. To understand the journal entries and flow of information in a cost accounting system, we need to recall how a perpetual inventory system works.

Chapter 13 demonstrated how a perpetual inventory system works for a merchandising business. The merchandise inventory account is increased for each purchase and decreased for each sale.

A manufacturing business has three inventory accounts: Materials, Work in Process, and Finished Goods. Inventory costs flow through all three of these accounts. This makes a manufacturing business's perpetual inventory system more complex than that of a merchandising business. The following four inventory movements and journal entries are illustrated in Figure 26-6:

> **LEARNING KEY** 🔑
>
> Manufacturing costs must be tracked through all three of the inventory accounts.

FIGURE 26-6 Flow of Costs Through Manufacturing Inventory Accounts

INVENTORY MOVEMENTS	JOURNAL ENTRIES
1 Materials are purchased.	Increase Materials Increase Accounts Payable
2 Materials are put into the manufacturing process.	Decrease Materials Increase Work in Process
3 Product is completed.	Decrease Work in Process Increase Finished Goods
4 Completed product is sold.	Decrease Finished Goods Increase Cost of Goods Sold

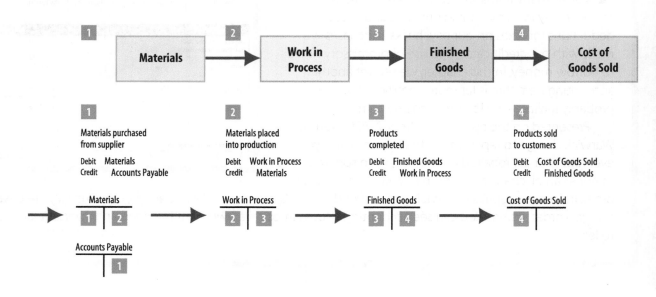

Accounting for Materials

When materials are purchased, their cost is debited to Materials. If materials costing $1,300 are purchased on account, the following journal entry is made:

4	Materials		1	3	0	0	00									4
5	Accounts Payable									1	3	0	0	00		5
6	Purchased materials on account															6

The materials account in the general ledger is a control account. A separate account for each type of material is kept in a subsidiary ledger called a materials ledger or stores ledger. Each subsidiary account shows the quantity and cost of the material received and issued and the resulting balance.

Materials are issued from the storeroom to production based on a form called a materials requisition. This form is both an authorization to the storekeeper to issue materials and a source document showing the movement of materials. Figure 26-7 illustrates one form of materials requisition.

FIGURE 26-7 Materials Requisition

MATERIALS REQUISITION

Requested by: **Susan Korman**   Req. No. **439**

Date: **January 19, 20--**   Approved: **C.D.**

Charge to: **Job No. 319 Materials**

Item No.	Description	Quantity	Unit Cost	Total Cost
SP10	16" Plastic Truck Body	500	$4.20	$2,100.00

Received By: *S.K.*   Date Received: **January 19, 20--**

If these are direct materials, the following journal entry is made:

The job number is placed after Work in Process.

8	Work in Process (Job No. 319)		2	1	0	0	00									8
9	Materials									2	1	0	0	00		9
10	Issued direct materials to production															10

Note that the debit to Work in Process also indicates the job to which the materials are charged. This job is in the job cost ledger, a subsidiary ledger for Work in Process. This ledger is explained later in the chapter.

Figure 26-8 shows Job No. 319 in the job cost ledger in T account form with $2,100 of direct materials charged to it.

FIGURE 26-8 Job No. 319 with Direct Materials

Job No. 319

Direct Materials, $2,100 ————▶ 2,100

Materials requisitions also are used to issue indirect materials. Since indirect materials are part of overhead, the following journal entry is made to issue $250 of indirect materials to production:

13	Factory Overhead	2 5 0 00		13
14	Materials		2 5 0 00	14
15	Issued indirect materials to production			15

Notice that no job number is indicated for these overhead costs. This is because overhead costs relate to many different jobs. These and other overhead costs are accumulated and will be applied to specific jobs. This application process is illustrated later in the chapter.

Accounting for Labor

Chapter 8 showed how to account for employee earnings and payroll deductions. A job order cost accounting system uses the same procedures, except more detail is involved. The earnings of workers whose services are direct labor are charged to the jobs on which they worked. The earnings of workers whose services are indirect labor are charged to the proper factory overhead accounts. This requires keeping a record of the time worked and labor cost incurred on each job. One way of doing so is to require the direct labor employees to complete a **daily time sheet** or **time ticket** like the one in Figure 26-9.

In businesses with computer-based timekeeping systems, a record of time and labor costs on each job can be generated automatically. Employees' barcode time cards (Chapter 8, Figure 8-2) are inserted into a computer at their workstations. The labor costs are then distributed by the computer system.

FIGURE 26-9 Daily Time Sheet

ToyJoy
Manufacturing Co.

DAILY TIME SHEET

Name __Charles Rhome__   Date __1/27/--__

Job No.	Start	Stop	Hours Reg.	Hours O.T.	Equiv. Hours	Rate	Amount Earned
319	8:00	12:00	4		4	10.00	40.00
319	1:00	5:00	4		4	10.00	40.00
							80.00

Approved __B.R.__

Time sheets normally are summarized by days, weeks, or months to provide the direct labor cost for each job. This summary is used to make the journal entry for the direct labor costs incurred. Based solely on the time sheet in Figure 26-9, the entry is as follows:

4		Work in Process (Job No. 319)	8	0	00				4
5		Wages Payable				8	0	00	5
6		Incurred direct labor costs							6

The debit to Work in Process also indicates the job to which the direct labor is charged.

Figure 26-10 shows Job No. 319 in T account form with $2,100 of direct materials and $80 of direct labor charged to it.

FIGURE 26-10 Job No. 319 with Direct Materials and Direct Labor

Employees who perform indirect labor also use time sheets. Since indirect labor is part of overhead, the following journal entry is made if indirect labor costs of $110 are incurred:

8		Factory Overhead	1	1	0	00					8
9		Wages Payable					1	1	0	00	9
10		Incurred indirect labor costs									10

As we saw with indirect materials, notice that no job number is indicated for these indirect labor overhead costs. They are accumulated and will be applied to specific jobs.

Accounting for Factory Overhead

Factory overhead includes all manufacturing costs other than direct materials and direct labor. The previous two sections showed how to charge indirect materials and indirect labor to Factory Overhead. Similarly, other overhead costs such as depreciation of factory buildings, utilities, and repairs are charged to Factory Overhead. For example, the factory lighting bill of $870 is recorded as follows:

12		Factory Overhead	8	7	0	00					12
13		Accounts Payable					8	7	0	00	13
14		Incurred factory lighting costs									14

The factory overhead account generally is a control account in the general ledger. Details of the different types of factory overhead costs are accumulated in a factory overhead ledger. This subsidiary ledger contains separate accounts for indirect materials, indirect labor, utilities, repairs, and other costs.

By using a factory overhead control account and subsidiary ledger, we can readily accumulate actual factory overhead costs. The major problem in a job order cost accounting system, however, is assigning a reasonable amount of overhead costs to each job. The nature of many factory overhead costs complicates the problem. Most factory overhead costs, such as depreciation of factory buildings, do not vary with the volume of production. Further, some types of overhead, such as heating costs, vacation pay, and repairs, are incurred irregularly throughout the year. These costs do not apply solely to the products manufactured in the months in which the costs occurred.

Predetermined Overhead Rate

Because of the difficulties of relating actual overhead costs to specific jobs, overhead is applied to jobs based on a **predetermined overhead rate**. The basic idea is that we estimate the total overhead costs and total production activity for the year. The overhead is then spread among the jobs based on the amount of production activity on each job. Common measures of production activity are direct labor hours, direct labor costs, and machine hours.

The predetermined overhead rate is computed as follows:

$$\text{Predetermined Overhead Rate} = \frac{\text{Estimated Factory Overhead Costs}}{\text{Estimated Production Activity}}$$

To illustrate, assume that ToyJoy Manufacturing Co. estimates its factory overhead costs at $366,000 and direct labor costs at $610,000 for the coming year. ToyJoy's predetermined overhead application rate based on direct labor costs is 60%.

$$\frac{\text{Estimated Factory Overhead Costs}}{\text{Estimated Direct Labor Costs}} = \frac{\$366,000}{\$610,000} = 60\%$$

As each job is completed during the year, 60% of the direct labor cost incurred on the job is added as the job's share of factory overhead. Assume that Job No. 319 had additional direct labor costs of $4,960, for a total of $5,040. Factory overhead applied to this job is $3,024.

Direct labor cost	$5,040
Application rate	× 60%
Overhead cost applied	$3,024

The entry to apply the overhead cost to Job No. 319 is as follows:

4	Work in Process (Job No. 319)	3 0 2 4 00		4
5	Factory Overhead		3 0 2 4 00	5
6	Applied overhead to work in process			6

The debit to Work in Process also indicates the job to which the overhead is charged.

Figure 26-11 shows Job No. 319 in T account form with $2,100 of direct materials, $5,040 ($80 + $4,960) of direct labor, and $3,024 of overhead charged to it.

FIGURE 26-11 Job No. 319 with Direct Materials, Direct Labor, and Overhead

Job No. 319

2,100
80
4,960
3,024
10,164

Direct Labor, $5,040

Overhead

Accounting for Work in Process—The Job Cost Sheet

In the three previous sections, we saw materials, labor, and overhead costs charged to a specific job (No. 319) that was part of work in process. For ease of presentation, the accumulation of the materials, labor, and overhead charges was illustrated in T account form in Figures 26-8, 26-10, and 26-11. In a job order cost accounting system, Work in Process is a control account with a subsidiary ledger (job cost ledger). This ledger is made up of job cost sheets. A **job cost sheet** is a document for recording the direct materials and direct labor costs incurred and factory overhead costs applied on a specific job. The job cost sheet for Job No. 319 is illustrated in Figure 26-12. As the direct

FIGURE 26-12 Job Cost Sheet

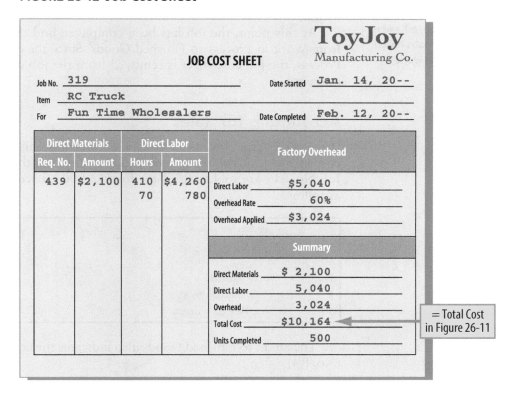

materials and direct labor costs are incurred on a specific job, they are entered on a cost sheet. When the job is completed, factory overhead is applied at the predetermined rate. Note that the total cost ($10,164) in Figure 26-12 is the same as in Figure 26-11.

Accounting for Completed Jobs

After a job has been completed, all of the costs accumulated on the job cost sheet are transferred to finished goods. For Job No. 319 (Figure 26-12), the entry is as follows:

The product number is placed after the inventory account title

9		Finished Goods (No. R4)		10	1	6	4	00						9
10		Work in Process (Job No. 319)								10	1	6	4	00	10
11		Transferred work in process to finished goods													11

The credit to Work in Process indicates the job that has been completed (Job No. 319). The debit to Finished Goods indicates the completed product number (R4). Finished Goods is a control account in the general ledger. A separate account for each product is kept in a subsidiary ledger called a **finished goods ledger**.

In T account form, product R4 would move from the job cost ledger as Job No. 319 to the finished goods ledger as Product R4 as follows:

Job No. 319			Product R4	
2,100	10,164	Job #297	13,400	
80		Job #319	10,164	
4,960				
3,024				
10,164				

> If jobs are in process when a financial statement is being prepared, overhead is applied to those jobs based on the amount of work completed.

Notice that the finished goods subsidiary ledger account shows the costs both by product and by job. Remember that in a job cost system, costs are accumulated by job.

At this point, the job has been completed and the costs have been transferred from Work in Process to Finished Goods. Since the costs are no longer in Work in Process, the job cost sheet is removed from the job cost ledger and filed for future reference.

Accounting for Sales

Using a perpetual inventory system, each time a sale occurs, both the sale and the cost of the goods sold are recorded. Assume that the 500 RC trucks produced in Job No. 319 are sold to RC Time for $13,900 on account. The entry for this sale is as follows:

4		Accounts Receivable	13	9	0	0	00							4
5		Sales						13	9	0	0	00		5
6														6
7		Cost of Goods Sold	10	1	6	4	00							7
8		Finished Goods (No. R4)						10	1	6	4	00		8
9		Made sale on account												9

The credit to Finished Goods also indicates the completed product that was sold (No. R4).

Flow of Job Order Cost Through the Accounts

In the preceding sections, we have made journal entries for events ranging from the purchase of materials through the sale of a finished product. We also used four different subsidiary ledgers. It might be helpful at this point to review the complete flow of costs in a job order cost system. Figure 26-13 summarizes the journal entries in T account form and ties in the subsidiary ledgers with the related control accounts for the following nine events:

1 Materials purchased from suppliers.

2 Direct materials issued to production (work in process).

3 Indirect materials issued to production (overhead).

4 Direct labor costs incurred (work in process).

5 Indirect labor costs incurred (overhead).

6 Other factory overhead costs incurred (e.g., utilities, depreciation).

7 Overhead applied to completed jobs at predetermined rate.

8 Jobs completed.

9 Finished goods sold to customers.

FIGURE 26-13 Flow of Job Order Costs

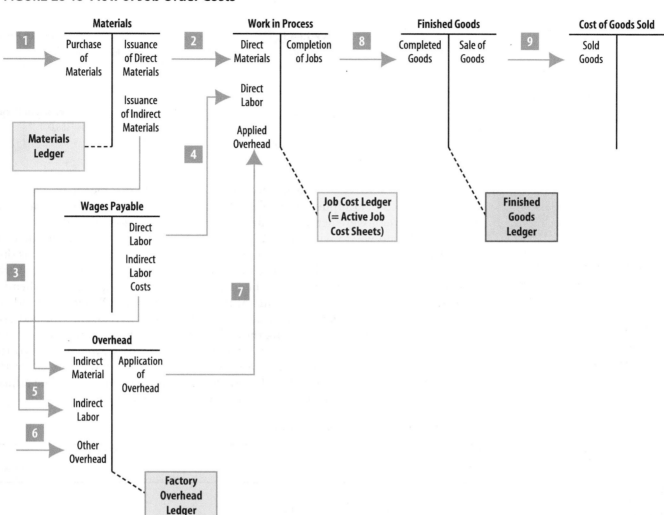

Note the linkage between each of the control accounts and its related subsidiary ledger. Each time an entry affects one of these control accounts, the related subsidiary ledger must be updated accordingly. All nine events require entries in both a control account and a subsidiary ledger.

Underapplied and Overapplied Factory Overhead

We apply factory overhead to completed jobs based on a predetermined rate. This rate is based on *estimates* of the total factory overhead costs and total production activity for the year. It is unlikely that these estimates will be exactly correct. When either estimate is too high or too low, the amount of factory overhead cost actually incurred will differ from the amount applied. If the amount of applied overhead is greater than actual overhead cost incurred, so that Factory Overhead has a credit balance, the difference is called overapplied overhead. If the amount applied is less than actual overhead cost incurred, so that Factory Overhead has a debit balance, the difference is called underapplied overhead.

Figure 26-14 shows two independent versions of Toy Joy's factory overhead account after entries for actual and applied overhead have been made for the year. In Case 1, factory overhead is *under*applied by $900 ($185,000 − $184,100). Overhead costs

FIGURE 26-14 Factory Overhead Account

CASE 1—Underapplied Overhead

of \$900 were incurred that were not applied to goods produced. In Case 2, factory overhead is *over*applied by \$1,000 (\$185,000 − \$186,000). Overhead costs of \$1,000 more than were actually incurred were applied to goods produced.

> If underapplied or overapplied overhead is a large amount, it should be spread among the work in process, finished goods, and cost of goods sold accounts, based on the relative size of these accounts.

What should we do with the underapplied or overapplied balance in the factory overhead account? Three accounts were affected by the overhead applications during the year: Work in Process, Finished Goods, and Cost of Goods Sold. First, overhead was applied to Work in Process. When the goods were completed, overhead was transferred to Finished Goods as part of the work in process. When the goods were sold, overhead was transferred to Cost of Goods Sold as part of the finished goods. We could spread the balance among these three accounts. This would require considerable cost and effort, and the accuracy achieved is generally viewed as not worth the trouble. Instead, unless the amount is large, the underapplied or overapplied overhead commonly is transferred to Cost of Goods Sold by an adjusting entry. The adjusting entries for each case shown in Figure 26-14 would be as follows:

CASE 1—Underapplied Overhead

4		Cost of Goods Sold				9	0	0	00				4
5		Factory Overhead								9	0	0	00	5

CHECKPOINT ✔

Complete Checkpoint-3 on page 1046 to test your basic understanding of LO4.

CASE 2—Overapplied Overhead

7		Factory Overhead			1	0	0	0	00				7
8		Cost of Goods Sold								1	0	0	0	00	8

LO5

Process Cost Accounting

Describe a process cost accounting system.

The job order cost system described in the previous section accumulates costs by job. This system is useful for costing separately identifiable products or batches of product. In a process cost system, costs are accumulated by process or department. This system is useful for costing similar or identical products. Good examples include basic models of most automobiles, or wooden bookshelves.

> **LEARNING KEY** 🔑
>
> In a process cost system, costs attach to products as the products move from one process to another.

As products move through the manufacturing process in a process cost system, costs of processing "attach" to the products. These costs are then passed on to the next processing operation where additional costs attach to the product. This sequence continues through the final production of finished goods.

The production of unassembled wooden bookshelves in a process cost system is illustrated in Figure 26-15. Notice how different manufacturing costs are added at different processing stages. Materials, labor, and overhead costs are incurred in

Process 1. In Process 2, only labor and overhead costs are added. In Process 3, materials, labor, and overhead costs are incurred again.

Also notice how the costs accumulate from process to process. The costs of the output from Process 1 are the materials, labor, and overhead incurred in Process 1. The costs of the output from Process 2 include both the costs transferred in from Process 1 and the additional costs incurred in Process 2. The costs of the output from Process 3 include the costs transferred in from Processes 1 and 2, plus the additional costs incurred in Process 3. Thus, the costs ultimately transferred to Finished Goods include costs incurred in and transferred through three different processing operations.

FIGURE 26-15 Process Cost System

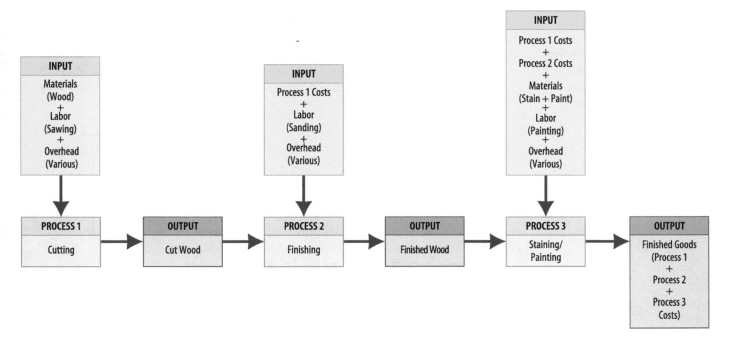

To function effectively, a process cost system must also have the following features:

- Work in process accounts. Each processing department has a separate work in process account.
- Overhead application rates. Each processing department has a separate predetermined overhead application rate.
- Costs per unit. Costs are calculated per unit to allocate costs to products moving through the processes.

The number of units is computed for each process based on:

1. units in process at the beginning of the period,
2. units started and completed during the period, and
3. units still in process at the end of the period.

The cost per unit must be computed separately for materials, labor, and overhead.

In general, process cost systems are more complicated than job order cost systems. Process cost systems are fully explained and illustrated in more advanced texts.

LEARNING OBJECTIVES	Key Points to Remember
LO1 Describe the three manufacturing costs.	The three primary elements of manufacturing cost are materials, labor, and factory overhead. These three costs come together in a conversion process to produce completed products, as shown in Figure 26-1.
LO2 Describe the three inventories of a manufacturing business.	Three inventories are needed in a manufacturing business: materials, work in process, and finished goods. Materials inventory consists of materials acquired to be used in production. Work in process inventory consists of products started but not yet finished. Finished goods inventory contains completed products.
LO3 Describe and illustrate how manufacturing costs and inventories affect the financial statements of a manufacturing business.	There are two main differences in the financial statements of a manufacturer and a merchandiser: (1) cost of goods sold on the income statement and (2) inventories on the balance sheet. Purchases on the merchandiser's income statement are replaced by cost of goods manufactured on the manufacturer's income statement. The manufacturer's balance sheet has three inventory accounts: Finished Goods, Work in Process, and Materials.
LO4 Define and describe how to operate a job order cost accounting system.	A job order cost system provides a separate record of the cost of each product or group of products that is produced. A cost accounting system with perpetual inventories is used to accumulate information about the cost of producing each product. Under this system, at least one of the three inventory accounts is affected every time (1) materials are purchased, (2) materials are placed in production, (3) products are completed, or (4) products are sold, as shown in Figure 26-6.
	Three important documents used in a job order cost system are the materials requisition, daily time sheet, and job cost sheet.
	Overhead is applied to jobs based on a predetermined overhead rate. Underapplied or overapplied overhead normally is transferred to Cost of Goods Sold.
	Four subsidiary ledgers are used in a job cost system: the materials ledger, factory overhead ledger, job cost ledger, and finished goods ledger. Figure 26-13 shows the use of these four ledgers.
LO5 Describe a process cost accounting system.	In a process cost system, costs are accumulated by process or department rather than by job.

DEMONSTRATION PROBLEM

Mantel Manufacturing Company uses a job order cost accounting system. The following is a summary of transactions completed during its first year of operations:

(a) Purchased materials on account, $435,000.

(b) (1) Issued *direct materials* to production.

Job No. 1	$55,000	Job No. 4	$119,000
Job No. 2	76,000	Job No. 5	65,000
Job No. 3	59,800	Job No. 6	18,000

   (2) Issued *indirect materials* to production, $11,900.

(c) (1) Incurred factory labor costs.

Job No. 1	$34,000	Job No. 4	$76,000
Job No. 2	40,000	Job No. 5	38,000
Job No. 3	29,000	Job No. 6	12,000

   (2) Incurred indirect labor costs, $10,000.

(d) Incurred other factory overhead costs, $96,000.

(e) Depreciation expense on factory equipment, $29,000.

(f) Applied factory overhead, 65% of direct labor cost incurred on jobs.

(g) Finished Job Nos. 1, 2, 4, and 5 as products A, B, D, and E, respectively.

(h) Shipped products A, B, and D and billed customers for $158,000, $210,000, and $362,000, respectively.

REQUIRED

1. Prepare general journal entries for the foregoing transactions. Make compound entries for (b), (c), and (f), but with separate debits for each job. (Use journal page numbers 7 and 8.)

2. Post the entries to the general ledger T accounts for Work in Process and Finished Goods, and determine the ending balances in these accounts.

3. Determine the balances in the job cost ledger to support the balance in the work in process account.

4. Verify that the balances in the finished goods ledger agree with the balance in the finished goods account.

5. Determine the amount of underapplied or overapplied overhead.

SOLUTION 1.

(a)
(b)

	GENERAL JOURNAL			PAGE 7	
	DATE	DESCRIPTION	POST. REF.	DEBIT	CREDIT	
1		Materials		435 0 0 0 00		1
2		Accounts Payable			435 0 0 0 00	2
3						3
4		Work in Process (Job No. 1)		55 0 0 0 00		4
5		Work in Process (Job No. 2)		76 0 0 0 00		5
6		Work in Process (Job No. 3)		59 8 0 0 00		6
7		Work in Process (Job No. 4)		119 0 0 0 00		7
8		Work in Process (Job No. 5)		65 0 0 0 00		8
9		Work in Process (Job No. 6)		18 0 0 0 00		9
10		Materials			392 8 0 0 00	10

(continued)

		Description	Debit	Credit	
	11				11
	12	Factory Overhead	11 9 0 0 00		12
	13	Materials		11 9 0 0 00	13
	14				14
(c)	15	Work in Process (Job No. 1)	34 0 0 0 00		15
	16	Work in Process (Job No. 2)	40 0 0 0 00		16
	17	Work in Process (Job No. 3)	29 0 0 0 00		17
	18	Work in Process (Job No. 4)	76 0 0 0 00		18
	19	Work in Process (Job No. 5)	38 0 0 0 00		19
	20	Work in Process (Job No. 6)	12 0 0 0 00		20
	21	Wages Payable		229 0 0 0 00	21
	22				22
	23	Factory Overhead	10 0 0 0 00		23
	24	Wages Payable		10 0 0 0 00	24
	25				25
(d)	26	Factory Overhead	96 0 0 0 00		26
	27	Accounts Payable		96 0 0 0 00	27
	28				28
(e)	29	Factory Overhead	29 0 0 0 00		29
	30	Accumulated Depreciation		29 0 0 0 00	30
	31				31
(f)	32	Work in Process (Job No. 1)	22 1 0 0 00		32
	33	Work in Process (Job No. 2)	26 0 0 0 00		33
	34	Work in Process (Job No. 3)	18 8 5 0 00		34
	35	Work in Process (Job No. 4)	49 4 0 0 00		35
	36	Work in Process (Job No. 5)	24 7 0 0 00		36
	37	Work in Process (Job No. 6)	7 8 0 0 00		37
	38	Factory Overhead		148 8 5 0 00	38
	39				39
(g)	40	Finished Goods (Product A)	111 1 0 0 00		40
	41	Work in Process (Job No. 1)		111 1 0 0 00	41
	42				42
	43	Finished Goods (Product B)	142 0 0 0 00		43
	44	Work in Process (Job No. 2)		142 0 0 0 00	44
	45				45
	46	Finished Goods (Product D)	244 4 0 0 00		46
	47	Work in Process (Job No. 4)		244 4 0 0 00	47
	48				48
	49	Finished Goods (Product E)	127 7 0 0 00		49
	50	Work in Process (Job No. 5)		127 7 0 0 00	50

GENERAL JOURNAL   PAGE 8

	DATE	DESCRIPTION	POST. REF.	DEBIT	CREDIT	
(h)	1	Accounts Receivable		158 0 0 0 00		1
	2	Sales			158 0 0 0 00	2
	3					3
	4	Cost of Goods Sold		111 1 0 0 00		4
	5	Finished Goods (Product A)			111 1 0 0 00	5

(continued)

6													6
7	Accounts Receivable	210	0	0	0	00							7
8	Sales						210	0	0	0	00		8
9													9
10	Cost of Goods Sold	142	0	0	0	00							10
11	Finished Goods (Product B)						142	0	0	0	00		11
12													12
13	Accounts Receivable	362	0	0	0	00							13
14	Sales						362	0	0	0	00		14
15													15
16	Cost of Goods Sold	244	4	0	0	00							16
17	Finished Goods (Product D)						244	4	0	0	00		17
18													18

SOLUTION 2.

Work in Process

(b) 55,000 / 111,100
76,000 / 142,000
59,800 / 244,400 } (g)
119,000 / 127,700
65,000 / 625,200
18,000

(c) 34,000
40,000
29,000
76,000
38,000
12,000

(f) 22,100
26,000
18,850
49,400
24,700
7,800
770,650
Bal. 145,450

Finished Goods

(g) 111,100 / 111,100
142,000 / 142,000 } (h)
244,400 / 244,400
127,700 / 497,500
625,200
Bal. 127,700

SOLUTION 3. In job cost ledger: Job No. 3 $107,650
Job No. 6 37,800
$145,450

SOLUTION 4. Product E: $127,700

SOLUTION 5.

Factory Overhead

11,900 / 148,850
10,000
96,000
29,000
146,900 / 148,850
1,950 (Overapplied overhead)

KEY TERMS

cost accounting system (1029)   A system for accumulating detailed information regarding the cost of producing a product.

daily time sheet (1032)   A record of the time worked and labor cost incurred on each job.

direct labor (1025)   The wages of employees who are directly involved in converting materials into finished goods.

direct materials (1025)   Those materials that enter into and become a major part of the finished product.

factory burden (1025)   See factory overhead.

factory overhead (1025)   All manufacturing costs other than direct materials and direct labor.

factory overhead ledger (1033)   The subsidiary ledger in which details of the different types of factory overhead costs are accumulated.

factory supplies (1025)   See indirect materials.

Finished Goods Inventory (1026)   The account that contains the costs of products that have been completed and are ready for sale.

finished goods ledger (1035)   The subsidiary ledger in which a separate account for each product is kept.

indirect labor (1025)   The wages and salaries of employees who devote their time to supervision or to work of a general nature.

indirect manufacturing cost (1025)   See factory overhead.

indirect materials (1025)   Those materials used in the manufacturing process that do not become a major part of the finished product.

job cost ledger (1034)   A subsidiary ledger for the work in process control account that is made up of job cost sheets.

job cost sheet (1034)   A document for recording the direct materials, direct labor, and factory overhead costs incurred on a specific job.

job order cost system (1029)   The system that provides a separate record of the cost of each individual product or group of products that is produced.

manufacturing overhead (1025)   See factory overhead.

Materials Inventory (1026)   The account that includes all the materials (both direct and indirect) acquired to be used in production.

materials ledger (1031)   The subsidiary ledger that shows the quantity and cost of material received and issued, and the resulting balance for each type of material.

materials requisition (1031)   A form used to issue materials from the storeroom to production.

overapplied overhead (1037)   The amount by which applied overhead is greater than the actual overhead cost incurred so that Factory Overhead has a credit balance.

predetermined overhead rate (1034)   The rate used to apply overhead, based on production activity such as direct labor hours, direct labor costs, or machine hours; used because of the difficulties of relating actual overhead costs to specific jobs.

process cost system (1030)   The system that accumulates manufacturing costs by process, such as cutting, painting, or finishing, and assigns each unit of product passing through the process a share of the costs.

stores ledger (1031)   See materials ledger.

time ticket (1032)   See daily time sheet.

underapplied overhead (1037)   The amount by which applied overhead is less than the actual overhead cost incurred so that Factory Overhead has a debit balance.

Work in Process Inventory (1026)   The account in which materials, labor, and overhead costs of producing a product are accumulated until the product is completed.

SELF-STUDY TEST QUESTIONS

True/False

1. **LO1**   Both direct and indirect materials enter into and become major parts of the finished product.

2. **LO1**   Factory overhead is also known as manufacturing overhead, indirect manufacturing cost, or factory burden.

3. **LO2**   Work in Process Inventory consists of three items: materials, labor, and factory overhead.

4. **LO2**   Finished Goods Inventory consists of only those items finished and sold during the period.

5. **LO5**   A process cost system is useful for costing separately identifiable products or batches of product.

Multiple Choice

1. **LO1**   Which of these would most likely be treated as an *indirect* material? (Assume you are manufacturing tables.)
   (a) wood   (c) glue
   (b) lacquer   (d) table legs

2. **LO3**   The cost of goods sold section of the income statement for a manufacturing company would contain which of the following?
   (a) purchases   (c) direct labor
   (b) cost of goods manufactured (d) no inventory account

3. **LO4**   When total anticipated factory overhead is $500,000 and budgeted direct labor hours are 200,000, what is the predetermined factory overhead rate based on direct labor hours?
   (a) $2.50/hour   (c) $10/hour
   (b) $5.00/hour   (d) It cannot be determined.

4. **LO4**   When direct labor hours for Job 101 are 30 and the predetermined factory overhead rate is $5/direct labor hour, what is the applied factory overhead amount?
   (a) $250
   (b) $500
   (c) $150
   (d) It cannot be determined.

5. **LO4**   Underapplied or overapplied factory overhead is normally charged or credited to which account?
   (a) Materials
   (b) Work in Process
   (c) Finished Goods
   (d) Cost of Goods Sold

Checkpoint Exercises

1. **LO2**   Different manufacturing costs and inventory accounts are listed in the left column below. For each cost or account, indicate the other manufacturing cost or inventory account into which it flows. Item (a) is completed as an example.

   a. Indirect materials   Factory Overhead
   b. Direct materials   _____
   c. Indirect labor   _____
   d. Direct labor   _____
   e. Factory overhead   _____
   f. Work in process inventory   _____

2. **LO3**   Prepare a schedule of cost of goods manufactured for the year ended December 31, 20--, based on the following information. (Assume that all materials inventory items are direct materials.)

Work in process, January 1	$29,700
Materials inventory, January 1	15,400
Materials purchases	16,800
Materials inventory, December 31	18,200
Direct labor	13,300
Overhead	7,700
Work in process, December 31	14,700

3. **LO4**   Prepare general journal entries for the following transactions.

   a. Purchased materials on account, $26,400.
   b. Issued direct materials to Job No. 6, $21,000.
   c. Issued indirect materials (factory overhead), $3,700.
   d. Incurred direct labor, Job No. 6, $12,900.
   e. Incurred indirect labor (factory overhead), $5,000.
   f. Incurred other indirect costs (factory overhead; credit Accounts Payable), $2,300.
   g. Applied factory overhead to Job No. 6, $7,740.

The answers to the Self-Study Test Questions are at the end of the chapter (page 1058).

APPLYING YOUR KNOWLEDGE

REVIEW QUESTIONS

LO1   1.   Why is the accounting for a manufacturing business more complicated than that for a merchandising business?

LO1   2.   What are the three primary elements of manufacturing cost?

LO1   3.   What are the two major types of materials, and how do they differ?

LO1   4.   Distinguish between direct and indirect labor.

LO1   5.   Describe and give three examples of factory overhead.

LO2   6.   What are the three inventories needed in a manufacturing business?

LO2   7.   Describe the flow of materials, labor, and overhead into Work in Process.

LO3   8.   What are the main differences between the financial statements of a manufacturing and a merchandising business?

LO4   9.   For what three reasons is product cost information needed by a manufacturing business?

LO4   10.   What two purposes are served by a materials requisition form?

LO4   11.   What information is provided by the daily time sheet?

LO4   12.   Explain how to calculate a predetermined overhead rate.

LO4   13.   What costs are entered on the job cost sheet?

LO4   14.   Describe underapplied and overapplied overhead. What is commonly done with the underapplied or overapplied balance in the factory overhead account?

LO5   15.   Briefly describe the difference between a job order cost system and a process cost system.

SERIES A EXERCISES

E 26-1A   **(LO3)**
✓ Cost of goods sold: $49,000

COST OF GOODS SOLD SECTION The following information is supplied for R&D Manufacturing Co. and WP West Co. (a merchandising company). Prepare the cost of goods sold sections for the income statements of both companies for the year ended 20--.

	R&D Manufacturing	WP West
Merchandise inventory, January 1		$57,000
Finished goods inventory, January 1	$57,000	
Merchandise purchases		36,000
Cost of goods manufactured	36,000	
Merchandise inventory, December 31		44,000
Finished goods inventory, December 31	44,000	

E 26-2A   (LO3)
✓ Total manufacturing costs: $108,000

SCHEDULE OF COST OF GOODS MANUFACTURED The following information is supplied for Maupin Manufacturing Company. Prepare a schedule of cost of goods manufactured for the year ended December 31, 20--. Assume that all materials inventory items are direct materials.

Work in process, January 1	$77,000
Materials inventory, January 1	31,000
Materials purchases	35,000
Materials inventory, December 31	26,000
Direct labor	48,000
Overhead	20,000
Work in process, December 31	62,000

E 26-3A   (LO4)
✓ Jan. 20 entry: Dr. Factory Overhead (Indirect Materials), $5,000

JOURNAL ENTRIES FOR MATERIAL, LABOR, AND OVERHEAD Hilburn Manufacturing Corporation had the following transactions for its job order costing operation. Prepare general journal entries to record these transactions.

Jan. 1   Purchased materials on account, $17,000.
15   Issued direct materials to Job No. 104, $11,000.
20   Issued indirect materials (factory overhead), $5,000.
31   Incurred direct labor, Job No. 104, $9,000.
31   Incurred indirect labor (factory overhead), $2,500.
31   Incurred other indirect costs (factory overhead; credit Accounts Payable), $2,000.

E 26-4A   (LO4)
✓ Entry for underapplied factory overhead: Dr. Cost of Goods Sold, $200

JOURNAL ENTRIES FOR FACTORY OVERHEAD Huang Company manufactures toys. It keeps a factory overhead account where actual factory overhead costs are recorded as a debit, and factory overhead applied is recorded as a credit. At the end of the month, under- or overapplied factory overhead is calculated and transferred to the cost of goods sold account. For the month of January, Huang had the following overhead transactions. Make appropriate general journal entries to record factory overhead and factory overhead applied, and to close the under- or overapplied factory overhead to the cost of goods sold account.

Jan. 1   Paid rent, $1,000.
10   Paid electricity bill, $250.
15   Paid repair expense, $1,500.
21   Vacation pay for machine operator, $500 (Wages Payable).
31   Depreciation expense for the month, $450.
31   Factory overhead applied was $3,500.

E 26-5A   (LO4)
✓ (1) $10.80/direct labor hour

PREDETERMINED FACTORY OVERHEAD RATE Millerlile Enterprises calculates a predetermined factory overhead rate so that factory overhead may be applied to production during the month. It calculates the overhead using three different methods and then decides which one to use. Total estimated factory overhead costs are $540,000. Total estimated direct labor hours are 50,000. Total estimated direct labor costs are $900,000. Total machine hours are estimated to be 80,000.

Calculate the predetermined overhead application rates based on (1) direct labor hours, (2) direct labor costs, and (3) machine hours.

E 26-6A   (LO4)
✓ 1st Apr. 30 entry: Dr. Finished Goods, $17,500

JOURNAL ENTRIES FOR MATERIAL, LABOR, OVERHEAD, AND SALES Micro Enterprises had the following job order transactions during the month of April. Record the transactions in the general journal, including issuance of materials, labor, and factory overhead applied; completed jobs sent to finished goods inventory; closing of the under- or overapplied factory overhead to the cost of goods sold account; and sale of finished goods.

Apr.   1   Purchased materials on account, $35,000.

     10   Issued direct materials to Job No. 33, $10,000.

     11   Issued direct materials to Job No. 34, $8,000.

     12   Issued direct materials to Job No. 35, $11,000.

     25   Incurred direct labor:

         On Job No. 33, $6,000
         On Job No. 34, $4,000
         On Job No. 35, $5,000

     25   Applied factory overhead:

         To Job No. 33, $1,500
         To Job No. 34, $1,200
         To Job No. 35, $1,600

     30   Transferred Job Nos. 33–35 to the finished goods inventory account as products F, G, and H, respectively.

     30   Sold products F, G, and H for $20,000, $16,000, and $22,000, respectively.

     30   Actual factory overhead for Job Nos. 33–35, $4,220.

SERIES A PROBLEMS

P 26-7A   (LO3)
✓ Cost of Goods Manufactured: $117,000

SCHEDULE OF COST OF GOODS MANUFACTURED AND COST OF GOODS SOLD SECTION The following information is provided for J. Klein Manufacturing Company. Prepare (1) a schedule of cost of goods manufactured, and (2) the related cost of goods sold section of the income statement for the company for the year ended December 31, 20--. Assume that all materials inventory items are direct materials.

Materials inventory, January 1	$26,000
Materials purchases for the year	39,000
Materials inventory, December 31	28,000
Direct labor for the year	58,000
Factory overhead for the year	30,000
Work in process, January 1	65,000
Work in process, December 31	73,000
Finished goods inventory, January 1	47,000
Finished goods inventory, December 31	42,000

P 26-8A   (LO4)
✓ (d): Dr. Work in Process: (Job No. 300), $8,000

JOURNAL ENTRIES FOR MATERIAL, LABOR, AND OVERHEAD Eto Manufacturing had the following transactions during the month:

(a) Purchased raw materials on account, $70,000.

(b) Issued direct materials to Job No. 300, $25,000.

(c) Issued indirect materials to production, $10,000.

(d) Paid biweekly payroll and charged direct labor to Job No. 300, $8,000.

(e) Paid biweekly payroll and charged indirect labor to production, $3,000.

(f) Issued direct materials to Job No. 301, $20,000.

(g) Issued indirect materials to production, $4,000.

(h) Paid miscellaneous factory overhead charges, $6,000.

(i) Paid biweekly payroll and charged direct labor to Job No. 301, $10,000.

(j) Paid biweekly payroll and charged indirect labor to production, $2,000.

REQUIRED

Prepare general journal entries for transactions (a) through (j).

P 26-9A　(LO4)

✓ 1. (h) Product L: Dr. Finished Goods, $17,200

JOB ORDER COSTING TRANSACTIONS Stonestreet Enterprises makes garage doors. During the month of February, the company had four job orders: 205, 206, 207, and 208. Overhead was applied at predetermined rates, while actual factory overhead was recorded as incurred. All four jobs were completed.

(a) Purchased raw materials on account, $44,000.

(b) Issued direct materials to production:

Job No. 205:	$8,500
Job No. 206:	9,600
Job No. 207:	8,000
Job No. 208:	9,000

(c) Issued indirect materials to production, $5,700.

(d) Incurred direct labor costs:

Job No. 205:	$5,400
Job No. 206:	4,600
Job No. 207:	5,200
Job No. 208:	5,500

(e) Charged indirect labor to production, $3,400.

(f) Paid electricity, heating oil, and repair bills for the factory and charged to production, $5,300.

(g) Applied factory overhead to each of the jobs using a predetermined factory overhead rate as follows:

Job No. 205:	$3,300
Job No. 206:	3,900
Job No. 207:	3,300
Job No. 208:	3,900

(h) Finished Job Nos. 205–208 and transferred to the finished goods inventory account as products L, M, N, and O, respectively.

(i) Sold products L, M, N, and O, on account, for $21,000, $20,300, $19,000, and $20,500, respectively.

REQUIRED

1. Prepare general journal entries to record transactions (a) through (i). Make compound entries for (b), (d), and (g), with separate debits for each job.

2. Post the entries to the work in process and finished goods T accounts only.

P 26-10A　(LO4)

✓ 3: Balance in job cost ledger, $66,600

JOB ORDER COSTING WITH UNDER- AND OVERAPPLIED FACTORY OVERHEAD M. Evans & Sons manufactures parts for radios. For each job order, it maintains ledger sheets on which it records direct labor, direct materials, and factory overhead applied. The factory overhead control account contains postings of actual overhead costs. At the end of the month, the under- or overapplied factory overhead is charged to the cost of goods sold account.

Factory overhead is applied on the basis of direct labor hours. For Job Nos. 101, 102, 103, and 104, direct labor hours are 12,000, 10,000, 11,000, and 18,000, respectively. The overhead application rate is $1.20/direct labor hour.

(a) Purchased raw materials on account, $50,000.

(b) Issued direct materials:

Job No. 101:	$10,000
Job No. 102:	8,000
Job No. 103:	9,000
Job No. 104:	15,000

(c) Issued indirect materials to production, $8,000.

(d) Incurred direct labor costs:

Job No. 101:	$22,000
Job No. 102:	19,000
Job No. 103:	20,500
Job No. 104:	30,000

(e) Charged indirect labor to production, $15,000.

(f) Paid electricity bill, taxes, and repair fees for the factory and charged to production, $8,000.

(g) Depreciation expense on factory equipment, $30,000.

(h) Applied factory overhead to Job Nos. 101–104 using the predetermined factory overhead rate (see above).

(i) Finished Job Nos. 101–103 and transferred to the finished goods inventory account as products N, O, and P.

(j) Sold products N and O for $50,000 and $45,400, respectively.

(k) Transferred under- or overapplied factory overhead balance to the cost of goods sold account.

REQUIRED

1. Prepare general journal entries to record transactions (a) through (k). Make compound entries for (b), (d), and (h), with separate debits for each job.

2. Post the entries to the work in process and finished goods T accounts only and determine the ending balances in these accounts.

3. Compute the balance in the job cost ledger and verify that this balance agrees with that in the work in process control account.

SERIES B EXERCISES

E 26-1B   (LO3)
✓ Cost of goods sold: $13,750

COST OF GOODS SOLD SECTION The following information is supplied for A&B Manufacturing Co. and JC Yoshino Co. (a merchandising company). Prepare the cost of goods sold sections for the income statements of both companies for the year ended 20--.

	A&B Manufacturing	JC Yoshino
Merchandise inventory, January 1		$15,750
Finished goods inventory, January 1	$15,750	
Merchandise purchases		11,000
Cost of goods manufactured	11,000	
Merchandise inventory, December 31		13,000
Finished goods inventory, December 31	13,000	

E 26-2B   (LO3)
✓ **Total manufacturing costs: $25,000**

SCHEDULE OF COST OF GOODS MANUFACTURED The following information is supplied for Sanchez Welding and Manufacturing Company. Prepare a schedule of cost of goods manufactured for the year ended December 31, 20--. Assume that all materials inventory items are direct materials.

Work in process, January 1	$20,500
Materials inventory, January 1	11,000
Materials purchases	12,000
Materials inventory, December 31	13,000
Direct labor	9,500
Overhead	5,500
Work in process, December 31	10,500

E 26-3B   (LO4)
✓ **Jan. 20 entry: Dr. Factory Overhead (Indirect Materials), $3,000**

JOURNAL ENTRIES FOR MATERIAL, LABOR, AND OVERHEAD Rich Manufacturing Corporation had the following transactions for its job order costing operation. Prepare general journal entries to record these transactions.

Jan.   1   Purchased materials on account, $22,000.
       15   Issued direct materials to Job No. 1, $18,000.
       20   Issued indirect materials (factory overhead), $3,000.
       31   Incurred direct labor, Job No. 1, $11,000.
       31   Incurred indirect labor (factory overhead), $4,000.
       31   Incurred other indirect costs (factory overhead; credit Accounts Payable), $1,500.

E 26-4B   (LO4)
✓ **Entry for underapplied factory overhead: Dr. Cost of Goods Sold, $500**

JOURNAL ENTRIES FOR FACTORY OVERHEAD Bandy Company manufactures toys. It keeps a factory overhead account where actual factory overhead costs are recorded as a debit and factory overhead applied is recorded as a credit. At the end of the month, under- or overapplied factory overhead is calculated and transferred to the cost of goods sold account. For the month of January, Bandy had the following overhead transactions. Make appropriate general journal entries to record factory overhead and factory overhead applied, and to close the under- or overapplied factory overhead to the cost of goods sold account.

Jan.   1   Paid rent, $2,000.
       10   Paid electricity bill, $500.
       15   Paid repair expense, $3,000.
       21   Vacation pay for machine operator, $500 (Wages Payable).
       31   Depreciation expense for the month, $500.
       31   Factory overhead applied was $6,000.

E 26-5B   (LO4)
✓ **(1) $20/direct labor hour**

PREDETERMINED FACTORY OVERHEAD RATE Marston Enterprises calculates a predetermined factory overhead rate so that factory overhead may be applied to production during the month. It calculates the overhead using three different methods and then decides which one to use. Total estimated factory overhead costs are

$600,000. Total estimated direct labor hours are 30,000. Total estimated direct labor costs are $1,200,000. Total machine hours are estimated to be 200,000.

Calculate the predetermined overhead application rates based on (1) direct labor hours, (2) direct labor costs, and (3) machine hours.

E 26-6B   (LO4)

✓ 1st Apr. 30 entry: Dr. Finished Goods, $18,800

JOURNAL ENTRIES FOR MATERIAL, LABOR, OVERHEAD, AND SALES Alert Enterprises had the following job order transactions during the month of April. Record the transactions in the general journal, including issuance of materials, labor, and factory overhead applied; completed jobs sent to finished goods inventory; closing of the under- or overapplied factory overhead to the cost of goods sold account; and sale of finished goods. Make compound entries for both transactions dated April 25, with separate debits for each job.

Apr. 1 Purchased materials on account, $28,000.
     10 Issued direct materials to Job No. 26, $11,000.
     11 Issued direct materials to Job No. 27, $9,000.
     12 Issued direct materials to Job No. 28, $7,000.
     25 Incurred direct labor:

> On Job No. 26, $6,000
> On Job No. 27, $4,000
> On Job No. 28, $5,000

     25 Applied factory overhead:

> To Job No. 26, $1,800
> To Job No. 27, $1,500
> To Job No. 28, $1,400

     30 Transferred Job Nos. 26–28 to the finished goods inventory account as products Q, R, and T, respectively.
     30 Sold products Q, R, and T for $20,600, $16,000, and $14,900, respectively.
     30 Actual factory overhead for Job Nos. 26–28, $4,500.

SERIES B PROBLEMS

P 26-7B   (LO3)

✓ Cost of Goods Manufactured: $45,000

SCHEDULE OF COST OF GOODS MANUFACTURED AND COST OF GOODS SOLD SECTION The following information is provided for WWE Manufacturing Company. Prepare (1) a schedule of cost of goods manufactured, and (2) the related cost of goods sold section of the income statement for the company for the year ended December 31, 20--. Assume that all materials inventory items are direct materials.

Materials inventory, January 1	$14,000
Materials purchases for the year	21,000
Materials inventory, December 31	13,000
Direct labor for the year	11,500
Factory overhead for the year	6,500
Work in process, January 1	20,000
Work in process, December 31	15,000
Finished goods inventory, January 1	32,000
Finished goods inventory, December 31	26,000

P 26-8B   (LO4)

✓ (d): Dr. Work in Process
(Job No. 200), $4,500

JOURNAL ENTRIES FOR MATERIAL, LABOR, AND OVERHEAD Shiar Manufacturing had the following transactions during the month:

(a) Purchased raw materials on account, $22,500.

(b) Issued direct materials to Job No. 200, $11,250.

(c) Issued indirect materials to production, $4,000.

(d) Paid biweekly payroll and charged direct labor to Job No. 200, $4,500.

(e) Paid biweekly payroll and charged indirect labor to production, $1,250.

(f) Issued direct materials to Job No. 201, $10,000.

(g) Issued indirect materials to production, $2,500.

(h) Paid miscellaneous factory overhead charges, $4,500.

(i) Paid biweekly payroll and charged direct labor to Job No. 201, $4,250.

(j) Paid biweekly payroll and charged indirect labor to production, $900.

REQUIRED

Prepare general journal entries for transactions (a) through (j).

P 26-9B   (LO4)

✓ 1. (h) Product W: Dr. Finished Goods,
$16,100

JOB ORDER COSTING TRANSACTIONS D & K Enterprises makes wicker baskets. During the month of August, the company had four job orders: 501, 502, 503, and 504. Overhead was applied at predetermined rates, while actual factory overhead was recorded as incurred. All four jobs were completed.

(a) Purchased raw materials on account, $44,000.

(b) Issued direct materials to production:

Job No. 501:	$8,200
Job No. 502:	9,100
Job No. 503:	7,300
Job No. 504:	8,500

(c) Issued indirect materials to production, $5,000.

(d) Incurred direct labor costs:

Job No. 501:	$4,800
Job No. 502:	4,100
Job No. 503:	4,800
Job No. 504:	5,000

(e) Charged indirect labor to production, $3,300.

(f) Paid electricity, heating oil, and repair bills for the factory and charged to production, $5,200.

(g) Applied factory overhead to each of the jobs using a predetermined factory overhead rate as follows:

Job No. 501:	$3,100
Job No. 502:	3,300
Job No. 503:	3,300
Job No. 504:	3,800

(h) Finished Job Nos. 501–504 and transferred to the finished goods inventory account as products W, X, Y, and Z, respectively.

(i) Sold products W, X, Y, and Z for $17,500, $18,000, $16,900, and $19,000, respectively.

REQUIRED

1. Prepare general journal entries to record transactions (a) through (i). Make compound entries for (b), (d), and (g), with separate debits for each job.

2. Post the entries to the work in process and finished goods T accounts only.

P 26-10B (LO4)
✓ 3: Balance in job cost ledger, $47,700

JOB ORDER COSTING WITH UNDER- AND OVERAPPLIED FACTORY OVERHEAD J. Bowen & Co. manufactures screen doors. For each job order, it maintains ledger sheets on which it records direct labor, direct materials, and factory overhead applied. The factory overhead control account contains postings of actual overhead costs. At the end of the month, the under- or overapplied factory overhead is charged to the cost of goods sold account.

Factory overhead is applied on the basis of direct labor hours. For Job Nos. 201, 202, 203, and 204, direct labor hours are 10,000, 11,000, 11,000, and 12,000, respectively. The overhead application rate is $1.50/direct labor hour.

(a) Purchased raw materials on account, $45,000.

(b) Issued direct materials:

Job No. 201:	$10,000
Job No. 202:	11,000
Job No. 203:	9,500
Job No. 204:	12,200

(c) Issued indirect materials to production, $7,500.

(d) Incurred direct labor costs:

Job No. 201:	$18,000
Job No. 202:	19,000
Job No. 203:	20,500
Job No. 204:	17,500

(e) Charged indirect labor to production, $11,000.

(f) Paid electricity bill, taxes, and repair fees for the factory and charged to production, $7,000.

(g) Depreciation expense on factory equipment, $40,000.

(h) Applied factory overhead to Job Nos. 201–204 using the predetermined factory overhead rate (see above).

(i) Finished Job Nos. 201–203 and transferred to the finished goods inventory account as products C, D, and E, respectively.

(j) Sold products C and D for $47,000 and $49,000, respectively.

(k) Transferred under- or overapplied factory overhead balance to the cost of goods sold account.

REQUIRED

1. Prepare general journal entries to record transactions (a) through (k). Make compound entries for (b), (d), and (h), with separate debits for each job.

2. Post the entries to the work in process and finished goods T accounts only and determine the ending balances in these accounts.

3. Compute the balance in the job cost ledger and verify that this balance agrees with that in the work in process control account.

CHECK LIST
- [ ] **Managing**
- [ ] **Planning**
- [ ] **Drafting**
- [ ] **Break**
- [ ] **Revising**
- [ ] **Managing**

MANAGING YOUR WRITING

Joan owns a print shop and has a difficult time figuring out what to bid on jobs. She knows how to estimate the cost of materials and labor on different jobs but is confused about how to handle many other costs she knows she incurs to run the shop. These include utilities, cleaning staff, property taxes on the building, and other expenses. Many of these types of costs vary from month to month. In addition, she often does not know the amounts until some time after jobs are completed.

Write a memo to Joan explaining how she should apply her overhead costs in developing bids on her jobs.

ETHICS ★

ETHICS CASE

Ben Reese is a painter for a small manufacturing plant. Sometimes he works directly on the product and sometimes he performs routine maintenance on the plant's three buildings. He is paid $11.50 an hour and fills out a time sheet at the end of each week. His supervisor then fills in the specific jobs that will be charged with Ben's time. On Friday afternoon, Ben's supervisor, Ralph Brooks, said he needed Ben to do a job off the plant site. Ralph explained that he had just installed a wooden garage door on his house and needed it painted. He told Ben to leave a couple of hours early and "just sign out as though you had stayed until quitting time." Even though this request made Ben uncomfortable, he did what the boss said.

1. What would you have done if you were Ben? Justify your answer.
2. How do you suppose Ralph will account for Ben's hours away from the plant?
3. Write a short paragraph explaining the difference between direct labor and indirect labor. Include how each is assigned to specific jobs.
4. In groups of two or three, come up with some suggestions on measures a company can take to prevent a situation like this from happening.

MASTERY PROBLEM

✓ 3: Balance in job cost ledger, $97,260

Forester Manufacturing Company uses a job order cost accounting system to keep track of finished jobs and jobs in process. All production is either to customer order or to specification. The following is a summary of transactions completed during the month of August:

(a) Purchased materials (direct and indirect) on account, $158,000.

(b) Requisitioned materials from storerooms, $149,000 (direct materials, $122,000; indirect materials, $27,000). Charged to jobs as follows:

Job No. 805:	$34,000
Job No. 806:	44,000
Job No. 807:	20,000
Job No. 808:	24,000

(c) Incurred factory labor cost for the month, $211,800 (direct labor, $150,000; indirect labor, $61,800). Charged to jobs as follows:

Job No. 805:	$25,500
Job No. 806:	39,800
Job No. 807:	51,400
Job No. 808:	33,300

(d) Incurred other factory overhead costs, $85,000 (depreciation expense, $10,000; miscellaneous factory expense on account, $75,000).

(e) Applied factory overhead, 120% of direct labor cost incurred on jobs. (Make a separate debit for each job.)

(f) Finished Job Nos. 805, 806, and 807 and placed them in stock as products X, Y, and Z, respectively.

(g) Sold products X, Y, and Z on account for $123,000, $150,000, and $168,000, respectively. Costs of products sold were $90,100, $122,000, and $140,000, respectively. (Products Y and Z included some items from the beginning inventory of finished goods and some from the current period's production.)

The beginning balances in the inventory accounts were as follows:

Work in Process	$0
Finished Goods	$76,000 (Product Y, $46,000; Product Z, $30,000).

REQUIRED

1. Prepare general journal entries for the foregoing transactions.

2. Post the entries to the general ledger T accounts for Work in Process and Finished Goods, and compute the ending balances in these accounts.

3. Verify that the balances in the job cost ledger agree with the balance in the work in process account.

4. Determine the amount of under- or overapplied factory overhead.

CHALLENGE PROBLEM

This problem challenges you to apply your cumulative accounting knowledge to move a step beyond the material in the chapter.

✓ 2: Net income = $75,750

For its most recent year of operations, Unovap Co. had sales of $950,000, cost of goods sold of $680,000, and operating expenses of $190,000. Its ending inventories were as follows:

Raw material	$30,000
Work in process	88,000
Finished goods	32,000

In addition, it has $5,000 of underapplied overhead which has not yet been transferred to any other accounts.

REQUIRED

1. Transfer the underapplied overhead to Cost of Goods Sold and calculate the net income for the year.

2. Spread the underapplied overhead among Work in Process, Finished Goods, and Cost of Goods Sold, and calculate the net income for the year.

3. (a) What is the difference in the net income based on the two different approaches to accounting for the underapplied overhead?

   (b) How would you recommend accounting for the underapplied overhead in this case?

ANSWERS TO SELF-STUDY TEST QUESTIONS

True/False

1. F (only direct materials)
2. T
3. T
4. F (items finished and not sold)
5. F (It is useful for costing similar or identical products.)

Multiple Choice

1. c   **2.** b   **3.** a   **4.** c   **5.** d

Checkpoint Exercises

1. a. Indirect materials   Factory Overhead
   b. Direct materials   Work in Process Inventory
   c. Indirect labor   Factory Overhead
   d. Direct labor   Work in Process Inventory
   e. Factory overhead   Work in Process Inventory
   f. Work in Process Inventory   Finished Goods Inventory

2. Work in process, January 1, 20-- $29,700
   Direct materials:
      Materials inventory, January 1, 20-- $15,400
      Materials purchases   16,800
      Materials available for use $32,200
      Materials inventory, December 31, 20--   18,200
         Cost of direct materials used $14,000
   Direct labor   13,300
   Overhead   7,700
   Total manufacturing costs   35,000
   Total work in process during period $64,700
   Work in process, December 31, 20--   14,700
   Cost of goods manufactured $50,000

3. a. Materials Inventory   26,400
         Accounts Payable   26,400
   b. Work in Process (Job No. 6)   21,000
         Materials Inventory   21,000
   c. Factory Overhead (indirect materials)   3,700
         Materials Inventory   3,700
   d. Work in Process (Job No. 6)   12,900
         Wages Payable   12,900
   e. Factory Overhead (indirect labor)   5,000
         Wages Payable   5,000
   f. Factory Overhead (miscellaneous)   2,300
         Accounts Payable   2,300
   g. Work in Process (Job No. 6)   7,740
         Factory Overhead   7,740

Chapter 27

Adjustments, Financial Statements, and Year-End Accounting for a Manufacturing Business

Throughout this text, we have emphasized how accounting is relevant to many aspects of our lives. It therefore seems fitting that we conclude with an example of its relevance even in dealing with natural disasters. When hurricanes, tornadoes, or earthquakes strike, someone needs to pick up the pieces. The government often is viewed as this someone. But the government must engage private businesses to do much of the actual work. SRS is one of those businesses.

SRS was founded in 2001 and has grown to become one of the premier construction management and disaster recovery organizations in the United States. SRS often works with FEMA (Federal Emergency Management Agency) and the U.S. Army Corps of Engineers. Their work includes projects like building construction, demolition, road building, and installation of underground utilities. Many of these projects involve millions of dollars and extend over long periods of time. It is common for SRS to end its fiscal year with many projects in process. The accounting for these projects can be challenging. In this chapter, you will learn how to make year-end adjustments for construction projects that are in process and the importance of making these adjustments correctly.

LEARNING OBJECTIVES

Careful study of this chapter should enable you to:

LO1 Prepare a 6-column spreadsheet for a manufacturing company.

LO2 Prepare adjustments to (1) apply factory overhead to ending work in process, (2) record additional actual factory overhead, (3) record under- or overapplied overhead, (4) record expected sales returns and allowances, (5) record other expenses not involving overhead, and (6) provide for corporate income taxes.

LO3 Prepare financial statements for a manufacturing company.

LO4 Prepare adjusting, closing, and reversing journal entries for a manufacturing company.

In Chapters 14 and 15, we learned how to use the spreadsheet to prepare end-of-period adjustments and the financial statements for a merchandising company. In this chapter, we use a spreadsheet to prepare end-of-period adjustments and the financial statements for a manufacturing company. Both the spreadsheet and financial statements of a manufacturer differ from those of a merchandiser.

LO1	The Spreadsheet for a Manufacturing Company

Prepare a 6-column spreadsheet for a manufacturing company.

The spreadsheet for a manufacturing company is similar to the one illustrated in Chapter 14 for a merchandising company. The same four steps are used to prepare both spreadsheets.

STEP 1   Prepare the trial balance.

STEP 2   Prepare the adjustments.

STEP 3   Prepare the adjusted trial balance.

STEP 4   Add all of the income statement accounts listed in the adjusted trial balance columns to compute the net income (loss) for the period.

Figure 27-1 shows only the Trial Balance and Adjustments columns of ToyJoy Manufacturing Co.'s spreadsheet, to help us focus on manufacturing company differences. We will use the full 6-column spreadsheet, including steps 3 and 4, later in the chapter. The Trial Balance columns were completed by copying the balances of all accounts from the general ledger (not shown). The following accounts and related adjustments are different from the Chapter 14 illustration and are highlighted in the spreadsheet:

1 Finished Goods Inventory, Work in Process Inventory, and Materials Inventory
2 Cost of Goods Sold
3 Factory Overhead
4 Income Tax Expense and Income Tax Payable

Inventories

Instead of a single merchandise inventory account, the manufacturer has three inventory accounts—Finished Goods, Work in Process, and Materials. The manufacturer purchases materials (Materials Inventory) and converts them (Work in Process Inventory) to completed products (Finished Goods Inventory) for sale to customers. These three inventories are shown as the first three boxes numbered 1, 2, and 3 in Figure 27-2 on page 1062.

Cost of Goods Sold

The cost of goods sold account is related to the inventory accounts. Cost of Goods Sold appears on the spreadsheet because ToyJoy uses a perpetual inventory system. With a perpetual inventory system, the movement of goods from materials to work in process to finished goods to cost of goods sold is recorded as the movement occurs. This movement of goods and the related journal entries were shown in Chapter 26 as Figure 26-6, which is reproduced as Figure 27-2. The use of a perpetual inventory system has two important effects on ToyJoy's spreadsheet compared with the one presented in Chapter 14 for a business using the periodic inventory method.

FIGURE 27-1 **Partial Spreadsheet**

	A	B	C	D	E	F	G	H
1			ToyJoy Manufacturing Co.					
2			Spreadsheet (Partial)					
3			For Year Ended December 31, 20--					
4	ACCOUNT TITLE		TRIAL BALANCE			ADJUSTMENTS		
5			DEBIT	CREDIT		DEBIT		CREDIT
6	Cash		25,843.00					
7	Government Notes		5,000.00					
8	Accounts Receivable		66,485.00					
9	Allowance for Doubtful Accounts			460.00			(i)	1,405.00
10	Finished Goods Inventory		35,614.00					
11	Work in Process Inventory	1	9,990.00		(a)	2,700.00		
12	Materials Inventory		9,275.00					
13	Estimated Returns Inventory		110.00		(g)	740.00		
14	Factory Supplies		5,542.00				(b)	5,020.00
15	Prepaid Insurance		8,060.00				(c)	6,520.00
16	Land		40,000.00					
17	Factory Building		178,000.00					
18	Accum. Depr.—Factory Building			30,000.00			(d)	7,500.00
19	Factory Equipment		155,000.00					
20	Accum. Depr.—Factory Equipment			40,640.00			(d)	13,500.00
21	Office Equipment		21,300.00					
22	Accum. Depr.—Office Equipment			4,925.00			(j)	2,000.00
23	Accounts Payable			39,685.00				
24	Customer Refunds Payable			180.00			(f)	1,020.00
25	Income Tax Payable	4					(k)	5,300.00
26	Interest Payable						(h)	800.00
27	Bonds Payable			100,000.00				
28	Capital Stock			75,000.00				
29	Paid-In Capital in Excess of Par			20,000.00				
30	Retained Earnings			132,690.00				
31	Cash Dividends		15,000.00					
32	Sales			840,458.00				
33	Sales Returns and Allowances		10,500.00		(f)	1,020.00		
34	Interest Revenue			430.00				
35	Factory Overhead	3	155,080.00	185,982.00	(b)	5,020.00	(a)	2,700.00
36					(c)	6,520.00		
37					(d)	21,000.00		
38					(e)	1,062.00		
39	Cost of Goods Sold	2	601,581.00				(e)	1,062.00
40							(g)	740.00
41	Wages Expense		91,316.00					
42	Advertising Expense		5,264.00					
43	Bad Debt Expense				(i)	1,405.00		
44	Utilities Expense—Office		5,690.00					
45	Depr. Expense—Office Equipment				(j)	2,000.00		
46	Interest Expense		8,800.00		(h)	800.00		
47	Income Tax Expense	4	17,000.00		(k)	5,300.00		
48			1,470,450.00	1,470,450.00		47,567.00		47,567.00
49			STEP 1			STEP 2		
50								

FIGURE 27-2 Flow of Costs Through Manufacturing Inventory Accounts

INVENTORY MOVEMENTS	JOURNAL ENTRIES
1 Materials are purchased.	Increase Materials Increase Accounts Payable
2 Materials are put into the manufacturing process.	Decrease Materials Increase Work in Process
3 Product is completed.	Decrease Work in Process Increase Finished Goods
4 Completed product is sold.	Decrease Finished Goods Increase Cost of Goods Sold

1. The costs of goods sold are accumulated in Cost of Goods Sold as sales occur during the year. Thus, Cost of Goods Sold is not computed by means of an adjustment process at the end of the period as we did in Chapter 14.

2. The inventory accounts (Materials, Work in Process, Finished Goods, and Estimated Returns Inventory) reflect ending rather than beginning balances.

As explained in Chapters 13 and 14, a physical count of the inventory still is necessary to verify the accuracy of the perpetual inventory records. If a difference is found between the physical count and the amount in the perpetual inventory records, the records must be corrected by an adjusting entry. The physical counts of ToyJoy's inventories agreed with the amounts in the books, so no adjustments for this purpose were necessary.

Factory Overhead

The factory overhead account appears solely because ToyJoy is a manufacturer. Factory overhead exists as part of the cost of manufacturing products. Both the debit ($155,080) and credit ($185,982) totals are shown for this account.

The debit represents the actual overhead costs incurred. The credit represents overhead applied to production. Both the debit and credit balances are shown for completeness of presentation, and because both amounts are useful in preparing financial statements.

Income Tax

Income Tax Expense and Income Tax Payable appear because ToyJoy is a corporation. As explained in Chapter 21, income taxes are an expense of doing business as a corporation.

LO2	Adjustments

Prepare adjustments to (1) apply factory overhead to ending work in process, (2) record additional actual factory overhead, (3) record under- or overapplied overhead, (4) record expected sales returns and allowances, (5) record other expenses not involving overhead, and (6) provide for corporate income taxes.

The second pair of amount columns in Figure 27-1 contains the adjustments labeled (a) through (k). Data for adjusting the accounts are as follows:

(a) Factory overhead to be applied to work in process ending inventory	$ 2,700
(b) Factory supplies consumed	5,020
(c) Insurance expired on factory building and equipment	6,520
(d) Depreciation on:	
factory building	7,500
factory equipment	13,500
(e) Overapplied factory overhead	1,062
(f) Estimate of this year's sales that will be returned next year	1,200
(g) Cost of goods expected to be returned	850
(h) Accrual of interest payable	800
(i) Estimate of uncollectible accounts, based on an aging of accounts receivable	1,865
(j) Depreciation on office equipment	2,000
(k) Provision for corporate income taxes	5,300

The adjustments that are similar to those illustrated in Chapter 14 will be explained very briefly. Adjustments (a), (b), (c), (d), (e), and (k) are new, and adjustments (f) and (g) are more complex. These adjustments will be explained more fully.

Apply Factory Overhead to Ending Work in Process

Adjustment (a)

As jobs were completed during the year, factory overhead was applied to them at a rate of 60% of direct labor costs. At the end of the year, several jobs are still in process. To correctly state the work in process ending inventory, factory overhead must be applied to these jobs. It should be applied using the same basis as for finished goods. The job cost ledger (not shown here) shows total direct labor costs of $4,500 on jobs in process at December 31. An adjustment is needed to apply $2,700 (60% of the direct labor costs) to work in process. Debit Work in Process Inventory and credit Factory Overhead.

Record Additional Actual Factory Overhead

Adjustment (b)

A physical count of factory supplies at the end of the year shows that $5,020 of factory supplies were used during the year. Since factory supplies expense is part of factory overhead, debit Factory Overhead and credit Factory Supplies for $5,020. The factory supplies expense account in the factory overhead ledger (not shown here) also is debited for this amount.

LEARNING KEY 🔑

Overhead must be applied to Work in Process at year end.

As explained later in the chapter, adjustment of individual jobs in Work in Process is unnecessary.

Adjustment (c)

A review of the insurance policy files shows that $6,520 of insurance on the factory building and equipment has expired. Since factory building and equipment insurance expense is part of factory overhead, debit Factory Overhead and credit Prepaid Insurance for $6,520. Also, debit the factory building and equipment insurance expense account in the factory overhead ledger.

Adjustment (d)

Depreciation expense for the year was $7,500 on the factory building and $13,500 on the factory equipment, a total of $21,000. Depreciation expense on the factory building and factory equipment is part of factory overhead. Therefore, debit Factory Overhead for $21,000, and credit Accumulated Depreciation—Factory Building for $7,500 and Accumulated Depreciation—Factory Equipment for $13,500. Also, debit the depreciation expense—factory building and equipment account in the factory overhead ledger for $21,000.

Notice that adjustments (b), (c), and (d) are *debited* to Factory Overhead. Recall from Chapter 26 that actual factory overhead expenses are debited to Factory Overhead.

Record Under- or Overapplied Overhead

Adjustment (e)

This adjustment is needed because overhead was overapplied during the year. Figure 27-3 shows the factory overhead account in T account form. The amounts shown are:

1. debit and credit "balances" from the December 31 trial balance (see Figure 27-1)

2. debits for adjustments (b), (c), and (d), for additional actual factory overhead

3. credit for adjustment (a), to apply factory overhead to jobs in process

4. total actual overhead and overhead applied

5. debit for adjustment (e), to adjust for overapplied factory overhead

FIGURE 27-3 Factory Overhead T Account

	Factory Overhead			
1		155,080		185,982 **1**
	(b)	5,020	(a)	2,700 **2**
2	(c)	6,520		
	(d)	21,000		
4 (Actual overhead)		187,620	(Overhead applied)	188,682 **4**
5 Overapplied overhead	(e)	1,062		
Totals		188,682		188,682

> **LEARNING KEY** 🔑
>
> A debit balance in Factory Overhead means overhead was underapplied. A credit balance means overhead was overapplied.

The two item **4** amounts in Figure 27-3 show that actual overhead for the year was $187,620, while overhead applied was $188,682. Thus, overhead was *overapplied* by $1,062. Debit Factory Overhead and credit Cost of Goods Sold for $1,062 to adjust for overapplied overhead.

Record Expected Sales Returns and Allowances

Adjustments (f, g)

As explained in Chapter 14, at the end of the year it is necessary to adjust for goods sold this year, but expected to be returned in the next year. ToyJoy estimates that customers will be granted $1,200 of refunds next year on the current year's sales, and that the goods expected to be returned will have cost $850 to manufacture. The Customer Refunds Payable and Estimated Returns Inventory accounts must be adjusted to equal these amounts.

The spreadsheet in Figure 27-1 shows that the unadjusted balances in these two accounts at December 31, 20--, are

Customer Refunds Payable	$180 (Credit)
Estimated Returns Inventory	$110 (Debit)

Recall from Chapter 14 that under the perpetual inventory system, when a customer returns goods sold in the prior year, the following entries are made:

Customer Refunds Payable	xxx	
Accounts Receivable (or Cash)		xxx
Finished Goods Inventory	xxx	
Estimated Returns Inventory		xxx

These entries would reduce the balances in the Customer Refunds Payable and Estimated Returns Inventory as returns occurred during the year. If last year's estimates of expected returns and costs were accurate, the ending balances in these accounts would be quite small. This is the case for ToyJoy.

To adjust these accounts for next year's expected returns of this year's sales, the following adjustments are needed:

(f) To increase the balance in Customer Refunds Payable to $1,200, debit Sales Returns and Allowances and credit Customer Refunds Payable for $1,020 ($1,200 − 180).

(g) To increase the balance in Estimated Returns Inventory to $850, debit Estimated Returns Inventory and credit Cost of Goods Sold for $740 ($850 − 110).

Record Other Expenses Not Involving Overhead

Adjustment (h)

Interest of $800 is accrued at the end of the year on the bonds payable. Debit Interest Expense and credit Interest Payable.

Adjustment (i)

The estimated amount of uncollectible accounts at the end of the year, based on an aging of accounts receivable, is $1,865. Allowance for Doubtful Accounts had a credit balance of $460, so the necessary adjustment is $1,405 ($1,865 − $460). Debit Bad Debt Expense and credit Allowance for Doubtful Accounts.

Adjustment (j)

Depreciation expense for the year on the office equipment was $2,000. Debit Depreciation Expense—Office Equipment and credit Accumulated Depreciation—Office Equipment.

Provide for Corporate Income Taxes

Adjustment (k)

Corporate income tax for the year is $22,300. As shown in Figure 27-1, income tax expense of $17,000 had been recorded during the year. Therefore, an adjustment of $5,300 is needed ($22,300 − $17,000 = $5,300). Debit Income Tax Expense and credit Income Tax Payable.

Completing the Spreadsheet

> **LEARNING KEY** 🔑
>
> The factory overhead account balances are not extended to the Income Statement or Balance Sheet Columns.

Figure 27-4 on page 1067 shows ToyJoy's full 6-column spreadsheet. Note the handling of the factory overhead account. Both the total debits and total credits of $188,682 appear in the Adjusted Trial Balance columns. But neither of these amounts is used in preparing the Income Statement or Balance Sheet. Figure 27-5 shows why this procedure is followed. Factory overhead costs are **1** incurred, **2** applied to Work in Process, **3** transferred to Finished Goods with completed products, and **4** transferred to Cost of Goods Sold when goods are sold.

The factory overhead amounts are not used in preparing the income statement or balance sheet because they have already been transferred to Work in Process, Finished Goods, and Cost of Goods Sold. These three account balances, which contain the factory overhead amounts, are used in preparing the Income Statement and Balance Sheet. As shown later in the chapter, both factory overhead amounts also are used in the closing process.

A BROADER VIEW

Work in Process Inventory—This Stuff Really Matters

When you study the year-end accounting procedures for a manufacturing company, you might question whether all the adjustments really matter in the real world. One way to answer that question is to consider the financial statements of a real company.

Boeing is a leading aircraft manufacturer and aerospace company. In 2017, Boeing reported net income of $8.2 billion. At the close of 2017, the ending inventory for Boeing included $67 billion of work in process. Think about the accounting implications of these figures. The work in process inventory for Boeing is 8 times ($67 billion ÷ $8.2 billion = 8+) the size of its net income. This means that a relatively small percentage error in work in process inventory could have a significant effect on the net income. Clearly, the year-end adjustments can be quite important for a company like Boeing.

VAALAA/SHUTTERSTOCK.COM

FIGURE 27-4 Spreadsheet

	A	B	C	D	E	F	G	H	I
1					ToyJoy Manufacturing Co.				
2					Spreadsheet				
3					For Year Ended December 31, 20--				
4	ACCOUNT TITLE	TRIAL BALANCE			ADJUSTMENTS			ADJUSTED TRIAL BALANCE	
5		DEBIT	CREDIT		DEBIT		CREDIT	DEBIT	CREDIT
6	Cash	25,843.00						25,843.00	
7	Government Notes	5,000.00						5,000.00	
8	Accounts Receivable	66,485.00						66,485.00	
9	Allowance for Doubtful Accounts		460.00			(i)	1,405.00		1,865.00
10	Finished Goods Inventory	35,614.00						35,614.00	
11	Work in Process Inventory	9,990.00		(a)	2,700.00			12,690.00	
12	Materials Inventory	9,275.00						9,275.00	
13	Estimated Returns Inventory	110.00		(g)	740.00			850.00	
14	Factory Supplies	5,542.00				(b)	5,020.00	522.00	
15	Prepaid Insurance	8,060.00				(c)	6,520.00	1,540.00	
16	Land	40,000.00						40,000.00	
17	Factory Building	178,000.00						178,000.00	
18	Accum. Depr.—Factory Building		30,000.00			(d)	7,500.00		37,500.00
19	Factory Equipment	155,000.00						155,000.00	
20	Accum. Depr.—Factory Equipment		40,640.00			(d)	13,500.00		54,140.00
21	Office Equipment	21,300.00						21,300.00	
22	Accum. Depr.—Office Equipment		4,925.00			(j)	2,000.00		6,925.00
23	Accounts Payable		39,685.00						39,685.00
24	Customer Refunds Payable		180.00			(f)	1,020.00		1,200.00
25	Income Tax Payable					(k)	5,300.00		5,300.00
26	Interest Payable					(h)	800.00		800.00
27	Bonds Payable		100,000.00						100,000.00
28	Capital Stock		75,000.00						75,000.00
29	Paid-in Capital in Excess of Par		20,000.00						20,000.00
30	Retained Earnings		132,690.00						132,690.00
31	Cash Dividends	15,000.00						15,000.00	
32	Sales		840,458.00						840,458.00
33	Sales Returns and Allowances	10,500.00		(f)	1,020.00			11,520.00	
34	Interest Revenue		430.00						430.00
35	Factory Overhead	155,080.00	185,982.00	(b)	5,020.00	(a)	2,700.00	188,682.00	188,682.00
36				(c)	6,520.00				
37				(d)	21,000.00				
38				(e)	1,062.00				
39	Cost of Goods Sold	601,581.00				(e)	1,062.00	599,779.00	
40						(g)	740.00		
41	Wages Expense	91,316.00						91,316.00	
42	Advertising Expense	5,264.00						5,264.00	
43	Bad Debt Expense			(i)	1,405.00			1,405.00	
44	Utilities Expense—Office	5,690.00						5,690.00	
45	Depr. Expense—Office Equipment			(j)	2,000.00			2,000.00	
46	Interest Expense	8,800.00		(h)	800.00			9,600.00	
47	Income Tax Expense	17,000.00		(k)	5,300.00			22,300.00	
48		1,470,450.00	1,470,450.00		47,567.00		47,567.00	1,504,675.00	1,504,675.00
49		STEP 1			STEP 2			STEP 3	
50	STEP 4							937,556.00	1,029,570.00
51	Net Income							92,014.00	

Balance Sheet Accounts

Income Statement Accounts

FIGURE 27-5 Flow of Overhead Costs in a Manufacturing Accounting System

① Actual overhead costs are accumulated as debits in the factory overhead account.

② Overhead is applied to products by debiting Work in Process and crediting Factory Overhead. This overhead application *transfers* overhead from Factory Overhead to Work in Process.

③ The portion of factory overhead related to completed products is transferred from Work in Process to Finished Goods.

④ The portion of factory overhead related to products sold is transferred from Finished Goods to Cost of Goods Sold.

CHECKPOINT ✔

Complete Checkpoint-1 on page 1083 to test your basic understanding of LO2.

LO3

Financial Statements

Prepare financial statements for a manufacturing company.

ToyJoy's financial statements include an income statement, statement of retained earnings, balance sheet, and statement of cash flows. The statement of cash flows is essentially the same in format as the one illustrated in Chapter 23, so it is not presented here. We will focus on the statements prepared from the 6-column spreadsheet for a manufacturing business.

Income Statement

LEARNING KEY 🔑

Both the remaining balance and December 31 balance of the estimated returns inventory are used in computing cost of goods sold on the income statement.

ToyJoy's income statement is presented in Figure 27-6. All income statement data were obtained from the Income Statement accounts on the spreadsheet, except for the cost of goods sold section. To prepare this section, the beginning finished goods inventory was taken from the finished goods account in the general ledger (not shown). The estimated returns inventory, January 1, remaining balance, is from this balance sheet account in the trial balance columns on the spreadsheet. The cost of goods manufactured was taken from the schedule of cost of goods manufactured (Figure 27-7, page 1070). The ending finished goods inventory and the ending estimated returns inventory are from the Balance Sheet accounts in the adjusted trial balance columns on the spreadsheet.

A manufacturer's income statement is commonly supported by a schedule of cost of goods manufactured like the one in Figure 27-7. The ending materials and work in process inventories are from the Balance Sheet accounts in the adjusted trial balance columns on the spreadsheet. Other data for this schedule, listed in the order in which they appear, were obtained from the following sources.

ToyJoy uses a perpetual inventory system, so cost of goods sold is already known, as shown in the spreadsheet in Figure 27-4. The procedures described here are simply to show the calculation of cost of goods sold on the income statement.

DATA	SOURCE OF DATA
Work in process inventory, January 1	Work in process account in general ledger
Materials inventory, January 1	Materials inventory account in general ledger
Purchases	Materials inventory account in general ledger
Indirect materials charged to production	Materials inventory account in general ledger
Direct labor	Work in process account in general ledger
Overhead	Factory overhead account in general ledger

FIGURE 27-6 **Income Statement**

ToyJoy Manufacturing Co. Income Statement For Year Ended December 31, 20--			
Sales		$ 840,458	
Less sales returns and allowances		11,520	
Net sales			$ 828,938
Cost of goods sold:			
Finished goods inventory, January 1	$ 24,569		
Estimated returns inventory, January 1, remaining balance	110	$ 24,679	
Cost of goods manufactured		611,564 ← From Schedule	
Cost of goods available for sale		$ 636,243	
Finished goods inventory, December 31	$ 35,614		
Estimated returns inventory, December 31	850	36,464	
Cost of goods sold			599,779
Gross profit			$ 229,159
Operating expenses:			
Wages expense		$ 91,316	
Advertising expense		5,264	
Bad debt expense		1,405	
Utilities expense—office		5,690	
Depreciation expense—office equipment		2,000	
Total operating expenses			105,675
Operating income			$ 123,484
Other revenue:			
Interest revenue			430
			$ 123,914
Other expense:			
Interest expense			9,600
Income before income taxes			$ 114,314
Income tax			22,300
Net income		To Statement of Retained Earnings	$ 92,014

Statement of Retained Earnings

The statement of retained earnings appears in Figure 27-8. The retained earnings balance at January 1 and the cash dividends for the year are taken from the Balance Sheet accounts in the adjusted trial balance columns on the spreadsheet. The net income for the year can be taken from the Income Statement accounts in the adjusted trial balance columns on the spreadsheet or from the income statement. The only distinctive feature of the statement of retained earnings arises from ToyJoy being organized as a corporation. As a corporation, ToyJoy pays dividends, in this case, $15,000.

Balance Sheet

ToyJoy's balance sheet is presented in Figure 27-9 on page 1071. Data for this statement were taken from the Balance Sheet accounts in the adjusted trial balance columns on the spreadsheet, except for the retained earnings. This amount was taken from the statement of retained earnings. Note that the retained earnings amount on the balance sheet ($209,704) also can be calculated from the spreadsheet. It is the sum of (1) the retained earnings balance shown on the spreadsheet ($132,690) plus

FIGURE 27-7 Schedule of Cost of Goods Manufactured

ToyJoy Manufacturing Co. Schedule of Cost of Goods Manufactured For Year Ended December 31, 20--			
Work in process, January 1			$ 11,940
Direct materials			
Materials inventory, January 1	$ 12,992		
Materials purchases	124,580		
Materials available	$ 137,572		
Materials inventory, December 31	9,275		
Cost of materials used		$ 128,297	
Less indirect materials included in overhead		3,200	
Cost of direct materials used		$ 125,097	
Direct labor		299,597	
Factory overhead		187,620	
Total manufacturing costs			612,314
Total work in process during the period			$ 624,254
Work in process, December 31			12,690
Cost of goods manufactured		To Income Statement →	$ 611,564

(2) the net income for the year ($92,014) less **(3)** the cash dividends for the year ($15,000), as follows:

(1)	Beginning balance	$132,690
(2)	Net income	92,014
(3)	Cash dividends	(15,000)
	Ending balance	$209,704

Two main differences in this balance sheet compared with those for merchandising companies are:

1. Since this is a manufacturing company, there are three inventory accounts listed: Finished Goods, Work in Process, and Materials.
2. Since ToyJoy is a corporation, the stockholders' equity section contains information regarding capital stock, paid-in capital in excess of par, and retained earnings.

FIGURE 27-8 Statement of Retained Earnings

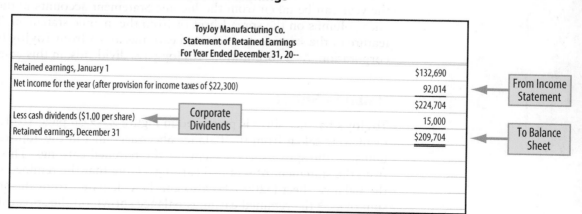

ToyJoy Manufacturing Co. Statement of Retained Earnings For Year Ended December 31, 20--		
Retained earnings, January 1		$132,690
Net income for the year (after provision for income taxes of $22,300)		92,014
		$224,704
Less cash dividends ($1.00 per share)	Corporate Dividends	15,000
Retained earnings, December 31		$209,704

From Income Statement

To Balance Sheet

FIGURE 27-9 Balance Sheet

ToyJoy Manufacturing Co.
Balance Sheet
December 31, 20--

Assets			
Current assets:			
Cash		$ 25,843	
Government notes		5,000	
Accounts receivable	$ 66,485		
Less allowance for doubtful accounts	1,865	64,620	
Inventories:			
Finished goods	$ 35,614		
Estimated returns inventory	850		
Work in process	12,690		
Materials	9,275	58,429	
Factory supplies		522	
Prepaid insurance		1,540	
Total current assets			$ 155,954
Property, plant, and equipment			
Land		$ 40,000	
Factory building	$ 178,000		
Less accumulated depreciation	37,500	140,500	
Factory equipment	$ 155,000		
Less accumulated depreciation	54,140	100,860	
Office equipment	$ 21,300		
Less accumulated depreciation	6,925	14,375	
Total property, plant, and equipment			295,735
Total assets			$ 451,689
Liabilities			
Current liabilities			
Accounts payable		$ 39,685	
Customer refunds payable		1,200	
Income tax payable		5,300	
Interest payable		800	
Total current liabilities			$ 46,985
Long-term liabilities:			
Bonds payable			100,000
Total liabilities			$ 146,985
Stockholders' Equity			
Common stock ($5 par value, 50,000 shares authorized;			
15,000 shares issued)		$ 75,000	
Paid-in capital in excess of par		20,000	
Retained earnings		209,704	
Total stockholders' equity			304,704
Total liabilities and stockholders' equity			$ 451,689

Three inventories →

Corporate section →

← **From Statement of Retained Earnings**

CHECKPOINT ✔

Complete Checkpoint-2 on page 1083 to test your basic understanding of LO3.

LO4 Journal Entries

Prepare adjusting, closing, and reversing journal entries for a manufacturing company.

Most of ToyJoy's adjusting, closing, and reversing entries are similar to those illustrated in Chapters 14 and 15 for a merchandising company. Only a few adjustments need explanation.

Adjusting Entries

The entries appearing in the Adjustments columns of the spreadsheet are journalized as shown in Figure 27-10 below. For ease of identification, each entry includes the coding letter from the spreadsheet.

FIGURE 27-10 Adjusting Entries

	DATE		DESCRIPTION	POST. REF.	DEBIT	CREDIT	
1			Adjusting Entries				1
2	20-- Dec.	31	Work in Process Inventory		2 7 0 0 00		2
3	(a)		Factory Overhead			2 7 0 0 00	3
4							4
5	(b)	31	Factory Overhead (Factory Supplies Expense)		5 0 2 0 00		5
6			Factory Supplies			5 0 2 0 00	6
7							7
8	(c)	31	Factory Overhead (Factory Building and Equipment,				8
9			Insurance Expense)		6 5 2 0 00		9
10			Prepaid Insurance			6 5 2 0 00	10
11							11
12	(d)	31	Factory Overhead (Depreciation Expense—				12
13			Factory Building and Equipment)		21 0 0 0 00		13
14			Accumulated Depreciation—Factory Building			7 5 0 0 00	14
15			Accumulated Depreciation—Factory Equipment			13 5 0 0 00	15
16							16
17	(e)	31	Factory Overhead		1 0 6 2 00		17
18			Cost of Goods Sold			1 0 6 2 00	18
19							19
20	(f)	31	Sales Returns and Allowances		1 0 2 0 00		20
21			Customer Refunds Payable			1 0 2 0 00	21
22							22
23	(g)	31	Estimated Returns Inventory		7 4 0 00		23
24			Cost of Goods Sold			7 4 0 00	24
25							25
26	(h)	31	Interest Expense		8 0 0 00		26
27			Interest Payable			8 0 0 00	27
28							28
29	(i)	31	Bad Debt Expense		1 4 0 5 00		29
30			Allowance for Doubtful Accounts			1 4 0 5 00	30
31							31
32	(j)	31	Depreciation Expense—Office Equipment		2 0 0 0 00		32
33			Accumulated Depreciation—Office Equipment			2 0 0 0 00	33
34							34
35	(k)	31	Income Tax Expense		5 3 0 0 00		35
36			Income Tax Payable			5 3 0 0 00	36

GENERAL JOURNAL

Aggregate → (a)

Identify subsidiary → (b)

Identify subsidiary → (c)

Identify subsidiary → (d)

Notice two things about these adjusting entries.

1. In adjustment (a), the application of factory overhead to ending work in process, no entries are made to the individual jobs in the job cost ledger. Aggregate work in process must be adjusted so that it is reported correctly on the financial statements. The individual jobs require no adjustment because they are not reported on any financial statements. The aggregate adjustment will be reversed at the beginning of the following period.
2. In adjustments (b), (c), and (d), the factory overhead account and the related subsidiary accounts are identified. Both the general ledger and subsidiary ledger accounts are adjusted for these actual overhead amounts.

Closing Entries

Six steps are used to close ToyJoy's temporary accounts.

STEP 1 Transfer the debit balance in the factory overhead account to Income Summary and close the subsidiary factory overhead accounts.

STEP 2 Transfer the credit balance in the factory overhead account to Income Summary.

STEP 3 Transfer the balances of the sales and interest revenue accounts to Income Summary.

STEP 4 Transfer the balances of the cost of goods sold and all expense accounts to Income Summary.

STEP 5 Transfer the balance of Income Summary to Retained Earnings.

STEP 6 Transfer the balance of Cash Dividends to Retained Earnings.

Figure 27-11 shows the journal entries corresponding to these six steps. Entries (3), (4), (5), and (6) are essentially the same as the ones we used for a merchandising company in Chapter 15. Entries (1) and (2) require explanation.

The T account in Figure 27-3 on page 1064 shows that the factory overhead account has a zero balance after all adjustments are entered. This account must still be "closed" to close the factory overhead subsidiary ledger accounts. This is the purpose of entries (1) and (2) in Figure 27-11.

Entry (1) closes the total debit amount in the factory overhead account to Income Summary. At the same time, the related factory overhead subsidiary ledger accounts are closed. (The detail for each subsidiary ledger account is omitted here.) Entry (2) closes the total credit amount in factory overhead to Income Summary.

> **LEARNING KEY** 🔑
> Both the debit and credit amounts in the factory overhead account must be closed to Income Summary.

Reversing Entries

ToyJoy reverses two of the adjusting entries made on December 31. Entry (1) in Figure 27-12 is related to the accrued interest on bonds payable. The purpose of this type of reversing entry was explained in Chapter 15. Entry (2) is unique to a manufacturing company. This entry reverses the adjusting entry to apply factory overhead to Work in Process. This reversal facilitates applying factory overhead to completed jobs in the following year. Recall that factory overhead is applied at a predetermined rate when a job is completed. If this reversing entry were not made, it would be necessary to keep track of which jobs already had a partial overhead application from a prior year's adjustment.

> **LEARNING KEY** 🔑
> Reverse the adjusting entry to apply overhead to Work in Process.

FIGURE 27-11 Closing Entries

	DATE		DESCRIPTION	POST. REF.	DEBIT	CREDIT	
1			Closing Entries				1
2	20-- Dec.	31	Income Summary		188 6 8 2 00		2	← Step 1
3	(1)		Factory Overhead (Subsidiary ledger accounts)			188 6 8 2 00	3
4							4
5	(2)	31	Factory Overhead		188 6 8 2 00		5	← Step 2
6			Income Summary			188 6 8 2 00	6
7							7
8	(3)	31	Sales		840 4 5 8 00		8	← Step 3
9			Interest Revenue		4 3 0 00		9
10			Income Summary			840 8 8 8 00	10
11							11
12	(4)	31	Income Summary		748 8 7 4 00		12	← Step 4
13			Sales Returns and Allowances			11 5 2 0 00	13
14			Cost of Goods Sold			599 7 7 9 00	14
15			Wages Expense			91 3 1 6 00	15
16			Advertising Expense			5 2 6 4 00	16
17			Bad Debt Expense			1 4 0 5 00	17
18			Utilities Expense—Office			5 6 9 0 00	18
19			Depreciation Expense—Office Equipment			2 0 0 0 00	19
20			Interest Expense			9 6 0 0 00	20
21			Income Tax Expense			22 3 0 0 00	21
22							22
23	(5)	31	Income Summary		92 0 1 4 00		23	← Step 5
24			Retained Earnings			92 0 1 4 00	24
25							25
26	(6)	31	Retained Earnings		15 0 0 0 00		26	← Step 6
27			Cash Dividends			15 0 0 0 00	27

FIGURE 27-12 Reversing Entries

	DATE		DESCRIPTION	POST. REF.	DEBIT	CREDIT	
1			Reversing Entries				1
2	20-- Jan.	1	Interest Payable		8 0 0 00		2
3	(1)		Interest Expense			8 0 0 00	3
4							4
5	(2)	1	Factory Overhead		2 7 0 0 00		5
6			Work in Process Inventory			2 7 0 0 00	6
7							7

CHECKPOINT ✓

Complete Checkpoint-3 on page 1083 to test your basic understanding of LO4.

Note that the adjustment for corporate income tax is not reversed. The purpose of reversing entries is to simplify the recording of routine transactions. Corporate income taxes are a specialized rather than routine transaction, so this adjustment is not reversed.

SELF-STUDY

LEARNING OBJECTIVES	Key Points to Remember
LO1 Prepare a 6-column spreadsheet for a manufacturing company.	Four steps are used to prepare a 6-column spreadsheet for a manufacturing company: 1. Prepare the trial balance. 2. Prepare the adjustments. 3. Prepare the adjusted trial balance. 4. Add all of the income statement accounts listed in the adjusted trial balance columns to compute the net income (loss) for the period. The new accounts and related adjustments on the spreadsheet are Finished Goods Inventory, Work in Process Inventory, Materials Inventory, Cost of Goods Sold, Factory Overhead, Income Tax Expense, and Corporate Income Tax Payable.
LO2 Prepare adjustments to (1) apply factory overhead to ending work in process, (2) record additional actual factory overhead, (3) record under- or overapplied overhead, (4) record expected sales returns and allowances, (5) record other expenses not involving overhead, and (6) provide for corporate income taxes.	Overhead must be applied to work in process at year-end. Adjustments for additional amounts of actual overhead are debited to Factory Overhead on the spreadsheet. After all adjustments are made for actual and applied overhead, an adjustment must be made for under- or overapplied overhead. Adjustments also are necessary for expected sales returns and allowances, other expenses not involving overhead, and corporate income taxes. The factory overhead account balances are extended to the Adjusted Trial Balance columns on the spreadsheet.
LO3 Prepare financial statements for a manufacturing company.	The main differences between a manufacturer's income statement and that of a merchandiser are the cost of goods sold section and the supplementary schedule of cost of goods manufactured. The only distinctive feature of ToyJoy's statement of retained earnings is the deduction for dividends, because ToyJoy is a corporation. Two main differences in ToyJoy's balance sheet are the three inventory accounts and the stockholders' equity section.
LO4 Prepare adjusting, closing, and reversing journal entries for a manufacturing company.	Each of the adjustments on the spreadsheet must be journalized. All revenue and expense accounts and both the debit and credit totals of Factory Overhead must be closed to Income Summary. Income Summary and Cash Dividends must be closed to Retained Earnings. Reverse the adjusting entry for Interest Expense and the adjustment to apply factory overhead to work in process.

DEMONSTRATION PROBLEM

Montgomery Manufacturing Co. manufactures and sells a limited line of products per customer order. Nothing is purchased for resale in its original form. The company rents offices and a factory building, and it owns neither real estate nor delivery equipment. It does have its own office and factory equipment. The company uses a perpetual inventory system and keeps its accounts on the calendar year basis. The trial balance of the general ledger as of December 31, 20--, is provided below. Data for the year-end adjustment of the accounts follow the trial balance.

	A	B	C
1	Montgomery Manufacturing Co.		
2	Trial Balance		
3	December 31, 20--		
4	ACCOUNT TITLE	TRIAL BALANCE	
5		DEBIT	CREDIT
6	Cash	46,275.00	
7	Accounts Receivable	95,928.00	
8	Allowance for Doubtful Accounts		1,800.00
9	Finished Goods Inventory	63,180.00	
10	Work in Process Inventory	41,256.00	
11	Materials Inventory	46,845.00	
12	Estimated Returns Inventory	70.00	
13	Office Supplies	2,916.00	
14	Factory Supplies	4,633.00	
15	Prepaid Insurance	5,589.00	
16	Factory Equipment	178,022.00	
17	Accum. Depreciation—Factory Equipment		34,956.00
18	Office Equipment	19,530.00	
19	Accum. Depreciation—Office Equipment		2,421.00
20	Notes Payable		27,000.00
21	Accounts Payable		38,590.00
22	Customer Refunds Payable		130.00
23	Income Tax Payable		
24	Interest Payable		
25	Capital Stock		135,000.00
26	Retained Earnings		38,131.00
27	Cash Dividends	10,000.00	
28	Sales		871,157.00
29	Sales Returns and Allowances	9,900.00	
30	Factory Overhead	44,212.00	60,585.00
31			
32			
33	Cost of Goods Sold	455,393.00	
34	Wages Expense	115,663.00	
35	Advertising Expense	24,680.00	
36	Office Rent Expense	13,180.00	
37	Office Supplies Expense		
38	Bad Debt Expense		
39	Insurance Expense—Office Equipment		
40	Depreciation Expense—Office Equipment		
41	Interest Expense	1,498.00	
42	Income Tax Expense	31,000.00	
43		1,209,770.00	1,209,770.00
44			

Data for year-end adjustments are as follows:

(a) Interest payable		$ 168
(b) Office supplies expense		900
(c) Factory supplies expense		1,870
(d) Depreciation of office equipment		960
(e) Depreciation of factory equipment		22,560
(f) Insurance expense on:		
office equipment	$ 120	
factory equipment	1,590	1,710
(g) Provision for bad debt expense (based on percentage of sales)		1,000
(h) Estimate of this year's sales that will be returned next year.		1,100
(i) Costs of goods expected to be returned.		600
(j) Provision for corporate income taxes		14,600
(k) Factory overhead to be applied to work in process		4,729

Physical counts of the inventories agreed with the amounts in the books.

Additional information needed to prepare the income statement and schedule of cost of goods manufactured is as follows:

Finished goods inventory, January 1	$219,692
Materials inventory, January 1	23,000
Purchases for the year	114,500
Direct labor	156,897
Work in process inventory, January 1	36,500
Indirect materials charged to production	4,500

REQUIRED

1. Prepare a 6-column spreadsheet for the year ended December 31, 20--. After the factory overhead account is adjusted, the total debits will differ from the total credits. Enter the under- or overapplied overhead on the spreadsheet by transferring it to Cost of Goods Sold. [Label this adjustment (l).]

2. Prepare an income statement with a supporting schedule of cost of goods manufactured.

3. Journalize the adjusting journal entries from the spreadsheet. [For parts (3), (4), and (5), use journal page numbers 15–17.]

4. Prepare closing entries.

5. Prepare reversing entries.

SOLUTION 1.

	A	B	C	D	E	F	G	H	I
1		Montgomery Manufacturing Co.							
2		End-of-Period Spreadsheet							
3		For the Year Ended December 31, 20--							
4	ACCOUNT TITLE	TRIAL BALANCE			ADJUSTMENTS			ADJUSTED TRIAL BALANCE	
5		DEBIT	CREDIT		DEBIT		CREDIT	DEBIT	CREDIT
6	Cash	46,275.00						46,275.00	
7	Accounts Receivable	95,928.00						95,928.00	
8	Allowance for Doubtful Accounts		1,800.00			(g)	1,000.00		2,800.00
9	Finished Goods Inventory	63,180.00						63,180.00	
10	Work in Process Inventory	41,256.00		(k)	4,729.00			45,985.00	
11	Materials Inventory	46,845.00						46,845.00	
12	Estimated Returns Inventory	70.00		(i)	530.00			600.00	
13	Office Supplies	2,916.00				(b)	900.00	2,016.00	
14	Factory Supplies	4,633.00				(c)	1,870.00	2,763.00	
15	Prepaid Insurance	5,589.00				(f)	1,710.00	3,879.00	
16	Factory Equipment	178,022.00						178,022.00	
17	Accum. Depreciation—Factory Equipment		34,956.00			(e)	22,560.00		57,516.00
18	Office Equipment	19,530.00						19,530.00	
19	Accum. Depreciation—Office Equipment		2,421.00			(d)	960.00		3,381.00
20	Notes Payable		27,000.00						27,000.00
21	Accounts Payable		38,590.00						38,590.00
22	Customer Refunds Payable		130.00			(h)	970.00		1,100.00
23	Income Tax Payable					(j)	14,600.00		14,600.00
24	Interest Payable					(a)	168.00		168.00
25	Capital Stock		135,000.00						135,000.00
26	Retained Earnings		38,131.00						38,131.00
27	Cash Dividends	10,000.00						10,000.00	
28	Sales		871,157.00						871,157.00
29	Sales Returns and Allowances	9,900.00		(h)	970.00			10,870.00	
30	Factory Overhead	44,212.00	60,585.00	(c)	1,870.00	(k)	4,729.00	70,232.00	70,232.00
31				(e)	22,560.00	(l)	4,918.00		
32				(f)	1,590.00				
33	Cost of Goods Sold	455,393.00		(l)	4,918.00	(i)	530.00	459,781.00	
34	Wages Expense	115,663.00						115,663.00	
35	Advertising Expense	24,680.00						24,680.00	
36	Office Rent Expense	13,180.00						13,180.00	
37	Office Supplies Expense			(b)	900.00			900.00	
38	Bad Debt Expense			(g)	1,000.00			1,000.00	
39	Insurance Expense—Office Equipment			(f)	120.00			120.00	
40	Depreciation Expense—Office Equipment			(d)	960.00			960.00	
41	Interest Expense	1,498.00		(a)	168.00			1,666.00	
42	Income Tax Expense	31,000.00		(j)	14,600.00			45,600.00	
43		1,209,770.00	1,209,770.00		54,915.00		54,915.00	1,259,675.00	1,259,675.00
44								744,652.00	941,389.00
45	Net Income							196,737.00	
46									

SOLUTION 2.

Montgomery Manufacturing Co.
Schedule of Cost of Goods Manufactured
For Year Ended December 31, 20--

Work in process, January 1			$ 36,500
Direct materials			
Materials inventory, January 1	$ 23,000		
Materials purchases	114,500		
Materials available	$ 137,500		
Materials inventory, December 31	46,845		
Cost of materials used		$ 90,655	
Less indirect materials included in overhead		4,500	
Cost of direct materials used		$ 86,155	
Direct labor		156,897	
Factory overhead		70,232	
Total manufacturing costs			313,284
Total work in process during the period			$ 349,784
Work in process, December 31			45,985
Cost of goods manufactured			$ 303,799

Montgomery Manufacturing Co.
Income Statement
For Year Ended December 31, 20--

Sales		$ 871,157	
Less sales returns and allowances		10,870	
Net sales			$ 860,287
Cost of goods sold:			
Finished goods inventory, January 1	$ 219,692		
Estimated returns inventory, January 1, remaining balance	70	$ 219,762	
Cost of goods manufactured		303,799	
Cost of goods available for sale		$ 523,561	
Finished goods inventory, December 31	$ 63,180		
Estimated returns inventory, December 31	600	63,780	
Cost of goods sold			459,781
Gross profit			$ 400,506
Operating expenses:			
Wages expense		$ 115,663	
Advertising expense		24,680	
Office rent expense		13,180	
Office supplies expense		900	
Bad debt expense		1,000	
Insurance expense—office equipment		120	
Depreciation expense—office equipment		960	
Total operating expenses			156,503
Operating income			$ 244,003
Other expense:			
Interest expense			1,666
Income before income taxes			$ 242,337
Income tax			45,600
Net income			$ 196,737

(*continued*)

SOLUTION 3.

	DATE		DESCRIPTION	POST. REF.	DEBIT	CREDIT	
1			Adjusting Entries				1
2	20–Dec.	31	Interest Expense		1 6 8 00		2
3	(a)		Interest Payable			1 6 8 00	3
4							4
5	(b)	31	Office Supplies Expense		9 0 0 00		5
6			Office Supplies			9 0 0 00	6
7							7
8	(c)	31	Factory Overhead		1 8 7 0 00		8
9			Factory Supplies			1 8 7 0 00	9
10							10
11	(d)	31	Depr. Expense—Office Equipment		9 6 0 00		11
12			Accum. Depr.—Office Equipment			9 6 0 00	12
13							13
14	(e)	31	Factory Overhead (Depr. Expense—Factory Equip.)		22 5 6 0 00		14
15			Accum. Depr.—Factory Equipment			22 5 6 0 00	15
16							16
17	(f)	31	Factory Overhead (Insurance Expense)		1 5 9 0 00		17
18			Insurance Expense—Office Equipment		1 2 0 00		18
19			Prepaid Insurance			1 7 1 0 00	19
20							20
21	(g)	31	Bad Debt Expense		1 0 0 0 00		21
22			Allowance for Doubtful Accounts			1 0 0 0 00	22
23							23
24	(h)	31	Sales Returns and Allowances		9 7 0 00		24
25			Customer Refunds Payable			9 7 0 00	25
26							26
27	(i)	31	Estimated Returns Inventory		5 3 0 00		27
28			Cost of Goods Sold			5 3 0 00	28
29							29
30	(j)	31	Income Tax Expense		14 6 0 0 00		30
31			Income Tax Payable			14 6 0 0 00	31
32							32
33	(k)	31	Work in Process Inventory		4 7 2 9 00		33
34			Factory Overhead			4 7 2 9 00	34
35							35
36	(l)	31	Cost of Goods Sold		4 9 1 8 00		36
37			Factory Overhead			4 9 1 8 00	37

GENERAL JOURNAL   PAGE 15

SOLUTION 4.

GENERAL JOURNAL   PAGE 16

	DATE		DESCRIPTION	POST. REF.	DEBIT	CREDIT	
1			Closing Entries				1
2	20-- Dec.	31	Income Summary		70 2 3 2 00		2
3			Factory Overhead			70 2 3 2 00	3
4							4
5		31	Factory Overhead		70 2 3 2 00		5
6			Income Summary			70 2 3 2 00	6
7							7
8		31	Sales		871 1 5 7 00		8
9			Income Summary			871 1 5 7 00	9
10							10
11		31	Income Summary		674 4 2 0 00		11
12			Sales Returns and Allowances			10 8 7 0 00	12
13			Cost of Goods Sold			459 7 8 1 00	13
14			Wages Expense			115 6 6 3 00	14
15			Advertising Expense			24 6 8 0 00	15
16			Office Rent Expense			13 1 8 0 00	16
17			Office Supplies Expense			9 0 0 00	17
18			Bad Debt Expense			1 0 0 0 00	18
19			Insurance Expense—Office Equipment			1 2 0 00	19
20			Depr. Expense—Office Equipment			9 6 0 00	20
21			Interest Expense			1 6 6 6 00	21
22			Income Tax Expense			45 6 0 0 00	22
23							23
24		31	Income Summary		196 7 3 7 00		24
25			Retained Earnings			196 7 3 7 00	25
26							26
27		31	Retained Earnings		10 0 0 0 00		27
28			Cash Dividends			10 0 0 0 00	28
29							29

SOLUTION 5.

GENERAL JOURNAL   PAGE 17

	DATE		DESCRIPTION	POST. REF.	DEBIT	CREDIT	
1			Reversing Entries				1
2	20-- Jan.	1	Interest Payable		1 6 8 00		2
3			Interest Expense			1 6 8 00	3
4							4
5		1	Factory Overhead		4 7 2 9 00		5
6			Work in Process Inventory			4 7 2 9 00	6
7							7

SELF-STUDY TEST QUESTIONS

True/False

1. **LO1**   Under the perpetual inventory system, Cost of Goods Sold is debited each time the finished goods inventory is sold.

2. **LO2**   At the end of the year, it is necessary to adjust for goods sold this year but expected to be returned in the next year.

3. **LO2**   On the spreadsheet, the factory overhead account shows both debit and credit totals in the Trial Balance columns.

4. **LO2**   The credit total of Factory Overhead represents actual factory overhead costs.

5. **LO2**   The adjustment for factory overhead applied to work in process at the end of the accounting period includes a debit to the factory overhead account.

Multiple Choice

1. **LO2**   The adjustment for the amount of factory supplies used during the year includes a
   (a) debit to Factory Supplies.
   (b) debit to Factory Overhead.
   (c) credit to Factory Overhead.
   (d) debit to Supplies Expense.

2. **LO2**   The adjustment for depreciation expense for the year on the factory building includes a
   (a) debit to Depreciation Expense.
   (b) credit to Factory Overhead.
   (c) credit to Accumulated Depreciation.
   (d) debit to Accumulated Depreciation.

3. **LO2**   At the end of the accounting period, a credit balance in the factory overhead account represents
   (a) overapplied factory overhead.
   (b) actual factory overhead.
   (c) underapplied factory overhead.
   (d) revenue earned.

4. **LO4**   During the closing process, the credit total in the factory overhead account is debited to
   (a) Work in Process Inventory.
   (b) Factory Overhead Expense.
   (c) Cost of Goods Sold.
   (d) Income Summary.

5. **LO4**   The adjusting entry to apply factory overhead to Work in Process is reversed at the beginning of the next accounting period and includes a
   (a) debit to Work in Process Inventory.
   (b) debit to Factory Overhead.
   (c) credit to Factory Overhead.
   (d) credit to Cost of Goods Sold.

CHECKPOINT ✔

Checkpoint Exercises

1. **LO2**   Prepare adjusting entries at December 31 for J P Company based on the following data.
   (a) Factory overhead is applied at a rate of 75% of direct labor costs. At the end of the year, the direct labor costs associated with the jobs in process totaled $8,000.
   (b) A physical count of factory supplies at the end of the year shows that $4,920 of factory supplies were used during the year.
   (c) Depreciation expense for the year on the factory building was $8,700 and on factory equipment was $11,600, a total of $20,300.
   (d) The factory overhead account has a debit balance of $186,500 and a credit balance of $183,900 [after recording adjustments (a) through (c)].

2. **LO3**   Prepare a schedule of cost of goods manufactured for Samo Company for the year ended September 30, 20-2, based on the following information.

Work in process, October 1, 20-1	$ 8,960
Materials inventory, October 1, 20-1	6,825
Materials purchases	96,530
Direct labor	196,420
Actual factory overhead	119,315
Work in process, September 30, 20-2	12,780
Materials inventory, September 30, 20-2	9,730
Indirect materials charged to production	5,040

3. **LO4**   Prepare closing journal entries for Adjent Company for the year ended December 31, based on the following data.

Factory overhead, debit and credit balances	$135,400
Sales	588,000
Cost of goods sold	395,400
Salaries expense	64,900
Office supplies expense	2,100
Depreciation expense—office equipment	4,000
Utilities expense—office	3,700
Bad debt expense	1,300
Income tax expense	23,000

The answers to the Self-Study Test Questions are at the end of the chapter (pages 1102–1103).

REVIEW QUESTIONS

LO1   1. What accounts and related adjustments are new in the spreadsheet of ToyJoy Manufacturing Co.?

LO1   2. How does the use of a perpetual inventory system affect the accounts on the spreadsheet?

LO2   3. Why must Work in Process Inventory be adjusted for factory overhead applied at year-end?

LO2   4. What is the relationship between the debit and credit balances in the factory overhead account when the overhead is said to be underapplied? Overapplied?

LO2   5. Why are the balances in the factory overhead account in the adjusted trial balance columns of the spreadsheet not used in preparing the Income Statement and Balance Sheet?

LO3   6. What are the distinctive features of ToyJoy's income statement? Its statement of retained earnings? Its balance sheet?

LO4   7. When the adjustment is made to apply overhead to ending work in process, why are no entries made in the job cost ledger?

LO4   8. Describe the procedures for closing the factory overhead account.

LO4   9. Which adjusting entries are reversed by ToyJoy?

SERIES A EXERCISES

E 27-1A (LO2)
✓ Factory overhead overapplied: $1,900

ADJUSTING ENTRIES INCLUDING ADJUSTMENT FOR UNDERAPPLIED/OVERAPPLIED FACTORY OVERHEAD Prepare the December 31 adjusting journal entries for Evanoff Company. Data are as follows:

(a) Factory overhead is applied at a rate of 60% of direct labor costs. At the end of the year, the direct labor costs associated with the jobs still in process totaled $8,000.

(b) A physical count of factory supplies at the end of the year shows that $5,100 of factory supplies were used during the year.

(c) A review of the insurance policy files shows that $6,500 of insurance on the factory building and equipment has expired.

(d) Depreciation expense for the year on the factory building was $9,000 and on factory equipment was $13,500, a total of $22,500.

(e) The factory overhead account has a debit balance of $187,600 and a credit balance of $189,500 [after recording adjustments (a) through (d)]. Use Cost of Goods Sold for this adjustment.

Was factory overhead under- or overapplied for the year?

E 27-2A   (LO3)

✓ Cost of goods manufactured: $287,500

SCHEDULE OF COST OF GOODS MANUFACTURED Prepare a schedule of cost of goods manufactured for Tomas Company for the year ended June 30, 20-2. Information to prepare the schedule is as follows:

Work in process, July 1, 20-1	$ 6,400
Materials inventory, July 1, 20-1	4,875
Materials purchases	68,950
Direct labor	140,300
Actual factory overhead	85,225
Work in process, June 30, 20-2	7,700
Materials inventory, June 30, 20-2	6,950
Indirect materials charged to production	3,600

E 27-3A   (LO4)

✓ Factory supplies adjustment, Dr. Factory Overhead (Factory Supplies Expense): $3,800

ADJUSTING JOURNAL ENTRIES Prepare the December 31 adjusting journal entries for Davis Company. Data for the end of the year adjustments are as follows:

Factory overhead to be applied to work in process ending inventory	$8,700
Estimate of this year's sales that will be returned next year (remaining balance from last year = 140)	800
Cost of goods expected to be returned (remaining balance from last year = 90)	530
Interest receivable	730
Provision for uncollectible accounts (based on percentage of sales)	4,200
Office supplies consumed	990
Factory supplies consumed	3,800
Insurance expired on factory building and equipment	3,100
Depreciation on factory building	8,000
Depreciation on factory equipment	6,300

E 27-4A   (LO4)

✓ Final closing entry, Dr. Income Summary: $129,670

CLOSING JOURNAL ENTRIES Prepare closing journal entries for Koehn Company for the year ended December 31. Data for the closing entries are as follows:

Factory overhead, debit and credit balances	$199,200
Sales for the year	877,400
Interest revenue	850
Cost of goods sold	581,000
Salaries expense	97,300
Office supplies expense	2,260
Depreciation expense—office equipment	6,040
Utilities expense—office	6,260
Bad debt expense	2,020
Advertising expense	9,100
Interest expense	9,900
Income tax expense	34,700

E 27-5A   (LO4)

✓ Final reversing entry, Dr. Factory Overhead: $3,180

REVERSING JOURNAL ENTRIES Prepare reversing journal entries for Rogerson Company on January 1, 20-2. The following year-end adjustments were made:

20-1				
Dec. 31	Interest Receivable		140	
		Interest Revenue		140
31	Interest Expense		930	
		Interest Payable		930
31	Work in Process Inventory		3,180	
		Factory Overhead		3,180

SERIES A PROBLEMS

P 27-6A **(LO1/2/3)**

✓ Net income: $104,045

SPREADSHEET, ADJUSTING ENTRIES, AND FINANCIAL STATEMENTS Lundberg Company had the following trial balance columns on its spreadsheet:

	A	B	C
1	**Lundberg Company**		
2	**Trial Balance**		
3	**December 31, 20--**		
4	ACCOUNT TITLE	TRIAL BALANCE	
5		DEBIT	CREDIT
6	Cash	30,300.00	
7	Government Notes	5,000.00	
8	Interest Receivable		
9	Accounts Receivable	34,000.00	
10	Allowance for Doubtful Accounts		530.00
11	Finished Goods Inventory	24,000.00	
12	Work in Process Inventory	9,000.00	
13	Materials Inventory	8,500.00	
14	Estimated Returns Inventory	60.00	
15	Office Supplies	3,100.00	
16	Factory Supplies	3,800.00	
17	Land	100,000.00	
18	Factory Building	120,000.00	
19	Accumulated Depreciation—Factory Building		10,000.00
20	Factory Equipment	40,000.00	
21	Accumulated Depreciation—Factory Equipment		5,000.00
22	Accounts Payable		13,800.00
23	Customer Refunds Payable		120.00
24	Income Tax Payable		
25	Interest Payable		
26	Bonds Payable		80,000.00
27	Capital Stock		50,000.00
28	Paid-in Capital in Excess of Par		30,000.00
29	Retained Earnings		92,820.00
30	Cash Dividends	30,000.00	
31	Sales		410,720.00
32	Sales Returns and Allowances	6,100.00	
33	Interest Revenue		300.00
34	Factory Overhead	78,630.00	89,300.00
35			
36			
37			
38	Cost of Goods Sold	190,700.00	
39	Wages Expense	70,000.00	
40	Office Supplies Expense		
41	Bad Debt Expense		
42	Utilities Expense—Office	4,400.00	
43	Interest Expense	7,000.00	
44	Income Tax Expense	18,000.00	
45		782,590.00	782,590.00
46			

Data for adjusting the accounts are as follows:

(a) Factory overhead to be applied to work in process ending inventory $3,100
(b) Estimate of this year's sales that will be returned next year   700
(c) Cost of goods expected to be returned   330
(d) Interest receivable   75
(e) Interest payable   610
(f) Estimate of uncollectible accounts, based on an aging of accounts
       receivable   2,930
(g) Office supplies consumed   2,900
(h) Factory supplies consumed   3,300
(i) Factory building depreciation   5,000
(j) Factory equipment depreciation   4,000
(k) Overapplied factory overhead   1,470
(l) Provision for corporate income taxes   6,100
(m) Physical counts of the inventories agreed with the amounts in the books

Additional information needed to prepare the financial statements is as follows:

Beginning inventories:
   Finished goods, January 1 $18,000
   Work in process, January 1   7,300
   Materials inventory, January 1   9,500
Materials purchases for the year   51,500
Direct labor   60,000
Actual factory overhead   90,930
Indirect materials charged to production   3,400

REQUIRED

1. Prepare a 6-column spreadsheet.

2. Prepare the following financial statements and schedule:
    (a) income statement
    (b) schedule of cost of goods manufactured
    (c) statement of retained earnings
    (d) balance sheet

P 27-7A   (LO1/3)
✓ 2. Retained Earnings, Dec. 31:
   $99,095

FINANCIAL STATEMENTS The adjusted trial balance columns of Braiden Company's spreadsheet are shown on the next page.

Additional information needed to prepare the financial statements is as follows:

Materials inventory, January 1 $ 4,140
Work in process inventory, January 1   5,730
Finished goods inventory, January 1   16,535
Estimated returns inventory, January 1, remaining balance   55
Materials purchases   136,665
Direct labor   76,000
Actual factory overhead   92,500
Indirect materials charged to production   5,400

(*continued*)

REQUIRED

1. Prepare an income statement and a schedule of cost of goods manufactured for the year ended December 31, 20--.

2. Prepare a statement of retained earnings for the year ended December 31, 20--.

3. Prepare a balance sheet as of December 31, 20--.

	A	B	C
1	**Braiden Company**		
2	**Spreadsheet (Partial)**		
3	**For the Year Ended December 31, 20--**		
4	ACCOUNT TITLE	ADJUSTED TRIAL BALANCE	
5		DEBIT	CREDIT
6	Cash	15,720.00	
7	Government Notes	3,500.00	
8	Interest Receivable	50.00	
9	Accounts Receivable	25,100.00	
10	Allowance for Doubtful Accounts		1,325.00
11	Finished Goods Inventory	18,430.00	
12	Work in Process Inventory	7,510.00	
13	Materials Inventory	4,650.00	
14	Estimated Returns Inventory	500.00	
15	Office Supplies	330.00	
16	Factory Supplies	480.00	
17	Prepaid Insurance	700.00	
18	Land	25,000.00	
19	Factory Building	90,000.00	
20	Accumulated Depreciation—Factory Building		20,650.00
21	Factory Equipment	100,000.00	
22	Accumulated Depreciation—Factory Equipment		29,000.00
23	Accounts Payable		17,000.00
24	Customer Refunds Payable		700.00
25	Income Tax Payable		3,550.00
26	Interest Payable		650.00
27	Bonds Payable		50,000.00
28	Capital Stock		55,000.00
29	Paid-in Capital in Excess of Par		15,000.00
30	Retained Earnings		80,200.00
31	Cash Dividends	20,000.00	
32	Sales		402,900.00
33	Sales Returns and Allowances	6,270.00	
34	Interest Revenue		250.00
35	Factory Overhead	92,500.00	92,500.00
36			
37			
38	.Cost of Goods Sold	295,135.00	
39	Wages Expense	45,200.00	
40	Office Supplies Expense	1,500.00	
41	Bad Debt Expense	2,150.00	
42	Utilities Expense—Office	1,700.00	
43	Interest Expense	2,850.00	
44	Income Tax Expense	9,450.00	
45		768,725.00	768,725.00
46		456,755.00	495,650.00
47	Net Income	38,895.00	
48			

P 27-8A   (LO1/2/4)

✓ 2. Final closing entry, Dr. Income Summary: $75,560

ADJUSTING, CLOSING, AND REVERSING ENTRIES A 6-column spreadsheet for Baldwin Company is shown on the next page.

Data for adjusting the accounts are as follows:

(a)	Factory overhead to be applied to work in process ending inventory	$3,600
(b)	Estimate of this year's sales that will be returned next year	1,250
(c)	Cost of goods expected to be returned	720
(d)	Interest receivable	140
(e)	Interest payable	1,200
(f)	Estimate of uncollectible accounts, based on an aging of accounts receivable	2,370
(g)	Office supplies consumed	3,700
(h)	Factory supplies consumed	4,200
(i)	Insurance on factory building and equipment expired	5,100
(j)	Factory building depreciation	5,000
(k)	Factory equipment depreciation	4,000
(l)	Underapplied factory overhead	1,300
(m)	Provision for corporate income taxes	5,900

REQUIRED

1. Prepare the December 31 adjusting journal entries for Baldwin Company.
2. Prepare the December 31 closing journal entries for Baldwin Company.
3. Prepare the reversing journal entries as of January 1, 20-2, for Baldwin Company.

SERIES B EXERCISES

E 27-1B   (LO2)

✓ Factory overhead underapplied: $3,500

ADJUSTING ENTRIES INCLUDING ADJUSTMENT FOR UNDERAPPLIED/ OVERAPPLIED FACTORY OVERHEAD Prepare the December 31 adjusting journal entries for Keiser Company. Data are as follows:

(a) Factory overhead is applied at a rate of 80% of direct labor costs. At the end of the year, the direct labor costs associated with the jobs still in process totaled $7,000.

(b) A physical count of factory supplies at the end of the year shows that $3,750 of factory supplies were used during the year.

(c) A review of the insurance policy files shows that $4,360 of insurance on the factory building and equipment has expired.

(d) Depreciation expense for the year on the factory building was $9,400 and on factory equipment was $11,600, a total of $21,000.

(e) The factory overhead account has a debit balance of $146,700 and a credit balance of $143,200 [after recording adjustments (a) through (d)]. Use Cost of Goods Sold for this adjustment.

Was factory overhead underapplied or overapplied for the year?

PROBLEM 27-8A

	A	B	C	D	E	F	G	H	I
1					Baldwin Company				
2					End-of-Period Spreadsheet				
3					For the Year Ended December 31, 20--				
4	ACCOUNT TITLE	TRIAL BALANCE			ADJUSTMENTS			ADJUSTED TRIAL BALANCE	
5		DEBIT	CREDIT		DEBIT		CREDIT	DEBIT	CREDIT
6	Cash	41,200.00						41,200.00	
7	Government Notes	6,000.00						6,000.00	
8	Interest Receivable			(d)	140.00			140.00	
9	Accounts Receivable	32,000.00						32,000.00	
10	Allowance for Doubtful Accounts		920.00			(f)	1,450.00		2,370.00
11	Finished Goods Inventory	21,000.00						21,000.00	
12	Work in Process Inventory	10,200.00		(a)	3,600.00			13,800.00	
13	Materials Inventory	9,100.00						9,100.00	
14	Estimated Returns Inventory	75.00		(c)	645.00			720.00	
15	Office Supplies	4,200.00				(g)	3,700.00	500.00	
16	Factory Supplies	5,100.00				(h)	4,200.00	900.00	
17	Prepaid Insurance	6,200.00				(i)	5,100.00	1,100.00	
18	Land	80,000.00						80,000.00	
19	Factory Building	120,000.00						120,000.00	
20	Accum. Depreciation—Factory Building		20,000.00			(j)	5,000.00		25,000.00
21	Factory Equipment	50,000.00						50,000.00	
22	Accum. Depreciation—Factory Equipment		8,000.00			(k)	4,000.00		12,000.00
23	Accounts Payable		16,400.00						16,400.00
24	Customer Refunds Payable		130.00			(b)	1,120.00		1,250.00
25	Income Tax Payable					(m)	5,900.00		5,900.00
26	Interest Payable					(e)	1,200.00		1,200.00
27	Bonds Payable		90,000.00						90,000.00
28	Capital Stock		60,000.00						60,000.00
29	Paid-in Capital in Excess of Par		40,000.00						40,000.00
30	Retained Earnings		46,780.00						46,780.00
31	Sales		406,445.00						406,445.00
32	Sales Returns and Allowances	6,300.00		(b)	1,120.00			7,420.00	
33	Interest Revenue		500.00			(d)	140.00		640.00
34	Factory Overhead	91,800.00	105,200.00	(h)	4,200.00	(a)	3,600.00	110,100.00	110,100.00
35				(i)	5,100.00	(l)	1,300.00		
36				(j)	5,000.00				
37				(k)	4,000.00				
38	Cost of Goods Sold	203,500.00		(l)	1,300.00	(c)	645.00	204,155.00	
39	Salaries Expense	80,000.00						80,000.00	
40	Office Supplies Expense			(g)	3,700.00			3,700.00	
41	Bad Debt Expense			(f)	1,450.00			1,450.00	
42	Utilities Expense—Office	6,700.00						6,700.00	
43	Interest Expense	8,000.00		(e)	1,200.00			9,200.00	
44	Income Tax Expense	13,000.00		(m)	5,900.00			18,900.00	
45		794,375.00	794,375.00		37,355.00		37,355.00	818,085.00	818,085.00
46								441,625.00	517,185.00
47	Net Income							75,560.00	
48									

E 27-2B   (LO3)
✓ Cost of goods manufactured: $685,956

SCHEDULE OF COST OF GOODS MANUFACTURED Prepare a schedule of cost of goods manufactured for Verdi Company for the year ended June 30, 20-2. Assume that all materials inventory items are direct materials. Information to prepare the schedule is as follows:

Work in process, July 1, 20-1	$ 20,760
Materials inventory, July 1, 20-1	12,348
Materials purchases	154,008
Direct labor	330,576
Actual factory overhead	201,384
Work in process, June 30, 20-2	17,940
Materials inventory, June 30, 20-2	15,180

E 27-3B   (LO4)
✓ Factory Supplies adjustment, Dr. Factory Overhead (Factory Supplies Expense): $4,160

ADJUSTING JOURNAL ENTRIES FOR A MANUFACTURING BUSINESS Prepare the December 31 adjusting journal entries for Ortiz Company. Data for the end of the year adjustments are as follows:

Factory overhead to be applied to work in process ending inventory	$7,780
Estimate of this year's sales that will be returned next year (remaining balance from last year = 130)	770
Cost of goods expected to be returned (remaining balance from last year = 85)	490
Interest receivable	435
Provision for uncollectible accounts (based on percentage of sales)	3,876
Office supplies consumed	750
Factory supplies consumed	4,160
Insurance expired on factory building and equipment	3,200
Depreciation on factory building	6,800
Depreciation on factory equipment	4,200

E 27-4B   (LO4)
✓ Final closing entry, Dr. Income Summary: $44,655

CLOSING JOURNAL ENTRIES Prepare closing journal entries for Armour Company for the year ended December 31. Data for the closing entries are as follows:

Factory overhead, debit and credit balance	$186,250
Sales for the year	930,600
Interest revenue	920
Cost of goods sold	710,500
Salaries expense	98,100
Office supplies expense	3,500
Depreciation expense—office equipment	6,130
Utilities expense—office	7,460
Bad debt expense	2,275
Advertising expense	9,250
Interest expense	8,300
Income tax expense	41,350

E 27-5B   (LO4)
✓ Final reversing entry, Dr. Factory
Overhead: $4,250

REVERSING ENTRIES Prepare reversing journal entries for Hendrix Company on January 1, 20-2. The following year-end adjustments were made:

20-1

Dec. 31	Interest Receivable	230	
	Interest Revenue		230
31	Interest Expense	875	
	Interest Payable		875
31	Work in Process Inventory	4,250	
	Factory Overhead		4,250

SERIES B PROBLEMS

P 27-6B   (LO1/2/3)
✓ Net Income: $73,270

SPREADSHEET, ADJUSTING ENTRIES, AND FINANCIAL STATEMENTS Woods Company's trial balance columns from its spreadsheet are shown on the next page. Data for adjusting the accounts are as follows:

(a)	Factory overhead to be applied to work in process ending inventory	$ 4,300
(b)	Estimate of this year's sales that will be returned next year	1,010
(c)	Cost of goods expected to be returned	490
(d)	Interest receivable	100
(e)	Interest payable	700
(f)	Estimate of uncollectible accounts, based on an aging of accounts receivable	4,110
(g)	Office supplies consumed	3,200
(h)	Factory supplies consumed	6,700
(i)	Factory building depreciation	10,000
(j)	Factory equipment depreciation	6,000
(k)	Underapplied factory overhead	7,690
(l)	Provision for corporate income taxes	8,100
(m)	Physical counts of the inventories agreed with the amounts in the books	

Additional information needed to prepare the financial statements is as follows:

Beginning inventories:	
Finished goods, January 1	$ 22,300
Work in process, January 1	12,400
Materials inventory, January 1	7,900
Materials purchases for the year	18,700
Direct labor	90,300
Actual factory overhead	104,290

Assume that all materials inventory items are direct materials.

REQUIRED

1. Prepare a spreadsheet.

2. Prepare the following financial statements and schedule:
   (a) income statement
   (b) schedule of cost of goods manufactured
   (c) statement of retained earnings
   (d) balance sheet

PROBLEM 27-6B (*continued*)

	A	B	C
1	**Woods Company**		
2	**Trial Balance**		
3	**December 31, 20--**		
4	ACCOUNT TITLE	TRIAL BALANCE	
5		DEBIT	CREDIT
6	Cash	28,400.00	
7	Government Notes	6,000.00	
8	Interest Receivable		
9	Accounts Receivable	32,800.00	
10	Allowance for Doubtful Accounts		610.00
11	Finished Goods Inventory	26,100.00	
12	Work in Process Inventory	10,200.00	
13	Materials Inventory	9,300.00	
14	Estimated Returns Inventory	65.00	
15	Office Supplies	4,200.00	
16	Factory Supplies	8,600.00	
17	Land	80,000.00	
18	Factory Building	160,000.00	
19	Accumulated Depreciation—Factory Building		30,000.00
20	Factory Equipment	60,000.00	
21	Accumulated Depreciation—Factory Equipment		20,000.00
22	Accounts Payable		16,000.00
23	Customer Refunds Payable		125.00
24	Income Tax Payable		
25	Interest Payable		
26	Bonds Payable		100,000.00
27	Capital Stock		60,000.00
28	Paid-in Capital in Excess of Par		20,000.00
29	Retained Earnings		111,400.00
30	Cash Dividends	40,000.00	
31	Sales		404,680.00
32	Sales Returns and Allowances	5,040.00	
33	Interest Revenue		500.00
34	Factory Overhead	81,590.00	92,300.00
35			
36			
37	Cost of Goods Sold	198,300.00	
38	Wages Expense	78,700.00	
39	Office Supplies Expense		
40	Bad Debt Expense		
41	Utilities Expense—Office	4,900.00	
42	Interest Expense	9,000.00	
43	Income Tax Expense	12,420.00	
44		855,615.00	855,615.00
45			

P 27-7B   (LO1/3)
✓ 2. Retained Earnings,
Dec. 31: $101,080

FINANCIAL STATEMENTS The adjusted trial balance columns of Wen Company's spreadsheet are shown on the next page.

Additional information needed to prepare the financial statements is as follows:

Materials inventory, January 1	$ 4,750
Work in process inventory, January 1	3,600
Finished goods inventory, January 1	14,990
Estimate returns inventory, January 1, remaining balance	100
Materials purchases	115,090
Direct labor	110,000
Actual factory overhead	96,850
Indirect materials charged to production	4,100

REQUIRED

1. Prepare an income statement and a schedule of cost of goods manufactured for the year ended December 31, 20--.

2. Prepare a statement of retained earnings for the year ended December 31, 20--.

3. Prepare a balance sheet as of December 31, 20--.

PROBLEM 27-7B (*continued*)

	A	B	C
1	**Wen Company**		
2	**Spreadsheet (Partial)**		
3	**For the Year Ended December 31, 20--**		
4	ACCOUNT TITLE	ADJUSTED TRIAL BALANCE	
5		DEBIT	CREDIT
6	Cash	16,450.00	
7	Government Notes	6,000.00	
8	Interest Receivable	210.00	
9	Accounts Receivable	19,700.00	
10	Allowance for Doubtful Accounts		1,600.00
11	Finished Goods Inventory	16,250.00	
12	Work in Process Inventory	7,600.00	
13	Materials Inventory	4,550.00	
14	Estimated Returns Inventory	530.00	
15	Office Supplies	465.00	
16	Factory Supplies	375.00	
17	Prepaid Insurance	700.00	
18	Land	30,000.00	
19	Factory Building	60,000.00	
20	Accumulated Depreciation—Factory Building		15,230.00
21	Factory Equipment	87,000.00	
22	Accumulated Depreciation—Factory Equipment		23,000.00
23	Accounts Payable		14,450.00
24	Customer Refunds Payable		720.00
25	Income Tax Payable		3,150.00
26	Interest Payable		600.00
27	Bonds Payable		40,000.00
28	Capital Stock		30,000.00
29	Paid-in Capital in Excess of Par		20,000.00
30	Retained Earnings		83,020.00
31	Cash Dividends	13,500.00	
32	Sales		409,860.00
33	Sales Returns and Allowances	5,900.00	
34	Interest Revenue		650.00
35	Factory Overhead	96,850.00	96,850.00
36			
37	Cost of Goods Sold	312,350.00	
38	Wages Expense	43,100.00	
39	Office Supplies Expense	2,250.00	
40	Bad Debt Expense	1,750.00	
41	Utilities Expense—Office	4,000.00	
42	Interest Expense	3,100.00	
43	Income Tax Expense	6,500.00	
44		739,130.00	739,130.00
45		475,800.00	507,360.00
46	Net Income	31,560.00	
47			

P 27-8B (LO1/2/4)
✓ 2. Final closing entry, Dr. Income
Summary: $65,190

ADJUSTING, CLOSING, AND REVERSING ENTRIES A 6-column spreadsheet for Milnor Company is shown on the next page.

Data for adjusting the accounts are as follows:

(a)	Factory overhead to be applied to work in process ending inventory	$4,400
(b)	Estimate of this year's sales that will be returned next year	700
(c)	Cost of goods expected to be returned	380
(d)	Interest receivable	190
(e)	Interest payable	1,420
(f)	Estimate of uncollectible accounts, based on an aging of accounts receivable	4,450
(g)	Office supplies consumed	4,200
(h)	Factory supplies consumed	3,800
(i)	Insurance on factory building and equipment expired	6,800
(j)	Factory building depreciation	8,000
(k)	Factory equipment depreciation	5,000
(l)	Overapplied factory overhead	4,340
(m)	Provision for corporate income taxes	6,400

REQUIRED

1. Prepare the December 31 adjusting journal entries for Milnor Company.

2. Prepare the December 31 closing journal entries for Milnor Company.

3. Prepare the reversing journal entries as of January 1, 20-2, for Milnor Company.

PROBLEM 27-8B (*continued*)

	A	B	C	D	E	F	G	H	I
1					Milnor Company				
2					End-of-Period Spreadsheet				
3					For the Year Ended December 31, 20--				
4	ACCOUNT TITLE	TRIAL BALANCE			ADJUSTMENTS			ADJUSTED TRIAL BALANCE	
5		DEBIT	CREDIT		DEBIT		CREDIT	DEBIT	CREDIT
6	Cash	39,600.00						39,600.00	
7	Government Notes	8,000.00						8,000.00	
8	Interest Receivable			(d)	190.00			190.00	
9	Accounts Receivable	40,000.00						40,000.00	
10	Allowance for Doubtful Accounts		1,250.00			(f)	3,200.00		4,450.00
11	Finished Goods Inventory	24,000.00						24,000.00	
12	Work in Process Inventory	12,300.00		(a)	4,400.00			16,700.00	
13	Materials Inventory	8,700.00						8,700.00	
14	Estimated Returns Inventory	90.00		(c)	290.00			380.00	
15	Office Supplies	5,500.00				(g)	4,200.00	1,300.00	
16	Factory Supplies	4,950.00				(h)	3,800.00	1,150.00	
17	Prepaid Insurance	7,450.00				(i)	6,800.00	650.00	
18	Land	90,000.00						90,000.00	
19	Factory Building	130,000.00						130,000.00	
20	Accum. Depreciation—Factory Building		40,000.00			(j)	8,000.00		48,000.00
21	Factory Equipment	70,000.00						70,000.00	
22	Accum. Depreciation—Factory Equipment		10,000.00			(k)	5,000.00		15,000.00
23	Accounts Payable		17,200.00						17,200.00
24	Customer Refunds Payable		150.00			(b)	550.00		700.00
25	Income Tax Payable					(m)	6,400.00		6,400.00
26	Interest Payable					(e)	1,420.00		1,420.00
27	Bonds Payable		120,000.00						120,000.00
28	Capital Stock		50,000.00						50,000.00
29	Paid-in Capital in Excess of Par		30,000.00						30,000.00
30	Retained Earnings		72,310.00						72,310.00
31	Sales		393,840.00						393,840.00
32	Sales Returns and Allowances	6,700.00		(b)	550.00			7,250.00	
33	Interest Revenue		800.00			(d)	190.00		990.00
34	Factory Overhead	84,560.00	108,100.00	(h)	3,800.00	(a)	4,400.00	112,500.00	112,500.00
35				(i)	6,800.00				
36				(j)	8,000.00				
37				(k)	5,000.00				
38				(l)	4,340.00				
39	Cost of Goods Sold	194,600.00				(c)	290.00	189,970.00	
40						(l)	4,340.00		
41	Wages Expense	90,000.00						90,000.00	
42	Office Supplies Expense			(g)	4,200.00			4,200.00	
43	Bad Debt Expense			(f)	3,200.00			3,200.00	
44	Utilities Expense—Office	7,200.00						7,200.00	
45	Interest Expense	9,000.00		(e)	1,420.00			10,420.00	
46	Income Tax Expense	11,000.00		(m)	6,400.00			17,400.00	
47		843,650.00	843,650.00		48,590.00		48,590.00	872,810.00	872,810.00
48								442,140.00	507,330.00
49	Net Income							65,190.00	
50									

CHECK LIST

☐ **Managing**
☐ **Planning**
☐ **Drafting**
☐ **Break**
☐ **Revising**
☐ **Managing**

MANAGING YOUR WRITING

You and a fellow student are arguing about the "value" of Chapter 27. She says that the chapter is mostly review. The spreadsheet and financial statements were fully covered in Chapter 15. Chapter 27 is a similar story with some cosmetic differences. You have just begun an impressive defense of Chapter 27 when your professor overhears the argument and decides to give the entire class the following assignment.

Prepare a report describing (1) the ways in which the manufacturer's spreadsheet differs from the merchandiser's and (2) the differences between the merchandiser's financial statements in Chapter 15 and the manufacturer's financial statements in Chapter 27.

ETHICS ♥★

ETHICS CASE

Kevin Ryan is an accountant for Warick Corporation, a medium-size manufacturing firm. One of his responsibilities is to review the adjusting entries at the end of each accounting period. Mary Sellers is a new accountant at Warick Corporation. She is a recent graduate and this is her first accounting job. One of the duties Kevin assigned Mary was to prepare the adjusting entries. After reviewing Mary's work, Kevin came to the conclusion that Mary did not understand the adjusting process for a manufacturing company. During their review meeting, Kevin told Mary that he was concerned about her ability to do the job. Mary admitted not having a sound knowledge of the adjusting and closing process but asked Kevin to give her another month to catch on. Kevin said he would have to think about it over the weekend and he would get back to her on Monday. That weekend, Kevin was offered a much better paying job with a large manufacturing company in the same city. He immediately accepted the position. When he gave his boss notice that he would be leaving Warick, his boss asked him how Mary was doing. Kevin said he thought she'd do just fine.

1. Do you think Kevin should have told his boss about Mary's poor performance? Why or why not?

2. How will Kevin's decision to not say anything affect Mary?

3. Write a short incident report concerning Mary's poor job performance and subsequent conference with Kevin. Assume Kevin writes the report and it will be placed in Mary's personnel file.

4. In groups of two or three, discuss what alternatives Kevin had in this situation. Come to a group consensus on the best alternative.

MASTERY PROBLEM

Reese Manufacturing Company manufactures and sells a limited line of products made to customer order. The company uses a perpetual inventory system and keeps its accounts on a calendar year basis. A 6-column spreadsheet is presented on page 1100.

Additional information needed to prepare the income statement and schedule of cost of goods manufactured is as follows:

Finished goods inventory, January 1	$ 85,454
Materials inventory, January 1	11,633
Purchases for the year	96,437
Direct labor	107,740
Work in process inventory, January 1	22,600
Indirect materials charged to production	3,200

REQUIRED

1. Prepare an income statement and schedule of cost of goods manufactured for the year ended December 31, 20--.

2. Prepare a statement of retained earnings for the year ended December 31, 20--.

3. Prepare a balance sheet as of December 31, 20--.

4. Prepare the adjusting, closing, and reversing entries.

MASTERY PROBLEM

	A	B	C	D	E	F	G	H	I
1		Reese Manufacturing Co.							
2		End-of-Period Spreadsheet							
3		For the Year Ended December 31, 20--							
4	ACCOUNT TITLE	TRIAL BALANCE			ADJUSTMENTS			ADJUSTED TRIAL BALANCE	
5		DEBIT	CREDIT		DEBIT		CREDIT	DEBIT	CREDIT
6	Cash	44,783.00						44,783.00	
7	Accounts Receivable	78,096.00						78,096.00	
8	Allowance for Doubtful Accounts		5,074.00			(g)	956.00		6,030.00
9	Finished Goods Inventory	42,675.00						42,675.00	
10	Work in Process Inventory	39,675.00		(k)	1,567.00			41,242.00	
11	Materials Inventory	22,353.00						22,353.00	
12	Estimated Returns Inventory	70.00		(i)	570.00			640.00	
13	Office Supplies	3,546.00				(b)	800.00	2,746.00	
14	Factory Supplies	1,878.00				(c)	1,389.00	489.00	
15	Prepaid Insurance	1,500.00				(f)	1,454.00	46.00	
16	Factory Equipment	186,674.00						186,674.00	
17	Accum. Depreciation—Factory Equipment		23,501.00			(e)	12,553.00		36,054.00
18	Office Equipment	46,986.00						46,986.00	
19	Accum. Depreciation—Office Equipment		2,916.00			(d)	923.00		3,839.00
20	Notes Payable		12,470.00						12,470.00
21	Accounts Payable		10,356.00						10,356.00
22	Customer Refunds Payable		120.00			(h)	1,040.00		1,160.00
23	Income Tax Payable					(j)	14,725.00		14,725.00
24	Interest Payable					(a)	132.00		132.00
25	Capital Stock		88,000.00						88,000.00
26	Retained Earnings		195,341.00						195,341.00
27	Cash Dividends	36,000.00						36,000.00	
28	Sales		537,137.00						537,137.00
29	Sales Returns and Allowances	9,800.00		(h)	1,040.00			10,840.00	
30	Factory Overhead	52,356.00	65,446.00	(c)	1,389.00	(k)	1,567.00	67,654.00	67,654.00
31				(e)	12,553.00	(l)	641.00		
32				(f)	1,356.00				
33	Cost of Goods Sold	281,407.00		(l)	641.00	(i)	570.00	281,478.00	
34	Wages Expense	58,380.00						58,380.00	
35	Advertising Expense	11,450.00						11,450.00	
36	Office Rent Expense	5,443.00						5,443.00	
37	Office Supplies Expense			(b)	800.00			800.00	
38	Bad Debt Expense			(g)	956.00			956.00	
39	Insurance Expense—Office Equipment			(f)	98.00			98.00	
40	Depreciation Expense—Office Equipment			(d)	923.00			923.00	
41	Interest Expense	1,289.00		(a)	132.00			1,421.00	
42	Income Tax Expense	16,000.00		(j)	14,725.00			30,725.00	
43		940,361.00	940,361.00		36,750.00		36,750.00	972,898.00	972,898.00
44								470,168.00	604,791.00
45	Net Income							134,623.00	
46									

CHALLENGE PROBLEM

This problem challenges you to apply your cumulative accounting knowledge to move a step beyond the material in the chapter.

✓ 2. Revised net income: $56,670

Drafts of the condensed income statement and balance sheet of Allofe Co. for the current year are shown below. Shortly after preparing these draft financial statements, Allofe discovered that an error had been made in the year-end adjustment process. Overhead of $2,500 had not been applied to the ending work in process.

Allofe Co.
Condensed Income Statement
For Year Ended December 31, 20--

Net sales	$501,570
Cost of goods sold	360,312
Gross profit	$141,258
Operating expenses	87,088
Net income	$ 54,170

Allofe Co.
Condensed Balance Sheet
December 31, 20--

Assets	
Current assets	$ 93,014
Property, plant, and equipment (net)	177,441
Total assets	$270,455
Liabilities	
Current liabilities	$ 28,671
Long-term liabilities	60,000
Total liabilities	$ 88,671
Stockholders' Equity	
Paid-in capital	$ 57,000
Retained earnings	124,784
Total stockholders' equity	$181,784
Total liabilities and stockholders' equity	$270,455

REQUIRED

1. Identify all adjusting and closing entries that would be affected by this error and prepare the missing portions of the entries.

2. Prepare a revised condensed income statement for Allofe.

(In solving this problem, assume that corporate income tax is not affected by the error.)

ANSWERS TO SELF-STUDY TEST QUESTIONS

True/False

1. T

2. T

3. T

4. F (debit total)

5. F (credit)

Multiple Choice

1. b   **2.** c   **3.** a   **4.** d   **5.** b

Checkpoint Exercises

1. (a) Work in Process Inventory   6,000

       Factory Overhead   6,000

    (b) Factory Overhead (Factory Supplies Expense)   4,920

       Factory Supplies   4,920

    (c) Factory Overhead (Depreciation Expense—Factory Building and Equipment)   20,300

          Accumulated Depreciation—Factory Building   8,700

          Accumulated Depreciation—Factory Equipment   11,600

    (d) Cost of Goods Sold   2,600

       Factory Overhead   2,600

2.

Work in process, October 1, 20-1			$ 8,960
Direct materials			
Materials inventory, October 1, 20-1	$ 6,825		
Materials purchases	96,530		
Materials available	$103,355		
Materials inventory, September 30, 20-2	9,730		
Cost of materials used		$ 93,625	
Less indirect materials charged to production		5,040	
Cost of direct materials used		$ 88,585	
Direct labor		196,420	
Overhead		119,315	
Total manufacturing costs			404,320
Total work in process during period			$ 413,280
Work in process, September 30, 20-2			12,780
Cost of goods manufactured			$ 400,500

3. Dec. 31 Income Summary   135,400
         Factory Overhead (Subsidiary ledger accounts)   135,400

    31 Factory Overhead   135,400
         Income Summary   135,400

    31 Sales   588,000
         Income Summary   588,000

    31 Income Summary   494,400
         Cost of Goods Sold   395,400
         Salaries Expense   64,900
         Office Supplies Expense   2,100
         Depreciation Expense—Office Equipment   4,000
         Utilities Expense—Office   3,700
         Bad Debt Expense   1,300
         Income Tax Expense   23,000

    31 Income Summary   93,600
         Retained Earnings   93,600

*Page references in **bold** indicate defined terms.

THE ACCOUNTING EQUATION

Assets = Liabilities + Owner's Equity

FINANCIAL STATEMENTS

Income Statement	**Revenues – Expenses = Net Income or Loss**
Statement of Owner's Equity	**Beginning Capital + Investments + Net Income – Withdrawals = Ending Capital**
Balance Sheet	**Assets = Liabilities + Owner's Equity**

T ACCOUNT

Title

Debit = Left	Credit = Right

EXPANDED ACCOUNTING EQUATION SHOWING RULES OF DEBIT AND CREDIT

Assets = **Liabilities** + **Owner's Equity**

Dr.	Cr.
+	–

Dr.	Cr.
–	+

Dr.	Cr.
–	+

Drawing

Dr.	Cr.
+	–

Expenses

Dr.	Cr.
+	–

Revenue

Dr.	Cr.
–	+

STEPS IN MAJOR ACCOUNTING PROCESSES

Steps in Journalizing a Transaction

1. Enter the date.
2. Enter the account title and debit amount.
3. Enter the account title and credit amount.
4. Enter the explanation.

Steps in Posting from the Journal to the Ledger

In the ledger:
1. Enter the date in the Date column.
2. Enter the amount of each transaction in the Debit or Credit column.
3. Enter the new balance in the Balance column under Debit or Credit.
4. Enter the page number of the journal from which each transaction is posted in the Posting Reference column.

In the journal:
5. Enter the ledger account number in the Posting Reference column in the journal.

Steps in Preparing the Work Sheet

1. Prepare the trial balance.
2. Prepare the adjustments.
3. Prepare the adjusted trial balance.
4. Extend adjusted balances to the Income Statement and Balance Sheet columns.
5. Complete the work sheet.

Steps in the Closing Process

1. Close the revenue accounts to Income Summary.
2. Close the expense accounts to Income Summary.
3. Close Income Summary to the owner's capital account.
4. Close the drawing account to the owner's capital account.

STEPS IN THE ACCOUNTING CYCLE

Source Documents

Steps in the Accounting Cycle

During Accounting Period:
1. Analyze source documents.
2. Journalize the transactions.
3. Post to the ledger accounts.

End of Accounting Period:
4. Prepare a trial balance.
5. Determine and prepare the needed adjustments on the work sheet.
6. Complete an end-of-period work sheet.
7. Journalize and post the adjusting entries.
8. Prepare an income statement, statement of owner's equity, and balance sheet.
9. Journalize and post the closing entries.
10. Prepare a post-closing trial balance.

Note: While for a specific company each account number used would have only one title, titles vary from company to company as needed. Particularly for the Owner's Equity accounts, the accounts used depend on the company ownership structure (proprietorship, partnership, or corporation).

Assets (100–199)

100s—Cash Related Accounts
101 Cash
105 Petty Cash

120s—Receivables
121 Notes Receivable
122 Accounts Receivable
122.1 Allowance for Bad Debts
123 Interest Receivable (Also Accrued Interest Receivable)

130s—Inventories
131 Merchandise Inventory
132 Raw Materials
133 Work in Process
134 Finished Goods
135 Estimated Returns Inventory

140s—Prepaid Items
141 Supplies (Specialty items like Medical, Bicycle, Tailoring, etc.)
142 Office Supplies
144 Food Supplies
145 Prepaid Insurance

150s—Long-Term Investments
153 Bond Sinking Fund

160s—Land
161 Land
162 Natural Resources
162.1 Accumulated Depletion

170s—Buildings
171 Buildings
171.1 Accumulated Depreciation—Buildings

180s—Equipment
181 Office Equipment (Also Store Equipment)
181.1 Accumulated Depreciation—Office Equipment (Also Store Equipment)
182 Office Furniture
182.1 Accumulated Depreciation—Office Furniture
183 Athletic Equipment (Also Tailoring, Lawn, Cleaning)
183.1 Accumulated Depreciation—Athletic Equipment (Also Tailoring, Lawn, Cleaning)
184 Tennis Facilities (Also Basketball Facilities)
184.1 Accumulated Depreciation—Tennis Facilities (Also Basketball Facilities)
185 Delivery Equipment (Also Medical, Van)
185.1 Accumulated Depreciation—Delivery Equipment (Also Medical, Van)
186 Exercise Equipment
186.1 Accumulated Depreciation—Exercise Equipment
187 Computer Equipment
187.1 Accumulated Depreciation—Computer Equipment

190s—Intangibles
191 Patents
192 Copyrights

Liabilities (200–299)

200s—Short-Term Payables
201 Notes Payable
201.1 Discount on Notes Payable
202 Accounts Payable (Also Vouchers Payable)
203 Customer Refunds Payable
204 Income Tax Payable
205 Common Dividends Payable
206 Preferred Dividends Payable
207 Interest Payable (Also Bond Interest Payable)
208 United Way Contributions Payable

210s—Employee Payroll Related Payables
211 Employee Income Tax Payable
212 Social Security Tax Payable
213 Medicare Tax Payable
215 City Earnings Tax Payable
216 Health Insurance Premiums Payable
217 Credit Union Payable
218 Savings Bond Deductions Payable
219 Wages Payable

220s—Employer Payroll Related Payables
221 FUTA Tax Payable
222 SUTA Tax Payable
223 Workers' Compensation Insurance Payable

230s—Sales Tax
231 Sales Tax Payable

240s—Deferred Revenues and Current Portion of Long-Term Debt
241 Unearned Subscription Revenue (Also Unearned Ticket Revenue, Unearned Repair Fees)
242 Current Portion of Mortgage Payable

250s—Long-Term Liabilities
251 Mortgage Payable
252 Bonds Payable
252.1 Discount on Bonds Payable
253 Premium on Bonds Payable

Owner's Equity (300–399)

311 Rohan Macsen, Capital
312 Rohan Macsen, Drawing
313 Income Summary
321 Common Stock
321.1 Common Treasury Stock
322 Paid in Capital in Excess of Par/Stated Value—Common Stock
323 Preferred Stock
323.1 Preferred Treasury Stock
324 Paid in Capital in Excess of Par/Stated Value—Preferred Stock
327 Common Stock Subscribed
327.1 Common Stock Subscriptions Receivable
328 Preferred Stock Subscribed
328.1 Preferred Stock Subscriptions Receivable
329 Paid in Capital from Sale of Treasury Stock
331 Retained Earnings
332 Retained Earnings Appropriated for…
333 Cash Dividends
334 Stock Dividends

Revenues (400–499)

400s—Operating Revenues

401 Delivery Fees
401 Appraisal Fees
401 Medical Fees
401 Service Fees
401 Repair Fees
401 Sales
401.1 Sales Returns and Allowances
401.2 Sales Discounts
402 Boarding and Grooming Revenue
403 Subscriptions Revenue (if main line of business)

410s—Other Revenues

411 Interest Revenue
412 Rent Revenue
413 Subscriptions Revenue (if not main line of business)
414 Sinking Fund Earnings
415 Uncollectible Accounts Recovered
416 Gain on Sale/Exchange of Equipment
417 Gain on Bonds Redeemed

Operating Expenses (500–599)

500s—Cost of Goods Sold

501 Purchases
501.1 Purchases Returns and Allowances
501.2 Purchases Discounts
502 Freight-In
504 Overhead
505 Cost of Goods Sold

510s—Selling Expenses

511 Wages Expense (Also Wages and Salaries Expense)
512 Advertising Expense
513 Bank Credit Card Expense
514 Store Supplies Expense
515 Travel and Entertainment Expense
516 Cash Short and Over
519 Depreciation Expense—Store Equipment and Fixtures

520s–40s—General and Administrative Expenses

521 Rent Expense
522 Office Salaries Expense
523 Office Supplies Expense (Also Medical)
524 Other Supplies: Food Supplies Expense (Also Medical)
525 Phone Expense
526 Transportation/Automobile Expense (Also Laboratory, Travel)
527 Collection Expense
528 Inventory Short and Over
529 Loss on Write Down of Inventory
530 Payroll Taxes Expense
531 Workers' Compensation Insurance Expense
532 Bad Debt Expense
533 Electricity Expense, Utilities Expense
534 Charitable Contributions Expense
535 Insurance Expense
536 Postage Expense
537 Repair Expense
538 Oil and Gas Expense (Also Automobile Expense)
540 Depreciation Expense—Building
541 Depreciation Expense—Equipment (Also Tennis Facilities, Delivery Equipment, Office Equipment, Furniture)
542 Depreciation Expense—Other Equipment (Medical Equipment, Exercise Equipment, Computer Equipment)
543 Depletion Expense
544 Patent Amortization
545 Organization Expense
549 Miscellaneous Expense

550s—Other Expenses

551 Interest Expense (Also Bond Interest Expense)
552 Loss on Discarded Equipment
553 Loss on Sale/Exchange of Equipment
554 Loss on Bonds Redeemed
555 Income Tax Expense

